Encyclopedia of
CRIMINOLOGY

Volume 2

Encyclopedia of
CRIMINOLOGY

Volume 2
H-P

Richard A. Wright
J. Mitchell Miller

Editors

ROUTLEDGE
New York • London

Published in 2005 by

Routledge
An Imprint of the Taylor & Francis Group
270 Madison Avenue
New York, NY 10016

Published in Great Britain by
Routledge
An Imprint of the Taylor & Francis Group
2 Park Square
Milton Park, Abingdon
Oxon, OX14 4RN, U.K.

10   9   8   7   6   5   4   3   2   1

Library of Congress Cataloging-in-Publication Data

Encyclopedia of criminology/Richard A. Wright, editor, J. Mitchell Miller, editor.
 p.   cm.
 Includes bibliographical references and index.
 ISBN 1-57958-387-3 (set: alk. paper) — ISBN 1-57958-465-9 (vol. 1: alk. paper) — ISBN 1-57958-466-7 (vol. 2: alk. paper) — ISBN 1-57958-467-5 (vol. 3: alk. paper) 1. Criminology—Encyclopedias. I. Wright, Richard A. (Richard Alan), 1953- II. Miller, J. Mitchell.

HV6017.E5295 2005
364'.03—dc22   2004004861

ADVISORY BOARD MEMBERS

DEDICATION

To Richard A. Wright, an outstanding scholar, colleague, and friend

CONTENTS

ALPHABETICAL LIST OF ENTRIES

Habeas Corpus

Habeas corpus literally means, "you have the body." In this case, the "body" being referred to is the living body of a prisoner. A writ of habeas corpus is a demand that a jailer or prison official bring the prisoner to court and defend the legality of the imprisonment. In other words, it provides a means for inmates to challenge their confinement. It is sometimes referred to as the "Great Writ."

The writ of habeas corpus dates back to the Middle Ages. In England, both by statute and under common law, a person who was in custody awaiting trial could demand to be brought before a judge, so that the judge could determine whether there had been legal authority to make the arrest and hold the prisoner. Therefore, habeas ensured citizens access to their right to bail, as well as a reasonably speedy trial. It was meant to protect people from arbitrary and illegal acts by the executive powers. This writ was considered so important that, just prior to the Revolutionary War, one of the American colonists' chief complaints against England was that the colonists were being denied the writ.

After the Revolutionary War, the writ of habeas corpus was adapted quickly into American law. Article I, Section 9 of the U.S. Constitution declared that the writ could not be suspended except when required during times of "rebellion or invasion." A federal statute enacted in 1789 explicitly gave federal courts the power to issue writs of habeas corpus.

The writ was, in fact, suspended by President Lincoln during the Civil War in order to imprison persons who aided or supported the Confederate rebellion. After the war, however, not only was the writ reinstated, it was strengthened. The Habeas Corpus Act of 1867 gave federal courts the right to hear habeas cases involving any person who was deprived of freedom. This included not only federal prisoners, but also newly emancipated slaves who had not yet been released by their former masters. It also included state prisoners who claimed their incarceration was a violation of federal law. It was this last group of cases that has proved most significant in the years since 1867.

Over the years, the Supreme Court interpreted the right of habeas corpus to include the right to postconviction relief. This means that people who had already been tried for and convicted of their crimes could bring habeas cases in which they could claim that some aspect of their incarceration violated federal law. In practice, this has usually meant that the petitioner alleges that some aspect of his or her trial or sentence was unconstitutional. For example, perhaps the prosecutor withheld exculpatory evidence, or a certain class of people was excluded from the jury, or the sentence constituted cruel and unusual punishment. Petitioners who win their habeas claims generally are not set free, but instead are given a new trial or sentence.

Some have criticized using the writ for postconviction relief. Why allow a prisoner to bring a case in federal court when he or she already has had ample opportunity to litigate any issues in the state courts? Furthermore, it is argued, the doctrine of federalism requires federal courts to give deference to state-court decisions; federal courts, it is claimed, should not be interfering with the trial process in state courts. And postconviction proceedings interfere with the finality of decisions. The most conservative critics also argue that this use of habeas goes far beyond the original intent of the Constitution's framers.

On the other hand, others argue that postconviction habeas proceedings are vital to ensure justice. Most significantly, habeas permits state prisoners to have their case considered by a federal court. This is significant because, although federal judges are appointed by the President, state judges are often elected. Thus, it is argued, state judges may be more sensitive to community sentiment, and may be tempted to overlook miscarriages of justice if they feel doing so is in their own political best interests. This might be particularly true in the last few decades, in which successful election bids usually require a "tough on crime" image.

The writ of habeas corpus becomes most vital in death penalty cases: over 40% of death sentences are overturned during habeas proceedings. Aside from a reliance on executive clemency (a chancy venture at best), habeas proceedings also may offer inmates their only chance to present newly discovered evidence of their innocence, such as the types of evidence made available through new DNA technologies. Again, however, critics argue that extensive use of habeas in capital punishment cases has led to decades-long delays in carrying out executions.

Even habeas proponents acknowledge that these proceedings are much more limited in scope than are direct appeals. To bring a habeas case, petitioners must be in custody and must have exhausted their direct appeals. They generally cannot raise an issue during habeas proceedings unless they raised that same issue during direct appeals. The petitioner's guilt or innocence is not at issue, but rather the constitutional adequacy of the trial proceedings and sentence. The Sixth Amendment right to an attorney does not apply in habeas cases, so indigent inmates may be forced to represent themselves. Furthermore, the Supreme Court held in *Stone v. Powell* (428 U.S. 465, 1976) that habeas cases cannot generally be used to raise Fourth Amendment issues. And in *Teague v. Lane* (489 U.S. 288, 1989), the Court ruled that habeas petitioners cannot take advantage of new federal rules of criminal procedure that were established after their convictions were final. Finally, in *Herrera v. Collins* (506 U.S. 390, 1993), the Court held that inmates are not entitled to habeas relief based solely on claims of actual innocence.

Despite all these limitations, some scholars and politicians believed that habeas corpus cases were still problematic, in that they were overly burdensome to the courts and caused cases to be drawn out for too long. As a result of these concerns, Congress in 1996 passed the Antiterrorism and Effective Death Penalty Act. This Act further restricted the Great Writ by limiting most prisoners to a single habeas petition, and by requiring that that petition be brought no more than 1 year after the prisoner has exhausted the state appeals. Although this Act was itself controversial, it is unlikely to be repealed. The right of habeas corpus, although still important, is likely to remain quite restricted.

PHYLLIS B. GERSTENFELD

References and Further Reading

Antieau, C.J. 1987. *The Practice of Extraordinary Remedies: Habeas Corpus and the Other Common Law Writs*. New York, NY: Oceana Publications.

Blume, J.H. and David, P.V. 1996. An introduction to federal habeas corpus practice and procedure, *South Carolina Law Review* 47.

Duker, W.F. 1980. *A Constitutional History of Habeas Corpus*. Westport, CT: Greenwood Press.

Leibman, J.S. and Randy, H. 1998. *Federal Habeas Corpus Practice and Procedure*, 3rd ed. Charlottesville, VA: LEXIS Law Publications.

O'Neill, M. 1996. On reforming the federal writ of habeas corpus, *Seton Hall Law Review* 26.

Tabak, R.J. 1996. Habeas corpus as a crucial protector of constitutional rights: A tribute which may also be a eulogy, *Seton Hall Law Review* 26.

See also **Supreme Court, U.S.**

Hackers: History, Motivations, and Activities

The terms "hacker" and "hacking" are now a common part of the public discourse on computer crime, but the definitions of these terms vary widely and have changed over the past several decades. The most general definitions of the terms refer to an expert computer programmer who understands and appreciates exploring the limits of computer systems and to individuals who use computer skills maliciously for some form of personal gain (Parker, 1983; Raymond and Steele, 1994; Grabosky and Smith, 1998). Conventional definitions of the words "hacker" and "hacking" common to mass media portrayals and computer security reports tend to equate the terms with "computer criminal" and "computer crime" (Chandler, 1996; Huss, 1998; Grabosky and Smith, 1998). Yet, hackers publicly dispute most negative characterizations and claim that media accounts and computer security professionals vilify most computer hobbyists unfairly (Platt, 1996; Huss, 1998). Hackers contend that a "true hacker" is an individual who enjoys the intellectual challenge of computer technologies, does little to harm computer systems, adopts the Hacker Ethic, and belongs to a loosely organized community known as the computer underground (Meyer, 1989; Levy, 1994; Raymond and Steele, 1994; Taylor, 1999). Further, hackers suggest that a more appropriate term, "cracker," should be used for those who break into computer systems (Raymond and Steele, 1994; Huss, 1998). These current differences in definitions derive from fundamental changes in the number of individuals who identify themselves as hackers and the alternative interpretations of the motives and activities of hackers over the past several decades.

The activities and motives of successive generations of early computer users played an important role in both the shifts in the meanings of the terms and the changes in the make up of the hacker community (Clough and Mungo, 1992; Chandler, 1996; Huss, 1998). The original use of the term hacker comes from the early work of computer enthusiasts of the late 1960s and early 1970s at the Massachusetts Institute of Technology and Stanford University, who would "hack" together programs (Levy, 1994). Heavily influenced by the counterculture movements at the time, these early hackers were motivated by a set of beliefs termed the "Hacker Ethic" (i.e., free access to information, mistrust of authority, status based on computer skill, and computer use for technological development) (Levy, 1994, 39–49; Taylor, 1999; Himanen, 2001). Although these hackers were perceived to be technological prodigies during this period, they often would engage in questionable activities such as breaking into locked offices or creating devices that allow unauthorized use of the telephone system (Clough and Mungo, 1992; Levy, 1994; Hafner and Markhoff, 1995; Chandler, 1996). Many of these hackers also began a practice of playing pranks on systems administrators and gaining unauthorized access to computer systems (Parker, 1983; Levy, 1994). Despite these activities, hackers of the earlier generations developed the hardware and software that would eventually create the computer industry. Thus, during this period, the term hacker was

considered a positive label associated with computer proficiency and many of these individuals would reap the benefits of financial rewards from their skills (Rheingold, 1991; Clough and Mungo, 1992; Sterling, 1992; Hafner and Markhoff, 1995; Chandler, 1996).

The technological innovations of the earliest hackers created opportunities for more individuals to identify themselves as hackers and for these newer cohorts to engage in the controversial activities now associated with the term (Chandler, 1996; Platt, 1997; Huss, 1998). The late 1970s and 1980s were characterized by the introduction of the microcomputer and the earliest forms of what would become the Internet. During this period, many computer users became the operating managers of Bulletin Board Systems, where others could access and share information or pirated games (Platt, 1997). But this period also is characterized by a divergence from a stricter interpretation of the motivations in the "Hacker Ethic," taking the form of on-line competitions to crash computer systems and virus development in what was claimed to be playful electronic competition (Platt, 1997). By the mid-1980s and through the early 1990s the motivations for hacking became more clearly malicious when some groups of hackers developed rivalries and began to report the activities of other hackers to authorities (Slatalla and Quitner, 1995; Platt, 1997). Others began to break into government systems to download files, began to alter phone systems to win radio contests, and began to steal proprietary software from corporations (Stoll, 1990; Littman, 1997). Some victims and law enforcement officials did not see these activities as game playing. Unrestricted activities in the electronic community came to an end when the media began reporting stories of hacking and legislators created the first of many forms of computer crime legislation (Platt, 1997; Hollinger and Lance-Kadduce, 1988).

Few estimates of the actual numbers of hackers or the extent of computer crime that can be attributed to hackers are available, and many estimates available typically come from mass media accounts that attribute all computer crimes to "hackers." Such media accounts often are unreliable and even disputed by computer security professionals who point to employees as the most common perpetrators of computer crime (BloomBecker, 1988; Hearden, 1989; Forester and Morrison, 1990; Winkler, 1997). Hackers themselves note that they often will exaggerate their abilities and exploits to provide reporters with exciting stories and to capitalize on a general fear the public has of them (Platt, 1997; Huss, 1998). Likewise, there is some debate over the real threat of hackers to computer systems within the computer security industry. Some experts contend that hackers are nothing more than a minor annoyance and their real threat is in sharing information on the Internet about weaknesses in systems (e.g., Winkler, 1997). Other computer security specialists, however, contend that hackers are a considerable threat and that their activities jeopardize both commerce and national security (Parker, 1983; Denning, 1996b; Grabosky and Smith, 1998). Despite the ambiguity over their numbers or the threat they pose, hackers are a concern of the now $13.5 billion computer security industry and more research is needed on hackers as a subject of criminological inquiry (Weintraub and Kerstetter, 2003).

Sean Huss, Heith Copes, and Sam Wallace

References and Further Reading

BloomBecker, J. 1988. *Introduction to Computer Crime*. 2nd ed. Los Angeles, CA: National Center for Computer Crime Data.

Chandler, A. 1996. The changing definition and image of hackers in popular discourse. *International Journal of the Sociology of Law*, 24: 229–251.

Clough, B. and Mungo, P. 1992. *Approaching Zero: Data Crime and the Computer Underworld*. London, UK: Faber & Faber.

Denning, D. 1996a. Concerning hackers who break into computer systems. *High Noon on the Electronic Frontier: Conceptual Issues in Cyberspace*, Ludlow, P. (Ed.), 1996. Cambridge, MA: MIT Press, pp. 137–160.

Denning, D. 1996b. Postscript to concerning hackers who break into computer systems. *High Noon on the Electronic Frontier: Conceptual Issues in Cyberspace*, Ludlow, P. (Ed.), 1996. Cambridge, MA: MIT Press, pp. 160–163.

Forester, T. and Morrison, P. 1990. Computer crime: New information for the information society. *Prometheus*, 8: 257–272.

Forester, T. and Morrison, P. 1994. *Computer Ethics: Cautionary Tales and Ethical Dilemmas in Computing*, 2nd ed. Cambridge, MA: MIT Press.

Grabosky, P. and Smith, R.G. 1998. *Crime in the Digital Age: Controlling Telecommunications and Cyberspace Illegalities*. New Brunswick, NJ: Transaction Publishers.

Hafner, K. and Lyon, M. 1996. *Where Wizards Stay Up Late: The Origins of the Internet*. New York, NY: Simon and Schuster.

Hafner, K. and Markoff, J. 1995. *Cyberpunk: Outlaws and Hackers on the Computer Frontier*. New York, NY: Touchstone.

Hearnden, K. 1989. Computer criminals are human, too. *Computers in the Human Context*, Forester, T. (Ed.). Cambridge, MA: MIT Press, pp. 415–426.

Himanen, P. 2001. *The Hacker Ethic and the Spirit of the Information Age*. New York, NY: Random House, Inc.

Hollinger, R.C. 1988. Computer hackers follow a Guttman-like progression. *Social Science Research*, 72: 199–200.

Hollinger, R.C. and Lance-Kaduce, L. 1988. The process of criminalization: The case of computer crime laws. *Criminology*, 26: 101–126.

Huss, S.T. 1998. *Hackers: Practices, Motivations, and Activities*. Master's Thesis, University of Tennessee, Knoxville.

Jordan, T. and Taylor, P. 1998. A sociology of hackers. *Sociological Review*, 46: 757–780.

Levy, S. 1984. *Hackers: Heroes of the Computer Revolution*. New York, NY: Dell Publishing.

Littman, J. 1997. *The Watchman: The Twisted Life and Crimes of Serial Hacker Kevin Poulson*. Boston, MA: Little, Brown and Company.

Ludlow, P. (Ed.) 1996. *High Noon on the Electronic Frontier: Conceptual Issues in Cyberspace*. Cambridge, MA: MIT Press.

Meyer, G. 1989. The social organization of the computer underground. Master's Thesis from Northeastern Illinois University made available through the Electronic Frontier Foundation Homepage; accessed September 1996. Available at http://www.eff.org/pub/Net_culture/Hackers/soc_org_of_comp-underground.paper.

Parker, D.B. 1983. *Fighting Computer Crime*. New York, NY: Charles Scribner's Sons.

Platt, C. 1996. *Anarchy Online*. New York, NY: Harper Collins.

Raymond, E.S. and Steele, G.L., Jr. 1994. *The New Hacker's Dictionary*, 2nd ed. Cambridge, MA: MIT Press.

Rheingold, H. 1991. *Virtual Reality*. New York, NY: Touchstone Books.

Statalla, M. and Quittner, J. 1995. *Masters of Deception: The Gang that Ruled Cyberspace*. New York, NY: Harper Collins.

Sterling, B. 1992. *The Hacker Crackdown: Law and Disorder on the Electronic Frontier*. New York, NY: Bantam.

Stoll, C. 1990. *The Cuckoo's Egg*. New York, NY: Simon and Schuster.

Stoll, C. 1995. *Silicon Snake Oil*. New York, NY: Anchor Books.

Taylor, P.A. 1999. *Hackers*. New York, NY: Routledge.

Winkler, I. 1997. *Corporate Espionage: What it is, Why it is Happening in Your Company, What You Must Do about It*. Rocklin, CA: Prima.

Weintraub, A. and Kerstetter, J. 2003. Cyber alert: Portrait of an ex-hacker. *Businessweek*, 3836: 116.

See also **Computer Offenses; Crimes against Consumers**

Halfway Houses and Day-Reporting Centers

Halfway houses and day-reporting centers are intermediate sanction programs that can stand alone or coexist with other forms of community corrections. They provide supervision that is intermediate between incarceration sanctions (jail or prison) and routine parole or probation in the community. The typical client referred to these programs is underemployed, undereducated, and has a history of alcohol, drug, and family disruption. Programs offered in these facilities are aimed at providing support for offender reintegration while maintaining safety for the community.

Day-reporting centers and halfway houses differ mainly in that the centers are nonresidential and more likely to have some clients who attend as a condition of probation (diversion) rather than postprison parole (early release). Day reporting is often combined with other intermediate sanctions such as electronic monitoring, home confinement, and intensive supervision forms of parole or probation. In contrast, halfway houses (also called Community Correctional Residential Facilities) provide 24-hour, 7-day-a-week service. Both kinds of facilities provide supervision that may vary according to the resident's parole conditions and needs. Both send most of their clients into the community to learn, work, and adjust.

Although both types of facilities have a long history, their emergence is usually traced to prototypes developed in the 1950s. Halfway houses of various kinds were first developed by community organizations to assist in aid to prisoners and to troubled youth. They were staffed by religious workers or volunteers, sometimes supplemented by professional staff. Although this model continues to exist, there is an increasing reliance on trained program staff and on government funding. Both voluntary agency and private for-profit facilities are mainly run according to government-set criteria.

Attendance centers preceded the day-reporting program. They grew out of a combination of youth probation initiatives and school programs for troubled students in the 1950s. In Britain, where this model originated, "at risk" youths are required to spend afternoons or a specified number of weekend hours in a police-supervised setting characterized by exercise and strict discipline. Two Canadian provinces experimented briefly with "attendance centers" for youths in the 1970s. These were staffed by social workers and used a group-work model.

Day-reporting facilities for adults were begun in Britain in the 1970s. Although originally used as an early release option, they came to be justified as ways of diverting prison-bound offenders prior to incarceration. The first day-reporting center in the U.S. was established in Hampden County (Massachusetts) in 1986, and there were over a 100 in more than 20 states by 1999. These are modeled partly on the British example, but are also influenced by similar U.S. facilities that served deinstitutionalized psychiatric patients. The U.S. model was more heavily influenced by public demands for the control of offenders in the community (safety) and reduction of prison costs.

Day-reporting centers and halfway houses provide highly structured and closely supervised programs that are offered "in house" or contracted out to other agencies. Typical programs include cognitive restructuring, problem-solving, anger management, life-skills training, educational and work skills upgrading, employment search skills, drug or alcohol treatment, and support for stronger families. Services range from the provision of basic needs to urinalysis, mental health evaluation, and referrals for employment or community participation. Offenders typically must have a schedule of approved hourly activities and show that they are meeting assigned responsibilities. If they are away from direct supervision, they can expect random checks by staff and be required to report (by phone) regularly. Violations can result in tighter rules (earlier curfew, for example) or revocation of the probation or parole.

Facilities vary in terms of clients served, types and expected length of programs, and other characteristics. Some are specialized to serve at risk youth, whereas others serve chronic nonviolent offenders, sexual offenders, women offenders, or DWI offenders. Some serve only one type of offender, whereas others handle (almost) any offender referred to them. The clients vary by gender, race, age, employment, and educational status, and the length and nature of their sentence. Programs may require 30 days to 2 years for completion. Day-reporting centers may have a capacity for a few dozen clients or, as in Harris County (Texas) be capable of serving thousands. Halfway houses may be small group-home types of facilities or much larger institutions bordering on an overlap with minimum-security prisons. They may be sited in a downtown, industrial, or neighborhood context. Other variations include the staff or client ratio and the working conditions, qualifications, and credentialing of staff. It is hardly surprising, then, that studies of the efficiency of such programs show mixed results.

Halfway houses and day-reporting centers are mandated to serve several major sentencing goals, including reduction of recidivism, incapacitation, retribution, rehabilitation, and restitution. In particular, they are expected to reduce prison populations and prison costs. The great variety within each of these forms, however, makes overall evaluation impossible. The very few studies that use a true experimental design have not shown impressive reductions in recidivism. Some programs show increased levels of restitution, community service, relapse avoidance, and sustained employment and some have shown reductions in rates of reoffending.

In the 1980s, halfway house and day-reporting options received much favorable attention from government and media, and expanded rapidly. In the 1990s, there was increasing recognition that they were not going to be the hoped-for panacea. In recent years, their expansion has been limited by "Not in My Back Yard" responses. There are not many neighbors who welcome having "criminals" next door, either as residents or as frequent visitors, despite the need and the assurance that there is little risk.

Although it might appear obvious that use of these options always reduces correctional expenditures, this is not necessarily true. In some cases, there is a demonstrable "net widening" effect. That is, offenders are being placed in these programs who might just as

effectively been assigned to less expensive, less controlled conditions. Greater surveillance means that individuals may be incarcerated for technical violations (such as lateness, rudeness, or failure to report) that would not be offenses if they were on ordinary parole or probation. It has also been suggested that close supervision may offset any rehabilitation that might occur from early release or diversion. Either way, overuse of these options may *increase* the use of prison and the costs of correction. Much work remains to be done to isolate the effective from the ineffective aspects of these two forms of community corrections.

LINDA B. DEUTSCHMANN

References and Further Reading

Clear, T.R. 1995. *Harm in American Penology: Offenders, Victims and Their Communities* (SUNY Series, New Directions in Crime and Justice Studies). New York, NY: State University of New York.

Clear, T.R and Harry, R.D. 1999. *The Offender in the Community*. Belmont, CA: Wadsworth.

Davies, M. 1993. *Punishing Criminals: Developing Community-Based Intermediate Sanctions*. Westport, CT: Greenwood Press.

Petersilia, J. 1998. Ed. *Community Corrections: Probation, Parole, and Intermediate Sanctions*. New York, NY: Oxford University Press.

See also **Alcohol Use: Prevention and Treatment; Child Abuse: Treatment and Prevention; Domestic Assault: Prevention and Treatment; Drug Policy: Prevention and Treatment; Rehabilitation or Treatment**

Hammurabi Code, The *See* Babylonian Legal Traditions

Hate Crime

The definition of hate crime is entirely dependent on time and place. Until approximately the 1980s, there was no legal definition of a hate crime, in spite of the fact that crimes motivated by hatred and bias have existed throughout time. In the past few decades, a majority of states and the federal government have created hate crime laws. Each law varies in the type of bias covered and the criminal justice system's

response to the crime. In some states, hate crimes are referred to as bias crimes.

Broadly speaking, hate crimes can be defined as crimes that are motivated by bias or prejudice. A hate crime consists of a predicate offense (an act, such as an assault or vandalism) combined with a prejudicial motivation for the predicate offense. Beyond this vague definition, the states and federal government each have defined their own ideas about what forms of bias and activities are included in this definition. These laws will be discussed shortly after a review of laws that set the stage for modern day hate crime laws.

The rise of the Ku Klux Klan after the Civil War provoked some state governments and the federal government to take action against the Klan. Freedom for slaves did not mean freedom from harassment, violence, and unfair treatment. Thirteenth and Fourteenth Amendment Rights were still being violated in Southern states and often these related crimes were ignored and not prosecuted. In an effort to curb Klan activities and protect the rights of Black citizens, the federal government passed the Enforcement Act of 1870 and the Ku Klux Klan Act of 1872. Although these laws were not hate crime laws *per se*, they were an attempt to protect civil rights and were one of the first efforts made by the federal government to stop harassment and violence based in prejudice. The Enforcement Act of 1870 (18 U.S.C. § 241) mandates:

[i]f two or more persons conspire to injure, oppress, threaten, or intimidate any person ... in the free exercise or enjoyment of any right or privilege secured to him by the Constitution or laws of the United States ... or;

If two or more persons go in disguise on the highway [i.e., the Ku Klux Klan], or on the premises of another, with intent to prevent or hinder [the] free exercise or enjoyment of any right or privilege so secured ... They shall be fined not more than $10,000, or imprisoned not more than 10 years or both ...

The Ku Klux Klan Act of 1872 (18 U.S.C. § 242) states:

Whoever, under color of any law, ... willfully subjects any person ... to the deprivation of any rights, privileges, or immunities secured or protected by the Constitution or laws of the United States, or to different punishments, pains, or penalties, on account of such person being an alien, or by reason of his color, or race, than are prescribed for the punishment of citizens, shall be fined ... or imprisoned ... (Jacobs and Potter, 1998).

Although these laws resulted in high arrests but many acquittals, the laws placed enough pressure on the KKK to reduce their membership and power.

The Klan did not die out completely and went through a series of rebirths including one during the civil rights movement of the 1960s. The next precursor to modern-day hate crime laws came at this time, when President Lyndon Johnson decided to fight back against the Klan uprisings. A major problem in curtailing Klan power and violence was the fact that some Klan groups included members of the criminal justice system; also, when charged with crimes against Black citizens the offenders would face sympathetic all-White juries. The result was that few Klansmen were getting punished for the harassment and violence against Black Americans. To combat this problem, President Johnson decided to use the 1872 KKK Act against Klan members, resulting in a number of guilty sentences for previously acquitted cases that diminished the power of some Klan groups. The federal government took one further step to protect the rights of citizens by creating the Federally Protected Activities Act of 1968. This act serves as a complement to the aforementioned civil rights acts by specifying protected activities under this act and serves as a precursor to modern hate crime law because it protects victims from violations based on race, color, creed, and national origin. It specifically states:

Whoever, whether or not acting under color of law, by force or threat of force willfully injures, intimidates or interferes with, or attempts to interfere with ... any person because of his race, color, religion, or national origin and because he is or has been enrolling in or attending public school or university; participating in any benefit, program, service or facility provided by a state or local government; applying or working for any state or local government or private employer; serving as a juror; traveling in or using any facility of any common carrier; or using any public facility, such as a bar, restaurant, store, hotel, movie theater, or stadium shall be punished.... [The statute provides a range of different punishments depending on the conduct, whether firearms or explosives are used, and the degree of injury to victims.]

In reality, federal civil rights acts serve only as protection against biased or faulty state and local criminal justice systems. As such, the need for federal and state hate crime laws eventually became apparent.

In addition to the aforementioned Civil Rights Acts, the federal government has also responded to the problem of hate crimes through four laws: The Hate Crime Statistics Act of 1990 (HCSA), The Hate Crimes Sentencing Enhancement Act of 1994 (HCSE) and the Violence Against Women Act of 1994 (VAWA) (both parts of the Violent Crime Control and Law Enforcement Act of 1994), and the Church Arson Prevention Act of 1996 (CAPA).

The 1990 HCSA (28 U.S.C. 534) orders the Department of Justice to monitor hate crime statistics. The resulting report provides hate crime statistics for racial, religious, sexual orientation, ethnicity or national origin, and disability biases. The Department of Justice decided to collect these statistics in a manner similar to the Federal Bureau of Investigation's (FBI) annual Uniform Crime Report (UCR) that presents statistics on major crimes across the U.S. As with the UCR, local law enforcement participation in this process is strictly voluntary. As a result, the hate crime statistics show only a partial picture of hate crime in America. For instance, in the most recent Federal Bureau of Investigation publication *Hate Crime Statistics, 1998*, the FBI reports that local law enforcement participation in hate crime statistics collection reflects about 80% of the population. The *Hate Crime Statistics* publications present hate crime data for murder, nonnegligent manslaughter, forcible rape, aggravated assault, simple assault, intimidation, arson, larceny-theft, robbery, burglary, motor vehicle theft and destruction, damage, or vandalism of property, among other crimes. The HCSA does not collect statistics on all types of hate crimes and omits data on crimes motivated by gender or age.

The Hate Crimes Sentencing Enhancement accompanied the Violent Crime Control and Law Enforcement Act of 1994. The HCSE requires the U.S. Sentencing Commission to enhance sentences by a minimum of three offense levels if an offender has committed a hate crime in national parks or on other federal property. Covering biases outside of the HCSA, the HCSE also defined hate crime by the intentional selection of a victim or victim's property based on the victim's actual or perceived race, color, religion, national origin, ethnicity, gender, disability, or sexual orientation. However, the U.S. Sentencing Commission excludes rape and sexual abuse as gender biases. Gender bias against women has often proven difficult to identify because of conflicting crime categories such as rape (which many believe is based on bias against women).

The Violence Against Women Act (VAWA)—also a part of the Violent Crime Control and Law Enforcement Act of 1994—can be considered to be a form of hate crime law. Although the HCSE acknowledged gender bias, the Violence Against Women Act provided the broadest legislation aimed at violence against women in U.S. history. VAWA created two new government offices, gave grants for shelters, provided rape counseling, facilitated interstate recognition of restraining orders, and made interstate travel to commit a crime against a spouse a federal felony. VAWA also states that victims of violence motivated by gender bias can recover damages from the offender.

The final piece of recent federal hate crime legislation is the Church Arson Prevention Act of 1996 (CAPA) (18 U.S.C. 247), enacted after a number of suspicious arson attacks against Black Southern churches. CAPA was intended to amend a U.S. Code from 1988 (18 U.S.C. 247) that gave the federal government jurisdiction in religious vandalism cases if the damage exceeded $10,000 or the offender crossed state or national borders. CAPA broadened this code by allowing for compensation to burned churches, enhancing penalties for damaging religious property, and

obstructing a person's right to exercise religious freedom if the offense has an affect on interstate commerce.

In addition to federal attempts at punishing hate crime, state governments have also made attempts to curtail hate crime. State hate crime laws began appearing in the 1980s and continued growing through the 1990s. According to the Anti-Defamation league, 43 states and the District of Columbia currently have statutes aimed at bias motivated violence and intimidation.

State laws vary by the type of bias they cover. The main biases covered are race, color, religion, national origin or ancestry, physical disability, gender, sexual orientation, and mental disability. However, one should note that some states have included other biases such as age and political affiliation. Thus, state laws can vary between no coverage of hate crime to coverage of multiple, specific biases. What may be considered a hate crime or bias crime in one state may not be considered a hate crime or bias crime in another state.

States also vary in their punishment of hate crime. Certainly, the actual punishment (e.g., sentence length or eligibility for probation) of any crime varies from one state to the next. However, the manner in which the punishment is defined for hate crimes also varies. The two main types of hate crime are substantive crime statutes and penalty enhancement statutes. Sentence enhancement statutes increase the regular penalty for a given crime motivated by bias. For instance, if a state had a 6-month penalty for assault, the crime would still be classified as an assault but the penalty would be increased beyond 6 months if the assault was motivated by bias. These state sentencing enhancement statutes operate in the same manner as the federal Hate Crimes Sentencing Enhancement Act described earlier.

A substantive hate crime statute treats the hate crime as a whole new category of crime. For example, if a person committed an assault against a Jew because of prejudice against the victim's religion, the incident would no longer be classified as an assault but would be classified as a hate crime. Under a substantive hate crime law, hate crimes would have their own set of punishments. Some substantive state hate crime laws have been challenged in court as unconstitutional for violating First Amendment rights. For instance, the finding in the Supreme Court case *R.A.V. v. St. Paul* (505 U.S. 377) suggested that some state hate crime laws violate the First Amendment when they criminalize only certain types of speech. Although sentencing enhancement statutes have not encountered as many challenges, substantive hate crime laws must be crafted carefully to avoid violating First Amendment rights.

Debate over the legitimacy and potential effectiveness of hate crime laws continues. Critics of hate crime laws suggest that it is difficult for law enforcement officials to identify hate crimes and difficult for prosecutors to prove the motive of bias. Some have suggested that hate crime laws will create further divisions in society. Proponents of hate crime laws note that hate crimes not only harm the immediate victim but also harm other members of the community who share the victim's status or beliefs.

As mentioned previously, the FBI collects hate crime statistics annually to create the *Hate Crime Statistics* report. The first report was published in 1993. It provides statistics on hate crime according to type of crime, type of bias, and jurisdiction. Drawing conclusions from these statistics and making cross-jurisdictional comparisons is difficult because the report does not give a full picture of hate crime. A partial picture exists owing to the fact that not all victims report hate crimes and not all law enforcement agencies participate in the report. In addition, some experts argue that both victims and police may not identify hate crimes as a hate crime but rather view it only as the predicate offense, perhaps because of misconceptions or apprehension about identifying a crime as a hate crime.

With these caveats in mind, it is interesting to note the statistical trends that exist. Based on the most recent report, *Hate Crime Statistics, 1998*, the FBI provides statistics on 9235 single-bias hate crime offenses in 1998. The most common type of bias among hate crimes is racial bias (58% of all hate crimes). Within this category, the most common racial bias is against Black citizens (67%). Religious and sexual orientation hate crimes are the second most frequent type of hate crime, each accounting for 16% of all hate crimes. The most common religious bias is anti-Jewish (78%) and the most common sexual-orientation bias is anti-male homosexual (66%). Ethnic or national origin hate crimes account for roughly 10% of all hate crimes. The most frequent ethnic or national origin bias is anti-Hispanic (65%). Finally, disability hate crimes account for less than 1% of all hate crimes and are split almost evenly between physical and mental disabilities. The FBI reports that in 1998, there were 15 multiple bias incidents.

According to the 1998 report, the most common form of hate crime is a personal offense (68%) and the most frequent personal offense is intimidation (55%). Among property hate crimes, the most common offense is destruction, damage, or vandalism (88%). The race of the offender is not always known in cases where the offender has not been apprehended. However, in cases where the offender is known, 66% of hate crimes were committed by White offenders. The data presented here reveal trends that are similar to the trends found in previous FBI *Hate Crime Statistics* reports.

Research on the causes of hate crime and criminal justice responses is minimal compared to other types of crime. The reason for the scant amount of research may be, in part, because of the fact that the legal definition of a hate crime did not exist until the 1980s. Furthermore, inaccuracies in hate crime statistics limit the scope of research. The causes behind the biases for committing hate crimes have yet to be uncovered, although the Bureau of Justice Statistics points to a number of possible factors, including unstable economic conditions, media racial stereotypes and racially biased discussions on TV, racial code language, individual experiences with certain minority groups, and scapegoating. In 1993, criminologists Jack Levin and Jack McDevitt published a book on hate crime, *Hate Crimes: The Rising Tide of Bigotry and Bloodshed*. This book outlined three types of hate crime offenders based on their motivations: thrill seeker hate crime offenders, reactive hate crime offenders (a protective or defensive act against "intruders"), and mission hate crime offenders (trying to rid the world of "evil").

Other research in the area of hate crime has focused on particular hate groups. For example, Mark Hamm's *American Skinheads: The Criminology and Control of Hate Crime* (1993) explored the inner workings of skinhead groups, along with the efforts of such organizations such as the Anti-Defamation League and Southern Poverty Law Center to monitor the location and membership of these groups. (In 1999, the Southern Poverty Law Center estimated that there were over 500 hate groups operating in the U.S., including Ku Klux Klan groups, neo-Nazis, Skinheads, the Identity Movement, and Black Separatists.)

The influence of hate groups has been enhanced by the Internet, where hundreds of different hate groups have started their own web pages displaying their racist beliefs. Many of these sites walk a fine line between directing violence against certain groups and merely hinting at violence. As long as the groups do not cross the line and direct individuals to commit criminal acts, their web sites remain protected by the First Amendment. However, some may argue that violent images and jokes about racist violence may encourage individuals viewing the page to commit hate crimes, even though they are not members of the group. The Internet has allowed hate groups to spread their racist messages worldwide.

In the wake of increasing legislation beginning in the 1980s, police, prosecutors, and community groups have tried to implement programs and policies to respond to hate crime. Local police departments have developed hate crime policies, and designated hate crime officers or hate crime units in an effort to attack hate crime. An essential element of law enforcement responses to hate crime is training. Officers must learn how to recognize a hate crime and how to respond.

The FBI has created a hate crime training model to guide police officers in identifying and responding to hate crimes. Some local police departments use the FBI training model whereas others may use their own version or a combination of an in-house training model and the FBI training model.

Similarly, some state attorneys' general offices have developed specialized approaches to handling hate crime cases, such as designating a special hate crime unit within the office. These special units often employ vertical prosecution. Vertical prosecution uses one prosecutor who is typically trained in a specific type of crime and is devoted to handling all cases within that given crime type. Vertical prosecutors handle the case from beginning to end (filing through sentencing), rather than having different staff handle the case at different phases.

At the community level, victim advocacy organizations often devote their time to encouraging hate crime victims to report hate crimes or to assist the victims. These groups also may support victims as their case moves through the criminal justice system and serve as go-betweens for victims and criminal justice agencies. Often, groups responding to hate crime cases tend to be specialized for specific hate crime victims (i.e., gay and lesbian victims, Jewish victims, or Black victims). Victim advocacy groups may also work to educate the community and create partnerships with criminal justice agencies such as the police to assist in their personnel training.

The present state of research on hate crime has been helpful in providing a foundation for understanding the nature of hate crime as well as how to respond to hate crime, but additional research is necessary in the area of hate crime policy and understanding hate crime offenders. In particular, improvements in the accuracy of hate crime statistics may help expand research aimed at assessing the effectiveness of hate crime policies and developing a theoretical understanding of hate crime offenders.

KATHERINE CULOTTA

References and Further Reading

Anti-Defamation League. *Hate Crimes Laws: State Hate Crimes Statutory Provisions*. Available at http://www.adl.org/frames/front_99hatecrime.html. Accessed on February 7, 2001.

Boyd, E.A., Berk, R.A., and Hamner, K.M. 1996. Motivated by hatred or prejudice: Categorization of hate-motivated crimes in two police divisions. *Law & Society Review, 3*: 819–850.

Bureau of Justice Assistance. 1999. *A Policymaker's Guide to Hate Crimes*. Washington, DC: U.S. Department of Justice.

Federal Bureau of Investigation. 1991. *Training Guide for Hate Crime Data Collection*. Washington, DC: U.S. Department of Justice.

Federal Bureau of Investigation. 1999. *Hate Crime Statistics, 1998*. Washington, DC: U.S. Department of Justice.

Hamm, M.S. 1993. *American Skinheads: The Criminology of Hate Crime*. Westport, CT: Praeger.

The History Channel. 1998. *The Ku Klux Klan: A Secret History.*

Jacobs, J.B. 1992. Rethinking the war against hate crimes: A New York City perspective. *Criminal Justice Ethics,* Summer/Fall: 55–60.

Jacobs, J.B. and Potter, K.A. 1997. Hate crimes: A critical perspective. In Tonry, M. and Morris, N. (Eds.). *Crime and Justice.*

Jacobs, J.B. and Potter, K.A. 1998. *Hate Crimes: Criminal Law and Identity Politics*. New York, NY: Oxford University Press.

Levin, J. and McDevitt, J. 1993. *Hate Crimes: The Rising Tide of Bigotry and Bloodshed*. New York, NY: Plenum Press.

Martin, S. 1995. A cross-burning is not just an arson: Police social construction of hate crimes in Baltimore County. *Criminology, 33*: 303–326.

Martin, S. 1996. Investigating hate crimes: Case characteristics and law enforcement responses. *Justice Quarterly, 13*: 455–480.

Russell, K.K. 1998. *The Color of Crime: Racial Hoaxes, White Fear, Black Protectionism, Police Harassment, and Other Macroaggressions*. New York, NY: New York University Press.

Southern Poverty Law Center. 1999. The Year in Hate. *Intelligence Report*, Winter Issue.

Walker, S. and Katz, C.M. 1995. Less than meets the eye: Police department bias-crime units. *American Journal of Police, 14*: 29–48.

Wexler, C. and Marx, G.T. 1986. When law and order works: Boston's innovative approach to the problem of racial violence. *Crime & Delinquency, 32*: 205–223.

See also **Genocide**

Health Care *See* **Crimes by Physicians and the Pharmaceutical Companies**

Heroin

Background and History

Heroin is a highly addictive and illegal drug. It is the most abused and fastest acting opiate, a class of drugs derived from the opium poppy. Heroin is also classified as a narcotic because of its pain-relieving effects. Other effects of narcotic use are euphoria, sedation, and slowed breathing. The best-known prescription narcotics in the U.S. include (trade names) Percocet, Talwin, Vicodin, Dilaudid, OxyContin, Percodan, Darvon, Sublimaze, and Demerol. The best-known illegal narcotic in the world is heroin.

Heroin originates from the milky fluid or sap that exudes from the base of the opium poppy when it is cut or lanced. After the milky fluid dries, it forms a thick brown mass of opium powder. The powder contains a number of alkaloids, including morphine, the earliest opium derivative, isolated in 1803 by the German chemist Friedrich Seturner and named after Morpheus, the Greek God of Sleep.

First synthesized in England in 1874 by Alder Wright, heroin is a morphine derivative three to five times more potent on a per weight basis than its parent drug. Its chemical name is diacetylmorphine. In 1898, Bayer and Company marketed heroin commercially under its own name (Heroin) as a patent medicine for coughs, chest pain, tuberculosis, pneumonia, and a variety of other ailments common in the late 19th century. Heroin was also marketed as a cure for morphine addiction. Users could swallow or inject heroin and purchase it over the counter. The first efforts to control heroin sales followed the passage of the Harrison Narcotic Act of 1914, giving the U.S. Treasury Department comprehensive powers to prosecute and convict drug suppliers and users. Heroin is currently listed under Schedule I of the Federal Controlled Substances Act, and is, therefore, considered a drug with a high potential for abuse and no accepted medical use.

Preparation and Production

The process of preparing heroin from opium is relatively simple and requires only elemental laboratory equipment. Raw opium is dissolved in water and purified by adding lime salts, ammonium chloride, alcohol, and ether. The mixture is filtered to extract organic wastes, leaving a pure morphine solution that is combined with hydrochloric and sulfuric acids, charcoal dust, and water. This solution is then filtered, heated, and filtered again to facilitate the complete separation of morphine. The process produces a brown morphine base ready for conversion to heroin.

The brown morphine base is treated with acetic acid, anhydride, and chloroform to remove impurities. The resulting brown heroin can be sold in its present form or bleached and treated with hydrochloric acid. Baked and sifted, it becomes a powder of differing colors and purity levels. "Black tar" heroin, from Mexico, has become increasingly available in the western U.S. Its consistency varies from sticky like roofing tar to hard like coal; its color varies from dark brown to black; and its purity level varies from 20 to 80%. Typically, black tar heroin is dissolved, diluted, and injected. The highest-purity heroin is referred to on the street as "China White."

When heroin is ready to be sold as a "bag"—a single dose of heroin—its quality and purity are usually greatly reduced. The drug is generally "cut" with different adulterants such as lactose and quinine. The former gives heroin a white tinge to signify greater purity. The latter gives heroin a bitter flavor, similar to the drug's actual taste. Adulteration is intended to confuse the buyer about the drug's quality and concentration level. Some heroin adulterants can be dangerous. For example, talcum powder, a common heroin adulterant, is insoluble when injected and can block the blood vessels leading to the heart, lungs, kidneys, and brain. Blockage often results in serious bacterial infections in these major organs.

Heroin has numerous street names, such as "junk," "horse," "smack," "dope," "hero," and "slag." It is sometimes mixed with other drugs to intensify or moderate its effects. For example, mixing heroin with cocaine (speedball) or amphetamines (bombitas) intensifies the immediate effects of the drug (the rush) and alleviates the sleepiness (the nod) that follows heroin injection. Heroin users often seek "good products," that is, those associated with overdoses and therefore regarded as more powerful quantities of the drug. Hence, heroin retailers frequently mark their merchandise with distinctive brand names that suggest purity and potency (e.g., "body bag," "poison," "dead on arrival"). Because heroin users are generally unaware of the actual strength or contents of the drug, they are at risk for overdose or death.

Worldwide heroin production was estimated at 313 metric tons in 1998; between 12 (4%) and 18

(6%) metric tons of heroin were made available for distribution in the U.S., where it originates entirely from four foreign supply sources: South America, Mexico, Southwest Asia (primarily Afghanistan), and Southeast Asia (primarily Burma). In the late 1990s, Latin American countries emerged as the leading supply sources of heroin in the U.S. Nearly two-thirds of the heroin seized in America is from Colombia. Since 1997, heroin from South America that is white and highly pure has become very common in the northeastern states, suggesting that cocaine distribution and sales networks are being employed to sell heroin.

Use, Prevalence, and Sales

Heroin can be ingested in one of four modes: smoked (chasing the dragon), snorted–sniffed, injected under the skin (skin popping), or injected intravenously (mainlining or shooting). A new form of heroin use consists of dissolving the drug in water and dripping it up the nose with a small plastic applicator, a mode of ingestion referred to as "shebanging." Intravenous injection is the most efficient means of ingestion, especially for low-purity heroin. The effects of injecting heroin are almost immediate (6–8 seconds), whereas the effects of smoking or sniffing heroin are less intense and usually appear 10–15 minutes after inhalation. All four modes of heroin ingestion can lead to addiction.

The increased availability of high-quality, white powder heroin has made snorting and smoking more popular modes of ingestion. With high-quality heroin, users can experience very potent effects without ever injecting the drug. Consequently, the smoking or snorting of heroin among users rose from 55% in 1994 to 71% in 1997. More recent users are more likely to smoke, snort, or sniff than to inject heroin because they perceive sniffing or smoking as much less stigmatizing, invasive, and dangerous than injection. Injection increases users' risk of HIV infection and other blood-borne diseases (e.g., hepatitis B and C, septicemia, endocarditis, and tetanus) that can be transmitted to their sexual partners and children. Heroin use typically progresses from inhaling or smoking to needle use because of increased tolerance to the drug's effects. Frequent exposure to the drug culture can diminish the stigma of injection and provide opportunities for intravenous drug use.

The intravenous use of heroin requires a set of "works" or injection equipment, which is also called a "fit" or "rig." Intravenous heroin use follows a discrete sequence of steps. The powdered heroin is first removed from its package and poured into a spoon or bottle cap. Water is squirted from a syringe into the spoon to liquefy the powder. The powder is then heated so it will fully dissolve and lose its adulterants. A piece of cotton or cigarette filter is used to draw the liquid from the spoon and filter it into a syringe. A tourniquet is applied to the upper arm when the injection site is the crook of the arm, and it is applied to the lower forearm when the injection site is the back of the hand. The needle is slowly and carefully inserted at a 45-degree angle into an engorged vein. Missing a vein or "blowing the shot" usually results in a painful swollen blister, an experience of little or none of the drug's effects and a desperate search for more heroin.

After the needle has pierced the skin, the user pulls up the syringe plunger. If blood trickles up into the syringe, a vein has been successfully located. The user loosens the tourniquet and administers the dose by pushing down on the plunger of the syringe. Some users "boot" several times after all the heroin is injected, that is, they pull back on the plunger, draw out blood, and reinject it into their veins. This practice is based on the mistaken belief that booting enhances the drug's effects.

The experience of "getting high" on heroin depends on many variables, including the purity of the drug, the mode of ingestion, users' tolerance to and expectations of the drug's effects, and other idiosyncratic factors. Heroin crosses the blood-brain barrier relatively quickly, is converted in the brain to morphine, and binds rapidly to the brain's opioid receptors, known as delta, mu, and kappa. Each of these receptors is important in different brain functions; mu, for example is responsible for the pain-relieving effects of morphine.

A typical high includes feeling an initial flush and warmth throughout the body. The pupils of the eyes constrict—the smaller the pupils become, the more powerful the heroin. In addition, the rate and depth of respiration sharply diminish, cardiac function slows, and users often sweat, itch, and become nauseated. At this point, users seem to be asleep, but they can be aroused and respond to conversation. The "nodding off" period is followed by several hours of euphoria and relaxation during which users can function normally and exhibit few signs of intoxication except for constricted pupils.

More than 3 million Americans have tried heroin at least once in their lifetimes. Heroin became increasingly available in many large cities in the late 1990s and has also been appearing in more affluent communities. The number of heroin users rose from 325,000 in 1997 to 456,000 in 2000, a 40% increase. The number of new heroin users averaged 140,000 throughout the 1990s. In 2000, the number was 146,000. From 1999 to 2001, the average percentage of Americans who reported lifetime heroin use was 1.3%. Fewer than 2% of 8th, 10th, and 12th graders reported in 2001 that they had used heroin at least once during their lifetimes.

In 2001, approximately 5% of male arrestees and 8% of female arrestees overall tested positive for heroin in

33 cities across the U.S. Also in 2001, agents of the Drug Enforcement Administration (DEA) made 3306 heroin-related arrests, representing 9% of the agency's total number of arrests for drug-law violations that year. In addition, the DEA and other federal agencies seized more than 4300 pounds of heroin in the U.S. in 2001.

Heroin users represent a variety of different ethnic groups, reflecting the racial and ethnic origins of local populations. Across the country, the typical user is a (relatively) older, white male, under-educated, unemployed, and living in a large metropolitan area. Heroin users usually live in the area in which they purchase and use the drug. Furthermore, a segment of heroin users participate in a wide range of criminal activities, and polydrug use among heroin users is common. Heroin sellers and users are frequently the same persons.

The average age of first-time heroin users has been declining steadily since the late 1980s. In 1988, for example, the average age of first-time heroin users was 27; in 1992, it was 23; and in 1997, it was 18. Younger users are lured by the availability of inexpensive, high-quality heroin that can be sniffed or snorted. Snorters or sniffers usually graduate to injection after they develop more tolerance to the drug's effects. A significant percentage (86%) of new heroin users are under the age of 26.

The young users across the country lured by inexpensive, high-purity heroin that can be sniffed or smoked instead of injected find the average retail price of heroin has recently become significantly lower (e.g., the price of 1 gram was $2650 in 1991 and $1799 in 1998), whereas the average purity level of retail heroin has become significantly higher (4% purity in 1980; 17% purity in 1990; 25% purity in 1997; 35% purity in 1998). In mid-1999, heroin purity was highest in east coast cities. For example, Boston's heroin was 68% pure, New York's and Newark's heroin were 66% pure, and Philadelphia's heroin was 76% pure.

Consequences of Heroin Use

Heroin addiction is a chronic, relapsing disease characterized by tolerance, physical dependence, intense cravings, drug-seeking behaviors, and compulsive drug use. Addiction results in neurochemical and molecular changes in the brain. The repeated use of heroin, apart from its significant potential for abuse and dependence, can produce a wide range of life-threatening complications, stemming mostly from impurities in the drug, unsterile needles, and unknown levels of purity that can result in accidental overdoses. Medical interventions to counteract the effects of overdose include the administration of a heroin antagonist (e.g., naltrexone or naloxone) to block the opiate receptor sites of the brain and oxygen to help the person resume normal breathing.

Without medical assistance, heroin overdose will eventuate in death within 20–30 minutes following ingestion.

Increases in the purity of heroin are related to increases in consumption and in users' appearances for treatment in hospital emergency departments. The numbers of heroin-related emergency department episodes have increased dramatically from 32,000 in 1990 to more than 60,000 in each year from 1993 to 1998. Heroin-related emergency department episodes doubled between 1991 and 1996—from 35,898 to 73,846. Most heroin users who appear for treatment in emergency departments have injected the drug (when the mode of ingestion is known). Most heroin-related emergency department visits also are made by older (35-year-old and up) men.

A large proportion of heroin-related deaths occur when heroin is used with other drugs, most commonly cocaine and alcohol. Hospital admissions data indicate that heroin is often combined with benzodiazepines, synthetic opiates, cocaine, and alcohol. Following cocaine, heroin is the most common drug involved in drug-related deaths. In 1998, for example, 17% of all drug-related visits to emergency departments involved heroin, and 43% of drug-related deaths involved heroin. Emergency room visits attributable to heroin overdoses increased 47% from 1994 to 2001. In 2001, heroin was the third most frequently mentioned drug (following cocaine and marijuana) during visits to hospital emergency departments for drug-related medical problems and overdoses.

Heroin overdose deaths are caused by respiratory failure and often accompany preexisting medical conditions and the use of needles for ingestion. The sharing of needles is particularly risky because of the threat of transmitting HIV, hepatitis, and other blood-borne viruses. Chronic heroin users can also experience a wide range of other adverse health consequences such as collapsed veins, skin abscesses, pneumonia, infection of the heart lining and valves, and liver disease.

Treatment

Heroin users accounted for 15% of the persons admitted to drug treatment programs in 2001. More than two-thirds of those admitted to treatment were men, and more than 80% of the persons admitted to treatment reported that they had used heroin daily. The treatment of heroin addiction usually begins with detoxification; that is, gradually and safely lowering the blood level of heroin in a user's system by administering an oral opiate, usually methadone, for 1 or 2 weeks. Detoxification is a useful first step in the recovery process only when it leads to long-term treatment and aftercare. During detoxification, other medications, for example, clonidine, are administered to alleviate painful withdrawal symptoms.

The symptoms of initial heroin withdrawal are rarely life threatening to otherwise healthy adults, but they can be very distressful, including sweating, tremors, fever, agitation, vomiting, diarrhea, muscle spasms, and elevated blood pressure. Abrupt heroin withdrawal by chronic users who are in poor health can sometimes be fatal, but heroin withdrawal is considered much less dangerous than withdrawal from alcohol or barbiturates. Initial heroin withdrawal usually begins within 12 hours after the last dose of heroin and can last as long as 72–96 hours, depending on the severity and duration of drug use. Secondary heroin withdrawal can last for several months and is accompanied by signs and symptoms such as intense cravings for the drug, lassitude, dilated pupils, and low blood pressure. Users sometimes endure the pain of withdrawal in order to reduce their tolerance to the drug and reexperience the heightened rush that occurs during early use.

Three of the best-known and most widely researched treatments for heroin addiction are therapeutic communities (TCs), methadone maintenance therapy, and narcotic antagonists. The first TC was formed in the early 1950s by a group of exaddicts. The program, located in Visalia, California, was called Synanon. TCs view heroin addiction as a symptom of deep-seated adjustment problems and attempt to help addicts pursue socially constructive and drug-free lives. The therapist in the TC is the community itself, composed of staff and peers who serve as surrogate family members, role models of successful recovery, and facilitators in the recovery process. TCs operate in regimented, drug-free, and segregated environments. TC models are generally implemented in three phases: orientation, primary treatment, and reintegration. To be most effective, treatment in a TC should last at least 3 months and incorporate a community-based aftercare component.

Methadone was originally synthesized in Germany at the end of World War II as a replacement for morphine. Its effectiveness as a detoxification agent was first demonstrated in 1946 at the U.S. Public Health Service Hospital in Lexington, Kentucky. Methadone is roughly equivalent to morphine in its actions and potency. Unlike morphine, methadone's effects are longer lasting and more continuous, and methadone is neither intoxicating nor sedating, allowing users to engage safely in ordinary activities, for example, driving a car. Hundreds of thousands of heroin addicts have successfully completed methadone maintenance programs and refrained from subsequent drug use and crime. Long-term methadone treatment appears to have no serious adverse consequences. In conjunction with comprehensive therapy and supportive services, methadone enables addicts to stop using heroin and to resume more stable and productive lives.

Synthetic narcotic antagonists such as naltrexone (Trexan) are drugs that bind to opiate receptor sites but do not activate them, producing a functional blockade of the brain's neurons and preventing heroin from producing its relaxing and euphoric effects. To be most useful, naltrexone that is nonaddictive and long lasting must be administered regularly and accompanied by rehabilitative and supportive services. After naltrexone is stopped, the use of heroin produces its usual high. Consequently, attrition rates from naltrexone treatment are significant. High doses of naltrexone can result in liver damage and are contraindicated for persons with preexisting liver or kidney problems. A new form of treatment for heroin addiction, termed "ultrarapid opiate detoxification under general anesthesia," uses naltrexone to instantly flush or rid patients' bodies of opiates. This procedure detoxifies patients within 6 hours, causing little discomfort and resulting in complete withdrawal.

Similar to naltrexone, levo-alpha-acetyl-methadol (LAAM) is a synthetic opiate that blocks the effects of heroin for up to 72 hours with minimal side effects. In 1993, LAAM received FDA approval for the treatment of heroin addiction. The drug is administered orally three times per week and has few side effects. However, LAAM is addictive and produces euphoria and sedation until the patient develops a tolerance to the medication. Studies have shown that LAAM reduces heroin use among patients by up to 90%.

Finally, buprenorphine is another medication that shows great promise in the treatment of heroin addiction. The drug acts as an antagonist and an agonist, a drug that mimics the actions of the brain's neurotransmitters. Buprenorphine is especially appealing, compared with other heroin medications, because it produces only moderate opiate effects, has few withdrawal symptoms, and is less likely to result in physical dependence or drug overdoses.

ARTHUR J. LURIGIO

References and Further Reading

Abadinsky, H. (2001). *Drugs: An introduction.* Belmont, CA: Wadsworth.

Adrade, X., Sifaneck, S.J., and Neaigus, A. (1999). Dope sniffers in New York City: ethnography of heroin markets and patterns of use. *Journal of Drug Issues*, 22, 271–298.

Drug Enforcement Administration. (1999). *Drugs of abuse.* Washington, DC: Government Printing Office.

Falkowski, C.L. (2003). *Dangerous drugs.* Center City, MN: Hazelden.

National Institute on Drug Abuse. (1997). *NIDA Research Report: Heroin abuse and addiction.* Rockville, MD: NIDA.

Scott, J.M. (1969). *The White Poppy: A History of Opium.* New York, NY: Funk and Wagnalls.

See also **Drug Use: Extent and Correlates; Drug Use: The Law**

Hindu Legal Traditions

Hinduism is estimated to have more than 800 million followers, and is currently the "third largest" and "second fastest growing" world religion (Esposito et al., 2002). It is most commonly identified with the republic of India and the neighboring kingdom of Nepal. However, more recently, it has spread to other parts of the world such as South East Asia, the U.K., the West Indies and North America by the Indian diaspora, and to a lesser extent, by picking up local adherents. Hinduism is the oldest religion and way of life that has been continuously practiced in the world and is said to date back 3500–4000 years (Glenn, 2000). The religion itself is generally thought to incorporate the beliefs of migrants to India of that period from west of the Khyber Pass along with those of the indigenous people of earlier local Indian civilizations. Precepts and ideas associated with its spiritual practices (for Hinduism is a combination of many related traditions) developed as a result of what believers claim to be revealed knowledge coupled with a continuous (oral and written) tradition that has carried it to the present day.

At the outset, it should be made clear that although it is possible to outline features of classical Hindu legal philosophy and related principles, it is difficult to connect them directly to contemporary Western criminal law and criminal justice as well as to criminological theory and debate. The reasons underlying this difficulty are twofold. First, India, the country with the most direct links to Hindu legal tradition, has as a matter of choice, following independence from the U.K. in 1947, opted to follow British legal traditions that after nearly two centuries of colonialism were well-embedded into Indian polity and society. (Coincidentally, both Mahatma Gandhi, the father of the movement for an independent India, and Jawaharlal Nehru, its first Prime Minister, were British trained barristers.) Consequently, it is difficult to find examples of the applications of Hindu legal thought to contemporary issues of crime and justice. Second, criminology as a formal discipline is essentially a creation of Western thought following the Enlightenment. Much of its theoretical development for the last two and a half centuries has also, until recently, taken place mostly in Western societies, reflecting, in terms of crime and punishment, their premises, concerns, and preoccupations. As a result, connecting Hindu legal traditions to contemporary crime and criminal justice

has to be carried out mostly by implication and connotation.

Hinduism, unlike many other world religions, welcomes, encompasses, and even encourages diversity and heterodoxy in belief, ritual, and practice. Esposito et al. (2002, 274) comment:

> What we label "Hinduism" ranges from monotheism to polytheism, from monism to materialism and atheism; from nonviolent ethics to moral systems that see as imperative elaborate blood sacrifices to sustain the world; from critical scholastic philosophical discussion to the cultivation of sublime, mystical, wordless inner experiences.

For example, Fernhout (1995) points out that both Mahatma Gandhi and his assassin Nathuram Godse were able to find in the *Bhagavad Gita* (one of Hinduism's most beloved sacred texts) justifications for their practice of nonviolence and violence, respectively. Hamilton (1998, 67) adds, "The sheer diversity of belief and practice encompassed by the term Hinduism in India has posed severe problems for the sociologist of religion." Given such variety, the lack of one divinely inspired prophet, and any accepted supreme leadership, it would be a mistake to suggest that a single unified strand of Hindu tradition exists. In the following discussion of Hindu legal traditions we point to three commonly acknowledged characteristics that scholars have examined for their relevance to contemporary discussions of crime and justice.

First, we pay attention to the source documents for Hindu law (all originally written in Sanskrit) and the earliest delineations of the rules and expectations that govern Hindu life. Scholars of Hinduism locate the origins of Hindu customs in the *Vedas* composed around 1500 BC. It is also customary to note that these precepts were explained and elaborated in the *Smritis* (composed around 500 BC) and the *Dharmasastras* (from around 100 AD). Among the latter (of which there are three) and in terms of law the most influential is the work of Manu (often described as the preeminent Hindu lawgiver). Traditional Hindu law, beginning with Manu, is divided into 18 areas identified by Glenn (2000, 258) as follows:

> Recovery of debt, deposit, sale without ownership, partnership, resumption of gift, non-payment of wages, non-performance of agreements, rescission of sale and

purchase, disputes between master and servant, boundary disputes, assault, defamation, theft, robbery and violence, adultery, mutual duties of husband and wife, partition and inheritance, and gambling and betting.

The areas of law set forth include both civil and criminal matters. Within the latter, they take into account what we would classify as violent offenses, property offenses, and public order offenses. The caste positions of the offender and the victim are explicitly invoked in calibrating both offense seriousness and official reaction with the usual resultant inequality. The other divergence from major, formal systems of law is that these rules and their interpretations were enunciated and applied through religious teaching and exhortation. "Hindu law is not official law, in its classic sources, nor did it tend to large institutions, or potentially corrupt institutions" (Glenn 2000, 257). Currently, only two of the 18 areas are operative (even in India) in a much modified form (although Menski, 2003, has argued vehemently that concepts from Hindu law continue to maintain their vitality under modern guises). The two surviving areas include the areas of partition and inheritance and mutual expectations of husband and wife.

Second, we consider two interrelated Hindu principles, that of *dharma* and *karma,* and their implications for criminal punishment. *Dharma* "is the totality of the duties of individuals in society according to their status and stage in life" (Neufeldt, 2001, 146), some of which, though not all, were traditionally attached to one's caste. The *karma* principle asserts "that each act results in a potency which survives the act itself, a potency which has the potential for either merit or demerit in this life or in future lives" (Neufeldt, 2001, 147). A simple linking of these two principles to the commission of crime by an individual would imply that he or she is acting in contravention of his or her *dharma* and that such negative action results in the attainment of a demerit in a system of cosmic accounting. Ordinarily, the burden of demerits accumulated in this life is to be endured in the next life. However, rather than leaving all consequences to future lives, and thereby, risking wholesale infringement of societal *dharma*, classical Hindu law allows that "for certain acts that contravene divinely ordained law, the legal or judicial authorities would exact punishment in this life" (Neufeldt, 2001, 147). The case being made here is for the state to intervene and practice general and specific deterrence. As Day (1982, 67) points out:

> This epitomizes the utilitarian expediency of criminal law through the investigation of crimes, the apprehension of criminals, the use of torture to elicit confessions, the infliction of bodily mutilations, and administration of capital penalties with or without torture, or prescriptions of fines and atonements as substitutes for them.

Thus, individual actions and their consequences (whether initiated by the state or the gods) are inexorably linked into the cycle of birth, death, and rebirth until the attainment of salvation through good karma and the correct performance of dharma. Individual and state through crime and punishment are inextricably connected to the eternal rhythms of the universe.

Third, although punishment was primarily meted to an individual with the aim of retribution, it "could be seen as a form of redemption or restoration in an ultimate sense. It had the kind of cleansing power that would guarantee entry into heaven" (Neufeldt, 2001, 155). There is a great deal of emphasis placed in Hindu law on the importance of penance (known as *prayaschitta*) and expiation, as punishment or as one part of it, for transgressions large and small. Following remorse, shame, and confession, there is scope for the individual offender to make efforts toward repentance and reconciliation with those who were victimized through apology and atonement for harms caused. This process, if engaged in with sincerity, reflects well on the offender's *karma*. In classical Hindu law, forms of penance can range from suicide (for killing a Brahmin, the highest caste and keepers of the religious or intellectual tradition) to fasting, reciting a certain number of prayers, giving gifts to the family of those offended against or to a temple, performing temple-related chores, going on a pilgrimage (which, in the days before mass travel, could be a hazardous undertaking) etc. depending on the seriousness of the offense. As an example, during the struggle for India's independence in the first half of the 20th century, several demonstrations resulted in mob violence. As a result, Mahatma Gandhi, because he was ashamed of what his nonviolent movement had come to, did penance (mainly through fasting, prayer, social withdrawal, and periodic vows of silence) to "gain more credit from God" (Klostermaier, 2000, 136). The process described earlier can be easily linked to Braithwaite's (1989) conception of reintegrative shaming. Stringent disapproval is placed on the offender's wrongful actions, yet hope is also held out for welcoming the offender back into society, following his or her personal experiencing of shame and acceptance of responsibility for the harm done.

Neufeldt (2001) believes that the Hindu spiritual roots of contemporary ideas regarding restorative justice are to be found within this penance–expiation attribute of its religious culture. While allowing the offender to gain karmic redemption (credit for the future life), the practice of penance and expiation also focused on the here and now:

> Specific penalties had built-in attempts at restitution. In the case of some forms of theft, a part of the punishment consisted of paying back to the victim the value of the

property stolen in addition to fines. In the case of injury, the assailant could be made to pay the cost of restoring the victim to health. In the case of the destruction of a pond, there was provision for having the perpetrator repair the pond in addition to paying a fine. (Neufeldt, 2001, 155)

The purpose of penance and expiation is truly comprehensive in that its concerns are for the transgressor, the victim, the social order, and the temporal present as well as the future.

Contemporary criminologists, surveying the welter of competing and contradictory criminological schools, theories, and explanations have reason for bewilderment. Similarly, criminal justice practitioners struggling with the multiplicity of sentencing and punishment objectives, claims and counter-claims about what works and what does not, have reason for puzzlement. For both groups, there may be some comfort in knowing that an ancient belief system contemplated the most profound questions of human existence and acknowledged that at the end of our quest for causal truths and functional pathways to change, pluralism, diversity, and all-encompassing concern are parts of the answers we will discover.

N. Prabha Unnithan

References and Further Reading

Braithwaite, J. (1989) *Crime, Shame and Reintegration.* Melbourne, Australia: Cambridge University Press.

Day, T.P. (1982) *The Conception of Punishment in Early Indian Literature.* Waterloo, Canada: Wilfred Laurier University Press.

Esposito, J.L., Fasching, D.J., and Lewis, T. (2002) *World Religions Today.* New York, NY: Oxford University Press.

Fernhout, R. (1995) Combating the Enemy: The use of Scripture in Gandhi and Godse. *Human Rights and Religious Values: An Uneasy Relationship?* An-Na'im, A.A., Gort, J.D., Jansen, H. and Vroom, H.M. (Eds.), pp. 120–132. Grand Rapids, MI: William B. Eerdmans Publishing Company.

Glenn, H.P. (2000) *Legal Traditions of the World.* New York, NY: Oxford University Press.

Hamilton, M.B. (1998) *Sociology and the World's Religions.* New York, NY: St. Martin's Press.

Klostermaier, K.K. (2000) *Hinduism: A Short Introduction.* Oxford, UK: Oneworld Publications.

Menski, W.F. (2003) *Hindu Law: Beyond Tradition and Modernity.* Oxford, UK: Oxford University Press.

Neufeldt, R. (2001) Justice in Hinduism. *The Spiritual Roots of Restorative Justice.* Hadley, M.L. (Ed.), pp. 143–160. Albany, NY: State University of New York Press.

See also **India, Crime and Justice in**

Hirschi, Travis

In 1960–61, Travis Hirschi was a teaching assistant for a statistics course at the University of California at Berkeley that was taught by Hanan Selvin. During the summer of 1961, Selvin asked Hirschi to be a research assistant on a project designed to catalog statistical techniques then in use in delinquency research. In 1962, Hirschi and Selvin submitted a manuscript entitled "The Methodological Adequacy of Delinquency Research" to The Free Press, which later became the classic work *Delinquency Research: An Appraisal of Analytic Methods.* The final book bore no resemblance to the original grant, and instead was a critique of quantitative delinquency research. This project gave Hirschi a familiarity with the field of delinquency, and gave him the skills necessary to work with the Survey Research Center at Berkeley starting in 1964. These events would prove essential to the development of Hirschi's classic explication of social control theory.

At this time, Hirschi became involved with the Richmond Youth Project as an unpaid worker. This project was a large-scale survey of western Contra Costa County (California), directed by Alan B. Wilson and Charles C. Glock. This project centered on occupational and career prospects in the community. Hirschi participated in the construction of the questionnaire for the schoolchildren and became deputy director of the project. Hirschi had read the work of F. Ivan Nye, Jackson Toby, Irving Piliavin (who also worked in the Survey Research Center), David Matza, and Erving Goffman. From these and other sources, he devised items relevant to comparisons of social control theory and the currently more popular theories of crime, theories he labeled "cultural deviance" and "strain." These comparisons are the major focus of his dissertation, entitled "Infraction as Action," better known to criminologists as *Causes of Delinquency. Causes of Delinquency* is an exposition and test of social control theory that is currently one of the most popular theoretical frameworks in the field. In 1966, Hirschi became an acting assistant professor at Berkeley and accepted a similar position at the University of Washington in 1967. He completed the dissertation in 1968 and that same year was cowinner of the C. Wright Mills Award for *Delinquency Research* with Selvin.

Hirschi accepted a position as professor of sociology at the University of California–Davis in 1971. In 1974, he was the Visiting Pinkerton Professor at the State University of New York at Albany, where he established a working relationship with Michael Hindelang and renewed his acquaintance with a former undergraduate student from Davis, Michael Gottfredson. While visiting Albany, Hirschi joined with Hindelang and Joseph Weis on a proposal to evaluate the psychometric properties of self-report measures of delinquency. A year later, he returned to Albany as a regular member of the faculty to work with Hindelang on the self-report project. While there, he collaborated with Hindelang on papers on the correlates of delinquency, such as the relationship between IQ and delinquency, and the book *Measuring Delinquency* (1981). This book is widely considered a major contribution to our understanding of the value and limitations of the self-report method of measuring delinquency.

At Albany, Hirschi also began the first of many collaborative efforts with Michael Gottfredson. Before leaving Albany in 1981 for the University of Arizona, Hirschi and Gottfredson drafted a paper on the age–crime relationship that argued that the relationship did not vary from one society or culture to another. This paper was the foundation for their later attack on longitudinal and criminal career research and laid the groundwork for the crime and criminality distinction that would be central in *A General Theory of Crime*, published in 1990. This book is an explication of self-control theory that argues that criminal acts result from the offenders' failure to consider their long-term consequences. Hirschi retired from the University of Arizona as Regents Professor in 1997.

Social control theory is an excellent example of Hirschi's ability to influence the research agendas of criminology. Hirschi did not invent social control theory, but he did outline and revive a theory that students of delinquency had ignored for decades. *Causes of Delinquency* was so successful in this respect that between 1969 and the early 1990s, 71 empirical tests of Hirschi's version of social control theory appeared in journals and doctoral dissertations. Social control theory has also influenced more recent theoretical work, particularly that dealing with change in delinquency over the life course. Self-control theory has been even more successful at influencing research in the 1990s. Research testing the general theory has been a prominent feature in the leading criminological journals during this period.

Unlike many leading criminologists during the formative years of the discipline, Hirschi had an iconoclastic stance toward the prevailing assumptions of sociology. Indeed, a consistent theme in his work is the tendency to question or attack the currently fashionable thinking in the study of crime. For example, at a time when many criminologists were skeptical about such arguments, Hirschi (with Michael J. Hindelang) published an article in 1977 showing a close association between low intelligence quotients (IQs) and juvenile offending. One source of this critical stance is Hirschi's belief that theoretical, substantive, and methodological considerations cannot be viewed in isolation. Thus, when he disputed longitudinal research, he did so on theoretical as well as methodological grounds. He has opposed theoretical integration and has argued for acceptance of individual differences between offenders and nonoffenders. Rather than relying exclusively on the tenets of contemporary sociology, Hirschi's work draws from a variety of sources dating back to the Enlightenment. On the one hand, Hirschi acknowledged acceptance of the underlying assumptions of Thomas Hobbes and Jeremy Bentham. On the other hand, Hirschi drew support from a particular interpretation of the work of Emile Durkheim and early sociologists in the U.S. whose work had fallen out of favor in the discipline. Hirschi's later work with Gottfredson shows that Gottfredson also was willing to break with contemporary thinking about crime. Working together, they moved even further from the taken-for-granted assumptions in social science.

Despite his sometimes controversial views, criminologists have recognized the excellence in Hirschi's work by electing him to the presidency of the American Society of Criminology in 1982–83 and awarding him the Edwin H. Sutherland Award (for outstanding contributions to the discipline of criminology) in 1986.

CHRISTOPHER J. SCHRECK

Biography

Born in Rockville, Utah, April 15, 1935. Educated at University of Utah, B.S., 1957; M.S., 1958; University of California, Berkeley, Ph.D. in Sociology, 1968; Assistant to Associate Professor, University of Washington, Seattle, 1967–1971; Professor, University of California–Davis, 1971–1977 (Chair, 1972–1974); Professor, State University of New York at Albany, 1977–1981; Professor to Regents Professor, University of Arizona, 1981–1997; C. Wright Mills Award from the Society for the Study of Social Problems for the book that best exemplifies outstanding social science research (for *Delinquency Research: An Appraisal of Analytic Methods*), 1968; president of the American Society of Criminology, 1982–83; Edwin H. Sutherland Award, American Society of Criminology, 1986.

Selected Works

Delinquency Research: An Appraisal of Analytic Methods (with Selvin, H.C.), 1967.

Causes of Delinquency, 1969.

Intelligence and delinquency (with Hindelang, M.J.), *American Sociological Review* 42, 1977.

Measuring Delinquency, 1981 (with Hindelang, M.J. and Weis, J.G.).

Age and the explanation of crime (with Gottfredson, M.R.), *American Journal of Sociology* 89, 1983.

The methodological adequacy of longitudinal research on crime (with Gottfredson, M.R.), *Criminology* 25, 1987.

A General Theory of Crime (with Gottfredson, M.R.), 1990.

References and Further Reading

Greenberg, D.F. 1985. Age, crime, and social explanation, *American Journal of Sociology* 91.

Hirschi, T. and Gottfredson, M.R. 1985. Comment on Greenberg, *American Journal of Sociology* 91.

Simons, R.L. 1978. The meaning of the IQ-delinquency relationship, *American Sociological Review* 43.

Hirschi, T. and Hindelang, M.J. 1978. Reply to Ronald L. Simons, *American Sociological Review* 43.

Blumstein, A., Cohen, J., and Farrington, D.P. 1988. Criminal career research: Its value for criminology, *Criminology* 26.

Gottfredson, M.R. and Hirschi, T. 1988. Science, public policy, and the career paradigm, *Criminology* 26.

Roshier, B. 1989. *Controlling Crime: The Classical Perspective in Criminology*. Chicago, IL: Lyceum Books.

Hirschi, T. and Gottfredson, M.R. 1995. Control theory and the life course perspective, *Studies of Crime and Crime Prevention* 4.

Sampson, R.J. and Laub, J.H. 1995. Understanding variability in lives through time: Contributions of life-course criminology, *Studies of Crime and Crime Prevention* 4.

Cohen, L.E. and Vila, B.J. 1996. Self-control and social control: An exposition of the Gottfredson-Hirschi/Sampson-Laub debate, *Studies of Crime and Crime Prevention* 5.

Taylor, C. 2001. The relationship between social control and self-control: Tracing Hirschi's criminological career, *Theoretical Criminology* 5.

See also **Juvenile Delinquency, History of; Juvenile Delinquency: Extent, Correlates, and Trends**

Historical Research

Public officials who project prison, court, and police budgets need to know the levels and types of crime to expect in future years, just as scholars who think carefully about the causes of crime need to know how it has been affected by social change in years past. Many experts need sound information about crime trends, and many groups develop such information. Historical research into crime attempts to discover the actual course of crime over the past 6 or 7 centuries, and to relate it to the vast changes that the West has undergone since the 15th century. Both sociologists and historians have embarked on these studies, and much has been learned. But the problems in determining precisely the distribution of crime in society as well as its historical trends need to be considered before an estimate of its historical course can be described.

Problems of Measurement

As the incidence of crime is largely unpredictable—like an earthquake—it can be measured only after it has already taken place. Some crimes are never uncovered and some cases that appear criminal, are not. All attempts to measure crime reflect not simply underlying criminal behavior but also biases inherent in the measurement process itself. Several modern sources of information about crime include data gathered and compiled after the fact by governmental officials (the Center for Disease Control and Prevention, police, coroners, the courts, and correctional departments), by researchers in contact with offenders (self-report studies), and data on victims collected by public and private survey groups. In earlier periods when village priests dealt with misbehavior, church records and coroner's rolls were also useful sources.

Most of what we know about crime today comes from at least one of these sources. Still each assesses a distinct facet of crime and encounters distinct problems. Crime data issued by the courts and police have become a rich source of information regarding criminality especially during the modern era, and the biases that creep into such data need to be taken into account. Only since the Great Depression have crime statistics cumulated by the FBI for the whole nation become available.

Police in particular are subject to several pressures that distort their crime data. Many large cities have more than one police department—one that patrols the parks, another that patrols the subways, another that handles street crime, another that polices university grounds, and another that focuses on white-collar crime. All these departments are independent and very loosely coordinated. At times, they refuse to cooperate with each other and do not always report their arrests to higher authorities. Thus, FBI data for the whole nation inevitably are incomplete and they must estimate the missing amount.

Some large departments with professional leadership, high morale, careful recruitment, and strong training programs are more effective in solving certain major criminal cases than others. The clearance rate of departments in major cities with homicide, for example, is slightly better than that with departments in cities with less than 1,000,000 citizens but more than 250,000. Eight police departments serving cities of at least 1,000,000 people regularly clear about 60% of their homicides, and departments in the next larger category clear about 55% (FBI, 1998, Table 25, 201–202).

Departments in small towns, however, often have better crime statistics too, thanks to local support and cooperation. They may not have much experience with major crimes, but they receive complaints and tips from local people about minor crimes and are able to solve a much larger portion of their minor crimes than departments in large cities. On this basis, they have a more accurate picture of what kinds of offenders they encounter. In towns with populations under 10,000, for example, 27.6% of the motor vehicle thefts were cleared by arrests in 1997, but in cities with populations of more than one million only 8.8% were (FBI, 1998, Table 25, 201–202).

Something should also be said about inaccurate population estimates and their impact on crime rates. It is very difficult to estimate population levels of certain neighborhoods today undergoing social upheaval. In 1990, for example, the census undercount of Blacks is estimated reliably at 4.6%, of American Indians on reservations at 12.2%, and of Hispanics at 5% (Harrison, 2001, 15). *All underestimates of a group's size result in overestimates of its crime rates.*

Taking this idea one step further, during the 1840s and 1850s a huge wave of impoverished Irish immigrants swept into Boston, New York, and Philadelphia, and during the Civil War large numbers of people were transplanted from place to place (armies, slaves, and refugees) so that local cities fluctuated wildly in size from one time to another. For many decades from 1840 onward, it was difficult to gauge accurately the population in major eastern cities, though crime as measured by police arrests suffered no such problem. The U.S. Census Bureau surveyed Massachusetts at the beginning of each decade and the state itself carried out another in the middle year. But with the vast influx of Irish immigrants and the social turmoil accompanying the Civil War many people were missed. A census undercount of major American cities existed for years, and although published arrest figures were probably accurate, arrests per 10,000 (as computed

in those days) were certainly inflated as a result of an undercount in the census.

By comparing genealogical records of the time with census returns, Adams and Kasakoff (1991, 529–530) have determined that in 1850 the national count of males in the U.S. Census was too low by 19% and of females by 23%, and *the undercount was greatest among mobile young men of 20–34 years*— about 26% were not counted (Adams and Kasakoff, 1991, Tables 1 and 4). Thus historical studies of cities that used census data to compute crime rates overestimated the rate of crime to a sizable extent (cf. Ferdinand, 1992, Ch. 5). An undercount of 26% meant that the crime rate was overestimated by at least 20.7% in major northeastern cities. Since New York, Philadelphia, and Boston absorbed a very large number of immigrants and experienced extreme turmoil during the Civil War, their undercount was even more than 26%—probably in the area of 33%.

Crime data must be presented as rates per unit of population to enable comparisons among large and small cities, but if the population is not counted accurately in major cities, crime rates are distorted and comparisons with less turbulent cities are misleading. Thus, crime rates for New York, Philadelphia, and Boston during the 1850s and 1860s probably overstate the crime rate by at least one-fourth.

A different kind of problem plagues comparisons of criminality during different historical epochs in the same city. It is common knowledge that police departments follow several different models and that these distinctive models operate at different levels of effectiveness. James Q. Wilson (1968) has identified three common patterns of operation among police departments. Service departments tend to be small, with low wages, but close to their community and informal with few authority levels and little specialization. Watchman departments tend to be larger, politically controlled, and serving ethnically diverse cities in an unaggressive fashion. They seek to dampen interethnic conflict and try above all to preserve stability in the community. Legalistic departments emphasize careful recruitment, thorough training, high morale, and political independence and favor a careful and dispassionate administration of the law (Wilson, 1968, Chs. 6–8).

This typology, though often criticized as outdated and oversimplified, has been widely used in police research. As the city a police department serves grows, the department often becomes more formal and more isolated from the community (Ferdinand, 1976). It evolves from a service to a legalistic or watchman pattern, and its rapport with the community—and therefore, its complaints, arrests, and clearance rates—declines. We have already seen that changes in clearance rates can have an impact on estimates of delinquency, but long-term changes in urban arrest rates over several generations may also reflect such changes. Long-term declines in violent crime in Boston and Salem, cited below, to some extent no doubt reflect such shifts in police style.

Court data must also be used with an eye to the peculiarities of a changing court system. Courts deal with defendants who have been arrested and charged with a crime, and all the biases and distortions of upstream phases are reflected in defendants in court. Even more importantly, different criminal courts normally have jurisdiction over narrow segments of the criminal spectrum. City, state, and federal courts address distinct crime segments and each follows different procedures. As different courts specialize in different types of crime, several courts at different levels in a city provide a fuller picture than any one of them can individually of the city's crime problem. Concentrating on just one court in a city can be misleading.

Pitfalls also await those who compare the activities of a single court over time. For example, the same court may change its name and jurisdiction with the result that historians might inadvertently compare a lower court with a higher court. Boston's Municipal Court was organized in 1800, but in 1859 it was renamed the Superior Court of Suffolk County. The Boston Police Court was founded in 1822, and in 1859 it became the Municipal Court of Boston. Thus, a comparison of the Municipal Court in 1850 with the Municipal Court in 1870 would compare a higher court with a lower one. Despite these problems, when used with appropriate cautions the courts and the police are very useful sources of information regarding crime, and for some historical periods, they offer virtually the only systematic data available.

In the last century, big-city police departments have become politicized and some have come under heavy fire for "managing" their crime data. Most large departments, from time to time, probably resort to "management," but it is possible to identify sharp increases (or decreases) as "political." It usually does not involve all crimes, and marked discrepancies among related crimes, e.g., murder versus aggravated assault, probably indicate an "adjustment."

Other problems of measurement are rooted in the changing character of the law and crime. In medieval times up to about the 17th century criminal violence was commonplace and was hardly regarded as a crime, but property crime was seen as serious and possibly indicating a "professional" criminal. Infanticide and forcible rape were hidden, aggravated assault and even murder in rural regions were not reported, and domestic violence was rarely noted.

On the other hand, many accidental deaths were regarded as homicide. The law did not recognize manslaughter or larceny until at least the 14th century; but as these legal distinctions took hold, the rate of murder over the last 200 years declined some (though not the rates and of manslaughter and larceny). Similarly refinements and improvements in medicine probably also led to reduced crime rates. We know that as medical practice became more effective it led to gradual shifts from homicide to aggravated assault. And better policing of domestic violence, forcible rape, infanticide, and aggravated assault led to more crime, at first, but as the likelihood of being charged went up, the incidence of crime probably went down. Yet just how these several changes have balanced out has never been carefully examined.

We do know, however, that the crime rate has dropped sharply since the medieval era, and that improvements in census taking, medicine, or policing cannot explain it all. Advancing urbanization and civilization have no doubt overwhelmed all the specific factors mentioned above, and produced a long-term decline in crime of large proportions throughout the West (see Garland, 1990, Ch. 10; Ferdinand, 1999).

Early Criminality

As the police did not exist before the modern era, our knowledge of premodern criminality is limited. It is based largely on early court records, church documents, or coroners' rolls, and research requires a painstaking effort, including mastering hand-written medieval Latin, to collect useful data from original documents. The completeness of these early records, however, is questionable. The early courts generally dealt with misbehavior among the gentry—an aristocrat involved in a vicious dispute with a high-ranking neighbor. But when the same aristocrat raped or physically abused a peasant, nothing happened. And as we have seen, actual accidents were sometimes treated as homicides. The medieval treatment of crime corresponds only very roughly to today's methods, and our studies of historical crime—whether of church records, court documents, or coroner's rolls—skim only the surface. Still there was plenty of surface to skim.

Studies of medieval towns often report very high levels of violent crime and low levels of property crime. For example, Scandinavian historians agree that the homicide rate in the 1500s was at least 20 times today's rate (see v. Hofer, 2000, 60), and Hanawalt's (2001, 98) study of coroner's rolls in 14th-century London revealed an annual homicide rate of about 44 per 100,000, 110 times the modern rate of 0.4 per 100,000 in London. Her findings incidentally included very few infanticide cases. Nearly all scholars agree that medieval communities from the Baltic to the Mediterranean were dangerous places. An historian, Given, estimates that "every person in England in the thirteenth century, if he did not personally witness a murder, knew, or knew of someone who had been killed. (Given, 1977, 40).

The end of the 16th century witnessed a mounting concern in England about crime. Judges and others regularly lamented the rising tide of lawlessness, though historical evidence suggests that violent crime had not increased significantly since the 14th century. In rural areas, crime was more typical of yeomen than peasants, whereas the gentry defied the local courts and were rarely punished. Justice may not have been sure in 16th-century England, but it was certainly swift. Those who were sentenced to die were, in the absence of a pardon or reprieve, marched out of the courtroom and promptly hanged. Nevertheless, many legal loopholes existed, including pardons, both special and general, and insanity, pregnancy, and a tender age. The most common loophole was benefit of clergy, which by the 16th century had been extended to all who could read (i.e., the upper classes) but was limited to cases of minor theft.

Moreover, medieval definitions of homicide embraced many forms of accidental death that today would not find their way into criminal court, and deadly weapons today can kill from afar without warning. But 500 years ago, poisons, arrows, spears, swords, fists, feet, and daggers playeda role in dangerous confrontations. High rates of homicide reported in the medieval period naturally reflect these differences, and infanticide, though common, was prosecuted haphazardly. All in all, however, the level of violence was most likely substantially greater in late medieval Europe than now.

Beattie's study of 17th-century Surrey and Sussex counties found a rate of 5.7 homicide indictments per 100,000 for 1663–1694, but with the growth of commerce in 17th-century England, violent crime receded generally. By 1780–1802 indictments had dropped to 2.3 per 100,000, whereas property crime increased slightly from 53 indictments per 100,000 in the 1690s to 65 by the 1760s. Indictments for both kinds of crimes were more common in urban than rural areas, but rural and urban areas both showed steep declines in violent crime and slight increases in property crime.

In colonial America, the crime rate was higher. The violent crime rate in Boston in the early decades of the 18th century was 37 indictments per 100,000 between 1703 and 1732, and property crime in Boston was nearly twice as high as England's at 123 indictments per 100,000 (Ferdinand, 1980). This contrast is striking in that puritan New England had a reputation among the colonies for sober conventionality and little crime.

Figures for lesser crimes are more difficult to evaluate. Many minor crimes were settled privately, and premodern records no doubt seriously underestimate their incidence. Moreover, many victims were reluctant to take their complaints to the courts. The prisons were disease-ridden and even short-term prison sentences often meant death. Unless there was a powerful reason for reporting a criminal offense to the court, many victims simply suffered in silence or settled matters in their own way.

Crime in the Modern Era

By the 18th century, English courts had achieved a high degree of independence and authority in an increasingly secular society, and estimates of criminality based upon court records were becoming more reliable. In the 18th century, early modern legal institutions were already at work fashioning the structures and procedures of a modern court system. By 1830, the training of lawyers and judges had improved, criminal procedures were rationalized, and new shortcuts for coping with a mounting volume of minor crime were invented (Ferdinand, 1992, 65–66). Thus as criminality changed in the modern period, legal institutions were also developing. As both processes occurred simultaneously, it is difficult to say which picture crime studies reflect. In most cases, the picture is a double exposure depicting both.

Criminality in the 19th Century

A number of studies relying heavily on court records have focused on 19th century cities and nations. Systematic police data first became available around the middle of the 19th century, and several investigators have made use of this important source. Virtually every study reports a steady, substantial decline in crime especially during the late 19th century. In France, serious crime fell by nearly 90% between 1826 and 1954 (Lodhi and Tilly, 1973). In England and Wales indictable offenses declined by 79% between 1842 and 1891, and in London they declined by 63% between the 1820s and 1870s (Gatrell and Hadden, 1972). Much of the decline in London reflects a sharp drop in violent crime of about 68% between the 1830s and the 1860s. Larceny indictments also decreased in London by 68% from about 220 per 100,000 in the 1830s and 1840s to about 70 per 100,000 in the 1850s. In Stockholm (Gurr, Grabosky, and Hula, 1977, 256–257) the rate of theft fell from 75 per 100,000 in the 1840s to about 22 in 1900, for a 71% decline, and the number of persons sentenced for assault or breach of the peace dropped from about 400 per 100,000 in the 1840s to about 60 in the 1920s, an 85% decrease.

One of the few studies to describe the opposite focused on the Black Country—an area around Birmingham, England, that became a major steel-producing region in the late 18th and 19th centuries. Larceny committals to trial rose substantially from 91 per 100,000 in 1835 to about 262 in 1860, and committals to trial for offenses against the person more than doubled from about 6 per 100,000 to about 14 (Philips, 1977, 143). This study shows that rural areas and small towns exhibited sharply higher levels of criminality as they industrialized, whereas studies of medieval cities such as London and Stockholm recorded declines in serious criminality as they and their surrounding regions developed.

Studies of criminality in 19th century American cities tend to agree with these broad findings (see Ferdinand, 1992, 1980, 1967). In Boston, the peak in recorded violent crime occurred in 1824. In 1824, shortly after the Boston Police Court was established, it recorded 1431 prosecutions per 100,000 for crimes against the person, a figure 1.67 times larger than the 853 arrests per 100,000 recorded by the Boston police in 1997. The year 1824 was relatively calm in Boston, and census undercounts were not so important as 30 years later. Fluctuations in crime corresponding to wars and economic cycles were apparent over the years, but the low mark in serious crime came during 1928–1930, when the rate, 650 per 100,000, was only 45% of the 1824 peak. Similar sharp declines in serious crime have been found during the 19th century in Buffalo, New York, and Salem, Massachusetts.

On the other hand, a study of crime in Rockford, Illinois, founded in the 1840s, revealed that violent crime rose sharply from 1882–1884 to 1905–1907 (Ferdinand, 1976, 309). After declining in the first half of the 20th century, it rose sharply again during the 1950s and 1960s. Thus, established cities like Boston, Salem, and Buffalo enjoyed declining violent crime rates as they modernized, whereas newly industrializing communities suffered rising violent crime.

The distinctive crime patterns of old European cities have been explored carefully by Zehr in a series of studies of German and French communities. Older medieval cities, though relatively low in violent crime, experienced substantial increases in violence as they industrialized. Low levels of property crime and high levels of violence were characteristic of premodern villages and rural areas, though industrialization transformed them into metropolitan centers with low levels of violent crime and high levels of theft. Four distinct patterns were discovered by Zehr: (1) low levels of violent crime in medieval cities, (2) very low levels of property crimes in medieval rural areas; and two transitional patterns, (3) old cities that were transformed into urban, industrial centers with initially rising levels of violence but ultimately declining levels, and (4) rural areas or villages that were transformed into new industrial centers with little violence but steep increases in theft. This pattern in Europe, however, does not seem to correspond closely to that found in the U.S.

Here legal institutions began to play a broad role in controlling public behavior in the 19th century. As criminal courts displaced the church, we often see a sharp increase in criminal cases, well beyond the volume handled by the church. At first, the courts kept to the church's standard and prosecuted many minor crimes. Some of the early rise probably reflects this zealousness. But it probably also derives from changes in urban life, as noted elsewhere (Ferdinand, 1999). As these changes (legal and social) do not act in close synchrony, the overall crime trends of different kinds of cities may fail to follow a consistent pattern.

Criminality in the 20th Century

During the late 19th and early 20th centuries, criminality in Western societies, particularly property crime, fluctuated in response to changing economic conditions and wars. Periods of economic distress usually resulted in higher levels of property crime, especially burglary and theft, whereas prosperity typically resulted in lower levels. But oddly enough juvenile delinquency rates followed a very different path during the 1930s and 1940s (Glaser and Rice, 1959). They rose during prosperity and fell during the Depression. During this period, juveniles constituted a small but growing part of the crime problem as peer groups and youth culture emerged in the public schools. Overall, however, the trend in property crime was downward through World War II.

This decline in criminality during the late 19th and early 20th centuries in America, a period of intense industrialization and urbanization, is somewhat surprising. Urbanization usually means rising crime rates as small towns become larger. This decline in criminality probably reflects two broad changes: an increasing sophistication in gathering census data and the gradual integration of urban immigrants from rural societies in their new urban communities (see Ferdinand, 1999). After settling into urban occupations and well-established neighborhoods, they were drawn into stable associations by temples and churches, ethnic clubs, labor unions, political groups, and informal groups of family, relatives, and friends. For the most part, it was the rootless poor who fell into crime. As growing numbers of newcomers were absorbed into neighborhoods, tramps and hoboes, common in the 19th century, began to disappear. During the 1930s, a mobile army of marginal men reappeared, but in the late 19th and early 20th centuries, their ranks had thinned in favor of a stable workforce that took its place in the cities. It is no coincidence that prostitution and public drunkenness also declined steadily during the 1920s, though Prohibition also had an impact on the latter.

Conclusion

This discussion has identified several patterns in Western criminal behavior. Evolving social and legal institutions in the West contributed basically to a long-term, secular decline in serious crime. During much of the 19th century and the early 20th century, crime trends, and particularly property crimes, were closely attuned to improving economic conditions. Moreover, criminality as recorded by the courts and police was largely a working-class or lower-class phenomenon.

THEODORE N. FERDINAND

References and Further Reading

Adams, J.W. and Kasakoff, A.B., Estimates of census underenumeration based on genealogies. *Social Science History* 15, 4: 527–539.

Beattie, J.M. 1986. *Crime and the Courts in England 1660–1800*. Princeton, NJ: Princeton University Press.

Federal Bureau of Investigation. 1998. *Uniform Crime Reports for the United States*. Department of Justice, GPO.

Ferdinand, T.N. 1999. Civic culture and criminal justice in the United States. *Criminal Justice Review* 24, 2: 119–144.

Ferdinand, T.N. 1992. *The Lower Criminal Courts of Boston: 1814–1850*. Newark, DE: The University of Delaware Press.

Ferdinand, T.N. 1980. Criminality, the courts, and the constabulary in Boston: 1702–1967. *Journal of Research in Crime and Delinquency* 17, 190–208.

Ferdinand, T.N. 1976. From a service to a legalistic style police department: A case study. *Journal of Police Science and Administration* 4, 3: 302–319.

Ferdinand, T.N. 1967. The criminal patterns of Boston since 1849. *American Journal of Sociology* 73, 1: 84–99.

Garland, D. 1990. *Punishment and Modern Society*. Chicago, IL: The University of Chicago Press.

Gatrell, V.A.C. 1980. The decline of theft and violence in Victorian and Edwardian England. *Crime and the Law: The Social History of Crime in Western Europe since 1500*. Gatrell, V.A.C., Lenman, B., and Parker, G. (Eds.), London, UK: Europa, 238–370.

Gatrell, V.A.C. and Hadden, T. 1972. Criminal statistics and their interpretation. *Nineteenth Century Society: Essays in the Use of Quantitative Methods for the Study of Social Data*. Wrigley, E.A. (Ed.). Cambridge, England: Cambridge University Press, 336–396.

Glazer, D. and Rice, K. 1959. Crime, age, and employment. *American Sociological Review* 24: 679–686.

Given, J.B. 1977. *Society and Homicide in Thirteenth Century England*. Stanford, CA: Stanford University Press.

Gurr, T.R., Grabosky, P.N., and Hula, R.C. 1977. *The Politics of Crime and Conflict: A Comparative History of Four Cities*. Beverly Hills, CA: Sage.

Hanawalt, B.A. 1979. *Crime and Conflict in English Communities, 1300–1343*. Cambridge, MA: Harvard University Press.

Harrison, R.J. 2001. Numbers running. *Crisis* 14–18.

Hofer, H. 2000. Criminal violence and youth in Sweden: A long-term perspective. *Journal of Scandinavian Studies in Criminology and Crime Prevention* 1, 1: 56–72.

Lane, R. 1979. *Violent Death in the City: Suicide, Accident, and Murder in Nineteenth-Century Philadelphia*. Cambridge, MA: Harvard University Press.

Lane, R. 1967. *Policing the City: Boston 1822–1885*. Cambridge, MA: Harvard University Press.

Lodhi, A.Q. and Tilly, C. 1973. Urbanization, crime, and collective violence in nineteenth-century France. *American Journal of Sociology* 79: 296–318.

Philips, D. 1977. *Crime and Authority in Victorian England: The Black Country, 1835–1860*. London, UK: Croom Helm.

Ruggiero, G. 1980. *Violence in Early Renaissance Venice*. New Brunswick, NJ: Rutgers University Press.

Wilson, J.Q. 1968. *Varieties of Police Behavior: The Management of Law and Order in Eight Communities*. Cambridge, MA: Harvard University Press.

Zehr, H. 1976. *Crime and the Development of Modern Society: Patterns of Criminality in Nineteenth-century Germany and France*. Totowa, NJ: Rowman & Littlefield.

See also **Criminology: Historic Development; Victimology**

Holocaust *See* **Genocide; Hate Crime**

Homelessness and Criminal Behavior

Two streams of research characterize criminological writings on homelessness. One area studies when and how authorities—kings, religious leaders, the state, and other social control agents—criminalize people for being homeless. Research in this tradition examines the use of criminal and civil law to penalize particular behaviors, such as sleeping in public places, begging, and being unemployed (Chambliss, 1964; Snow et al., 1989;

Duneir, 1999; Wardhaugh, 2000). Penalties for violating these laws range from forced relocation, fines, and incarceration to police executions (as in the case of Brazilian street children).

A second area of research, and the one that this essay reviews, focuses on factors that influence offending once someone becomes homeless. Researchers use a variety of definitions when studying the homeless, but most definitions are similar to the following: the homeless are people who do not have access to permanent housing that meets the minimum housing standards of their community; many of the homeless find temporary accommodations with relatives or with friends and in relief shelters, but others live on the street. By definition, the homeless are a diverse group and criminological research has studied several subgroups including hoboes, tramps, and youth variously described as runaways, throwaways, and street youth. Researchers have also studied mental illness among the homeless, but these works are not reviewed here.

We begin our summary with an overview of criminological interest in the homeless in North America. We then consider contemporary studies, examining their approach to one of four questions: Do the homeless commit more crimes than others? Is crime among the homeless a reflection of the type of people who become homeless or a consequence of homelessness itself? Which aspects of homelessness have the greatest consequences for crime? What can crime among the homeless tell us about offending in general?

Homelessness in North American Criminology

In North American research, the connection between homelessness and crime was first suggested in the ethnographies conducted during the 1920s and the Great Depression. In one of the classic works of the "Chicago school" of sociology, Anderson (1923) spent time with homeless males who stole aboard trains and traveled across the U.S. Although some of these men blamed their homelessness on a lack of stable work or a personal crisis, many of these men, or "hoboes," claimed that they had willingly abandoned the comfort, security, and boredom of conventional life for the adventures of "riding the rails." Anderson describes several minor crimes common among these men, ranging from petty theft and graft to "jack-rolling" (stealing from a "drunk"); however, he provides little systematic information on the extent of offending or on the factors that encourage crime.

A little more than a decade later, Sutherland and Locke (1936) studied the lives of 20,000 homeless, unemployed men living in Chicago relief shelters during the Great Depression. Unlike the hoboes that

Anderson met, the majority of these men did not flee their familial homes because of their wanderlust; instead, the dire economic situation of the 1930s left these men no alternative but to take to the road in search of work. Sutherland and Locke (1936) provide few details of these men's involvement in crime; however, Sutherland (1937) drew upon this research in his work on professional thieves, arguing that a crisis, particularly an economic one, was a key factor in the development of a career in theft.

Another work from the Great Depression offers more in-depth information on the link between homelessness and crime. In 1932–33, Thomas Minehan (1934) traveled the western U.S., speaking with 500 "boy and girl tramps," who had left their familial homes in search of work, companionship, and adventure. Minehan's book provides a stark portrayal of these adolescents' lives: their familial poverty and the strains it engendered; the combination of the necessity of leaving home to search for work and the desire for independence and excitement; their relationships with other travelers; their loneliness and their victimization. For many, the traumas and deprivations of life on the road were worse than the poverty from which these youth fled. Minehan describes these adolescents' need to "get wise" and accept theft and prostitution as legitimate means of obtaining food, shelter, and other necessities.

The economic recovery of the late 1930s and the ensuing prosperity of subsequent decades encouraged criminologists to consider factors other than homelessness and adversity in their work on crime. For example, theories that focus on strain, differential association, sub-cultures, and differential opportunities all acknowledge that economic circumstances or class conditions contribute to crime; however, these theories downplay the causal consequences of abject poverty, concentrating instead on dominant cultural goals and the limited means to achieve them; exposure to other offenders; class-related values; and access to illegal opportunities. Although anthropologists and sociologists continued to study the homeless, by the 1970s, most criminologists focused on other groups, particularly the men who lived on "skid row." It became increasingly common for criminologists to argue that class and economic status were all but irrelevant for understanding crime.

A methodological change accompanied these theoretical developments; self-report surveys replaced ethnographies as the dominant mode of data collection. At the same time, criminologists shifted their focus from people on the margins of society to those at its heart. Thus, by the 1970s and 1980s surveys of school youth were the norm, a trend that reflects the ascendancy of "school criminology" over a "criminology of the street"

(Hagan and McCarthy, 1997). School criminology continues to dominate criminological research; however, the number of poor and homeless people has risen dramatically in the last two decades and criminology has witnessed a revival in "street" studies of those on the economic margins.

Do the Homeless Commit More Crime Than Others?

Several studies indicate that the homeless are disproportionately involved in and arrested for illegal behavior; however, most of this crime is victimless. In their examination of Austin, Texas, police records, Snow, Baker, and Anderson (1989) discover that about 80% of homeless adult male arrests were for substance use and public order offenses (e.g., trespassing, sleeping in public). This is about six times higher than the rate for the nonhomeless. Although only a small percentage of homeless arrests were for more serious crimes, Snow et al. find that the homeless were disproportionately arrested for these offenses: the property crime arrest rate among homeless adult males is more than 35% higher than the rate for males with a permanent address, and it was about 24% higher for violent crimes (although most of this is for less serious offenses such as threatening or common assault). Studies of homeless adults in other cities and of homeless youth are consistent with Snow et al.'s findings. For example, in a study described in greater detail below, Hagan and McCarthy (1997) report that of the homeless youth they studied, 46% sold drugs, 49% committed a serious theft, and 27% broke into a home or business since becoming homeless (also see Kipke et al., 1997). These proportions far exceed those for youth surveyed in schools or in their homes.

The homeless also experience higher rates of criminal victimization. Studies of adults (e.g., Snow and Anderson, 1993) and of youth (e.g., Whitbeck and Hoyt, 1999) reveal that the homeless are more often assaulted, sexually abused, raped, and murdered than the nonhomeless; they also have their belongings stolen more frequently. Consistent with other groups, victimization among the homeless is strongly related to offending.

Is Crime a Product of Homelessness or of Who Becomes Homeless?

Some social critics argue that crime among the homeless has more to do with who becomes homeless than with homelessness itself. They claim that homeless individuals who resort to crime would have done so regardless of their living situation. McCarthy and Hagan (1992) address this issue with self-report survey data from a sample of 390 male and female youth

living on the streets of Toronto, a Canadian city of approximately 3 million. They combine these data with information from a sample of 562 students who attended high school in the same city during the same period (1987–88). Using statistical techniques that correct for problems associated with bias in samples, McCarthy and Hagan find that several characteristics of homelessness influence theft and prostitution independently of the background variables that distinguish youth who become homeless (e.g., high levels of parental strain and abuse, problems with school, and criminal involvement before leaving home). In effect, their research suggests that any individual who remains homeless for more than a short period of time faces a heightened risk of criminal involvement regardless of his or her background.

Which Aspects of Homelessness Contribute to Crime?

Contemporary research on the homeless demonstrates that homelessness involves several conditions, and variation in these may have important implications for crime. For example, extending conventional concerns with class backgrounds, McCarthy and Hagan (1992) argue that the living conditions of the homeless place them at the bottom of the class hierarchy, a position characterized by extreme levels of economic adversity and powerlessness. In their analysis, McCarthy and Hagan find that for homeless youth, involvement in serious theft increases with hunger (i.e., the frequency of going without food for a day or more), inadequate shelter (e.g., sleeping in parks, abandoned buildings), and the length of time since leaving home, independent of other variables. As well, involvement in the sex trade increases with an individual's lack of shelter and employment.

In a subsequent study, Baron and Hartnagel (1997, 1998) explore in greater detail how individual unemployment contributes to crime among the homeless. In 1993, they interviewed 200 street youth in Edmonton, a Canadian city of approximately 800,000 people. Drawing on attribution theory, Baron and Hartnagel propose that the negative consequences of unemployment and loss of income are exacerbated for youth who are angry about their predicament and who blame it on external factors (e.g., market conditions), rather than their own shortcomings (e.g., failure to finish high school).

Baron and Hartnagel find several interactions that are consistent with their predictions: property crime increases for youth who had been unemployed for long periods and who believe that their willingness to work would not necessarily increase the chances of their success; drug selling and violent crime are more common for youth who had been without a job for a long period and who think that their unemployment was the fault of government and industry's failure to create sufficient jobs; and drug selling is highest among youth who experienced a succession of jobs and are angry about their unemployment. They also find that both property and violent crime decrease as income rises. In a subsequent paper, Baron and Hartnagel (1998) demonstrate that for homeless youth, the ameliorative effect of employment income decreases their involvement in robbery and other violent crimes even after controlling for variables specified by theories more commonly used to study violence (i.e., culture of violence and routine activities).

In 1997, Hagan and McCarthy published their second study of homeless youth, adding further insights into the ways homelessness influences offending. In this study, Hagan, McCarthy, and a team of researchers collected interview and self-report survey data from 482 homeless male and female youth (16–24 years old) who were living on the streets of Toronto or Vancouver, Canada, in 1992. Hagan and McCarthy note that municipalities vary in their responses to homelessness. For example, during the time of the second study Toronto provided an array of services for homeless youth that included counseling agencies, health care, legal services, meals, and access to several hundred beds in various shelters, some exclusively for homeless youth. During the same period, Vancouver offered many of these services; however, it did not provide any shelter for youth who lived on its streets. Moreover, provincial laws allowed Toronto's police force greater flexibility with street youth who could legally leave home at 16 years of age; in contrast, provincial laws required Vancouver police to apprehend and contact the families of homeless youth under the age of 19. Hagan and McCarthy find that the many benefits then provided by Toronto's "social welfare" approach to homelessness include lower crime rates among its homeless youth. In contrast, Vancouver's "crime control" perspective appears to increase crime. Hagan and McCarthy find that compared to homeless youth in Toronto, those in Vancouver spent more nights on the street without shelter, committed more nonviolent street crime (i.e., theft, drug selling, and sex trade), and faced greater risks of arrest, independent of their involvement in crime.

Hagan and McCarthy's analysis also demonstrates how police arrests contribute to crime in other ways. They note that a large number of homeless youth flee from homes where they were victims of parental physical or sexual abuse. Many of these youth feel considerable "shame" as a result of their victimization. Hagan and McCarthy suggest that an arrest can escalate these feelings, triggering other emotions, particularly anger, rage, and defiance. The combination of emotions may encourage youth to strike out on a post-arrest "crime spree." Consistent with this hypothesis, Hagan and McCarthy find that parental physical and sexual abuse and police arrest have sizable interaction effects on involvement in a range of street crimes, including violent and nonviolent offenses.

Several U.S. studies have also explored how homelessness contributes to crime. In 1995–96, Whitbeck and Hoyt (1999) collected data from 602 youth they encountered on the street and in shelters in a variety or urban and rural centers in several midwestern states. Their analyses of drug selling and property crimes supports many of the findings from earlier studies and draws attention to the long-term consequences of problematic home environments. They find significantly greater levels of drug dealing among youth whose parents were heavy drug or alcohol users and significantly higher levels of theft among youth whose parents had committed a serious crime.

What Do Studies of the Homeless Tell Us About Broader Theoretical Issues?

Criminologists who study the homeless argue that their research has implications beyond this group. They note that many theories of crime focus on variables that figure prominently in the lives of the homeless (e.g., illegal opportunities, exposure to other offenders) and that research on homelessness can test existing theories and develop new ones. For example, Hagan and McCarthy (1997) argue that research on the homeless has several advantages over studies of people located in more conventional and commonly studied environments of home and school: the homeless commit more crime, are more often the victims of crime, and have more diversity in their backgrounds. In essence, the homeless have greater variation in the factors central to key theoretical perspectives.

Hagan and McCarthy (1997) illustrate this point with an analysis of the effects of parental violence on offending among homeless youth. General strain theory suggests that parental physical abuse should have strong positive effects on an individual's violent and nonviolent offending; however, many studies find that parental use of force has small or nonsignificant effects on crime. Hagan and McCarthy argue that these findings reflect the limited variation in parental aggression among youth surveyed in schools and at home. In contrast, their studies indicate that parental abuse increases the likelihood of leaving home, directly increases involvement in violent crime (also see Baron and Hartnagel, 1997, 1998), and indirectly increases involvement in nonviolent crime (also see Whitbeck and Hoyt, 1999).

Hagan and McCarthy's (1997) data also raise a key, but typically neglected aspect of Sutherland's theory of differential association. Combining Sutherland's work with ideas on the effects of conventional human and social capital, Hagan and McCarthy argue that both "conventional" and "criminal" capital play key roles in offending. Specifically, conventional human capital, namely skills and information valued in the legal economy, is typically obtained through one's conventional social capital (i.e., productive relationships with family, friends, and others). In contrast, knowledge about offending (e.g., techniques) or "human criminal capital" is often obtained through relationships with other offenders that operate as "criminal social capital." Hagan and McCarthy argue that these two types of capital typically affect crime in opposite ways: that is, crime decreases with conventional capital and increases with its criminal counterpart. Consistent with Sutherland's theory, they find that tutelage (offers of illegal assistance and teaching) significantly increases drug selling, theft, and prostitution among homeless youth.

In two subsequent papers, McCarthy, Hagan, and Cohen (1999) and McCarthy and Hagan (2000) use data on homeless youth to examine the role of criminal capital in offending. McCarthy et al.'s work focuses on co-offending and argues that conventional theories of crime (e.g., general theory of crime and rational choice theory of offending) are inadequate explanations of the processes that encourage offenders to work together. Drawing on game theory and social dilemma research, McCarthy et al. argue that co-offending is influenced by an individual's criminal social capital; that is, co-offending is most likely when two or more individuals inspire mutual trust and the belief that co-operating with others will provide greater rewards than offending alone. Consistent with their hypothesis, McCarthy et al. find that involvement in serious theft increases with a willingness to co-offend, whereas those who offend on their own commit fewer thefts.

Extending McCarthy et al.'s research, McCarthy and Hagan (2001) demonstrate that homeless youth who are willing to collaborate in their drug selling earn more money than other young drug dealers: youth who score high on measures of competence (i.e., efficacy and academic abilities) increase their illegal earnings only when they are willing to co-offend, enjoy taking risks, or have a strong desire to make money. In essence, McCarthy and Hagan's analysis suggests that illegal success is influenced by many of the same factors that increase prosperity in the legal economy.

The number of homeless people has escalated dramatically since 1980. Researchers from an array of disciplines responded to this increase and we have now accumulated a sizable amount of knowledge about the causes, conditions, and consequences of homelessness. It is clear that various elements of homelessness contribute to crime and that research on the homeless had contributed significantly to criminology. It remains to be seen, however, if this research will reduce homelessness and its negative results.

BILL MCCARTHY AND JOHN HAGAN

References and Further Reading

Anderson, N. 1923. *The Hobo: The Sociology of the Homeless Man*, Chicago, IL: University of Chicago Press.

Baron, S.W. and Hartnagel, T.F. 1997. Attributions, affect, and crime: Street youths' reactions to unemployment, *Criminology* 35.

Baron, S.W. and Hartnagel, T.F. 1998. Street youth and criminal violence, *Journal of Research in Crime and Delinquency* 35.

Chambliss, W. 1964. A sociological analysis of the law of vagrancy, *Social Problems* 12.

Duneier, M. 1999. *Sidewalk*, New York, NY: Farrar, Straus and Giroux.

Hagan, J. and McCarthy, B. 1997. *Mean Streets: Youth Crime and Homelessness*, Cambridge, UK, and New York, NY: Cambridge University Press.

Kipke, M.D., Unger, J.B., O'Connor, S., Palmer, R.F., and LaFrance, S.R. 1997. Street youth, their peer group affiliation and differences according to residential status, subsistence patterns, and use of services, *Adolescence* 32.

McCarthy, B. and Hagan, J. 2001. When crime pays: Capital, competence and criminal success, *Social Forces* 79.

McCarthy, B., Hagan, J., and Cohen, L.E. 1998. Uncertainty, cooperation and crime: Understanding the decision to co-offend, *Social Forces* 77.

Minehan, T. 1934. *Boy and Girl Tramps of America*, New York, NY: Farrar & Rinehart.

Snow, D.A. and Anderson, L. 1993. *Down on Their Luck: A Study of Homeless Street People,* Berkeley, CA: University of California Press.

Snow, D.A., Baker, S. and Anderson, L. 1989. Criminality and homeless men: An empirical assessment, *Social Problems* 36.

Sutherland, E. 1937. *The Professional Thief: By a Professional Thief.* Annotated and Interpreted by Edwin, S. Chicago, IL: University of Chicago Press.

Sutherland, E.H. and Locke, H. 1936. *Twenty Thousand Homeless Men: A Study of Unemployed Men in the Chicago Shelters*, Philadelphia: J.B. Lippincott.

Wardhaugh, J. 2000. *Sub City: Young People, Homelessness and Crime*, Ashgate, UK, and Brookfield, VT: Aldershot.

Whitbeck, L.B. and Hoyt, D.R. 1999. *Nowhere to Grow: Homeless and Runaway Adolescents and Their Families*, New York, NY: Aldine de Gruyter.

See also **Sociological Theories of Criminal Behavior**

Homicide: Mass Murder and Serial Killings

Both mass murders and serial killings share the characteristic of being one of the most frightening forms of homicide. One of the greatest fears of urban dwellers is that they will be subject to a random unpredictable attack by strangers, people whom they do not know, but must interact with on a daily basis.

> Life in metropolitan areas ... involves a startling paradox: we fear strangers more than anything else, and yet we live our lives among strangers. Every time we take a walk, ride a subway or bus, shop in a supermarket or department store, enter an office building lobby or elevator, work in a factory or large office, or attend a ball game or the movies, we are surrounded by strangers. The potential for fear is as immense as it is unavoidable. (Charles E. Silberman, *Criminal Violence, Criminal Justice*, 1978, p. 11)

Stereotypes of mass and serial killers reflect the fear. Mass killers are typically portrayed as disgruntled or deranged White males in their 30s or 40s who suddenly "go berserk" and kill a number of randomly chosen targets, then conclude the event by committing suicide (Petee, Padgett, and York, 1997). Serial killers, on the other hand, are modern day equivalents of demons, werewolves, and vampires (Jenkins, 1994). In the mind of the public, there is a supernatural element to serial killers: (1) their motivation is demonic or satanic; (2) they possess superhuman powers, particularly in their ability to avoid capture; (3) the case will be solved by miraculous means (Fisher, 1997).

Electronic and print media play a large role in describing, interpreting, and explaining phenomena such as mass and serial killers. Of course, there are other components that promote a particular image as a social problem. Organizations devoted to handgun control argue that easy access to deadly weapons is part of the cause; politicians argue that more severe penalties will solve the problem; and experts weigh in with explanations and demands for money to do more research (Best, 1999).

But for the media to sustain audience attention and appeal, mass and serial murders have to be portrayed in detailed, dramatic, and compelling form. For example, a mass murder where a man kills his wife, three children, and himself is shocking and a tragedy. Such an incident will make headlines, but it will fade from public attention relatively quickly (Petee et al., 1997). On the other hand, suppose an individual enters a fast food restaurant with an automatic weapon, opens fire, kills four people, and escapes. This will receive far more media attention for a longer period of time than the man who killed his family.

The reason the latter is framed in media accounts differently and sustains public attention better is a fear factor. If a stranger can enter any fast food restaurant and kill people, how do I know it will not happen to me? The incident in which the person kills his family is localized; we do not know what the circumstances were within that family and, furthermore, the offender is dead.

Similarly, vulnerability and defenselessness is what makes serial murders newsworthy. Serial murders are repetitive, appear to be random, and lack closure.

In a solitary murder, the deed is done and the offender arrested. By definition, serial murders are repetitive; the horror of one act is compounded by recognizing that others will follow. Because the serial murderer is not arrested quickly, and sometimes not at all, there is a lack of closure. The lack of closure allows the fear to continue and healing to be postponed (Riedel, 1998).

If further evidence is needed of media impact, consider the consequences of the terrorist attacks on the World Trade Center on September 11, 2001. If the mood of the country following the attack can be characterized at all, it is one of fear. If the terrorists can destroy an important landmark in one of our largest cities and kill over 4000 people, where will they attack next? Is anybody safe? Although most of the media have acted to reduce widespread panic, their coverage of this event has been extensive and continuing. The accuracy of their accounts is not immediately known.

If the imagery projected by media serves their needs, what are the characteristics of mass and serial murders uncovered by objective researchers? I begin by distinguishing the two types of killings.

Generally, mass murders involve the killing of several people in a short period of time (hours) whereas serial murders involve killing of several people over a long period of time such as months and years. Beyond that very general definition, disagreement abounds.

How many is "several"? Although there is some disagreement among researchers, the range is between three and four or more victims. Mass murders are also typically carried out in one location or two locations within minutes or hours of each other, whereas serial killings may occur at widely scattered locations over a long period of time (Holmes and Holmes, 1994).

Mass Murders

Indicative of how little is actually known about mass murders are the many attempts to classify types of mass murders and mass murderers. For example, Levin and Fox (1996) classify by type of motive; Dietz (1986) distinguishes between family annihilators, pseudocommandos, and set-and-run killers (bombings or poisonings that allow for the possibility of escape); Holmes and Holmes (1994) add two additional categories: disciples, such as followers of Charles Manson, and disgruntled employees; and Petee, Padgett, and York (1997) developed a classification of nine offender motivations. The major conclusion that can be drawn from these thoughtful approaches is that mass murder is a very diverse offense. To remain reasonably brief, this essay will discuss four types of mass murders.

Disgruntled Employees

This category corresponds to the most commonly held view of mass murders. Sadly, the term, "going postal" has entered the lexicon for someone who goes berserk and kills a number of people. The term originated in a mass murder of 15 employees in a post office in Edmond, Oklahoma, by Patrick Sherrill (Nicolletti, Zinna, and Spencer-Thomas, 1999).

The targets of such attacks may be specific locations that contain individuals representing a source of frustration or anger for the offender. But the offender may also target specific individuals. Petee, Padgett, and York give the example of Gang Lu, who killed five people on the University of Iowa campus in 1991. Gang Lu was

> livid over what he perceived to be a slight by faculty members in the Department of Physics for not having nominated his doctoral dissertation for a prestigious award. His anger led him to shoot two professors who were on his dissertation committee, the department chair, a university administrator, and a rival student, who had won the prestigious award. (Tom Petee, Kathy G. Padgett, and Thomas S. York, "Debunking the Stereotype: An Examination of Mass Murder in Public Places," 1997, p. 324.)

Domestic or Romantic Relationships

One of the more interesting examples of mass murders involving domestic relationships is the New Jersey case of John List, who killed his wife, three children, and 85-year-old mother in 1971. List was extremely religious, had a history of failed jobs, and was badly financially overextended. In addition, List felt that his wife and daughter were turning away from God. He insisted that he was killing them for their own good and they would be safe in heaven. As is usually the case for the type Holmes and Holmes (1994) call the family annihilator, List felt that his life was out of control and he had no way of correcting things short of murdering his family and starting over.

List escaped to Colorado where he met another woman and married her, saying that his previous wife had died of cancer. But in May 1989, the New Jersey case was aired on *America's Most Wanted*. This led to a series of leads, followed by the FBI, that led to List's arrest on June 1. He was subsequently convicted and sentenced to five consecutive life terms (Ramsland).

Another type of mass murder results from a romantic obsession with a person who does not return the affection, a type of "fatal attraction." One of the better known instances of this is Richard Farley, who romantically pursued Laura Black for 2 years. She did not return his affections and that eventually led to the murder of seven employees and the wounding of three others, including Black (Petee et al., 1997).

Mass Murders Involving Another Felony

Although previous types of mass murders generally involve solitary White offenders in their 30s who sometimes attempt suicide, mass murders involving another felony, such as robbery, are different. The majority of offenders are non-White, in their 20s, never attempt suicide, and may include more than one offender (Petee et al., 1997). The motivation is to acquire property, and people are killed either to prevent identification or because offenders lose control of the situation.

An instance of this type of mass murder occurred in the robbery of a Popeye's Chicken Restaurant in Gadsden, Alabama, in 1994. Richard Melson and Cuhuatemoc Peraita entered the building through a rear door with the intent of robbery. After collecting the money, they herded the employees into a walk-in freezer, opened fire, killed three, and wounded one. By killing the employees, Melson and Peraita hoped to avoid detection. (Petee et al., 1997).

Terrorism

The final type of mass murders are very similar to what Dietz has classified as set-and-run mass murders. These types of mass murders are politically motivated and occur after the offender has left the scene. Until the September 11, 2001, destruction of the World Trade Center, the largest terrorist act committed in the U.S. was the attack on the Albert P. Murrah building on April 19, 1995, in Oklahoma City, Oklahoma. More than 500 people were injured and 168 people were killed.

The perpetrator was Timothy McVeigh. Timothy McVeigh apparently had a conventional upbringing in rural New York towns and joined the army in 1988.

He was a model soldier, was awarded the Bronze Star among other decorations, during the Persian Gulf War, and was invited to join the Green Berets. McVeigh was not prepared for the rigorous evaluation program and left the Green Berets after the third day. Shortly thereafter, he resigned from the army.

McVeigh then wandered from state to state buying and selling firearms. Three events seemed to solidify his hatred of the government. First, he was moved by the book *The Turner Diaries*, which is a fictional account of Andrew McDonald, who reacts to the increasing restriction against the use of firearms by bombing a federal building. Second, in 1992, the FBI went after White supremacist Randy Weaver, in what became known as the Ruby Ridge incident. Weaver's wife, Vicky, was killed by an FBI sniper and the incident became a rallying cry for the militia movement. Finally, McVeigh was outraged at the FBI attack on the Branch Davidians, a religious group led by David Koresh, who perished with his followers in the subsequent fire.

Beginning in 1994 and working with Terry Nichols, McVeigh decided something had to be done to curb the tyrannical power of the government. They began building a truck bomb that would eventually weigh 400 pounds. McVeigh drove the rented truck to Oklahoma city on April 19, 1995, and put it in a parking lot next to the Murrah building where it detonated a few minutes later. McVeigh was subsequent convicted and executed by lethal injection on June 11, 2001 (Ottley, 2001).

Conclusions

Perhaps the major conclusion drawn from the preceding is that mass murders are an extremely diverse group. Although there certainly are mass murders committed by madmen, they are hardly an accurate description of most mass murders. Most of the mass murderers considered here had identifiable motivations for their violence. Further, whereas many mass murders are committed by strangers, there is little evidence of random selection of victims. Even where disgruntled employees pick specific targets, bystanders do not become victimized unless they interfere with the goals of the shooter.

Serial Murders

Prior to the 1980s, most experts believed that serial murders comprised 1% or 2% of total murders. During the 1980s, the most widely quoted claims were that serial murders were 20–25% of all murders. How did this enormous, and largely false, statistic gain credence among otherwise rational and thoughtful people?

Although there were a number of events propelling the popularity of serial homicide in the 1980s, the belief that serial murders made up a fifth of all murders received an enormous amount of legitimation from the Behavioral Sciences Unit and congressional hearings on serial murders. It was in these hearing that William Webster, FBI Director, described large numbers on "patterns of murders committed by one person in large numbers with no apparent rhyme, reason or motivation" (U.S. Senate, 1984, cited in Jenkins, 1994, 59).

Although it is not difficult to conclude that stranger murders were patterns of murder committed with no apparent rhyme, reason, or motivation, it is somewhat more difficult to conclude that they were committed by serial offenders rather than solitary ones. Cases from the "unknown" category were factored in to the serial killer estimate because "unknown" was interpreted to mean "no apparent motive," which meant it was "motiveless," and therefore belonged to the serial homicide category. "Unknown" in homicide data simply means that the police did not know the circumstances: it is a confession of ignorance rather than an affirmation of serial homicide (Jenkins, 1994).

Serial murders are an extremely rare offense. If serial murders are about 1% as suggested by Jenkins, there were 127 serial murder victims of 1268 murder and nonnegligent homicides reported to the FBI in 1999 in a U.S. population of over 280 million people. If each serial offender killed two victims, we are left with 64 offenders (Riedel and Welsh, 2001). Alternatively, Fisher (1997) estimates there are ten serial killers operating in the U.S. every year—which is an even smaller number of offenders.

In addition to their rarity, the traditional image of serial killers has been shaped by case studies done by forensic psychiatrists of offenders held by the court and media presentations. In more recent decades, criminologists using a social science perspective have examined social and cultural forces underlying serial killings (Fox and Levin, 1999).

Given their late start, criminologists have labored to correct many of the myths and misconceptions of serial offenders. These can be divided into myths about their psychological characteristics and social and demographic myths.

Psychological Characteristics

One of the myths discussed by Fox and Levin (1999, 167) is that serial killers are unusual in appearance and lifestyle. Nearly all researchers on the subject agree that serial killers are "extraordinarily ordinary" (Jenkins, 1994; Fisher, 1997; Egger, 1998; Holmes and Holmes, 1998; Hickey, 2002). What makes serial killers so difficult to identify and apprehend is that they do an excellent job of blending in with the crowd and not drawing attention to themselves. They frequently hold full-time jobs, are involved in stable relationships, and are members of various community groups.

Fox and Levin (1999) enumerate several other psychological myths about serial killers. They list and describe beliefs that serial killers are all insane, sociopaths, products of bad childhoods, sexual sadists, select victims who somehow resemble their mothers, and really want to get caught—none of which are generally true.

Social and Demographic Myths

The most popular image of the serial killer is the lone White male, a mad slasher or ripper. In actual fact, from 10 to 20% of serial killings can be attributed to two or more individuals working together (Jenkins, 1994).

Not all serial killers are males; Hickey (2002) studied 337 male and 67 female serial killers who were responsible for a minimum of 2526 murders between 1800 and 1995. The 67 female killers were 16% of the total pool of offenders. Its important to note the 67 female killers represent *known* cases. Jenkins (1994) and Hickey (2002) point out the number of female offenders may be underrepresented because they are more likely to use asphyxiation or poisoning, which were less likely to be noticed prior to the emergence of modern forensic medicine.

Until the arrest of Wayne Williams, claims were made that no serial killers were African Americans. However, Hickey found that African Americans constitute 20% of the offenders in his study.

Finally, serial killers do not generally move about the country. The claims in the 1980s that the typical killer moved through about 10–20 states were made to justify increased federal involvement. Although there is a minority of serial offenders who do move about, the majority tend to operate in one city or even in one neighborhood (Jenkins, 1994).

Are Serial Murders Increasing?

Hickey (2002) found that of the 337 cases studied, 94% began their killing since 1900. More offenders (45%) were identified between 1975 and 1995 then during any previous 25-year span. But are serial murders increasing or are they just being reported more reliably? (Fox and Levin, 1999).

There are three problems that have an impact on studying serial murders and determining the number of serial murders. First, there is no publicly available source of homicide data that record serial murders. The estimates given are drawn from stranger homicide records and newspaper accounts that are useful, but of unknown validity and reliability.

Second, until recently it has been possible for a serial offender to move among jurisdictions, killing one or two victims in each place, without ever alerting law enforcement that a serial offender was active. That serial offenders could be mobile and kill with impunity was possible because of linkage blindness, that is, the "nearly total lack of sharing or coordinating of investigative information and the lack of adequate networking by law enforcement agencies" (Egger, 1998, 180).

Finally, even if communication between law enforcement agencies has improved, serial killers can and do alter their mode of operation. What links seemingly unrelated killings to one offender is the *modus operandi*; such things as the same type of victim, same method of killing and disposing of the remains, etc. link the offender to the event. If the serial offender decides to change his or her mode of operation, then the offense will not be linked to this individual.

Conclusions

Serial and mass murders share one characteristic: the portrayal of them is calculated to frighten the public rather than inform them. Both types of murders are described by the media in ways that are calculated to appeal to the public fascination for violence. This process leads to a one-sided picture of the phenomena: mass murders in the workplace are more interesting than mass murders of a family.

Serial and mass murders are also extremely diverse. With respect to mass murders, I provided one version of a classification. As I tried to make clear, there are a variety of classifications, each emphasizing a different element. Serial murders are also extremely diverse: offenders are of different ages, races, and genders.

Finally, serial and mass murders are extremely rare. The rarity makes it difficult to generalize about a phenomenon that appears so seldom. Perhaps more importantly, they are difficult to prevent and in the case of serial murders offenders are difficult to apprehend.

MARC RIEDEL

References and Further Reading

Best, J. 1990. *Random Violence: How We Talk about New Crimes and New Victims*, Berkeley, CA: University of California Press.

Dietz, P.E. 1986. Mass, serial, and sensational homicides, *Bulletin of the New York Academy of Medicine* 62, 477–491.

Egger, S.A. 1998. *The Killers among Us*, Upper Saddle River, NJ: Prentice-Hall.

Fisher, J.C. 1997. *Killer among Us: Public Reactions to Serial Murder*. Westport, CT: Praeger.

Fox, J.A. and Levin, J. 1999. Serial murder, Smith, M.D. and Zahn, M.A. (Eds.), *Homicide: A Sourcebook of Social Research*, pp. 165–175, Thousand Oaks, CA: Sage Publications.

Hickey, E.W. 2002. *Serial Murderers and Their Victims* (3rd ed.), Belmont, CA: Wadsworth.

Holmes, R.M. and Holmes, S.T. 1994. *Murder in America*, Thousand Oaks, CA: Sage Publications.

Holmes, R.M. and Holmes, S.T. 1998. *Serial Murder*, Thousand Oaks, CA: Sage Publications.

Jenkins, P. 1994. *Using Murder: The Social Construction of Serial Homicide*. New York, NY: Aldine de Gruyter.

Levin, J. and Fox, J.A. 1996. A psycho-social analysis of mass murder, O'Reilly-Fleming, T. (Ed.), *Serial and Mass Murder: Theory, Research and Policy*, pp. 55–76, Toronto: Canadian Scholars Press.

Nicoletti, J., Zinna, K., and Spencer-Thomas, S. 1999. *Violence Goes to School: Lessons Learned from Columbine*, Lakewood, CO: Nicolletti-Flater Associates.

Ottley, T., *The Timothy McVeigh Story: The Oklahoma Bomber*. Available at http://www.crimelibrary.com/serial9/mcveigh/index.htm. Retrieved on October 29, 2001, from the World Wide Web.

Petee, T.A., Padgett, K.G., and York, T.S. 1997. Debunking the stereotype: An examination of mass murder in public places, *Homicide Studies* 1, 317–337.

Ramsland, K., *John List*. Available at http://www.crimelibrary.com/classics/list/index.htm. The Crime Library. Retrieved on October 29, 2001, from the World Wide Web.

Riedel, M. 1998. Serial murder, communities, and evil: A review essay, *Criminal Justice Review* 23, 220–232.

Riedel, M. and Welsh, W.N. 2001. *Criminal Violence: Patterns, Causes, and Prevention*, Los Angeles, CA: Roxbury Publishing Co.

U.S. Senate 1984. *Serial Murders: Hearings Before the Subcommittee on Juvenile Justice of the Committee of the Judiciary*, On patterns of murders committed by one person in large numbers with no apparent rhyme, reason, or motivation, Washington, U.S. Senate, 985th Congress, 1st Session.

See also **Genocide; Homicide: Nature, Extent, and Correlates; Terrorism**

Homicide: Murder-for-Hire

In 1993, Lawrence Horn hired James Edward Perry to kill his son so that he could collect the $1.7 million medical malpractice insurance the boy would receive (Mobilio, 1999; Goodwin, 2001). After reading *Hit Man: A Technical Manual for Independent Contractors*, Perry followed the book's pointers to kill Horn's ex-wife, her son, and the boy's nurse. The book was found in Perry's home after his arrest. Perry was sentenced to death and Horn to life imprisonment. The book is no longer available from its publisher, Paladin Press.

Hiring someone to kill another person has been the subject of a large number of fictional works and movies. In fact, there are relatively few instances of contract killings or murder-for-hire and very little factual national or international data about hired killers. According to 1999 reports from the FBI, there were 391 murders in Tennessee; by comparison, Black (2000) found 30 convicted murder-for-hire cases in the same state during the entire decade of the 1990s. Black's research covers murders, attempted murders, and solicitations to commit murder.

Black has suggested that murder-for-hire has gone through a three-stage process in the U.S. In the *entrepreneurial* stage, killers were hired for economic and racially motivated reasons and not personal and private reasons. For example, Lane in *Murder in America* describes the use of the Pinkerton agency "and other

hired guns" to protect striking workers against minorities who wanted their jobs. As organized underworld organizations emerged in the early 20th century, there was a need for more of a *professional* or *independent* hired gun. Mob-based "hit men" emerged because violence is a means of internal control as well as protection from outside interference.

Though professional hit men still offer their services in support of political and economic corruption in developing market economies (especially in the former communist nations in Eastern Europe and Asia), there is evidence in the U.S. that this type of killer is being replaced by *personalized* murder-for-hire. This personalized hit man is more amateurish, but also is more accessible to a wider range of people. In addition, the person who wants the killing done, the solicitor, is changing. Increasingly, solicitors have problems in their personal intimate domestic lives that they believed can be resolved by killing.

In their murder-for-hire project, Black and Cravens define the event as a "continuous sequence of interactions by one or more persons in which one person solicits another person to have a third person killed for gain, monetary or otherwise. An event begins with the initial exploration of the possibility of having someone killed, and terminates with a murder, attempted murder, or police intervention." These authors obtained information on 30 cases of murder-for-hire using court

Table 1. Comparisons of Homicide and Murder-for-Hire Events*

Participants	Homicide Events			Murder-for-Hire Events	
	Variable		Percent	Variable	Percent
The solicitor	Sex	Male	90	Male	53
	Race	Black	58	White	93
	Age	15–34	78	19–41	75
	Prior Offenses	Yes	68	Yes	55
The hit man	Sex			Male	97
	Race			White	90
	Age			16–30	70
	Prior Offenses			Yes	50
Victim	Sex	Male	77	Male	65
	Race	Black	49	White	90
	Age	20–34	74	26–49	70
Circumstance	Time	8:00 PM–1:59 AM	49	2:00 AM–7:59 AM	43
	Place	Home	49	Home	63
	Method	Firearm	75	Firearm	35
	Results	Murder	100	Murder	45
				Attempted murder	10
				Murder and attempted murder	3
				Police intervention	41

*Table taken from Cravens and Black.

and Department of Corrections records, presentence reports, state historical archives, and interviews. Table 1 compares the characteristics of homicide and murder-for-hire events.

Considering the solicitor, almost all (93%) are White whereas in ordinary homicide events, 42% are White and 58% Black. Although ordinary homicide is considered a male offense (90%), in murder-for-hire events almost as many females (47%) as males (53%) solicit the death of another. Solicitors tend to be somewhat older than homicide offenders; slightly over three-fourths (78%) of homicide offenders are between 15 and 34 whereas three-fourths of offenders in murder-for-hire events range between 19 and 41. The majority of both homicide offenders (68%) and solicitors (55%) have prior arrest records.

Table 1 suggests that the hit men (one was a woman) are predominantly White (90%) and male (97%). Thirty-seven percent of the hit men were undercover law enforcement agents who learned the solicitor's intention and posed as killers (the lone female hit man was an undercover agent). Seventy percent of the hit men were between the ages of 16 and 30 and 50% had a prior arrest record.

Comparing victims of ordinary homicide and murder-for-hire events, it is clear that murder-for-hire is a White person's offense. In addition to a predominance of White solicitors and hit men, 90% of the victims

were White. By comparison, less than half (49%) of homicide events described by Black and Cravens were Black. Male victims were in the majority for both homicides (77%) and murder-for-hire events (65%). As was the case for solicitors, targets or victims of murder-for-hire events tend to be somewhat older than victims of homicides. Seventy percent of murder-for-hire victims were between 26 and 49 whereas 74% of homicide victims were between 20 and 34.

Comparison of the circumstances in Table 1 indicates that about half of homicides occurred between 8:00 PM and 2:00 AM; 43% of murder-for-hire events occurred between 2:00 AM and 8:00 AM. Although the home was the preferred location for both types of homicide, murder-for-hire events (63%) occurred in the home more often than other types of homicides (49%). Firearms were used much more frequently (75%) in ordinary homicides than in murder-for-hire events (35%). Police intervention prevented homicides in 41% of the murder-for-hire events.

Elsewhere, Black and Cravens reported that solicitors contacted strangers in 31% of the cases that they examined. In 24% of the cases, the solicitors were friends. Sixty-three percent of the solicitors and victims were married.

The vast majority of murders involve one offender and one victim owing to the seriousness of the offense, the severity of sanctions, and the ever present possibility that others with foreknowledge will inform authorities. This raises the question for contract murders of how solicitors go about the task of finding someone to do the killing, getting that individual to agree to do the task, and then actually completing it.

Black and Cravens describe the interactional process between solicitor and hit man using a theory of "scripted behavior." Scripted behavior begins with "a stable cognitive representation of the particular script." "Scripts," or contracts to kill, originate in the minds of solicitors who have decided they have some insurmountable problem that can be resolved by having someone kill the target of their problem. The decision to have someone killed is not a spur-of-the-moment decision, but is the product of considerable reflection. The motives offered for the killing often include greed, revenge, jealousy, and sex, but the process by which solicitors conclude that murder is the only strategy available to them to resolve these problems is unclear.

Once the decision to kill is made by solicitors, the cognitive script must be transformed to a participatory script to commit murder. At this point, there are two tracks; the first involves solicitors and hit men that know one another and is called the *intimate track*. The second, the *staged track*, involves solicitors seeking the help of experienced strangers who turn out to be undercover law enforcement agents posing as hit men.

Focusing only on the intimate track, the participatory script begins by exploring the possibility of a murder using friends, acquaintances, or relatives as offenders. These kind of "priming scripts" include an offer of money, sex, or continuing intimacy and an approach that can be brushed off as humor in case the individual being solicited reacts negatively. If the idea of killing is not rejected out of hand, considerable coercion or manipulation might be used by solicitors to promote cooperation.

Once the hit men have agreed to the killing, the interaction changes to contracting and plotting how the killing will be accomplished. In the contracting stage, the hit men's rewards are discussed. Black and Cravens find that contracts with women solicitors and between solicitors and hit men with close interpersonal relationships tend to be more implicit in indicating the nature of rewards for the hit man. There appears to be little order in any of these scripts with regard to when the murder should occur or the costs of killing.

The same looseness prevails with respect to how the contract killing is going to be carried out. Decisions about weapons, time, location, and strategies for hit men interactions with solicitors do not adhere to any particular pattern. However, pressure is applied to hit men who take too long to complete the murder.

The outcome, of course, is murder or attempted murder. The intimate track is particularly lethal because in the staged track, the police often arrest solicitors for the crime of solicitation to commit murder.

MARC RIEDEL

References and Further Reading

Black, J.A. 2000. Murder-for-hire: An exploratory study of participant relationships, in *The Varieties of Homicide and its Research*, Blackman, P.A., Leggett, V.L., Olson, B.L., and Jarvis, J.P. (Eds.), Washington: U.S. Government Printing Office.

Black, J.A. and Cravens, N.C., Murder for hire: Characteristics and casual implications, University of Tennessee—Knoxville, unpublished.

Black, J.A. and Cravens, N.M., Contracts to kill as scripted behavior, University of Tennessee—Knoxville, unpublished.

Goodwin, J., *The "Hit Man" Manual*. Northwestern University. Available at http://faculty-web.at.northwestern.edu/commstud/freespeech/cont.../hitman.htm. Retrieved on January 28, 2001.

Lane, R. 1997. *Murder in America: A History*, Columbus, OH: Ohio State University Press.

Mobilio, A. 1999. The criminal within: A genre of how-to manuals indulges our darkest fantasy, *Harpers* 298.

See also **Homicide: Nature, Extent, and Correlates; Homicide: Law**

Homicide: Nature, Extent, and Correlates

Introduction

Homicide is the killing of one human being by another. Whether the homicide is considered criminal or not varies according to legal codes of given jurisdictions at given points in time. Criminal homicides are frequently considered first-degree murder when one person causes the death of another with premeditation and intent. They are considered second-degree murder when the death involves malice and intent but is not premeditated. Noncriminal homicides can also be of different types, including those that occur in self-defense and justifiable homicides, as when a convicted offender is executed by the state.

When using statistics on homicide it is important to know what forms of killing are included in the definitions of agencies that are reporting. For example, the U.S. Federal Bureau of Investigation, in its Uniform Crime Reporting Program, defines homicide as the willful, nonnegligent killing of one person by another. This data source is most frequently used to chart trends in criminal homicide in the U.S. Another U.S. data source on homicide is the National Center for Health Statistics, which classifies homicide according to the International Classification of Diseases, 9th ed. (1979–1998). This definition of homicide is somewhat broader than the one used by the Federal Bureau of Investigation.

International Comparisons

Both the United Nations (UN) and the World Health Organization (WHO) collect international data on homicide. Like the National Center for Health Statistics, these organizations report mortality data according to the International Classification of Diseases, 9th ed., used from 1979 to 1998. Homicide is defined as a death from injury purposely inflicted by another person, excluding legal interventions and acts of war. Both the UN and WHO depend on reporting agencies within each nation to submit homicide numbers. As a result, we lack information for many nonreporting nations, particularly those in the Middle East and Africa, and must be cautious about data reported by other countries, such as those in the former Soviet Bloc. In any case, examining international rates over time makes general comparisons between different countries more reliable.

According to WHO data published in 1998, the South American nation of Colombia has the highest rate of homicide, topping the world at 78.5 homicides per 100,000 people. The Russian Federation has the second highest rate, 30.8. Other South and Central American nations, and nations formerly part of the Soviet Union are also very high. European nations, Australia, Canada, and Asian nations typically have much lower rates of homicide. Many have homicide rates of less than 2.0 per 100,000 people. For example, according to the WHO, Canada has a homicide rate of 1.7 and Great Britain has a rate of 0.8. Japan is at the bottom of the list, with a rate of 0.6 homicides per 100,000. The U.S., although similar to these nations in terms of economic development, has a relatively high homicide rate, recorded as 9.4 by the WHO (1998).

Researchers offer several explanations for international differences in homicide rates (see LaFree, 1999). These explanations often focus on the make-up of a country's population or a nation's economic characteristics. For example, some social scientists suggest that the presence of numerous racial or ethnic or religious groups in a nation affect the homicide rate, but there is little evidence to support this. One population characteristic associated with the homicide rate is a fast-growing population. Increasing population growth in a country is related to a higher homicide rate.

Differences in economic development across countries partially explain differences in homicide rates. Generally, the less economic development that exists in a nation, in terms of a lower per capita gross national product, less energy use, and the amount of industry and technology, the higher the homicide rate. For instance, Japan and most Western European countries have high levels of economic development and low homicide rates. The U.S. is an exception to this pattern, as it has high levels of development and a relatively high homicide rate.

Another national economic characteristic linked to differences in homicide rates is the amount of divergence between the rich and poor in a country. Inequalities based on income and education have the greatest effect on a nation's homicide rates, and account for differences between countries (Gartner, 1995). The larger the difference between the rich and the poor in a nation, the higher the nation's homicide rate; this fact is one of the most enduring findings of cross-national comparisons of homicide rates.

Homicide Trends in the U.S.

The U.S. Bureau of Justice Statistics compiles and presents information regarding homicide trends (see Fox and Zawitz, 2001). These data are based on the FBI's publication *Crime in the United States*, called the Uniform Crime Reports, and its *Supplementary Homicide Reports*. Between the early 1930s, when homicide statistics reported to the FBI became more reliable, and 1950, the homicide rate declined, although this decline was interrupted briefly in the 3 years following World War II (Zahn and McCall, 1999). From the 1950s to the mid-1960s, homicide rates remained relatively stable, ranging between 4.0 and 5.1 homicides per 100,000 people. Starting in 1964, when the rate was 4.9, the homicide rate steadily increased through the 1970s, reaching an all-time high of 10.2 in 1980. By 1984, the rate decreased to 7.9, but rose again through the 1980s into the early 1990s, topping at a rate of 9.8 in 1991. In the mid-1990s, the rate decreased, hitting a 30-year low of 5.7 homicides per 100,000 people in the U.S.

in 1999. Overall, the homicide rate more than doubled between the 1950s and 1980, peaked again in the 1990s, but declined in the late 1990s, attaining rates not seen since the 1960s.

Homicide in Different Demographic Groups in the U.S.

Age

Historically, homicide is a young adult's crime (see Fox and Zawitz, 2001). Rates for homicide victimization and offending are consistently highest for those ages 18–35. Beginning in the mid-1980s, conventional trends in homicide for certain age categories were defied. Prior to this time, those under 18 and over 50 had the lowest rates of both victimization and offending, whereas those between 18 and 35 had the highest rates, with 35–49-year-olds falling in the middle. Then, in 1985, although those under 14 still remained lowest in victimization and offending, 14–17-year-olds surpassed those over 50 and 35–49-year-olds as victims of homicide, and surpassed all groups but the 18–24-year-olds as perpetrators of homicide. Although there was a gradual decline in this trend for 14–17-year-olds in the mid to late 1990s, rates for victimization and offending remained higher than 1980s levels.

Race

African Americans are much more likely than Whites to be victims and perpetrators of homicide (see Fox and Zawitz, 2001). For example, in 1999 African Americans were six times more likely than Whites to be victims of homicide, and seven times more likely than Whites to be perpetrators of homicide. Homicide trends for African Americans reflect national homicide trends. However, the race distribution for homicide victimization and offending differs by homicide type. For the years 1976–1999 combined, African American victims were overrepresented in homicides involving arguments and drugs, whereas Whites were more likely to be victims of gang-related, felony, and workplace violence. As offenders, African Americans were overrepresented in homicides involving felonies, drugs, and arguments, whereas Whites were more likely to be perpetrators of sex-related, gang-related, and workplace homicide (see Fox and Zawitz, 2001).

The majority of homicides are intraracial (see Fox and Zawitz, 2001). From 1976 to 1999, 94% of African American victims were murdered by African Americans; 86% of White victims were murdered by Whites. Although intraracial homicides are predominant, when homicides are interracial, the perpetrator is more likely to be a stranger to the victim. Three in ten homicides committed by strangers are interracial, whereas only one in ten homicide committed by a friend or acquaintance is interracial.

Much of the research on race and homicide investigates how racial inequalities are likely to be a particularly potent source of criminal violence (see Messner and Rosenfeld, 1999). Some studies explain racial differences in homicide with reference to income inequality between racial groups. That is, because Blacks, as a group, have lower incomes than Whites and economic inequality is related to homicide rates, Blacks are more likely to be offenders and victims of homicide. Others explain racial differences in homicide with reference to the characteristics of the communities. On one hand, Blacks are disproportionately restricted to communities that provide their members with few economic resources (e.g., jobs) and restricted social opportunities (e.g., education) (Wilson, 1996). This leads to feelings of frustration and hostility that may increase violence or lead people to seek illegal means to make money. On the other hand, the social isolation created by racial segregation in housing may increase violence, because this isolation undermines the ability of the community to obtain adequate police protection or to mobilize community residents for crime prevention activities (Peterson and Krivo, 1993). Both economic and segregation explanations have empirical support.

Gender

Perpetrators and victims of homicide are predominately male (see Fox and Zawitz, 2001). For instance, in 1999 males were 3.2 times more likely than females to be murdered and were nearly nine times more likely to commit murder. On a nationwide basis, homicide involving a male offender and a male victim is most common (65.1% of homicides between 1976 and 1999), followed by homicides involving a male offender and a female victim (22.4%). About 10% of homicides involved female offenders and male victims, and only 2.4% of homicides involved female offenders and female victims.

The gender distribution of homicide offenders and victims differs by victim–offender relationship (see Fox and Zawitz, 2001). For example, in the years 1976–1999 combined, females were more likely than males to be murdered by an intimate and had a similar risk to males of being murdered by another family member. Although males maintain higher offense rates than females in all relationship categories, females tend to murder people within an intimate or family relationship.

As depicted by the UCR data, females are generally underrepresented in homicide incidents (see Messner and Rosenfeld, 1999). Much more research attention has been given to females as victims of homicide than to females as homicide offenders. Female homicide victimization is sometimes attributed to gender inequality. One approach theorizes that as women gain higher levels of education as well as occupational, employment, and income attainment, they are more "protected" from victimization, but there has been little to no support for this theory (Messner and Rosenfeld, 1999).

On the other hand, some researchers have proposed that women's increasing participation in society puts them at greater risk for victimization because their activities are expanded outside the home where there can be greater opportunity for a would-be assailant or because their activities are threatening to men's advantageous position in society (Messner and Rosenfeld, 1999). This perspective has limited empirical support as well. In general, research shows that women's increased participation in the labor force has not resulted in an increase in female homicide victimization or offending. Thus, women's low rates of victimization and offending remain to be adequately understood.

Age, Race, and Gender

As might be inferred from the above discussion, the "typical" homicide offender and victim in the U.S. is a young African American male. Indeed, statistics between 1976 and 1999 consistently indicate that African American males ages 18–24 have the highest rates of homicide victimization and offending (see Fox and Zawitz, 2001). For both races and genders, homicide victimization and offending for those over 25 declined from 1976 to 1999. Between the mid-1980s and mid-1990s, victimization and offending rates for males ages 14–24, young African American males in particular, increased markedly. Since the mid to late 1990s, victimization and offending rates for these groups have decreased. The pattern for young African American females was similar but not as dramatic. Patterns for young White females remained relatively stable.

Homicide and Economic Deprivation

Economic deprivation is often cited as a social condition leading to homicide. Economic deprivation is generally categorized and linked to homicide in two ways (see Messner and Rosenfeld, 1999). First, absolute deprivation, analogous to poverty, refers to a situation in which people have difficulty securing, because of lack of resources, the basic necessities for healthy living. In this argument, poverty produces

strains that can push or pressure people to commit violent acts. Poverty demoralizes people, weakening social controls that inhibit violent expression. Accordingly, when poverty in an area increases, homicide rates increase. Some studies directly link poverty in an area to its homicide rate. Other studies show it is not poverty alone but poverty in concert with other social conditions related to it, such as low educational attainment, inadequate housing, and family breakdown that contribute to high levels of homicide (Messner and Rosenfeld, 1999).

The second type of economic deprivation, relative deprivation, which is analogous to income inequality, refers to people's relative lack of material goods compared to others, and their subjective experiences of deprivation. This line of argument proposes that the subjective feeling of deprivation motivates or frees people to engage in violence. On this account, as income inequality in an area increases, feelings of relative deprivation become more widespread and acute, resulting in rising homicide rates. For areas like cities or states, research evidence is mixed with some studies finding the hypothesized relationship between income inequality and homicide, but other studies finding no relationship. As noted above, at the national level, evidence consistently links income inequality and violence. Despite this documentation that economic deprivation is related to homicide, further research is needed to conclusively link this social condition to lethal violence in other geo-political units.

Circumstances of Homicide

Through the *Supplementary Homicide Reports*, information is available regarding victim or offender relationships and the primary circumstances of homicides. Victim–offender relationship is categorized in several ways, such as acquaintance, intimate, family, stranger, and unknown. Intimates include spouses, ex-spouses, boyfriends, and girlfriends. Circumstance is broken into four categories: felony type, suspected felony, other than felony, and unknown. Felony-type homicides are those in which a murder occurred during the commission of a felony such as robbery or drug trafficking. In the "other-than-felony" category are circumstances like arguments, gang killings, and romantic triangles. Although the most common type of homicide involves men who are acquaintances in an argument (UCR, 1999), two special categories of homicide are discussed here: homicide between intimates and homicides committed during another felony.

Historically, most victims of homicide have known their offenders. For example, in 1999, strangers committed only 12% of homicides. Homicides in which the offender and victim are acquaintances constituted the largest proportion of murders from the mid-20th century until 1990. Homicides committed by intimates and family member were smaller proportions by comparison. Beginning in the mid-1970s, victims' murders by intimates or family members declined, whereas homicides in which the victim–offender relationship was unknown sharply increased and became the second largest category (see Zahn and McCall, 1999). In fact, by 1990 unknown relationships surpassed acquaintance homicides, which began to decline as well. According to the 1999 UCR, in 40% of homicides the relationship between the victim and offender was unknown, whereas victims and offenders were acquaintances in 25% of homicides.

In 1999, homicides between intimates accounted for 10% of cases. Female victims are much more likely than male victims to be murdered by an intimate (see Fox and Zawitz, 1999); indeed, women are more likely to be killed by their male partners than any other perpetrator (Browne et al., 1999). About one-third of female victims are killed by intimates, compared to 4% of male victims. Further, it is in this category of homicide that females' offending rates approach that of males; nonetheless, women are two times more likely to be killed by their male partners than men are by their female partners (Browne et al., 1999). According to Block and Chrisakos (1995), women are at particular risk of being murdered by their intimate partners when trying to leave relationships. They are also more likely to be killed by partners with violent arrest records or by partners who are suicidal. Women are particularly likely to be offenders in cases that involve alcohol or in cases that involve knives. Other researchers have noted similar results (Browne et al., 1999). There is clear link between women leaving their partners and men responding with rage and violence leading to murder. Men who eventually murder their partners have a history of physically abusing and threatening their partners. Women's violence against their partners is often in response to aggression and threat.

Although the proportion of homicides resulting from arguments has declined since 1980, arguments still remain the most common factor precipitating homicide (see Fox and Zawitz, 1999). Starting in 1990, homicides owing to arguments, felonies, narcotics violations, and gang violence slowly declined, whereas homicides with unknown circumstances continued to increase, nearly doubling since the mid-1970s (Fox and Zawitz, 1999; Zahn and McCall, 1999). By 1999, homicides resulting from arguments comprised 31% of cases, followed closely by homicides of unknown origins (30%). Felony-related homicides constituted

about 17% of cases; of these, half were the outcome of robberies, and a quarter were because of narcotics violations (about 5% of total homicides). Gang violence was responsible for 6% of homicides in the U.S. in 1999.

Homicides resulting from arguments are often so-called "crimes of passion," murders that take place in the heat of the moment. Felony-related homicides, many of which are "robberies gone bad," are the subject of some speculation by scholars. Philip Cook (1987) has offered an interpretation of robbery-based homicides. Cook argues that robbery-related homicides are very similar to nonfatal robberies. Rather than being a separate act from the robbery, robbery murders are an intrinsic by-product of the robbery itself. That is, the murder is unplanned: the victim is accidentally killed by a robber who is responding to the victim's resistance or who has a momentary impulse. A major factor is the robber's choice of weapon. When the weapon is a gun, the encounter is much more likely to be fatal for the victim (Cook, 1987).

Homicide and Juveniles

Teen involvement in homicide, as both victims and perpetrators, increased dramatically in the U.S. in the latter half of the 1980s and early to mid-1990s (see Fox and Zawitz, 2001). Although victimization and offending rates for 14–17-year-olds declined in the late 1990s, the 1999 rates remain higher than levels before 1985 and still represent the second highest offending rate. Blumstein and his colleagues (1995, 2000) contend that the increase in homicides in the late 1980s and the subsequent decline can be attributed to gun violence by juveniles and young adults.

Scholars have tried to explain the explosive increase that occurred in juveniles' participation in homicide. These explanations focus on individual and social factors. Among the individual characteristics contributing to juvenile homicide are low self-esteem, inability to deal with strong negative feelings, boredom, and poor judgment (Heide, 1997, 1998). Juveniles involved in homicide are often involved with drugs and alcohol as well (Heide, 1997, 1998). Violent victimization of children, child abuse and neglect, and witnessing violence in and out of the home play roles in juvenile homicide (Howell et al., 1995; Heide, 1997, 1998).

Broader social conditions also contribute to juvenile homicide. One important impact on youth violence is the availability of guns to juveniles whether obtained from a family member or friend or on the street (Blumstein, 1995; Howell et al., 1995; Heide, 1997, 1998;

Blumstein et al., 2000). Youths who commit murder are also affected by a lack of positive, especially male, role models in their families and communities, and by what Heide terms a crisis in leadership in the U.S., both in the government and private sectors (Heide, 1997, 1998). There has been a decline in income among families with young children, and increasing numbers of children are growing up in single parent families, both conditions that put children at greater risk for experiencing poverty and other deleterious consequences (Howell et al., 1995).

Poverty itself is an important social factor contributing to juvenile homicide (Howell et al., 1995; Heide, 1997, 1998). Experiencing poverty puts youths at greater risk for physical and mental health problems, low academic achievement, unemployment, and delinquency. These youths are also likely to grow up in disorganized neighborhoods that lack resources and provide few opportunities. Additionally, Blumstein and his colleagues (1995, 2000) have linked rising homicide rates in the 1980s and the flourishing illicit drug market in American cities. The drug trade provided teens and young adults opportunity for illegitimate work in a declining job market, and drug markets were associated with the increase in violence. Heide (1997, 1998) suggests that the cumulative effect of these individual and social factors is a negative one. In essence, youths that turn to violence have little or nothing left to lose. The declining youth violence seen in the mid to late 1990s may be partially attributed to the national economic growth that occurred during this time, but achieving further declines in youth violence requires addressing the conditions that lead to hopelessness among youth.

Homicide and Firearms

Firearms are an important factor in violence. The great majority of homicides are committed with guns, particularly handguns (see Fox and Zawitz, 2001). Mirroring the national trend for homicides, the number of homicides committed with guns increased dramatically in the late 1980s then dropped in the late 1990s. During the same time period, homicides committed with other weapons, such as knives, blunt objects, and poison, slowly decreased. In 1999, firearms accounted for 65% of all homicides; in nearly 80% of these cases, handguns were the weapon of choice (UCR, 1999). As noted above, some researchers argue that the increase in homicides in the late 1980s and the subsequent decline can be attributed to gun violence by juveniles and young adults. Although gun homicides committed by those 25 and older slowly declined from 1976 to 1999, gun homicides by 14–24-year-olds spiked beginning in the mid-1980s and decreased slightly in the latter half of the 1990s.

Scholars point to two explanations for the prevalence of firearms, particularly handguns, in U.S. murder rates. Cook and Moore (1999) argue that the fact that violent crimes in the U.S. are so deadly and the homicide rate so high (compared to other nations) has very much to do with the availability and use of guns. Research suggests that the overall availability of guns in a community influences weapon choice in violent events. Where gun ownership is prevalent in a community, guns tend to be prevalent in violent events. Research also shows that acquiring a gun is little challenge to those who are motivated to acquire one, either by legal or illegal means. The willingness to use guns is also important: Guns provide the power to intimidate other people and gain control of a situation. When the offender's main intent is robbery, intimidation, or self-defense (rather than inflicting injury), a gun is more effective in achieving that purpose without the actual use of violence. But when violence does erupt, the end result is more likely to be fatal when the offender wields a firearm as opposed to another type of weapon.

Preventing Homicide

The U.S. government's *Healthy People 2010* initiative, a cooperative effort of numerous federal and state agencies headed by the Department of Health and Human Services, considers homicide a public health issue (DHHS, 2001). Homicide is the second leading cause of death for 15–24-year-olds and the third leading cause of death for 5–14-year-olds. Because homicide is a public health concern, one of the goals of the *Healthy People 2010* initiative is violence prevention.

Several intervention strategies for preventing youth violence have been shown to be effective. One group of strategies aims to change individual behavior by addressing educational achievement or the development of techniques and skills to avoid expressing violence (Mercy and Hammond, 1999). These strategies include reducing classroom size in elementary schools; tutoring; vocational training and employment; mentoring relationships that include behavior management techniques; behavioral monitoring and reinforcement of school attendance, progress, and behavior; and curricula focused on conflict resolution and violence prevention (Brewer et al., 1995). Another type of intervention program focuses on building healthy interpersonal relationships through intervening with parents and children early in life (Mercy and Hammond, 1999). These programs involve parent training, family therapy, and home visitation by counselors and health practitioners

(Brewer et al., 1995). Other strategies concentrate on environmental factors (Mercy and Hammond, 1999). Such interventions include structured after-school recreation, restricting and regulating firearms, and community policing (Brewer et al., 1995).

Any policy aimed at preventing violence should have three organizing principles (Thornberry et al., 1995). To have the greatest effect, intervention programs should start early in life, should be comprehensive in design, and should be available on a long-term continuing basis. Additionally, programs should extend far beyond the criminal justice system, applying multiple interventions reaching individuals, schools, communities, and the public at large (Zimring and Hawkins, 1995). In considering homicide prevention, it is important to keep in mind that violence is not just an individual problem, but also the outcome of many socially determined causes (Zimring and Hawkins, 1995). Preventing homicide requires attention to individuals, communities, and larger social influences.

MARGARET A. ZAHN

References and Further Reading

Block, C.R. and Christakos, A. 1995. Intimate partner homicide in Chicago over 29 years. *Crime and Delinquency* 41: 496–526.

Blumstein, A. 1995. Youth violence, guns, and the illicit-drug industry. *The Journal of Criminal Law and Criminology* 86 (1): 10–36.

Blumstein, A., Rivara, F.P., and Rosenfeld, R. 2000. The rise and decline of homicide—And why. *Annual Review of Public Health* 21: 505–541.

Brewer, D.D., Hawkins, J.D., Catalano, R.D., and Neckerman, H.J. 1995. Preventing serious, violent, and chronic juvenile offending: A review of evaluations of selected strategies in childhood, adolescence, and the Community, pp. 61–141, Howell, J.C., Krisberg, B., Hawkins, J.D., and Wilson, J.J., Eds., *Serious, Violent, and Chronic Juvenile Offenders: A Sourcebook*. Thousand Oaks, CA: Sage.

Browne, A., Williams, K.R., and Dutton, D.G. 1999. Homicide between intimate partners: A 20-year review, pp. 149–64, Smith, M.D. and Zahn, M.A., Eds., *Homicide: A Sourcebook of Social Research*. Thousand Oaks, CA: Sage.

Cook, P.J. 1987. Robbery violence. *Journal of Criminal Law and Criminology* 78: 357–376.

Cook, P.J., and Moore, M.H. 1999. Guns, gun control, and homicide: A review of research and public policy, pp. 277–296, Smith, M.D. and Zahn, M.A., Eds., *Homicide: A Sourcebook of Social Research*. Thousand Oaks, CA: Sage.

Department of Health and Human Services. 2001. *Healthy People 2010*. Available at www.health.gov/healthypeople.

Federal Bureau of Investigation. 1999. *Crime in the United States: Uniform Crime Reports*. Washington, DC: Government Printing Office.

Fox, J.A. and Zawitz, M.W. 2001. *Homicide Trends in the United States*. Available at www.ojp.usdoj.gov/homicide/homtrnd.htm#contents.

Gartner, R. 1995. Methodological issues in cross-cultural large-survey research on violence, pp. 7–24, Ruback, R.B. and Weiner, N.A., Eds., *Interpersonal Violent Behaviors: Social and Cultural Aspects*. New York, NY: Springer Publishing Company.

Heide, K.M. 1997. Juvenile homicide in America: How can we stop the killing. *Behavioral Sciences and the Law* 15: 203–220.

Heide, K.M. 1998. *Young Killers: The Challenge of Juvenile Homicide*. Thousand Oaks, CA: Sage Publications.

Howell, J.C., Krisberg, B., and Jones, M. 1995. Trends in juvenile crime and youth violence, pp. 1–35, Howell, J.C., Krisberg, B., Hawkins, J.D., and Wilson, J.J., Eds., *Serious, Violent, and Chronic Juvenile Offenders: A Sourcebook*. Thousand Oaks, CA: Sage.

International Classification of Diseases, 9th ed. 1979–1998. Available at www.cdc.gov/nchs/icd9.htm.

LaFree, G. 1999. A Summary and review of cross-national comparative studies of homicide, pp. 125–148, Smith, M.D. and Zahn, M.A., Eds., *Homicide: A Sourcebook of Social Research*. Thousand Oaks, CA: Sage.

Messner, S.F. and Rosenfeld, R. 1999. Social structure and homicide: Theory and research, pp. 27–41, Smith, M.D. and Zahn, M.A., Eds., *Homicide: A Sourcebook of Social Research*. Thousand Oaks, CA: Sage.

Mercy, J.A. and Hammond, W.R. 1999. Combining action and analysis to prevent homicide: A public health perspective, pp. 297–310, Smith, M.D. and Zahn, M.A., Eds., *Homicide: A Sourcebook of Social Research*. Thousand Oaks, CA: Sage.

Peterson, R.D. and Krivo, L.J. 1993. Racial segregation and Black urban homicide. *Social Forces* 71: 1001–1026.

Wilson, W.J. 1996. *When Work Disappears: The World of the New Urban Poor*. New York, NY: Alfred A. Knopf.

World Health Organization. 1998. *World Health Statistics Annual, 1996*. Geneva: World Health Organization.

Zahn, M.A. and McCall, P.L. 1999. Trends and patterns of homicide in the 20th century United States, pp. 9–23, Smith, M.D. and Zahn, M.A., Eds., *Homicide: A Sourcebook of Social Research*. Thousand Oaks, CA: Sage.

Zimring, F.E. and Hawkins, G. 1997. *Crime is Not the Problem: Lethal Violence in America*. New York, NY: Oxford University Press.

See also **Homicide: Mass Murder and Serial Killings; Homicide: Murder-For-Hire; Homicide: Law**

Homicide: The Law

Of all crimes, murder is the least common, the most often cleared, and the one that receives the greatest attention from law enforcement and the media. In homicide investigations, the crime scene is often the greatest source of information about the offense and the offender. Most homicides that are murders involve people who know each other, occur in the heat of passion, and result in an arrest from within the circle of spouses, friends, associates, and relatives. It is this familiarity that makes murders easier to clear than other offenses. Investigations of stranger-on-stranger and serial murders must depend on evidence found at the scene of the crime. It is axiomatic in the world of homicide investigation to say that if the crime is not cleared in the first 24 hours it may not be cleared at all. It should be borne in mind that a clearance is an arrest, not a conviction. Arrest data is the foundation for much of the crime reports generated by the U.S. government.

Not all homicides require the attention of the police. A homicide is the taking of a human life by another human. The circumstances of the homicide will determine if the homicide was justifiable or murder, the killing of another with malice aforethought. Justifiable homicides would be those occurring in situations involving self-defense against persons intending to cause death or serious bodily injury or in police shootings where the use of deadly force was justified. Such homicides are not considered murder for investigation purposes, and once a determination of justifiable homicide is made, the case is closed.

Criminal homicide is defined by state statute and may be further subdivided into categories such as capital murder (murder of a police officer and other specific circumstance murders), murder (with malice aforethought), and manslaughter (murder with the absence of malice aforethought). Many states still use degrees to distinguish one type of homicide from another; first-degree murder is murder with malice aforethought (premeditated), second-degree murder is manslaughter (murder in the heat of passion), and third-degree murder is negligent homicide (murder with an automobile). To that list of degreed homicides many states have added capital murder to the scheme.

Capital murder is murder with accompanying "aggravating circumstances." In order for a capital punishment law to be constitutional there are some considerations that must be reflected in the specific language of the law. A state may not elect to execute all murderers. There must be some characteristics that differentiate the capital murderer from the noncapital murderer. In most states murder or first-degree murder is homicide with "malice aforethought." Spontaneous emotional outbursts, wherein murder occurs in the "heat of passion," are often referred to as second-degree murder or manslaughter. The penalty for manslaughter is less than that for premeditated murder in that the people of the states through their representative state governments see murder in the heat of passion as less grievous or heinous than murder that has been premeditated. Most states have a different characterization and penalty for death resulting from the heat of passion (manslaughter) versus death occurring as a result of preplanning and implementation of that plan (premeditation—malice aforethought). Therefore, murder with "aggravating" characteristics should be treated differently than premeditated murder of one person. All states that have a capital punishment law define capital murder as murder with one of the following accompanying circumstances:

- Murder of more than one person;
- The knowing and intentional murder of a police officer, judge, or firefighter;
- The knowing and intentional murder of a witness;
- Murder in the course of another felony;
- Murder of children or the elderly;
- Murder in a correctional institution;
- Murder for hire.

In addition to proving at least one of the above aggravating circumstances the state must prove in each capital prosecution that the defendant poses a "continuing threat of violence to the community." This is usually accomplished by having a state psychologist or psychiatrist mentally evaluate the defendant prior to trial. The state must address the issue of guilt or no guilt separately from the question of punishment. Once a determination is made of murder with one of the above aggravating characteristics the trial will go into a second stage where issues regarding sentencing are addressed. It is important that the defendant have an opportunity to submit any mitigating circumstances he or she feels are applicable to the sentencing.

It is the aggravating circumstances that make a capital offense subject to more severe penalty. It should be noted that the term capital offense is a vestige of our English and common law roots. Under English and

American colonial law, any person found to be guilty of an offense that carried with it the penalty of death could only be executed in the colonial capital wherein the offense occurred. Hence, the name "capital punishment" and "capital offense."

Every murder has specific elements that must be proven at the time of trial; these elements are referred to as the *corpus delicti* of the offense. Often confused by the public and the media as requiring the state to produce a corpse in order to convict for murder, it is simply a reminder that there are specific and unique proofs submitted to the court in support of a prosecution for murder. All criminal homicides require that the state prove (1) that there has been a death of a human being (this may be difficult to prove absent a body, hence the prevalence of premeditated murderers' attempting to dispose of the body), (2) that the death was the cause of another person's illegal act or failure to act, and (3) that the illegal act caused the death.

The legal questions that often plague a homicide investigation usually revolve around proximate cause and causation. The question of proximate cause deals with the conduct and the consequences of that conduct. The illegal act must be close in time and space to the death of another. There is no problem in determining that a person who shot a gun was responsible for the consequences of that act when the projectile struck the person he or she was aiming at. Proximate cause may become an issue, however, in more convoluted scenarios. For example, a shot fired into a construction site intended for a personal enemy could cause an individual on the construction site to jump instinctively and drop a concrete block onto another individual two stories below. The result may be tragic, but the person firing the shot has not committed murder of the person upon whom the block has fallen. The chain of cause and effect is too tenuous to establish the cause element of the *corpus delicti* of murder.

The question of causation most often arises in those situations where an individual is seriously injured by another but does not die immediately or shortly after the assault. The greater the time from the illegally caused injury until death the more attenuated becomes the relationship between the injuring act and the death. Most states address the causation question by statute requiring that the death occur within a particular timeframe after the illegal act causing the injury.

Closely related to "causation" is the issue of "limitations." When one speaks of "limitations" it generally refers to the time within which the state may prosecute a particular offense. It is the consensus of people in the U.S. that a person should not be pursued indefinitely for a crime that has been committed. All states have a "statute of limitations" in criminal cases that requires the state to employ due diligence in the pursuit, capture, indictment, and conviction of a criminal offender. That "limitation" of any offense is determined by the legislature and all states have statutes of limitation for all offenses. Less serious crimes have shorter "statutes of limitation"—for example in most states the "limitations" for theft are anywhere from 3–5 years. The statute of limitation runs day for day during the time that the offender remains within the state in which the crime was committed. Any time the offender remained outside the state would not be counted as to apply to the associated "statute of limitations" and is said to "toll" (stop the counting) the statute. As the crime becomes more severe the limitations period is longer until we reach the crime of murder, which has no "statute of limitations." A murderer can be arrested, indicted, tried, and convicted for a murder committed at any time.

Investigating a Homicide

When homicides are reported they receive a degree of attention that lesser crimes are not afforded. Part of that "selectivity" has to do with the limitations on manpower and resources. A police agency must decide where its priorities lie and allocate its manpower and resources accordingly. The most prevalent crimes against property are most difficult to clear and the cost of manpower to investigate these crimes would be astronomical. Property crime is so prevalent that most people will be the victim of a property crime in their lifetime. The prevalence and relative seriousness relegates their investigation somewhere close to the bottom in terms of manpower allocations. Conversely, the number of homicides occurring nationally can be managed by an appropriate allocation of manpower and resources. Not all countries value life the way it is valued in the U.S. The standard of living in the U.S. is high as is the relative value we give to human life. That cultural perspective is reflected in how homicides are investigated. Bodies are treated with the greatest dignity, not for any convenience for the deceased but because of the sensibilities of friends, relatives, and the public at large. It is the most heinous of crimes and is thereby accorded the most investigative attention. Crime scenes are protected, witnesses and suspects constrained. All the power and abilities are theoretically brought to bear on investigations of homicides. Protocols are involved in criminal investigations; those for homicides are the most universally recognized: cordoning off the crime scene, assessing the potential location of evidence within a crime scene, photographing the crime scene, locating the evidence (marking the locations), constructing a crime scene sketch (reflecting relevant measurements), photographing the marked evidence, tagging the evidence (for later identification), and bagging the evidence (in a way that will preserve it and prevent contamination). The investigation will include talking to those who may have been witnesses and canvassing the neighborhood to discover what might have been seen or heard that was unusual. It is said that the majority of investigative work happens on the bottom of the shoe (walking and talking). Not all homicides can be solved, but if the crime scene has been properly processed, witnesses intelligently interviewed, and suspects interrogated, if all paperwork has been accurately completed and all leads followed, that investigation is a success, whether or not it results in an arrest and conviction.

Defense and Prosecution

Because of concerns of "proportionality" as contained in the Eighth Amendment's prohibition against "cruel and unusual punishment" those states with death penalties were responsible to assure that:

- No race is disproportionately subject to the death penalty;
- The penalty fits the crime.

It was this latter concern that prompted the states to identify murder with aggravating circumstances rather than simply murder. The responsibility of the state rests on the shoulders of the attorney for the state in deciding what offense to charge and whether or not the available evidence is sufficient to sustain the state's burden to establish "aggravating circumstances." Often the state will charge capital murder in the hopes of soliciting a plea agreement wherein the defendant will plead guilty to murder with the state's guarantee that they will not seek the death penalty. It is expensive for a state to pursue the death penalty for a defendant. The associated costs run into the millions for each defendant who does not waive his or her appellate rights.

Each state in its capital punishment statute not only has to address issues of proportionality, thereby listing aggravated circumstances, but it also has to address issues of continuing danger to the community and guarantee that any conviction that carries the death penalty is assured of appeal to the highest court within the state. It should also be apparent that every capital trial has some built-in appellate issues beginning with allegations of "cruel and unusual punishment." In addressing the notion that the death penalty is "cruel and unusual" the defense generally offers two arguments:

1. The death penalty is "cruel and usual punishment" *per se* (in itself) and,
2. The evolving standards of society have made the death penalty an unacceptable sanction.

It is the state's position that neither of these arguments is applicable. Media focus, generally, is on the impending death of the defendant and generally couched in favor of abrogation of the death penalty. The constitutional arguments are seldom addressed in the media; consequently it is an emotional issue mediated through passion rather than logical discourse. From a legal perspective the state's position is fairly simple: if the death penalty is *per se* unconstitutional, there should be some evidence that the founders of our nation abhorred the death penalty and considered it unacceptable from the inception of this country. However, a careful examination of the Constitution and its Amendments reveals just the opposite. The Fifth Amendment to the Constitution has a due process clause that include in part the idea that no person shall be deprived of life, liberty, or property without due process of law. It would appear on its face that the men who wrote the Amendments to the Constitution had in mind the legitimacy of the death penalty when it was implied that the government could take someone's life as long as that government provided "due process of law."

The state must also contend with the "evolving standards of decency" argument espoused by not only the defendant's lawyers but most of the media reporting the event. This issue is fairly easily resolved in favor of the state and the solution to the argument is available through empirical evidence. No state is required to have a death penalty. A state that chooses to have one must provide certain statutory assurances against "disproportionality." So it is fair to say that those states that have a death penalty were free to make that decision. If standards of decency have evolved to render the death penalty no longer a legitimate sanction, it should be borne out by simply counting the number of states that have a death penalty and comparing it to the number of states that do not. For Justices on the U.S. Supreme Court it is not a matter of convenience or simply applying one's personal preferences or philosophy to an issue to resolve it. They have been tasked, and fairly abide by that task, to apply constitutional precedent and interpretation to the resolution of constitutional disputes. The constitutional scholars among them will recognize the "evolving standards of decency" argument the day there are more states without a death penalty than there are states with a death penalty. Until that time, it would be specious to claim we have evolved as people to the point of refusing to accept capital punishment as an acceptable sanction.

In most cases, the state has the burden of proof. That burden includes:

- Proof that the defendant committed the crime within the area over which the court has authority;
- Proof that the court has the subject matter authority to hear the case; and
- The elements of a crime.

To prove capital murder, the state must prove the intentional, premeditated taking of another human life. Once they have proven that the defendant in fact premeditatedly murdered the victim, the state must prove one of the "aggravating circumstances" that make up the laundry list of accompanying characteristics to murder. They must prove that the defendant poses a continuing threat of violence and danger to the community. If the state's prosecutor proves these things beyond a reasonable doubt, the state's job is finished.

The defendant traditionally must prove "nothing." There is but one burden of proof in a criminal case and that rests squarely on the shoulders of the prosecution. The defendant may present evidence in his or her behalf but is not required to do so. The defendant may choose to take the stand and offer testimony but is not required to do so and in most cases is advised by competent counsel not to take the stand. It is the defense lawyer's job to ensure that rules of procedure, rules of evidence, and the constitutional rights of the client are defended. A defense lawyer's sole responsibility is to ensure that the efforts on the part of the state to convict his client are in conformity with the rules of the court and the Constitution of the U.S. If a capital defendant is convicted, the jury expects the defendant to take the stand, show remorse, and provide testimony that disputes his proclivity for violence. A variety of defense witnesses including a defense mental health expert will attempt to convince the judge or jury that the defendant, although guilty, is not deserving of the death penalty because of certain mitigating circumstances and is not an inherently violent person. For the defendant this is a stage where it is necessary for him or her to participate. With nothing from the defense in mitigation the probability is that the defendant will be sentenced to death.

Justification

Many states have statutes that describe the circumstances under which a person is justified in using deadly force. Because there are justifications in certain cases of homicide, not all homicides are considered criminal. When considering whether a death is caused by murder, the evidence of the offense must be present but there must also be no "justification." Most states recognize that citizens under certain circumstances have the right to use deadly force to protect themselves, others, their property, and the property of others. Those circumstances are specifically provided for by statute. The Texas Penal Code contains a common example of legislative efforts to recognize this right:

> ... a person is justified in using force against another when and to the degree he reasonably believes the force is immediately necessary to protect himself against the other's use or attempted use of unlawful force ... (Texas Penal Code Ch. 9. Justifications Excluding Criminal Responsibility, Subchapter C. Protection of Persons, Section 9.31 Self-defense)

A person is justified in using deadly force against another:

1. If he would be justified in using force against the other as described in Section 9.31;
2. If a reasonable person in the actor's situation would not have retreated; and
3. When and to the degree he reasonably believes the deadly force is immediately necessary; (a) to protect himself against the other's use or attempted use of unlawful deadly force; or to prevent the other's imminent commission of aggravated kidnapping, murder, sexual assault, aggravated sexual assault, robbery, or aggravated robbery ... (Section 9.32 Deadly Force in Defense of Person)

States vary as to justifications for using deadly force to protect others or property but all jurisdictions recognize self-defense and the use of a deadly weapon when confronted with the prospect of deadly force.

Window of Death Determinations

Most criminal homicide investigations attempt to establish a "time of death." The time at which the crime was committed is important in investigative efforts to (1) establish the victim's movements prior to death, (2) establish the victim's activities prior to death, (3) establish a suspect and witness pool, (4) corroborate the suspect's alibi, (5) establish some parameters for the investigation, and (6) clarify anomalies at the crime scene.

In attempting to determine the time of death in most investigations the best that can be hoped for is an approximation. No methods have been discovered that independently or in conjunction with others can establish the moment of death precisely. The best case scenario is a "window of time" in which it is determined the death must have occurred. It is through the constant reduction of the time frame in this window of opportunity that investigators can best approximate the time of death. In attempting to frame this "window" the investigator must discover the people and events that the victim encountered before death. That discovery is based on tracing the movements of the victim and those the victim had encountered from the last time he or she was seen until the body was discovered. In addition to the information gathered by investigators, valuable insight can be gained from the information provided by medical examiners, pathologists, entomologists, autopsy (a medicolegal internal and external examination of the body of the deceased), and toxicology reports.

The only time that can be determined for sure at the outset of a criminal homicide investigation is the time the body was discovered. Establishing and narrowing the "window of death" is a process that begins from the discovery of the body and moves backward in time. The broadest window that the investigator will be able to establish is from the last time anyone saw or heard the victim until the body is found. The assessment of time of death begins here and becomes even narrower as a result of additional evidence from the crime scene and the body of the deceased. Medical data, along with information gathered from people and events preceding the slaying, can gleaned from help to narrow the "window."

The medical examiner determines cause of death (accident, suicide, or criminal homicide) and he or she or a forensic pathologist may determine mechanism and manner of death (e.g., brain damage resulting from blunt trauma or loss of blood from a gunshot wound).

There are a number of methods employed by the medical examiner and forensic pathologists to assist the investigator in narrowing the "window of death." These methods are based on the principle of using sequential changes in the deceased as a postmortem clock. The evaluation may include physicochemical changes evident upon direct examination of the body such as changes in body temperature, rigor mortis, and decomposition and generally include:

1. Post mortem cooling (algor mortis)
2. Ocular changes
3. Postmortem lividity (livor mortis)
4. Postmortem rigidity (rigor mortis)
5. Cadaveric spasm
6. Stomach contents
7. Putrefaction.

RONALD BECKER

References and Further Reading

Bray, M. 1985. The eye as a chemical indicator of environmental temperature at the time of death. *Journal of Forensic Science*, 29:389–395.

Breitenecker, R. 1969. Shotgun wound patterns. *American Journal of Clinical Pathology*, 52:258.

Bugliosi, V. 1992. *And the Sea Will Tell*. New York, NY: Ivy Books.

Coe, J. and Curran, J. 1980. Definition and time of death. Curran, W.J., McGarry, A.L., and Petty, C.S., *Modern Legal Medicine, Psychiatry, and Forensic Science*. Philadelphia, PA: Davis Co.

Federal Bureau of Investigation Laboratory: Gunpowder and shot pattern tests. 1970. *FBI Law Enforcement Bulletin*, September.

Hall, D. 1948. *The Blowflies of North America*. Baltimore, MD: Monumental Printing Co.

Knight, B. 1988. The evolution of methods for estimating the time of death from body temperature. *Forensic Science International*, 36:47.

Miller, L.S. and Brown, A.M. 1990. *Criminal Evidence Laboratory Manual*, 2nd ed. Cincinnati, OH: Anderson.

Pepper, J. 1993. Time of death and changes after death: Anatomical considerations. Spitz, W.U. (Ed.), *Medicolegal Investigation of Death*, 3rd ed. Springfield, OH: Charles C. Thomas.

Saferstein, R. 1990. *Criminalistics: An Introduction to Forensic Science*. Englewood Cliffs, NJ: Prentice Hall.

Smith, K. 1986. *A Manual of Forensic Entomology*. London, UK: British Museum.

Spitz, W.U. 1993. *Drowning. Medicolegal Investigation of Death*, 3rd ed. Springfield, OH: Charles C. Thomas.

See also **Homicide: Nature, Extent, and Correlates**

Homosexuality

Centuries before the term homosexuality was invented to describe sexual activity between two people of the same sex and the identity of those engaging in such sexual activity, it was deemed criminal and deserving of sanction by governments in North America, Europe, and parts of the Middle East. Historical records of homosexual activity in ancient Egypt, Greece, North America, China, and Japan exist as far back as 5000 BC—yet such activities were not deemed criminal or even inappropriate until several thousand years later. Boswell (1980) identifies a 12th century law drafted in Jerusalem by Europeans that punished "sodomites" with death by fire as the earliest official state action against homosexuals (specifically gay men). Others have found proscriptions against homosexuality as early as 700 AD, at which time it was punishable by castration in Spain. Later, in 14th century France, the legal school of Orléans also adopted a law requiring that male homosexual conduct be punished with castration on the first offense, dismemberment of one's limbs on the second offense, and death by fire on the third offense. Female homosexuals were punished with dismemberment on the first as well as second offenses.

Similar punishments comprised the official state reaction to homosexuality in colonial America. In his historical account of the treatment of gay men and lesbians in North America from 1566 to 1966, Katz (1976) documents state-imposed sanctions for homosexual conduct or even gender inappropriate behavior of any kind that included death by hanging, drowning, and other means. In the earliest codified law of colonial America, the Plymouth colony in 1636 placed sodomy in a list of eight offenses punishable by death. Although their definition of sodomy required penetration, lesser punishments, including whipping, burning, and banishment, were imposed on same-sex conduct that did not involve penetration. Yet, even then, there were no references to homosexuals as a specific group of people.

The word "homosexual" is a 19th century invention, coined by Karoly Maria Kertbeny to describe sexual activity between two people of the same sex, or the inability to achieve physical arousal with a member of the opposite sex. Many theories have been posited to explain the etiology of homosexuality. They range from biological and genetics explanations involving a "gay gene" and hormonal differences that are thought to predispose a person to homosexuality to psychosocial explanations emphasizing upbringing and environment. Until the 1970s, homosexuality was largely thought of as not just a moral flaw, but a psychophysiological aberration. Building on the works of Sigmund Freud, the psychiatric community medicalized homosexuality in the early 20th century, defining it as an illness rather than as a sin or a crime. It was not until the American Psychiatric Association removed homosexuality from its Diagnostic and Statistical Manual of psychiatric disorders in 1973 that it ceased to be defined as a mental ailment. Yet the medicalization and demedicalization of homosexuality did not change its status as a form of deviance in the eyes of many, including lawmakers.

In the modern U.S., attention to homosexuality as a form of criminality surfaced as part of the temperance and neo-Victorian reform movements of the late 19th and early 20th centuries. This political development in the U.S. was complemented in Europe by the sensational trial of poet and playwright Oscar Wilde. Wilde was convicted in 1895 for homosexual offenses

by a British court, sentenced to hard labor, and exiled. This high profile case, along with the wave of neo-puritanical sentiments in the U.S., led to a renewed concern for the criminal status of homosexuality. This concern was not uniform in its content, however—the seeds of an oppositional movement, which would criticize the criminalization of homosexuality, were planted.

The first known gay rights organization, aimed at educating the public and reforming laws criminalizing homosexuality, was formed in Germany in 1897, in the wake of the Oscar Wilde trial. Its first U.S. counterpart was founded in 1924, and aimed to combat public prejudice against homosexuals. The organization was short lived, however, and the gay rights movement did not resurface in any significant form until the post-World War II era. In the late 1940s, Alfred Kinsey and his associates began their path-breaking research, developing the first epidemiological portrait of homosexuality in the U.S. Although his findings—namely, that 10% of the population was gay or lesbian—have since been critiqued, the study was instrumental in initiating a meaningful public and academic dialogue about homosexuality and revealing that it was far more common than previously thought. Yet, even once the gay rights movement gained considerable strength and visibility in the 1950s and 1960s, significant reform of sodomy laws in the U.S. came slowly.

Following the compilation of the Wolfenden Report in Great Britain and the American Law Institute's Model Penal Code, both advocating the legalization of consensual homosexual conduct, Illinois became the first state to decriminalize sodomy in 1961. Still, most states continued to categorize sodomy, including anal as well as oral sex, as a felony, punishable by as much as a 20-year prison term. In 1969, Connecticut followed suit, becoming only the second state to completely decriminalize sodomy. Around the same time, New York responded to the Model Penal Code proposal by reducing sodomy from a felony to a misdemeanor, and, thereby, lowering the punishment significantly. Throughout the late 1960s, 1970s, and into the 1980s, several cases were brought before state and federal courts challenging the constitutionality of sodomy laws. Some resulted in the decriminalization of sodomy in certain states by ruling of the state supreme court, such as those in New York and Pennsylvania.

The U.S. Supreme Court, however, did not issue any written decisions on gay rights or sodomy until the 1986 landmark case of *Bowers v. Hardwick* (478 U.S. 186). *Bowers v. Hardwick* involved the arrest of an adult gay man, Michael Hardwick, for consensual oral sex with another man in the privacy of his own bedroom. Hardwick was arrested for violating Georgia's sodomy law (which was subsequently ruled invalid in 1998 by the Georgia Supreme Court), after a policeman entered the room to serve a warrant on an unrelated allegation. Challenging the constitutionality of the Georgia statute with the help of the American Civil Liberties Union, the case was appealed by Hardwick to the U.S. Supreme Court. The court eventually ruled against Hardwick, stating in effect that the constitutional right to privacy, guaranteed in *Griswold v. Connecticut* (381 U.S. 479, 1965), did not extend to homosexual sodomy, and that the "promotion of public morality" is a sufficient justification for laws criminalizing such conduct. As the first U.S. Supreme Court ruling dealing with gay rights and sodomy laws, *Bowers* had a tremendous impact on the homosexual community. It effectively reinscribed the criminal status of gay men and lesbians by outlawing their most defining feature. This occurred despite the fact that several state legislatures had repealed their sodomy statutes in the 1970s and 1980s. As of 2001, 17 states continue to criminalize sodomy: Alabama, Arizona, Arkansas, Florida, Idaho, Kansas, Louisiana, Massachusetts, Michigan, Minnesota, Mississippi, Missouri, North Carolina, Oklahoma, South Carolina, Utah, and Virginia. In four states (Oklahoma, Kansas, Missouri, and Arkansas), sodomy laws apply to only same-sex activity.

It has been argued that the gay rights movement's opposition to sodomy laws inaccurately highlights sodomy as the essence of homosexuality and of gay or lesbian identity. Indeed, the *Bowers* decision did not make it illegal to *identify* as homosexual, or to *say* that one is homosexual; it outlawed only the sexual act associated with homosexuality. Therefore, it could be argued that homosexuality as a status is not a crime if the person in question remains celibate. More recently, gay rights advocates such as Janet Halley have argued for a "personhood" definition of homosexuality, which defines homosexuals as a class according to their shared form of personality, rather than by their commission of sodomy (an illegal and "deviant" sexual behavior). This argument is particularly salient in those 13 states having sodomy laws that technically criminalize both homosexual and heterosexual sodomy; by virtue of the fact that the law recognizes that people of all sexual orientations can and do engage in sodomy, it cannot be solely a marker of homosexuality.

Yet the reality is that the criminal status of sodomy has regularly been used as a justification to deny homosexuals certain rights, such as the right to privacy and equal protection rights in employment. In *Padula v. Webster* (261 U.S. App. D.C. 365, 1987), a lesbian woman was denied employment by the Federal Bureau of Investigation on the basis of her sexual orientation. In deciding against her claim, the court held that the *Bowers* ruling foreclosed any effort to apply equal protection and due process guarantees to

homosexuals since the earlier decision had upheld the criminalization of the "behavior that defines the class" of people. In other words, because sodomy is seen as the defining feature of homosexuality as an identity, any homosexual person is a potential criminal in states that outlaw sodomy—even if she or he has not been proven to have engaged in sodomy. This has proved to be a significant impediment for the gay rights movement in many legal and social arenas.

A major effort in the gay rights movement that has been significantly affected by the *Bowers v. Hardwick* ruling and by the continued existence of sodomy laws has been the establishment of antidiscrimination laws protecting against antihomosexual bias in employment, housing, the military, and other realms of public life. These laws rely on the Fourteenth Amendment's due process and equal protection clauses, and take the same form as laws protecting against racial and religious bias. The standard of "strict scrutiny" in these laws dictates that racial and religious minorities constitute "suspect statuses," making them prime targets for discrimination. Therefore, the government must afford them affirmative protection against bias by subjecting any case in which a person of one of these statuses feels his or her equal protection rights have been violated to *strict scrutiny*, in order to make sure that such discrimination has not taken place. In cases such as *Padula*, courts have denied such status to gay men and lesbians, arguing that "It would be quite anomalous, on its face, to declare status defined by conduct that states may constitutionally criminalize as deserving of strict scrutiny under the equal protection clause." Yet, on the local government level and even in some state legislatures, the homosexual minority has been successful in applying equal protection doctrine to their civil rights, affording gay men and lesbians the classification of a "suspect status," or protected class, and enacting laws that prohibit discrimination based on sexual orientation in the public sphere. Just as quickly as these laws are enacted, though, antigay activists often have proposed bills and referendums to invalidate such statutory protections.

In the 1990s, these two positions on the antidiscrimination law debate clashed in Colorado, and later in the U.S. Supreme Court. In 1992, conservative groups in both Oregon and Colorado introduced ballot initiatives that prohibited any governmental agency from enacting antidiscrimination laws aimed at protecting the civil rights of gay men and lesbians. The Oregon initiative, Measure 9, ultimately failed at the polls; but Colorado's Amendment 2 was successful, gaining the votes it needed to be enacted into law. This law would effectively nullify the antidiscrimination ordinances that had been enacted in Denver, Boulder, and Aspen. After the vote, Amendment 2 was challenged in court in the case of *Romer v. Evans* (517 U.S. 620, 1996). Gay rights attorneys argued that the law was unconstitutional in that it singled out a specific group of people—homosexuals—for the purpose of barring them from certain fundamental rights and equal protection of the law. This argument proved successful, and Colorado's Amendment 2 was struck down by the U.S. Supreme Court. The court reasoned that the Colorado legislature did not have the right to classify a specific group in order to deny them rights afforded to everyone else. This meant that, depending on the jurisdiction and the circumstances, homosexuals could draw on the protections of the Fourteenth Amendment in pursuing equal rights—or at least in combating overt discrimination in the public sphere.

Although seen as a victory for gay rights, *Romer* was not inconsistent with *Bowers*, and it did not significantly change the status of gays and lesbians; it merely gave them back what they once had in the municipalities that had enacted antidiscrimination legislation. The justices writing the majority opinion in *Romer* did not consider their decision to be an overruling of *Bowers*. Although the two cases had completely different outcomes in terms of gay rights implications, their justifications were quite compatible. In *Bowers*, the justices reasoned that privacy rights could not be extended to a class or activity that had previously not enjoyed those rights because of its illegality (homosexual activity or sodomy). In *Romer*, the justices were not extending a previously nonexistent right to a new class of people; rather, they were returning rights to a group whose rights had been selectively removed by the state. Therefore, the *Romer v. Evans* decision has the capacity to extend basic civil rights protection to homosexuals in jurisdictions that decide to enact such laws, but has not had the effect of eliminating the criminal status of homosexuality or making gay rights universal in the U.S.

The fact that gay men and lesbians are not uniformly afforded the same rights and protections as other minority groups, and that they are still defined by a conduct that is considered criminal in 17 states, has a broad impact—both political and personal—on homosexuals, bisexuals, and their families. This impact is most significant in two areas of personal and legislative concern: the family and antigay violence. With regard to the former, there are several factors that make it particularly difficult for gay men and lesbians to form and maintain families. The most obvious and hotly debated of these is the prohibition of same-sex marriage. In 2000, legislation in Vermont for the first time anywhere in the U.S. allowed legal partnerships or "civil commitments" between two people of the same sex—essentially tantamount to an official marriage, but not so named. Before that, only Hawaii had taken any steps toward the

recognition of gay and lesbian marriages. In *Baehr v. Lewin* (74 Haw. 645, 1993), the Hawaii Supreme Court became the first high court in the nation to officially sanction same-sex marriages. This decision met considerable resistance on the federal level. First, in response to the *Baehr* decision and pressure from conservatives in Congress, President Clinton in 1996 signed into federal law the Defense of Marriage Act (DOMA), which defined legal marriages as only those unions between a man and a woman, and prohibited the states from recognizing any other form of marriage. Later, in 1997, the Hawaii legislature adopted a similar statute, and in 1999, the *Baehr v. Lewin* decision was overturned on remand from the federal circuit court (*Baehr v. Miike,* 92 Haw. 634, 1999).

Because gay couples do not have the option of marriage available to them, they have often been barred from many other facets of family life, including public recognition as spouses, inheritance, health benefits, adoption, and child custody. Until fairly recently, many states prohibited unwed couples from jointly adopting a child. In some states today, such as New Hampshire and Florida, where adoption by heterosexual unmarried couples or by single people is allowed, there are express prohibitions against adoption by homosexuals—whether as a couple or individually. Many gay and lesbian couples now opt to have children by way of reproductive technology, either with a surrogate mother or by artificial insemination. Yet, in the event of a partner's death or a break up of the relationship, there are no guarantees that the nonbiological parents will have any parental rights, because there is no legal bond between the two partners owing to their inability to marry. When combined with the presumption in many family courts that being raised by a homosexual parent may be harmful to a child, the issue of child custody proves to be a persistently difficult one for gay men and lesbians who wish to parent. This difficulty is especially salient when one takes into account the fact that approximately half of all lesbians and one-third of all gay men are parents.

Perhaps an even more pressing concern for the homosexual community and lawmakers is the recent proliferation of high profile acts of antigay and lesbian violence. Although "gaybashing" has long been a part of American life, it has not received widespread media attention or been systematically measured until recently. Following a number of well-publicized antigay hate crimes in the late 1990s, including the gruesome murders of Matthew Shepard, a young college student in Wyoming, and 39-year-old Billy Jack Gaither in Alabama, lawmakers and activists across the country began to push harder for additional hate crime laws and for the inclusion of sexual orientation on the list of protected statuses in existing hate crime laws. By the year 2000, 22 states had hate crime laws on the books that included violent acts based on sexual orientation; ironically, neither Wyoming nor Alabama are on this list.

With the recent attention to antigay hate crimes, homosexuality as a topic of criminological inquiry has come full circle. Whereas violence was once the official legal response to homosexuality in colonial America, it is now considered criminal in the eyes of the state and unacceptable to a majority of the public. Under current hate crime laws in many states, the punishment for a violent crime is enhanced if it can be proven that the act was motivated by antigay prejudice. Ironically, both the public and the federal government are willing to add measures to protect homosexuals from criminal victimization—yet, they are not willing to completely decriminalize homosexuality itself.

KIMBERLY D. RICHMAN

References and Further Reading

Boswell, J. 1980. *Christianity, Social Tolerance, and Homosexuality*, Chicago, IL: University of Chicago Press.

Cain, P.A. 2000. *Rainbow Rights: The Role of Lawyers and Courts in the Lesbian and Gay Civil Rights Movement*, Boulder, CO: Westview Press.

Davis, N. and Geis, G. 2001. *Encyclopedia of Criminology and Deviant Behavior: Sexual Deviance*, Philadelphia, PA: Brunner-Routledge.

Eskridge, W.N. Jr. and Hunter, N.D. 1997. *Sexuality, Gender, and the Law*, Westbury, NY: The Foundation Press, Inc.

Greenberg, D. 1988. *The Construction of Homosexuality*, Chicago, IL: University of Chicago Press.

Herek, G. and Berrill, K.T. 1992. *Hate Crimes: Confronting Violence against Gay Men and Lesbians*, Newbury Park, CA: Sage Publications.

Katz, J.N. 1976. *Gay American History: Lesbians and Gay Men in the U.S.A.*, New York, NY: Thomas Y. Crowell Company.

Richardson, D. and Seidman, S. 2001. *Handbook of Lesbian and Gay Studies*, Beverly Hills, CA: Sage Publications.

Rubenstein, W.B. 1993. *Lesbians, Gay Men, and the Law*, New York, NY: The New Press.

Vaid, U. 1995. *Virtual Equality: The Mainstreaming of Gay and Lesbian Liberation*, New York, NY: Doubleday.

Warner, M. 1993. *Fear of a Queer Planet: Queer Politics and Social Theory*, Minneapolis, MN: University of Minnesota Press.

See also **Hate Crime**

Hoover, John Edgar

The Federal Bureau of Investigation's headquarters in Washington, DC represents simultaneously the legacy of the most prominent police executive of the 20th century and many law and order conflicts of grand proportions. In important ways, also, the J. Edgar Hoover building symbolizes constructive advances in criminology, criminal justice administration, and crime fighting, particularly the rising standards of police professionalism and training, commitment to scientific techniques of investigation, and developments in record keeping and analysis. Practitioners and scholars alike will grant Hoover significant credit in these areas. By contrast, however, Hoover's legacy attracts critics who charge the FBI with unlawful investigations of agency opponents and left-leaning political dissidents. Additionally, critics note Hoover's stubborn and consistently vengeful agency protectionism. Fans of the FBI praise the director's 48-year reign, recognizing that he transformed an inept agency into a world-class investigative organization. Detractors respond that Hoover was responsible for restricting the FBI's administrative progress, thereby contributing to contemporary accusations of mismanagement, obsolescence, and inappropriate agent conduct.

Despite the FBI's record of achievement since Hoover's death, any historical overview of American crime fighting is incomplete if the life and work of J. Edgar Hoover is not mentioned. Posthumous characterizations of Hoover find him a complex man, an engaging powerhouse of administrative leadership. His persona is virtually inseparable from the FBI's reputation in the field of law enforcement. His long career at the FBI extends from the era of new social scientific studies of crime causation and the modern era of crime prevention, critical criminology, and policy evaluation. His contributions to these worthy endeavors derives mainly from dedication to building a center of excellence in the war on crime, indeed transforming the FBI from a bureaucratic agency to an institution.

The private and public lives of J. Edgar Hoover have been exhaustively evaluated from diverse perspectives. Research on Hoover's life and achievements has been partly aided by the FBI's voluntary participation. Discovery of important documents concerning agency misdeeds, however, has followed from aggressive litigation under the Freedom of Information Act and from interviews with current and former insiders. Informed journalists, including Fred Cook, Ovid Demaris, Curt Gentry, Hank Messick, and Anthony Summers, have probed deeply behind the headlines of Hoover's well-orchestrated public image. Historians, such as Richard Powers and Athan Theoharis, have published an extensive collection of articles and books addressing, in part, the connections between Hoover's ideological reference points and FBI policies and practices. Hoover, too, supplied a considerable collection of writings to promote his views on crime and the evils of communism. Hoover's publications were partly crafted by trusted lieutenants, thus reducing their value as historical records. The corpus of documentation on his life and work has supplied important trace evidence of an intensely dedicated, enigmatic, and almost machine-like bureaucrat. Generally, the written record has revealed Hoover as a man who invented and controlled his own universe, energized by a drive to inject crime control into the mainstream of American governance processes, and with equal determination to win and maintain support for his beloved FBI.

Attorney General Harlan F. Stone appointed J. Edgar Hoover as director of the Bureau of Investigation (BOI) in 1924. Created by Congress in 1907 and implemented in 1908, the BOI struggled for identity and a formal role in a small but expanding federal law enforcement sector. At a critical juncture in the scandal-racked Justice Department, Stone consulted with Secretary of Commerce Herbert Hoover (no relation to director Hoover) and others in President Calvin Coolidge's administration. All advice emphasized J. Edgar Hoover's dedication and integrity, some recognizing his achievements in the Bureau's General Intelligence Division under Attorney General A. Mitchell Palmer and the 1919 Red Scare roundup of anarchists and communists. Following his appointment, Hoover worked in relative seclusion for most of the 1920s, focused mainly on recruiting trustworthy agents, molding agency units, and conducting discrete investigations of individuals and groups. As the decade ended, he was not entirely secure in his job. He responded by broadening Bureau affiliations with the scattered policing community and by giving special attention to new developments in investigative techniques. Quietly, Hoover secured the support of many federal and state politicians and police leaders. He called on that support when FBI resources were needed for advancing the science of fingerprinting, for uniform crime statistics and reports to local police and the public, and for developments in wiretapping devices. In time, Hoover's emphasis on technologies, perfection of administrative practices, and cooperation with local and state police organizations enlarged his network of interpersonal and political influence. Among law enforcement practitioners no government official commanded more influence and respect in articulating the anticrime agenda than J. Edgar Hoover.

The presidencies of Herbert Hoover (1929–1933) and Franklin Roosevelt (1933–1945) presented opportunities for J. Edgar Hoover to ride a new wave of political and social interest. Public support encouraged Hoover to fight common gangsters, build Bureau resources, and achieve recognition for the Bureau as one of the world's best agencies of investigations and domestic intelligence. In 1935, the formal title of the agency was changed to the Federal Bureau of Investigation. Hoover had achieved a clear but guarded national mandate. Increasingly, Roosevelt relied on the FBI for reports on international intrigues, domestic policy in-fighting, and intelligence relevant to tensions in Asia and Europe. As hostilities escalated after 1939, the climate of war mobilization drew Hoover back to his philosophical roots in anticommunism. The FBI was accused of excessive actions against opponents of American involvement in the war, but by then the agency was known in every household in America, a status won in previous years when agents rounded up notorious bank robbers, embezzlers, kidnappers, and spies. During World War II, Hoover attempted to overshadow the work of William Donovan, a World War I hero and the World War II director of the Office of Strategic Services. His goal was to capture the position of intelligence chief in the postwar years. Aside from Roosevelt's affinity for paring off equally ranked bureaucrats, Donovan was the clear winner over Hoover in the race for Roosevelt's ear on intelligence advice. Hoover's narrow educational record and limited knowledge of international politics were no match for Donovan or any likely successor. Congress cut short Hoover's intentions in 1947 when it created the Central Intelligence Agency, insistent on maintaining a sharp distinction between the CIA's jurisdiction in overseas intelligence gathering and the FBI's domestic intelligence and investigative assignments. Quietly, however, Hoover targeted opportunities for expanding the mission of the FBI, and part of his success came from aligning with right-wing politicians who controlled the Bureau's budget.

From the late 1940s to 1961, Presidents Harry Truman and Dwight Eisenhower valued the stability that Hoover and the FBI brought to federal law enforcement in a time of cold war tensions. Hoover maneuvered congressional support for funds to expand investigations of Soviet espionage, to assist Senator Joseph McCarthy's anticommunist campaign, and to make modest efforts to investigate organized crime. Hoover strengthened his popular image as a crime and spy hunter extraordinaire, greatly enhanced by television crime series, effective public relations, and the director's portrayals of good and evil in the world. *Masters of Deceit* and *On Communism*, for example, represented Hoover's attempt to perpetuate the anticommunist theme at a time when public support for McCarthy-era paranoia had faded. Despite widespread publicity about organized crime and warnings about significant international drug trafficking, Hoover remained uninterested in widespread actions against mafia leaders. Historians and others have argued that Hoover's obsessions with FBI credibility, compromise of the director's personal integrity, and inadequate legal jurisdiction justified inattention to the mob.

Hoover had served for nearly three decades when John Kennedy took office in 1961. The new Kennedy administration marked the first real challenge since the 1920s to Hoover's base of power. Attorney General Robert Kennedy pressured Hoover to depart from comfortable methods of crime fighting. Hoover was asked to weigh the value of building even more mountains of agency statistics when the intentions of mobsters like the three Joe's (Bonanno, Columbo, and Gallo) had not been confronted. Indirectly, he was also urged to compare the sophistication of criminal enterprises with the relatively simple techniques employed in bank robbery and in tracking spies. The Kennedy White House proved to be a special kind of intrusion into Hoover's rigid control over agency priorities. The director countered by delivering his standard response that the Bureau had minimal legal authority to pursue organized crime. Unwilling to accept Hoover's less-than-forthright actions, Attorney General Robert Kennedy shifted resources to U.S. attorneys and to special multiagency investigative teams. Hoover's carefully worded public announcements proclaimed the sinister nature of organized crime, declaring the FBI's full intentions to make arrests and convictions where federal authority existed. He adamantly refused to allow agents to work on joint agency missions, but it was not uncommon for field agents to supply other agencies with intelligence. Within 6 months of John Kennedy's assassination, the *DePaul Law Review* published Hoover's detailed defense of his agency's actions. Hoover, of course, was not alone in confronting new challenges in a changing environment of crime. Criminologists encountered a sharply rising juvenile and youth crime rate in the early 1960s. Their main data source, i.e., FBI-produced information from police agencies, became less useful for analyzing crime trends and for support of new anticrime policies. Hoover seemed unwilling to participate in debates among criminologists about methods for improving data sources, particularly acquisition of information on crime victims.

Hoover's private life manifested significant contradictions. His aura of confidence and personal control contrasted with a rarely acknowledged pleasure in gambling. A man who was obsessed with possible compromises of the FBI's image was also a man who maintained a life-long private and unexplained companionship with his chief deputy director, Clyde Tolson. And Hoover's no-nonsense public persona was not easily reconciled with his love of art and antique collecting. Perhaps the paint-by-numbers rendition that hung in the Eisenhower White House suggested an inescapable subconscious boundary: a life influenced so deeply by self-control that even in the attempt to find limited artistic expression the imagination was fettered by predetermined lines on canvas and specified colors schemes.

In the late 1960s, Hoover began to lose control of the political high ground. The FBI he had invented faced a constant barrage of domestic turmoil associated with the war in Vietnam. Media coverage took aim at the Bureau's practice of surveilling "enemies" of the Nixon administration, and it encountered charges of agency excesses and obsolescence. The Lyndon Johnson and Richard Nixon administrations had delayed asking Hoover to resign. Each recognized that the director had overstayed his effective time in the office. Undoubtedly, they wished that Hoover would go quietly into retirement, perhaps to write his memoirs about the glory days of crime fighting. Until the bitter end, however, Hoover controlled the terms and the timing of his departure, ingenious in his ability to contrive justifications for stalling the inevitable result. The end came in the privacy of Hoover's home in northwest Washington. The housekeeper found his body sprawled on the bedroom floor, an end not unlike so many tragedies depicted in thousands of FBI files.

J. Edgar Hoover's life in law enforcement paralleled the evolution and major advances in criminology. In the same year as his appointment, Edwin H. Sutherland published *Criminology*, the first textbook in a long series of modern approaches to crime research. Hoover devoted his early career to creating a federal investigative organization that would capture the admiration and support of ordinary citizens while allaying the fears of critics in the Congress, the federal courts, the Justice Department, and the White House. His writings added little to scientific assessments of crime causation, but they articulated a narrow frame of reference that remains a prominent element in the modern discussions about crime control policy. For a long period in the 20th century, Hoover was a necessary force of stability in a climate of economic disarray, world war, and cold war tensions. His passing brought new attention to years of missed opportunities in the FBI, but it also created opportunities for the post-Hoover leadership to introduce the agency to streams of modern criminological research and research applications.

JAMES D. CALDER

Biography

Born in Washington, DC, January 1, 1895; son of a civil servant. Educated through high school in Washington, then George Washington Law School, L.L.B., 1916; L.L.M., 1917; clerk and indexer, Library of Congress, 1913–1917; investigator, Department of Justice War Emergency Division, 1917–1918; assistant to the U.S. Attorney General and head of the General Intelligence Division, 1918–1921; assistant director of the Bureau of Investigation, 1921–1924; director of the Bureau of Investigation, 1924–1935; director of the Federal Bureau of Investigation, 1935–1972. Member of the board of directors, George Washington University, National Presbyterian Church, Boys Clubs of America. Died Washington, DC, May 2, 1972.

Selected Writings

Organized protection against organized predatory crimes, *Journal of the American Institute of Criminal Law and Criminology*, 24 (July–August 1933).
The real public enemy no. 1, *American Magazine*, 121 (April 1936).
Amazing Mr. Means, *American Magazine*, 122 (December 1936).
Some legal aspects of interstate crime, *Minnesota Law Review*, 21 (1937).
Persons in Hiding, 1938.
Hitler's spying sirens, *American Magazine*, 138 (December 1944).
How the Nazi spy invasion was smashed, *American Magazine*, 138 (September 1944): 20–21.
The spy who double-crossed Hitler, *American Magazine*, 141 (May 1946).
A comment on the article, Loyalty among government employees, *Yale Law Journal*, 58 (February 1949).
Role of the FBI in the federal employee security program, *Northwestern University Law Review*, 49 (1954–1955).
The confidential nature of FBI reports, *Syracuse Law Review*, 8 (Fall 1956).
Masters of Deceit, 1958.
A Study of Communism, 1962.
The U.S. businessman faces the Soviet spy, *Harvard Business Review*, 42/1 (January 1964).
The war on organized crime, *De Paul Law Review*, 13 (Spring–Summer 1964).
How Red-China spies on U.S., *Nation's Business*, 54 (June 1966).
J. Edgar Hoover on Communism, 1969.
J. Edgar Hoover Speaks, 1971.
J. Edgar Hoover Speaks, 1971.

References and Further Reading

Cook, F.J. 1964. *The FBI Nobody Knows*, New York, NY: Macmillan.
Demaris, O. 1975. *The Director: An Oral Biography of J. Edgar Hoover*, New York, NY: Harper's Magazine Press.
Garrow, D.J. 1981. *The FBI and Martin Luther King, Jr.: From "Solo" to Memphis*, New York, NY: Norton.
Gentry, C. 1991. *J. Edgar Hoover: The Man and the Secrets*, New York, NY: Norton.
Lowenthal, M. 1950. *The Federal Bureau of Investigation*, New York, NY: William Sloane.
Messick, H. 1972. *John Edgar Hoover*, New York, NY: David McKay.
O'Reilly, K. 1983. *Hoover and the Un-Americans*, Philadelphia, PA: Temple University.
Powers, R.G. 1983. *G-Men: Hoover's FBI in American Popular Culture*, Carbondale, IL: Southern Illinois University.
Powers, R.G. 1987. *Secrecy and Power: The Life of J. Edgar Hoover*, New York, NY: Free Press.
Sullivan, W.C. 1979. *The Bureau: My Thirty Years in Hoover's FBI*, New York, NY: W.W. Norton.
Summers, A. 1993. *Official and Confidential: The Secret Life of J. Edgar Hoover*, New York, NY: G.P. Putnam's Sons.
Theoharis, A.G. and Cox, J.S. 1988. *The Boss*, Philadelphia, PA: Temple University.
Williams, D. 1981. They never stopped watching us: FBI political surveillance, 1924–1936, *UCLA History Journal*, 2: Spring.
Williams, D. 1981. The Bureau of Investigation and its critics, 1919–1921: The origins of federal political surveillance, *Journal of American History*, 68: December.

See also **Federal Bureau of Investigation (FBI)**

Hostage Taking and Negotiations

The taking of hostages has a long history as a tool of diplomacy. Exchange of hostages ensured that both sides would respect any alliance, and treaties usually contained "hostage clauses" (Crelinsten and Szabo, 1979). The earliest *criminal* forms of hostage taking were probably the activities of bandits and pirates, such as the Barbary pirates who tormented the early American Republic (Buhite, 1992). During the late 17th century and throughout the 18th century, pirates were used by maritime powers to attack the ships of competing states while sparing their own—a foreshadowing of state-sponsored terrorism in the 20th century. Taking hostages was an integral part of this phenomenon. When the interests of more powerful states, such as Great Britain, were seriously harmed, however, international regulation resulted. Until then, piracy was seen as a useful alternative to war (Chambliss, 1989).

In more recent times, hostage taking has taken a variety of forms, both criminal and political. In the context of international terrorism, it is one of the favorite tactics of insurgents, rebels, and revolutionary terrorists. Embassy seizures and airline hijackings or skyjackings are the two most common forms, the latter amounting to a siege when the aircraft has ultimately landed and is surrounded on the tarmac. Skyjackings were almost unknown before the 1960s, but increased dramatically after 1967. Ships have also been seized, the most notable case being the 1985 takeover of the *Achille Lauro* by Palestinian terrorists. Embassy seizures were quite common during the 1970s and 1980s, the most traumatic in recent U.S. history being the seizure of the U.S. Embassy in Teheran, Iran in 1979. Such incidents can become major international crises whose resolution can be extremely complex. A more recent example is the seizure of the Japanese embassy in Lima, Peru in December 1996, which involved several countries besides Japan and Peru and lasted almost 4 months (Murakami, 1999). Hostage takings have occurred in the context of peacekeeping, peacemaking, and humanitarian assistance in time of war and conflict. During the Bosnian conflict, for example, Canadian peacekeepers were taken hostage by Serbian forces and chained to military installations to deter NATO bombings. Aid workers in conflict-ridden hot spots in developing countries, especially in Africa, have been taken hostage by insurgents and criminal gangs, where the distinction between the two is not always clear in any case.

In the criminal context, the most common situations are prison hostage takings or the taking of hostages during the commission of a criminal act, such as a bank robbery, as a means to escape capture when police arrive on the scene. A classic film, *Dog Day Afternoon*, starring Al Pacino, depicts an example of the latter situation, and was based on an actual incident. Hostage takings also occur in the domestic context, usually when a man takes his wife or children hostage when police are called to a domestic dispute. Such emotionally-driven hostage takings have also occurred in workplaces, when individuals take coworkers hostage as an expression of frustration or anger. Law enforcement officials often call these kinds of domestic or interpersonal incidents "pseudo-hostage incidents," because there are usually no explicit demands and the seizing of hostages is usually a desperate act by an emotionally distraught individual. There are other kinds of incidents in which there are technically no hostages, but an armed individual barricades himself somewhere and threatens to harm himself or others or to commit suicide in such a way as to endanger others. The term "barricaded subject" is preferred to the term "hostage-taker" in such situations, whereas the term "crisis negotiations" has replaced the narrower term "hostage negotiations."

Hostage taking should be distinguished from kidnapping. In the former, the site of sequestration is known and the situation amounts to a siege, with the authorities and other relevant actors on the outside and the hostage takers and their hostages barricaded on the inside. For this reason, they are often called barricade or hostage-barricade situations. In a kidnapping, the site of sequestration is unknown and the hostage takers can often circulate freely, while their hostages remain in captivity. The dynamics of the two situations are quite different, including the negotiation process. Two factors that differ are the element of danger and the element of time (MacWillson, 1992). In the hostage siege, the danger for both hostage taker and hostage is the same, because they are in effect both prisoners to the situation. By contrast, the danger factor for the kidnap victim is greater than that of his or her captor, as the latter can escape the situation and his whereabouts remain unknown to the police. In the hostage siege, the passage of time creates an advantage for the authorities doing the negotiation, whereas it creates a disadvantage for the besieged hostage taker, who becomes increasingly exhausted and frustrated. In the kidnapping, the situation is the reverse, with the advantage going to the kidnapper as time passes and the police become increasingly exhausted and frustrated. Of course, such distinctions are not always clear-cut. In very long sieges, the exhaustion and frustration can occur on both sides or primarily with the police. In the 1993 Waco siege, involving the FBI and the Branch Davidian religious sect under the leadership of David Koresh, it was the FBI's hostage-rescue team that became increasingly frustrated with the negotiations, ultimately leading to a deadly assault (Wright, 1999). In this case, it was not even clear that hostages were involved, because most members of the sect remained inside voluntarily, whereas the authorities justified their assault by arguing that many, especially the children, were held against their will.

The central elements of any hostage taking are the identity and motive of the hostage takers, the identity of the hostages, the demands of the hostage takers, the target of those demands, and the setting where the siege takes place (e.g., bank, embassy, prison, or airliner). Politically motivated hostage takers tend to be rational actors open to negotiation and bargaining. The same can be said for many criminal hostage takers, including even rioting prisoners holding correctional staff or officers. Pseudo-hostage takers are less rational, but can often be persuaded to surrender if dealt with patiently and empathetically. Once they are calmed down by trust building and de-escalating techniques, they can then deal rationally with the situation. It is when the hostage taker has nothing to lose, has a completely different vision of reality, or possesses different ideological or cultural beliefs that negotiation can be problematic. The cross-cultural dimension of crisis negotiation has become much more salient as police have encountered situations involving immigrants, refugees, native peoples, and subcultural groups or religious communities with distinct belief systems that are often antithetical to dominant cultural values.

The role of the hostage can be crucial in determining the outcome of an incident. Law enforcement traditionally considers the hostage to be a passive figure who should do as little as possible to provoke the hostage taker and let the police do their job. Contrary to this expectation, many hostages become actively involved, sometimes trying to escape or bargain with the hostage takers. In some cases, they come to identify with the hostage taker and take sides with him or her against the authorities. This is known as the "Stockholm Syndrome" after a 1973 bank robbery turned barricaded hostage situation in Stockholm, where the hostage taker had sexual relations with one of the female hostages, who continued to visit him in prison after he was caught and convicted.

The demands and the target of those demands are important, as some demands are impossible to grant, and some targets cannot grant demands even if they wanted to. Here, it is important to differentiate between negotiation and concessions. Though many states have declared a "no negotiation" policy, in practice even the most hard-line states have negotiated, although sometimes in secret, as seen when Iran and the U.S. bargained during the Iran-Contra affair in the 1980s. Negotiation allows the authorities to gain its most precious commodity, time. It also permits the gathering of information and intelligence that can help in the resolution of the incident. Concessions usually involve granting the hostage takers' demands and, in certain contexts, this is either impossible or extremely undesirable. Political terrorists holding hostages in one country may, for example, demand the release of prisoners held in another country over which the negotiating government has no influence. Sometimes hostage takers demand more weaponry and authorities never accede to such a demand for obvious reasons. Concessions that increase the comfort of the hostages and their captors, such as provision of food, water, and medicine, is usually a good idea, as it facilitates the negotiation process and increases the possibility of building trust between hostage takers and authorities.

The setting or context of a hostage taking is an important variable as it often determines the feasibility of a negotiated solution or the possibility of a successful assault if negotiations fail. Negotiation and assault are two complementary poles in the overall approach to resolving hostage crises. Negotiation can be the primary strategy or it can merely be a delaying tactic in a strategy that relies on force. When assault is not feasible, negotiation can be the only strategy available, even if other factors make it undesirable. In the 1977 case where an Israeli airliner was hijacked to Entebbe airport in Uganda, the Israelis seriously considered releasing prisoners in exchange for freeing the hostages—a concession antithetical to declared policy—until a plan for a long-distance assault was found to be practical. In a political hostage taking, good-faith negotiations are preferable, as there is usually a wide audience watching and media coverage can be intensive. The political consequences of bad-faith negotiations can be damaging in the long run. In criminal contexts, promises can more easily be broken without serious consequences, though in a prison context, this is not desirable as it can sow the seeds for future incidents. In some cases, there can be disagreements between the negotiation team and the tactical team responsible for assault. This occurred during the Waco siege in 1993, and some argue that the tactical team never took the negotiations seriously. This is why crisis management units typically include a command team, whose job it is to coordinate the operations of the negotiation and tactical teams and to determine when communication and persuasion should prevail and when to resort to force.

Hostage sieges typically run through a series of phases and the most dangerous one is the initial phase, when emotions are running high and the hostage takers are trying to gain control over the hostages and to assert their power and authority. A good negotiator can cool the situation down and make the hostage taker feel comfortable. Key elements of a good negotiation strategy include building trust, de-escalating stress, avoiding provocation, threats, or insults, and using patience and empathy to develop a common interest in resolving the incident peacefully. Before that, however, the incident must be contained and a perimeter set up to keep onlookers and the media away from the scene. The media can play a particularly disruptive role if crisis managers do not provide regular updates and try to understand the needs of the media in covering a breaking story. The same is true for relatives and friends of the hostages, who should be provided with psychological support and "handholding" during and often after the incident.

The ideal resolution of a hostage incident involves the safe release of the hostages in return for the surrender and successful prosecution of the hostage takers. Whether or not this is possible depends on a variety of factors that themselves vary according to context. The art of hostage negotiations was developed in the 1970s by Harvey Schlossberg and Frank Bolz of the New York Police Department, as well as by others such as the Dutch psychologist Dick Mulder. Today, it is a sophisticated tool that has often served to resolve incidents peacefully and without loss of life. Assault is a last resort that can be successful but can often result in the deaths of hostages as well as their captors. Hostages die more often at the hands of the authorities than at the hands of their captors. This is why negotiations are preferred whenever feasible.

RONALD D. CRELINSTEN

References and Further Reading

Barkun, M. 1994. Millenarian groups and law enforcement agencies: The lessons of Waco, *Terrorism and Political Violence* 6.

Buhite, R.D. 1995. *Lives at Risk: Hostages and Victims in American Foreign Policy*, Wilmington, DE: Scholarly Resources Inc.

Chambliss, W.J. 1989. State-organized crime—The American society of criminology, 1988 Presidential Address, *Criminology* 27.

Clutterbuck, R. 1993. Negotiating with terrorists, in *Western Responses to Terrorism*, Schmid, A.P. and Crelinsten, R.D. (Eds.), London and Portland, OR: Frank Cass.

Crelinsten, R.D. and Szabo, D. 1979. *Hostage-Taking*, Lexington, MA, and Toronto: D.C. Heath.

Lambert, J.L. 1990. *Terrorism and Hostages in International Law—A Commentary on the Hostages Convention 1979*, Cambridge, UK: Grotius Publications Ltd.

Lanceley, F.J. 1999. *On-Scene Guide for Crisis Negotiators*, Boca Raton, FL: CRC Press.

MacWillson, A.C. 1992. *Hostage-Taking Terrorism: Incident-Response Strategy*, New York, NY: St. Martin's Press.

McMains, M.J. and Mullins, W.C. 2000. *Crisis Negotiations: Managing Critical Incidents and Hostage Situations in Law Enforcement and Corrections*, Cincinnati, OH: Anderson Publishing, 1996; 2nd ed., *Crisis Negotiations: Managing Critical Incidents and Hostage Situations in Law Enforcement and Corrections*, McMains, M.J. and Mullins, W.C., Cincinnati, OH: Anderson Publishing.

Murakami, Y. 1999. *El Espejo del Otro: el Japan ante la Crisis de los Rehenes en el Peru*, Lima: Instituto de Estudios Peruanos, and Osaka: Japan Center for Area Studies.

Poland, J.M. and McCrystle, M.J. 1999. *Practical, Tactical, and Legal Perspectives of Terrorism and Hostage-Taking*, Lewiston, NY: E. Mellon Press.

Rogan, R.G., Hammer, M.R., and Van Zandt, C.R., Eds., 1997. *Dynamic Processes of Crisis Negotiation: Theory, Research, and Practice*, Westport, CT: Praeger.

Wright, S.A. 1999. Anatomy of a government massacre: Abuses of hostage-barricade protocols during the Waco standoff, *Terrorism and Political Violence* 11. [See also in the same issue the three replies to Wright by Eugene V. Gallagher, Jayne Simare Docherty, and Kerry Noble, as well as Wright's rejoinder to these articles.]

See also **Kidnapping; Terrorism**

House Arrest and Electronic Monitoring

The use of homes as an official place of criminal confinement had its origins in antiquity. Two instances are found in the Bible. The first, in the Old Testament, involved Shimei, who was executed by King Solomon (I Kings 2, 36–46) for disobeying an order to not leave his home. Later in Rome St. Paul dwelt 2 years under arrest in a rented house (Acts 28, 16–31). Recent years witnessed a dramatic explosion of interest in the development of "house arrest." This term is often used loosely and it is probably preferable to refer to this correctional policy alternative as *home confinement*, a term that has the virtue of covering more specific practices such as *home detention* and *home incarceration*. The term "house arrest" tends to imply police action without much in the way of judicial process.

Home confinement has been both praised and damned. It has been praised as more humane and less "corrupting" than traditional incarceration and as an economical alternative to building more prisons and jails. It has been condemned, or at least seriously questioned, because it seems to turn the home into a prison, setting a dangerous precedent and violating the sanctity of one's home as one's "castle," a last refuge from governmental intrusion.

In its modern form, both the *idea* and *practice* of connecting home confinement with electronic monitoring (EM) of offenders began its initial stage in the U.S. between the 1960s and the mid-1970s. By this time it had become clear that the policy of exclusion—punishing offenders by incarceration within secure penal facilities—was ill-conceived because such facilities were plagued by idleness, overcrowding, and inadequate financial support (Lilly and Ball, 1987). Early advocates of EM saw it as an idea that could radically alter the conventional wisdom of traditional imprisonment; little actual EM occurred between the mid-1970s and the early 1980s. By 1983, interest in the merits of EM expanded to include experimentation, implementation, the creation of legislative guidelines, and evaluative research.

The surge of interest in home confinement was closely associated with the confluence of political conservatism and the development of new technologies that were capable of various forms of surveillance and monitoring that previously had been confined to science fiction. One of the first of these tools used by courts in the early 1980s was based on radio frequencies (RF) and a bracelet or anklet that emitted an electronic signal that was picked up by a receiver placed in an offender's home telephone. If an offender moved more than approximately 150 feet from the home telephone, the transmission signal would be broken, alerting authorities that the offender had left the premises.

Today, in addition to RF home monitoring technology—the major EM technology used worldwide—there are three additional monitoring product categories: geophysical positioning systems (GPS), random programmed contact (based mostly on voice verification technology or wrist-worn devices), and unsupervised alcohol testing (Conway, 2003). GPS offers the greatest leap forward since 1983 because of the its ability to report the movements of offenders in "real time"—approximately 1 dozen GPS systems are in various stages of experimentation and implementation in the U.S.

By its 20th anniversary, 2003, EM in the U.S. had witnessed two trends, one of initial growth that accelerated through 1995. The other trend was and continues to be a decline in EM usage that appears to have leveled off to what experts in late 2003 estimated to be approximately 100,000 individuals monitored daily. At no time has EM been used at the level of enthusiasm and with the expected impact proposed by its earliest U.S. supporters.

The picture of EM in parts of Europe is different from the one in the U.S., in part because of the ability of centralized governments and various national interest groups therein to create vigorous debates about nation wide criminal justice policies. The case of EM in Britain is informative though by no means representative of the varying degrees of enthusiasm and resistance that EM has generated in Sweden, the Netherlands, Switzerland, Portugal, Spain, Germany, and France (Nellis, 2003b).

EM in Britain was initiated in 1989–90 largely as the result of lobbying by the Offender Tag Association and two major companies in the security and telecommunications business (Nellis, 2003b). Then it was vigorously opposed by a wide spectrum of organizations that were concerned that EM posed a threat to the humanistic traditions that had historically informed penal reform and social work. Over the next decade its use was gradually expanded, often confirming earlier concerns about the government's managerialism-based hostility toward probation and social work. Within this context—and also because research indicated EM could be used with (a) rehabilitative programs and to (b) reduce the need for prison places—opposition to EM was forced to reconsider. Today for a variety of reasons—research findings, generational change in criminal justice-related organizations, influx of staff who are not technophobic, and rising prison populations—EM has little opposition. It remains unclear whether it will be used mostly for surveillance and control or for traditional social work values, or both.

The short-term U.S.–European future of EM will be shaped by salient shifts in social context including (1) a continued shift to the right on a number of issues (immigrants, rise of surveillance, declining support for social work and probation), (2) increased concern about cost effectiveness and technological solutions within criminal justice, (3) and the growing influence of private business on criminal justice policies and practices (Lilly, 2003). These factors will have greater or lesser impact on EM in other parts of the world, depending on local social contexts. Efforts to ward development of EM in South Africa thus far have been driven far more by prison overcrowding than anything else, but nonetheless are hampered by the lack of needed technological infrastructure, adequate housing, and corruption.

J. ROBERT LILLY

References and Further Reading

Ball, R.A., Huff, R.C., and Lilly, J.R., 1988. *House Arrest and Correctional Policy: Doing Time at Home*, Newbury Park, CA: Sage.

Conway, P., 2003. Survey of agencies using electronic monitoring reveals a promising future, *Journal of Offender Monitoring*, 16, 2.

Lilly, J.R., 2003. From an American point of view: Does electronic monitoring have a future in Europe?, *Will Electronic Monitoring Have a Future in Europe?* Mayer, M., Haverkamp, R., and Levy, R. (Eds.), Freiberg, Germany: Max-Planck-Institut.

Lilly, J.R. and Ball, R.A. 1987. A brief history of house arrest and electronic monitoring, *Northern Kentucky Law Review*, 13, 3.

Lilly, J.R., 1990. Tagging reviewed, *Howard Journal of Criminal Justice*, 29, 2.

Nellis, M., 2003. Electronic monitoring and social work in England, *Will Electronic Monitoring Have a Future in Europe?* Mayer, M., Haverkamp, R., and Levy, R. (Eds.), Freiberg, Germany: Max-Planck-Institut.

Neillis, M. 2003. They don't even know we're there: The electronic monitoring of offenders in England and Wales, *The Intensification of Surveillance*, Webster, F. and Ball, K., London, UK: Pluto.

Nellis, M. 1991. The electronic monitoring of offenders in England and Wales: Recent developments and future prospects, *British Journal of Criminology*, 31, 4.

Whitfield, D. 1997. *Tackling the Tag: The Electronic Monitoring of Offenders*. Winchester, CT: Waterside Press.

Whitfield, D. 2001. *The Magic Bracelet: Technology and Offender Supervision*. Winchester, CT: Waterside Press.

See also **Diversion and Diversion Programs; Electronic Surveillance and Wiretapping; Intensive Supervision Programs (ISP); Probation**

I

Identity Theft *See* **Consumers, Crimes Against; Computer Offenses**

Immaturity as a Defense to Criminal Liability *See* **Defenses to Criminal Liability: Justifications and Excuses**

Immigration and Naturalization Service (INS)

The Immigration and Naturalization Service (INS) was founded in 1891 to regulate immigration in response to an increase in hostile American sentiment toward the increasing numbers of immigrants. The first federal immigration station opened on Ellis Island, New York on January 2, 1892, serving as the busiest port of entry for immigrants for several decades (Smith, 1998). As immigration numbers and legislation increased over the years, the INS evolved to keep pace with the demands of these ever-increasing numbers.

Initially a division of the Treasury Department, the INS was first transferred in 1940 to the Justice Department and then in 2002 was incorporated into the Department of Homeland Security (DHS), which was formed because of terrorism concerns following the attacks on September 11, 2001 (Department of Homeland Security, 2004). On March 1, 2003, the INS became the U.S. Citizenship and Immigration Services (USCIS), a division of the DHS. This transformation and union with the DHS was an important step forward

for the INS, allowing for improved administration of benefits and immigration services through an exclusive focus on immigration and citizenship services.

The former INS included the U.S. Border Patrol, responsible for protecting national borders, but the transition created a separate Directorate of Border and Transportation Security within DHS. Now, the mission of the USCIS is to promote national security, provide prompt immigration rulings, and provide immigration and citizenship customer services. The bureau is responsible for processing naturalization, asylum, and residency applications, as well as supervising immigrant and visitor entry into the U.S. and identifying illegal immigrants. In addition, the USCIS investigates illegal alien employment and issues benefits to legal immigrants (Bureau of Citizenship and Immigration Services, 2004).

The USCIS is also responsible for an array of benefits and services to both citizens and immigrants. Helping relatives of citizens gain permanent residency and work in the U.S. through *family-based petitions* is one responsibility of the USCIS. Similarly, *employment-based petitions* aid current and prospective employees to immigrate and remain in the U.S.

In addition to employment-related assistance, the USCIS also provides naturalization services and asylum to refugees. *Naturalization* provides citizenship to eligible persons who wish to become U.S. citizens. *Asylum and refugee processing* adjudicates asylum and the processing of refugees, whereas the *special status programs* more specifically focus on adjudication eligibility for U.S. immigrants as a form of humanitarian aid to foreign nationals. Finally, the USCIS *document issuance and renewal* division verifies eligibility and produces and issues immigrant documents.

Some of the long-term goals and strategies of the USCIS include the ability annually to: process and adjudicate more than 6 million applications, serve nearly 20 million customers through various outlets (such as National Customer Service Call Centers [NCSC] and information counters at local offices), process approximately 90,000 asylum cases, and perform nearly 100,000 refugee interviews. An additional responsibility of the USCIS is to provide public information to former INS customers regarding miscellaneous customer service issues, for example, informing the public that official forms and documents issued by the former INS are still valid and processed in the same manner as in the past, and that local USCIS offices remain in former INS offices. Achieving the goals and objectives of the USCIS, especially with regard to expediting the immigration process and issuing immigration benefits, involved expanding the staff personnel, analyzing and implementing new immigrant benefits, and increasing the annual budget to over three quarters of a billion dollars (U.S. Citizenship and Immigration Services, 2004).

The last few years have been very successful for the INS/USCIS. Most recently, an expansion of the NCSC provides toll-free, automated, or live information about immigration services and benefits to customers from anywhere in the U.S., the Virgin Islands, Puerto Rico, and Guam. Implementation of Naturalization Quality Procedures (NQP) and the establishment of Application Support Centers (ASCs) have standardized the processing and fingerprinting (for use by the FBI in criminal background checks) of all applicants for naturalization. Most impressively, the USCIS has reduced the number of pending naturalization application backlogs from over 2 million in 1998 to less than 622,000 in 2003.

The Office of Citizenship, within the USCIS, encourages and aids legal immigrants to integrate into the American culture by providing information and training on the responsibilities of American citizens and immigrants. Specifically, the Office of Citizenship's goals are to emphasize community identity and American values by encouraging educational enhancement of the English language, American history, citizens' responsibilities, community involvement, and, most importantly, by issuing information about the process of naturalization. The USCIS requirements for naturalization include a continuous residence and physical presence in the U.S., the ability to read, write, and speak English, and an understanding of U.S. history and government structure. In addition, naturalization also requires the candidate to exhibit good moral character, demonstrate respect for constitutional principles, and embrace a favorable temperament to U.S. and American values. Certain requirements are waived for applicants with spouses who are American citizens or for those who are members of the U.S. armed forces (U.S. Citizenship and Immigration Services, 2004).

Congress, however, constantly amends and modifies the laws regarding naturalization and immigration. Recent developments in immigration policies include the Immigration Act of 1990, which granted naturalization jurisdiction solely to the office of the Attorney General and included residency requirement reductions and English language exceptions for those seeking naturalization. Following the terrorist attacks of September 11, immigration policies have stiffened and the DHS and other departments have implemented many new policies (U.S. House of Representatives, 2004).

Most recently is President Bush's January 2004 Fair and Secure Immigration Reform proposal to Congress, which recommends a temporary match of foreign workers with U.S. employers when no American employee is available for the position, in an effort to allow legal foreigner contributions to the American economy. He claims that border protection would increase while exploitation of foreign workers would decrease as agreements are made with participating countries. The reform would not give foreign workers preference over legal documented immigrants nor provide connections to obtaining a green card or citizenship, but it would not preclude them from following the procedures to obtain these benefits. However, the proposal also includes incentives for the employees to return to their native country after completing the temporary position.

Despite its many transformations, U.S. nationality law seeks to maintain uniformity in naturalization by establishing policies and procedures that are consistent and fair to all who seek U.S. citizenship.

JESSICA MCGOWAN AND SEAN C. STUCKER

References and Further Reading

Bureau of Citizenship and Immigration Services, *Encyclopedia Americana* (Grolier online, 2004). Available at http://ea.grolier.com (January 19, 2004).

Department of Homeland Security, *Encyclopedia Americana* (Grolier online, 2004). Available at http://ea.grolier.com (January 19, 2004).

Smith, M.L. 1998. Overview of INS history. In Kurian, G.T. (Ed.), *A Historical Guide to the U.S. Government*. New York, NY: Oxford University Press.

United States Citizenship and Immigration Services (USCIS). 2004. Welcome to U.S. Citizenship and Immigration Services. Available at http://uscis.gov. United States House of Representatives. (2002). H.R. 5005, Homeland Security Act. Washington, DC: Government Printing Office.

See also **Customs Service, U.S.**

Incapacitation (Collective and Selective)

Incapacitation is one of many strategies to restrain criminals from committing further crimes (Wilson, 1975). Prior to the 18th century, banishment, mutilation, and dismemberment were among the practices used to control criminals. Following the design and implementation of the penitentiary as a more humane form of punishment, physical isolation from the free-world community through incarceration replaced dismemberment as one of the primary methods of controlling criminal behavior throughout most of the world. In the U.S., the increased use of incarceration via jails for short-term and prisons for long-term incapacitation began in the early 1970s following disillusionment with the effectiveness of rehabilitation and deterrence as crime control strategies (Zimring and Hawkins, 1995).

According to Cohen (1983), the practice of incapacitation has the following assumptions:

- All active offenders are susceptible to being arrested and punished;
- An incarcerated offender cannot harm the community;
- Incarceration prevents crime by interrupting criminal careers (or the period of time from the first to the last criminal offense);
- Incapacitated offenders are not replaced by another offender on the streets;
- Incarceration is neutral—it neither rehabilitates nor debilitates a criminal career.

The degree to which these assumptions are met in reality is debated by researchers (Cook, 1986; Zimring and Hawkins, 1995).

Collective Incapacitation

Two ways that incapacitation is used to achieve a reduction in crime are collective and selective incapacitation (Greenberg, 1975; Visher, 1987). Collective incapacitation attempts to prevent crime overall by requiring similar sentences for similar offenses. Collective incapacitation begs the question: Given the same amount of jail and prison space we have now, is it better to sentence 100 offenders to 10 years each, or 50 offenders to 20 years each? Equity and "just desserts" for all offenders is the aim of this strategy, with the duration of punishment based on the seriousness of the crime, as well as the offender's prior criminal record (von Hirsch, 1984). First-time offenders who commit a more serious crime (e.g., a violent crime) will theoretically serve a longer sentence than property offenders. Also, repeat offenders, or those who continue criminal behavior, will be incapacitated longer if convicted. Proponents of collective incapacitation believe that an increase in the use of incarceration will decrease crime.

The length of an offender's sentence under the collective incapacitation model is also dependent on available jail and prison bedspace and the crime rate. Areas with higher crime rates typically have higher levels of arrests and a greater likelihood of prison crowding. To alleviate crowding, offenders in these jurisdictions serve shorter sentences compared to areas with lower crime rates.

Two examples of collective incapacitation include mandatory minimum sentences and sentencing guidelines. Mandatory minimum sentences are typically statutes that require a certain minimum percent of one's sentence for certain crimes to be spent in prison before a prisoner is eligible for discretionary release. For example, many "truth-in-sentencing" laws require that a person convicted of a violent crime serve at least 85% of the original sentence imposed by the judge.

Sentencing guidelines exist at the federal and state levels, and require judges to impose a predefined sentence length based on crime severity and the offender's criminal history. The method by which criminal history is measured varies by jurisdiction; for example, in the federal system, a criminal history score is obtained through sentence length and the recency of the past and current offenses. Although there are opportunities for judges to depart from these prescribed ranges, sentencing guidelines generally narrow judicial discretion and produce increased consistency in sentencing than other more discretionary methods.

Collective incapacitation does not predict future criminality, but focuses instead on how sentences (either past sentencing practices or hypothetical sentences) affect the overall crime rate. Langan (1991) found that the U.S. prison population increased nationwide from the mid-1970s to the 1980s owing to changes in sentencing. The subsequent rise in the number of prisoners coincided with a reduction in crime. One U.S. study estimated that over one-third of violent crimes in 1975 were prevented owing to incapacitation alone (Cohen and Canela-Cacho, 1994). Based on her extensive review of sentencing practices during the 1970s and mid-1980s, Visher (1987) estimated that these polices "reduced crime by 10 and 30 percent…[with] a near doubling of the U.S. prison populations in less than 10 years" (Visher, 1987, 519). Other researchers estimated that prison populations in the 1980s must rise between 10% and 20% for every *one* percent reduction in the rate of crime (Blumstein, Cohen, Roth, and Visher, 1986).

Increasing prison time for offenders has had only a "modest impact" on the crime rate at the expense of large increases in jail and prison populations (Cohen, 1983). In the 1990s, researchers in other countries estimated that doubling the size of the prison population reduced crime by only 10% (Chan, 1995) or virtually none at all (Tarling, 1993). Swelling prison populations have continued throughout the U.S. in the 1990s and into the 21st century and are believed by some to be among the most significant contributions to the decrease in crime (Conklin, 2003). With the unprecedented building of correctional facilities in the last few decades, this modest decrease in crime has come at quite a social and financial price.

Selective Incapacitation

Selective incapacitation is based on the premise that a small number of people commit a disproportionately large share of crimes in society (Loeber and Farrington, 1998). Wolfgang and his colleagues (1972) found that over half of all police arrests for that age group were committed by only 6% of the general population (or 18% of active offenders). Selective incapacitation is concerned with early prediction and incarceration of the "career criminal" or the "habitual offender" (offenders who persistently commit a disproportionately large number of crimes over the life course) for a longer

time period than a "low-risk offender" for the same offense. Selective incapacitation seeks to prevent crime by using predictive criteria to incarcerate the career criminal for an extended period, while at the same time, reducing penalties for lower-risk offenders. Unlike collective incapacitation that tries to equalize sentencing for low- and high-risk offenders who commit the same crime, selective incapacitation "encourages different sentences for the same offense to take account of differences in anticipated future crimes among offenders" (Visher, 1987, 524). The key question in selective incapacitation, therefore, is to determine on an individual level and before it happens, who will become a career criminal versus who will desist from crime on their own.

The idea of selective incapacitation seemed valuable initially because researchers thought at the time that it would decrease crime, improve public safety, and reduce cost because prison resources would be used more efficiently (Blumstein, Cohen, and Nagin, 1978).

Peter Greenwood of the RAND Corporation attempted to identify future rates of offending behavior for robbery and burglary using calculated rates of self-reported offending behavior of incarcerated state prisoners (Chaiken and Chaiken, 1982). Greenwood also used the knowledge from mathematical and computer-simulated models to predict the prevalence of high-rate offenders over their "criminal careers" (Shinnar and Shinnar, 1975), and Hoffman and Beck's (1974) "Salient Factor Score" that determined levels of risk on parole. Greenwood (1982, 94) used the RAND data to construct a seven-variable prediction and classification scheme in which an affirmative answer to four or more of the following seven indicated a "high-risk" offender:

1. Priors of the same type as the offense;
2. Conviction before age 16;
3. Juvenile drug use of heroin and barbiturates;
4. Served juvenile facility time;
5. Heroin or barbiturate use in last 2 years;
6. Incarcerated more than half of the last 2 years;
7. Employed less than half of last 2 years.

Based on his classification instrument, Greenwood found that crime could be reduced without any change in the California prison population simply by reallocating space and how long we confine certain offenders. Robbery could be reduced by 15–20% and burglary by 11% if the incarceration rates of "high-rate" offenders (as Greenwood defined them) were doubled from their current terms (to 8 years for robbers and 3.5 for burglars), whereas other "low-risk" robbers and burglars were imprisoned for no more than 1 year. Reanalysis of the same data indicated that only a 13–14% reduction in robbery would occur using the same assumptions (Cohen, 1983; Visher, 1986). All three of these studies, however, assumed that criminals do not slow down, desist, or "age out" of crime (which we now know is inaccurate for the vast majority of even the most active criminals). When aging out of crime was considered with Greenwood's data, Cohen estimated that robbery would decrease by 6–10% if we assume that a criminal career lasts an additional 5–15 years beyond an offender's first adult conviction (as cited in Visher, 1987).

Another criticism aimed at Greenwood's research was the use of prisoner self-report crime data, which seemed to overestimate the crime reduction effect of incarceration because it did not account for the fact that once an offender was removed from the streets, another offender would take his or her place. This phenomenon was called the "replacement factor" and occurs with certain types of crimes, such as drug sales or other vice crimes (Spelman, 1994). A related criticism of Greenwood's use of incarcerated prisoners to generalize to all criminals is the assumption that incarcerated criminals and active "free" criminals commit crimes at the same rate. Incarcerated criminals average a far greater number of (10 to 50 times more) crimes than offenders who are not incarcerated, thereby, inflating the impact of an incapacitation policy offending rates of free offenders are overlooked (Canela-Cacho, Blumstein, and Cohen, 1997).

Incarceration via selective incapacitation was found to lack the crime reduction power it initially promised (Bernard and Ritti, 1991). Part of the problem was that the Greenwood scale was later found unreliable (Cronbach's alpha of 0.48) and thus unacceptable to use in policy decisions (Auerhahn, 1999). Clearly, the results of the initial selective incapacitation studies depended on the inaccurate assumptions researchers had about criminal career length, the replacement factor, and the frequency of crimes committed by active and incarcerated criminals.

Selective incapacitation has been criticized on ethical grounds, particularly on the errors that might be made when predicting future propensity to crime. On the one hand, offenders whose score happens to label them as "high-risk offenders" may actually be good risks and incarcerating them based on crimes they may never commit is a denial of their liberty and who are thus called "false positives" (Cohen, 1983; Visher, 1987; Tarling, 1993). Studies using the RAND data reported a false positive rate of 48% (Greenwood, 1982) and as high as 55% (Cohen, 1983; Visher, 1986). A "false negative," on the other hand, is a person who is misidentified as a low-risk offender, when in reality, that person becomes more criminally active in the future. Selective incapacitation does not account for the harm done by the offender to the victim or the community at large (von Hirsch, 1984).

Researchers provide further evidence against selective incapacitation by arguing that recidivism is difficult to predict, there is no proof that incarcerating a small number of chronic offenders reduces cost, and that selective incapacitation is a "setback," but it does not necessarily end one's criminal career (Haapenan, 1990; Zimring and Hawkins, 1995).

Finally, selective incapacitation is believed to be overly simplistic in that it fails to consider that humans alter their behavior on the basis of perceived costs and benefits. In other words, "active criminals are well informed about sentencing policies and tend to adapt their behavior to the severity of the punishment" (Cook, 1986, 212). Selective incapacitation is based on the assumption that offenders will not alter their "predetermined criminal careers" by desisting from crime at an earlier age than predicted; or that low-rate offenders will increase their propensity to crime. Philip Cook believes that selective incapacitation methods do not use prison resources more efficiently and may even *increase* the total crime rate because "the increase in offending by the low-rate group outweighs the reduction in offending by the other groups" (Cook, 1986, 210).

Studies indicate that too severe a sentence may have more of a negative result than researchers first believed. The longer the confinement, the more likely it was that prisoners developed procriminal attitudes and rationalizations that led to a greater chance of recidivism (Bondeson, 1989).

Greenwood's (1982) research spawned increased scientific inquiry into the duration of criminal careers and whether specific risk factors can differentiate or predict serious habitual offenders from lower-risk offenders. Police-initiated "repeat offender programs" are an example of such a practice. Police use information they have through official records and informants to identify and increase the apprehension rate of chronic offenders by working with prosecutors to ensure a severe sentence or case enhancement. The Phoenix Repeat Offender Program (ROP) used nine criteria to identify ROP offenders, including role played in crime, lifestyle and peers, felony convictions, family background, and past informant activity. The ROP program could be considered a form of selective incapacitation because an identified offender in the program was significantly more likely to be committed to prison, and that offender also served an average of 18 months longer than other chronic offenders not in the ROP program (Abrahamse, Ebener, Greenwood, Fitzgerald, and Kosin, 1991).

Selective incapacitation strategies have been used to pass and uphold laws targeting specific offenders for longer sentences. Various versions of selective incapacitation include California's Three Strikes and civil commitment of dangerous sexual predators.

California's "Three Strikes" law in 1994 is a form of "retrospective" selective incapacitation for repeat offenders because it based "the quanta of punishment on some characteristic of the offender—in this case, the criminal history of the offender" (Auerhahn, 2002, 358). Individuals convicted of their second felony offense received a mandatory doubling of their sentence for that crime, whereas individuals who are convicted of their third felony offense must serve the longer of the two options: either a minimum of 25 years before becoming eligible for release, or three times the rate of the presumptive sentence for that same crime. Third Strike commitments currently average nearly 50 years that offendess must serve prior to being considered for release (Austin, Clark, Hardyman, and Henry, 1999).

The bulk of offenders affected by Three Strikes are *not* violent offenders, but drug offenders who are older and are purportedly aging out of crime. The impact of Three Strikes on crime and public safety was less than originally anticipated. California crime rates decreased along with the rest of the nation, but it is difficult to say whether California's crime decrease was or was not because of Three Strikes, or some other factor (Stolzenberg and D'Alessio, 1997). In a view of one researcher, it appears that the constellation of changes to criminal sentencing policies associated with the "War on Drugs" and other sweeping legislative reforms aiming to "get tough on criminals" that have resulted in massive expansion of the prison population have had the net effect of making our incapacitation policies *less* selective (Auerhahn, 1999, 725).

Civil commitment of sexual predators is a second example of selective incapacitation policies. Sexual predator acts allow for the indefinite civil commitment of habitual sex offenders to a mental institution following a prison term. If the offender is deemed to be a chronic sexual predator and a team of psychiatrists and other treatment specialists predict, using various risk assessment scales, that the offender is likely to continue committing predatory sexual offenses if released, the offender will be transferred from prison directly to a treatment facility. The passage of the law was to protect the public from sex offenders who sexually prey on vulnerable victims. The problem with this law, critics say, is that sexual offenders are being committed for what could be the rest of their lives for crimes that they *might* do in the future. Variables used in many of the risk assessments include the offender's age, prior criminal history, age and gender of the victim(s), offender's marital status, and compliance to treatment.

The public perceives that sex offenders have high recidivism rates, when according to researchers, sex offenders actually "demonstrate relatively low levels of sexual re-offending," or about 20% continue to reoffend 4 or 5 years after release from prison (Grubin and Wingate, 1996).

In 1990, Washington State was the first to have a "Special Commitment Center" for sexual predators operated by the Department of Social and Health Services. The U.S. Supreme Court upheld civil commitment statutes in 1997 based on the Kansas model. At least 15 states currently have sexual predator laws, but most apply this law to a small number of sex offenders. Washington has used this law to incapacitate over 130 sexual predators at the SCC, and the numbers are growing. Critics contend that civil commitment statutes are a denial of due process based on rudimentary and imperfect risk assessment instruments that need more evaluation before they are used to civilly commit someone and remove their freedom.

Given what we currently know at this time about predicting chronic criminality, the use of prediction or identification instruments for selective incapacitation strategies may be better used for evaluation, rather than making decisions about an individual's future criminality (Haapenan, 1990; Auerhahn, 1999). When making new sentencing legislation or changing existing law, it is recommended that legislators first use forecasting and simulation models to predict how the new sentence would impact prison populations, and that legislators use "sunset" laws that would automatically expire unless readopted (Mauer, 2002). This removes the problem that California has right now with their requirements for altering or amending Three Strikes (either two-thirds of both legislative houses or another voter ballot). Finally, given the problems with implementing selective incapacitation, researchers believe that multiple strategies such as prevention, rehabilitation, and a more uniform sentencing strategy are ultimately more effective for crime control (Cook, 1986; Visher, 1987).

LEANNE FIFTAL ALARID

References and Further Reading

Abrahamse, A.F., Ebener, P.A., Greenwood, P.W., Fitzgerald, N., and Kosin, T.E. 1991. An experimental evaluation of the Phoenix Repeat Offender Program, *Justice Quarterly*, 8.

Auerhahn, K. 2002. Selective incapacitation, Three Strikes, and the problem of aging prison populations: Using simulation modeling to see the future, *Criminology & Public Policy*, 1.

Auerhahn, K. 1999. Selective incapacitation and the problem of prediction, *Criminology*, 37.

Austin, J., Clark, J., Hardyman, P., and Henry, D.A. 1999. The impact of 'Three Strikes and you're out,' *Punishment and Society*, 1.

Bernard, T. and Ritti, R. 1991. The Philadelphia birth cohort and selective incapacitation, *Journal of Research in Crime and Delinquency*, 28.

Blumstein, A., Cohen, J., and Nagin, D. 1978. *Deterrence and Incapacitation: Estimating the Effects of Criminal Sanctions on Crime Rates*, Washington, DC: National Academy Press.

Bondson, U.V. 1989. *Prisoners in Prison Societies*, New Brunswick, NJ: Transaction.

Canela-Cacho, J.A., Blumstein, A., and Cohen, J. 1997. Relationship between the offending frequency of imprisoned and free offenders, *Criminology*, 35.

Chaiken, J.M. and Chaiken, M.R. 1982. *Varieties of Criminal Behavior*, Santa Monica, CA: RAND.

Chan, J. 1995. The limits of incapacitation as a crime control policy, *Crime and Justice Bulletin*, 25, Sydney: New South Wales Bureau of Crime Statistics and Research, NSW Department of Attorney General.

Cohen, J. 1983. Incapacitation as a strategy for crime control: Possibilities and pitfalls. pp. 1–48 in *Crime and Justice: An Annual Review of Research*, Vol. 5, Tonry, M. and Morris, N. (Eds.), Chicago, IL: University of Chicago Press.

Conklin, J.E. 2003. *Why Crime Rates Fell*, Boston, MA: Allyn and Bacon.

Cook, P.J. 1986. Criminal incapacitation effects considered in an adaptive choice framework. *The Reasoning Criminal: Rational Choice Perspectives on Offending*, Cornish, D.B. and Clarke, R.V. (Eds.), pp. 202–216. New York, NY: Springer-Verlag.

Greenberg, D. 1975. The incapacitative effect of imprisonment: Some estimates, *Law and Society Review*, 9.

Greenwood, P. 1982. *Selective Incapacitation*, Santa Monica, CA: RAND Corporation.

Grubin, D. and Wingate, S. 1996. Sexual offence recidivism: Prediction versus understanding, *Criminal Behaviour and Mental Health*, 6.

Haapenan, R.A. 1990. *Selective Incapacitation and the Serious Offender: A Longitudinal Study of Criminal Career Patterns*, New York, NY: Springer-Verlag.

Hoffman, P.B. and Beck, J.L. 1974. Parole decision making: A salient factor score, *Journal of Criminal Justice*, 2.

Langan, P.A. 1991. America's soaring prison population, *Science*, 251.

Loeber, R. and Farrington, D.O. (Eds.), 1998. *Serious and Violent Juvenile Offenders: Risk Factors and Successful Interventions*, Thousand Oaks, CA: Sage.

Mauer, M. 2002. Analyzing and responding to the driving forces of prison population growth, *Criminology & Public Policy*, 1.

Shinnar, R. and Shinnar, S. 1975. The effect of the criminal justice system on the control of crime: A quantitative approach, *Law and Society Review*, 9.

Spelman, W. 1994. *Criminal Incapacitation*, New York, NY: Plenum.

Tarling, R. 1993. *Analyzing Offending: Data, Models, and Interpretations*, Home Office Research and Planning Unit, London, UK: HMSO.

Visher, C.A. 1987. Incapacitation and crime control: Does a 'Lock 'Em Up' strategy reduce crime? *Justice Quarterly*, 4.

Visher, C.A. and Roth, J.A. 1986. Participation in criminal careers. *Criminal Careers and Career Criminals*, Vol. 2, Blumstein, A., Cohen, J., Roth, J.A., and Visher, C., Washington, DC: National Academy Press.

Von Hirsch, A. 1984. The ethics of selective incapacitation: Observations on the contemporary debate, *Crime and Delinquency*, 30.

Wilson, J.Q. 1975. *Thinking about Crime*, New York, NY: Basic Books.

Wolfgang, M., Figlio, R., and Sellin, T. 1972. *Delinquency in a Birth Cohort*, Chicago, IL: University of Chicago Press.

Zimring, F.E. and Hawkins, G. 1995. *Incapacitation: Penal Confinement and the Restraint of Crime*, New York, NY: Oxford University Press.

See also **Prisons and the Rule of Law**

Incarceration   *See* **Jails; Prisons**

Incest

Incest is a form of child sexual abuse and child molestation. Incest occurs when family members other than married couples touch private parts, engage in oral, anal, or vaginal penetration, or touch other body parts of other family members to achieve personal sexual gratification. Incest occurs between biological children and their parents or grandparents, stepchildren and their stepparents or step-grandparents, uncles or aunts and nieces or nephews, siblings, and first cousins. Some studies have found that uncles are common perpetrators of incest, in addition to parents, stepparents, and grandparents.

Incest occurs in every country. Estimates of incest rates, however, are difficult to obtain because it is substantially underreported and young victims may forget or suppress the abuse. Data obtained from the U.S. National Incident-Based Reporting System representing sex offenses from 1991 to 1996 in 12 states provide the most recent estimates of incest. Of all sex offenses reported to law officials, about 27% of all sex offenders were family members of their victims, and family members committed just over one-third of all sex crimes against children. Family members preyed the most on very young children (below the age of 6) and prepubescent children (between the ages 6 and 11); adolescents were less likely to be victims.

Child sexual abuse by caretakers received much media attention in western countries in the 1980s, and reports of suspected child sexual abuse to child protective services increased dramatically in the 1980s. However, in the U.S., reports of child sexual abuse gradually decreased from 1992 to 1998, resulting in a decline in reported suspected cases of 37%. (The number of suspected cases that were proven also decreased 31% during this time period.) Because child protective service data primarily focuses on incest cases and caretaker cases (babysitters and teachers), these declines provide estimates of known incest cases. There are many possible explanations for the decline in child sexual abuse involving caretakers. Media attention in the 1980s focused on caretaker sexual abuse, but in the 1990s the media highlighted cases of strangers sexually assaulting young children. Mandated reporters (physicians and teachers) may have become more lax in detecting signs of sexual abuse owing to the media attention surrounding stranger assault or may have become more guarded in reporting suspected cases because of concerns that they may falsely accuse an innocent parent. Thus, the decline may not represent a true decline in the incident of incest, but rather a change in the reporting behavior of mandated reporters.

Does the criminal justice system treat incest cases similarly to other sex offense cases? A few studies have found that incest offenders are less likely to be arrested and formally charged in the criminal justice system, but if convicted, they receive similar sentences as child molesters who victimize children outside of their family. Incest victims are more reluctant to disclose the abuse than victims where offenders are strangers or acquaintances. Stroud et al. (2000) found that only 59% of suspected incest victims disclosed the abuse to authorities compared to 95% of the children victimized by strangers. Police are less likely to arrest in reported cases involving parents or stepparents as alleged offenders than in cases involving strangers. Prosecutors are less likely to pursue formal charges in cases where the offender is a family member or acquaintance than where the offender is a stranger. Levesque (2000) found that incest and child molesters of victims outside the family received similar sentences (in the actual amount of prison time to be served), although the study did not examine whether incest offenders were less likely to be sentenced to prison. In a sample of Canadian incarcerated child molesters, incest offenders were more likely to receive parole than child molesters of children outside their own family or rapists of adult women.

Incest offenders vary substantially in their demographic, criminal history, and social and mental health adjustment. Studies have found that reported incest occurs in all socioeconomic levels and ethnic groups, and have not found a consistently higher risk for lower-income groups or ethnic minorities. Moreover, incest offenders often victimize children outside of their family and participate in other forms of sexual offending. For example, some incest offenders also develop child pornography, and others force their children into the sex trade or prostitution. Many incest offenders have been caught or have admitted to purchasing and viewing child pornography. Incest offenders also are very tenacious repeat offenders. For example, in an anonymous survey, 159 of the 561 incest offenders that violated girls reported 12,927 sexual abuse acts against 286 victims who were either family members or acquaintances. Between 40% and 50% of sex offenders arrested for incest crimes have no conscience or empathy for others, focus only on their desires and needs, and meet the criteria for psychopathic deviancy. There also are few differences between offenders arrested for victimizing acquaintances and incest offenders, though incest offenders are less likely to be sexually aroused by children. Given all of these findings, some scholars question whether there is a category of sex offenders who only victimize children in their own families.

Research has also revealed inconsistent findings of whether children with stepparents are at a higher risk of being an incest victim. Some research suggests that child victims are at a higher risk of incest if their mothers have been victims of sexual abuse and are abusing illicit drugs. A substantial proportion of reported incest offenders have also violated children outside of their own family, which challenges the myth that incest offenders are only dangerous to their own family members. Some incest offenders are sexually aroused by children whereas other incest offenders are only sexually aroused by adult women but revert to children for external reasons such as marital dissatisfaction or alcohol abuse. Some incest offenders are physically as well as sexually abusive to their wives and children and feel entitled to abuse their children or "teach" their children about sex. However, incest offenders compared to adult rapists and child molesters of children outside of the family generally have lower rates of committing new sex crimes. Only a few studies have focused on which offender and offense characteristics predict whether incest offenders will commit a new crime. Alcohol abuse, psychopathic deviancy, and prior arrests for sexual offenses predicted new sexual recidivism in one study.

Are victims of childhood sexual abuse more likely to commit sex crimes as adults? The research indicates that most victims of childhood sexual abuse do not grow up to become sex offenders. However, in the criminal population, offenders who have been sexually or physically abused as children are about four times more likely to commit sex crimes. Most prison inmates convicted of violent or sexual offenses against children do not report that they are victims of prior physical or sexual abuse. Only one-third of incarcerated sex offenders reported a history of being sexually or physically abused as a child. Moreover, sodomy (anal penetration) increases the risk that victims will begin to commit sex crimes on other children as juveniles and as adults. Boys are at a much higher risk of anal penetration and researchers believe that this abuse is so traumatic that victims may attempt to obtain control over this trauma through selecting similar victims and performing similarly abusive acts.

Furthermore, incest may be more traumatic than other forms of sexual abuse. Research has found that incest involving penetration compared to other child molestation events involving penetration can have a greater negative impact on the child victim's long-term psychological and social adjustment. Incest victims generally feel a more profound violation of trust that disrupts their ability to form healthy attachments with other people and produces anxiety, depression, and other maladjustments. The media, criminal justice professionals, and the public must not assume that incest offenders are less harmful than sexual predators; these two categories have considerable overlap and are not mutually exclusive. Apparently, when they have the opportunity to groom child acquaintances to trust and admire them, sex offenders are dangerous to their own family members as well as other children.

LORETTA J. STALANS

References and Further Reading

Abel, G.G., et al. 1987. Self-reported sex crimes of nonincarcerated paraphilics. *Journal of Interpersonal Violence*, 2, 3–25.

Firestone, P., Bradford, J.M., McCoy, M., Greenberg, D.M., Larose, M.R., and Curry, S. 1999. Prediction of recidivism in incest offenders, *Journal of Interpersonal Violence*, 14(5), 511–531.

Groff, M.G. and Hubble, J.M. 1984. A comparison of father–daughter and stepfather–stepdaughter incest, *Criminal Justice and Behavior*, 11(4), 461–475.

Jones, L. and Finkelhor, D. 2001. The decline in child sexual abuse cases, Washington, DC: Department of Justice, (NCJ 184741), January.

Levesque, R.J.R. 2000. Sentencing sex crimes against children: An empirical and policy analysis, *Behavioral Science and the Law*, 18, 331–341.

Margolin, L. 1994. Child sexual abuse by uncles: A risk assessment, *Child Abuse & Neglect*, 18(3), 215–224.

Myers, J.E.B. 1997. *A Mother's Nightmare—Incest: A Practical Legal Guide for Parents and Professionals*, Thousand Oaks, CA: Sage Publications.

Stroud, D.D., Martens, S.L., and Barker, J. 2000. Criminal investigation of child sexual abuse: A comparison of cases referred to the prosecutor to those not referred, *Child Abuse & Neglect*, 24(5), 689–700.

Snyder, H. 2000. *Sexual Assaults of Young Children as Reported to Law Enforcement: Victim, Incident, and Offender Characteristics*, Washington, DC: U.S. Department of Justice, (NCJ 182990), July.

Widom, C.S. 1995. *Victims of Childhood Sexual Abuse Later Criminal Consequences*, Washington, DC: U.S. Department of Justice, (NCJ 151525), March.

See also **Child Abuse: Extent and Correlates; Child Molestation**

Incivilities Theory

Incivility can be defined as the social and physical disorder resulting from the disinterest of residents within a particular neighborhood. The term incivility has evolved from the "broken windows" hypothesis, a concept introduced by James Q. Wilson and George Kelling in the *Atlantic Monthly* in March of 1982. Wilson and Kelling used this phrase to explain how criminogenic neighborhoods evolve from physical decay and the inattention of residents. They argued that if an office or factory window is broken and not repaired, passersby take notice and conclude that no one cares enough to fix that window. In time, people

begin to throw rocks at the building to break more windows. Eventually, all the windows will be broken and people will conclude that not only is no one in charge of the building, no one is in charge of the neighborhood. Residents will subsequently begin to abandon the neighborhood, and unsupervised youth, prostitutes, drug addicts, and other marginalized groups will take over the neighborhood. Thus, small disorders, left unrepaired, evolve into larger and larger disorders, and eventually breed crime.

Skogan (1990) suggests that incivility involves both social and physical disorder. Social disorder is a matter of experiences and perceptions within a neighborhood. Signs of social disorder include public drinking, prostitution, catcalls, and sexual harassment experienced by female neighborhood residents, and the continued presence of unsupervised youth and other marginalized groups on the streets of the neighborhood. Physical disorder, on the other hand, involves visual signs of decay and negligence, including abandoned or deteriorating buildings, empty trash-filled lots, broken streetlights, abandoned cars, and alleys filled with garbage and litter. As Skogan suggests, social disorder appears as a series of relatively episodic events, whereas physical disorder refers to ongoing conditions within a neighborhood.

Neighborhoods exhibiting signs of incivility have a number of problems not found in neighborhoods that are more civil, centering around a sense that residents have lost control of their surroundings. This in turn creates increased levels of fear of crime; this fear of crime causes residents to fear strangers and others whom they do not know. This fear subsequently increases the social isolation of each neighborhood resident, resulting in fewer social controls, both formal (churches and schools) and informal (adult supervision of a neighbor's children). This loss of controls leads to further deterioration within the neighborhood. Offenders from other neighborhoods are then increasingly attracted by the area's vulnerability to crime and other deviant acts. Nearly all the studies testing incivilities theory report a significant positive relationship between neighborhood incivility and fear of crime (Bursik and Grasmick, 1993; Taylor and Covington, 1993; Will and McGrath, 1995).

Incivilities theory falls under the larger ecological school of criminology and sociology that originated at the University of Chicago in the 1930s and 1940s, pioneered by Robert Park, Ernest Burgess, Henry Shaw, and Clifford McKay. These theorists were the first to examine the impact of neighborhood characteristics and location on crime, as they determined that certain neighborhoods in Chicago had higher crime rates than others. Theorists from this school argued that urbanization, migration, and immigration have created conditions that bring about social disorganization in certain neighborhoods. These conditions bring about crime and delinquency in those areas.

Kelling and Coles (1996) argue that combating incivility is the first step to reducing the crime problem. They suggest that responsibility for crime control should be shifted from the exclusive purview of criminal justice agencies to the broader idea that crime control is most effective when accomplished in a collaborative effort between neighborhood residents and criminal justice agencies in that community. Kelling and Coles argue that because reducing disorder and fear are as important in crime control as efforts to reduce serious crime, restoring and maintaining order are as important as combating crime. They point out that citizens are the key element in the effort to reduce disorder, fear, and crime. Following incivility theory, Kelling and Coles suggest that if citizens set standards for their neighborhood and work with the police and other community agencies to enforce those standards, neighborhood incivility and the subsequent crime resulting from it can be controlled. In the crime control model that they propose, police act in conjunction with the community as its representatives instead of against the community as representatives of the state.

A wide array of crime control policies has been attributed to incivility theory. Examples of these policies include the establishment of housing regulations that require proper maintenance and upkeep of houses and buildings within a neighborhood, swift repair or removal of deteriorating buildings or cars within a community, and finally, the broader ideas of order maintenance and community policing. Both order maintenance policing (increased emphasis on enforcing laws pertaining to crimes against public order, such as arresting individuals for open containers of alcohol and loitering, offenses frequently unenforced under other models of policing) and community policing (police working as partners with citizens to reduce crime and disorder in a community) are predicated on the idea that curing minor problems prevents the development of more serious problems (such as crime) within a community. Both styles of policing require substantial decentralization and the allocation of considerable discretion to line officers. A number of critics of order maintenance policing suggest that the focus on enforcement of laws against less serious crimes leads to increased violations of individual rights of citizens by police. In New York City, often cited as an example for its use of order maintenance policing to reduce incivility, serious violent crimes have dropped dramatically throughout the 1990s, but the number of citizen complaints against police in that same period increased threefold (Greene, 1999). Other cities (e.g., San Diego) using models of community policing have experienced similar reductions in serious violent crime without similar increases in citizen complaints.

Additionally, order maintenance policing has become a popular style of law enforcement in other countries as well. Newburn and Hayman (2001) discuss recent strategies adapted in London, England that use closed circuit television (CCTV) in the management and surveillance areas throughout the city. Cities in the U.S. have also begun implementing CCTV to observe certain areas and neighborhoods in their areas as well. The idea that CCTV will deter individuals from engaging in minor crimes and offenses against public order evolves directly from the "broken windows" thesis.

Although some suggest that as more and more criminal justice agencies switch to policies designed to combat incivility, increase in quality of life may occur together with decreases in crime, this approach is not without its critics. These critics counter that order maintenance policing, designed to reduce neighborhood incivility, may be in fact increasing racial bias and discrimination among some police departments, particularly in New York City where this style of policing is credited with dramatically reducing crime in the 1990s but also drastically increasing complaints against the police department for false arrest and racial discrimination. Thus, law enforcement strategies designed to reduce incivility have the potential to dramatically change the interaction between police and the community in the U.S.

DAVID C. MAY

References and Further Reading

Bursik, R.J., Jr. and Grasmick, H.G. 1993. *Neighborhoods and Crime: The Dimensions of Effective Community Control*, New York, NY: Lexington Books.
Greene, J.A. 1999. Zero tolerance: A case study of police policies and practices in New York City, *Crime and Delinquency* 45.
Kelling, G.L. and Coles, C.M. 1996. *Fixing Broken Windows: Restoring Order and Reducing Crime in Our Communities*, New York, NY: The Free Press.
Newburn, T. and Hayman, S. 2001. *Policing, Surveillance and Social Control: CCTV and Police Monitoring of Suspects*, United Kingdom: Willan Publishing.
Shaw, C.R. and McKay, H.D. 1942. *Juvenile Delinquency in Urban Areas*, Chicago, IL: University of Chicago Press.
Skogan, W.G. 1990. *Disorder and Decline: Crime and the Spiral of Decay in American Neighborhoods*, New York, NY: The Free Press.
Wilson, J.Q. and Kelling, G.L. 1982. Broken windows: The police and neighborhood safety, *Atlantic Monthly* 249.

See also **Fear of Crime**

Indeterminate Sentences *See* **Sentences and Sentencing**

India, Crime and Justice in

India's more than one billion people are diverse in every sense of the term. There are 17 officially recognized languages, and more than 5000 dialects are spoken. Almost every major religion has its followers—Hinduism and Islam being the two most prominent. Confrontation and harmonization are almost constant processes of India's history. The inhabitants, varying in intellectual and material development, have nevertheless always shared a sense of oneness in the country.

History of the Criminal Justice System

Despite diversity, the criminal justice system has been uniform for most of India's history. There have been three distinct systems: (1) the ancient system based on the principle of Dhamma (Dharma) or righteousness, (2) the Mughal system based on the Sharia ("Islam-derived" law), and (3) the British system based on common law.

Kautilya's *Arthshastra* (Shamashastry, 1951) best describes the ancient justice system (in the Mauryan period) suggesting that cases must be interpreted according to the customs of the prevailing society and for this, learned men must be trusted to do so correctly. There was no rigidity in the authority of any texts and it appears that the ancient Indian society did take into account changing customs, new knowledge, and philosophies. The king had overriding authority over all judicial functions but he was not considered the source of laws nor did he have divine rights. The system also recognized the diversities and dissimilarities in the society. However, it was based upon an unequal power base and biased in favor of the ruling elite. The caste system was unjust and cruel in its treatment of the Sudra (untouchables). The system was local and justice as understood was emphasized and well regulated; there was no absolutism and philosophers guided the society and the king. Justice in this system was inexpensive and swift and so helped to keep the society in order.

The Mughals ruled India for almost 300 years and introduced a centralized single model based on the Sharia. However, in view of the large Hindu population, the Panchayat and the lower administration were allowed to follow their own customs. Policing in towns was entrusted to the Kotwal (town inspector) who provided watch and ward duties and regulated prostitution, distillation of liquor, and public gatherings. The inspector also kept a census of all the residents and had to compensate any victim for the loss of the stolen property if he was unable to find the thief. Despite its long reign, the Mughal administration can only be remembered for its mixture of great pomp and show combined with benevolent and despotic intervention (Cohn, 1961).

The British came as traders to India in the 17th century and over the course of a century became its rulers. The primary objectives of the British were the exigencies of trade and profit, but unchallenged authority helped establish the British Raj symbolized by "glamour and snobbery" of the rulers. The British saw the prevailing system as backward and created new criminal justice institutions. New criminal laws, like the Code of Criminal Procedure (1862), the Indian Penal Code (1860), and the Evidence Act (1872) replaced all the previous laws. The police were designed as an instrument of control over the vast lands and diverse people at an economic cost. They were to hold India as the brightest jewel in the British crown, and the personnel, ill-trained and ill-qualified, were still given extraordinary discretionary powers to "rule with a firm hand and ruthlessly, if necessary" (Gupta, 1979). A serious consequence of the British rule was the total destruction of indigenous systems and upheaval in the Indian society. The English never invested in extending their institutions to cover the vast country. Thus courts, police stations, and government offices were generally miles from the *muffasi* (rural areas), forcing people to find intermediaries to approach distant judges. The resulting class of middlemen and lawyers corrupted the system and made justice difficult to find.

The Constitution

India's independence from British rule in 1947 marked a fresh beginning. A new constitution guaranteed citizens social, economic, and political justice; liberty of thought, expression, belief, faith, and worship; equality of status and opportunity; and the dignity of the individual. Many fundamental rights were also guaranteed to the citizens, such as the rights to equality, freedom of speech, assembly and movement, life and liberty, and freedom of religion.

The federal parliament consists of the Lok Sabha (House of the People) and the Rajya Sabha (Parliament). The members of the Lok Sabha are elected by the people directly; some members of parliament are

elected by the legislatures of the states and some are nominated by the president. A central council of ministers is formed by the political party that wins the majority in the elections and the leader, the prime minister, is the chief executive. On a similar pattern, state legislatures are elected by an adult franchise and headed by the chief minister. Municipalities and Panchayats are also elective bodies. A fiercely independent judiciary and media have emerged as important institutions keeping check over the executive. Further, a permanent bureaucracy, an independent Election Commission, a Human Rights Commission, a commission for Scheduled Castes and Tribes, and a Minority Commission are other forms of balancing power in the present system.

The Indian constitution began what some have described as the greatest political adventure since the creation of the U.S. constitution in Philadelphia in 1787. In a country where inequality was a historical and social reality for thousands of years, the stroke of a pen gave equal status to everyone. The impoverished millions suddenly had power that they never enjoyed for thousands of years. Women have status and voting rights equal to those of men, a situation unique in the patriarchal society of India. The rights of free movement, vocation, education, and freedom of religion have unshackled the caste and class privileges, unthinkable developments just a few years before independence.

The Court System

The judicial system in India is established as a unitary body with the Supreme Court at the apex, high courts at the state level, and lower courts at the district level. The Supreme Court—with 25 judges and 1 chief justice—is the highest court under Article 124 (1). The president appoints the justices after consultation with the chief justice of the Supreme Court and high courts. The judges hold office until they are 65 years of age and a superior judge can only be removed after an extraordinary session of the parliament. The salaries and perks of the judges are also protected under the constitution to assure judiciary independence.

The Indian Supreme Court exercises three kinds of powers: original, appellate, and consultative or advisory jurisdiction. The Supreme Court is the final court of appeal for a judgment of any subordinate court of India. Generally, all death sentences can be appealed. Article 32 (1) of the constitution provides the means to approach the Supreme Court directly for enforcement of the fundamental rights. The courts have used this provision for extended judicial actions that have come to be known as public interest litigation. Such judicial activism has opened new doors of justice to the poor, rectified several structural problems, and forced the chief executive to show responsibility to the rights of the citizens (Verma, 2001).

The Police

The Indian police are governed by Act V of 1861 that provides for a single department at the state level headed by the director general of police. States are divided into administrative units, called districts, in which the superintendent is the head of the police force. Each district has 20–30 police stations staffed by 15–20 constables and 4–6 investigating officers. Each station also has an armed force, and reserves exist at the district and state levels. These armed forces are meant only for law and order duties and are not involved in public dealings. Senior police officers control the Directorate of Prosecution, and decisions to prosecute are usually made by the superintendent.

Policing is a state duty, although the federal government also maintains large police units. There has been a phenomenal growth of armed and paramilitary police on the grounds of escalating violent conflicts, terrorism, and threats to stability. Many specialized units have been created to deal with communal problems, to provide security to important people (politicians and military officials), and to prevent cross-border smuggling and terrorism. A women's battalion in the Central Reserve Police Force has also been created to deal with the increasing number of female agitators. The Central Bureau of Investigation is the premier investigation agency and enjoys much respect. Other specialized units, like the National Police Academy, the Bureau of Research and Development, and the National Crime Records Bureau (NCRB) provide auxiliary support. Yet, the criminal justice system remains essentially unchanged from the British design. The police continue to be a ruler's force and "politically useful" (GOI Report I–VIII 1979–1983), especially in the sphere of combative elections. Partisan performance, brutality, corruption, and inefficiency remain as problems of the police institution in the country.

Prisons

Like the police, the prison system is also a state subject controlled directly by the Home Ministry. Indian prisons are notorious for being overcrowded, unsanitary, and lacking any provisions for the rehabilitation of the detainees. The long delays in conducting trials have also affected the prisons because the majority of inmates are awaiting trial. As their detention is temporary (although it may last more than a year) few resources are set aside for them. In 1994, Kiran Bedi, an Inspector General of Tihar Jail at Delhi, won the prestigious Ramon Magsaysay award for innovative schemes she introduced, such as mass meditation and special training programs. Another prison in the state of Rajasthan runs an "open jail" for those showing good behavior. They are allowed to live with their families during the day and must report back to the prison at night. However, these have been the exceptions. Most prisons in India continue to function unchanged from British days with the objectives of punishment and retribution.

Order Maintenance and Crime

Despite the national slogan of "unity in diversity," modern India is besieged by social strife of every kind. The communal division between Hindus and Muslims that led to the partitioning of the land into India, Pakistan, and Bangladesh still simmers. The caste system within the Hindu community frequently erupts violently between the so-called backward and forward castes (Sinha, 1991). There are many ethnic and regional conflicts, too. The nascent democracy is also threatened by serious political conflicts, left-wing terrorism, and externally supported mercenary activities in Kashmir and in the northeastern parts of India. Elections are marred by violence and "booth-capturing" while industrial strikes, labor problems, and job reservation issues continually test the functioning of the criminal justice system.

Despite the large population and growing conflicts, the general crime situation does not seem to be as alarming. Around 6,411,259 crimes were officially reported in 1997, of which property crimes like burglary and theft form the bulk of incidents. These have been showing a declining trend over the past two decades. Property disputes and class and caste conflicts are some of the main reasons for murders. The number of rape cases has increased by 79.1% from 1987 to 1997. Kidnapping cases increased 43.6% in the same time span. Police performance in investigating crimes has been poor by its own records. Between 1987 and 1997, about 20% of the reported cases remain pending police action.

The Indian police remain notorious for their misbehavior, corruption, and misuse of force. In 1997, there were six cases of rape under police custody, and deadly force was used on 790 occasions, resulting in the deaths of 467 civilians. During 1997, there were also 123,523 citizen complaints filed against police officers, of which 1501 cases were found to be serious and went to trial. The Indian police strength remains low, and the workload of the investigators is heavy. There are 1.3 personnel per 1000 population and the national average workload for an investigator is approximately 60.7 cases per year (NCRB 1998).

Future Trends

At the beginning of the 21st century, terrorism, and social and political conflicts appeared to be serious threats to the stability of the Indian society. The criminal justice system, unaltered from the British design, needed drastic reform to address issues of civilian accountability, corruption, and misuse of force by the police. Computer crimes, money laundering, and financial irregularities were real and emerging challenges to the developing economy. However, the cumbersome nature of legal procedures delayed the judicial processes and made the system virtually unworkable. In view of the country's large population, a more decentralized system of courts and police seemed to be required. Yet reforms were difficult to implement because of a politicized bureaucracy, rampant corruption, and lack of political will.

ARVIND VERMA

Further Readings

Bayley, D.H. 1969. *The Police and Political Development in India*. Princeton, NJ, Princeton University Press.

Cohn, B.S. 1961. *The Development and Impact of British Administration in India*. New Delhi: Indian Institute of Public Administration.

Government of India. 1979–1983. *Report I–VIII of the National Police Commission*. Ministry of Home Affairs. Faridabad, India: Government of India Press.

Gupta, A. 1979. *The Police in British India: 1861–1947*. New Delhi, India: Concept Publishing Company.

National Crime Records Bureau. 1998. *Crime in India—1997*. Faridabad, India: Government of India Press.

Kohli, A. 1990. *Democracy and Discontent: India's Growing Crisis of Governability*. New York, NY: Cambridge University Press.

Potter, D.C. 1986. *India's Political Administrators: 1919–1983*. Oxford, UK: Clarendon Press.

Raghavan, R.K. 1999. *Policing a Democracy: A Comparative Study of India and the U.S.* New Delhi, India: Manohar Publications.

Saxena, N.S. 1987. *Law and Order in India*. New Delhi, India: Abhinav Publications.

Sinha, A. 1991. *The Struggles of the Poor*. London, UK: Oxford University Press.

Shamasastry, R. 1951. (translated), *Kautilya's Arthasastra*, Sri Raghuveer.

Verma, A. 2001. Taking justice outside the courts: Judicial activism in India. *The Howard Journal of Criminal Justice* 40, 2: 148–165.

Woodruff, P. 1954. *The Men Who Ruled India: The Guardians*. New York, NY: Schocken Books.

Indictment (Filing an Information)

In most U.S. jurisdictions, there are two methods of formally charging an individual with a crime: by indictment and by information. The purpose of both formal charges is the same; a defendant is put on notice of the charges, the defendant is provided with the information that is needed to prepare a defense, and the proper court is made a part of the process.

An indictment is a formal criminal charge issued by a grand jury. In the early history of the U.S., grand juries were used to guard against government abuse and to minimize the harm to an innocent individual's reputation. These two goals were advanced by interposing a group of citizens, who met in secret to determine if probable cause to believe a crime was committed, between the Crown and the accused. The framers believed so strongly in the grand jury that they included a right to grand jury review in the Fifth Amendment to the U.S. Constitution. That Amendment reads, "[N]o person shall be held to answer for a capital, or otherwise, infamous, crime, unless on a presentment or indictment of a Grand Jury." Crimes punishable with a prison term are "infamous," as are crimes that may be punished with a term of hard labor. (See *Mackin v. U.S.*, 117 U.S. 348 (1886) and *U.S. v. Moreland* 258 U.S. 433 (1922)). In the federal system, defendants are permitted to waive indictment by grand jury in all but capital cases.

The Supreme Court of the U.S. has rejected the proposition that grand jury review is a fundamental right. Accordingly, grand jury review is not required in state proceedings. See *Hurtado v. People of State of California*, 4 S.Ct. 111 (1884). Regardless, grand juries are used by many states. If state law does not provide for grand jury review, another method of determining whether probable cause exists to continue a prosecution must occur. The preliminary hearing is the alternative used in such instances.

Individuals suspected of committing crimes who are investigated by grand juries are commonly known as targets. The objective of grand jury review is to determine if probable cause exists to believe that a target has committed a crime. Grand juries are typically larger than *petit juries* (juries that make the guilty or not guilty determination). In the federal system, grand juries are composed of 16–23 persons (F.R. Crim. P. 6(a)). The procedures of the grand jury also differ from that of the *petit jury* in several regards. First, grand jury proceedings are closed. Members of the public may not attend grand jury sessions (F.R. Crim. P. 6(d)). Even more, targets are not entitled to attend. Second, not only are the proceedings closed, but they are secret (F.R. Crim. P. 6(e)). Every person who attends a grand jury session is instructed not to disclose what transpires during the session. Third, a judge does not oversee the daily operations of the grand jury. In most jurisdictions, it is the prosecutor who oversees the proceedings. However, even the prosecutor is excluded from the grand jury room during deliberations and voting (F.R. Crim. P. 6(d)). Fourth, witnesses do not possess a right to counsel while testifying before a grand jury. However, the Fifth Amendment's privilege against self-incrimination is applicable. It is a common practice to permit a witness to leave the grand jury room to confer with counsel who is waiting in an adjacent room or hallway. In support of the investigative function, grand juries have the authority to compel people to appear, to subpoena documents, and to hold people in contempt.

After a grand jury has completed its investigation, the grand jury determines if probable cause exists to charge someone. The formal charge is known as an indictment or a true bill. In the federal system, at least 12 members of the grand jury must vote to charge an individual before an indictment may be issued. The indictment is to be written in plain and concise language, it shall state the law upon which the charge is predicated, it shall present the essential facts of the offense charged, and it shall address all the essential elements of the crimes charged (F.R. Crim. P. 7(c)). If more than one crime is charged, each crime shall be detailed separately. Multiple defendants may be charged in the same indictment so long as the alleged crimes arose from a common set of facts and each defendant is charged in a separate count. In the federal system, the decision whether to prosecute rests with the U.S. Attorney of the district where the grand jury sits. As such, the U.S. Attorney may refuse to prosecute individuals who have been indicted by a grand jury. The states differ on this point. Some states follow the federal model. Other states require prosecutors to sign the indictment and to prosecute the named defendants.

The second method of formally charging a person with a crime is by information. An information is filed by a prosecutor without grand jury review. Information is the default charging method. It may be used in all cases where grand jury indictment is not required.

The technical requirements of an information are the same as that of the indictment. The document is to be written in plain and concise language, it shall state the law upon which the charge is predicated, it shall present the essential facts of the offense charged, and it shall address all the essential elements of the crimes charged. If more than one crime is charged, each crime shall be detailed separately.

An indictment or information that does not cite the law that is alleged to have been violated, that does not include one of the essential elements of the charged crime, or that charges multiple defendants in one count may be invalidated by the reviewing court. Technical errors, such as misspellings, are not fatal to the document unless they jeopardize the defendant's ability to prepare a defense.

In some instances, an indictment or information may be legally sufficient, but still lacking in a description of the underlying facts that a defendant needs to prepare a defense. In such cases, a defendant may move for a Bill of Particulars (F.R. Crim. P. 7 (f)). If granted, the government will file a Bill of Particulars detailing the underlying facts of the alleged crimes. Bills of Particulars not only assist the defendant in the preparation of a defense, but also facilitate plea negotiations and permit the reviewing court to prepare better for trial.

Complaints are to be distinguished from indictments and information. Complaints are not filed in all cases. When used, a criminal complaint precedes an indictment or information. Often filed by law enforcement officers, and occasionally by prosecutors and citizens, the complaint is a written statement that is used to support a warrantless arrest at an initial appearance or to support an application for an arrest warrant. In such cases, the complaint is eventually replaced by an indictment or information as the formal charging instrument. It is common under state and local law for the complaint to act as both the formal charge and as a summons to appear in court in minor misdemeanor and infraction cases. In such instances, no indictment or information is filed.

DANIEL E. HALL

References and Further Reading

Hall, D.E. 2004. 4th ed., *Criminal Law and Procedure*, Delmar/West Publishing. Ch. 14.
Lafave, W., Israel, J., and King, N. 2000. 3rd ed., *Criminal Procedure Hornbook*, Eagan, MN, West Group Publishing, Ch. 8, 15, and 19.
41 Am. Jur. *Indictments and Informations*. 2003.
42 C.J.S. *Indictments and Informations*. 2003.

See also **Arraignments; Due Process**

Infancy as a Defense to Criminal Liability *See* Defenses to Criminal Liability: Justifications and Excuses

Inmates *See* Prisons: Inmate Populations and Subcultures

Inquisitorial Justice

Inquisitorial procedure governs the official investigation of crime, arrest, prosecution, trial, sentencing, and appeals of accused criminals in many countries that are historically characterized as civil code jurisdictions.

Civil code jurisdictions include most Western European countries, most states of the former Soviet Union, parts of Latin America, and parts of Asia, amounting to almost half of the legal systems in countries of the world. Civil codes usually cover both criminal law and civil (tort) law in these countries. Some jurisdictions are divided so that they may include civil-inquisitorial courts along with other systems such as common law, Islamic, or customary courts.

Early inquisitorial courts (notably, the Spanish Inquisition of the 15th and 16th centuries) were characterized by the use of torture to extort confessions and a total lack of protection against false accusations. Virtually all modern states using inquisitorial procedures have modified them by including basic human rights protections and procedures to ensure the accountability of court personnel to those above them and to the public. Many reject the term *inquisitorial* for this reason. No other term has been widely adopted, however.

The inquisitorial procedures of the civil code (Romano–Germanic) family of legal systems are often contrasted with the adversarial procedures of countries such as England and the U.S., which rely on a common law tradition. Criminal law in civil code countries is legislatively enacted (i.e., political) and is found in comprehensive, systematized, and logically ordered documents that emphasize legal principles rather than case precedents. The civil law tradition favors a hierarchically organized and highly educated judiciary that interprets the law as written, referring to prior cases only as a check on consistency.

In most civil law jurisdictions prosecution is required unless it can be shown to be in the public interest to avoid it. A prosecutor's discretion is severely limited by bureaucratic supervision and the right of citizens to appeal nonprosecution.

Inquisitorial procedure relies heavily on a lengthy, free-ranging, and relatively intrusive process of pretrial investigation. There are few impediments to active police and judicial questioning of anyone with potential information and few restraints on search, seizure, and pretrial investigatory detention. An investigative judge (*juge d'instruction*) in France can be authorized by the prosecutor's office to undertake control of any complex investigation. This judge interrogates witnesses and the accused (individually or together) as part of the pretrial phase. The defendant cannot escape being repeatedly brought before the judge and confronted with the emerging evidence. The investigative judge or prosecutor creates a file (dossier) that includes all the evidence (including hearsay and character evidence). The defense has access to the record that is being developed against the accused so that misinformation can be challenged and surprise at trial is unlikely.

Typically, the inquisitorial trial is a single, focused, dramatic event. A mixed bench including a presiding professional judge or president, flanked by two or three assessors (lay or professional judges), is a common form. The presiding judge will use the dossier (read prior to trial) as a guide to ensure that all the relevant evidence is heard orally in open court. The presiding judge is expected to take an active, dominating role in examining and cross-examining the participants. The questions tend to be open-ended, calling upon the individuals to explain themselves fully. The prosecutor assists in the presentation of evidence, whereas the defense counsel is mainly restricted to advising the defendant on what is happening, not how to resist it. The defense can object on limited grounds—such as pointing out that evidence that has been shown to be false should not be presented. In some jurisdictions (such as Germany) victims may be granted the right to participate or to be represented by their own lawyer as adjunct prosecutors (*Nebenkläger*).

After the testimony has been heard, the judge and assessors retire together to chambers to deliberate. They decide by a simple majority on both the legal and the factual issues of the trial. In theory, it is possible for the assessors to outvote the presiding judge, with respect to verdict and sentence. In practice, the presiding judge has vastly superior influence. The governing standard for conviction or acquittal is persuasion (personal belief or conviction) based on understanding of the evidence that has been presented in court. Appeals can be grounded in legal-procedural or factual claims and can result in an entirely new trial.

Inquisitorial courts almost always convict, and appeals are relatively rare, partly because the pretrial phase weeds out weak cases and partly because there is no tradition of avoiding trial through a plea bargain. In inquisitorial systems, the confession is treated as evidence, but not as termination of the inquiry.

Inquisitorial processes have been dramatically influenced by the expansion of democracy and the impact of globalization. Modern human rights codes (modeled by the UN, the European Court of Human Rights, and the International Court of Justice) have encouraged the incorporation of adversarial procedures that protect against improper arrest, unwarranted search and seizure, lengthy pretrial detention, or self-incrimination. Agencies such as Amnesty International have highlighted human rights abuses and increased the pressure for change. In response, defense lawyers are becoming more active and more respected as participants in civil law trials, and rights receive more attention than before. It is no longer true, if it ever was that inquisitorial procedure contrasted with the common law presumption of innocence. Both civil and common law maintain the legal fiction that the defendant is innocent until proven guilty. The inquisitorial system, however, retains a strong expectation that accused persons should cooperate with authorities in the pursuit of truth, rather than defend themselves by any legal means.

Some civil law countries have adopted many adversarial elements (Italy since 1988), whereas others have taken on relatively few (France). Even so, almost all countries participate in discussions with neighboring countries toward more uniform and compatible systems. The European Court of Justice and the proposed *Corpus Juris* encourage a standardization of procedures not only in individual civil law countries, but also in nations having other legal traditions. An example of this convergence is England, where there have been controversial adjustments to traditional common law features such as the right to remain silent. The increasing tendency for cooperative international initiatives with respect to drugs, terrorism, and organized transnational crime has also fed into the demand for greater procedural uniformity among the nations.

LINDA B. DEUTSCHMANN

References and Further Reading

Barak, G., (Ed.) 2000. *Crime and Crime Control: A Global View,* Westport and London: Greenwood Press.

Ebbe, O.N.I., (Ed.) 1996. *Comparative and International Criminal Justice Systems.* Boston, MA: Butterworth–Heinemann.

Fairchild, E. and Dammer, H.R. 2001. *Comparative Criminal Justice Systems,* 2nd ed., Belmont, CA, and London: Wadsworth/Thomson Learning.

Fennell, P., Harding, C., Jorg, N., and Swart, B. 1995. *Criminal Justice in Europe: A comparative Study,* New York, NY: Oxford.

Goldstein, A.S. 1997. Converging criminal justice systems: Guilty pleas and the public interest. *Israel Law Review* 31.

Hatchard, J., Huber, B., and Vogler, R., (Ed.) 1996. *Comparative Criminal Procedure,* London, UK: The British Institute of International and Comparative Law.

Nelkin, D., (Ed.) 2000. *Contrasting Criminal Justice: Getting from Here to There*, Aldershot and Burlington: Ashgate Publishing Company.

McDonald, W.F., (Ed.) 1997. *Crime and Law Enforcement in the Global Village,* Cincinnati, OH: Anderson Publishing.

Reichel, P.L. 1999. *Comparative Criminal Justice Systems,* 2nd ed., Englewood Cliffs, NJ: Prentice-Hall.

Rounds, D. 2000. *International Criminal Justice: Issues in a Global Perspective,* Boston, London, and Toronto: Allyn and Bacon.

See also **Medieval Europe, Crime and Justice in; Spain, Crime and Justice in**

Insanity and Diminished Responsibility as Defense to Criminal Liability

Societies have always made exceptions for criminal responsibility. Societies have always allowed for mental disorder as an excuse for blame. Societies have always avoided punishing the mentally disordered for their misdeeds. History suggests that insanity defense law was simply giving name to standard legal practice. Despite this, modern societies continue to argue and fret over the legitimacy of the insanity defense. Rather than accept it as part of traditional legal history, as having a place in society, much discussion and legal wrestling continues in trying to craft the perfect, but fair, insanity defense. In some corners, there are calls for abolishing the special defense altogether.

The underlying philosophical foundation for the insanity defense is that individuals who are so seriously mentally ill that their behavior is irrational or that they cannot control their behavior should not be punished. Punishment should be not meted out to those who cannot control their behavior (deterrence), that they should not be the object of our revenge (retribution), and that they should be treated with compassion (rehabilitation). The proponents of abolition of the insanity defense argue that no one, including a seriously mentally ill person, is completely without reason. Underlying the debate is what constitutes individual or criminal responsibility.

The insanity defense has achieved nearly mythological status in the U.S., equating it with what is "wrong" with the criminal justice system, leading many from the general public to legal professionals to highly overestimate the rate of pleas. Highly publicized cases often lead to a dissection of the insanity defense, contributing to the belief that insanity pleas frequently occur. Insanity is among criminal defenses that raises questions about the defendant's mental state at the time of the offense. Others include affirmative defenses such as self-defense, entrapment, duress, and provocation; defenses of substance abuse; diminished capacity; and guilty but mentally ill. This chapter is largely devoted to the insanity defense, but the defenses of diminished responsibility and guilty but mentally ill will also be briefly covered.

The case most often cited as the beginning of the modern common law insanity defense is that of Daniel McNaughtan, a Scotsman who mistakenly killed Sir Robert Peel's secretary, Edward Drummond, thinking

Drummond was Prime Minister Peel. In McNaughtan's 1843 trial, the judge ordered the jury to determine if at the time of the offense McNaughtan could distinguish right from wrong. McNaughtan was found not guilty "on the ground of insanity." There was suspicion from the outset that the verdict was predetermined, noting that the jury never left the court room and briefly deliberated in the corner. The acquittal caused much outcry and discussion in England, prompting Queen Victoria to speak to Parliament, expressing her dissatisfaction with the outcome of the trial. This case established the McNaughtan test of insanity, also known as the "right/wrong" test.

What is often unexamined is that the holding in McNaughtan simply restated existing law. In 1800, James Hadfield had been acquitted by reason of mental defect in England of attempting to assassinate King George III while attending the Drury Lane Theatre. Hadfield's aim was less than perfect, and he was subdued while at the same time pledging his allegiance to the King. What is notable about Hadfield's case is that it is one of the first instances in which the psychiatric concept of "delusion" was used. Further, Hadfield had suffered significant and disfiguring head wounds that may have persuaded the jury to render an acquittal on the grounds of insanity. Owing to the fact that Hadfield was charged with treason, British law provided him with a lawyer of his choosing. Wisely, Hadfield chose Thomas Erskine, one of the most admired legal minds of the time. His talented legal counsel most likely also contributed to his successful acquittal. Following Hadfield's acquittal, the British Parliament passed the 1800 Criminal Lunatics Law that allowed for automatic, involuntary hospitalization of persons acquitted by reason of insanity. Insanity acquittees were confined until the Crown approved their release. This law is the foundation for U.S. psychiatric commitment standards in practice yet today (Moran, 1985). Both McNaughtan and Hadfield spent their remaining years confined at Bethlem Psychiatric Hospital (AKA Bedlam Hospital).

The McNaughtan and Hadfield cases owe their decisions to yet earlier cases in English common law in which the mental health of the defendant was raised. Walker (1985) examined London's Old Bailey court records and documented over 100 cases in which the insanity defense was used in the 18th century; it is unclear why it was so popular and had a 50% success rate. Two especially noteworthy cases are *Rex v. Arnold* (16 How. St. Tr. 684, 1724) and *Rex v. Ferrers* (19 How. St. Tr. 886, 1760). In *Arnold* the "wild beast test" was used, a phrase attributed to the historian Henrici Bracton in the 1200s, establishing that defendants could be found not guilty only after being found completely insane, "....no more than a brute, or a wild beast." In 1736, the influential legal scholar Lord Hale wrote that where there is "total defect of the understanding," there is no free will. In *Ferrers* (1760), the court ruled that the defendants could be found not guilty by reason of insanity (NGRI) only if they lacked reason to restrain themselves and if there was the ability to tell "moral good from evil." The legal question in both cases was the extent of impairment necessary to be acquitted by reason of insanity, not whether it was a legitimate defense.

The McNaughtan rule remains the primary test of insanity in the U.S. although it has been revised, first by introducing the "irresistible impulse" defense in 1887. In such cases, mentally ill defendants who acted without prior contemplation would potentially qualify for an insanity defense. The central question is whether the defendant could exercise self-control. Another defense that sought to clarify the McNaughtan rule was the "product-test" established in *Durham v. U.S.* (214 F.2d 862 D.C. Cir., 1954). The D.C. Circuit Court found that defendants were not guilty by reason of insanity if their criminal behavior was "the product of mental disease or defect." For this period, the courts were taking into account the advances made in psychiatry and, thus, allowing broader testimony. Thus, McNaughtan was viewed as too restrictive as it provides an "either/or" outcome, not allowing for degrees of impairment.

The American Legal Institute's (ALI) Model Penal Code (MPC) test of insanity was an attempt to modernize the emerging variations of McNaughtan and to incorporate more clinical input. The ALI test of insanity includes a cognitive "prong" and a volitional "prong." The ALI states that "[a] person is not responsible for criminal conduct if at the time of such conduct as a result of mental disease or defect he lacks substantial capacity either to appreciate the criminality of his conduct *or* [emphasis added by author] to conform his conduct to the requirements of the law" (MPC, 1962). The ALI is a more liberal test of insanity in that it allows for acquittal on cognitive or volitional grounds, but it exempts repeated criminal behavior as a qualifying mental defect.

One of the concerns raised by some judges and other legal scholars is that the ALI test (as well as the *Durham* product test) gave too much influence to psychiatric and psychological experts. Many cases have wrestled with the definition of nonclinical terms such as "mental disease," "mental defect," and "mental disturbance." Most agree that major psychoses such as schizophrenia and major affective disorders are the intended mental disorders included in those broad terms where the insanity defense is considered. Some debate exists, particularly under the ALI volitional prong, concerning what other disorders would be considered serious enough to excuse a defendant. Under most state laws, personality disorders fail to meet the criteria. The role of the clinical expert, then, is pivotal in most insanity cases whether the case is tried before a jury or judge or is disposed of with a plea bargain. Much of the concern about the role of the clinical expert focused not only on their ability to determine state of mind at the time of the offense. Public safety issues became a new issue from the 1960s to 1980s once courts mandated the release of persons previously held, for all intents and purposes, for the remainder of their lives (see cases discussed below). Prior to the 1960s, most insanity acquittees were hospitalized forever. As the result of a number of court decisions, hospital-based psychiatrists had responsibility for discharging insanity acquittees who they believed to be no longer dangerous and mentally ill. Public scrutiny of these decisions remained minimal. As a consequence of what were perceived as too lax release standards, many states passed legislation in the 1980s that required the approval of the committing criminal court judge and district attorney prior to the release or discharge of persons acquitted as insane. The treating clinician would make a recommendation to the court, but the court would retain jurisdiction over the acquittee.

The importance of the clinical professional in court is amplified in the broad issue of "diminished capacity," which differs from "diminished responsibility." The latter is a pseudo-insanity defense that allows clinical testimony on volition and cognition and enjoyed only brief acceptance in California. Diminished capacity, however, allows psychiatric testimony on the degree of culpability or *mens rea* as a mitigation strategy. A defendant can introduce clinical testimony on *mens rea* without entering an insanity defense, for example, as to whether the defendant acted knowingly or purposefully. This may reduce his or her degree of blameworthiness from an intentional crime to one of negligence. This is especially critical in death penalty cases. Rules of evidence vary by state as to the degree to which clinical professionals can testify on *mens rea* issues without raising the insanity defense.

There is little doubt that the insanity defense is among the most controversial aspects of the nexus between law and mental health. Language alone serves as a mutual irritant between the two professions. What gives insanity acquittees unique status among persons with mental disorders is that they also have been found legally innocent of crimes for which they are factually guilty. In a comprehensive U.S. study on the insanity defense completed in the early 1990s, researchers found that although most crimes for which defendants are acquitted are felonies involving a victim, nearly 30% were acquitted of a property or less serious offense. Additionally, they found that nearly 90% NGRI acquittees were diagnosed as having psychosis (e.g., schizophrenia or bipolar disorder) or other major impairment (e.g., mental retardation), and most (82%) had a history of psychiatric hospitalization, helping to dispel the myth that many are "malingerers" and not really mentally ill. This study also set the benchmark that an insanity defense is raised in approximately 1% of felonies and is successful about 26% of the time (Callahan, McGreevy, Steadman, and Robbins, 1991).

Thus, in addition to a diagnosis of a serious mental disorder, insanity acquittees are often viewed by the public, court, and often clinicians as dangerous. The dual roles have given insanity acquittees their own legal history that has at times intersected with persons civilly committed under state jurisdictions. The insanity defense raises jurisprudential issues of individual rights versus society's rights. And given the dismal state of risk assessment leading up to the 21st century, U.S. courts experimented with expansion of constitutional rights, followed by a constriction. In states with an insanity defense, it is an affirmative defense, meaning that when raised, the defendant has the burden of proving insanity. This is different from other mental health defense strategies mentioned above.

Popular misconception about the insanity defense is likely aided by the excessive media coverage in the U.S. of a few insanity defense cases, most notably John Hinckley who was acquitted by reason of insanity in 1983 for attempting to kill then President Reagan. Following the Hinckley acquittal, public support for the insanity defense in the U.S. plummeted. This was followed closely by insanity defense reforms in a majority of states that aimed to restrict the use and success of the insanity defense (Callahan, Mayer, and Steadman, 1987). Misinformation about the insanity defense persists, despite extensive research on the topic. Most often, the public believes that the insanity defense is raised often; that it is usually successful; that defendants who are acquitted are quickly released from custody; that insanity acquittees are faking mental illness; and that insanity defendants are dangerous. Continued misperception is counterproductive in that it can lead to misallocation of scarce mental health resources, to inappropriate institutionalization of non-dangerous persons, and to unintended legal consequences when laws are changed.

For example, in most states insanity acquittees are involuntarily committed for evaluation upon acquittal in a maximum security forensic hospital, regardless of their offense. The mandatory, automatic evaluation period is normally followed by involuntary hospitalization, often in forensic hospitals although most Americans believe acquittees leave the court "scot free." Research is inconsistent in establishing whether insanity defendants spend more or less time confined than their convicted counterparts. These varying findings are likely owing to methodological differences among studies. Making comparisons across populations is additionally difficult because the nature and context of the offenses vary between NGRI acquittees and convicted offenders.

Although many states reformed their insanity defense following the Hinckley acquittal, Montana moved to limit its used in 1976 by becoming the first state to abolish the affirmative defense of insanity. Idaho and Utah later adopted similar laws. Montana's new law returned mental disorder to the *mens rea* stage of trial and added it to the sentencing phase. There is no doubt that Montana eliminated insanity acquittals in their state. However, an unanticipated consequence of Montana's abolition was a dramatic increase in defendants being found incompetent and never going to trial, eventually falling under less strict civil commitment standards once their charges were dropped (Callahan, Robbins, and Steadman, 1995). Montana's experiences raise the ethical and legal question as to whether numerous defendants in other states are going to trial or pleading to an insanity acquittal without having the competency to do so. By accepting an NGRI plea, the defendant is forfeiting rights and liberties that might have been retained had the question of competency (to stand trial, to enter a plea, to waive jury trial) been seriously raised. An insanity acquittal is so often seen as a "win," that the issue of competency is usually given a minor status; go for the acquittal.

The insanity defense began to fall into disfavor well before the 1982 insanity acquittal of Hinckley; however, there is little doubt that his successful insanity defense continued, and perhaps increased the velocity of the decline in pleas and acquittals nationwide. What likely began the downward trend was an overall move toward more conservative criminal justice policies in the late 1980s. Changes in the 1970s as a result of a number of federal court decisions in the late 1960s and early 1970s placed the insanity defense in a state of ambiguity and change, eventually resulting in a return to a restrictive approach toward persons found NGRI.

During a very brief period from 1966 to 1983, the federal courts addressed a range of insanity defense issues, ranging from how insanity was defined to how insanity acquittees could be institutionalized and released. The natural starting point for challenging the legal status of insanity acquittees was to compare them with persons who were civilly committed. The early cases, then, addressed civil commitment and were generalized to insanity acquittees. Beginning with *Baxtrom v. Herold* (383 U.S. 107, 1966) and concluding with *Jones v. U.S.* (463 U.S. 354, 1983), the legal status of insanity defendants underwent major shifts in judicial attitudes and decisions, first moving from being ignored to one in which this class of defendants were given expanded considerations and rights, followed by a return to restrictive, conservative decisions.

Though not a case involving an insanity acquittee, *Baxtrom* is the crucial starting point for tracing the U.S. legal history of the insanity defense. The U.S. Supreme Court unanimously held that a convicted defendant transferred to a mental hospital and whose criminal sentence was about to expire was subject to the more lenient civil commitment standards. Prior to *Baxtrom* persons found NGRI were held indefinitely with few if any constitutional protections. One year later in 1967, the U.S. Supreme Court held in *Specht v. Patterson* (386 U.S. 605, 1967) that a "habitual dangerous sex offender" (not NGRI) was denied equal protection when he was committed to a mental institution without a meaningful hearing. Although neither case involved a person acquitted NGRI, they raised two critical questions that eventually were considered for NGRIs: commitment standards and the right to a hearing.

Finally, in *Bolton v. Harris* (395 F.2d 642 D.C. Cir., 1968) Judge Bazelon and the D.C. Court of Appeals ruled that insanity acquittees must be given approximately the same procedural protections as persons civilly committed. What immediately followed were all but ten states changing their laws to prohibit automatic, involuntary commitment upon an insanity acquittal; defendants would be subject to periodic reviews of present mental state and dangerousness.

Although not a federal case, the Michigan Supreme Court's ruling in *People v. McQuillan* (392 Mich. 511, 1974) is critical for two reasons: first, the court held that although insanity defendants could be held for evaluation following trial, they had to be held to the less-stringent civil commitment standards; and second, as a consequence, Michigan passed the first guilty but mentally ill (GBMI) law in the U.S. The *McQuillan* decision led to the release of over 100 insanity defendants, two of whom were later convicted of murder; the aftermath of *McQuillan* led to the first GBMI law. The GBMI laws seemed to placate the public into believing they were being compassionate yet tough. Research on these laws has shown that they have generally failed to live up to their promise of reducing the volume of insanity acquittals. It is important to note that in every state with a GBMI law, it coexists with the NGRI law; it does not replace it.

Although defendants can enter a plea of "guilty but mentally ill," it is more often the case that a defendant is found GBMI following an unsuccessful insanity plea.

The intent of the GBMI was to increase public safety by reducing the use of the insanity defense; early research suggested that it did not live up to its objectives (Smith and Hall, 1982). However, Keilitz (1987) found that the GBMI may have drawn the less seriously mentally ill and more violent offenders away from the NGRI cohort. There is evidence that GBMI siphons from the insanity defense the more violent, or socially repugnant offenders and that persons found GBMI who are imprisoned serve longer sentences than either those acquitted NGRI or found guilty (Callahan, McGreevy, Cirincione, and Steadman, 1992). The legal criticisms of the GBMI law involve its use of the conjunction "but" rather than "and" mentally ill. Additionally, the law also misleads juries and perhaps judges into believing that defendants who are found GBMI are more likely than others to receive mental health care in prison, which is untrue. The law allows for juries and judges to render what they might believe is a benevolent punishment that guarantees public safety.

Lastly, in *Benham v. Edwards* (678 F.2d 511, 1982) the U.S. District Court struck down Georgia's NGRI laws as they did not provide equal protection similar to persons civilly committed. *Benham* was the last case that expanded the legal rights of persons acquitted by reason of insanity and was ultimately vacated during its appeal owing to the decision in *Jones v. U.S.* (1983). The period of expanding the rights of insanity acquittees came to an abrupt end the year after *Benham* and the 1982 Hinckley acquittal with the 1983 U.S. Supreme Court decision in *Jones*. As discussed earlier, the Hinckley acquittal was the watershed event in the modern insanity defense in the U.S. The Court's 5-4 decision in Jones signaled an end to regarding insanity acquittees in any way similar to persons civilly committed. What is remarkable about the *Jones* decision is that while Jones was involuntarily hospitalized as an insanity acquittee for shoplifting a jacket, the Court held that this crime demonstrated that he was dangerous under civil commitment standards. At the heart of this decision is the priority given to public safety at the expense of equal protection. Now states could return to practices of involuntary, automatic commitment of insanity acquittees who were mentally ill in that their acquittal was *per se* evidence of dangerousness.

Although the *Jones* decision had a major impact on insanity defense legislation throughout the U.S., the U.S. Supreme Court had yet another avenue they wanted to retrace. In 1997, the Court held in *Hendricks v. Kansas* (117 S.Ct. 2072, 1997) that prisoners who are predatory sex offenders and have a "mental disturbance" or a personality disorder can be involuntarily transferred to psychiatric facilities after their prison sentence has expired. They may be detained in the hospitals until they are no longer "mentally disturbed." There is no consideration as to whether repeat sex offending is a mental disorder, treatable or not. Although the Court held in *Hendricks* that states could detain sex offenders in psychiatric facilities, it is up to individual states to change their laws. Many states have *de facto* Hendricks' laws by allowing the involuntary civil commitment of sex offenders, holding that their repeat sex offending is a mental disorder and that they are dangerous. Although repeat sex offending is not an acceptable mental disorder to meet the McNaughtan and ALI tests of insanity, it is once again a mental "abnormality" to meet involuntary civil commitment standards.

All states in the U.S. have revised their insanity defense laws to adhere to minimal constitutional standards. In the past 20 years, no states have expanded the scope of its application. Although the number of NGRI acquittals has dwindled nationwide since the 1970s, there has not been a proportionate reduction in NGRIs in state custody. Procedures for releasing and supervising NGRIs in the community have become more strict and clinicians are more cautious in recommending discharge. Many states have a type of mental health parole for NGRIs; this differs considerably from outpatient commitment or assisted outpatient treatment. Much like parole, conditional release of insanity acquittees includes specific behavioral and therapeutic conditions that must be followed to remain in the community. In most states, there is no mandated maximum period of supervision. And in most states, individuals have minimal rights if the release is revoked. Thus, constitutional provisions guaranteed to individuals serving a criminal sentence are not extended to persons acquitted by reason of insanity. A 1992 U.S. Supreme Court decision in *Foucha v. Louisiana* (563 So. 2d 1138, 1992) failed to clarify the standards under which states may hospitalize an insanity acquittee. The question was whether a state could continue the commitment of an insanity acquittee who was dangerous but no longer mentally ill. The Court, citing *Jackson v. Indiana* (406 U.S. 715, 1972), ruled that the basis of continued commitment of insanity acquittees must parallel their offense. In other words, insanity acquittees who have been acquitted of less serious offenses and do not meet both of the criteria for commitment—dangerousness and mental illness—cannot be involuntarily hospitalized.

A few states, notably Oregon and Connecticut, have established a psychiatric parole board to supervise insanity acquittees in the community. These two boards vary, but they are more autonomous than most other forms of supervision. It is ordinarily the case that state departments of mental health have responsibility for supervising insanity acquittees in the community although judges have legal jurisdiction for release and discharge. Many persons who were acquitted by reason of insanity and conditionally released into the community spend many years under state supervision.

It is likely that the insanity defense has been constricted to its most constitutionally minimal level. Without eliminating the special defense altogether, which would be a significant rewriting of legal history, courts have made it an unattractive defense to most mentally disordered defendants. For defendants who are suspected of having committed serious violent offenses, the insanity defense remains a reasonable legal option. If acquitted or convicted, the defendant is likely to be hospitalized or incarcerated for a lengthy period of time. For seriously mentally ill yet not dangerous offenders, the insanity defense may be too costly a defense. The expressed intolerance of the legislatures, judiciary, and public toward most violent offenders would suggest that the limited insanity defense will be enduring. At least two professional conditions are prerequisites for an expansion of the insanity defense: empirically valid and reliable risk assessment tools and an increased public understanding of mental disorder. The first would restore confidence in the clinical professions and the second would provide the social climate for tolerating and perhaps treating people who have mental disorders and commit crimes.

LISA A. CALLAHAN

References and Further Reading

Callahan, L., Mayer, C. and Steadman, H.J. 1987. Post-Hinckley insanity defense reforms in the United States, *Mental and Physical Disabilities Law Reporter* 11.

Callahan, L., McGreevy, M., Cirincione, C., and Steadman, H.J. 1992. Measuring the effects of the GBMI verdict: Georgia's 1982 GBMI Reform, *Law and Human Behavior* 16.

Callahan, L., Robbins, P., and Steadman, H.J. 1995. The effect of Montana's insanity defense abolition, *Psychiatric Quarterly* 66.

Callahan, L., Steadman, H.J., McGreevy, M., and Robbins, P. 1991. The volume and characteristics of insanity defense pleas: An eight state study, *Bulletin of the American Academy of Law and Psychiatry* 19.

Eigen, J.P. 1995. *Witnessing Insanity: Madness and Mad-Doctors in the English Court*, New Haven, CT: Yale University Press.

Keilitz, I. 1987. Researching and reforming the insanity defense, *Rutgers Law Review* 39.

Model Penal Code, Section 4.01 (1962).

Moran, R. 1981. *Knowing Right from Wrong: The Insanity Defense of Daniel McNaughtan*, New York, NY: Free Press.

Moran, R. 1985. The modern foundation for the insanity defense: The case of James Hadfield (1800) and Daniel McNaughtan (1843), *Annals of the American Academy of Political and Social Science* 477.

Robinson, D.N. 1996. *Wild Beasts and Idle Humours: The Insanity Defense from Antiquity to the Present*, Cambridge, MA: Harvard University Press.

Smith, G.A. and Hall, J.A. 1982. Evaluating Michigan's guilty but mentally ill verdict, *16 U. Mich J.L. Ref. 77*, 94.

Steadman, H.J., McGreevy, M.A., Morrissey, J.P., Callahan, L.A., Robbins, P.C., and Cirincione, C. 1993. *Before and After Hinckley: Evaluating Insanity Defense Reform*, New York, NY: Guilford Press.

Walker, N., Crime and Insanity in England. 1968. *The Historical Perspective*, Vol. 1, 25–26.

See also **Defenses to Criminal Liability: Justifications and Excuses**

Institutional Corrections

All persons convicted of felonies in the U.S. face the possibility of incarceration in a correctional institution. In most cases, these sentences are suspended and replaced with some form of supervision by a legal authority in a community-based setting, although the threat of incarceration always exists for persons who fail to abide by the rules of community supervision. There are currently 1.8 million persons incarcerated for felony offenses in state and federal correctional institutions for adults in the U.S. Although the term "correctional" institution implies an attempt to treat or "correct" an offender's criminal behavior, the term is used more generally in the U.S. to refer to all institutions where convicted felony offenders are *incarcerated*, regardless of the reasons for (philosophies underlying) their incarceration. These facilities are distinct from places of confinement for persons *suspected* of committing crimes as well as convicted misdemeanor offenders. Criminal suspects are housed in either temporary holding facilities or jails, whereas convicted misdemeanants are placed in jails or local detention facilities.

Adult felons in the U.S. can be incarcerated in either state or federal institutions depending on whether they are convicted in state or federal courts. Several philosophies underlie the incarceration of convicted offenders: punishment, deterrence (general and specific), incapacitation, and rehabilitation. These philosophies are applied in varying degrees by different judges, and the extent of each philosophy's influence on sentencing decisions changes over time and is determined by a host of social and political factors. Suffice to say that inmates of correctional facilities today are incarcerated for different reasons depending on the particular philosophy considered by a single judge for a specific offender.

The purpose of *punishment* is to deprive an individual of personal freedoms enjoyed by citizens who abide by societal rules (e.g., liberty and autonomy). Therefore, the "pains" inflicted on an incarcerated person are not physical in nature. (Physical pains that are endured by inmates, such as those resulting from victimization by other inmates, are not "intended" by the state.) Moreover, incarceration for this purpose can only be imposed after establishing that the person was responsible for their actions, although the definition of "responsibility" varies across cultures. For this reason, punishment is *not* a goal of incarceration when imposed by juvenile court because of the assumption that juveniles are not fully responsible for their actions because of their immaturity and lack of social development. Juveniles can only be imprisoned for the purpose of punishment when they are bound over to and convicted in an adult criminal court.

The length of confinement under punishment is determined by the state and generally follows the seriousness of the crime committed, where longer periods coincide with more serious crimes (defined in terms of the harm inflicted on society). When the length of confinement is graded according to offense seriousness and the purpose is symbolic in nature (i.e., condemnation is involved), the term "retribution" is often used in place of "punishment." Regardless of the term used, the purpose of punishment for the sake of punishment is *nonutilitarian* in nature. That is, there is no interest on the part of the state in the actual or predicted consequences of the punishment (such as reducing the offender's or others' likelihoods of engaging in future crime). It simply reflects the idea that persons who harm society by violating legally proscribed rules will have harm (deprivations) inflicted back on them by society. Society is viewed as the "victim" of a crime.

Any act in violation of a legal rule advocated by all citizens is, symbolically, an act that victimizes all members of a society. When incarceration is imposed on offenders by the state, the state is acting as the voice of the people in condemning the offenders for their actions.

The remaining goals of incarceration are *utilitarian* in nature as each involves the ultimate function of reducing crime. Each utilitarian goal involves predictions made by the state regarding the potential *future* benefits of incarcerating offenders. Inherent in any of these predictions is the possibility of error owing to imprecision in the information used for evaluation.

The utilitarian goal of general deterrence involves punishing an individual for the purpose of making an example of that individual to society. Persons who have not yet engaged in crime may refrain from doing so because they do not wish to endure the same punishment as the "example" offender. Therefore, making the public aware of an offender's confinement is a key element of general deterrence. In his *On Crimes and Punishments*, Beccaria argued that public awareness of society's laws and the sanctions for violating those laws should be enough to achieve general deterrence, although his logic rests on the assumption that all offenders convicted of a particular crime necessarily face the same sanction (see Paolucci (1963) for a translation). This would leave no question regarding the magnitude of punishment for a convicted criminal. In reality, however, the length of incarceration varies somewhat for different individuals convicted of the same offense, prohibiting a shared understanding of what punishments offenders "must" face when convicted of specific crimes. Legal systems interested in general deterrence, therefore, face the task of periodically publicizing the sanctions for particular offenders, where these choices are driven predominantly by political movements to reduce certain types of crimes (e.g., publicizing an unusually long sentence of incarceration for a drug dealer). The goal of general deterrence has been criticized when the sentences imposed are unusually severe relative to the offense committed. The criticism is that relatively more severe sanctions are not intended to punish offenders for what they have done, but rather for the *tendencies* of others to engage in similar illegal activities.

In contrast to general deterrence, the goal of *specific (special) deterrence* involves punishing an offender in order to deter that offender from engaging in the same types of behavior. Similar to general deterrence, this goal rests on the assumptions that individuals are rational in their decisions to engage in crime, and that all persons make choices that serve to maximize their pleasure and minimize their pain. If the "pains" of engaging in crime (i.e., the punishment) outweigh the benefits to an offender, that person will alter his or her behavior in the future to avoid similar pains (Bentham, 1823). Yet, critics of this idea argue that many offenders do not calculate their actions in the same fashion as nonoffenders, and their decisions to engage in crime are often spontaneous (e.g., violent criminals who engage in crime in the "heat of passion").

Incarceration for the purpose of *incapacitation* is intended to eliminate an individual's opportunities for engaging in similar crimes in the future by separating the offender from the rest of society. Incapacitation is more often a goal for offenders at the highest risk of engaging in more criminal activity and for offenders at *any* risk of engaging in more serious types of crimes (e.g., homicide, rape, and armed robbery). This is because of a belief that a fixed term of incarceration will produce the greatest benefit to society when it is reserved for the most habitual or most dangerous offenders. Length of confinement is dictated more by the time deemed necessary by the state for protecting society from the offender rather than the seriousness of the offense convicted for (although the two criteria may be necessarily related). Therefore, the length of confinement can be much longer than the specific crime dictates, as in the case of an offender who has been convicted several times previously for the same type of offense. Confining individuals for this purpose rests on the assumption that the state can adequately determine whether an offender will engage in more criminal activity if released back into society.

Advocates of *rehabilitation* as a goal of incarceration are critical of deterrence strategies because of a belief that criminal behavior is a product of influences that are outside the control of offenders. Rehabilitation or *reform* rests on the assumption that the causes of criminality can be identified and "corrected" in order to change future behavior. These causes may be psychological in nature (having to do with the psychological make-up of individuals such as personality disorders or learning disabilities), environmental (related to the social climates of individuals such as being raised by abusive parents or having friends who also engage in crime), or a combination of both (e.g., abusive parents may contribute to antisocial personality disorders). Rehabilitation underlies most sentencing in juvenile court owing to a belief that juveniles are less "set in their ways" and are more amenable to treatment compared with adults. This was the philosophy that led to the creation of separate institutions for juveniles across the U.S. in the late 1800s and early 1900s, an era during which punishment and deterrence philosophies guided the sentencing of most adult offenders.

Not all advocates of rehabilitation believe that behavior can be changed in an institutional setting via incarceration, but some argue that a controlled environment is needed to effect change in an individual in order to separate the person from the negative stimuli causing the deviant behavior. There is a lack of consensus across legal systems regarding definitions of effective institutional programming, resulting in different foci across systems operating under the principle of reform. For example, eastern cultures focus more on the importance of hard work and structure in a person's daily life for conditioning offenders whereas western cultures place a greater emphasis on counseling, education, and other socialization techniques. (A more detailed discussion of incarceration philosophies is offered by Duffee (1989).)

Despite the fact that incarceration is one of the most common sanctions handed down by state and federal courts today, "doing time" is a relatively new concept. Throughout human history, societies have always specified rules of appropriate conduct that include sanctions for persons who fail to abide by them. Simpler and smaller societies concerned only with day-to-day survival had very few rules, all of which related to the survival of the society. A simple "system" of punishment developed whereby persons who threatened survival of the group were put to death. With economic and population growth came greater complexity in rules, generating greater complexity in punishments. Monetary systems enabled the forfeiture of personal property (fines) as sanctions, the degree to which varied according to the seriousness of the offense. Geographic stability also allowed the exile of criminals from society, a form of "civil death." Enslavement was also used where criminals were put to work building homes for growing populations. In addition to the above, brutal forms of punishment were used in many agrarian societies such as Rome and, subsequently, France, Spain, and England. This was in part owing to the influence of religious ideology on attitudes toward criminals and a belief that deviant behavior was a manifestation of evil spiritual influences. Various forms of torture were used either to drive evil influences out of a person's body or to serve as penitence for one's sins. For example, Western European governments and the Catholic Church were virtually indistinguishable, resulting in a combination of state and religious laws. Confinement (incarceration) was used during this period, but only to hold offenders until physical punishment could be inflicted on them. The barbarity of these punishments demanded confinement to prevent offenders from escaping their brutal fate. Places of confinement were harsh (e.g., cages) because incarceration involved very short periods.

Incarceration as punishment in and of itself did not take place until after the "Age of Enlightenment" (around 1700 AD), an era sparked by advancements in scientific thought leading to a recognition of humanity's essential dignity and imperfection. Among other issues, French and Italian philosophers criticized (1) the role of religion in affairs of the state, (2) the need for brutal punishments exceeding the seriousness of the crimes, (3) the arbitrariness of sanctions, and (4) the absence of rights for persons accused but not yet convicted of crimes. These debates had an enormous influence on the political development of the North American colonies because of the correspondence in time between the emergence of these more liberal ideas and the political independence of the colonies from England, and the fact that the colonies were initially founded by individuals fleeing Western Europe to escape the tyranny of the English government.

This era sparked a separation of government and religious laws and a movement toward retribution (proportionality in punishment) as the guiding philosophy of punishment. This movement occurred in both Western Europe and North America, although the new philosophies were easier to translate into practice in the U.S. because state and federal governments were in their initial stages of development. William Penn brought the idea of treating convicted criminals more humanely to America. Incarceration became the dominant mode of punishment in these cultures because it lacked the physical brutality of previous punishments and it could be graded (in length) to the seriousness of crimes.

In the North American colonies, incarcerated inmates engaged in hard labor during confinement. The Protestant work ethic ("no resting place this side of the grave") contributed to the development of "workhouses" where inmates would work all day. After the colonies became politically independent from Great Britain, a system of classification was developed to separate offenders based on the seriousness of their crimes, and to separate adult males from women and children. Some of the earliest of such prisons involved converting underground mine shafts into places of confinement for felons. However, the Walnut Street Jail (built in Philadelphia in 1789) was the first institution with a separate wing designated for convicted felons except those sentenced to death. Inmates housed in this unit worked alone in their cells under the condition of solitary confinement at night. This practice was based on the idea that inmates would be more quickly reformed if they were isolated from others like themselves because they would have time to reflect on their misdeeds.

During the late 1700s and early 1800s, facilities for confinement in the U.S. were still physically harsh by today's standards, with little to no natural light, cramped cells or living quarters, and unsanitary conditions. Most of these physical traits were not intended to be cruel but, instead, reflected ignorance regarding proper sanitation and the ill effects of physical isolation and darkness on mental health. Subsequent developments in medicine and psychology led to changes in these conditions of confinement, but many inmates died as a consequence of being housed in these primitive facilities.

Increase in crime resulting from industrialization and population growth led to crowded prison conditions in both Pennsylvania and New York State. This demand for more facilities led to the Penitentiary Movement during the early 1800s, a period marked by a rapid growth in facilities, a change in administrative ideologies, and the introduction of the "penitentiary." Administrators of these new prisons believed that a criminal could be reformed by breaking his spirit. This process involved hard labor for 10–12 hours each day, isolation, noncommunication, and physical abuse to enforce the rules of the prison (although physical abuse was, at least initially, supposed to only be a means of achieving "reform"). These methods were abandoned after the Civil War in the U.S. because treatment was so harsh that many inmates either became physically or mentally ill, or died as a consequence.

Scientific developments in the areas of psychology and medicine changed our philosophies about how to effectively reform criminals between 1870 and 1910. The first facility to reflect these new ideas was the Elmira Reformatory (established in New York state in 1876). Administrators at Elmira adopted "good time" (a concept first developed by Walter Croften of Ireland related to reducing an inmate's sentence for good behavior) and "indeterminate sentencing" (developed by Alexander Maconochie of Great Britain related to an indefinite period of confinement for inmates until they are deemed "reformed"). Not until the early 1900s were more of these facilities built in the U.S. This marked the beginning of an era focusing on rehabilitation, although confinement conditions as well as many of the earliest attempts at reform were quite punitive by their nature. For example, the use of electric shock and frontal lobotomies were not uncommon, and operations were performed on many female offenders so they could not have children. Further scientific advancements led to a more widespread use of more humane treatment techniques, but not until the 1950s and 1960s.

A trend throughout the 20th century was the implementation of more humane living conditions and methods of treatment in "correctional facilities" (the term that eventually replaced "penitentiary" to reflect the goal of rehabilitation). The conditions were improved even further in the 1960s across the U.S. because of what is now called the "inmate rights movement," a period during which inmates legally challenged conditions of confinement that, they argued, were in violation of their civil rights. Courts became relatively sympathetic to this litigation because of the more liberal social and political environment that existed during this time (as described by Jacobs (1980)). The most significant changes occurring during this period involved granting inmates certain rights and privileges not previously available (e.g., freedom of religion, speech, personal property, dress, and access to medical services). Correctional facilities could no longer be seen as places of confinement where individuals lost all the rights of free citizens. Advocates of retribution tended to view this evolution in institutional corrections as undermining the punitive aspects of incarceration. However, improvements in the confinement conditions for adult males have been more significant and widespread compared to improvements for women, and incarcerated females today still face deprivations not experienced by males (such as a lack of adequate medical care, fewer opportunities for educational advancement, poor job training, and limited resources for recreation). Disillusionment with the success of institutional treatment programs in the U.S. led to a greater focus on the punishment of offenders throughout the 1970s and continuing to the present. Regardless, the improved conditions of confinement and the substantive rights granted inmates during the 20th century remain in place. Punishment is now defined more in terms of sentence length and solitary confinement (isolation) rather than in terms of confinement in harsh environments and the denial of particular rights (although the deprivation of liberty will always exist by the very nature of incarceration).

The U.S. currently leads the world in it use of incarceration. The inmate population is six times the amount it was 30 years ago. Incarceration rates outside of the U.S. dwindle in comparison. The current rate of incarceration is 702 inmates per 100,000 population—a rate that is 5–8 times higher than in Canada and most European nations. Russia and South Africa also have high rates of incarceration, whereas Iceland, Japan, and India have some of the lowest rates. Crime rates alone cannot explain the differences across countries. Public attitudes toward offenders and the criminal justice system best explain variations in sentencing severity. Individuals in countries with large disparities in wealth tend to express more punitive attitudes toward offenders compared to individuals residing in countries with more advanced social welfare programs. America's current "war on drugs" policy initiative has significantly increased its prison population. Many European countries as well as Australia, view substance abuse from a medical model perspective and offer more in the way of treatment to offenders. The U.S. also incarcerates more property offenders and for longer periods of time compared to other European countries.

(See Johnson and Wolfe [1996] for a thorough discussion of the evolution of institutional corrections in Western cultures.)

In the U.S., "serious" offenders (convicted of felony offenses punishable by one or more years of incarceration) are confined in either state or federal institutions. These facilities are intended to be physically secure places of confinement, but security levels will vary across institutions according to the actual or perceived dangerousness of the inmate population as well as whether the goals of the institution involve punishment, deterrence, incapacitation, or rehabilitation. At the state level, one-fourth of all inmates are incarcerated in maximum-security prisons. Characterized by high walls, double fences, and guard towers, these facilities are designed to make escapes difficult. Emphasis is placed on security and control, and inmates are subject to a regime of discipline and order that resembles a military model. Movement within the institution is limited and constantly supervised. More recently in the U.S., facilities designed as "high-close supervision" are being constructed to provide maximum security through the use of electronic surveillance. The increasing popularity of the "super-maximum security prison" has also resulted in more facilities where inmates spend 23 hours each day confined to their cells and have no contact with other inmates. In these facilities, visitation with outsiders is either forbidden or restricted to nonphysical contact.

One-half of all state inmates are serving time in medium security institutions. Inmates in these facilities have typically committed a serious offense but are not considered to be "hardened" criminals. These institutions resemble maximum-security prisons in appearance, but inmates do have more internal freedom and greater contact with the outside world through visitation and mail privileges. The remaining inmates at the state level are confined in minimum-security prisons. Designed for nonviolent offenders or offenders near the completion of their sentence, these institutions grant inmates more freedom to move about the facility. Inmates reside in dormitories or small private rooms as opposed to barred cells. Opportunities for educational and vocational training are greatest in a minimum-security prison and inmates may even have the opportunity to work outside of the prison prior to their actual release. Some facilities are also classified as "mixed security," predominantly medium–maximum or minimum–medium institutions. These prisons are more likely to confine women, because many states only have one or two facilities for all adult female offenders. (Allen and Simonsen [2001] offer more detailed discussions of U.S. facilities as well as differences between institutions for men and those for women.)

Once an inmate has been assigned to a particular type of institution, a second classification system is used within a facility to determine the appropriate housing unit. Housing assignments are made according to security needs, medical or mental health needs, and treatment or program needs. Most inmates begin their incarceration as part of the general population and if they maintain good behavior, may be reassigned to an honor block. These inmates are given more freedom and privileges within the institution, sometimes have larger living units, and usually have more options in terms of work assignments. Inmates who are likely to become victimized by other inmates, for example, child molesters and police officers may be assigned to protective custody. Inmates in protective custody are isolated from the general population at all times. These inmates have the same privileges as those in the general population, but access to particular jobs and prison facilities may be limited to avoid contact with other inmates. Inmates who are violent in prison or violate prison rules may be temporarily assigned to punitive segregation, formerly known as solitary confinement or "the hole." Inmates in punitive segregation are kept separate from other inmates, lose all privileges, and are only permitted to leave their cell for 1–2 hours of solitary exercise. Death row inmates are also housed separately from the general population in conditions that resemble punitive segregation.

The use of incarceration for so many convicted criminals has created numerous problems that threaten the security of institutions and the safety of inmates. These include inmate riots and escapes; lack of resources for effective treatment; limited medical resources for the proper care and treatment of pregnant inmates and their newborn (or recently born) children; suicides and homicides among inmates; physical attacks on staff; and the creation and persistence of criminal gangs and other illegitimate activities. The extent of these problems varies across institutions, although their mere existence highlights the need to reconsider the use of incarceration as one of the most common sentences for offenders.

AMY THISTLETHWAITE

References and Further Reading

Allen, H. and Simonsen, C. 2001. *Corrections in America*, Upper Saddle River, NJ: Prentice Hall.

Beccaria, C. 1963. *On Crimes and Their Punishments*, translated by Paolucci, H. Englewood Cliffs, NJ: Prentice-Hall.

Bentham, J. 1962. The rationale of punishment. *The Works of Jeremy Bentham*, Vol. 1, Bowring, J. (Ed.), New York, NY: Russell and Russell.

Cullen, F.T. and Gilbert, K. 1982. *Reaffirming Rehabilitation*, Cincinnati, OH: Anderson.

Duffee, D.E. 1989. *Corrections: Practice and Policy,* New York, NY: Random House.

Jacobs, J.B. 1980. The Prisoners' Rights Movement and its impacts, 1960–80, *Crime and Justice,* Vol. 2, Morris, N. and Tonry, M. (Eds.), Chicago, IL: University of Chicago Press.

Johnson, H. and Wolfe, N.T. 1996. *History of Criminal Justice,* Cincinnati, OH: Anderson.

Marquart, J.W. and Sorensen, J.R. 1997. *Correctional Contexts: Contemporary and Classical Readings,* Los Angeles, CA: Roxbury Publishing Company.

See also **Prisons: Administration and Organization; Prisons: Correctional Officers and Staff; Prisons: Women's Facilities**

Integrated Theories of Criminal Behavior

Discussions of integrated theory frequently focus on the process of theoretical integration, rather than on integrated theory itself. The process of theoretical integration has been variously defined or described as "a combining of elements of historically divergent theories into more inclusive and powerful theoretical models," "an activity that involves the formulation of linkages among different theoretical arguments," "the act of combining two or more sets of logically interrelated propositions into one larger set of interrelated propositions in order to provide a more comprehensive explanation of a particular phenomenon," or "the combination of two or more pre-existing theories, selected on the basis of their commonalities, into a single reformulated theoretical model with greater comprehensiveness and explanatory value than any one of its component theories" (Elliott, 1985, 123; Messner et al., 1989, 2, 52, 95). All of these descriptions or definitions effectively assume preexisting, less comprehensive theories or partial theories, which can be combined in some way to produce a potentially better, more comprehensive theory of crime, delinquency, or deviance. Given the above definitions of theoretical integration, and much of the literature on integrated theory, one can be forgiven if one gets the mistaken impression that the field of criminology began with a set of pristine, single-factor theories which, beginning with the work of Elliott et al. (1979), were finally combined into more comprehensive theoretical models.

Definitions of integrated theory itself, the product as opposed to the process, are harder to find, and for good reason. As noted by Vold et al. (1998, 300), "Most theories 'integrate' at least some previously existing material in their arguments, so there is no firm and fast line between integrated theories and other theories." Additionally, in defining integrated theories, one common thread in the above definitions can profitably be ignored: there is no need to assume preexisting theories that require a process of "integration" in order to be combined. In fact, historically, more comprehensive theories were commonplace, and the only way in which they would be distinguished from "integrated" theories, based on the definitions of theoretical integration, would be the absence of clearly stated and preexisting "pure" theories that could have been combined to produce the more comprehensive theories.

The term *integrated theory* is used here to refer most broadly to theoretical perspectives that incorporate in some way elements (concepts, variables, propositions, or assumptions) from two or more theoretical perspectives, whether those perspectives were formulated before the integrated theory, or perhaps "dis-integrated" from some more comprehensive perspective at a later date. The rough test is whether, if the theory were published for the first time today, it would be regarded as an integrated theory. This definition avoids artificially limiting integrated theories to theories constructed after a certain period (specifically after World War I, when many of the apparently "pure" forms of strain, control, labeling, learning, and other theories were first proposed). At the same time, however, it permits some distinctions in the processes that produce more comprehensive theories, including but not limited to integrated theories.

Constructing Integrated Theories

There are several processes by which a more comprehensive theory may be constructed from two or more simpler theories. One can (1) simply mix elements of different theories based on empirical relationships; or (2) take a single theory and "elaborate" that theory, possibly incorporating elements of other theories that are compatible with the original theory, and even possibly changing the original theory to accommodate elements of other theories that prove too valuable to exclude; or (3) take two or more preexisting theories that share some common features, resolve whatever differences exist in the theories, possibly by modifying or rejecting less useful elements of one or more of the theories, to produce a truly integrated theory (Elliott, 1985; Messner et al., 1989).

The first approach is consistent with the pattern of construction of the earliest comprehensive theories, and is also consistent with the suggestion that it may be better for criminologists to shift their focus from theories to variables (Vold et al., 1998, 311) in order to produce more useful predictive models. The second approach is taken by several of the authors in Messner et al. (1989). The third approach has been advocated by Delbert S. Elliott (1985), and his integration of strain, social control, and social learning theories (Elliott et al., 1979) has stimulated much of the debate about how and whether to integrate criminological theories (Vold et al., 1998, 303). In practice, there seems to be little more than a semantic difference between the second (elaboration) and third (integration) approaches, and even advocates of theoretical elaboration admit that the outcome may be the same for elaboration and integration.

Once the broad process for combining theories has been selected, the specific form of integration must also be considered. First at what level are the theories to be combined: (a) macro-level, explaining crime in terms of societal-level characteristics, as in Marxian theory or the macro-level component of anomie theory; (b) micro-level or individual-level, as in social control and social learning theories; (c) intermediate, for example, explaining crime rates in regions, cities, or neighborhoods, as in social disorganization theory; or (d) cross-level, combining two or all three levels into a single theory, as is done in Robert K. Merton's (1938) anomie theory? Second, is the integration to be (a) conceptual, in which concepts from one theory are shown to overlap in meaning with concepts from another theory, or (b) propositional, in which the same predictions are made despite different assumptions of the two theories? Third, will the integration be (a) up-and-down, or deductive, in which one theory is shown to be a special case of another, or two theories are shown to be special cases of a larger theory; (b) side-to-side, or parallel, in which different theories explain the outcomes for different cases; or (c) end-to-end, or sequential, in which a distinction is made between more remote and more immediate causes of the outcome (Elliott, 1985; Messner et al., 1989, 5–15; Akers, 1997, 208-09). Note that in end-to-end or sequential integration, it is possible for only one variable (the most proximate cause) to have a direct effect on crime, and all of the others affect crime only indirectly, via their

effects on each other and on the most proximate cause; but this pure model is rare in practice, and it is more common to allow for the possibility that even less proximate causes may have direct effects on crime.

Once the theories have been integrated, the question remains whether the integrated theory represents any improvement over the separate theories from which it was derived. What criteria should be used to compare the original theories with the integrated theory? Elliott (1985) proposes a straightforward and objective criterion: how well the integrated theory explains the variance in the endogenous variables, including not only the final dependent variable (crime or delinquency), but also the variance in intervening variables (variables that predict crime and are themselves predicted by other variables in the integrated model). Other authors (in Messner et al., 1989) have argued that it is almost inevitable that by combining theories, some additional variance will be explained. They suggest instead that the success of the integration should be judged by how much our understanding of crime is improved by the integrated theory. "Understanding," however, is a highly subjective criterion, more esthetic than scientific, and unlikely to produce any consensus on the value of the theory. One can also argue that the ability of the model to explain variation in the variables is itself an indication of increased understanding of the causal process.

From a contemporary perspective, one of the major issues has been how to reconcile the contradictory assumptions of different theoretical perspectives. From a longer historical perspective, a more interesting question is how strain and control theories became *disintegrated* in the first place. Initially viewed as complementary parts of a general explanation of crime, strain, and social control seem to have become separated as theorists after World War I focused on parts, rather than the whole, of earlier theoretical work.

A Brief History of Integrated Theories

The idea that there may be multiple causes or multiple pathways that result in illegal behavior may be most strongly associated with Elliott et al. (1979), but it goes back at least to the 19th century, to some of the earliest attempts at scientific theories of crime, delinquency, and deviance (hereafter simply crime). For example, Adolphe Quetelet identified severe inequality in wealth and poverty, opportunity to commit crime, social organization, and moral character as influences on crime, with opportunity and moral character the more immediate causes of crime (Vold et al., 1998, 29–32). By contemporary standards, this could be a cross-level (social organization at the societal level; inequality at the intermediate level; opportunity to commit crime and moral character at the micro-level), end-to-end integration of strain or anomie (wealth, poverty, and opportunity), social disorganization (social organization), and social control (moral character) theories.

Similarly, the early Italian positivists proposed what could be considered integrated theories. As described in Martin et al. (1990), they identified different causes of crime, often specifying different causes for different types of crime. In addition to the "born criminal" or atavism for which he is most famous, Lombroso also suggested defects in mental functioning (the insane criminal), emotional control (the criminal by passion), and more minor weaknesses in emotional or moral control (the occasional criminal) as causes of crime. His student, Enrico Ferri, largely retained these types of criminals, and further described the habitual criminal (a subcategory of the occasional criminal in Lombroso's theory) as the result of poverty, poor education, and bad companions. Again applying contemporary standards, this would suggest an individual level and side-by-side or parallel integration of biological (atavisms or born criminals), psychological (insane criminals), and social control (criminal by passion and occasional criminals); and for Ferri's (but not Lombroso's) habitual criminals, even strain plus social learning theories (poverty and bad companions).

Emile Durkheim as an Integrated Theorist

Another 19th century theorist, claimed by both strain and control theorists as a theoretical predecessor (Vold et al., 1998), was Emile Durkheim. Durkheim's work on strain and social control theory appears in several of his most important publications. It is most directly applied to deviant behavior in his analysis of suicide (Durkheim, 1897). He emphasized that there were broad differences in general reasons for committing suicide, and used these differences to define four types of suicide: egoistic, anomic, altruistic, and fatalistic. Regarding the parallel to control theory, note that in contrast to Travis Hirschi's (1969) natural motivation to crime (which is not included in all variants of control theory; see Vold et al., 1998, 202–207), Durkheim assumes no "natural motivation" for suicide.

Egoistic suicide refers to suicide by individuals who are so weakly bonded to a society that cultural or social prescriptions against suicide are ineffective. Durkheim describes this type of suicide as one of excessive individuation (as opposed to integration) of the individual, and egoistic suicide exemplifies the failure of social control at the *individual* level as a cause of suicide. Egoistic suicide is the form of suicide most consistent with contemporary control theory. A second type, *anomic* suicide, also represents a failure of social control,

but at the aggregate rather than the individual level. Anomic suicide occurs as a result of the failure of the society or culture to regulate the aspirations of its members, thus producing strain at the individual level. The idea that structural level anomie produced individual level strain was later incorporated into Merton's (1938) anomie theory. Suicide is one (but by no means the only) possible consequence of or reaction to this individual level strain.

Altruistic suicide is a form of suicide that, from the perspective of the society, is not deviant, but instead represents conformity to the cultural norms of the society. Examples listed by Durkheim include culturally obligatory suicides of wives at the deaths of their husbands, followers at the deaths of their leaders, military suicides in which soldiers sacrifice their lives to save their comrades, and the religiously motivated suicides of early Christian martyrs, and of Jainists in southern India. Altruistic suicide may be regarded with strong social approval if the circumstances and motivations for the act are regarded as appropriate. According to Durkheim, altruistic suicide is the opposite of egoistic suicide, and involves insufficient individuation. Another way of expressing this is to say that altruistic suicide occurs as a result of adequate, or arguably excessive, social control. Again, however, the existence of strain is implicit, at least in the general sense in which Robert Agnew (1992) describes strain as the inability to avoid an aversive situation (the death of a husband or leader, the threat to the lives of one's comrades, religious persecution). Although the behavior remains the same, however, the character of altruistic suicide is much different from the other forms of suicide discussed by Durkheim, and its inclusion as a form of *deviant* behavior here may justifiably be questioned.

Durkheim (1897 [1951], 276) describes fatalistic suicide as "the suicide deriving from excessive regulation, that of persons with futures pitilessly blocked and passions violently choked by oppressive discipline." The conditions described by Durkheim for fatalistic suicide thus correspond closely with Agnew's (1992) description of general strain. Durkheim regarded this form of suicide as being of minor interest, but it rounds out his typology of suicides and, importantly, illustrates a form of deviance that arises from strong rather than weak social controls, a situation opposite to what we would expect from contemporary control theories of crime. Durkheim also noted the possibility of mixed types of suicides, suicides having components of more than one of the four basic types described above.

In summary, Durkheim may legitimately be claimed as an intellectual forefather by both strain and control theorists. Both must acknowledge that Durkheim's theory of suicide combines elements of what we today call strain and control theory, and Vold et al. (1998) note the intellectual influence of Durkheim not only on strain and control, but also on labeling theories of crime. This places Durkheim clearly within the ranks of proponents of integrated theory (cross-level and side-by-side integration of strain and control theories). Like the Italian positivists, Durkheim also presages Elliott et al.'s (1979) suggestion that there are multiple etiological paths to crime.

Merton's Anomie Theory as an Integrated Theory

About 40 years after Durkheim first published his analysis of suicide, Robert K. Merton (1938) borrowed and modified Durkheim's concept of anomie and used it to account for deviant behavior, including but not limited to crime. Merton's approach is usually classified as a strain theory, although it is integrated in two respects. First and most obviously, Merton integrates a macrosocial theory of differences in rates of crime with a microsocial theory of individual differences in crime. He does this by tracing the microsocial consequences (modes of adaptation) of the tension between universally prescribed cultural goals and differential access to the legitimate means of achieving those goals, and the different emphases placed on the goals and the legitimacy of the means used to achieve them.

Less obviously, Merton integrates elements of strain and social control theories. Specifically, Merton's modes of adaptation are defined by acceptance of (or in control theory parlance, commitment to) the culturally prescribed goals, and acceptance of (or again in control theory terms, belief in) the social institutional restrictions that define some means of attaining those goals as legitimate, but other means as illegitimate. The first part of this conceptual link between strain and control theory is clearly recognized by Hirschi (1969), who in his criticism of strain theory treats aspirations as indicators of both commitment (control theory) and acceptance of cultural goals (anomie theory). In anomie theory, selection of a mode of adaptation other than conformity represents a failure of commitment, a failure of belief, or both. Rejection of the restrictions on some means as illegitimate is most clearly linked to crime. Rejection of the cultural goals, in the absence of rejection of the restrictions on the means, may lead not to deviance, but to overconformity or lower rates of actual deviant behavior. Merton explicitly rejected individual predisposition to deviance as an adequate motivation for deviant behavior. Like Durkheim, Merton insisted that motivation for deviance is variable, and that society has much to do with shaping that motivation. Also like Durkheim, Merton asserted that anomie does not explain all deviant behavior, and

suggested that anomie theory might profitably be combined with other theoretical perspectives to better explain crime. This latter suggestion was followed by Richard Cloward (1959), (see also Cloward and Ohlin, 1960) in the development of differential opportunity theory.

Modern Integrated Theory: Cloward (1959) and Cloward and Ohlin (1960)

Although Richard Cloward and Lloyd Ohlin (1960) are often treated simply as strain theorists, they are more appropriately viewed as the first of the modern (post–World War II) integrated theorists, and some recognition of this is now evident in textbook treatments of their work. Cloward (1959), two decades after the first publication of Merton's anomie theory, began by combining Merton's anomie theory, which focused on the problematic nature of access to *legitimate* means of attaining culturally prescribed goals, with human ecological or social disorganization theory and differential association theory, both of which focused on the problematic nature of access to *illegitimate* means. Cloward described his theoretical integration as an extension (perhaps in contemporary terminology, it would be an elaboration) of Merton's anomie theory, although it is better viewed as an integrated theory because of the very prominent roles social disorganization (or differential social organization) and differential association play in the theory. Cloward (1959) applied his theory to explain individual illegal behavior in general. Cloward and Ohlin (1960) modified the theory and applied it to the explanation of the onset and persistence of delinquent subcultures among lower class, inner-city males.

It should be noted that in combining Merton's anomie theory with the social disorganization perspective of the Chicago school, Cloward and Ohlin integrated two theoretical perspectives that already involved the integration of strain and control theory. The strain and control components of Merton's theory are discussed above. The Chicago school or social disorganization perspective saw inadequacies in social control, especially at the neighborhood level, as arising from conditions of inadequate access to resources, a condition akin to anomie in Merton's theory, but at least as closely related to Agnew's (1992) conception of general strain. Where the theories differed was in level of aggregation and the relative focus on legitimate and illegitimate opportunities. Merton's focus alternated between the macrosocial level (societies or similarly large social aggregates as units of analysis) and the microsocial (individual modes of adaptation) level. The social disorganization theorists focused at the intermediate level, on neighborhoods, families, and small groups. Thus by integrating the social disorganization and anomie perspectives, Cloward and Ohlin blended two compatible theories to provide a more continuous transition from macrosocial to microsocial levels of explanation, and broadened the perspective of each to recognize as problematic issues of access to legitimate means (for social disorganization) or illegitimate means (for anomie) that had previously not been considered as problematic within the respective theories.

A major problem for both Merton's and Cloward's versions of anomie theory was the tendency by some criminologists to oversimplify both the theoretical framework and the operationalization of that framework when purporting to test the theory. As detailed in a review by Menard (1997), the theories were sometimes reduced to a single variable, for example poverty, income, or at the social psychological level, perceived low opportunities or the discrepancy between aspirations and opportunities. Most conspicuously missing from attempts to test anomie theories was any operationalization of the mode of adaptation and, for tests of Cloward's or Cloward and Ohlin's differential opportunity theory, any operationalization of illegitimate learning and performance structures. Inadequate operationalizations of the theories produced results that, not surprisingly, generally failed to support the theories. In a series of tests that incorporated all of the major concepts of the theories, Menard (1997) however found stronger support for Cloward's more highly integrated differential opportunity theory than for either control theory or Merton's anomie theory.

Theoretical Integration in the 1970s

Twenty years later, in the seminal paper that set off the current series of debates on theoretical integration in criminology, Delbert Elliott, Suzanne Ageton, and Rachelle Canter (1979) proposed an integrated theory that combined strain, social control, and social learning theories of criminal behavior. According to the integrated theory as described in Elliott et al. (1979) and elaborated in subsequent work by Elliott and his colleagues, social and demographic background variables may influence perceived and objective opportunities to attain academic, occupational, and other goals, and may also be associated with differences in socialization. As a result of these differences, some individuals enter adolescence with weak bonds to social institutions (external controls) and weak personal beliefs or commitment to conventional, conforming, or law abiding behavior (internal controls). Other individuals, particularly from disadvantaged social backgrounds, may enter adolescence with strong bonds to conventional society, but the experience or anticipation of failure

(strain) attenuates those bonds. Still other individuals enter adolescence with strong conventional bonds, experience and anticipate success, and maintain strong conventional bonds throughout adolescence.

With weak conventional bonding, individuals become more susceptible to the development of external bonds to unconventional, deviant, or delinquent peers. To the extent that a person associates with others who engage in delinquent behavior, there is more opportunity to learn (learning theory) about opportunities for illegal behavior, ways of successfully committing illegal acts (and getting away with them), and reasons or rationalizations for committing illegal acts. As a result, individuals with low levels of conventional bonding are more likely to develop unconventional or delinquent bonding, especially in the peer group, and as a result of this delinquent bonding are more likely to engage in more frequent and more serious illegal behavior than individuals with weaker delinquent bonds and stronger conventional bonds. The influences of strain and social control thus operate, according to the theory, primarily indirectly, through their influences on delinquent peer group bonding.

Thalia Roitberg and Scott Menard (1995) report the most recent test, and also list and summarize the results of past tests, of the integrated theory, noting that the tests of the integrated theory have produced consistent results. In Roitberg and Menard (1995) and in previous tests of the theory, the learning component of the theory (delinquent peer group bonding) has the strongest direct influence on illegal behavior, and males have higher rates of delinquency than females (but when males and females are analyzed separately, there is little or no apparent difference between them in the etiology of illegal behavior). Variables from strain and control theories have either weak or no direct effects on illegal behavior other than substance use. Belief that it is wrong to violate the law (control theory) has the second strongest influence, after delinquent peer group bonding, on substance use (alcohol, marijuana, and polydrug use, considered separately), but has no consistent direct effects on minor, serious, or violent offending. Most of the influence of strain and control theory variables on illegal behavior is indirect, via delinquent peer group bonding, consistent with the predictions of the theory.

It should be noted, however, that in the tests of the integrated theory, the "strain" variables were not adequate operationalizations of either Merton's or Cloward's anomie theory. (Control theory variables are better operationalized than anomie theory variables in the tests of the integrated theory.) Once Cloward's differential opportunity theory is fully operationalized, including learning and performance structures as well as Merton's modes of adaptation, the explanatory power of differential opportunity theory is comparable to that of the integrated theory (Menard, 1997). Upon detailed examination of the fully operationalized differential opportunity model, this result is not surprising. As noted by Menard, many of the same variables are included in both the differential opportunity and integrated theory models, and the distinction between the two lies to a large extent in the postulated causal order of the variables and in the incorporation of the belief variable as one component of the mode of adaptation in the differential opportunity model (rather than being a stand-alone predictor in the integrated theory).

From Integrated Theory to Developmental Theory

As noted earlier, Elliott et al.'s (1979) (see also Elliott, 1985; Roitberg and Menard, 1995) introduction of the term "integrated theory" and their attempt to reconcile and combine strain, social control, and social learning theories, was seminal, both in stimulating discussion of the process of theoretical combination (whether mixing, elaborating, or integrating theories) and in leading to other attempts to combine theories to better predict, explain, and understand illegal behavior. Reviews by Delbert Elliott (1985) and Ronald Akers (1997) identify literally dozens of attempts at theoretical integration since 1970, some predating Elliott et al. (1979). There is little question that mixing, elaborating, and perhaps even integrating theories will continue for the foreseeable future. More importantly, however, these integrated theories are increasingly incorporating or being incorporated into developmental perspectives as an integral component of the theory, thus introducing the life cycle as a new dimension along which theories can be integrated.

The extent to which integrated theory and developmental theory represent convergent trends may to some extent be judged by the contributions to two recent (as of this writing) anthologies of theories of crime and delinquency. Of the seven chapters in Hawkins (1996), six address developmental issues and four of the six explicitly deal with developmental patterns in crime and delinquency in the context of integrated or elaborated or mixed theories (chapters by: Loeber; Elliott and Menard; Catalano and Hawkins; and Thornberry). The eight chapters in Thornberry (1997) all pertain (as the title would suggest) to developmental theory, and they range from relatively "pure" theoretical perspectives (chapters by Agnew; Matsueda and Heimer) to mixed or elaborated or integrated models involving different pathways to crime and delinquency (chapters by: Moffitt; LeBlanc).

The conjunction of developmental and integrated theories has occurred in at least two ways. First, integrated theories have been tested at different ages or stages of life. Evidence from such tests suggests, for example, that Cloward's (1959) anomie theory and Elliott et al.'s (1979) integrated theory provide relatively weaker explanatory power for early adolescent delinquency, but stronger explanatory power for illegal behavior in later adolescence (Roitberg and Menard, 1995; Menard, 1997). Such findings do not transform integrated theories into developmental theories, but they do lay the groundwork for a restatement of integrated theories in a developmental framework, or to put it another way, for the integration of a developmental perspective into (already) integrated theories. Second, using longitudinal data, it has been possible to examine the sequencing and causal relationships involving the onset or initiation, continuity, and desistance in illegal behavior (see for example Chapters 1 and 2 in Hawkins, 1996, and Chapters 1 and 4 in Thornberry, 1997). Here, integrated theories are in some sense in competition with "pure" theories to explain developmental patterns. Where the first line of research involved incorporation of developmental considerations into integrated theories, this second line of research involves the (at least tentative) incorporation of integrated theoretical perspectives into developmental theory and research.

Conclusions

As noted by Vold et al. (1998, 298) (see also Hawkins, 1996; Thornberry, 1997), "Although developmental psychology has been around for a long time, developmental criminology is fairly new and it will take some time to assess how much support for it is garnered within the criminological community." Integrated theories of crime are not new. If, by integrated theory, we understand the combination of elements of different theoretical traditions (possibly including an attempt at reconciliation of contradictory assumptions), then integrated theories have been with us since the 19th century. In historical perspective, it is the disintegrated, "pure" strain, control, and learning theories that are new, and these "pure" theories are largely artificial, more a result of a classification system in criminology textbooks than of a real disagreement about what influences crime. Perhaps especially in the anomie tradition, theoretical integration has been the rule, not the exception, from the outset. If we have failed to recognize this, it may be a failure to give a close reading to the original sources through an excessive reliance on secondary sources to describe and classify theories.

On a practical level, this has implications for instruction, theory construction, and the general discussion of theory in criminology. The classification of theories as "strain," "control," "learning," and so forth may be a useful heuristic device for textbook authors attempting to condense a broad range of material in an accessible way, but it should be recognized that these classifications reflect differences in emphasis, not real distinctions among "pure" theoretical perspectives. With respect to theory construction, it suggests that arguments over whether the assumptions of different theories can be reconciled is largely sterile, based on an unrealistic view of different theoretical perspectives as well-defined and mutually exclusive. The ultimate test is not whether a theory is "really" a strain, control, or learning theory, but how well it works. In this light, the move toward theoretical integration (or elaboration or combination) in criminology seems inevitable. Integrated theories simply do a better job of explaining illegal behavior than artificially "pure" theories, both conceptually, in terms of the complexity of crime, delinquency, and deviance, and empirically, in terms of tests of explained variance. In contrast to simpler theories, integrated theories seem to come closer to matching the richness of the phenomena we study by the richness of our theoretical explanations.

SCOTT MENARD

References and Further Reading

Agnew, R. 1992. Foundation for a general strain theory of crime and delinquency, *Criminology* 30.

Akers, R.L. 1997. *Criminological Theories: Introduction and Evaluation*, Los Angeles, CA: Roxbury.

Cloward, R.A. 1959. Illegitimate means, anomie, and deviant behavior, *American Sociological Review* 24.

Cloward, R.A. and Lloyd, E.O. 1960. *Delinquency and Opportunity*, New York, NY: Free Press.

Durkheim, E. *Suicide* 1897, translated by Spaulding, J.A. and Simpson, G. New York, NY: Free Press, 1951.

Elliott, D.S., 1985. The assumption that theories can be combined with increased explanatory power: Theoretical integrations, *Theoretical Methods in Criminology*, Meier, R.F. (Ed.), Beverly Hills, CA: Sage.

Elliott, D.S., Ageton, S.S., and Canter, R.J. 1979. An integrated theoretical perspective on delinquent behavior, *Journal of Research in Crime and Delinquency* 16.

Hawkins, J.D., (Ed.) 1996. *Delinquency and Crime: Current Theories*, Cambridge, UK: Cambridge University Press.

Hirschi, T. 1969. *Causes of Delinquency*, Berkeley, CA: University of California Press.

Martin, R., Mutchnick, R.J., and Austin, W.T. 1990. *Criminological Thought: Pioneers Past and Present*. New York, NY: Macmillan.

Menard, S. 1997. A developmental test of Cloward's differential-opportunity theory, *The Future of Anomie Theory*, Passas, N. and Agnew, R. (Eds.), Boston, MA: Northeastern University Press.

Merton, R.K. 1938. Social structure and anomie, *American Sociological Review* 3.

Messner, S.F., Krohn, M.D., and Liska, A.E., (Eds.) 1989. *Theoretical Integration in the Study of Deviance and Crime: Problems and Prospects*, Albany, NY: SUNY Press.

Roitberg, T. and Menard, S. 1995. Adolescent violence: A test of integrated theory, *Studies on Crime and Crime Prevention* 4.

Thornberry, T.P. 1997. (Ed), *Developmental Theories of Crime and Delinquency*, New Brunswick, NJ: Transaction Publishers.

Vold, G.B., Bernard, T.J., and Snipes, J.B. 1998. *Theoretical Criminology*, 4th ed., New York, NY: Oxford University Press.

See also **Durkheim, Emile; Merton, Richard K.; Strain Theories: From Durkheim to Merton**

Intelligence (IQ) and Criminal Behavior

Historically, a relationship between intelligence and crime was suggested as early as 1876 by Cesare Lombroso, who suggested that at least some criminals were atavisms, biological throwbacks to an earlier stage of human evolution, inferior to normal, law-abiding individuals both physically and mentally. In 1905, Alfred Binet and Theodore Simon developed a test of general intelligence for use in the public schools, then revised the test in 1908 to incorporate the concept of mental age. Subsequent revisions of Binet's intelligence test, with the addition of the concept of mental age and the

intelligence quotient (IQ), equal to the mental age divided by the chronological age and multiplied by 100, produced the familiar IQ test. (For a general review of early studies of intelligence and crime, see Vold et al., 1998, Chapt. 5.)

Henry Goddard translated the Binet intelligence test and administered it to all of the inmates of the Training School for the Feeble-Minded at Vineland, New Jersey, where he was the director of the research center. Goddard found that none of the inmates had a mental age over 13. Based on this, he concluded that mental age 12 (IQ 75) marked the upper limit of feeblemindedness. He also examined studies of feeblemindedness in institutionalized criminals, and found that 28–89% were feebleminded by this criterion. In his 1914 book *Feeble-Mindedness: Its Causes and Consequences,* he estimated that 70% of the criminal population was feebleminded. In a related finding, W. Healy and A.F. Bronner in their book *Delinquency and Criminals: Their Making and Unmaking,* published in 1926, showed that 37% of tested delinquents in Chicago and Boston were subnormal in their intelligence, and concluded that delinquents were 5–10 times more likely to be mentally deficient than nondelinquents. Later research using Goddard's criterion for feeblemindedness, however, found that 37% of white and 89% of black draftees during World War I were feebleminded. Subsequently, the definition of feeblemindedness was revised downward to an IQ of 50 (mental age 8) or below, and Goddard abandoned not only his original criterion for feeblemindedness but also some of his more extreme positions, in which he had denied the possibility of ameliorating feeblemindedness through education, and in which he had espoused segregating feebleminded individuals in institutions and preventing them from reproducing.

Measuring Intelligence and Measuring Crime

IQ became the principal criterion used in studies of the relationship between intelligence and crime for the remainder of the 20th century. The early researchers in the field of intelligence and crime generally contended (or assumed) that IQ was an innate, genetic characteristic of individuals. Critics of the IQ-delinquency or IQ-crime hypothesis argue that despite strong test–retest correlations for IQ, there is extensive evidence indicating that IQ scores are responsive to social environmental factors (Simons, 1978; see also Menard and Morse, 1984, 1352, note 7). In evaluating the relationship between intelligence and crime, this is a peripheral issue. The assumption that IQ is "constant" over the life span, or "innate," or predominantly "genetic," is *not* critical to the hypothesis that intelligence affects illegal behavior. Instead, the combination of constancy (at least in *differences* in IQ scores) and innateness of IQ, plus the correlation between IQ and crime, is used to argue that some individuals are innately (and by implication genetically) more predisposed to crime than others.

A second, more critical question that has been raised in studies of the relationship between IQ and crime is, what exactly is the IQ test measuring? Advocates of IQ testing argued that it measured a general ability for abstract reasoning and problem solving.

Detractors argued that it measured social learning rather than native intelligence, and also noted that IQ tests were sensitive to conditions of administration of the test and to the motivation and stress level of the test takers. To the extent that IQ tests systematically measure something other than or in addition to intelligence, differences in IQ between criminals and noncriminals (and also, incidentally, between members of higher and lower socioeconomic groups, or majority and minority ethnic groups) may be attributable to that "something else": testing conditions, motivation, or cultural bias. Although this does not invalidate the existence of a correlation between the *IQ test* and crime, it may not reflect a correlation between *intelligence* and crime. Instead, the relationship between IQ test scores and crime may reflect, for example, differences between criminals and noncriminals in how well they have learned mainstream culture. In the context of comparing incarcerated criminals with nonincarcerated individuals, it may reflect differences in how benign or hostile the test environment is in a criminal justice institution as opposed to an educational institution, rather than differences in intelligence. In the latter case, moreover, because the condition of test administration may occur *after* one has been arrested or otherwise processed by the justice system, it would be more reasonable to interpret any correlation between IQ test scores and crime as indicating that involvement in the justice system is a cause of lower IQ test scores, rather than indicating that lower IQ is a cause of involvement in the justice system.

In addition to issues regarding the measurement of intelligence, studies of the relationship between intelligence and crime have been beset with problems in how to measure illegal behavior. The use of official data on arrests and convictions has been criticized by Scott Menard and Barbara Morse (1984, 1348), among others, who suggest that self-reported illegal behavior is a more valid measure of illegal behavior. Menard and Morse based their criticisms on an extensive literature on the reliability and validity of self-report as opposed to official measures of illegal behavior, which generally indicated a much higher validity for self-report studies than for official data on most offenses (about 80% accuracy for self-reports, about 25–50% for official data on more serious offenses, and less than 5% for official data on illicit drug use and some less serious offenses; but official homicide and motor vehicle theft data are probably over 90% valid). Comparisons between incarcerated offenders and the general population are especially problematic, first because the general population includes criminals who are not presently incarcerated (offenders who are undetected, or on probation or parole), and second because incarcerated offenders may disproportionately consist of offenders unintelligent enough (low IQ) to get caught. This latter possibility is made all the more plausible by the finding that low IQ scores are more highly correlated with official than with self-reported crime and delinquency (Hirschi and Hindelang, 1977).

Richard J. Herrnstein and his associates (Wilson and Herrnstein, 1985; Herrnstein and Murray, 1994) and other proponents of the hypothesis that intelligence is a risk factor for crime have acknowledged that incarcerated offenders may have lower intelligence than offenders who are not incarcerated. Possible explanations include: the simple proposition that more intelligent criminals are less likely to get caught; the possibility that more intelligent offenders have the opportunity to commit crimes such as embezzlement and other white-collar crimes that pose less risk of detection and apprehension than "street crimes" like robbery and burglary; the possibility that more intelligent respondents are more likely to conceal their illegal behavior on self-reports; and the assertion that incarcerated offenders account for most of the crime anyway, so there is little left to be accounted for by the nonincarcerated offenders. The first two propositions are plausible. There is no evidence to support the third (and it could be argued with equal force that less intelligent respondents might underreport or over-report their illegal behavior because of their inability to fully understand the questions). The last assertion is highly suspect, relying on official statistics' underestimates of the actual amount of illegal behavior that occurs.

Research Evidence on the IQ–Crime Relationship

Evidence contrary to the hypothesis that low intelligence leads to crime began to accumulate not long after the publication of the studies by Healy and Bronner and by Goddard. (Again, see Vold et al., 1998, Ch. 5, for a review of earlier studies of the relationship between intelligence and crime.) In his book *Brothers in Crime,* published in 1938, Clifford R. Shaw reported that delinquents generally were not different, with respect to intelligence, from people in conventional society. Evidence from a longitudinal study of treatment outcomes for boys, the Cambridge–Somerville Youth Study, published in William and Joan McCord's (1959) *Origins of Crime,* indicated that intelligence was not strongly related to crime. Similarly, the research of Sheldon and Eleanor Glueck, later reanalyzed by Robert J. Sampson and John H. Laub in their (1993) *Crime in the Making,* indicated no consistent relationship between intelligence and delinquency.

Other research indicated that there was a weak-to-moderate relationship between intelligence and delinquency. Marvin E. Wolfgang, Robert M. Figlio, and

Thorsten Sellin's (1972) *Delinquency in a Birth Cohort* found that in their cohort of Philadelphia boys, the IQ scores for delinquents were 8–11 points lower than for nondelinquents, controlling for black or white ethnicity and higher or lower social class. In England, D.J. West (1982) in *Delinquency: Its Roots, Careers, and Prospects* found a six-point difference in IQ at ages 8–10 between boys who did and did not become delinquent during their teen years. Robert Gordon (1987) reported consistency in several studies of modest negative correlations (in the low-to-high 0.20s) between IQ and delinquency in populations whose average IQ would be close to 100. Reviews by Herbert Quay (1987) and by Travis Hirschi and Michael Hindelang (1977) indicate that IQ differences of 8–12 points, and correlations of 0.17–0.27, are commonly found in studies of IQ and delinquency or crime, with the delinquents consistently having lower IQ scores than the nondelinquents.

More detailed examination of the IQ–crime relationship indicates that there is a difference between verbal intelligence and nonverbal or performance intelligence. Using the Wechsler IQ test, which distinguishes between verbal and performance IQ, delinquents disproportionately had higher performance IQ than verbal IQ scores, a result that is more evident for boys than for girls (Quay, 1987). Although the results reported by Quay are somewhat mixed, it appears that the discrepancy between verbal and performance IQ is attributable primarily to lower verbal IQ scores for delinquents. This once again raises the issue of social learning as opposed to innate ability, as language learning is dependent on socialization.

In a variant of the intelligence–crime relationship, learning disabilities have also been found to be related to illegal behavior (Keilitz et al., 1979). Although learning disabilities should not be equated with intelligence, the pattern of the relationship is the same, with learning disability being correlated with illegal behavior, more so for official than for self-report data. Keilitz et al. (1979) reported that learning-disabled children were more likely to be official delinquents than children in the general population (and official delinquents were twice as likely to be learning disabled as children in the general population), but there were no differences in self-reported illegal behavior between learning-disabled children and children who were not learning disabled.

Several possible explanations of the relationship between intelligence and crime have been proposed, and are stated here as hypotheses.

Hypothesis 1: Intelligence has a direct influence on crime, with criminal behavior resulting from an inability to understand or conform to norms and laws, or from lower levels of moral reasoning or development that result from lower intelligence (Wilson and Herrnstein, 1985, 169).

Hypothesis 2: Low intelligence has an indirect influence on crime, with criminal behavior resulting from a weakening of social controls or from strain, where the weakened controls or strain are caused by low intelligence. One variation on this theme is suggested by Hirschi and Hindelang (1977), who argue that low IQ leads to school failure and negative attitudes toward the school and teachers, producing a lower level of social control, which in turn results in delinquency. Keilitz et al. (1979, 101) describe a similar "school failure rationale" that has been used to explain the relationship of learning disabilities to delinquency.

Hypothesis 3: Low intelligence is a risk factor, not for crime itself, but for getting caught if you commit a crime, as discussed above (Wilson and Herrnstein, 1985; Herrnstein and Murray, 1994).

Hypothesis 4: Low intelligence is a source of social discrimination, which in turn may produce strain and weaken social controls (Menard and Morse, 1984). In this explanation, it is not low intelligence itself, but the negative social response to low intelligence, that would properly be regarded as the cause of crime, and which would need to be modified in order to reduce illegal behavior. This explanation parallels the differential treatment hypothesis suggested by Keilitz et al. (1979) as an explanation for the relationship between learning disabilities and illegal behavior. It is also consistent with differences between official and self-report data in intelligence-delinquency and learning-disability– delinquency correlations.

Hypothesis 5: The relationship between intelligence and illegal behavior is spurious. In particular, low social class and ethnic minority status produce both lower IQ scores and higher rates of illegal behavior.

Hypothesis 6: Low intelligence may be an indirect effect of, rather than an indirect cause of, illegal behavior. For example, Deborah Denno (1985) suggests that there is no direct link between mental ability and delinquency, and raises the possibility that delinquency leads to low school performance, which in turn is reflected in low IQ scores.

Hypothesis 7: Although low intelligence may not be a risk factor for crime, high intelligence is a protective factor, not in the sense that it reduces crime for everyone, but in the sense that it reduces criminal behavior in individuals *who are otherwise at risk* for committing crimes (Werner and Smith, 1982).

Hypotheses 1, 2, and, more indirectly, 3 and 4, have been tested in empirical research on the "school failure" model. Both Menard and Morse (1984) and David A. Ward and Charles R. Tittle (1994) tested variants of the model suggested by Hirschi and Hindelang, incorporating measures of IQ, school performance, school attitudes, and self-reported delinquency. For all of the models tested (two by Menard and Morse, three—one with

two different methods of estimation—by Ward and Tittle), the explained variance was small, with IQ accounting for only 4–5% of the differences in delinquency. Menard and Morse (1984) also tested two pairs of models (one each for minor and serious delinquency), one of which included only variables from an integrated theory of illegal behavior, and the other of which added IQ, scholastic aptitude (the Differential Aptitude Test or DAT), and school performance (grade point average or GPA). The integrated theory used by Menard and Morse suggested that lack of access to desirable social roles could lead to premature and inappropriate negative labeling, which could in turn exacerbate the lack of access to desirable social roles. Taken together, lack of access plus negative labeling could lead to alienation from conventional social contexts (home and school) and association with delinquent peers, which in turn led to delinquency.

The models with only the variables from the integrated theory explained 20% of the variance (differences) between individuals in serious delinquency, and 29% of the variance in minor delinquency. The addition of IQ, scholastic aptitude, and school performance resulted in a negligible increase (less than 1%) in explained variance. None of these models indicated a direct effect from IQ to delinquency, as suggested in Hypothesis 1, and the results from Menard and Morse (1984) suggest that there is no need to include even an indirect effect as suggested by Hypothesis 2. Menard and Morse interpreted their results as being consistent with a differential reaction model, as described by Keilitz et al. (1979).

In general, the suggestion in Hypothesis 5 that the relationship between intelligence and crime is spurious, and in Hypothesis 6 that illegal behavior affects intelligence, is speculative, with little or no basis in empirical research. Studies have examined socioeconomic status or race as explanations for both intelligence and crime with the finding that IQ is more closely related to crime than race or social class, and that IQ is related to crime even controlling for social class or ethnicity (Hirschi and Hindelang, 1977; Gordon, 1987), findings contrary to the suggestion that the relationship is spurious with social class or ethnicity. Neither race nor social class is terribly strongly related to illegal behavior to begin with, however, especially when illegal behavior is measured by self-reports (Menard and Morse, 1984, 1348), so the persistence of a relationship between IQ and illegal behavior controlling only for these variables is insufficient to establish the importance of intelligence as a cause of crime. There is some limited research evidence in support of Hypothesis 7 that higher intelligence may reduce the probability of involvement in crime for individuals who are otherwise at high risk for illegal behavior (Werner and Smith, 1982; Herrnstein and Murray, 1994).

Conclusion

Most criminologists would probably agree that there is a small, consistently replicated correlation between intelligence and crime. Some would suggest that there is a direct influence of intelligence on illegal behavior, either as a risk factor for crime or as a protective factor, reducing the probability of illegal behavior for individuals otherwise at risk. Still others would argue that the relationship between intelligence and crime, although causal, is indirect. None of these positions, however, receives strong support from research, especially when self-report data and adequate controls for theoretically important variables are included. A serious limitation on this research, however, is the focus on juvenile delinquency. Comparable research has not been done on adults, not surprisingly, given the dearth of self-report data on adult respondents. On balance: (1) a good case can be made that intelligence is weakly correlated with illegal behavior; (2) the evidence is inadequate to support the contention that low intelligence *causes* criminal behavior, and in fact is more consistent with the contention that intelligence is neither a direct nor an indirect cause of crime; but (3) it would be advisable to conduct further research into the relationship between intelligence and crime for adults, and also the possible contribution of intelligence as a protective factor for individuals who are otherwise (based on characteristics other than intelligence) at high risk of involvement in illegal behavior.

SCOTT MENARD

References and Further Reading

Denno, D. 1985. Sociological and human developmental explanations of crime: Conflict or consensus, *Criminology* 23.

Gordon, R.A. 1987. SES versus IQ in the Race-IQ-Delinquency Model, *International Journal of Sociology and Social Policy* 7.

Herrnstein, R.J. and Murray, C. 1994. *The Bell Curve: Intelligence and Class Structure in the United States,* New York, NY: Free Press.

Hirschi, T. and Hindelang, M.J. 1997. Intelligence and delinquency: A revisionist review, *American Sociological Review* 42.

Keilitz, I., Zaremba, B.A., and Broder, P.K. 1979. The link between learning disabilities and juvenile delinquency: Some issues and answers, *Learning Disability Quarterly* 2.

Menard, S. and Morse, B.J. 1984. A structuralist critique of the IQ-delinquency hypothesis: Theory and evidence, *American Journal of Sociology* 89.

Quay, H.C. 1984. Intelligence, *Handbook of Juvenile Delinquency*, Quay, H.C. (Ed.), New York, NY: Wiley.

Simons, R.L. 1978. The meaning of the IQ-delinquency relationship, *American Sociological Review* 43.

Vold, G.B., Bernard, T.J., and Snipes, J.B. 1998. *Theoretical Criminology,* 4th ed., New York, NY: Oxford University Press.

Ward, D.A. and Tittle, C.R. 1994. IQ and delinquency: A test of two competing explanations, *Journal of Quantitative Criminology* 10.

Werner, E.E. and Smith, R. 1982. *Vulnerable but Invincible: A Longitudinal Study of Resilient Children and Youth,* New York, NY: McGraw-Hill.

Wilson, J.Q. and Herrnstein, R.J. 1985. *Crime and Human Nature,* New York, NY: Touchstone.

See also **Biological Theories of Criminal Behavior; Genetic Theories of Criminal Behavior; Neurophysiological Theories of Criminal Behavior**

Intensive Supervision Probation

Intensive supervision probation is simply a sentence received by an individual who has been convicted of a crime. This punishment is classified as a community-based intermediate sanction because the requirements are not as lenient as traditional probation and not as restrictive as incarceration. Intensive supervision probation's basic function is to strictly monitor individuals who would otherwise be placed in prison. Although the majority of intensive supervision programs today are viewed as diversion programs some may also function as enhancements. Enhancement programs are provided to those who have been sentenced to traditional probation but have not had much success or whose committing offense is deemed by administration to warrant increased supervision levels. This entry will explore intensive supervision probation with regards to its daily function and the success of implementation.

Function

This sentencing option involves more stringent guidelines and constraints than regular probation, although there is a lack of agreement over what constitutes "intensive" supervision. Fundamentally, intensive supervision probation means more control over the offender occurs through increased contacts, restrictions, or service requirements that are accomplished by reducing case-load size among the assigned probation officers. The contacts are increased both in terms of frequency and the type of interaction (i.e., direct personal contact and indirect contact). The restriction and service requirements may include community service, electronic monitoring, drug screening, employment, counseling, and restitution. The logic behind the greater frequency of contacts and requirements is simply to increase the exchange between the client and probation officer as a means to assure for compliance with program demands and public safety.

It is important to recognize that the use of intensive supervision probation is not a new phenomenon, in fact, it has been noted that there have been two waves of this sanction. The common elements of the two models are smaller caseloads and increased contacts, however, the early models operated with the goal of improved treatment in order to reduce recidivism; whereas, the current programs are more inclined to stress enhanced monitoring and supervision in order to reduce the prison population. Therefore, the earlier versions' emphasis was on increased control of the offender in an attempt to enhance treatment services to the client whereas current programs are more likely to function as an opportunity to reduce prison crowding.

Regardless of the goal of the intensive supervision program there are two philosophies that emerge when examining the structure of enforcing the requirements of the sanction. The two philosophies are derived from a control model and a treatment model. The control model focuses on the concept of enforcing all conditions of supervision and emphasizes surveillance, community service, and restitution. And the treatment model is concerned with helping offenders become more independent and contributing members of society by requiring employment or education, community service, and a treatment agenda.

A final issue to consider is variations in case management. Some jurisdictions simply have one officer assigned to a client and others use a team approach that incorporates two officers: one is the surveillance officer and the other the probation officer. This dual officer approach is applied in order to compare the progression or regression of an offender's progress with the intention not only to assist the offender but also to reduce officer burnout.

Evaluation

Although the implementation of intensive supervision probation varies by jurisdiction, there have been a variety of studies conducted to examine the two primary goals of the program (Pearson 1985; Erwin, 1987;

Erwin and Bennett, 1987; Byrne and Kelly, 1989; Jones, 1991; Latessa, 1992, 1993; Petersilia and Turner, 1990, 1993). Intensive supervision programs have been implemented and evaluated in almost every state—the results have been modest, at best.

One basic assumption of intensive supervision probation is reduced recidivism rates. Latessa and Allen (1997, 318–19) provide a summary table that can be recapitulated as showing variations in the number of contacts received by the clients and the type and methods in which comparison group and intensive groups were selected. The contacts for intensive clients ranged from five times per week to ten per month. The percentage of intensive clients who recidivated ranged from as little as 12% to as high as 48% and among these same studies the recidivism for the control groups were 4% and 28%, respectively (Petersilia and Turner, 1993). An issue that must be considered when examining recidivism regarding the comparison of intensive clients to those who did not receive intensive supervision probation is the fact that the intensive clients are monitored more closely, thus increasing the likelihood of a technical violation. Likewise, each evaluation of intensive supervision probation will be conducted to capture the specific goals and objectives found within the given jurisdiction, making cross-comparisons difficult.

Another basic principle of intensive supervision probation is that such programs will divert individuals from prison. Several studies show that diversion of offenders from incarceration is not occurring (Erwin, 1986; Baird and Wagner, 1991; Jones, 1991) and other research supports the fact that offenders are being diverted (Pearson and Bibel, 1986; Clear and Latessa, 1990; Noonan and Latessa, 1997). It appears that the differences found in the results are partially because of the way in which the offender is admitted to intensive supervision probation. To illustrate, in New Jersey and Ohio the program is structured to select from only those who have received a sentence of incarceration (Pearson and Bibel, 1986; Clear and Latessa, 1990; Noonan and Latessa, 1997), whereas other models allow individuals to be placed into intensive supervision probation either as a direct sentence, split sentence, as part of revocation proceedings, or as an amended sentence (Erwin, 1986; Baird and Wagner, 1991; Jones, 1991). From this, it is apparent that in order to meet the intended goal of prison diversion the jurisdiction must limit admissions to intensive supervision probation to only those offenders sentenced to a period of incarceration. It must be pointed out, however, that Petersilia (1990) illustrates that if given a choice convicted offenders may prefer shorter periods of incarceration over longer restrictions while in the community.

Summary

In summary, intensive supervision probation involves more restrictive monitoring of convicted offenders while they remain in the community rather than receiving a period of incarceration. This sanction is used across the country but there fails to be uniformity in the elements a program should encompass in order to effectively assist the client, protect the community, and reduce imprisonment rates. Research indicates that programs vary in the ability to achieve the intended goals; to reduce prison commitments or to reduce recidivism. In spite of these issues, intensive supervision probation is the most widely used community-based intermediate sanction and is supported by the public.

JILL A. GORDON

References and Further Reading

Baird, C., and Wagner, D. 1990. Measuring diversion: The Florida community control program. *Crime and Delinquency* 36: 112–125.

Byrne, J. 1986. The control controversy: A preliminary examination of intensive supervision programs in the United States. *Federal Probation* 50: 4–12.

Byrne, J. and Kelly, L. 1989. Restructuring probation as an intermediate sanction: An evaluation of the Massachusetts intensive supervision program. *Final Report to the National Institute of Justice.* Washington, DC: U.S. Department of Justice.

Byrne J., Lurigio, A., and Petersilia, J. 1993. *Smart Sentencing.* Beverly Hills, CA: Sage.

Clear, T. and Latessa, E. 1990. Probation officer roles in intensive supervision. *Federal Probation* 54: 1–20.

Erwin, B. 1987. *Final Report: Evaluation of Intensive Probation Supervision in Georgia.* Atlanta, GA: Georgia Department of Corrections.

Erwin, B. 1986. Turning up the heat on probationers in Georgia. *Federal Probation* 50: 17–24.

Erwin, B., and Bennett, L. 1987. *New Dimensions in Probation: Georgia's Experience with Intensive Probation Supervision.*

Washington, DC: National Institute of Justice, U.S. Department of Justice.

Fulton, B., Stone, S. and Gendreau, P. 1994. *Restructuring Intensive Supervision Progams: Applying 'What Works'."* Lexington, KY: American Probation and Parole Association.

Jones, M. 1991. Intensive probation supervision in Georgia, Massachusetts, and New Jersey. *Criminal Justice Research Bulletin,* 6: 1–9.

Latessa, E. 1993. An Evaluation of the Lucas County Adult Probation Department's IDU and High Risk Groups. Cincinnati, OH: Department of Criminal Justice, University of Cincinnati.

Latessa, E. 1992. A Preliminary Evaluation of the Montgomery County Adult Probation Department's Intensive Supervision Program. Cincinnati, OH: Department of Criminal Justice, University of Cincinnati.

Latessa, E. and Allen, H. 1997. *Correction in the Community.* Cincinnati, OH: Anderson Publishing Company.

Noonan, S. and Latessa, E. 1987. Intensive probation: An examination of recidivism and social adjustment. *American Journal of Criminal Justice.* 12: 45–61.

Pearson, F. 1985. New Jersey's intensive probation supervision program: A progress report. *Crime and Delinquency* 31: 393–410.

Pearson, F. and Bibel, D. 1986. New Jersey's intensive supervision program: What is it like? How is it working? *Federal Probation* 50: 24–31.

Petersilia, J. 1987. *Expanding Options for Criminal Sentencing.* Santa Monica, CA: Rand Publishing.

Petersilia, J. 1990. When probation becomes more dreaded than prison. *Federal Probation* 54: 23–27.

Petersilia, J. and Turner, S. 1990. *Intensive Supervision for High-Risk Probationers.* Santa Monica, CA: Rand Publications.

Petersilia, J. and Turner, S. 1993. *Evaluating Intensive Supervised Probation/Parole Results of a Nationwide Experiment.* Washington, DC: U.S. Department of Justice.

Petersilia, J. and Turner, S. 1993. *Evaluating Intensive Supervised Probation/Parole Results of a Nationwide Experiment.* Washington, DC: U.S. Department of Justice.

Petersilia, J. and Turner, S. 1993. *Evaluating Intensive Supervised Probation/Parole Results of a Nationwide Experiment.* Washington, DC: U.S. Department of Justice.

See also **Probation; Sentences and Sentencing: Types**

Intermediate Sanctions

The use of intermediate sanctions in the criminal justice system challenges the notion that prison is the "yardstick for all punishments." Whereas in reality, probation is the most frequently used sentencing option in America, public perceptions are that prison is the only "real" punishment.

Intermediate sanctions can be defined as a continuum of punishments that lay between probation and prison. Examples of intermediate sanctions include restitution, substantial fines, community service, day centers, house arrest and electronic monitoring, intensive supervision programs, residential programs or halfway houses, and boot camps. Intermediate sanctions do not exist in isolation from one another, but may be combined so that a judge for example, may sentence someone to house arrest *and* restitution.

All of these practices are less severe than prison custody, but require more of the offender than basic probation. Treatment orders may be considered under this term as well, if it is acknowledged that treatment is often intrusive and unpleasant. What the various forms of intermediate sanctions have in common is that they are an alternative to collective incapacitation, are more punitive than regular probation, and provide greater control over the offender. Intermediate sanctions received the greatest enthusiasm and support from practitioners and academics in the 1980s and early 1990s.

Intermediate sanctions evolved from the community corrections movement in the 1960s. The goal of traditional community corrections was to avoid the stigma and other collateral damage inflicted on those detained in prison. Those who championed community corrections also argued that effective rehabilitation could not occur in a prison setting.

Intermediate sanctions place the offender in the community, but were developed for different reasons. Primary objectives included the need to enhance community protection, relief from the economic costs of mass incarceration, and the desire to provide a better match between the severity of crime and the punishment.

In 1985, the RAND Corporation published a study that generated support for intermediate sanctions based on the important issue of community safety. Joan Petersilia and others studied a group of felony probations in two California counties. They found that over two-thirds of the probationers in the sample were rearrested, and of those, one-third was sentenced to prison or jail for crimes committed while on probation. Seventy-five percent of the charges were for burglary, robbery, and other violent crimes. Mindful of the costs incurred by incapacitating a greater proportion of felony offenders, intermediate sanctions were recommended as a method to more efficiently increase control over felony probationers. A subsequent study showed that in a comparison sample, offenders released from prison had a higher recidivism rate than those sentenced to probation. This supported the recommendation that intermediate sanctions be employed at the back end as well as the front end of the system.

A second development that contributed to support for intermediate sanctions was the increase in crime in the 1960s and the public and political response to it. Beginning in the 1980s, "get tough on crime" polices were introduced including truth in sentencing laws, longer prison sentences, and mandatory minimum sentences for habitual offenders and certain crimes such as drug offenses. Largely as a result of changes in sentencing policies, incarceration rates increased dramatically. Between 1980 and 1990, incarceration rates increased from 220 to 457 per 100,000.

The initial government response to a mammoth increase in the prison population was to build more facilities. Between 1980 and 1988 state correctional costs increased by almost 60%. At the same time, costs for elementary and secondary education declined by 2%. It was clear that the imprisonment binge, as some called it, could not continue at the same rate without bankrupting state budgets or seriously impacting spending on other sectors such as education. The policy of collective incapacitation (locking up any offender considered to be a crime risk) would need to be returned to one of selective incapacitation where only the most serious and risky offenders would be imprisoned. Intermediate sanctions offered great promise to those who wanted to decrease the cost of government, adequately punish offenders, and protect the community. At the same time, those concerned with the more humanitarian treatment of offenders were encouraged by the practice of intermediate sentencing.

Governments began experimenting with various forms of intermediate sanctions in the 1980s, but it was not until 1990 that a cohesive, principled, and rational argument for intermediate sanctions was offered. Norval Morris and Michael Tonry authored a well-received book explaining how intermediate sanctions would further the principle of just deserts, which means that a convicted person should receive the punishment he or she deserves based on the seriousness of the offense and his or her criminal record. Convicted offenders would be evaluated according to their risk to the community and the nature of the crime. Prison would be reserved for *only* the most serious offenses and the most dangerous offenders. Punishments would be introduced that could be served in the community, and these intermediate sanctions could be scaled to fit the crime and the offender. A policy of sentencing guidelines was recommended so that like cases would be treated alike. According to the just deserts model, probation was too weak and prison was too severe a punishment for most cases that come before the courts. The introduction of intermediate punishments would cure this problem.

The nature of intermediate sanctions is illustrated with the examples of home confinement with electronic monitoring, intensive supervision programs, and boot camps. Home confinement requires the offender to remain in his or her place of residence for specified times each day. Typically, the offender is allowed to leave home for certain purposes such as work, school, or church attendance. Home confinement can be enhanced with an electronic monitoring device, which permits more rapid detection of violations. It is clear that home confinement is less punitive and less costly than incarceration, but more harsh than traditional probation. The goal of electronic monitoring was to better control the offender's whereabouts, thereby providing greater protection to the public. By 1990, all states had implemented house arrest with electronic monitoring.

Intensive supervision programs (ISPs) impose close monitoring and rigorous conditions on lawbreakers. The program was originally implemented in Georgia in 1982. It required multiple face-to-face contacts between probation officers and offenders (four to seven per week in contrast with regular probation that typically imposed only one contact per month), a curfew, community service hours, and frequent random urinalysis and breathalyzer tests.

The popular and controversial boot camp movement originated in Oklahoma in the early 1980s. The target population for boot camps was young offenders. As the name suggests, boot camps involve a short (usually 3-month) session in residence with rigorous military style training that focuses on order and discipline. Boot camp is usually followed by a period of intensive supervision. By 1990, almost half of the states had boot camp programs.

Many of the same pressures that led to the adoption of intermediate sanctions in the U.S. are present around the world. The rediscovery of the just deserts philosophy gained ground in Europe, Australia, and Canada where the overuse of the prison sentence received attention. Furthermore, the increase in the prison population that began in the U.S. in the mid-1970s occurred in other nations as well. For example the prison population in Canada increased by 10.6% between 1975 and 1979 and rose another 10.3% between 1979 and 1982. Much of this growth was owing to the increased length of prison sentences. In Switzerland, a country with a relatively low rate of crime, the average prison sentence length increased by 50% between 1982 and 1991.

Although electronic monitoring, ISP, and boot camps were the most popular adoptions in the U.S., the British made more frequent use of day-reporting centers. The day-fine system, which reflects the seriousness of the offense and the financial position of the offender, has been used much more widely in Europe than in the U.S. The use of restitution is widespread in Canada. In Europe, community service is often used as a stand-alone sentence, whereas in the U.S. it is usually an add-on to another sanction.

Outside of western nations, the use of intermediate sanctions is rare. On the African continent, there is a perception that prison is counterproductive and prison

overpopulation ranges from about 30–200%. A major obstacle to the use of intermediate sanctions in African countries is the lack of enabling legislative measures. This can be explained in part by an inherited legal system from colonial times, which has become rigid and difficult to change. In addition, African nations have no tradition of allowing social science knowledge to guide government policy in the field of criminal justice.

Prison is the most frequently imposed sanction in Arab countries, but there is also agreement about the negative effects of imprisonment, and hence the need to apply other sanctions. Much of the slow progress in applying new punishment methods is because of a resistance to trying "modern" methods and skepticism that if such methods do work, they may not be appropriate for Arab societies.

Intermediate sanctions are not common in Asia and the Pacific region. Fines and community service are used in some countries. Finally, in Latin America the prison rate is growing faster than the population rate. Overcrowding in some countries is up to 200, 300, and as much as 900%. Furthermore, some of the worst human rights violations in the region can be attributed to prison conditions. The criminal justice systems in many Latin American countries are described as "systems in crisis." Fines and community service are used in some nations, and house arrest is limited mainly to political crimes. Many Latin American countries have neither the legal nor the administrative infrastructure to implement a policy of intermediate sanctions.

After 20 years' of experience with intermediate sanctions, what does the evaluation literature tell us? For the most part, intermediate sanctions have fallen short of the goals of relieving prison crowding and enhancing public safety, all at a lower cost. Two practices explain this assessment. First is the practice of net widening. This occurs when an intermediate punishment is imposed on an offender who would normally receive a lesser punishment. Thus, judges have typically imposed intermediate sanctions on those who would merit regular probation. Second, as intermediate sanctions involve closer monitoring and control of the offender, probation and parole officers have detected more technical violations (for example, curfew), increasing the numbers of offenders sent to prison. If technical violations are indeed a proxy for future criminal behavior, then it can be argued that intermediate punishments have achieved the goal of protecting the public. But the net effect has been an increase in the prison population. In 2002, U.S. prisons and jails reached a historical high of 2 million inmates.

The availability of sentencing options clearly promotes the principle of just desserts. However, for this goal to be realized, discretion needs to be guided so that judges and parole boards do not simply enhance punishment and control for the sake of being tough on crime, resulting in "over control" and escalating costs.

One of the more interesting research findings is that when intermediate sanctions are combined with treatment orders, drug offenders are less likely to relapse and recidivate. Early on, intermediate sanctions focused largely on supervision and control. This research suggests that in the future, community control *and* rehabilitative efforts should be used together.

The promoters of intermediate sanctions may have expected too much. In corrections, there is no "free lunch." Intermediate sanctions are clearly on solid ground in promoting the principle of just desserts, and evidence suggests they have the potential to reduce recidivism among certain types of offenders. Recent studies recommend the continued use of intermediate sanctions because they have the potential to promote a more rational allocation of resources. But, the devil is in the details of implementation. Policies would need to be developed to better govern the ways that intermediate sanctions are used.

CHERYL SWANSON

References and Further Reading

Crouch, B. 1993. Is incarceration really worse? An analysis of offenders' preferences for prison over probation, *Justice Quarterly*, 10.

Johnson, K. 2002. States use of GPS offender tracking systems, *The Journal of Offender Monitoring* 15.

Junger-Tas, J. 1994. *Alternatives to Prison Sentences: Experiences and Developments*, Amsterdam/New York: Kugler Publications.

Mauer, M., and Chesney-Lind, M., (Eds.) 2002. *Invisible Punishment: The Collateral Consequences of Mass Imprisonment*, New York, NY: The New Press.

McCarthy, B.R., McCarthy, B.J., Jr., and Leone, M.C. 2001. *Community-Based Corrections*, 4th ed., Belmont, CA: Wadsworth.

Morris, N. and Tonry, M. 1990. *Between Prison and Probation: Intermediate Punishments in a Rational Sentencing System*, New York, NY: Oxford University Press.

Parent, D., Dineworth, T., McDonald, D., and Rhodes, W. 1997. *Key Legislative Issues in Criminal Justice: Intermediate Sanctions*, Washington, DC: Department of Justice.

Palumbo, D.J., Clifford, M., and Snyder-Joy, Z.K. 1992. From net widening to intermediate sanctions: The transformation of alternatives to incarceration from benevolence to malevolence, *Smart Sentencing: The Emergence of Intermediate Sanctions*, Byrne, J.M., Lurigio, A.J., and Petersilia, J. (Eds.), Newbury Park, CA: Sage.

Petersilia, J., et al. 1985. *Granting Felons Probation*, Santa Monica, CA: RAND Corporation.

Tonry, M. 1998. Evaluating intermediate sanction programs, *Community Corrections: Probation, Parole, and Intermediate Sanctions*, Petersilia, J. (Ed.), New York and Oxford: Oxford University Press.

Von Hirsch, A. 1976. *Doing Justice: The Choice of Punishments*, New York, NY: Hill and Wang.

Zvekic, U. 1994. (Ed.), *Alternatives to Imprisonment in Comparative Perspective*, Chicago, IL: Nelson-Hall.

See also **Intensive Supervision Programs; Probation; Sentences and Sentencing: Types**

Internal Revenue Service (IRS)

The Internal Revenue Service (IRS) is a federal U.S. government agency located within the Treasury Department. The IRS is responsible for overseeing the administration and enforcement of regulatory tax laws and for collecting the fair and accurate amount of taxes owed from each citizen. Since Congress passed the IRS Restructuring and Reform Act of 1998, the IRS has refocused its mission, goals, and organizational structure. The IRS now views taxpayers as customers and places priority on customer service in a fair, reasonable, and effective manner to help taxpayers meet their tax responsibilities. To provide better service, the IRS has structured its divisions around groups of taxpayers with similar needs. There are four operating divisions: (1) wage and investment taxpayers, (2) small business and self-employed taxpayers, (3) large and midsize business, and (4) tax-exempt organizations and government entities. Each division focuses on the unique tax laws and circumstances affecting its taxpayers and is responsible for education and the enforcement and collection of taxes. Each division has specific operating units, such as taxpayer education before filing, investigation, and collecting delinquent payments. Other units specialize in a narrower group of taxpayers, such as financial services and health care businesses, natural resources, or international businesses. In addition to these divisions, Criminal Investigation is a line unit reporting to the commissioner and is solely responsible for investigating criminal violations. IRS agents in only a small minority of cases allege criminal tax violations. Information Systems and the Chief Counsel provide support to all divisions. Information Systems runs such programs as e-filing and matches tax returns and third-party information, as well as performing other important functions. The Chief Counsel unit provides overall guidance through tax advice and legal counsel and representation to the IRS. The Chief Counsel unit represents the IRS in tax court and drafts regulations, rulings, and published legal guidance manuals to educate taxpayers and their representatives. An independent oversight board for the IRS made up of private-sector representatives also provides a watch on IRS investigations and dealings with taxpayers.

Taxpayers can seek help in protecting their rights from the National Taxpayer Advocate (NTA) program. The NTA is an independent agency outside of the IRS organization, but its employees are very familiar with IRS procedures. Service center advocates act as representatives and advocates for the taxpayer and attempt to resolve difficult issues. The advocates primarily address procedural and organizational issues that have hindered a resolution. The program assisted approximately 200,000 taxpayers in 1999. In addition, the NTA is proactive and attempts to identify systemic problems with the IRS's handling of education, investigations, and collections. The NTA, without IRS review, provides Congress with two annual reports that describe plans for the next year, the top 20 problems facing taxpayers, and the top ten litigated issues for each category of taxpayers.

Another channel for taxpayers who believe IRS decisions are unfair is the independent nationwide Appeals organization. It attempts to resolve tax disputes without litigation. It offers fast-track mediation where a third party facilitates discussions between the IRS and the taxpayer in an attempt to resolve disputes within 30 days.

Most taxpayers dread receiving correspondence from the IRS. The IRS sends out about 2 million CP-2000 letters every year that require taxpayers to explain a discrepancy between third-party information and the information on their tax return or pay the additional taxes. In its move toward customer-friendly service, the IRS now only sends threatening letters after taxpayers refuse to cooperate with a tax audit. In addition, IRS agents conduct face-to-face audits with about 1.19 million returns, or 0.99% of all returns filed. Self-employed persons and corporations have a much higher audit rate. The IRS uses a formula (Discriminant Function System) to determine which tax returns to audit. IRS agents also review tax returns in certain professions and industries. The Market Segment Specialization Program has written guidelines on how to select and audit returns from 53 professions or industries, such as attorneys and contractors.

The IRS has often received unfavorable press suggesting that agents consider politics or other irrelevant issues in their audit investigations. Such allegations have not been supported with evidence. However, research suggests that individuals in high-prestige professions who represent themselves in audits have a lower burden of proof and receive more favorable outcomes than do taxpayers in lower-prestige jobs (Kinsey and Stalans, 1999). Interestingly, the advantage for high-prestige taxpayers in audits disappears if they use a professional representative, suggesting that representation may sometimes be ill advised. To improve its image and conduct, the IRS has taken a proactive role in attempting to catch and correct problems at an early stage and to coordinate and evaluate all suggestions for improvements through a new program called the Taxpayer Treatment and Service Improvements Program (TTSIP). The IRS also now allows taxpayers to use credit cards to pay their tax bills. The IRS reserves a lien against property for taxpayers owing over $25,000 in back taxes; those who owe less can enter an installment payment plan that charges 8% annual interest.

LORETTA J. STALANS

References and Further Reading

Conoboy, H.B. 2000. A wrong step in the right direction: The National Taxpayer Advocate and the 1998 IRS Restructuring and Reform Act, *William and Mary Law Review,* 1401, 41(4).

IRS, Modernizing America's tax agency: IRS organization blueprint, *Department of the Treasury Internal Revenue Service Document 11052* (Rev. 4-2000) Catalog Number 27977p, 2000. Available at www.irs.ustreas.gov.

Karnegis, T.P. 1999. The impact of the 1998 IRS Restructuring Act, *Trusts & Estates,* 66, 138(1).

Kinsey, K.A. and Stalans, L.J. 1999. Leveling the playing field: Prestige and representation in regulatory enforcement, *Law & Society Review,* 993, 33(4).

Russell, R. 2000. IRS fine tunes e-file program; E-signature a barrier no more. *Accounting Today,* 3, 14(19).

Sean, P. 1999. But the agency says it will reform itself, *Insight on the News,* 23, 15(15), April 26.

Worsham, J. 1998. IRS overhaul is good news for small-business owners, *Nations Business,* 8, 86(9), September.

Also see on the Internet: www.irstreas.gov

See also **Tax Evasion and Tax Fraud**

International Court of Justice (World Court)

The International Court of Justice

For centuries, jurists defined international law solely in terms of relations between states. World leaders acted with impunity because international law did not hold them accountable. But this has begun to change. The UN tribunals for Rwanda and the former Yugoslavia address the legal responsibilities of individuals who have committed war crimes and crimes against humanity. National courts, too, have exercised jurisdiction over world leaders, and some, such as former Chilean dictator Augusto Pinochet, have been charged by courts in many countries. The International Court of Justice takes this process even further.

The International Court of Justice (ICJ), which sits at The Hague (the Netherlands), acts as a world court and is distinguished from its predecessor, the Permanent Court of International Justice (1922–1946). The International Court of Justice is the principal judicial organ of the UN and operates under a Statute similar to that of its predecessor, which is an integral part of the Charter of the UN. The ICJ decides cases in accordance with international law and rules on disputes of a legal nature submitted to it by States. In addition, certain international organs and agencies are entitled to call upon it for advisory opinions. The Court was established in 1946 under the Charter of the UN to be the principal judicial organ of the Organization, and its basic instrument, the Statute of the Court, forms an integral part of the Charter.

Functions of the Court

The Court has a dual role: (1) to settle in accordance with international law the legal disputes submitted to it by States, and (2) to give advisory opinions on legal questions referred to it by duly authorized international organs and agencies.

Composition

The Court is composed of 15 judges elected to 9-year terms of office by the UN General Assembly and Security Council sitting independently of each other. It may not include more than one judge of any nationality. Elections are held every 3 years for one-third of the seats, and retiring judges may be re-elected. The Members of the Court do not represent their governments but are independent magistrates.

The judges must possess the qualifications required in their respective countries for appointment to the highest judicial offices, or be jurists of recognized competence in international law. The composition of the Court should also reflect the main forms of civilization and the principal legal systems of the world (e.g., civil law, common law, etc.). When the Court does not include a judge possessing the nationality of a State party to a case, that State may appoint a person to sit as a judge *ad hoc* for the purpose of the case.

The Registrar of the Court is Philippe Couvreur, of Belgian nationality, and the Deputy-Registrar is Jean-Jacques Arnaldez, of French nationality.

Cases between States

The Parties

Only States may apply to, and appear before, the Court. The Member States of the UN (at present numbering 191) are so entitled.

Jurisdiction

The Court has jurisdiction to hear a dispute only if the States concerned have accepted its jurisdiction in one or more of the following ways:

1. by the conclusion between them of a special agreement to submit the dispute to the Court;
2. by virtue of a jurisdictional clause, i.e., typically, when they are parties to a treaty containing a provision whereby, in the event of a disagreement over its interpretation or application, one of them may refer the dispute to the Court. Several hundred treaties or conventions contain a clause to such effect;
3. through the reciprocal effect of declarations made by them under the Statute whereby each has accepted the jurisdiction of the Court as compulsory in the event of a dispute with another State having made a similar declaration. The declarations of 63 States are at present in force, a number of them having been made subject to the exclusion of certain categories of dispute.

In cases of doubt as to whether the Court has jurisdiction, it is the Court itself that decides.

TABLE 1. Present Composition of the Court

President	Vice-President	Judges
Shi Jiuyong (China)	Raymond Ranjeva (Madagascar)	Gilbert Guillaume (France)
		Abdul G. Koroma (Sierra Leone)
		Vladlen S. Vereshchetin (Russian Federation)
		Rosalyn Higgins (UK)
		Gonzalo Parra-Aranguren (Venezuela)
		Pieter H. Kooijmans (the Netherlands)
		Francisco Rezek (Brazil)
		Awn Shawkat Al-Khasawneh (Jordan)
		Thomas Burgenthal (USA)
		Nabil Elaraby (Egypt)
		Hisashi Owada (Japan)
		Bruno Simma (Germany)
		Peter Tomka (Slovakia)

Procedure

The procedure followed by the Court is defined in its Statute, and in the Rules of Court adopted by it under the Statute. The latest version of the Rules was updated on December 5, 2000. The proceedings include a written phase, in which the parties' file and exchange pleadings, and an oral phase consisting of public hearings at which agents and counsel address the Court. As the Court has two official languages (English and French), everything written or said in one language is translated into the other.

After the oral proceedings, the Court deliberates *in camera* and then delivers its judgment at a public sitting. The judgment is final and without appeal. Should one of the States involved fail to comply with it, the other party may have recourse to the Security Council of the UN.

The Court discharges its duties as a full court but, at the request of the parties, may also establish a special chamber. The Court constituted such a chamber for the first time in 1982, formed a second in 1985, constituted two in 1987, and two more in 2002. A Chamber of Summary Procedure is elected every year by the Court in accordance with its Statute. In July 1993, the Court also established a seven-member Chamber to deal with any environmental cases falling within its jurisdiction.

Since 1946, the Court has delivered 76 judgments on disputes concerning *inter alia* land frontiers and maritime boundaries, territorial sovereignty, the non-use of force, noninterference in the internal affairs of States, diplomatic relations, hostage taking, the right of asylum, nationality, guardianship, rights of passage, and economic rights.

Sources of Applicable Law

The Court decides in accordance with international treaties and conventions in force, international custom, the general principles of law and, as subsidiary means, judicial decisions and the teachings of the most highly qualified jurists.

Advisory Opinions

The advisory procedure of the Court is open solely to international organizations. The only bodies at present authorized to request advisory opinions of the Court are five organs of the UN and 16 specialized agencies of the UN.

On receiving a request, the Court decides which States and organizations might provide useful information and gives them an opportunity to present written or oral statements. The Court's advisory procedure is otherwise modeled for contentious proceedings, and the sources of applicable law are the same. In principle, the Court's advisory opinions are consultative in character, and are therefore, not binding as such on the requesting bodies. Certain instruments or regulations can, however, provide in advance that the advisory opinion shall be binding.

Since 1946, the Court has given 24 Advisory Opinions concerning *inter alia* admission to UN membership, reparation for injuries suffered in the service of the UN, territorial status of South-West Africa (Namibia) and Western Sahara, judgments rendered by international administrative tribunals, expenses of certain UN operations, applicability of the UN Headquarters Agreement, the status of human rights, and the legality of the threat or use of nuclear weapons.

Pending cases

1. Application of the Convention on the Prevention and Punishment of the Crime of Genocide (*Bosnia and Herzegovina v. Serbia and Montenegro*): Bosnia and Herzegovina filed an application instituting proceedings against then Yugoslavia in respect to a dispute concerning allegations of performing genocide, which goes against a December 9, 1948 convention. Bosnia and Herzegovina has asked the court to declare that Yugoslavia performed genocide against its citizen and rule that the practice stop and that they pay reparations. Serbia and Montenegro submitted a counterclaim asking the court to declare Bosnia and Herzegovina guilty of committing genocide against their citizens. They requested that Bosnia and Herzegovina punish the individuals responsible and take the necessary measures that these acts will not be repeated in the future.

2. Gabcikova-Nagymaros Project (*Hungary v. Slovakia*): Hungary and Slovakia jointly notified the Court in 1993, regarding issues that have arisen owing to the implementation and termination of the Budapest Treaty of 1977, which concerned the construction of the Gabcikova-Nagymaros barrage system. Hungary abandoned the project in 1989 citing that it entailed grave danger to the Hungarian environment, including their water supply. Slovakia denies these allegations and insists that Hungary is held to the obligations of the treaty. Slovakia put into operation an alternative project within only Slovakian borders, whose operation had effects on Hungary's water access via the Danube River. In 1997, the Court decided that both parties had breached their contractual obligations and ruled for them to enter good faith negotiations to achieve the objectives of the 1977 Budapest Treaty.

3. Ahmadou Sadio Diallo (*Republic of Guinea v. Democratic Republic of the Congo*): The Republic of Guinea instituted proceedings against the Democratic Republic of the Congo asking the Court to condemn the Congo for "grave breaches of international law perpetrated on a of Guinean national," Ahmadou

Sadio Diallo, a 32-year-old business man. Guinea alleges that Ahmadou Sadio Diallo was unlawfully imprisoned, "divested of his investments, companies, bank accounts, movable and immovable properties then expelled" in February of 1996 when he attempted to collect sums owed to him by the government of the Congo and oil companies operating in the country.

4–11. Legality of Use of Force (*Serbia and Montenegro v. Belgium*), (*Serbia and Montenegro v. Canada*), (*Serbia and Montenegro v. France*), (*Serbia and Montenegro v. Germany*), (*Serbia and Montenegro v. Italy*), (*Serbia and Montenegro v. the Netherlands*), (*Serbia and Montenegro v. Portugal*), (*Serbia and Montenegro v. UK*): Serbia and Montenegro instituted proceeding before the court against the above States as well as against Spain and the U.S. (the Court later removed Spain and the U.S. from the list because of a lack of jurisdiction) alleging that the bombing on the Yugoslav territory violated their international obligations. Serbia and Montenegro alleged that the defending States had violated international obligations that assert that no country can use force against another on matters involving only internal issues of that particular country, therefore violating its sovereignty; States have an obligation to protect civilian population and objects as well as the environment during wartime; obligations relating to free navigation on the internal rivers; obligations of fundamental rights and freedoms were also violated; and accusations of targeting a particular national group for destruction. They are asking that these acts cease as well as for compensation for these acts.

12. Armed activities on the territory of the Congo (*Democratic Republic of the Congo v. Uganda*): The Democratic Republic of the Congo alleges that Uganda has perpetrated acts of armed aggression on the territory of the Democratic Republic of the Congo, violating the terms of the UN Charter and of the Charter of the Organization of African Unity.

13. Application of the Prevention and Punishment of the Crime of Genocide (*Croatia v. Serbia and Montenegro*): Croatia maintains that the Yugoslavian government is liable for the "ethnic-cleansing" of Croatian citizens as the Yugoslavian government established military control of the region in which the alleged cleansing took place. They are asking for reparation from the genocide and extensive property damage that took place.

14. Maritime Delimitation between Nicaragua and Honduras in the Caribbean Sea (*Nicaragua v. Honduras*): Nicaragua maintains that there has never been a maritime border with Honduras. Honduras claims that the border is set. The court is asked to determine the maritime border. The right to ask for compensation for natural resources is reserved as well.

15. Certain Property (*Liechtenstein v. Germany*): Liechtenstein claims that Germany seized the property of Liechtenstein nationals as reparation or restitution, or as a result of war: three-fourths without ensuring any compensation to the owners or Liechtenstein itself. Liechtenstein requests reparation.

16. Territorial and Maritime Dispute (*Nicaragua v. Colombia*): Nicaragua has instituted proceedings against Colombia in regard to Territorial and Maritime disputes. They have asked the ICJ to award sovereignty over numerous islands to Nicaragua, in addition to establishing a single maritime border between the two nations. Nicaragua has reserved the right to seek compensation from missed economic opportunities from these areas in dispute.

17. Frontier Dispute (*Benin v. Niger*): The two parties to the dispute jointly asked the ICJ to determine boundaries of the States. The Court is given the responsibility to determine the course of the Boundaries between the Republics of Benin and Niger, which state owns which river islands, and where is the boundary in the river.

18. Armed Activities on the Territory of the Congo (New Application, 2002) (*Democratic Republic of the Congo v. Rwanda*): The Democratic Republic of the Congo has alleged that the Republic of Rwanda has committed serious human rights violations on the territory of the Congo. They maintain that these violations go against the UN and OAU charters and request provisionary measures.

19. Application for revision of the judgment of 11 September 1992 in the Case concerning the Land, Island, and Maritime Frontier Dispute (*El Salvador v. Honduras*: Nicaragua intervening) (*El Salvador v. Honduras*): The Court is asked to determine the land, island, and maritime boundaries between primarily El Salvador and Honduras. Nicaragua has invested interest in this case as well. One primary issue is that over time a former bordering river has shifted its course.

20. Avena and other Mexican Nationals (*Mexico v. USA*): Mexico has asked the ICJ to hear a case concerning 54 Mexican nationals who have been sentenced to death in the U.S. Mexico maintains that carrying out theses sentences will violate the Vienna Convention. They ask the Court to take provisionary measures to ensure that future capital sentences do not occur.

22. Criminal Proceedings in France (*Democratic Republic of the Congo v. France*): The Democratic Republic of the Congo has asked the Court to annul the investigations and prosecution set forth by French judicial authorities against leaders of the Congolese government involving complaints of crimes against humanity against their own peoples. They maintain that this violates their rights as a sovereign nation and the immunities against foreign Heads of State. In addition, the Republic of the Congo requests provisional measure against future such instances.

23. Sovereignty over Pedra Blanca or Pulau Batu Puteh, Middle Rocks, and South Ledge (*Malaysia v. Singapore*): Both Malaysia and Singapore petitioned the ICJ requesting resolution as to the sovereignty of the above-mentioned territories. In advance, both parties jointly agree to accept the ruling that is to be delivered by the Court.

NATHAN R. MORAN AND GABRIEL THRASHER

References and Further Reading

Hudson, M.O. 1972. *The Permanent Court of International Justice 1920–1942*, reprint, New York, London.

Rosenne, S. 1985. *The Law and Practice of the International Court*, 2nd ed. (revised), Dordrecht.

Rosenne, S. 1995. *The World Court—What It is and How It Works*, 5th ed. (revised), Dordrecht.

See also **International Crime and the U.S.; International Criminal Tribunals**

International Crime and the UN

The Definition of International Crimes

An international crime is a crime that has been legally defined by an international agreement (such as a convention, treaty, or protocol) or by customary international law.

The mere fact that a crime has been defined by an international agreement does not mean that any person committing that crime anywhere in the world can be convicted. In general, international agreements are binding only on the signatory countries, which are required to enact the necessary legislation and take the other measures necessary to bring offenders to justice. Furthermore, countries will usually take action only if the crime was committed in the country in question or by a citizen of that country. However, in time, international agreements may contribute to the evolution of customary international law, as defined by article 38 of the Statute of the International Court of Justice. Once the definition of a crime becomes part of such customary international law, it is binding on all countries and all persons. Even persons from countries that have not signed any of the relevant international agreements may be convicted by the courts of any other country that claims jurisdiction, or by an international tribunal, in the very rare cases that such a body has been established for the crime in question.

International agreements not only define international crimes but also contain provisions on the exercise of jurisdiction, in other words, on which country has the right or duty to place international offenders on trial. The agreements also generally include provisions on the right or duty of signatory countries to extradite suspected offenders to another country for trial, and on what forms of mutual legal assistance may or should be extended among the signatories. Increasingly, the agreements also contain provisions that seek to protect certain fundamental human rights.

The list of international crimes has emerged slowly. During the 1800s, only slavery and piracy were widely recognized as international crimes, and most notably the British Navy often intervened when its ships encountered such activity on the high seas. During the first half of the 1900s, various conventions added a motley collection of other crimes to the list: international traffic in obscene publications, the unlawful use of the mails, unlawful interference with submarine cables, and falsification and counterfeiting. In particular, the 1907 Hague Convention and the 1929 Geneva Convention helped to define what became known as "war crimes."

These 1907 and 1929 conventions were much cited in the aftermath of World War II, when *ad hoc* international military tribunals were established to deal with war crimes committed by the Axis powers in the European Theatre of Operations (the Nuremberg War Crimes Trials) and in the Far East (the Tokyo War Crimes Trials). The charges in Nuremberg also contributed to the evolution of the definition of two additional international crimes, crimes against peace (essentially, waging a war of aggression) and crimes against humanity (essentially, certain serious crimes against civilians, such as genocide, forced sterilization, or forced transfer of segments of the population). Subsequently, new conventions were adopted on war crimes (such as the 1949 Geneva Convention and additional protocol) and on crimes against humanity (the 1948 Paris Convention).

In the half century since World War II, the list of international crimes began to expand more rapidly. The following were added to the nine offenses already noted: unlawful use of weapons and unlawful emplacement of weapons; the recruitment, use, financing, and training of mercenaries; racial discrimination and apartheid; torture; unlawful medical experimentation; aircraft hijacking; unlawful acts against maritime navigation; threat and use of force against internationally protected persons; the taking of civilian hostages; drug trafficking; the destruction or theft of national treasures; unlawful acts against the environment; theft of nuclear materials; bribery of foreign officials; and crimes against the UN and associated personnel.

Although there are different views on which international crimes have moved from being based (solely) on international agreements to becoming part of customary international law, the prevailing view is that this is the case at least with war crimes, crimes against peace, crimes against humanity, genocide, piracy, slavery, and torture.

One offense that is conspicuously absent from the list of international crimes is terrorism. No single definition of terrorism has gained universal acceptance, although a number of conventions have entered into force on specific features of terrorism.

A concept that is closely related to international crime is "transnational crime," which refers to crimes that extend into two or more countries. (It is quite possible for an international crime, in turn, to be committed in only one country.) Some examples of transnational crime are when an offender steals a car in country A and takes it to country B, a computer hacker in country A destroys files located in a computer system in country B, an offender in country A organizes the smuggling of illegal aliens into country B, and a factory illegally disposes of its wastes by dumping them into a river flowing from country A to country B on its way to the sea.

Because of, for example, the ease with which offenders can elude the police by jumping from one country to the next, or use the telephone or the Internet to direct activities on the other side of the globe, transnational crime is becoming more prevalent.

The Role and Work of the UN

Article 55 of the UN Charter states that one of the main purposes of the UN is to create the conditions for stability and well-being that are necessary for peaceful and friendly international relations, based on mutual respect, equality, and self-determination. The UN is also specifically charged with the promotion of universal respect for, and observance of, human rights and fundamental freedoms.

Crime, in general, and international crime in particular, is a major concern of all countries. Within the UN system, the primary responsibility for crime prevention and criminal justice lies with the Economic and Social Council (ECOSOC). Within the UN Secretariat, these issues are dealt with by the International Center for the Prevention of Crime, although related issues are also dealt with by, for example, the Center for Human Rights and the UN International Drug Control Program. Many politically sensitive issues, such as war crimes, genocide, and terrorism, are often debated directly in the General Assembly of the UN. In addition, the General Assembly sets up special bodies to deal with specific issues, such as the drafting of new international agreements.

The specific mandate of the UN in this field is discussed and determined by the UN Commission on Crime Prevention and Criminal Justice, which is a functional commission of ECOSOC. The Commission consists of 40 Member States, and meets annually.

Because the crime and criminal justice sector is wide and complex, the Commission has established priority themes as the basis for the work of the UN. There are three such themes: (1) national and transnational crime, including organized crime, economic crime, money-laundering, and environmental crime; (2) urban crime, juvenile crime, and violent crime; and (3) the management and administration of the criminal

justice system. The Commission has also decided that the immediate priority is the prevention and control of transnational organized crime.

In order to promote training, research, and regional cooperation, the UN has established a network of interregional and regional institutes. Every five years, a global Congress is held on the prevention of crime and the treatment of offenders. These Congresses have served to provide the overall political framework for the evolution of UN activities.

The work of the UN in this field takes a number of different forms. The most important are the collection and exchange of information; research and training; technical assistance; the development of international standards and norms; the drafting of new international agreements or model agreements; and assistance to Member States in the implementation of international agreements.

Given the universal nature of crime and also of international crimes, countries can learn considerably from one another's experience with crime and with the effectiveness of various responses. The UN Secretariat has therefore sought to improve its capacity for the collection and exchange of information, in line with guidelines laid down by the Commission. For example, the Secretariat has established a Global Program on Transnational Organized Crime for the collection and analysis of information on this subject.

The Secretariat and in particular the UN network of institutes have been active in promoting research and training, in particular in order to assist developing countries that have not yet been able to sufficiently develop their own research and training capacity. Training has been provided not only to criminal justice professionals for duties in their own countries, but also to professionals (such as police officers) who are taking up peacekeeping and peace-building duties.

In the area of technical assistance, the UN is assuming, to an increasing degree, the role of coordinator or facilitator in the development of bilateral and multilateral model projects. Priority areas at present include preventing and controlling money laundering, corruption, terrorism, and trafficking in women and children. The UN International Drug Control Program has been very active in carrying out a variety of model projects around the world, designed to both reduce the demand for and reduce the supply of illegal drugs.

Over the years, the UN has developed a large number of standards and norms, beginning with the Standard Minimum Rules for the Treatment of Prisoners (1956). These standards and norms cover a range of issues, from the independence of the judiciary, a code of conduct for law enforcement officials, the role of lawyers and the role of prosecutors, to the administration of juvenile justice, the treatment of victims of crime, and capital punishment. Currently, the emphasis is on providing technical assistance to help member states apply the existing standards.

The UN has prepared a number of model international agreements. These have dealt with mutual assistance in criminal matters, extradition, the transfer of proceedings, the transfer of foreign prisoners, the transfer of supervision of offenders conditionally sentenced or conditionally released, and the prevention of crimes that infringe on the cultural heritage of peoples in the form of movable property. The purpose of the model agreements has been to provide a basis for the development of agreements between two or more countries, in particular if the countries represent different legal traditions

Over the years, various actual international agreements have been prepared within the framework of the UN. Among the more influential ones has been the 1988 Vienna Convention against illicit traffic in narcotic drugs and psychotropic substances. This Convention has contributed to increased uniformity in the definition of drugs crimes, to the introduction of money laundering legislation, and to improved mutual assistance in drug crime cases. The UN International Drug Program has worked extensively on helping signatory countries to implement the Vienna Convention.

The 1988 Convention also served as the basis for the recently concluded work on the UN Convention against Transnational Organized Crime, which was signed at the end of 2000 in Palermo by over 120 states. This Convention, and two protocols, will enter into force when they have been ratified by 40 countries, possibly already during 2002. The Convention and protocols serve to define additional international crimes: participation in an organized criminal group, corruption, laundering of the proceeds of crime, obstruction of justice, trafficking in migrants, and trafficking in persons. Further work is underway on a third protocol to the UN Convention, on illegal trafficking in firearms. Work is also underway on an international instrument specifically devoted to corruption.

The Palermo Convention has been enthusiastically supported not only by the U.S., the Russian Federation, and China as well as the European Union countries, but also by many other countries around the world. The U.S., for example, has noted that although it already has in place the laws required by the Convention as well as an intensive network of bilateral agreements, the Convention nonetheless serves to establish global norms, criteria, and standards. Some experts suggest, in fact, that the crimes defined in the Convention may soon become part of customary international law.

In anticipation of the entry of the Palermo Convention into force, the UN is gearing up to assist signatory countries in its implementation. A considerable amount of work needs to be done in both developing and developed countries to adopt new legislation, improve the performance of criminal justice agencies and provide mutual legal assistance. Much of this work—such as the training of the police in the investigation of money laundering, responding to international requests for mutual legal assistance, and providing victims and witnesses with appropriate protection is expensive. The Convention includes a novel provision according to which signatory countries may contribute part of any proceeds of crime that they have confiscated to an international fund set up for the provision of technical assistance to developing countries and countries in transition. For example, Italy has already made a political commitment to do so. In time, illegal assets confiscated from Italian *Mafioisi*, Colombian drug lords, or Russian migrant smugglers may be used to strengthen the police force in Haiti, streamline prosecutions in Zambia, and provide training to judges in Bangladesh.

The Establishment of International Tribunals and an International Criminal Court

Work on the Palermo Convention proceeded relatively quickly, despite the complexity of the issues involved. The work on the establishment of an international criminal court has proceeded much more slowly, largely because of the political sensitivities involved.

The origin of the international criminal court lies in the Nuremberg and Tokyo War Trials. The Nuremberg trials followed a mixed procedure, as elements of the common law systems of the U.S. and the UK, the civil law system of France, and the socialist law system of the USSR had to be taken into consideration. The Tokyo trials, in turn, largely followed the legal system of the U.S. The organization of both war trials was simplified by political agreement of all the Allied powers to conduct the trials, the occupation of the territories in question, the fact that the defendants were already in custody, ready access to witnesses, and the good record keeping of the Axis powers.

A half century later, the commission of corresponding war crimes and crimes against humanity in the territory of former Yugoslavia and in Rwanda also led to demands that the offenders be brought to justice.

In 1993, the Security Council of the UN set up the *ad hoc* International Criminal Tribunal for the former Yugoslavia. The tribunal is located in The Hague in the Netherlands and deals with such "serious violations of international humanitarian law" as war crimes, genocide, and crimes against humanity. This time, there were considerable problems to be overcome, ranging from inadequate funding, the lack of evidence and the logistical problems associated with holding the trial outside of the former Yugoslavia, to the fact that the competence of the court has not been recognized by Serbia–Montenegro or by the Serbian part of Bosnia–Herzegovina.

One year later, the Security Council set up the *ad hoc* International Criminal Tribunal for Rwanda. This tribunal operates in Arusha, Tanzania, and deals with genocide and crimes against humanity. (As the war in Rwanda was a civil war, the treaties defining war crimes are not applicable.) The tribunal's jurisdiction extends to crimes committed by either side of the conflict (Tutsi and Hutu). It is beset by many of the same problems as the *ad hoc* tribunal in The Hague.

Since 1947, the International Law Commission (which is connected with the UN) has been working on a general codification of offenses against the peace and security of mankind, as well as a draft statute for a permanent international criminal court. The idea has been supported by many countries and by many experts, but has run up against the concerns of some of the major powers (in particular the U.S. and the former USSR) that the work of the court may violate their sovereignty. The end of the Cold War, the adoption of the 1988 UN drug convention, and in particular, the horrors committed in former Yugoslavia and in Rwanda were factors in changing the attitudes of governments toward the work. As a result, the charter on the International Criminal Court (ICC) was finally approved in Rome in 1998.

The ICC was created to prosecute persons guilty of war crimes, genocide, and crimes against humanity. The ICC would specifically not supersede national judicial systems but would be used only when national tribunals are unavailable or deemed unable to function in accordance with generally accepted international standards. Charges can be brought by a member State, the Security Council, or the independent prosecutor of the Court, and the case can be heard only with the permission of the state where the alleged crime took place or of the suspect's home state. The Security Council can postpone the consideration of charges by 1 year at a time. The concept of war crimes was defined to include (as new elements) rape, enforced pregnancy, and the conscription of children as soldiers. Charges cannot be brought against persons below the age of 18 years. The maximum sentence that can be imposed by the Court is life imprisonment. The charter will enter into force after ratification by 60 countries, possibly already during 2002.

Although the ICC would solve many problems of jurisdiction and would be based on an international criminal code now under preparation, it remains a politically sensitive issue, especially for the U.S. and the People's Republic of China. However, the U.S. decided to sign the charter at the end of the year 2000, primarily in order to preserve its role in the continued negotiations over the practical work of the ICC.

MATTI JOUTSEN

References and Further Reading

Bassiouni, C.M. 1998. *The Statute of the International Criminal Court. A Documentary History*, Ardsley, NY: Transnational Publishers.

International Criminal Court 2000. Ratification and National Implementing Legislation. *International Review of Penal Law*, 71, 1, 2, Paris.

Newman, G. (Ed.) 1998. *Global Report on Crime and Justice*, New York and Oxford: Oxford University Press.

Paust, J.J., Bassiouni, M.C., Williams, S.A., Scharf, M., Gurulé, J., and Zagaris, B. 1996. *International Criminal Law. Cases and Materials*, Durham, NC: Carolina Academic Press.

Van den Wyngaert, C. (Ed.) 1996. *International Criminal Law. A Collection of International and European Instruments*, The Hague, London, and Boston: Kluwer Law International.

See also **International Court of Justice; International Crime Tribunals; International Criminal Law; International Policing: Cooperation among Nations in the European Union; International Policing: Coordinated Efforts against Crime in Europe**

International Crime Statistics: Data Sources and Interpretation

What Is International Data? Who Collects It and Why?

Collecting crime statistics at the international level and making cross-national comparisons are longstanding topics in criminology and criminal justice. The first two major efforts were made at the General Statistical Congress held in Brussels in 1853, and the International Congress on the Prevention and the Repression of Crime held in London in 1872. In 1947, the UN Secretariat started collecting and disseminating international crime statistics and information on crime trends (see Newman, 1999). The early rationale for collecting and comparing statistics beyond the national level was to gain some insight about patterns of crime causation across countries. Over time, this focus shifted toward the workings and management of criminal justice systems.

Although many nations today collect crime and criminal justice statistics, there are two noted limitations that have implications for comparative research. First, there are countries that do not participate in international data collection projects. To illustrate, a total of 203 countries were surveyed for the seventh UN Surveys of Crime Trends and Operations of Criminal Justice Systems (1998–2000), however, only 82 nations responded to it (UNODC, 2003). Second, most international crime data sources rely on statistics reflecting primarily the Western Hemisphere. Developing nations, particularly those in Africa and Asia, are underrepresented in international crime data reports.

A number of international organizations, such as the UN (UN), the World Health Organization, the International Police Organization, and the Council of Europe, collect and publish official crime (crimes known to and recoded by the police) and criminal justice statistics. These organizations rely on criminal justice or vital statistics agencies within each individual country for these data. National statistics from member countries are collected and published periodically. Most international organizations, at least until recently, made no attempt to validate the data they received from different nations (Killias, 2000). The lack of validity checking also limited the usefulness of these data for cross-national comparisons.

Victimization and self-report of offending data represent another source of information on crime and criminal justice cross nationally. To obtain better estimates of the "true" amount of crime, offenses that have not been reported to or recorded by police are collected using random samples of individuals in several nations. Two examples include the international victimization survey (ICVS) and the international self-report delinquency (ISRD) study.

Whether official or victimization data, international crime, and criminal justice statistics are collected at various levels, by either international organizations (i.e., the UN, The European Commission), or governmental agencies of individual nations that work in cooperation with such international organizations. Data are then gathered at national (one country), regional (more than one country in a geographical region), and continental (countries within a continent) level. In 1998, for example, the UN Developing Program (UNDP) funded a national victimization survey in South Africa (Statistics South Africa, 1998). The UN's research institute, UNICRI, provided technical advice and constructed the questionnaire used in the survey (Statistics South Africa, 1998). Similarly, in 2002, the European Commission sponsored a public opinion survey on safety and exposure to crime, covering the 15 member states (EORG, 2003).

Data are also collected at the continent level. In addition to its Centre for International Crime Prevention (CICP), the UN has established a network of research institutes worldwide. Operating under the joint auspices of the UN and the governments of the respective countries, these agencies collect crime statistics and conduct research, thereby aiding local governments in the implementation of crime preventive services (UN Note, 1970). For example, the UN, in collaboration with the government of Japan, established in 1962 the UN Asia and Far East Institute for the Prevention of Crime and the Treatment of Offenders, a regional institute whose goals include criminal research in Asia and the Pacific region (see UNAFEI, http://www.unafei.or.jp/). Another such UN regional institute, The European Institute for Crime Prevention and Control (HEUNI) was established in cooperation with Finland in 1981 (see HEUNI, http://www.heuni.fi/).

The UN Latin American Institute for the Prevention of Crime and the Treatment of Offenders has collected crime statistics in Latin America and the Caribbean since 1975 (see ILANUD, http://www.ilanud.or.cr/). Finally, The UN African Institute for the Prevention of Crime and the Treatment of Offenders, in operation since 1989, gathers crime data and promotes crime prevention in the African region (see UNAFRI, http://www.unafri.or.ug/).

International Data: Specificity and Methodological Rigor

As legal definitions and recording practices across nations vary considerably, international data sources have developed broad definitions of different types of crimes and criminal justice categories to ease comparative research. Although standardization offers important advantages for comparisons among a large number of countries, there might be instances where the data reported by a given country will not accurately describe the particular situation in that country. Rape, for example, is a crime defined within a specific cultural context.

Attempts to compare crime and criminal justice data globally are also characterized by methodological difficulties related to data collection, survey organization, and implementation issues, to name a few. Many countries lack the appropriate infrastructure, experience, and expertise to conduct national surveys, or to produce high quality statistics on crime and criminal justice (van Kesteren, 2003). Only a few countries—England or Wales, Scotland, the Netherlands, U.S., and Sweden—regularly administer national crime-related surveys (Barclay, 2003). Compared to national level data, international statistics are then less sensitive to specific national contexts and, therefore, are forced to employ less rigorous methodological standards than those used by the best single-country surveys.

Sources of International Crime Data: Official Data

1. The International Police Organization (Interpol)

   • Interpol has collected police and judicial statistics from member countries since 1950 (see http://www.interpol.int/). The organization sends a standard form to each nation. Crime statistics from 181 member countries are collected and published in four languages (Arabic, English, French, and Spanish) annually in the organization's publication entitled *International Crime Statistics* (Interpol, 2003).

   • The Interpol database contains information on (1) the volume of crime; (2) offender information in general "number" categories of crime; (3) and other information related to offenders, such as total number, and percentage of known female or youth offenders. The uses of these data are limited because they are not checked for validity. The data reflect differences in legal definitions of offenses and statistical methods employed by individual member countries.

2. The UN survey of crime trends and operations of criminal justice systems (UNCJS)

   • The UN Center for International Crime Prevention (CICP) has conducted the UNCJS every 5 years since 1970 through 1994, and biannually through 2000, to its member countries (see http://www.unodc.org/unodc/crime_cicp_surveys. html). The 2001–02 represents the eighth wave of UNCJS data collection.

   • The main purpose of the UNCJS is to "provide an accounting of crime and the governmental response to it" and to improve the dissemination of qualitative and quantitative crime-related information to international researchers and policy makers, across national boundaries (UNODC, 2003). Unlike Interpol, which receives data from police organizations in member countries, the UN collects its information from Ministers of Foreign Affairs, and other government respondents or institutions.

   • Crime counts are collected for (1) items related to intentional and nonintentional homicide, (2) assault, (3) rape, (4) robbery, (5) theft, (6) burglary, (7) fraud, (8) embezzlement, (9) drug-related offenses, and (10) bribery crimes. Information on the number of crimes recorded by police, and demographic characteristics of those arrested are also provided. Once collected, the information is validated. A standard definition for each crime is provided to each participating country and any discrepancies between national definitions and those of the UN are noted (see UNODC, 2003).

3. World Health Organization (WHO)

   • The WHO collects national mortality data from 192 member countries (see http://www.who.int/en/). This information has been published regularly in its *World Health Statistics Annual*. As of July 2000, mortality statistics are provided online, on the WHO web site.

   • One of the external causes of death recorded by national vital statistics agencies is "homicide and injury purposely inflicted by other persons"

(WHO, 2003). Detailed information is collected about the specific cause of death (e.g., diseases, accidents, suicide, and self-inflicted injuries, homicides, etc.) as well as the age category (e.g., less than 1 year of age, 1–4 years, 5–14, 15–24, etc.) and sex of the victim (see WHO, 2003).

Sources of International Crime Data: Victimization Data

The International Victimization Survey was initiated in 1987 by the Ministry of Justice of the Netherlands, and was further developed with the help of the UN Interregional Crime and Justice Research Institute (UNICRI). The ICVS is a global project that covers all continents. The survey provides the comparative measure of crime at international level as it asks questions about information about the victims and crime incidents that are not asked in other data sources. The first ICVS was completed in 1989 and covered 15 industrialized countries and two cities, Surabaja (Indonesia) and Warsaw (Poland) (van Kesteren, Mayhew, and Nieuwbeerta, 2000). To date, 24 industrial nations and 46 cities in developing countries and countries in transition, took part in the project (van Kesteren et al., 2000).

In the developed countries, nationwide samples are drawn, and computer-assisted interviews are employed to collect the data. In developing countries and countries in transition, the samples are drawn from the largest city (usually the capital city) and the respondents are picked through random walk techniques, and are interviewed face to face. The sample size differs from country to country, but typically consists of at least 1000 persons.

The survey asks one respondent from each sampled household about (1) household victimization and (2) own personal victimization, experienced in a 5-year period. Household victimization includes theft of and from cars, car vandalism, theft of motorcycles or bicycles, and burglary. Personal victimization includes robbery, theft of personal property, sexual incidents and assaults, and assaults with or without threats or force.

Similar to national victimization surveys, when victimization is reported to the interviewer, the respondents are asked more detailed questions about the incident. Demographic information and attitudes about crime, sentencing, and police are also elicited from all respondents.

Sources of International Crime Data: Self-Report Data

Unlike police recorded crime data or estimates of crime from victimization surveys, self-report data convey information about offenders, as well as victimless crimes. These surveys ask respondents about their own criminal behavior, and are especially useful in gathering information about juvenile populations.

Starting in the early 1990s, a series of self-reported delinquency studies that used a common instrument was conducted in several countries. The International Self-Report Delinquency (ISRD) study has been through one sweep, conducting self-report surveys among young males and females (ages 14–21) in 12 countries—11 European nations, one American state, and one region in New Zealand. Comparative analyses of data from 11 countries have been completed, and are soon to be published; New Zealand's and the Greek sample were excluded, as their data were not sufficiently comparable (see Junger-Tas and Ribeaud, 2003).

Random samples of young people aged 14–21, including both males and females, were drawn nationally, citywide, and within schools in the participant countries. A standardized instrument was developed to measure: (1) prevalence and frequency of delinquent behavior, (2) circumstances surrounding the event, (3) reactions of the third parties, including police, (4) social and demographic measures, and (5) theoretical variables pertaining to social control theory. Data collection was initiated in 1992, using both face-to-face interviews and self-administered questionnaires (Junger-Tas, Terlouw, and Klein, 1994).

The ISRD study gathered information about respondents and their delinquent behavior, as well as about their family, school, and peers. Several Central and Eastern European countries in transition have adopted and are currently using the survey instrument (Neapolitan, 1997 cited in Howard; Newman and Pridemore, 2000). The self-report method appears to be both reliable and valid; it is a useful and important tool for measuring criminal behavior and testing theory (Thornberry and Krohn, 2002).

Sources of International Crime Data: Problems of Interpretation

Comparing crime statistics cross-nationally, whether official figures or victimization and self-report data are employed, is a challenging task. In addition to the limitations inherent in official and unofficial crime data, comparative research is fraught with unique problems including: (1) the lack of standardized definitions of crime across and within countries; (2) different police recording and public reporting practices; (3) incomplete statistics or data that cannot be disaggregated; (4) sampling problems such as coverage; (5) problems that arise when data collection instruments are translated into different languages; and (6) other methodological problems inherent in victimization or self-report offending surveys, such as memory decay or interviewer bias.

As to standardized definitions of different types of crime, the legal definition of the same type of crime may vary across nations (European Sourcebook of Crime and Criminal Justice Statistics, 2003, Appendix II). Even across different jurisdictions within a given country in the case of federal systems, such as the U.S. with its 50 states, there are different legal definitions of the same crime (e.g., stalking). Counting crime varies widely across individual countries, as no international set of standards in defining crime has been developed yet (see Alvazzi del Frate, Hatalak, and Zvekic, 2000). When homicide figures are compared internationally, wide differences could be observed depending on the source that was used (e.g., the UN, Interpol, WHO). Although all three sources collect the same data from individual nations, without editing the information beyond checking it for anomalies, the homicide figures they report vary significantly for many countries.

Comparing cross-national data becomes problematic, as certain offenses are country specific. Some countries have crimes that others do not (e.g., drug possession). Even when nations do share the same offense, what constitutes a typical robbery in England, for example, might not, conceptually, be the same as a robbery in the U.S. For example, approximately half of robberies that occurred in the U.S. between 1993 and 2001 involved a firearm (Perkins, 2003). By contrast, firearms were used in only 4.5% of robberies that took place in England and Wales during 2001–02, and this figure is similar to the previous 5 years (Flood-Page and Taylor, 2003). As much as one would like to think that basic concepts, such as robbery or burglary, are understood roughly similarly everywhere, subtle differences, in the least, in how crimes are legally defined or perceived worldwide, will affect the results of cross-national comparisons.

Another set of problems with international crime data relates to differences in police recording and public reporting practices. It has been widely accepted that police recorded statistics are not a true indicator for the amount of crime that takes place in a given country. Many crimes go unreported, or the police may decide not to record certain offenses until they can also record that they have solved them. Cross-national comparisons using police data are not always valid for a variety of reasons that include different counting procedures, the varied size and structure of the police force, differences in standards and administrative practices, and level of professionalism and efficiency.

The difference in public reporting further impacts cross-national comparisons. Research has shown that crime reporting to the police depends on cultural,

social, political, and economic factors. For example, in countries with developed telecommunication systems, the public will report more crime; where telephones are less common, however, less crime will be reported.

One other important difficulty in interpreting international data pertains to the samples drawn, their size, and structure. Cross-national research is limited to working with a convenience sample—data that reflect only the countries that collect and report national crime statistics to international organizations. It is very possible that the sample of countries used will impact on the findings of comparative research. For example, the ICVS covers a limited number of countries. The reliability of the ICVS data becomes questionable when observations about a limited sample, often drawn from the largest city of a given country, are generalized to the population of that entire nation and subsequently used in cross-national comparisons. Pertaining to sample size, Killias (1990) suggested that samples of at least 5000 persons should be employed in most European countries, owing to their relatively low victimization rates. The ICVS sample sizes are on average 2000 persons, with some samples as low as 700 persons (i.e., Macedonia, in 1996).

When data collection instruments are translated from English into different languages, the validity and reliability of the results might be further threatened. Very little attention has been paid to the issue of the quality of translation in conducting comparative research. Data that cannot be disaggregated, or incomplete data, represent yet other limitations for cross-national comparisons. Data are often unavailable for all crimes, all countries, over an extended period.

Finally, there are also other methodological problems that affect this type of data-gathering effort that extend from single country research, such as difficulties associated with asking delicate questions, respondent memory decay, telescoping, and interviewer bias. Respondents' willingness to report sexual victimization, for example, is a sensitive issue, and this will probably vary across nations, in function of their cultural norms. Memory decay and telescoping are also problematic with victimization and self-reported data. For example, the ICVS interviews ask people to remember victimization that occurred over a period of 1–5 years. These reports depend on the respondents' ability to remember, perceive, and reconstruct crime events. Problems of interviewer bias, and cultural differences in the ways people convey information, are also inevitable whenever interviews are conducted.

International crime and criminal justice measurement is one of the major challenges to the discipline in the 21st century. There is an increasing need for valid and reliable data at the international level, both for the purpose of monitoring differences in crime rates and in the operation of criminal justice systems as well as for the purpose of theoretical development and hypothesis testing. At the moment, researchers and policymakers must be mindful in their selection of data sources and in the interpretation of the data used.

ELENA LICU, ROSEMARY BARBERET, AND BONNIE S. FISHER

References and Further Reading

Alvazzi del Frate, A., Hatalak, O., and Zvekic, (Eds.) 2000. *Surveying Crime: A Global Perspective*. Roma: Istituto Nazionale di Statistica (ISTAT).

Barclay, G.C. 2003. *Global Crime Trends*. Paper presented at the United Nations Expert Meeting on the World Crime and Justice Report, 2004-2005. Turin, Italy, 26–28 June.

European Sourcebook of Crime and Criminal Justice Statistics. 2003. *Appendix II: Offence Definitions*. Available at http://www. europeansourcebook.org/esb/chapter_0/app2.pdf. Retrieved on October 21, 2003 from the World Wide Web.

Flood-Page, C. and Taylor, J. 2003. *Crime in England and Wales 2001/2002: Supplementary Volume*. Measuring Crime Programme: Home Office, RDS. Available at http://www. homeoffice.gov.uk/rds/pdfs2/hosb103.pdf. Retrieved on October 21, 2003 from the World Wide Web.

Howard, G.J., Newman, G., and Pridemore, W.A. 2000. Theory, method, and data in comparative criminology. *Criminal Justice: Measurement and Analysis of Crime and Justice* 4: 139–211. Available at http://www.ojp.usdoj.gov/nij/ criminal_justice2000/vol4_2000.html. Retrieved on 25 September 25, 2003 from the World Wide Web.Junger-Tas, J. and Ribeaud, D. 2003. The international self-report delinquency study. *Newsletter of the European Society of Criminology*. 18–20 March.

Junger-Tas, J., Terlouw, G.J. and Klein, M.W. 1994. *Delinquent Behavior among Young People in the Western World*. Amsterdam: Kugler Publications.

Killias, M. 1990. New methodological perspectives for victimization surveys: The potential of computer assisted telephone surveys and some related innovations. *International Review of Victimology* 1:153–167.

Killias, M. and Rau, W. 2000. The European sourcebook of crime and criminal justice statistics: A new tool in assessing crime and policy issues in comparative and empirical perspective. *European Journal on Criminal Policy and Research* 8:3–12.

Newman, G. (Ed.) 1999. *Global Report on Crime and Justice*. New York, NY: Oxford University Press.

Perkins, C. 2003. *Weapon Use and Violent Crime: National Crime Victimization Survey, 1993–2001*. NCJ 194820. Washington, DC: U.S. Department of Justice, Bureau of Justice Statistics. Available at http://www.ojp.usdoj.gov/bjs/pub/pdf/wuvc01.pdf. Retrieved on October 21, 2003 from the World Wide Web.

Statistics South Africa. 1998. *Victims of Crime Survey*. Available at http://www.statssa.gov.za. Retrieved on October 20, 2003 from the World Wide Web.

The European Opinion Research Group (EORG). 2003. *Public Safety, Exposure to Drug-Related Problems and Crime: Public Opinion Survey*. Available at http://europa.eu.int/comm/justice_home/eucpn/docs/eurobarometer. 20052003.pdf. Retrieved on October 20, 2003 from the World Wide Web.

The European Institute for Crime Prevention and Control (HEUNI). 2003. *About Us*. Available at http://www.heuni. fi/12441.htm. Retrieved on October 20, 2003 from the World Wide Web.

The International Police Organization (Interpol). 2003. *The Official Interpol Site*. Available at http://www.interpol.int. Accessed on October 20, 2003 from the World Wide Web.

The United Nations Asia and Far East Institute for the Prevention of Crime and the Treatment of Offenders (UNAFEI). 2003. *History*. Available at http://www.unafei.or.jp/english/aboutus/history.html. Retrieved on October 20, 2003 from the World Wide Web. The United Nations Latin American Institute for the Prevention of Crime and the Treatment of Offenders (ILANUD). 2003. *ILANUD Activities in 2002 and 2003 Work Programme*. Available at http://www.ilanud.or.cr/InformeING2002.doc. Retrieved on October 20, 2003 from the World Wide Web.

The United Nations African Institute for the Prevention of Crime and the Treatment of Offenders (UNAFRI). 2003. *About UNAFRI*. Available at http://www.unafri.or.ug/index.php?option=displaypage&Itemid=85&op=page&SubMenu=85. Retrieved on October 20, 2003 from the World Wide Web.

Thornberry, T.P. and Krohn, M.D. 2002. *Comparison of Self-Report and Official Data for Measuring Crime*. Measurement Problems in Criminal Justice Research: Workshop Summary. Available at http://www.nap.edu/openbook/0309086353/html/43.html. Retrieved on October 21, 2003 from the World Wide Web.

United Nations Office on Drugs and Crime (UNODC). 2003. *The Seventh United Nations Survey on Crime Trends and the Operations of Criminal Justice Systems (1998–2000)*. Available at http://www.unodc.org/unodc/ crime_cicp_survey_seventh.html. Retrieved on October 20, 2003 from the World Wide Web.

United Nations Note. 1970. Available at http://www.unafei.or.jp/english/aboutus/agreement.html. Retrieved on October 20, 2003 from the World Wide Web.

van Kesteren, J. 2003. *Victimisation*. Paper presented at the United Nations Expert Meeting on the World Crime and Justice Report, 2004–2005. Turin, Italy, 26–28 June.

van Kesteren, J., Mayhew, P., and Nieuwbeerta, P. 2000. *Criminal Victimisation in Seventeen Industrialised Countries: Key-findings from the 2000 International Crime Victims Survey*. The Hague, Ministry of Justice: WODC. Available at http://www.unicri.it/icvs/publications/pdf_files/key2000i/index.htm. Retrieved on October 20, 2003 from the World Wide Web.

World Health Organization (WHO). 2003. *WHO Mortality Database*. Available at http://www3.who.int/whosis/menu.cfm?path=whosis,mort&language=english. Accessed on October 20, 2003 from the World Wide Web.

See also **International Crime Statistics: Juvenile Delinquency and Youth Crime; International Crime Trends**

International Crime Statistics: Juvenile Delinquency and Youth Crime

The terms "juvenile delinquency" and "youth crime" are used interchangeably in the criminological and criminal justice literature although they have different definitions. Juvenile delinquency is the more traditional term and includes acts considered criminal as well as other kinds of youthful antisocial behavior, such as truancy, bullying, and running away from home. Youth crime is a term of more recent usage and refers to only acts considered criminal committed by young people (Muncie, 1999, 37–38). International youth crime has received less attention by criminologists than international adult crime statistics, although it is widely acknowledged that young people, particularly young males, commit a disproportionate amount of crime.

Measurement Issues

Juvenile delinquency and youth crime statistics present their own validity and reliability problems, in addition to those that are common to international crime statistics (see International Crime Statistics: Data Sources and Problems of Interpretation, this volume). Overall, these problems make it very difficult to compare juvenile delinquency and youth crime rates cross-nationally.

The first problem inherent in the juvenile delinquency and youth crime rate data is the difference across nations in ages of criminal responsibility. This issue involves both a minimum age (at which a young person is responsible for a crime as a minor) and a maximum age (at which a young person may be, or must be, tried as an adult).

In nations with federal systems, such as Australia, this age range can vary within the country. It can also vary in certain countries according to the offense. Although the majority of countries attribute full adult responsibility to age 18 and over, ranging from 15 (St. Vincent) to 21 (Hong Kong), minimum age limits are much more variable, ranging from 6 (Sri Lanka) to under 21 (Indonesia) (Newman, 1999, 79). This makes comparisons of official statistics difficult, as some countries, because of age limits, count much more—or less—crime as committed by minors as opposed to adults.

The difficulty can be resolved to some extent if countries can disaggregate their statistics by age for the purpose of international comparison. To obtain official measures of youth crime and victimization, one must be able to access either statistics of youthful offenders (those detected by the authorities) or statistics of youthful victims reporting crimes. This is so for two reasons. First, official statistics that are event-based (that count the number of crimes) rarely note the age of the offender as reported by the victim, unless the offender has been arrested. Second, official statistics do not always report the age of the victim. As such, much crime committed or experienced by young people is hidden in official crime statistics.

The age range issue is much less problematic when surveys are used as the method to obtain data, as survey designers can limit the sample of young people to be interviewed to an agreed-upon age range. This agreed-upon age range is not common to all studies, however. The International Self-Report Delinquency (ISRD) included a sample of young people aged between 14 and 21 years old in 13 western countries (Junger-Tas, Terlouw, and Klein, 1994). However, the most recent Youth Lifestyles Survey of the British Home Office (1998–99 sweep) included a nationally representative sample of young people aged between 12 and 30 years living in private households in England and Wales (http://www.homeoffice.gov.uk/rds/offendingyls.html). It is likely that the age range in future international self-report surveys may increase, given the interest of criminologists in examining precursor behavior to crime and desistence, as well as the acknowledgement that modern youth extends further beyond the typical "teenage" years.

The second problem is the variability in definitions of what constitutes a crime for minors. Countries vary in terms of what antisocial behavior may fall within the legal jurisdiction of their juvenile justice systems. Some may include acts that would be punishable as an adult, and others may include a wide range of antisocial behavior, such as running away from home, disobedience to parental authority, etc. Again, this is a problem with aggregated official statistics, and less of a problem with surveys, which can clearly delineate a list of behavior agreed by the research team or sponsoring agency that can be aggregated or disaggregated depending on whether one wishes to analyze criminal or antisocial behavior.

Sources of International Youth Crime Data: Official Data

The three major official sources of international crime statistics on juveniles are (1) International Police Organization (Interpol), (2) the World Health Organization (WHO), and (3) the UN Survey of Crime Trends and Operations of Criminal Justice Systems (UNCJS).

1. The International Police Organization (Interpol) collects information about juvenile offenders (http://www.interpol.int). "Persons responsible for offenses" are reported for each of the seven crime categories: murder, sex offenses (including rape), serious assault, all theft (including aggravated theft, robbery, and violent theft, breaking and entering, theft of motor cars, other thefts), fraud, counterfeit currency offences, and drug offenses. Total offenders are further disaggregated into three categories: percent juveniles, percent females, and percent aliens. Criteria for juvenile status are also presented for each country. For example, England and Wales reported that in 2001, 24% of offenders were juveniles (defined as 10–17-year olds). For the same year, Argentina reported that 17.87% of offenders were juveniles (defined as 16–18-year olds).

2. World Health Organization (WHO) collects detailed information about the specific cause of death (for our interests, Code E55, "homicide and injury purposefully inflicted by other persons") as well as the age category (e.g., less than 1 year of age, 1–4, 5–14, 15–24, etc.) and sex of the victim (http://www3.who.int/whosis/menu.cfm?path= whosis,mort&language=english). In 2000, an estimated 199,000 youth (ages 10–29) homicides occurred in the world. The rates vary greatly by region. In the higher income countries of Europe, parts of Asia and the Pacific, rates are low (0.9 per 100,000 aged 10–29), whereas in Africa and Latin America, rates are generally higher (17.6 per 100,000 aged 10–29 and 36.4 per 100,000 aged 10–29, respectively). Between 1984 and 1994, youth homicide rates increased in many parts of the world. Rates increased more for those young people aged 15–24 than those aged 10–14, and male rates rose more than female rates. Rates increased most in developing and transitional countries (Krug, Dahlberg, Mercy, Zwi, and Lozano, 2002, 25–26).

These data reveal clear gender- and age-related patterns. The proportion of male and female victims of homicide is roughly equal up to 4 years of age (WHO, 2001). From 5 years onward, males begin to outnumber female homicide victims.

Although most infants and children are killed by older perpetrators, from 10 years of age onward, both victims and perpetrators of homicide tend to be of equivalent age groups (WHO, 2001).

3. The UN Survey of Crime Trends and Operations of Criminal Justice Systems (UNCJS) collects information on "persons brought into formal contact with the criminal justice system by sex and age" (http://www.unodc.org/pdf/crime/seventh_survey/7sv.pdf). It breaks down juvenile suspects into: total juveniles, juvenile female suspects, and juvenile male suspects. Each country is asked for its definition of juvenile and adult, and the responses are publicly available.

These official statistics on juvenile delinquency indicate that during the 1990s, with the exception of the U.S., youth crime increased in many nations around the world. Many of the criminal offenses committed by young persons are drug and alcohol related. In Western Europe, between mid-1980s and the late 1990s, arrests of juvenile delinquents and underage offenders rose on average by 50%. In England and Wales, for example, around 580 out of 100,000 young offenders aged 14–16 years were either "convicted or cautioned" by the police for violent crimes in 1994. In Western Germany in 1995, the number of 14–18-year olds suspected of violent crime was about 760 per 100,000. Nonviolent crimes committed by young people also increased dramatically. For example, property crimes committed by Italian youth (ages 14–17) more than doubled between 1986 and 1993 (Pfeiffer, 1998).

Although nations with more urbanized populations have higher registered crime rates than those where rural lifestyles and communities are predominant, countries in transition have also experienced a dramatic increase in delinquency rates during the 1990s. In many Eastern European countries, for example, juvenile crime increased by more than 30% since 1995. Juvenile delinquency in the Eastern European region is most often linked to high unemployment of both young people and their parents, poverty in the family, and the inability of overworked parents to successfully monitor children (Salagaev, 2003).

When disaggregating available delinquency and youth crime data (police records) by gender, the crime rates of male juvenile and young adult offenders are more than double compared to those of females. And conviction rates for male youths are six or seven times higher. Overall, the data clearly suggest that, throughout the world, more young men than women are involved in violent or criminal behavior (Salagaev, 2003).

Although many of the causes or correlates for juvenile delinquency and crime are universal, several aspects related to youth crime vary across different cultures and regions of the world. In Africa, for example, delinquency is primarily attributed to "hunger, poverty, malnutrition and unemployment, which are linked to the marginalization of juveniles in the already severely disadvantaged segments of society" (Salagaev, 2003, 10). Juvenile crime and delinquency are on the rise. This trend is related to the dramatic changes Africa has experienced in recent decades in the social, political, and economic spheres. The main offenses committed by young Africans during the 1990s are theft, robbery, smuggling, prostitution, drug use, and drug trafficking (UN, Centre for Social Development and Humanitarian Affairs, 1993).

In Asian countries, juvenile crime and delinquency are primarily urban phenomena (Salagaev, 2003). Youth violence is also on the rise throughout this region. An increase in both drug-related offenses and female juvenile delinquency represent the main trends for the 1990s (UN, Centre for Social Development and Humanitarian Affairs, 1993).

In Latin America, juvenile delinquency is often associated with homelessness among both children and adolescents. The youth have been the hardest hit by the economic crisis in the region, which resulted in significantly high unemployment rates affecting this age group (Salagaev, 2003).

In the Arab world, problems related to juvenile delinquency differ across nations. In more prosperous countries, delinquency may occur as a result of migrants seeking employment, continued urbanization, sudden prosperity, rapid changes in the economy, and increased heterogeneity among individuals (Salagaev, 2003).

Sources of International Youth Crime Data: Survey-Based Crime Statistics

Survey-based crime statistics, such as the International Crime Victimization Survey (ICVS) and the International Self-Report Delinquency (ISRD) study, are another important source for international crime statistics on juvenile delinquency and youth crime. Victimization surveys are useful in finding out about crimes experienced by people that may or may not have been reported to officials. Self-report surveys ask young people about their own antisocial or offending behavior that may or may not have come to the attention of the authorities. The self-report method may be one of the more valid and reliable ways of obtaining international statistics in juvenile delinquency. Self-report surveys elicit information confidentially from samples of young people. These surveys establish comparable age limits for the sample and definitions for offenses or antisocial behavior within and across countries, and include a host of explanatory variables that aid researchers in theory development and hypothesis testing.

1. International Crime Victimization Survey (ICVS)
   • The ICVS includes persons aged 16 or over. Victims are not questioned as to the age of the perpetrator. As such, the ICVS can only provide estimates of the extent of victimization among young people aged 16 years onward. The ICVS covers crimes against property (car thefts, burglaries, and attempts and petty crimes), contact crimes (robberies, assaults, and threats) and sexual incidents (women only). Not surprisingly, young people (aged 16–24) have the highest victimization rates in all categories. Overall, for victimization that occurred in 1999 in 16 countries, 32% of young people age 16–24 were victimized, compared to 22.9% of those aged 22–54 and 13.1% of those aged 55 or older (van Kesteren et al, 2000, 55).

2. The International Self-Report Delinquency (ISRD) Study
   • To date, the ISRD study is the only one of its kind that exists. A common instrument was developed and used in five country samples (England and Wales, the Netherlands, Spain, Switzerland, Portugal) and eight city samples (Mannheim, Germany; Belfast, North Ireland; Liege, Belgium; Helsinki, Finland; Turin, Messina and Siena, Italy; Athens, Greece; Dunedin, New Zealand; Omaha, Nebraska, USA) in the early 1990s. A second sweep of the ISRD is in the planning stages.
   • The ISRD includes a sample of young men and women aged 14–21 years old. Samples of varying size were drawn nationally, citywide, and within schools in the participant countries. The survey was administered either face to face or self-administered. Each country that participated had to secure a funding source, which accounts for the lack of uniformity in the sampling frame and size.

The questionnaire was translated into the languages of the countries participating in the study, but had a large core element to which national researchers could add their own questions. The core included measures of the prevalence and frequency of delinquent behavior, circumstances surrounding the event, reactions of the third parties, including police, social and demographic measures, and theoretical variables pertaining to social control theory. Types of delinquent behavior included were property offenses (theft, purse snatching, pickpocketing, burglary, buying and selling stolen goods), violence against objects (graffiti and vandalism), violence against persons (carrying a weapon, injuring with a weapon, threats, assaults, arson, engaging in riots), drug offenses (soft and hard drug use and sale), youth-related offenses (fare dodging and driving without a license) and problem behavior (truancy, running away, and alcohol use). Data were entered at the national level, and then sent to the coordinating body at the Dutch Ministry of Justice who generated a combined dataset.

The ISRD results overall suggest that self-reported offending rates are broadly similar, except for drug use, which did not seem to have penetrated as much to Southern Europe as to Northern Europe. The correlates of self-reported offending are very similar across countries. Girls are much less delinquent than boys, the peak age of offending is 16–17 years, there is little relationship between educational level and offending, or between socioeconomic status and offending. Strong parental supervision and liking school are factors related to less participation in self-reported offending (Junger-Tas, Terlouw, and Klein, 1994, 370–379).

International Juvenile Delinquency Studies

Statistics on juvenile delinquency and youth crime are also available through smaller scale published research that is conducted nationally or cross-nationally. First, there are incipient efforts to put together international working groups of the researchers who are involved in longitudinal youth studies within one country. Second, there is a longstanding tradition in criminology of conducting single country or comparative research in juvenile delinquency. This research supplements some of the gaps in international statistics available, as well as supplying the discipline with important theoretical inroads.

1. Longitudinal Youth Studies

• There are a growing number of single country longitudinal self-report studies of juvenile delinquency and youth crime, in such countries as England, (Farrington, 1995), the U.S. (http://ojjdp. ncjrs.org/ccd/ index.html), New Zealand (Moffitt, 1993), Scotland (Smith and McVie, 2003), and Canada (Janosz, LeBlanc, Boulerice, and Tremblay, 2000). To date, these studies have all been conducted with little regard for the cultural differences inherent in them, but their growing number shows that comparative analyses are possible and fruitful, despite differences in sampling, questionnaire design and time frames (see for example, International Collaborative Studies, http://www.scopic.ac.uk/studies.htm; Broidy, Nagin, Tremblay, Brame, Dodge, Fergusson, Horwood, Loeber, Laird, Lynam, Moffitt, Bates, Pettit, and Vitaro, in press).

2. Comparative Studies

• Small scale comparative studies are another source of statistics on juvenile delinquency and youth crime. They range from single country studies that are implicitly comparative, to explicitly comparative studies that examine juvenile delinquency in two or more countries. These studies often combine sources of data such as self-report data and official statistics, and usually have a strong theoretical focus. There is a longstanding tradition of this kind of research in criminology (see for example, Rosenquist and Megargee's study of psychological and sociological variables among Anglo-Americans, Mexican-Americans, and Mexican Nationals (1969); DeFleur's analysis of strain theory in Argentina (1970); Hartjen and Kethineni's, 1996 study of control theory in India and the U.S.; Finckenauer's 1995 study of legal socialization of Russian and American youths; Vazsonyi et al.'s test of a general theory of crime (2001) and routine activities theory (2002) with samples of American, Dutch, Hungarian and Swiss youth; and Friday, Ren, Weitekamp, Kerner and Taylor's analysis of social integration using Wolfgang's original 1973 Chinese cohort data (in press)).

Implications

Future research as to the extent of international youth crime should be directed at improving the validity and reliability of these measures, with attention given to the comparability of these statistics across countries. Given the difficulties in comparing official statistics, as well as the positive results achieved when using the self-report method with young people, it may be beneficial in the future to rely more extensively on the self-report method when gathering youth crime statistics and conducting research on juvenile delinquency and crime. In addition, future research should study both the offending of young people as well as their victimization.

ROSEMARY BARBERET, ELENA LICU, AND BONNIE S. FISHER

References and Further Reading

Broidy, L.M., Nagin, D.S., Tremblay, R.E., Brame, B., Dodge, K., Fergusson, D., Horwood, J., Loeber, R., Laird, R., Lynam, D., Moffitt, T., Bates, J.E., Pettit, G.S., and Vitaro, F. (in press). Developmental trajectories of childhood disruptive behaviors and adolescent delinquency: A six site, cross national study. *Developmental Psychology.*

DeFleur, L.B. 1979. *Delinquency in Argentina: A Study of Córdoba's Youth.* Washington State University Press.

Farrington, D. 1995. The development of offending and antisocial behaviour from childhood: Key findings from the Cambridge Study in delinquency development. *Journal of Child Psychology and Psychiatry* 36:929–64.

Finckenauer, J.O. 1995. *Russian Youth: Law Deviance and the Pursuit of Freedom.* New Brunswick, NJ: Transaction Publishing.

Friday, P.C., Ren, X., Weitekamp, E., Kerner, H-J., and Taylor, T. (in press) A Chinese birth cohort: Theoretical implications. *Journal of Research in Crime and Delinquency.*

Hartjen, C.A. and Kethineni, S. 1996. *Comparative Delinquency: India and the United States.* New York, NY: Garland Publishing.

Home Office, Research Development Statistics. 2004. *Youth Lifestyles Survey.* Available at http://www.homeoffice.gov.uk/rds/offendingyls.html. Accessed on January 5, 2004 from the World Wide Web. The International Police Organization (Interpol). 2003. *The Official Interpol Site.* Available at http://www.interpol.int. Accessed on October 20, 2003 from the World Wide Web.

Janosz, M., LeBlanc, M., Boulerice, B., and Tremblay, R.E. 2000. Predicting different types of school dropouts: A typological approach on two longitudinal samples. *Journal of Educational Psychology* 92 (1):171–190.

Junger-Tas, J., Terlouw, G.J., and Klein, M.W. 1994. *Delinquent Behavior among Young People in the Western World.* Amsterdam: Kugler Publications.

Krug, É.G., Linda, L.D., Mercy, J.A., Anthony, B.Z. and Rafael, L. (Eds.) 2002. *World Report on Violence and Health.* Geneva: World Health Organization.

Moffitt, T.E. 1993. Adolescence-limited and life-course-persistent antisocial behavior: A developmental taxonomy. *Psychological Review*, 100:674–701.

Muncie, J. 1999. *Youth and Crime: A Critical Introduction.* London, UK: Sage.

Newman, G. (Ed.). 1999. *Global Report on Crime and Justice.* New York, NY: Oxford University Press.

Office of Juvenile Justice and Delinquency Prevention. 2004. Causes and Correlates of Delinquency Program. Available at http://ojjdp.ncjrs.org/ccd/index.html. Accessed on January 2, 2004 from the World Wide Web.

Pfeiffer, C. 1998. *Trends in Juvenile Violence in European Countries.* Washington, DC: U.S. Department of Justice, NIJ. Available at http://www.ncjrs.org/pdffiles/fs000202.pdf. Accessed on January 4, 2004 from the World Wide Web.

Rosenquist, C.M. and Megargee, E.I. 1969. *Delinquency in Three Cultures.* Austin, TX: University of Texas Press.

Salagaev, A. 2003. Juvenile Delinquency. In *World Youth Report 2003.* Report of the Secretary-General (document E/CN.5/2003/4): The United Nations. Available at http://www.un.org/esa/socdev/unyin/wyr/index.html. Accessed on January 4, 2004 from the World Wide Web.

Social Contexts of Pathways in Crime (SCoPiC), the Economic and Social Research Council (ESRC) Cambridge Network. 2004. *The Studies.* Available at http://www.scopic.ac.uk/studies.htm. Accessed on January 5, 2004 from the World Wide Web.

Smith, D.J. and McVie, S. 2003. Theory and method in the Edinburgh study of youth transitions and crime, *British Journal of Criminology* 43:169–195.

United Nations, Centre for Social Development and Humanitarian Affairs. 1993. *The Global Situation of Youth in the 1990s: Trends and Prospects.* New York, NY: UN, ST/CSDHA/21.

United Nations Office on Drugs and Crime (UNODC). 2003. *The Seventh United Nations Survey on Crime Trends and the Operations of Criminal Justice Systems (1998–2000).* Available at http://www.unodc.org/unodc/crime_cicp_survey_seventh.html. Accessed on October 20, 2003 from the World Wide Web.

van Kesteren, J., Mayhew, P., and Nieuwbeerta, P. 2000. *Criminal Victimisation in Seventeen Industrialised Countries: Key-findings from the 2000 International Crime Victims Survey.* The Hague, Ministry of Justice: WODC. Available at http://www.unicri.it/icvs/publications/pdf_files/key2000i/index.htm. Accessed on October 20, 2003 from the World Wide Web.

Vazsonyi, A.T., Pickering, L.E., Junger, M. and Hessing, D. 2001. An empirical test of a general theory of crime: A four-nation comparative study of self-control and the prediction of violence. *Journal of Research in Crime and Delinquency.* 38,2:91–131.

Vazsonyi, A.T., Pickering, L.E., Belliston, L.M., Hessing D., and Junger, M. 2002. Routine activities and deviant behaviors: American, Dutch, Hungarian and Swiss Youth. *Journal of Quantitative Criminology.* 18,4:397–422.

World Health Organization (WHO), Department of Injuries and Violence Prevention, Noncommunicable Diseases and Mental Health. 2001. *Prevention of Child Abuse and Neglect: Making the Links between Human Rights and Public Health.* Submission from the WHO to the Committee on the Rights of the Child, September 28, 2001, Geneva, Switzerland. Available at http://www.crin.org/docs/resources/treaties/crc.28/WHO1.pdf. Accessed on January 3, 2004 from the World Wide Web.

World Health Organization (WHO). 2003. *WHO Mortality Database.* Available at http://www3.who.int/whosis/menu.cfm?path=whosis,mort&language=english. Accessed on January 5, 2004 from the World Wide Web.

See also **Juvenile Delinquency and Youth Crime throughout History; Juvenile Delinquency: Extent, Correlates, and Trends**

International Crime Trends

Whether measured by official crime statistics (crimes known to and recorded by the authorities), victimization or self-report offending data, international crime rates are not static from year to year. Macro-level researchers compare rates of a single set of offenses (for example, homicides, assaults, or thefts) longitudinally, typically for several time periods (for example, months or years), within individual countries. Many then compare these crime rate trends cross-nationally and cross-regions of the world (see LaFree, 1999; Newman, 1999; Van Kesteren, Mayhew, and Nieuwbeerta, 2000).

Sources of International Crime Trend Data

Among the most important organizations that have been collecting and publishing international official crime and criminal statistics over the years are the UN, the World Health Organization (WHO), and the International Police Organization (Interpol). These three data sources are reviewed elsewhere (see International Crime Statistics: Data Sources and Problems of Interpretation, this volume). The UN has collected crime counts for specific categories of offenses from member countries since 1970 (see http://www.unodc.org/unodc/crime_cicp_surveys.html). The WHO has gathered annual national mortality data from participating countries since 1951 (see http://www.who.int/en/). Similarly, the Interpol has collected police and judicial statistics from member countries since 1950 (see http://www.interpol.int/).

The International Crime Victimization Survey (ICVS) is another source of information on crime and victimization trends cross nationally. The ICVS, however, offers a more limited use for longitudinal analyses. Only four ICVS sweeps (1989, 1992, 1996, and 2000) have been conducted to date.

International Crime Trends

International Crime Victimization Survey Data

Van Kesteren, et al. (2000) summarized the results from four sweeps of the ICVS data. In general, the ICVS data suggest that crime increased between 1988 and 1991, remained steady or fell in 1995, to fall back once again in 1999. This pattern seems to be the dominant trend in several European countries.

The crime rate trend in North America, however, is different from that in Europe. The ICVS victimization rates in the U.S. have fallen consistently since 1988. In Canada, crime has increased slightly in 1991, but went down in both 1995 and 1999. In the three European countries that took part in all four ICVS sweeps (England and Wales, The Netherlands, and Finland), crime levels in 1999 were higher than in 1988, although victimization risks were falling in 1999. And compared with 1991, victimization risks in 1999 fell more in North America than in five of the seven European nations experiencing decreases (Sweden and Poland were the exceptions during 1995 and 1999).

There is much variation in ICVS crime rates within one country across years. For example, in France, Scotland, and Switzerland the ICVS rates rose from 1988 to 1995, with Switzerland experiencing the largest increase. In Sweden between 1991 and 1995 the ICVS rates significantly increased. The ICVS rates in France, The Netherlands, and Switzerland significantly decreased during 1995–1999.

Variation in violence (robberies, assaults and sexual incidents such as sexual assault, rape, and indecent assault) and property (burglaries, car-related crimes, and thefts of bicycles and motorcycles) crime are also evident. Between 1988 and 1991, both violence and property offenses increased in all seven countries (England and Wales, The Netherlands, Finland, Australia, Canada, Belgium, and the U.S.) that participated in the ICVS during those years. Between 1991 and 1995, violence rose slightly more than property offences in a majority of the seven countries. Property offences have consistently fallen since 1995. The general pattern for violent crimes is represented by a sharp increase between 1988 and 1999, with the exception of two countries, Poland and the U.S., where violence decreased significantly during this time (see Lamon, 2002).

The UN Survey of Crime Trends and Operation of Criminal Justice Systems Data

The UN Survey of Crime Trends and Operation of Criminal Justice Systems (UNCJS) data, representing police records of crime, suggests the following general crime patterns during the 1990s. On average, crime has continued to rise during the 1990s, following a similar course from the previous decade. Reported crime rates varied significantly by country, for all offense categories (homicide, assault, rape, robbery, theft, burglary, fraud, embezzlement, drug-related offenses, and bribery crimes). Arab nations reported, in general, very low rates for almost all types of crime. The most commonly reported crimes were theft and burglary, violent offenses such as, homicide, assault, and robbery representing around 10–15% all reported crime. Theft rates were higher for industrialized countries than less developed countries. Finally, although most cities show similar trends for homicide and robbery rates, several Latin American cities, New York, and some cities in Northern Europe reported high rates of homicides. Some nations, such as Andorra and France, Albania, Belarus, and Macedonia, and England, Wales, and Scotland evidence a much higher proportion of nonfatal violence and homicide than others, such as Luxembourg, Norway, Sweden, Northern Ireland, and

Spain; Armenia and Poland; and the U.S. (see Aromaa and Leppa, 2003).

Homicides—the World Health Organization (WHO)

The WHO collects annual homicide victimization rates. LaFree and Drass (2001) assembled these annual rates beginning in 1955 until 1994. Thirty-four countries (including Finland and 25 other industrialized nations, three Latin American countries, four Eastern European countries, five countries from the Western Pacific region, and one from the African region) are included in their data set.

Because Finland has an exceptionally high rate of homicide compared to other Western European nations, they chose to examine Finnish homicide trends after World War II, and compare these to trends for other nations. LaFree and Drass estimated a total homicide rate for all the countries they had homicide trend data for ("world" homicide rate), except Finland. They then compared Finnish homicide rates to those of the "world" total. The total homicide rate for the "world" was rather low and flat during the 1950s and 1960s, it went up sharply starting in 1969, and it peaked around 1992, when it was 72% higher than at its lowest point, in 1963. The authors recognize, however, that this estimate of the "world" rates was inflated significantly by Mexico, Venezuela, and the U.S. because each of these countries has a relatively high homicide rate.

When compared to other European Union (EU) nation homicide rates, the Finnish trend was consistently higher. The same conclusion was drawn when the homicide rate trend for the Nordic countries (excluding Iceland, owing to its low rate of homicide), and the Finnish homicide rate trend were compared.

LaFree and Drass (2001) concluded that over time Finnish homicide rates are converging with rates for other Nordic countries, such as Denmark, Sweden, and Norway. One possible explanation they offered was that over time social, economic, and political predictors of homicide (such as economic inequality) are becoming more similar for those countries. As a result, the homicide rates of these countries are converging.

Explanations for International Crime Trends

Explaining why there are changes or no change in crime rates over time is one challenge faced by both researchers and policy makers. Researchers have attempted to account for such differences both over time within a country and between or among countries.

The earliest and most common theoretical perspective explored in cross-national studies, *modernization*

or *social disorganization theory,* originated with Durkheim's (1947) assessment of social modernization. According to this theory, crime occurs as a result of a social breakdown or disruption in normative order. Normative guidelines become ambiguous and traditional support mechanisms are disrupted (LaFree, 1999). Crime, thus, will more likely occur in societies that suffer rapid changes, where traditional social patterns are disrupted. Economic growth, urbanization, or changes from agricultural to industrial and service economies are related to these processes (Shelley, 1981). Tests of this theory have received mixed results (for a synthesis of research results, see Neuman and Berger, 1988).

Economic hardship, a second theoretical perspective used to explain cross-national crime trends, is the view that crime results from the stress caused by inequality, poverty, and unemployment. This perspective focuses on how economic conditions directly impact crime rates. The mechanism suggested here is that economic inequality causes alienation, despair, and aggression, which in turn, materialize in frequent conflicts, including criminal violence (Blau and Blau, 1982), or that it weakens the "moral authority of conventional society" (Chamlin and Cochran, forthcoming) a macro-social intervening process that directly influences violence. According to world system theory, the world market economy creates conditions of uneven development across time and between nations, with economically stronger nations exploiting weaker ones (Chirot and Hall, 1982), and subsequent effects on crime rates. Related, *economic variables,* low levels of unemployment and high economic growth in both North America and Western Europe, may "have depressed the levels of property crime by reducing the need for the proceeds of crime." (Field, 1990; cited in Lamon, 2002, 46). The trading value of some stolen goods (TVs, VCRs, and car stereos) has also declined as the real price of these items decreased (Van Kesteren et al., 2000).

Situational theories are linked to the work of Cohen and Felson (1979) and are primarily concerned with how changes in "routine activities" such as spending more time away from one's home, for example, heighten opportunities for certain types of crime. Routine activities theory predicts lower crime rates for societies with "active guardianship norms, decentralized populations, low levels of youth mobility and independence, and women engaged in homemaking roles rather than involved in the paid labor market" (LaFree, 1999, 140). Bennett (1991), Kick and LaFree (1985), and Gartner (1990) have tested this perspective with cross-national data. Killias and Aebi (2000) found that the differences in crime trends in Europe in the early 1990s, when compared to those from the U.S., were best explained by situational theory.

Finally, and perhaps most theoretically of all, changes in the legitimacy of social institutions of a given country could also explain changes in crime (Lamon, 2002). Using crime data that span five decades, LaFree (1998) suggested that social institutions are the key to understanding the U.S. crime wave. The postwar American crime boom occurred as a result of a crisis in institutional legitimacy characterized by growing political distrust, economic stress, and family disintegration. Racial minorities were particularly affected by these changes. As a result, American society began investing in the areas of criminal justice, education, and welfare. He concluded that the increased support for criminal justice and educational institutions, as well as the increase in economic well-being account for the decline in crime the U.S. has been experiencing during the 1990s.

Researchers have offered other plausible explanations for international crime trends (see Van Kesteren et al., 2000; Lamon, 2002). *Demographic factors* such as the general "aging" of the population in both Western Europe and North America, as well as the decline in the number of young males in the crime-prone age groups, influenced, to some extent, crime rate trends. The role of *drugs*, particularly the use of hard drugs and its relationship to offending, has been clearly attested. *Police performance* has improved significantly in many countries around the world, although many current policing strategies have been in place since the 1980s, when crime trends were less favorable. Changes in criminal justice and policing such as proactive policing, and the use of CCTV and forensics, to name a few, could explain changes in crime trends.

Limitations of International Crime Trend Data

Ideally, crime trend comparisons require analyses of multiple crime observations over time for each individual country, as well as availability of crime trend data for all countries of the world, whose trends are ultimately to be compared. Conducting longitudinal cross-national comparisons of crime rate trends across time is a challenging task for two major reasons. First, crime and criminal justice statistics have been collected internationally only recently, victimization data, in particular. Second, as it is the case in crime and criminal justice cross-national research, trend data are available primarily for industrialized countries with less developed countries often failing to report crime statistics to international organizations. And when they do choose to report, their figures have been deemed unreliable owing to questionable recording practices or incomplete registers (Gartner, 1990). Finally, some countries fail to report crime and criminal justice

statistics to international agencies on a consistent basis, across time. This leads to the exclusion of these countries from longitudinal cross-national analyses.

The two primary limitations of trend data mentioned above affect to a greater extent the victimization data collected by the ICVS, and to a lesser extent the official crime statistics collected and published by the UN, the WHO, and the Interpol, respectively. Cross-national victimization data are severely limited in terms of the number of years and countries that could be analyzed and compared. The ICVS allows crime rate estimates for a total of 4 years preceding each of the four surveys that have been conducted. Furthermore, only five countries have taken part in all four sweeps (England and Wales, Finland, the Netherlands, Canada, and the U.S.), and only 13 nations, all industrialized, have participated in the ICVS at least three times (see Van Kesteren et al., 2000; Lamon, 2002).

Unlike ICVS data, official crime and criminal justice statistics are more suitable for longitudinal comparative studies but may entail a sacrifice in validity (see International Crime Statistics: Data Sources and Problems of Interpretation, this volume). The UN has been collecting and disseminating crime and crime rates in member countries for over three decades, the WHO and the Interpol for five decades. These longitudinal data—homicides, violent offenses, and property crimes—however, are available for only a limited number of countries as it is up to each individual nation to report crime statistics to international organizations. Not every UN or Interpol member country reports crime statistics every year (see UNODC, 2003; Interpol, 2003). For example, in April 2001, the UN requested information for its seventh survey on crime trends and the operations of criminal justice systems from 203 nations. Only 82 nations responded, providing data for this UN survey (UNODC, 2003).

Some countries, such as South Africa, Japan, Poland, Russia, Finland, the Netherlands, Australia, and the U.S., did not report crimes to the Interpol in 1991. All these countries did, however, report crime statistics to the Interpol in either 1995 or 1999 (Interpol, 2003). Some countries fail to report statistics for certain crime categories in a given year. Spain, for example, did not report to the UN any burglaries for the years 1986, 1987, and 1990 (UNODC, 2003).

Among those who report crime statistics, there are countries that fail to do so in a consistent manner. The UN Center for International Crime Prevention (CICP), in charge of the UN Survey of Crime Trends and Operations of Criminal Justice Systems (UNCJS) data collection, records annually, among other categories, total "major" or aggravated thefts (rates per 100,000 population) for each participating country (UNODC, 2003). For instance, Norway reported crimes in this category between 1990 and 1994. This country reported no aggravated thefts for the years 1995–1997, but resumed reporting for the period between 1998 and 2000 (UNODC, 2003). Inconsistent reporting on the part of some countries leads researchers to discount these nations altogether when engaging in cross-national longitudinal comparisons.

Finally, some countries report only certain crime categories and not other crime categories. For example, in 1995, and again in 1999, South Africa reported to the UN thefts, burglaries, and assaults, but no robberies (UNODC, 2003). It is highly unlikely that indeed no robberies occurred in this country during these 2 years. All these specific limitations and other more general problems inherent in cross-national comparisons, which have been presented in detail elsewhere (see International Crime Statistics, Data Sources and Problems of Interpretation, in this volume), make it difficult to analyze differences in crime rates over time and to compare crime trends across nations. Despite the scarce and problematic trend data criminological cross-national research is faced with, information on international crime trends does exist and it warrants inspection.

Implications for Future Research Using International Crime Trends

International crime trend research is hampered by the discontinuity of data, missing data from a large number of countries, and a lack of national as well as international advocacy and coordination as to the need for investing in the gathering of good international trend data. Nevertheless, scrupulous researchers have been able to form a limited body of knowledge that reconciles data with explanations for parts of the world in the latter half of the 20th century. In this field there are more theories than data, and a lack of not only dependent variables but also independent variables; in fact, two promising theories—civilization and world system theory—have not received the empirical attention deserved owing to a lack of data (see Howard, Newman, and Pridemore, 2000). Future research in this area thus needs to concentrate on the gathering of good data from more nations (a good example is the European Sourcebook initiative), as well as imaginative ways of using available data such as regrouping countries by cultural domain as opposed to the more conventional method of geography (see Marshall, 2003).

ELENA LICU, BONNIE S. FISHER,
AND ROSEMARY BARBERET

References and Further Reading

Aromaa, K. and Leppa, S. 2003. Crime Trends: Europe and North America. *Crime and Criminal Justice in Europe and North America 1995–1997: Report on the Sixth United Nations on Crime Trends and Criminal Justice Systems.* Aromaa, K., Leppa, S., Nevala, S., and Ollus, N. (Eds.) Helsinki: HEUNI . Available at http://www.heuni.fi/uploads/0gyxd5c8.pdf. Retrieved on January 3, 2004 from the World Wide Web.

Bennett, R. 1991. Routine activities: A cross-national assessment of a criminological perspective. *Social Forces* 70(1): 147–163.

Blau, J.R. and Blau, P.M. 1982. Metropolitan structure and violent crime. *American Sociological Review* 47: 114–128.

Chamlin, M.B. and Cochran, J.K. 2003. Ascribed economic inequality and homicide among modern societies: Toward the development of a cross-national theory. *Homicide Studies.*

Chirot, D. and Hall, T.D. 1982. World system theory. *Annual Review of Sociology,* 8: 81–106.

Cohen, L.E. and Felson, M. 1979. Social change and crime rate trends: A routine activity approach. *American Sociological Review* 44:588–608.

Durkheim, E. 1947. *The Division of Labor in Society.* Translated by Simpson, G. Glencoe, IL: Free Press.

Gartner, R. 1990. The victims of homicide: A temporal and cross-national comparison. *American Sociological Review* 55 (February): 92–106.

Howard, G.J., Newman, G., and Pridemore, W.A. 2000. Theory, Method and Data in Comparative Criminology. *Criminal Justice 2000* (Vol. 4). Washington, DC: National Institute of Justice.

Kick, E.L. and LaFree, G. 1985. Development and the Social Context of Murder and Theft. *Comparative Social Research,* 8: 37–58.

Killias, M. and Aebi, M.F. 2000. Crime trends in Europe from 1990 to 1996: How Europe illustrates the limits of the American experience. *European Journal on Criminal Policy and Research,* 8: 43–63.

LaFree, G. 1998. *Losing Legitimacy: Street Crime and the Decline of Social Institutions in America.* Boulder, CO: Westview Press.

LaFree, G. 1999. A Summary and Review of Cross-National Comparative Studies of Homicide. *Homicide: A Sourcebook of Social Research.* Smith, M.D. and Zahn, M.A. (Eds.) London, UK: Sage.

LaFree, G. and Drass, K.A. 2001. Homicide trends in Finland and 33 other nations since 1955: Is Finland still exceptional? *Homicide in Finland: Trends and Patterns in Historical and Comparative Perspective.* Lappi-Seppälä, T. (Ed.). Helsinki: National Research Institute of Legal Policy. Available at http://www.om.fi/optula/11873.htm. Retrieved on January 3, 2004 from the World Wide Web.

Lamon, P. 2002. Crime trends in thirteen industrialized countries. *Crime Victimization in Comparative Perspective: Results from the International Crime Victims Survey, 1989–2000.* Nieuwbeerta, P. (Ed.). The Hague: Boom Juridische Uitgevers (BJU).

Marshall, I.H. 2003. *Crime in Europe in Global Perspective.* Presentation at the Annual Conference of the European Society of Criminology, Helsinki, August 27–30.

Neuman, W.L. and Berger, R.J. 1988. Competing perspectives on cross-national crime: An evaluation of theory and evidence. *Sociological Quarterly,* 29: 281–313.

Newman, G., (Ed.). 1999. *Global Report on Crime and Justice.* New York, NY: Oxford University Press.

The International Police Organization (Interpol). 2003. *The Official Interpol Site.* Available at http://www.interpol.int. Accessed on December 18, 2003 from the World Wide Web.

Shelley, L. 1981. *Crime and Modernization: The Impact of Industrialization and Urbanization on Crime.* Carbondale, IL: Southern Illinois University Press.

United Nations Office on Drugs and Crime (UNODC). 2003. *The Seventh United Nations Survey on Crime Trends and the Operations of Criminal Justice Systems (1998–2000).* Available at http://www.unodc.org/unodc/crime_cicp_survey_seventh.html. Retrieved on December 18, 2003 from the World Wide Web.

Van K., John, P.M., and Nieuwbeerta. P. 2000. *Criminal Victimisation in Seventeen Industrialised Countries: Key-findings from the 2000 International Crime Victims Survey.* The Hague, Ministry of Justice: WODC. Available at http://www.unicri.it/icvs/publications/pdf_files/key2000i/index.htm. Retrieved on December 18, 2003 from the World Wide Web.

World Health Organization (WHO). 2003. *WHO Mortality Database.* Available at http://www3.who.int/whosis/menu.cfm?path=whosis,mort&language=english. Accessed on December 18, 2003 from the World Wide Web.

See also **International Crime Statistics: Data Sources and Problems of Interpretation; International Crime Statistics: Juvenile Delinquency and Youth Crime**

International Criminal Law

Modern international criminal law has two main sources: (1) the laws and customs of war, and (2) international humanitarian law, which prohibits crimes against humanity and genocide. The laws of war are mostly concerned with regulating the means of warfare and human conduct during the course of armed conflict; they focus on the participants in battle. Crimes against humanity and genocide are not restricted to periods of armed conflict and focus on the victims of such crimes.

For the most part these laws have evolved during the course of the 19th and 20th centuries, although the laws of war go back to earlier times. International criminal law is still in its infancy, but it has developed more since World War II than at any previous time in history.

Criminal law is often thought of as a means of maintaining human order within the confines of a specific community. The courts apply criminal law to a specific geographical area referred to as a "jurisdiction." However, notions of what constitute the boundaries of a community are relative, and have changed over time.

As human intercourse and communication have moved from the primitive printing press to satellite-conveyed television images and cyberspace, so too has the concept of what constitutes a community. Instead of criminal law being the exclusive business of a local community such as a region, town, city, or state, the question of regulating human conduct beyond the nation–state becomes an issue as human activities and concerns have extended beyond the nation state. Community support for the international rule of law progressively has increased because of a perceived need to regulate and control the conduct of persons whose acts have repercussions beyond the boundaries of their nation states.

War Crimes

National war crimes codes regulating the conduct of armies have existed for centuries. However the first significant national modern war crimes code that went beyond matters of strict military discipline was drafted by Francis Lieber in 1863. Lieber drafted this code for use in the American civil war and parts of it are still to be found in the U.S. military code.

The creation of international war crimes is a much more recent phenomenon. About the same time as Leiber was drafting his code, on the other side of the Atlantic Ocean, Henry Dunant, a Swiss banker, observed the cruelty of war first hand at the Battle of Solferino in northern Italy. This was a war between France–Italy and Austria. There were about 40,000 casualties to the conflict, and what struck Dunant most was the total lack of regulation concerning removal of the dead and wounded after the battle. He returned to Switzerland and 1862 wrote *Memory of Solferino.* The book suggested that neutral relief societies should be formed to care for the sick and wounded in times of war. He further suggested that an international conference should be held to enable representatives of different countries to consider and adopt an international agreement on how to care for the soldiers wounded in battle.

Such a conference was held in Geneva, Switzerland in 1864 and was attended by the representatives of 16 countries. The international conference concluded by agreeing upon a short convention that focused on providing a means by which medical attention could be provided to the soldiers wounded in battle. It also saw the creation of the Red Cross Society, with its distinctive emblem and the Red Cross principles of neutrality, humanity, impartiality, and respect for the individual.

At the same time that Henry Dunant was promoting the Red Cross, Czar Alexander II of Russia proposed the idea of holding an international conference to ban the use of lightweight bullets that exploded upon contact with human flesh. Accordingly the Declaration of St. Petersburg in 1868 prohibited the use of explosive projectiles under 400 grams in weight. This was the first international convention in modern times to prohibit the use of a particular weapon of war. The Declaration provided that the unnecessary use of weapons that "uselessly aggravate suffering" were contrary to the "laws of humanity."

In 1899, Czar Nicholas II of Russia proposed another conference in The Hague, the Netherlands, to consider banning the dropping of bombs from balloons, the use of poisonous gases and expanding (dumdum) bullets during war. The Hague Rules of 1899, which were the result of this conference, adopted these prohibitions but, significantly, also introduced the "Laws and Customs of War on Land." This code (further modified in 1907) provided guidelines for the care of prisoners of war, flags of truce, and the treatment of civilians and property in occupied territories and prohibited rape and pillage. The 1899 and 1907 Convention on the Laws and Customs of War expressly recognized that these standards were not exhaustive and provided for the development of further laws according to "usages established among civilized peoples, from the laws of humanity, and the dictates of the public conscience."

Other agreements settled upon at The Hague in 1907 included conventions dealing with Enemy Merchant Ships at the Outbreak of Hostilities; Merchant Ships into War Ships; Laying of Automatic Submarine Contact Mines; Bombardment by Naval Forces; and Neutrality. Unfortunately, the dropping of bombs from balloons was only prohibited for 5 years, the ban against exploding bullets did not prevent the development of much more devastating ammunition, and poisonous gases continued to be used extensively throughout the 20th century.

Although often more recognized in their breach than their observance, the Laws and Customs of War settled upon at The Hague Peace Conferences of 1899 and 1907 have now been enshrined as customary international rules of war applicable to this day. Thus the killing of innocent civilians, the use of poisonous weapons, killing the enemy after they have laid down their arms, declaring that no quarter be given, sentence without trial, employing weapons causing unnecessary suffering, mistreatment of prisoners of war, and deceptive use of flags of truce or distinctive emblems are all prohibited.

This attempt to contain the use of excessively destructive weapons of war spawned a proliferation of similar conventions and declarations during the course of the 20th century including the Geneva Gas Protocol of 1925, which banned the use of poisonous gases as a weapon of war. This protocol was replaced by the Biological Weapons Convention of 1972. Other arms control conventions included The Conventional Weapons Convention of 1980 and the additional protocols of 1995 and 1996; The Chemical Warfare Convention of 1993, and the 1997 Ottawa Treaty banning the use of antipersonnel land mines.

Parallel with the development of The Hague Rules of war, the Geneva Conventions first proposed by Henry Dunant of Switzerland were also modified and updated during the 20th century. The Geneva Conventions of 1906 made greater provision for the care of wounded and sick soldiers. In 1929, the Geneva Conventions Relative to the Treatment of Prisoners of War and for the Amelioration of the Condition of the Wounded and Sick in Armies in the Field included provisions for the protection of medical aircraft and the adoption of red crescent and red lion emblems for Muslim countries.

Following the horrors of World War II the Geneva Conventions were again extensively overhauled at a Conference in 1949. As a result of this Conference, four new Geneva Conventions were adopted each dealing with a specific subject area: (1) wounded and sick in armed forces; (2) wounded and sick at sea; (3) treatment of prisoners of war; and (4) treatment of civilians. However, as World War II was an international armed conflict, the 1949 Geneva Conventions were primarily directed at the regulation of conduct in the course of international wars.

This limitation on the application of the 1949 Geneva Conventions was modified in 1977 to protect civilians in both internal and international armed conflict. Thus the 1977 additional protocols on International Armed Conflict and Internal Armed Conflict, when coupled with the 1949 Conventions, now constitute the most important source of Geneva law.

The Laws of War prohibiting the use of excessively destructive weapons (e.g., gas, bombs, and bullets) during armed conflict and the conduct of soldiers (e.g., rape, murder, and pillage) were not originally intended to apply to individuals but only to the responsible state as a basis of claiming compensation or reparation. Thus, although this conduct was prohibited, the laws did not give rise to individual criminal responsibility at the international level. The notion that the state could be held responsible in terms of its collective guilt and be ordered to pay reparations for its wrong doings rarely did anything to redress the pain and suffering caused to the victims of such atrocities. Reparation payments went to the injured state, not to the individuals concerned.

Prior to the 20th century, there were occasional international trials for war crimes, but at no time was a sovereign head of state seriously considered as a candidate for war crimes prosecutions. International laws of war were not originally meant to make the head of state criminally liable for the breach of the laws and customs of war by their armies. Historically, sovereigns viewed themselves as above the law. They were the manifestation of the law itself, so they were not bound by criminal law. Eventually, the position of the sovereign was extended to the sovereign state and this immunity from criminal liability passed on to the sovereign state as well. Accordingly, states and their human representatives were immune from the criminal law both at a national and international level. The head of a sovereign state could not be brought to trial for domestic or international crimes, no matter how egregious their crimes might have been.

The state of the law on individual responsibility and sovereign immunity at the international level changed in the 20th century. Kaiser Willhelm II of Germany was supposed to be tried by an international tribunal for the atrocities his armies committed during World War I, but this call for prosecution soon passed when the Kaiser took asylum in the Netherlands (ironically, now the seat of the new International Criminal Court) and no prosecutions followed.

Dramatic changes relating to the concepts of individual responsibility and sovereign neutrality occurred after World War II because of the extensive violation of the laws of war. The Nuremberg Charter of 1945 introduced, for the first time, the concept of individual criminal responsibility for violation of the laws and customs of war and ensured that sovereign heads of state could not hide behind sovereign immunity.

Although the Nuremberg Charter and the Charter for the International Military Tribunal for the Far East (the Tokyo Tribunal) abolished sovereign immunity, this did not ensure that the sovereign Emperor of Japan, Hirohito, was prosecuted for war crimes. Indeed, no sovereign head was prosecuted following World War II because of the wartime deaths of Adolf Hitler and Italian dictator Benito Mussolini.

The principle of sovereign immunity was to remain relatively untested until 1998 when General Augusto Pinochet of Chile went to London for back surgery. Pinochet found himself defending a Spanish extradition warrant for his arrest for committing crimes against humanity. After two hearings, the British House of Lords accepted the argument that for crimes against humanity, which attracted universal jurisdiction, there can be no immunity from prosecution. However, Pinochet was later found unfit to stand trial owing to illness and was allowed to return to Chile. Other heads of state now charged with crimes against humanity, including former Serbian presidents Slobodan Milosevic and Radovan Karadzic, offer additional tests for this seldom used legal principle.

Crimes against Humanity

A crime against humanity is an international crime that is distinguished from a domestic crime because the offense is the concern of the whole of the international community and as a consequence invokes international jurisdiction. The concept of humanity as the victim, rather than individual victims, characterizes crimes against humanity. The perpetrator of a crime against humanity must know that his or her act is part of a widespread or systematic attack against a civilian population.

Crimes against humanity have their origins in the laws of war. The "Martens Clause" of the 1907 Hague Convention first noted "laws of humanity" in the context of developing international customary law. Although addressed around the time of World War I, it was not until the end of World War II that these vague and undefined references were crystallized into a new form of international criminal law.

The Charter of the International Military Tribunal for Nuremberg, adopted by the International Law Commission of the UN in 1950, expressly created Crimes against Humanity and provided a sanction for their breach. The crimes were to attract individual criminal liability for the perpetrator. Those who drafted the Nuremberg Charter had to grapple with the then applicable but outmoded principle that international law had no application to events that occurred within the national boarders of a country. In other words, international law only applied to events that had occurred during the course of an international armed conflict. This meant that the atrocities committed by the Nazi's against the Jews of Germany could not be punished by an international tribunal. The Nuremberg Charter enabled courts to prosecute and punish Nazi criminals for the genocidal crimes they had committed.

Genocide

The Genocide Convention of 1948 was one of the most significant steps forward in the development of international humanitarian law. Prior to 1948, international law did not prohibit genocide in peacetime. The term genocide itself was coined during the course of the Second World War.

Genocide is the intentional destruction of a national, ethnic, racial, or religious group of people. The crime could be committed by killing, seriously harming (physically or psychologically), inflicting conditions on life calculated to bring about the whole or partial destruction of the group, or by imposing measures intended to prevent births, or forcibly transferring children from the group, with the intention of completely or partially destroying the targeted group of people.

Cultural genocide was expressly excluded from the Convention at the behest of Australia, Canada, and the U.S. as a means of ensuring that they would not be liable for what they had done to their indigenous peoples. However, the implementation of assimilation policies did in fact bring about the partial physical destruction of the group, and it is hard to see why such assimilation policies would not offend the prohibition on "inflicting measures on the group calculated to bring about its physical destruction." If given the opportunity, it is unlikely that an international court would interpret the provisions nowadays so narrowly as to exclude liability for cultural genocide such as that which was practiced in Canada, the U.S., and Australia against the indigenous peoples.

Genocide is now generally recognized as a norm of *jus cogens*; in other words, it forms part of customary international law binding upon all states (See *Barcelona Traction Case Belgium v. Spain* 1970 ICJ Reports 3 at 32), although the court did not expressly state that genocide was a norm of *jus cogens*, evidence of *opinio juris* and general State practice, support the conclusion that the rule against genocide is part of customary international law (and most probably *jus cogens* as well).

Tragically, acts of genocide are not limited to what occurred in Europe during the course of the World War II. Genocidal crimes have been committed since 1945 in places such as Cambodia, Rwanda, and Bosnia.

Today the Laws and Customs of War, Crimes against Humanity, and Genocide are not seen as separate crimes but instead as part of International Criminal Law. The effect of the Nuremberg Charter was to incorporate all these laws into the one instrument and make them criminal offenses. This method of presentation was carried on in the criminal provisions of Statutes for the International Criminal Tribunal for the former Yugoslavia, Rwanda, and the International Criminal Court. They are collectively referred to as breaches of international humanitarian law, for which a criminal sanction applies.

International Criminal Law is still very much in its infancy. In some cases, crimes such as torture and slavery, which are the subjects of their own International Conventions, are picked up and applied in the interpretation of traditional crimes against humanity. This has been especially so with respect to sexual assaults including rape, where sexual slavery during armed conflict has been characterized as both sexual slavery and torture. However because customary international law develops alongside or in addition to statute or treaty law it is likely that other crimes such as torture and slavery will form part of the body of International Criminal Law in their own right.

Aspirations ran high after the formation of the UN in 1945 that the International Law Commission (ILC) would effectively undertake the task of formulating principles of international law including a code of offences against the peace and security of humankind. Sadly, the "cold war" delayed much of this work by the ILC. However, after 50 tortuous years from 1947 to 1996, the ILC did eventually produce a comprehensive code that incorporated general principles of International Criminal Law. This code covers much the same territory as the laws discussed above, but what makes the ILC code of great importance is that this code is now considered as general principles of customary international law.

With the ever-increasing number of transnational issues affecting the world as a single global community, International Criminal Law will inevitably have to expand to address new questions that extend beyond the borders of any one sovereign state. Such issues may well include illegal international financial manipulation—"globalization of the world economy;" global environmental vandalism—the "green house effect" and the international drug trade, just to mention a few.

Crimes such as these threaten the peace and security of humankind as much as war threatens human peace and security. Accordingly as a body of laws, the international community may come to depend very heavily on International Criminal Law as a means of preserving the global community much the same way as traditional national criminal law protected the society of the nation state.

GRANT NIEMANN

References and Further Reading

Kelly, D.A. 1999. *War Crimes against Woman*. Martinus Nijhoff.

Cherif, M.B. 1992. *Crimes against Humanity, Criminal Law*. Martinus Nijhoff.

Cherif, M.B. 1987. *A Draft International Criminal Code and a Draft Statute for an International Criminal Tribunal* Martinus Nijhoff.

Cherif, M.B. 1986. *International Crimes: Digest/Index of International Instruments* Oceana.

Cherif, M.B. 1986. *International Criminal Law* Transitional Publ.

Antonio, C. 1988. *Violence and Law in the Modern Age.* Cambridge

Antonio, C. 1986. *The Current Legal Regulation of the Use of Force* Martinus Nijhoff.

Antonio, C. 1990. *Human Rights in a Changing World.* Cambridge: Polity Press.

Antonio, C. 1991. *The International Fight against Torture.* Baden-Baden: Nomos.

Benjamin, B.F. 1980. *An International Criminal Court: A Step Toward World Peace.* Oceana.

Misha, G. 1993. *The fall of Yugoslavia: The third Balkan War.* Penguin Books.

Roy, G. 1993. *A Witness to Genocide.* MacMillan Pub. Co.

Jean, S.P. 1960. *The Geneva Conventions of 1949 Commentry.* ICRC Geneva.

Richard, G. and Roberts, A. 1994. *Documents on the Laws of War,* Vol. 2. Clarendon Press.

Gretchen, K. 2000. *Even Wars Have Limits,* Vol. 2. Australian Red Cross.

McCormack, T.LH. and Simpson, G.J. 1997. *The Laws of War.* Kluwer Law International.

Geoffrey, R. 2000. *Crimes against Humanity: The Struggle for Global Justice.* Penguin Books.

Telford, T. 1993. *The Anatomy of the Nuremberg Trials.* Bloomsbury Publ.

International Criminal Tribunals

An international criminal tribunal is an *ad hoc* court of law, where the judges are especially selected from a number of different countries to distinguish it from the criminal court of a single nation state. The crimes traditionally tried before an international criminal tribunal are those that concern the international community and are considered sufficiently serious so that they threaten humanity itself. International criminal tribunals generally consist of a panel of trained judges who try both questions of fact and of law.

International criminal tribunals have primarily developed since World War II, although international criminal law tribunals are recorded to have existed as far back as 1474 when the Governor of Breisach, Peter von Hagenback, was tried before an international tribunal made up of judges from the Holy Roman Empire. He was held responsible for the crimes committed by his troops during the occupation of Breisach. His troops had killed, raped, and pillaged innocent civilians; crimes described as being "against the laws of God and humanity." His defense of superior orders was dismissed and he was sentenced to death. This is the first case where liability was based on "command responsibility" and the defense raised was "superior orders."

Following World War I an attempt was made to establish an *ad hoc* international criminal tribunal to try the crimes perpetrated by defeated armies during the war. A commission of enquiry investigated crimes committed by German troops who came under the supreme command of the Kaiser Wilhelm II. The crimes included the bombardment of undefended cities and towns, attacks against hospital ships, and the wholesale slaughter of the Armenians by the Turks. A total of 896 German defendants were identified including the Kaiser himself. However, the Kaiser secured sanctuary in the Netherlands, and interest in prosecutions waned because the Allied Powers were more preoccupied with extracting reparations than enforcing international justice.

In an effort to circumvent the international trials, the Germans jumped in and tried the war criminals themselves. This turned out to be a complete farce. Only 12 of the 896 persons were eventually prosecuted at the German city of Leipzig. Out of the 12 accused, only 6 were convicted, and the sentences imposed were so light as to make a mockery of the whole affair.

In 1937, an attempt was made to extend the jurisdiction of the International Court of Justice so as to give it an international criminal division, which would be empowered to prosecute individuals. However, this initiative did not succeed because the U.S. had not joined the League of Nations and the other members of the League were distracted by the rise of Nazi Germany.

In October 1943, the Allies set up a commission of enquiry to investigate crimes being committed by Nazi Germany and Japan during World War II. Called the UN Commission (but not to be mistaken for the present UN in New York), it was charged with the responsibility of investigating both political and military leaders responsible for waging aggressive war, for war crimes, and crimes against humanity. The commission then issued a Declaration in Moscow warning Germany and Japan that those responsible for these crimes would be prosecuted following the conclusion of the war.

True to their word, on August 8, 1946, the victorious Allies (the U.K., the U.S., France, and the Soviet Union) signed the Agreement for the Establishment of the International Military Tribunal, at London (the London Agreement). The Tribunal was to sit in the German city of Nuremberg and became known as the Nuremberg Tribunal.

The Charter for the Nuremberg Tribunal provided for three types of offences: (1) crimes against peace, (2) war crimes, and (3) crimes against humanity. A crime against peace occurred when persons were responsible for planning, preparing, initiating, or waging a war of aggression.

War crimes, namely violations of the laws or customs of war, included the ill-treatment of prisoners of war, deportation, plunder, and the wanton destruction of cities, towns, or villages, not justified by military necessity. Although war crimes predated Nuremberg, they were not previously considered applicable to acts perpetrated against civilian populations (or part thereof) during the course of an internal armed conflict nor were they enforceable against the sovereign leaders of a nation state.

Crimes against humanity included murder, extermination, enslavement, deportation, and other inhumane acts committed against any civilian population before or during the war, or persecution on political, racial, or religious grounds. These attacks must be widespread or systematic. Though such acts may be war crimes, they become crimes against humanity when the acts (murder, extermination, or enslavement) are committed against particular political, racial, or religious groups. The motivational element of a crime against humanity is a policy that requires that a certain group be targeted.

The development of international criminal tribunals progressed in tandem with the growth of individual criminal responsibility for the perpetrators of international crimes. Under the Nuremberg Charter it was no defense to show that such a crime was permitted under the local law of the particular country where the offender committed the crime, or that the offender was acting under superior orders. What the Nazi Government had done to the Jewish people of Germany was permitted under German law. Previously this would have excluded the operation of international criminal law. However, this principle was overturned by the Nuremberg Charter. Therefore, the state of German law at the time of commission of the crime did not excuse the offender under the Nuremberg principles.

One criticism leveled at the Nuremberg Tribunal was that it dispensed "victor's" justice, in that only perpetrators on one side of the conflict were prosecuted. This was a particular problem because there is no doubt that war crimes had been committed by both sides of the conflict, especially when the Soviet Union invaded Germany.

Another criticism was the fact that superior orders was no defense, but could be taken into account in mitigation of the penalty. This whole area was controversial during the Nuremberg Trials because the totalitarian nature of the Nazi state left the offender with little option but to obey orders. It was argued that it was unjust to hold a person criminally liable because in a life or death situation they chose to live when reduced to commit atrocities under the threat of death.

Following the Nuremberg Trials in 1950, the International Law Commission (ILC) adopted the "Principles of International Law Recognized in the Charter of the Nuremberg Tribunal and in the Judgement of the Tribunal." The ILC consists of a body of legal experts who are charged with the responsibility of assisting the UN on matters of international law.

The Nuremberg principles were also adopted by the International Military Tribunal for the Far East, often referred to as the Tokyo Tribunal. This Tribunal was established to prosecute Japanese war criminals. The Nuremburg Tribunal was considered to be more authoritative than the Tokyo Tribunal because it was established pursuant to the agreement of a number of states. The Tokyo Tribunal was established through the orders of General Douglas MacArthur, who appointed the judges. A shadow was also cast over the Tokyo Tribunal's impartiality when a French jurist criticized its lack of procedure. Still another factor that weakened the Tokyo Tribunal was General MacArthur's interference in its functions. MacArthur prohibited the investigation and prosecution of the Japanese Emperor Hirohito. Hirohito as supreme commander of the Japanese military forces clearly should have been prosecuted on the basis of his "command responsibility." MacArthur prevented this from happening for political reasons, largely because the Japanese public venerated the Emperor.

International criminal law may be enforced by international criminal tribunals, such as the Nuremberg and Tokyo Tribunals or by state courts exercising universal jurisdiction. One of the early examples of a state tribunal exercising universal jurisdiction was the trial of General Tomoyuki Yamashita by a U.S. Military Tribunal. Following the Japanese invasions of the Philippines under the command of Yamashita, General MacArthur promised the people of the Philippines that Yamashita would be held accountable for the appalling crimes committed by the Japanese troops during the invasions and subsequent occupation of the Philippines by Japan. MacArthur did not want to leave this "important" prosecution to the vagaries of the Tokyo Tribunals, so he subjected Yamashita to trial by Military court marshal. These proceedings have been criticized because Yamashita was held liable for the crimes of his troops notwithstanding that it was clearly proven that he had no knowledge of the fact that they were committing such crimes. However, despite such criticism the Supreme Court of the U.S. held on appeal that the exercise of jurisdiction by the military tribunal was nevertheless valid.

Similarly, trials by the Netherlands in Batavia (now Java, Indonesia) were considered an appropriate exercise of international jurisdiction by a state tribunal. The Netherlands's military trials of Japanese war criminals was in response to the widespread use of young women as sex slaves by Japanese soldiers during the war. Apart from these very few minor trials, the so-called "comfort women" crimes committed by the Japanese forces before and during World War II have never been addressed, despite the fact that over 200,000 women were brutally enslaved for this purpose. This is an enormous crime that could and should have been addressed, but again the Tokyo Tribunal failed in this regard.

Perhaps a better example of state tribunals exercising international criminal jurisdiction occurred in occupied Europe following World War II. Thousands of prosecutions followed the Nuremberg Trials in occupied zones by military tribunals of the occupying state. Some of these prosecutions, particularly those pursued in the American sector, were of great importance to the development of international criminal law. Sometimes these prosecutions were for a particular group of crimes; these are referred to as "theme" prosecutions. For example, the Einsatzgruppen Case concerned the prosecution of members of an elite German SS Unit established for the sole purpose of exterminating the Jews of Europe.

When a state court applies international criminal law to an offender present within its borders, it claims universal jurisdiction. Universal jurisdiction applies when the international criminal law concerned has reached the status of *jus cogens* and applies universally notwithstanding national or domestic law of that state.

A good example of a state exercising universal jurisdiction was in the Eichmann Case. In 1961, Adolf Eichmann, who was wanted for Nazi war crimes and had taken refuge in Argentina, was forcibly taken by Israeli agents covertly operating in Argentina. Israel no doubt had a considerable political interest in prosecuting this case, but could not claim that Eichmann had committed his offenses on Israeli territory or against Israeli citizens. The court found jurisdiction on the basis that Eichmann was charged with international criminal offenses. In the absence of an international criminal tribunal to deal with these crimes, the Israeli court expressly stated that it was exercising universal jurisdiction.

In 1968, the "Non Applicability of Statutory Limitations to War Crimes and Crimes against Humanity Convention" (Article IV) obliged states not to have any statute of limitations provisions for war crimes and crimes against humanity. As a result, when a person is charged with a war crime or crime against humanity, the charges will only lapse with the person's death, or when the person is tried.

During the 1980s, a wave of investigations and subsequent prosecutions were initiated against war criminals who fled continental Europe following World War II to take residence in such countries as the U.K., the U.S., Canada, and Australia. Domestic legislation was introduced in the U.K., Australia, and Canada so that the national laws could be applied to any Nazi War criminals found in these countries. In the U.S., persons suspected of these offenses were not subjected to criminal trial but were deprived of their citizenship and deported. These were civil proceedings and the courts decided the issues according to civil standards. The cases were based on the falsification of immigration papers when offenders entered the U.S. The standard U.S. immigration questionnaire specifically questions the entrant on whether they were connected with the war crimes or crimes against humanity on behalf of the Nazi Government of Germany or other associated entities during the course of World War II. If suspects lied on these forms, they were subjected to decitizenship and deportation proceedings.

An important example of international criminal tribunals was the creation of the International Criminal Tribunal for the former Yugoslavia (ICTY). In 1991, the Federal Republic of Yugoslavia collapsed as Serbian President Slobadan Milosevic attempted to exert Serbian domination over Slovenia and Croatia. Eventually these provinces, along with Bosnia–Herzegovina, withdrew from the Federation precipitating a major Balkan war. One of the main features of this war was the ruthless interethnic struggle that ensued. Because "ethnic cleansing" became the central focus of the military objective, the consequences for the civilian population was especially brutal. Not since World War II had Europe experienced such widespread barbarity directed against segments of the civilian population based entirely on racial, ethnic, or religious prejudice.

The modern worldwide news media depicted the scale of the cruelty directed against civilians, causing the international community to clamor for intervention. The U.S., Britain, and other western democracies, fearful of a European "Vietnam," were slow to take decisive action. In desperation, the UN intervened but could do little to stop the human carnage.

Seemingly as an afterthought, perhaps in a half-hearted attempt to disguise its impotence, the Security Council established an International Criminal Tribunal to try the perpetrators of these grisly crimes. Accordingly, by Resolution 808 of 1993 and Acting under the Authority of Chapter VII of the UN Charter (which allows the Security Council to go behind the "sacred sovereign shield" in circumstances where international peace and security are threatened), the Security Council adopted Resolution 808 in 1993, creating the tribunal.

Until this time, doubt existed as to whether this was a legally justified response by the Security Council. Although the Tribunal was limited in its geographical and temporal jurisdiction, the statue of the Tribunal was a bold and innovative step forward for international justice. The Tribunal was given sweeping powers to prosecute persons responsible for serious violations of international humanitarian law committed in the territory of the former Yugoslavia since 1991. The Tribunal enjoyed concurrent jurisdiction with national courts, although it was deemed to have primacy, so that it could formally request that national courts defer to its rulings.

The International Criminal Tribunal for the former Yugoslavia (ICTY) was given jurisdiction over war crimes, crimes against humanity, and genocide. Although it has no police force or law enforcement mechanism, other than the "rule of law" itself, it has successfully gained the support of nation states that have assisted it with ensuring that indicted war criminals are arrested and brought to The Hague for trial. Though many skeptics questioned whether it could succeed so long as the major perpetrators of Balkan war crimes remained at large, those critics have now been silenced since the arrest of the major perpetrator, Slobodan Milosevic.

Perhaps the single most important achievement of the ICTY is that its success has been the major catalyst for the establishment of the International Criminal Tribunal for Rwanda (ICTR). In addition, it has paved the way for the creation of a permanent International Criminal Court. The only way that international justice can be assured is if there is a permanent international criminal tribunal charged with the responsibility of enforcing international criminal law.

The one significant valid criticism that can be made against *ad hoc* tribunals of ICTY and ICTR are that they represent selective justice because they can only investigate and punish war crimes and crimes against humanity committed within specific geographical and temporal jurisdictions. The consequence of this is that other equally heinous crimes committed in other places

such as Cambodia go completely unpunished. This glaring deficiency in international criminal justice has increased the pressure for the creation of a permanent court, which would not be limited in time and place.

The first proposal for a permanent international criminal court occurred in 1937 under the auspices of the now defunct League of Nations. The idea was shelved during World War II but was briefly reenergized in the UN following the war only to stall once more during the Cold War. When the ICTY was created by the Security Council, efforts were again resumed by the UN to reintroduce a permanent international criminal court. In 1992, the General Assembly for the UN requested the International Law Commission to begin drafting a statute for the permanent international criminal court. The draft statute was completed by the International Law Commission in 1994, and serious international lobbying commenced to bring about its creation.

On July 17, 1998, representatives from 120 nations met in Rome and voted to adopt a treaty creating a permanent International Criminal Court. Although 21 nations abstained from the vote, only 7 nations actually opposed the creation of the Court. The Rome treaty is now going through the slow and tortuous process of ratification by individual nations. Some criticism could be made against the proposed permanent International Criminal Court because it does not enjoy total freedom on who or what it can investigate, and there are doubts about whether influential countries such as the U.S., China, and India will ratify the treaty. It undoubtedly must be hailed as the greatest step forward in the development of International Criminal Law.

In due course, the International Criminal Court that has now commenced operations in The Hague in the Netherlands, may one day be called upon to investigate acts other than war crimes and crimes against humanity. The continued existence of humankind is not only threatened by the horrors of war, but as we move into the 21st century, other equally devastatingly destructive clouds are gathering on the horizon. Environmental crimes (e.g., acts that cause the "greenhouse" effect and thereby threaten human existence) and international terrorist offenses may one day be prosecuted by this court.

GRANT NIEMANN

References and Further Reading

Bassiouni, M.C. 1991. *The Time Has Come for an International criminal Court. Indiana International and Comparative Law Review.*
Cassese, A. 1988. *Violence and Law in the Modern Age.* Polity Press, Cambridge.
Roling, B. and Cassese, A. 1993. *The Tokyo Trial and Beyond: Reflections of a Peacemonger.* Polity Press.

Morris, V. and Scharft, M. 1995. *An Insider's Guide to the International Criminal Tribunal for the Former Yugoslavia.* New York.

ELSA. 1997. *Handbook on the International Criminal Court.* Belgium: European Law Students Association.

Ferencz, B. 1992. An international criminal code and court: Where they stand and where they are going, *Colombia Journal of Transnational Law.*

Ferencz, B. 1980. *An International Criminal Court: A step towards would peace.* Oceana Publications. 2 Vols.

Maogoto, J.N. June 2001. International Justice under the Shadow of Realpolitik: Revisiting the Establishment of the Ad Hoc International Criminal Tribunals. *Flinders Journal of Law Reform.* 161.

Robertson, G. 2000. *Crimes against Humanity* New York, NY: Penguin Books.

Schwarzenberg, G. 1968. *International Law as Applied by International Courts and Tribunals.* Stevens and Sons, London.

Taylor, T. 1992. *The Anatomy of the Nuremberg Trials.* New York, NY: Knopf.

Report of the Secretary General Pursuant to Paragraph 2 of Security Council Resolution 808 (May 3, 1993) UN Document s/25704.

See also **International Court of Justice (World Court); International Crime and the UN; International Criminal Law**

International Imprisonment: Rates and Conditions

No society is completely free of crime and criminality and every society has in place some type of penal system to deal with those who violate the law. Prisons are universally used to incarcerate and punish offenders, although the structure and conditions of detention vary greatly internationally. Some nations use prisons extensively to confine virtually all types of offenders, violent and nonviolent offenders sentenced and those awaiting trial, but other nations are more cautious in their use. Overcrowding, poorly trained and inadequate staff, and substandard facilities contribute to generally deplorable prison conditions universally, and in even the richest and most developed countries one finds overcrowding, outmoded and decaying physical structures, a lack of minimal medical care, staff abuse and corruption, and violence.

In 2000, there was an estimated 8.6 million people incarcerated in penal institutions around the world, including both pretrial detainees and those convicted of and sentenced for crimes. Almost half of these offenders were incarcerated in the U.S., China, and Russia. Although a nation's crime rate is obviously related to its use of incarceration, official crime statistics and victimization surveys indicate that differential crime levels cannot adequately explain the differences in prison populations and incarceration rates between nations.

The U.S. has the highest incarceration rate in the world (calculated per 100,000 residents) at 690. Russia follows at 680 (prior to a general amnesty in 2000 it was approximately 730) with the Cayman Islands third at 665. Most countries have incarceration rates of 150 or less, but these figures vary significantly between different regions globally as well as between different regions on the same continent. In Europe, the median incarceration rate for southern European countries is 70, but 220 for those in central and eastern European countries. In Africa, western and central African countries have a median incarceration rate of 50, and as for southern African countries, it is 260. South central Asian countries have a low incarceration rate of 45 whereas in central Asian nations (including former Soviet-bloc nations) it is approximately 260. In Australia, New Zealand, and the rest of Oceania, the median incarceration rate is 120. In the Americas, South American countries have a median incarceration rate of 155 and in the Caribbean, it is 330 (based on 1999 figures).

In the U.S., the high prison population and incarceration rate is a direct result of the recent "get tough" sentencing policies, especially regarding violent and drug offenders. Several states (notably California) enacted some form of habitual offender, "three strikes and you're out" legislation within the last ten years and prison systems are now beginning to feel the effect of these laws. At the end of 1999, over 1.2 million inmates were in the custody of state and federal prison authorities nationwide, an average yearly increase of 6.5% since 1990. Violent offenders constitute 48% (545,200) and drug offenders 21% (236,800) of those incarcerated in American prisons. In some of the former Eastern Bloc, Caribbean, and Central American nations with very high rates of incarceration, it has been noted that this is primarily owing to the imprisonment of drug traffickers who are not residents or citizens of those countries.

Worldwide, the number of women serving prison sentences has increased dramatically in recent years. In the U.S. since 1985, the women's prison population has almost tripled, and this trend is also noted in several other countries. In Sweden, for example, it has almost quadrupled, primarily because of increases in general property crimes, shoplifting, forgery, and drug offenses. Only about 5% of women were incarcerated for violent crimes (compared to 17% for men) but increases are occurring here as well. Other general trends among women prisoners are evident. First, their average age is increasing. More middle-aged women are going to prison who, in many cases, would formerly have been dealt with either outside the system (e.g., in psychiatric care) or with probation. Another trend is the increasing number of women sentenced to prison for drug offenses; in many countries, women are twice as likely as men to be incarcerated for these crimes.

Women prisoners, especially in the U.S. and some European systems, are disproportionately racial or ethnic minorities and are overwhelmingly poor. In American prisons, 46% are African American and 14% are Hispanic, and 53% were unemployed prior to incarceration. Because there are typically fewer facilities for convicted women, they are usually incarcerated much farther away from home than they average male prisoner. As almost 70% of women incarcerated in state prisons in the U.S. have children under the age of 18, this increased distance causes a number of problems for children of inmates and deprives women prisoners of contact with their children. Women prisoners are particularly vulnerable to sexual assault and abuse. Amnesty International reported in 1999 that sexual abuse is "virtually a fact of life" for women prisoners in the U.S., and in some nations the situation is even more common. In the Philippines, the situation is probably the most acute. A large number of women in custody have reported being subjected to various degrees of sexual violence and degradation but only a small number of officials have been convicted. Although it is a capital offense for officials to sexually assault a woman in custody, this does not seem to deter this behavior.

Incarcerated juveniles in many countries continue to be dealt with harshly by the prison regime, routinely housed with adult prisoners and detained for several months or even years while awaiting trial. Many nations, including the U.S., are abandoning efforts to rehabilitate child offenders and are increasingly dealing with them through the adult court and correctional systems. In Jamaica, children—some as young as 12 or 13—are reported to remain in police lockups for up to 6 months before trial. Human Rights Watch reported in 1998 that juvenile offenders are routinely beaten and tortured while in custody, even though international standards and Jamaican law prohibit it. In many correctional systems, children share their cells with adult prisoners, and are subjected to various forms of torture and abuse.

Almost since its inception, the UN has been involved in overseeing and monitoring member nations' compliance in a number of areas, including prison conditions and other penal practices. In 1955, the First UN Congress on the Prevention of Crime and the Treatment of Offenders adopted a major resolution setting minimum standards and rules for the treatment of prisoners. Although not intended to describe in detail a model system of standards for penal institutions, it did attempt to outline what was generally accepted as good principles and practices in the treatment of prisoners and the management of prisons. Noting that penal practices and philosophies (legal, social, and economic) vary greatly around the world, this resolution recognized that not all of these rules and standards were capable of being met in all places at all times. In recent years, numerous resolutions have been passed by the General Assembly regarding torture and other cruel, inhumane, or degrading punishment (e.g., UN Resolution 37/193 (December 18, 1992)), summary or arbitrary executions (e.g., UN Resolution 44/159 (15 December, 1989)), and specific circumstances of juveniles and children in detention (e.g., UN Resolution 50/181 (22 December, 1995)). The UN, Amnesty International, and Human Rights Watch are foremost among agencies and groups that periodically observe and inspect penal institutions in the international arena. Although these entities have little or no enforcement power, the fact that they bring abuses to light in the international arena can affect, albeit informally, the practices and conditions within a country's penal institutions and detention facilities.

Prison overcrowding is prevalent in almost every country and the problem is most severe in smaller pretrial facilities where, in many countries, inmates are packed together so closely that there was no space to move around. Human Rights Watch reported in 1999, for example, that in some Brazilian police lockups, where a large percentage of the approximately 180,000 inmates were held awaiting trial, overcrowding was so severe that inmates had to tie themselves to the bars of the cells to sleep. Rioting and inmate disturbances in prisons in numerous countries have increased in recent years primarily because of overcrowding and the conditions that that arise from it.

Institutionalized torture continues to exist in various prison systems around the world. In 2000, the European Committee for the Prevention of Torture (CPT), the Council of Europe's official prison monitoring body, inspected prisons in 12 countries. They found torture and physical abuse widespread in many prisons, more often for those incarcerated for committing political crimes. Some countries continue to permit corporal punishment and the use of leg irons, chains, and shackles is not uncommon. In Japan, Amnesty International reports that inmates routinely are subjected to systematic cruel, inhumane, and degrading treatment. Cases have been documented where prisoners have been severely beaten by guards for minor rules infractions, detained in solitary confinement for long periods, restrained in leather belts and cuffs, and held in special protection cells as punishment.

The "protection cells" (hogobo), common in all Japanese prison facilities, are used for detaining prisoners who: (1) act violently, committing harm to themselves or others; (2) persist in making noise despite orders to stop; (3) exhibit repeated abnormal behaviors such as damaging their cells; or (4) are deemed inappropriate to hold in a normal cell. These cells contain no furniture except for a bed, sink, and toilet built into the floor. The walls are wooden and the interior of the cell is subjected to 24-hour video monitoring. Leather or metal restraints are used and are not removed at any time (including mealtimes) except when the prisoner sleeps or needs to use the toilet. Prisoners are normally kept in these cells for periods of 2–3 days.

It is estimated that in Peru there are over 5000 political prisoners accused of supporting insurgency who are singled out for the harshest treatment. Basic essentials are so scarce that many of these inmates survive only by having friends and relatives bring them food, medicine, and clothing. Amnesty International reported that in 1999, at least 50 inmates died in Pakistani prisons because of torture and ill-treatment. Worldwide, political prisoners under sentence of death are especially susceptible to torture and inhumane conditions of confinement and, in some cases, extrajudicial execution.

Another major human rights issue concerns unsentenced prisoners: those who have not been convicted and sentenced for a crime, but who were detained at some stage of the trial process. In several countries (primarily in Central and South America), unsentenced prisoners make up the majority of the incarcerated population. In Honduras, Paraguay, and Uruguay, almost 90% of incarcerated inmates are unsentenced. In Nigeria, over 60% of prisoners were pretrial detainees; some have been held for over 4 years before release. In eastern and central European prisons, approximately 25% were unsentenced, primarily because of the limited use of bail, the length of criminal investigation procedures, and the length of time awaiting trial after the investigation process is completed.

Health and medical care is inadequate or almost nonexistent in numerous prisons around the world.

Because of the unsanitary conditions and overcrowding, communicable diseases are widespread and difficult to control. Tuberculosis is one of the serious diseases affecting incarcerated populations and continues to increase, primarily in prisons in developing countries. In March 2000, the International Committee of the Red Cross reported that in the prisons of the Commonwealth of Independent States (CIS), the prevalence of TB was on the average 50 times greater than in the general population. In Russia, with an inmate population of over 1 million, one of every hundred inmates had active TB, with more than 10% of them affected by multidrug resistant strains. It is estimated, that TB may be 34 times greater among Russian prisoners than in the general population. In several countries, many offenders entering prison already have the disease, so it is difficult to prevent TB from spreading to other inmates. Where there are shortages of medicine and medical equipment, and where the equipment is old and outdated, the problem is especially serious.

The spread of HIV/AIDS has affected prisons and jails in many countries with particular severity. In the U.S., there are approximately 5.5 cases of AIDS per 1000 prisoners, which is nearly six times the incidence found in the general population. Inmates in French prisons are estimated to be HIV-positive at a rate almost ten times that of other adults in the country. In South American prisons (especially those in Brazil and Argentina), the rates are even higher. Not only are offenders entering prison with high incidences of HIV, but the prison environment itself provides a perfect breeding ground for the transmission of the virus. High-risk behaviors, such as intravenous drug use and unprotected sexual contact (including forced sex), are common in prisons around the world. In many cases, rather than providing prisoners with protection and prevention means (e.g., condoms for safer sex and liquid bleach for sterilizing needles and syringes), officials frequently bar the entry of these items into the prisons. Since 1993, however, prison authorities in Switzerland have made sterile needles available to prisoners in a number of Swiss prisons. More recently, Germany has followed suit.

In the U.S., prisoners have a constitutional right to health care that people on the outside do not necessarily have; under the Eighth Amendment, inmates are entitled to a "safe and humane environment" and since the mid-1970s, prison health care has improved dramatically. Regarding AIDS, however, prisons have historically approached the problem in two somewhat contradictory ways: either segregation and quarantine or education. Currently, a number of state and federal prisons segregate all inmates with AIDS or who are HIV-positive. A majority of systems have instituted extensive education programs for inmates. In recent years, a few prisons in the U.S. have granted a small number of terminally ill inmates with advanced AIDS conditional release from prison before the expiration of their sentences. Usually released to families or hospices with access to community health services, these prisoners typically had no history of violence although incarcerated or were originally convicted for nonviolent offenses.

Many prison systems use some form of inmate labor, either using physically fit convicts to take part in vocational training and meaningful rehabilitative work for pay, or forcing inmates to work in inhumane or degrading conditions. In Cuba, an extensive prison labor and agricultural camp system exists, and clothing assembly, construction, furniture, and other factories are operated in institutional prisons throughout the country. The system's reliance on malnourished prisoners, nonexistent or extremely low wages, and work without rest, violate several international standards relating to penal conditions and rules. It has been reported that in a factory that primarily manufactures mattresses, inmates are paid the equivalent of 1¢ (U.S.) per day and must pay food and clothing costs. Although not challenging the principle of employing prisoners to engage in meaningful work, many nations prohibit the importation of any goods or merchandise produced or manufactured in another country by convict or forced labor. U.S. law in this area, for example, is based on fair trade and human rights concerns; goods and services produced in federal prisons can only be sold to other government agencies within the U.S. In recent years, China and several Latin American countries have come under close scrutiny from the U.S. State Department and Customs concerning imports that were suspected of being produced by inmate labor under inhumane conditions. A number of trends in penology will seriously impact prisons and prison conditions internationally. For example, the emergence of private prisons marks a significant transformation in the development of penal system in the late 20th century. Nations are examining privatization as a mechanism to economically and efficiently deal with burgeoning prison populations. Some commentators believe that privatization will lead to a deterioration of prison conditions.

In the U.S., there are more than 20,000 inmates, nearly 2% of the prison population, held in several supermaximum security prisons. These facilities were designed for what prison officials call the "worst of the worst"—inmates so violent, disruptive, and dangerous that they cannot be kept in regular custody.

Prisoners in these facilities typically spend 23 hours a day locked in their cell without contact with others. Politicians who want to be seen as "tough on crime" have supported the construction of these institutions that cost considerably more to build and operate than regular prisons. Supermaximum security prisons are coming under increased scrutiny in lawsuits and official investigations regarding allegations of serious human rights violations. Originally designed to house only violent and dangerous inmates, many inmates confined in these facilities do not meet these criteria.

Model prisons have opened in a few nations, notably Scandanavia. Nevertheless, criminologists and penologists predict that correctional systems around the world will continue to experience rapid changes and emerging problems, including: (1) increasing prison populations and incarceration rates; (2) eroding conditions of pretrial confinement, specifically overcrowding, and length of detention; (3) the need for new prisons to replace old, outdated structures; (4) shortages of noncustodial alternatives to imprisonment; (5) recruitment and retention of sufficient and quality staff; and (6) finding suitable employment for prisoners. These problems continue to compromise the prospect for humane confinement.

CHARLES B. FIELDS

References and Further Readings

Amnesty International, 2000. *Annual Report 2000*, London, UK: Amnesty International, International Secretariat.

Carlie, M.K. and Minor, K.I. 1992. *Prisons around the World: Studies in International Penology*, Dubuque, IA: William C. Brown, Publishers.

Human Rights Watch, *The Human Rights Watch Global Report on Prisons*, New York, NY: Human Rights Watch Publications.

Stern, V. 1998. *A Sin against the Future: Imprisonment in the World*, Boston, MA: Northeastern University Press.

Van Zyl Smit, D. and Dünkel, F. (Ed.) 1991. *Imprisonment Today and Tomorrow: International Perspectives on Prisoners' Rights and Prison Conditions*, Deventer, the Netherlands: Kluwer Law and Taxation Publishers.

Wamsley, R. 2000. *World Prison Population List (Research Findings, No. 116)*, London, UK: Home Office Research, Development and Statistics Directorate.

Wamsley, R. 1996. *Prison Systems in Central and Eastern Europe: Progress, Problems and the International Standards*, Helsinki, Finland: European Institute for Crime Prevention and Control.

Weiss, R.P. and South, N. (Eds.) 1998. *Comparing Prison Systems: Toward a Comparative and International penology*, Amsterdam, The Netherlands: Gordon and Beach, Publishers.

See also **International Crime and the UN**

International Police Cooperation, History of

International police activities are not the invention of the recent age of globalization. The historical roots of international policing today go back to at least the 19th century expansion of national states. Over the course of history, international police activities have taken on different forms in pursuit of a variety of objectives. Broadly, the historical trend has been for police institutions to gradually abandon political police tasks to focus on distinctly criminal goals and to move from momentary and limited forms of cooperation to the creation of more permanently structured arrangements of cooperation. International police organizations with broad international representation were not formed until police institutions had become sufficiently autonomous from the political centers of their respective national states to function as relatively independent professional bureaucracies. When this structural condition of institutional autonomy was fulfilled, police institutions began to collaborate across the borders of their respective national states on the basis of shared conceptions concerning the development and enforcement of international crime. Thus, the forms of international police cooperation that throughout the 19th century were oriented at protecting established autocratic political regimes, especially on the European continent, would ultimately lead to the establishment in 1923 of the International Criminal Police Commission, the organization known today as Interpol.

The 19th-Century Origins of International Policing

During the 19th century, U.S. police institutions did not play any significant role in international police practices. At that time, police duties with international dimensions in the U.S. were related to specifically American circumstances, such as enforcement tasks associated with slavery, immigration, and the founding of national borders on the North American continent. In Europe, however, international police practices were from the middle of the 19th century onward comparatively much more developed. Most European police cooperation then concerned political tasks related to the protection of established conservative rule from suspected subversive activities. Such was most clearly the case with the Police Union of German States, an international police organization that was active from 1851 until 1866 to suppress the political opposition,

consisting of democrats, anarchists, and socialists. The Union was especially oriented at instituting systems of information exchange among participating police in the form of the circulation of information through printed materials and at police meetings. But the Police Union was able to attract cooperation from police of only seven German-language nations that were ideologically closely akin and politically united in a federal union. Because the organization remained closely tied to political conditions, it was no surprise that the Police Union's activities gradually began to decline with mounting hostilities among the governments of the countries whose police institutions were a member of the Union. The Union was finally disbanded when war broke out between the countries of its two primary members, Prussia and Austria, in 1866.

Policing Anarchism

Although there was during the second half of the 19th century already a noticeable trend toward criminal duties in international police activities, political objectives continued to dominate most police work across national borders. In the final decade of the 19th century, violent incidents inspired by radical political ideas once again shook the foundations of established autocratic regimes in Europe and accelerated international police activities. On September 10, 1898, Empress Elisabeth of Austria was murdered by the Italian anarchist Luigi Lucheni, further intensifying concerns over the anarchist menace. A few weeks later, on September 29, 1898, the Italian government organized an international conference in Rome to organize the fight against anarchism.

The International Conference of Rome for the Social Defense against Anarchists was held from November 24 to December 21, 1898, and was attended by 54 delegates from 21 European countries. In the final protocol of the Conference, anarchism was defined as any act that used violent means to destroy the organization of society. On matters of practical policing, the Rome protocol included plans to encourage police to keep watch over anarchists, to establish in every participating country a specialized surveillance agency to achieve this goal, and to organize a system of information exchange among these national agencies. Also, the countries that signed the final Conference protocol agreed to adopt the *"portrait parlé"* method of criminal identification. A technically more sophisticated version of the bertillonage system that was invented by Alphonse Bertillon, the *portrait parlé* (spoken picture) was a method of identification that classified criminal suspects on the basis of numerically expressed measurements of parts of their head and body. The Conference also approved a provision to extradite persons who had attempted to kill or kidnap a sovereign or head of state.

In November 1901, Russian authorities invoked the assassination of U.S. President McKinley by an anarchist in September of that year as a basis to revive the antianarchist program of the Rome Conference. The initiative led to a second antianarchist meeting, in March 1904 in St. Petersburg, Russia, where the representatives of ten countries agreed upon a Secret Protocol for the International War on Anarchism.

The Limits of Political Policing

The 19th-century fight against anarchism was evidently a matter of a decidedly political nature, especially when it included policies reaching beyond the control of criminal incidents inspired by anarchist motives. Aware of the politically sensitive nature of anarchism, the antianarchist meetings in Rome and St. Petersburg purposely conceived of anarchism as a strictly criminal matter, the enforcement of which was to be handled at the administrative level by police institutions. Nonetheless, only a few countries actually passed new legislation based on the provisions of the Rome and St. Petersburg protocols. The aspiration to treat anarchism as a criminal matter could not be maintained at the level of the national governments where the international treaties had to be ratified. Ideological divisions in international political affairs also posed limits to the international police cooperation plans that were developed in function of formal intergovernmental treaties. Most clearly, the participants of the Rome and St. Petersburg meetings could not agree on the creation of a central antianarchist intelligence bureau for information exchange across various nations.

Another special focus of international police activities from the early 20th century onward was international prostitution or the white slave trade, as it was called then. An international conference on white slavery was first organized by the French authorities in Paris on July 15, 1902. At a follow-up meeting in Paris in 1904, the International Agreement for the Suppression of White Slave Traffic was signed by the governments of 12 European countries. Some non-European states, among them the U.S., did not sign the accord but nonetheless agreed to adhere to its provisions. At a subsequent meeting in Paris on May 4, 1910, the International Convention for the Suppression of the White

Slave Traffic was signed by 13 nations, including most of the countries that signed the 1904 Agreement. The U.S. was among the countries that no longer adhered to the new treaty.

Although the international agreements on white slavery dealt with a nonpolitical issue, the agreements reached in Paris were like those on anarchism decided upon at the intergovernmental level and framed in the language of formal international law. In consequence, the white slavery accords did not significantly influence the course and outcome of international police strategies and other practical aspects of prostitution policy. Instead, police activities in the area of white slavery developed as part of national policies. Efforts to control the trafficking of prostitutes into the U.S., for example, were largely conducted on the basis of national U.S. legislation, specifically the White Slave Traffic Act of 1910.

International Policing and the Bureaucratic Autonomy of Police

During the 20th century, certain structural conditions and operational motives were met that would determine the further development of international policing. Structural conditions ensure that national police agencies are in a position to move beyond the confines of their respective national jurisdictions. When these structural conditions are met, international police organizations need an additional motivational basis to become operational. Historical evidence shows that international police organizations with broad international representation were formed because and when police institutions had become sufficiently autonomous from the governments of their respective national states to function as relatively independent bureaucracies. Police institutions achieved this position of autonomy on the basis of the development of a purposive-rational logic to employ the most efficient means given certain objectives of crime control. When the structural condition of institutional autonomy was fulfilled, police institutions started to collaborate across the borders of their respective national jurisdictions on the basis of a shared system of knowledge concerning the development and enforcement of international crime. To be sure, variable sociohistorical circumstances impact the degree of bureaucratic autonomy of police institutions during periods of momentous societal change. Intense social disturbances typically lead to attempts to redirect bureaucratic activity to again play a role intimately related to the political goals of national states.

In the early decades of the 20th century, efforts to formally organize international police cooperation increased in number. Most of the plans were not successful, but the remarkable increase in attempts to structure international police work clearly manifests a more general globalization that took place in many areas of society. International police cooperation also gradually depoliticized in terms of its goals, although there were also momentary returns to political police duties. Next to the disruptive impact of World War I, a striking example of the momentary shifts brought about in the autonomy of police during sudden crises occurred after the Bolshevik Revolution, when police institutions in Europe, the U.S. and elsewhere turned attention to the spread of a global communist movement. Yet in the 20th century, such politically motivated international police activities would be only temporarily relevant. Efforts to repoliticize police and other social institutions during moments of intense societal change are not surprising. What is ironic is that these politicization efforts can still occur at times when police institutions continue to expand and solidify a position of autonomy, enabling them to better resist such attempts at political control.

The first 20th century initiative to formally establish an international police organization on matters of a nonpolitical nature was taken at the First Congress of International Criminal Police in Monaco in 1914. As indicated by the name of the Congress, the meeting focused on distinctly criminal law enforcement duties, a development that was anticipated since the late 19th century. However, the Congress nonetheless failed to institute an international police organization, mostly because the meeting was not organized by police officials but by politicians and legal officials. The discussions at the Congress took place exclusively within a legal framework, including debates about arrangements of international law, such as extradition procedures. Proposals that concerned police measures were discussed only in function of legal principles, which police institutions had by then already abandoned.

On the American continent, the main counterpart to European police cooperation in the early 20th century first originated in Latin America, where arrangements were made to structure international police cooperation at international police conferences in Buenos Aires in 1905, in Sao Paolo in 1912, and in Buenos Aires in 1920. But these efforts were largely inconsequential, because they were mainly oriented at professional objectives, namely to foster better relations among the police of different countries, but not to control international crime.

In September 1922, the International Police Conference (IPC) was established at a police meeting in New York City. Explicitly conceived as an organization to promote and facilitate international cooperation among police, the Conference would remain a predominantly American organization that was mostly concerned with promoting an ideal of professionalism among local U.S. law enforcement agencies. In 1932, the IPC was brought under the direction of Barron Collier, a wealthy retired businessman, who tried to put new life in the organization, but to no avail. The IPC was independently organized by police officials, especially from within the New York City Police Department, and cooperation among the Conference's members was attempted to be accomplished outside the context of formal legal systems. However, what the International Police Conference missed were any realistic concerns with international crime. An internationalization of crime that could justify the establishment of an international police organization was at this time still missing in the U.S. Especially because of the distance from Europe and other parts of the world and because the U.S. did not yet have a well-developed federal police, U.S. policing operations at this moment in time still remained insulated from the rest of the world.

The Birth of Interpol

The International Criminal Police Commission (ICPC), the organization currently known as Interpol, was founded in 1923 and exists until this day as the most enduring international police organization. The ICPC was formed at the International Police Congress in Vienna as the result, not of a diplomatic initiative, but of an initiative independently taken by police officials from various, mainly European countries. The Commission was set up without the signing of an international treaty or legal document. The ICPC activities were planned at police meetings and through correspondence among police officials, without control from their governments. For a long time since its founding, also, the ICPC had no internationally recognized legal status and no legal procedure was formalized for a police agency (rather than a nation–state) to acquire membership in the Commission.

The ICPC headquarters were initially located in Vienna, which had the technically most accomplished police facilities. The headquarters contained specialized divisions on the falsification of passport, checks and currencies, fingerprints and photographs, and other systems of police knowledge and police technique. Various means of direct police-to-police communication, such as a radio network and publications, were the most important achievements of the ICPC.

The motivational basis for police to cooperate through the structures of the ICPC was in the first instance provided by a cross-national rise and an internationalization of crime that had taken place at the end of World War I. What police officials organizing and participating in the ICPC argued to justify collaboration across national borders were new types of crime that took place across countries undergoing rapid social change and technological progress. Therefore, the Commission established new systems of technologically advanced means for international police communication. Also in opposition to the cumbersome legal procedures of extradition, the ICPC advocated direct police-to-police communications to more efficiently cooperate across national borders.

The Dynamics of International Policing

Among the implications of the fact that police institutions historically began to cooperate on the basis of their achieved position of bureaucratic autonomy is that cooperation could take place among police of national states that may be very different in political, legal, and other respects. The strength of survival of the ICPC is remarkable in this respect, in the light of the political and cultural heterogeneity that marks the various countries in Europe and elsewhere. The bureaucratic autonomy of police accounts for the fact that police institutions can transcend their jurisdictional authority and move beyond the function assigned to them by their respective governments. International police cooperation efforts were set up on the basis of standards of efficiency and systems of knowledge about international crime that could be shared among police professionals. Therefore, the ICPC was able to found and expand its organizational structures and facilities despite the fact that among the Commission members no clear-cut definition of international crime was agreed upon.

The apolitical nature of the ICPC has ironically brought about that the organization could be exploited by the police of nations that hold extreme political ideologies and consequently engage in police activities for political purposes. The potential to politicize international police work is in the case of the ICPC most tragically revealed when the organization was taken over by the Nazi regime after the annexation of

Austria in 1938. In that year, the ICPC presidency was assigned to a Nazi police official and, a few years later, the headquarters were brought over to Berlin, where they were organizationally aligned with the SS police. Although the practical consequences of the Nazification of the ICPC are not clear, the organization was evidently vulnerable to be used for political purposes. After the end of World War II, the ICPC was reformed in 1946 at a gathering of police in Brussels, Belgium. Since then, the ICPC headquarters have been located in France. The organization's membership has continued to expand and presently comprises police institutions from 181 nations.

MATHIEU DEFLEM

References and Further Reading

Anderson, M. 1989. *Policing the World: Interpol and the Politics of International Police Cooperation*, Oxford, UK: Clarendon Press.

Deflem, M. 2002. *Policing World Society: Historical Foundations of International Police Cooperation*, Oxford and New York: Oxford University Press.

Deflem, M. 2002. Technology and the internationalization of policing: A comparative-historical perspective, *Justice Quarterly* 19.

Deflem, M. 2002. The logic of Nazification: The case of the International Criminal Police Commission ('Interpol'), *International Journal of Comparative Sociology* 43.

Fijnaut, C. 1997. The International Criminal Police Commission and the fight against communism, 1923–1945, *The Policing of Politics in the Twentieth Century: Historical Perspectives*, Mazower, M. (Ed.), Providence, RI: Berghahn Books.

Jensen, R.B. 1981. The International Anti-Anarchist Conference of 1898 and the origins of Interpol, *Journal of Contemporary History* 16.

Liang, H.-H. 1992. *The Rise of the Modern Police and the European State System*, New York, NY: Cambridge University Press.

See also **International Criminal Tribunals; International Policing: Coordinated Efforts among Nations of the European Union; International Policing: Interpol**

International Police Organizations *See* **International Policing:**
Interpol

International Policing: Cooperation among Nations in the European Union

---

International policing in what is now the European Union has been in existence since the beginning of the 20th century. Cooperation among European nations laid the foundation for Interpol, which is the largest international policing organization in the world. More recently, the European Union has initiated other cooperative policing efforts. They include the TREVI (Terrorism, Radicalism, Extremism, Violence, and Internationalism) group, Schengen, and Europol. Each of these cooperative efforts has strengths and weaknesses, which have played a part in subsequent efforts to battle international criminality. With the ever-increasing sophistication of international criminal enterprises such as trafficking in drugs, humans, and weapons, it has become necessary for countries to work together more and more frequently.

Interpol

The first international meeting of policing agencies took place in Rome in 1898. Twenty-five years later in 1923, the initial foundation for Interpol was laid when 20 countries met in Vienna and established the International Criminal Police Commission (ICPC). By 1938, the time of the Nazi takeover in Austria, 34 countries had joined what was initially a European organization. After the end of World War II, 19 of the previous member countries met in Paris and became known as Interpol (International Criminal Police Organization). Interpol is a mutual assistance organization of police forces. Day-to-day operations are handled at Interpol headquarters, which was located in Paris until 1989 when the organization moved its headquarters to Lyon, France. Major policy decisions are made at annual meetings of the general assembly of all members.

Each member nation maintains a domestic clearing-house that processes data on international criminals and their activities, especially smuggling, counterfeiting, and trade in narcotics. Members cooperate by detaining suspects within their borders and by providing information on criminals, missing property, and unidentified human remains. Interpol has its own agents, but they may not pass freely from one country to another; and arrests and investigations are the responsibility of each country's own police force. Involvement in political, religious, military, or racial matters is strictly prohibited.

The historical development of Interpol followed a distinct pattern. Although the first meeting was in 1898, it was not until after World War I that an actual organization was built. This may have been owing to the desire of countries after the war to illustrate their goodwill to other nations and the world. It was a time when cooperation was viewed as the key to maintaining the peace they had fought so hard to obtain. This pattern was mirrored after World War II in 1946. Again, each nation sought to prove it was willing to work in conjunction with its neighbors. The organization was reborn and throughout the Cold War nations flocked to join, perhaps in part to show that the West stood united against the Communist states.

The strengths of Interpol include the organization's ability to compile and disseminate information, its broad membership, and its universal acceptance throughout the world. The ability to compile and disseminate information was enhanced in 1989 with the relocation to Lyon. A state-of-the-art complex was erected that included the latest in computer technology. This aided Interpol's efforts to help not only member states but also a number of the cooperative policing organizations that will be discussed here later. The membership of Interpol is more extensive than that of any other multinational policing organization. At the beginning of the 21st century it had 173 member countries from all over the world. Interpol has received a great deal of support since its inception. Unlike other European efforts at cooperative policing, Interpol has met with little resistance to its activities.

Interpol is not without its critics. Its ability to collect information has been questioned. All 173 countries have made a commitment to pass along any information that concerns international policing or criminal activities, however, there is no policy that requires a country to provide any specific information. This creates problems for many countries that question the integrity of states that support terrorism. Terrorist-friendly member states are not likely to provide information on terrorists supporting their cause. Similar arguments have been made for Latin American countries regarding information pertaining to the drug trade.

Although Interpol is now composed of 173 different countries, 85% of all inquiries are intra-European. This raises doubts as to how many countries are providing complete cooperation. The truth may be that some countries join in an effort to bolster their international image when in fact they have limited motivation to aid in the capture and prosecution of international criminals.

Interpol is widely accepted by the world's nations, although it has no policing authority. Furthermore, the organization has no jurisdiction and no police or enforcement personnel of any kind. In other words, it has no power of arrest and can only inform members of the location of dangerous criminals. Interpol is purely an information exchange system. This provides another source of tension between members. Returning to the terrorism example, Interpol could inform a European government as to the country a man who planted a bomb near the Eiffel Tower was known to be residing. That government might be frustrated to know that Interpol could track the terrorist but could not bring him to justice if the government of the country he was living in chose not to act.

TREVI

The second group, designed as a cooperative effort, is known as TREVI. TREVI was organized originally in 1976 by a meeting of the ministers of the interior from the nine European Community (now European Union) members. The first TREVI working group was constructed in 1986 to combat terrorism. This group was composed of senior police and civil servants from various organizations and was responsible for gathering and coordinating information about terrorists and terrorist activities. Since that time, several other TREVI groups were organized to deal with specific issues. TREVI II was initiated to deal with equipment and aspects of public order, and TREVI III was designed to fight international crime and drug trafficking. In 1989, another group, TREVI 1992, was initiated to look at the implications of a single European market on Policing.

The strengths of the TREVI groups include the creation of a forum in which members of the European Union can exchange information and experiences on dealing with specific problems, greater effectiveness of policing, and support by police officials in member states for TREVI's efforts to build police cooperation. Unlike Interpol, the TREVI groups are composed solely of European countries with very similar interests. In addition, the groups include police officials in each country. This adds significantly to cooperative efforts to curtail international criminal activity.

TREVI was not without faults. The organization did not have a single organizational complex but was basically adrift in the European Community, meeting only at conferences to identify problems or to confront specific issues. This greatly hindered the organization's effectiveness in the transfer of information and in policing certain activities. TREVI was organized as an intergovernmental group within the European Community but had no tie to European Community treaties. This laid the foundation for questions that arose regarding the accountability of the TREVI groups.

Schengen

The Schengen agreement (1990) deals with opening internal borders of the signatory states within the European Community. The intention was to ease transport of individuals, goods, and services across borders, to increase police cooperation in those matters, and to develop the Schengen Information System (SIS). The SIS would be an information exchange system targeted at immigration. The Schengen treaties were originally signed in 1990 by Belgium, France, Germany, Luxembourg, and the Netherlands; later in that same year, Italy signed as well. The following year, Spain and Portugal signed the agreement. Four European Community members are therefore not part of the agreement, Britain, Denmark, Ireland, and Greece. Greece, however, has agreed to join in the future.

The general agreement provides for an increased policing effort at the external borders and is specifically targeted at aliens attempting to enter the Schengen territory. An alien is defined as anyone who is not a legal resident of one of the member states. There are also agreements in place for a common Schengen visa, allowing anyone holding a Schengen visa to travel freely within those countries. The strengths of Schengen are generally in the intentions of the accords. The idea of having a common visa that allows an individual passage in a number of countries is appealing. Similarly, increased police cooperation between countries in regard to immigration matters is helpful. Schengen has been praised in the European Community for exactly those reasons, but in actual practice, the agreements may have caused more harm than good.

One argument against the Schengen agreements was proposed by the Dutch and reiterated by other European Community members who refused to sign the agreement. They argued that the Schengen treaty violated Article 14 of the Universal Declaration of Human Rights in regard to asylum. That article states that any person has the right to seek refuge in any country in an attempt to flee persecution. This argument can be clarified through an examination of the Schengen agreements. Schengen stipulates that anyone seeking asylum in the member states must submit an application in their country of origin. One can logically assume that persons fleeing persecution are unlikely to have the means to submit an application in their own country. This limits an individual's ability to reach the Schengen borders legally; in turn policing agents within Schengen borders cannot allow such refugees entry into the country.

Another problem with the Schengen agreements is in the processing of information through the SIS. Applications for a visa come from the country of departure; thus, the SIS collects information on individuals from immigration offices all over the world. The technological advances made in the last years of the 20th century increased the transfer of information exponentially. The SIS has consequently been flooded with lists of undesirable people. These undesirables are then transferred to a list that will deny them access into the Schengen territories. The problem that arose is that the SIS had no system installed to access information on those individuals who were removed from the list. For example, a girl who is accused of theft will temporarily be added to the list of undesirables in France. This information is relayed to the SIS and categorized accordingly, thus banning her entry into the entire Schengen territory. Officials in France drop the charges based on mistaken identity and remove her from the French list. She is now capable of transit across the French border. The early SIS, however, had no means of collecting this information, and would not remove her from their list, and she would subsequently be forbidden entry into any of the other signatory states.

Europol

Europol was instituted in 1995 to fulfill the mandate set forth in the Maastricht treaty, which specified that each country would create a national unit that would designate a liaison officer representing their interests in Europol. The convention also mandated the creation of a computer database that regulated access so as to protect personal information. Europol has been designed to work within the framework of intergovernmental cooperation. To this effect, Europol was structured to act as an information exchange center with emphasis on supporting national criminal investigation, creating a database, analyzing and assessing information, evaluating training practices, and conducting research. The strengths and weaknesses of Europol are yet to be seen. As in previous cooperative efforts, the outset looks promising.

DAVID JENKS

References and Further Reading

Anderson, M., and Den Boer, M. 1994. *Policing across National Boundaries,* New York, NY: Pinter Publishers.

Barker, T. 1994. *Police Systems and Practices: An Introduction,* Englewood Cliffs, NJ: Prentice Hall.

Benyon, J., Morris, S., Toye, M., Willis, A., and Beck, A. 1995. *Police Forces in the New European Union: A Conspectus,* University of Leicester: Center for the Study of Public Order.

Bossard, A. 1993. *Law Enforcement in Europe: Building Effective Cooperation,* Chicago, IL: Office of International Criminal Justice.

Bresler, F. 1992. *Interpol,* London, UK: Sinclair Stevenson.

Fijnaut, C., (Ed.) 1993. *The Internationalization of Police Cooperation in Western Europe,* Boston, MA: Kluwer Publications.

Guyomarch, A. 1995. Problems and prospects for European police cooperation after Maastricht, *Policing and Society 5.*

Kangaspunta, K. (Ed.) 1995. *Criminal Justice Systems in Europe and North America 1986–1990.* HEUNI Publication 25, Monsey, New York, NY: Criminal Justice Press.

King, M. 1995. The impact of Western European border policies on the control of 'refugees' in Eastern in Central Europe, *New Community, 19, 2.*

McDonald, W. (Ed.) 1997. *Crime and Law Enforcement in the Global Village,* Cincinnati, OH: Anderson.

See also **International Policing: Interpol**

International Policing: Coordination against Organized Crime in Europe

Introduction

Although informal cooperation has long been a feature of police and customs operations within Western Europe, the expansion of terrorism in the early and mid-1970s created the need for more formal collaborative structures. In 1976, the Justice and Interior Ministers of the member states of the European Economic Community (EEC) established the TREVI Group (a French acronym for Terrorism, Radicalism, Extremism, and International Violence). By 1989, one of the four TREVI working groups focused exclusively on organized crime, the others on police cooperation, terrorism, and the free movement of persons.

With the end of the Cold War, organized crime groups were quick to take advantage of the new opportunities presented by globalization. Even more efficiently than legal operators, they exploited the internationalization of commercial and financial markets, the relaxation of international boundaries, the free movement of labor and goods, and scientific and technological advances—particularly in the field of telecommunications.

Criminal groups already operating in Eastern Europe and the former Soviet Union expanded their activities and began cooperative arrangements with West European, Asian, and South American criminals to smuggle illicit goods across borders and overseas in reciprocally beneficial arrangements. War in the former Yugoslavia resulted in arms and oil embargoes that were flouted by criminal syndicates, often with political collusion and to considerable profit. The mass migration of displaced persons through ethnic cleansing or economic hardship provided a labor force for organized crime that could be coopted into narcotics smuggling and prostitution, and exploited for the fastest growing criminal activity of the 1990s—illegal immigrant smuggling.

Today's organized crime is characterized by multiservice agencies based on fluid networks and functional cooperation. Ethnic ties remain important because criminal diasporas across continents facilitate the establishment of trust relationships. In the absence of formal contracts, such bonds reduce the risk of doing business transnationally. However, ethnicity is functional within increasingly multiethnic criminal partnerships: in Germany, 77% of all organized crime groups investigated in 1999 had international links, with Spanish investigations showing a similar level. In that year, of 437 organized crime investigations in Germany with international links, offences had been committed in 92 countries.

Indigenous organized crime groups in Western Europe now face serious competition from Eastern Europe. The most powerful of them, the Sicilian Cosa Nostra, has kept a lower profile after sustained law enforcement efforts dismantled its top echelons in the mid-1990s, in the wake of a high-level assassination campaign. Italian organized crime, comprising the Calabrian n'Ndrangheta, the Camorra (around Naples), and the Sacred Holy Crown (Apulia) as well as Cosa Nostra, remains active in narcotics and arms traffic, extortion, loansharking, and money laundering. It exercises considerable influence over political and administrative affairs at the local level and is adept at the infiltration of large-scale public works, particularly in construction and in infrastructure maintenance.

Albanian organized crime groups have expanded and consolidated their presence in Europe, and now control a significant share of the illicit traffic in narcotics, arms, and human beings, including children for adoption and women (and young girls) for prostitution. Criminals from the former Soviet Union are involved in money laundering, narcotics, and counterfeit currency and documents. Chinese criminal gangs run transcontinental illegal immigration networks and are particularly strong in the UK and the Netherlands. Nigerian syndicates are involved in prostitution networks and narcotics.

Narcotics are still the principal illicit activity of organized crime across Europe. Colombian cocaine enters through the ports of Lisbon, Malaga, and Marseille as well as the airports of Madrid, Frankfurt, London, and Rome. Heroin arrives via a variety of routes: along the Balkan route by road from Turkey, and from Afghanistan and the Central Asian republics into Russia; in containers from Thailand and Hong Kong. Synthetic drugs are primarily produced and trafficked within Europe, with the Netherlands as the primary source country. The efforts to stop terrorist funding after 9/11 has made money laundering more difficult, and criminals have been forced to outsource this activity to specialized operators. Faced with these daunting challenges from transnational organized crime, European law enforcement authorities have tried to match the response to the threat.

The Schengen Agreement

The signing in 1985 by France, Germany, Belgium, Luxembourg, and the Netherlands of the Schengen Agreement, followed by an implementing Convention in 1990, established freedom of movement within this group of countries in advance of the single European Market, which came into being on January 1, 1993. The increase in cross-border movements of persons, goods, and capital, combined with the gradual elimination of frontier controls and identity checks was compensated by a strengthening of external borders and by a greater degree of police collaboration within the Schengen area. The Schengen Information System (later renamed the European Information System) was set up to maintain records of "undesirable aliens" barred from entry to the Schengen area. Data were stored on refugees, asylum seekers, criminals, firearms, and persons under surveillance. Provisional arrest and extradition procedures among Schengen countries partially circumvented the rigidity of mutual legal assistance requests based on an exchange of rogatory letters. The right of cross-border pursuit and surveillance was established, though has been applied differently from one country to another. A "safety clause" permits the temporary restoration of border controls in exceptional cases. With the Treaty of Amsterdam of 1999, the Schengen Agreement and implementing Convention became part of the European Union *acquis*, with special provisions allowing non-Schengen members of the UK and Ireland to retain external border controls.

Maastricht and Europol

Under the terms of the Maastricht Treaty, signed in 1992 and ratified the following year, a clear framework was established for police cooperation between the member states of the European Union in the Third "Pillar" or Title VI of the Treaty, concerning Justice and Home Affairs. Because Third Pillar matters involve delicate areas of national sovereignty such as policing and criminal justice, they require intergovernmental agreement and must be negotiated by conventions. Title VI, Article K.1 no. 9 of the Maastricht Treaty states that:

Police cooperation should take place for the purposes of preventing and combating terrorism, unlaw-

ful drug trafficking and other serious forms of international crime with a view to establishing a Union-wide system for exchanging information within a European Police Office (Europol).

Member states were obliged to set up structures for police cooperation in areas of "common interest" although policing itself remained a sovereign issue. A Declaration on Police Cooperation, annexed to the text of the Treaty of Maastricht, outlined Europol's future functions as:

Support for national criminal investigation and security authorities;
Creation of databases;
Central analysis and assessment of information;
Analysis of national prevention programs; and
Measures relating to further training, research, forensic matters and criminal records departments.

The preparatory work for Europol began in 1992 with the establishment of a European Drugs Unit in Strasbourg, later renamed Europol Drugs Unit and relocated to The Hague, where it began to operate on January 1, 1994, on a limited basis of bilateral exchanges of information and intelligence. The Europol Convention was signed in October 1995, and came into force on October 1, 1998, but only became fully operational on July 1, 1999. Europol was empowered to:

Exchange operational information and intelligence between two or more member states;
Make operational and strategic analyses;
Support operational law enforcement activities such as controlled deliveries, and give other forms of support to the Member States such as training;
Draft strategic reports.

Europol's areas of competence initially comprised illicit drug trafficking, illegal immigration, trafficking in human beings, illicit trafficking in vehicles, trafficking in radioactive and nuclear substances, and associated money laundering activities. Terrorism, plus the forgery of money and other means of payment, were added to the mandate from July 1999.

Prior to the formalization of Europol's structure there was much debate over whether the mandate should cover not only supportive tasks but also executive police powers, enabling the agency to investigate international organized crime either on its own initiative or in close cooperation with the police of member states. In the late 1980s, German Chancellor Helmut

Kohl had argued strenuously, but in isolation, for a fully operational "European FBI," and Europol was assigned supportive tasks only.

Intensified EU Cooperation against Organized Crime

By the early 1990s, investigations had shown that Italian Mafia groups were operating in every continent and were exploiting the possibilities offered by the single market and the collapse of Communism. Conversely, powerful mafia-type groups from the former Soviet Union were profiting from the liberalization of financial and commercial controls and from the opening of new European trade routes to extend their activities across the continent. An *ad hoc* Working Group on Organized Crime was set up by the TREVI Group in September 1992, composed of senior police and legal experts. It prepared two reports that reviewed the available information on the extent and nature of organized crime within the Community and made recommendations for improving the response. A standard methodology for collecting and analyzing information relating to organized crime was adopted by member states in November 1993.

In December 1996, a high level group of experts of the 15 EU member states was set up to devise an Action Plan against Organized Crime. This plan, with 15 political guidelines and 30 recommendations designed to promote practical cooperation between police, customs, and judicial authorities through the adoption of conventions and other legal instruments, was adopted in June 1997, by the European Council (the Heads of State or Government of the EU plus the EU Commission President). These initiatives have been implemented through a series of programs. The *Falcone Programme* (1998–2002) provides training for judges, public prosecutors, officials of police and customs departments, and of financial and public procurement supervisory bodies who have responsibilities for combating organized crime.

The *Oisin Programme* (1997–2000) has encouraged cooperation between police and customs services in the area of prevention. In 1999, it financed 51 projects concerning drug trafficking, terrorism, violence, and urban crime and the use of technology for combating crime. The *Stop Programme* (Sexual Treatment of Persons, 1996–2000) was concerned with training officials in the fight against trafficking in human beings and the sexual exploitation of children.

The European Commission and the Council of Europe (a pan-European body based in Strasbourg) financed the *Octopus Programme* (1996–1998) to extend cooperation to the countries of Central and Eastern Europe, whereas *Octopus II* (1999–2000) facilitated the adoption of new constitutional and legislative measures in Eastern European countries by providing training and assistance to those responsible for combating corruption and organized crime.

In May 1998, the Ministers for Justice and Home Affairs of the member states and of the applicant countries signed a preaccession pact to combat organized crime. This involves the preparation of legislation and provision of training to police forces in EU applicant countries.

The Treaty of Amsterdam

With the entry into force of the Treaty of Amsterdam on May 1, 1999, an important distinction was created between the free movement of persons and the establishment of an area of freedom, security, and justice. As a result, policies on asylum, visas, immigration, and judicial cooperation in civil law are now dealt with under the First Pillar or community matters, whereas police and judicial cooperation in criminal matters remain within the Third Pillar. According to Article 29 of Title VI, Provisions on Police and Judicial Cooperation in Criminal Matters, the Union's objective is "to provide citizens with a high level of safety within an area of freedom, security and justice." This is to be achieved by "preventing and combating crime, organized or otherwise, in particular terrorism, trafficking in persons and offenses against children, illicit drug trafficking and illicit arms trafficking, corruption, and fraud." Article 30 states that:

> [c]ommon action in the field of police cooperation shall include:
>
> (a) Operational collaboration between police, customs and other specialized law enforcement services of member states in relation to the prevention, detection and investigation of criminal offenses;
> (b) the collection, storage, processing, analysis, and exchange of relevant information, including information held by law enforcement services on reports on suspicious financial transactions [...];
> (c) cooperation and joint initiatives in training, the exchange of liaison officers, secondments; the use of equipment and forensic research;
> (d) the common evaluation of particular investigative techniques in relation to the detection of serious forms of organized crime.

Important modifications to Europol were also envisaged by this Treaty. Article 30 no. 2 states that the Council of the European Union (the representatives of member state governments at ministerial level) "shall promote cooperation through Europol" and, within a period of 5 years after the date of entry into force of the Treaty, shall:

(a) Enable Europol to facilitate and support the preparation, and to encourage the coordination and carrying out, of specific investigative actions by the competent authorities in the Member States, including operational actions of joint teams comprising representatives of Europol in a support capacity;

(b) Adopt measures allowing Europol to ask the competent authorities of the Member States to conduct and coordinate their investigations in specific cases and to develop specific expertise which may be put at the disposal of Member States to assist them in investigating cases of organised crime;

(c) Promote liaison arrangements between prosecuting/investigating officials specializing in the fight against organised crime in close cooperation with Europol;

(d) Establish a research, documentation, and statistical network on cross-border crime.

The Tampere European Council meeting in Finland on October 15 and 16, 1999, specifically addressed the problems of cooperation against organized crime and money laundering. The meeting proposed that Europol's powers be extended to all money laundering activity whatever the origin, and that joint investigative teams be set up, possibly with the support of Europol, to combat terrorism and trafficking in drugs and human beings. An operational liaison structure may be set up as part of this initiative to promote the exchange of experiences, best practices, and information. Council members also agreed to set up a European Police College to train senior law enforcement officials, including those from applicant countries, and to establish a unit called *Eurojust*, composed of national prosecutors, magistrates, or other investigative officers, to facilitate the coordination of prosecutions of organized crime within the EU.

Conclusions

The extent to which Europol's powers and the new forms of police cooperation envisaged by Tampere will be enhanced was uncertain in early 2001. This process would come close to endowing Europol with the operational capacity that some EU members have hitherto rejected, and might involve a reconsideration of the immunity protocol that functionaries currently enjoy under the Europol Convention. During 1999, however, a gradual shift of Europol's activities from strategic to operational activities did take place, according to Director Jürgen Storbeck. Of 2180 enquiries initiated by Member States, 58% related

to drugs, with priority given to combating the production and trafficking of synthetics such as ecstasy and amphetamine. Twelve "strategic projects" were begun on specific crime phenomena from an EU perspective, such as drug production and drug trafficking, illegal immigration, and trafficking in human beings. Operational analysis was provided to assist particular investigations against major criminal organizations. For the first time, two applicant countries, Hungary and Lithuania, helped Europol in supporting an operation to disrupt illicit vehicle trafficking by organized criminal groups in the Baltic area. The number of controlled deliveries coordinated by Europol, allowing law enforcement officers to track shipment of drugs or other illegal goods through different jurisdictions, rose from 46 in 1998 to 121 in 1999.

The signing in December 2000 by 125 states, including all EU members, of the UN Convention against Transnational Organized Crime and the two accompanying Protocols against the Smuggling of Migrants and against the Trafficking of Persons, gave international policing a further boost. At the heart of these new instruments is the recognition that transnational organized crime has expanded in the years since the end of the Cold War, and that only a transnational approach can provide the necessary response. Signatories of the Convention are required to establish in their domestic laws four criminal offenses—participation in an organized criminal group; money laundering; corruption; and the obstruction of justice. They impose obligations for police and judicial authorities to assist one another, both in general and in specific cases. Once ratified by 40 nations, the Convention will enter into force and will also become part of the *acquis* of the European Union.

There can be no doubt that police cooperation in Europe against organized crime has made significant advances in the last ten years, although many problems remain. These include Europol's cumbersome practice of working in eleven languages, issues of data protection or privacy, and the additional burdens that will be imposed by EU enlargement. Yet with political will, these problems can and should be resolved.

ALISON JAMIESON

References and Further Reading

Consiglio Europeo di Tampere 15 e 16 ottobre 1999: Conclusioni della Presidenza. Available at http://www.eurooparl.eu.int/summits/tam_it.htm.

Cooperation in the Field of Justice and Home Affairs. Available at http://ue.eu.int/jai/pres.asp?lang=en.

Area of Security: Current Area and Outlook. Available at http://europa.eu.int/scadplus/leg/en/lvb/l33002.htm.

Europol Annual Report for 1999, The Hague, April 2000.

United Nations Convention against Transnational Organized Crime, United Nations, New York, 2000 (advance copy of authentic text).

Protocol to Prevent, Suppress and Punish Trafficking in Persons, especially Women and Children, supplementing the United Nations Convention against Transnational Organized Crime, United Nations, New York, 2000 (advance copy of authentic text).

Protocol against the Smuggling of Migrants by Land, Sea and Air, supplementing the United Nations Convention against Transnational Organized Crime (advance copy of authentic text).

Jamieson, A. 1999. *The Antimafia, Italy's Fight against Organized Crime*, Macmillan/Palgrave.

Findlay, M. 1999. *The Globalisation of Crime*, Cambridge University Press, UK.

See also **International Policing: Cooperation among Nations in the European Union; Organized Crime: Activities and Extent; Organized Crime: Enforcement Strategies**

International Policing: Interpol

Brief History

The International Criminal Police Organization held its first International Criminal Police Congress in Monaco from April 14 to 18, 1914. The meeting was attended by delegates from 14 different countries and territories. On September 7, 1923, Dr. Johannes Schober, Chief of Police in Vienna, Austria, organized the second International Criminal Police Congress, setting up the International Criminal Police Commission (ICPC) with its headquarter in Vienna. The organization was created in response to the postwar financial disruption in Europe and an increase in internationally mobile forgers, swindlers, and black marketeers after the First World War. There were two main unofficial goals at the onset of the organization: (1) to develop methods for the rapid exchange of information about international criminals; and (2) to improve procedures for arresting and returning those international criminals to the country in which they could stand criminal trial.

In 1946, after the Second World War, a conference was held in Brussels to revive the ICPC and the whole concept of international police cooperation. New statutes were adopted and the Commission's Headquarters moved to Paris. "Interpol" was chosen as the telegraphic address of the Headquarters. In 1956, the ICPC became the International Criminal Police Organization-Interpol, abbreviated to ICPO-Interpol. In 1966, the Interpol General Secretariat moved to Saint Cloud, outside Paris. On November 27, 1989, the Organization's new Headquarters building in Lyons was officially inaugurated. By 2000, Interpol had 178 official members worldwide, making it one of the largest international organizations in the world, second only to the UN.

Vision, Values, and Mission

Interpol currently states its vision as "It exists to help create a safer world. Our aim is to provide a unique range of essential services for the law enforcement community to optimize the international effort to combat crime." As to its values, Interpol supports the following: a respect for human rights and integrity, commitment to quality, availability, cooperation, value for money, and accountability in the delivery of services. Finally, Interpol makes great attempt to be the world's preeminent organization in support of all organizations, authorities, and services whose mission is preventing or detecting international crime. Specifically, Interpol will achieve these missions by (1) providing both a global perspective and a regional focus; (2) exchanging information that is timely, accurate, relevant, and complete; (3) facilitating international cooperation; (4) coordinating joint operational activities of the member countries; and (5) making available know-how, expertise, and good practice.

Structure

The General Assembly of Interpol is run by its Executive Committee with a president, four vice presidents, eight delegates, and a secretary general. The eight delegates are appointed by the governments of Member States. As Interpol's supreme governing body, it meets once a year and makes all the major decisions affecting general policy, the resources needed for international cooperation, working methods, finances, and programs of activity. It also elects the Organization's officers. Generally speaking, the Assembly makes decisions by a simple majority in the form of resolutions. Each member state represented has one vote only. Further, Interpol has eight Directorates in charge of Executive Office, Information System, Strategic Planning, Administration and Finance, Legal Affaires, Criminal Intelligence, Regional Coordination and Development, and Finance Control. Finally, Interpol coordinates its routine operations through a National Central Bureau (NCB) in each member state.

The 69th Interpol General Assembly in November 2000, has elected the following officials in the Executive Committee: President Jesus Espigares Mira (Spain); Vice President for Africa Augustine Chihuri (Zimbabwe); Vice President for Americas Neal Parker (Canada); Vice President for Asia Kim Joong Kyoun (Korea); Vice President for Europe John Abbott (U.K.); and Secretary General Ronald K. Noble (U.S.). The eight delegates are from Australia, China, Germany, Greece, Nigeria, Sudan, U.S., and Uruguay.

New Initiatives and Strategies

At the present stage, Interpol's General Secretariat handles approximately two million messages a year. Its database contains over 300,000 criminal files. Through the Automated Search Facility (AFS) about 140 member states can automatically have access to 125,000 files out of the 30,000 files. Yet, Interpol is facing new challenges. Its 178 member countries have different expectations of service levels, different needs, and various capacities in electronic information systems. Further, its 178 members have huge differences in wealth, culture, languages, and political systems. It is obviously a challenging task to fulfill the needs and demands from its member countries. With the increase in international travel, liberalized immigration policies, global marketing through expansion of free trade, and high-tech communications, crime is becoming international. To face the new challenges, Interpol has established several regional organizations, such as Europol, ASEANAPOL in Southeast Asia, and SARPCCO in Southern Africa.

In March 1993, the General Secretariat set up an Analytical Criminal Intelligence Unit (ACIU) and 1 year later, the Unit became operational. Thus, Interpol became the first international organization to provide crime analysis on an international scale to develop cooperation within the international law enforcement community. With the Microsoft Windows™ environment, three analytical methods are used: case analysis, comparative analysis, and offender group analysis. An analysis result is in the English language version with table, graphics, text, and analytical charting. Since 1994, several projects have been completed, including Project Mandrax on traffic in methaqualone (mandrax) between India and South Africa, Project Transal on traffic in cocaine between South America and Europe, Project Nuclear on traffic in radioactive substance in Europe, Project Noah on worldwide traffic in protected species, and Project Admiral on international money laundering.

In 1999, the General Secretariat changed the name of the Organized Crime Branch (OCB) to the Organized Crime Projects Branch (OCP). Since the early 1990s, both OCB and OCP have been implementing four new projects, targeting organized crimes worldwide. Project Rockers (1991) was aimed at outlaw motorcycle gangs. At present, 4000 criminal files on individuals connected to outlaw motorcycle gangs have been stored in the database in terms of membership, hierarchy, and criminality. Project Millennium (1998) was conducted to facilitate the centralized collection, collation, and analysis of sensitive intelligence concerning East European and Russian organized crime groups. Project Bridge (1999) was initiated to collect more information on illegal immigration and trafficking of people. This project focuses on criminal intelligence information regarding smuggling routes, methods of smuggling, locations of safe houses, method of escorts, forged documents, and visas used in smuggling. Project Mercosur (1999) was proposed to promote the exchange of operation and strategic information regarding organized crime members and groups within Mercosur. (Mercosur is the South American Common Market created in 1994, with Argentina, Brazil, Paraguay, and Uruguay as official members, and Bolivia and Chile as associated countries.) Finally, the idea of an international police force has been a recurring theme within Interpol in recent years because of the globalization of crime we face today.

Publications

One of the first ICPC decisions was to create an official publication to form a bond among member countries. The official journal *International Public Safety* was adopted in November 1924, focusing on international arrest warrants and reports on criminals. The first issue of today's *International Criminal Police Review* appeared in September 1946 in French and English. Its Spanish version started in 1954 and Arabic version in 1978. Other publications under Interpol include *International Crime Statistics, Counterfeit and Forgeries Review, The Smart US & Checker, Annual Passport Guide*, and *Vehicle Registration Documents*.

Websites

Interpol offers two websites, first initiated in July 1999. The first is designed for the general public with no restrictions (http://www.interpol.int). Both yellow (used to help locate missing persons, especially minors) and red (used to seek arrests with a view of extradition of subjects wanted upon an arrest warrant) notices can be accessed at the website. Another function of the website is to provide the electronic versions of the journal of *International Criminal Police Review*, summaries of recent issues, abstracts of the articles published, and selected articles published. The second website (https://www.interpol.int) provides password holders with more restricted information, such as *modus operandi* of drug trafficking, the database of counterfeiting credit cards, and investigation techniques. The Interpol's General Secretariat has effectively used its websites to circulate information about its day-to-day operations worldwide. In 2000, its monthly individual visitors were around 52,000.

More than ever Interpol has been faced with many major challenges as it strives to improve the level, intensity, and quality of investigative cooperation and information sharing. Specifically, its member countries expect Interpol to play a greater role in facilitating data sharing, providing criminal intelligence, conducting operational information analysis, sponsoring training on subjects concerned, and promoting cooperation among its 178 member countries in the world.

JOHN Z. WANG

References and Further Readings

Babovic, B. 1990. Interpol and human rights, *International Criminal Police Review*, 256.

Babovic, B. 1997. An international police force, *International Criminal Police Review*, 464.

Berouiguet, B. 1986. Interpol and the fight against art theft, *International Criminal Police Review*, 205.

Berouiguet, B. 1987. The crimal records sub-division at the Interpol general secretariat, *International Criminal Police Review*, 230.

Kawada, A. 1987. Interpol and the fight against drug traffic—60 years of international experience, *International Criminal Police Review*, 224.

McClure, G. 2000. The role of Interpol in fighting organized crime, *International Criminal Police Review*, 481.

Taconis, I.J. 1956. Interpol takes a hand, *International Criminal Police Review*, 32.

Valleix, C. 1985. Interpol, *International Criminal Police Review*, 177.

See also **International Criminal Law**

International Policing: Role of the U.S.

In matters of international policing that involve police activities transcending the borders of national states, police agencies from the U.S. play a role more significant than police from any other nation. Historically, U.S. law enforcement was by and large insulated from international activities and cooperation with police from other nations, but since World War II and, particularly, over the past few decades, U.S. police institutions have taken on a dominant role in international operations. Reviewing the involvement of U.S. police agencies in international practices and cooperation efforts, the goals that such international police strategies are aimed at, as well as the forms in which they occur, are manifold and complex.

International Dimensions of U.S. Law Enforcement

International police activities radiating from the U.S. are predominantly planned and executed by several U.S. federal law enforcement agencies. Among the U.S. federal police agencies with international orientations, the Federal Bureau of Investigation (FBI) and the Drug Enforcement Administration (DEA) stand out because of their wide-ranging global presence. Various other U.S. law enforcement agencies also

have distinctly international tasks. The terrorist incidents of September 11, 2001, furthermore, have sharply amplified the U.S. role in international police activities in recent years.

As the principal investigative arm of the U.S. Department of Justice, the Federal Bureau of Investigation is responsible for the enforcement of various federal violations of criminal law that have distinct international dimensions, including the policing of terrorism and drug trafficking, the organization of a system of liaison agents abroad, and the administration of international police training programs. The FBI's system of legal *attachés* (or *legats*) is operative in all continents of the globe, currently covering 52 countries. The FBI *attachés* can engage in criminal investigations abroad and assist foreign police in making arrests, but they cannot make arrests on foreign soil. Among the most interesting recent expansions of the FBI's international role are the elaboration of its international training programs and the increase in attention to the fight against international terrorism. The FBI administers training programs for foreign police at the FBI National Academy in Quantico, Virginia, as well as at the International Law Enforcement Academy in Budapest, Hungary. Opened in April 1995, the Budapest Academy offers to students from Russia, Eastern

Europe, and the Baltic states courses in advanced techniques to combat modern crime while respecting human and civil rights. The FBI's work on terrorism is coordinated through the Counterterrorism and Counterintelligence division, which oversees antiterrorism activities both at home and abroad.

The DEA is the primary agency responsible for the enforcement of U.S. drug laws. Among its internationally oriented tasks, the DEA engages in antidrug policing activities at the U.S. borders and abroad. The DEA also serves in a liaison capacity with international organizations involved with drug control. The DEA's Operations Division comprises an Office of International Operations that is in charge of organizing the administration's international missions. In terms of border-related activities, the DEA is particularly active along the U.S.–Mexico border. The DEA's foreign liaisons system is even more extensive than the FBI's, maintaining 78 offices in 56 countries throughout the world.

The Objectives of U.S. International Policing

U.S. participation in formally established multinational structures of police cooperation is not very well developed. Typically, police agencies from the U.S. tend to prefer unilaterally planned and executed international police work and, to a somewhat lesser extent, bilateral cooperation strategies. Among the exceptions is the participation by the U.S. in the International Criminal Police Organization, better known as Interpol. Presently providing cooperation among police agencies of 181 nations, Interpol is represented in the U.S. by the U.S. National Central Bureau, also called Interpol-Washington, which is directed by the Department of Justice and jointly managed with the Treasury Department. Interpol-Washington consists of five divisions: the Alien or Fugitive Enforcement Division, which oversees activities involving international fugitives from justice; the Financial Fraud or Economic Crimes Division, which focuses on economic crimes; the Criminal Investigations Division, which centers on various forms of international crime; the Drug Investigations Division, which specializes in drug crimes; and the State Liaison Division, which maintains relations with various police agencies within the U.S. All agents working for Interpol-Washington are drawn from various U.S. states and federal police agencies.

The War on Drugs

The fight against illegal drugs has been a major factor in the internationalization of U.S. policing, influencing the work of a multitude of agencies to take on international dimensions. Not only the DEA is affected by the war on drugs, but so are some of the activities of the Bureau of Customs and Border Protection (formerly called the U.S. Customs Service), the U.S. Marshals Service, and the U.S. Coast Guard. Importantly, U.S. military forces have also begun to participate in the enforcement of antidrug crimes, especially in the U.S.–Mexico border region. Additionally, the U.S. State Department is increasingly involved in international police matters inasmuch as the international drug trade is also conceived of as a component of foreign policy, not only a police matter.

The Office of National Drug Control Policy develops U.S. efforts to control illegal drugs. The Office specifies among its goals certain distinctly international tasks, such as the protection of America's borders, the control of foreign sources of drug supply, and the promotion of international drug control cooperation. U.S. drug policies are also tied in with multilateral initiatives, such as those taken by the UN General Assembly and, more importantly still, a series of antidrug efforts agreed upon in the Organization of American States. Because of shifts in the drug trade toward Mexico since the early 1990s, furthermore, a series of bilateral antidrug efforts have been taken by the governments of the U.S. and Mexico.

Protecting the U.S. Border

In terms of the control of the U.S. borders, the Bureau of Citizenship and Immigration Services (formerly called the Immigration and Naturalization Service) is primarily responsible for enforcing U.S. laws on immigration. Border control operations are especially oriented at the prevention of smuggling, the entry of illegal aliens into the U.S., and the apprehension of smugglers and illegal aliens after they enter the country. The most important police strategy in this respect since the 1990s has been to increase the number of agents stationed at the borders. Alongside of the stationing of a high number of patrol agents drawn from various federal and local agencies, another major strategy has been the use of advanced technologies, such as computerized fingerprint tracking systems, as well as the deployment of military forces in the fight against border crimes.

International Terrorism

The terrorist attacks in the U.S. on September 11, 2001, have not only brought about a considerable expansion of police powers in the U.S. (as well as elsewhere in the world), it has also particularly influenced significant developments in international police activities. In the U.S., the USA Patriot Act (the "Uniting and

Strengthening America Act by Providing Appropriate Tools Required to Intercept and Obstruct Terrorism" of 2001) places special emphasis on foreign investigative work and the investigation of aliens engaged in terrorist activities. At the international level, also, the September 11 attacks have motivated an expansion of cooperation efforts among the police of various countries. Considering the centrality of the U.S. as the politically and economically most powerful nation in world affairs, the policing of international terrorism heightens the centrality of the role played by U.S. police agencies in international activities surrounding terrorism. In order to accomplish effective cooperation among police institutions across the world, including counter-terrorist cooperation efforts involving the FBI (the leading U.S. antiterrorism agency), the target of terrorism is at the level of cooperating police institutions typically redefined in a language that can be shared across the world. To accomplish this goal, police institutions typically depoliticize terrorism to view it as a crime problem with global implications that is stripped of any ideological justifications. As such, longstanding developments in the creation and expansion of a global police culture are seen to outweigh the sudden political disruptions caused by the terrorist attacks of September 11.

The Limits of International Policing

Participation of the U.S. in international police activities does not always proceed smoothly. The preference among U.S. law enforcement to work unilaterally or only in limited cooperative form can create resentment on the part of foreign police, in turn leading U.S. police to avoid broad cooperative forms of international policing. Typical in this respect is the uneasy membership of the U.S. in Interpol, for the international organization is judged to be too slow and dependent on national governments, some of whom U.S. police officials can place no trust in.

Also, the U.S.-controlled war on drugs is not always judged to have brought about intended effects in terms of the production and distribution of illegal drugs. International efforts to curb the flow of illicit drugs have been seen to bring about a mere dispersion of the problem: the drug trade moves away from locales with heightened police activities to regions where the police presence is less pronounced. Some critics, also, have argued that the very strategy of prohibition is inefficient and costly as well as an unintended cause of criminal activity, especially because well-organized criminal enterprises take control of the drug trade. With respect to the control of drug trafficking at the U.S. border with Mexico, also, serious issues are posed because of the militarization of police work and the redefinition of police duties as national security issues.

In matters of border control, there are indications of a differential enforcement at the U.S. borders with Mexico and Canada. The expansion of border policing activities since the 1980s has almost exclusively implied an enhancement of the protection of the U.S. economy from a Mexico invasion of illegal workers, targeting the U.S.–Mexico border as a "war zone." Because the drug production and trade in Latin America has shifted toward Mexico, the U.S. border with that country has received most police attention. Recent developments in the fight against international terrorism, however, have shifted some attention toward Canada, because the country has been used by suspected members of terrorist groups to enter the U.S.

The Future of International Policing

Police efforts undertaken in terms of globally understood crime issues that transcend the borders of national states can be expected to continue to be a major part of law enforcement in the coming decades. Especially because of continued problems surrounding illegal immigration, the international drug trade, and, arguably most important of all, international terrorism, attention toward international crime problems among police of many countries will remain a crucial factor in worldwide police relations. A central question for the future is whether the U.S. dominance that currently characterizes many international police activities will continue to be a determining factor in the future or whether there will be increasing tension with and possible resentment from the police agencies of other nations. For as U.S. police forces are typically unilaterally involved in international activities, foreign police may in turn decide to prefer to work without participation from U.S. police, effectively diminishing the scope of international cooperation.

Different perceptions of and difficulties in international policing operations reaffirm that the various participants in cooperation efforts remain the key players in the international arena. For instance, the impact of the drug trade and of international terrorism affects nations on a global scale, but at the same time it is clear that national police systems are differently influenced by these global processes and react to them in terms of their own national repercussions. Therefore, it is not only useful to discuss the domestic consequences of global processes, it is clearly not meaningful to analyze international processes of policing without investigating the local dynamics of the various police agencies that are involved in those international activities.

The case of the U.S. dominance in international policing shows clearly that international police work is typically conceived of and engaged in as an extension of nationally defined police duties. Unilaterally enacted police operations that are prevalent in U.S. international police operations are an expression of the relatively high degree of autonomy of U.S. police agencies in planning and instigating such operations, irrespective even of political and legal considerations. Relatedly, an emphasis is placed in international police work on principles of efficiency, such as direct police-to-police communications, that may operate in international activities irrespective of concerns related to legality, justice, and civil and human rights. The efficiency-oriented nature of international police activities underscores the perspective that police institutions are relatively autonomous in setting their own agendas on the basis of acquired knowledge and expertise in matters of international crime. This process of achieving a high degree of autonomy in international policing does not mean that participating police institutions can successfully absolve themselves from concerns over legality and rights, but instead that they are subject to evaluations in moral terms precisely because of their primary reliance on efficiency standards. Internationally oriented police activities are guided by expert conceptions of international crime and its enforcement, but in consequence of such conceptions of international crime, police institutions often seek to accomplish efficiency in their work with little regard for issues of legality, due process, and justice.

The Centrality of Policing Terrorism

The relative independence of police from politics is presently also revealed in the case of counter-terrorism policing. Indeed, although counter-terrorism has clearly moved center stage to the policies of the governments of national states, in the U.S. and elsewhere in the world, antiterrorist police operations on an international level continue to operate relatively independently from the politically enacted policies of counter-terrorism. In the case of the U.S., a remarkable militarization of the judicial processing of foreign terrorists and new legislation and policies aimed to broaden counter-terrorist police strategies (especially the passing of the PATRIOT Act and the creation of the Department of Homeland Security) are among the most concrete political efforts to control the work done by the manifold U.S. security agencies involved in the "war on terror." However, the level of professional autonomy of modern U.S. police institutions, especially the FBI, is now at an unparalleled high level, so that police can effectively resist political influences to remain involved with police work that harmonizes with professional standards of expertise and knowledge with respect to the means and objectives of counter-terrorism. With respect to the means of antiterrorist policing, technological advances and concerns of efficiency are observed to be the primary considerations in establishing police practices against terrorism. This technological emphasis is shown in a concern with interagency communications, computerized information, linguistic issues, the financing of terrorism, and the use of special techniques such as wire-tapping. And in terms of the objectives of social control, the bureaucratization of policing involves most noticeably a depoliticization of the target of counter-terrorism. A criminalization of terrorism is accomplished by defining terrorism very vaguely, for instance as a "crime against humanity," and by dissociating the distinctly criminal elements, such as bombings and killings, from the complex occurrence of terrorist attacks.

The dynamics of international policing, much like many other dimensions of world-historical processes of globalization, corroborate the viewpoint that international events have differential effects on the institutions of different nations. Importantly, the political conditions of foreign policy and international diplomacy do not explain the dynamics of international police work. Among the most important implications in the case of international policing with U.S. involvement is that cooperation among U.S. police and agencies from other countries can be accomplished or can fail irrespective of political and legal conditions. Given the globally recognized centrality of international crime problems, presently no more than international terrorism, the U.S. dominance in international police relations will likely remain an important factor in the future, putting U.S. law enforcement at a distinct advantage relative to other police institutions in the world.

MATHIEU DEFLEM

References and Further Reading

Deflem, M. 2001. International police cooperation in Northern America, in *International Police Cooperation: A World Perspective*, Koenig, D.J. and Das, D.K., (Eds.). Lanham, MD: Lexington Books.

Deflem, M. 2002. *Policing World Society: Historical Foundations of International Police Cooperation*, Oxford and New York: Oxford University Press.

Deflem, M. 2003. The boundaries of international cooperation: Problems and prospects of U.S.–Mexican policing, in *Corruption, Police, Security & Democracy*, Amir, M. and Einstein, S. (Eds.). Huntsville, TX: Office of International Criminal Justice.

Dunn, T.J. 1996. *The Militarization of the U.S.–Mexico Border, 1978–1992*, Austin, TX: CMAS Books.

Koenig, D.J. and Das, D.K. (Eds.) 2001. *International Police Cooperation: A World Perspective,* Lanham, MD: Lexington Books.

Marenin, O. 2001. United States international policing activities: An overview, in *International Police Cooperation: A World Perspective*, Koenig, D.J. and Das, D.K. (Eds.). Lanham, MD: Lexington Books.

McDonald, W.F., (Ed.) 1997. *Crime and Law Enforcement in the Global Village,* Cincinnati, OH: Anderson Publishing.

Nadelmann, E.A. 993. *Cops across Borders: The Internationalization of U.S. Criminal Law Enforcement,* University Park, PA: Pennsylvania State University Press.

See also **International Criminal Tribunals; International Policing: Interpol**

Internet Resources in Criminology and Criminal Justice

To understand the role of the Internet in criminology and criminal justice, it is necessary to understand the history of the Internet. These disciplines of study and the Internet have matured together over the same number of years. Not only has the Internet become a vehicle for communication, information gathering, online databases, collaboration, and a tool for efficiency and investigation, but it is poised to become a major platform for distance learning for criminology and criminal justice. Some would say that criminology and criminal justice are late entrants to the possibilities for distance learning, and that is probably true. History shows that other uses were explored first.

Definition and History of the Internet

The Internet is a worldwide collection of computers with permanent or temporary IP (Internet Protocol) addresses that are connected to one another through telephone lines, TV cable lines, close proximity cables (Ethernet), or wirelessly to a series of transit or backbone supercomputer networks that are themselves interconnected via fiber optic cables. The internet prior to 1990 was known as ARPANET, and provided communication between a small number of scientific, military, university, and corporate institutions. Back then, Internet communication was accomplished via a command line interface on computer screens that displayed telnet and FTP (file transfer protocol), both programs allowing computers to emulate or mimic one another. E-mail, chat, and USENET (news groups) also existed for communication purposes, but those programs were based on time-sharing technology instead of remote emulation technology. In 1990, the year the Internet was born, ARPANET ceased operation owing to overwhelming growth in the handful of FREENET experiments

that were set up in various North American, European, and Australian cities to allow public access. By 1991, all restrictions on public access to the backbone networks were removed and, also in 1991, the World Wide Web (WWW) was born, officially releasing the Internet to the public along with some protocols developed in Switzerland called HTML and HTTP (hypertext markup language and hypertext transfer protocol). This "great renaming" of the Internet as the web (WWW) established the look and feel of the Internet as it exists today and probably always will. In 1992, the Clinton administration made the web, or "information superhighway" one of the nation's highest priorities, and over the next few years, numerous fiber optic upgrades were made to the nation's carrier lines and infrastructure, most notably involving the wiring of schools across the U.S. The Clinton administration also ordered the web deregulated in 1993. By 1994, computer manufacturers were making browsers for people to "surf" the web, and by 1995, Internet access providers, such as CompuServe, AOL, and Prodigy, started business. Today, nobody "owns" the Internet, except for a few companies that lease out pieces of the infrastructure, such as carrier lines. The Internet is overseen and maintained by a professional cooperative called the Internet Society (http://www.isoc.org/), and another group, InterNIC (http://www.internic.net/) manages the registration of IP addresses and domain names.

Overview of Internet Usage in Criminology and Criminal Justice

The Internet has grown exponentially, and so have the number of websites devoted to criminology and criminal justice. The time has long passed when bulletin board services (BBS) dominated the landscape (Jacobs, 1995). Criminology and criminal justice have a rapidly expanding knowledge base, vibrant professional organizations, numerous scholarly journals, hundreds of academic programs, and large student populations, as well as topics of interest to the general public who frequently look for information about those topics on the web. A "web presence" is also evident among the hundreds of institutes, centers, think tanks, interest groups, government organizations, and private agencies that have some connection to the fields of criminology and criminal justice. A general tendency is for such sites to be comprehensive, and maintain a list of many links to other sites, sometimes annotated with comments about the usefulness of those links. A good example would be the *Pinellas County Department of Justice Coordination* at http://www.co.pinellas.fl.us/bcc/juscoord/explore.htm. On the other hand, when an online journal is involved, such as the *Western Criminology Review,* at http://wcr.sonoma.edu/, the tendency is to be quite focused.

It seems that the primary use of the Internet by criminology and criminal justice is for the dissemination of information to the general public via web pages. The most frequently found result when one types a crime or justice keyword into a search engine is a personal or organizational website where the public is informed about matters pertaining to a topic. When the website is personal, the author's ideas, research, or publications are presented. When the website belongs to an organization, the goals and operational structure of the agency or organization are usually presented. Typically, an organization's website contains the mission statement, a personnel list, press releases, annual reports, and some other publications, either free or available for purchase. If the website belongs to a police-related organization, as is often the case, there may also be crime reports, fugitive lists, and crime prevention tips. It is interesting that some police agencies have also experimented with Internet technology for management purposes, as online crime reporting, crime responding, report writing, record keeping, complaint handling, and personnel recruitment can often be found, but these things are more frequently handled via a secure intranet. An example of academic websites that reach out to the public would be this author's one at http://faculty.ncwc.edu/toconnor/ or Cecil Greek's at http://www.criminology.fsu.edu/cj.html. An example of an organization's website accomplishing the same thing would be the *Nassau County Police* at http://www.police.co.nassau.ny.us/.

Criminology and criminal justice organizations have historically made use of list servers and bulletin boards where one can join a discussion and have others participate by group e-mails or by posting comments to the comments of others. For example, one of the oldest list servers in the field is *Critical Criminology* at http://critcrim.com/. The contemporary trend is for such organizations to have e-mail newsletters that one can subscribe to for a fee or for registration only. Some of these discussion boards, list servers, and chat rooms are restricted to working professionals, and others are operated by members of the general public with an interest in crime and justice issues. Still other discussion boards, list servers, and chat rooms are operated by faculty who teach in criminology and criminal justice. Many of these, however, are generally restricted to registered students only. The criminology and criminal justice field has also embraced Internet technology in such areas as distance education, training, and online higher education. Indeed, distance learning is probably the fastest growing area where the Internet is put to use in criminology and criminal justice. For example and to name only a few, *Florida State* at http://www.criminology.fsu.edu/dlstudents/ and *Tiffin University* at http://www.tiffin.edu/livepages/203.shtml both offer an online master's degree in criminal justice.

On average, most websites in criminology and criminal justice are free and easily accessible to the public. There are only a small number of restricted sites, and more frequently, one finds a site where some sort of user registration is required. Registration is typically required to subscribe to a newsletter site, and some online journal sites, but if the goal is to obtain official statistics, numbers, or data on crime and justice topics, then criminology and criminal justice Internet resources in that respect are easily obtainable free. A number of research guides, for example, have been published, which are intended to help students do research over the Internet or enhance their learning by providing stimulating Internet exercises (O'Connor and Barr, 2003; Dennis and Chipman, 2003). Legal research has also been easily done over the web, for example, with *FindLaw* at http://www.findlaw.com/ or *Cornell's Legal Information Institute* at http://www.law.cornell.edu/. For data gathering, two websites are significant enough to mention as perhaps the most popular places to obtain crime and justice statistics: the *National Criminal Justice Reference Service* (NCJRS) at http://www.ncjrs.org/; and the *Sourcebook of Criminal Justice Statistics* at http://www.albany.edu/sourcebook/.

In recent years, the Internet has also become recognized as a technology that produces crime and provides objects of study. Computer crime, cyber-crime, and cyber-terrorism have led many in the field of criminology and criminal justice to study exactly how Internet security or network security works. For example, Michigan State has an online master's degree program in Internet Security at http://www.cj.msu.edu/~outreach/secdist.html and a number of other schools have either established courses, minors, or training modules in computer forensics.

Classification of Websites in Criminology and Criminal Justice

It is possible and to some degree preferable to classify all the Internet resources available according to some logical, rather than topical, scheme. Far too often, a topical scheme fails to hold up because websites disappear or change the topics they are devoted to. Much more favorable is a scheme that allows classification on the basis of purpose or design characteristics. What follows is a working typology of the types of websites one can find that are related to criminology and criminal justice.

1. Comprehensive, "portal"-like sites
2. Agency websites
3. Academic websites
4. Publisher websites
5. Information clearinghouses
6. Law and legal research sites
7. Current events and news sites
8. Personal, "home" page websites

Comprehensive, or "mega" websites usually have the most content among all websites available, but this content may only be in the form of links, with or without any comments or annotations by the author of that website. For example, one of the largest websites in criminal justice is Ira Wilsker's *Law Enforcement on the Web* at http://www.ih2000.net/ira/ira.htm. To view such a site is amazing in its breadth and depth, but a common problem is that these kinds of sites are simply designed to have more and more links added onto them. There is little concern demonstrated over maintenance of those links, and little concern over the load time of content-heavy pages or navigational aids for the viewer. Far more useful is a design approach that focuses upon the "best" of the best, such as Frank Schmalleger's *Cybrary* at http://talkjustice.com/cybrary.asp that features the Top 100 websites in criminal justice or a Top Ten List such as the author has put together for academic sites at http://faculty.ncwc.edu/toconnor/linklist.htm, or CrimeLynx at http://www.crimelynx.com/ that is very selective. A so-called "portal" website is designed with the intent of becoming one's start-up page when a browser is launched. It is bad form, but sometimes a pop-up window will appear, asking the viewer if they want to make this website the "home" page in their browser. For example, *Officer.com* at http://www.officer.com/ and *CourtTV* at http://www.courttv.com/ both seem clearly designed to be one-stop shopping places for anything to do with policing or the courts. At Officer.com, you can browse through the nation's police department websites any way you want, geographically, by special operations, or by individual officer home pages. Look no further if you want to learn about specialized police units like air support, bomb squads, horse patrol, and SWAT teams. Of course, there are lots of other sites that index police departments by state, size, or employment opportunities, but Officer.com is perhaps the number one, most popular law enforcement site in the world, and it is so precisely because of its large and well-maintained size.

Agency websites can be easily found by typing in the name of the agency one is looking for into a search engine. When following this route, it is best to be as specific as possible when naming the agency or the division of it one is interested in. The reason for this is that it is often frustrating to drill down the many layers of government bureaucracy that stand between the home page of the agency and what the Internet user might be looking for. Try to drill or tunnel down to the *FBI's Behavioral Science (Profiling) Section*, for example, at http://www.fbi.gov/hq/isd/cirg/ncavc.htm and you will see that it is not listed on the site map for the agency, and from the URL alone, one can easily see at least three layers of bureaucracy represented by root directories in the URL pathway. As an alternative, directories like Yahoo.com, which are not really search engines, but directories, or human-generated index of what is available on the web, may be useful. Similarly, many websites can be found that index or maintain lists of agencies, like *CopNet* at http://www.copnet.org/directory.html for police agencies, *AllLaw* at http://www.alllaw.com/ for courts, and the largest site for corrections, the *Corrections Connection* at http://www.corrections.com/. Agency websites should be considered the bedrock of the Internet for criminology and criminal justice because they are not supposed to move, and only do so when they host or install new server equipment. By exploring agency sites, one can find out what they are up to and what they have done lately, but a typical research assignment for students is not to extract specific information but to assess the overall "style" of the agency from its website. There are approximately 18,000 police agencies in the U.S., roughly 17,000 courts, and about 4500 prisons and jails, but do not expect every one of them to have a website. Agencies are posting their websites for the first time every day. It takes search engines about a month to index a new site that is submitted, suggested, or found by them. Sometimes, a knowledgeable person in the agency creates an unofficial web page, and then that web page is later transferred to an official agency server. Sometimes, the unofficial web page exists alongside the official site, typically for union or personal reasons.

Academic websites refer to the kinds of Internet resources maintained by a college or university department of criminology and criminal justice, by a group of faculty in that department, or by individual faculty members themselves. Some departments have their own webmaster, others have a faculty member assigned by the IT department to be a "pagemaster," and others rely upon the time-honored tradition of giving each faculty member their own personal web space on the school's server. In addition, some faculties prefer to host their website on private domain space. One would expect that, logically, the websites of the larger institutions in the field would be more informative than the smaller institutions, but that is not always the case. Some of the best, hidden "gems" in criminology and criminal justice are academic websites maintained by faculty members in rather small schools. For example, a large school in the field, such as New York's John Jay College at http://www.jjay. cuny.edu/ seems somewhat reserved with its informative online resources when compared to say, Charles Dreveskracht's *Criminal Justice History Resources* at http://arapaho.nsuok.edu/~dreveskr/ from the Tahlequah campus of Northeastern State in Oklahoma. The author's own website, *MegaLinks in Criminal Justice*, at http://faculty.ncwc.edu/toconnor/, is another example of a small school website, as is John Fuller's *Peacemaking & Crime* at http://www.westga.edu/~jfuller/ peace.html. Numerous other examples exist, especially at the community college level. It appears that many large school academic websites are designed to highlight faculty publications that are frequently offered for sale, but there are exceptions, such as the sociology professor, Gary Marx, who posts online, accessible versions of what he publishes at http://web.mit.edu/gtmarx/www/garyhome.html or the "hybrid" variety of book promotion characterized by Internet excerpts or Internet link supplements, such as Matt Robinson's *Justice Blind* at http://www.justiceblind.com/. One is likely to encounter some frustration when surfing academic websites. There is a need for a guide or directory to individual faculty sites, and school websites are infamous for being difficult to navigate.

Publisher websites were once known for not providing very much content, but all that has changed in recent years. There are a number of good publishing companies in the field of criminology and criminal justice, and they regularly roll out new Internet applications every year at professional conferences. Wadsworth, for example, at http://www.wadsworth.com/criminaljustice_d/ conducts monthly live lecture series that classroom instructors can log into and have their students chat with an expert. Sage, at http://www.sagepub.com/ maintains links to archived issues of journals. Roxbury, at http://www.roxbury.net/ offers some complete works online as Adobe Acrobat files, and many other publishers maintain a variety of supplements, teacher aids, student aids, and lists of Internet resources. Some of the best collections of Internet resources in criminology and criminal justice are maintained by publishing companies. The trend is for them to display, as Amazon.com does, some excerpts from books published, and to go further in creating multimedia-rich "companion websites" for books. They generally construct their Internet resources by contracting on a work-for-hire basis with faculty in the field of criminology and criminal justice. Publishing companies are also in the forefront of distance learning, and produce ready-made content, such as syllabi, lesson plans, PowerPoint slides, etc., which plug into online course management systems. With the Blackboard course management system, these content packages are called "cartridges," and with the WebCt course management system, they are called "e-Paks." Other course management systems also exist, such as PageOut from McGraw Hill, at http://www.pageout.net/, which helps an instructor design online course supplements from ready-made templates.

Information clearinghouses consist of informative profit and nonprofit centers with websites that provide quick access to perspective, ideas, facts, and figures on some particular topic. The concern of the user in seeking such information is not so much to get "official" data, but instead, to discern patterns and trends that are frequently not tracked by anybody but a "cause-based" organization or center. Many government-funded information clearinghouses exist, and in the overview, two of them were mentioned as the best sources for crime and justice statistics: the *National Criminal Justice Reference Service* (NCJRS) at http://www.ncjrs.org/; and the *Sourcebook of Criminal Justice Statistics* at http://www.albany.edu/sourcebook/, and others exist, targeting more practitioner than academic, such as the *National Consortium for Justice Information and Statistics* (SEARCH) at http://www.search.org/ and *Justice Technology Information Network* (JUSTNET) at http://www.nlectc. org/. However, what is usually meant by clearinghouse in the government sense is "database," and sometimes the Internet user is seeking information that stands alone as an analysis, interpretation, or perspective on a topic. For example, one will find an enormous number of nongovernmental clearinghouses on the web devoted to victims and lesser known victimizations. In most cases, these are reform sites, and *Justice for All*, at http://www.jfa.net/, is one of the largest and most popular. One of the more well-financed and politically influential sites in this category is the *Children's Defense Fund*, at http://www.childrensdefense.org/. Data at such sites are typically presented as "key facts" which may or may not correlate exactly with "official" data as it is presented in a novel or interesting way; for example, "Every day, 3,585 babies are born to unwed mothers" whereas a government site would report "The U.S. out-of-wedlock birth rate jumped from 32% to 34% last year." Another common subtype of the reform site deals with sentencing and punishment issues. For example, *Families against Mandatory Minimums*, at http://www.famm.org/, or the *Sentencing Project*, at http://www.sentencingproject.org/, are sites that have been around a long time and commonly thought of as useful Internet sites for criminology and criminal justice, as is *Stop Prisoner Rape*, at http://www.spr.org/, the latter being part of the IGC (Institute for Global Communications) Network, at http://www.igc.org/ that hosts over 250 nonprofit organizations with something to say on crime and justice issues. Other "causes" that one will discover many Internet resources for are First Amendment, or privacy, issues. Here, both the American Civil Liberties Union (ACLU) at http://www.aclu.org/, as well as the American Bar Association (ABA) at http://w3.abanet.org, have excellent thought pieces on those issues. For racial matters and the fairness of justice, there are few substitutes for resources available from the Vera Institute of Justice at http://www.vera.org/, and for policy matters on immigration, drugs, and homeland security, think tanks like the Rand Corporation at http://www.rand.org/ are quite useful. One will find about an equal number of "conservative" and "liberal" Internet resources in criminology and criminal justice, and one would, of course, have to assess the quality of those websites for themselves.

Law and legal research sites, as well as law schools, law school clinics, centers, and institutes have a big Internet presence. Some people say the practice of legal research can be done almost entirely by Internet these days. There is a trend for some of the more sophisticated sites that contain advanced citation tools to be subscription and fee based, such as *LexisNexis* at http://www.lexisnexis.com/, but the average Internet user will find the many free sites, like *FindLaw*, at http://www.findlaw.com, and *Cornell's Law School* at http://www.law.cornell.edu/ are designed for a variety of audiences, including the general public and beginners at the study of law. Legal dictionaries even exist online, for example, by *Duhaime and Company* at http://www.duhaime.org/. Only a few guides and directories for law and legal sites can be found on the Internet, however, but the few that do often direct researchers, on an "as-is" basis to certain legal sites depending upon how that site is perceived as having a "strong" wealth of content on a particular topic.

For example, the Jurist website of the University of Pittsburgh School of Law at http://jurist.law.pitt.edu/ is frequently regarded as a good source for information about cyberspace law and terrorism law. Almost every law school has some institutional venture, center, institute, or interdisciplinary program with an informative website supporting it, frequently containing the transcripts of a recorded lecture series. Many law schools, such as Washburn at http://washburnlaw.edu/wlj/ also provide online archives of past issues of their law journal. One of the more impressive law-related websites is the Virtual Tour of the Supreme Court at http://www.oyez.org/oyez/tour/ that offers a panoramic, 360° view.

Current events and news sites exist that are dedicated to the field of criminology and criminal justice. One host that keeps pop-up ads down to a minimum is About.com that has a site for crime and punishment at http://crime.about.com/ and another one for civil liberties at http://civilliberty.about.com/. CrimeNews 2000 at http://www.crimenews2000.com/ does a good job of extracting headlines and stories about crime from the U.S. newspapers. Top stories in crime are collected by Yahoo News at http://news.yahoo.com/, and CourtTV's Daily Crime News at http://www.crimelibrary.com/news/ provides interesting coverage of ongoing trials. Some owners of websites in criminology and criminal justice have paid for the services of companies like Moreover.com at http://w.moreover.com/ to provide their sites with a "news feed" that extracts the headlines and links to relevant news items. For international news, the World Justice Information Network (WJIN) at http://www.wjin.net/ is a good source, and free, but requires registration. Also, to keep on top of the news, some prefer to subscribe to a list server, and one of the major list servers in criminal justice is CJUST-L that you join by sending an e-mail to LISTSERV@LISTSERV.CUNY.EDU. Two major newsgroups that one can also join are alt.crime and alt.true-crime. In recent years, a phenomenon known as a "blog" (which stands for web log) has emerged. A blog consists of persons expressing their stream of consciousness in a fairly irreverent way toward some topic or news event. Only a few blogs exist on the Internet for criminology and criminal justice. Perhaps the largest one is TalkLeft at http://www.talkleft.com/ that is dedicated to the politics of crime. Another blog is at http://blindjustice.blogspot.com/ that deals with how the media covers crime, and yet another is at http://offenderreentry.blogspot.com/ that deals with the problem of reintegrating exoffenders back into society. Many of the major police-related websites also have news feeds.

Personal "home" pages related to criminology and criminal justice tend to be eclectic, ever-changing in the content that can be found there, and sometimes it is unclear exactly who the author is. For example, a website calling itself the *Internet Crime Archives* at http://www.mayhem.net/ appears to be about serial killers, mass murderers, and cult crimes, but no one knows exactly who exercises maintenance over the site. It appears to be simply a demonstration of someone's ability to create flashy web pages. Other "home" pages combine interests in criminology and criminal justice with things like wedding photos, such as with *Sherri's Home Page* at http://www.soc.umn.edu/~overall/index.html that appears to be a remnant of a former student at a university. Sometimes, alumni of an academic program in criminology and criminal justice create a home page, such as *Kevin Atterbury's Home Page* at http://www.angelfire.com/ak/honeymnster/ that is a good example of former students speaking out about their instructors. There is a tendency for "home" pages to be built by criminology and criminal justice students in the context of student clubs or organizations. The club site for Chico State, at http://www.csuchico.edu/cjsu/, has photos, links, messages, and promises to make assessments about the teaching effectiveness of instructors there. The club site for NC Wesleyan, at http://students.ncwc.edu/LKB/, has photos, links, announcements, and other strange experiments with Javascript running on it. Clearly, there is a need for more direction and support if personal "home" pages are to become a useful and informative part of resources in criminology and criminal justice.

Top Topical Internet Resources in Criminology and Criminal Justice

What many people think of when they think of Internet resources are topics or specialty areas in criminology and criminal justice, which can be categorized a number of different ways. What follows are some select resources on various topics.

Computer Crime

Center for Democracy and Technology (http://www.cdt.org/)—A news-oriented site that focuses upon encryption and other government initiatives related to ensuring a future of safer computing.

Cybercrimes (http://www.cybercrimes.net/)—An informative site from the University of Dayton law school.

Electronic Frontier Foundation (http://www .eff.org/)—One of the most influential sites on the Internet. It discusses the future of Internet technology and its many promises and pitfall; and contains special features on government-driven hacker crackdowns.

International Association of Computer Investigative Specialists (http://cops.org/)—An extensive site consisting of members and their interests who work in law enforcement or the private sector regarding bugs, viruses, and other alerts.

PedoWatch (http://pedowatch.org/)—A citizen safety-oriented comprehensive site on pedophilia and Internet child pornography.

Virtual Gumshoe: Investigative Resources on the Internet (http://www.virtualgumshoe.com/)—A site set up by a private investigator with extensive resources for finding anybody.

Cyber-crime, Justice, and Law (http://www.infosyssec.com/infosyssec/cybercrim1.html)—A comprehensive security portal for IT professionals.

Corrections

The Other Side of the Wall (http://www.prisonwall.org/)—A nicely done site focusing on prison law and a whole lot more.

New York State Correctional Officer's Home Page (http://www.geocities.com/MotorCity/Downs/3548/index.html)—An extensive prison site maintained by a New York corrections officer and union advocate. Go here for prison news, gang info, and issues.

Human Rights Watch: Prisons (http://hrw.org/prisons/) — They monitor conditions and do research.

Rick's Prison Links (http://links.prisonwall.org/)—Contains information on the hard-to-find topics like health and religion with state-by-state links.

JailNet (http://www.jail.net/)—A site with links and resources on issues affecting jail administration, including the law and mandatory jail services. There is a state-by-state directory of jail links.

Courts

Tennessee Criminal Law (http://www.tncrimlaw.com/)—A well-done site that is primer oriented with an excellent set of resources.

Administrative Offices of the U.S. Courts (http://www.uscourts.gov/)—An exhaustive amount of information on the federal court system.

ADR and Mediation Links (http://adrr.com/)—This is a very extensive site on all things related to alternative dispute resolution and mediations, from its philosophy to its actual operations. The site features a topical guide and online essays.

American Judges Association (http://www.theaja.org)—A central clearinghouse of information designed to assist judges and judicial staff. The AJA offers conferences, seminars, and research resources for its member.

Courtroom 21 (http://www.courtroom21.net/)—A site at William & Mary College demonstrating the advantages of technology-augmented adjudication and modern courtrooms.

Crime Analysis

International Association of Crime Analysts (http://www.iaca.net/)—This association has an extensive and useful website. There are tutorials on crime mapping, what crime analysis is, a list of job openings, a newsletter, and related links of interest.

Tempe (AZ) Police Department Crime Analysis Unit (http://www.tempe.gov/cau/default.htm)—Informative site about police analysis of crime data.

Crime Mapping and Analysis (http://gislounge.com/ll/crimemapping.shtml)—An informative site about GIS and its applications toward crime.

Crime Prevention

National Crime Prevention Council (http://www.weprevent.org/)—This site contains content dealing with the history of public education campaigns in crime prevention.

Security Management Online (http://www.security-management.com)—A site for the online counterpart of a magazine that also has extensive online resources relating to the area of private security.

Criminalistics or Forensic Science

Kruglick's Forensic Law Resources (http://www.kruglaw. com/)—A law and forensic science mega-site.

Zeno's Forensic Site (http://forensic.to/forensic.html)—A directory of Internet resources in forensic science, including forensic psychology.

American Academy of Forensic Sciences (http://www.aafs.org/)—An association website that is very informative, especially to young scientists who want to become forensic scientists.

Knowledge Solutions (http://www.corpus-delicti.com/)—A site that provides online coursework in forensic science, computer forensics, and criminal profiling. Some of the content is free.

Criminal Procedure

Anatomy of a Prosecution (http://www.co.eaton.mi.us/ecpa/process.htm)—This is one of the best criminal justice sites on the Internet, as it walks the viewer through the whole criminal justice process from arrest to final appeal.

Grand Jury Information (http://www.udayton.edu/~grandjur/)—An informative website dealing with all sorts of questions one may have about grand juries.

Fully Informed Jury Association (http://nowscape.com/fija/fija_us.htm)—A website chock full of information about regular, petit, or trial juries.

Criminological Theory

Australian Institute of Criminology (http://www.aic.gov.au/)—A source for worldwide, and particularly Australian literature on the possible policy implications of criminological theory.

CrimeTheory.com (http://www.crimetheory.com/) —A well-designed website with a historical timeline of criminological thought.

Demelo's Criminological Theory (http://home.comcast.net/~ddemelo/crime/crimetheory.html)—A series of lecture notes providing an overview of almost all schools of thought and theory in criminology.

Crime Times (http://www.crime-times.org/)—A resource for almost all things related to the biology of crime.

Robert Keel's Sociology of Deviance website (http://www.umsl.edu/~rkeel/200/200lec.html)—A useful site for sociological explanations of crime.

Death Penalty

Death Penalty Links (http://www.derechos.org/dp/)—Probably the best death penalty site, with links to all the others.

Drugs/Alcohol and Crime

Forfeiture Endangers American Rights (http://www.fear.org/)—A site that is critical of policies regarded asset forfeiture.

Web of Addictions (http://www.well.com/user/woa/)—Accurate and complete information about drugs and people who use drugs.

Gangs and Juvenile Justice

National Youth Gang Center (http://www.iir.com/nygc/)—An excellent place to begin gang research.

The Coroner's Report (http://www.gangwar.com/) — A website that contains many links to other gang sites.

Police and Policing

Broken Windows (http://www.theatlantic.com/unbound/flashbks/crime/crime.htm)—An Atlantic Monthly reprint of the famous article, Broken Windows.

Community Policing Consortium (http://www.communitypolicing.org)—A site with online lectures and other material.

CopSeek.com (http://www.copseek.com/)—A rather large and police-oriented site.

Organized Crime

Crime Magazine (http://www.crimemagazine.com)—A site devoted to organized crime, celebrity crime, and justice issues.

Prisons

Departments of Corrections for All States (http://www.geocities.com/MotorCity/Downs/3548/docs.html)—A comprehensive mega-directory.

Prof. Logan's Private Prisons Page (http://www.ucc.uconn.edu/~logan/)—An excellent resource site from this expert on the topic.

THOMAS O'CONNOR

References and Further Reading

Dennis, C. and Chipman, T. 2003. *Internet Activities for Criminal Justice*. Belmont, CA: Wadsworth.

Jacobs, S. 1995. Online criminal justice resources. *Journal of Criminal Justice Education* 6(2): 259–280.

Kurland, D. and Polsenberg, C. 2002. *Internet Guide for Criminal Justice*. Belmont, CA: Wadsworth.

O'Connor, T. and Barr, L. 2003. *i-Search: Criminal Justice*. Boston, MA: Allyn & Bacon.

Schmalleger, F. 2002. *The Definitive Guide to Criminal Justice and Criminology on the World Wide Web*, 2e. Upper Saddle River, NJ: Prentice Hall.

Strutin, K. 2002. *The Insider's Guide to Criminal Justice Resources on the Internet*. Albany, NY: New York State Defender's Association.

See also **Educational Programs in Criminology and Criminal Law; National Crime Victimization Survey (NCVS); Publications in Criminal Law; Uniform Crime Reports (UCR)**

Interrogation and Confessions

The institution and practice of police interrogation raises numerous descriptive, explanatory, and normative questions for practitioners, scholars, and policy makers. How do police interrogate? What is the psychological logic of their techniques, methods, and strategies? Why do individuals confess to crimes that may carry lengthy sentences, life imprisonment, or even the death penalty? Why do some individuals confess falsely? How does the law regulate interrogation and confession? How important is confession evidence in the criminal justice system? And what reforms have been suggested to improve the quality of police interrogations and the reliability of confession evidence they produce?

The modern institution of policing emerged in England in the early part of the 19th century and in America in the mid to late 19th century. Police interrogation at the station house is therefore a relatively recent practice. In the early years of modern policing, there were no established interrogation techniques. Instead, officers either interrogated by intuition or learned how to question suspects as part of their job or did not interrogate at all. In America, the "third degree"—the infliction of physical pain and psychological distress to extract confessions of guilt—was common (Leo, 1992). Through at least the early 1930s, American police routinely beat, tortured, and threatened criminal suspects during interrogation (especially for more serious crimes), sometimes employing methods that left external signs of abuse, but more commonly using physical force in ways that did not (Lavine, 1930; Hopkins, 1931). Not only was the "third degree" common inside the interrogation room, but the confessions police elicited were often admitted into court.

As a result of the influential Wickersham Commission Report in 1931 (National Commission on Law Enforcement and Observance, (1931)), a number of Supreme Court cases beginning with *Brown v. Mississippi*, 297 U.S. 278 (1936), and the movement toward police professionalization, the "third degree" began to decline in the 1930s and, less than three decades later, appeared to be rare in America (Leo, 1992). In its place, American police developed increasingly subtle and sophisticated psychological methods of interrogation that they and others came to believe were more effective at eliciting confessions than the old "third degree." In 1940, W.R. Kidd published *Police Interrogation*, the first American police interrogation manual, exhorting American police in the new science of modern interrogation. In 1942, Fred Inbau published the first edition of his seminal interrogation manual, *Lie*

Detection and Criminal Interrogation. With John Reid, Inbau published successive versions of this training manual in 1948 and 1953. In 1962, Inbau and Reid reorganized and expanded their teachings on police interrogation and confessions into the first edition of *Criminal Interrogation and Confessions.*

Inbau et al.'s *Criminal Interrogation and Confessions,* now in its fourth edition (Inbau, Reid, Buckley, and Jayne, 2001), is the bible of modern police interrogation training; it has virtually defined the teaching and practice of interrogation in America. The Inbau and Reid manual spawned the "Reid Method" of interrogation, and in 1974, the Chicago-based firm Reid and Associates began training police across America in the Reid Method of interrogation. Since 1974, Reid and Associates boast that they have trained more than 100,000 police in the Reid Method of interrogation; undoubtedly, many more police have either read one or more versions of the Inbau et al. manual or have encountered the Reid Method without any formal training. Inbau et al.'s influential training manual conceives of interrogation as the successful undoing of deception to elicit incriminating statements, admissions, or confessions of guilt. According to Inbau et al., prior to interrogation, the detective should administer the "Behavioral Analysis Interview" (a set of 15–20 questions) in response to which the detective, acting as a human lie detector, evaluates the suspect's verbal and nonverbal (i.e., body language) responses. If the detective judges the suspect guilty, he then launches into the nine-step method of interrogation. The first step involves accusing the suspect of committing the crime and confronting him with the evidence of his guilt. Launching into a monologue, the interrogator then develops "themes" (psychological, moral, or legal excuses or justifications) to give the suspect an "out" with which to minimize or eliminate his culpability (step 2), cuts off any denials (step 3), overcomes objections by using them to advance "theme" development (step 4), recaptures the suspect's attention (step 5), handles the suspect's now passive mood by reducing the successful theme to its essential elements (step 6), presents the theme as a two-choice situation in which both choices (one better for the suspect, one worse) still incriminate him (step 7), obtains the oral confession (step 8), and then reduces it to writing (step 9).

The Reid Method presumes that the suspect under interrogation is guilty and will, at least initially, steadfastly deny his guilt. Indeed, Inbau et al. caution that the Reid Method of interrogation should only be used when a detective is certain of the suspect's guilt. Inbau et al. admonish detectives that interrogation—as distinct from mere interviewing—should not be used either to gather general information as a part of a "fishing expedition." Interrogation is a highly strategic and goal-directed activity whose sole purpose is to elicit confessions of guilt. Inbau et al. theorize that the act of interrogation is the undoing of deception and that the Inbau/Reid techniques succeed in eliciting confessions because they simultaneously increase the anxiety a normally socialized (yet deceptive) suspect experiences during interrogation while decreasing his perception of the material, psychological, and legal consequences of confessing. The social science research literature confirms that many of the Inbau/Reid techniques are commonly used by detectives in America (Wald et al., 1967; Simon, 1991; Leo, 1996a). However, there is, as yet, no empirical support for the Inbau/Reid theory about why suspects confess.

Social scientists and psychologists have researched the interrogation process and proffered empirically supported theoretical models to explain how and why contemporary psychological techniques lead to the decision to confess (Kassin and Wrightsman, 1985; Gudjonsson, 1992; Ofshe and Leo, 1997a, 1997b). Modern interrogation techniques and strategies are designed to break the resistance of a rational person who knows he is guilty, manipulate him to stop denying his culpability and persuade him, instead, to confess (Ofshe and Leo, 1997a, 1997b). Police interrogators elicit the decision to confess by influencing the suspect's perception of (a) the nature and gravity of his immediate situation, (b) his available choices or alternatives given his situation, and (c) the consequences of each of these choices. By continuously manipulating the suspect's perception of his situation and his available alternatives, the interrogator labors to persuade the suspect that he has few options but to confess and that the act of admitting culpability is the most optimal, and thus most sensible, course of action.

American police interrogation is essentially a two-step process (Ofshe and Leo, 1997a, 1997b). The goal of the first step of modern interrogation is to break the suspect's resistance by causing him to perceive that he is caught and that his situation as hopeless. The interrogator seeks to accomplish this by leading the suspect to believe that his guilt can be objectively demonstrated to the satisfaction of any reasonable person; that this fact is indisputable and cannot be changed; that there is no way out of his predicament; and that, as a result the suspect is trapped and his fate is determined. Detectives often strive to create the perception that the suspect is dependent on the interrogator's help and can only be released from the pressures of interrogation through confession.

Presuming that the suspect is guilty, the interrogator is likely to rely on several well-known interrogation techniques and strategies to successfully communicate the message that the suspect is caught and persuade him that his situation is hopeless. The interrogator is likely to (repeatedly) accuse the suspect of having committed the crime. The interrogator is likely to express unwavering confidence in these repeated assertions of guilt, ignoring or rolling past any of the suspect's objections. This is likely to have the effect of causing the unknowing suspect to believe that he bears the burden of proving his innocence. Yet the interrogator may seek to prevent the suspect from issuing denials or asserting his innocence. If the suspect offers an alibi, the interrogator may attack it as inconsistent, implausible, contradicted by all the case evidence, or simply impossible, even if none of these characterizations is true.

The most important and effective technique that police use to convince the suspect that his situation is hopeless is to confront him with objective and irrefutable evidence of his guilt, whether or not any actually exists. American law permits interrogators to pretend they have evidence when they do not, and American police often confront suspects with fabricated evidence such as nonexistent eyewitnesses, false fingerprints, make-believe videotapes, false polygraph results, etc. (Leo, 1992, 1996a, 1996b). Because they are legally permitted to lie about the evidence during interrogation, police may also exaggerate the nature, type, amount, and strength of evidence they already have. The purpose of this technique is to convince the suspect that the case against him is so objectively irrefutable that his guilty will be established beyond any possible doubt, that his conviction and imprisonment are inevitable, and, therefore, that he has no choice but to confess to the crime.

In the second phase of interrogation, the detective seeks to influence the suspect to perceive that the only way to improve his otherwise hopeless situation is by admitting to the offense. The interrogator's general strategy is to persuade the suspect that the benefits of admitting guilt clearly outweigh the costs of continuing to assert innocence. To accomplish this goal, the interrogator presents the suspect with inducements that are intended to communicate that he will receive some personal, moral, communal, procedural, material, legal, or other benefit if he confesses to the offense. These inducements, which can be arrayed along a continuum that ranges from obtaining legally permissible benefits to explicitly coercive harms, convey to the suspect that, given his immediate situation and limited choices, it is in his self interest to confess.

For analytic purposes, researchers have classified these inducements into three categories: *low-end, systemic*, and *high-end* inducements (Ofshe and Leo, 1997a, 1997b). *Low-end* inducements refer to self-image, interpersonal, and moral appeals that suggest the suspect will feel better and/or improve his social

standing if he confesses (Ofshe and Leo, 1997a, 1997b). *Systemic* inducements are intended to focus the suspect's attention on the discretionary ability of criminal justice officials to positively influence his case and the systemic benefits for confessing and the systemic costs for continuing to deny guilt. The interrogator's goal is to lead the suspect to reason that his case is likely to be processed more favorably by all actors in the criminal justice system if he accepts responsibility, demonstrates remorse, cooperates with authorities, and admits guilt, but that he will be treated less favorably if he continues to deny any involvement in the offense. *High-end* inducements communicate the message that the suspect will receive less punishment, a lower prison sentence and some form of investigative, prosecutorial, judicial, or juror leniency; or clemency if he complies with the interrogator's demand that he confess, but that the suspect will receive a higher charge, higher sentence, or longer prison sentence if he does not comply with the interrogator's demand that he confess (Ofshe and Leo, 1997a, 1997b). *High-end* inducements may either be implicit or explicit: the important question is whether the interrogation technique communicates the message, or is understood to communicate the message, that the suspect will receive a lower criminal charge or lesser punishment if he confesses (minimization) as opposed to a higher criminal charge or greater amount of punishment if he does not (maximization) (see Kassin and McNall, 1991).

Effective psychological interrogation is a gradual, yet cumulative process. As he progresses through the two phases of interrogation, the detective works to structure the suspect's perceptions about the nature of his immediate situation, the limited choices available to him, and what follows from these choices. Through techniques that rely on deception, manipulation, and sometimes coercion, the interrogator seeks to transform the psychological context within which the suspect comes to perceive his situation and make the decision about whether or not to confess. At the beginning of the interrogation, when the suspect's subjective confidence of leaving the interrogation without incriminating himself is high, the suspect may have thought he would never agree to make an admission. At that point, the suspect would have had nothing to gain and everything to lose by making an admission, and thus he may not have even thought it possible that he would be made to confess. However, once the suspect has been convinced that he will almost certainly be arrested, convicted, and punished, his evaluation of his immediate situation and his decision-making calculus are likely to change. Once the suspect has been persuaded that he is caught and that his situation is hopeless, the act of confessing may, given how he now views his circumstances and limited alternatives, now appear to be in his rational self-interest (Ofshe and Leo, 1997a, 1997b).

The process of psychological interrogation in America often results in incriminating statements, admissions, or confessions from custodial suspects. In some instances, however, contemporary interrogation methods have resulted in confessions from the innocent. Most people do not appear to know that the phenomenon of police-induced false confession even exists (Ainsworth, 1995; Johnson, 1997; Kassin and Neumann, 1997) and along with many criminal justice officials (especially police and prosecutors) appear to believe that an innocent person will not falsely confess to police unless he is physically tortured or mentally ill (Ainsworth, 1995; Johnson, 1997; White, 1997). The social science research has amply documented that contemporary methods of psychological interrogation can, and sometimes do, cause cognitively and intellectually normal individuals to give false confessions to serious crimes of which they are entirely innocent (Gudjonsson, 1992; Kassin, 1997; Leo and Ofshe, 1998). The central research issue is no longer whether police-induced false confessions exist, but why they occur and what can be done to prevent them.

Kassin and Wrightsman (1985) first identified three conceptually distinct types of false confession: voluntary, coerced-compliant, and coerced-internalized. Kassin and Wrightsman's typology or classification scheme has offered a useful framework for scholars of interrogation and confession (Gudjonsson, 1992), though it has also been criticized (Davison and Forsaw, 1993; Ofshe and Leo, 1997a,; McCann, 1998). Synthesizing the existing research literature, Ofshe and Leo (1997a) have extended and modified Kassin and Wrightsman's initial typology to include five distinct types of true and false confession: voluntary, stress-compliant, coerced-compliant, noncoerced persuaded, and coerced-persuaded. A *voluntary* false confession is offered either in the absence of police interrogation or in response to minimal police pressure. A *stress-compliant* false confession is given when the stresses and pressures of custodial questioning overwhelm the suspect and he comes to believe that the only way to terminate the punishing experience of interrogation is by confessing (Ofshe and Leo, 1997a, 1997b). As Kassin (1997, 225) states, "Coerced-compliant false confessions occur when a suspect confesses in order to escape or avoid an aversive interrogation or to gain a promised reward." A *coerced-persuaded* false confession occurs when the interrogator's use of coercive influence techniques causes a suspect to temporarily doubt the reliability of his memory, to come to believe that he probably did, or logically must have, committed the crime under question, and to confess to it, despite having no memory or knowledge of participating in or committing the offense (Ofshe and Leo, 1997a). A *non-coerced persuaded* false confession follows the same structure, sequence and logic as a coerced-persuaded false confession, but is not elicited in response to coercive interrogation techniques.

Police-induced false confessions have always been one of the primary causes of miscarriages of justice in America (Borchard, 1932; Bedau and Radelet, 1987; Leo and Ofshe, 1998). Although it is not presently possible to provide a valid quantitative estimate of the incidence or prevalence of police-induced false confession (Gudjonsson, 1992; Kassin, 1997; White, 1997), it is well-established in the social science research literature that police-induced false confessions occur with troubling regularity and are highly likely to lead to unjust deprivations of liberty and the wrongful conviction of the innocent (Gudjonsson, 1992; Wrightsman and Kassin, 1993; Leo and Ofshe, 1998a). Psychologists, criminologists, and others have documented so many examples of police-induced false confession by now that there is no longer any dispute about their occurrence. However, because most police-induced false confessions are likely to go unnoticed by researchers, unacknowledged by police and prosecutors, or unreported by the media, they are not easily discovered and are rarely publicized. As a result, the documented cases likely represent only the tip of a much larger false confession (and wrongful conviction) iceberg.

Historically regarded as a form of self-conviction, false confessions are highly likely to lead to miscarriages of justice because of the extreme biasing effect that they exert on the perceptions and decision making of criminal justice officials and lay jurors (Wrightsman and Kassin, 1993; Kassin and Sukel, 1997; Leo and Ofshe, 1998). Except for the rare instance in which a perpetrator is caught *in flagrante* (more common in cinema than real life), a confession is regarded as the most powerful, persuasive, and damning evidence of guilt that the state can bring against the accused (Kassin and Wrightsman, 1985; Leo, 1996a; Leo and Ofshe, 1998). A *false* confession is therefore the most powerful, persuasive, and damning *false* evidence of guilt that the state can bring against an accused, more prejudicial than virtually any other potential source of evidence.

A suspect who confesses to police, whether truthfully or falsely, will not only be presumed guilty from the start, but will also be pressured to plead guilty and treated more harshly by every legal official and at every stage of the criminal process (Leo, 1996a). Police typically "clear" the case as solved once they elicit a confession, even if it is not supported by any independent evidence, is internally inconsistent, or was obtained under questionable conditions. Criminal justice officials typically will not believe a suspect's retractions, which they may interpret as further evidence of his deceitfulness. Suspects who confess, especially in serious cases, will experience greater difficulty making bail, a disadvantage that significantly reduces a criminal defendant's likelihood of acquittal (Walker, 1994; Leo and Ofshe, 1998). Prosecutors will be more likely to charge suspects who confess and charge them with more counts, whereas defense attorneys will pressure these suspects to concede guilt and accept a plea bargain (Leo and Ofshe, 1998). If the case goes to trial, the jury will treat the confession as more probative of the accused's guilt than any other type of evidence (Miller and Boster, 1977; Kassin, 1997), and the suspect is more likely to be convicted of more serious crimes (Leo and Ofshe, 1998). And if convicted, a suspect who has falsely confessed is likely to be sentenced more harshly for failing to show remorse.

In America, the Fifth, Sixth, and Fourteenth Amendments to the U.S. Constitution regulate the admissibility of confession evidence in courts. According to the Fourteenth Amendment, a confession is inadmissible if police interrogation methods overbear the suspect's will and thus cause him to make an "involuntary" confession. Under this standard, the trial judge evaluates the voluntariness (and hence admissibility) of a confession case by case based on the totality of the circumstances (i.e., the facts of the case, the suspect's personality and background characteristics, and the specific police interrogation methods). It is well-established in American law that any techniques involving physical assault, incommunicado or excessively lengthy interrogation, threats, promises; or deprivations of essential necessities such as food and water will be regarded as involuntary and thus suppressed from evidence at trial. The Fourteenth Amendment additionally permits courts to exclude as "involuntary" any confessions obtained by fundamentally unfair police methods, regardless of the confession's voluntariness (Dressler and Thomas, 1999). In practice, trial judges in America suppress very few confessions.

According to the Sixth Amendment to the U.S. Constitution a conression may be excluded from evidence if after a suspect has been indicted he is questioned outside the presence of his attorney. In practice this is rarely an issue as virtually all interogation in America occurs prior to indictment.

The most well-known law regulating the admissibility of confession evidence in America derives from the Fifth Amendment's privilege against self-incrimination. According to the well-known Supreme Court decision of *Miranda v. Arizona*, 384 U.S. 436 (1966), American police are required to inform suspects of their "*Miranda*" rights, to remain silent, to have appointed counsel, and to be informed that anything they say can be used against them in court, before interrogation can legally commence. The U.S. Supreme Court declared that the purpose of the *Miranda* warnings was to dispel the coercion that, it believed, was inherent in police-dominated custodial interrogation. In addition, the prosecution bears the legal burden of demonstrating that the detectives obtained the *Miranda* waiver "knowingly, voluntarily, and intelligently" before any confession can be admitted into evidence. If the police fail to properly inform the suspect of his *Miranda* rights or to properly obtain a waiver from the suspect, then, in theory, any statement that the suspect makes to police is excluded from evidence at trial.

American police initially feared that *Miranda* would handcuff their investigative abilities, not only causing them to lose numerous essential confessions and convictions, but also returning rapists and killers to the streets only to prey again. Police chiefs predicted chaos, believing that the new *Miranda* requirements were the equivalent of a virtual ban on interrogation (Baker, 1983). Contrary to these dire predictions, however, American police have successfully adapted to *Miranda* in the last four decades. The overwhelming majority of suspects (some 78–96%) waive their rights and thus appear to consent to interrogation, whether explicitly or implicitly. They have devised multiple strategies to avoid, circumvent, nullify, or simply violate *Miranda* and its invocation rules in pursuit of confession evidence. These strategies include recasting a custodial interrogation as a noncustodial interview (so *Miranda* warnings are no longer necessary), eliciting "implicit" waivers, deemphasizing the significance of the *Miranda* warnings, persuading suspects to waive *Miranda*, and interrogating suspects "outside *Miranda*" (i.e., after invocation, even though it is not permissible to do so). Because American police have learned how to "work *Miranda*" to their advantage, i.e., to issue (or avoid having to issue) *Miranda* warnings in strategic ways that will result in legally acceptable waivers, *Miranda* operates as a weak or minimal restraint on police interrogation, contrary to the intentions and beliefs of the Warren Court as well as its many contemporary liberal and progressive supporters. It does little, if anything, to protect suspects against abusive interrogation tactics. Perhaps because, *Miranda* has not changed the nature or tactics of American police interrogation, it has not caused a significant decline in confession rates and thus has not affected the ability of police to clear cases or prosecutors to obtain convictions. Despite the constitutional protections offered by the Fifth, Sixth, and Fourteenth amendments to the U.S. Constitution, American defendants continue to allege that their interrogators used psychologically coercive methods, they continue to dispute the legality and reliability of their confessions, and, on occasion, they get convicted on the basis of confessions that subsequently are proven false (Leo and Ofshe, 1998). Despite the great constitutional protections of American law, virtually all confessions in America are admitted into evidence and used against the accused at trial. Nevertheless, police interrogation continues to be a controversial subject in courtrooms across the country, in the television shows that fuel the popular imagination, and in American law and legal doctrine.

As a result, several reforms have been proposed to improve the quality of interrogation, that is, to assist police in using interrogation techniques that are legal and increase the number of true confessions while decreasing, if not eliminating, the number of false ones. One prominent reform is the mandatory electronic recording of the entirety of police interrogations. In America, two states require that police record the entirety of all police interrogations (Alaska since 1985, Minnesota since 1994), though many police departments in other states voluntarily record interrogations (Geller, 1992). In England, police have been required to contemporaneously record all interrogations since 1986. There are numerous advantages to recording interrogations. Perhaps most significantly, video-taping creates an objective, comprehensive, and reviewable record of the interrogation so that it is no longer necessary to rely on subject credibility judgments to resolve any "swearing contests" between the police and the defendant about what occurred during the interrogation, thus rendering the fact-finding process more accurate and reliable (Kamisar, 1980; Johnson, 1997; Westling and Waye, 1998). In addition, video-taping leads to a higher level of scrutiny (by police officials as well as by others) that many believe will deter police misconduct during interrogation, improves the quality of interrogation practices, and thus increases the ability of police to separate the innocent from the guilty. Finally, videotaping creates the opportunity for various criminal justice officials to more closely monitor both the quality of police interrogation and the reliability of police statements. As a result, detectives, police managers, prosecutors, and judges should be able to detect false confessions and thus prevent their admission into evidence against innocent defendants more easily.

RICHARD A. LEO

References and Further Reading

Ainsworth, P. 1995. *Psychology and Policing in a Changing World*. New York, NY: John Wiley & Sons.

Baker, L. 1983. *Miranda: Crime, Law and Politics*. New York, NY: Athenum Press.

Bedau, H. and Radelet, M. 1987. Miscarriages of justice in potentially capital cases. *Stanford Law Review*. 21–179.

Borchard, E. 1932. *Convicting the Innocent: Errors of Criminal Justice*. New Haven, CT: Yale University Press.

Davison, S.E. and Forshaw, D.M. 1993. Retracted confessions: Through opiate withdrawal to a new conceptual framework. *Medicine, Science and the Law*. 285–290.

Dressler, J. and Thomas, G.C. III. 1999. *Criminal Procedure: Principles, Policies and Perspectives* St. Paul, MN: West Group.

Geller, W. 1992. *Police Videotaping of Suspect Interrogations and Confessions*. A Report to the National Institute of Justice. Washington, DC: United States Department of Justice.

Gudjonsson, G. 1992. *The Psychology of Interrogations, Confessions and Testimony*. West Sussex, England: John Wiley & Sons.

Johnson, G. 1997. False confessions and fundamental fairness: The need for electronic recording of custodial interrogations. *The Boston University Public Interest Law Journal*. 719–751.

Kamisar, Y. 1980. *Police Interrogation and Confessions: Essays in Law and Policy*, Ann Arbor, MI: University of Michigan Press.

Kassin, S. 1997. The psychology of confession evidence. *American Psychologist*. 221–233.

Kassin, S. and Neumann, K. 1997. On the power of confession evidence: An experimental test of the fundamental difference hypothesis. *Law and Human Behavior*. 469–483.

Kassin, S. and Sukel, H. 1997. Coerced confessions and the jury: An experimental test of the "Harmless Error" rule. *Law and Human Behavior*. 27–46.

Kassin, S. and McNall, K. 1991. Police interrogation and confessions: communicating promises and threats by pragmatic implication. *Law and Human Behavior*. 233–251.

Kassin, S. and Wrightsman, L. 1985. Confession evidence, *The Psychology of Evidence and Trial Procedure*, Kassin, S. and Wrightsman, L. (Eds.), Thousand Oaks, CA: Sage Publications.

Kassin, S. and Kiechel, K. 1996. The social psychology of false confessions: Compliance, internalization, and confabulation, *Psychological Science*, 125–128.

Hopkins, E.J. 1931. *Our Lawless Police: A Study of the Unlawful Enforcement of the Law*. New York, NY: Viking Press.

Inbau, F., Reid, J., Buckley, J., and Jayne, B. 2001. *Criminal Interrogation and Confessions*. 4th ed. Gaithersburg, MD: Aspen Publishers, Inc.

Lavine, E. 1930. *The Third Degree: A Detailed and Appalling Expose of Police Brutality*, New York, NY: Garden City Publishing Co.

Leo, R.A. 1996b. The impact of *Miranda* revisited. *The Journal of Criminal Law and Criminology*. 621–692.

Leo, R.A. 1996a. Inside the interrogation room. *The Journal of Criminal Law and Criminology*. 266–303.

Leo, R.A. 1992. From coercion to deception: The changing nature of police interrogation in America. *Crime, Law and Social Change: An International Journal*. 35–59.

Leo, R.A. and Ofshe, R.J. 1998. The consequences of false confessions: Deprivations of liberty and miscarriages of justice in the age of psychological interrogation, *The Journal of Criminal Law and Criminology*. 429–496.

McCann, J. 1998. A conceptual framework for identifying various types of confessions. *Behavioral Sciences and the Law*. 441–453.

Miller, G.R. and Boster, F.J. 1977. Three images of the trial: Their implications for psychological research, Sales, B. (Ed.), *Psychology in the Legal Process*. New York, NY: Pocket Books.

Ofshe, R.J. and Leo, R.J. 1997. The social psychology of police interrogation: The theory and classification of true and false confessions. *Studies in Law, Politics and Society.* 189–251.

Ofshe, R.J. and Leo, R.A. 1997. The decision to confess falsely: Rational choice and irrational action, *Denver University Law Review.* 979–1122.

National Commission on Law Observance and Enforcement. 1931. *Report on Lawlessness in Law-Enforcement.* Vol. 11. Washington, DC: U.S. Government Printing Office.

Simon, D. 1991. *Homicide: A Year on the Killing Streets.* Boston, MA: Houghton Mifflin Company.

Wald, M., Ayres, R., Hess, D.W., Schantz, M., and Whitebread, C.H. 1967. Interrogations in New Haven: The impact of *Miranda. The Yale Law Review.* 1519–1648.

Walker, S. 1994. *Sense and Nonsense about Crime and Drugs: A Policy Guide.* Belmont, CA: Wadsworth, Inc.

Westling, W. and Waye, V. 1998. Videotaping police interrogations: Lessons from Australia. *American Journal of Criminal Law.* 493–543.

White, W.S. 1997. False confessions and the constitution: Safeguards against untrustworthy confessions, *Harvard Civil Rights-Civil Liberties Law Review.* 105–157.

Wrightsman, L. and Kassin, S. 1993. *Confessions in the Courtroom.* Newbury Park, CA: Sage Publications.

See also **Due Process; Police Detectives; Police Investigation**

Intoxication as a Defense to Criminal Liability

Intoxication is a limited defense to criminal liability. According to the Model Penal Code, intoxication "is a disturbance of mental or physical capacities resulting from the ingestion of a foreign substance, such as alcohol or a drug." However, for intoxication to serve as a defense to criminal liability, the intoxication must be involuntary. Voluntary intoxication is not a defense to criminal liability.

What is *involuntary* intoxication? There are basically four ways by which a person can become involuntarily intoxicated. The first is coercion. If a person is coerced to ingest an intoxicant, then that person will succeed with an intoxication defense if he or she commits a crime under the influence. The second way to become involuntarily intoxicated is by mistake. In the case of *People v. Penman* (110 N.E. 894, IL 1915), the defendant was tricked into taking cocaine in tablet form, after being told that it was a breath purifier. This constituted involuntary intoxication. The third way to become involuntarily intoxicated is by a condition known as "pathological intoxication." If a person suffers from a grossly disproportionate intoxication in light of the amount of intoxicant ingested, that person will succeed with an intoxication defense, so long as the person does not know that he or she is susceptible to such a reaction. Finally, involuntary intoxication occurs when a person becomes unexpectedly intoxicated from ingestion of a medically prescribed drug (e.g., *City of Minneapolis v. Altimus*, 238 N.W.2d 851, MN 1976).

If a person becomes involuntarily intoxicated, there are two means by which such a condition reduces culpability. First, involuntary intoxication can cause a person to lose the required *mens rea* (criminal intent) to commit the offense for which he or she is charged. For example, if a defendant is charged with the robbery of a victim, but the robbery was a result of the defendant's involuntary intoxication, the defendant will succeed with an intoxication defense. Another way to view involuntary intoxication is that it causes a person to become "temporarily insane," a condition that diminishes or eliminates intent to commit a crime.

Involuntary intoxication can do more than negate *mens rea*. It can also influence the *actus reas* (the criminal act) component of criminal liability. If a person is involuntarily intoxicated to the point of incapacitation or unconsciousness but is later charged with a crime that was presumably committed while the person was in this condition, the defendant may argue that he or she could not have physically performed the act. For example, if the defendant passed out from involuntarily consuming too much alcohol, the defendant could introduce evidence to show that he could not have committed the voluntary act of the charged offense.

Is all hope lost if a person becomes voluntarily intoxicated? No, but a voluntarily intoxicated person cannot succeed with a formal intoxication defense. Instead, such a person will argue that criminal intent was absent or that he or she could not have physically performed the act in question. This may appear strikingly similar to the discussion of involuntary intoxication in the previous paragraphs. It is not. Involuntary intoxication is an affirmative defense (one that is actually raised in trial) recognized by the courts. *Voluntary* intoxication is not an affirmative defense. Instead, if the defendant wants to raise the intoxication issue, he or she will have to show that *mens rea* or *actus reas* (or both) were compromised under the circumstances.

It is useful at this point to distinguish between specific- and general-intent offenses. Specific-intent offenses have as one of their elements a requirement that the defendant commit the crime with a certain level of intent (i.e., willingly, knowingly, and aforethought). General-intent offenses involve a broad disregard for propriety and public safety (as with recklessness and negligence), but do not formally require a specific type of intent as part of the statute. This distinction is important because at common law a person would not be found guilty of a specific-intent offense if, as a result of *voluntary* intoxication, she lacked the capacity or failed to form the specific intent required in the definition of the offense (e.g. *People v. Low*, 732 P.2d 622, CO 1987). This rule did not apply, however, to general intent offenses.

The *Model Penal Code*, which departs in many ways from common law practices, does not distinguish between general- and specific-intent offenses. Under the *Model Penal Code*, voluntary intoxication will exculpate the defendant if it negates any element of the offense (*mens rea* or *actus reas*). The code does state, however, that if persons are charged with specific crimes of recklessness, they cannot avoid conviction by proving that, because of their intoxication, they were unaware of the riskiness of their conduct. Assume, for example, that a man becomes voluntarily intoxicated, drives a car, and kills a pedestrian. He is charged with reckless homicide (manslaughter). He argues that he was drunk at the time of the killing and was unaware that he was acting recklessly. Under the *Model Penal Code*, he will not succeed with this argument. Because of this "intoxication rule," he will be found guilty of reckless homicide. Had the man been charged with first-degree murder, however, he might succeed in arguing that he did not intend for the homicide

to occur. As controversial as this sounds, the *Model Penal Code* does not prohibit people from arguing that they could not have committed or did not intend to commit a criminal act.

What if a person is an alcoholic or a drug addict? Intoxication that is the result of alcoholism or drug addiction is viewed as voluntary for purposes of the intoxication defense. In some cases, heavy consumption of alcohol over an extended period of time can result in organic brain damage. If this occurs, a person may succeed with an insanity defense if the condition is "settled" or "fixed," but not an intoxication defense. In the absence of permanent, physical brain damage, there is little medical consensus on whether alcohol can truly "compel" a person to drink, thereby reducing culpability. Interestingly, the Supreme Court has implicitly held that a person cannot be punished for the *status* of chronic additcion (*Robinson v. California*, 370 U.S. 660, 1962), but that the defendant may still be punished for conduct involving the use of drugs if the behavior was not a symptom of alcoholism or chronic addiction.

JOHN L. WORRALL

References and Further Reading

Anderegg, S.A. 1988. The voluntary intoxication defense in Iowa. *Iowa Law Review* 73:935.

Brookman, H.J. 1997. To drink or not to drink: The Supreme Court delivers a sobering blow to the intoxication defense by placing due process on the rocks. *Seton Hall Law Review* 28:514.

Keiter, M. 1997. Just say no excuse: The rise and fall of the intoxication defense. *Journal of Criminal Law and Criminology* 87:482.

Layton, C.J. 1997. No more excuses: Closing the door on the voluntary intoxication defense. *John Marshall Law Review* 30:535.

Mandiberg, S.F. 1984. Protecting society and defendants too: The constitutional dilemma of mental abnormality and intoxication defenses. *Fordham Law Review* 53:221.

See also **Defenses to Criminal Liability: Justifications and Excuses**

Investigative (Psychological) Profiling

Criminal profiling, referred to as offender profiling, psychological profiling, or criminal personality profiling is the derivation of inferences about a criminal from

aspects of the crime(s) that he or she has committed. Available information from a crime and crime scene theoretically should point to a psychological portrait of the unknown perpetrator inferring such things as the offender's motivation for the crime and production of a description of the type of person likely to be responsible. The profiler, based on his or her technique and investigative experience, examines pertinent data from a specific crime scene including crime-scene photographs, detailed photos of bodily injuries to victims, photos of any mutilation evidence, information related to the condition of the victim's clothing or absence there of, information regarding whether the crime scene was altered or unaltered, types of weapons employed, the medical examiner's report and opinion, and any other relevant information concerning the crime. Additional information used in criminal profiling can involve geographical analysis of the crime and the areas beyond the immediate crime scene, including maps of the area, tracking data on how the perpetrator got to and from the crime scene, and relevant aspects of the residential location of the victim. Depending on the profiling technique, specific data collected is then categorized to produce predictive information regarding the suspect's likely age, sex, race, weight, height, physical, mental, or psychological condition, and likely area of residence; as well as whether the victim was known to the offender, whether the suspect had a prior criminal record, and other details. Despite differences in profiling, the goal of the profiling process is to deduce enough behavioral, personality, and physical characteristics about an offender so that he or she may be apprehended by authorities. Rarely will a profile be so accurate that it points to a particular individual, rather it helps the police by narrowing down the list of possible suspects who may have committed the crime (Bennett and Hess, 1991; Muller, 2000).

Popular films such as *Silence of the Lambs* or television programs such as *Profiler* or *Millennium* depict horrible crimes such as serial murder, rape, and kidnapping committed by calculating pathological offenders who appear unable to be apprehended by traditional law enforcement methods. As a last act of desperation and usually under protest by local detectives, a criminal profiler (e.g., an agent from the Federal Bureau of Investigation [FBI] or a psychologist) is brought in to help catch the offender before he or she can commit other grisly crimes. Unfortunately, the role of the profiler and the techniques depicted by the media suggest that criminal profiling is more of a science than it is in actual practice. Many law enforcement agencies remain skeptical of the work of profilers and do not fully understand how the techniques work. Most criminologists who study criminal profiling likewise question the validity and reliability of profiling techniques in the identification and apprehension of violent offenders and point to the lack of scientific studies to support the claims of profilers. Nevertheless, criminal profiling has great potential and is believed by many

to be an aid to understanding the make-up of offenders who commit certain types of criminal behaviors and to guiding investigations leading to the apprehension of criminal perpetrators of these crimes.

According to some experts, criminal profiling is not applicable to all types of criminal situations but rather lends itself to cases where the offender is unknown and has recurring patterns of violent behaviors. In particular, profiling has proven useful in cases involving lust and mutilation murder, serial murder, rape, sadistic torture in sexual assaults, satanic and ritualistic crime, bombings, and pedophilia (Holmes and Holmes, 1996).

Types of Profiling

Criminal profiling is not one specific type of technique. Two major types of criminal profiling, crime scene analysis (CSA) and investigative psychology (IP), have developed rather independently albeit employing somewhat similar procedures. Crime scene analysis, made popular by the Behavioral Science Unit of the FBI in its efforts to solve particularly violent crimes such as serial murders, rapes, and child-molesting cases in the 1970s, is what most people probably think of when they hear of criminal profiling. Law enforcement agencies who desired a criminal personality profile from the FBI had to meet certain criteria for a case to be analyzed. The case had to involve a crime of violence, the offender had to be unknown, and all major investigatory leads had to be exhausted.

Investigative psychology, an approach developed by British psychologists such Dr. David Canter, links the dominant themes in an offender's crimes to characteristic aspects of their lifestyles and offending history (Muller, 2000). British profilers have worked closely with the police and have sought to establish an empirical, rather than intuitive, basis for offender profiling (Grubin, 1995).

Two lesser techniques, diagnostic evaluation and geographical analysis are in the early stages of development. Diagnostic evaluation as a form of criminal profiling relies exclusively on the clinical judgment or assessment of a practitioner (e.g., trained psychiatrist) and has therefore, remained eclectic in its presentation of significant behavioral manifestations and associated interpretations. Very early efforts at profiling were based primarily on psychoanalytic principles and conclusions based on a practitioner's clinical intuition. Geographical profiling examines the spatial decision making process of offenders in relation to their selection of crime victims and crime scene locations. Clues to how offenders select their victims and seek suitable targets can be derived by developing geographical profiles (Holmes and Holmes, 1996).

Crime Scene Analysis

The written works of several former FBI profilers such as Robert Ressler (1988, 1992), Roy Hazelwood (1993), and John Douglas (1997, 1999) have publicized the use of criminal personality profiling in the investigation of serial and spree killers, mass murderers, bombers, rapists, and hijackers. Although these books make for exciting reading, and give some insight into the types of data that the profilers collected and examined, they offer very little detail of the precise methodology or technique employed. Hazelwood and his colleagues report that successful profilers are experienced in criminal investigations and research but that they also possess common sense, intuition, and have the ability to isolate their feelings about the crime, the criminal, and the victim. In addition, they are able to think and reason like the criminal who committed the crime (1993). This description of a profiler suggests that some things other than the scientific method are at root in deriving psychological profiles of offenders that might be of use in their eventual apprehension. In essence, FBI profilers do not suggest that their techniques are exclusively scientific, rather they describe investigative profiling as a strategy enabling the police to narrow the field of options and generate educated guesses about the perpetrator (Douglas, et al, 1992). Early efforts of the FBI Behavioral Science Unit, however, did incorporate techniques based on the systematic collection of large amounts of information about known violent offenders and their crimes. The study of violent offenders by the FBI's National Center for the Analysis of Violent Crime in Quantico, Virginia has also resulted in efforts to refine the investigation of major crimes by the examination of clues and crime scene indicators common to each type of crime. The publication of the *Crime Classification Manual: A Standard System for Investigating and Classifying Violent Crimes* by John Douglas and his associates (1992) formally classifies the critical characteristics of the perpetrators and victims of three major violent crimes—murder, arson, and sexual assault.

The crime-scene analysis approach to profiling assumes that the crime scene reflects the personality of the offender. Through their work, FBI profilers have identified the characteristics of *organized* and *disorganized* murders, particularly those murders that involve sex as a primary motive (Ressler et al., 1988). By using information gathered at a crime scene and by examining the nature of the crime itself, agents have constructed psychological profiles of the offenders that are in turn classified as organized and disorganized. An organized murderer is often profiled as being highly intelligent, socially competent, and charismatic, whereas the disorganized murderer is profiled as being of average intelligence, socially immature, and a loner. The level of planning of crimes including the selection and treatment of victims, method of death, and crime scenes of organized and disorganized offenders likewise suggests significant differences between the two types of offenders. Organized murderers reflect more methodical patterns of behavior and well-organized plans, involving the careful selection of strangers as victims, demanding victims to be submissive, taking great care in the actual methods of death, leaving little evidence at the crime site, and even killing at one site and dumping the body at another site. On the other hand, disorganized murderers commit their crimes more spontaneously with little planning; they may actually know or be aware of their victims, and they often kill in surprise or blitz attacks which result in crime scenes that reveal a great deal of physical evidence.

A well-accepted description of the crime scene analysis profiling technique applied to murder is given in an early work written by Robert Ressler, Ann Burgess, and John Douglas (1988). The authors describe the criminal profiling techniques according to a six-stage process. In the first stage, *profiling inputs*, profilers collect all information connected with the case including such things as crime scene photographs and diagrams, police reports, victim data, and forensic data. The second stage, *decision process models*, all data and information are examined and organized and a preliminary analysis is completed. At this stage the nature of the homicide is categorized (e.g., single, mass, or serial murder) along with other information such as the intent of the offender (e.g., whether the crime was the primary objective or whether it was committed while conducting another crime), the nature of the victim (e.g., whether the victim was a high or low risk target), and the degree of risk that the offender subjected himself or herself to in committing the crime. The location(s) of the crime and other pertinent information are also determined (e.g., where the victim was abducted and where the victim was murdered) as well as the possible length of time that was taken to carry out the offense (s).

In the third stage, *crime assessment*, the profiler attempts to place himself or herself in the role of the offender and, so to speak, think like the offender or use the offender's reasoning processes. The crime is categorized as organized or disorganized and the profiler addresses such things as the motivation of the offender, the selection of the victim, whether the crime was planned or spontaneous, how the crime was executed, whether aspects of the crime scene were staged (i.e., aspects of the crime scene were altered to confuse or fool the police), the nature and the types of wounds on the victim, and any ritualistic actions such as displaying or positioning the body of the victim in a certain manner. In the fourth state, *criminal profile*, the investigator coalesces all of the information and data heretofore collected as well as drawing upon his or her experiences with other crimes and constructs a criminal profile. The report, ranging from a few paragraphs to several pages, describes the type of person who most likely committed the crime; including physical features such as age, gender, race, and appearance of the offender as well as possible occupation and employment, military service, education, residence, familiarity with the crime scene area, and relationship history with other individuals. Projections about the offender's personality (e.g., psychopathic or special fetishes or pornographic interests) are made. In addition, the profiler offers strategies for identifying, interrogating, and apprehending the criminal.

The fifth stage, *investigation*, is the submission of the profile report to the respective law enforcement agency that is investigating the crime. The profile is judged to be successful if an offender is identified and confesses the crime. If, on the other hand, new information is obtained about a case, the profile is considered open and a reevaluation of the original profile takes place. *Apprehension* of the perpetrator makes up the sixth stage. The accuracy of the profile is assessed and the case data are added to the existing body of knowledge for use by future profilers (Muller, 2000).

Investigative Psychology

Pioneered by British environmental psychologists such as Dr. David Canter at the University of Liverpool, investigative psychology attempts to introduce a scientific basis to previously subjective aspects of criminal detection, crime scene analysis, investigation, apprehension, and prosecution of the offender. Rather than offering a comprehensive methodology, investigative psychology represents a collection of theories, hypotheses, and results of studies of the history and patterns of behavior as they relate to certain individual characteristics. Canter (1989) argues that crime is an interpersonal transaction, usually between the criminal and the victim, within a social context. To this extent, criminals are performing actions that are direct reflections of the sorts of transactions they have with other people in more normal circumstances. The role of investigative psychology is to determine which aspects of those criminal transactions can be linked to other aspects of the offender's past and present life. In particular, investigative psychology searches for behavioral characteristics that are clearly unique to the individual offender as opposed to the social groups that he or she is a member of. Canter proposes five approaches based on psychology that can be used to profile offenders and hopefully lead to their successful apprehension. These include: (1) interpersonal coherence; (2) significance of time and

place; (3) criminal characteristics; (4) criminal career; and (5) forensic awareness.

The first approach, *interpersonal coherence*, is based on the hypothesis that offenders select victims with key characteristics similar to significant people in their lives outside of crime. For example, American research results on serial murders suggests that serial murderers generally select victims sharing their same ethnicity. Similarly, targeted victims may have special other personal significance for the offenders. For instance, Mark Essex, an African American seaman, perceived himself unable to move through the ranks in the U.S. Navy because he was black. His killing spree targeted types of individuals, chiefly whites, resembling those who discriminated against him. The second approach, *significance of time and place*, suggests that the time and place for a violent crime has special meaning for the perpetrator. Prime hunting grounds are jobs or occupations that allow offenders to observe potential victims over time in their own settings. Additionally, offenders' knowledge of the geography or spatial patterns of an area has a particular bearing on their perception of where it is possible to commit certain types of crimes and even dispose of victim's bodies. Canter believes that individuals make such decisions based on "mental maps" or internal representations of the terrains that they inhabit.

The third approach, *criminal characteristics*, involves empirically examining categories of crimes and offenders and developing typologies or classification schemes based on psychological, behavioral, *modus operandi*, and other factors. Many current classifications of offenders such as serial murderers (Holmes and DeBurger, 1988), pedophiles (Knight, 1988), and rapists (Groth and Birnbaum, 1979) rely heavily on psychological clinical-categorical underpinnings. The fourth approach, *criminal career*, looks at the longitudinal sequence of offenses committed by an offender over time in an effort to see various aspects of the crime (e.g., target selection, method of committing the crime, and location) change over time or remain stable. Canter notes that a later crime may differ based on what happened to the offender in the commission of earlier crimes. The progression or evolution of criminal careers makes it possible to extrapolate back to earlier crimes certain offenders committed and to examine evidence that can be of use in solving more current crimes. The fifth approach, *forensic awareness*, points to the fact that offenders who have committed prior crimes and have direct contact with the investigative techniques of the police may be very astute, leaving little forensic evidence at a crime scene. Canter reports on cases where rapists force their victims to take baths after the crime, or who comb their victim's pubic hair, as is done in a forensic investigation, so that no incriminating evidence will be left. The significance of these practices tells the profiler that this particular offender has had past contact with the police that may be found in official records.

The Success of Profiling

Research on the validity and reliability of criminal profiling is mixed. According to the FBI, in a study of 192 cases where profiling was performed, 88 cases were solved. In 15 cases (only 17% of the solved cases and 8% of the total cases) profiling turned out to be useful in the actual identification of a suspect (Holmes and Holmes, 1996). In one of the few studies that empirically tests profiling techniques, Pinizzotto and Finkel (1990) asked groups of profilers, detectives, psychologists, and college students to examine closed police cases to determine whether professional profilers were more accurate than nonprofilers in generating personality profiles and correctly identifying known offender characteristics for one sex offense and one homicide case. Although the professional profilers scored significantly higher in the number of correct responses for the known sex offender, there were no significant differences for the homicide case. The profilers did, however, appear to process all of the information given to them differently from the other groups, suggesting that experience is an important ingredient for profiling. A great deal more social scientific research is necessary, especially research that is carried out in collaboration with law enforcement agencies.

WILLIAM E. THORNTON

References and Further Reading

Bartol, C.R. 1995. *Criminal Behavior: A Psychosocial Approach*, Englewood Cliffs, NJ: Prentice Hall.

Canter, D. 1989. Offender profiles, *Psychologist*, 2.

Canter, D. 1994. *Criminal Shadows: Inside the Mind of the Serial Killer*, London, UK: Harper-Collins.

Canter, D. 2000. Offender profiling and criminal differentiation, *Legal and Criminological Psychology*.

Douglas, J.E., Burgess, A.W., Burgess, A.G., and Ressler, R.K. 1992. *Crime Classification Manual: A Standard System for Investigating and Classifying Violent Crimes*, New York, NY: Lexington Books.

Douglas, J. and Olshaker, M. 1999. *The Anatomy of Motive*, New York, NY: Scribner.

Douglas, J. and Olshaker, M. 1997. *Journey into Madness: The FBI's Premier Investigator Penetrates the Minds and Motives of the Most Terrifying Serial Killers*, New York, NY: Pocket Books.

Groth, N., and Birnbaum, J.H. 1979. *Men Who Rape: The Psychology of the Offender*, New York, NY: Plenum.

Grubin, D. 1995. Offender profiling, *The Journal of Forensic Psychiatry*, 6.

Hazelwood, R.R., Ressler, R.K., Depue, R.L., and Douglas, J.E. 1993. Criminal personality profiling, *Practical Aspects of Rape Investigation*, Hazelwood, R.R. and Burgess, A.W. (Eds.), Boca Raton, FL: CRC Press.

Hickey, E.W. 1997. *Serial Murderers and Their Victims*, Belmont, CA: Wadsworth.

Holmes, R.M. and Holmes, S.T. 1996. *Profiling Violent Crimes: An Investigative Tool*, Thousand Oaks, CA: Sage.

Holmes, R.M. and DeBurger, J. 1988. *Serial Murder*. Newbury Park, CA: Sage.

Knight, R.A. 1988. A taxonomic analysis of child molesters, *Human Sexual Aggression: Current Perspectives*, Prentky, R.A. and Quinsey, V.L. (Eds.), New York, NY: New York Academy of Science.

Ormerod, D.C. 1996. The evidential implications of psychological profiling, *Criminal Law Review*.

Pinizzotto, A.J. and Finkel, N.J. 1990. Criminal personality profiling, *Law and Human Behavior* 14.

Ressler, R. and Shachtman, T. 1992. *Whoever Fights Monsters*. Lexington, MA: Lexington.

Ressler, R., Burgess, A., and Douglas, J. 1988. *Sexual Homicide*. Lexington, MA: Lexington.

Salfati, G.C. and Canter, D. 1999. Differentiating stranger murders: Profiling offender characteristics from behavioral styles, *Behavioral Sciences and the Law* 17.

Voigt, L., Thornton, W.E., Barrile, L., and Seaman, J. 1994. *Criminology and Justice*, New York, NY: McGraw Hill.

See also **Classification of Offenders; Federal Bureau of Investigation (FBI); Police: Detectives; Police Investigation; Psychoanalytic Theories of Criminal Behavior; Psychological Autopsies; Psychological Theories of Criminal Behavior; Psychopathy and Crime**

Islamic Legal Traditions

Islamic legal traditions have a long history behind their development. The world of Islam in which these traditions have occupied a central place until very recent times covers many nation-states, the majority of which adhere to the Sunni brand of the faith. Sunni jurists have produced four legal traditions. Each tradition has its top jurist (Imam) credited with having given to the tradition its most evolved jurisprudential format. These are: (1) the Hanefi tradition of Imam Abu Hanifah (died 767 AD), (2) the Shafei tradition of Imam Shafei (died 820 AD), (3) the Hanbali tradition of Imam Ibn Hanbal (died 855 AD), and (4) the Maliki tradition of Imam Malik Ibn Anas (died 795 AD). The Shii legal tradition is of a minority status and was established by Imam Jafar al-Sadiq (died 765 AD). Both traditions follow Islam's main sources from which each school has constructed its principles of jurisprudence. These are: (1) the Koran, (2) the traditions of the Prophet Muhammad, (3) the consensus of the community, or, of Muslim jurists, over legal matters, and (4) appeal to analogy. In Shii Islam, next to these principal sources, the so-called "news" pertaining to the lives and deeds of 12 Shii Imams have played a role in the formation of the Shii legal tradition. The technical field that has historically concerned itself with the study of the Sacred Law is known as the "science of jurisprudence" (*Ilm al-Fiqh*). Adjudication was called then, and now, *Qaza*, a term that denotes the process through which the judge, that is, the *qazi* (anglicized as kadi) determines the guilt and innocence of the accused. The *qazi* has historically played a central investigatory role in Islamic Qaza. The field of study that concerns itself with adjudication and its principles is known as the science of adjudication (Ilm al-Qaza). A synopsis of the first four principal sources are provided below. It is customary to denote the legal traditions under the *sui generis* term of *Shariah* that stands for the Sacred Law of Islam. A synopsis of each principal source is provided below with the proviso that throughout this article legal traditions are synonymous with the term *Shariah* unless otherwise stated.

The Koran comprises the most important source of the legal traditions. The text is believed to be the verbatim word of God revealed upon the Prophet Muhammad gradually through a period of 23 years (610–632 CE). Muslims believe that the revelation process commenced in 610 CE in Mecca, and came to its eternal end in 632 CE in Medina. At the same year Muhammad passed away.

There are 114 chapters in the Koran. The content of the text is believed to be in a Heavenly Protected Source (*Luh Mahfuz*) based on (lxxxv: 21-22) in the Koran. Muslims believe that the Koran is not a man-created text but it is the word of God that has been revealed for guidance, salvation, and for peace in this world and the next world to come when death takes us from our bodily abode. It also contains what is known as God's Commandments (*Ahkamallah*) and God's Boundaries and Punishments (*Hududallah*).

The Traditions (*Sunna*) of the Prophet Muhammad comprise the second principal source. These are utterances that Muslim jurists have attributed to Prophet Muhammad. They have been subjected to what is know as the authentication (*isnaad*) process gradually developed and systemized after Muhammad passed away in 632. Most western legal scholars, following Joseph Schacht, have argued that by the 10th century CE, the four Sunni legal traditions reached their established format closed to further interpretive process through what is known as the "closure of the gates of interpretation" (*ijtihad*). Since then no Sunni jurist has supposedly been able to point to a jurisprudential issue that needs reinterpretation. The situation of Shii legal tradition is different because other Shii Imams, who followed al-Sadiq, built further upon the Shii principles of jurisprudence, and therefore, the tradition was not subjected to the closure process.

The communal, or juristic, consensus on legal matters constitutes the third source of legal traditions. The rationale for using this source stems from a saying (*Hadith*) attributed to Prophet to the effect that an Islamic community will not agree on error. C. Snouk Hurgronje has taken this to mean that the communal consensus provides the base of the truth concerning a matter in legal disputation. Whether this was intended by the Prophet or not, what is certain is the fact that by the passage of time, the communal consensus was replaced by the consensus among the learned men of the law, the jurists, because the Sacred Law, as the base of the legal traditions, went through an intertwined canonization, elaboration, and sophistication process making it too specialized a field of knowledge upon which the community could reach consensus.

The fourth source is analogy. When a jurist faces a matter that neither the Koran, nor the Prophetic Traditions have addressed, the jurist is allowed to appeal to human rationality and analogical reasoning. Both

Sunni and Shii jurists have used human rationality and analogical reasoning in finding legal solution to matters that have not lent themselves to a precedent-based process.

In the Islamic legal traditions the legitimacy of an act has to be measured against the general thrust of the Koran as to whether it is prohibited by the "explicit word" (*nas-i sarih*) of the text. For example, murder is explicitly condemned, so are adultery, thievery, unprovoked aggression, and mayhem, the consumption of alcoholic beverages, or of mind-altering substances. The more severe an act, the more severe the punishment for that behavior is the logic followed. For example, unjustified homicide for which retributory (*qisaas*) forms of punishment applies is known as *qatl-i nafs*; adultery for which both stoning (*rajam*) and flogging (*jild*) applies, is known as *zinaa*; thievery for which the amputation (*qat*) of (from one to four) finger(s) applies, is known as *Sirqat*; battery and injury for which retribution in kind (*qisas-i `uzw*) and compensatory monetary punishments apply, are known as *zarb wa jarh*; false witness for which flogging (*jild*) applies, is known as *shahadat-i kizb;* drinking of alcoholic beverages for which flogging applies, is known as *khamr*; and finally, the use of mind altering substances for which flogging applies, is known as *maysar.*

Another classification, the so-called *ifsad*, describes acts that corrupt the soul and the body of the believer and of the community. The most important among these has been the *harb* crimes that involve rebellion against the "just" state, rejection of Allah, of the Koran, and of Muhammad's Prophecy. For these crimes, the punishments have varied from no punishment (in the case of rebellious person(s) who repent (*tawbah*)), to the most severe punishments that range from flogging, to beheading with a sword, or to hanging and crucifixion of the unrelenting rebels.

With the rise of the four Sunni and the Shii jurisprudential schools in the second century of Islam, each school developed its own penology allowing the judges to take into consideration the aggravating and the mitigating circumstances. This consideration led the jurists to the recognition of the traditions and local customs (*urf wa adaat*) that prevailed among the many cultures and peoples who came under Islamic rule. In the juristic texts, the *Shariah* is conceived as the main vehicle through which the community of believers is enabled to follow the moral and legal injunctions of the faith in their daily conduct. For the law to engender a long-term anti-criminogenic impact, it has to operate in unison with other structures in society such as family, education, and community. In the classical juristic texts, punishments are covered under captions such as *kitaab al-hudud* that covers the corporal (*hadd)* punishments; *kitaab al-qisaas* that covers retributory

punishments; *kitaab al-diyaat* that covers the procedural and substantive laws of blood money.

Traditionally, it has been argued that Islam's legal traditions represent a tripatriate system of law, morality, and justice, the core of which has emanated from a divine authority, Allah. Therefore, both legal traditions strive to achieve these sublime purposes of the Sacred Law. The legal theory behind this tripatriate system has conceived of the law as more than an abstract instrument of power *per se*, but as a reflection of Allah's will. Accordingly, Allah has created men and women for a lofty purpose: to live as Allah's deputies on earth (*khalifatallah fi al-ard*), to prosper, to multiply, to do good and refrain from evil, and to leave God's bounty for the next generation. To achieve this, the so-called fundamentalist Muslim circles argue that the Sacred Law ought to be applied in its totality to both legal and social affairs of life in a true Islamic society. Other circles (more liberal) argue that the Sacred Law has to be adapted to the modern world in relation to crime, justice, and punishment.

Western legal scholars of Islam as, for example, Noel J. Coulson, argue that Islam's Sacred Law has a dual nature. The Law purports to be divine and yet it has to be applied to temporal and even mundane issues, a situation that has had led to an inherent tension in the application of it: a divine revelation that has to lend itself to human reasoning when it comes to both enforcement and application. Ignaz Goldziher and Joseph Schacht argue that early Muslim jurists adopted, although quite unconsciously, various concepts, maxims, and legal principles from various sources. Schacht, following Goldziher, gives four sources: (1) the Roman and Byzantine law, (2) the Canon law of the Eastern Churches, (3) Talmudic law, and (4) Persian Sassanid law. It was in the second century of Islam that these incubating concepts and legal borrowing gave rise to what Schacht considers to represent a doctrine of law. In the same line of reasoning, J.N.D. Anderson argues that the distinctive characteristics of the Islamic law is in its religious nature, a view that finds expression as well among some scholars of Islamic law such as Fazlur Rahaman, Parviz Sanei, and Mustapha Azmai to name but a few.

There is no doubt that the *Shariah*-based legal traditions went through a gradual canonization process in order to respond to an expanding world of Islam's more sophisticated social, economic, and legal problems. This was only natural considering that the Koran gives this distinct impression that Islam was destined, from its early inception, to become a world religion. Not only it declares Islam as the last hope for humanity in so far as salvation is concerned as for instance in Chapter (xxxi, 3), or (xxxii, 3), it also proclaims that Islam is the most complete and perfect culmination of

God's everlasting messages vouchsafed upon other prophets from Adam all the way to Noah, Moses, Jesus, and Muhammad in (xli, 43). This is the claim of the Koran that it is a perfect totality (*al-Kamil*) that is nothing less than a divine miracle (*al-I'jaz*); it is the inspired sign(s) (*al-Ayah*) of God, an eternally valid (*Sahih*) revelation (*Wahy*) that reflects God's Will.

In conclusion, it can argued that to the Muslim mind set, the argument that the Koran is inadequate is unacceptable because it implies that Allah, as a universal deity, is inadequate unless one is to accept the argument that the text is of an anthropocentric, and not a theocentric, nature. Once reduced to this level, then all other claims of the Koran of being a divine text become meaningless, reducing the faith of Islam and its legal traditions to the status of what 19th century Orientalist scholars depicted Islam of being: a hodge-podge of borrowings from other religions and especially from Christianity and Judaism and their legal traditions. In the Islamic legal genera, it is the Koran that gives to the legal traditions their past-historical legitimacy notwithstanding the fact that most Islamic countries have now adapted secular laws and jurisprudential systems. The only states that adhere to the *Shariah* are the Kingdom of Saudi Arabia, the Islamic Republic of Iran, and Afghanistan.

HAMID R. KUSHA

References and Further Reading

Anderson, J.N.D. 1959. *Islamic Law in the Modern World*, Westport, CT: Green Wood Press Publishers.
Azmi, M.M. 1987. *Studies in Early Hadith Literature: With a Critical Edition of Some Early Texts*, Indianapolis, IN: American Trust Publication.
Coulson, N.1969. *Conflicts and Tensions in Islamic Jurisprudence*, Chicago, IL, The University of Chicago Press.
Fazlur, R. 1979. *Islam*, Chicago, IL: The University of Chicago Press.
Goldziher, I. 1981. *Introduction to Islamic Theology and Law*, translated by Hamori, A. and Hamori, R. Princeton, NJ: Princeton University Press.
Hallaq, W.B. 1995. *Law and Legal Theory in Classical and Medieval Islam*, Norfolk, Great Britain, Asghate Publishing Ltd.
Masud, M.K., Messick, B., and Powers, D.S., (Eds) 1996. *Islamic Legal Tradition: Muftis and their Fatwas*, Cambridge, MA: Harvard University Press.
Kusha, H.R. 2002. *The Sacred Law of Islam: A Case Study of Women's Treatment in the Islamic Republic of Iran's Criminal Justice System*, Norfolk, Great Britain: Ashgate Publishing Limited.
Liebesny, H. 1975. *The Law of the Near and Middle East: Reading, Cases and Materials*, Albany, NY: SUNY Press.
Hurgronje, S., Le Driot Musulman. *The Law of the Near and Middle East.*
Sanei, P. 1995. *Huquq-e Jaza-ye Umumi*, Tehran, Iran: Ganj-e Danesh Publications.
Schacht, J. 1964. *An Introduction to Islamic Law*, Oxford, England: Clarendon Press.

See also **Babylonian Legal Tradition**

Israel, Crime and Justice in

Israel, approximately the size of the state of Massachusetts, is home to a diverse population from many cultural, socioeconomic, ethnic, and religious backgrounds. Since its founding in 1948, the country has absorbed an enormous influx of immigrants from over 70 different countries. By the early 1950s, the new country had already absorbed more than 1 million new immigrants—survivors of the Nazi holocaust in Europe and Jewish refugees from such Arab countries as Yemen, Iraq, Syria, Egypt, Morocco, Tunisia, and Algeria. In recent years, almost 1 million Jews from the former Soviet Union have settled in Israel. At the present time, of its more than 6 million people, over 80% are Jewish; the rest are Moslem and Christian Palestinian Arabs, and other minorities, such as the Druze. The difficulties in absorbing large numbers of immigrants from so many different backgrounds as well as trying to integrate them into a diverse society was problematic from the beginning. This has affected greatly the problem of crime. The traditions, values, customs, and habits of many immigrants, especially those who came from Moslem countries, conflicted sharply with the reality of the new state of Israel, dominated by Jews of European origin. The problem of integration was aggravated when, out of necessity and ignorance, the government of Israel decided to first house many of the immigrants in makeshift transit camps and later in so-called development towns. In too many instances, even at the present time, the inhabitants of these towns or their descendants remain poorly educated and unable to take advantage of the country's growing industrialization and high-tech employment opportunities. Indeed, as income inequality between the wealthiest and poorest households in

Israel widened, many of the country's "have-nots" have become alienated and resentful of the rest of Israeli society. It is, therefore, not surprising that the great majority of Jewish inmates in Israel's prisons belong to this socioeconomically disadvantaged group. In addition to the social inequalities that contribute to the crime problem, other factors such as drug addiction, the proliferation of firearms, and the tendency to resort to violence to solve personal and social problems aggravate the situation.

All sorts of criminal activity, especially violent crime committed by youth, has been rising steadily in Israel. Armed robbery, rape, unlawful entries into homes, businesses and cars, and the vandalism of property have become common occurrences. White-collar crime, drug-related and organized crime-related offenses, as well as domestic violence and child abuse characterize the growing problem of crime and delinquency in Israel.

Although the streets of Israel's major cities still are relatively safe by day and night (there were 136 murders in 1999), violence among Israelis is of growing concern to many of the country's citizens. Of special concern are the many reports of increasing violence among Israel's youth. School violence in the U.S. has sparked fears of similar violence in Israel. A recent study, for instance, found that over 10% of the students surveyed in May and June of 1998 had brought either a knife, gun, or stick with them to school. According to a survey conducted on behalf of the World Health Organization, 43% of Israeli students admitted bullying other students, ranking Israel 11th among the 28 countries surveyed. The concern over the level of violence among youth has prompted the Ministry of Education to sponsor antiviolence and conflict resolution classes in Israel's schools. Moreover, the police recently added 160 detectives to its juvenile-crime units. A contributing factor to the general rise of crime and its consequences is the drug problem. Israel's Anti-Drug Authority, the organization that coordinates the nation's war on drugs, estimates that there are approximately 250,000 drug abusers in the country. In Israel, drug education and prevention as well as treatment and rehabilitation are emphasized over law enforcement.

The institutional basis of Israel's criminal justice system was formed before the founding of the state, during the time Great Britain ruled over Palestine (1918–1948). More recently, however, as Israel has come to resemble the U.S., American concepts and ideas about crime and justice have started to shape Israel's own war on crime.

The Police

The Israel Police (IP) is a national police force of some 25,000 officers. Created when Israel gained its independence, the newly formed police force was modeled after the police that had been established by the British in Palestine. Like any traditional police department, the IP is a semimilitary, centralized organization, characterized by specialized operational functions, investigative and forensic services, administrative and technical support functions, and an hierarchical command structure headed by a chief of police (commissioner). The police commissioner commands the IP from National Police Headquarters in Jerusalem. The IP is divided geographically into six districts. Each police district has a district headquarters, which organizationally duplicates the national headquarters. Each district is subdivided further into subdistricts and these, in turn, exercise organizational control over police stations. The major task of the IP is to control and prevent crime and maintain public order. However, unlike most police departments, the IP also is responsible for maintaining internal security related to Israel's conflict with the Palestinians and its neighboring countries. Along with the Army and other security agencies, the IP is deployed to counter and prevent terrorist activities inside Israel. The constant pressure on the IP to mount security-related operations has impaired its ability to wage war against traditional crime. Consequently, in an effort to compensate for the limited resources at its disposal to fight crime, the IP in 1995 created a Community Policing Unit charged with involving the community more actively in prevention and suppression of crime and delinquency on the local level through problem solving strategies conceptualized in the U.S.

The Judicial System

Criminal and civil jurisdiction in Israel is exercised by magistrates' and district courts. Magistrates hear nonserious offenses, primarily misdemeanors, and certain civil claims. Serious criminal offenses, usually felonies, as well as civil cases not heard by the magistrates' courts come before the district courts. As there are no jury trials in Israel, cases in the Magistrates' courts are usually tried before a single judge, though some cases are tried by three-judge panels. Most criminal cases in the District courts also are tried before a single judge, but three-judge panels try criminal offenses that carry a prison sentence of 10 years or longer. Appellate jurisdiction in both criminal and civil cases lies with the District courts. All appeals are heard before three-judge panels. Cases from the District Courts can be appealed to Israel's Supreme Court in Jerusalem. In addition to exercising jurisdiction as the court of last resort in all criminal and civil matters, the Supreme Court serves as the nation's High Court of Justice providing judicial review of government policies and actions. Israeli citizens often petition the court to issue injunctions against what they may perceive as abusive or illegal administrative initiatives. As Israel has no formal constitution, the High Court of Justice has become the most important legal body to defend the rights of citizens against the power of the state.

Israel's judicial system, like its police, was created by the British. In addition to organizing magistrates and district courts, Britain maintained religious courts originally established in Palestine in the 19th century by the Ottoman Turks. These courts were modified only slightly after the founding of the State of Israel. At the present time, the religious courts include rabbinical, Moslem, Christian, and Druze religious courts. These courts apply the religious law of their respective communities in matter of personal status, especially marriage and divorce.

In Israel, as in many other countries, there are too many defendants for the court system to work effectively and efficiently. Court backlogs have plagued the system for a long time, forcing too many cases to be dropped, continued, or plea bargained. There is a general consensus in the legal community that the country's court system must be overhauled and modernized in order to provide better justice for all.

Sentencing and Penalties

Under Israeli law, judges enjoy judicial discretion and can impose on offenders a wide range of penalties. After conviction, a court may sentence an offender to prison, impose a suspended sentence, a term of probation, house arrest, a fine or community service; or sentence the offender to a combination of these penalties. A person convicted of murder can receive a life sentence. Capital punishment is allowed but was imposed only once, namely, when Adolf Eichman, the man responsible for the extermination of Jews in the holocaust, was brought to Israel and was tried and executed in 1961. Any offender sentenced to prison for a term that exceeds 6 months (except a life term) may be released on parole after serving two-thirds of the sentence.

Community Corrections

Israel's probation system serves both adults and juveniles. Organizationally and philosophically probation is part of the country's social services system rather than the criminal justice system. There are two distinct probation departments organized on a national basis: the Adult Probation Service and the Juvenile Probation Service. Probation officers prepare presentence reports in which they evaluate a person's chances to be rehabilitated; they broker services, provide treatment through individual and group counseling, and supervise offenders released on parole.

Detention and Imprisonment

Israel's prisons hold pretrial detainees (as such, they serve the function of American jails) and convicted criminals. There are 15 prisons in Israel, three of which house pretrial detainees.

The most recent rules that govern the detention of suspects were enacted in 1997. Any person detained by the police is entitled to an initial court hearing within 24 hours of arrest. A judge may then order that the suspect be released either unconditionally or on bail or that the person be jailed for up to 15 days. Although detention may be extended by order of the court, no suspect may be detained for over 90 days from the day of arrest without formal charges being filed. Israeli law stipulates that a person may be detained before trial if he or she poses a danger to the public and the process of justice. Suspects detained by the police enjoy the right to consult their private attorney or, when called for, a public defender immediately after their arrest.

Israel's incarceration rate (100 per 100,000 population) is much lower than the incarceration rate in the U.S. but higher than the incarceration rates of many European countries. Israeli law provides that prison inmates be separated on the basis of age, sex, and custodial risk and that first-time offenders be housed separately from repeat offenders. Also, mentally ill and drug-addicted offenders are to be kept segregated from the general prison population. Although the law is specific about the classification and segregation of inmates, these procedural regulations are not always adhered to. In fact, prison conditions in Israel have been criticized repeatedly over the years, but because of overcrowding and lack of adequate resources many of the documented abuses have not been rectified. There exists, however, a national master plan for prison construction under which new prison facilities have been built and several older structures have been upgraded. As many of the inmates are addicted to drugs, rehabilitation and drug treatment programs are provided within the prisons. Inmates willing to undergo drug treatment are offered an array of therapeutic interventions, including medical treatment, group and family therapy, the "12-steps program," and other modalities.

Israel has been preoccupied with defense and immigrant absorption ever since it became an independent state. Because of wars and constant security threats, too many internal needs, including better law enforcement, were overlooked. In recent years, however, Israel has raised its standard of living and has begun to pay greater attention to long-neglected domestic matters, including the problem of crime and the administration of justice.

GAD J. BENSINGER

835

References and Further Reading

Bensinger, G.J. 1998. *Justice in Israel: The Criminal Justice System*, Chicago, IL: Office of International Criminal Justice, The University of Illinois at Chicago.

Bensinger, G.J. 1999. The emulation and adaptation of American criminal justice concepts in Israel, *International Journal of Comparative and Applied Criminal Justice* 23, 1.

Friedman, R. 1998. *Crime and Criminal Justice in Israel: Assessing the Knowledge Base Toward the 21st Century*, Albany, NY: State University of New York Press.

Kedmi, J. 1997. *The Law of Criminal Procedure*, Tel-Aviv, Israel: Tel-Aviv University. (in Hebrew)

Shetreet, S. 1994. *Justice in Israel: A Study of the Israeli Judiciary*, Boston, MA: Martinus Nijhoff Publishers.

State of Israel, *Laws of State of Israel, Special Volume. Penal Law, 5737-1977.*

Authorized translation from Hebrew prepared by the Ministry of Justice, Jerusalem, Israel: Government printer, nod.

J

Jails: Purposes, Populations, and Problems

Jails are unique institutions in the criminal justice system of the U.S. Recent institutional surveys have found that currently there are between 3300 and 3400 jails in the U.S., nearly one for every county in the nation. They are not correctional institutions in the strictest sense, but they are expected to perform some correctional functions. They are not law enforcement entities, but a great many of the jails in this country are operated by police or sheriff's departments. They are not prisons, but they have many of the problems prisons have, plus some more. Most of all, aside from police lockups, jails are the most pervasive facilities for incarcerating people in the U.S. and they hold the most undifferentiated populations of any type of secure confinement institution. They may be called county, city, metropolitan, or regional jails, but increasingly they are becoming known as local detention centers or houses of detention. Jails can be loud, smelly, and incredibly difficult to manage. This makes both the study and operation of jails fascinating and challenging.

Purposes

It would seem that this is the one area where there would be the greatest agreement about jails: describing the purposes they serve. However, as with many factors associated with jails, this turns out not to be the case. Part of the confusion and outright disagreement over the functions of jails comes from their long history of development.

Jails can be traced back to the periods of earliest recorded history. Dungeons often were the predecessors of jails, and in early England the word *gaols* (thought to be pronounced jails) first appeared over 500 years ago. These first gaols were not necessarily places of punishment, but places where criminals, paupers, debtors, and the mentally ill might be held until they could be punished. Frequently the forms of punishment included corporal punishment (that is, flogging, branding, or placing people in the pillories and stocks) or capital punishment. Thus the *common jail*—so designated because all offenders typically were housed in one room—was the temporary place of confinement until the offender went to court or until the appropriate punishment could be meted out.

The living conditions in the early jails, especially the sanitary conditions, normally were nothing short of atrocious. These facilities were places of pestilence and perversion. The jailers frequently were not paid for their services and they engaged in extortion from the families of inmates. Unfortunately, this legacy of jails in England was transferred to the colonies in North America. From the founding of the Jamestown colony in Virginia, jails were part of the development of the English colonies. Nearly every community of any size had a jail, and as the colonies gave way to the founding of the U.S., states frequently mandated in their new constitutions that the sheriffs would be responsible for maintaining and operating the county jails.

This tradition of control by the county sheriff has continued in most parts of the U.S. until today. In fact, of the slightly more than 3300 jails in the U.S., county sheriffs operate roughly 70%. Some large city police departments also operate jails, some large metropolitan areas have local corrections departments, and one state (Kentucky) has an elected jailer system. These different organizational and operational arrangements can have profound implications for the nature of jails, as well as their problems and the prospects for improvement.

As jails have evolved they have assumed more responsibilities and taken on more functions. At the most basic level the jail is designed to incarcerate people who have been accused of violating the law. Individuals who have been arrested by various police agencies are transported to the jail to be "booked." The booking process usually involves taking fingerprints and photographs of the suspect and completing a form with personal information on it. Some jails also do cursory screening for drug and alcohol problems, medical conditions that may need treatment, an assessment of communicable diseases, and mental health or suicide profiles. Whereas this type of screening is by no means universal, it has become increasingly common among medium- to large-sized jails because of the threat of lawsuits.

Roughly half of the people booked into jails will be able to make bail and will be released on their own recognizance, under a property or cash bond, or through the services of a bail-bonding agency. Another way to look at the people housed in jails in the U.S. is to consider that half of them have not been convicted of any crime yet, but they remain in jail because a judge has not set bail or, more frequently, they cannot make bail even in fairly modest amounts. Thus, a primary function of the jail is to house the pretrial detainee population, or those people awaiting trials or other court appearances.

A second function of jails is to house people who have been convicted of crimes. Two classes of inmates are included here. First, there are inmates who have been convicted of misdemeanors or infractions involving local ordinances. If these individuals are to be confined, they serve their sentences in local jails. In most states, ordinance infractions and misdemeanors provide for periods of incarceration of less than one year. However, jail sentences often average 90 to 100 days. Periods of confinement for longer than six months are considered long jail sentences. Second, there are inmates in jails who have been convicted of felonies. The vast majority of these prisoners (in 1997 there were nearly 34,000 nationwide) are awaiting transportation to a state or federal prison for intake, classification, and assignment. As a result of prison crowding in nearly two-thirds of the states, during the past 25 years convicted felons have occupied an increasingly larger proportion of local jail bed space. In fact, some states practically treat jails as if they are overflow space for state prisons. The crowding that has occurred in many state prison systems has caused some states to reconsider the nature and length of incarceration. The result has been that a few states now permit inmates serving sentences of more than one year, but less than two years, to serve their time in local jails. The inmates are not always amenable to this situation, since most jails have fewer programs and services for inmates than prisons. The positive feature of this situation is that it keeps inmates near their home communities and family ties. The negative feature is that it causes jails to function as something they were not intended to be: long-term confinement facilities.

Jails also house other groups of offenders. One of the most common of these includes probation and parole violators. Most states give probation and parole officers the authority to incarcerate—on a short-term basis—clients suspected of having violated conditions of their probation or parole orders. These individuals might be held for 48 to 72 hours, or until a judge or other appropriate hearing authority can decide if a condition of community supervision was violated, if the violation is sufficiently serious, and, if so, what should be done to the probationer or parolee. Whereas this population might be confined for a relatively short time period, the numbers of such detainees have become conspicuous over the past two decades. For example, in 1996 nearly 3% of the average daily jail population in the U.S. was composed of probation or parole violators.

Material witnesses occasionally are detained in jails also. These are individuals whose testimony is essential in a trial but who, for a variety of reasons, might be inclined not to show up in court. In those rare instances, a judge may order the material witness detained in a local jail until the trial is completed.

In addition to this, jails often serve as transfer points. Occasionally inmates may be extradited from one state to another and they may be held in jail until extradition processes are complete. Inmates awaiting transfer to a state prison, or those being transferred from one prison to another, or from state to federal custody (or vice versa) also may pass through local jails on the way to their ultimate destination. These responsibilities further illustrate the transient nature of jail populations.

Some groups or individuals are held in jails for other reasons, and one of the most common is that there is no other facility in which to house them. Among these groups are juveniles who have run away from home and have been apprehended in another location. Many jurisdictions maintain separate juvenile detention facilities, but for those that do not the local jail is the default option for temporary secure confinement. Furthermore, increasingly local jurisdictions are discovering that jails are being used to house the mentally ill. In fact, a number of observers have labeled jails the "new" mental health clinics for many communities. As should be readily apparent, having mentally ill individuals in jails makes a difficult situation even more difficult.

Populations

Previously it was said of jails that they house undifferentiated populations. In this section that designation will be explained more fully. However, it is useful to first distinguish prisons from jails in terms of their populations. Prisons incarcerate convicted felons for periods from one year up to life (or, in some circumstances, until the inmate is executed). Prison inmates are housed in single-gender institutions in virtually every case in the U.S. Most of these inmates range in age from their late 20s to their late 40s. A few are older and very few are younger. In recent years the state and federal prison population in the U.S. has grown to nearly 1.3 million inmates, but there are two very important considerations. First, this count frequently does not include prison inmates housed in local jails. In fact, a recent population survey by the U.S. Bureau of Justice Statistics found nearly 64,000 state prison inmates housed in local jails. Second, the number of prison inmates, while increasing, is relatively stable within a given year. Some inmates are admitted and some are released, but prisons seldom deal with rapid or massive turnovers in populations.

By contrast, as previously mentioned, jails house both those convicted of crimes (misdemeanors and felonies) and those awaiting trial. At the end of 1999, local jails in the U.S. confined nearly 606,000 people. At first glance, this number would appear to be less than one-half of the number of inmates confined in prisons. However, jails process more than 13 million admissions and releases each year, and although we do not have any way to control for multiple processing situations, this means that possibly as many as 5 million people pass through jails annually. The result is that jails come into contact with a significant number of individuals, and they house most of their inmates for short time periods (frequently, 2–3 days).

The numbers of inmates in the nation's jails tell part of the story, but distinguishing the population by gender, age, and race or ethnicity tells much more about the nature of jails and the inmates they house. For instance, like most parts of the criminal justice system in the U.S., jails overwhelmingly deal with male offenders. Recent population surveys have found that although the female jail inmate population has been growing, women still constitute only about 10% of the nation's jail inmates. Unlike with state and federal prisons, most of these women are held in separate housing units of mixed-gender institutions.

Nevertheless, there are slightly more than a dozen all-female jails in the U.S., and most of these are in large urban counties and in cities such as New York, Miami, Los Angeles, and San Diego. Because 90% of the jail inmates are male, this too has profound implications for jail operations. In fact, research has indicated that the smaller numbers of female inmates often cause their health care and programming needs to be minimized.

When we consider inmates' ages, jails have a much broader age range than prisons. Some localities still detain juveniles in adult jails, and recent surveys have found around 9000 juveniles housed in the nation's jails. A substantial number of these youngsters—perhaps all but about 1000—are awaiting trial as adults. Once again, the presence of this small population can create a multitude of administrative problems for jail managers.

The ethnic or racial composition of jails, like prisons, presents something of dilemma for criminal justice system officials. Recent surveys show that White, non-Hispanic and Black, non-Hispanic inmates comprise roughly equal portions of the nation's jail inmate population: both groups comprise slightly over 41% each. Hispanics account for between 15% and 16% of the jail inmate population. Blacks and Hispanics both are present in jail inmate populations (and prisons as well) in greater proportions than their numbers in the general population. Two explanations have been offered, and both are unsatisfying and controversial. One explanation is that racial and ethnic minorities simply commit more crimes and are apprehended more frequently. The other explanation is that the criminal justice system in the U.S. targets minorities, thus bringing more of them into the system. In the end, some of both of these explanations seem to be at work. Whatever reason or reasons might bring them into the system, we must recognize that Blacks and Hispanics are disproportionately represented in our jail inmate populations. Further compounding this situation is the vastly disproportionate overrepresentation of low-income individuals, most of whom cannot make bail.

Several groups comprise what might be called "special needs" inmates. Among these, three groups are most conspicuous: drug and alcohol dependent inmates, inmates with communicable diseases (especially tuberculosis and HIV/AIDS), and the mentally ill. Each of these groups will be addressed briefly.

Annual research conducted by the federal government has revealed that a significant number of inmates enter jails with drug and alcohol problems. Although the estimates vary from one location to another, a profile of jail inmates completed by the U.S. Department of Justice found that as many as 82.4% of inmates used drugs before they entered jail, and 64.2% used drugs regularly. Furthermore, 19.6% had used drugs only, 24.5% had used alcohol only, and 16.1% had used both at the time they committed their crimes. These inmates may suffer withdrawal symptoms and require a great deal of medical attention as a result of problems associated with their dependency. These inmates may be sick or disruptive. Since they may have decreased inhibitions under the influence of drugs or alcohol, special care also must be taken when drug and alcohol dependent inmates express suicidal ideations.

Inmates with communicable diseases typically require additional staff attention and special handling. Additional staff attention may involve closer supervision to protect these inmates from others, and it certainly is likely to involve more medical care. Special housing may be required, particularly for inmates who have highly contagious diseases like tuberculosis (TB) and human immunodeficiency virus (HIV). Often these diseases have been contracted as a result of risky behaviors like needle sharing among intravenous (IV) drug users and unprotected sex. Also, poverty, unemployment, and lack of medical care (added to drug and alcohol use) increase the risks of contracting certain contagious diseases. Jail inmates and staff members are especially susceptible to these diseases because of the crowded conditions and close quarters found in many jails. Jails may have closed ventilation systems, and this makes the transmission of airborne diseases like TB especially likely. As we will see in the section on jail problems, dealing with inmates who carry communicable diseases has become a major challenge for jails.

Finally, inmates with a variety of mental illnesses are appearing with regularity in most of the nation's jails. One of the primary reasons for this has been a change in the way we have delivered mental health services in the U.S. Beginning in the 1960s, largely as a result of class action lawsuits filed around the nation, states deinstitutionalized their residential mental health populations. As a result, some states closed all or substantial portions of their psychiatric hospitals and relied instead on community mental health programs. Unfortunately, many of the people who should have been served by community mental health agencies are not able to get into these programs or they choose not to participate. Substantial numbers of them receive no treatment whatsoever, and many of them live on the streets. When they begin to exhibit bizarre behavior, especially in public places, law enforcement agencies are called to take them away. Unfortunately, in many instances the only place these people can be housed on a short-term basis is in the local jail. Therefore, jails find themselves called on to provide mental

health services to a conspicuous part of their inmate population. The mentally ill may have committed no crime, other than being publicly disruptive, but some communities do not provide alternative services that would keep them from being jailed.

Mentally ill inmates must be protected from harming themselves. They may be so withdrawn that other inmates can provoke them into attempting suicide or retaliating as a result of taunting. They also may be assaultive toward the jail staff. Therefore, extra care must be taken to keep mentally ill inmates from harming themselves or others. The chief goal typically is to keep their condition from deteriorating while they are in jail.

Problems

Jails present virtually an endless array of problems, most of which continue to plague jails of all sizes around the country. To make this area more manageable, seven of the most persistent problems have been chosen as a focus. First, a critical problem with which most jails have to deal is the architecture of the facility. Despite the abuse they suffer, jails tend to be particularly enduring facilities. Thus, we find jails in the U.S. that are between 50 and 100 years old. The traditional layout of most jails has been designated the linear design. That is, cellblocks are constructed along hallways that meet at right angles. This type of construction gives the custody staff limited (what has been called intermittent) supervision over inmate activities. In linear jails the staff must make regular rounds to observe the inmates. Between the periods of officer rounds the inmates are relatively free to do whatever they desire. Since linear jails suffer from deficiencies in inmate control by the staff, some jails instituted what might be called second-generation supervision techniques. This type of supervision involves the use of close circuit television cameras and monitors to keep an eye on inmates. However, even in these types of facilities there are blind spots and places in housing units that are not monitored by cameras. As a result, in the 1980s many communities built new jails under what has been labeled a "new-generation" design. The new-generation jails are built around inmate housing pods that contain between 24 and 48 inmates, and each pod has one or more custody officers placed in the pod. Thus, the custody staff has direct inmate supervision, in contrast to the intermittent supervision they have in linear jails. Direct supervision jails hold the promise of revolutionizing jail administrative practices in the U.S., but these facilities can be expensive to build and operate. They also require a period of transition for the staff, who, in the past, had limited direct contact with the inmates.

The second major problem with which jails have been faced for nearly three decades is crowding. In the late 1980s and early 1990s jails nationwide were operating at between 101% and 108% of their rated capacities. Today that number has come down, but the most recent figures show that jails still are operating at about 97% of their rated capacities. There is some regional variation in these numbers, and urban jails in many locations still are operating above capacity.

So, what has changed? At least three things have changed. In many states additional prison space has been added or prison populations have been reduced to conform to capacity. This has caused some prison inmates to be sent back to local jails. Also, like prisons, the most crowded jails have been subjected to lawsuits by advocacy groups and inmates complaining of conditions of confinement, and crowding has been a major point of contention in these suits. Finally, many jurisdictions have engaged in vigorous building campaigns for both prisons and jails. Thus, from 1983 to 1998 the rated capacity of the nation's jails increased from 262,000 to 613,000. A number of counties have raced to build their way out of their crowding crisis. Nevertheless, localities often find that jail population size may be a function of rated capacity. In other words, the shoe decides how big the foot can grow.

The third problem plaguing jails in the U.S. is the combined influence of local politics and local funding. Many jail administrators have come to recognize that this can be a deadly combination. Politicians, local and otherwise, publicly often take a get-tough-on-crime approach at election time. They promise that new laws will be passed, the existing laws will be enforced to the fullest extent, and violators will receive the severest punishments. What they fail to account for is the fact that locking people in jail costs money (probably on the order of $15,000 to $25,000 per inmate per year). Quite often, law-and-order politics have met head-on with the financial realities of jail operations. The politicians and the public may believe that the inmates incarcerated in jail deserve whatever conditions they may be faced with. However, the courts may believe otherwise and order jails to be improved, new jails built, or inmates to be released. Therefore, the notion of locking the most people up at the lowest possible cost may be unreasonable and unworkable.

The fourth problem facing contemporary jails is related to the third one. Many observers have come to recognize that jails are particularly enduring facilities. There are jails operating in the U.S. today that are more than 100 years old, and a substantial number that are more than 50 years old. Even with the wear and tear they face from high numbers of inmates and rapid turnovers in populations, jails just seem to last. This is partly a result of the high security standards to which most jails are built. But whatever the reason may be, jails keep getting older, and older jails are difficult to maintain and operate.

As a result communities have had to build new jails. Often the jails are significantly bigger, but in every case they are expensive. The high security standards to which most jails are built result in cost estimates along the order of $50,000 per bed space to construct. If that sounds expensive, it is. However, the greatest expense is not building a jail, but operating it. Over the life cycle of a jail, 90% of the total cost will involve operations, and much of that cost is related to the personnel employed by the jail. Therefore, the next problem to which we turn our attention is jail personnel.

Personnel issues constitute a fifth problem area for jails. It has been said that jail personnel problems are easy to summarize: too few staff members, low qualifications, low pay, and a woeful lack of training. Custody officer positions in jails—whether they are called guards, detention officers, or jail deputies—are not ones to which many people aspire. In fact, the assumption has been for a long time that if you cannot do anything else, at least you can be a jail officer. Most jurisdictions require only a high school diploma or GED, and, because of the pay schedule, they seldom attract applicants with higher educational credentials. Even with minimal qualifications required, local governments still have a difficult time attracting individuals to the detention officer position, particularly when fast food restaurants may pay more for a less dangerous work environment. There continue to be jurisdictions in the U.S. where a jail officer working full time still may be classified as below the poverty level because of his or her family size. The result is that jails often operate short-handed and, as a consequence, many officers work substantial amounts of overtime. Although this increases their income, it frequently contributes to occupational stress, burnout, and employee turnover.

Lack of training has been a sore spot for jails for a long time. Police departments and correctional agencies both have pursued increased training opportunities aggressively. The same cannot be said for most jails. What we have come to recognize is that jail training is not police training, nor is it correctional officer (prison) training. Jails represent a unique organizational and operational environment. Nevertheless, most of the staff members working in jails in the U.S. have been trained as law enforcement officers, typically sheriff's deputies. This fact creates another unique personnel problem for jails.

In counties where the sheriff operates the jail, the pay for jail officers may be better (since they are deputies), but assignments to the jail are not especially sought after by sworn law enforcement personnel.

Most individuals trained in law enforcement typically rate jail service as among their lowest preferences in job assignments. Therefore, sheriffs sometimes take one of two paths in filling jail custody staff positions. First, in some counties it is expected that every deputy who graduates from the academy will be assigned to jail duty for up to one year. Deputies frequently look at this assignment as a rite of passage that must be endured, but not one that is appreciated. The choice assignment for sworn personnel (those certified as peace officers) is as "road deputies," or uniformed patrol officers. Second, in some sheriff's departments it still is a practice to use jail assignments as a punishment detail. Fortunately this is a declining custom, since individuals who may not be fit to interact with the general public may not be fit to interact with people in custody either. Some departments have discovered that the use of sworn personnel in the jail as punishment duty has increased their litigation potential.

The sixth problem area facing jails is the delivery of programs and services to inmates. As has been indicated previously, inmates come into jail with a variety of problems. A substantial number need medical and dental services. Some will need prescriptions for their on-going medical conditions. More and more need mental health services, including suicide screening and perhaps medication. A significant portion of the jail inmate population needs drug and alcohol screening and counseling. Additionally, some jails now provide chaplaincy services to help inmates with spiritual needs (especially when a family member has died during the inmate's period of incarceration). Jails may attempt to provide constructive activities such as books and arts and crafts materials. Inmates also need the types of services that we frequently associate with prisons, such as education in basic literacy and job training and other life skills. Up until the 1980s most of these issues were not addressed or were simply ignored. During the past two decades jail administrators have started to recognize—sometimes as a result of lawsuits—that most jail time is dead time. Inmates do nothing during most of their waking hours, and this contributes to mental and physical deterioration during long periods of incarceration. Idle inmates also became control problems when they have time on their hands to concoct mischief for the staff and other inmates. Therefore, meeting inmate program and service needs has become a major priority for a number of jails.

One of the difficulties in implementing these changes in many jails results from inaccurate public perceptions. Members of the public (and many politicians as well) perceive that inmates are receiving something not available to the general populace, or they are receiving more or better than they deserve. In the field of corrections this is known as the principle of less eligibility. The truth is that in many jails relatively few taxpayer dollars pay for inmate programming. For instance, chaplaincy services frequently are provided by religious organizations or local churches. Programming supplies (including arts and crafts materials, exercise equipment, and even televisions) may be paid for out of "inmate welfare" funds. In many counties these monies are generated by items purchased at the commissary and telephone charges paid by the inmates and their families. Nevertheless, the area of inmate programs and services represents a hard sell to a tax-weary public.

Finally, a major problem (or prospect, depending on one's perspective) involves inmate litigation against jails and the people who operate them. During the 1980s and 1990s there was a significant increase in the number of class action lawsuits filed by inmates challenging the conditions of their confinement (see, for example, *Duran v. Elrod*, 713 F.2d 292, 7th Cir., 1983; *Hamm v. DeKalb County*, 774 F.2d 1567, 11th Cir., 1985; and *Shelby County Jail Inmates v. Westlake*, 798 F.2d 1085, 8th Cir., 1986). Suits have addressed concerns such as crowding (see especially *Bell v. Wolfish*, 441 U.S. 520, 1979), medical treatment (*Fields v. Garner*, 734 F.2d 1313, 8th Cir., 1984; *Whisenant v. Yuam*, 739 F.2d 160 4th Cir., 1984; *Matzker v. Herr*, 748 F.2d 1142, 7th Cir., 1984), contact visits (*Block v. Rutherford*, 468 U.S. 576, 1984; *Rutherford v. Pitchess*, 710 F.2d 572, 3rd Cir., 1983), and access to the courts (*U.S.USA ex rel. George v. Lane*, 718 F.2d 226, 7th Cir., 1986; *Love v. Summit County*, 776 F.2d 908, 10th Cir., 1985). The standards applied by most appellate courts include the "totality of circumstances" and—in cases of medical care—the notion of deliberate indifference (in addition to the previously cited cases also see *Estelle v. Gamble*, 429 U.S. 97, 1976). The courts have continued to defer to jail authorities on a number of issues, but inmate lawsuits have heightened concern over state jail standards and the professionalization of jail operations.

Jails in Other Nations

Jails, as we know them in the U.S. and the U.K., typically do not exist in many other nations. There are some exceptions to this statement in other North, Central, and South American countries. For example, Brazil, Colombia, and Mexico also have jails, many operated by municipal governments, and these facilities are for detaining suspected offenders as well as for incarcerating those convicted of less serious crimes. France maintains what are called "stop houses," which hold offenders sentenced to less than one year, and in other nations, such as Australia and New Zealand, as well as Belgium, Germany, Sweden, and most other continental European countries, accused offenders may be held for short periods in what might be classified as police lockups. If accused offenders are going to be held for any length of time, they will be transferred to "remand centers." These remand centers frequently are part of the prison system, and inmates may be housed in separate quarters or assigned to the prison's general population. In most European Union countries these inmates actually appear in the prison inmate population numbers.

The Future of Jails

Three particular trends seem promising for improving a lot of jails in the U.S. First, the American Correctional Association has developed standards (now in their third edition) for designing and operating local detention facilities. Furthermore, some states have enacted mandatory jail standards into state law. One of the positive features of this approach is that meeting the standards provides a jail with a defense when inmates file lawsuits. By contrast, a negative feature is that if the standards are not met, the jail is vulnerable to successful litigation. Thus, it appears that litigation will continue to be a part of the future of jails.

Second, the number of jails in the U.S. has been steadily declining since the 1970s. Several small jails, which seem to be especially problematic to manage, have closed and some jurisdictions have cooperated in the building of regional jails. Virginia has been one state that has pioneered the use of regional jails in order to achieve economies of scale in operations.

Third, the states of Alaska, Connecticut, Delaware, Hawaii, Rhode Island, and Vermont have a tradition of state run jails or combined jail or prison systems. Other states have examined this option, and the State of Texas has built a number of state jails to meet some of the problems associated with prison overflow populations backed up in local jails.

These three approaches provide a broader funding base, greater operational efficiency, and increased governmental oversight into jail policies and practices. The end result could be improvements in jail facilities that seem to be especially resistant to change and reform.

G. LARRY MAYS

References and Further Reading

Carlson, P.M. and Garrett, J.S. 1999. *Prison and Jail Administration*, Aspen Publishers, Gaithersburg, MD.

Goldfarb, R. 1975. *Jails: The Ultimate Ghetto of the Criminal Justice System*, Anchor Press/Doubleday, Garden City, NY.

Irwin, J. 1985. *The Jail: Managing the Underclass in American Society*, University of California Press, Berkeley.

Kerle, K.E. 1998. *American Jails*, Butterworth-Heinemann, Boston, MA.

Maguire, K. and Pastore, A.L., Eds., 1999. *Sourcebook of Criminal Justice Statistics—1998*, Bureau of Justice Statistics, U.S. Department of Justice, Washington, DC.

Moynahan, J.M. and Stewart, E.K., 1980. *The American Jail*, Nelson-Hall, Chicago.

Thompson, J.A. and Mays, G.L., Eds., 1991. *American Jails: Public Policy Issues*, Nelson-Hall, Chicago.

Welsh, W.N. 1995. *Counties in Court: Jail Overcrowding and Court-ordered Reform*, Temple University Press, Philadelphia.

Zupan, L.L., 1991. *Jails: Reform and the New Generation Philosophy*, Anderson Publishing Co., Cincinnati, OH.

See also **Prison Riots; Prisons, Problems and Recent Developments in; Prisons: Inmate Populations and Subcultures**

Japan, Crime and Justice in

Japan was and still is famous for its low crime rate. A number of people have tried to find the reasons for this mysterious phenomenon. In the last quarter of the 20th century heinous offenses began to happen intermittently, and the myth of a safe society started to erode, although the crime rate was still relatively low in comparison with other countries.

Statistically, the number of penal code offenses reported to the police has consistently shown an upward trend since 1975 and in 1998 hit a record high for the post war era with 2,690,267 offenses—an increase of 6.8% over the previous year. Of these, larceny was the most prevalent offense (66.5%), followed by traffic professional negligence (24.4%). These two offenses together account for about 90% of all penal code offenses.

So-called "special law offenders" processed by the public prosecutors' offices numbered 1,143,714 in

1998, a decrease of 2.1% over the previous year. Among these offenses, road traffic violations were the largest in number, accounting for more than 90%. Drug offenses, including violations of the Stimulant Drugs Control Law and of the Law for Control of Poisonous and Powerful Agents, were the second largest category of special law offenses, followed by violations of laws regulating foreigners (such as the Immigration-Control and Refugee-Recognition Act) and offenses against public safety (such as violations of the Firearms and Swords Control Law).

Statistically, there was no substantial change in the general crime situation at the end of the 20th century. On the other hand, heinous offenses, such as murder cases against ordinary citizens using firearms and robberies against financial institutions, were on the rise. This indicates a trend toward increased handgun possession in Japan. The Firearms and Swords Control Law has been revised several times and preventive measures against the possession of handguns have been taken. In addition, greater international cooperation is needed to prevent handguns from being smuggled into Japan. Crackdowns on organized crime are also effective means of controlling handguns, since these groups are often involved as suppliers.

Drug abuse has become a serious social issue and violations of the Stimulant Drug Control Law, especially involving foreigners, have increased. It is notable that stimulant drug offenses have spread among juveniles. Moreover, organized criminals contribute to drug offenses, and secondary crimes and accidents influenced by drug abuse continue to occur. A variety of measures have been enacted to reduce drug use, including the Narcotics Law Concerning Special Provisions.

With regard to organized crime, the enactment of the Anti-Boryokudan Law in 1991 (the Law for Preventing Gangsters' Unlawful Actions) has caused a rapid drop in confrontations between organized criminal forces and members. On the other hand, organized criminal gangs have invested more heavily in legitimate businesses and continued their traditional involvement in stimulant drug offenses, extortion, and bookmaking. In 1997, in order to deter extortion, the Law for Preventing Gangsters' Unlawful Actions was revised.

As part of the internationalization of Japanese society, illegal entry offenses (such as smuggling of foreigners and the illegal stay by foreigners looking for employment) have increased, as have crimes committed by foreigners. These crimes have become a serious social concern and have caused bitterness among the citizens. In addition, criminals have internationalized their operations with connections to one or more foreign countries. These problems demand greater inter-national collaboration in the investigation and the extradition of criminals, especially relating to organized crimes (e.g., drug distribution and money laundering). International activities for crime prevention also are needed.

As for juvenile delinquency, the number of juvenile penal code offenders cleared by the police exceeded 300,000 in 1984, declined until 1996, but appears to be on the rise again (numbering 221,410 offenders in 1998). Since when, heinous offenses such as homicide and robbery have increased among juveniles. The latter trend suggests that efforts made by criminal justice agencies are no longer sufficient to tackle the problem of juvenile delinquency.

The Japanese criminal justice system is composed of five segments: police, prosecution, courts, institutional corrections, and noninstitutional corrections (probation or parole and aftercare services). These segments are managed by the national government, except for the police, which is administered at the prefectural (local) level under the guidance and supervision of the national government. There are different proceedings for juveniles (under 20 years of age) and adults. All juvenile cases are referred to family courts and adjudicated therein, except for those cases that involve juveniles over 14 years accused of serious crimes.

In regard to adult criminal processing, the present Code of Criminal Procedure was enacted in 1948, borrowing the best features of Anglo-American law. Some due process features that were adopted include the strict requirement of judicial warrants for compulsory measures, an emphasis on the principle of party presentation and the adversary system, state-appointed counsel, the rejection of hearsay evidence in courts, and the requirement of evidence corroborating confessions.

The family courts that process juvenile offenders stress rehabilitation principles (education and correction). Corrective measures include decisions to dismiss the case with or without a hearing, to place the child under probationary supervision, or to commit the juvenile to a reform or training school. If the family court finds that the juvenile should be treated as an adult in view of the nature of the offense and the circumstances of the case, the case is turned over to the public prosecutor. In these circumstances, the public prosecutor is generally compelled to prefer indictment before a criminal court.

In the Japanese criminal justice system, only strictly selected serious offenders are imprisoned; others are screened at the different stages of processing and diverted into other criminal justice procedures. During 1997, a total of 1,120,010 persons were given final judgment by the court. Of these, only 64,635 persons

(5.8%) were sentenced to imprisonment with or without forced labor. Moreover, of these 64,635 persons, the rate of suspension of their sentences was 63.4%. Thus, only a small portion of offenders is ever imprisoned.

Looking at juvenile cases, the number of defendants adjudicated by the family courts (excluding predelinquency cases, traffic professional negligence offenders, and road traffic violators) was 145,474 in 1997. Of these, only 3% were referred to juvenile training schools. Only 0.2% of the cases that were initiated in the family courts were sent to a public prosecutor for due criminal proceedings.

In Japan, the collective term "penal institutions" denotes prisons, juvenile prisons, and detention houses. Prisons and juvenile prisons mainly accommodate convicted prisoners and implement correctional treatment. Detention houses are mainly for those who are awaiting trial.

The prototype of the current prison can be traced to the establishment of Ishikawajima "Ninsokuyoseba" (Workhouse) in 1790. This facility was founded on a humanitarian philosophy, and various rehabilitation programs, such as vocational training and lectures by intellectuals, were implemented to assist in the rehabilitation of vagrants and offenders who committed repeat offenses. This fundamental ideal of effective rehabilitation and resocialization continues in the present prison system. For over two centuries, affectionate humanitarian principles have always been a key element in Japanese corrections.

The present Prison Law was enacted in 1908 and needs revisions to reflect changing social circumstances and advances in correctional administration and treatment. Improvements are needed in the clarification of the rights and duties of inmates, the living conditions and health services provided for inmates, and the implementation of additional treatment modalities for resocialization.

The modern correctional system faces many problems associated with changes in the inmate population. The increase of female and foreign inmates requires different treatments from those delivered to Japanese male offenders. In addition, a steady aging of the inmate population has occurred, and gangster-group members and habitual stimulant abusers and recidivists have occupied a larger portion of the inmate population.

Prisons are asked to accomplish three major objectives: modernization, internationalization, and legalization. Modernization means that contemporary prisons must sensitively adjust offender treatment and programs must be reformed to reflect the needs of an ever-changing society. Internationalization means that better accommodations must be made in the treatment and confinement of foreign offenders. Legalization means that a humane perspective and fundamental

human rights must be ensured by law so that confinement is more humane.

Despite dramatic changes mainly because of rapid industrialization and urbanization, Japanese society has remained relatively stable and secure. Japan has enjoyed a strong economy; low unemployment; high educational standards; deep-seated informal social controls at work in local communities; much cooperation from citizens toward the criminal justice administration; the strict control of firearms, swords and drugs; and a high clearance rate of crime. This combination of factors has helped to build a secure society with little crime.

But these positive factors have been weakened in recent years. Rapid internationalization has caused Japan, as a small island nation, to lose some of its homogeneity. In addition, because of the urbanization and destruction of traditional communities, informal controls have weakened. With the diffusion of individualism, cooperation with the criminal justice administration has deteriorated. Moreover, the economic situation in Japan got worse in the early years of the 21st century. It is likely that these factors will cause crime and delinquency to increase in Japan.

The end of World War II brought terrible economic hardships and social turmoil to Japan, resulting in an unprecedented high rate of crime. Facing this serious situation, stringent dispositions and harsher punishments were leveled, chiefly against property offenders. With an improvement in social conditions, penal code offenses later decreased, while violations against drug-related laws fluctuated over the years.

The return of instability and change in Japan has brought with it an increase in heinous offenses. This has created a to movement to consider issues relating to the economic, psychological, and emotional suffering of victims that has led to the beginnings of victims' rights advocacy in Japan. The status and sentiments of victims will be an important issue in the future of Japanese criminal justice.

NORIYOSHI TAKEMURA

References and Further Reading

Correction Bureau, Ministry of Justice, Japan, Correctional Institutions in Japan, 1990.

Fairchild, E. and Dammer, H.R. 2001. *Comparative Criminal Justice Systems*, 2nd ed., Belmont, CA: Wadsworth/ Thomson Learning.

Fujimoto, T. 1994. *Crime Problems in Japan*, Tokyo: Chuo University Press.

Government of Japan, 1998. *Summary of the White Paper on Crime 1997*, Tokyo: Research and Training Institute, Ministry of Justice.

Human Rights Watch/Asia Human Rights Watch Prison Project, 1995. *Prison Conditions in Japan*, New York, NY: Human Rights Watch.

Johnson, D.T. 1996. The Japanese Way of Justice: Prosecuting Crime in Japan, Ph.D. dissertation, University of California, Berkeley, CA.

Johnson, E.H. 1996. *Japanese Corrections: Managing Convicted Offenders in an Orderly Society*, Carbondale and Edwardsville, IL: Southern Illinois University Press.

Johnson, E.H., Johnson, C.H. 2000. *Linking Community and Corrections in Japan*, Carbondale and Edwardsville, IL: Southern Illinois University Press.

Miyazawa, S. 1992. *Policing in Japan: A Study on Making Crime*, Albany: State University of New York Press.

Murayama, M. 1992. Postwar Trends in the Administration of Japanese Criminal Justice: Lenient but Intolerant on Something Else? *Journal of the Japanese-Netherlands Institute*, 4.

Shikita, M. and Tsuchiya, S., Eds, 1990. *Crime and Criminal Policy in Japan from 1926 to 1988: Analysis and Evaluation of the Showa Era*, Tokyo: Japan Criminal Policy Society.

Terrill, R.J. 2000. *World Criminal Justice Systems: A Survey*, 4th ed, Cincinnati, OH: Anderson Publishing Co.

Yokoyama, M. 1997. Juvenile Justice: An Overview of Japan, in Winterdyk, J.A., Ed., *Juvenile Justice Systems: International Perspectives*, Toronto: Canadians Scholars' Press.

See also **Organized Crime: Japanese Mobsters**

Jeffery, Clarence Ray

Dr. C. Ray Jeffery was trained as a classical sociologist and was a student of Edwin Sutherland and Jerome Hall while at Indiana University in the early 1950s. This was also the time period when B.F. Skinner was the chair of the psychology department at Indiana and, although Jeffery did not take psychology courses at that time, the impact of Skinner's ideas on the intellectual community of the campus, and Jeffery in particular, was to have far reaching consequences. It was during this period that Jeffery first began to consider that symbolic interaction might not be the key factor in understanding criminal behavior, as was the criminological dogma of the time.

After receiving his Ph.D. he took an academic position at Arizona State University and then went on to Chicago for a postdoctoral fellowship. There he studied with such notable law professors as Francis A. Allen and Karl Llewellyn, who imparted a strong interest in the sociology of law, adding to his view of criminology as more than just a sociological field of study. Once freed from the chains of a strictly sociological view of behavior, he started to see behavior as having multiple causes. It was during this period that Jeffery called for a more integrated approach to criminology, one that integrated sociology, psychology, and the law. As an astute observer and historian of the early development of criminology, he advocated a return to a more interdisciplinary approach to criminal behavior, an approach more philosophically aligned with the early positivists before the 20th-century fragmentation of criminology into separate disciplines dominated by the field of sociology.

In the early 1960s, while working on a project attempting to educate older delinquent boys who had dropped out of school in Washington, DC, he developed a greater appreciation of the true value of psychological factors, particularly positive reinforcement, in the etiology of delinquency and crime in general. The project sought to monetarily reward, i.e., positively reinforce, the boys for staying in school and completing their GEDs. However, the boys easily earned more money from their criminal activities than they earned from the project. Thus, the project generally failed to keep the boys in school or away from crime. The project's failure only served to bolster his view that behavior and its control are complex. His research and scholarly work during the 1960s reflected this growing interest in the contributions of behavior modification, genetics, psychiatry, and, most importantly, the physical environment in the study of crime. His 1965 article on learning theory and crime argued that crime and many criminological concepts could be explained by learning theory, and a year later Burgess and Akers (1966) followed with an article that reinterpreted Sutherland's theory as *differential association-reinforcement*.

In 1970 Jeffery moved to Tallahassee, Florida, to take a position at the Florida State University's School of Criminology. It was while at Florida State that he developed his reputation as a champion of interdisciplinary, scientific criminology. As the founding editor of *Criminology,* he tried to encourage a wider frame of reference concerning crime and criminals than the prevailing sociological perspective. His own writings included topics such as genetics, neurophysiology, behavioral conditioning, environmental design, psychosurgery, sociobiology, and multimodel preventive and treatment strategies. These were topics that, at the time, were seen as irrelevant by mainstream, sociologically trained criminologists. During this period he wrote *Crime Prevention Through Environmental Design*, a 1971 text that challenged the very foundation of the established views on criminology. The 1977 revised version of the text was less about crime prevention or environmental design, for that matter, and more about the potential criminological contribution of the fields of chemistry, biology, psychology, neurobiology and all the other hard and social sciences. It proposed an interdisciplinary approach to the study of crime and the criminal, one that bridged the paradigmatic differences that had long separated them. Another important aspect of the book was his use of the concept of interaction: behavior was the result of the biological organism's constant interaction with its environment. Jeffery used this model, originally a mainstay of the early positivist, to explain how and why a wide variety of disciplines were needed in the study of crime and the criminal. The social environment, he wrote, was no longer the only environment of import and the actors were now filled with malleable neurons, chemical process, and the like, as well as norms, beliefs, definitions, and other social contextual factors.

Despite his controversial views on criminology, he was elected president (1977–1978) of the American Society of Criminology (ASC) after also receiving several of that organization's most prestigious awards. These accolades from his peers did not guarantee acceptance of his views, however. At a mid-1970s national meeting in which several prominent criminologists shared the dais, he was nearly shouted off the stage by those who objected to the inclusion of more biological considerations in criminology. At another large national conference in the early 1980s, he organized a panel with a decidedly biological theme. Not only was it given an unappealing, early Sunday morning time slot, but only a former doctoral student, who was on the panel, and one lone attendee were in the room. When it was time to begin and Jeffery announced the title of the panel, the lone attendee got up to leave, explaining that he was at the wrong presentation! These rebuffs of his insistence on a more interdisciplinary approach did not dissuade him from organizing more panels, putting together conferences, and generally speaking about the need to integrate these nonsociological disciplines into criminological thought. Sociological criminologists of the day did not understand the nature of this type of interaction, and, instead, incorrectly labeled his views as a type of biological determinism.

He steadfastly maintained the belief that our real understanding of behavior was in its infancy and, although still holding on to the value of the interaction model, he came to see the central nervous system, especially the brain, as the key to any hope the criminal justice system would have in controlling crime. This commitment is perhaps best illustrated by a chance encounter he had with a promising young doctoral student at Florida State in 1980. The student, wondering about the direction for his own dissertation, asked Jeffery what he would study if he had it all to do over again. Jeffery replied succinctly, "I would study the brain," and then quickly disappeared into his office.

In 1990 he published *Criminology: An Interdisciplinary Approach*, the first modern criminology text that provided students with an accurate discussion of the value of a scientific criminology based on all of the sciences. The text also explored the problems of a criminal justice system based on the principle of *legality* and containing such concepts as insanity. The text questioned the usefulness of continuing to employ the legal fictions of the rational man, *mens rea,* and legal guilt. All behavior, even criminal behavior, he argued, was a product of a physical being in constant interaction with its environment. Prevention and treatment were more important than guilt and punishment.

His enduring contribution to criminology will be that he made it possible for other disciplines (e.g., psychology, neuroscience, genetics) to legitimately study topics that had traditionally been under the almost exclusive purview of sociologically dominated criminology. He opened venues in criminological arenas for basic behavioral science researchers to publish their findings in the field of criminology and helped forge working partnerships between a wide variety of investigators. As a result of Jeffery's persistence and scholarship, the study of criminal behavior is now an interdisciplinary task.

ALLAN R. BARNES

Biography

Born in Pocatello, Idaho, May 14, 1921. Educated at Indiana University, A.B. in economics, 1949; Ph.D. in sociology and political philosophy, 1954. Lecturer, Southern Illinois University, 1954–1957; Assistant and Associate Professor, Arizona State University, 1957–1963; Lecturer in Criminology, New York University Law School, 1964–1967; Professor of Public Administration, Graduate School of Public Administration, New York University, 1967–1970; Professor of Criminology, Florida State University, 1970–present. Senior Fellow, "Law and Behavioral Science Project," Law School, University of Chicago, 1958–1959; Senior Social Scientist, "Law and Psychiatry in the District of Columbia," National Institute of Health Project, Washington School of Psychiatry, 1963–1964;

Director, "Project for the Social and Educational Rehabilitation of Drop-outs and Delinquents," US Office of Education Grant, Washington School of Psychiatry, 1965–1967; Member, "Ford Foundation Project on the Administration of Justice," Law School, New York University, 1968–1970; Director, "Crime Prevention Through Environmental Design," HUD Grant, Albany, Georgia, 1990–1991; Director, "Biochemical Aspects of Antisocial Behavior," Thomasville and Albany, Georgia, 1990–1991; Director, "Crime Prevention and Crime in Tallahassee," Florida, 1991–1992. Founder and editor of *Criminology*, 1969–1974; Vice-President, ASC, 1972–1973; Herbert Bloch Award, ASC, 1973; Edwin H. Sutherland Award, ASC, 1975; President-Elect, ASC, 1976; President, ASC, 1977–1978; Emeritus Professor of Criminology and Criminal Justice, 1998. Currently resides in Tallahassee, Florida.

Selected Writings

"The Structure of American Criminological Thinking," *Journal of Criminal Law, Criminology, and Police Science* 45 (1956).

"The Historical Development of Criminology," in *Pioneers in Criminology*, edited by H. Mannheim (1960).
"Criminal Behavior and Learning Theory," *Journal of Criminal Law, Criminology, and Police Science* 56 (1965).
Criminal Responsibility and Mental Disease: The Durham Rule, 1967.
Crime Prevention Through Environmental Design, 1971; substantially revised in 1977.
"Criminology as an Interdisciplinary Science," *Criminology* 16, 1978.
"Sociobiology and Criminology: The Long Lean Years," in *Taboos in Criminology*, edited by E. Sagarin (1980).
Attacks on the Insanity Defense: Biological Psychiatry and New Approaches to Criminal Behavior, with R. del Carmen and J. White, 1985.
"An Interdisciplinary Theory of Criminal Behavior," in *Advances in Criminological Thought*, edited by W.S. Laufer and F. Adler (1988).
Criminology: An Interdisciplinary Approach, 1990.

See also **Biological Theories of Criminal Behavior**

Judeo-Christian Legal Traditions

There may be a number of countries whose legal traditions were influenced by Judeo-Christian teachings on crime and justice. However, it seems more evident that the U.S., from the beginning, has implemented much of the biblical concept in the legal arena. From the Declaration of Independence to the Pledge of Allegiance and the Constitution, the biblical influence is embedded in the essence of these historical documents. Although the attitudes and perceptions toward crime and justice have changed over the years, remnants of the biblical influence are still detectable in the legal arena. The changes we have made may be the indication of either diversity in beliefs or a trend to minimize "religious" tones. For the Puritans, the latter trend must have been a somewhat familiar one.

Historical Background

After the arrival of the Pilgrims, the Puritans came to the New World to pursue the religious freedom they so yearned for in England. As the persecution against the Puritans gained momentum, a large number of those who had a deep covenant with God migrated to the New World (Marshall & Manuel, 1977). Naturally, their purpose in migrating to a new country where no civil government or any other types of governing agen-

cies existed was to establish societies that were based on biblical principles. The Puritans must have thought it a tremendous opportunity to serve God, even though their predecessors had suffered much of their lives in the New World. Nonetheless, their faith in God and deep relationship with Jesus Christ had kept them focused on their faith, the faith that God would provide for them, just like He provided for the Pilgrims by sending them the Indians, who showed the Pilgrims how to cultivate the land. Therefore, it is no wonder that the Bible became the source of the Puritans' ethical and moral foundations. Christian faith was protected in the colonies, acting as a supreme guide to the people who set foot on the land. Two of the concepts, free will and individual accountability, were directly attributable to the Bible (McHugh, 1978). Inevitably, these two concepts had played a significant part in formulating a view on crime and justice during colonial times.

During these embryonic stages of the country, a number of acts were considered crimes, some of which nowadays are no longer considered criminal behaviors. For example, blasphemy was a crime in the colonies of Massachusetts, New Hampshire, Virginia, and Delaware (Freeman, 1993). The Sabbath was also a serious matter (Freeman, 1993). Adultery and fornication were also strongly frowned upon, inviting a united effort by the community to handle what is now considered a private matter. The Puritan colony of Massachusetts set aside heresy as a crime, thereby allowing the community to banish those guilty of such a crime in an attempt to save the rest of the community from further destruction of the Christian faith (Freeman, 1993).

The focus of criminal codes during the colonial times was on the offense, rather than on the offenders (McHugh, 1978). This is because the Bible, the source of the colonial criminal codes, commands people not to engage in such acts as murder and theft, along with other potentially destructive actions. What is usually misunderstood about the biblical influence on criminal justice is that offenders were viewed as sinners who desperately needed mercy from God. Hence, offenders themselves were not the focus of condemnation, but rather their actions were called into question because, ultimately, sinful actions by a person could corrupt another if not dealt with swiftly and appropriately.

The Puritans' attitude towards sin was crystal clear: those who went astray needed proper and loving discipline. They "felt that the entire fabric of their covenant life together depended on living in proper order and in joint obedience to the laws of God. Thus when one sinned, it affected them all" (Marshall & Manuel, *The Light and the Glory: Did God Have a Plan For America?* 1977, p. 172). Repentance on the part of sinners (offenders) was desired, followed by forgiveness of their actions. However, it is safe to assume that the concept of repentance and forgiveness was not always practiced. As the migration to the New World increased, there must have been migrants who did not profess the Christian faith, at least not in the form the Puritans had practiced. Much of the Puritan ideal of civil society was based on biblical teachings. As a result, a society with a deep foundation in biblical teachings did not survive in later generations. Instead, remnants of their effort to establish a truly Christian nation with liberty were carried through the history of crime and justice in the U.S.

A Caution for Judeo-Christian Legal Practice

It is unfortunate that the good and godly intentions of the colonists to establish a biblically based legal system was largely distorted or misused in some areas in the criminal justice system. When the area invites much controversy and debate, as in capital punishment, it is inevitable to dismiss the historical events as mere happenings in the past. They are the message from our predecessors to be cautious about the issues they themselves faced decades ago.

It is documented that public executions took place during the 18th and 19th centuries in this country. Whatever people thought about the public executions, the intentions of the authorities for making the executions public were to encourage order and conformity in society by warning people that God alone is the ultimate judge of any criminal behavior (Masur, 1989). The public executions served as a reminder of religious purification by executing a sinful soul from the community, and thus saving the rest of the community members who acted according to God's law (Masur, 1989).

As the public executions permeated people's lives, some committed murder in much the same way as the condemned criminals had done on the very day the execution was held. Disorderly citizens engaged in unlawful acts, some resulting in death (Bessler, 1997). Sometimes the scenes of public executions were filled with an atmosphere of gaiety, often ending in fighting or even rioting (Costanzo, 1997). This may partly be because of a low degree of sympathy felt by the spectators for those executed. Although the public executions seemed to have lost the intended effects of the maintenance of order in the community by stirring up violence (Costanzo, 1997), the executions may have served not only as a satisfactory closure to the survivors of victims, but also as a demonstration of the power of the authorities to protect the community and its people (Kronenwetter, 1993). In the end, because of widespread disorderly acts by citizens during and after the public executions, most people seemed to start questioning the idea of carrying out the executions publicly (Bessler, 1997).

This may be one example of a godly intention gone awry. Hopefully, this portion of history will not be repeated, but rather will act as a reminder that godly intention without empathy or sympathy toward other human beings can result in cruelty in people's hearts. This is quite the opposite of the Christian principle to love one another. In fact, the Bible reminds us that to do anything without love, even having faith, is death.

Influence of Judeo-Christian Traditions on Modern Criminal Justice

Although it is fragmented, the influence of earlier Judeo-Christian ideas remains in our criminal justice system. Witnesses are asked to give oaths to God for telling the truth while placing their hand on the Bible in court. There has been a movement toward restorative justice rather than punitive justice that may have plagued our criminal justice system by using excessive force to enforce the law. On the other hand, restorative justice that has been employed primarily for juvenile justice and minor offenses emphasizes personal responsibility, restitution, and community integration. Instead of sending offenders to jail or prison for their crime, offenders are provided with the opportunity to participate in mediation with their victims to repair the harm. Offenders are expected to return to the community after completion of restorative justice programs. The philosophy of restorative justice can be traced to the New Testament in the Bible, where Jesus repeatedly said to forgive those who wrong us and to love them. In cases of criminal offense, it must be difficult to forgive the offender, especially for those who are directly affected by the crime. The Puritans must have thought of themselves as examples of God's love toward one another, even for those who committed crimes. After all, they were viewed as uncommon in their practice of purifying themselves of any sinful nature, even before coming to the colonies.

Unlike the colonists' close-knit community, where enforcing Judeo-Christian principles was without many obstacles, the modern criminal justice system lacks one vital participant: the victim. Since the establishment of a state agency to handle all criminal cases, private prosecution, where victims take initiative to bring their offenders to justice, no longer exists in our society. Crime is an offense against the state, and for that matter, the victim's part in criminal justice is reduced to mere evidence. This is quite a deviation from the early practices of crime and justice, where the victim's voice was heard and the community was involved in the entire process of healing the wound, whether physical or emotional. The core of restorative justice is to have victims involved with their family members and the community, and that means revisiting the tradition this country exercised so long ago. Criminal justice professionals may gain insight from the core of restorative justice for possible utilization in the current system, this time adjusting to our ever-changing ideology without compromising the foundations of Christian principles.

Future Directions for Judeo-Christian Principles in Crime and Justice

Judeo-Christian values can be helpful in various areas in criminal justice. Victims can be comforted by community members in the aftermath of victimization and receive adequate emotional and spiritual support in the midst of criminal justice proceedings. Church communities, therefore, must reach out to their own community in the event of tragedy, ideally making a concerted effort to help alleviate the pain the victims and the community experience. In this sense, leadership from the church community is vital to the success of utilizing Christian principles. Because crime victims, more often than not, feel they are being left out of the proceedings without much opportunity to express the harm the offense caused, it is essential that their needs be met somewhere in the criminal justice system. Although the victim impact statement is employed for some types of offenses in court, the role of victims may need to be much broader in scope in order to fully repair the harm they have suffered. In essence, there may be a wider usage of restorative justice concepts in the future.

It is equally important to note that condemning the offender is not based on Judeo-Christian values in crime and justice. As the Bible commands us to love one another and to have peace with others whenever possible, resorting to vengeful feelings toward those who commit crimes is considered equally damaging to one's soul. Forgiveness, one of the fundamental philosophies of Christianity, may seem far-fetched for those who suffer the unthinkable loss of family members or those who are the dear to them. Victims of violent crimes may experience difficulty forgiving the offender. The question is not whether forgiveness should be exercised or not, but rather, how can we create a society where forgiveness is possible? If we are to preserve our Judeo-Christian heritage in crime and justice, we ought to think about how and why we have strayed from the original intent of establishing biblically based criminal codes. They were to correct the wrong behavior and restore peace in a community that included offenders, victims, and the rest of the community members. In other words, each individual must take part in restoring community peace. This is, after all, what Christianity is about; demonstrating God's love by supporting one another and by bearing the burdens of those around us.

YUMI SUZUKI

References and Further Reading

Bessler, J.D. 1997. *Death in the Dark: Midnight Executions in America*, Boston, MA: Northeastern University Press.

Bianchi, Herman, 1994. *Justice as Sanctuary: Toward a New System of Crime Control*, Bloomington, IN: Indiana University Press.

Costanzo, M. 1997. *Just Revenge: Costs and Consequences of the Death Penalty*, New York, NY: St. Martin's Press.

DeMar, G. 1995. *America's Christian History: The Untold Story*, Atlanta, GA: American Vision, Inc.

Federer, W.J., 1994. *America's God and Country Encyclopedia of Quotations*, Coppell, TX: FAME Publishing.

Friedman, L.M. 1973. *A History of American Law*, 2nd. ed., New York, NY: Touchstone Book.

Friedman, L.M. 1993. *Crime and Punishment in American History*, New York, NY: BasicBooks.

Kronenwetter, M. 1993. *Capital Punishment: A Reference Handbook*, Santa Barbara, CA: ABC-CLIO, Inc.

Marshall, C.D. 2001. Beyond Retribution: A New Testament Vision for Justice, *Crime and Punishment*, Grand Rapids, MI: William B. Eerdmans Publishing Company.

Marshall, P. and Manuel, D. 1977. *The Light and the Glory: Did God Have a Plan for America?* Grand Rapids, MI: Fleming H. Revell.

Masur, L.P. 1989. *Rites of Execution: Capital Punishment and the Transformation of American Culture, 1776—1865*, New York, NY: Oxford University Press.

McHugh, G.A. 1978. *Christian Faith and Criminal Justice: Toward a Christian, Response to Crime and Punishment*, New York, NY: Paulist Press.

Vann Ness, D. and Heetderks, K.S. 1997. *Restoring Justice*, Cincinnati, OH: Anderson Publishing Co.

See also **Colonial America, Crime and Justice in; Israel, Crime and Justice in**

Judges

Introduction

A judge is a public official who is authorized to conduct tribunals and decide questions of law. Judges are responsible for ensuring that laws are impartially administered; unsurprisingly, the fairness of a tribunal depends largely on a judge's character. There are as many different judge types as there are tribunal types; the most common judicial types handling criminal matters are magistrate (that includes municipal court judge), state circuit court judge, family court judge, federal district court judge, and appellate judge (although administrative hearing judges and arbitrasors or mediators will handle criminal matters on occasion). In 1998, there were approximately 9000 judges serving in the 71 statewide trial court systems with general jurisdiction and nearly 1500 appellate court judges, 75% of whom served on intermediate appellate courts (Bureau of Justice Statistics, 1998). In 2000, nearly 45,000 people worked as judges, magistrates, or judicial workers.

Judges work within a federalist court system. Court power is distributed between federal, state, and local courts, each often with overlapping jurisdictions. Particularly in the state and local systems, the court system is decentralized and disunified, with each court maintaining its own independent docket. Most criminal cases are handled in magistrate or municipal courts, which likewise keep their own dockets. The decentralized nature of the court system prevents the reallocation of court cases between courts and, unsurprisingly, leads to disparate burdens among courts.

Judges typically are generalists who must handle a wide variety of cases, both civil and criminal. Judging is a high-prestige occupation that is relatively well compensated. Trial court judges are often the most prominent members of the local bar. In 2002, the mean salary for a general-jurisdiction trial court judge was $111,000 (National Center for State Courts, 2002). Even magistrate judges, who often lack college degrees, typically make at least $50,000 when full-time employees. Despite the benefits, judging is often a lonely business, with judges separated from the other courtroom players by distance and ethical proprieties.

Magistrates

The magistrate is the most common type of judge, and magistrates handle more criminal matters than any other judges. Magistrates are typically appointed and preside over limited-jurisdiction tribunals that do not handle felony cases. Magistrates typically set bonds, issue warrants, try cases, and sentence offenders. Requirements for magistrates are not as exacting as those for other judges: magistrates are frequently non-lawyers. In some states, such as South Carolina, magistrates need only have high school degrees. Magistrates frequently are former police officers, lawyers, or politically connected individuals. Despite the relatively low requirements for magistrate service, magistrates are responsible for applying complex statutory, constitutional, and common laws. A magistrate must, for example, apply the reasonable doubt standard, allow for indigent representation, and adjudge search and seizure laws. Magistrates typically handle high caseloads and must administer justice at a rapid pace. They often operate in small, makeshift courtrooms such as trailers, portables, and small buildings.

State Circuit Court Judge

Circuit court judges handle general-jurisdiction criminal cases that often include felonies. Such judges are typically distinguished lawyers with considerable professional experience. Circuit courts handle the vast majority of felony cases nationwide; in 2000, circuit courts handled 920,000 felonies, compared to just 60,000 in federal courts (Bureau of Justice Statistics, 2003). Circuit court judges are typically elected officials who are capable politicians. Most states use citizen-based elections, although some states appoint judges through representative elections, with judges serving definite terms.

Family Court Judge

Family court judges handle criminal cases involving juveniles. Like their circuit court counterparts, these judges are typically lawyers with practical experience handling family court matters, and they serve terms of definite duration. The family court orientation is decidedly conflicted between proceduralism and paternalism (Sanborn, 2001). On one hand, family court judges, after *In re Gault*, 387 U.S. 1 (1967), must formally respect a defendant's constitutional rights through an adversarial process, just as if the defendant were an adult. The defendant must, for example, be proven guilty beyond a reasonable doubt. On the other hand, family court judges must act in the juvenile's best interests while ruling on the case without the use of a jury. Often it is in a juvenile's best interests to find the juvenile guilty in order to connect the juvenile with necessary services. After gaining adult rights, juveniles increasingly receive adult punishments; society has become more punitive over the last three decades (Garland, 2001). Family court judges may waive certain juveniles to adult courts, particularly based on offender history and offense severity (Snyder, Sickmund, and Poe, 2000). Like circuit court judges, family court judges are typically elected officials.

Federal District Court Judges

Federal district court judges head federal tribunals of general jurisdiction. These judges are typically distinguished, experienced lawyers. The selection of federal judges is a transparently political process. The Department of Justice searches for qualified lawyers by consulting political leaders, partisan supporters, and senators (Neubauer, 2002, 199). The president then submits a nomination, which is considered by the Senate Judiciary Committee, and ultimately either approved or disapproved by the Senate. Federal judges serve for life.

Appellate Judge

Appellate judges sit on intermediate or high courts of appeals in both state and federal systems. These judges sit either individually or in groups and hear appeals of the decisions of lower courts. These judges have the power to reverse or affirm lower court decisions. In considering lower court cases, appellate judges frequently create new common law, which is binding on the lower courts. There is no uniform procedure for the selection of appellate judges. In nearly half the states (21), judges are selected by gubernatorial appointment, whereas other states find judges through nonpartisan elections (14), partisan elections (8), or by legislative appointment (3) (Bureau of Justice Statistics, 2001).

The Judge as Public Figure

The criminal court system is part of society's formal mechanism of social control. In their roles as heads of tribunals, judges maintain order, but also a particular power structure and values (Crystal, 2001). Social theorists have noted that the power of the laws is strongest when the legal power is coupled with legitimacy (see, e.g., Parsons, 1962; Weber, 1954). Judges help ensure legal power through legitimacy by conducting fair proceedings according to established laws.

As the most visible figures in criminal courts, judges are public figures, and judicial decisions may be widely scrutinized. Court actions that are perceived as unfair harm the court system's legitimacy and may even destabilize communities. Under the concept of judicial independence, judges should be free of outside influences when rendering decisions and must focus solely on the law and facts of the individual case, according to the American Judicature Society (2004).

Judicial independence is a concept that expresses the ideal state of the judicial branch of government. The concept encompasses the idea that individual judges and the judicial branch as a whole should work free of ideological influence. Scholars have broken down the general idea of judicial independence into two distinct concepts: decisional independence and institutional, or branch, independence. Decisional independence refers to a judge's ability to render decisions free from political or popular influence based solely on the individual facts and applicable law. Institutional independence describes the separation of the judicial branch from the executive and legislative branches of government.

Unfortunately, a judge's prominence may occasionally undermine judicial independence. As public figures often depending on politics to maintain their positions, judges' decisions may be influenced by political factors, including threats of impeachment, recall, or lost election. Empirical research suggests that judicial decision-making is plagued by the influence of extralegal factors, such as race and socioeconomic status (Amnesty International, 2001; Black, 1994; Steffensmaier and Demuth, 2001). Research further suggests that procedural injustice may be invisible to, although strongly perceived by, minority groups; for example, procedural injustices are most strongly perceived when legal hierarchies appear illegitimate and impermeable, and when injustices are directed at a particular group with shared relevant identities (Clay-Warner, 2001). Blacks perceive courts as less fair than do their white counterparts (Rottman and Hansen, 2001).

Commensurate with their central place in the criminal justice system, judges have their own ethical canons that tend to promote the judiciary's appearance of fairness. Judges are ethically obligated to uphold the judiciary's integrity and independence, be impartial and diligent in performing judicial duties, avoid impropriety as well as the appearance of impropriety in judicial activities, refrain from inappropriate political activity, and conduct extra-judicial activities in a manner that minimizes risks of conflict with judicial obligations (see, e.g., South Carolina Judicial Code of Conduct). These judicial ethical requirements are in addition to ethical requirements already imposed on attorneys in all states. In most states, these judicial canons have been extensively interpreted by ethical opinions issued by state ethics commissions. In order to avoid impropriety or its appearance, judges must avoid *ex parte* communication, i.e., they cannot discuss case-related details of a pending case without both sides being present. Judicial misconduct is usually punished by a state judicial commission, and sanctions may include public reprimand, suspension, or disbarment.

Despite the judge's centrality, the judicial selection system is typically haphazard, characterized by self-promotion and political pull. Magistrate selection is often a political plum, given in return for prior political service. Circuit court and family court judges often become judges through a political process spearheaded by self-selection: A lawyer may decide that the time is right for a judgeship and initiates the appointment process. Consequently, the applicant pool tends to be disproportionately politically connected self-promoters, typically white and male. Judges generally receive little formal preparation for judging. Magistrates, for example, typically need no legal experience prior to appointment. Circuit court and family court judges, by contrast, have often been steeped in law and court procedures through formal law school education and professional experience. However, there is virtually no formal judge training prior to receiving an appointment.

Judicial selection is potentially problematic in that the system works like dice-rolling: Little is known about the predictors of future good judging, and a judge's eventual performance will be realized only postappointment. By that time, considerable harm may have ensued. Compounding the problem is the fact that incumbent judges, even if incompetent or abusive, are frequently difficult to unseat.

In an effort to select better judges, many judicial candidates now undergo a preselection character screening test. Such a test may help reduce the robing of candidates with poor judicial temperaments. Additionally, many states have judicial rating systems, wherein attorneys appearing before a particular judge can give feedback that will become part of the judge's permanent record. Even so, the current system of popular elections is ill suited for choosing the ablest future judges, and the stresses of waging a political campaign may discourage good candidates.

The Changing Face of Judging

Historically, the judicial role has been characterized by broad discretion, but the scope of judicial discretion has been rapidly shrinking. Even so, judges wield immense authority. Like an anachronistic monarch, judges have immediate power over everyone within their court. A judge's position within the courtroom often mimics a king's throneroom: A judge often sits on an elevated seat, separated from courtroom players by a desk or bench, and further separated from observers by a bar. A judge controls who sits or stands where and may silence any speaker. The police and bailiff are at a judge's immediate command, and judges may jail or fine disrupters through their contempt power. The judge's decisions typically have the binding authority of law. A judge may issue warrants, rule on legal matters, accept pleas, dismiss cases, and sentence offenders. Like a monarch, a judge often exerts powers over courtroom players, even though such powers are not expressly authorized. For example, a judge often decides which types of cases will be heard and the times for their hearings. A judge also frequently issues written orders relating to courtroom behaviors and schedules.

Court dockets have burgeoned over the last two decades, even as crime rates have decreased. State court felony filings increased 65% between 1984 and 1998 (Ostrom and Kauder, 1999), leading to clogged court dockets. To keep the court system moving, judges must frequently make more and faster decisions than ever before. The most effective judges must also engage in considerable administrative planning. The vast majority of all cases are disposed by plea bargaining (see Fisher, 2000). Judges may either accept or reject prosecutorial recommendations. However, as a practical matter, judges who frequently reject prosecutorial recommendations will move fewer cases.

Judges must now know more rules than ever before. As laws, guidelines, and restrictions have proliferated, judging has become increasingly technocratized, with a corresponding decrease in judicial discretion. Rationalization processes are affecting every aspect of judgeship, but are particularly evident in sentencing, evidentiary laws, and jury charges. Rationalization leads to more detail and structure in decision-making, with a corresponding reduction in judicial discretion.

Historically, a judge's sentencing discretion was absolute: a judge had unfettered discretion to impose any sentence within the minimum and maximum sentencing ranges supplied by law. Typically, judges sentenced based on severity of offense, history of offender, and the presence of any aggravating or mitigating circumstances. Judges, being human, ruled in context, according to their prejudices. Unsurprisingly, researchers noted racial disparities in sentencing, such as black burglars receiving longer sentences than their white counterparts (Kelly, 1976). Discrimination varied by judge (Gibson, 1978; Hagan, 1975), locale (Pope, 1975), race of the victim (Myers, 1979), and offender-victim-race triad (LaFree, 1980). Adding to the sentencing problem, politicians of the 1970s increasingly blamed high crime rates on judicial leniency. Parole procedures were also deemed overly lenient and disparate. In Massachusetts, for example, an individual receiving a prison sentence in Concord would typically be released after serving one-tenth of the prison term, though an individual sentenced in Walpole would serve either one-third or two-thirds of the sentence (Sparks, 1983).

In response to the twin problems of leniency and disparity, the federal government moved to rationalize federal judicial sentencing by establishing the U.S. Sentencing Commission (Sentencing Reform Act of 1984). The Commission, in turn, created the Federal Sentencing Guidelines. Under the Guidelines, a judge must apply a two-dimensional sentencing grid in sentencing an individual. The grid itself only factors in the seriousness of the offense and the criminal history of the offender; downward departures from the Guidelines are only allowed under rigidly defined exceptions. The Guidelines greatly restricted judicial discretion: A federal judge could no longer consider factors such as race and socioeconomic status. The Guidelines also technocratized the sentencing process, as a judge needed specialized training to apply the sentencing grid. Regulations relating to the Guidelines have reached over 1000 pages in length.

The advent of the Guidelines has been a decidedly mixed blessing. Savelsberg (1992) interprets the Guidelines as part of a neoclassical movement aiming to reverse the substantivization of law while reducing due process failures, disparities, and discrimination. Indeed, there is evidence that the Guidelines have reduced sentencing disparities, particularly concerning race and socioeconomic status (Dixon, 1995), although judges still have (to a lesser degree) displayed bias toward personal characteristics (Hanbury, 2000). The Guidelines have likewise reduced inter-judge disparities (Hofer, Blackwell, and Ruback, 1999). The Guidelines

certainly have affected leniency: Sentencing has become more punitive and a greater percentage of individuals are going to jail than ever before. However, the Guidelines have limited a judge's discretion to make exceptions in extraordinary circumstances. Consequently, Guidelines sentences have occasionally made for draconian results, and often for first-time offenders. Critics have further charged that the Guidelines' byzantine complexity undermines the goals of sentencing reform (Ruback & Wroblewski, 2001) and renders sentencing decisions incomprehensible to the layperson. Perhaps in response to harsh outcomes and spiraling complexity, mandatory sentencing guidelines have spread to only a handful of state courts.

Although states have generally declined to impose mandatory sentencing guidelines, many states have passed a variety of punitive sentencing laws that have caged judicial discretion. Many offenses now call for mandatory minimum sentences or no suspended sentences. In some cases, such as life-without-parole statutes, there is no sentencing discretion. Many states have given the jury sentencing discretion for felony convictions at trial.

New evidentiary laws have made judges the gatekeepers of expert testimony. Judges frequently must distinguish between accepted scientific practice and junk science. Under the old law of *Frye v. U.S.*, 54 App. D.C. 46, 293 F. 1013, 1014 (1923), expert testimony was inadmissible unless based on a scientific technique that was "generally accepted" as reliable in the relevant scientific community. The *Frye* rule allowed judges to assess experts by asking other experts about the scientific community's relevant practices. Under *Daubert v. Merrell Dow Pharmaceuticals*, 509 U.S. 579 (1993), the general acceptance requirement is eliminated and the judge must make a more individualized determination; under the *Daubert* rule, the judge must ensure that expert opinions "rest on a reliable foundation ... relevant to the task at hand ... [and] based on scientifically valid principles." Even as *Daubert* relaxed admissibility requirements, scientific evidence is becoming increasingly common in serious criminal cases. Judges must somehow strike the appropriate balance between individual rights and the truth-seeking function of the tribunal: Improper scientific claims may jeopardize an individual's right to a fair trial, whereas excluding proper scientific claims may lead to a verdict that does not speak the truth. Researchers have found, however, that judges lack the scientific literacy necessary to apply *Daubert* (Gatowski et al. 2001); for example, only 5% of judges understood the concept of falsifiability, and just 4% the concept of error rate (ibid).

Compounding the difficulty of correct judging is the error-based due process model that increasingly technocratizes the judging process. Every courtroom keeps a record of its activities. For magistrate or municipal courts, frequently the record is just an audiotape. In higher courts, however, a court reporter generally records every word of every proceeding. The court reporter can then produce a court transcript that can be reviewed by appellate courts. Upon appeal, an appellate court will review the court transcript for errors by the trial judge. Serious errors will result in reversals. In any event, the consideration of error continuously produces a common-law jurisprudential literature. Year by year, this literature becomes more nuanced, and judges are responsible for incorporating each new requirement. There is often one best, correct procedure to be employed. This process is clearly exemplified in jury instructions. Judges typically prepare jury charges prior to trial and invite supplements and suggestions from the prosecutor and the defense attorney. These charges are based on constitutional, statutory, and common-law sources, and are often directly copied from a pattern jury instructions sourcebook. The correct wording for a murder charge, for example, is exact, and small mistakes of wording can lead to reversals. The judge's discretion in giving charges or explaining the law is minimized in favor of a hyper-technical, rationalized approach to due process.

Along with new sentencing and evidentiary approaches, new courts are being created with newly specialized judges that go beyond the Beccarian model of punishment (see, e.g., Berman & Feinblatt, 2001). Some criminologists have noted that the present deterrence-based system fails to appeal to an offender's non-rational emotions (see, e.g., Sherman, 2003). Research has shown that specialized therapeutic courts are effective in treating particular types of crime problems (in drug addiction contexts, Belenko, 1998; in domestic violence contexts, Gover et al., 2003). In these new therapeutic courts, judges must learn new sets of skills. In drug courts, for example, judges must educate themselves about drug addiction studies to understand the drug addiction types, as well as successful treatment models for various addiction types.

J. EAGLE SHUTT

References and Further reading

American Judicature Society. 2004. *What is Judicial Independence?* Available at: http://www.ajs.org/cji/cji_whatisji.asp. Retrieved on January 24, 2004.

Amnesty International. 2001. *Racism and the Administration of Justice.* New York, NY: Amnesty International.

Belenko, S. 1998. Research on Drug Courts: A Critical Review. *National Drug Court Institute Review,* 1(1), 1–42.

Berman, G. and Feinblatt, J. 2001. Problem-solving Courts: A Brief Primer. *Law and Policy,* 23(2), 125–140.

Black, D. 1994. *The Social Structure of Right and Wrong.* San Diego, CA: Academic Press.

Bureau of Justice Statistics. 2001. *Court Organization Statistics.* Available at: http://www.ojp.usdoj.gov/bjs/courts.htm#judges. Retrieved on January 24, 2004.

Bureau of Justice Statistics. 2003. Criminal Case Prosecuting Statistics. Available at: http://www.ojp.usdoj.gov/bjs/cases.htm.

Clay-Warner, J. 2001. Perceiving Procedural Injustice: The Effects of Group Membership and Status. *Social Psychology Quarterly,* 64(3), 224–238.

Crystal, J. 2001. Criminal Justice in the Middle East. *Journal of Criminal Justice,* 29(6), 469–482.

Dixon, J. 1995. The Organizational Context of Criminal Sentencing. *American Journal of Sociology,* 100(5), 1157–1198.

Fisher, G. 2000. Plea Bargaining's Triumph. *Yale Law Journal,* 109(857), 868–1086.

Garland, D. *The Culture of Control: Crime and Social Order in Contemporary Society.* Chicago, IL: University of Chicago Press.

Gatowski, S.I., Dobbin, S.A., and Richardson, J.T. 2001. Asking the Gatekeepers: A National Survey of Judges on Judging Expert Evidence in a Post-'Daubert' World. *Law and Human Behavior,* 25(5), 433–458.

Gibson, J.L. 1978. Race as a Determinant of Criminal Sentences: A Methodological Critique and a Case Study. *Law & Society Review,* 12, 455–478.

Gover, A., MacDonald, J., and Alpert, G. Combating Domestic Violence: Findings from an Evaluation of a Local Domestic Violence Court. *Criminology and Public Policy,* 3(1), 109–132.

Hagan, J. Law, Order and Sentencing: A Study of Attitude in Action. *Sociometry,* 38(2), 374–384.

Hanbury, B.M. 2000. Are Judges Downwardly Departing from the U.S. Sentencing Guidelines Based on the Offenders' Personal Characteristics? PhD Dissertation, University of Maryland. Ann Arbor, MI, University Microfilms International.

Hofer, P.J., Blackwell, K.R., and Ruback, R.B. 1999. The Effect of the Federal Sentencing Guidelines on Inter-judge Disparity. *Journal of Criminal Law and Criminology,* 90(1), 239–321.

Kelly, H.E. 1976. Comparison of Defense Strategy and Race as Influences in Differential Sentencing. *Criminology,* 14, 241–249.

LaFree, G. 1980. The Effect of Sexual Stratification by Race on Official Reactions to Rape. *Criminology,* 14, 241–249.

Myers, M.A. 1979. Offended parties and Official Reactions: Victims and the Sentencing of Criminal Defendants. *Sociological Quarterly,* 20, 529–540.

National Center for State Courts. 2002. *Survey of Judicial Salaries,* 27(2). Available at: http://www.ncsconline.org/courtinfoportal/search/search1.html. Retrieved on January 24, 2004.

Neubauer, D.W. 2002. *America's Courts and the Criminal Justice System,* 7th ed. Belmont, CA: Wadsworth.

Ostrom, B. and Kauder, N. 1999. *Examining the Work of State Courts, 1998.* Williamsburg, VA: National Center for State Courts.

Parsons, T. 1962. The Law and Social Control, in Evan, W.M., Ed., *Law and Sociology.* pp. 56–72. New York, NY: The Free Press.

Pope, C.E. 1975. The Judicial Processing of Assault and Burglary Offenders in Selected California Counties. National Criminal Justice Information Statistics Service. Washington, DC: U.S. Department of Justice.

Rottman, D.B. and Hansen, R.M. 2001. *How Recent Court Users View the State Courts: Perceptions of Whites, African-Americans, and Latinos.* Unpublished report to the National Institute of Justice.

Ruback, R.B. and Wroblewski, J. 2001. The Federal Sentencing Guidelines: Psychological and Policy Reasons for Simplification. *Psychology Public Policy and Law*, 7(4), 739–775.

Sanborn, J.B. 2001. A Parens Patriae Figure or Impartial Fact Finder: Policy Questions and Conflicts for the Juvenile Court Judge. *Criminal Justice Policy Review,* 12(4), 311–332.

Savelsberg, J.J. 1992. Law that does not fit Society: Sentencing Guidelines as a Neoclassical Reaction to the Dilemmas of Substantivized Law. *American Journal of Sociology*, 97, 1346–1381.

Sentencing Reform Act of 1984. S. Rep. No. 225, 98th Cong., 1st Sess. 52, 56.

Sherman, L.W. 2003. Reason for Emotion: Reinventing Justice with Theories, Innovations, and Research–The American Society of Criminology 2002 Presidential Address. *Criminology,* 41(1), 1–38.

Snyder, H.N., Sickmund, M., and Poe, Y.E. 2000. *Juvenile Transfers to Criminal Court in the 1990's: Lessons Learned from Four Studies.* Washington, DC: Office of Juvenile Justice and Delinquency Prevention.

Sparks, R.F. 1983. The Construction of Sentencing Guidelines: A Methodological Critique. in Blumstein, A., Cohen, J., Martin, S.E., and Tonry, M.H., *Research on Sentencing: The Search for Reform.* pp. 194–264. Washington, DC: National Academy Press.

Steffensmeier, D. and Demuth, S. 2001. Ethnicity and Judges' Sentencing Decisions: Hispanic-Black-White Comparisons. *Criminology,* 39(1), 145–178.

Weber, M. 1954. *On Law in Economy and Society.* Translated by Rheinstein, M. and Shils, E., Cambridge, MA: Harvard University Press.

See also **Courts in the U.S.; Criminal Justice System: Models of Operation; Law and Legal Services: Careers**

Juries and Juror Selection

Jurors are key participants in the American criminal justice system because most cases are plea bargained "in the shadow of the jury," that is, with great concern for what a jury might think if the matter came to trial. Prosecutors' decisions about whether to pursue a case often reflect assessments of how jurors would respond should a case make it to trial. For this reason, the influence of the jury system extends far beyond the actual verdicts rendered in particular trials.

The opportunity for ordinary citizens to participate in the legal process as jurors is a key aspect of American government. But why should we have juries composed of ordinary citizens, especially when so many people would prefer not to take the time to serve as jurors? The answers lie in the role that jurors play in the legal system.

Juries in colonial America were intended to be a bulwark against government oppression of citizens, and this central role of juries continues today. Historically, jurors in America were empowered to decide both the law and the facts in a given case. In contrast, modern-day jurors are restricted to deciding only the facts in a case, while judges determine the law. Thus, jurors must determine whether the prosecutor in a criminal trial has proven the government's case beyond a reasonable doubt. Does the evidence support the state's version of events—or that of the defense?

But jurors are not simply or solely fact finders. If this were the only function of juries, why not use people with expertise in investigation, or people known for their logical thinking or their specialized knowledge? The use of laypeople as jurors illustrates the democratic role of the jury.

The framers of the Constitution considered trial by jury to be an important constitutional right because of the unique status of jurors as amateurs—rather than hired officials. In essence, jurors play the role of "the conscience of the community" in the court system (*Witherspoon v. Illinois*, 391 U.S. 510, 1968), bringing community values to bear on the process of justice. This is how jurors can help protect against government oppression, because jurors can send a message about public attitudes toward the law and the way it is applied. For example, jurors once acquitted a defendant on gun charges after intense deliberation revealed that they favored the gun law in question, but they did not support its application in this particular case.

Jury Selection

The Sixth Amendment provides the right to trial by an "impartial" jury, but conceptions of impartiality have changed considerably over time. Historically the concept of juror impartiality referred to the ability to make a fair, unbiased decision. Impartiality was seen as distinct from juror knowledge of the case, and if a juror was personally familiar with the parties and events in the case, this was seen as an asset.

In contrast, the modern conception of impartiality is manifested by the search for jurors who know as little as possible about the case and, some critics argue, as little as possible about anything. A major problem with equating lack of knowledge and impartiality is that this fails to recognize that knowledge can be a source of competence rather than partiality. In essence, this equation represents a "false opposition between knowledge and impartiality" (Abramson, 1994). It can be argued that not only is it possible to be highly knowledgeable yet impartial, but also there is a greater probability that being informed helps individuals to be open-minded and unbiased. This issue is highlighted by the fact that increasingly broad media coverage of crime stories raises the probability that prospective jurors may be familiar with important details of most notorious cases.

The right to trial by an impartial jury raises many questions concerning jury selection and composition. A common method of jury selection before 1968 was the "key man" system, relying on prominent citizens in the community to serve. This meant many qualified citizens were excluded from jury duty, despite the fact that as early as 1880 the Supreme Court found that the exclusion of African American jurors violated equal protection provisions in the Constitution (*Strauder v. West Virginia*, 100 U.S. 303, 1880). However, in practice the exclusion of minorities from jury service continued unacknowledged by the Court, as illustrated by its decision in *Swain v. Alabama* (380 U.S. 202, 1965). Similarly, although women became jury eligible between 1870 and 1940 (depending on locale), most states failed to summon women for jury service until a U.S. Supreme Court ruling that this violated equal protection (*Taylor v. Louisiana*, 419 U.S. 522, 1975).

In 1968, Congress enacted the Jury Selection and Service Act, requiring that federal jury pools be comprised of citizens drawn at random "from a representative cross section of the community." In *Taylor,* the court extended this requirement to states. The random selection requirement substantially changed the methods used to summon citizens for jury duty. In *Holland v. Illinois* (493 U.S. 474, 1990) the Court clarified that the *process* of selecting the jury pool, rather than juries themselves, must be representative. This is a crucial distinction to note. Many people mistakenly believe that a "jury of your peers" means that some jurors should share the defendant's demographic characteristics. Instead, a jury of peers refers to the idea that defendants should be tried by fellow community members.

The Goal of Representativeness

Why does the modern process of jury selection strive for representativeness in jury selection? One assumption is that drawing jurors from a representative cross section of the community will lead to a more diverse jury and, in turn, that jurors from different demographic groups may have significantly different perspectives on the case. Yet research shows that jurors' demographic characteristics, although having significant influences on the verdict in some cases, are less important than the evidence in most cases. The assumption that jurors' verdict choices can be neatly parsed along demographic lines is not supported by research. Juror behavior is difficult to predict based on demographic characteristics for a number of reasons. For example, jurors' attitudes are not necessarily predictive of their behavior (e.g., in verdict choice). This is in fact legally appropriate, given that verdicts should reflect only the evidence presented at trial.

However, it should not be assumed that demographics have nothing to do with verdict choices; we are a product of our experiences, so diversity matters. If a juror shares the same ethnicity as the defendant, it may increase the likelihood that the juror will acquit—or convict. Members of a given demographic group cannot be assumed to share the same perspective, attitudes, or experiences. Although they may indeed share some common experiences, individual differences will exist. Thus, assumed "group loyalties" often may not exist in reality.

Another assumption underlying the representativeness goal is that the existence of diverse views within the jury may improve the group's decision-making abilities. This "deliberative" model of jury decision making posits that the existence of contrasting perspectives may increase the likelihood that various arguments on the issues will be presented, rather than group members taking a uniform approach to the issues in the case (Abramson, 1994). A related theoretical argument for the importance of representativeness is the "balancing biases" model, which assumes that recruiting jurors who represent a variety of viewpoints increases the likelihood that biases held by jurors cancel each other out during deliberations (Abramson, 1994). Greater jury diversity may reduce the possibility of prejudice tainting the jury. For example, a juror inclined to make derogatory comments about a given ethnic or gender group might gain a new perspective if members of that group are also on the jury. For these and other reasons, representativeness in the jury selection process may help ensure due process protection for defendants.

Public controversy surrounding high-profile criminal cases, especially those that raise questions about the relationship between race, ethnicity, and the fairness of the legal process, suggest another rationale for representativeness. Verdicts from relatively homogenous juries may be greeted with skepticism by significant segments of the public, whereas verdicts from more diverse juries are more likely to be perceived as legitimate.

Steps in the Process of Jury Selection

Using voter registration and Department of Motor Vehicles roles, each county creates a master list of county residents, from which the names of people who will receive a jury summons are randomly drawn. To be eligible to serve as a juror, one must be an adult citizen with no felony convictions who is able to understand English. Individuals whose names are not on these lists have no chance of being called for jury service, leading to an underrepresentation of people who are homeless or move frequently, such as students or seasonal employees.

After the summonses are sent out, more prospective jurors are in effect "weeded out" of the jury selection process: nonrespondents, persons ineligible for jury duty, or those who are exempt or excused. The people left after this stage comprise the *venire* (the jury panel). The next step is *voir dire*, during which the judge and the attorneys question prospective jurors under oath to determine whether they should be seated on the jury. In some cases, prospective jurors fill out questionnaires about their attitudes and experiences with the issues in the case.

Voir dire provides an interesting contrast to earlier steps in the process of jury selection, where the focus on the representativeness of the selection process requires *random* selection of prospective jurors. In contrast, jury selection during *voir dire* is anything *but* random; instead, attorneys attempt to select favorable jurors and exclude those they believe could be biased against their side.

Attorneys have two major tools for "striking" a prospective juror from the panel. Attorneys have unlimited opportunities to challenge a potential juror "for cause," which means they ask the court to excuse the juror from service because of a potential bias (e.g., the person was a crime victim or is a relative or acquaintance of the accused). The judge has discretion to grant or refuse the request. The attorneys also have a limited number of "peremptory challenges" that they can exercise without specifying a reason. Peremptory challenges allow attorneys to strike an unwanted juror who could not be challenged for cause. Historically, the attorney's reason was legally irrelevant; perhaps the attorney had a "gut hunch" that the person would favor the opposition. However, questions about the role of peremptory challenges in jury selection came into sharper focus after *Duncan v. Louisiana* (391 U.S. 145, 1968), reflecting the new emphasis on inclusiveness in jury selection. Controversy focused on the question of whether prosecutors were using peremptory challenges to exclude African American jurors in cases with an African American defendant. The "race-based" use of "peremptories" raises equal protection and due process concerns because it directly conflicts with the goal of representativeness.

Supreme Court decisions until recently supported the use of peremptory challenges in ways that could block representativeness, as illustrated in *Swain*. *Swain* challenged the prosecutor's use of peremptories to strike all African American jurors from the panel, arguing that this violated due process. The Supreme Court disagreed, questioning whether the prosecutor's challenges of African American jurors at Swain's trial occurred solely on the basis of race. The court noted that if defendants could present evidence establishing a pattern of race-based use of peremptory challenges across several cases, this would reveal bias by the state and thus an impermissible violation of equal protection. However, defendants found such evidence impossible to obtain, either because these records were not kept by courts or could not be accessed.

However, the court reversed its position in *Batson v. Kentucky* (476 U.S. 79, 1986), holding that the prosecutors' use of peremptory challenges to exclude potential jurors solely on the basis of race violated the defendant's right to equal protection. The court discussed the potential harm to the representativeness ideal through the use of peremptories to strike members of a "cognizable group" (a group of people recognizable as having a high likelihood of sharing common experiences and attitudes).

The court forbade the use of race-based peremptories in civil cases in *Edmonson v. Leesville Concrete Company* (500 U.S. 614, 1991). In *Georgia v. McCollum* (505 U.S. 42, 1992), the court ruled that the use of race-based peremptories by defense counsel in criminal cases is unconstitutional. In 1994, the court's reasoning on peremptory challenges was extended to gender in a case arising out of a child custody dispute (*J.E.B. v. Alabama ex rel. TB*, 114 S.Ct. 1419, 1994). If an attorney appears to be using peremptory challenges in an impermissible manner, the court can require an explanation of how this does not represent a race- or gender-based pattern. Critics contend, however, that this has not prevented the continued use of peremptory challenges for race-based reasons.

Although the Supreme Court's logic banning peremptories for race- or gender-based reasons has not thus far been applied to other potential "cognizable groups," it may be only a matter of time. In 2000, the California Supreme Court ruled that sexual orientation defines a cognizable group, and thus in California peremptory challenges cannot be used to remove prospective jurors solely on the basis of their sexual orientation (Chiang, 2000).

After *voir dire*, the remaining persons comprise the jury. The fact that so many potential jurors are "weeded out" at various steps in the selection process leads some to protest the "myth of representativeness" (Abramson, 1994).

Jury Selection Strategies

Traditionally, attorneys use their experience, intuitions, and implicit personality theories in selecting who they believe will be the best jurors for their side, and in deciding how to challenge jurors they perceive as least favorable. In the 1960s, "scientific jury selection" (SJS) techniques were first put to use in the trial of the Chicago Seven, a group of antiwar protestors.

Scientific jury selection refers to the use of social science techniques to assist attorneys in selecting jurors and developing persuasive case presentations. SJS techniques include surveying community members and holding discussion groups to gauge their attitudes and reactions on issues crucial to the trial. The key assumption underlying scientific jury selection techniques is that individuals' demographic characteristics and attitudes are correlated with their views on case-relevant issues. In theory, research with community members (although not the actual prospective jurors themselves, for legal and ethical reasons) should help identify the characteristics and attitudes of citizens who would make the most favorable jurors. However, much research also demonstrates that the attitudes of potential jurors are not necessarily linked to demographic characteristics, and that attitudes do not necessarily predict behavior.

Scientific jury selection is controversial and employed relatively rarely in criminal trials compared to its use in complex civil trials. Some proponents of SJS believe it is quite effective, and it may be particularly useful in certain kinds of cases (e.g., those involving political crimes or certain types of civil cases). The results of research on the effectiveness of scientific as compared to traditional jury selection strategies are mixed. The use of SJS techniques together with traditional methods may be the most promising approach to juror selection. Scientific jury selection techniques may be most valuable when used to develop trial presentation strategies (e.g., how to present complex legal and scientific information in the most comprehensible fashion, or the most effective way to structure the sequence of arguments).

There are also ethical questions raised by the use of SJS. To the extent that SJS is an effective tool, does this provide an unfair advantage to wealthy defendants and litigants who employ SJS in comparison to those without access to such techniques? This question raises broader issues related to the old and persistent problem of equal access to resources throughout the legal system.

Jury Service: Participation in Democracy

The central role that jurors play in the American legal system is highlighted in the controversy surrounding the question of how many people are required on a jury. Although juries of twelve people are traditional, a series of court cases established that smaller juries are acceptable in certain circumstances, depending upon whether the case is a civil or a criminal trial (see the entry on "Right to Trial"). A related issue that is arguably even more controversial is the question of whether jury verdicts must be unanimous, or whether majority verdicts (such as 10 to 2 decisions) are acceptable in certain cases (see the entry on "Right to Trial").

At the core of the arguments over jury size and decision rule are concerns about representativeness and due process. Proponents of traditional juries assert that having twelve person juries that are required to return a unanimous verdict is critical to safeguarding the rights of the accused and preventing potential miscarriages of justice. Others argue in rebuttal that smaller juries are more economical for states to convene, and that requiring unanimous verdicts means that one holdout juror can create a hung (deadlocked) jury. Both jury size and decision rule remain controversial issues, but most jurisdictions continue to use traditional juries in criminal cases, while civil cases often involve smaller juries and majority verdicts.

Juries: A Comparative Look

The modern jury system has ancient roots, but the most visible ones are reflected in the English jury system. The practice of trial by jury accompanied the rise of the British Empire and traveled to the American colonies. Today, over forty nations use jurors in one capacity or another, including countries from almost every continent (Vidmar, 2000: 3), yet beyond that commonality there is remarkable variation between nations in the roles that juries have in each legal system. Despite common English roots, jury systems in different nations have been adapted to fit specific legal and cultural contexts in each society. Such diversification reflects political, legal, and cultural factors and influences every aspect of the jury system. Thus, nations vary widely in how jurors are selected, the degree of autonomy they have, the procedures they must follow in coming to a decision, and the legal functions that juries have (Vidmar, 2000).

Another illustration of the diversification of jury systems is that today, even the English and American jury systems have distinct differences. Juries are convened in a much wider range of cases in the U.S., compared to England. Jury selection differs significantly between the two countries; for example, in England there are no peremptory challenges, although the government has the power to ask a juror to "stand aside." The juror then returns to the jury pool and may be called again later if more suitable jurors are not seated (Vidmar, 2000). The most conspicuous difference between the American and English jury systems, however, is that the right to trial by jury is firmly entrenched as a fundamental right only in America. In contrast, in England the right to trial has been "progressively eroded" through legislation that restricts the circumstances under which a criminal defendant can receive a jury trial. Thus, most English defendants are tried by magistrates (lay judges) rather than citizens serving as jurors (Lloyd-Bostock and Thomas, 2000).

Conclusion

In their role as key legal decision makers, jurors have an impact that extends beyond the boundaries of individual cases; jurors' decisions both *reflect* and *shape* societal attitudes about the legal system and legal processes. Jury selection thus raises important legal and social questions about who serves and how they are selected to fill this essential role in the legal system—issues to think about when you receive a jury summons.

DIANA GRANT

References and Further Reading

Abramson, J. 1994. *We, the Jury*. Basic Books,
Chiang, H. 2000. Ruling Protects Gay Juror Rights. *San Francisco Chronicle,* p. A-1.
Finkel, N.J. 1995. *Commonsense Justice: Jurors' Notions of the Law.* Cambridge, MA: Harvard University Press.
Fukurai, H. and Butler, E., and Krooth. R., 1993. *Race and The Jury.* New York, NY: Plenum Publishing.
Geller, L.H. and Hemenway, P. 1997. *Last Chance for Justice: The Juror's Lonely Quest.* Dallas, TX, NCDS Press.
Hans, V. and Vidmar, N. 1987. *Judging The Jury.* New York, NY: Plenum Publishing.
Levine, J. 1992. *We, the Jury.* Pacific Grove, CA: Brooks/Cole Publishing Company.
Lloyd-Bostock, S. and Thomas, C. The Continuing Decline of the English Jury, in Vidmar, N., Ed., *World Jury Systems.* Oxford, UK: Oxford University Press.
Vidmar, N. 2000. A Historical and Comparative Perspective On the Common Law Jury, in Vidmar, N., Ed., *World Jury Systems.* Oxford, UK: Oxford University Press.

See also **Trial, The Right to**

Juvenile Delinquency and Youth Crime Throughout History

Juvenile delinquency is broadly defined as "any action by someone designated a juvenile (nonadult) that would make such a young person subject to action by the juvenile court" (Kratcoski and Kratcoski, 1996, 2). This definition is somewhat problematic and poses problems for a historical discussion of juvenile delinquency and youth crime. Thus, the following discussion will focus on crime among those under the age of 18 throughout history, and how that criminal activity has created what we call "juvenile delinquency" today.

The present system of juvenile justice in the U.S. emerged at the turn of the 20th century. Nevertheless, juvenile delinquency and youth crime trace their roots much further back than the past two centuries. Juveniles have always committed acts that we now label as "delinquency" or "status offenses" (acts that are presently defined as crimes for children only, such as incorrigibility or truancy). Thus, children have always fought, drank alcohol, skipped school, and rebelled against their parents. It was only with the creation of the juvenile court that some of these acts became crimes in the U.S. The emergence of the juvenile court traces its roots back to Europe and, particularly, Great Britain, but to understand where our present system comes from, one must understand how the concepts of "childhood" and "juvenile delinquency" emerged.

Because they have historically been society's most powerless members (even in democracies, children are not allowed to vote, hold political office, or sign contracts), children have historically endured numerous hardships. In the ancient Roman, Greek, and Chinese empires, children were often killed for offenses committed by their parents. Even law-abiding children were often treated harshly by their parents with little recourse available. Cruelty to animals was a punishable offense, both in England and in the U.S., before cruelty to children was. In fact, the first child removed from her home because of abuse by parents (New York, 1874) had to be removed under a law preventing cruelty to animals. Thus, only recently in the larger historical scheme has the welfare of children became a concern throughout the world (Regoli and Hewitt, 1997). As such, until the Middle Ages, children were seldom mentioned in legal codes. There are exceptions to that rule, however.

The Code of Hammurabi is the oldest known set of written laws, and was created during King Hammurabi's reign in Babylon between 1792 and 1750BC. This set of laws made some differentiation between children and adults, as one of the 282 rules that Hammurabi created was specifically aimed at children who disobeyed their parents, stating that sons who struck their father should have their hands cut off. Some 1000 years later, the Greek empire responded to misbehavior by children by passing laws that held parents responsible for the misbehavior of their children, a precursor of the parent-liability laws of the 20th century U.S. discussed below.

We have more information about childhood in the Middle Ages. Historical evidence indicates that the children of that time period were often allowed many of the freedoms that adults had, including the ability to drink at home and in taverns, the ability to wear sidearms, and the choice not to attend school. Law regulating the behavior of children began to emerge in the tenth century, when King Aethelstan of England (reign 924–939) ruled that a thief over 12 years of age should be executed if he or she stole more than eight pence. Although such laws made a distinction between very young children and adults, they made little distinction between what we now call adolescents and adults (Regoli and Hewitt, 1997).

Aries (1962) agrees that, in medieval society, childhood did not exist. As soon as a child could live without the constant supervision of its mother, he or she became an adult. Infants who were too fragile to take part in everyday life, with the exception of their mother or caregiver, were simply ignored. Aries argues that children were not "coddled" or protected as they are today, and this "coddling attitude" toward children began to meet staunch resistance from adults in the 17th century. This staunch resistance to coddling, as well as a concerted effort by the church in the 18th century, changed the child from one who was to be coddled to one who was to be safeguarded and reformed.

The education of children impacted the creation of juvenile delinquency as well. Prior to the 15th century, the most common form of education for children was apprenticeship, where a child (typically around the age of 7) was sent to live and work with a skilled craftsman to learn that trade. Starting in the 15th century, however, public schools began to emerge, and thus children began to stay with their families through childhood and attend public schools. This changed the relationship between the family and the child as well, making the family much more concerned about the well being of the child after age 7 than it had been previously. Parents now began to keep their children at home for as long as possible (Aries, 1962).

Historical Development of Juvenile Delinquency in Europe

Prior to the 19th century, existing law in England assumed that children under age 7 were incapable of having the ability to develop criminal intent and, as such, were exempt from criminal penalties. Children between the ages of 7 and 14 were also presumed to lack the ability to develop criminal intent but could, in some cases, be held liable for their actions that were criminal.

Schwedinger and Schwedinger (1985) argue that the emergence of capitalism in England introduced the concept of youth crime. They review English developments in the 15th and 16th centuries that resulted from capitalism's replacement of older modes of production, arguing that the move away from apprenticeship created a number of unemployed children who went throughout the country, either alone or in bands, and committed crimes against the population at large. Further, because capitalism stabilized criminal populations such as prostitutes and thieves, their children were brought up as criminals as well. This state of unsupervised children throughout the country brought about the creation of workhouses in the late 17th century to deal with these problematic children. Despite the establishment of workhouses throughout England, the problem of youth crime continued.

Muncie (1999) reviews a number of historical works that discuss the prevalence of youth crime in Europe, particularly in England. He contends that the number of individuals under 17 years of age imprisoned in England grew from 9500 in 1838 to 14,000 in 1848, but argues that this almost 50% increase was due more to changes in the law in England rather than increased "lawlessness" among young people. He points out that the Vagrancy Act of 1824 and the Malicious Trespass Act of 1827 broadened categories of crime to include gambling on the street and stealing apples from orchards and gardens, prevalent behaviors among the youth of that period. Further, the police in London began to "crack down" on youthful offenders with arrests, rather than turning a blind eye to the youthful misbehavior as they had done in the past.

Muncie (1999) reveals that the residents of these juvenile facilities primarily came from poor and working-class families in England. He argues that reformers during this time wanted to recognize that youth were fully responsible for their actions and emphasized the role of the state to intervene when families were incapable of controlling their children. This idea that the state could intervene when the family failed was known as *parens patriae*. Under this concept, the state acted *in loco parentis* (in lieu of the parent) on behalf of the child. These two intertwined ideas dramatically changed the nature of the relationship between the criminal justice system and juvenile offenders.

Historical Development of Juvenile Delinquency in the U.S.

The treatment of children in early America was comparable to the treatment children received in England. As in England, child labor was widely popular until the turn of the 20th century, but there were laws specifically designed to regulate the behavior of children in America as well. In 1641, the Massachusetts Bay Colony passed the "stubborn child law," which stated that children who disobeyed their parents would be put to death. Historical evidence indicates the Massachusetts Bay Colony (due largely to the Puritan influence) punished children more harshly than other colonies; caning was the most common punishment for children who rebelled against parents or the law in other colonies.

Despite the harsh punishment often given children in the colonies, Americans by the turn of the 20th century appeared to have mixed feelings about the role of the child in society. Childhood was viewed as a period of life when children needed discipline and guidance, yet they were viewed as innocent and fragile as well. Upper class people appeared to have thought that childhood was a "special" status, and children should be treated differently than adults, nurtured into adulthood and punished less harshly when they did run afoul of the law.

At the same time, societal changes were taking place that impacted the concept of juvenile delinquency as well. Schwedinger and Schwedinger (1985) suggest that many of the aforementioned criminal and impoverished groups in London and other parts of England settled in the American colonies, thus bringing delinquency to America with them. Authors of the early 19th century described the behavior of adolescents in urban areas such as Boston, Philadelphia, and Baltimore as very similar to that of London in the 17th and 18th centuries. In the U.S., at the turn of the 19th century, the first public body to investigate crime among youth, the Society for Investigating the Causes of the Alarming Increase of Juvenile Delinquency in the Metropolis, was formed. The society concluded that the main cause of juvenile delinquency was improper conduct of parents and a shortage of educational and employment opportunities for children (Muncie, 1999). The society suggested a separate system for dealing with young offenders, one that would be used to encourage the rehabilitation of young offenders, not strictly punishment, as was the case with adults. It was during this time that the first statistics on numbers of juvenile offenders emerged. Rapid industrialization in the 19th century also brought an increase in leisure time for many wealthy people, an increased emphasis on public education, and a deterioration of the close-knit communities that existed during agrarian America. Many wealthy people became concerned (and fearful) about the plight of lower class children and their misbehavior. Out of this concern came a group called the child savers.

The child savers were a group of upper class reformers who believed that children were inherently good and delinquency and other forms of misbehavior were caused by bad environments. Thus, they felt that the state should intervene under the doctrine of *parens patriae* (defining the state as the ultimate guardian of every child) and incarcerate "problem" children, particularly those from the lower class (Regoli and Hewitt, 1997). This group actively pursued legislation that would give the state more power to intervene in the lives of children who violated the law (or in many cases, "street urchins" and unruly or rebellious children who violated their upper class norms of behavior). Although the intentions of the child savers may have been noble, the results of their movement were not, as many institutions (called houses of refuge) emerged to house these "problem" children, primarily in the East.

The first house of refuge was opened in 1825 in the state of New York. While the house was originally designed to save children from a life of crime and rehabilitate them before they reached adulthood, it soon became a vehicle for the child savers to "save society from children" (Regoli and Hewitt, 1997). The managers of the New York house of refuge and others like it thus emphasized repentance and punishment; children accused of crimes not only were to be persuaded not to commit those crimes again, but were also harshly punished for their behavior. Fox (1970) argues that by the turn of the 20th century, these houses of refuge primarily existed because of the upper class's fear of immigrants, the poor, and their children, and were used to control rather than to rehabilitate problem children. Thus, the houses of refuge were America's way of dealing with problem children throughout the 19th century.

At the end of the 19th century, reformers realized that the houses of refuge were not the panacea for youth crime many originally thought they would be. Thus, in a continuous effort to look for new solutions to the problem of juvenile delinquency, other measures were explored. The most significant of these measures began in 1899, when the juvenile court system was established in Cook County (Chicago) Illinois. Legislators in Illinois passed a statute that defined a delinquent child as someone under the age of 16 who violated any law of the state or any village or city ordinance. Legislators also defined dependent and neglected children as children who were homeless, abandoned, dependent on public support, living in a house of disrepute, or who habitually begged or received alms (Abbot 1938). This new court segregated juvenile offenders from adult offenders and hired probation officers to supervise most juvenile offenders in the community. By the early 20th century, most states had adopted a juvenile court system similar to the one begun in Illinois (Elrod and Ryder, 1999).

In the original design of the juvenile court system, trials (referred to as hearings to avoid the stigma of the adult court) were overseen by special judges who ensured that the hearings were closed. Judges had wide discretion, and proof of guilt was not necessary for a judge to intervene in a child's life. In practically all states, however, the juvenile courts did not function as designed. Reformatories and penal institutions were still filled with hundreds of children, and in many jurisdictions, children were still confined in jails with adults. Despite evidence that the juvenile court was not entirely successful in meeting its goals, the juvenile court system that emerged at the turn of the 20th century continued relatively unchanged until the 1960s.

In the 1960s, legal and public concerns with juvenile delinquency changed dramatically. Baby boomers (those born immediately after World War II, generally considered to be those born between 1946 and 1964) began to reach their teenage years in the first part of the 1960s. This dramatic increase in the proportion of the population who were in their teenage years caused delinquency rates to soar well above any previous levels. Adolescents were not only being arrested for status offenses and traditional minor property crimes,

such as larceny, theft, and burglary, they also were being arrested for murder, rape, and robbery at unprecedented levels.

Many states responded with new policies that gave more severe punishments to violent juvenile offenders, whereas many also lowered the age at which individuals could be tried as adults from 18 to 17 or 16. Other states rewrote their statutes so that *any* offender guilty of certain offenses (e.g. murder, forcible rape) could be tried as an adult. Additionally, a number of important court decisions (e.g., *Kent v. U.S.* (1966), *In re Gault* (1967), and *In re Winship* (1970)) caused the juvenile court to more closely resemble adult courts by insuring a number of procedural protections not previously available to juveniles. This trend has continued until today.

The 1970s also brought about changes in how noncriminal behavior of juveniles was defined. Statutes were written to replace the vague distinctions between status offenses, neglect, and dependency. Most states moved to separate juvenile delinquents from status offenders, and status offenders from neglected and dependent children.

The 1970s and early 1980s were a period of relative calm in the area of juvenile delinquency. The number of juvenile arrests for arson, larceny-theft, and the serious violent crimes (e.g. murder, rape, robbery, and aggravated assault) leveled off and remained relatively constant until the late 1980s.

In 1989, however, for serious violent crimes, the juvenile arrest rate began a dramatic increase that continued until it reached its peak in 1994, when this rapid increase was followed by a rapid decline that has continued until present. Motor vehicle theft followed a similar pattern, with a dramatic increase in the juvenile arrest rate that began in 1984 and continued until 1991, when the rate began to steadily decline. Larceny-theft arrest rates for juveniles have remained relatively stable from 1980 until today, and the burglary rate declined over 50% in the decade of the 1990s (Snyder and Sickmund, 1999; Federal Bureau of Investigation, 2000).

DAVID C. MAY

References and Further Reading

Agnew, R. 2001. *Juvenile Delinquency: Causes and Control*, Los Angeles, CA: Roxbury Publishing.

Aries, P. 1962. *Centuries of Childhood*, New York: Alfred A. Knopf.

Elrod, P. and Ryder, R.S. 1999. *Juvenile Justice: A Social, Historical, and Legal Perspective*, Gaithersburg, MD: Aspen Publishing.

Federal Bureau of Investigation, 2000. *Crime in the U.S.: The Uniform Crime Reports*, Washington, DC: U.S. Government Printing Office.

Kratcoski, P.C. and Kratcoski, L.D. 1996. *Juvenile Delinquency*, 4th ed., Upper Saddle River, NJ: Prentice Hall.

McCord, J., Widom, C.S., and Crowell, N. Eds. 2000. *Juvenile Crime, Juvenile Justice*, Washington, DC: National Academy Press.

Muncie, J. 1999. *Youth and Crime: A Critical Introduction*, Thousand Oaks, CA: Sage.

Regoli, R.M. and Hewitt, J.D. 1997. *Delinquency in Society* 3rd ed., New York, NY: McGraw Hill.

Schwedinger, H. and Schwendinger, J. 1985. *Adolescent Subcultures and Delinquency: Research Edition*, New York, NY: Praeger.

See also **International Crime Statistics: Juvenile Delinquency and Youth Crime; Juvenile Justice: History and Philosophy**

Juvenile Delinquency, Girls and

Introduction

Juvenile delinquency is considered to be a serious problem in many communities. Yet, explanations of the causes of delinquency have focused on males and largely ignored the female population, perhaps because there has been a tendency to view crime and delinquency as a predominantly male driven issue. However, a growing body of research continues to develop in an effort to explain the factors that may lead female youth down the road of delinquent behavior. Despite this growing body of research, Smith and Paternoster (1987) suggest that variables derived from traditional criminological theories are equally applicable to female delinquency, and that male-female variations in delinquency reflect "differential exposure" to "gender-neutral" factors (Smith and Paternoster, 1987, 153). Supporting this view, Steffensmeier and Streifel (1993) reported that both male and female delinquency is influenced by the same variables, such as learning processes, desire for peer acceptance, search for excitement, lack of sufficient stakes in conformity, and availability of illicit opportunity. Still others have made compelling arguments against the use of theories that have been constructed based on male delinquency and have responded by developing gender specific theories to address female criminality (Cain, 1989).

Some researchers have refuted theories that have been developed as the result of male behavior, and suggest that these theories should not be utilized to explain the gap between male and female crime. Studies have shown that some concepts originally used in explaining male delinquency, such as family relationships, peer involvement, and attitudes toward school, are equally important variables in developing a conceptual view of female crime (Rankin, 1980; Canter, 1982). If in fact these factors are gender neutral, strong ties to the family unit, positive experiences in school, and positive attachment to peers may serve as buffers against delinquent behavior. Conversely, the absence of these buffers, or a weak attachment to them, may increase the likelihood that one will engage in criminal activity.

Female Criminality

Despite the fact that the majority of crimes in this country are committed by males, there are categories of crime where females are statistically more active than their male counterparts. According to the Federal Bureau of Investigation (FBI), female juveniles account for a significantly lower percentage of the nation's total juvenile crime but have historically accounted for the majority of arrests for running away and prostitution (Federal Bureau of Investigation, 2000). In 2000, the Federal Bureau of Investigation reported that 36,255 juvenile males and 52,061 female juveniles were runaways, and 336 juvenile males and 443 juvenile females were arrested for prostitution and commercialized vice. In addition to these offenses, a trend has begun to emerge that indicates female youth have increasingly been arrested for the crimes of larceny-theft, embezzlement, gambling, and vagrancy, although not as often as juvenile males (Federal Bureau of Investigation, 2000).

Although the majority of violent criminal activity continues to be dominated by the male population (approximately 90%), the Federal Bureau of Investigation reported in 2000 that there has been an increase in violent offenses committed by female youth. For example, between 1999 and 2000, the arrest rate for female offenders charged with the crimes of murder and nonnegligent manslaughter increased 9% (67–73%). In addition to murder and nonnegligent manslaughter, there was also a 2% increase in female arrests during the same time period for the crime of robbery (Federal Bureau of Investigation, 2000). However, changing societal reactions and increased official labeling of young female offenders have often been cited as the cause for the increases in these statistics (Berger, 1996). For example, the position of women in contemporary society, increased media attention with regard to female crime, concerns with equality and sexual discrimination, and increased police professionalism have all been identified as possible factors that may account for increased female crime and delinquency (Steffensmeier and Streifel, 1992).

Despite the increased attention that has been given to female delinquency and adult female crime, questions remain as to why females engage in this type of behavior. Do males and females respond in a similar fashion to the same environmental circumstances? Do familial controls account for the differences in juvenile male and female arrest rates? Can traditional theories (in whole or in part) be utilized to explain this population's behavior? The answers to all of these questions are not readily available, but some explanations appear to have greater utility than others do.

Delinquency Theories

Hirschi's Control Theory

Travis Hirschi, in his 1969 book *Causes of Delinquency*, linked delinquent behavior to the bond an individual has to society. According to Hirschi, when this bond is weak or broken, the person is more likely to break the law. The major component of Hirschi's theory is that a person's social bond to society has four primary elements: attachment to others, commitment to conventional activities, involvement in conventional activities, and a belief in widely shared values (Siegel and Senna, 2000).

In an attempt to test his theory, Hirschi administered a self-report survey to 4000 junior and senior high school students in Contra Costa County, California. He found that strong attachment to parents, commitment to family values, involvement in school, attachment to peers, and respect for the police and law enforcement all reduced the chances of delinquency (Siegel and Senna, 2000). With regard to female delinquency, the family unit has the potential to control access to others outside of the family unit, regulate the activities that may pose increased risk of victimization or delinquency, and teach and instill values that are shared by family members.

Nye's Social Control Theory

Nye's theory of social control specifies three different kinds of controls: indirect control, direct control, and internalized control. *Indirect control* is the attachment the adolescent has to parents and his or her affection for them. When adolescents are emotionally attached to others, they refrain from delinquency to avoid disappointing or hurting these people. *Direct controls* are punishments that are imposed or threatened for misbehavior, and compliance is rewarded by parents or caregivers. According to Nye's theory, parents can reduce the likelihood that their child will engage in delinquent behavior if they control who their child interacts with, how long they spend away from home, and the activities they choose to allow their child to engage in. The last of these controls is *internalized control*. The parent-child relationship and the child's acceptance of his or her parents form this method of control (Seydlitz, 1993; Akers, 2000).

Therefore, the degree to which the "family" protects or buffers the adolescent from delinquent behavior appears to be directly proportional to the amount of affection that is shared between the parent and child, the connection that the child feels with his or her parents, and the controls that are utilized by the family unit to influence positive behavior. With regard to female delinquency, this theory is significant in that, as young girls begin to mature, the family may no longer be able to satisfy their personal needs, and disappointing parents may slowly become secondary to one's own needs and wants. Like most teenagers, the need for separation from their parents becomes greater with age, and it is at this point that rebellion against family rules and expectations is possible. Furthermore, it is at this time in most young people's lives that testing the limits of parental and societal rules is likely to occur. Therefore, it is possible that one will become involved in deviant or delinquent activity because of increased freedom and individual opportunity.

Differential Association

Edwin Sutherland's theory of differential association can also be utilized to explain why girls may become delinquent. According to Sutherland, people learn criminal behavior from regular interaction with intimate groups. In addition, the process of learning criminal behavior by association with criminals involves the same methods that are involved in any other type of learning (Siegel, 2003).

As teenagers move through adolescence into young adulthood, the quest for independence becomes increasingly important. Freedom to be with friends, the need to experience new things, and the urge to go to new places sets the stage for constant interaction with other young people who seek the same experiences and freedom. However, the values and behaviors that are learned in the home, or the lack thereof, may be transmitted between youth by constant contact and interaction. This interaction between close friends has the potential to teach negative and even delinquent behavior to the group's members. Reiss and Roth (1993), however, do not believe this is the norm for most children and have suggested that positive family values are not forgotten or disregarded when youth begin to interact with other children outside of the home. In fact, they believe that children conform to parental expectations and tend to shy away from interacting with deviant and aggressive youth. Therefore, it is possible that only youth who share similar characteristics or views (both deviant and nondeviant) will be attracted to each other.

Strain Theory

According to sociologist Robert Agnew's general strain theory of crime and delinquency, individuals engage in delinquent acts because of the influences of stress (i.e. anger, frustration, depression, and fear) that emerge in the wake of negative and destructive relationships (Siegel, 2003). These stressors include failure to achieve positively valued goals, removal of positively valued stimuli, and the presentation of negative stimuli. According to Agnew, the greater the intensity, frequency, and duration of these stressors, the more likely the individual will become involved in delinquent activity (Akers, 1997).

One application of the general strain theory as it relates to female delinquency is in situations where abused youth are involved. The negative emotions that are described in Agnew's theory are typical emotional responses of youth who have been subjected to the negative stimuli that are presented in abusive homes. For youth (particularly young girls) who have been subjected to physical and sexual abuse at the hands of a perceived loved one, the stress induced may cause the victim to take steps that are statutorily criminal, but nonetheless necessary for survival. Chesney-Lind (1989) defined these types of behaviors as "survival strategies," and explained that victims of sexual and physical abuse may commit crimes such as running away, which in most states is classified as a status offense. What becomes increasingly problematic in situations like these, however, is that the victimization forces many young people into the streets, where they may begin to use drugs and alcohol to escape from their problems. In addition, young girls who choose, or who are forced, to run away are often left with little choice but to steal or engage in prostitution in order to survive.

In addition to physical and sexual abuse, it is possible that the pressure to conform to female gender roles in male dominated households may produce sufficient enough stress to cause deviant or delinquent behavior. This stress, which may increase as the female grows older and moves through adolescence into young adulthood, can result in rebellious behavior when the child is free from the watchful eyes of parents. For example, some young girls have been raised in homes that have been primarily dominated by males (father and male siblings). Often there is a double standard in place that prohibits certain acts by females and encourages or does not punish males for similar behavior. Some of these behaviors include staying out late, dating several people in a short period of time, recreational use of alcohol or tobacco products, skipping school, and fighting. Although several of these are normally discouraged for both males and females, young girls tend to have rules for behavior more strictly enforced, thereby restricting opportunity. This may be because the parent(s) fear that the young girl will be victimized or that her reputation as a young lady will be tarnished. The end result, however, may be increasing amounts of stress that can influence the choice to engage in deviant or delinquent behavior when unsupervised.

Maslow's Hierarchy of Needs

Many feel that one of Abraham Maslow's greatest contributions to the study of crime and delinquency was his hierarchical theory of human needs that was developed in the 1960s (Crews and Montgomery, 2000). Maslow believed that humans strive to reach the highest levels of their capabilities and he explained that through five levels. These five levels or needs, starting with the most basic needs, include *physiological needs*, which include the need for oxygen, food, and water, and *safety needs*, which address the need to feel secure and safe from harm. Additionally, *love and belonging needs* are addressed, which include both giving and receiving love and affection. *Esteem needs*, which are near the top of the hierarchy, explain the need people have to receive respect and have self-respect. At the top of Malsow's hierarchy is *self-actualization*, which is arguably a life-long process that is never fully obtainable. Nonetheless, this level focuses on the constant struggle to be the best that one can be (Crews and Montgomery, 2000, 95).

Maslow's perspective has been utilized along with other theories to help determine the root cause(s) of delinquency and criminal behavior. Additionally, this theory has raised many questions. Are juvenile delinquents criminal because one or more of their basic needs have not been met? If so, other issues such as societal values must be considered. For example, is it wrong for a child to break into a vacant home or building to seek shelter from the cold or to steal food when they are hungry? The law emphasizes that stealing and breaking and entering are unlawful, but who is really to blame for this child's desperate attempt to feed and shelter him- or herself (Crews and Montgomery, 2000)?

Maslow's hierarchy points out that a person cannot progress effectively toward *self-actualization* without successfully moving through or obtaining success in the previous stages. If this is so, the causes of criminal behavior may become increasingly clear. In keeping with Maslow's theory, society must consider all social ills that create significant amounts of stress (Crossen-Tower, 1999; Crews and Montgomery, 2000). The basic human needs that are outlined in this theory appear to be gender, class, and racially neutral. Failure of family or society to provide these basic needs, particularly to children, may force youth to take steps similar to those who have been victims of physical or sexual abuse (i.e., prostitution or theft) to ensure their survival.

Labeling Theory

The labeling theory is based on the concepts developed by Frank Tannenbaum in 1938, Lemert in 1951, Becker in 1963, Turk in 1969, and Quinney in 1970 (Fox, 1985, 131). This theory is defined as the assigning of a classification such as "delinquent" to an individual by groups in society who both define and react to deviant behavior (Vito and Holmes, 1994). According to this theory, the act itself is less important than society's reaction to the event. According to Tennenbaum (1938), labeling can be defined as "the process of making the criminal by tagging, defining, segregating, describing, emphasizing, making conscious and self-conscious.... The person becomes the thing he or she is described as being" (Vito and Holmes, 1994, 189).

Adding to this evolving theory, Lemert included *primary* and *secondary* deviance. *Primary deviance* involves norm violations or crimes that have little influence on the individual and are usually forgotten. *Secondary deviance*, however, occurs when the deviant or illegal act comes to the attention of significant others or social control agents who apply the negative label (Siegel, 2003, 235). It is when this label is internalized by the individual that the change takes place.

With regard to females and delinquency, an example of this labeling would be a young college student who steals a calculator from a local department store, is caught by a store employee, and is subsequently arrested. As a result, her dreams of being a teacher are no longer probable. People who know her and have heard about her shoplifting believe her to be untrustworthy. In response to this, she begins to steal and pawn things of increasing value on a more regular basis.

Female Liberation and the Influence of Other Variables on Delinquency

One theory that has received considerable attention is the female liberation hypothesis. This theory, also known as the "emancipation hypothesis," links the increasing equality of women to the rise in female crime rates. The increased opportunity for women in the contexts of education, family, politics, and occupations is believed to be significant in trying to explain the closing gap between male and female crime (Chesney-Lind, 1997). The basis of this theory explains that the increasing opportunity of women in the workforce and elsewhere in society has provided women with not only the same legitimate occupational, social, educational, and political opportunities, but also the same criminal opportunities. (Adler, 1975). However, other variables such as parental divorce and economic hardship may also influence female crime rates.

The increasing trend of divorce, and subsequently the increase in single-parent homes in this country, can arguably set the stage for future delinquency. For example, in many situations, custody of young girls in divorce cases are granted to mothers who undoubtedly are required to work one or more jobs to provide for themselves and their child or children. Depending on the availability of family members, friends, and neighbors, these mothers may have little choice but to leave the child alone for extended periods of time. This unsupervised time may lead to several problems, including alcohol and drug use, association with deviant peers, falling academic performance, and poor nutrition. Despite these possibilities, it has been argued that this logic is flawed because it suggests that mothers' workforce participation leads to daughter's delinquency (Chesney-Lind, 1989). Instead of directly causing delinquency, it is more likely that the conditions that arise in response to female occupational involvement (by opportunity or necessity) cause a decrease in the protective factors or buffers that typically prevent delinquent behavior, for example, having a parent or guardian to supervise behavior, assist with homework, regulate and supervise peer involvement, as well as other activities that usually take place after school.

Conclusion

There are several potential theories that can be utilized to help explain why female juveniles may engage in delinquent activity. Feminist criminologists, however, have made significant arguments against the use of male-based theories to address female crime. Despite the fact that there are few gender specific theories that are geared toward addressing this important issue, some existing theories that were created from research with delinquent males appear to have utility. For example, theories that address both risk and protective factors such as school, positive peer relationships, attachment to family and community institutions, and economic stability can be used because of their gender neutrality.

In addition, as female crime continues to be reported and the gap between male and female crime closes, criminologists will be increasingly encouraged to develop theories that are geared specifically toward the female offender population. Today it is unclear why female youth engage in delinquent behavior. What is clear, however, is that the arrest rate for females is increasing, and if this trend continues, research as well as gender specific theories will be needed in order to provide appropriate services to this unique population of offenders.

JEFFREY A. TIPTON

References and Further Reading

Adler, F. 1975. *Sisters in Crime: The Rise of the New Female Criminal*, New York, NY: McGraw-Hill.

Adler, P.A. and Adler, P., (2000). *Construction of Deviance*, Belmont, CA: Wadsworth Publishing Company.

Akers, R.L. 1997. *Criminological Theories: Introduction and Evaluation*, 2nd ed., Los Angeles, CA: Roxbury Publishing Company.

Akers, R.L. 2000. *Criminological Theories: Introduction and Evaluation* 3rd ed., Los Angeles, CA: Roxbury Publishing Company.

Berger, R.J. 1996. Explaining Female Delinquency: Does Gender Make a Difference? in Berger, R.J., Eds., *The Sociology of Juvenile Delinquency*, pp. 282–291, Chicago, IL: Nelson-Hall.

Cain, M. 1989. *Growing Up Good: Policing the Behavior of Girls in Europe*, Thousand Oaks, CA: Sage Publications.

Canter, R.J. 1982. Family Correlates of Male and Female Delinquency, *Criminology*, 20(2), 149–167.

Chesney-Lind, M. 1989. Girls' Crime and Woman's Place: Toward a Feminist Model of Female Delinquency, *Crime and Delinquency*, 35(1), 5–29.

Chesney-Lind, M. 1997. *The Female Offender: Girls, Women, and Crime*, Thousand Oaks, CA: Sage Publications.

Chesney-Lind, M. and Shelden, R.G. 1998. *Girls' Delinquency and Juvenile Justice*, 2nd ed., Belmont, CA: Wadsworth Publishing Company.

Crews, G.A., and Montgomery, R.H. Jr., 2000. *Chasing Shadows: Confronting Juvenile Violence in America*, Upper Saddle River, NJ: Prentice Hall.

Crossen-Tower, C. 1999. *Understanding Child Abuse and Neglect*, 4th ed. Needham Heights, MA, Allyn and Bacon.

Eder, D. 1995. *School Talk: Gender and Adolescent Culture*, New Brunswick, NJ: Rutgers University Press.

Federal Bureau of Investigation 2000. *Crime in the U.S.* Washington, DC: U.S. Government Printing Office.

Fox, V. 1985. *Introduction to Criminology*, 2nd ed., Englewood Cliffs, NJ, Prentice Hall.

Gelsthorpe, L. and Morris, A. 1990. *Feminist Perspectives in Criminology*, Philadelphia, PA: Open University Press.

Hagan, J. and McCarthy, B. 1997. *Mean Streets: Youth Crime and Homelessness*, Cambridge, MA: Cambridge University Press.

Heimer, K. and De Coster, S. 1999. The Gendering of Violent Delinquency, *Criminology*, 37(2), 277–313.

Mazerolle, P. and Maahs, J. 2000. General Strain and Delinquency: An Alternative Examination of Conditioning Influences, *Justice Quarterly*, 17(4), 753–777.

Rankin, J.H. 1980. School Factors and Delinquency: Interactions by Age and Sex, *Sociology and Social Research*, 64(3), 420–435.

Reiss, A.J. Jr. and Roth, J.A. 1993. *Understanding and Preventing Violence*, Washington, DC: National Academy Press.

Seydlitz, R. 1993. Compared to What? Delinquent Girls and Similarity or Difference Issue, in Culliver, C., Ed, *Female Criminality: The State of the Art* pp. 133-168, New York, NY: Garland Publishing, Inc.

Siegel, L.J. 2003. *Criminology*, 8th ed., Belmont, CA: Wadsworth Publishing Company.

Siegel, L. and Senna, J. 2000. *Juvenile Delinquency: Theory, Ractice, and Law*, 7th ed., Belmont, CA: Wadsworth Publishing Company.

Smith, D.A. and Paternoster, R. 1987. The Gender Gap in Theories of Deviance: Issues and Evidence. *Journal of Research in Crime and Delinquency*, 24(2), 140–172.

Steffensmeier, D.J., and Streifel, C. 1992. Time-Series Analysis of the Female Percentage of Arrests for Property Crimes, 1960–1975: A Test of Alternative Explanations, *Justice Quarterly*, 9(1), 77–103.

Steffensmeier, D.J. and Streifel, C. 1993. Trends in Female Crime 1960–1990. in Culliver, C., Ed., *Female Criminality: The State of the Art*, pp. 63–101. New York, NY: Garland Publishing Inc.

Vito, G.F. and Holmes, R.M. 1994. *Criminology: Theory, Research, and Policy*, Belmont, CA: Wadsworth Publishing Company.

See also **Gender and Criminal Behavior; Juvenile Delinquency: Theories of; Gangs, Girl**

Juvenile Delinquency, Theories of

Theories of delinquency are generalizations about why young people engage in behavior that would be defined as criminal if committed by an adult. Efforts to explain why young people engage in criminal behavior vary across as well as within academic disciplines. Theories of delinquency reflect different assumptions about human nature as well as cultural and social values. Historically, society made no distinction between juveniles who committed criminal offenses and adult offenders. It was not until the creation of the first juvenile court system in Cook County, Illinois in 1899 that the criminal behavior of the young would be defined as "delinquent."

The earliest explanations of crime were rooted in spiritualism. Those who failed to live according to the standards set forth by society were thought to be possessed with evil spirits. Distinctions were not made between sin and crime. In the 18th and 19th centuries, two schools of thought emerged to explain why individuals committed crimes. The classical school of criminology located the causes of crime within the legal system itself. The classical school refers primarily to the works of Cesare Beccaria (1738–1794) and Jeremy Bentham (1748–1832), both of whom were advocates for reforming the legal systems of Italy and England. Beccaria and Bentham were critical of the overly severe and arbitrary methods of punishment administered by the state against those who failed to live according to society's laws. Punishment should deter individuals from illegal behavior, but punishment would only deter if administered in a swift and certain fashion (Vold et al., 1998). Out of the classical school grew rational choice theory. According to this perspective, individuals choose to engage in crime when the benefits derived from crime outweigh the consequences (punishment). Individuals exercise free will in their choices, and, according to modern day rational choice theorists, punishment must also be severe as well as swift and certain before an individual will make the choice to refrain from illegal behavior. Proponents of rational choice theory today argue that delinquency is a product of a juvenile justice system that is too lenient with its offenders and fails to hold juveniles accountable for their crimes.

In the 19th century, the positivist school of criminology signified the first attempt to explain crime from a multifaceted and scientific approach. In contrast to classical school thinking, members of the positivist school believed criminal behavior to be a product of factors beyond an individual's control. Cesare Lombroso (1835–1909), the founder of the positivist school, argued that criminals inherit their negative behavioral traits from their parents and that criminal tendencies manifest themselves through physical characteristics (Lombroso referred to these individuals as *atavists*). Today, efforts to locate the causes of crime within an individual are primarily carried out by biologists in pursuit of a possible genetic, chemical or hormonal link to crime and by psychologists, who search for developmental and personality causes (Wolfgang, 1973). Recently, scientists have uncovered a genetic link between impulsivity and delinquency.

Beginning in the 20th century, a new theme in the study of criminal behavior began to emerge. In 1892, the first sociology department in the U.S. was established at the University of Chicago and sociology as an academic discipline was born. Chicago school sociologists were primarily interested in studying the impact of a growing industrial and urban society upon the lives of individuals. Sociologists interested in studying criminal behavior could locate the causes of crime within an individual's social environment. Sociological theories can either explain why some areas have higher rates of crime (macro-level theories) or why certain individuals (micro-level theories) engage in criminal behavior.

The Chicago School of Criminology grew out of the research being conducted by Chicago sociologists. The faculty and students were interested in studying the criminogenic quality of life in an urban environment. Criminologists also turned their attention to the illegal behaviors of juveniles in the hope that if the causes of delinquency could be identified, then through early intervention, delinquents would not grow up to become adult criminals (Bulmer, 1984). Two Chicago School members—Clifford R. Shaw and Henry D. McKay (1943)—were interested in mapping out the city according to officially recorded rates of delinquent behavior. They discovered that rates of delinquency from 1900 to 1933 varied geographically according to the structural characteristics of the neighborhoods in which the delinquents lived. Neighborhoods characterized by high rates of poverty, population density, urban decay, residential mobility, and heterogeneous populations tend to become socially disorganized and have high rates of delinquency. Shaw and McKay were impressed by the fact that, regardless of who lived in these types of neighborhoods, delinquency was always high. They speculated that there was something about the neighborhood structure itself that was pushing young people into a life of delinquency.

According to Shaw and McKay's theory, socially disorganized neighborhoods are often lacking in effective informal social control institutions. Families, churches, schools, and neighborhood organizations lose their ability to impart upon the youth of the community conventional values and behaviors. Community members residing in socially disorganized neighborhoods become unable or unwilling to solve commonly experienced problems and delinquency flourishes. The neighborhood itself becomes the cause of delinquency. In an effort to combat the consequences of neighborhood social disorganization, Shaw organized the Chicago Area Project (CAP) in the 1930s. The goals of CAP included providing resources to residents of economically disadvantaged neighborhoods in an effort to develop community groups that would provide constructive youth activities and foster a cooperative relationship between the community, schools, and police. Social disorganization theory remains today one of the most influential theories of delinquency because of the recognition that the structural characteristics of a community can influence behavior. Most criminologists today, however, assert that community factors alone are insufficient to explain the deterioration of informal social control networks (Akers, 2000).

Social disorganization theory fits within the larger theoretical framework of "social structure theories." Social structure theories assert that delinquent behavior is primarily a product of socioeconomic conditions and cultural values. Two other theoretical traditions also fall into this category: strain theory and subcultural theory.

About the same time Shaw and McKay proposed their social disorganization theory, Robert K. Merton (1938) put forth a version of strain theory called anomie theory. Merton wanted to provide a coherent, systematic approach to the study of sociocultural sources of crime and delinquency. The term "anomie" was borrowed from the French sociologist Emile Durkheim (1897). *Anomie* refers to a collective state of "normlessness" that occurs whenever society is unable to exert control over the wants or desires of its members. Individuals share several common perceptions, including a sense of futility, a sense that life goals are receding, and the feeling that one cannot count on others for support (Cullen, 1984).

All social structures contain cultural goals that define success as well as the socially acceptable means of achieving these goals. Merton applied the concept of anomie to the U.S. because of its competitive economic system that can be alienating for some members. The U.S. places a great deal of importance on material wealth and all members of society are expected to achieve this goal. The problem is that not everyone has the education or economic resources needed to achieve success as defined by material wealth. The opportunity structure is stratified along socioeconomic lines, where individuals in the lower classes may be without the necessary resources to acquire wealth and material possessions. This disjuncture between society's goals and means will produce feelings of frustration or strain for some members.

Merton described five possible ways that an individual will adapt to feelings of strain. The *conformist* accepts society's goals and the acceptable means of achieving that goal. This individual will work hard, obey the law, and obtain an education. Individuals who *innovate* also accept the goals put forth by society, but reject the conventional means of achieving the goals and instead substitute their own means. Innovation is a reason why a young person may resort to delinquency as a way of acquiring something that would otherwise be unobtainable. Individuals who adopt the conventional behaviors of working hard and pursuing an education but have given up trying to achieve material success fall into the *ritualism* mode. Other individuals will *retreat* from both society's goals and means by becoming outcasts. Finally, some individuals will *rebel* against society by rejecting conventional goals and means and substituting their own definition of success and way(s) of achieving it (Jacoby, 1993).

Merton's strain theory offers a useful approach to understanding the concentration of delinquency in economically disadvantaged communities where educational and employment opportunities may be scarce. The government funded the Job Core program and student loan programs try to expand opportunities for disadvantaged youth.

More recently, Robert Agnew (1985 and 1992) extended Merton's theory to include two additional sources of strain that can be related to delinquency. According to Agnew's general strain theory, strain can result from the removal of positively valued stimuli; delinquent behavior becomes a way to retrieve what was lost or to cope with the loss. Strain can also result from being presented with negatively valued stimuli, such as physical or emotional abuse. Young people may react to the abuse by becoming violent with others (Agnew, 2000). Agnew's theory builds upon the ideas of Merton, rendering the strain theory a viable explanation for delinquency across all socioeconomic classes.

The third group of social structure theories is known as "cultural deviance" theory. According to this perspective, delinquent behavior may contradict the norms and values of conventional society, however, it conforms to the norms and values of particular groups that run counter to those of the larger society. Shaw and McKay recognized that much of the delinquency found in lower class communities was committed by groups of young people who shared the belief that delinquency was acceptable behavior. Building on this perspective, several criminologists during the 1950s and 1960s began exploring the concept of a delinquent subculture.

Albert K. Cohen (1955) observed that delinquent subcultures emerge in lower class neighborhoods as a response to middle class values that disadvantaged youth are unable to meet. In 1960, Richard A. Cloward and Lloyd E. Ohlin added a further contribution to subcultural theory with their theory of differential opportunity. Delinquency is primarily a product of lower class youth who are faced with the "strain of status discontentment." Lower class youth will begin to explore nonconformist alternatives, but will find that, just as the legitimate opportunity structure is stratified, so is the *illegitimate* opportunity structure. Not all youth will be able to join a subculture where members are "successful" delinquents who make money from their criminal activities. Youth residing in disorganized neighborhoods may seek support from a violent subculture or retreat into drug use (Jacoby, 2000).

Walter Miller's (1958) lower class culture theory asserts that lower class youth subscribe to a group of focal concerns that encourage delinquent behavior. Miller's lower class focal concerns include trouble, toughness, smartness, excitement, fate, and autonomy (Empey et al., 1999). It is the devotion to these delinquent values that produces delinquency.

Subculture theories are useful for explaining why young people join criminal gangs. Membership in a gang affords individuals who may feel rejected by conventional society the opportunity to achieve status and acceptance. Delinquency prevention programs like the Boston Mid-City Project attempt to provide prosocial role models and mentors to work with juvenile gang members in the hopes of reducing violence and delinquency.

Social structure theories are useful for explaining why delinquency is highly concentrated within communities characterized by economic disadvantage. Early explanations of delinquency relied primarily upon official sources that tend to underestimate the amount of delinquency committed by middle and upper class youth. When criminologists started collecting self-report data from juveniles in the 1940s it was recognized that middle and upper class youth were involved in delinquency at much higher levels than the official measures were indicating. Possible reasons include an overconcentration of police resources in lower class communities as well as police officers in middle and upper class communities using their discretion to informally handle juvenile offenders.

Given that delinquency is not solely a phenomenon of lower class culture and that a majority of the youth living in economically disadvantaged communities do not become delinquents, many criminologists reject the notion that the causes of delinquency are found within the structural characteristics of a young person's environment.

"Social process theories" attribute delinquency to the inadequate or improper socialization of young people. Certain youth, regardless of social class, are not socialized to become law-abiding members of society. Two major variations of social process theories are social learning theory and social control theory.

According to social learning theory, delinquent behavior, like all behavior, is learned through a process of interaction with others. In 1939, Edwin H. Sutherland, one of the preeminent American criminologists of the 20th century, put forth his differential association theory. The theory was revised several times with the help of Sutherland's long-time associate, Donald R. Cressey, and appeared in its final form in 1947. Differential association theory consists of the following postulates. Delinquent behavior is learned; the learning occurs by interacting with others through a process of communication; and the learning occurs within primary social groups. Delinquents learn the techniques for committing crimes, how to rationalize their behavior, and the motivations and drives involved in delinquency. The specific direction of motives and drives is learned from definitions that are either favorable or unfavorable to delinquency, and a young person becomes delinquent because of exposure to an excess of definitions favorable to delinquent behavior (the principle of differential association). Differential associations may vary in frequency, intensity, duration, and priority. The learning process itself involves the same mechanisms by which all behavior is learned. Finally, criminal behavior may be an expression of general needs and values, however, it cannot be explained by those needs and values because noncriminal behavior is also an expression of general needs and values (Sutherland et al., 1992). Differential association theory is considered to be one of the most useful explanations of delinquency today, primarily because of the recognition that peer associations play an important role in the behavior of young people. Juveniles who have close friends who are involved in delinquency are also likely to become delinquent themselves.

Ronald L. Akers (1979) reformulated the concept of differential association to provide an explanation of exactly how individuals acquire behavior with his theory of differential reinforcement. Borrowing ideas from operant behavioral theory and cognitive learning theory, Akers argues that delinquency is a product of behavior that has been reinforced. Reinforcement can be either positive or negative. Behavior becomes reinforced through rewards or a lack of punishment. Like Sutherland, Akers believes that a juvenile's peer group constitutes a primary source of reinforcement and is responsible for shaping both delinquent and nondelinquent behavior (Akers 2000).

Another variation of social learning theory is the neutralization approach. In the 1950s, Gresham M. Sykes and David Matza argued that there are five "techniques of neutralization" that delinquents use to protect themselves from self-blame. The techniques of neutralization allow free youth to commit delinquency and weaken the ability of social control agents to effectively control behavior. These techniques include the denial of responsibility (the delinquent attributes his or her conduct to forces beyond his or her control, for example, a bad neighborhood or delinquent peer influences), denial of injury (the delinquent fails to see the harm done by his or her conduct because the harm is indirect, for example, vandalism), denial of victim (the delinquent views his or her conduct as a form of punishment or rightful retaliation), condemnation of condemners (the delinquent focuses attention away from his or her conduct to the motives of authorities by arguing that "everyone is picking on me"), and the appeal to higher loyalties (the delinquent makes the argument that his or her conduct was not a form of self-interest but was for the benefit of an individual's peer group or for some higher cause) (Lilly et al. 1994).

A few years later Matza (1964) incorporated these techniques of neutralization into his drift theory of delinquency. Matza argued that delinquency is a matter of drift in which juveniles are no more committed to delinquency than they are to conformity. Rather, they are "transiently, intermittently, and casually" involved in delinquent conduct. Drift lies midway between freedom and control. The techniques of neutralization only make delinquency possible. There are two triggering factors that explain the actual occurrence of delinquency: preparation and desperation. Preparation is the process in which the juvenile realizes that a particular delinquent act is possible, that he or she is capable of the act, and that he or she can deal with any fear of apprehension. Desperation refers to a deep feeling of fatalism in which the juvenile attempts to assert his or her own individuality by committing a crime (Lilly et al., 1994).

The second group of social process theories is known as the social control theory. Social controls are the perceived benefits and punishments that are likely to result when an individual either conforms to, or deviates from, a system of consensually agreed upon definitions of what constitutes conformist and deviant behavior. There are two types of social control: formal and informal. Formal social control refers to those actions taken by the criminal justice system (i.e., arrest, prosecution, and sanctioning). Informal social control refers to social and social-psychological processes that inhibit delinquent behavior. According to control theorists, all controls are social in the sense that they develop and are maintained through a process of social interaction (Kornhauser, 1978). Furthermore, it is through a process of social interaction with an individual's primary social groups that social control originates and becomes strengthened.

The idea that crime is caused by a breakdown in informal social control represents a dominant theme in the field of criminology. Not only do several variations of control theory exist, but elements of control theory are found in other sociological theories as well. There are several dimensions of informal social control. The concept of informal social control was first mentioned by Durkheim (1897) in his theory of anomie. Durkheim defined anomie as relative normlessness in society that occurs from the destruction of the fundamental bonds that unite individuals in a collective social order. Control theory per se grew out of the work of Shaw and McKay (1943) from the Chicago School. According to their theory of social disorganization, one of the consequences of social disorganization is a breakdown of informal social control that contributes to high rates of delinquency.

Control theories offer a different approach to delinquency causation compared to traditional theories (strain and differential association). Control theorists attempt to explain conformity to the rules and norms of society, not delinquency. Delinquent behavior is a given fact, whereas conformity must be explained. The first sociologist after Shaw and McKay to pick up on the idea of crime resulting from a breakdown in control was Albert J. Reiss in 1951. Reiss argued there are two types of control: personal and social. Personal or internal control refers to the ability of an individual to resist meeting his or her needs in ways that conflict with society's norms and values. Social or external control refers to the ability of social institutions and groups to make rules and norms binding on the individual members. Delinquency is a product of a breakdown of either type of control or both.

In the early 1960s, Walter C. Reckless proposed his version of control theory known as the containment theory. Reckless (1961) observed that not everyone who is exposed to a disease actually catches that disease. The same is true for delinquency. Not all individuals exposed to delinquent influences become delinquent. Immunity is a matter of control, of being "contained" or "restrained" from the temptation of crime. These control or containment factors are of two orders: outer containment and inner containment.

Outer containment refers to social pressures to conform and includes training in roles, affiliation with a community, and a sense of tradition. Outer containment serves as a defense against delinquency where community standards condemn antisocial values and misconduct. Reckless further stressed the importance of meaningful activities, reasonable limits and support, reinforcement, and acceptance from personal relationships.

Inner containment refers to self-control over an individual's behavior. The presence of self or internal control is indicated by four factors: a perception of one's self as a law-abiding citizen; reasonable goals; an ability to handle frustration constructively; and the acceptance and internalization of conventional norms and values (Lilly et al., 1994).

In 1969, the most influential variation of the control theory was put forth by Travis Hirschi in his *Causes of Delinquency*. Hirschi's social bond theory asserts that conformity can be explained by an individual's bond to society. This bond is comprised of four related elements. A weakness of any one element is sufficient to explain delinquency. However, if an individual is weak on one bond, they will tend to be weak on all bonds. The elements are attachment, commitment, involvement, and belief. *Attachment* refers to the extent that an individual is emotionally invested in his or her family and friends and cares about their opinions. *Commitment* refers to the extent of an individual's investment in conventional activities or stakes in conformity. *Involvement* refers to the amount of time and resources an individual invests in conventional activities and with his or her family and friends. Finally, *belief* refers to the extent to which a youth subscribes to and adopts the rules and norms of society. Hirschi stressed family relationships in his theory by emphasizing the importance of spending time with children, intimate communication, and affection. He also believed that strong bonds prevent delinquency, regardless of social class, race, or delinquent peer influences.

The dimensions of informal social control have been called by different names by different criminologists, although these terms all have in common an emphasis on two specific elements: direct and indirect social control (Kornhauser, 1978). A breakdown in either type is sufficient to explain delinquent or criminal behavior. Direct control encompasses attempts

made by such social institutions as the family, school, and work to restrain an individual's behavior through supervision. Supervision is an important component of social control and is exercised by these social groups in two ways. Parents may impose a curfew upon a child to restrict that child's behavior, monitor their child's behavior, and finally punish their child for failing to abide by the curfew. The degree of supervision exercised by parents over their children has a direct influence on a child, diminishing the likelihood of risk-taking and subsequent delinquency.

Supervision is also exercised in the form of restricting an individual's opportunity to engage in delinquency. If a child is involved in conventional activities, their opportunity to engage in unconventional behavior becomes limited. The same social institutions responsible for exercising direct control over the behavior of its members are also responsible for providing indirect social control. Indirect social control involves an internalization of conventional values and norms, emerging through the process of socialization. The strength of social relationships within families and schools explains delinquency. Further, youths who have strong social bonds possess the needed social and psychological resources (such as conformist self-identity and emotional support) to resist the temptation of illegal behavior. Indirect social controls need not be overt and intentional—youths can become attached to those whom they admire, even when there is limited contact with this role model (Elliott et al., 1985). Efforts to assist parents in their child-rearing practices and programs that encourage parents to involve their children in constructive activities are intended to strengthen a juvenile's social bond.

Social reaction theories differ from social process and social structure theories in the sense that they focus attention on the role society plays in producing delinquent behavior. Social reaction theories became popular in the 1960s when many Americans started to question the legitimacy of various governmental institutions, including the juvenile justice system. There are two major social reaction perspectives—labeling theory and conflict theory.

The labeling perspective explains delinquent behavior as the result of stigmas that emerge through social interactions. Behavior does not become delinquent until it is defined as such. These definitions are not inherent in the behaviors themselves, but are a product of the laws created by those with political power. Labeling theorists concern themselves with two basic issues: how the delinquent label is applied and the consequences resulting from the label. Labeling theorists are generally not concerned with explaining why youths originally commit delinquent acts, but why they continue their delinquent conduct. Secondary delinquency refers to the continued occurrence of illegal behavior after an individual comes into contact with a social control system that applies the delinquent definition. Factors that influence the process of being labeled delinquent include the visibility of the behavior, an individual's status (e.g., race or social class), the degree to which others are tolerant of a particular behavior, and the ability of those who apply the label to reinterpret past behavior based on the applied label (Schur, 1971).

The second issue addressed by labeling theorists is the consequences of being labeled a delinquent. Negative labels produce stigmas that adversely affect an individual's social status. Once labeled a delinquent, the individual becomes a social outcast who may be denied access to higher education and good jobs. Being labeled a delinquent influences future social interactions. Interpersonal relations and structural opportunities are blocked, increasing the likelihood that the delinquency will continue. A second consequence of being labeled a delinquent is the individual acknowledgment of the label as a personal identity. As the juvenile justice system, parents teachers, and friends react to the labeled delinquent, his or her self-concept may suffer. C. H. Cooley (1902) referred to this process as the "looking glass self" in which individuals look to others for an interpretation and evaluation of their own behavior. Secondary delinquency is an outcome of this changed self-concept.

Research on labeling theory can be categorized in two ways. The first examines the characteristics of those individuals selected for labeling and the second attempts to determine the consequences of being labeled. Most labeling theorists will agree that it is the poor and powerless who are selected for processing by the juvenile justice system and that labels are not equally divided among class and racial groups. Labeling theory has come under attack because of its failure to explain primary delinquency and differences in crime rates across jurisdictions (Paternoster and Iovanni, 1989). Although some delinquent acts may be the product of a negative label, certain other illegal acts, such as homicide and rape, are universally sanctioned, indicating that these offenses are inherently wrong. Despite these criticisms, labeling theory contributes to an understanding of delinquency if its application is limited to explaining minor types of delinquency and status offenses (offenses that are only illegal because of the person's age).

From a policy perspective, the juvenile court system in the U.S. was founded on the premise that youthful offenders should be protected from stigmatizing labels that would follow them through their lives. Juvenile offenders who are under the jurisdiction of the juvenile court system are protected with confidentiality in the media and their criminal records are sealed once they become an adult. Increasing the due process rights afforded to juveniles beginning in the 1960s was seen as a way to protect young people from being unjustly labeled as delinquent. The courts also try to ensure that juveniles who are convicted of status offenses are not housed in facilities designed for juvenile delinquents. Many juveniles are protected from the stigmatization associated with a criminal record through some type of diversionary program where charges are dismissed against the juvenile for participating in a treatment program or staying out of trouble.

Conflict (also called radical) theories focus attention upon the struggles between individuals and groups in terms of power differentials. Conflict theories can be traced back to the political economy of Karl Marx (1818–1883). Marxian philosophy grew out of a period of history when capitalism was at its peak in Western Europe. The oppressive conditions that accompanied industrialization created a large population whose existence was completely determined by their capitalist employers. Marx believed that in capitalism there are two dominant social classes: those who own the means of production (capitalists) and those who work for these owners (the proletariat). Conflict naturally exists between these two classes, and it is this conflict that determines the structure of social relations and institutions. As capitalism becomes successful, the working class expands while the ruling class's size diminishes. The values maintained by capitalism (competition, individualism, and expansion) exploit the working class, leaving them with feelings of alienation and worthlessness. When technology advances, fewer individuals are needed to perform labor. A surplus of labor creates a capital-intensive society in which the working class will either blame themselves for their failures or become "class conscious" and challenge the existing social order (Spitzer, 1975).

Modern conflict criminology developed out of the ideas developed by Marx. This approach sees the criminal justice system as a political mechanism designed to protect the power and status of the ruling class. Those in power decide which behaviors are proscribed and enforced. The behaviors frequently designated as delinquent show the willingness among "problem populations" to question and potentially confront the social institutions maintained by the ruling class (Spitzer, 1975). The extent to which these problem populations are considered criminal is influenced by their relationship with the control structure. In his *The Child Savers*, Anthony Platt (1969) describes the creation of the juvenile justice system around the turn of the 20th century as a way for wealthy reformers (the child savers) to control the unconventional behavior of young people. Greenberg

(1977) argues that in a capitalistic society, youth are placed in a vulnerable position. Juveniles are faced with peer pressures to possess material goods, but for the most part they are denied access to the labor market and have to rely upon their parents for economic support. If parents are financially unable or unwilling to support these consumptive styles, some youths will turn to delinquency (Empey et al., 1999).

Conflict theory provides useful insight into the differential application of the law for certain classes of individuals, like juveniles, who are relatively powerless. Many of the assumptions underlying conflict theory are difficult to empirically evaluate. Conflict theories offer little in terms of realistic programs to reduce delinquency because of the notion that delinquency is a product of a capitalistic economic system.

In an effort to integrate ideas from social learning, social control, structural, and social reaction theories, criminologists have recently proposed a variety of integrated or multifactor theories. One such integrated approach is self-control theory proposed in Michael Gottfredson and Travis Hirschi's *General Theory of Crime* (1990). These authors integrate concepts from control theory and rational choice theory with ideas drawn from the psychological literature of crime. They argue that delinquency is a product of low self-control, causing some youths to be susceptible to the enticements of illegal behavior. Individuals who are deficient in self-control often seek immediate gratification of their wants and desires, lack long-term commitments, and often take unnecessary risks. Low self-control primarily results from poor child-rearing practices (especially insufficient supervision and discipline) within the family.

A second integrated theory proposed by Delbert S. Elliott and his colleagues David Huizinga and Suzanne S. Ageton (1985) includes ideas drawn from strain, differential association, and control theory. According to this perspective, young people who are improperly socialized are likely to experience feelings of strain. These frustrated individuals are not likely to develop strong social bonds. Feelings of strain can lead to the rejection of conventional standards of conduct, pushing youths toward delinquent subcultures where they will be exposed to an excess of definitions favorable to delinquency (Elliott et al., 1985).

Most of the theories discussed above were developed using samples of male delinquents and leave two important unanswered questions. First, can the same theories explain both male and female delinquency and, second, why are delinquency rates lower for females? Feminist theory attempts to shed light on these issues. According to Freda Adler (1975), as society becomes more egalitarian, women will have greater freedom and opportunities in the schools, work place,

and politics. Opportunities for crime will also increase. Recently, society has experienced larger increases in female criminality compared to males; however, the rates for females are still lower than for their male counterparts. John L. Hagan's (1989) power-control theory asserts that the convergence in rates between male and female rates of delinquency can be attributed to an egalitarian socialization process within the home. Middle class girls are now given more freedom by their parents and are just as likely as some males to develop a preference for taking risks that might include engaging in illegal behaviors (Akers, 2000).

Theories of delinquency offer explanations as to why young people engage in illegal behavior. Theories of delinquency are dynamic and evolve through a process of empirical research. No single theory exists to explain all types of delinquency, but each of the theories mentioned above plays an important role in helping to understand why some juveniles become delinquent and what can be done to remedy the problem.

AMY THISTLETHWAITE

References and Further Reading

Agnew, R. 2000. *Juvenile Delinquency: Causes and Control*, Roxbury, Los Angeles, CA.

Akers, R.L., 2000. *Criminological Theories: Introduction, Evaluation, and Application*, Roxbury, Los Angeles, CA.

Beirne, P. and James Messerschmidt, W. 2000. *Criminology*, Westview Press, Boulder, CO.

Bulmer, M. 1984. *The Chicago School of Sociology*, University of Chicago Press, Chicago, IL.

Cullen, F.T. 1984. *Rethinking Crime and Deviance Theory: The Emergence of a Structuring Tradition*, Rowman and Allenheld, Totowa, NJ.

Elliott, D.S., Huizinga, D., and Ageton, S.S., 1985. *Explaining Delinquency and Drug Use*, Sage, Newbury Park, CA. Empey, L.T., Stafford, M.C., and Hay, C.H., *American Delinquency: Its Meaning and Construction*, 4th ed., Wadsworth Publishing, Belmont, CA.

Gottfredson, M.R. and Hirschi, T., 1990. *A General Theory of Crime*, Stanford University Press, Palo Alto, CA.

Jacoby, J.E., Ed., 1994. *Classics of Criminology, Second Edition*, Waveland Press, Prospect Heights, IL.

Kornhauser, R.R., 1978. *Social Sources of Delinquency: An Appraisal of Analytical Models*, University of Chicago Press, Chicago, IL.

Lilly, J.R., Cullen, F.T., and Ball, R.A. 1984. *Criminological Theory: Context and Consequences*, Sage, Newbury Park, CA.

Maguire, M., Morgan, R., and Reiner, R., Eds. 1998. *The Oxford Handbook of Criminology*, 2nd ed., Oxford University Press, New York.

Paternoster, R. and Bachman, R., Eds. 2000. *Explaining Criminals and Crime: Essays in Contemporary Criminological Theory*, Roxbury, Los Angeles, CA.

Paternoster, R. and Iovanni, L.A. 1989. The Labeling Perspective and Delinquency: An Elaboration of the Theory and An Assessment of the Evidence, *Justice Quarterly*, 6, 379–394.

Rojek, D.G. and Jensen, G.F., Eds. 1996. *Exploring Delinquency: Causes and Control (An Anthology)*, Roxbury, Los Angeles, CA.

Schur, E.M. 1971. *Labeling Deviant Behavior*, Harper and Row, New York.

Spitzer, S., 1975. Toward a Marxian Theory of Deviance, *Social Problems*, 22, 638–651.

Sutherland, E.H., Cressey, D.R., and David Luckenbill, F. 1992. *Principles of Criminology*, 11th ed., General Hall, New York.

Vold, G.B., Bernard, T.J., and Snipes, J.B., 1998. *Theoretical Criminology*, 4th ed., Oxford University Press, New York.

Williams, F.P. and McShane, M.D. 1998. *Criminology Theory: Selected Classic Readings*, 2nd ed., Anderson, Cincinnati, OH.

Wolfgang, M.E., Cesare Lombroso (1835–1909), in Hermann Mannheim (editor), 1972. *Pioneers in Criminology*, 2nd ed. (Enlarged), pp. 232–291, Patterson Smith, Montclair, NJ.

See also **Juvenile Delinquency and Youth Crime Throughout History; Juvenile Delinquency, Girls and; Juvenile Delinquency: Definitions and the Law; Juvenile Delinquency: Extent, Correlates, and Trends; Schools and Delinquent Behavior**

Juvenile Delinquency: Definitions and the Law

Historically few societies made little distinction of criminal responsibility between an adult and a child. Early Greek and Rome civilizations made no distinction between crimes committed by adults or children, although Roman law eventually made some distinctions beginning in the 5th century. Adults who committed theft, for instance, could be put to death; in contrast, children under the age of puberty who committed theft were flogged or beaten. Both civilizations perceived children as being legally culpable but provided for different punishments based on the age of the child.

Later in the Middle Ages Europe recognized that children under a certain age did not understand the concept of right and wrong, referred to as the *age of reason*. As a result most societies in Europe did not hold children under the age of 7 legally responsible. Similarly, in England, judicial decisions (referred to as common law) also reflected the philosophy that there was a relationship between criminal culpability and age.

English common law also served as the foundation for the legal thought and practice in colonial America. Thus, only children between the ages of 7 and 14 in Europe, England, and in colonial America were viewed as legally responsible for their crimes and were dealt with less harshly depending on the severity of the crime and the judge. However, in reality many children who committed crimes were subjected to "adult" punishments, such as being sentenced to jails or prisons, floggings, or binding them into apprenticeships. Other children who were considered *wayward* (begging, or dependent children without a legal guardian) were placed in over-crowded and filthy orphanages, poor-houses, or asylums. Thus, the criminal adult code often applied to both adults and children and rarely viewed children differently unless they were younger than 7 years old. It wasn't until the early 1800s that societies, particularly in England and in the U.S., began to recognize that children should be treated as a separate entity.

In the U.S. in the early 19th century there was a rapid influx of immigrants and rural families gravitating to the urban areas of America to find employment and a better way of life. However, the sudden increase in population also created havoc on the urban social and economic systems that were unprepared to handle such a huge increase of population. As a result of too many people and too few jobs, poor wages ensued and it was necessary for both parents to work in factories, which often meant leaving their children to fend for themselves. These children were often found roaming the streets committing petty crimes of theft, vandalism, and vagrancy.

Members of the middle and upper class noted this increase in wayward children and became increasingly concerned about the societal implications of these changes. These individuals (known as the *child savers*) believed that it was the children's poor living conditions and lack of parental moral guidance that caused them to commit crimes. The *child saving movement* set out to remove children from their poor environments and place them in healthier situations with adult supervision and moral guidance. This movement forwarded the view that children who were no longer associated with poverty, were well supervised, and were versed on proper morals would not commit more crimes.

The child savers were largely responsible for convincing state legislatures to separate delinquent and wayward children from adult criminals. In addition the child savers argued that these children's parents were not appropriate moral role models and therefore the state should legally intervene by becoming the children's parents. This philosophy was based on English common law's *parens patriae* doctrine. Thus, the children were removed from their parents' custody and legally committed to institutions designed to instill morals and values. The most famous was the House of Refuge in New York, built in 1825. England and Scotland also developed child-saving reformatories during the same period. The House of Refuge and other institutions that followed were marked by strict discipline and harsh labor conditions, and as a result many children ran away.

By the late 1800s the child savers become more convinced that children needed to be decriminalized (from the adult system) and dealt with in a separate system. The child savers' efforts were rewarded when the Illinois Juvenile Court Act was passed in 1899. This act established the first juvenile court in Chicago. During the next two decades most other states created separate juvenile court systems.

The juvenile justice system continued to rely on the *parens patriae* doctrine. This meant that when states determined that it was in the *best interest of the child*, it could legally become the guardian of children in need. The court had jurisdiction of three types of children: (1) *delinquent offenders,* those children who committed crimes; (2) *status offenders*, those children who committed crimes that would not be crimes if committed by adults, such as truancy, curfew, alcohol consumption, running away, or incorrigibility; and (3) *neglected, abused, and dependent*, those children whose parents failed to provide for their basic needs or used corporal punishment to an extreme. The backbone of the juvenile justice system was the philosophy embraced by the rehabilitation model. Rather than focusing on punishment and the crime (as the adult system mandated) the juvenile justice system stressed individualized justice and treatment for these children.

Initially the juvenile justice system was an informal process that tried children without providing them due process rights (right to counsel, trial by jury, and appeal.) It was not until the 1960s that this lack of legal rights and informal court proceedings was scrutinized and legally challenged. A series of Supreme Court decisions would ultimately change the juvenile justice system forever. The first case to address juveniles' due process rights was *Kent v. U.S.* (1966). Morris Kent, a 16-year-old juvenile who admitted to committing burglary, robbery, and rape was held in a juvenile *detention facility* (similar to an adult jail) for approximately one week. The judge then transferred jurisdiction (allowable under state statute) of Kent's case to the adult court without a hearing or notice to Kent's attorney. Kent was later found guilty in adult court and sentenced to 30–90 years in prison. Had Kent's case remained in juvenile court he would have only been institutionalized for a maximum of five years (i.e., until he turned 21). In reviewing Kent's case the U.S. Supreme Court found that although the practice of waiver of juvenile jurisdiction in favor of adult jurisdiction was allowed under the statute, the lower court had acted arbitrarily by failing to provide Kent a hearing, access of probation reports by Kent's attorney, and a written statement from juvenile court explaining the rationale of the waiver. Kent's case was remanded to the lower court for a new waiver hearing.

A year later the U.S. Supreme Court rendered its most significant case relating to juvenile law, a case that was responsible for reforming the *adjudication process* (the juvenile court's procedures in determining whether the juvenile committed the offense). *In re Gault* (1967) involved 15-year-old Gerald Gault, who was on probation for stealing a wallet. Gault, was arrested again for making lewd telephone calls. Gault was taken to a detention home and held there for several days. Gault's parents were not informed of their son's location. Gault's mother later arrived at the detention home and was informed that there would be a hearing the next day. During the *adjudicatory hearing* (fact finding hearing) a petition was filed but did not provide specific facts of the alleged delinquent act. Neither the complainant (the alleged victim) nor Gault's attorney were present; no one was sworn in; and no transcript was made of the proceedings since such an informal hearing was not "on the record." Gault *agreed to* (the equivalent of pleading guilty in adult court) the petition.

Soon after a *dispositional hearing* (the equivalent of a sentencing hearing in adult court) was held. Once again Gault was not legally represented, his parents did not receive the copy of the probation dispositional report or recommendation, and no transcript of the hearing was available. Gault was committed to the state industrial school for six years; however, had he been an adult he would have only been fined or sentenced to a maximum of two months in jail.

Gault's case was appealed to the U.S. Supreme Court and created a great deal of outrage among the majority of Supreme Court justices as well as by society. Justice Abe Fortas, who wrote the majority opinion, stated that "under our Constitution, the condition of being a boy does not justify a kangaroo court." Thus, the court ruled adjudication hearings must afford juveniles four specific due process rights: (1) timely notice of a hearing (usually 24 to 72 hours in most states); (2) notification' of the right to counsel and the right to counsel if the juvenile's family cannot afford an attorney; (3) protection against self-incrimination; and (4) the right to confront sworn testimony and witnesses.

Subsequent U.S. Supreme Court decisions further impacted the juvenile justice system. In *In re Winship* (1970) the court held that the standard of proof in juvenile proceedings must be "beyond a reasonable doubt" (generally considered requiring at least 90% certainty that the youth committed the delinquent act) rather than the less stringent standard used in civil cases of "preponderance of evidence" (generally considered requiring over 50% certainty that the youth committed the delinquent act).

How close the juvenile system had to follow the adult system became a very significant issue, with some advocates claiming that juveniles should be afforded the very same protections provided to adults in adult courts. The Supreme Court rejected this proposition the year following *In re Winship* in the case of *McKeiver v. Pennsylvania* (1971). In the *McKeiver* case the U.S. Supreme Court held that juveniles did *not* have the constitutional right to a jury of their peers. The court did not perceive the right to a jury trial as a constitutionally necessary aspect of fact finding in juvenile cases and concluded that juvenile courts should not become as fully adversarial as the adult courts. In addition the court believed that allowing a jury trial in juvenile cases might cause unnecessary delays as well as make the proceedings public.

These landmark cases served as a catalyst to the federal government's interest in addressing the treatment of children in the juvenile justice system. Particular interest focused on detaining juveniles in adult jails. In the early 1970s many organizations, such as the National Council on Crime and Delinquency and the Children's Defense Fund, as well as other expert testimony before the senate judiciary committee reported that many children were experiencing brutal beatings, rapes, suicides, and unsanitary cell conditions during their detention in adult jails. As a result the Juvenile Justice and Delinquency Prevention Act was passed in 1974. The act proved to be an extremely important and controversial piece of legislation because of its two goals. The first goal was to deinstitutionalize *status offenders* and abused, neglected and dependent children by diverting them away from juvenile and adult offenders and placing them in more appropriate programs. The second goal was to separate juvenile delinquents from adult criminals when detaining the juveniles in adult jails. The act called for "sight and sound separation" between juvenile and adult offenders in every jurisdiction.

The act encouraged states to follow these mandates by providing funding for delinquency prevention programs and for establishing separate detention facilities.

However, most states did not initially comply with the act because it only provided block grants, thereby leaving much of the economic burden to the communities. In addition, many jurisdictions varied drastically in the number of juveniles detained. In rural jurisdictions particularly it did not make economic sense to build a separate detention facility or establish preventive programs if they did not have the number of juveniles to justify it. Thus, many jurisdictions were not in compliance with the act until the mid to late 1980s and the only penalty states received was not receiving the federal funding. The act has been understandably criticized for its weakness in that it did not have any backbone to enforce its mandates.

Finally, in reference to the legality of detaining juveniles at all, the U.S. Supreme Court in *Shall v. Martin* (1984) concluded that it was constitutional and not unreasonable to detain juveniles for their own protection.

Today, most states are now in compliance with the federal act requiring separate detention facilities (or at least the separation of juveniles from adults in the same facilities). Perhaps more importantly, most states generally recognize that merging adult, juvenile, and status offenders can often result in serious consequences. In addition, most states have statutes that strictly prohibit placing status offenders in detention facilities (unless they violate a court order).

Two things occurred that have increased states' compliance with the federal requirement of separation. First, several amendments to the act (1980, 1985, 1988, and 1996) have addressed some of the weaknesses of the act. For example, Congress has added the "rural exception rule." This rule allows juvenile offenders in rural areas to be held in an adult jail facility (with sight and sound separation) for up to 24 hours, until the juvenile can be transported to a detention facility in another jurisdiction.

Second, civil lawsuits on behalf of children who experienced abuse, neglect, and in some cases even death (years after the act was passed) have motivated states to establish separate facilities. Some of these cases include *Doe v. Burwel* (1984), which involved a 15-year-old female status offender who left home without her parents' permission. As result of committing the status offense the judge ordered that she be detained in the adult county jail for five days. On her fourth night she was raped by a correctional officer. Doe's parents brought a civil law suit against Ada County and won $38,000. In *Yellen v. Ada County* (1985), a 15-year-old Idaho boy died in an adult jail after being detained in jail for traffic fines after his parents refused to pick him up. Over a 14-hour period Yellen was tortured by other inmates and eventually beaten to death. His parents sued and received $30,000.

Today the majority of jurisdictions have adopted legal procedures forbidding the placement of status offenders in detention facilities. However, most jurisdictions make an exception to this general rule if the status offender violates a court order. This "loop hole" in confining status offenders who fail to go to school, who are incorrigible, and who run away from home has caused a great deal of controversy. One of the main arguments against juvenile courts even having jurisdiction over status offenders (instead of using a social services entity or a private agency) is that these courts typically do not have adequately trained staff or resources to deal with these types of offenders, many of whom have complex problems. Further, if juvenile courts divest themselves from status offenders they would have more time to deal with the more serious and repetitive juvenile offenders, and by diverting status offenders to private agencies they can receive the psychological and other interventions they need.

Today, juvenile courts are no longer purely civil proceedings as they initially were. Much of the juvenile court proceedings resemble adult criminal court proceedings. In addition, much of the juvenile justice system has become adversarial in nature by providing due process rights of legal representation to the juveniles. Juvenile courts no longer use preponderance of evidence (used as the legal standard in civil proceedings) but now use "beyond a reasonable doubt" for the legal standard of fact finding, just as the adult court system does. In addition, approximately 12 states also allow jury trials in juvenile courts for certain offenses. In summary, juvenile court proceedings were initially designed to be informal and casual, but because of the landmark court decisions (previously discussed) that challenged the justice, fairness, and procedural due process rights of juveniles, juvenile courts have become more formalized in their proceedings.

The get tough on crime policies established in the 1980s have continued to flourish and have also influenced the merging of civil and criminal procedures in juvenile court. This get tough on crime focus has continued unabated despite the fact that the overall juvenile crime rate decreased in the U.S. between 1995 and 1999. Still, juvenile offenders today are improperly depicted as more serious, less remorseful, and less amenable to treatment. In addition, because of the recent surge of school shootings, the media portray juvenile courts as lacking effective punishment and failing to deter violent juvenile offenders. Thus, the juvenile justice system in many ways moved from a rehabilitative, protective parental model to a more punitive, punishment model used in the adult system. As a result, one of the most recent and controversial issues facing the juvenile justice system today is society's demand for harsher treatment of juvenile offenders who commit heinous offenses (i.e. murder, rape, kidnapping, and arson.) Twenty-eight states have enacted statutes setting minimum age standards and type of offenses for when juveniles can be legally transferred (sometimes referred to as a waiver or certified as an adult) to adult court and tried as an adult. In 1997 Vermont and Wisconsin had the lowest age limit of 10 years of age. Some states even allow the death penalty to be imposed on juveniles (as well as the mentally infirm).

Many states have been critical of the juvenile court's discretionary decision making regarding which juveniles should be transferred to adult court and that juveniles should be adjudicated in the juvenile court system. Much of the juvenile court's decisions are based on subjective standards and each case varies according to the judge's view of the law and the information provided to him or her. In addition, because juvenile courts only have the power or jurisdiction to confine juveniles in secure lock-ups until their 18th or 21st birthday (depending on the state statutes) and cannot impose harsher sentences (such as longer sentences or the death penalty) waiving or transferring violent juvenile offenders to adult court was seen as the answer to society's demand to impose harsher punishments. As a result of this, many states have rebelled against the traditional policies and decision-making processes of juvenile courts, and have passed legislative waiver laws that abolish juvenile court waiver hearings. In these states juveniles do not have the right to waiver hearings as was mandated in the *Kent* decision. Under the recent state laws some juvenile courts only have to verify that the youth is of the minimum age and is charged with a certain violent crime as required by state statute. Essentially, these states have overruled the requirements set forth in *Kent* (that required a waiver hearing), thereby abrogating the power and authority that the juvenile court once had over these to determine which juveniles can be tried in the adult court system.

The courts have begun reviewing the constitutionality of such laws, focusing primarily on the variables associated with such laws. For instance, the U.S. Supreme Court held in *Eddings v. Oklahoma* (1982) that a defendant's age should be considered a mitigating factor in deciding whether to apply the death penalty. Six years later the U.S. Supreme Court examined whether the death penalty imposed on a juvenile was cruel and unusual punishment. In *Thompson v. Oklahoma* (1988), the court found that imposing the death penalty on a 15-year-old murderer violated his eighth amendment rights prohibiting cruel and unusual punishment. Yet, just a year later in *Stanford v. Kentucky* (1989) the U.S. Supreme Court held that it was not cruel and unusual punishment to impose the death penalty on juveniles who committed a crime between the ages of 16 and 18.

These new statutes end the policies and procedures as articulated in *Kent* even though the U.S. Supreme Court has not overruled that decision. Unless the state or the Supreme Court finds these statutes permitting automatic waiver to be unconstitutional, the states are able to side step the rights of juveniles that were originally granted by the Supreme Court. The question still remains, however, whether judicial waivers versus legislative waivers are meeting the goals of punishing juvenile offenders and, more importantly, deterring other potential violent juvenile offenders.

Some experts argue that given the recent political demands for punishment regardless of age and in light of the fact that more than one half of the states allow for juveniles to be transferred to adult courts, there is at least the potential of the juvenile justice system coming to full swing and treating children in the same way as adults, as was done centuries ago. In some jurisdictions there is a demand to abolish the juvenile justice system altogether and leave everything to the traditional criminal system. Some experts may view this as having merit since more and more juveniles are being waived into the adult criminal justice system. Indeed, these experts may argue that because the juvenile justice system is becoming more of a criminal proceeding focused on punishment rather than a civil proceeding (particularly with the increase of more serious sanctions that can be imposed on juveniles), the juvenile justice system should adopt more procedural formality providing *all* due process rights afforded to adults and essentially mirror the adult criminal justice system.

As it stands today, though, the courts and legislatures continue to extol the importance of the *parens patriae* doctrine and at least claim that the concept of rehabilitation remains at the heart of the juvenile justice. Whether this is truly the case remains to be seen. Some jurisdictions are making efforts to implement prevention programs (such as Teen Courts) that reduce the risks of delinquency by targeting first-time juvenile offenders and requiring more community and parental involvement.

In other countries legal approaches in dealing with juvenile delinquency vary from country to country, yet most countries recognize a minimum age when children are considered to be capable of understanding the consequences of their actions as well as being culpable for their actions. Currently no nation has an age below 7 years old. But in other countries the age is much higher (in Italy and Japan the age of legal culpability is 14 years old). Currently most countries either have a juvenile justice system or are in the process of establishing juvenile justice systems. In some countries this may mean developing a separate system or developing

programs and safeguards for juveniles within the adult criminal system. Some countries, such as Germany and Scotland, have also instituted get-tough policies similar to the U.S. that focus less on treatment and more on punishment. Other countries have been noted to take punishment to an extreme. For example, South Africa and Singapore have in recent years sentenced juveniles to corporal punishment.

Terms and Definitions

Below is an overview of the steps in processing juveniles through the juvenile justice system in the U.S. Corresponding to these steps are the common terms and definitions associated with each step. This overview of the juvenile court process will be preceded by an outline of the types of children over which the juvenile courts have jurisdiction.

The U.S. Juvenile Court System has jurisdiction over these children:

[Note: Juvenile offenders and status offenders often fit into more than one category]

Juvenile offender: A juvenile who commits a criminal offense.

Status offense: An act committed by a juvenile that if committed by an adult would not be criminal (curfew, truancy, consumption of alcohol, smoking tabacco).

Neglected child: A child who has not been afforded by her or his legal guardian(s) the basic needs in life (food, water, shelter, clothing, supervision, medical, or educational needs).

Abused child: A child who has suffered from physical injury that did not result from accidental means, or a child sexually exploited through some form of sexual activity.

Dependent child: A child who has been abandoned by his or her legal guardians

Steps in the U.S. Juvenile Court Process

1. Preadjudicatory Stage

Take into custody: Similar to arrest in adult system; intake hearing or interview; probation officer interviews the juvenile to determine whether the case should be petitioned to court;

Petition: Similar to indictment in adult court; agree with petition; an adult would plead guilty;

Deny petition: An adult would plead not guilty;

Adjustment to petition: Similar to a plea bargain;

Detention: Similar to adult jail (for juvenile offenders);

Shelter care facility: Similar to foster care (for status offenders);

Detention hearing: To determine whether to release juveniles to their parents or to hold them for protective custody until their adjudication hearing.

2. Adjudication Stage

Transfer, waiver hearing: Statutes that allow juveniles to be tried as adults depending (Certification Hearing) on the offense; a hearing must be conducted to determine if the juvenile meets the legal criteria to be transferred to adult court;

Adjudication hearing: A fact-finding hearing to determine if there is sufficient evidence (proof beyond a reasonable doubt) that the allegations in the petition are true;

Adjudication: The juvenile is found to be a delinquent.

3. Postadjudicatory Stage

Dispositional report: Similar to a presentence investigation in adult court; prepared by the probation officer, who provides details of the offense, the juvenile's criminal and social history, and makes a dispositional (sentencing) recommendation;

Dispositional hearing: Hearing to impose a sentence on the juvenile;

Probation: Placing juveniles on court supervision; commitment juveniles are placed in a locked facility (either therapeutic or correctional facility);

Youth corrections: Similar to adult prison or correctional system;

Parole: Juveniles who are released from youth corrections may be released on parole.

LANETTE P. DALLEY

References and Further Reading

Binder, A., Geis, G., and Dickson, B.D. 2001. *Juvenile Delinquency Historical, Cultural and Legal Perspectives*, 3rd ed., Anderson Publishing Company, Cincinnati, OH.

Champion, D. 2001. *The Juvenile Justice System*, 3rd ed., Prentice Hall, Upper Saddle RIver, NJ.

Clement, M.J. 2002. *The Juvenile Justice System,* Butterworth Heinemann, Boston, MA.

Decker, S.H. 1980. The Impact of the Juvenile Justice and Delinquency Prevention Act in Missouri, *Juvenile and Family Court Journal*, 31(4).

Isralowits, R.E. 1979. Deinstitutionalization and Serious Juvenile Offender, *Juvenile and Family Court Journal*, 30(3).

Krisberg, B. and Austin, J. 1978. *The Children of Ishamael*, Mayfield Publishing Company, CA.

Krisberg, B., Schwartz, I., Litsky, I.P., and Austin, J. 1986. The Watershed of Juvenile Justice Reform, *Crime and Delinquency,* 32(1).

Sarri, R. and Hansenfeld, Y. 1976. *Brought to Justice? Juveniles, Courts, and the Laws*, University of Michigan, Ann Arbor, MI.

Siegel, L. and Senna, J. 2000. *Juvenile Delinquency Theory, Practice, and the Law*, 7th ed. Wadsworth, Standford, CT.

Solar, M. 1988. Litigation on behalf of children in adult jails, *Crime and Delinquency*, 34(2).

U.S. Department of Education and U.S. Department of Justice, 2000. *1999 Annual Report on School Safety*, Washington, DC.

Whitehead, J. T., Lab, S. 1999. *Juvenile Justice* (3rd ed.), Anderson Publishing, Cincinnati, OH.

See also **Juvenile Delinquency and Youth Crime Throughout History; Juvenile Delinquency: Extent, Correlates, and Trends; Juvenile Delinquency: Theories of**

Juvenile Delinquency: Extent, Correlates, and Trends

Juvenile delinquency is broadly defined as " … any action by someone designated a juvenile (nonadult) that would make such a young person subject to action by the juvenile court" (Kratcoski and Kratcoski, 1996, 2). This definition is somewhat problematic, particularly because the meaning of the word "juvenile" often changes from one jurisdiction to the next. Internationally, the age at which countries make the distinction between juveniles and adults varies widely. In Saint Vincent, individuals achieve full adult status at age 15 (the minimum age internationally) whereas individuals in Hong Kong become adults at 21 (UN Office for

Drug Control and Crime Prevention, 1999). Even within the U.S., definitions of juveniles vary widely from state to state. Only six states have established a minimum age at which a person may be referred to the juvenile court while one state set the upper age limit for original juvenile court jurisdiction (the age at the time the offense was committed) at 18; the federal system, the District of Columbia, and 38 states use the age of 17; eight states use 16; and three states use 15 (Kratcoski, 1996).

Additionally, all states and most countries allow juveniles to be tried as adults under certain circumstances. In a number of states and countries, if the offense is a serious violent crime such as murder, the juvenile court does not have original jurisdiction as the statute for punishment for that offense specifies that everyone who commits that crime must be tried as an adult. The predominant means through which juveniles are tried in adult courts, however, is through judicial waiver, or transfer from the juvenile court that has original jurisdiction (Kratcoski, 1996). The number of juveniles waived to adult court annually has remained relatively unchanged since 1988, with less than 1% of the juvenile delinquency cases waived to adult court every year. Nevertheless, since 1993, cases involving crimes against persons have been more likely to be judicially waived in greater numbers than other offenses (Puzzanchera, 2000).

The present system of juvenile justice in the U.S. emerged at the turn of the 20th century. Until 1899, when the juvenile court system was established in Cook County (Chicago), Illinois by a group of reformers known as the "child savers," juveniles who were found guilty of crime were treated in much the same manner as adults. The child savers were a group of conservative, well-educated, middle-class Protestant women of Anglo-Saxon descent who sought to alleviate jail and reformatory conditions in Illinois. Their examination of these problems led them to believe that the legal system should intervene in the lives of juveniles in order to prevent them from living immoral and criminal lives. The juvenile court was thus predicated on the idea that juveniles could be rehabilitated, and that the state should aid in that rehabilitation. By the early 20th century, most states had adopted a juvenile court system similar to the one begun in Illinois (Elrod and Ryder, 1999).

In the original design of the juvenile court system, trials (referred to as hearings to avoid the stigma of the adult court) were overseen by special judges who ensured that the hearings were closed. Judges had wide discretion, and proof of guilt was not necessary for a judge to intervene in a child's life. The juvenile justice system continued relatively unchanged until the 1960s, when a number of important court decisions (e.g., *Kent*

v. U.S. (383 US 541, 1966); *In re Gault* (387 US 1, 1967); and *In re Winship* (397 US 358, 1970)) caused the juvenile court to more closely resemble adult courts by ensuring a number of procedural protections not previously available to juveniles. This trend has continued until today, with some critics even questioning the need for a separate juvenile court (Elrod and Ryder, 1999).

Juveniles are considered delinquent when they commit any act whose violation by an adult would also be a crime (e.g., homicide, burglary, and larceny). In many states, however, juveniles can also be arrested for acts that are legal for adults. As these acts are criminal only for those who have the status of juvenile, they are called "status offenses." The most commonly committed status offenses are truancy (failure to attend school), incorrigibility (failure to obey parents), and drinking alcoholic beverages (Agnew, 2001).

There are three different methods through which we obtain information about the number of juvenile delinquents in the U.S. The most commonly cited data source from which we obtain the number and type of people who violate the law is called Crime in the U.S.: The Uniform Crime Reports (UCR), published annually by the Federal Bureau of Investigation. The UCR provides data for eight serious crimes (so-called "index" crimes, including aggravated assault, arson, burglary, larceny-theft, motor vehicle theft, murder, rape, and robbery) and 22 less serious crimes. In 1999, 10% of the offenders arrested for murder, 17% of those arrested for rape, 25% of those arrested for robbery, and 14% of those arrested for aggravated assault were under the age of 18. Additionally, 34% of those arrested for burglary, 32% of those arrested for larceny, 35% of those arrested for motor vehicle theft, and 55% of those arrested for arson were under the age of 18 (Federal Bureau of Investigation, 2000). Although these percentages vary slightly from year to year, they present a general picture of the proportion of criminals who are juvenile delinquents each year. Generally, juveniles are responsible for around one in five serious violent crimes and one in three serious property crimes.

Juvenile crime trends in the U.S. generally match those in other countries as well. Crime statistics collected by the UN from many countries (within the limitations of the data) reflect that young people are overrepresented as offenders and victims in most crimes and male juveniles are more likely to be arrested for and be victimized by crime than female juveniles (UN, 1999; Shaw, 2001). Further, a very small number of juvenile offenders is responsible for a disproportionate amount of juvenile crime in both the U.S. and other countries (Shaw, 2001). Finally, most countries throughout the world experienced increases in officially recorded crime by young people from the 1980s until the mid-1990s and have experienced a decline in crimes among young people from the mid-1990s until present (Shaw, 2001).

Although juvenile crime in the U.S. generally mirrors juvenile crime throughout the world, there are some distinctive differences, however, particularly as it relates to gender. The ratio of male juvenile crime suspects per female juvenile crime suspects is far lower in the U.S. (3.02) than in most other countries throughout the world (the mean being 15.64, with a maximum of 79.44 in the nation of Georgia). This may be because of the more egalitarian social treatment of females in the U.S. and other industrialized countries (UN, 1999).

Juvenile delinquents, both in the U.S. and other countries, are frequently involved in less serious offenses as well. In 1999, 18% of those arrested for assaults other than aggravated assault, 43% of those arrested for vandalism, and 24% of those arrested for weapons violations were under the age of 18. Additionally, there were 96,586 arrests for curfew and loitering law violations and 81,236 arrests for runaways. As both crimes are status offenses, all of those arrested were under the age of 18 (Federal Bureau of Investigation, 2000).

Violent and property crime arrest rates among juveniles have followed somewhat dissimilar paths over the last three decades. From the early 1970s through 1988, the number of juvenile arrests for arson, larceny-theft, and the serious violent crimes outlined earlier (e.g., murder, rape, robbery, and aggravated assault) remained relatively constant. In 1989, however, for arson and the serious violent crimes, the juvenile arrest rate began a dramatic increase that continued until it reached its peak in 1994, when this rapid increase was followed by a rapid decline that has continued until present. Motor vehicle theft followed a similar pattern, with a dramatic increase in the juvenile arrest rate that began in 1984 and continued until 1991, when the rate began to steadily decline. Nevertheless, the larceny-theft arrest rate for juveniles has remained relatively stable from 1980 until today, while the burglary rate declined by more than 50% during that same time period (Federal Bureau of Investigation, 2000).

The last two decades have also brought about a significant change in the juvenile arrest rates for females. The juvenile arrest rate among females for serious property crime increased approximately 30% from 1980 to 1999, while the juvenile arrest rate for serious violent crimes among females increased almost 100% in that same time period. Nevertheless, as detailed below, juvenile males remain much more likely than juvenile females to be arrested for serious violent and property crimes (Federal Bureau of Investigation, 2000).

Official statistics such as the arrest data presented above are not completely reliable, however, as the reports are based on data gathered from police departments throughout the U.S. and thus underestimate the actual amount of crimes that juveniles commit. These limitations have motivated criminologists to attempt to develop more valid measures of crime and victimization to provide a more thorough picture of crime in the U.S. by uncovering much of the crime not reported to the police. One of these alternate sources of crime data is the National Crime Victimization Survey (NCVS).

The NCVS originated in 1972 and is conducted every six months by the Bureau of Justice Statistics. The NCVS measures six of the eight index crimes examined by the UCR (excluding murder and arson). The NCVS presents data from surveys of approximately 60,000 households, involving about 130,000 people, seven times over a 3-year period. Annually, the NCVS uncovers over twice as many victimizations as the UCR (O'Brien, 1985).

When compared to other age groups, data from the NCVS reveal that juveniles are disproportionately victimized by violence as well. Youths aged 16–19 have the highest victimization rates for violent crime (77.4 per 1,000) of any age group, followed by those youths aged 12–15 (74.4 per 1,000). Youth in these age groups are also more likely to be robbed and assaulted than members of any other age group. Although half of the older age group (15–19) would be considered adults in most jurisdictions, it is apparent that juveniles are disproportionately at risk of violent victimization as well (Rennison, 2001).

Although UCR data offer a variety of information about criminal offenders, and the NCVS offers a wide variety of information about crime victims, neither offers any insight into the reasons that people commit crimes. Because of this, another method of data collection has emerged: the self-report survey.

Use of self-report surveys became an acceptable criminological research design in the 1950s, largely as a result of the work of James Short and F. Ivan Nye. Self-report surveys ask samples of respondents about their own participation in criminal activities, as well as a number of other background and contextual questions that have allowed researchers to identify a number of factors associated with involvement in juvenile delinquency. Since the studies of Short and Nye, the self-report survey has been the primary source of data for examination of the causes of juvenile delinquency (O'Brien, 1985).

Each of the aforementioned methods of data collection has problems that make it impossible to use that method as an absolute measure of the amount of crime in the U.S., making it virtually impossible to determine the exact amount of juvenile delinquency in the U.S. It is important to understand, however, that there are several areas of agreement among the three sources of data. Thus, much time and effort have been expended in an attempt to determine some of the correlates and causes of juvenile delinquency. The following is a review of the major patterns of juvenile delinquency in the U.S.

A number of demographic factors have a significant association with juvenile delinquency. Arrest, victimization, and self-report data all confirm that males are more likely than females to commit most delinquent acts; the disparity between the two groups is even greater when focusing solely on violent crime. Males were approximately 12 times more likely to be arrested for murder, 10 times more likely to be arrested for robbery, approximately eight times more likely to be arrested for burglary and arson, and five times more likely to be arrested for motor vehicle theft in 1999. Even for larceny, the Index Crimes, where gender differences are the smallest, males were almost twice as likely to be arrested as females. In fact, for only two crimes, the majority of those arrested were females—prostitution (57.8%) and running away (59.4%) (Federal Bureau of Investigation, 2000).

Victimization data, in which the respondent is required to identify the gender of the perpetrator in their victimization incident, strongly resemble the UCR data for robbery as most crimes. Self-report studies also indicate that males are more likely to be involved in delinquency, particularly violent delinquency.

Just as males commit the vast majority of delinquent acts, males are also more likely to be victimized by crime. Males were three times more likely to be murdered (75.5% as compared to 24.4%) than females in 1999 (Federal Bureau of Investigation, 2000), and were twice as likely as females to be victims of robbery or aggravated assault. On the other hand, females were 7.5 times more likely to be victimized by rape or sexual assault than were males (Rennison, 2001).

Another important demographic predictor of juvenile delinquency offending and victimization is race or ethnicity. Although approximately 12% of the population in the U.S. is Black (U.S. Bureau of the Census, 2002), 49% of those under the age of 18 arrested for murder in 1999 and 54.4% of those arrested for robbery were Black. Additionally, Blacks were disproportionately arrested for every other delinquent act except drunkenness, driving under the influence (DUI), and liquor law violations (Federal Bureau of Investigation, 2000).

Critics of official statistics argue that self-report studies and victimization surveys should be used in lieu of arrest statistics to study the impact of race on juvenile delinquency. The findings from self-report surveys seem to support this argument, as a number of self-report studies indicate that Whites and Blacks commit the same range of delinquent behaviors, although Blacks often offend at a higher frequency, particularly for serious violence (see Hindelang et al., 1981). Victimization studies further support the idea that blacks are disproportionately involved in delinquency, although at lower levels than those found in arrest statistics (U.S. Department of Justice, 2000).

As with gender, the group most likely to be the offender in juvenile delinquency is also most likely to be the victim. In 1999, there were 41.6 violent crime victimizations per 1000 Black persons aged 12 and over compared to 31.9 per 1000 for Whites. For robbery, there were even larger discrepancies in the rates, with 7.7 robbery victimizations per 1000 for Blacks and only 3.1 per 1000 for Whites (Rennison, 2001).

The association between social class and crime has fascinated criminologists for many years. Most aggregate level research using UCR data indicates an inverse relationship between social class and delinquency; in other words, the lower the socioeconomic status of a neighborhood, the higher is its rate of delinquency (Shaw and McKay, 1942). Many researchers argue, however, that reliance on official data for measures of class and crime/delinquency may bias the results against members of the lower class as official law enforcement agents are more likely to concentrate their efforts in lower class neighborhoods and thus uncover more crime and delinquency. For this reason, many researchers suggest using self-report data to measure the relationship between social class and crime (Tittle and Meier, 1990).

Studies at the individual level that use self-report data often uncover contradictory findings about the relationship between social class and delinquency. Whereas some theorists argue that socioeconomic status is an important predictor of delinquency, others disagree. After reviewing numerous studies using both official and self-reported data, Tittle and Meier (1990) concluded that " ... there is no pervasive relationship between individual SES and delinquency ... " (Tittle and Meier, 1990, 292).

Although it may be impossible to say without doubt that an empirical relationship between social class and delinquency does or does not exist, the relationship between victimization by violent crime and social class is much more conclusive. Juveniles from the lowest income households ($7,500 or less) are much more likely to be victimized by violent crime than any other income group (Rennison, 2001).

As Agnew (2001) suggests, it is difficult to disentangle the interaction between race and class when it comes to the area of delinquency. Blacks are more likely to be members of the lower class than whites, and lower class adolescents are more likely to engage in serious delinquency than their counterparts from other classes. Thus, many researchers suggest that the reason blacks are more likely to engage in delinquency is because of their disproportionate representation in the lower class. Agnew (2001) tentatively concludes that much of the racial differences in serious delinquency are because of the fact that blacks are more likely to be poor and live in impoverished communities.

Another variable that has a significant association with juvenile delinquency is gang membership. Gang members are much more likely than nongang members to use alcohol and marijuana regularly, participate in violent crime, sell drugs, and own and carry weapons (Shelden, Tracy, and Brown, 1997).

Sanchez Jankowski (1991) suggests a number of reasons why gang members are more likely to engage in delinquency. He points out that gangs are most prevalent in lower class neighborhoods; thus, the relationship between gang membership and delinquency may be similar to the relationship between race and delinquency, with socioeconomic status conditioning the effects.

Jankowski (1991) also indicates that there are two reasons besides financial distress that explain why youths join gangs: natural association—youths often join gangs because the people that they associate with join gangs; and problems in identity construction—kids join gangs in search of social status.

A number of individual traits exhibiting a strong relationship with delinquent activity, particularly serious, violent delinquency, have also been identified. Youth with low verbal IQ scores and youth with learning disabilities are significantly more likely to engage in delinquency than their counterparts, as are youth who are hyperactive, impulsive, and suffer from attention deficit disorder. Further, those youth who have a greater need for excitement, those who are more irritable than their counterparts, and those who are insensitive to others exhibit greater tendencies toward delinquency (for review, see Agnew, 2001). Additionally, youth whose parents were criminals, who were abused as children, who were separated from one or more parents, and who live in communities that are disorganized and where drugs and firearms are readily available are most prone to serious delinquency. As Agnew (2001) points out, however, there are many youth with these traits who do not engage in delinquency. Agnew suggests that delinquency occurs when one or more of these traits is combined with social environmental influences. When considering theories of delinquent behavior, Agnew (2001) argues that there are three important points to keep in mind. First, criminologists have been unable to identify any single cause of delinquency. Agnew argues that at the most general level,

delinquency is caused by both features of the social environment and individual traits. Thus, individuals in certain environments (e.g., abusive families and poor communities) are more likely to engage in delinquency than as are individuals with certain individual traits (e.g., low intelligence or irritable temperaments). Second, most of the causes of delinquency are related to one another in some manner. Thus, individuals in abusive families are more likely to have irritable temperaments, whereas youth from poor communities are more likely to join gangs. Finally, theoretical predictors influence, but do not absolutely determine, behavior. Consequently, whereas youth from lower socioeconomic neighborhoods are more likely to join gangs and engage in delinquency, there are far more youths from poor neighborhoods who neither join gangs nor engage in delinquency.

Although there is disagreement among criminologists regarding which theories best explain delinquency, there is little disagreement that the three leading explanations of delinquency are strain theory, social learning theory, and social control theory.

According to strain theory, juveniles sometimes engage in delinquency when they become upset because of the strain or stress that they experience in their lives (Agnew, 2001). There are a number of versions of strain theory, the most prominent being those proposed by Robert K. Merton, Albert K. Cohen, Richard Cloward and Lloyd Ohlin, and Richard Agnew. All of these theorists suggest that failure to achieve goals, especially money (Merton, Cloward and Ohlin's versions of the theory) or status and respect (Cohen and Agnew) results in strain. Empirical research shows that when youths fail to achieve any or all of these goals, they experience strain, and are more likely to engage in delinquency.

Agnew (2001) has recently expanded traditional strain theory to encompass other forms of strain. He suggests that some individuals experience strain when they want or expect something, but do not get it. Additionally, youth may also experience strain when they lose something of value (positive stimuli) or are presented with noxious or negative stimuli. Examples of these negative situations include strain that results from insults, physical assault, undeserved discipline or punishment, and rejection from others. A number of studies have determined that these experiences make adolescents more likely to engage in delinquency.

Agnew (2001 and 1992) suggests that not all individuals who experience the aforementioned strains engage in delinquency. He argues that strain is more likely to lead to delinquency when the situation bringing about the strain: (1) involves areas of the individual's life that he or she considers important (e.g., challenges to masculinity of adolescent males); (2) involves individuals with poor coping skills and resources (e.g., those with few verbal or problem-solving skills); (3) involves individuals with few conventional social supports (e.g., little support from family, friends, and teachers); (4) occurs in situations where the benefits of delinquency are high and the costs are low (e.g., delinquency is more likely to occur when the chances of being caught and punished are small); and (5) occurs among individuals "disposed" to delinquency (e.g., those with low intelligence or irritable temperaments) (Agnew, 2001).

The second leading explanation of delinquency is social learning theory that emerged primarily from the works of Edwin H. Sutherland and Ronald Akers. These theorists argue that juveniles learn to engage in delinquency primarily through association with intimate acquaintances. In this process, adolescents learn beliefs favorable to delinquency and are rewarded by other adolescents when they engage in delinquency. As a result, these adolescents come to view juvenile delinquency as an activity that is desirable and rewarding and continue to engage in delinquent activities.

Social learning theorists claim that juveniles learn to engage in delinquent behavior in much the same way they learn to engage in conformist behavior: through association with others, particularly intimate groups such as the family and close friends. As Agnew (2001) notes, association with delinquent peers is generally one of the best predictors of delinquency. There are at least three avenues through which adolescents learn to engage in delinquency from their peers and family. Peers and family may teach juveniles beliefs favorable to delinquency, they may reinforce or fail to punish delinquent acts of juveniles, or they may provide models of delinquent behavior for the youth to imitate (Agnew, 2001).

In his differential association theory, Sutherland (1947) argues that people engage in deviant activity because of "...an excess of definitions favorable to violation of law over definitions unfavorable to violation of law" (Sutherland, 1947, 6). Sutherland suggests that individuals learn these definitions from intimate personal groups; thus, according to Sutherland, individuals learn to engage in criminal behavior through interactions with others (commonly referred to as peer groups or cliques) who have values and beliefs that encourage breaking the law.

Recently, Akers has introduced the ideas of operant conditioning into a broader theoretical perspective called social learning theory. Akers argues that delinquent conduct is more likely to develop when the peers of an adolescent define delinquent behavior as appropriate and reward that individual for delinquent behavior. He suggests that delinquent behavior is more likely to occur in three situations: (1) when it is infrequently punished and frequently rewarded; (2) when it results in large amounts of reinforcement (e.g., a lot of money or social approval); and (3) when delinquent behavior is more likely to be reinforced than other behaviors. Akers (1998) calls this the concept of differential reinforcement, because different behaviors have different probabilities of being reinforced.

Akers also differentiates between positive and negative reinforcements and positive and negative punishments. Positive reinforcements occur when the behavior results in something good (e.g., if a juvenile robs a liquor store successfully, he has two positive reinforcements: the money he gained from the robbery and the approval of his delinquent peers). Negative reinforcement, on the other hand, occurs when a behavior results in the removal of something negative or bad (e.g., a youth viewed as a "sissy" by his peers may lose that stigma if he shoots a gun at a rival gang member). Positive punishment involves the introduction of something bad (e.g., a youth who commits a delinquent act is apprehended and sent to boot camp). Finally, negative punishment involves the removal of something good from one's environment (e.g., an adolescent who breaks curfew may have the car keys taken away) (Akers, 1998).

Finally, Akers (1988) also demonstrates the importance of modeling. This occurs when people imitate the behavior of others, especially when they feel that this will result in reinforcement. Unlike the previously discussed aspects of social learning theory, modeling does not have to involve direct contact with those whom an adolescent imitates. Thus, a number of researchers have suggested that juveniles model the behavior presented in the media, particularly television.

Control theorists, unlike their strain and social learning counterparts, do not ask why adolescents engage in deviance, but rather why some juveniles conform. They argue that delinquency requires no explanation; rather, the important question becomes what factors restrict individuals from engaging in delinquency. According to control theory, those adolescents who do not engage in delinquency are those who believe it is wrong or fear what will happen to them if they are caught and sanctioned in some way. Specifically, those adolescents with the most to lose from engaging in delinquency (e.g., scholarship opportunities, social status, and respect from parents) will avoid delinquency; those adolescents without those same constraints will be most likely to engage in delinquency.

Social control theory is most often associated with Travis Hirschi's *Causes of Delinquency* (1969),

886

although numerous authors have contributed to the argument (e.g., Albert J. Reiss, Walter C. Reckless, and Jackson Toby). Hirschi argues that all youth are motivated to commit delinquent acts; only those individuals who have strong social bonds to society refrain. According to Hirschi (1969), there are four elements of the social bond: commitment, attachment, belief, and involvement. Hirschi (1969) argues that the more committed an adolescent is to the rules of society, and the stronger the attachment between the adolescent and parents, teachers, and peers, the less likely it is that the juvenile will become delinquent. He further argues that those adolescents who believe in the conventions and behavior restrictions placed upon them by the larger society and those youth involved in conventional activities (jobs and extracurricular activities at school) will be less likely to commit delinquent acts (Hirschi, 1969).

Gottfredson and Hirschi (1990) present a more recent version of control theory, commonly known as self-control theory. Self-control is defined as the idea that people "differ in the extent to which they are vulnerable to the temptations of the moment" (Gottfredson and Hirschi, 1990, 87). In other words, youth with low self-control lack the ability to restrain themselves, so they are more likely to engage in delinquency. Delinquency is attractive to individuals with low self-control because it brings immediate gratification, is exciting and risky, and requires little skill or planning (Gottfredson and Hirschi, 1990).

In recent years, reflecting the conservative political climate regarding crime in general, a number of "get-tough" policies have been implemented in the U.S. in an effort to control juvenile delinquency. Some states have established mandatory sentencing guidelines for juvenile offenders, stiffened penalties for adjudicated juvenile offenders, and increased the number of juveniles incarcerated in juvenile and adult facilities (Elrod and Ryder 1999). Despite these trends, research shows that treatment and rehabilitation programs can reduce recidivism among juveniles, especially in programs that directly address the dynamic characteristics associated with offending (e.g., attitudes, cognitions, employment behaviors, education, peers, authority, substance abuse, and interpersonal relationships) (Mackenzie, 1997). Mackenzie concludes that programs that work can be identified and should be implemented to reduce juvenile delinquency, not just in isolated instances, but throughout society in general.

DAVID C. MAY

References and Further Reading

Agnew, R. 2001. *Juvenile Delinquency: Causes and Control*, Roxbury Publishing, Los Angeles, CA.

Agnew, R. 1992. Foundation for a General Strain Theory of Crime and Delinquency, *Criminology,* 30.

Akers, R.L. 1998. *Social Learning and Social Structure: A General Theory of Crime and Deviance*, Northeastern University Press, Boston, MA.

Elrod, P. and Ryder, R.S. 1999. *Juvenile Justice: A Social, Historical, and Legal Perspective*, Aspen Publishing, Gaithersburg, MD.

Federal Bureau of Investigation, 2000. *Crime in the U.S.: The Uniform Crime Reports*, U.S. Government Printing Office, Washington DC.

Gottfredson, M.R. and Hirschi, T. 1990. *A General Theory of Crime*, Stanford University Press, Stanford, CA.

Hawkins, J.D., Herrenkohl, T.I., Farrington, D.P., Brewer, D., Catalano, R.F., Harachi, T.W., and Cothern, L. 2000. *Predictors of Youth Violence*, Office of Juvenile Justice and Delinquency Prevention, NCJ 179065, Washington, DC.

Hindelang, M.J., Hirschi, T., and Weis, J.G. 1981. *Measuring Delinquency*, Sage Publications, Inc., Beverly Hills, CA.

Hirschi, T. 1969. *Causes of Delinquency*, University of California Press, Berkeley, CA.

Jankowski, S.M. 1991. *Islands in the Street: Gangs and American Urban Society*, University of California Press, Berkeley, CA.

Kratcoski, P.C. and Kratcoski, L.D. 1996. *Juvenile Delinquency*, 4th ed., Prentice Hall, Upper Saddle River, NJ.

MacKenzie, D.L. 1997. Criminal Justice and Crime Prevention, Ch 9, in Sherman, L.W., Gottfredson, D., MacKenzie, D., Eck, J., Reuter, P., and Bushway, S., *Preventing Crime: What Works, What Doesn't, and What's Promising*, Department of Criminology and Criminal Justice, University of Maryland, MD.

O'Brien, R.M. 1985. *Crime and Victimization Data*, Sage Publications, Beverly Hills, CA.

Puzzanchera, C.M., 2000. *Juvenile Court Placement of Adjudicated Youth, 1988–1997*, U.S. Department of Justice, OJJDP Fact Sheet, Washington DC.

Rennison, C.M. 2001. *Criminal Victimization 2000: Changes 1999– 2000 with Trends 1993–2000*, U.S. Department of Justice, Bureau of Justice Statistics, NCJ 187007, Washington DC.

Shaw, M. 2001. *Investing in Youth: Preventing Crime and Victimization*, International Centre for the Prevention of Crime, Montreal, Quebec, Canada.

Shaw, C.R. and McKay, H. 1942. *Juvenile Delinquency in Urban Areas*, University of Chicago Press, Chicago, IL.

Shelden, R.G., Tracy, S.K., and Brown, W.B. 1997. *Youth Gangs in American Society*, Wadsworth, Belmont, CA.

Sutherland, E.H. 1947. *Principles of Criminology*, 4th ed., Harper and Row, Publishers, New York.

Tittle, C.F. and Meier, R.F. 1990. Specifying the SES/Delinquency Relationship, *Criminology*, 28(2), 271–299.

U.S. Census Bureau, 2002. *U.S. Summary: Census 2000 Profile*, Department of Commerce, Washington, DC, U.S.

U.S. Department of Justice 2000. *Criminal Victimization in the U.S., 1998 Statistical Tables*, Bureau of Justice Statistics, NCJ 181585, Washington, DC.

UN Office for Drug Control and Crime Prevention 1999. *Global Report on Crime and Justice*, Oxford University Press, New York.

Williams, F.P. III and McShane, M.D. 1999. *Criminological Theory*, 3rd ed., Prentice Hall, Upper Saddle River, NJ.

See also **Juvenile Delinquency, Theories of**

Juvenile Justice: Corrections

The dilemma is one that we face every day: how should we handle children who commit crimes and are considered a danger to their communities, to their families, or to themselves? When justice demands action, what should we do with delinquent youth? To treat them as adults and to imprison them with adult inmates fails to account for the very fact of their youth, their potential malleability, and their relative immaturity. Yet, to do nothing makes light of the offense and the victim's suffering, and it leaves the youth free to reoffend. How then do we balance justice with the conflicting goals of crime control and rehabilitation when dealing with delinquent youth?

The juvenile justice system was founded on the ideal of *parens patriae,* the belief that the state—in the form of the juvenile court—should act as a "super-parent" to its troubled youth, treating them sternly but kindly, and always attempting to act in the best interests of the individual child. In the early stages of the juvenile justice system and juvenile corrections, delinquent children were treated and housed alongside neglected children and those who were dependent on the state for their basic needs. In the original juvenile court, judges had full discretion in deciding how to sentence each of the children who came before them. In deciding what to do with such children, judges tried to get the most complete picture they could of each child. They took into account not just the offense, but the circumstances of the child's life—his or her family, friends, education, and community. Judges then decided the placement and the length of the sentence based on how long they believed it would take to rehabilitate the youth. Because the court was created to act in the best interest of the child, children had few rights; in real ways, delinquent and dependent youth were subject to the judges' whims and idiosyncrasies.

Juvenile corrections really began when houses of refuge were established in large cities in the U.S. in the early 1800s. These institutions were built to house all children in need of the state's supervision. Shortly after the creation of houses of refuge, the first reformatories or training schools were built. Reformatories were basically the juvenile version of adult prisons. Delinquent children, along with abused, neglected, and abandoned children, were sent to reformatories in the hopes that the institutions could instill in them strong work ethics, staunch morals, and conforming values.

Reformatories were generally located in rural areas, far away from the problems and temptations of the cities. Most reformatories used a cottage system in which juveniles lived in fairly intimate settings; cottages generally housed 20–40 youths. Within the reformatories, youths were required to attend school and to labor within the institutions. It was not a perfect system, however. One common critique of reformatories was that they became "crime schools" as status offenders (who committed acts illegal for juveniles but not adults, such as truancy or underage smoking and drinking) and children who were neglected or abandoned were confined along with those who had committed serious crimes. In time, juvenile reformatories or training schools began to closely mirror their counterparts, the adult prisons. Juvenile residents or inmates of such institutions found themselves serving time amidst violence, victimization, and harsh punishment. Inmate subcultures developed to provide a familiar context for the offenders and a way to deal with the pains of imprisonment.

Juvenile corrections were significantly altered when the Juvenile Justice Delinquency and Prevention (JJDP) Act was passed in 1974. The JJDP Act offered financial incentives for states to decriminalize status offenses and to deinstitutionalize status offenders. Most states chose to follow the money and revamp their systems; from then on, secure juvenile institutions became the agency of last resort reserved for the most serious juvenile offenders. Many alternative programs were developed to provide supervision and care for less serious delinquent children.

These days, when children commit crimes, the state is responsible for sentencing juvenile offenders to programs that will hold them accountable for their crimes, provide for the safety of the community, and, hopefully, rehabilitate or "resocialize" the wayward youth. Similar to the medical doctor's creed of "first do no harm," a primary goal of juvenile corrections is to work in the best interest of the child and to place him or her in the least restrictive, least harmful setting.

Juvenile corrections is an umbrella term for the agencies charged with supervising juvenile offenders after they have been adjudicated delinquent, which is equivalent to an adult being convicted of a crime. Juvenile offenders may be treated in the community or they may be placed in secure facilities—in essence, they may get probation; they may be placed in a group home, halfway house, or foster care; or they may be sentenced to serve time in a secure facility such as a training school, a wilderness program, or a boot camp. Together, these agencies share responsibility for "correcting" or reforming delinquent children.

Many youths are sentenced to community-based corrections. Such treatment includes probation, counseling, community service, and any number of non-secure residential placements such as foster care, group homes, forestry camps, or boot camps. Probation is the most common disposition of juvenile court cases and it is generally reserved for less serious offenders—juveniles on probation are assigned to the supervision of an officer in the community and they are given a list of rules and conditions to live by. Probation is generally viewed as an alternative to institutionalization, but it is not a free ride. If offenders violate any of the terms of their probation, they can be immediately incarcerated in a detention center or a state training school. If, on the other hand, they finish their sentences without committing a new offense or violating the terms of their probation, juvenile offenders will remain free in the community and can avoid the negative impact of incarceration.

In the 1990s, probation practices in juvenile corrections drew criticism for being too lenient and for not effectively controlling the behavior of delinquent youth. New emphasis was then placed upon restitution, electronic monitoring, and shock incarceration programs. Probation frequently includes an element of restitution—a disposition in which juveniles are ordered to repay their victims or the community or both for the damage they caused. Juveniles who hold jobs can pay for their crimes monetarily; for others, work restitution or community service is a possibility. With electronic monitoring, juvenile offenders are fitted with a wrist or ankle cuff that tracks their position for the agency monitoring them. Authorities can then tell if the offender is within range of where he or she is supposed to be. Offenders on house arrest or placed on electronic monitoring may also have to call their probation officer at prearranged times during the day and night to check in and show that they are at their residences.

Probation may also be given in conjunction with shock incarceration treatments. Boot camps are generally one of the most popular forms of shock incarceration; such programs are often seen as an intermediate sanction for younger offenders and those who violated their probation. The idea is to shock juvenile offenders with a rigorous program of physical exercise and military ceremony and discipline. Youths are sentenced to from 30 to 120 days in boot camps and the hope is that the experience will deter them from committing further crimes, while instilling them with a

sense of self-pride in accomplishment, discipline, and responsibility. Another form of shock incarceration that enjoyed great popularity in the 1970s and 1980s were "Scared Straight" programs. In intense confrontation sessions, inmates painted a vivid picture of the horrors of life in prison, attempting by intimidation to make the juveniles think twice before committing crimes and possibly ending up in prison themselves. The popularity of such shock programs declined significantly after rigorous scientific studies found that scared straight seemed to do more harm than good, as youth who had gone through the program ended up more criminal than those who had not.

One of the pressing issues with shock incarceration programs and with juveniles returning to the community after serving their sentences in training schools is the lack of follow-up treatment. Some youth are allowed to finish their sentences in group homes or halfway houses. In these intermediate placements, they can ease back into daily life in the community while still under the close supervision of trained house parents and staff members. Not all juvenile offenders are able to make such a transition, however. Instead, many youths released from training schools are assigned to aftercare and reentry programs. Aftercare is generally the youth equivalent to parole. Juvenile offenders are assigned to the supervision of a parole or aftercare officer, and they are usually required to attend school, to hold jobs, and to participate in appropriate counseling. If they violate the terms of their parole or aftercare, they can be sent back to the institution for the remainder of their sentence.

These days, the trend is towards accountability and punishment rather than rehabilitation as the political climate has become severe for delinquent youth. States are spending large amounts of money to build more reform or training schools and to house increasing numbers of juvenile offenders in secure facilities. Juvenile inmates suffer many of the pains of imprisonment that adults do. They spend their days in strictly regimented routines consisting of school and educational programming; vocational training; work and chores within the institution; individual and group counseling; structured recreation and programs; group meals; and set times for waking up, taking care of their personal hygiene, and lights out. They have very little privacy and are effectively disconnected from the outside world except for the occasional visit or phone call from home.

In addition to state training schools, the privatization of juvenile corrections is also becoming more popular as companies see the potential profit in handling the country's problem children. Indeed, some argue that the U.S. system of juvenile corrections is a two-tiered system—a state-run system for poor minorities, and private facilities for children whose parents can afford alternative placements.

The U.S. is not alone in its struggle to care for, to hold accountable, and to rehabilitate its criminal youths. Other countries also strive to safeguard the well being of their youths and to treat juvenile offenders fairly and without prejudice. Nearly all industrialized nations have a wide range of facilities and institutions that house juvenile offenders. Like the U.S., other countries also have trouble with a disproportionate confinement of minority youths. In Canada, Native Indians are over-represented in the juvenile justice system; in Australia, Aboriginal children seem to be singled out for especially harsh treatment.

To look at the current trends in incarcerating juveniles, one might well wonder if and when we'll ever find acceptable alternatives to imprisoning our youth. Perhaps the best example of bucking trends and employing alternative strategies in juvenile corrections came in the early 1970s in Massachusetts. Under Jerome Miller's direction, the state of Massachusetts systematically closed down its reform schools and replaced them with a wide range of alternatives. Miller took proposals from the community to create alternative residential and nonresidential programs for reform school youths. He eventually contracted with over 175 different private programs. Formerly incarcerated youths were sent back to their families, sent to private boarding schools and universities, put in specialized foster care, and given access to counseling in their home communities. The key to the Massachusetts experiment was flexibility—youths were assigned to programs, but were able to request different placements and to be moved until they found the one that

worked best for them. In the end, recidivism rates stayed roughly the same after the closing of the reform schools. The Massachusetts experiment stands today as a reminder that incarcerating more juveniles in youth prisons is not the only choice when it comes to "correcting" our young offenders.

MICHELLE INDERBITZIN

References and Further Reading

Bartollas, C. and Miller, S.J. 2001. *Juvenile Justice in America, Third Edition*, Prentice Hall, Upper Saddle River, NJ.

Bortner, M.A. and Williams, L.M. 1997. *Youth in Prison: We the People of Unit Four*, Routledge, London.

Drowns, R.W. and Hess, K.M. 2000. *Juvenile Justice*, 3rd ed., Wadsworth/Thomson Learning, Belmont, CA.

Elrod, P. and Ryder, R.S. 1999. *Juvenile Justice: A Social, Historical, and Legal Perspective*, Aspen Publishers, Inc., Gaithersburg, MD.

Feld, B.C. 1999. *Bad Kids: Race and the Transformation of the Juvenile Court*, Oxford University Press, New York.

Feld, B.C., Ed. 1999. *Readings in Juvenile Justice Administration*, Oxford University Press, New York.

Finckenauer, J.O. and Gavin, P.W. 1999. *Scared Straight: The Panacea Phenomenon Revisited*, Waveland Press, Inc., IL.

Goffman, E. 1961. *Asylums*, Anchor Books, New York.

Miller, J. 1998. *Last One Over the Wall: The Massachusetts Experiment in Closing Reform Schools*, 2nd ed., Ohio State University Press, Columbus, OH.

Platt, A. 1977. *The Child Savers: The Invention of Delinquency*, 2nd ed., The University of Chicago Press, Chicago, IL.

Schwartz, I.M. and Barton, W.H. 1994. *Reforming Juvenile Detention: No More Hidden Closets*, Ohio State University Press, Columbus, OH.

See also **Boot Camps and Shock Incarceration; Community Service and Restitution Programs**

Juvenile Justice: Due Process

The Fifth and Fourteenth Amendments to the U.S. Constitution guarantee "due process of law" to "any person." Although these words are, arguably, among the most important in the Constitution, the Constitution itself does not specify what sorts of process are due; that job has been left to the courts. The Fifth and Fourteenth Amendments also make no distinctions according to age, but over a hundred years of American jurisprudence has made it clear that juveniles are due a different process than adults.

Juveniles haven't always had a separate system of justice. In England, children younger than 7 couldn't be tried for their crimes, because it was presumed that they were too young to understand what they were doing. Children between 7 and 14 could be tried, but only if it was proven that they had the mental capacity to comprehend the nature and consequences of their behaviors. Children age 14 and older were treated as adults. Any child who was tried for a crime was tried in the same courts as were adults, and was treated essentially the same. By the middle of the 16th century, there were special correctional institutions for poor or wayward youths (in England, these were called the Bridewells), but there was no special process for sending children there.

In the colonial era and for many years following the Revolutionary War, jurisdictions in America largely followed the British model of juvenile justice. The primary method of controlling children wasn't the courts, but rather the family: a father had nearly absolute control over his children and could punish disobedience with physical punishment, forced apprenticeship, expulsion from the family (that would mean a life of extreme poverty or even starvation for the miscreant), or even death. When the legal system did step in, minors were treated, by and large, like adults.

By the mid-19th century, conditions had changed drastically in the U.S. Immigration, urbanization, and industrialization were booming, and so were crime and delinquency. Families no longer could assert sufficient authority over their children, and those in power sought alternate methods of control. Youth correctional facilities were constructed; the first, The House of Refuge, opened in 1825 in New York City. But legal authority had to be found to send children to these facilities when their parents couldn't or wouldn't do it themselves. Such authority was found in the doctrine of *parens patriae*.

Parens patriae literally means "the state as parent." Under this doctrine, a court could step in and act in a child's best interests. Because houses of refuge were meant to help reform youths and set them on the path to righteousness, productiveness, and obedience to the law, sending wayward children to these places was often seen to be in their best interests.

In reality, however, the conditions in the houses of refuge were often terrible, and the children were frequently used as simply a source of cheap labor. Moreover, delinquency continued to increase, and members of the more privileged classes felt that juvenile crime presented a real threat. Calls for reform finally resulted in the creation of courts especially for juveniles. The first juvenile court was founded in 1899 in Chicago, and by the 1920s, all but two states had juvenile courts of their own.

Juvenile courts operated on the *parens patriae* principle. Rehabilitation, rather than punishment, was the goal. The process was informal: ideally, a juvenile court judge should sit down with the child and his family and determine the causes of his misbehavior, and, together, they would find a way to "save" that child. This model is very different from the adult model, which is considerably more formal, and in which the court focuses on guilt and punishment.

In the adult criminal justice system, the main purpose is to punish those who violate the laws. There may be some ancillary goals, such as rehabilitation and incapacitation, but punishment was the primary purpose a hundred years ago, and it remains so today. From a philosophical and moral point of view, it is entirely inappropriate to punish an innocent person; the extent to which we have adopted this view is demonstrated in the oft-repeated phrase that it is better to let ten guilty people go free than to punish a single innocent person. It is this belief coupled, perhaps, with a cultural mistrust of government that has led to the creation of a myriad of due process rights for the accused. These include the right to be found guilty beyond a reasonable doubt, the right to assistance of an attorney, the right to confront and cross-examine witnesses, the right against self-incrimination, the right to a jury, the right to appeal, and so on. All of these rights serve as shields from the mighty arm of the state.

In juvenile cases, however, the arm of the state was meant to be protective rather than punitive. Thus, it was believed, juveniles did not need those due process rights. In fact, it was argued, due process rights and the entire adversarial approach of the criminal justice system would actually interfere with helping these children. Therefore, youths in juvenile court were not afforded those rights. The juvenile justice system was to offer a trade-off: in exchange for their due process rights, children were to have their best interests looked after.

In theory, this might have made sense, but in practice, it never really worked. Juvenile courts were almost immediately overburdened, and the staff was undertrained. Many juvenile court judges had no formal training in either law or dealing with children, and many juvenile court workers were simply unpaid volunteers. Although a wide variety of treatment alternatives for youths was supposed to be available, it rarely was. As a result, children were often simply rushed through a sham proceeding, and were placed either back in the environment they'd come from or in state training schools that had improved little since the 19th century.

By the middle of the 20th century, criticism of the juvenile justice system was widespread. The first real legal change, however, did not occur until 1966, when the U.S. Supreme Court decided the case of *Kent v. U.S.* (383 U.S. 541, 1966). Sixteen-year-old Morris Kent was accused in Washington, DC, of committing rape. His mother hired an attorney for him, and despite the lawyer's claims that Kent needed psychiatric care, and that with such care he could be rehabilitated, the juvenile court judge transferred his case to adult court without a hearing. Presumably, the judge made this decision on the basis of the contents of Kent's social service and probation files, but the actual reasons are unknown, as the judge never stated them. Kent's attorney was also never allowed to see his files, so there was no way for him to know if they were accurate. When Kent's lawyer tried to appeal and also tried to file a *habeas corpus* petition (that claimed Kent's constitutional rights had been violated), the courts ruled that these proceedings were not available. Kent was eventually tried as an adult, and though the jury found him not guilty by reason of insanity on the rape charge, he was convicted of six related counts of breaking and entering, and sentenced to 30 to 90 years.

The Supreme Court reversed the decision, holding that the procedures followed by the juvenile court were invalid. The actual legal impact of the case was minimal, because the Court relied on District of Columbia statutory law, rather than on constitutional principles, for its decision. More important, however, was the Court's dicta: its nonbonding commentary on the state of the juvenile justice system. Justice Fortas wrote, "[T]he admonition to function in a 'parental' relationship is not an invitation to procedural arbitrariness." Furthermore, he wrote, in many juvenile courts, "There is evidence, in fact, that there may be grounds for concern that the child receives the worst of both worlds: that he gets neither the protections accorded to adults nor the solicitous care and regenerative treatment postulated for children." If *Kent* served as a portend for the future of due process in juvenile courts, its promise was fulfilled only a year later in the landmark case of *In re Gault* (387 U.S. 1, 1967).

Gerry Gault, 15 years old, was accused of making prank calls to a neighbor. He was taken into custody and held at a juvenile detention center. Two hearings were held before a juvenile court judge. During these hearings, no witnesses were sworn, the original complainant was not present, Gault was not represented by an attorney, and no record of the proceedings was kept. Gault and his parents were not allowed to see the referral report made by juvenile probation officers. At the end of the hearing, without explaining his reasons, the judge committed Gault to the state industrial school until he reached the age of 21. Had Gault been charged as an adult, the maximum penalty he would have faced was a $50 fine or two months in jail. Gault was not permitted to appeal the judge's decision.

Gault subsequently filed a writ of *habeas corpus* that eventually made its way to the U.S. Supreme Court. In its opinion, the Court traced the history of the American juvenile justice system. While the Court found that the original goals of the system may have been laudable, it also found that, in practice, the actual operation of the juvenile justice system was often far from just. The *quid pro quo* that the system promised youths—a denial of their due process rights in exchange for special individualized treatment—was often not delivered. Children were denied due process but often, as with Gerry Gault, received only a charade of a hearing. This was a significant deprivation, given the importance of due process. Justice Fortas wrote in *In re Gault*, "Due process of law is the primary and indispensable foundation of individual freedom. It is the basic and essential term in the social compact that defines the rights of the individual and delimits the powers that the state may exercise."

Furthermore, the Court felt, granting of due process rights would not necessarily preclude the juvenile court from reaching its goals. In fact, it was arguable that providing the appearance of fairness would actually result in increased rehabilitation of young offenders; an unfair system would merely result in resentment and, perhaps, further defiance of authority.

It was disingenuous of the state to argue that Gault was not entitled to due process rights because the juvenile court proceedings were civil, rather than criminal, the Court concluded. Gault was facing several years of being locked up in a secure facility, and to call that facility a state industrial school rather than a prison made little difference.

Justice Fortas concluded, "The condition of being a boy does not justify a kangaroo court." Accordingly, the Court ordered that juveniles who were facing possible incarceration be provided with several important due process rights: adequate notice of the charges, representation by an attorney, privilege against self-incrimination, confrontation and cross-examination of witnesses, a transcript of the proceedings, and the right to appeal.

There was not complete agreement on these matters among the members of the Court. Justice Harlan felt that some procedural protections were due, but also felt that the Court went too far in granting the rights against self-incrimination and for confrontation and cross-examination. And Justice Stewart, while acknowledging that the juvenile justice system had serious problems, felt that the actions of the majority would only make those problems worse.

The decision in *Gault* had a profound and lasting influence on the operation of juvenile courts. However, it also left several questions unanswered. Were juveniles to be entitled to other rights as well? If full due process protections were granted juveniles, would the distinction between juvenile and adult courts become meaningless? The Court responded to these issues in the several years following *Gault*.

In 1970, the Supreme Court decided *In re Winship* (397 U.S. 358, 1970). Samuel Winship, who was 12, was accused of stealing $112 from a woman's locker. A juvenile court judge found him delinquent and committed him to a reformatory, perhaps until his 18th birthday. The judge admitted that, although the evidence did not prove Winship's guilt beyond a reasonable doubt, it did prove it by a preponderance of the evidence, which was all that was required under state law in juvenile cases.

Interestingly, prior to this case the Supreme Court had never explicitly held that the standard of proof in criminal cases must be proof beyond a reasonable doubt. Citing the importance of reducing the risk of convicting the innocent, the Court in *Winship* did hold that this standard was to apply in criminal cases. Furthermore, the Court held, the same rationale applies in juvenile cases as well, and so the standard in juvenile cases must also be proof beyond a reasonable doubt. As in *Gault*, the Court asserted that this requirement would not interfere with the juvenile justice system's goals. As Justice Harlan wrote in his concurring opinion, "Although there are no doubt costs to society (and possibly even to the youth himself) in letting a guilty youth go free, I think here, as in a criminal case, it is far worse to declare an innocent youth a delinquent."

One additional due process right was accorded juveniles in 1975, in *Breed v. Jones* (421 U.S. 519, 1975). Seventeen-year-old Gary Jones was accused in a California juvenile court of armed robbery; after an adjudication hearing (the juvenile court version of a trial) he was adjudicated delinquent (in effect, he was found guilty). Prior to a dispositional hearing, however, another hearing was held in which the juvenile court judge found that Jones was not amenable to treatment within the juvenile justice system, and ordered that he be prosecuted as an adult. After a trial in adult criminal court, he was found guilty of the armed robbery.

Jones claimed that to try him first in juvenile court and then in adult court for the same crime violated the protection against double jeopardy. The state argued that it did not, as juvenile court proceedings are civil rather than criminal, and the double jeopardy clause applies only to criminal proceedings. A unanimous Supreme Court sided with Jones. Justice Burger wrote, "[I]n terms of potential consequences, there is little to distinguish an adjudicatory hearing such as was held in this case from a traditional criminal prosecution." Once again, the Court wrote, this due process requirement would not cripple the juvenile justice system: to avoid double jeopardy problems, a hearing as to a minor's fitness for the juvenile system could simply be held before his adjudicatory hearing.

Taken as a whole, the four cases—*Kent*, *Gault*, *Winship*, and *Jones*—clearly demonstrate the Supreme Court's commitment toward providing substantial due process protections to juveniles. They also demonstrate the Court's skepticism about whether the juvenile justice system is achieving its intended goals in any significant way. However, the Court has not been willing to provide juveniles all the protections that adults enjoy, perhaps out of the fear that to do so would erase any meaningful distinctions between the two systems.

In *McKeiver v. Pennsylvania* (403 U.S. 528, 1971), in 1971, the Court decided that fundamental fairness did not require jury trials for juveniles. To require a jury, the majority felt, would be to turn the juvenile court into a fully adversary process, thus destroying whatever hope there was of the system achieving its rehabilitative goals. The Court remained deeply dubious about the success of the system, but it was unwilling to give up on it.

In two additional cases, the Court also refused to give juveniles certain due process rights. In *Schall v. Martin* (467 U.S. 253, 1984), the Court held that it was constitutional to hold accused juveniles in preventative detention. That is, a juvenile accused of a crime could be kept incarcerated while he was waiting his adjudicatory hearing if the court found that there was a risk he might commit additional crimes in the meantime. And in *Fare v. Michael C.* (442 U.S. 707, 1979), the Court held that no special rules applied to the interrogation of juveniles. Therefore, there was nothing unconstitutional about interrogating a minor outside the presence of his parents or a lawyer, so long as he had been informed of his Miranda rights.

Although most of the case law on juveniles' due process rights was decided some years ago, that does not mean that all questions on this issue have been answered. In fact, conditions in more recent years have raised new questions. Perhaps the most substantial of these is the continuing viability of the juvenile justice system itself. Most commentators see the system as a failure, and have called for either its abolishment or, at the very least, a substantial overhaul. Legislatures have turned increasingly to widening the circumstances under which juveniles can be tried as adults, making juvenile dispositions more punitive and eliminating some of the special protections that juveniles have enjoyed, such as confidentiality. The place of due process rights within this scheme is unclear.

An example of a specific issue that has arisen concerns jury trials. In some states, such as California, juvenile court adjudications can count as the first two of a person's "three strikes." Thus, a person with two juvenile adjudications for violent offenses need commit only one (violent or nonviolent) adult offense to qualify for drastically increased penalties.

Some have argued that if juvenile adjudications are to be counted as "strikes," then juveniles ought to be accorded juries in those cases. As of yet, most courts have not been convinced. However, it does seem inevitable that other important due process questions will need to be addressed in the near future.

PHYLLIS B. GERSTENFELD

References and Further Reading

Ayers, W. 1997. *A Kind and Just Parent: The Children of Juvenile Court*, Beacon Press, Boston, MA.

Melton, G. 1989. Taking Gault Seriously: Toward a New Juvenile Court, *Nebraska Law Review*, 68.

Schwartz, I. 1989. *Injustice for Juveniles: Rethinking the Best Interests of the Child*, Lexington Books, Lanham, MD.

See also **Juvenile Justice: The Courts**

Juvenile Justice: History and Philosophy

In most states, juvenile justice is the center of a whirlwind of conflicting policies and ideals. The juvenile court is still a child-oriented, rehabilitative institution in a society that is more and more punitive. The court itself is usually guided by *parens patriae*, or the notion that governments must serve as parents of last resort. This doctrine puts redeeming delinquents as its first priority. The court often works with a system of juvenile facilities that are oriented mainly to custodial routine, and it utilizes a whole web of rehabilitative groups (group homes, private treatment programs, wilderness programs) in the community that are trying to help wayward juveniles. The community itself—the schools, the police, community leaders, churches, business groups—is often progressive and working earnestly to help children move beyond delinquency, but it is also conservative by endorsing punishment to control misbehavior. Each purpose gains the upper hand from time to time, and communities as well as many states follow cycles in dealing with delinquents—selecting a punitive policy at first, but when excesses dictate a change, moving to a redemptive policy. Some communities, however, rarely alternate their stance, mainly following a conservative policy vis-à-vis delinquency and crime.

The picture is further complicated by the fact that a child may obviously need help, but delinquency is not the problem. In the past many children came to the court who refused to obey their parents or teachers. They were incorrigible. *Parens patriae* permitted the court to take custody of such children if necessary, even if the child had committed no crime. But the court itself was ill equipped to provide help, and it routinely began sending "status offenders" to the same facilities that accepted delinquents. Since many status offenders were head-strong and unruly, some families didn't want them back, and many girls spent long periods in institutions waiting for someone to accept them. In 1947–1950 several criminologists discovered that female status offenders usually spent longer periods in custody than all but the most serious delinquents. This obvious injustice led many states to eliminate custody for status offenders. As a result some came to believe that *parens patriae* was unconstitutional, but that is incorrect. In Illinois as elsewhere *parens patriae* is still in force in the juvenile court, but most status offenders are handled today in social agencies as dependent or neglected children. The move clarified the juvenile court's mission, but it did not solve the problems of status offenders.

Children who get into trouble as delinquents come in many forms. Some are simply testing the waters. What is it like to shoplift, to break into a store, or to bully another juvenile? When their parents step in punitively, they accept restrictions willingly and avoid further delinquency. The court only spurs the family to closer control. But some are very troubled children, who are avoided, feared, and even mocked by parents, teachers, and other juveniles. In their own way these children need help. Other delinquents feel good about themselves, their esteem, and wish to be left alone with their antisocial friends. They have no obvious problems, but they indulge in violence against schools, minorities, and rival groups. Their problem is mainly their peers and the invitation they embody to vandalism and mayhem. Had their families lived in a different neighborhood, they probably would have had different friends and behaved differently.

All of these children break the law, but all are different. They need different responses from the court to become constructive adults, and the wise judge and probation officer must recognize both the source of their troubles and the kind of response needed to correct them. The juvenile court and the community cannot afford to treat all kids alike, but can they provide the kind of help that each needs? Most often the court wisely leaves the matter up to the youngster and his family (about 65% are boys). But with serious cases the court may need a more formal, longer-term approach, and the judge must be familiar with alternatives available both in the community and the state as a whole. Until the 1940s the juvenile court attempted to provide for the juveniles' needs by itself, but that required a psychological expertise far beyond the court's capability, and communities stepped in to organize programs for troubled juveniles—alternative schools, group and individual therapy, drug or alcohol programs, and group homes—and the state provided juvenile institutions.

The Beginning of Juvenile Justice

The first juvenile institutions were established in the 1820s as houses of refuge or reform in New York, Boston, and Philadelphia. They were small and organized benevolently along religious lines. But before long all of them had evolved into custodial institutions—shedding their visionary leaders and becoming routine, one-size-fits-all institutions. In the 1850s Boston's House of Reform was phased out in favor of a secular, state-run institution, but the rest continued until the mid-1930s. The transformation of these houses of refuge into stern, punitive institutions took about 15 years and is often seen as a failure of vision, i.e., nothing works, but it may also have been simply a result of growth. As houses of refuge took in more and more children, they became very large, often with more than 150 kids. Keeping a kindly staff in a sea of unruly children is very difficult. Only disciplinarians could manage these institutions effectively and keep the children under control. Humanitarians were forced out.

Some may ask, what's wrong with a little disorder? Persistent disorder (runaways, fights, riots, suicides) is unacceptable to most if not all immediate communities. To gain local support the boys must be under control, and without discipline among them, the staff often becomes deeply demoralized. But the answer is not simply firm discipline, because it evokes fear, suspicion, and hatred. The answer is to keep juvenile facilities small with a benevolent staff that interacts easily with young people. Familiarity between staff and children fosters an informal discipline on both sides that thins out and becomes ineffective when the institution involves more than 90–100 children.

Juvenile institutions preceded the juvenile courts by about 75 years. In the early 19th century serious delinquents were also dealt with in the criminal courts and in penal institutions along with serious adult criminals (clearly a very poor policy). But when large juvenile institutions became available during the antebellum period, serious delinquents were sent there along with many minor delinquents from the civil courts. Large, disciplinary training schools were well established in most states, long before the juvenile court itself was inaugurated. Moreover, these institutions were organized and governed at the state level, whereas juvenile courts were a regional or county institution. Individual courts were powerless to shape the juvenile training schools. Reform usually depended on an initiative by a governor who could appoint the kinds of leaders needed in custodial institutions to carry out desired reforms. But even here the difficulties were daunting.

The first state juvenile institution was established in Massachusetts in 1847, and in 25 years most of the populous states and large cities in the Midwest and North had similar juvenile institutions. Nearly all were large, punitive, and criminogenic and were very effective at turning problem-plagued juveniles into bitter, antisocial adolescents and young adults. Equally important their staffs became a strong base of support in the state for discipline and punishment in juvenile justice. Their approach to delinquency urged a traditional philosophy, and it seemed to work with some—the more mild delinquents—who wanted nothing further to do with juvenile institutions. But it probably aggravated the delinquency of many troubled kids who could not contain their destructiveness. These institutions immersed them in very hostile environments wherein their only hope was an alliance with a group of juveniles who were usually very antisocial. The record of these early institutions was nothing to be proud of.

Between 1856 and 1861, 250 girls were admitted to the Lancaster School for Girls in Massachusetts (see Brenzel, 1983). Ten years after returning to the community 51.1% had married and made a good adjustment; 19.6% were leading a lawful but dissolute life; and 13.0% were "grossly antisocial." The rest were missing or dead. Later the Gluecks (1943) gathered follow-up data on 418 boys and girls discharged from Massachusetts juvenile institutions in 1921–22. They found that 38.6% were nearly crime free after 15 years. Another 32.9% were serious offenders, and 29.8 were minor offenders—that is, only about 39% had reformed. By 1968, on the eve of major reforms, the record of Massachusetts' juvenile institutions was slightly better—five years after release 53% had avoided serious crime (Coates et al., 1976). From about 40% to 55% of the children in Massachusetts juvenile institutions made good adjustments after release from traditional juvenile institutions. Studies in Japan and Germany show roughly similar results with their juvenile institutions.

The Juvenile Court

When a *parens patriae* juvenile court finally made its appearance in this country, it encountered a formidable adversary in the very system, juvenile corrections, with which it needed to work. In most states both coexisted in an uneasy alliance. By the turn of the century political factions had already formed regarding crime and punishment, and 30–40 year cycles began to take shape during the 1880s. Reformatories for youthful offenders focused on improving work skills, indeterminate sentences gave them added authority, and the dominant philosophy became rehabilitative. Today we are again in a phase of punishment and discipline, and critics call for the abolition of the juvenile court. They point out that the juvenile court cannot make effective therapy available as its parens *patriae* credo demands. The ineffectiveness of most treatment programs both in institutions and in the community is well established, and their ability to reduce recidivism is often slight. Some have no positive effect at all. Even more basically however, under *parens patriae* the court regularly denies equitable justice and due process to juveniles. Unacceptable disparities appear between males and females, and blacks and whites. Critics claim it would be better to have strict due process, if that's all we can reasonably expect of a *parens patriae* court. But the critics ignore several facts.

The small treatment effects and slight reductions in recidivism shown in careful meta-analytic studies, when computed for large numbers of delinquents translate into sizable savings of misery and funds. About 1.8 million juveniles answer charges annually in America's juvenile courts, and about half of them are there for at least the second time. A 5% reduction in recidivism could mean 45,000 fewer delinquents in court every year. Can we afford to reject treatment in the face of such numbers?

Moreover, rehabilitation can work even in the formal justice system. In Illinois a graduated system of treatment programs for juveniles has now been operating for more than 30 years. In the 1970s it achieved truly surprising reductions in posttreatment arrests (see Murray and Cox, 1979), and after Massachusetts reformed its antiquated juvenile system in 1972–1975, it also achieved remarkable results. By 1986 juveniles discharged from juvenile justice in Massachusetts were being arraigned for serious crimes at only half their earlier rate before entering the system. In 1972, i.e., before reform was well under way, dischargees from juvenile institutions made up 35% of the adult correctional population, but by 1985 this figure had declined to 15%, and recidivism among dischargees as measured by rearrests dropped from 74% in 1974 to 5% in 1985. When a systematic effort to redeem juveniles is made within the juvenile justice system, considerable success is possible. Too often we accept failure in juvenile justice as normal, but in Massachusetts and now elsewhere too (Pennsylvania, Hawaii, and Missouri) intensive efforts are being made to redeem serious delinquents, and the results though still unfolding are encouraging.

Critics of the juvenile court have also ignored the fact that the criminal court, county jail, and the adult correctional system could hardly prove a useful experience for most juveniles. They review the juvenile court's failures, but fail to consider those of the adult system. Minor offenders are plea bargained in nonadversarial proceedings in criminal court. And consider that the prisons are not wholesome places for adults let alone juveniles. Indeed juvenile justice was designed in the 19th century to eliminate this very situation. Too many children were finding their way into adult institutions.

Sentencing teenagers according to the criminal law would no doubt result in institutions designed solely for juveniles, but such institutions would contain several hundred children who would stay in them for years. And they would be administered by adult correctional officials with all the "tender mercies" that felons receive in departments of correction. It's hard to imagine any good coming from such an arrangement. Thus far no state governor has accepted the critics' argument and abolished the juvenile court, and only Washington state has introduced a fully due process juvenile court.

Juvenile justice also works closely with the community—especially schools and families, both of which enjoy special protections based on substantial constitutional doctrine. Families and schools carry out near-sacred responsibilities that are closely monitored by the courts to ensure equitable treatment (see *Brown v. Board of Education*, 347 US 483, 1954), and the family socializes children, a function that is protected by law and the Supreme Court (see *Tinker v. Des Moines School District*, 393 US 503, 1969, and *Wisconsin v. Yoder*, 406 US 205, 1972).

The juvenile court can counsel schools and guide parents, but it cannot coerce them as long as they remain lawful. Families, schools, and the juvenile court must use persuasion with one another, but the responsibility here lies mainly with the court. The court must be sensitive to the proper functions of the school and the family, while encouraging flexibility and reforms. Juvenile justice must balance a wide range of conflicting publics, philosophies, and institutional systems, as it pursues its *parens patriae* mission in the community and the state.

A Hub, Spokes, and Wheel

One way of getting a grip on juvenile justice is to view the juvenile court and its *parens patriae* mission as the hub of a great wheel. The spokes are the various philosophies and the constituencies it serves—the redemptive model, the justice model, federal justice agencies, teenagers, families, schools, community programs, and penal or treatment facilities. Thus, juvenile justice is the wheel, the juvenile court is its hub, and the philosophies and constituencies of juvenile justice are its spokes. The spokes should be closely aligned with one another and to the hub, but they are clearly not in at least six fundamental ways, making for a very uneven ride for wayward youngsters through juveniles justice.

Six Vexing Problems

First, the philosophies that guide practitioners directly contradict one another. The court's *parens patriae* doctrine means that it works with boys and girls who need distinctive programs and methods specifically tailored to their situation. They are not overtly punished, but in avoiding a punitive focus, the court falls into conflict with the just deserts philosophy of the criminal courts in which each offense must be punished in proportion to the crime. If the juvenile court provides a program tailored to each child, it has difficulty in fulfilling justice. We must nonetheless find a way to do both without undermining either, if we truly want to control juvenile delinquency. Our nation will not abandon due process and equity in the name of helping juveniles—especially if the result is not clearly benefiting juveniles. If an effective treatment-oriented system is to endure, conservatives and progressives must both be satisfied that it respects their ideals and goals.

The Supreme Court attempted to help by issuing several rulings in the 1960s and 70s that codified the due process responsibilities of the juvenile court, while also supporting its *parens patriae* mission. In 1966 the Supreme Court ruled in *Kent v. U.S.*, 383 US 541, 1966) that juvenile waiver hearings had to be adversarial, which is, that the child's attorney must be allowed to present arguments regarding both the grounds for and the value of waiver to a criminal court. Previously judges could waive a child's case to the criminal court without any input from the defendant or his attorney. *In re Gault* (387 US 1, 1967) held that juvenile hearings that could result in confinement must

be based upon a written statement of charges, the right to an attorney, the right to cross-examine witnesses, and the right to remain silent. In this decision Judge Abe Fortas explained that such rights were routinely available to adults in the criminal court but that they need not hamper the juvenile court's *parens patriae* mission. Indeed, he expected they would strengthen it. Three years later the Supreme Court ruled (*In re Winship*, 397 US 358, 1970) that the standard of proof in the criminal courts (guilt beyond a reasonable doubt) was also required in the juvenile court when a juvenile faced confinement, but in *McKeiver v. Pennsylvania* (403 US 528, 545, 1971) the Supreme Court held that a juvenile in juvenile court did not have the *right* to a jury trial. The decision did not forbid jury trials, but it held that a jury trial would encourage a full adversarial process in the juvenile court and thereby hamper its *parens patriae* mission. A jury trial was not essential to a just decision in the juvenile court. Finally, in *Turman v. Morales* (383 F. Supp. 53, 120 E.D. Tex., 1974) the Supreme Court ruled that a juvenile court that sent a child to confinement with the promise that he or she would receive helpful treatment must ensure that the treatment is in fact provided. Clearly the Supreme Court was dismayed at the swashbuckling style of some juvenile courts and was determined to tighten up their adjudicatory hearing. At the same time it was not ready to abandon the court's *parens patriae* mission during its dispositional hearing. Some have found the Supreme Court's decisions inconsistent, but in fact these decisions simply confirm the dual mission of the court—it must seek justice in its adjudicatory phase, and it must rehabilitate juveniles in its dispositional phase. Most courts and judges have several important goals in dealing with defendants, and the Supreme Court was simply reminding juvenile judges that they were no exception.

Second, broad discretion in juvenile justice and especially in the juvenile court opens the door to conflict with the individual families and schools. Juvenile justice must work closely and diplomatically with each as it copes with delinquency. The family and school are fundamentally important social institutions, and the court must not undermine their effectiveness as each of them attempts to cope with troubled teenagers. Delinquents pose heart-wrenching problems for families and schools, and both welcome balanced, responsible *advice* from justice officials. But delinquents also arouse powerful emotions in families and schools, and probation officers in particular must tread lightly lest raw emotions take over.

Third, as we have seen, juvenile custodial institutions have long been a problem in juvenile justice. They must control a herd of very difficult children, and they have developed a variety of custodial measures over the years that do just that. These same methods, however, often make little provision for rehabilitation. We must find ways of reorganizing custodial rules and methods so that children and staff feel less antagonism toward one another. Size is certainly a factor and so is the quality of staff recruited to such institutions. Custodial facilities must become rehabilitative centers instead of centers for punishment, violence, and crime. The time spent by delinquents in custody must be used productively so that recidivism is minimized. To do otherwise is to squander a golden opportunity to confront crime at the beginning.

Fourth, even if custodial institutions become instruments of rehabilitation, juveniles must still return to their community where stressful families, gangs, reckless peers, rigorous or boring schools, and hopelessness abound. The courts may lift them for a while out of these very difficult situations for rehabilitative purposes, but often it returns them to these same conditions with only stern warnings to avoid contact with criminogenic surroundings and other delinquents. Success in redeeming juvenile delinquents depends fundamentally on the ability of juvenile justice to ease its most antisocial youngsters from rehabilitative facilities into constructive communities that encourage prosocial behavior. As difficult as this may seem, we are beginning to see how it can be done.

These programs must offer juveniles who cannot return to their families a comfortable, pleasant place to live that provides warm support, sensible discipline, mature guidance, and attractive recreational opportunities, that is, the same kind of supportive environment that most adolescents enjoy with their own parents. In the absence of such placements reformed children will only sink back into criminal groups. Foster care can provide them advantages, but without such care, all bets are off. Furthermore, effective aftercare is most important to those youngsters who are extreme—more violent, more experienced, and more delinquent. These children are the core of the problem. Since they have few noncriminal opportunities, the community must step in to supply them with the qualities that most adolescents enjoy in their families. Sound aftercare programs have never been a priority in the justice system, but without such programs, all that is worthwhile before release is reversed as if it had never happened. Juvenile parolees need the same kind of family support that most nondelinquents see as normal. They also need solid schools where their teachers and peers offer constructive, essential knowledge, and they need beneficent employers who are willing to train them patiently in productive tasks. These needs are normally provided in the family, and it may be utopian to ask juvenile justice to offer them to serious juvenile delinquents.

But the fact remains that ignoring them only encourages more serious crime. Without effective aftercare programs juvenile justice is nearly helpless to reform serious delinquents.

Fifth, each juvenile court as a local court usually has jurisdiction over only a small region of the state, and as the hub it must lead juvenile justice in its community toward treatment and justice. Yet its main spokes include national institutes in the U.S. Department of Justice; statewide public agencies such as juvenile corrections and social welfare; private agencies such as psychiatric hospitals, wilderness-adventure programs, and community centers; and local departments such as the police and public health. Each is administered by a distinctive staff and adheres to distinctive ideals and goals. It is very difficult for the juvenile court to assert decisive influence over all of these. In most cases it can offer only gentle persuasion.

A statewide office is needed that can gather all the political and social agencies that constitute juvenile justice and provide them with leadership on behalf of delinquency control. It could also muster all branches of juvenile justice—the courts, probation, juvenile institutions, and community programs—in developing a clear empirical picture of juvenile justice in the state, much as the Criminal Justice Information Authority does in Illinois, and the Office of Juvenile Justice and Delinquency Prevention in Washington, DC, and the National Center for Juvenile Justice in Pittsburgh do for the federal government. Such an office could help fill the leadership void while fending off temporary, spiteful moods that sweep the justice system from time to time. Such an office could anticipate inquiries and criticism from the political arena and answer them with solid facts and information regarding juvenile justice. It would be invaluable to legislators and the interested public. In some states a Department of Youth Services performs such a function, and they play a pivotal role in charting the course of juvenile justice in their state.

But in most states the juvenile justice system is a loosely coupled system that has great difficulty in moving as a unit. It is more like an unruly mob than a team. A mob has weak consensus and goals, and there is little agreement about which goals to pursue or how to cope with changing circumstances. Mobs are impulsive and moody. They are irrational, one-sided, and self-defeating. An agency that could coordinate the broad range of philosophies, groups, facilities, and publics involved in juvenile justice is badly needed to bring order and balance to the several constituencies that make up juvenile justice.

Such an initiative is well underway in Massachusetts, where the Department of Youth Services has assumed statewide responsibility for rehabilitating delinquents, and Missouri and Hawaii are moving in this direction too. But these states still lack an information authority that can provide a close, objective view of juvenile justice in the state. A state's justice authority need not be aligned with its information authority but at the very least they should work hand in hand.

Sixth, delinquency has changed considerably in the last century—as the whole nation has—and juvenile justice must adapt to these changes. Before World War I delinquents were rebellious and predatory. They exploited their immediate neighborhoods, and they formed cliques, instead of gangs. They were troublesome but on the whole not dangerous. Crime by young adults was often bloody and fearsome, but juveniles were less violent. After World War II however, young people became more iconoclastic and suspicious of adults in Europe as well as in America. The Rolling Stones in Britain and Bob Dylan in this country reflected some of these values, and the same kind of shift had a remarkable impact in Britain on the rehabilitation of delinquents.

Around the turn of the century Great Britain established its Borstals—a system of some 21 small institutions scattered around Britain that provided a variety of educational and vocational programs for troubled adolescents and young adults. By all accounts they were highly effective in molding the bulk of their young people into constructive British citizens, but after World War II their effectiveness dwindled until the Borstals were finally abolished in the early 1980s.

Massachusetts also adapted to changing conditions in the mid-1970s but in a different way. Jerome Miller, the new director of DYS, stirred up a fire-storm as he replaced the old training schools with community-based programs and a single, small custodial facility. Punitive methods were not working in the training schools and were replaced with more rehabilitative methods geared to the variegated needs of different delinquents. Miller was in tune with criminological thinking but not with conservatives in criminal justice. To be effective however, his kind of broad revolution requires several preliminary steps.

The public as a whole and juvenile justice in particular must be alert to fundamental changes in adolescents' values and ideals. Such changes must be documented, and their implications for delinquency spelled out. Moreover, the condition of the traditional system needs to be examined honestly so that the public can determine if change is needed. Open debate on both old and new approaches should be encouraged so that plans can take both sides into account. Ultimately Massachusetts evolved a plan that places rehabilitation at the center of juvenile justice but that also acknowledges its responsibility for controlling serious delinquency.

Miller's vision of the path ahead was clear, but his mistake was to proceed roughshod without demonstrating the broad need for change. Not only did his reforms threaten the jobs of many people, they also addressed serious delinquency with treatment and tolerance. He polarized the issues and provoked wide-spread anger and resistance. In Missouri things unfolded more peacefully, perhaps because the Missouri people learned from events in Massachusetts.

Conclusion

Few governmental agencies ever solve all of these six most vexing problems, but ignoring them means that juvenile justice must endure challenges dictated neither by the shifting nature of delinquency nor by the failings of juvenile justice but by external political forces. In the absence of sound information on the history of juvenile justice, and in its whirlwind of conflicting constituents, it will be buffeted by politics, and instead of steering a steady course, it will be forced into an aimless tracking of irrelevant ideologies and short-sighted sentiments.

THEODORE N. FERDINAND

References and Further Reading

Andrews, D.A. and Bonta, J. 1998. *The Psychology of Criminal Conduct*, Anderson Publishing Co., Cincinnati, OH.

Bernard, T.J. 1992. *The Cycle of Juvenile Justice*, Oxford University Press, New York.

Brenzel, B.M. 1983. *Daughters of the State*, MIT Press, Cambridge, MA.

Coates, R.B., Miller, A.D., and Ohlin, L. 1976. *Diversity in a Youth Correctional System*, Ballinger Publishing, Cambridge, MA.

Dawley, D. 1973. *A Nation of Lords*, Anchor Books, Garden City, NY.

Feld, B.C. 1999. *Bad Kids: Race and the Transformation of the Juvenile Court*, Oxford University Press, New York.

Ferdinand, T.N., History Overtakes the Juvenile Justice System, *Crime & Delinquency*, 37(2), 204–224.

Garlock, P.D., 'Wayward' Children and the Law, 1820–1900: The Genesis of the Status Offense Jurisdiction of the Juvenile Court, *Georgia Law Review*, 13(2), 341–447.

Glueck, S. and Glueck, E. 1943. *Criminal Careers in Retrospect*, The Commonwealth Fund, New York.

Gold, M., and Osgood, D.W. 1992. *Personality and Peer Influence in Juvenile Corrections*, Greenwood Press, Westport, CT.

Hirsch, A.V. 1985. *Past or Future Crimes*, Rutgers University Press, New Brunswick, NJ.

Krisberg, B., Austin, J., and Steele, P.A. 1989. *Unlocking Juvenile Corrections: Evaluating the Massachusetts Department of Youth Services*, The National Council of Crime and Delinquency, San Francisco, CA.

Mennel, R.M. 1973. *Thorns & Thistles*, University Press of New England, Hanover, New Hampshire.

Miller, J. 1991. *Last One Over the Wall*, Ohio State University Press, Columbus, OH.

Murray, C.A. and Cox, L.A. 1979. *Beyond Probation*, Sage Publications, Beverly Hills, CA.

Palmer, T. 1994. Issues in Growth-Centered Intervention with Serious Juvenile Offenders, *The Legal Studies Forum XVIII*, 3, 263–298.

Pisciotta, A.W., Treatment on Trial: The Rhetoric and Reality of the New York House of Refuge, 1857–1935, *American Journal of Legal History*, 29, 151–181.

Rosenheim, M.K., Ed. 1974. *Pursuing Justice for the Child*, The University of Chicago Press, Chicago, IL.

Sutton, J.R. 1988. *Stubborn Children*, California, University of California Press, Berkeley, CA.

See also **Juvenile Justice: The Courts; Juvenile Justice: Due Process**

Juvenile Justice: The Courts

Juvenile justice is not simply a matter for the specialized juvenile courts; it concerns the whole criminal justice system. Nevertheless, the primary responsibility for dispensing juvenile justice rests with the juvenile courts and the associated agencies within the juvenile justice system. We will examine the forces that lead to the creation of the juvenile court in the U.S., the elements that defined the first juvenile courts, age jurisdiction considerations, the subject matter of the cases with which they must deal, and the types of hearings they conduct. We will conclude with a consideration of the juvenile courts' due process revolution beginning in the 1960s and the directions in which the juvenile courts seem to be headed.

Creation of the Juvenile Court

The juvenile court is a uniquely American legal innovation. However, today we find juvenile courts in operation in a variety of countries around the world. Several factors lead to the creation of the first juvenile court, and the establishment of that court cannot be fully understood without considering the context in which it was originated.

During the mid-19th century a number of forces profoundly affected the social fabric of the U.S. During this time period the effects of the Industrial Revolution began to be felt as the U.S. moved from a rural, agrarian society to one based more on manufacturing and industrial development. The Civil War hastened the Industrial Revolution, and it took many young and old men from different parts of the country and placed them into a great conflict. Additionally, before and after the Civil War the great tides of immigration also were sweeping the U.S. All of these factors taken together changed the fundamental nature and character of cities, especially those along the East Coast.

The chaos brought about by movement into the cities, large numbers of European immigrants, and the tendency for both mothers and fathers to work in factories altered family structures and child-rearing practices. Couples that moved to the cities for factory work no longer had daily contacts with their extended families. Grandparents and aunts and uncles no longer were available to assist with child-rearing and providing additional supervision for youngsters growing up. Children who moved to the cities no longer had their freedom constrained by farm chores. This time period also predated the implementation of mandatory school attendance laws. The result was that many children roamed the streets and some of them got into trouble.

To respond to these "wayward" children wealthy philanthropists, religious and benevolent societies, and organizations composed of middle class, Protestant women emerged as the "child saving" movement and began to express their concerns over child welfare in the U.S. As a result, during the last decade of the 19th century four factors converged to bring about a separate juvenile justice system. First, throughout many parts of the country the Progressive Movement began to emerge. The Progressives were concerned about a just society, safe streets, pure foods, and good government. Second, an outgrowth of the Progressive Movement was the creation of a social welfare system, and the emergence of social work as a profession. Women such as Jane Addams and Julia Lawthrop in cities like Chicago had a particular impact in this regard. Third, beginning with Colorado, and soon spreading to other states, was the movement to create mandatory school attendance laws. One of the chief aims of this legislation, aside from the obvious educational intent, was to use the force of law to keep children from roaming loose on the streets. Finally, in 1899 the Illinois legislature passed a statute creating the nation's first juvenile court in Cook County. This court combined elements of the law with those of the nation's emerging social welfare philosophy.

The Nature of the Original Juvenile Courts

There are some elements of the nation's juvenile justice system that seem to have been lost in the mists of time, and some of these are cause for dispute among juvenile justice historians. However, three principal characteristics of the first juvenile courts are almost universally agreed on. These first courts, unlike their adult criminal court counterparts, were to hold confidential hearings. These hearings were to be informal, and they were to be nonadversarial. Each of these elements needs to be considered.

First, juvenile hearings were to be confidential. This meant that outsiders, casual observers, and particularly members of the news media were excluded from virtually all juvenile court hearings. Juvenile court judges would enforce this rule scrupulously, and would announce at the beginning of each case that persons not involved in the case should leave the courtroom. This authority, although somewhat informal, was reinforced by most state juvenile codes that prohibited publishing the names of accused juvenile offenders in the newspapers.

Second, juvenile court hearings were to be informal. At the most basic level this meant that the rules of procedure typically associated with adult criminal trials were absent or severely minimized. Therefore, in most instances there was no jury, accusing witnesses might or might not be present, and hearsay evidence might be admissible. The assumption was that the youngster was not in legal jeopardy since all parties were there in "the best interests of the child." Since jeopardy was assumed not to exist the child did not need the legal protections typically associated with constitutional due process.

Third, hearings in juvenile courts were to be nonadversarial. This suggested that under most circumstances neither side—prosecution or defense—was represented by an attorney. In some courts attorneys were not present simply by legal custom. In other courts they were not present because of the wishes of the judges.

These three features need to be understood in the context of the primary legal principle—*parens patriae*—that was at the heart of the juvenile court. The notion of *parens patriae* developed under the English common law tradition. Historically, under English law children were not legal persons, so they could not transact business or assume certain responsibilities. When a child was orphaned the king's chancellor, one of the chief court officials, would intercede

on the child's behalf to make certain that the child's property interests were maintained. From this position it was assumed that the king would act as the "father of the country" (a liberal translation of *parens patriae*) assuring the rights of the least powerful of his subjects. The intercession of the king's chancellor led to what is now known as chancery (or equity) law, and this concept was transferred to the American colonies. *Parens patriae* becomes the legal premise upon which the juvenile court and the first juvenile judges could act in the child's best interests: the judge was the ultimate father (or mother) of the children coming before the court.

Age Jurisdiction Considerations

Age is the ultimate factor defining the reason for the existence of juvenile courts. A key premise, beginning with the first juvenile court, was that children were not fully culpable for their acts. At best they could form limited criminal intent and, under some circumstances, they could not form criminal intent at all. Therefore, rather than basing the court's jurisdiction on a vague notion such as "maturity," state legislatures used different ages to define the cases in which the juvenile court could, and could not, act. Before discussing the three age points that are essential for juvenile courts, it is important to consider the traditional common law age distinctions in relation to *mens rea* (or criminal intent).

Under English common law, descended from earlier Roman law, there were three age categories that courts examined in relation to deciding criminal intent. First, children under the age of 7 were deemed incapable of forming criminal intent. This is the affirmative defense of infancy. Second, children between the ages of 7 and 14 were presumed incapable of forming criminal intent. However, with this group the state could present factors such as (1) the child knew the difference between right and wrong, and (2) the child had an appreciation for the consequences of his or her actions in establishing the capacity to form criminal intent. The final group, those over the age of 14, were presumed capable of forming criminal intent, and, up until the juvenile court's creation, these individuals were accounted as adults by the law.

In terms of age considerations, the juvenile courts traditionally have addressed three different thresholds. The first significant age is the age at which juvenile courts can take jurisdiction over a case. Some states continue the common law tradition of 7 as the minimum age of juvenile court intervention. This age varies from state to state, with some states using 10 as the minimum age and a few states not specifying a minimum age for the court. The second age consideration for juvenile courts is the maximum age. This is a point of much greater agreement. The vast majority of states (about three-fourths) use 17 as the maximum age of juvenile court jurisdiction. Saying this another way, in most states, once a person turns 18 the adult criminal courts gain jurisdiction over alleged offenses. Finally, transfer age is perhaps the most controversial part of juvenile court age jurisdiction. Since the creation of the first juvenile court, states have provided that there are certain ages at which, and certain offenses for which, juveniles could be tried as adults. The most common age at which transfer becomes possible is 16, but for certain offenses (such as murder) states sometimes provide transfer ages as young as 14. Five states (Connecticut, Massachusetts, Nebraska, New Mexico, and New York) now have eliminated discretionary judicial transfer provisions for juvenile offenders, but they still allow for youngsters to be tried and sentenced as adults.

Subject Matter Considerations

The first juvenile courts had jurisdiction over three types of cases: delinquency, dependency, and neglect. For the most part, these are still the issues with which juvenile courts contend today. What has changed is the definition of what may constitute any one of these three categories of cases.

Delinquency can be defined fairly simply. However, there are a great number of subtleties and complexities associated with the definitions of delinquency. Perhaps the easiest definition is to say that delinquency results from any act committed by a child (a person under the legal age of majority) that would be a crime if committed by an adult. This means that state juvenile codes may not distinguish felonies from misdemeanors for juveniles, since any violation of the law—from shoplifting to murder—is delinquency. As originally constituted, most juvenile courts also considered status offenses as a part of delinquency. Status offenses are those violations (such as truancy and running away) that are against the law for juveniles, but not for adults.

Dependency involves situations in which juveniles are found, much more than anything they have done. In most states dependency cases arise when children are found in a condition of want or need (for example, food, clothing, and shelter) that is not a direct result of something the parents have done. In other words, because of poverty or some other deficiency, the parents simply are unable to provide for the children. As a result of numerous legal changes—both case law and legislative changes—occurring in the juvenile courts since the 1960s many states now include status

offenses in the category of dependency or some other nondelinquency classification.

In contrast to dependency, where the parents or guardians fail to provide for the children as a result of circumstances beyond their control, in neglect cases the parents deliberately fail to provide for the children. The results of dependency and neglect may not be distinguishable, but the motivations are.

The recent trend has been for states to move from the traditional juvenile court structure to more broadly based family courts. Family courts may include the types of cases originally heard in juvenile courts plus paternity, domestic relations (divorce), and child support cases. The assumption is that children who violate the law or who are found in situations of dependency or neglect cannot be treated in isolation. In most circumstances the family situation must be addressed and family remedies must be crafted. The family court movement has caught on in certain parts of the U.S., but many states still maintain separate juvenile courts.

Types of Hearings

Juvenile courts conduct at least four types of hearings as a part of their responsibilities. At the time a child is taken into custody a preliminary decision will be made by the juvenile court intake officer concerning whether the child will be detained until a hearing on the petition's merits, or whether the child will be released into the custody of parents or guardians. If the child is to be detained, a juvenile court judge must hold a detention hearing to determine whether detention is warranted. After the detention hearing is held, but before a decision can be made on whether the child is delinquent, the state may ask the juvenile court to hold a transfer hearing to determine whether the child should be tried as an adult. The traditional and most common method for transferring juveniles to adult courts is through the judicial waiver system, where the juvenile court judge is the ultimate authority in the decision making process.

As previously mentioned, today all but five states (Connecticut, Massachusetts, Nebraska, New Mexico, and New York) provide for judicial transfers—also called waivers, remands, or certification—for certain youngsters, depending on their age, offense history, and the crime with which they have been charged. Some states (Florida being the notable example) allow prosecutors to bypass the juvenile courts and direct-file certain juvenile cases in the adult criminal courts. Many states also legislatively exclude certain very serious crimes like murder from juvenile court jurisdiction. Additionally, a small number of states (New Mexico currently is the best example) have moved to "blended sentencing" systems, where youngsters are adjudicated without knowing in advance whether their final penalty will be juvenile or adult in nature.

After the preliminaries are completed, the remaining youngsters whose cases are not handled informally will be scheduled for an adjudicatory hearing. Adjudicatory hearings for juveniles are the equivalent of adult trials. In most jurisdictions there are some procedural differences between the two. For instance, only 16 states provide for jury trials for accused juvenile offenders. The remaining states conduct adjudicatory hearings before a judge with no jury. Once the adjudicatory hearing is completed and the child is found to be delinquent, the juvenile probation office will prepare a predisposition report. The predisposition report is the juvenile counterpart of the adult presentence investigation report. The predisposition report will give the judge information on the child's family and school situations, prior offenses, and recommendations for disposition and treatment. In the vast majority of delinquency cases in the U.S. the youngster will receive probation as the final disposition.

Juvenile Courts in Other Nations

As previously mentioned, the juvenile court is a uniquely American innovation that has been widely copied throughout the world. Many nations use 18 years of age as the point at which full criminal liability attaches, although in Sweden it is 15. Some countries also extend juvenile court age jurisdiction through the age of 20 for certain offenses. Among the nations that have adopted juvenile court models similar to the U.S. are Australia (with each of the states and territories having juvenile or children's courts), Brazil (which has regional child and juvenile courts), France (where there are Courts for Children, for minor offenses, and Assize Courts for Minors, which handle more serious offenses), Germany, Italy, and Spain (with 70 juvenile courts nationwide). By contrast, other nations (Sweden being one of them) do not maintain separate courts for juvenile and adult offenders. In most instances the same laws apply to both groups, although more lenient penalties are provided for youngsters.

Changes in the Legal Environment

In some ways today the juvenile court still resembles the court that was created at the end of the 19th century. The *parens patriae* legal philosophy still is very much alive, and many courts try to emphasize the best interests of the child.

However, in other ways the juvenile court is vastly different today. The changes that have occurred are a result of changing social and political values, changes in legislation, and a series of Supreme Court cases that

began with *Kent v. U.S.*, 383 U.S. 541 (1966). In *Kent*, for the first time, the U.S. Supreme Court was willing to take on a juvenile court issue. The result of this case was that the Supreme Court held that juveniles had a right to a transfer hearing before being tried as adults, that they had the right to an attorney at transfer proceedings, and that the attorneys should have access to all social records used in the juvenile court's disposition process.

The year after *Kent* the Supreme Court decided its most sweeping juvenile justice case: *In re Gault*, 387 U.S. 1 (1967). The *Gault* case provided a full frontal assault on traditional juvenile court proceedings. In effect, the Supreme Court said that youngsters were persons before the law and that they had most, but not necessarily all, due process rights that were extended to adults accused of crimes. These protections included notification of charges, the right to counsel in delinquency proceedings, the right to confront and cross-examine witnesses, and the privilege against self-incrimination. For the first time the Supreme Court explicitly noted that many juvenile court proceedings, where they differed from adult proceedings, were constitutionally deficient.

Following *Gault* there was a series of less sweeping, but still important, cases decided by the Supreme Court in regard to constitutional due process for juvenile offenders. The case of *In re Winship*, 397 U.S. 358 (1970) provided that juveniles must be adjudicated on the same standard of proof as adults—guilt beyond a reasonable doubt—not on the less stringent civil standard of the preponderance of the evidence. Unlike the cases that had gone before, *McKeiver v. Pennsylvania*, 403 U.S. 528 (1971) held that states did not have to provide jury trials to accused delinquents; they could do so if they chose to, but the Court's reading of the Constitution was it was not compelled. Two other cases clarify the juvenile court's due process guarantees. In *Davis v. Alaska*, 415 U.S. 308 (1974) the U.S. Supreme Court upheld the right of a juvenile accused of delinquency to confront his accuser. The prosecution witness in this case was another youngster who was on probation, and the state asserted that a confidentiality statute shielded the accusing witness from being required to appear in court. The Supreme Court rejected this argument and came down on the side of the defendant's interest in a fair trial. *Breed v. Jones*, 421 U.S. 519 (1975) asked the Supreme Court to decide whether protection against double jeopardy applied to juveniles the same as it did to adults. This case was unique in that the juvenile defendant was first a fully adjudicated delinquent (rather than the court merely holding a transfer hearing), and then the court decided that the youngster actually should be tried as an adult. In this instance, the Supreme Court believed that the child had been placed in jeopardy twice.

Taken together, these cases, along with others on school searches and related issues, have established a juvenile court that closely resembles adult criminal courts. The juvenile court today is both formal and adversarial. In most jurisdictions court proceedings are no longer confidential. In fact, in some jurisdictions adult courts have become more like juvenile courts in their use of diversion programs, and juvenile courts have become more like adult courts in their legal proceedings and their orientation toward punishment. With so little distinction, the eventual question may be: do we retain the juvenile court as a separate entity or simply merge the juvenile court back into the adult adjudication system?

G. LARRY MAYS

References and Further Reading

Bernard, T.J. 1992. *The Cycle of Juvenile Justice*, Oxford University Press, New York.

Bortner, M.A. 1982. *Inside a Juvenile Court: The Tarnished Ideal of Individualized Justice*, New York University Press, New York.

Champion, D.J., and Mays, G.L. 1991. *Transferring Juveniles to Criminal Courts: Trends and Implications for Criminal Justice*, Praeger Publishers, New York.

Feld, B.C. 2003. *Juvenile Justice Administration*, West Group, St. Paul, MN.

Gardner, M.R. 2003. *Understanding Juvenile Law*, 2nd ed., Matthew Bender, New York.

Platt, A. 1977. *The Child Savers: The Invention of Delinquency*, Revised edition, University of Chicago Press, Chicago, IL.

Rubin, H.T. 1985. *Behind the Black Robes: Juvenile Court Judges and the Court*, Sage Publications, Beverly Hills, CA.

Schwartz, I.M., In *Justice for Juveniles: Rethinking the Interests of the Child*, Lexington Books, Lexington, MA,

Singer, S. 1996. *Recriminalizing Delinquency: Violent Juvenile Crime and Juvenile Justice Reform*, Cambridge University Press, New York.

Snyder, H.N., Sickmund, M., and Poe-Yamagata, E., 2000. *Juvenile Transfers to Criminal Courts in the 1990s: Lessons Learned from Four States*, Office of Juvenile Justice and Delinquency Prevention, Washington, DC.

Torbet, P., Griffin, P., Hurst, H., Jr., and MacKenzie, L.R., 2000. *Juveniles Facing Criminal Sanctions: Three States That Changed the Rules*, Office of Juvenile Justice and Delinquency Prevention, Washington, DC.

See also **Juvenile Justice: Due Process**

Juvenile Justice: The Police *See* **Juvenile Delinquency: Definitions and Laws; Juvenile Justice: Corrections**

K

Kidnapping

Losing one's child to a stranger or ex-spouse is a parents' worst fear, and is a crime in all 50 states in the United States. This crime has raised the concern of both legislators and members of society alike and is a type of crime "for which only limited statistical information has been available" (Hammer et al., 2002). In May 2002, "… police entered 59,600 missing children … into a database, and removed 57,998 who had been found or were the subject of a custody battle between parents; furthermore, during the first eight months of 2002, 62 kidnapping cases were opened by the FBI; 93 cases were opened for all of 2001; 103 in 2000, and 134 in 1999" (*Law Enforcement News,* 2000). It is evident from these FBI statistics that kidnappings have decreased over the past five years, but those individuals who have had their child kidnapped have taken a more aggressive stance with law enforcement to assist them when attempting to find their child or child's abductor.

Kidnapping Laws

The case law in the United States governing kidnapping has grown considerably since the first law was created in the 1930s. This law was known as the Lindbergh Law and defined a kidnapper as one "who unlawfully seizes, confines, inveigles, decoys, kidnaps, abducts, or carries away and holds for ransom or reward or otherwise any person …" (Gill, 1981, 31). This law has since been modified, and current laws such as The Missing Children Act of 1982 and The National Child Search Assistance Act of 1990 have

been implemented to control the crime of kidnapping in the most efficient and effective way possible.

The Missing Children Act of 1982 requires the FBI to post information about kidnapping victims into the National Crime Information Center (NCIC). This system allows law enforcement officers across the nation to access detailed information about a child they believe has been kidnapped.

The National Child Search Assistance Act of 1990 requires any law enforcement agency that receives information about a missing child to enter it into the NCIC computer system immediately. The 1990 Act strictly prohibits agencies from utilizing a waiting period to enter information about a kidnapping victim once a report of such an offense has been given to the police. It even requires police departments to enter the information without the officer knowing if a criminal violation has occurred.

Amber Alert

The Amber Alert program was initially utilized by only five states when it was established in 1996. Today, 45 states have implemented the system, which broadcasts nationwide and simultaneously on radio and television detailed descriptions of children who are believed to have been kidnapped by either a stranger or family member. Because of its recent inception, the effectiveness of this system is not yet known; however, it is believed by many in the criminal justice system that such a program will only increase the odds of kidnappers being apprehended and children being returned to their families.

Kidnappers: Identified Offender Types

In 1988, the FBI began relying on state and local law enforcement agencies to voluntarily report crimes committed within their communities and states. This system of data collection was named the National Incident-Based Reporting System or NIBRS. Within this nationwide reporting system, the FBI collects data on the occurrence of a kidnapping when it is reported to law enforcement officials.

Three distinct categories of perpetrators have been created and identified when looking at kidnapping data from the NIBRS. The first category is entitled "family kidnappers," and generally involves a parent taking a child from their home or yard when involved in a custody dispute. Hammer et al. (2002) found this crime to be prevalent among children who were 6 years of age or younger and lived with one parent, and in 53% of the kidnapping cases they examined, the abductor was the child's father, typically between the ages of 30 and 40. They also found that "46% of family abducted children were gone less than 1 week, and 21% were gone 1 month or more" (Hammer et al., 2002).

The second identified category is entitled "acquaintance kidnappers," and often involves someone that the child knows, such as a friend of the family, taking them from their home and family against their will. Finkelhor et al. (2000) found this category of kidnappers to have the greatest number of juvenile offenders, and further found that in 84% of the cases they examined, the abductor was male.

The third and final category of identified kidnappers is entitled "stranger kidnappers," and often involves someone unknown to the child taking them from their family against their will. Finkelhor et al. (2000) found perpetrators in this category were overwhelmingly adult males who kidnapped children from outside locations, such as parks, streets, or public areas.

It is important to note that the motive of perpetrators in family abductions is to get their child back, because they are typically involved in a custody dispute with their ex-spouse. In situations where the perpetrator is an acquaintance or stranger to the child, the motives of these individuals are quite different. Their intentions, when kidnapping a child, are typically to sexually assault them. As a result of their sexual experience with the adolescent, the offender, more often than not, is compelled to take the child's life to prevent them from talking to their parents or police about their experience with the kidnapper.

Conclusion and Future Suggestions

It is impossible to accurately determine if kidnappings are on the rise because it is currently not mandatory for police departments to report the prevalence of this crime in their city to the FBI. However, Grasso (2001) notes it is imperative that members of society, as well as law enforcement officers, realize that kidnapping is a serious crime and must be investigated and prosecuted in the most efficient way possible. "Getting a clear picture of how many children become missing, and why, is an important step in addressing the problem" (Hammer et al., 2002). It would benefit children and law enforcement officers if police departments were to "establish specialized units made up of law enforcement personnel and prosecutors skilled in investigating and prosecuting the crime of parental abduction" (Grasso et al., 2001), stranger abduction, and acquaintance abduction.

The future of our children mandates the need for more research to better understand this social phenomenon, for more police resources to return abducted children to healthy environments, and for resources to help better educate the public on the frequency and long-range impact of child abductions on our communities.

W. WESLEY JOHNSON AND MISTI TOBIAS

References and Further Reading

Child-snatchings are news, but a problem? 2003. *Law Enforcement News*, Vol. XXVIII, 2002, John Jay College of Criminal Justice/CUNY, August 12. 2003.

Finkelhor, D., Hammer, H., and Sedlak, A. 2002. *Nonfamily Abducted Children: National Estimates and Characteristics*, Office of Juvenile Justice and Delinquency Prevention.

Finkelhor, D., and Ormrod, R. 2000. *Kidnaping Juveniles: Patterns*, NIBRS Office, of Juvenile Justice and Delinquency Prevention.

Gill, J.E. 1981. *Stolen Children: How and Why Parents Kidnap Their Kids—And What to Do About It*, 1st ed., Seaview Books, New York.

Grasso, K., Sedlak, A., Chiancone, J., Gragg, F., Schultz, D., and Ryan, J. 2001. *The Criminal Justice System's Response to Parental Abduction*, Office of Juvenile Justice and Delinquency Prevention.

Hammer, H., Finkelhor, D., and Sedlak, A. 2002. *Children Abducted by Family Members*, National Estimates and Characteristics, Office of Juvenile Justice and Delinquency Prevention.

See also **Child Abuse: Extent and Correlates; Victimization, Crime: Characteristics of Victims**

L

Labeling and Symbolic Interaction Theories

Labeling Theories

The study of crime is an analysis of being, becoming, and experiencing difference. More appropriately crime is the articulation of trouble in the maintenance of moral rules and ordered worlds. Crime as a legal judgment negotiates between the more micro-politicized processes and the more macro-structures of politics. Juxtaposed against the backdrop of crime as judgment, we examine labeling and symbolic interactionism theories in order to assess their respective theoretic influences, arguments, criticisms, and contributions to criminology.

The labeling perspective directs attention away from the causes of crime, focusing instead on the relationship between the power to label (Schur, 1971) and the inability to challenge the social repercussions of the label. Crime is defined specifically as an interactive process of typification and designation between at least two kinds of people: those who commit or are said to have committed a crime, and the rest of society. Central to the labeling perspective is the reaction of "some" toward "others," that is, the response to crime that transforms people into criminals (Kitsuse, 1962, 253). Accordingly, labeling theory asks the following questions. How are designations of crime constructed and applied to individuals and practices? What are the origins of these designations and how have they become institutionalized? And, what is the process by which agents of the criminal justice system attach official designations? There are two analysts who are particularly well known for their work in this labeling tradition—Edwin Lemert and Howard Becker.

Edwin Lemert's (1951) inquiry into primary and secondary deviance represents a formidable shift in criminology—a move away from a highly deterministic etiology of crime to a more comprehensive investigation of the problematic nature of societal reactions. Primary or original deviance is the violation of a certain rule caused by a variety of "external" factors and arises in a variety of social, cultural, and psychological contexts (Lemert, 1967, 17) occurring prior to any reaction. On the other hand, secondary deviance is related to a processual or social control explanation, emphasizing both how deviant acts are symbolically attached to persons and the effective consequences of such attachment for subsequent deviation for the person. It is precisely in Lemert's analysis of secondary deviation that we witness a radical reappraisal of deviance. Social control leads to deviance, that is, the process of negative reactions creates negative role engulfment as Lemert notes:

> When a person begins to employ his deviant behaviour or a role based upon it as a defense, attack, or adjustment to the overt and covert problems created by the consequent societal reaction to him, his deviation is secondary (1951, 76).

In effect, the original causes of crime recede and give way to the central importance of disapproving, degradational, and isolating reactions of society. The sequence of interaction leading to secondary deviation is as follows: (1) primary deviation; (2) social penalties; (3) further primary deviation; (4) stronger penalties and rejections; (5) further deviation, perhaps with hostilities and resentment beginning to focus upon those doing the penalizing; (6) crisis reached in the tolerance quotient, expressed informal action by the community stigmatizing the deviant; (7) strengthening of the deviant conduct as a reaction to the stigmatizing and penalties; and (8) alternate acceptance of deviant social status and efforts of adjustment on the basis of the associated role (1951, 77).

Lemert's analysis is concerned with actors moving from primary to secondary deviance based on societal reactions. For Lemert, when a person begins to employ a deviant behavior or a role based on it as a means of defense, attack, or adjustment to the overt and covert problems created by the consequent, societal reaction to one's deviation is secondary. Specifically, Lemert (1967, 40) elaborates: "The secondary deviant, as opposed to his actions, is a person whose life and identity are organized around the fact of deviance." Secondary deviation then, is a product of the interaction between primary deviation and negative social reaction.

Similar to Tannenbaum's "dramatization of evil" that segregates an actor, secondary deviation traumatizes the self concept and encourages the continuation of criminal or deviant acts. Tannenbaum adds (1938, 19):

> The process of making the criminal is a process of tagging, defining, identifying, segregating, describing, emphasizing ... The person becomes the thing he is described as being.

Howard Becker's (1963) early theoretical formulations confronted traditional approaches to crime by politicizing Lemert's conceptions. Becker's work addressed the following: the nature of labels; the power of some to impose labels; and the acceptance or rejection of labels by the affected targets. In the *Outsiders*, Becker (1963, 8) provides us with the principle element of the labeling perspective—crime as a creation of society. Becker states:

> From this point of view, deviance is not a quality of the act the person commits, but rather a consequence of the application by others of rules and sanctions to an "offender." The deviant is one to whom that label has successfully been applied; deviant behaviour is behaviour people so label (1963, 8–9).

Likewise, Kai Erikson points out that:

> Deviance is not a property inherent in certain forms of behaviour; it is a property conferred upon these forms by the audiences which directly or indirectly witness them. The critical variable in the study of deviance, then, is the social audience which eventually determines whether any episode of behaviour or any class of episodes is labelled deviant (1964, 11).

Definitions of crime are arrived at and constructed in negotiations between deviants and moral entrepreneurs.

The latter are politically powerful audiences, persons, or groups who attempt to criminalize certain acts and individuals by influencing law makers and law enforcers and their attendant welfare measures, police practices and prevailing ideologies. Differences in the ability to define crime and deviance are inherently power differentials, the relative power of groups involved and their channels of publicity. Consequently, socially distant or marginal people are treated in a way that exacerbates and exploits their vulnerability. A label once affixed by powerful interests not only crystallizes identity but also remains so sticky that it becomes difficult to remove. Furthermore, when these individuals fail to shed the designation, they often "personalize" or internalize the labels as "master status" by organizing their lifestyles around the assumptions associated with the labels.

In the second part of his text *Outsiders*, Becker examines crime as constituted by actors in an active, conscious, and intentional process. The process of becoming a secondary deviant, the steps by which a person moves from primary to secondary deviation, is related to the notion of "career." Herein Becker contributes significantly to the study of labeling by clarifying the concept of "career" as an analytic tool. The concept of career refers to the progression of related experiences and identity changes through which one moves during his or her working life. As Becker elucidates (1963), a career is a socially recognized process involving a relatively orderly "sequence of movements." Within the interpretive paradigm, a career, therefore, is not only a way of being but also a way of knowing. Careers consist of forms of sociation that impose some intelligibility on the actor's world. The concept of career provides a hitherto neglected focus on the processes of, and stages in, choice, development, and transformation, discerning major components and relations that incorporate both formal and informal links between stages as well as various contingencies affecting the nature of interactions. Career stages are characterized by identifiable and organized sets of relations and social meanings. Stages are essentially procedures that individuals use in making sense of their immediate situations. With increased and continued interactions, these career categories evolve so that stage identifications follow and are considered by others in future encounters. These categorizations establish routine rules for interaction and serve as directives for future involvements. The social organization of careers consists of various forms that typically plot biographies and relationships. They include different features of: (1) the initial "getting connected" or "becoming" stage that involves various aspects of exposure, exploration, entry (recruitment or induction), trial and initiation, or training and apprenticeship; (2) the "staying connected" or "being" established in roles that concerns the maintenance of identity, achievement, stability, and clarification, and also advancement, promotion, or specialization; (3) the "disconnecting" or decline stage of a career pursuit characterized by graduation, expulsion, termination, retirement as well as transformation, conversion, or greater induction into another orientation (Rock, 1979; Visano, 1987). Actors create stages that in turn are used to justify degrees of involvements. Three related factors are fundamental in building and maintaining the symbolic worlds of careers: constituting skills of actors, reactions of others, and self-identity.

Critiques of Labeling Perspectives

Despite the contributions of labeling theory, there are a number of weaknesses. For Jack Gibbs (1966, 12), not only is causality imprecise but the application of labels presents highly relativistic moral statements, failing to specify the conditions that must exist before an act or individual is labeled deviant. Likewise, Ronald Akers notes that labeling approaches fail to ask why people commit the initial deviant act, and do not deal adequately with personal decision making in the crime or deviance process (Akers, 1968, 463). According to Akers, there is only an overemphasis on the importance of official labeling. Furthermore, what is important, yet often downplayed, is that much crime goes undetected and is never labeled. The assumptions of labeling theory do not fully address most macro-sociological concerns. For example, labeling theory examines how the deviant responds to the label applied, but fails to address the process by which the larger society has come to define him or her as deviant. The "deviant" in this instance is portrayed as a submissive, passive victim of a one-sided process. Moreover, labeling approaches neglect issues of social structure and class. The crimes of powerful corporations are often ignored (Chambliss, 1969). Similarly, Alvin Gouldner (1968) has shown that the attacks on the discriminatory or discretionary practices of social control agencies have served in some measure to effectively divert attention from the fundamental underlying disparities in the social structure. By overemphasizing the causal aspects of labeling, the social reaction approach creates a somewhat insidious role inversion that promotes an "ideology of the underdog" (Gouldner, 1968) within a liberal ethos.

Symbolic Interactionism (SI)

It was the well-established social theory of symbolic interactionism that succeeded in advancing labeling perspectives in criminology, especially in terms of the following concepts: stigma, secondary deviance,

sequential processes, master status, moral entrepreneurship, negotiations, and career. Unlike the deterministic explanations characteristic that are of mainstream criminology, symbolic interactionism (SI) abandons the practices of predefining or predetermining causalities of crime and instead interprets all reality as socially constructed, tentative, and problematic. SI challenges the following normative claims of conventional criminology: crime as given and static; crime as constructed by external forces (beyond the control of the individual) that propel criminal behavior; and crime defined by fixed norms and values. For SI, on the other hand, criminals and policing authorities are creators of their environments, engaging in a continual process of meaning construction in relation to their social realities, actively and reflectively shaping their experiences and the experiences of those with whom they routinely interact. Through interaction, individuals collectively define situations and participate in negotiating and reconstituting meanings. This paradigm calls for a criminology characterized by what Max Weber (1969) terms *verstehen*—an empathic and interpretive understanding of the subjective meanings that actors attach to social action. The only way to contextualize social action is to know the subjective meanings of actors, that is, how actors take into account the actions of others and are guided by these subjective meanings. SI recognizes the importance of the inner and outer perspectives of the human agency. The inner perspective emphasizes the ability of actors to know themselves and to understand others through "sympathetic introspection" and "imaginative reconstructions" of "definitions of situations" (Filstead, 1970, 4).

Symbolic interaction refers to the peculiar and distinctive character of interaction as it takes place between human beings. The social world is constructed out of shared symbolic universes that shape interactions. SI goes back to the ideas first presented by George Herbert Mead (1863–1931) and later elaborated by his student, Herbert Blumer (1900–1987), who coined the term "symbolic interactionism". For Mead, ones social life is a dynamic, continuing social process, governed by ongoing, changing, and renegotiated interactions among mind, self, and society. The self, as object and subject, is "essentially a social process" (Mead, 1934, 178) occurring within social situations. The self emerges in reference to others, in projections, and rehearsals of roles. As Mead (ibid, xxv) noted, the "individual constitutes society as genuinely as society constitutes the individual." Charles Horton Cooley (1864–1933), a student of John Dewey, argued that humans have a capacity for self-consciousness that emerges out of interaction with others. Communication is the mechanism through which human relations exist, develop, and recognize themselves as objects, (Codey, 1956). Cooley stressed the indissoluble relation between self and society through his looking-glass self concept. Individuals come to regard themselves as others see them, a perception of self that is analogous to a "looking glass." Images people have of themselves are reflections of meanings assigned by the primary groups (1902, 84–87).

Influenced by Weber, Mead, and Cooley, Herbert Blumer (1969) reiterates the significance of the subjective meanings of individuals. Blumer argues that no comprehension of human behavior and social life can be obtained without taking account of the process of forming and transforming the self. Blumer stresses the importance of considering the subjective experience, behavior, and observable conduct of actors. Meanings, therefore, are social constructions that serve to anchor, orient, and indicate action to the self. Symbolic interactionism stresses the importance of others in shaping one's self-concept and draws attention to the central role of self-evaluation in validating and sustaining one's self-concept. By attending to others, for example, the actor learns both favorable definitions of self and guides for interaction. This "joint action" refers to the collective unit, the fitting together of different participants (Blumer, 1979, ix) which is a frame of reference that aids in organizing experiences. This clarification of individuals as actors is a process of "self-indication, a moving communicative process in which individuals note things, assess them, give them meaning, and decide to act on the basis of the meaning" (Blumer, 1962, 181). SI encourages theoretical pursuits that directly confront the time-honored distinctions between process and structure. In general, the priority of micro-social constructions acknowledges elements of social structure. Interactionists however, have moved judiciously in unraveling macro-conditions from the plethora of their detailed observations (Lyman, 1984). Processes of group life are articulated as generic (Couch, 1984) and alternatively recast within socio-historical influences (Hall, 1987). Although SI defies systemization, the subject of recurring regularities within diverse temporal and spatial domains has emerged as a more heightened focus of study, especially in reference to generic concepts. Briefly, the generic concept is a panoptic tool that imposes order on diverse findings. Generic concepts are abstract categories or invariant properties of human life (Blumer, 1969, 86; Couch, 1984). The task for SI, therefore, is to delve into universal forms of processes that make group life possible. The above discussion of SI approaches highlights the significance of agency, intentionality, and subjectivity. Interactionism mediates and opens space for the hitherto neglected subject; the constituting capacity of the social agent consistent with the SI's emphasis on the more immediate everyday patterns of social interactions in situations that characterize crime incidents rather than the attributes of offenders is routine activities theory (Cohen and Felson,

1979; Felson, 1994). For example, street crime is a product of opportunity that arises from ongoing activities. In general, the convergence of the following three routine activities of everyday life contributes to criminal opportunity: motivated perpetrators or offenders, suitable targets, and the absence of capable guardians (surveillance). Drawing upon SI, especially ideas about social construction, the criminal event perspective, and interactionism, the focus is on the informal systems of social control that grow out of our everyday relationships with other people. For Kennedy and Forde (1989, 127), the structure of the situation, such as the location or the presence of a third party, plays a significant role in the outcome of the event. In these situations meanings are created through socialization, the active participation of all parties in the interaction, especially in terms of the ways in which individuals react to others and the situation itself. Routine activities theory is closely related to rational choice theory (opportunity theory) or what Garland (1996; 2001) calls the "criminologies of everyday life" Like routine activities theory, rational choice theory views criminal behavior as reflecting the offenders' exploitation of perceived opportunities.

Despite the above contributions to micro-criminology, SI has been criticized as too liberal, too relativistic, too voluntaristic, and too easily accommodating to state interests. The depoliticized elements of labeling and SI, for example, have been appropriated by the state. In discussions of human agency of the criminal, these approaches ignore structural features of class crimes and state reactions. The traditional text of labeling and SI reduce too much to actor–reactor relations lodged in the interactions at a micro-level of inquiry. The textured language of agency forecloses an examination of more global political struggles.

On the one hand, the more dubious value of labeling has been inherent in the more recent state practices of racial profiling concomitant with the "war on terrorism." On the other hand, labeling and symbolic interactionist theories have been easily appropriated by liberal democratic states in advancing more progressive policies on juvenile justice, especially community-based corrections and neighborhood policing. Labeling perspectives have contributed to more effective rehabilitative strategies such as reintegrative shaming and restorative justice. Traditionally, labeling is a shaming practice that stigmatizes offenders as outcasts and engulfs them permanently in humiliating criminal identities. But, in addition to this disintegrative shaming there are also reintegrative shaming efforts that reconnect offenders to more conformist community bonds and discourage further participation in criminal subcultures (Braithwaite, 1989). Reintegrative shaming is a deterrent form of disapproval that invokes remorse (repentance) in the shamed offender but communicates to the offender that the crime is condemned and not the criminal (Brathwaite, 1994). Shaming of the offender's significant others (networks, colleagues, family, friends, or corporation) can be very effective, especially when collective punishments, in turn, are imposed by those groups or individuals meaningful to an offender. As an example of restorative justice, reintegrative shaming contributes to greater accountability, more direct participation of supporters of both victims and offenders, enhanced learning opportunities, and increased ties to legitimate social institutions. Interestingly, countries that culturally support reintegrative shaming enjoy relatively low crime rates.

DAVID BAKER AND LIVY VISANO

References and Further Reading

Akers, R. 1968. Problems in the sociology of deviance, *Social Forces*, 46 (June), 455–465.

Becker, H. 1963. *Outsiders: Studies in the Sociology of Deviance*, Free Press, New York, NY.

Becker, H. 1974. Labelling theory reconsidered, in *Deviance and Social Control*, Paul, R. and Maureen, M., Eds., Tavistock, London, UK.

Blumer, H. 1962. Society as symbolic interactionism in *Human Behavior and Social Processes*, Rose A.M., Ed., Houghton-Mifflin, New York, UK.

Blumer, H. 1969. *Symbolic Interactionism*, Prentice-Hall, Englewood Cliffs, NJ.

Blumer, H. 1979. Introduction, in *Stations of the Lost*, Wiseman J., Ed., University of Chicago Press, Chicago, IL.

Braithwaite, J. 1989. *Crime, Shame and Reintegration*, Cambridge University Press, Cambridge U.K.

Braithwaite, J. 1994. Conditions of successful reintegration ceremonies, *British Journal of Criminology*, 34, 2.

Chambliss, W. 1969. *Crime and Legal Process*, McGraw-Hill, New York, NY.

Cohen, L. and Marcus, F. 1979. Social change in crime rate trends: A routine activity approach, *American Sociological Review*, 44, 588–608.

Cooley, C.H. 1956. *Human Nature and the Social Order*, Charles Scribner's Sons, New York, NY.

Couch, C. 1984. Symbolic interactionism and generic principles, *Symbolic Interactionism* 7, 1–14.

Erikson, K. 1964. *Wayward Puritans*, Wiley and Sons, New York, NY.

Felson, M. 1994. *Crime and Everyday Life*, Pine Forge Press, Thousand Oaks, CA.

Filstead, W. 1970. *Qualitative Methodology*, Rand McNally, Chicago, IL.

Garland, D. 2001. *The Culture of Control*, Oxonian University Press, Oxonian.

Garland, D. 1996. The limits of the sovereign state: Strategies of crime control in contemporary society, *British Journal of Criminology*, 36, 445–471.

Gibbs, J. 1966. Conceptions of deviant behaviour—The old and the new, *Pacific Sociological Review*, 9, 9–14.

Gouldner, A. 1968. The sociology as partisan: Sociology and the welfare state, *American Sociologist*, 3(May), 103–116.

Hall, P. 1987. Interactionism and the study of social organization, *Sociological Quarterly*, 28(1), 1–22.

Kennedy, L.W. and Forde, D.R. 1999. *When Push Comes to Shove: A Routine Conflict Approach to Violence*, State University of New York Press, Albany, NY.

Kitsuse, J. 1962. Societal reaction to deviant behavior, *Social Problems*, 9 (Winter), 247–256.

Lemert, E. 1951. *Social Pathology*, McGraw-Hill, New York, NY.

Lemert, E. 1967. The concept of secondary deviation, *Human Deviance, Social Problems and Social Control*, Prentice-Hall, Toronto, Canada.

Lyman, S. 1984. Interactionism and the study of race relations at the microsociological level: The contribution of Herbert Blumer, *Symbolic Interaction*, 7, 107–120.

Mead, G. 1934. *Mind, Self and Society*, University of Chicago Press, Chicago, IL.

Rock, P. 1979. *The Making of Symbolic Interactionism*, Macmillan, London, UK.

Schur, E. 1971. *Labelling Deviant Behaviour*, Harper and Row, New York, NY.

Schur, E. 1980. *The Politics of Deviance*, Prentice-Hall, Englewood Cliffs, NJ.

Tannenbaum, F. 1938. *Crime and Community*, Ginn, Boston, MA.

Visano, L. 1987. *This Idle Trade Concord*, Vita Sana.

Visano, L. 1983. Tramps, tricks and trouble: Street transients and their controls, in *Deviant Designations*, Thomas, F. and Livy V., Eds., Butterworth, Toronto, Canada.

Weber M. 1969. *Max Weber on Law in Economy and Society*, Harvard University Press, Cambridge, MA.

See also **Becker, Howard; Chambliss, William**

Larceny and Theft: Extent and Correlates

The common law crime of "larceny" was developed to address a rightful owner's loss of a legal interest in property. Legal interest involves the "ownership, possession, or custody" an individual has in an item. For example, a taxi company purchases a taxi and becomes the owner of the taxi. A taxi driver is given possession of the taxi for specific periods of time in exchange for an agreement to return both the taxi and profits earned through use of the taxi. A taxi passenger pays the taxi driver for the right to direct the taxi to the destination of his choice. The company owns the car (has title), the driver has the legal right to use the car without interference from others (has possession), and the passenger has purchased a more limited right to direct the car to the destination of his choice (has temporary custody of the back seat). Each party has purchased a different legal interest in the car.

At common law larceny was comprised of six separate elements. Those elements were: taking, carrying away, personal property, of another, with intent to permanently deprive, by trespass. The first four elements describe the prohibited act. The term "taking" required a nonowner to assume dominion and control over an item for at least a brief period of time. "Carrying away" referred to the action of removing an item from its location. Only a slight movement was necessary, but merely picking an item up to look at it was not enough to show a "carrying away." The third element, "personal property" limited the type of property that the crime of larceny was intended to deal with. Thus, neither real property nor intangible property could be the subject of a larceny at common law. The fourth element, "of another," restricted the crime to acts involving property clearly owned by another person. The fifth element set forth the general intent of the nonowner at the time he took the item. For a "taking" to be labeled "larceny" the "taker" must have had the intent to deprive the true owner of the use of the item permanently. Intent to merely cause a temporary deprivation was not larceny.

The sixth element, "by trespass," is the defining element of the crime of larceny. "By trespass" meant the item was taken by a nonowner without the rightful owner having any knowledge of the taking. Knowingly receiving stolen goods also qualifies as a trespass. If a nonowner took property of another by mistake, no trespass occurred. If that person later learns, however, that the property is not their own and they fail to return it, they have then committed a trespass.

The element of trespass, although clearly defining the prohibited act, also narrowed the scope of the crime of larceny. Thus, several different types of larceny were developed to address situations involving forms of loss not involving a trespass.

"Larceny by false pretenses" had six elements at common law. The first five elements were identical to those of general larceny: taking, carrying away, personal property of another, with intent to permanently deprive. The sixth element, however, replaced the element of trespass with the element of "false pretenses." False pretenses were defined as "obtaining possession and title to property with the consent of the owner through deception." Accordingly, to allege larceny by false pretenses the rightful owner had to prove that the transfer of title and possession to the accused thief was owing to substantial reliance on the thief's false

statements. The accused thief could not claim the taking was by consent because the consent was gained through deceit.

"Larceny by trick or device" addressed situations in which an owner had lost rightful possession but had not relinquished title to property at issue. There was no trespassory taking because the victim voluntarily gave the property to the thief believing the thief would return the property. The first five elements of this crime were identical to the general form of larceny: taking, carrying away, personal property of another, with intent to permanently deprive. The sixth and defining element was called "trick or device." To prove that a loss was because of trick or device, the rightful owner needed to show that the thief gained possession of the item through deception. Again, consent was no defense to this crime because the consent was obtained by deceit.

A fourth type of larceny, "Larceny by embezzlement," developed to address issues of a nonowner, rightfully in possession of an item, unlawfully assuming a greater legal interest in the property. The first five elements of the crime of larceny by embezzlement were identical to the other three types of common law larceny. The sixth element of this crime, however, was called "unlawful conversion." Unlawful conversion required that a person with lawful possession of an item assume an increased legal interest in the property without authority of the rightful owner. Unlawful conversion included selling property and keeping the proceeds, keeping property for personal use, or even giving property away. To prove larceny by embezzlement a rightful owner was required to show that the property was "taken" and "carried away," beyond the permitted geographical area or beyond the permitted time allowed by the lawful possession.

A fifth type of larceny developed at common law was "robbery." This crime had seven elements. The first five were the same as the other types of common law larceny. The sixth element required that the owner be aware, someone was unlawfully taking property because the item was taken from their immediate presence. "Immediate presence" meant that the item was under the immediate control of the victim at the time it was taken. The seventh element required that the item be taken by force or fear. Force included both threat of force and actual physical harm that compelled the victim to relinquish possession owing to fear.

Today, approximately 30 states and the District of Columbia have integrated the various types of common law larceny into a consolidated "theft" statute. A consolidated theft statute typically includes a clear legislative intent to consolidate the different types of common law larceny into a single criminal act called "theft." (See e.g., Alaska Stat. § 5-36-102 [2003]; Md. Code Ann.

§ 7-102 [2002]; Neb Rev. Stat. § 28-510 [2002]). States integrate most of the common law elements of the various types of larceny into consolidated theft statutes. Thus, most statutory definitions of "theft" include the elements of obtaining control over the property of another by trespass, by threat, or by deception. Additionally, these statutes often require proof that the thief had the intent to permanently deprive the owner of the possession of the property.

Most states using a single statute to consolidate the various forms of common law larceny have adopted the term "theft" to describe the criminal act of taking the property of another. A few consolidated state statutes, however, use other terms, including "larceny" and "stealing." (See e.g., Conn. Gen. Stat. §53a-119 [2003]; Mo. Rev. Stat. §570.030 [2003]). Regardless of the chosen language, a close inspection of these laws shows legislative intent to consolidate the various forms of common law larceny into a single criminal act.

Fewer than 20 states continue to use any of the separate types of common law larceny. Many of these states have partially consolidated the common law forms of larceny but maintained a few as separate crimes. (See e.g., Ga. Code Ann. § 16-8-2 through 16-8-4 [2002]). It should also be noted that the word "theft" or "steal" may be used in place of the word "larceny." By itself, this change in title affects neither the distinctness nor the nature of the various crimes as they were established at common law. (See e.g., Del. Code Ann. title 11 § 841-844 [2003]; Ky. Rev. Stat. Ann. § 514.030 and 514.040 [2002]).

The concept of "theft of services" is recognized by all of the states. It may be found in a consolidated theft statute or set forth as a separate criminal act. Theft of services differs from other types of theft in that the item alleged to be taken is a service rather than an identifiable piece of property.

The Federal Bureau of Investigation (FBI) includes larceny–theft in its crime measurement index, The Uniform Crime Reporting Program. Within that crime reporting program the concept of larceny–theft is defined as "[t]he unlawful taking, carrying, leading, or riding away of property from the possession or constructive possession of another" (Federal Bureau of Investigation, Crime in the U.S., Section VII, 2002 [Washington, DC: Government Printing Office, 2003] at 454 [hereinafter, Uniform Crime Reports]). This definition is broader in scope than the definitions used at common law, and adopted by most state and local jurisdictions in that it does not require the taking to be permanent. Thus, the Uniform Crime Report includes crimes within its definition of larceny–theft that other jurisdictions have defined as some form of temporary deprivation. At the same time, it should be noted that the definition of larceny–theft used by the Uniform Crime Reports is also narrower in scope than the definition used by many state and local jurisdictions. The Uniform Crime Reports specifically exclude embezzlement, confidence games, forgery, worthless checks, and theft of motor vehicles from the definition of larceny–theft (Uniform Crime Reports, §VII, 454). Although this limiting language serves a purpose in narrowing the scope of acts that may be reported as larceny–theft, it also excludes a portion of the larceny–theft crimes recognized both at common law and by many states' consolidated theft statutes.

In 2002, the offense of larceny–theft accounted for 59.4% of all crime recorded in the Uniform Crime Reports (Uniform Crime Reports, §II, 9). This category was by far the largest. The second largest category was burglary representing slightly more than 18% (Uniform Crime Reports, §II, 11). Robbery, a form of larceny at common law, is classified separately within the Uniform Crime Reports and accounted for less than 4% of the total crimes reported in 2002. Motor vehicle theft, another separate category, comprised 10.5% of the total crimes reported that year (Uniform Crime Reports, §II, 11).

In 2002, a total of 70.5% of larceny–theft arrestees were of persons 18 years and older (Uniform Crime Reports, §IV, 242). Almost 68% of persons arrested for larceny–theft were White, slightly more than 29% were Black, and the remainder were of other races (Uniform Crime Reports, §IV, 52). Females accounted for 37% of the total number of larceny–theft arrestees. (Uniform Crime Reports, §IV, 251). An examination of the 10-year trend of crimes reported from 1993 to 2002, however, showed a decline in the total number of larceny–theft related arrests for all ages, races, and both sexes (Uniform Crime Reports, §IV, 239).

Larceny–theft is divided into categories by the Uniform Crime Reports. In 2002, private property removed from motor vehicles accounted for the largest defined group of larceny–thefts at 26.5% of the total (Uniform Crime Reports, §II, 50). Shoplifting was the second largest category, accounting for 14% (Uniform Crime Reports, §II, 217). Thefts from buildings comprised 12.5% of the larceny–theft total, whereas larceny–thefts of motor vehicle accessories were 10.7% of the total. Thefts of bicycles equaled 3.9% of all larceny–thefts. Pocket-picking, purse-snatching, and theft from coin operated machines each represented less than 1% of the total (Uniform Crime Reports, §II, 217). All other larceny–thefts were compiled into an "other" category representing slightly more than 30% of the total.

ALISON MCKENNEY BROWN

References and Further Reading

Black, H.C., et al. 1979. *Black's Law Dictionary*, 792 and 1324, 5th ed., West Publishing, St. Paul, MN.

Federal Bureau of Investigation 2003. Crime in the United States, 2002, Government Printing Office, Washington, DC.

Hails K.J. 1997. *Criminal Law*, Copperhouse Publishing, Incline Village, NV.

See also **Larceny and Theft: The Law; Receiving Stolen Goods**

Larceny and Theft: The Law

Introduction

Although crimes against the person receive the bulk of media and public attention, the reality is that crimes against property are far more common. The oldest and most common property crime is the theft of property. Theft is a general term used to describe a variety of crimes involving the misappropriation of property. The law of theft has a long and convoluted history. At early common law only the crime of larceny existed, but, as society developed and criminals devised new ways to deprive people of their possessions, the law responded by creating numerous theft-related offenses. These offenses were confusing and often difficult to distinguish from one another. Today many states have done away with the variety of theft offenses and lump together all crimes involving the unlawful obtaining of property as *larceny.*

The elements of larceny at early common law included the unlawful taking and carrying away of another's personal property with the intent to permanently deprive the rightful owner of its possession. This definition encompassed takings by force, later known as *robbery*, and takings without the knowledge of the owner, commonly referred to as *stealing*. Only larceny by force or stealth was considered a criminal act. Those who chose to lend their property to others were not protected by the law if the borrower refused to return the property.

As society evolved and people began to rely on others to do business, personal property was placed in the custody of another for a limited purpose. Thus, Jane Doe might give a bank clerk $100 to deposit in person Jane Doe's bank account. If the clerk instead kept the money for himself, it was not larceny at early common law because there was no wrongful taking as Jane Doe willingly handed over the money to the clerk. Courts soon responded by enlarging the definition of larceny and creating other offenses such as conversion, embezzlement, and false pretenses. Today larceny is defined broadly and includes takings by stealth, force, and fraud.

The Elements of Larceny

The elements of larceny, at early common law, included the unlawful taking and carrying away of another's personal property with the intent to permanently deprive the rightful owner of its possession. Each of these, and their development over time, are discussed below.

Taking

The taking requirement means that the thief must gain at least brief control over the property of another. Examples include picking someone's pocket, taking items from a store, or stealing a car. Common law courts often stated that there must occur a "trespass in the taking." This merely meant there must be an unlawful taking of property from another's possession.

Carrying Away

The carrying away requirement means that the actor must transport the item taken at least some distance from its original location. One only need carry the item a short distance, such as taking a wallet out of someone else's pocket.

Property

At common law, larceny included only personal property. Larceny was, therefore, limited to the misappropriation of goods and chattels. Real property and anything attached to it were not eligible for larceny. Negotiable paper (such as checks, stocks, and bonds) was also excluded as subject matter of common law larceny. This is because negotiable paper is not seen as actual property, but only as a representation of property. Gas, oil, and electricity were also excluded, as were services and labor. Modern larceny includes virtually all property, regardless of its classification as real or personal.

"of another"

The "of another" requirement means that one cannot commit larceny of property they either own or possess, so long as they came into possession of the property in a lawful manner (meaning neither by force nor stealth). Originally, a person could not commit larceny of property given to them to hold for another. This changed as society changed. Custodians for a particular purpose (commonly known as bailees) can wrongfully take and carry away property in their possession, thereby committing larceny. A bailee is a person to whom goods are entrusted. If that person refuses to return an item given to them for a particular purpose, under modern larceny law that is a crime. An example is a dry cleaner. John Doe gives the drycleaner his shirts to launder, and returns the next day to pick them up. If the dry cleaner refuses to return the shirts, and instead claims they are now his, a larceny may have occurred.

Possession secured by trick is a wrongful taking. At common law this was known as larceny by trick. If someone lies to get your property, even though you gave it up voluntarily, it is larceny. Additionally, keeping property you find on the street is larceny, if you do so with the intent to deprive the owner permanently—there is no such thing as "finders keepers, losers weepers" in the law.

Intent to Permanently Deprive

The intent requirement means that the prosecution must prove that the defendant intended to permanently deprive the rightful possessor of the property when he or she took it away. A temporary misappropriation does not constitute larceny. Modern statutes have filled the gap this creates in the law. An example is joyriding—someone who takes another's car for the limited purpose of using it for a short time and then returning it or abandoning it has not committed larceny, but has committed the lesser offense of joyriding.

Conclusion

All the elements of larceny have been significantly broadened over the years. The taking element is satisfied when an actor gains brief control over an item, either directly or indirectly. The carrying away element is satisfied if the item is moved even a slight distance from its original location. The personal property element has been expanded to cover both personal and real property. Finally, there must still be an intent to deprive permanently.

Until the 1960s, a variety of common law larceny-related crimes existed in every jurisdiction. These included larceny by stealth, by trick, or by force; conversion; and false pretenses. In 1962, the Model *Penal Code* consolidated many common law theft crimes; many states have since also done so. Consolidated theft statutes eliminate the largely artificial need to decide whether property was "taken and carried away" or "converted" or "swindled." Joining all the common law theft offenses under one statute deals with the common social problem—criminal property misappropriation—while simplifying the law regarding larceny.

CRAIG HEMMENS

References and Further Reading

Brickey, K.F. 1980. The jurisprudence of larceny: An historical inquiry and interest analysis, *Vanderbilt Law Review*, 33:1101.

Dressler, J. 1995. *Understanding Criminal Law*, Matthew Bender, New York, NY.

Fletcher, G. 1978. *Rethinking Criminal Law*, Little, Brown, Boston, MA.

Tigar, M.E. 1994. The right of property and the law of theft, *Texas Law Review*, 62:1443.

See also **Larceny and Theft: Extent and Correlates; Receiving Stolen Goods**

Law and Legal Services: Careers

There are a range of career opportunities in the legal arena, including careers that are focused on working in court and those that provide more of a support service to the judicial system. Regardless of the actual job, however, it is important to remember that the judicial system is one built on strict rules, consideration of competing arguments, and a long history of highly valued tradition. As such, the courts are usually thought of as the most formal of areas of the criminal justice system and the sets of careers that have both the strictest rules and perhaps the most intricate procedures.

When most people think of a career in the legal arena, they think about being a lawyer. Attorneys are the individuals who actually make arguments in and to courts on behalf of either the government or individuals. Some attorneys, such as many criminal prosecutors, will spend a great deal of their time actually in court, whereas some attorneys will never set foot in a courtroom.

In the criminal justice system attorneys fulfill two basic types of roles. First, some lawyers work for the government as prosecutors. A criminal prosecutor's job includes determining what charges to file against suspected criminals, deciding when they have enough evidence to proceed with a case, presenting evidence to the court in support of the charges against defendants, and recommending sentences for convicted offenders. In larger communities, individual prosecutors often specialize in certain types of crimes (violence, domestic violence, traffic offenses, drugs, etc.) whereas in smaller communities prosecutors handle any and all cases that come to them. The second type of attorney in the criminal justice system is the defense attorney. The job of the defense attorney is—contrary to the popular assumption that her job is to "get the defendant off"—to represent individuals charged with crimes in such a way as to ensure that their legal rights are respected and provided. This means that the defense attorney argues against the prosecutor, and tries to refute the evidence and testimony offered against his client, as well as provides any evidence to show that his client is not guilty.

Some attorneys also work for the courts themselves, acting in administrative roles that facilitate the processing and review of cases. These lawyers do not try cases, but provide background information for judges, review cases and materials to determine whether cases are ready for further processing, and sometimes try to divert cases to alternative dispute resolution mechanisms.

All attorneys need to be licensed in order to practice. Attorneys need to have a college degree and a juris doctorate degree. In addition, in order to be licensed they must pass the bar exam in the state(s) where they wish to practice; this is usually also accompanied by a background investigation to ensure that they are "of good character."

Paralegals fulfill a number of different tasks, but are usually thought of as assistants to attorneys. In this role, paralegals work under the supervision of an attorney and do legal research, prepare legal documents, conduct interviews with witnesses and other persons involved in a case, file documents with courts, and generally provide any and all types of tasks that assist attorneys in preparing for a trial, deposition, arbitration, or negotiations in a case. Paralegals are professional staff that have specialized training in legal research and legal writing. Their educational requirements are not as strict as attorneys, but they are expected to have working understandings of the basics of legal research, writing, and the structure and processes of the court system.

Judges, or, as they are sometimes called, "magistrates," are the individuals with the responsibility for seeing that the law is applied to cases. Judges are the individuals who receive, hear, and review information (in the form of witness testimony and written legal briefs) to decide how the law actually applies to particular cases. Judges are required to be impartial and to make decisions on the merits of the evidence or arguments presented to them. In criminal cases, judges either decide the outcome or direct a jury, determine and apply sentences, determine whether evidence is legally permitted to be introduced, and hear and decide legal maneuverings (motions) filed by the prosecution and the defense. In some jurisdictions, judges are elected and in others they are political appointees. Judges' terms vary across jurisdictions. In smaller communities judges often hear all cases that come to the court, and in larger jurisdictions some judges specialize, at least for designated "terms," hearing only arraignments, criminal trials, family disputes, or other civil lawsuits. Judges almost always are required to be licensed attorneys, and usually are expected to have some experience as a practicing attorney.

Court administrators are the individuals who actually oversee the business, flow of cases, and staffing of the court as a workplace. Usually the court administrator's office works jointly with a chief judge to oversee the preparation of reports about the court's activities, case scheduling, and personnel matters concerning other court staff members.

In addition to the jobs that are directly focused on the legal process itself, there are also a number of different types of social service careers that work in and around the court system. These include individuals who work for the court system itself, those who work for other government agencies, but do most of their work in or at the court, and those who are actually employed by nonprofit agencies but work in and at the courts. Social service types of jobs include victims' advocates, whose responsibilities include providing emotional and social support to crime victims as they see their cases work their way through the court system. Victim advocates often collaborate with prosecutors to assist victims in sharing their experiences with the prosecutor and being prepared for testifying in court. Victim advocacy groups originally grew out of the battered woman's movement, and today have been expanded into child abuse cases and, in most large communities, to all types of personal or violent crimes.

Social service workers are also present in the court system to assist individuals involved in legal proceedings access necessary services—including child care, psychological counseling, educational programs, financial assistance, etc.—that are also often considered important in ensuring that the individuals do not need to return to court in the future (in any role). Social service workers are also sometimes used in criminal courts to assist in the preparation of presentence investigations and make recommendations to both judges and the corrections system about a convicted offender's programming needs.

RICHARD TEWKSBURY

References and Further Reading

Damp, D.V. 2002. *The Book of U.S. Government Jobs*, Bookhaven Press, Ashland, OH.
Eckert, J. and Kathy, M. 2003. *Ask the Career Counselors …Answers for Lawyers on Their Lives and Life's Work*, American Bar Association, Chicago, IL.
Justice Research Association. 2000. *Your Criminal Justice Career: A Guidebook*, Prentice-Hall, Upper Saddle River, NJ.
Munneke, G.A. 2003. *The Legal Career Guide: From Law Student to Lawyer*, 4th ed., American Bar Association, Chicago, IL.
Wadsworth Publishing. 2003. *Wadsworth's Guide to Careers in Criminal Justice*, 2nd ed., Wadsworth Publishing, New York, NY.

See also **Criminology and Criminal Justice: Careers in Research and Training; Defense Lawyers; Judges; Law Enforcement: Careers**

Law Enforcement

It is important to note that in both the past and the present, law enforcement agencies have only contributed minimally to social control; ordinary citizens and informal social institutions such as families, churches, and schools play a larger and more comprehensive role in regulating citizen behavior in society. It is only when these informal institutions break down that formal social control agencies, such as the police, must step in. Historically, the makeup, organization, and behavior of these agencies have been shaped by societal factors, including the political, economic, and social climate present in a particular time and place.

Many characteristics of policing in contemporary society can be traced to the London Metropolitan Police force (established in 1829), and its father, Sir Robert Peel. Three elements of this style of policing, also known as the London Model, provide the foundation for modern police practices: a mission of crime prevention, a primary strategy of patrol, and a quasi-military organizational structure. Several traditions that originally emerged in England continue to figure in the practice and organization of policing in western societies. First, there has been a tradition of limited police authority; each police agency may exercise its police power only within its proscribed physical and legal jurisdictions. Second, a tradition of local control means that the administration and management of a police agency are carried out under the guidance and direction of its governing body (be it at the city, county, state, or federal level). The above traditions contribute to enormous variety among police departments in terms of size, governing body, influence by local history and politics, and relationships with the communities they serve.

American policing during the 19th century fell far short of the ideals originally outlined by Sir Robert Peel, for example, that police should be carefully selected and trained, focus on the prevention of crime, and deal with citizens in a respectful and nonviolent manner. To quote the noted police historian Samuel Walker, "the modern police were created to deal with the problems of crime and disorder, but they succeeded primarily in becoming a social problem themselves …" (1999, 27). The negative attributes of early American police can be grouped into two broad categories. First, problematic internal personnel practices included hiring based on political connections, the corresponding lack of job security for officers hired and fired according to political whim, and no formal training for officers. Second, extremely limited supervision of officers caused major corruption problems, most notably resulting in widespread nonenforcement of the law. For example, the Tenderloin district of New York City was so named because of the juicy payoffs that officers could receive for overlooking gambling, prostitution, and alcohol offenses.

These problems tended to differentially affect certain groups—the poor, immigrants, and racial minorities. Personnel and corruption problems among the police traditionally have most affected those with the lowest social status.

During the early part of the 20th century in the U.S., the professional movement attempted to rectify some of the problems plaguing American policing. Police leaders noted for their reform efforts included August Vollmer, O.W. Wilson, and William H. Parker. Wilson promoted a theory of management that emphasized police efficiency and identified the primary mission of policing as crime control. Known as the professional model, this style of policing includes a reliance on centralized control and bureaucratic organization within departments, efficient use of police resources such as personnel and equipment, more training of officers, and greater use of technology in police work.

With the developments of the patrol car, two-way radio, telephone, and uniform crime reports (UCR), the police embraced a reactive role of controlling crime, rather than a proactive role of preventing crime. These technological advances changed the nature of police work and police-citizen contacts. Good police performance came to be viewed as providing faster response times and increased amounts of service to the public via telephone and emergency response systems. The nature of these technological advances, however, was paradoxical, skewing officers' perceptions of those they served. Technology brought police into more contact with the most needy and desperate elements of society rather than an even distribution of all types of citizens. Subsequently, intimacy between police and citizens was reduced rather than enhanced. Initiated by citizen demand, policing occurred in private residences, and no amount of technology could prepare officers for the myriad social problems they encountered—addiction, family disturbances, mental illness, and poverty— which they could do little about.

As a result of the professional movement, the crime control function of police was given dominance over all other police functions, such as service, peacekeeping, and order maintenance. To a large extent, contemporary performance measures continue to reflect and maintain a crime-oriented conception of the police role; for example, most police continue to be evaluated using crime rates, arrests, response times, and clearance rates. An exclusive focus on crime control unfortunately prohibits police from establishing a mandate they are able to fulfill—because the causes and consequences of crime are often beyond police control. Ironically, traditional indicators like arrest may be viewed as either police successes (e.g., by engaging in productive crackdowns on crime) or failures (e.g., by

not decreasing or preventing crime). Furthermore, these indicators represent only a small proportion of what police do on a daily basis (it is estimated that fewer than 25% of calls to police deal with a criminal law violation).

Technology not only plays a central role in the nature of modern policing, it also continues to play an important role in efforts to improve policing. For example, the use of computers, sophisticated crime-mapping and data analysis, and advanced surveillance technology have emerged as necessary tools for officers to control crime. With enough advanced technology, it is hoped that the police can be effective at solving complex social problems. It is often ignored that these problems have taken decades to develop and simply are not amenable to quick solutions or technological advances.

Of the three components comprising the criminal justice system of the U.S.—police, courts, and corrections—the police system is the largest. The local level is by far the most dominant level of the police system, both numerically (the number of law enforcement agencies) and symbolically (most citizen contacts are with local law enforcement agents). The reason for this is that a large proportion of police officers are assigned to patrol the streets: 65% in the U.S., 65% in Canada, 56% in Britain, 54% in Australia, and 40% in Japan (Bayley, 1994, 16). Law enforcement agents at this level deliver four types of service: law enforcement, crime prevention, order maintenance, and social services. Although most police research is done on very large departments employing thousands of officers, the typical local department in the U.S. has fewer than ten officers. It is important, therefore, to resist applying findings from large, urban departments to their smaller, often rural, counterparts. Critics consider the local system to be fragmented, lacking in cooperation and coordination between agencies, and suffering from a lack of uniform standards. Others contend that arrangements have been worked out between local agencies that reduce the likelihood of duplication of services. Compared to other western countries, however, there is little doubt that local law enforcement in the U.S. can be considered decentralized, fragmented, and various.

The state level is the second largest component of the U.S. police system, and includes agencies such as the highway patrol and state police. These agencies provide policing to areas not covered by local agencies. The federal level is the third and numerically the smallest in the U.S. police system. The role and mission of federal agencies are much more specific and clearly defined. Federal agents are charged with enforcing federal criminal laws, whereas their state and local counterparts are charged with "policing"—a more nebulous responsibility including order maintenance, peacekeeping, and providing general assistance. Federal law enforcement agencies are recognized for their higher entry requirements, more extensive training, and more competitive salaries than state and local agencies.

The police role in society, for many reasons, is more complex than is often supposed. One feature of the police role that contributes to its complexity is that it comprises two often conflicting functions: law enforcement activities such as making arrests, and harder to define order maintenance activities involving keeping the peace, agency referrals, and social work activities. On a daily basis, most policing is of the order maintenance variety, where citizen and supervisor expectations of the appropriate response may be conflicting, arbitrary, or even unknown to the officer.

Another factor contributing to the complexity of the police role is that officers are confronted with a wide variety of tasks, only a few of which require criminal law enforcement. For example, officers may be called upon to provide medical assistance, arrange for the removal of abandoned vehicles, deal with the mentally ill, or ticket people for minor violations. Many of these tasks are extremely vague and may even conflict with one another. For example, the classic tension in police work is that of maintaining order in the community while protecting the constitutional rights of individual citizens. The police focus on "law" versus "order" has shifted many times over the years owing to societal changes and demands. Furthermore, society has not reached a consensus regarding exactly what situations require police intervention, and how the police should respond to those that do. The recent domestic violence policy shift away from informal police responses (such as mediation, separation, or counseling), toward a formal arrest response is a clear example of the ever-changing nature of police roles and responsibilities.

Discretion is a defining feature of police work that also contributes to the complexity of the police role. Discretion refers to the unwritten rule that police officers have the right to be selective in how they do their jobs as long as they stay within widely prescribed departmental guidelines. Discretion is an intrinsic element of police work and considered by most police scholars to be normal, beneficial, and unavoidable. Police organizations are unique because discretion increases as one moves down the organizational chart; in other types of work, middle and upper managers have more discretion than those they supervise.

Because financial as well as societal factors prohibit officers from full enforcement of the law, police have to use discretion on a daily basis to determine which laws to enforce and for which people. The law, and whether it has been violated, only comprises a small fraction of the information officers consider when making decisions. Order maintenance situations are more often faced by patrol officers, and produce even more discretionary behavior because officers must interpret laws, determine appropriate standards of conduct, and assign blame.

Research investigating the impact of discretion on police decision making has shown that police discretion is *not* random, but rather patterned and somewhat predictable. Several categories of factors influence the exercise of discretion: situational features of the incident; the officer's work environment; individual characteristics of the officer; and, departmental policies. Situational features, such as the seriousness of the crime, the strength of the evidence, or the victim's preference for or against a certain police response, tend to exert the strongest influence on police decisions. For example, the best predictors of the arrest decision are situational rather than the responding officers' attitudinal or social background characteristics. Features of officers' immediate work environment also influence their decisions, for example, whether they are assigned to work in high- or low-crime areas. Neighborhood context has been shown to be important for understanding levels of police activity and use of force. Research has shown that individual officer characteristics, such as race, gender, or education, do not appear to have a major influence over discretionary decisions. When predicting police use of force, for example, it is more important to know the characteristics of the beat in which an officer works rather than his or her individual characteristics.

Departmental policies (e.g., those limiting the use of high-speed pursuits or physical force against citizens) have had a powerful influence over police discretion. Known as administrative rule making (ARM), this is the preferred method of control over police discretion used in contemporary policing. The goal of ARM is to structure or guide police discretion rather than attempt its elimination. To control the use of discretion, departments attempt to have clearly prescribed policies and procedures for various incidents so that officers know exactly what is expected of them at the scene, and can act accordingly.

In short, the police role is complex because the average officer on the street must deal with a wide variety of ill-defined and conflicting tasks, and must use his or her discretion to determine the appropriate response to these cases. The desired response to certain incidents may also change over time and vary according to what groups in society the officer is serving.

Models or styles of policing in the U.S. have attempted to shift away from "professional" police practices and toward "community-oriented" policing. Several events precipitated this shift in the police mandate. First, civil unrest during the 1960s challenged police legitimacy and brought questionable police practices into the national spotlight. Second, recognition of the isolation of the police from the public led to interest in creating police–citizen partnerships and forging better relationships with citizens, especially those in minority communities. Third, the community-policing movement arose from research findings that the assumptions underlying the professional movement were erroneous. As research indicated that "nothing works," reformers attempted to identify and adopt policing strategies that might make a difference, such as foot patrols, permanent beat assignments, and neighborhood mini-stations.

The underlying premise of the community-policing philosophy is that the police and various individuals, agencies, organizations, or community groups should work together to accomplish mutual goals. Accordingly, the police and the public ought to become "co-producers" of public safety, because "together, police and public are more effective and more humane co-producers of safety and public order than are the police alone" (Skolnick and Bayley, 1988). Proponents of community policing consider it vital, therefore, that the police and the public create meaningful, working partnerships to identify and address community problems. Community-policing officers are urged to respond creatively to community problems, increase citizen involvement in crime control, and improve community relations. Community policing also attempts to empower officers by giving them greater discretionary power through organizational changes such as decentralization and reduction of bureaucratic controls. Officers are encouraged to use their own initiative and skill to solve problems and build positive relationships within the communities they serve.

Performance indicators used to assess police performance have been expanded as a result of the broadened police mandate under community policing. Today, the object of the game is to reduce disorder, solve problems, and build relationships with the community in addition to enforcing the law. In this way, law enforcement "is not an end in itself, but only one of several means by which the police can deal with the problems they are expected to handle" (Goldstein, 1990). Police continue to rely disproportionately on traditional or crime-related measures of performance, although some progress has been made in using other performance indicators, including citizen fear of crime, public satisfaction with and confidence in police, the reduction of disorder, and solving community problems.

Although community policing is currently widespread and embraced by politicians, police administrators, and the public, some critics note that contemporary American policing represents an "iron fist within a velvet glove," that is, increased militarism and aggressive police tactics are couched in softer rhetoric emphasizing police and community partnerships as part of the community-policing ideology. There is substantial variation in the tactics and strategies deployed by police departments as part of a community-policing strategy. For example, in a study of community-policing programs in eight U.S. cities, Skolnick and Bailey (1988) concluded that there were more differences than similarities among the programs; some focused on aggressive street enforcement and drug crackdowns as part of community policing whereas others attempted community organizing and interagency cooperation. This has led police scholars to question whether community policing is more rhetoric than reality.

A related criticism of community policing is that it tends to work the best where it is needed the least. In other words, poor, crime ravaged, socially disorganized, and minority communities often experience little or no benefit from this new policing movement. This could in part be a function of the "face" of community policing that a community receives; if police espouse a new community-policing mandate and then engage solely in traditional crime fighting (involving tactics of patrol, surveillance, and arrest), they may confront a crisis of legitimacy. This may decrease a community member's desire to work with police, assuming they wanted to in the first place.

Not only has policing changed philosophically over the past 25 years, but it has also changed demographically. For example, the proportion of female officers in the U.S., Australia, and Britain has grown from less than 2% (confined to specialized units) to 10% (present in varying degrees in all ranks and units). Some believe that the community-policing philosophy reflects these gender changes in police organizations. Whereas previously police work emphasized the stereotypically masculine traits of suspicion, cynicism, and aggression, now the importance of interpersonal skills and mediation are recognized as valid police characteristics. Despite these changes, female officers have yet to be fully accepted into the police profession. The negative relationship between traditional masculinized gender roles that continue to dominate policing and the experiences of female officers has been well-established, propagating sexual harassment and restriction of promotional opportunities, among other workplace stressors. This is despite the fact that most studies find only minor performance differences between male and female officers, and some research suggests that female officers may be viewed more favorably by the public.

Police departments have also become more heterogeneous in terms of race. In the U.S., Black officers comprise about 12% of the total officers, but this proportion varies widely, with larger departments employing more African Americans. Hispanics nationally constitute 6% of police officers, but are much better represented in communities with large Hispanic populations. Minority employment in police departments began to increase during the 1970s, and with some important implications for the culture of policing. For example, some studies have shown that minority officers are more likely to speak out on police use of force or in other ways criticize their departments. Other research suggests high levels of intergroup conflict based on the sex and race of officers. Because the demographic makeup of many police organizations has changed, we may need to question the notion that there is a unified police "subculture." Indeed, many police experts now favor the idea of a heterogeneous or fractured police subculture, rather than one all-encompassing "blue wall."

Issues that will challenge police agencies during the 21st century include improving the technological training of officers, promoting effective community-policing practices, evaluating officer and departmental performance, and promoting a work environment that is supportive of all officers, regardless of their backgrounds.

AMANDA L. ROBINSON

References and Further Reading

Bayley, D. 1994. *Police for the Future*, Oxford, New York, NY.
Bittner, E. 1990. *Aspects of Police Work*, Northeastern University Press, Boston, MA.
Crank, J. 1998. *Understanding Police Culture*, Anderson, Cincinnati, OH.
Goldstein, H. 1990. *Problem-Oriented Policing*, McGraw-Hill, New York, NY.
Greene, J.R. and Mastrofski, S.D. 1988. *Community Policing: Rhetoric or Reality?* Praeger, New York, NY.
Manning, P.K. 1997. *Police Work*, 2nd ed., Waveland, Prospect Heights, IL.
Martin, S.E. 1980. *Breaking and Entering: Policewomen on Patrol*, University of California Press, Berkeley, CA.
Rubinstein, J. 1973. *City Police*, Noonday Press, New York, NY.
Skolnick, J.H. 1975. *Justice without Trial: Law Enforcement in a Democratic Society*, 2nd ed., John Wiley and Sons, New York, NY.
Skolnick, J.H. and David, H.B. 1988. *New Blue Line: Police Innovation in Six American Cities*, Free Press, New York, NY.
Walker, S. 1999. *The Police in America*, 3rd ed., McGraw-Hill, Boston, MA.

See also **Police: Administration and Organization; Police: Community Policing; Police: Municipal or Urban; Police: Patrol; Police: Rural**

Law Enforcement Assistance Administration

The Law Enforcement Assistance Administration (LEAA) represented the federal government's major foray into providing assistance (including funds) and guidance to the states in combating the nation's crime problem. Born in the turbulent 1960s in the wake of riots, civil disturbances, large increases in street crime, and political assassinations, the LEAA had a short life, but its more successful programs were merged into the U.S. Department of Justice (DOJ) bureaucracy. By the 21st century, the National Institute of Justice (NIJ), the Bureau of Justice Statistics (BJS), and the National Criminal Justice Reference Service (NCJRS) were the major remnants of the LEAA legacy.

The genesis of the LEAA can be traced to President John Kennedy's measure sent to Congress on March 8, 1963, which resulted in the Criminal Justice Act of 1964 and creation of the Office of Criminal Justice in the DOJ. This office, in turn, prepared the Law Enforcement Assistance Act of 1965 (Harris, 1968). President Lyndon Johnson proposed the new Act in his March 8, 1965 Message on Crime to Congress and on September 22,

1965, Johnson signed the Act into law (Law Enforcement Assistance Act of 1965). Under it, $10 million was appropriated for the fiscal year ending June 30, 1966, to improve "the capabilities, techniques, and practices of state and local agencies engaged in law enforcement; the administration of criminal laws; [and] the correction of offenders or the prevention of crime" via training and educating personnel; grants for special projects, stipends, and allowances for trainees; and special studies and technical assistance. In other words, it provided a small amount of funding for pilot projects and training and technical assistance (Stephens, 1976).

In his 1965 Message on Crime, President Johnson also announced the appointment of his President's Commission on Law Enforcement and Administration of Justice to deal with the "malignant enemy" of crime in America. In its report in 1967, the commission held: "The Federal Government can make a dramatic new contribution to the national effort against crime by greatly expanding its support of the agencies of justice in the states and in the cities" (Stephens, 283).

On February 6, 1967, President Johnson delivered a new message on crime to Congress, detailing the findings of his commission and proposing the Safe Streets and Crime Control Act of 1967, which included creation of the LEAA to oversee this federal assistance (U.S. Congress, 1967). Despite the seeming urgency of the crime and disorder problem, it took 16 months to gain passage, as legislators voiced concern about the creation of the new administrative agency, the type of grants it would dispense, and the fear this federal agency would be a major step leading to creation of a national police state in the U.S. By the time it did pass, the bill had been renamed the Omnibus Crime Control and Safe Streets Act of 1968.

In the Omnibus Act, the purpose was stated as "to assist state and local governments in strengthening and improving law enforcement at every level by national assistance," specifically through the creation of comprehensive state and local planning for law enforcement, federal grants to improve and strengthen local and state law enforcement, and research and development to improve law enforcement (Public Law 90-351). The LEAA was created and placed under the "general authority" of the attorney general within the Justice Department, with a "troika" administrative structure—an administrator and two deputy administrators, all appointed by the president and confirmed by the Senate, with no more than two from the same political party as the president.

The LEAA was established to oversee the planning and grant procedure, which included creating a State Planning Agency (SPA) in each state and providing 90% federal-funded grants to develop an "annual comprehensive state-wide law enforcement plan to receive federal assistance." It also provided block grants to states to carry out state plans, as well as discretionary grants for pilot and demonstration projects (Stephens, 1976). The block grants became the cornerstone of federal revenue sharing, whereas the discretionary grants led to many of the crime-prevention programs (e.g., neighborhood watch, operation ID, home and business security surveys) established in local police and sheriffs' departments nationwide. Also established under the LEAA was the National Institute of Law Enforcement "to encourage research and development to improve and strengthen law enforcement (i.e., now NIJ). Another major provision that led to massive expansion of law enforcement or criminal justice curricula in the higher education community was the "academic assistance" section that initially provided up to $1800 in loans per year to preservice law enforcement students (to be forgiven at 25% per year for the total loans acquired via service as a law enforcement officer) and up to $300 per semester grants to law enforcement officers in college or university programs.

Later designated the Law Enforcement Education Program (LEEP), the assistance was expanded both in loan or grant amounts and in eligibility—later including preservice and in-service corrections, juvenile, and eventually court personnel.

Throughout its short history, the LEAA was judged by no less than 17 published critiques, ranging from the original "Law and Disorder" appraisal issued 6 months after the agency's establishment by the Urban Coalition and Urban America (with "Law and Disorder II, III, and IV" issued within a decade) and including three by the General Accounting Organization (GAO), two by the National Conference of State Criminal Justice Administration, and individual evaluations by groups such as the Twentieth Century Fund and the Brookings Institute (Anderson, 1981). The judgments were often harsh, given the difficult goals established for the LEAA by Congress: "(a) to assist state and local governments in reducing the incidence of crime, and (b) to increase the effectiveness, fairness, the coordination of law enforcement and criminal justice systems at all levels of government" (Stephens, 293). To accomplish these goals, the LEAA never had more than $895 million a year (FY1975), after beginning with $63 million (FY1969), and dipping under $650 million by FY1978 (Anderson, 340).

The LEAA lost most of its programs during restructuring in 1979–80 and met its demise in 1984, a victim of President Ronald Reagan's revised definition of "new federalism," returning criminal justice programs for the most part to the state and local governments for funding and administration (Justice Assistance Act of 1984). The more successful LEAA programs were kept on a diminished scale by DOJ under a newly established Office of Justice Programs (OJP). Besides NIJ, BJS, and NCJRS, the programs included the Bureau of Justice Assistance (BJA), to operate formula and discretionary grant programs; the Office of Juvenile Justice and Delinquency Prevention (OJJDP); and the Office of Victims of Crime (OVC).

The LEAA had several successes during its decade and a half, including: (1) expanding the view of "criminal justice" as a "system" that required coordination to succeed in its goals of preventing and reducing crime; (2) creating crime specific planning under which each program was to be judged by its effectiveness in meeting quantitative goals (e.g., reduce burglary by 15% in 12 months; increase percentage of college graduates in a specific agency by 20% in 4 years); (3) establishing a clearinghouse (NCJRS) for criminal justice research and literature; (4) developing a massive data base (BJS) on criminal justice; (5) expanding criminal justice scholarship via research (coordinated by NIJ) and education and training facilities and programs; and (6) establishing standards and goals for criminal justice agencies via a two-year commission effort (1971–1973) resulting in *A National Strategy to Reduce Crime.*

R. EUGENE STEPHENS

References and Further Reading

Anderson, P.R. 1981. *An Examination of Published Evaluations and Their Relationship to Legislative Activity Regarding the Law Enforcement Assistance Administration*, PhD dissertation, Florida State University.

Brookings Institution. 1976. *Where Have All the Dollars Gone? Implications of General Revenue Sharing for the Law Enforcement Assistance Administration*, National Institute of Law Enforcement and Criminal Justice, Washington, DC.

Harris, R. 1969. Annals of legislation: The omnibus crime control and safe streets Act of 1968, *The New Yorker,* November 6.

Justice Assistance Act of 1984. 1984. *Statutes at Large*, 98 (P.L. 98-473).

Law Enforcement Assistance Act of 1965. 1965. *Statutes at Large*, 79 (P.L. 93-83).

Law Enforcement Assistance Act of 1965. 1966. *US Code Congressional and Administrative News*, 89th Cong., 1st Session, 1965, Vol. 2, West Publishing, St. Paul, MN.

National Advisory Commission on Criminal Justice Standards and Goals. 1973. *A National Strategy to Reduce Crime*, US Government Printing Office, Washington, DC.

Omnibus Crime Control and Safe Streets Act of 1968. 1969. *Statutes at Large,* 82 (P.L. 90-351).

Omnibus Crime Control and Safe Streets Act of 1968. 1969. *US Code Congressional and Administrative News*, 90th Cong., 2nd Session, 1968, Vol. 2, West Publishing, St. Paul, MN.

President's Commission on Law Enforcement and Administration of Justice. 1967. *The Challenge of Crime in a Free Society*, US Government Printing Office, Washington, DC.

Stephens, R.E. 1976. The Law Enforcement Assistance Administration: An Analytical, Descriptive Overview of Its Origin, Legislative Mandate, and Federal Administration, PhD dissertation, Emory University.

US Congress 1965. President Johnson's Message on Crime, *Congressional Record 111.*

US Congress 1967. President Johnson's Message on Crime, *Congressional Record 113.*

US General Accounting Office. 1974. *Difficulties of Assessing Results of Law Enforcement Assistance Administration Projects to Reduce Crime*, US Government Accounting Office, Washington, DC.

US General Accounting Office. 1977. *Overview of Activities Funded by the law Enforcement Assistance Administration*, US General Accounting Office, Washington, DC.

The Urban Coalition and Urban America, Inc. 1969. *Law and Disorder: State Planning Under the Safe Streets Act*, Urban Coalition, Washington, DC.

See also **Police Administration and Organization; Police: History in the U.S.**

Law Enforcement: Careers

Children aspire to become various types of professionals, and typically, becoming a police officer is near the top of the list. For those who maintain the desire to be a police officer, an important career decision has to be made—"In what capacity do I want to enforce law?" When policemen are mentioned, most people envision a person in uniform driving black and white marked police cars. The reality of police careers is that there are many other aspects of law enforcement other than the frontline patrol officer. Fundamentally, there are three layers of law enforcement—local, state, and federal. Each layer maintains officers conducting the duties of various functions. According to the Bureau of Justice Statistics (BJS), 17,784 full-time law enforcement agencies were operating in the U.S. in 2000. This article is written to introduce the reader to the multitude of careers within the law enforcement profession, beginning with local law enforcement organizations and progressing through federal law enforcement agencies.

Local level law enforcement duties primarily lie within the domain of municipal police departments, county sheriffs' departments, and special police agencies. Of the 12,666 local police agencies, 76.8% employ fewer than 25 sworn officers, whereas 62.6% of the 3070 sheriffs' departments have fewer than 25 sworn officers. Primary duties of sworn personnel in local police and sheriffs' departments include enforcing traffic and criminal laws, responding to calls for service, taking reports, and proactive patrol of jurisdictions. The majority of the officers within these agencies are uniformed officers; however, depending on the size and resources, the department may have specialized units to include: investigations, bike patrol, crime prevention, community-oriented policing, warrant service, traffic enforcement, and drug enforcement.

Generally, there are many mobility opportunities within local law enforcement agencies. Most have established rank structures for upward mobility, but lateral mobility is also possible in departments with multiple functions. Entry-level salary ranges vary depending on location, candidate experience and credentials, but typically fall between $15,900 and $64,500. According to the Bureau of Labor Statistics (BLS), national median earnings for local law enforcement officers in 2000 were $39,790. Although many local agencies are beginning to require some college credit, the majority only require a high school diploma or equivalent. Candidates must be at least 21 years old, have a valid driver's license, be of good moral character, and have limited driver and criminal histories. Generally, candidates for local law enforcement positions will experience a battery of preemployment screenings and, upon selection, must successfully complete training at a police academy.

The realm of state law enforcement agencies generally comprises a state police, or highway patrol. Some states also maintain a forensic investigative agency, investigators in the attorney general's office, and a wildlife enforcement bureau. The most visible of state police agencies is the highway patrol. Every state, excluding Hawaii, operates a highway patrol, or state police, division. Some states have separate agencies for highway patrol and state police, but most operate a single uniformed state authority. Highway patrol officers, or state troopers, are primarily tasked with assisting motorists, enforcing traffic laws, and investigating traffic collisions. Some state troopers perform patrol duties for unincorporated areas that do not have local police forces.

State police agencies generally offer services in the capacity of investigation assistance and forensic services. Typically, state police agencies employ many fewer agents than the highway patrol. Agents are stationed throughout the state, but have a centralized headquarters. The attorney general in each state is the chief prosecuting officer for that state. As such, attorneys general maintain an investigations squad to assist in case preparation, and to investigate incidents reported to the attorney general. Typically, such cases involve wrongdoing by a public official; however, investigators of the office of the attorney general may also investigate white-collar crimes, financial security fraud, and threats to public security. Game wardens, or wildlife enforcement officers or conservation officers, are responsible for enforcing hunting and fishing laws, incidents involving endangered species, and boating law infractions on public waters. Game wardens in some states also provide security at state parks and recreation centers.

Entry-level salaries for state level law enforcement officers typically range from $15,900 to $59,000, depending on location and qualifications. The BLS reported that the median salary for state law enforcement officers in 2000 was $44,400. Excluding highway patrol agencies, most state law enforcement agencies prefer some college credit and previous law enforcement experience. Candidates for state law enforcement positions must be at least 21 years old, have a decent driving history, and no criminal background. Competing for a state-level law enforcement position is typically more challenging than for a local department; therefore, interested candidates should gain experience and complete college degrees prior to pursuing a law enforcement career on the state level. Upward mobility is more limited and slower within a state law enforcement agency; however, most do promote primarily from within, when positions are available. Selected candidates must complete police academy training, if necessary, and many require further instruction for specific job task training.

There are numerous federal law enforcement agencies responsible for a vast array of obligations. The most popular of federal law enforcement agencies is the Federal Bureau of Investigations (FBI). The FBI employs approximately 11,500 agents deployed throughout the U.S. and the world. Aside from being a forensic investigations resource, the FBI is responsible for enforcing over 260 federal laws and investigating incidents including civil rights violations, terrorism and counterterrorism, organized and white-collar crime, and violent crimes.

A division of the Department of Justice, the Drug Enforcement Administration (DEA) is the leading drug enforcement and investigations agency in the country. The DEA investigates the illegal drug trade, as well as prescription drug diversion, particularly in relation to drugs categorized as controlled substances. DEA agents often work in partnership with local and state agencies through established task forces to accomplish initiatives. The DEA has over 4100 sworn personnel dispersed in 22 domestic field offices and various foreign extension offices.

The U.S. Secret Service (USSS) was developed as an investigative bureau for the Department of the Treasury and remained under the Treasury Department umbrella until 2003, when the USSS was moved to become a division of the Department of Homeland Security. Among the responsibilities of the Secret Service is protection of federal political leaders, specifically the president, vice-president, former presidents, former vice-presidents, and their immediate families, as well as major political party presidential and vice-presidential candidates and foreign dignitaries during visits to the U.S. The Secret Service continues to be the primary investigative agency for counterfeiting and other financial security crimes. It coordinates security initiatives for national security events and maintains a threat assessment center. The Secret Service staffs 125 offices worldwide with approximately 4039 sworn law enforcement officers—special agents and uniform patrol officers.

The Bureau of Alcohol, Tobacco, Firearms and Explosives (ATF) was originally founded as a tax collecting bureau of the Department of the Treasury; however, in accordance with the Homeland Security Act of 2002, the ATF today is a division of the Department of Justice. The ATF not only operates tax-collecting operations, but also performs regulatory and enforcement missions in an effort to reduce violent crime and to protect the public. The ATF employs approximately 2000 agents who are tasked with enforcing federal alcohol, tobacco, firearms, explosives, and arson laws and regulations, often working in partnership with other federal agencies, as well as state and local law enforcement departments.

The U.S. Marshals Service is the oldest of the federal law enforcement agencies. Headed by a director, deputy director, and 94 U.S. marshals, who are appointed by the president or U.S. attorney general, the U.S. Marshals Service is fundamentally tasked with the protection of elements of the federal government and services to federal courts in 95 districts. Deputy U.S. marshals conduct investigations of fugitives from the federal prison system and provide courtroom security and witness protection in the federal court system. The service employs approximately 2735 deputy marshals in over 350 locations in the U.S. and abroad.

As part of the Homeland Security Act of 2002, the border protection agencies, including U.S. Customs, U.S. Border Patrol, Department of Agriculture, and the Immigration and Naturalization Service, were combined to form the Customs and Border Patrol (CBP) agency as a division of the Department of Homeland Security. The CBP is headed by a director nominated by the president and confirmed by Congress. The CBP is responsible for enforcing federal laws and regulations in relation to illegal aliens, drug smuggling, agricultural cargo, and general trade. CBP agents are stationed throughout the nation, especially along the borders and ports of entry. The CBP employs over 40,000 agents and investigators to carry out the agency's initiatives.

The U.S. Postal Inspection Service is empowered by Congress to enforce over 200 laws and regulations in relation to the nation's mail as well as civil matters involving the postal service. The service employs approximately 2000 postal inspectors and 1400 uniformed postal police officers to perform these duties.

Law enforcement positions in federal agencies are prestigious, and as such, there is a considerable amount of competition among candidates to fill position openings. Bachelor's degrees are required for federal positions, and some prefer graduate level credit and previous law enforcement and investigative experience. Candidates must be at least 21 years old, but less than 37 years old at the time of appointment to a position. All selected candidates must complete 11 to 20 weeks of training prior to being deployed. Salaries are based on a general schedule (GS), an index of salaries based on job position and candidate dynamics such as education, experience, and background criteria, but typically range from $25,000 to $70,000.

Another aspect of law enforcement that is present on all three levels is that of corrections. Local, state, and federal jails, prisons, penitentiaries, and other correctional facilities are staffed by sworn officers to ensure the security of the facility as well as the safety of inmates, facility staff, and the visiting public. Correctional officers conduct searches of personnel at the facility, both incarcerated and civilian, and physical areas within the facility to locate contraband and bring appropriate charges, if necessary. The Federal Bureau of Prisons employs approximately 13,557 correctional officers, whereas approximately 457,000 correctional officers staff state-level prisons. Local jails and detention facilities are often staffed with local officers who have been described above. Candidates for correctional officer positions must have a high school diploma or equivalent for state-level positions, and a bachelor's degree for federal positions, and should have limited driver and criminal histories. Entry-level salary ranges from $11,000 to $50,000, depending on location, position applied for, experience, and educational background. Another aspect of the correctional system is that of probation and parole officers. These officers are responsible for maintaining records of individuals released from prison on probation and parole. They are tasked with making periodic contact with clients and bringing charges on those who fail to comply with probation or parole conditions. Requirements for these positions are similar to those for federal correctional officers, and entry-level salary ranges widely from $20,000 to $70,000.

Aside from sworn law enforcement positions at all levels, agencies employ great numbers of civilians to assist in carrying on day-to-day tasks, such as records keeping, data entry, support functions, forensic and lab tasks, and a plethora of other responsibilities. A requirement for any candidate in a law enforcement agency is that of U.S. citizenship. As previously stated, education and experience background requirements vary among law enforcement agencies in the three governmental levels, as do salary ranges. Most agencies have mobility opportunities; however, in some agencies, mobility is limited.

This article briefly describes some of the basic dynamics and issues concerning careers in law enforcement on the local, state, and federal levels. This listing is not all-inclusive; therefore, individuals interested in law enforcement careers should not depend solely on this article. Interested candidates are encouraged to search for and review Internet web sites for local and state agencies using a search engine. Internet web sites for federal agencies are listed below for readers to obtain more information.

M. PATRICK LONG

References and Further Reading

Echaore-MdDavid, S. 2000. *Career Opportunities in Law Enforcement, Security, and Protective Services*, Checkmark Books, New York, NY.

Smith, G. 2000. Keeping the law and order, *Career World, a Weekly Reader Publication*, 29 (1), 12.

Stinchcomb, J. 2003. *Opportunities in Law Enforcement and Criminal Justice Careers*, McGraw-Hill Companies, New York, NY.

The Kiplinger Washington Editors Inc. 1984. Careers in law enforcement, *Changing Times*, 38, 50.

U.S. Department of Justice, Bureau of Justice Statistics. 2001. *Census of federal law enforcement agencies, 2000. Bureau of Justice Statistics Bulletin, NCJ 187231*.

U.S. Department of Justice, Bureau of Justice Statistics. 2002. *Census of state and local law enforcement agencies, 2000. Bureau of Justice Statistics Bulletin, NCJ 194066*.

U.S. Department of Labor, Bureau of Labor Statistics, *Occupational Outlook Handbook*, 2002–2003, Available at www.bls.gov.

World Wide Web Resources

Bureau of Alcohol, Tobacco, Firearms and Explosives (ATF) (www.atf.treas.gov)

Customs and Border Patrol (CBP) (www.cbp.gov)

Department of Homeland Security (www.dhs.gov)

Drug Enforcement Administration (DEA) (www.dea.gov)

Federal Bureau of Investigations (FBI) (www.fbi.gov)

U.S. Marshals Service (www.usdoj.gov/marshals)

U.S. Postal Inspection Service (www.usps.com/postalinspectors)

U.S. Secret Service (www.ustreas.gov/usss)

See also **Legal Careers**

Law Enforcement: Community Policing

Community policing is a modern approach to policing that represents a paradigm shift in the way police deliver services to their citizenry. Since the early 1980s, police agencies in the U.S., Canada, the U.K., Australia, New Zealand, and throughout Western Europe have adopted new, broad principles that govern the structure, function, and operations of their contemporary police organizations.

The first section of this essay presents a summary of the literature that depicts the primary conceptual dimensions and effectiveness of community policing. The second section describes several policing concepts and approaches that are related to community policing, including crime prevention, problem-oriented policing, third-party policing, and zero tolerance.

Conceptual Dimensions

David Bayley, in his seminal book *Police for the Future*, depicts four elements of community policing: consultation, adaptation, mobilization, and problem-solving (CAMPS). Changes in the strategic, tactical, and programmatic operations of a police organization logically flow from adoption of Bayley's "CAMPS" community-policing principles. Bayley's four community-policing principles are depicted below.

Consultation refers to the police reaching out to their communities. Under a community-policing model, the police discuss priorities and strategies with the community by deepening their community contacts, meeting regularly with existing community groups, or creating entirely new councils or committees. Consultation may occur on a geographical basis or according to interests.

Adaptation refers to the efforts that the police make to:

reshapecommandstructuressothatlocalcommanders canuseresourcesmoreflexibly.Thisinvolvesdecentralizingcommandsgeographicallyaswellasplacingdecision-makingresponsibilityfartherdowntherankhierarchy … the new initiatives call upon local commanders todeviseplansandadaptresourcestolocalneeds(Bayley, 1994, 107).

Mobilization refers to direct efforts by the police to mobilize citizens, business owners, residents, community groups, government agencies, industry representatives, and victims to play a critical role in crime prevention. Herman Goldstein (1990), Lorraine Green Mazerolle and her coauthor Jan Roehl (1998), and the National Crime Prevention Council (1996) identify a myriad of strategies, people, and agencies that the police can mobilize to augment their crime-prevention activities. Neighborhood watches youth patrols, multi-agency response teams, drug nuisance abatement, and crime prevention through environmental design (CPTED) initiatives comprise just a few examples of mobilization programs.

Problem-solving refers to activities that the police undertake to solve community problems. As an important component of community policing, problem solving requires the police to reorient their efforts away from merely responding to crime events to studying the conditions that underpin persistent crime and disorder problems, developing responses to correct these crime-inducing conditions, and then implementing and evaluating these responses. Herman Goldstein (1990), as the founding scholar of the problem-solving approach to policing, coined the term "problem-oriented policing." Others, such as John Eck and Bill Spelman (1987), have operationalized the concept of problem-oriented policing and are the proponents of the SARA approach to problem solving. The acronym SARA refers to scanning, analysis, response, and assessment. More details about problem-oriented policing are provided in the next section.

Bayley's CAMPS model for community policing provides a broad umbrella under which to conceptualize and understand the vast array of activities that need to take place to move a department toward adopting, implementing, and practicing the principles of community policing.

Like Bayley, George Kelling and Mark Moore (1988) define community policing very broadly and differentiate community policing from earlier eras in policing: the political era and the reform era (also known as the professional era). Kelling and Moore's community problem-solving era comports with Bayley's CAMPS depiction of community policing. They identify eight categories that define police organizations that have adopted community policing as their corporate strategy. These eight categories, as they relate to community policing, are as follows:

Sources of Legitimacy and Authority

Police departments that adopt community policing as their corporate strategy emphasize a balance between the law and the community as the major legitimating basis for police function. The law defines basic police powers, but it is community support and involvement that shape the way that the police maintain order, negotiate conflicts, and solve community problems.

Police Function

Community policing, as a corporate strategy, places equal weight on crime control and crime prevention as the two central functional objectives of a police organization. Rapid response, preventive patrols, and investigations continue to play a role in community-oriented police organizations, but crime prevention becomes at least an equal partner, if not a priority, for the police organization.

Organizational Design

Participative management, decentralized tactical decision making, increased line-officer discretion, and fewer levels of authority comprise the essential organizational ingredients of community-oriented police departments. Community-oriented policing agencies are typically organized such that the functions of police (e.g., patrol, investigations, and traffic management) are geographically decentralized, and local area commanders make important resource allocation decisions for their individual neighborhoods, precincts, or districts.

External Relationships

Successful implementation of community policing relies upon the police forging positive working relationships with nonpolice entities such as community groups (e.g., neighborhood and block watch groups), business associations (e.g., local merchant groups), corporations (e.g., insurance agencies), nongovernment agencies (e.g., the Salvation Army, homeless shelters, soup kitchens), as well as other government agencies (e.g., housing, family welfare, public works). Buerger and Mazerolle refer to this mode of policing as "third-party policing." Third-party policing is defined as:

> … police efforts to persuade or coerce non-offending persons to take actions which are outside the scope of their routine activities, and which are designed to indirectly minimize disorder caused by other persons or to reduce the possibility that crime may occur (Buerger and Mazerolle, 1998, 301).

Demand Management

Old-school (Reform Era) policing relies on centralized systems to manage citizen demands for police service. Centralized systems refer to 9-1-1 or emergency call centers that receive, handle, and dispatch citizen calls for police service. In the past, emergency call centers comprised the most common way that citizens could get into contact with the police and thus most police work (e.g., patrol officers responding to calls for service) was generated through these central dispatch systems.

In the community-policing era, citizens are encouraged to work with their local police to identify and solve localized crime and disorder problems. Emergency call centers (e.g., 9-1-1) are "demarketed" and the police and communities are encouraged to develop new avenues for reporting crime and disorder problems.

The City of Baltimore in the State of Maryland on the east coast of the U.S. implemented a high-tech approach to redirecting calls away from 9-1-1 call centers. In Baltimore, citizens can call a nonemergency number (3-1-1) to report problems in their communities. These problems are then handled using a problem-oriented policing approach where the police can systematically assess the problems and strategically allocate resources to solve the problem.

In essence, under a community-policing model, the demand for scarce police resources is managed with a long-term focus (to solve the problem) rather than from a short-term focus (to provide immediate police presence).

Programs and Technologies

George Kelling and Mark Moore identify foot patrols, problem solving, victim counseling, community organizing, education, and knock-on-door programs as examples of programs that are consistent with the principles of community policing as a corporate strategy. These types of programs and tactics are typically implemented under a model of community policing in conjunction with traditional patrol tactics, such as preventive patrolling and rapid response. Traditional policing tactics are simply deemphasized, rather than abandoned, within a community-policing environment.

Measured Outcomes

During the reform or professional era of policing the performance of a police agency was measured using officially-reported crime rates for serious crimes such as murder and rape and serious property crimes such as burglary. Performance measurement for a community-oriented police agency, by contrast, includes indicators that assess the quality of life in neighborhoods, problem solution, reduction in fear, and citizen satisfaction with police services as well as crime control.

This section has emphasized the all-encompassing breadth of community policing. As should be clear from these descriptions of community policing, a police agency that implements a foot patrol program, for example, is not necessarily embarking on community policing unless other fundamental reforms accompany the adoption of the foot patrol program. Organizational reforms, demand management reforms, and efforts to systematically consult with community groups are some important indicators of a police department that is dedicated to the process of implementing community policing.

Evaluation Evidence

The amorphous nature of community policing makes it exceptionally difficult to evaluate the overall effectiveness, efficiency, and equity of community policing. Nonetheless, researchers across the world have embarked on major research programs to assess whether or not community policing reduces crime, makes people less fearful, improves police–community relations, improves citizen satisfaction with the police, and generally improves people's quality of life. Although the evidence is difficult to interpret and generalize, the research tends to suggest that fear of crime can be reduced by community-policing programs (see Skogan, 1994; Skogan and Hartnett, 1997) and that people are generally more satisfied with the police and feel that their quality of life has been enhanced as a result of community-policing programs (see Skogan and Hartnett, 1997). Some research has also accredited community policing with a decline in calls for service and reductions in some categories of crime (see Greene, Bergman, and McLaughlin, 1994; Skogan, 1996).

Related Strategies

Implementation of all aspects of community policing is a daunting proposition for many police departments. Some scholars argue that community policing requires such fundamental changes to every aspect of policing that very few, if any, police agencies can claim to have truly adopted community policing. Against this backdrop, many police departments have opted to establish specialist problem-solving units and to implement operational law enforcement strategies that are at least complementary to the ideals of community policing. In this section, I describe four organizational approaches that, for various reasons, have been associated with community policing.

Crime Prevention

One of the core functions of community-oriented policing agencies is to prevent crime. Over the last 20 years or so, many police departments have established crime-prevention units and introduced preventive programs into many operational aspects of police life. For example, crime-prevention units are typically responsible for disseminating crime-prevention literature, coordinating neighborhood watch groups, attending community meetings, and working with other specialist units within the police organization to design and implement education programs (e.g., the DARE program in schools, drug abuse education programs, and domestic violence awareness campaigns).

Police departments that are heavily vested and committed to community policing tend to integrate crime-prevention programs, like those identified above, more directly and systemically into the organizational life of the police agency than those police departments that are less committed to community policing. For example, general patrol officers within a community-oriented police department are likely to attend community meetings, coordinate neighborhood watch activities and disseminate crime-prevention literature as part of their day-to day job. In these community-oriented departments there is often no need for a specialist crime-prevention unit.

Problem-Oriented Policing

Problem-oriented policing (POP) is a *tactic* of a police organization. The problem-oriented policing approach seeks to identify crime problems, *analyze* the factors contributing to the problems, develop appropriate *responses* to directly eliminate or reduce the magnitude of the problems, and then *assess* the effectiveness of the strategies (see Eck and Spelman, 1987; Goldstein, 1990).

POP involves a four-step intervention process: scanning, analysis, response, and assessment. A police department that is traditionally organized can use a problem-oriented policing approach and a police department that is decentralized and community oriented does not necessarily have to use problem-solving tactics (although most of them do).

The POP approach is characterized by police officers taking responsibility for developing and implementing a range of solutions depending on their assessments of the causes of a specific problem.

The POP approach goes beyond simply reacting to problem places or situations and attempts to solve a broad spectrum of crime and disorder issues.

The problem-solving approach to crime control, unlike traditional policing tactics, is information-dependent: for example, scanning for problems and analyzing factors contributing to problems require a concerted effort by problem-solving teams to gather information pertinent to solving the problem.

The problem-oriented policing method can be applied to a vast array of crime problems such as street gangs, shopper victims, prostitutes, motor vehicle crime, and street-level drug markets.

The four-step SARA model of problem-oriented policing provides straightforward guidelines for implementing POP. *Scanning* involves identifying neighborhood crime and disorder problems. A "problem" is defined as involving two or more incidents that are similar in nature, that are capable of causing harm, and that the public expects the police to do something about.

The initial scanning or identification stage is the most developed in existing problem-oriented policing programs. In many departments that have implemented problem-solving methods, line officers are trained to look at the chronic crime problems on their beats with an eye toward the nature of the problem, how widespread it is, and what connections might exist between the environment and crime problems.

A common deficiency in the scanning stage is the lack of exploratory and analytic techniques that would facilitate this process. For example, although officers can note characteristics of problem neighborhoods, they often lack the expertise to develop data collection or analysis tools, such as computer mapping, that would help their identification of the complex causes of a specific problem.

The *analysis* stage of problem solving involves linking the crime events with the social context and the physical setting and creating an understanding of the underlying conditions that cause the problem to occur. The analysis stage asks:

Who are the actors? (offenders, victims, and third parties)
Where are the crimes happening? (physical location and characteristics)
What is the sequence of events surrounding the incidents and results of incidents?
Why are the activities occurring here?
How is the illegal activity being done?

The analysis stage has been identified by problem-oriented scholars as the main weakness in the problem-solving model, sometimes resulting in an inferior response to the problem under study (Eck and Spelman, 1987).

Many of the tools used to conduct accurate analyses are the same ones that are helpful in the initial scanning stage. They include: complainant or victim interviews, formal or informal surveys of area residents, personal observations, conversations with fellow officers, interviews with social service agency representatives, interviews with private agency representatives, meetings with community or business leaders, and examination of arrest reports (Eck and Spelman, 1987).

After problem solvers identify the problem and analyze the nature of the problem, they set about developing an effective *response*.

The response stage of the problem-solving process is very much dependent on the quality of the problem identification and analysis stages.

The response may be dramatic, as with the Newport News Police Department's decision to raze a deteriorated building plagued with burglaries and find safe housing for the residents elsewhere (Eck and Spelman, 1987). Other responses may be as simple as painting the curb in an open-air drug market orange to discourage customers from parking and buying drugs.

The number of solutions to problems is as varied as the problems they seek to address. Herman Goldstein (1990) identifies the following categories of typical POP responses: (1) concentrating attention on those individuals who account for a disproportionate share of the problem; (2) connecting with other government and private services (e.g., referral to another agency); (3) coordinating police responses with other agencies; (4) correcting inadequacies in municipal services and pressing for new services (e.g., eliminating zoning violations or removing garbage); (5) conveying accurate and sound information to reduce fear and anxiety, enable citizens to solve their own problems, to elicit conformity with laws and regulations that are not known or understood, to warn potential victims about their vulnerability and advise them of ways to protect themselves, to demonstrate to individuals how they unwittingly contribute to problems, to develop support for addressing a problem, to acquaint the community with the limitations on the police and to define realistically what can be expected of the police; (6) making use of existing forms of social control in addition to the community (e.g., parents, friends, apartment managers, contractors in controlling behavior of their workers, and university officials); (7) changing the environment; (8) coordinating civil ordinance enforcement with other agencies, for example, increased regulation, through statutes and ordinances, of conditions that contribute to problems, for example, youth curfews; (9) using mediating or negotiation skills in domestic disputes; (10) mobilizing the community to take back a drug infested street corner; (11) more discriminate use of the criminal justice system (i.e., more selected use of investigation, arrest, and prosecution); (12) enforcing criminal laws that, by tradition, are enforced by another agency (e.g., the violation of building codes by landlords and illegal business schemes for maximizing profits and avoiding taxes); (13) defining, with greater specificity, the types of behavior that should be subject to criminal prosecution; (14) intervention without making an arrest; use of arrest without intention to prosecute; (15) attaching new conditions to probation or parole; (16) increasing regulation at traffic problem spots; and (17) using the civil law to control public nuisances, offensive behavior, and the conditions contributing to crime.

Third-Party Policing

According to Buerger and Mazerolle, "third-party policing" refers to police efforts to convince or coerce nonoffending persons to take actions that are outside the scope of their routine activities, and that are designed to indirectly minimize disorder caused by other persons, or reduce the possibility that crime may occur. In practice, third-party policing invokes formal, noncriminal controls imported from the regulatory wing of civil law. Though the ultimate target of police action remains a population of actual and potential offenders, the *proximate* target of third-party policing is an intermediate class of nonoffending persons who are thought to have some power over the offenders'

primary environment. The police encourage these third parties to manipulate the environment in such a way as to discourage criminal and disorderly behavior, or to impose noncriminal penalties for such behavior.

Zero Tolerance

The fundamental principle of zero-tolerance policing is to aggressively enforce selective laws in an effort to maintain order at the street level. Zero-tolerance policing, for example, entails police using legal tools, such as youth curfew laws, drug nuisance abatement statutes, and local rules and regulations to aggressively target street-level drug dealing, prostitution, panhandling, vandalism, and other disorderly behavior. Police use existing legal tools to aggressively issue citations and arrest people who are in violation of the law with little, if any, regard to the social context of the incident; hence the term zero tolerance.

Zero-tolerance policing is generally seen as a manifestation of James Q. Wilson and George Kelling's "Broken Windows" thesis, which proposes that serious crime is the result of neighborhood decay and the inattentiveness of the police in addressing disorderly conduct and minor offenses.

Community Policing in an International Context

Community policing has proliferated across the world over the last 20 years. Indeed, even in emerging, democratic societies efforts have been made to reestablish public policing with the principles of community policing in mind (see Dziedzic, 1998). Although the desire may be great across the world to institutionalize the principles of community policing, different countries place different emphasis on the various aspects of community policing. The police in the U.S., with direct funding from the U.S. COPS (Community-Oriented Policing Service), have placed considerable emphasis on institutionalizing problem-oriented policing. In Queensland, Australia, the police refer to this approach as "Problem-Oriented and Partnership Policing" and place an emphasis on police building partnerships with "third parties" in an effort to reduce crime.

Different countries face different challenges in their attempts to decentralize police services. In Australia, for example, police services are delivered at the state level, challenging the police to regionalize their commands and decentralize police organizations to provide locally relevant services. Similarly, the police in Britain have worked hard to decentralize their police services and devolve decision-making authority to commanders of basic police units (BPUs).

LORRAINE GREEN MAZEROLLE

References and Further Reading

Bayley, D.H. 1994. *Police for the Future*, Oxford University Press, New York, NY.

Buerger, M.E. and Lorraine, G.M. 1998. Third party policing: A theoretical analysis of an emerging trend, *Justice Quarterly*, 15(2), 301–328.

Eck, J.E. and William, S. 1997. *Problem Solving: Problem-Oriented Policing in Newport News*, Police Executive Research Forum, National Institute of Justice, Washington, DC.

Goldstein, H. 1990. *Problem-Oriented Policing*, McGraw-Hill, New York, NY.

Greene, J. R., Bergman, W. T., and McLaughin, E. J. 1994. Implementing community policing: Cultural and structural in police organizations, in D. P. Rosenbaum (Ed.), *The Challenge of Community Policing: Testing the Promises.* Sage, Thousand Oaks, CA.

Jack R.G. 2000. Community policing in America: Changing the nature, structure and function of the police, in *Criminal Justice 2000: Policies, Processes, and Decisions of the Criminal Justice System*, Vol. 3, U.S. Department of Justice, Washington DC, July. pp. 299–370.

Kelling, G. and Catherine, M.C. 1996. *Fixing Broken Windows: Restoring and Reducing Crime in Our Communities*, Free Press, New York, NY.

Kelling, G. and Mark, H.M. 1988. The Evolving Strategy of Policing, *Perspectives on Policing*. No 4. Washington DC

National Institute of Justice, U.S. Department of Justice, and the Program in Criminal Justice Policy and Management, John F. Kennedy School of Government, Harvard University, June.

Mazerolle, L.G. and Jan, R., Eds. 1998. *Civil Remedies and Crime Prevention: Crime Prevention Studies*. Vol. 9, Criminal Justice Press, Monsey, NY. pp. 1–20.

National Crime Prevention Council. 1996. *New Ways of Working with Local Laws to Prevent Crime*, National Crime Prevention Council, Washington, DC.

Skogan, W. 1994. The impact of community policing on neighborhood residents: A cross-site analysis, in D.P. Rosenbaum (Ed.), *The Challenge of Community Policing: Testing the Promises.* Sage, Thousand Oaks, CA.

Skogan, W. 1996. Paper Presented to the Conference on Problem-Oriented Policing as Crime Prevention, Stockholm, Swedish National Police College.

Skogan, W. G. and Hartnett, S. M. 1997. *Community Policing, Chicago Style.* Oxford University Press, Carey, NC.

Tonry, M. and Norval, M., Eds. 1992. *Modern Policing. Crime and Justice: A Review of Research*, Vol. 15, The University of Chicago Press, Chicago, IL, and London, UK.

Wilson, J.Q. and George, K. 1982. Broken windows: The police and neighborhood safety, *The Atlantic* 249, 29–38.

See also **Community Corrections; Police: Municipal or Urban; Police: Patrol; Police: Rural**

Lawyers   *See* **Defense Attorneys; Prosecuting Attorneys**

Left Realism

A variant of critical criminology, left realism originated in the context of trenchant criticisms leveled against radical and mainstream criminologies and criminal justice policies in the U.K. in the late 1970s. The architects of left realism, most notably Ian Taylor, Paul Walton, and Jack Young (Taylor, Walton, and Young, 1975; Taylor, Walton, and Young, 1973), pointed to several concerns. First, they were sharply critical of Prime Minister Margaret Thatcher's conservative political regime, which emphasized a harsh "law and order agenda." This approach to criminality stressed correctionalism, harsh punishment, "getting tough" on crime, and a commitment to the principles of deterrence consistent with classical criminology. The difficulty with this strategy, left realists felt, was that it ignored the social context of crime and, in particular, the notion that capitalist, market societies breed crime.

Second, left realists maintained that Marxist-inspired radical criminologists (whom they termed left idealists) had reacted to conservative law and order politics unsat-

isfactorily. They accused left idealists of subscribing to an outdated instrumentalist conception of the state, in which state power merely reflected the interests of the ruling class. Instrumentalism implied that the state was a monolithic handmaiden to capitalism, and was therefore impervious to reform. Rather than explore the potential for reform, idealism endorsed a revolutionary role for the oppressed and exploited, in which the illogical nature of free markets would eventually create the structural conditions in which a more humane approach to justice issues could emerge, a transformation in which the disenfranchised proletariat would play a pivotal role.

Instead, realists argued that the state was a crucible of competing interests, which suggested that reform of state policies, including those addressing law and order, was possible. Realists were in agreement with left idealists that mainstream (conservative) criminology was a "state-sponsored" ideology that focused attention away from the crimes of the powerful, ignored gender oppression, and disproportionately punished racial minorities. However, realists criticized the "criminology of the old left" for dwelling excessively on the victimization of the working classes by capital, at the expense of recognizing that a substantial amount of crime is indeed conducted by the working class against the working class. In effect, realists charged that left idealists had erroneously portrayed working-class criminality as a form of proto-revolutionary activity.

For left realists, the central consequence of the old left's idealistic approach was that there could be no practical and socialist solution to reduce the harm caused by crime. Thus, realists argued that idealists had romanticized working-class crime, that their solutions were largely utopian, but that at the same time, conservative solutions were both ineffective and excessively punitive. Thus, one of the central objectives of left realism is to redress the balance between a focus solely on crimes of the powerful and the realities of street crime while advocating policies that promote greater race, class, and gender equality.

In opposition to old left radical criminologists, then, proponents of left realism contended that "crime really is a problem for the working class" and that crime control should be taken seriously. A crucial idea underpinning this approach is that left realists should continually reflect on their roots in critical criminology. In other words, left realists contend that any analysis of crime should understand crime as a process rooted in fundamental social, economic, and political inequalities. Chief among these is a commitment to understanding the intersections (or interrelations) among race, class and gender, criminal behavior, and crime control responses. Importantly, realists were also influenced by criticisms emerging from feminists who rightly complained that mainstream criminology had ignored women altogether and that left idealist criminology had ignored women as the victims of crime.

Left realists use the metaphor of the "square of crime," which emphasizes that criminologists should study: (1) victims, (2) offenders, (3) the state (or formal agents of social control), and (4) the general public (who react to crime, exerting informal social control). Understanding the interrelationships among these four points of the square is essential in explaining rates of criminal behavior (Young, 1992).

Further, though realism emphasizes the seriousness of street crime, it rejects the proposition that greater sanctions will win the war on crime. Instead, realists advocate minimal coercive sanctions for minor and "victimless" crimes (e.g., marijuana use and minor property offenses), and an extension of social control for more harmful crimes such as corporate malfeasance, industrial pollution, and child and woman abuse (Young, 1991).

In addition, left realists maintain that one of the great shortcomings of idealist criminology was that it had remained primarily theoretical and abstract in its orientation, and had thus neglected empirical research on the dimensions of crime. Further, in opposition to traditional methods of gathering crime data, realists emphasize methodological approaches that increase an empirical understanding of crime from the perspective of victims and provide a better approximation of actual levels of crime that were not possible from official crime statistics. Hence, studies informed by left realism in Britain, Canada, and the U.S. have gathered victimization data via a series of local crime surveys. In each of these surveys, the objective was not only to provide empirical justification for the claims of left realism, but also to give weight to the roles, voices, and experiences of the victims of crime. Significantly, and as predicted by left realist theory, these early surveys showed that the victims of crime were most likely to be those in the community who experience race, class, and gender oppression.

As a theoretical perspective on criminal behavior and the social reactions to crime, realism represents a synthesis of several theories, including strain, labeling, subcultural, radical Marxist, and feminist approaches. It maintains that people living in societies characterized by gross inequality will undergo strain, and that they may consequently develop subcultures of alternative values to cope with the frustration of "relative deprivation." Relative deprivation refers to the notion that people will feel oppressed compared to those classes in the social structure with whom they identify and who they aspire to be. For instance, poor people may not view themselves as worse off than others if everyone around them is poor, but in the midst of a society with blatant socioeconomic inequality, they will feel deprived. It is "poverty experienced as unfair that creates discontent" (Lea and Young, 1984, 88).

Left realists also believe that political marginalization is a key factor contributing to criminal behavior. Political marginalization consists of two components: "isolation from the effective channels of pressure-group politics, and isolation from processes whereby political interests can be clearly and instrumentally formulated" (Lea et al., 1984, 214). Lea and Young (1988) argue that the causes of crime can be understood by the following model:

Relative Deprivation = Discontent;

Discontent + Political Marginalization = Crime.

Left realism has been subject to a number of criticisms. In keeping with the original split between left realists and left idealists, some critics have questioned whether there is anything "left" about left realism, contending that the perspective strays too far from its roots in radical Marxist philosophy, and that consequently, left realism is nothing more than liberal theory in a new guise. There is also the criticism that realists focus too much on working-class crime and not enough on crimes of the powerful, a problem exacerbated by the use of victimization surveys that highlight crime and victimization of the poor and the most vulnerable segments of society (Einstadter and Henry, 1995). A related concern is that in claiming to offer a realistic strategy for reducing crime and the harm it causes, realists sometimes embrace the same punitive control strategies advocated by conservatives (Schwartz, 1991). Finally, even though left realism owes a debt of gratitude to the arguments put forth by feminist scholars it has been accused of failing to account fully for the gendered nature of crime, the role of patriarchy in oppression, and women's experiences as victims of street, corporate, and "privatized" crime (i.e., violence in intimate relationships) (DeKeseredy, 1992). This is an accusation that left realists have taken seriously, and efforts are under way to incorporate an understanding of feminist issues into realist theory and empirical inquiry (see Young, 1999).

Numerous policy implications emerge from left realism in its concerns for striking a balance between the crimes of the powerful and the realities of street crime. A left realist justice agenda focuses on creating social justice through democratic and fair reform of the socioeconomic milieu (e.g., the right to safe, remunerative, and fulfilling work; satisfactory and affordable housing; childcare; support for families and communities; universal health care; and adequate transportation). It also seeks to provide progressive and effective solutions to the realities of street crime, including demarginalization of offenders through alternatives to prison that serve to integrate the offender into the community, preemptive deterrence (deterring crime before it is committed), and, in light of evidence that prison generally creates cynical, bitter criminals with reduced chances of "going straight," the minimal use of incarceration. Realists also maintain that a policy goal should be to democratize mechanisms of social control, particularly the police, in order to foster a more proactive (rather than reactive) approach to law and order.

As a relatively new perspective on crime, much empirical work remains to be done before we can evaluate the efficacy of left realism. Left realism's strengths lie in its willingness to merge some of the key insights of radical criminology with a pragmatic but progressive approach to the problem of law and order. It promises to remain a fruitful area of inquiry, practicing theoretical and policy debates within criminology.

SHAHID ALVI

References and Further Reading

DeKeseredy, W. 1992. Confronting woman abuse in Canada: A left realist approach, in Lowman, J. and MacLean, B., Eds., *Realist Criminology: Crime Control and Policing in the 1990s*, University of Toronto Press, Toronto, Canada, pp. 264–282.

Einstadter, W. and Henry, S. 1995. *Criminological Theory: An Analysis of Its Underlying Assumptions*, Harcourt Brace, Fort Worth, TX.

Lea, J. and Young, J. 1984. *What is to be Done about Law and Order?* Penguin, New York, NY.

Schwartz, M.D. 1991. The future of critical criminology, in MacLean, B.D., Ed., *New Directions in Critical Criminology*, Collective Press, Vancouver, Canada, pp. 119–124.

Taylor, I., Walton, P., and Young, J. 1973. *The New Criminology*, Routledge and Kegan Paul, London, UK.

Taylor, I., Walton, P., and Young, J. 1975. *Critical Criminology*, Routledge and Kegan Paul, London, UK.

Young, J. 1991. Asking questions of left realism, in MacLean, B.D., and Milovanovic, D., Eds., *New Directions in Critical Criminology*, Collective Press, Vancouver, Canada, pp. 15–18.

Young, J. 1992. Ten points of realism, in Young, J., and Matthews, R., Eds., *Rethinking Criminology: The Realist Debate*, Sage, London, UK, pp. 24–68.

Young, J. 1999. *The Exclusive Society*, Sage, London, UK.

See also **Feminist Theories of Criminal Behavior; Marxist Theories of Criminal Behavior; Radical Theories of Criminal Behavior; Sociological Theories of Criminal Behavior**

Life-Course and Developmental Theories

The Life-Course Concept

According to Glenn Elder (1994), the life course generally refers to the interweaving of age-graded trajectories that are subject to changing conditions and future options and to short-term transitions over time. Trajectories refer to long-term patterns of behavior that are marked by a sequence of transitions, where transitions are marked by life events (first crime, first marriage, etc.) that are embedded in trajectories and evolve over shorter time spans. As the normative timing of life events is important, "life-course analyses are often characterized by a focus on the duration, timing, and ordering of major life events and their consequences for later social development" (Sampson and Laub, 1993, 8). The study of the life course necessitates a prospective, longitudinal research design.

The life-course perspective encompasses four key themes. The first theme is the study of patterns of change and the stability between childhood behavior and adult behavior. The second theme concerns the social meanings of age throughout the life course. The third theme refers to the intergenerational transmission of social patterns. The final theme espouses the effects of macro-level events on individual life histories. Of all four themes, the most difficult to come to grips with has been the extent of stability and change in behavior and personality attributes over time (Sampson and Laub, 1993). Nowhere is this more controversial than in the application of stability and change to the study of criminal behavior over the life course.

Stability and Change in Criminal Offending

At the core of the controversy is the interpretation of a statement by prominent social scientist Lee Robins (1978): "adult antisocial behavior virtually requires childhood antisocial behavior," but not all juvenile delinquents become adult offenders. This statement implies that an offender's criminal career is marked by both stability and change.

There is considerable evidence that antisocial behavior is remarkably stable over the life course. In fact, most scholars accept some element of stability in criminal offending; however, the decisive factor concerns the element of change, especially the life events that are believed to produce a change in criminal offending. For example, Sampson and Laub (1993), whose age-graded informal social control theory blends elements of both stability and change, argue that modifying life events and socialization in adulthood can change the course of an offender's criminal trajectory. For these scholars, life events such as marriage and employment generally, and the strength of informal ties to these events specifically, are believed to propel offenders away from continued participation in criminal behavior and place them on a smoother path toward eventual desistance from crime.

On the other hand, Gottfredson and Hirschi (1990, 238) argue that ordinary life events, such as marriage and employment, have little effect on criminal behavior because crime declines with age "whether or not these events occur." For Gottfredson and Hirschi, the tendency to commit crime appears early in life, much before sociological variables appear. Therefore, sociological variables cannot be important in changing life trajectories. To be sure, these scholars do not contend that individuals cannot and do not change; in fact, they recognize that within-individual change is possible because socialization continues to occur throughout life. The key point for them is that such change is not owing to the effect of some sort of life event on criminal behavior. For Gottfredson and Hirschi, relative stability refers to between-individual differences over time in the propensity to offend, and it is this type of stability that characterizes their approach to stability and change.

Several theories have been developed to account for patterns of stability and change in criminal offending. These approaches, integrative in nature, are commonly referred to as life-course, or developmental, theories.

Developmental Theories

Recently, criminologists have been witness to several theories that attempt to understand stability and change in criminal offending over the life course. Theoretical research in this area has been so strong that a subdiscipline of criminology, life-course criminology, has developed to take stock of the relevant theoretical and empirical research (Piquero and Mazerolle, 2001). These theories have attempted to integrate elements from several social science disciplines including biology, psychology, and sociology. Four prominent examples will be discussed here.

In 1993, psychologist Terrie Moffitt outlined a developmental taxonomy that set out to account for antisocial behavior over the life course. Arguing that the aggregate age or crime curve hides (at least) two distinct types of offenders, Moffitt's theory contends that groups of offenders differ in offending etiology as well as life-course patterns of offending.

The first group of offenders, termed life-course-persistent, begins offending early in life, offends more while active, and desists much later (if at all) in the life course. The proximate cause of crime for these offenders lies in the interaction between neuropsychological deficits and disadvantaged neighborhood and familial environments. These individuals do not have the privilege of being born into environments that can help them overcome their neuropsychological deficits. As a function of continuing and interactional problems, these individuals fail across several of life's domains including school, employment, and interpersonal relationships. This cumulative continuity results in a varied antisocial repertoire that begins early in the life course with hitting and stealing, continues in early adolescence with drug use and other aggressive acts, and continues into early adulthood with more person-oriented offenses. As these offenders do not have the social skills to deal with difficult situations, they are likely to react in negative fashions and further their downward spiral. As can be deduced, intervention strategies for life-course-persistent offenders are difficult, but prevention techniques administered early in the life course could be successful.

The second group of offenders under Moffitt's scheme, adolescence-limited, begin offending during the adolescent period of the life course, engage in acts that symbolize adult social status, and likely desist as early adulthood approaches. The proximate cause of criminal behavior for these offenders lies in the maturity gap: the recognition that they look like adults but are not allowed to engage in adult-like behaviors. When this recognition is met with the peer social context of adolescence, these offenders attempt to break free from the maturity gap and demonstrate their autonomy. The antisocial repertoire of adolescence-limited offenders includes minor thefts, vandalism, early sexual experiences, smoking, and other rebellious acts of delinquency. As these offenders do not possess the neuropsychological deficits of life-course persisters, adolescent-limited offenders possess the requisite social skills to contemplate and recognize that with ensuing adulthood, they will be able to engage in the adult behaviors that they so much wanted to partake in as juveniles. Therefore, desistance is the modal response for these offenders, and only a handful are expected to be ensnared by negative life experiences and continue their antisocial offending. Intervention efforts for adolescent-limited offenders are plentiful and revolve around the tempering of the felt maturity gap.

A similarly situated developmental theory was developed by psychologist Gerald Patterson and his colleagues (1989). Also encompassing two distinct types of offenders, Patterson et al. anticipate an early-start and late-start offender. Early starters, individuals who engage in delinquency during early adolescence, are viewed as having serious deficits in social skills as a result of inept parenting. These individuals are believed to be aggressive and defiant in their interactions with others, and therefore become rejected by conventional peers. Early starters are believed to be at risk for chronic offending during adolescence and continued criminal and antisocial behavior through adulthood. Late starters, individuals who experiment with delinquency during mid to late adolescence, largely offend because of the aid, comfort, and encouragement of delinquent peers. These youths may have experienced a decline in the quality of parenting because of

the turbulence of parent–child relationships during adolescence. As a result of this strain, late starters tend to drift or gravitate toward delinquent peers and thus experiment with delinquency.

A third developmental theory was constructed by sociologist Terence Thornberry (1987). Termed interactional theory, the underlying causes of crime are hypothesized to include a person's weak bond to conventional society and the existence of an opportunity to learn and practice criminal behavior, which results primarily as a function of exposure to delinquent peers. Once criminal activity has occurred, it leads to additional criminal behavior by weakening one's attachments to convention, commitment to others, and involvement in conventional institutions. Because these inhibitions are curtailed, persons are more likely to become more involved with both delinquent peers and continued criminal activity.

Loeber and Hay's (1994) three pathways to problem behavior and delinquency model have also been advanced as a developmental theory. This model specifies three specific pathways. The first, the overt pathway, begins with childhood aggression such as annoying and bullying others as the first step, followed by physical fighting, and then violent crime. The second, the covert pathway, begins with minor covert behaviors such as frequent lying and shoplifting, and then progresses to property damage such as fire setting and vandalism, and then to moderate or serious delinquent acts such as fraud, serious theft, and burglary. The third, the authority conflict pathway, progresses from stubborn behavior in childhood to acts of disobedience and defiance, to more serious authority-avoidance acts such as truancy, staying out late, and running away.

Research on Developmental Theories

The publication of developmental theories has generated a renewed interest in the study of criminal offending over the life course. By employing advanced methodological techniques, many of these empirical tests have contributed important information that probably otherwise would not have been generated.

In an early study, Daniel Nagin and Ken Land (1993) were able to provide evidence that there are distinct groups of offenders underlying the aggregate age–crime curve. Their analysis supports the various developmental perspectives and lies in stark contrast to the expectations made by Gottfredson and Hirschi. In a follow-up study, Nagin and his colleagues (1995) were able to distinguish the characteristics that separated the distinct groups of offenders. Their results also suggested that although most of the adolescent-limited offenders refrained from being convicted, they continued to drink heavily, use drugs, get into fights, and commit criminal acts.

Several studies pit the developmental models against Gottfredson and Hirschi's perspective. Consistent with developmental theory, Bartusch and her colleagues (1997) found that separate latent factors underlie childhood and adolescent antisocial behavior. Supporting Moffitt's developmental taxonomy, they found that childhood antisocial behavior was related more strongly than adolescent antisocial behavior to neuropsychological functioning whereas adolescent antisocial behavior was related more strongly than childhood antisocial behavior to peer delinquency. Tibbetts and Piquero (1999) also found support for Moffitt's hypothesis that the interaction between neuropsychological deficits and disadvantaged environments would predict early but not late onset of criminal offending. Paternoster and Brame (1997), however, did not find support for an either–or approach between the developmental and Gottfredson and Hirschi theories. Their analysis reported evidence for a middle-ground approach that combined elements from each of the two approaches.

Simons and his colleagues (1994) found strong support for Patterson's early or late starter theory. Specifically, they reported that, for late starters, quality of parenting predicted affiliation with deviant peers, which in turn was associated with criminal justice system involvement. Importantly, oppositional or defiant behavior was unrelated to deviant peer affiliation and to involvement with the criminal justice system among late starters. For early starters, quality of parenting predicted oppositional or defiant behavior, which in turn predicted delinquent peer affiliation as well as criminal justice involvement.

Jang (1999) tested Thornberry's interaction theory with data from the National Youth Survey. His analysis showed that the direct as well as the total effect of delinquent peers and school on delinquency tended to increase from early to middle adolescence. In addition, he found that both direct and total effects of family on delinquency were significant throughout the period of adolescence. Jang's analysis is important because it represents the first attempt to examine whether the effects of family, school, and delinquent peers on delinquency are age-variant, and if so, what patterns of those age-varying effects follow during the most crime-prone periods of adolescence.

Loeber, Wei, Stouthamer-Loeber, Huizinga, and Thornberry (1999) tested Loeber and Hay's three-pathway model with data from three ongoing longitudinal studies. Although their data were limited in several respects, their analysis revealed that steps two and higher in the overt and covert pathways were observed across all three sites.

Prevention or Policy Proscriptions from the Developmental Approach

Life-course or developmental approaches present numerous opportunities for developing and implementing age-appropriate interventions for preventing and reducing criminal and antisocial behavior over the life course. For example, identification of the risk factors associated with early problem behaviors represents an important opportunity to focus directed efforts at individual and parent functioning. Several research studies have been initiated in order to prevent criminal behavior over the life course.

In a study designed to curb early onset of delinquency, Richard Tremblay and his colleagues (1992) implemented a parent- and child-training program to a sample of kindergarten boys from low socioeconomic areas of Montreal. The parent portion of the program involved (1) giving parents a reading program, (2) training parents to monitor their children's behavior, (3) training parents to give positive reinforcement for prosocial behavior, (4) training parents to punish effectively without being abusive, (5) training parents to manage family crises, and (6) helping parents to generalize what they learned. The child portion of the program involved a social skills training component that was aimed at problem solving and the development of self-control. Their results showed that the treated disruptive boys were less physically aggressive in school, that they were more often in an age-appropriate regular classroom, that they had less serious school adjustment problems, and that they reported fewer delinquent behaviors.

Olds and his colleagues (1998) examined the long-term effects of nurse-home visitation on children's criminal and antisocial behavior. The nurse-home visits were designed to promote three aspects of maternal functioning: (1) positive health-related behavior during pregnancy and the early years of the child's life, (2) competent care of their children, and (3) maternal personal development, such as family planning, educational achievement, and workforce participation. The nurses linked families with needed health care and human services and attempted to involve other family members and friends in the pregnancy, birth, and early care of the child. Results showed that adolescents born to women who received the nurse visits and who were unmarried and from households of low socioeconomic status, in contrast with those in the comparison groups, reported fewer instances of running away, fewer convictions and violations of probation, fewer lifetime sex partners, fewer cigarettes smoked per day, and fewer days having consumed alcohol in the past 6 months.

Future Directions in Life-Course or Developmental Research

Given the recency of life-course or developmental theories of crime, research is just starting to provide information about the causes of criminal and antisocial behavior. Much more remains to be learned.

One of the most important components necessary for testing life-course or developmental theories concerns the collection of the requisite data. As discussed earlier, many of the life-course or developmental theories posit several neuropsychological and environmental variables that are not part and parcel of many existing data sets in the social sciences. The collection of such key pieces of information is necessary for more complete tests of these theories, and also for substantiation of public policies aimed at improving the lives of children.

Second, future research efforts should attempt to collect information from various sources. For example, criminal and antisocial behavior is typically collected from the respondent via self-report surveys and from official criminal justice agencies. But, as noted above, several life-course or developmental theories suggest that antisocial behavior begins early in the life course, before the criminal justice process is likely to be initiated. Thus, collection of data from other sources such as parents, peers, and teachers will provide additional information to researchers in testing these developmental models.

Third, the collection of adult life experiences will be central to testing developmental models against the Gottfredson and Hirschi approach. The collection of these data will be complex, however, as researchers probe respondents for more in-depth information concerning the strength of the attachment to life events such as marriage and employment. Fortunately, methodological advances have allowed researchers to provide reasonable answers to the life-event hypotheses.

Fourth, future research directions will also begin to integrate contextual information into empirical models. To date, few studies have examined the extent to which the developmental models described above have differing effects across neighborhood contexts. As race is highly correlated with certain neighborhood contexts, future research should also attempt to examine if the developmental processes vary across groups defined by race and gender.

Fifth, evidence awaits the extent to which research conclusions are sensitive to the modeling assumptions made by the estimation procedures employed by researchers. As more advanced methodological techniques become developed, researchers should reanalyze previous studies to determine which modeling techniques are most appropriate for the research question at hand.

Finally, researchers should also begin to consider more fully the public policy implications of life-course or developmental models. For example, some of these models attribute importance to early family functioning. Assessing the extent to which public policy efforts should be targeted very early in the life course is one issue that has yet to be answered. Another related issue that warrants attention is the cost factor of implementing prevention and intervention policies. Many of the policies advanced by developmental models are extremely costly. Determining who will bear the cost of these programs remains an unanswered question, one that should be at the forefront of public and private discourse on crime control efforts.

ALEX R. PIQUERO

References and Further Reading

Bartusch, D.R.J., et al. 1997. Is age important? Testing a general versus a developmental theory of antisocial behavior, *Criminology*, 35.
Elder, G.H., Jr. 1994. Time, human agency, and social change: Perspectives on the life course, *Social Psychology Quarterly*, 57.
Gottfredson, M.R. and Hirschi, T. 1990. *A General Theory of Crime*, Stanford University Press, Stanford, CA.
Jang, S.J. 1999. Age-varying effects of family, school, and peers on delinquency: A multilevel modeling test of interactional theory, *Criminology*, 37.
Loeber, R. and Hay, D.F. 1994. Developmental approaches to aggression and conduct problems, in *Development Through Life: A Handbook for Clinicians*, Hay, D.F. and Rutter, M., Eds., Blackwell Scientific, Oxford, UK, and Boston, MA.
Loeber, R., et al. 1999. Behavioral antecedents to serious and violent offending: Joint analyses from the Denver youth survey, Pittsburgh youth study, and the Rochester youth development study, *Studies on Crime and Crime Prevention*, 8.
Moffitt, T.E. 1993. Adolescence-limited and life-course-persistent antisocial behavior: A developmental taxonomy, *Psychological Review*, 100.
Nagin, D.S., and Land, K. 1993. Age, criminal careers, and population heterogeneity: Specification and estimation of a nonparametric, mixed-poisson model, *Criminology*, 31.
Nagin, D.S., Farrington, D.P., and Moffitt, T.E. 1995. Life-course trajectories of different types of offenders, *Criminology*, 33.
Olds, D., et al. 1998. Long-term effects of nurse home visitation on children's criminal and antisocial behavior, *Journal of the American Medical Association*, 280.
Paternoster, R., and Brame, R. 1997. Two routes to delinquency? A test of developmental and general theories of crime, *Criminology*, 35.
Patterson, G., DeBaryshe, B., and Ramsey, E. 1989. A developmental perspective on antisocial behavior, *American Psychologist*, 44.
Piquero, A.R. and Mazerolle, P., Eds. 2001. *Life Course Criminology: Contemporary and Classic Readings*, Wadsworth Thomson Learning, Belmont, CA.
Robins, L.N. 1978. Sturdy childhood predictors of adult antisocial behavior, replications from longitudinal studies, *Psychological Medicine*, 8.
Sampson, R.J. and Laub, J.H. 1993. *Crime in the Making: Pathways and Turning Points through Life*, Harvard University Press, Cambridge, MA.

Simons, R.L., et al. 1994. Two routes to delinquency: Differences between early and late starters in the impact of parenting and deviant peers, *Criminology* 32.

Thornberry, T.P. 1987. Toward an interactional theory, *Criminology* 25.

Tibbetts, S.G. and Piquero, A.R. 1999. The influence of gender, low birth weight, and disadvantaged environment in predicting early onset of offending: A test of Moffitt's interactional hypothesis, *Criminology* 37.

Tremblay, R.E., et al. 1992. Parent and child training to prevent early onset of delinquency, in *Preventing Antisocial Behavior: Interventions from Birth through Adolescence*, Tremblay, R.E. and McCord, J., Eds., Guilford Press, New York, NY.

See also **Biological Theories of Criminal Behavior; Integrated Theories of Criminal Behavior; Psychological Theories of Criminal Behavior; Sociological Theories of Criminal Behavior**

Loan-Sharking

Since the Middle Ages loan-sharking has been a criminal practice (Layman and Potter, 2000, 195). For the last half a century, Americans have become intensely conscious, dependent, and vulnerable to the phenomenon of loan-sharking. The practice of loan-sharking embodies two central features: "the assessment of exorbitant interest rates in extending credit and the use of threats and violence in collecting debts" (Goldstock and Coenen, 1978, 2). Whether in times of economic slowdown or economic boom, this practice of lending money at excessive interest rates persists in spite of government regulations. Loan-sharking clearly still is a social and legal problem that warrants considerable attention.

In contemporary American society, there are many situations in which individuals and businesses may need to find illegitimate forms of capital. Unfortunately, an individual may face an immediate financial burden incurred such as a gambling debt or may require money to satisfy a drug addiction. These demands typically overextend extant sources of legitimate or conventional lines of credit. Alternatively, a business may have all its available sources of legal credit dried up and thus is unable to secure more money from a lending institution or extended credit from suppliers, a common occurrence in some industries, such as fur trades (Simon and Witte, 1982, 229). For these interests, loan-sharking provides a ready source of cash. Goldstock and Coenen elucidate:

> Contemporary loan-sharking is marked by the dominance of organized crime. This pervasive influence is hardly surprising. Syndicate access to rich stores of capital allows the underworld to pour substantial amounts of cash into the credit market. The strength and reputation of organized operations lends credence to threats of reprisals, thus augmenting the aura of fear critical to success in the loan-shaking business (Goldstock, Ronald, and Dan T. Coenen, *Extortionate and Usurious Credit Transactions: Background Materials*, 1978, 4).

However, it is important to note that contemporary loan sharks are not in the "muscle business" (Abadinsky, 2003, 239), they are in the credit business and as such "they lend money to customers whom they expect will pay off and eventually return as customers" (Abadinsky, 2003, 239). This can take the form of an old practice known as "salary lending which thrived in the U.S. between 1880 and 1915" (Abadinsky, 2003, 238). Currently this form of salary lending is frequently known as "payday loans" (Wahl, 1999, 2000).

There has been a proliferation of "payday loan" businesses across the U.S. and Canada. Although the interest rates vary from state to state and country to country, the basic lending principle remains the same. The payday lender takes advantage of the people who are willing to pay high interest rates to get a small, short-term loan, usually for a period of 2 weeks. This is a service that many banks no longer offer in light of the boom in credit card services. Interestingly, users of this service are low-income earners or individuals with tarnished credit histories.

Predatory lending institutions (loan-sharking) are prevalent throughout the U.S. and Canada. They include advanced check-cashing outlets, second mortgages—loan consolidation, high-cost loan products, credit repair, and unsolicited credit cards for low-income individuals. Interest rates on some of these loans range from 300 to 800%, and there are often processing fees that further add to the total impact of such quick cash transactions. Consequently, these transactions lead to further financial instability rather than to financial stability.

Financial stability can lead to homeownership and neighborhood improvement. For families and individuals, homeownership is a source of stability and the way most citizens save for their futures and that of their children. For communities, homeownership provides continuity, civic investment, and a source of communal wealth. Conversely, the reliance on fast cash institutions devastates families and communities, indentures low-income residents, promotes impulse buying, and can even contribute to increased violence and crime, as quick cash facilitates the purchase of guns in moments of anger and enables the quick purchase of drugs. Increasing the debt on an individual or family also pressures the beleaguered borrowers toward theft and other lawless behavior as they struggle to overcome their economic dilemma.

There are extensive documented instances and too many credible theories to dismiss loan-sharking as a mere issue that resurfaces at times of economic slum. The underlying question lingers: what can the U.S. and Canada do to effect major changes in law and the enforcement of those laws? Over the past 2 years, there have been numerous laws and regulations promulgated by the federal government, many state governments, and some county and state governments to curb predatory lending practices (Franzen and Howell, 2001; Obara, 2001). These laws and regulations have supporters and detractors depending upon lobbying and support or advocacy groups and the political party that introduces the legislation and controls the legislature.

It is clear that loan-sharking takes different forms and poses important new threats to the social fabric of society. There are many who argue that loan-sharking or predatory lending is a criminal activity entirely devoid of informed consent. Despite its bad reputation, loan-sharking or predatory lending is a business in which individuals engage and in many cases self-victimize. It is within this context that more research is needed.

A research agenda that incorporates the following elements is long overdue as well as a fertile beginning: problem identification, development of data sources, possible methodologies for empirical and theoretical analyses, and assessment of the consequences of regulation and control. Such an agenda would draw on divergent views, allowing for alternative emphases among and within the various topics, such as predatory lending, which is closely related to loan-sharking.

DAVID BAKER

References and Further Reading

Abadinsky, H. 2003. *Organized Crime*, 7th ed., Belmont, CA: Wadsworth/Thomson Learning.
Conklin, J.E. 1973. *The Crime Establishment: Organized Crime and American Society*, Englewood Cliffs, NJ: Prentice-Hall.
Goldstock, R. and Coenen, D.T. 1978. *Extortionate and Usurious Credit Transactions: Background Materials*, Ithaca, NY: Cornell Institute on Organized Crime.
Johnson, C. 2002. Payday loans: Shrewd business or predatory lending? *Minnesota Law Review* 87.
Lyman, M.D. and Potter, G.W. 2000. *Organized Crime*, 2nd ed., Upper Saddle River, NJ: Prentice-Hall.
McCaguh, C.H. and Cernkovich, S.A. 1987. *Crime in American Society,* New York, NY: Macmillan.
Potter, G.W. 1994. *Criminal Organizations: Vice, Racketeering, and Politics in an American city*, Prospect Heights, IL: Waveland Press, Inc.
Reuter, P. 1983. *Disorganized Crime: The Economics of the Visible Hand*, Cambridge, MA: MIT Press.
Rubinstein, J. and Reuter, P. 1978. Facts, fancy, and organized crime, *Public Interest* 53.
Simon, C.P. and Witte, A.D. 1982. *Beating the System: The Underground Economy*, Boston, MA: Auburn House.
Wahl, M. 2000. Surge puts payday loans under scrutiny, *Chicago Tribune* 1, 11.
Wahl, M. 1999. Payday loans hit pay dirt *Chicago Tribune* 1, 6.
Walsh, M.E. 1977. *The Fence*, Westport, CT: Greenwood.

See also **Crimes against Consumers; Organized Crime: Activities and Extent**

Lombroso, Cesare

Cesare Lombroso (1835–1909) is known as the father of positivist criminology. He underwent formal medical training at universities in Pavia and Greece, where he developed his lifelong interest in psychology and psychiatry (Pelfrey, 1980). While serving in the army he began his research on the physical features of over 3000 soldiers. He then used these data to draw connections between physical features and personality traits of the soldiers. He eventually took this information and used it to form one of the major principles of his theory of criminal behavior. In his book, *Crime Its Causes and Remedies*, he wrote "… crime is caused almost entirely by the anthropological characteristics of the criminal" (Lombroso, 1911, xii). He believed that all criminals were atavistic, meaning criminals were throwbacks to a previous generation of mankind. He claimed that criminals have physical deformities of the skull and facial features, unusual extremities, and usually have tattoos (Lombroso, 1911). Atavistic criminality is a return of those influenced by a morbid nature to the violent means of struggle for existence now suppressed by modern civilization (e.g., rape, robbery, homicide) (Lombroso, 1911).

Not only did he associate physical features to criminal behavior, he also believed that social and environmental factors can influence or cause criminal behavior. He claimed that more crimes are committed in the summer months, believing that excessive heat had an effect upon the mind (Lombroso, 1911). One's socioeconomic status was also believed to contribute to criminality, being that the lower class supposedly contained the majority of the atavistic criminals. He accurately predicted that an increase in population density will elevate the level of crime. Another important social factor that he believed contributes greatly to crime is the prison system. Lombroso wrote, "We think that we are protecting and avenging society by imprisoning criminals, whereas, on the contrary, we are not only furnishing them with the means of associating with one another and giving mutual instruction, but we are giving them real enjoyment besides" (Lombroso, 1911, 209). Reform of the prison system was viewed as the only way to remedy this problem.

Lombroso believed there were three types of criminals: born criminals, insane criminals, and criminaloids. Born criminals exhibited the majority of the physical deformities that Lombroso associated with criminality. Born criminals have great physical deformities, often mimicking animal-like features (Lombroso-Ferrero, 1972). Most born criminals have an abnormal fondness for strangers and animals, and have an inability to distinguish between right and wrong. Another interesting feature that Lombroso attributed to born criminality is tattoos. In Lombroso's *Criminal Man* (translated to English by his daughter, Gina Lombroso-Ferrero) it states, "This personal decoration so often found on great criminals is one of the strangest relics of a former state" (Lombroso-Ferrero, 1972, 45). Lombroso did not believe that just one characteristic, such as incorrigible laziness, creates a born criminal. He wrote, "Just as a musical theme is a result of a sum of notes, and not of any single note, the criminal type results from the aggregate of these anomalies, which render him strange and terrible, not only to the scientific observer, but to ordinary persons who are capable of an impartial judgment" (Lombroso-Ferrero, 1972, 49).

A second category of criminals is the insane criminal. Lombroso-Ferrero wrote, based on her father's classifications, "… there is an important series of offenders, who are not criminals from birth, but become such at a given moment of their lives, in a consequence of an alteration of the brain, which completely upsets their moral nature and makes them unable to discriminate between right and wrong" (Lombroso-Ferrero, 1972, 74). Lombroso felt that many types of people fall into this category, such as the idiot, the imbecile, and those suffering from dementia. The insane criminal tends to commit crimes because of emotional or psychological impulses or other unpremeditated factors. Lombroso also believed that there were special forms of the criminally insane. Lombroso viewed alcoholics with great disdain and believed, "All substances which have the power of exciting the brain in an abnormal manner drive one more easily to crime and suicide, as well as to insanity, with which last the other two are often inextricably linked" (Lombroso, 1911, 93). Those who would not normally commit any type of crime might be temporarily mentally incapacitated and, therefore, unable to make rational decisions. Lombroso also believed that those suffering from alcoholism end up having general pseudo-paralysis or complete dementia further contributing to their criminally insane behavior (Lombroso-Ferrero, 1972). A second special form of insane criminals is those suffering from hysteria. Women were viewed to suffer from this catalyst to crime. Those with hysteria tend to have extreme mood swings, be influenced by hypnotic suggestions, and have an irresistible tendency to lie (Lombroso-Ferrero, 1973). These unstable emotions and mental functioning would cause a normal law-abiding female to commit criminal acts.

The last type of criminal classified by Lombroso was the criminaloid. These criminals have no physical anomalies, in contrast to the born criminal, and usually commit their first crime later in life. Criminaloids are usually hesitant to commit crimes and feel guilty and confess to their wrongdoings more easily than the other two types of criminals. The criminaloid breaks the law by accident, for example, by committing involuntary homicide or arson, and are is categorized as a criminal by public opinion (Lombroso-Ferrero, 1972). Criminaloids also tend to commit offenses that do not cause social harm or damage (e.g., atheism, obscene language) (Lombroso-Ferrero, 1972). Criminals of passion were also considered criminaloids by Lombroso. These criminals break the law for pure altruistic purposes, have noble qualities, and are usually found in homicide cases (Lombroso-Ferrero, 1972).

Lombroso, in line with the positivistic modern school, felt that crime can be prevented, and efforts should be focused on this area, instead of the punishment of criminals. He believed the reformatory system should be specialized in order to deal with each type of offender. It was believed that juvenile and female offenders should be isolated from the general prison population, in line with the prison systems of today. Lombroso felt that criminals of passion should never be imprisoned for their crimes. Criminaloids should be punished with fines and other probationary measures and only sent to prison as a last resort. The probation system as opposed to the prison system "… seeks to encourage in them habits of integrity and to check the growth of vices by means of a benevolent but strict supervision" (Lombroso, 1911, 188). Lombroso viewed the prison system as one that fosters and encourages increased criminality once released into society. However, even penitentiaries could ultimately aid in the prevention of future crime. Lombroso wrote, "Even the adult offender should be looked upon in the light of a child or a moral invalid, who must be cured by a mixture of gentleness and severity, but gentleness should predominate since criminals are naturally prone to vindictiveness and are apt to regard even slight punishments as unjust tortures" (Lombroso, 1911, 198). In order to prevent crime, punishments must be tailored to each type of offender in order for the criminal to benefit from the justice system.

In summation, Lombroso contributed greatly to the modern field of criminology. He was not only the founder of the positivist school, but he also created theories of evolution, degeneracy, moral insanity, racism, and physical anthropology. Although some of the major principles of his theory on the atavistic criminal have been refuted today by modern science, he still bought forth a new way of studying and examining crime and its causes.

JENNIFER TATUM

References and Further Reading

Lombroso, C. 1911. *Crime Its Causes and Remedies.* Montclair, NJ: Patterson Smith Publishing Corporation.

Lombroso, C. 2003. The criminal man. In Cullen, F.T. and Agnew, R. (Eds.), *Criminological Theory: Past to Present* (pp. 23–25). Los Angeles, CA: Roxbury Publishing Company.

Lombroso-Ferrero, G. 1972. *Criminal Man: According to the Classification Of Cesare Lombroso.* Montclair, NJ: Paterson Smith Publishing Corporation.

Pelfrey, W.V. 1980. *The Evolution of Criminology.* Cincinnati, OH: Anderson Publishing Company.

See also **Biological Theories of Crime; Body-Type Theories of Crime**

Loitering: *See* Trespass

Lynching

Lynching as a form of criminal behavior assumes two forms. The first is the strict legal meaning of the term found in state penal codes throughout the U.S., which define lynching as the unauthorized taking by riot of another person from the lawful custody of a peace officer. It is not essential to the legal definition of lynching that the victim be harmed in any way; the elements of unauthorized taking from the custody of a law officer and the plurality requirement of three or more persons are sufficient to commit the offense (Schmalleger, 2002, 438).

The second, more familiar definition of "lynching" is less a legal than a sociological phenomenon, possessing a nimbus of connotations that include the infliction of death on (typically) African American men in the South without due process of law. We are chiefly concerned here with the second definition of the term.

A criminological understanding of lynching must be informed by the sociohistorical context in which it arose, a context that nourished the practice of lynching from its late 19th century origins until the present day. The reconstruction period following the War Between the States was the milestone in the history of lynching. Although "extralegal" justice certainly existed in the antebellum period, it seldom went beyond beatings, whippings, tarring and feathering, or ostracism of offenders from the community. Such unofficial sanctions were meted out in both the North and the South prior to the war. In the Western territories, particularly in the 1850s, vigilante groups resorted to hanging as a means of "frontier" justice, whereas Southern slave owners imposed harsh punishment on rebellious slaves. Not until the era of Reconstruction, however, did lynching emerge as a common method of "punishing" African Americans with lethal violence (Brundage, 1993; Johnson and Wolfe, 2003).

The crucial prelude to lynching violence occurred in the years immediately following the Civil War, when Congress enacted a series of civil rights laws— including the Fourteenth and Fifteenth Amendments— to grant full rights of citizenship to African Americans. The first, the Civil Rights Act of 1866, provoked a backlash from Southerners, who responded by forming "black codes" (enabling local officials to "hire out" unemployed blacks to private employers) and unleashing murderous violence on African Americans. Congress reacted by passing the Enforcement Act of 1870, which guaranteed African Americans their Fourteenth Amendment rights of due process and equal protection and their Fifteenth Amendment right to vote. The Ku Klux Klan Act followed in 1871, empowering the federal government to prosecute interferences with rights guaranteed to blacks by the Constitution. Four years later, Congress passed the Civil Rights Act of 1875, which made it illegal for anyone to deny access to places of public accommodation (inns, public transit, theaters) based on race (Lawrence, 1999, Historical Appendix).

As some scholars of lynching have noted, the passage of these laws created a "boundary crisis" in the minds of many Southerners. Prior to 1865, the superior civil status of white Southerners was assured under the law. After 1865, unabridged civil rights were, for a time at least, conferred on Southern African Americans. The net effect of the Civil Rights Act of 1866 and its progeny was to place blacks on an equal legal footing with whites. The elevation of African Americans from the status of chattel to that of citizens eroded the boundary between whites and blacks, thereby endangering the centuries-old institution of white supremacy in the American South. White Southerners responded to this boundary crisis by seeking to recreate the conditions of white dominance that existed prior to 1865 (Wiegman, 1990; Mills, 1997).

Southern whites faced legal obstacles to the restoration of white supremacy, especially the Fourteenth and Fifteenth Amendments. These obstacles were significantly overcome by two momentous events in the history of lynching: the withdrawal of federal troops in 1876–77 and the evisceration of federal civil rights laws by the U.S. Supreme Court between 1876 and 1883. Once federal military occupation of the South ended, whites were free to terrorize their black populations with virtual impunity. The persecution of Southern

blacks was greatly facilitated when the Supreme Court held in 1883 that the Fourteenth Amendment forbade only state actors, and not private individuals, from discriminating on the basis of race. The High Court's holding signaled federal disengagement from prosecuting racially motivated crimes against blacks by private actors like the Ku Klux Klan and lynch mobs. Given the refusal of white law enforcement authorities in the South to hold these private actors criminally liable under state law for their assaults on blacks, federal abdication gave Southern whites license to brutalize their black population, free from the strictures of the criminal law. White Southerners meanwhile nullified African Americans' Fifteenth Amendment rights through subterfuges like poll taxes, literacy texts, and "grandfather" laws (Lawrence, 1999).

It is in this context of reinstituting racial apartheid in the American South that the practice of lynching is best understood. Along with stripping Southern blacks of their recently won civil rights, whites employed lynching as a means of renewing the inferior status of blacks that had prevailed before the war. Between 1880 and 1930, the percentage of American lynchings tilted further toward the South, increasing from 82 to 95%, whereas the proportion of black lynching victims in the South mounted from 68 to 91%. Scholars have estimated that 4587 lynchings were committed in the U.S. between 1880 and 1930, a figure that includes 3943 in the South alone. Of the Southern total, 3220 of the victims were African American. The worst decade in the 50-year meridian of lynching was the 1890s, in which 187 lynchings occurred on average each year. Eighty percent of lynchings were perpetrated in the South; 75% of these victims were black (Brundage, 1993; Brinkley, 1999; Litwack, et al., 2000). (Even after the horrific decade of the 1890s, when lynchings began to decline, the proportion of black victims grew from 75 to 91%.)

Several distinct events could trigger the lynching of African Americans. Typically, the victims were accused of a crime, most commonly murder or physical assault. In other cases, victims were alleged to have behaved insubordinately toward whites. The range of "insubordination" offenses is deeply revealing of the psychology of lynching perpetrators, and includes:

- Using "incendiary" language (i.e., speech that is interpreted as slanderous, insolent, or prideful);
- Adopting an inappropriate manner with whites, such as smiling ironically or failing to respond immediately when questioned;
- Failing to demonstrate proper deference toward whites, like failing to remove one's hat or step aside when a white approached on a sidewalk;
- Defending oneself against an assault by whites;

- Suing or testifying against whites;
- Defending one's property against white confiscation;
- Displaying wealth;
- Seeking to behave like a white.

The literature teems with accounts of Southern blacks tortured, dismembered, castrated, set afire, and hanged for these and other "offenses" (Litwack et al., 2000).

A notorious triggering "event" of lynchings was alleged sexual depredations by black men on white Southern women. Any real or imagined sexual advance by a black man toward a white woman exposed him to being lynched. Frequently, allegations of sexual assault by black men proved on further inspection to be violations of the system of total white hegemony. Where accusations were not entirely fabricated by hysterical white women, the underlying "offense" was often relatively trivial: whistling or even looking at white women "with lustful eyes" (as a contemporary Little Rock journalist averred), spending time with a white woman or having consensual sex with her were all sufficient to provoke—and did in fact provoke—the formation of lynch mobs to redeem "Southern virtue." A boundary had been breached, and the wall between the races could be mended only by inflicting the ultimate subordination on the "presumptuous" black man: physical destruction (Litwack et al., 2000).

Many lynchings during the heyday of the practice took place in urban areas, where large mobs of whites broke into jail cells, seized black prisoners, and subjected them to agonizing indignities before finally hanging them. Such well-attended lynchings, often in broad daylight with the explicit or implied support of local law enforcement, are referred to in the literature as "public spectacle lynchings." Sometimes newspapers informed the public of the date and time of the lynching; special transport (like "excursion trains") was arranged for out-of-towners; parents asked their children's teachers to excuse them from class to attend; and a generally festive air characterized the event (Brundage, 1993; Brinkley, 1999; Litwack et al., 2000).

It is important for the student of lynching to understand that lynching was not merely, or even primarily, an instance of vigilante justice, expressing the public's outrage over a crime and its impatience with the plodding speed of the judicial system. In this respect, conventional definitions of lynching can be misleading. The *Oxford English Dictionary* (OED), for example, describes lynching as "the practice of inflicting summary punishment upon an offender, by a self-constituted court armed with no legal authority." This definition indicates that lynchers seek to "punish" an "offender"

without "legal authority." The dense phenomenological texture of real lynchings, however, resists such an interpretation. The OED's definition fails to account for the extreme brutality and sadism of public lynchings, often deliberately prolonged for several hours while the perpetrators tortured, dismembered, exoculated, shot, or burned their victims prior to hanging them. A 1904 account from the *Vicksburg Evening Post*, relating the execution of a black man and his wife, is illustrative:

> The blacks were forced to hold their hands while one finger at a time was chopped off. The fingers were distributed as souvenirs. The ears of the murderers were cut off. Holbert was beaten severely, his skull fractured and one of his eyes, knocked out with a stick, hung by a shred from the socket. ... The most excruciating form of punishment consisted in the use of a large corkscrew in the hands of some of the mob. This instrument was bored into the flesh of the man and woman, in the arms, legs and body, and then pulled out, the spirals tearing out big pieces of raw, quivering flesh every time it was withdrawn.

Accused of murdering his white employer, the only evidence against the lynched man was an argument between the two before the murder. His wife was lynched because she was married to an alleged "murderer" (excerpted in Litwack et al., 2000).

The breathtaking ferocity of this case is by no means unusual in the annals of lynching. Two conclusions may be drawn that have application to the phenomenon as a whole. First, lynchings were not so much designed to punish criminal offenders as to reinscribe the racial subordination of blacks to whites in the American South of the postbellum era. The actual guilt or innocence of the victim was immaterial. Rather, the lynched body of the African American operated semiotically: by inflicting grievous pain and physical dismemberment on the suffering black body, the perpetrators created a powerful sign directed at all members of the community. The message was unmistakable, written in the castrated genitals, the burning flesh, and the helpless, animal agony of the black body: blacks are legally and socially inferior, and any black who forgets this basic truth will suffer a similar fate. Second, the widespread practice of distributing body parts from the victim among the crowd recreated the prewar chattel status of African Americans. Where black bodies circulated among whites as commodities before 1865, after 1865 they circulated as inanimate trophies for whites. Whether as chattel or as souvenirs, black bodies existed for the pleasure of white Southerners. The reaffirmation of this "truth" was the chief aim of lynching (Mills, 1997, 56–57; Litwack et al., 2000).

Activists sought to mobilize public opinion against lynching, among them the black journalist Ida Wells and the NAACP. The Association of Southern Women for the Prevention of Lynching was established in 1930 as an advocacy group calling for federal antilynching laws. Franklin Roosevelt, fearing loss of white voters in the South, declined his support of the proposed legislation (Lawrence, 1999). Although the incidence of lynching declined precipitously after 1930, it continued well into the post-World War II period. As the 1998 lynching-style murder of James Byrd in Jasper, Texas, reminds us, lynching violence has not disappeared from American criminality, but slumbers like a dormant virus in the bloodstream of the culture, reawakening when racial boundaries are threatened.

MICHAEL BRYANT

References and Further Reading

Allen, J. et al. 2000. *Without Sanctuary: Lynching Photography in America*, Santa Fe, NM: Twin Palms Publishers.

Brinkley, A.1999. *American History: A Survey*, Vol. II, Boston, MA: McGraw-Hill.

Brundage, W.F. 1993. *Lynching in the New South*, Urbana and Chicago, IL: University of Illinois Press.

Cutler, J. 1969. *Lynch-Law*, Montclair, NJ: Patterson Smith.

Ginzburg, R. 1962. *100 Years of Lynchings*, New York, NY: Lancer Books.

Johnson, H.A. and Wolfe, N.T. 2003. *History of Criminal Justice*, Cincinnati, OH: Anderson Publishing Co.

Lawrence, F.M. 1999. *Punishing Hate: Bias Crimes under American Law*, Cambridge, MA: Harvard University Press.

Litwack, L.F., Allen, J., Als, H., and Lewis, J. 2000. *Without Sanctuary: Lynching Photography in America*, Santa Fe, NM: Twin Palms Publishers.

Mills, C. 1998. *Blackness Visible*, Ithaca, NY: Cornell University Press.

Mills, C. 1997. *The Racial Contract*, Ithaca, NY: Cornell University Press.

Schmalleger, F. 2002. *Criminal Law Today: An Introduction with Capstone Cases*, Upper Saddle River, NJ: Prentice-Hall.

Wiegman, R. 1990. The anatomy of lynching, in *American Sexual Politics*, Fout, J. and Tantillo, M., Eds., Chicago, IL: University of Chicago Press.

See also **Hate Crimes**

Lysergic Acid Diethylamide (LSD)

LSD (D-lysergic acid diethylamide) was first synthesized in 1938 by Albert Hofmann, a chemist working at the Sandoz Research Laboratories in Basel, Switzerland, while looking for a substance that might be useful in the treatment of vascular problems such as migraine headache and postpartum hemorrhage. As LSD did not prove to be particularly useful in this regard compared with other ergot alkaloids, the compound was dropped from further study. However, 5 years later, Hofmann somehow ingested an unknown amount of the drug accidentally (probably by absorbing it through the skin) and described what happened thereafter as follows:

Last Friday, April 16, 1943, I was forced to stop my work in the laboratory in the middle of the afternoon and to go home, as I was seized by a peculiar restlessness associated with a sensation of mild dizziness. Having reached home, I lay down and sank in a kind of drunkenness which was not unpleasant and which was characterized by extreme activity of imagination. As I lay in a dazed condition with my eyes closed (I experienced daylight as disagreeably bright) there surged upon me an uninterrupted stream of fantastic images of extraordinary

plasticity and vividness and accompanied by an intense, kaleidoscope-like play of colors. This condition gradually passed off after about two hours (Reprinted from Hofmann, A., *Psychotomimetic Agents*, 1968, pp. 184–185, courtesy of Marcel Dekker, Inc.).

Hofmann was so interested in this experience that he tried to repeat it by taking a controlled amount of LSD the following Monday. He later described the symptoms of his second experiment:

I had great difficulty in speaking coherently, my field of vision swayed before me, and objects appeared distorted like images in curved mirrors. ... vertigo, visual disturbances; the faces of those around me appeared as grotesque, colored masks; marked motor unrest, alternating with paresis; an intermittent heavy feeling in the head, limbs, and the entire body ... Moreover, all objects appeared in unpleasant, constantly changing colors, the predominant shades being sickly green and blue ... all acoustic perceptions (e.g., the noise of a passing car) were transformed into optical effects, every sound causing a corresponding colored hallucination constantly changing in shape and color like pictures in a kaleidoscope. (Reprinted from Hofmann, A., *Psychotomimetic Agents*, 1968, pp. 185–186, courtesy of Marcel Dekker, Inc.).

It should be noted that the dose Hofmann ingested (0.25 mg) was 5–8 times the amount usually taken to produce the altered subjective or perceptual effects (state of consciousness) that later came to be known as an LSD "trip."

Because LSD is a semisynthetic compound, derived from the plant *Claviceps purpurea* and diethylamide, it has both an old and a new history, both of which are noteworthy, if not notorious. *Claviceps purpurea* is a parasitic fungus that grows on grain, especially rye, the eating of which can cause a disease called ergotism or Saint Anthony's fire. This disease has two forms, the first of which, convulsive ergotism, is characterized by tingling sensations in the skin, muscular spasms that may develop into convulsions, and disturbances of consciousness and thinking. In the second form of the disease, gangrenous ergotism, the limbs become swollen and inflamed before becoming numb (gangrenous) because of the vasoconstrictive effect of the fungus.

Although infected grain is not difficult to detect and destroy, it might have been used throughout history to make bread, especially during periods of famine or particularly inclement weather. It is known that at least 20 outbreaks of ergotism occurred in France between the years 945 and 1600 CE. Perhaps more interestingly, at least to American readers, the delusions reported at the Salem witch trials of 1692, which resulted in the execution of 20 women, have been linked to an outbreak of convulsive ergotism in Massachusetts (Caporael, 1976; Ray and Ksir, 2002). Thus, the effects of LSD-like and related "hallucinogens," which were also known to the indigenous populations encountered by the Spanish *conquistadores* throughout the Americas (North, Central, and South), caused medical, legal, psychological, and social problems long before LSD was synthesized in the 20th century.

At this point, it should be understood that the use of the term "hallucinogen" to characterize the effects of LSD and other indole and phenylethyl amines should not be interpreted to imply that these drugs have effects that are indistinguishable from (or are even very similar to) endogenous hallucinations such as those that occur in patients suffering from schizophrenia. In fact, the subjective effects of LSD and related drugs differ in many ways from those that occur during psychosis or in response to (other) stressors; they are, for example, usually much more visual than auditory and are not accompanied by serious distortions of, or dissociation from, reality. Nevertheless, the term "hallucinogen" has become commonplace and will be used throughout this article to distinguish the effects of LSD and related drugs from those of other substances, which can also cause alterations in perception and consciousness but do so only at much higher doses and usually in conjunction with a plethora of other physiological changes.

LSD did not have much of an impact on European and American society until the 1960s, except perhaps among a few clinicians who claimed that the drug, which was also called "psychedelic" (mind-viewing) or "psychotomimetic" (psychosis mimicking), could be a useful adjunct to psychotherapy (Osmond, 1957) and several researchers who argued, for a variety of reasons (below), that LSD might affect consciousness by altering normal biological processes such as neuronal transmission (Giarman and Freedman, 1965). In view of developments in the biomedical sciences at that time (which included the birth of modern psychopharmacology and the transformation of psychiatry into a considerably more biochemical or molecular science), the importance of the second of these insights cannot be overemphasized.

Some of the notoriety associated with LSD stems from its use by the military and the CIA during the 1950s. According to many writers, this episode (in which "research subjects" were never informed of what was given to them or why it was given) was characterized by the complete absence of any ethical considerations as well as by low scientific standards. However, it was probably the Harvard psychologist Timothy Leary and his colleague Richard Alpert (who later became known as Baba Ram Dass), along with the writer Ken Kesey (*One Flew over the Cuckoo's Nest*), who did the most to popularize LSD and to promote its recreational use among a generation of young people that was already seriously alienated from the mainstream of American society by, among other things, the war in Vietnam. Indeed, Leary became famous, if not infamous, by encouraging some of America's most promising students to use drugs such as LSD and psilocybin to "turn on, tune in, and drop out," which, in fact, many of them did (or pretended to do) during the "psychedelic 1960s." This can be seen in even the most cursory examination of the music and "pop" culture of the era (e.g., the Beatles song "Lucy in the Sky with Diamonds"). By 1970, not coincidently the year that witnessed the passage of the Comprehensive Drug Abuse Prevention and Control Act (more commonly known as the Controlled Substances Act), more than 2 million people in the U.S. were estimated to have used LSD at least once (Maisto et al., 1999).

A variety of factors contributed to a decline in the use of LSD during the 1970s, including: (1) claims that the drug causes chromosome damage, insanity, acts of violence, homicidal behavior, and suicide (most of which proved to be unfounded); (2) the decreased availability of the drug owing to its changed legal status; (3) an increased interest in other substances such as marijuana and MDMA (methylenedioxymethamphetamine or "ecstasy"); (4) a changing political and social climate; and (5) the increasing realization that the "benefits" promised by the advocates of the recreational use of LSD was a false hope (Thompson, 1971).

Although the self-administration of LSD and related hallucinogens has by no means disappeared in the 21st century, such use no longer seems to be major public health problem. The recreational use of so-called "club" drugs such as MDMA, which is in some respects similar to but far more dangerous than LSD is, however, of serious concern to several agencies of the federal government, including the Department of Justice and the National Institute on Drug Abuse (Leshner, 1999). Nevertheless, LSD (like marijuana and MDMA) is classified as a Schedule I substance under the Controlled Substances Act of 1970 (which is still in effect), meaning that, according to the U.S. Department of Justice (which usually acts on the recommendation of the U.S. Department of Health and Human Services), the substance has a high potential for abuse and no generally accepted medical use. Simple possession or distribution of even small amounts of Schedule I substances can be punished by up to 1 year's imprisonment and/or a fine of $1000–$5000. The penalty for illegally manufacturing or distributing such "narcotics" was 15 years and $25,000 but became much more complicated in 1986, depending on the individual drug and the amount sold. Under the Omnibus Drug Act of 1988, which was aimed at reducing the demand for drugs, the consequences of possessing small amounts of Schedule I substances (for personal use) were increased and now include a fine of up to $10,000, forfeiture of the car, boat, or plane conveying the substance, and loss of federal benefits, including student loans and grants. One interesting consequence of all this legislation (and of the expensive "war on drugs") was that the number or prisoners per 1000 inhabitants of the U.S. increased from less than 1 from 1930–1970 to almost 5 in the year 2000.

LSD is one of the most potent psychoactive substances known; when taken orally, it has effects at doses as low as 10–15 μg. Yet, surprisingly, in light of all the negative publicity it has endured, LSD is remarkably safe in the sense that doses hundreds of times higher than those that elicit profound physiological and psychological effects (such as those described by Hofmann) are unlikely to be fatal.

Once ingested, LSD travels rapidly through the body and causes vasomotor and sympathomimetic effects such as dilated pupils, elevated body temperature, blood pressure, and salivation, tachycardia, sweating,

chills, and sometimes headache, nausea, and vomiting. Interestingly, only about 1% of the drug enters the central nervous system (brain and spinal cord), where it is distributed unevenly to receptors located in the midbrain, pons, limbic cortex, median forebrain bundle, hypothalamus, thalamus, cortex, cerebellum, and other areas.

LSD is degraded rapidly in humans, with a half-life of 2–3 hours, and is excreted in the bile and feces. Nevertheless, a "trip" may last from 6–9 hours and "flashbacks" may occur many months after ingestion of a single dose, suggesting that the drug acts by altering endogenous neuronal processes.

Users of LSD report that during a "trip" they experience both visual and auditory synesthesias, which are mixed sensations such as "seeing" smells or "hearing" colors. The sense of touch is magnified, time is distorted, and thoughts do not proceed in logical sequences. During "bad" trips, confusion, panicky feelings, paranoia, depression, and even psychotic-like symptoms may also occur. It is unclear, however, whether these are direct effects of the drug or reflect a drug-induced "unmasking" of existing emotional problems or mental illness. In any event, the psychological effects of LSD are extremely variable, even in a single individual.

Tolerance develops to many (but not all) the effects of LSD in 3–4 days. Cross-tolerance also occurs to other indole and phenylethylamines, but not to other compounds that are sometimes said to be "hallucinogenic" (e.g., anticholinergics and PCP), suggesting that different subclasses of hallucinogens not only exist but act through different neuronal or receptor mechanisms. This hypothesis is supported both by subjective reports in humans and behavioral (drug discrimination) experiments in animals (in which only indole and phenylethylamines have effects that cannot be differentiated from those of LSD).

Although the mechanism of action of LSD is not entirely clear, it has been argued since the 1950s that the diverse effects of the drug involve the neurotransmitter serotonin (5-hydroxytryptamine; 5-HT). Such arguments were initially based on structural similarities between LSD and, to an even greater extent, other hallucinogens, which, like 5-HT, contain an indole nucleus (Figure 1).

Considerable anatomical, biochemical, electrophysiological, and behavioral evidence not only supports this hypothesis (Feldman et al., 1997), but refines it further by suggesting that many, if not most, of the actions of LSD are the result of direct (agonist) actions of the drug at one or, possibly, two of the many different kinds of (postsynaptic) serotonin receptors (5-HT2A, 5-HT2C). Such evidence includes but is not limited to the following considerations: (1) 5-HT receptors are distributed heterogeneously in the brain and are the binding sites for

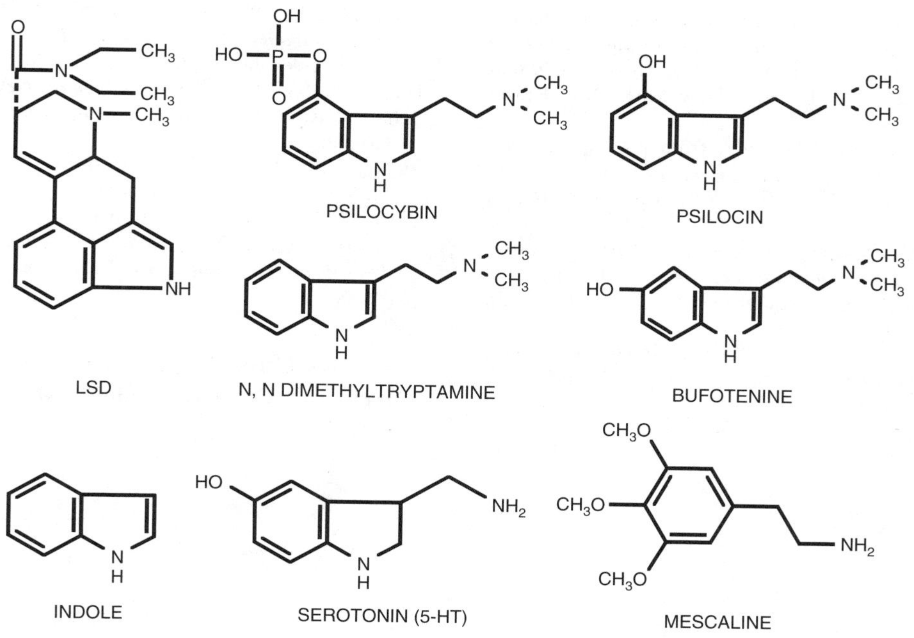

FIGURE 1 Structures of LSD and related hallucinogens. Notice that LSD, psilocybin, psylocin, DMT (*N,N*-dimethyltryptamine), and bufotenine all contain an indole nucleus, as does the neurotransmitter serotonin (5-hydroxytryptamine; 5-HT)). Although mescaline is a phenylethylamine, structurally more similar to dopamine (DA) and norepinephrine (NE) than to 5-HT, it is known to act *in vivo* primarily through serotonergic neuronal mechanisms (Appel and Callahan, 1989).

a variety of hallucinogenic drugs (Bennett and Snyder, 1975); (2) reducing the density or functional activity of 5-HT receptors reduces sensitivity to LSD in both humans and other animals (Lucki and Frazer, 1981); (3) 5-HT antagonists block the behavioral (discriminative stimulus) effects of LSD, the most potent of which act at 5-HT2A receptor subtypes; (4) tolerance to LSD is correlated with a loss of 5-HT2A receptors in the cortex (Buckholz et al., 1990); and (5) the relative potencies of 22 drugs in producing behavioral effects similar to those of the hallucinogen DOM (3,4-dimethoxymethamphetamine) are correlated with both 5-HT2A receptor binding potency in rats and hallucinogenic potency in humans (Glennon et al., 1984).

JAMES B. APPEL

References and Further Reading

Appel, J.B. and Callahan, P.M. 1989. Involvement of 5-HT receptor subtypes in the discriminative stimulus properties of mescaline, *European Journal of Pharmacology* 153.

Bennett, J.P. and Snyder, S.H. 1975. Stereospecific binding of d-lysergic acid diethylamide (LSD) to brain membranes: Relationship to serotonin receptors, *Brain Research* 94.

Buckholtz, N.S., Zhou, D., Freedman, D.X., and Potter, W.Z. 1990. Lysergic acid diethylamide (LSD) administration selectively down-regulates serotonin receptors in rat brain, *Neuropsychopharmacology* 3.

Caporael, L.R. 1976. Ergotism: The Satan loosed in Salem, *Science* 192.

Feldman, R.S., Meyer, J.S., and Quenzer, L.F. 1997. *Principles of Neuropsychopharmacology*. Sunderland, MA: Sinauer.

Giarman, N.J. and Freedman, D.X. 1965. Biochemical aspects of the actions of psychotomimetic drugs, *Pharmacological Reviews* 17.

Glennon, R.A., Titeler, M., and McKenney, J.D. 1984. Evidence for 5-HT2 involvement in the mechanism of action of hallucinogenic agents, *Life Sciences* 35.

Hofmann, A. 1968. Psychotomimetic agents, in *Drugs Affecting the Central Nervous System* (Vol. 2), Burger, A., Ed., New York, NY: Marcel Dekker.

Leshner, A.I. 1999. What are club drugs? *NIDA Notes* 14.

Lucki, I. and Frazer, A. 1981. Prevention of the serotonin syndrome by repeated administration of monoamine oxidase inhibitors, but not tricyclic antidepressants, *Psychopharmacology* 205.

Maisto, S.A., Galizio, M., and Connors, G.J.1 999. *Drug Use and Abuse*, 3rd ed., Orlando, FL: Harcourt Brace.

Osmond, H. 1957. A review of the clinical effects of psychotomimetic agents, *Annals of the New York Academy of Sciences* 66.

Ray, O. and Ksir, C. 2002. *Drugs, Society and Human Behavior*, 9th ed., New York, NY: McGraw-Hill.

Thompson, H.S. 1971. *Fear and Loathing in Las Vegas*, New York, NY: Random House.

Further Reading

Abraham, H.D. 1983. Visual phenomenology of the LSD flashback. *Archives of General Psychiatry*, 40.

Appel, J.B. and Rosecrans, J.A. 1984. Behavioral pharmacology of hallucinogens in animals: Conditioning studies, in *Hallucinogens: Neurochemical, Behavioral, and Clinical Perspectives*, Jacobs, B.L., Ed., New York, NY: Raven Press.

Freedman, D.X. 1984. LSD: The bridge from human to animal, in *Hallucinogens: Neurochemical, Behavioral, and Clinical Perspectives*, Jacobs, B.L., Ed., New York, NY: Raven Press.

Glennon, R.A. 1996. Classical hallucinogens, in *Pharmacological Aspects of Drug Dependence: Toward an Integrated Neurobehavioral Approach*, Schuster, C.R. and Kuhar, M.J., Eds., Berlin: Springer-Verlag.

Hofmann, A. 1968. Psychotomimetic agents, In *Drugs Affecting the Central Nervous System* (Vol. 2), Burger, A., Ed., New York, NY: Marcel Dekker.

Hollister, L.E. 1984. Effects of hallucinogens in humans, in *Hallucinogens: Neurochemical, Behavioral, and Clinical Perspectives*, Jacobs, B.L., Ed., New York, NY: Raven Press.

Huxley, A. 1954. *The Doors of Perception*, New York, NY: Harper.

Schultes, R.E. 1976. *Hallucinogenic Plants*, New York, NY: Golden Press.

Siegel, R.K. 1992. *Fire in the Brain: Clinical Tales of Hallucination*. New York, NY: Dutton.

Siegel, R.K. 1984. The natural history of Hallucinogens, in *Hallucinogens: Neurochemical, Behavioral, and Clinical Perspectives*, Jacobs, B.L., Ed., New York, NY: Raven Press.

See also **Club Drugs; Drug Use: Extent and Correlates; Drug Use: The Law**

M

Mandatory Sentencing *See* **Sentences and Sentencing**

Marijuana

Introduction

What is Marijuana?

Marijuana is the most commonly used illicit drug in the U.S., with Americans spending over $10 billion on marijuana each year. According to the 2001 National Household Survey on Drug Abuse, approximately 83 million Americans have tried marijuana at least once in their lifetime, and 14 million people used marijuana in the last month. Of all illicit drug users, over half use marijuana only and 17% use marijuana and another illicit substance, making marijuana the obvious drug of choice for illegal drug users (Office of Applied Studies, 2002).

Marijuana is a greenish-brown mixture of dried leaves, stems, and flowers of the *Cannabis sativa* plant. The main active chemical in marijuana is delta-9-tetrahydrocannabinol, or THC. Marijuana is a psychoactive drug that produces a sense of euphoria and a pleasant state of relaxation. Within a few minutes of inhalation, marijuana users experience elevated heartbeat, loss of coordination and balance, and slower reaction times. Although typically smoked in the form of marijuana cigarettes called joints, in pipes, bongs, or hollowed out cigars, marijuana can also be orally ingested as it is mixed into foods or used to brew a tea.

Marijuana potency typically ranges from 4 to 6% THC for commercial-grade marijuana and up to 15 to 22% THC for sinsemilla, a type of stronger marijuana. Today's marijuana is much more potent than that smoked during its peak in the 1970s.

Under the Controlled Substances Act, marijuana is classified as a Schedule I drug, which means that it has a high potential for abuse, no currently accepted medicinal purpose, and a lack of accepted safety for its use. Recently, in the U.S. Supreme court case of the *U.S. v. Oakland Cannabis Club*, it was ruled that marijuana has no medical benefits worthy of an exception to the Controlled Substances Act. As recently as May 2002, the U.S. Court of Appeals for the District of Columbia upheld the position that marijuana is to remain a Schedule I drug.

Prevalence and Trends in Marijuana Use

Marijuana use peaked in the U.S. during the late 1970s, with over 60% of 12th graders reporting that they had tried marijuana at least once. The prevalence of marijuana use began to decline each year for more than a decade, reaching a low of 33% in 1992. However, since then, the proportion of high school students admitting to marijuana use has been gradually on the rise again, reaching a peak in 1997 and remaining at similar rates for the past 5 years (Johnston et al., 2003). Approximately 2 million people in the U.S. tried marijuana for the first time in 1999, and the vast majority (two-thirds) were under the age of 18. Although the percentage of high school students using marijuana is lower than its peak in the late 1970s, the potency of the marijuana smoked by today's youth is up to five times more powerful than that typically smoked two decades ago (NIDA, 2002).

Youth

The average age of initiation for marijuana users is approximately 17 years of age and has steadily declined since 1965 (SAMHSA, 2002). The 2002 Monitoring the Future Study found that among 8th, 10th, and 12th grade students, 19%, 39%, and 48% had used marijuana in their lifetime, respectively. Additionally, in 2002, 21.5% of high school seniors were current users, reporting that they had used marijuana at least once in the 30 days prior to the survey. Despite increases in the prevalence of marijuana use during the 1990s, illicit drug use by high school students has since leveled off in the past few years.

Gateway Theory

Drugs that often lead to the use of more serious substances of abuse are referred to as "gateway" drugs. Marijuana can be seen as a gateway drug in that many users of more serious drugs such as cocaine and heroin used marijuana prior to their use of harder drugs. Other factors lending support to this theory are that marijuana users are much more likely than nonusers to progress to harder drugs and the greater the frequency of marijuana use, the greater the likelihood of using harder drugs later. However, there is only a small percentage of marijuana users who ever progress to harder drugs and there are also data indicating that for some, there is an underlying propensity to use drugs, and it is not specific to any particular substance. Proponents of this theory also feel that one reason that marijuana is used prior to trying other illicit drugs is simply because of its availability for younger drug users. In other words, there are more opportunities to initiate marijuana use than there are for more serious drugs. If marijuana is truly a gateway drug that will lead to the use of more dangerous substances, then it is necessary to maintain current policies and laws regarding possession and use of the drug. However, if marijuana is not a gateway drug, then perhaps drug laws are too harsh for marijuana offenders.

Effects of Marijuana

Physiological Effects

Acute effects of marijuana use include impairment of short-term memory, attention, and judgment. Short-term effects of marijuana, those that persist beyond intoxication, but are not necessarily permanent, include problems with memory and learning, diminished critical thinking and problem solving skills, and anxiety. Long-term, chronic marijuana use leads to increased risk of bronchitis, emphysema, and cancers of the mouth, neck, and lungs. Psychological problems such as depression, anxiety, and personality disturbances have also been found to be associated with marijuana use (NIDA, 2002). Over the past decade, the number of emergency-room mentions for marijuana has more than tripled in the U.S. According to the Drug Abuse Warning Network (DAWN; Office of Applied Studies, 2001), marijuana contributed to an estimated 110,000 emergency room visits in 2001.

Personal Effects

In addition to the acute and long-term physiological effects of its use, marijuana users also often experience a variety of consequences resulting from chronic use. Studies have shown that compared with their peers who abstain from marijuana, high school students who smoke marijuana get lower grades and are less likely to graduate. Another study found that in a sample of high school students with previous comparable test scores, heavy marijuana smokers scored significantly lower on standardized verbal and mathematical tests (NIDA, 2002). Negative consequences experienced by adult users of marijuana often appear in the workplace, as those workers who smoke marijuana are more likely to have problems on the job such as excessive absences, tardiness, accidents, workers' compensation claims, and job turnover.

Marijuana Dependence

There are numerous models and definitions of addiction, yet there are several basic processes that are consistent throughout: psychological dependence, physical dependence, and tolerance. Psychological dependence refers to the need to use the drug to think, feel, or function normally. Physical dependence is when the body requires the drug to function normally, often characterized by withdrawal syndrome. Tolerance refers to a phenomenon in which increasing doses of a drug are required to achieve the same effects as obtained from the original dose. Numerous studies have established that a tolerance to some of the effects of *Cannabis* builds in animals. There is debate as to the addictive properties of marijuana. In a recent nationwide survey, over 2 million people met the diagnostic criteria for *Cannabis* dependence, recognized by the *Diagnostic and Statistical Manual of Mental Disorders*, 4th edition (DSM-IV). Some individuals will use marijuana compulsively despite its interference with family, school, or work, thus leading to its label as an addictive substance. Also, symptoms such as craving and withdrawal often make it hard for long-term marijuana smokers to stop using the drug. Common withdrawal symptoms seen among marijuana users include irritability, sleeping difficulties, and anxiety. Experience of withdrawal symptoms is often reported among those attempting to reduce their marijuana use, especially for long-term users.

Prevention and Treatment

Risk and Protective Factors

In order to develop effective programming to curb marijuana use among youth, it is necessary to have an understanding of those factors leading to the initiation and persistence of its use. Especially among youth, both risk (factors that increase likelihood of substance use) and protective factors (factors that offset risk factors) become a necessary component of all prevention programming. Other factors associated with a teenager's decision on whether or not to use illicit drugs include perceived risk, disapproval, and availability of drugs. Historical trends have shown an inverse relationship between perceived risk and marijuana use, with increases in perceived risks associated with decreased rates of marijuana use. In 2002, over half of all 12th graders believed it to be harmful to smoke marijuana regularly and 78% disapproved of regular use (Johnston et al., 2003). These numbers are consistent with use in that, even though more than one-third of high school seniors smoked marijuana in the past year, only 6% reported daily use. The perceived risks of marijuana use are also decreasing among younger high school students. Another major contributing factor to the high rate of use is that 89% of high school seniors reported marijuana as being accessible. Numerous studies funded by the National Institute of Drug Abuse have yielded consistent findings identifying the opportunity to use illicit substances as a major risk factor for illegal drug use among youth (NIDA, 2002). During the rise in marijuana use that occurred in the 1990s, the availability of marijuana for young adults increased as well.

LifeSkills Training Program

One school-based prevention strategy that has been shown to be effective at reducing drug and alcohol use among youth is called the *LifeSkills Training* program (Botvin et al., 1994). This SAMHSA model program targets three primary factors leading to drug and alcohol use: the development of drug resistance skills, personal self-management, and overall social skills. Although originally developed for elementary and junior high school students, a recent study found that the *LifeSkills Training* program reduced new marijuana use among college students as well.

ONDCP, National Youth Anti-Drug Media Campaign

As mentioned previously, perceived benefits and risks associated with taking illicit drugs influence a young person's decision of whether or not to use a specific drug. However, the benefits or positive effects of taking a drug typically will spread much faster among youth than information on the negative consequences of using that drug. From one point of view, this makes marijuana that much more dangerous because the perceived risks, both short- and long-term, are much lower for marijuana than most other illicit substances. As such, the Office of National Drug Control Policy's National Youth Anti-Drug Media Campaign attempts to reduce marijuana use among adolescents and young adults by increasing the perceived risks of using the drug and raising awareness of the negative consequences associated with its use. This campaign uses a variety of media outlets including television, radio, magazines, newspapers, and the Internet. The majority of the messages for this campaign target the teens themselves, however, other aspects of this media campaign focus on the parents by reinforcing those skills necessary to talk to their children about drugs.

Treatment

There are relatively few treatment programs that specifically target marijuana use, primarily because those individuals in need of treatment use marijuana in combination with other substances. Typically, these other substances are either cocaine or alcohol, which are deemed more harmful than marijuana and thus become the primary focus of the treatment regimen. Studies have found that extensive group therapy and brief, individualized motivational interviewing are both effective strategies in reducing marijuana use among adults. Currently, there are no accepted pharmaceutical medications available for treating marijuana abuse.

According to the Treatment Episode Data Set, in 1999 there were more than 220,000 admissions to publicly funded substance abuse treatment in which marijuana was the primary drug of abuse (SAMHSA, 2001). That number increased in 2000 to 243,000, which accounted for almost 15% of all treatment admissions. Treatment admissions for marijuana have increased dramatically during the past decade. Between 1993 and 1999, marijuana admission rates increased in most states, and 18 states reported at least a 100% increase in marijuana treatment admission rates. In 1993, the treatment admission rate for marijuana abuse in the U.S. was 55 admissions per 100,000 persons aged 12 or older. From 1993 to 1999, almost one-third of all marijuana treatment admissions were under the age of 18, and two-thirds were between the ages of 12 and 25. By 1999, the admission rate had increased to 103 per 100,000 persons. The majority (76%) of those admitted for treatment for marijuana abuse were male, and slightly over half were white. One factor behind the recent surge in marijuana treatment admissions is the criminal justice system, as over half (57%) of the admissions were the result of a judicial decision in 1999.

Marijuana and Crime

Production, Trafficking, and Distribution

The primary sources of marijuana in the U.S. are Mexico, Canada, and domestically grown, in both indoor and outdoor operations. According to the Federal-wide Drug Seizure System (FDSS), over 1200 metric tons of marijuana were seized in 2000, up slightly from the previous year. In 2001, there were over one and a half million arrests for drug abuse violations in the U.S. and almost half involved marijuana (5% for sales or manufacturing and 40% for possession). The Arrestee Drug Abuse Monitoring (National Institute of Justice, 2000) program, which collects drug-use data from arrestees in the U.S., revealed that marijuana is the drug of choice for arrestees born since 1970. Contrary to the argument that there is little association between marijuana and crime, ADAM also reported that 43% of adult male arrestees and 28% of adult female arrestees tested positive for marijuana.

Legalization and Decriminalization

Even though support for the legalization of marijuana is at its highest level in 30 years, recent initiatives by several states to legalize small quantities, reduce penalties for possession, or provide treatment instead of jail have all failed.

Medical Marijuana

In addition to the intoxicating effects caused by marijuana use, the main active ingredient in marijuana, THC, also produces effects that are useful in treating various medical problems. For example, THC is currently being used to treat nausea, increase appetite, and relieve pain for cancer patients undergoing chemotherapy, and those suffering from AIDS and glaucoma. Current investigations are exploring the potential of other medical uses of marijuana for neurological disorders such as Parkinson's disease and Tourette's syndrome. In such cases where medicinal marijuana is allowed, there is debate as to whether smoked marijuana is more or less effective than pills containing THC. Problems such as the physical damage to the respiratory system caused by inhaling marijuana as well as the unknown additives present in marijuana leave scientists wary of classifying the illicit drug as having medicinal value (NIDA, 2002).

Using marijuana for legitimate medicinal purposes, sometimes referred to as "medipot," already exists in the form of a pharmaceutical product called Marinol. Marinol is available through a prescription in pill form and current studies are testing its delivery through an inhaler or patch. Marinol relieves nausea and vomiting for cancer patients undergoing chemotherapy, and assists with loss of appetite for AIDS patients. Currently, the Food and Drug Administration does not approve of any medications that are smoked as an acceptable method to deliver medicine. Also, the harmful chemicals and tar in marijuana cigarettes are likely to create new health problems for the patient, causing even greater discomfort.

Across the U.S., various states have sought to ease the penalties and restrictions for marijuana possession. Eight states have passed initiatives allowing marijuana to be used for medicinal purposes, and one state has enacted such legislation. Despite the failure of recent efforts in some states to decriminalize possession of marijuana in small amounts, it is anticipated that similar measures will be sought, especially by those states with medicinal marijuana initiatives.

Future Directions

Marijuana is the most widely used illicit drug in the U.S., and prevalence rates have remained consistent over the past decade. Both emergency room visits and treatment admissions in which marijuana is the primary drug of abuse have been gradually increasing. Although the rise in treatment admissions are partly owing to the increasing number of courts offering treatment instead of incarceration for nonviolent offenders, there is still cause for concern. Despite recent prevention efforts, the perceived risk of marijuana use remains low for teens and young adults, leading to the persistence of its use and the low age of initiation. However, much of society feels that marijuana should not be seen in the same light as harder illicit drugs and the penalties associated should reflect this. Scientists are divided as to the dangers associated with marijuana, and more research and clinical trials are needed to determine appropriate medicinal uses of the drug as well as specific consequences, both short- and long-term, associated with its use. Taken together, the gradually decreasing age at which people first try marijuana, the nearly 2 million new marijuana users each year, and the increasing options of treatment instead of incarceration for nonviolent offenders all lead to an increased demand for substance abuse treatment services for marijuana.

STUART L. USDAN AND LAURA TALBOTT

References and Further Reading

Botvin, G.J., Schinke, S.P., Epstein, J.A., and Diaz, T. (1994). Effectiveness of culturally focused and generic skills training approaches to alcohol and drug abuse prevention among minority youths. *Psychology of Addictive Behaviors*, 8, 116–127.

Hanson, G.R., Venturelli, P.J., and Fleckenstein, A.E. (2002). *Drugs and Society,* 7th ed. Sudbury, MA: Jones and Bartlett Publishers.

Johnston, L.D., O'Malley, P.M., and Bachman, J.G. (2003). *Monitoring the Future: National Results on Adolescent Drug Use. Overview of Key Findings, 2002.* NIH Pub. No. 03-5374. Bethesda, MD: National Institute on Drug Abuse (NIDA).

Miller, J.M. (2001). Marijuana as social common denominator: Reconsidering the use and academic success relationship, *Humanity and Society* 24 (4).

National Institute on Drug Abuse (NIDA). (2002). *Marijuana Abuse. Research Report Series*. Rockville, MD: NIDA.

National Institute of Justice, Arrestee Drug Abuse Monitoring Program. (2000). *1999 Annual Report on Drug Use among Adult and Juvenile Arrestees*. Washington, DC: U.S. Department of Justice.

Office of Applied Studies. (2002). *Results from the 2001 National Household Survey on Drug Abuse: Volume II. Technical Appendices and Selected Data Tables*. NHSDA Series H-18. DHHS Pub. No. (SMA) 02-3759. Rockville, MD: SAMHSA.

Office of Applied Studies. (2001). *Year-End 2000 Emergency Department Data from the Drug Abuse Warning Network* (Table 24). DAWN Series D-18; DHHS Pub. No. (SMA) 01-3532. Rockville, MD: SAMHSA.

Substance Abuse and Mental Health Services Administration. (2001). *Treatment Episode Data Set (TEDS): 1994–1999, National Admissions to Substance abuse Treatment Services*. DASIS Series: S-14, DHHS Pub. No. (SMA) 01-3550. Rockville, MD: DHHS.

Substance Abuse and Mental Health Service Administration. (2002). *Initiation of Marijuana Use: Trends, Patterns and Implications*.

Supreme Court of The U.S., Syllabus. (2001). *U.S. v. Oakland Cannabis Buyers' Cooperative et al.* Available at http://a257.g.akamaitech.net/7/257/2422/14may20011055/www.supremecourtus.gov/opinions/00pdf/00-151.pdf.

Weisheit, R.A. (1992). *Domestic Marijuana: A Neglected Industry*, Westport, CT: Greenwood Press.

See also **Criminalization and Decriminalization; Drug Use: Extent and Correlates; Drug Use: The Law**

Maritime Offenses: Crime at Sea

Crime at sea can be divided into two distinct offenses: piracy and trafficking. Piracy, though typically associated with the 17th and 18th centuries, still occurs in the 21st century and is defined as "an act of boarding or attempting to board any ship with the intent to commit theft or any other crime and with the intent or capability to use force in the furtherance of that act" according to the International Marine Bureau. Although typically interpreted as a private act for personal gain, this view is not historically accurate, as privateers were often employed by nations as a substitute defense tactic when lacking in naval power. A clear distinction between pirates and privateers exists, though the generalization of pirating is most commonly associated with maritime offenses. Trafficking, of both drugs and human cargo, also takes place in the

modern world, though it does not have as long a history as piracy. These two offenses typify crimes at sea, with illegal fishing also a concern for those who patrol coastal waters.

Piracy can be traced as far back as the Phoenician and Roman eras; whenever trade at sea existed, the act of piracy accompanied it. Acts of piracy are typically reduced to that of pirating legends, especially those concerning the most notoriously known pirates of the 17th and 18th centuries. However, nations often employed licensed pirates, known as privateers, to secure and protect their own coastal borders. As trade and imperialism grew, the need for privateers grew exponentially as well, in order to prevent the commerce and colonization efforts of rival powers. This tactic avoided warfare, and at the same time deflected blame away from European countries. Queen Elizabeth I of England employed such defenses during her reign, primarily because her nation lacked naval power. The American colonies also engaged in such behavior in the War for Independence against Britain and continued to use this force until their naval force superceded the effectiveness of pirating in the late 19th century. Since this time, piracy has decreased, though the act still existed in recent history.

In the past decade, an alarming number of pirate attacks have occurred throughout the southern hemisphere. A study published in 2000 by the Woods Hole Oceanographic Institute reports of 469 piracy attacks, 307 boardings, and 8 hijackings with 72 killed and 99 injured. These attacks occurred in waters off South America, South East Asia, the Middle East, and Africa. The increase, advancement, and availability of weaponry make such attacks possible, whereas coastal law enforcement lacks the manpower to monitor all waters. Also, the value of modern commerce has increased, turning large cargo ships, which typically sail at low speeds, into ideal targets for this crime. With microcosmic crews and foreign vessels, regulating and monitoring piracy remains a difficult task. Nations are able to exert legislation over waters within their borders and the territorial waters 12 nautical miles beyond their coast lines, according to international law, which allows for the prosecution of these modern privateers. However, when such attacks occur further than 200 nautical miles from the coast (known as international waters), even the nation to which the ship is registered is unable to arrest and prosecute the offenders. High-threat waters have been located and announced as such, warning both cruise vessels and privately owned vessels to avoid such areas.

Combating piracy at sea is not the sole concern in maritime security, as both human and drug trafficking also constitute a majority of maritime offenses. The U.S. encounters security issues when monitoring illegal aliens from Haiti, Cuba, the Dominican Republic, and Latin America via territorial waterways. Immigrants from these areas typically use water transit as one method for entering the country and officials fear the possibility of mass migration from other nations through cargo ships. Drug trafficking has increased in recent years because of the demand for illicit drugs. Nations with low economies become enablers of this offense, both cultivating the crops and transferring the product. Human trafficking is usually a result of labor situations in which immigrants make for ideal workers because they are considered to be of low value and are therefore paid less, in addition to working and living in inhumane circumstances. On December 19, 2003, President George W. Bush intensified the effort to combat global human trafficking in both the arenas of wage slavery

and child prostitution. With 200 million dollars in funding, the Trafficking Victims Protection Reauthorization Act of 2003 has committed itself to eradicating the crime of human trafficking throughout the world. The U.S. government estimates that between 18,000 and 20,000 humans are trafficked into the U.S. each year and plans to use the new funding to provide assistance to these victims. As far as the maritime offense of trafficking, this legislation is the most ambitious, providing victims the opportunity to bring federal civil suits against their traffickers. The legislation operates under the notion that these humans are victims and not criminal offenders.

Drug trafficking constitutes a key concern for the U.S. Customs Service, which estimates that 6 million come to the U.S. by water each year. Nearly 90,000 ships dock at U.S. ports each year and another 157,000 ships locate themselves in smaller coastal towns. Given the influx of people and ships via waterways, both the Drug Enforcement Agency and the U.S. Customs Service (USCS) have an enormous amount of cargo holdings to approve and search. Because of these numbers and limited manpower, drugs often enter the U.S., which has one of the most competitive drug markets in the world, through this medium. The illegal drugs that penetrate U.S. borders range from marijuana, cocaine, and heroin to methamphetamines and amphetamines and have been more apparent in the U.S. since the 1970s. The ships that enable this offense are often based in Mexico and the Caribbean, allowing the DEA and USCS a better chance of determining the key location of this maritime offense. Although Middle Eastern and European drug trafficking does exist, especially with the trafficking of MDMA (also known as ecstasy), these cartels do not nearly preoccupy coastal law enforcements in the manner that Caribbean and Mexican cartels do.

ABBIE E. VENTURA

References and Further Reading

Blakesley, C.L. 1992. *Terrorism, Drugs, International law, and the Protection of Human Liberty: A Comparative Study of International Law.* Ardsley-on-Hudson, NY: Transnational Publishers.

Fasulo, L.M. 2004. *An Insider's Guide to the U.N.* New Haven, CT: Yale University Press.

Mueller, Gerhard. 1985. *O. W. Outlaws of the Ocean: The Complete Book of Contemporary Crime on the High Sea.* New York, NY: Hearst Marine Books.

Smith, P.J. 1997. *Human Smuggling: The Challenge to America's Immigration Tradition.* Washington, DC: Center for Strategic & International Studies.

United States Congress House. 1995. Committee on Transportation and Infrastructure. Subcommittee on Coast Guard and Maritime Transportation. Coast Guard Drug Interdiction Mission. Washington. U.S. GPO: Supt. of Docs., Congressional Sales Office.

Marshals Service, U.S.

The U.S. marshals service is recognized as the "First Federal Law Enforcement Agency." The service's headquarters is located in Arlington, Virginia, and 94 U.S. marshals conduct law enforcement and protection duties in each judicial district of the U.S. federal court system. The mission of the service begins with its oath to defend the constitution of the U.S. Operationally, the service is responsible for protecting federal court facilities and for assuring unimpeded and safe operations associated with the important civil and criminal justice work of the judicial system. It protects federal judges, transports federal prisoners, protects endangered federal witnesses, and manages assets seized from criminal enterprises. Upholding standards of modern law enforcement professionalism, deputies pursue and arrest 55% of federal fugitives. The service employs approximately 4000 deputy marshals and career employees who carry out essential tasks: fugitive investigations; court security; prisoner custody and transportation; witness security; asset seizure; special operations and programs; missile escort protection; and international investigations. State-of-the-art training is conducted at the Federal Law Enforcement Training Academy in Glynco, Georgia. Training ranges from personal fitness and computer applications to electronic surveillance.

In 1789, Congress passed the First Judiciary Act to create the Office of U.S. marshal. The statute introduced the first elements of a federal justice system by providing for justices of the U.S. Supreme Court, federal circuit court judges, a clerk for each court, the U.S. attorney, and the office of U.S. marshal. Congress intended to provide a structure of criminal justice reflecting some characteristics of the British admiralty courts. The marshal's job was to serve as a functionary of the admiralty court, reaching beyond general law enforcement duties. Some writers have suggested that this development introduced the title of "marshal" rather than sheriff or constable. Marshals were authorized to support the U.S. courts within specified judicial districts and to execute all lawful orders issued by federal judges, Congress, or the president.

The first 13 U.S. marshals were appointed by President George Washington. One marshal was appointed for each of the original 11 states and one for each of the districts of Maine and Kentucky. Each marshal was required to obtain a performance bond of $20,000, and he and his deputies took an oath to faithfully and honestly execute their duties, all lawful precepts, and to uphold the laws of the U.S. Marshals were appointed to serve a term of 4 years at the pleasure of the president. They were authorized to disburse government money by paying the fees and expenses of court clerks, U.S. attorneys, jurors, and witnesses. They procured courtrooms, housed government prisoners in local jails, and employed bailiffs, criers, and janitors. The efficiency of federal courtrooms was aided by delivering prisoners, witnesses, and jurors in a timely fashion to the court. Marshals employed deputies on a fee basis to assist in the service of subpoenas, summonses, writs, warrants, and other legal documents. Important law enforcement work included the execution of warrants of arrest, and sometimes they traveled long distances over difficult terrain. From its earliest days the a U.S. marshals were responsible for enforcing laws in a manner that sometimes ended in tragedy. In January 1794, for example, a U.S. marshal for the district of Georgia, Robert Forsyth, a veteran of the Revolutionary War, was killed by gunfire while attempting to serve civil process. Marshal Forsyth became the first federal law enforcement officer killed in the line of duty. In 1801, Congress codified the authority of the president to appoint and remove marshals. The decision served to establish the marshal as a political appointee. Early marshals were directed by Congress to perform many types of duties associated with federal administration, including census taking, facing off rebels during the Pennsylvania Whiskey Rebellion of 1794, enforcing the Fugitive Slave Act of 1850, and preventing cruelty to animals in interstate transportation.

Through succeeding decades the leadership, management, and organization of the U.S. marshals developed into a modern and prestigious law enforcement agency. Beginning in 1861 a presidential executive order granted the attorney general supervisory authority over the budget of the marshals. Congress formalized and extended this authority by statute in 1870. No headquarters or central administration existed to supervise the work of the marshals until the late 1950s, when the Executive Office of the U.S. Marshals was established. This office held no appreciable authority over district operations but it did retain control over budgets for district activities.

In 1962, the first hint of a U.S. marshals service emerged when President John F. Kennedy appointed James J.P. McShane to the new position of chief

U.S. marshal. McShane had served as a New York City policeman, security provider for President Kennedy, and U.S. marshal for the District of Columbia. He provided leadership during the tumultuous years of the early 1960s. He used his fiscal authority to establish special assignments for deputy marshals at key locations in the South in support of federal desegregation efforts. To minimize hostilities he provided civilian law enforcement in place of the military, a practice that had been used effectively in disturbances in Little Rock, Arkansas. McShane's efforts were ambitious and commendable especially because deputy marshals lacked radio communications, riot gear, and the proper training for civil disturbances. Furthermore, it was not uncommon for deputy marshals to borrow equipment and supplies from other agencies. McShane's involvement, however, provided the necessary motivation to advance the skill and success of the service in the performance of traditional and new tasks. In October 1967, the DOJ ordered marshals to provide support to the military during street protests against the war in Vietnam. Deputies responded with antiquated white helmets, homemade riot batons, personal pistols, and personal vehicles. They were confronted with near riot conditions for 2 days and there was no plan for relief or meals. They were successful, however, in denying the protestors access to the Pentagon building and in arresting several violent protestors.

Statutory and other changes continued to affect the development of the marshals service. In November 1967, supervision of the Executive Office of the U.S. Marshals was removed as a responsibility of the deputy attorney general and placed within the organization of the assistant attorney general for administration. In 1969, the attorney general selected Carl C. Turner as the new Chief Marshal. Turner's military background had provided him with an inclination toward organization and strong leadership, two characteristics needed to establish the U.S. marshals service. During his short and troublesome tenure, Turner guided development of the DOJ's office of the director for the U.S. marshals service. This office reported to the deputy attorney general and it established the authority of the director over all personnel issues and field support units. Headquarters staff was also authorized for marshals service. Regrettably, Turner's career ended when he resigned while under indictment for crimes alleged to have been committed in earlier years.

In 1970, the U.S. marshal for the southern district of California, Wayne B. Colburn, was sworn in as director. As a former police officer and marshal he was aware of the diversity of missions and talents within the service. He developed career ladders and established new and lasting opportunities for the service as part of his management objectives. Colburn identified

judicial security, air piracy, and witness security as proper efforts to incorporate and to enhance the responsibilities of the marshals. He was successful in obtaining civil service status for the deputies, but he could not persuade Congress and his DOJ superiors to remove the 94 marshals from the process of political appointments. Two years later Colburn was granted a new charter to establish the service as a bureau of the department of justice, an achievement that was withdrawn in 5 months' time by a new attorney general. Colburn was successful in obtaining departmental authority to create a paramilitary-style organization known as the special operations group (SOG). This new organizational resource strengthened the government's ability to respond to serious law enforcement situations when a decision was made under appropriate legal direction that the local authority could not respond. The SOG was deployed effectively in the government's response to the Wounded Knee situation in South Dakota in 1973. In 1976, Colburn retired to California.

William E. Hall was named director in May 1976. He had worked in private law practice following previous employment as a special agent with the Federal Bureau of Investigation, as general counsel to the marshals service, as assistant director for operations, and as deputy director of the service. Hall benefited from experience under Carl Turner and Wayne Colburn. His administrative style preferred consensus and refinement of the service mission to extend operational effectiveness and responsibilities. Hall was judged by many people to have excellent interpersonal skills and adroitness in retaining high quality staff personnel. He provided resources to the 94 districts to improve communications, equipment, and transportation facilities. He mandated improvements in training for new deputies and he established a new training facility for the SOG in Louisiana. Hall held the first retreat for senior management of the service at Leesburg, Virginia, and he held annual conferences of the U.S. marshals. Two major innovations were accomplished during Hall's tenure. First, the federal fugitive program, an initiative that had been generally ignored by the FBI, was provided with the resources to make it successful. Second, the court security program was strengthened by increasing the number of court security personnel through contracts with private agencies.

In October 1983, President Ronald Reagan appointed Stanley E. Morris as director. Morris was an experienced government manager who had closely examined the service from other positions he held in the DOJ. He was known as a "quick study" and was inclined toward candid remarks about administrative and operational conditions. He obtained funding, established and expanded the court security program, and established the National Asset Seizure and Forfeiture program.

He modernized the prisoner airlift program and he authorized a system of vans and buses to support prisoner transportation. Morris encouraged staff to innovate new approaches to fugitive investigations, resulting in three successful task force operations and in two operations to arrest felony narcotics fugitives. He directed operational improvements throughout the service, including higher quality official vehicles, establishment of data systems, pay and grade increases, office space and appearance, and establishment of a fitness program. He was always available to the district marshals, and he found time to streamline all service communications. Morris was also skillful in the legislative arena, exhibited by his ability to persuade Congress to permanently raise the service to a DOJ bureau and to make the director a presidential appointee. Morris was at the helm when the marshals service celebrated its bicentennial year in 1989 with a series of events and a Smithsonian exhibit that traveled the nation. He reconfirmed the bureau's commitment to personnel diversity by emphasizing its constitutional mandate, thus preparing this venerable law enforcement agency for the challenges of the 21st century.

The recent directors of the service have exhibited significantly different management styles. K. Michael Moore was appointed by President Bush from his position as U.S. attorney. His leadership style was generally friendly and low profile. He soon left the job to become a U.S. District Judge in Miami, Florida. Henry Hudson, also a former U.S. attorney and candidate for Congress, served as director through the 1992 election. Eduardo Gonzalez, chief of police of Tampa, Florida, was the first director appointed by President Bill Clinton but upon his resignation was replaced by John Marshall, a Virginia state police sergeant and son of Supreme Court justice Thurgood Marshall. Louie T. McKinney served as the acting director until Benigno G. Reyna was appointed by President Bush.

Despite the generally high quality appointees to serve as U.S. marshals, the first federal law enforcement function, several deficiencies still inhibit the service's ability to carry out duties in the best possible manner. The general accounting office conducted a comprehensive review of the service when William E. Hall was director, finding a major obstacle to management being that of serving two masters, the courts and the attorney general. Future congresses and presidents will be expected to address issues of compensation, the need for more deputy marshals, operational readiness for emergencies, and additional staff support. Unquestionably, however, the legacies, traditions, and human resource strengths of the marshal service will sustain its professional performance.

WILLIAM JONAS

References and Further Reading

Calhoun, F.S. 1989. *The Lawmen, United States Marshals and Their Deputies, 1789–1989*, Washington, DC: Smithsonian Institution.

Cohen, M.L. 1998. *Bibliography of Early American Law*, New York, NY: W.S. Hein & Co.

Goldstein, N. 1991. *Marshal, the Story of the U.S. Marshals Service*, New York, NY: Dialogue Systems.

Henderson, D.F. 1985. *Congress, Courts, and Criminals*, Westport, CT: Greenwood.

Mitchell, G. 1982. The new federal fugitive hunt: The U.S. Marshals take on a new role, *Police Magazine*, 5.

Sherrard, R. 1995. *Badges of the United States Marshals*, Garden Grove, CA: RHS Enterprises.

Slate, R.N. 1997. The federal witness protection program: Its evolution and continuing growing pains, *Criminal Justice Ethics* 16.

Sommer, R.L. 1993. *The History of the U.S. Marshals*, Philadelphia, PA: Courage.

See also **Law Enforcement; Law Enforcement: Careers; Police History: U.S.**

Marxist Theories of Criminal Behavior

Marxist criminology finds its roots in the basic notions of Karl Marx's political economic theory, itself a stinging attack on capitalism. Marx, born in 1818 to Jewish parents in Treves, Germany, argued that throughout the history of humankind, the "haves" and the "have nots" have been pitted against each other in a series of class struggles. Under capitalism, those who own the means of production subjugate those who work for them. The former are often referred to as the bourgeoisie, and the latter as proletariats, or the working class. Marx believed that under capitalism, the bourgeoisie are able to accrue a great deal of wealth on the backs of the proletariats. The notion of surplus labor comes into play here, as does that of alienation.

Marx argued that, unlike earlier economic systems, for example, the mercantile system, where individuals often bartered for the exchange of commodities, in a capitalist system the workers are paid a wage that is much less than the profits being put in the pockets of the bourgeoisie. All of the profit that is above and beyond the wage paid to the worker is referred to as surplus labor. In a system where individuals must sell their labor to the capitalists, the workers become alienated from their true natures, and are locked into a sort of false consciousness. This sets up a situation in which the more powerful class is able to control the major institutions of society, especially the political and the economic institutions. In this type of society, conflict and exploitation of the weaker class are the norm. In an often-cited quote by Marx, he sums this point up in the following manner:

> The mode of production in material life determines the general character of the social, political, and spiritual processes of life. It is not the consciousness of men that determines their existence, but, on the contrary, their social existence determines their consciousness (Marx, 1981, 20–21).

Marx's two major works consisted of *The Communist Manifesto*, published in 1848, and *Das Kapital*, published in three volumes, the first in 1867 and the second and third completed after his death in 1885 and 1894, respectively, by his long-time friend, benefactor, and coworker, Friedrich Engels. In *The Communist Manifesto*, Marx provided a thorough description of what he meant by "The history of all human society, past and present, has been the history of class struggles" (as cited in Ruhle, 1928, 131). Marx argued that the 19th century developing capitalist society did not bring an end to the class system found under earlier economic systems, for example, the feudal society. Rather, as stated above, the new bourgeois age ushered in two opposing classes that were ripe with disdain one for the other. During a time of a great revolution, Marx believed that the proletariat would rise and loose itself of the yoke of capitalism, and that history would usher in this revolt of the workers of the world. Toward that end, he argued, the capitalists are sowing the seeds to their own destruction.

Almost 20 years later, in the first volume of *Das Kapital*, Marx began a scathing critique of the capitalist economy. He began with an analysis of the commodity system, exchange value, and with an in-depth look at the issues of profits and the accumulation of capital that the proletariats, through the sale of their labor, provided the capitalists. Although humankind had been freed from the chains of the feudal system, they were met with a new set of chains under capitalism. As Ruhle (1928, 327) argues, "He is blessed with the gift of freedom; but, should he try to use that freedom for any other purpose than to sell his labour power, he is condemned to irretrievable starvation." Individuals truly had no choice but to sell their labor to the capitalist class in order to purchase the certain "commodities" needed to survive (e.g., food, shelter, and clothing). Marx talks further about the fetishistic nature of money under capitalism, and about the competitive, individualistic nature of the bourgeois society, subsuming all of these concepts under his theory of historical materialism, that was developed earlier in *The Communist Manifesto*.

In sum, Marx developed a political economic theory that argues that the outcrops of any civil society, for example, its very nature as seen through the interaction of its citizens, one with the other, through its social and political institutions, is determined by its base: the economic system on which it is situated. Economics, from a Marxist perspective, is the moving force of history (Ruhle, 1928) and, as such, determines the actions and the ideas of individuals situated within society.

Whither a Marxist Criminology

If Marx is right, then one could argue that different economic systems will produce different ideas and behaviors. Although Marx wrote very little about crime, he did allude to the fact, in *Das Capital*, that the "free" proletariats who found it difficult to adapt to the new conditions of capitalism became "beggars, vagabonds, robbers," and "in accordance with a newly inaugurated and barbarous legal code, they are flogged, branded, racked, and in the end, are handed over like beasts of burden for use in the manufactories and the factories" (Ruhle, 1928, 347).

A Dutch socialist, Willem Bonger, developed the roots of modern-day Marxist criminology (sometimes referred to as critical or radical criminology) in his work *Criminality and Economic Conditions* in 1916. The earlier arguments of Marx can be seen in Bonger's notion that capitalism sets up a society that is ripe for crime in that altruism, actions undertaken by individuals in the pursuit of what is best for the whole of society, takes a backseat to egoism. He argued that the criminal class is a backlash of capitalism because individuals are taught to engage in cutthroat competition, and to exploit others to get ahead. Coupled with the deplorable conditions in which many of the working class are forced to live, it is no wonder that crime is the result.

In the U.S., primarily beginning in the 1960s, there appeared a group of theorists who questioned the mainstream theories of criminology under positivism, the scientific study of crime from such perspectives as social disorganization, strain, and subculture of deviance theories, many of them grounded in the writings of the late 19th century writer, Emile Durkheim. Under positivism is the view that society functions out of a consensus of sorts, with give and take as the pendulum swings to the left, to the right, and then back to the middle, reaching, in the end, an equilibrium. In such places as the University of California at Berkeley, theorists (e.g., Tony Platt, Herman and Julia Schwendinger, and Paul Takagi) turned consensus theory on its head, arguing that, in fact, society was organized around conflict, not consensus.

Marxist theorists attempted to focus attention on the fact that under capitalism, power was deeply embedded in the hands of a few, those who were able to accrue a vast amount of financial resources for their use. The laws of society and the criminal justice system that enforced them are little more than instruments of the powerful put in place to further their own interest at the expense of the lower classes with very few resources, financial or political. In *Critique of the Legal Order*, Richard Quinney (1974, 16) argued that, "The criminal law is an instrument of the state and ruling class to maintain and perpetuate the existing social and economic order."

At its core, however, Marxist theory seeks to divert attention away from the *crimes of the powerless* and toward the *crimes of the powerful*. Under capitalism, *street* crimes of the lower classes might be an unintended consequence of competition, rugged individualism, and the fetishism of money gone amok, but ignored for too long are the behaviors committed by the ruling classes. Among these are violations of basic human rights, unsafe working conditions, pollution of the air and water, substandard living conditions, deprivation of basic human needs, police brutality, and waging war. The few laws that are in existence to deal with some of these violations, according to such writers as Herman and Julia Schwendinger (1970), Friedrichs (1980), Michalowski (1985), and Quinney (1980), are rarely enforced even though they are much more likely to cause greater harm to society than the crimes of the powerless.

Critique of Marxist Criminology

From a pure Marxist perspective, the only solution to the type of crime associated with a capitalist society is to replace the capitalist system entirely, a notion that parallels nicely with Marx's basic argument that the end of the exploitation of the proletariat will come only when capitalism has taken its last breath upon the earth. For this reason, many critics view Marxist criminology as utopian in nature and not applicable to society in the 21st century, especially 21st century American society. The great revolution of the proletariat seems a distant dream of dead political and economic theorists, and is not likely to come to fruition anytime soon. Theorists, therefore, have a responsibility to work within the present-day capitalist society to provide policy makers and criminal justice practitioners with sensible approaches to the crime problem.

Further, critics of Marxist criminology argue that theories that are based primarily on *class* ignore *individual* differences and the role those differences play in the production of crime. Why is it, they ask, that all lower class individuals, living under repressed conditions, do not become criminals? In fact, most do not.

Marxist criminologists respond to these criticisms by using their own arguments against them. For example, so-called mainstream theories have, at some time or another, been considered utopian in nature. After all, how can, the blocked opportunities important to strain and anomie theories, be removed from society? How can the social institutions that are important for social disorganization theory, be revamped in such a way as to be able to exercise a certain amount of control over society's members? Why is it that all strained individuals, as well as individuals living in communities that are broken down and in vast disarray, do not turn to crime?

These questions are not easily answered, but it could be that the answers lie somewhere in the notion that neither individual traits nor social characteristics of the environment are constant, and it could be a matter of tipping the balance in favor of more risk factors than protective factors. For Marxist theorists, there is no direct contradiction between the arguments of consensus theorists and those of Marxists. Rather, Marxist theorists argue that the relative deprivation experienced by differentially situated individuals in a class system, a notion inherent in mainstream criminology, does not happen in a vacuum. To get to the source of the problem, theorists must explain the contradictions of a capitalist system, and to do this, the works by Marx provide a rich and invaluable foundation.

In sum, modern-day Marxist theorists are viewed by many of their colleagues as holding fast to a theory that has long been placed on the shelves of history as the great revolution, as stated previously, but has not occurred. Marx could not have envisioned the machinery of capitalism that exists today, nor could he envision the uplifting of the sea of workers into such a prosperous middle class. Instead of calling for a direct overthrow of the capitalist state, many radical or critical theorists (preferring a different title than that of "Marxist") push for reforms in the system instead, primarily in the criminal justice system (see Lynch and

Groves, 1989, for an excellent handling of this issue). They call for making the meting out of "justice" more fair and equitable, erasing such atrocities as the disproportionate representation of minorities in the system, the failed "wars" on crime and drugs, mandatory minimum sentences, etc. True Marxists, however, and in the spirit of Marx himself, see the dialectic spirit of historical materialism marching forward every time even a shred of ground is reclaimed by the masses. The capitalist system is evolving because it has to. It cannot escape that fact any more than could the economic systems that came before it.

BARBARA SIMS

References and Further Reading

Bonger, W. 1916. *Criminality and Economic Conditions*. Boston, MA: Little, Brown and Company.

Friedrichs, D.O. 1980. Radical criminology in the United States: An interpretive understanding. Inciardi, J. (Ed.) *Radical Criminology: The Coming Crisis*. Beverly Hills, CA: Sage.

Lynch, M.J. and Groves, W.B. 1989. *A Primer in Radical Criminology*. 2nd ed. Albany, NY: Harrow and Heston.

Marx, K. Crime and capital accumulation. Greenberg, D. (Ed.) *Crime and Capitalism*. Palo Alto, CA: Mayfield.

Michalowski, R.J. 1985. *Order, Law, and Crime: An Introduction to Criminology*. NY: Random House.

Quinney, R. 1974. *Critique of Legal Order*. Boston, MA: Little, Brown and Company.

Quinney, R. 1980. *Class, State and Crime*. NY: Longman.

Ruhle, O. 1928. *Karl Marx: His Life and Work*. New York, NY: Viking Press.

Schwendinger, H. and Schwendinger, J. 1970. Defenders of order or guardians of human Rights? *Issues in Criminology* 7(1):71–81.

See also **Bonger, Willem; Chambliss, William; Radical Theories of Criminal Behavior; Social Class and Criminal Behavior; Sociological Theories of Criminal Behavior**

Masculinity Theory

Among the many statistics produced by criminologists, none has appeared more consistently than this one: By far, men are responsible for a disproportionate share of crime. This correlation between gender and criminal behavior has been produced and reproduced over time and across cultures. Interestingly, this correlation begs a question that until recently has been largely overlooked: Why are men so much more likely than women to engage in crime? Unfortunately, as noted by Allen (1989), the discipline of criminology has been woefully inadequate in addressing this question, primarily because of the tendency throughout its history to unequivocally accept males as the normative subject of study. But masculinity theory, rooted in feminist and critical criminology and gender studies in sociology, seeks to address directly what one might call the "maleness" of crime.

The theory's current favor among criminologists can be traced to James Messerschmidt's *Masculinites and Crime* (1993). (In addition, see *Just Boys Doing Business?*, a collection of essays on masculinities and crime edited by Tim Newburn and Elizabeth Stanko, 1994). Structured action is the key concept of the theory. It involves both the situational antecedents of crime and crime itself (i.e., violent action). In relation to gender,

Messerschmidt (1993) argues that all of us engage in "doing gender"—the form of action that this will take is dependent on both the social settings and situations in which we find ourselves. In this sense, gender is not only an ascribed status, but also something that is achieved in day-to-day interactions with other people. The relevant form of structured action to this theory is "doing masculinity." Beginning at an early age, boys learn both to develop and reinforce their masculine identities, as well as to reinforce other boys' masculinity through actions taken in specific social settings (e.g., schoolyards or baseball diamonds).

Messerschmidt (1993, 2000) employs R.W. Connell's (1987) conceptualization of three such "masculinities": hegemonic, subordinated, and oppositional. Hegemonic masculinity refers to the cultural ideal of masculinity in a society; in the U.S., for example, hegemonic masculinity would entail values such as strength, aggression, heterosexuality, independence, and the need for control (of oneself and others). As Kimmel (2001) notes, this form of masculinity is as much a statement of masculinity as it is a rejection of feminine traits and values. Set apart from hegemonic masculinity are subordinated masculinities, which are more likely to be accomplished by men and boys who belong to society's marginalized groups (e.g., gay and minority group males). Finally there are oppositional masculinities whose adherents strongly eschew the hegemonic norm and seek to "do masculinity" on their own terms.

The theory itself frames "structured action" (i.e., doing masculinity) within an overarching set of social (gender) relations and social structures that encourage and constrain such actions. Put simply, Messerschmidt (1993) argues that doing masculinity is situational: whether masculinities are accomplished or what type of masculinity is done depends on a number of factors. Violence by males is often preceded by some sort of challenge to the eventual offender's masculinity, or, as Polk (1994) describes it, an "honor confrontation." This challenge provides the situational motivation for violence, but whether this situation will in fact involve an act of lethal or criminal violence depends on a number of factors: (1) the opportunities available for such violence, which are often determined by (2) the power or status of actors to promote or defuse a situation (e.g., individuals with higher status are more likely to have resources at their disposal to help them avoid physical confrontations); and (3) the particular form of masculinity that the potential offender adheres to (hegemonic, oppositional, or subordinated—Messerschmidt 2000). The theory makes clear that masculinity is not only implicated in the foreground of criminal behavior, but that the form of masculinity that is practiced by males also will vary depending on the situation.

Messerschmidt (2000) provides a test of the theory in his *Nine Lives: Adolescent Masculinities, the Body, and Violence*. The book contains life history data based on Messerschmidt's interviews with nine adolescent boys representing three groups: violent sexual offenders, assaultive offenders, and nonoffenders. Based on these interviews, Messerschmidt finds that all three major forms of masculinity are constructed and reproduced in the major socializing contexts of family and school. He concludes that fathers and other male figures in the household, as well as male adolescent peers, clarify these forms and share in the process of doing masculinity. Overall, masculinities are heavily implicated in the social process leading to violence by adolescent males in the U.S. The lesson learned from the non-violent offenders, Messerschmidt (2000) notes, is that we should encourage a more "democratic manhood" to evolve—particularly in schools—that allows young males a way out of violence.

Messerschmidt's (2000) findings lend support to Polk's (1994) research, which demonstrated the strong correlation between masculinity and lethal violence in Australia. They complement other findings in criminology as well, including Schwartz and DeKeseredy's (1997) arguments and research linking male peer group support to violence against women and Anderson's (1999) interpretation of inner-city violence as a male-based "code of the street." In addition, the theory supports more psychological treatments of male aggression and violence (Campbell, 1993).

Masculinity theory is a unique, alternative theory in criminology—one that supports the overall call for attention to the gendered nature of violence (Danner and Carmody, 2001). The most obvious criticism of the theory is that it fails to address crime committed by girls and women, but as Messerschmidt (1993) notes, masculinity theory is not intended to be a general theory of crime. Gender may be relevant in certain social settings, but not others. Masculinity also has been used to explain mostly street crime, but Schwartz (1996) contends the theory may be more generalizable than it first appears, with possible use in explaining white-collar and corporate crime.

Masculinity theory currently holds increasing favor in criminology, with more sessions devoted to the topic every year at the annual conferences (Collier, 1998). Further, the theory has a strong international presence, particularly among researchers in North America, the U.K., and the Australian continent. In future, it will be exciting to see the theory applied cross-culturally and across various social contexts.

MICHAEL O. MAUME

Further Reading

Allen, J. 1989. Men, crime and criminology: Recasting the questions, *International Journal of the Sociology of Law* 17.

Anderson, E. 1999. *Code of the Street: Decency, Violence, and the Moral Life of the Inner City*, New York and London: W.W. Norton and Company.

Campbell, A. 1993. *Men, Women, and Aggression*, New York, NY: BasicBooks.

Collier, R. 1998. *Masculinities, Crime and Criminology: Men, Heterosexuality and the Criminal(ised) Other*, London; Thousand Oaks, CA; and New Delhi, India: Sage.

Connell, R.W. 1987. *Gender and Power: Society, the Person, and Sexual Politics*, Stanford, CA: Stanford University Press.

Danner, M.J.E. and Carmody, D.C. 2001. Missing gender in cases of infamous school violence: Investigating research and media explanations, *Justice Quarterly* 18.

Kimmel, M.S. 2001. Clarence, William, Iron Mike, Tailhook, Senator Packwood, Spur Posse, Magic…and us, in *Men's Lives*, 5th ed., Kimmel, M.S. and Messner, M.A. (Eds.) Boston. MA: Allyn and Bacon.

Messerschmidt, J.W. 1993. *Masculinities and Crime: Critique and Reconceptualization of Theory*, Lanham, MD: Rowman & Littlefield Publishers.

Messerschmidt, J.W. 2000. *Nine Lives: Adolescent Masculinities, the Body, and Violence*, Boulder, CO, and Oxford: Westview Press.

Newburn, T., and Stanko, E.A. (Eds.) 1994. *Just Boys Doing Business? Men, Masculinities and Crime* London, UK, and New York, NY: Routledge.

Polk, K. 1994. *When Men Kill: Scenarios of Masculine Violence*, Cambridge, UK, and Melbourne, Australia: Cambridge University Press.

Schwartz, M.D. 1996. The study of masculinities and crime, *The Criminologist* 21.

Schwartz, M.D. and DeKeseredy, W.S. 1997. *Sexual Assault on the College Campus: The Role of Male Peer Support*, Thousand Oaks, CA; London, UK; and New Delhi, India: Sage.

See also **Critical Criminology; Feminist Theories of Criminal Behavior; Sociological Theories of Criminal Behavior**

Mass Media and Crime and Justice

Crime and justice are socially defined in a process in which news and entertainment media are major contributors. The relationship between media and the agencies of the criminal justice system is interactive in the milieu within which this social reality is created.

Crime and justice are what we say they are, and what we say they are is primarily a product of media. "Americans learn what they know about crime and justice from the popular media—commercial news and entertainment, especially. And what they know—what they think they know—can often be but a distorted version of reality, for the popular media are not as interested in informing us as in commanding our attention, not as interested in 'the truth' as in good stories" (Bailey and Hale, 1998, ix–x).

These public perceptions of crime and justice that lead to social reality and later constructive reality (after policies are made based on social reality) are often the product of "myths" that are unsupported by research and physical reality. Popular culture's entertainment is escapism, not realism, whereas popular culture's news is voyeurism (Bailey and Hale). To maintain readers' and viewers' attention, popular culture has to be different from reality—more interesting.

Media in the U.S. has a long history of storytelling within an established framework of good versus evil, right versus wrong, heroes versus villains—entertainment and news cloaked in a never-ending morality tale in a simplistic, dualistic world (Barak, 1994). Crime and justice news fits nicely into this mold and has become a staple of media, often the number one topic of both nightly news and entertainment.

The relationship between media and public and private agencies that deal with crime and justice is usually one of symbiosis (Bailey and Hale). Media need access to a constant flow of highly entertaining and (in the case of television) highly visual events; crime and justice agencies need to frame these events in a manner that provides public support for their activities. In exchange for access, the media generally agree to a formula that stresses the heroic work of law enforcers and the importance of retribution and deterrence supposedly obtained through prosecution and imprisonment—thus, a symbiotic relationship. Usually the formula works for all, as the fear and blood lust created by the media both entices readers and viewers that feed media budgets and leads to calls for more support of police, courts, and corrections that feed criminal justice agency budgets. There are, of course, exceptions, such as when camcorder and now cell picturephone evidence indicates police brutality and (because it is highly visual and entertaining) is used by media, or when a court issues a "gag" order in an attempt to keep pretrial publicity from prejudicing a community before a trial.

Mass media has expanded significantly in the 21st century—beyond 19th century books, magazines, and newspapers, and 20th century movies, radio, and television, to video and computer games, the Internet, music CDs, DVDs, popup advertisements, proliferation of channels via cable and satellite, etc. The explosion of media sources should bring a pluralism that would negate or at least mitigate the mythmaking power of a uniform media message. Barak (1994), however, argued that media pluralism (many channels, many outlets) had not led to message pluralism (diversity of content). For the most part, the major mass media sources continued to homogenize the news to fit into its set format of sound bites within the morality tale framework.

The Internet, however, has become a "wild card" (a new and unpredictable medium) as "blogs" (personal web sites that allow individuals to express their own opinions and provide their own evidence on any matter) and a worldwide diversity of organized groups with web sites (e.g., www.kukluxklan.net, www.stormfront.com, www.hatewatch.org, www.unitedagainsthate.com, www.crimevictims.org, www.prisonreformtrust.org, www.hackers.com, www.cops.com, www.tvcops.com, www.clumsycrooks.com, www.terrorismanswers.com, www.bestlawyers.com) have changed the process of acquiring news and entertainment for millions of Americans and others worldwide. This is particularly true of the young and is a phenomenon that well may change the impact of media in the formulation of perceptions and influence on policy.

Media as a Socializing Influence

Media historically has played a major role in the creation of social structure and the socializing of inhabitants of society. Possibly the oldest form of enduring media is art, beginning with the cave paintings that point to communication that served itinerant clans and was preserved for future generations. Paintings of fierce animals and scary tribesmen surely reinforced clan bonds for protection and willingness to harm others to enhance their own well-being. Even after written language developed, most were uneducated and still got their messages from pictures. On a recent trip to view the Notre Dame Cathedral in Paris, this writer asked the tour guide why the stone-carved pictures around the main entrances were so elaborate and detailed, and he replied: "That's so all who come would get the message. Most couldn't read and many could not understand the priest, but the stories were clear and graphic in the paintings by the doors. They got the message of the wages of sin and the powers of redemption."

In colonial times in America, one major form of mass media was the "broadside" or "pamphlet" that often included an essay or a fiery message in support or opposition to a current or proposed policy, such as independence from Great Britain. It was public reaction to these messages (such as Thomas Paine's *Common Sense*) that is credited in large part for events such as the Boston Tea Party, the confrontation with the British at Concord and Lexington, and The Declaration of Independence (printed, distributed, and read by town criers) that led to the Revolutionary War. The U.S. Constitution received the same treatment, as media was crucial to the creation of the new nation.

As Euro-Americans searched for land and a new life in the 19th century, Horace Greeley urged them on with editorials in his *New York Tribune* in 1841, declaring: "Do not lounge in the cities! There is room and health in the country, away from the crowds of idlers and imbeciles. Go west...." Thousands, and later millions, took his advice, and the media that went with them played a role in both conquering and "civilizing" the frontier while simultaneously vilifying the Native Americans and later Mexican Americans who stood in the way of white settlement. The pioneer media—usually town newspapers started as a way to make a living by a settler—were known for supporting the townsfolk against outside threats although seeking desirable development and financial support from outside interests. The other media, primarily correspondents for penny papers and dime novels back east, acted as today's supermarket tabloid reporters, sensationalizing the battle for the frontier between "savages" (sometimes "noble") and settlers and between gunslingers and law enforcers. Some see this period as the beginning of the everlasting morality play in American media; more likely it was a period in which this framework was honed and exaggerated, impacting media and crime and justice to this day.

In a study of the media's impact on the Civil War, Ratner and Teeter (2003) examined the treatment of several major events—e.g., John Brown's raid at Harpers Ferry (1859), Abraham Lincoln's election (1860), the firing on Fort Sumter (1861)—and concluded media rhetoric inflamed passions and, to pursue their own agendas, newspapers north and south "played fast and lose with facts and logic" and "stoked the fires that heated tensions." They also contended that because of advancing technology—use of the telegraph, printing presses, and the railroad for acquiring and distributing the news—this was the first example of truly "mass media" in the U.S. It was this newfound power and its use that might also have led to Lincoln's assassination, as he was portrayed as everything from saint and savior to devil and demon but seldom as just a struggling president in dire times.

Before the Civil War, the "Black Press" began to emerge in the north and extended to the south during reconstruction. These media were active in supporting abolitionists and the underground railroad and later in protesting lynching and the rise of the Ku Klux Klan. One female Black editor, Eda Wells Barrett, documented abuses of Black citizens, including lynching, which resulted in the firebombing of her paper, the *Memphis Free Speech*.

After the Civil War, the new mass media turned its attention to profits over politics, and often became an amoral observer of events as scandal and sensationalism ushered in the "yellow journalism" period. Among other events of this Reconstruction Period, the media often reported lynching as more of a spectator sport than a brutal crime (West, 2004). Reporters of this period were said to be poorly educated, and prone to rush from one crime scene to another seeking blood and gore to fill the penny press and dime novels. It was, however, also a period when the media was at a low in its influence on public opinion and policy-making.

In the West during this period, profits also drove correspondents and writers who were usually paid only for what was published or sold. Entertainment couched as news sold best; thus gunfighters versus marshals and sheriffs and frontiersmen versus Native Americans and Mexicans became the stuff of legends. Gunfighters turned lawmen, such as Wyatt Earp and Bat Masterson, and gunfighters supposedly driven by dire circumstances, for example, Billy the Kid and Jesse James, became heroes and part of American folklore (Eisfeld, 1995). This fascination with the flawed but colorful lawbreaker as an essential element of the nation's psyche continued with the gangsters of the 1930s and beyond.

Near the end of the 19th century, attention began to focus on improving the quality of those who gathered the news, as in 1875 Cornell University offered a Certificate of Journalism for completion of a liberal arts curriculum and some hands-on work in printing, and in 1878 the University of Missouri offered the first course in journalism. By 1885, several press clubs were formed and a trade publication, *The Journalist*, was begun. Still these earliest "professional journalists" were the ones who led the "yellow journalism" era, and it was not until the early 20th century that a full-fledged School of Journalism with a full degree curriculum was founded at Columbia University—in 1902 under the guidance of newspaper magnate Joseph Pulitzer (Boyland, 2004). In 1909, the Sigma Delta Chi professional journalism fraternity (today the Society of Professional Journalists) was founded at DePauw University "to improve and protect journalism" and to stimulate high standards of ethical behavior among its practitioners. With education and standards in place, the media became a more influential force in American society, although a complaint voiced in *The Galaxy* magazine in 1867 still resonates well over a century later: "The Alpha and Omega of (journalism's) sins and failings amount to just this...that it is not yet enough a profession, in remuneration, public repute, or special training" (Overholser, 2004, online).

Branded sensationalists and muckrakers, Pulitzer, William Randolph Hearst, and other media giants of the period turned the media from partisan voices for a single political party or commercial venture toward reporting the news relatively objectively and spearheading projects for the "public good"—such as a campaign to raise $300,000 to provide a pedestal for the Statute of Liberty that was being presented to the U.S. by France (West, 2004). The money was raised via donations by 120,000 contributors, many giving 5 or 10 cents. Corruption in government and child labor violations were also subjects embraced by the new media. Technology greatly enhanced the ability of the media to reach mass audiences as the telephone soon joined telegraph lines and the Associated Press, born in 1848, had enough customers by the turn of the century to provide stories from around the world at low cost to its newspaper clients.

The Spanish American War of 1898 provided a good example of the media's newfound power of persuasion. Called by many "The Newspaper War," the events surrounding the conflict were covered daily by *Hearst's New York Journal,* the *San Francisco Examiner,* and Pulitzer's *New York World*; they sensationalized a derogatory remark about the president by a Spanish minister and the probable accidental sinking of the U.S. battleship *Maine* into a moral panic, where the public literally demanded the war that was declared by President William McKinley, despite his feelings that the situation could have been handled by diplomacy. With war declared, the *Examiner* ran the headline: "The Triumph of New Journalism" (Baker, 2004).

Although there were photographs in the media in the 19th century, it was not until the 20th century that sound and pictures really began to have a major impact in the media as influences on public perceptions, public opinion, and public policy. Movies, then radio, and finally television joined books, magazines, and newspapers as major mass media.

In the early part of the century, newspapers still reigned and were influential in creating an isolationist atmosphere for the U.S., but when thrust into World War I, the media was equally important in garnering support for the troops and the cause. It was the power of the photograph that led to increased government interference with media decision making during this period, as the Office of War Information (OWI) was given the responsibility to censor words and pictures from the battlefront (Print and War, 2004, online). For example, it banned publication of any picture of a dead American soldier, a ban that lasted through the first 2 years of World War II. It also prepared and assisted the media in creating positive images of Americans in these wars and spearheaded campaigns to keep the public busy and supportive of the war (such as "Rosie the Riveter" posters and newsreels). In 1943, fearing that Americans at home were weary of the exhausting war, the OWI authorized the first images of dead Americans to be published and shown on film, including one on the cover of *Life* magazine. Designed both to incense the public and to encourage support for completing the task, the pictures were nevertheless not to show any blood and guts or allow identification of any individual, but sterile images of the dead only.

A good example of the power of images to create social reality can be seen in D. W. Griffith's filming of *Hearts of the World* during the waning days of World War I. Given access to the battles themselves, Griffith became frustrated with the messiness of trench warfare, so he scripted battles and put actors and soldiers together to stage them in a visual manner that could be more easily captured on film. Thus, the images of World War I that dominate today were largely the result of images in the head of a movie director of how war "ought to look." The same approach was later taken to depict gangsters and lawmen in the Prohibition and Depression eras. During Prohibition, unpopular with the public, gangsters like Al Capone were often pictured in newspapers and on film as Horatio Alger types—taking advantage of the times to make their fortunes by providing a marketable product (liquor)—and became folk heroes, as did the outlaws on the road, such as Bonnie and Clyde, who were portrayed as poor people driven by desperation. For the gangsters, however, much changed after their excesses, culminating in the St. Valentines' Day Massacre of 1929, after which "in the cultural catharsis of the early Depression [the gangster] became a scapegoat villain, threatening the survival of social order and American values" (Maltby, 2003, online).

Once Prohibition ended, Assistant Prohibition Commissioner Harry J. Anslinger spearheaded an effort to find another drug to "demonize" in order to keep the drug enforcement movement alive. In 1932, the Alcohol Unit of the Treasury Department was abolished and the Federal Bureau of Narcotics was born with Anslinger as its commissioner. Although marijuana was not under his jurisdiction, Anslinger had an intense interest in the drug. An alliance with Hearst papers and sensational testimony before Congress led to the passage of the Marijuana Tax Stamp Act in 1937, effectively prohibiting the possession or use of the drug. In testimony before a Senate hearing, headlined in the newspapers, Anslinger invoked fear with claims that: "Marijuana is the most violent-causing drug in the history of mankind.... You smoke a joint and you're likely to kill your brother.... Marijuana is an addictive drug which produces in its user insanity, criminality, and death." He also invoked racism, saying most marijuana smokers "are Negroes, Hispanics, Filipinos, and entertainers," and declaring, "This marijuana causes white women to seek sexual relations with Negroes, entertainers, and any others....the primary reason to outlaw marijuana is its effect on the degenerate races (Father of the Drug War, 2004, online). A movie released in 1936, *Reefer Madness*, complemented Anslinger's campaign, as White youth joined Blacks and entertainers in the film to smoke marijuana and commit criminal and sexually promiscuous acts. The opening crawl of the film included warnings that marijuana is "The Real Public Enemy Number One" and "is destroying the youth of America in alarmingly increasing numbers" (Maltby). Anslinger has been called the first czar in a war on drugs that has never ended.

Soon after the end of World War II, the balance of power in the media as a purveyor of perceptions shifted from newspapers to television (Print and War, 2004). Whereas newspapers played a significant role in forming public opinion, it did so via words, with the reader left to visualize the scene and form a perception. Television brought the scene right into the home, forcing the visuals on the viewer. The real power of television was demonstrated during the Vietnam War, where horrific scenes of burning children and mangled bodies of American soldiers were instrumental in turning the nation against the conflict. Despite assurances from government sources the war was going well and was necessary, the public, seeing the death and destruction in this "living room war," began to side with the protesters and withdrew support, forcing the war to an end without victory. It was these debacles that led the military in subsequent conflicts to closely monitor the media and try to limit their mobility in war zones—such as embedding reporters with troops in Iraq in the belief the interaction of media with soldiers would create a symbiotic relationship, resulting in more favorable coverage of the military and the war policies.

The visual media also brought crime and violence into the living room, especially during the social revolution beginning in the 1960s. A combination of body bags from Vietnam and body counts in urban ghettos graphically portrayed on the nightly news and in movie and television shows led to numerous federal commissions to study the violence and disorder and recommend ways to stem it. Because television is driven by ratings and sound bytes, the visuals were often without real context, leading to often draconian solutions to crime, some of which actually exacerbated the problem.

By the beginning of the 21st century, two other factors were of major importance in the role of the media in the process of creating social reality, especially about crime and justice: (1) media conglomerates threatened to reduce both media pluralism and message pluralism, and to give a few voices enormous power in perception and policy making, but (2) the diversity of opinion expressed on web sites and "blogs" on the Internet and the emergence of the cell picturephone as a major communicator, combined with evidence that these were the "main" source of news for those under 25 years of age, might provide a counter for the concentrated power of the mainstream media.

Social Science or Popular Culture Perspectives

As the social sciences emerged in the 20th century and, more specifically, as popular culture studies proliferated late in that century, the impact of the media on crime and justice became an important phenomenon for speculation and research. Attention was first given to the connection between media content and the effect on reader, listener, or viewer perception. Most agreed (as did research findings later) that the media is where the average persons learn about the world outside their immediate experience. As most events are outside the experienced reality of the individual, the media play a significant role in creating a social reality (Chermak, 1994). Attention was also spent on trying to determine the impact of social reality—especially when shared by a large segment of society—on the formulation of law and policy. Again the role of the media was found to be significant; some concluded it was the most significant factor.

Specific attention to crime and justice can be traced to the numerous studies of the impact of media violence—first in the movies and then on television—on violence in society, especially among youth. The study of the relationships between media and crime and justice gained its theory base in the 1970 work of Richard Quinney, *The Social Reality of Crime*. It was, however, the late 1980s and the 1990s before this interest proliferated. Among the significant events that precipitated this increased interest: (1) publication of "myth" articles and books, calling into question the perceptions Americans have about crime and justice (Walker, 1985; Bohm, 1986; Pepinsky and Jesilow, 1992; Kappeler, Blumberg, and Potter, 1993); (2) publication of popular culture books specifically concerned with crime and justice (Barak, 1994; Bailey and Hale, 1998; Freeman, 2000); and (3) the founding in 1993 of the *Journal of Criminal Justice & Popular Culture* at the School of Criminal Justice, State University of New York-Albany.

The "myths" literature took public perceptions of crime and justice issues found in national opinion polls and presented research pro and con, usually concluding that these beliefs, formulated largely from media presentations, were not supported by empirical evidence.

Among the "myths" still prevalent in the media: White-collar crime is nonviolent. Crime in the U.S. is primarily violent. Crime is increasing. Some groups are more law abiding than others. Most crime is committed by poor, young males. Police are primarily crime fighters. Police solve most crimes (Bohm, 1986). Child abduction, serial murders, and stalking are frequent occurrences. Organized crime is a major threat imposed by outsiders. Corporate crime is minor compared to street crime. Illegal drugs are our most serious social problem. Violence by youth is out of control. The criminal justice system is far too lenient (Kappeler et al., 2000).

In *Media, Process, and Social Construction of Crime: Studies of Newsmaking Criminology*, Barak and his contributors examined the chicken and egg question—does media promote crime and violence or does it just reflect crime and violence in society?—and concluded that, on balance, the tendency of the media to report the unusual and the sensational, combined with the failure of the media to put news in context, has the effect of misinforming the public and spreading unreasonable fear of crime and violence. Other conclusions usually based on content analysis or research synthesis were: (1) mass media has created a "social reality" of crime that supports the "war on crime" paradigm or "mean world view" characterized by "mistrust, cynicism, alienation, and perceptions of higher-than-average levels of threat and crime in society"—also called the "retributive justice perspective" (p. 21); (2) tabloid journalism "is close to fascism" (p. 23) in its reporting of crime and crime control; it creates a "world is out of control" hysteria; (3) there is a "tendency of the [media] to prefer individual to societal and cultural explanations of crime" (p. 26), resulting in little concern with social and cultural problems associated with crime; and (4) crime news is so out of perspective with other events that, according to content analysis, half or more of time and space in newspapers and on radio and television news reports is devoted to it. Barak called on criminologists to become newsmakers and "straighten out" news media editors and reporters by presenting them the empirical evidence on crime and justice issues, holding optimistically that journalists' personal values and practices are "not fixed rigidly but are rather fluid."

Bailey and Hale and their contributors in *Popular Culture, Crime & Justice* examine how the criminal justice system (police, courts, and corrections) and its participants (practitioners, witnesses, victims, and offenders) are portrayed in popular culture. In the prologue, Ray Surette holds "subjective" social reality is created and becomes the basis for "objective" social behavior and policy. "The media's role is that of [being the] playing field for the social construction competition between *claimsmakers* [who] compete for media attention, and the media tend to favor those who are dynamic, [are] sponsored by powerful groups and [are] related to established cultural themes" (p. xvi). Surette found that the media make "it difficult for those outside the popular media mainstream to access the media and establish their claims" (p. xvii). Those who win in this battle for media attention set the social reality that leads to policies favoring their positions and increasing their access to the media.

Both public and private criminal justice agencies not only have access to the media, but have an interactive, often symbiotic, relationship with the media. Police, for example, provide a significant amount of content for the media and thus have constant access, which can be used to obtain resources and support for police actions and activities. The media also interact on a regular basis with court officials, especially filing clerks, prosecutors, and defense attorneys, and public interest in courts has been enhanced by the advent of *Court TV* and *Judge Judy* and her imitators. The interaction is not as frequent with either adult or youth corrections agencies; thus the focus is more likely to be negative in media reports (e.g., escapes, riots, and charges of abuse or corruption) (Bailey and Hale, 1998). Other agencies that gain generally favorable media interaction are victims' advocacy groups, anticrime associations (e.g., Mothers against Drunk Drivers), and quasi-vigilante organizations (e.g., Take Back the Streets). On the other hand, proponents of the rights of accused and convicted offenders (ACLU, Amnesty International, Prisoner's Rights) are likely to have difficulty in getting positive media attention.

The relationship between the media and crime and justice has proven to be fertile ground for social science research for several decades. Five areas of particular fruitfulness include: violence, moral panics, image of police, fear of crime, and youth.

Violence

Concern about the impact of violent images on public perceptions can be traced to early movie days, when in 1930, the Motion Picture Production Code established rules for movie content that "may be directly responsible for spiritual or moral progress, for higher types of social life, and for much correct thinking." (The Motion Picture..., 2004, online). Although violence was not one of the 12 "Particular Applications" of the code (e.g., crime, sex, vulgarity, obscenity), it was included in the prohibitions: "Brutal killings shall not be explicitly presented" and "The technique of murder must be presented in a way that will not inspire imitation." Required to be treated "within the careful limits of good taste" were hangings or electrocutions, third-degree methods, brutality and possible gruesomeness, and apparent cruelty to children or animals. The code lasted until 1968, when it was replaced by the current age-based movie or television ratings. Since then, graphic violence has proliferated on the screen and more than 1000 studies and investigations have found a correlation between viewing violence and aggressive behavior (Decade by Decade..., 2004; Research on..., 2004; Mediascope..., 2004; Tepperman, 2004). A preponderance of evidence indicates that, although there is no proven direct link between viewing violence and violent crime, it appears viewing violence has a significant impact on certain groups— already aggressive young males, emotionally unstable individuals, and individuals who watch more than normal amounts of television. Content analysis of television has found violence is a staple of programming; the national television violence survey (1997) found 61% of programs contain some violence, 44% involve perpetrators with some attractive qualities worth emulating, 43% of violent scenes involve humor, 75% feature no immediate punishment or condemnation of the violence, and 40% feature "bad" characters who are never or rarely punished for aggressive actions. Some researchers compared television societies with nontelevision cultures and found simply introducing television into a community was associated with an increase in violence, providing support for the law of imitation. Other researchers found media violence desensitizes people to real violence and makes violence in society more acceptable; conversely, other researchers found that media violence served as a catharsis and might actually prevent violence in society. Still, a continuing mantra of the broadcast media is: *If it bleeds, it leads.*

Moral Panics

The term "moral panic" was coined by sociologist Stanley Cohen in 1972 to depict an "episode, condition, person, or group of persons defined as a threat to societal values and interests" (p. 9). The media was seen as the main perpetrator of moral panics, with headlines such as: "Town on Pedophilia Alert," "Serial Killer on the Loose," "Crime Soars" (Sands, 2004). More recently sniper shootings by a couple of individuals created a panic in an entire metro area and less than a dozen letters containing anthrax panicked a nation. Moral panics often occur with the cooperation of criminal justice practitioners who feed information and opinion to the media, which then use "exaggerated attention, exaggerated events, distortion, and stereotyping" to garner readers and viewers. To become a full-fledged moral panic, there must be creation of "folk devils" and the development of a "disaster mentality." Failure to act in such a case would be deemed morally irresponsible and thus government officials create task forces and increase police presence to cope immediately, whereas lawmakers rush through legislation to "solve" the problem. A final element is "disproportionality," as often the situation creating the panic is "normal," or at least no different from the recent past. For example, there was no indication of increased use of marijuana or a link between the drug and crime when Anslinger and the Hearst newspapers and the movie industry (*Reefer Madness*) created the panic that led to Senate hearings and the beginning of the war on drugs that has never ended. Media-induced "crime waves" have been as likely to occur in times of crime decrease as in times of increase (Killingbeck, 2001).

Image of Police

Although sheriffs and marshals were portrayed as folk heroes in the penny press and dime novels of the frontier period, the local media often painted police in a less favorable manner, and early movies often treated them as buffoons—Keystone Kops. It was the anger of police chiefs that was instrumental in getting this changed with the passage of the Motion Picture Production Code (see Violence above). In response to police demands to be treated with respect and honor, the code required that "Law, natural or human, shall not be ridiculed, nor shall sympathy be created or its violation," and crime "shall never be presented in such a way as to throw sympathy with the crime as against law and justice…" (Motion Picture…, 2004, online). For a while after the code was established, police were seldom major players in films that focused instead on gangsters and detectives or federal agents. The film *Naked City* (1948) ushered in an era when police were depicted as professionals who followed procedure and solved crimes. In the 1950s, Marshal Matt Dillon on *Gunsmoke* and Sgt. Joe Friday on *Dragnet* became models for the depiction of law enforcers in this "crime doesn't pay" era. With the relaxing and then demise of the code in the late 1960s a new era of "crime out of control" began (Crawford, 1999) as a moral panic atmosphere called for violent enforcers to quell violent crime and disorder. Clint Eastwood's *Dirty Harry* (1971) and Gene Hackman's Popeye Doyle in *The French Connection* (1971) became the vigilante-style, rules-breaking, tough-cop model for the times. With censorship softened and a civil liberties movement under way, cops like Harry were seen first as superheroes and later as less sympathetic, following movies such as *Serpico* (1974) and *Dog Day Afternoon* (1976) and late 1970s television shows such as *Starsky & Hutch, SWAT, The Rookies*, and *Police Woman*. With the 1980s came the War on Crime policies in Washington and across the nation. Police were portrayed as complex human beings, sometimes plagued by the same problems as the offenders they sought, such as the movie *To Live and Die in LA* (1985) and the television series *Hill Street Blues* and later *NYPD Blue*, but most were still willing to either ignore or seek a way around policies that might thwart their quest for "justice" as they saw it. Even Dirty Harry became more complex and less sympathetic in *Sudden Impact* (1983) and *Tightrope* (1984). Comedy also returned to depictions of police with the *Lethal Weapon* and *Beverly Hills Cop* series of movies and television shows such as *Barney Miller*. Even edgier and bordering on return to Keystone Kops in the 21st century was Fox TV's *Reno 911* and movies such as the *Police Academy* series and *Me, Myself, and Irene*. With decreasing crime and concern focused more on terrorism, the media lightened up a little on police, but did not afford them much respect in the entertainment sector.

Fear of Crime

One of the earliest findings of studies of the media and crime was that those who got their news primarily from the media were more fearful of being victims of crime than those who either did not read or watch the mass media or those who balanced media reports with other sources (e.g., research, personal experience). Fear of crime polls have become a staple of criminologists, especially moral panic theorists and media scholars (Maguire and Weatherby, 1999; Altheide, 2002; Dowler, 2003; Research on…, 2004). Having conducted a statewide fear poll for more than a decade, this writer found fear was consistently higher than was the threat of harm from crime; that fear was higher among the elderly and women—the least likely victims of serious crime; that fear decreased with increased years of education and higher levels of income; and that fear increased both in times when crime increased and when the media indicated crime was increasing when it was not. Under retributive justice, fear has been considered a "good" reaction by many criminal justice practitioners, as it makes the citizen more vigilant and it provides more support for budgets and continued development of the criminal justice–industrial complex. Under the new restorative justice system, fear is seen as a serious problem that needs to be alleviated, as fear impoverishes relationships in communities, hampers economic development, and leads to physical and mental health maladies. The media gain much from fear—increased attention to news reports and news magazine offerings, higher ratings and the accompanying higher revenues, and a perennial audience reading or watching for "fear" of missing important messages. People who fear crime have been found to have more punitive attitudes toward suspected lawbreakers and be more likely to support increased use of imprisonment and longer sentences—law and order answers to the complex problems of crime and justice.

Youth

The media have not been kind to young people (Killingbeck, 2001; Huesmann et al., 2003; Dorfman and Schiraldi, 2004; Schiraldi, 2004; Tepperman, 2004; Youth Violence…, 2004). Although stories of academic, social, athletic, and other types of achievement can be found within the pages of the newspaper or occasionally within the newscast on television, front page or lead broadcast stories on youth are usually reserved for the child in trouble. In its 2001 report, "Off Balance: Youth, Race & Crime in the News," the Building Block for Youth initiative reported: "Despite declines in youth crime, the public expresses great fear of its own young people," noting that while youth crime was at historic lows "62% of poll respondents felt that juvenile crime was on the increase" (Dorfman and Schiraldi, 2004, online). Other polls found a majority of Americans felt juveniles were responsible for most violent crime and most adults were fearful of youth, especially children of color. The results of this media-driven fear, based on perceptions created by news presented without context (e.g., a child is charged with murder of a neighbor, headlined without any indication of the rarity of this type of crime), are support for harsher penalties for youth convicted of crime. In one poll, 70% of the respondents favored treating teenagers the same as adults when convicted of a violent crime—"if you're old enough to do the crime, you're old enough to do the time." A substantial number of citizens and public officials have expressed support for abolishing the juvenile justice system altogether. Meanwhile, considerable social science research indicates juveniles are not just little adults; children, even young adults (up to age 25), have been found to think differently from mature adults, partly because of the years it takes for the "hard-wiring" of the brain to be completed. Prior to this completion, youth make decisions quicker, based more on emotion than rationality, and with more attention to immediate rather than future consequences.

Conclusion

The complex relationship between the media and crime and justice is both interactive and often symbiotic. The media need easy access to criminal justice practitioners in order to quickly gather data for timely news and entertainment presentations; practitioners need the media to constantly remind the public and others of their important roles and their need for public assistance and monetary support. Out of this interaction comes a media-borne perception of crime based more on the needs of the actors in the process than on the actual occurrences. Both the media and practitioners choose what information to divulge and how to divulge it. The media want readers and viewers and have found that exciting stories that (in the case of movies and television) are accompanied by interesting visuals draw an audience. The more sensational and graphic the presentation, the more likely the readership or viewership will be large. Access to the media also becomes a factor as groups in the mainstream of popular culture—criminal justice agencies, victims' advocates, anticrime

associations—have greater access than less popular groups—ACLU, prisoners' rights groups. A popular media mantra—*If it bleeds, it leads*—also explains the frequent appearance of violence in media presentations and the emphasis on crime coverage.

In terms of social problems, crime may not be in the top tier in terms of harm to individuals, but it remains at or near the top in terms of media coverage and thus is disproportionally displayed. Citizen fear of crime and support of repressive policies is a result of this presentation of crime out of context. Often the disproportion is further skewed by moral panics that are driven by events (sniper shootings) reported beyond their objective importance to society; on other occasions it is created intentionally to support a position favored by the media and other interest groups, such as the war on drugs begun in the 1930s and renewed every generation since.

The media can be expected to remain a dominant player in the creation and maintenance of citizen attitudes toward crime and justice and the resultant policy and action decisions. The media in the 21st century, however, have been undergoing significant and contradictory changes. Traditional mass media—newspapers, radio, television—have become more assimilated via merger and joint ownership; fewer owners usually mean less pluralism of messages. New media—Internet web sites and blogs, cell picturephones, music CDs, DVDs, and more to come—have begun to expand the outlets and message. It remains to be seen whether this expanded media access will result in more accurate reporting or will simply modify the "myths" established in popular culture.

GENE STEPHENS

References and Further Reading

Altheide, D.L. 2002. *Creating Fear: News and Construction of Crisis*, New York, NY: Aldine de Gruyter.

Bailey, F. and Hale, D. (Eds.) 1998. *Popular Culture, Crime & Justice*, Belmont, CA: Wadsworth.

Baker, J., *Effects of the Press on Spanish—American Relations in 1898*. Available at http://www.humboldt.edu/~jcb10/spanwars.html. Retrieved on January 21, 2004.

Barak, G. (Ed.) 1994. *Media, Process, and the Social Construction of Crime*, New York, NY: Garland.

Bohm, R.M., Crime, criminal and crime control policy myths, *Justice Quarterly* 3(2), June 1986. Boyland, J. Pulitzer's school. Available at http://www.columbia.edu/cu/cup/catalog/data/023113/0231130902.HTM. Retrieved on January 21, 2004.

Brown, R., *Newspaper Production 1892–1992*. Available at wysiwyg://79/http://www.historybuff.com/library/refnew1892.html. Retrieved on January 21, 2004.

Chermak, S.M. 1994. Crime in the news media: A refined understanding of how crimes become news, in *Media, Process, and the Social Construction of Crime*, Barak, G. (Ed.) New York, NY: Garland.

Chermak, S.M. 1998. Police, courts, and corrections in media, in *Popular Culture, Crime & Justice,* Bailey F. and Hale, D. (Eds.). Belmont, CA: Wadsworth.

Cohen, S. 1972. *Folk Devils and Moral Panics,* London, UK: MacGibbon and Kee.

Crawford, C. 1999. Law enforcement and popular movies: Hollywood as a teaching tool in the classroom, *Journal of Criminal Justice and Popular Culture* 6(2).

Decade by Decade: Media Violence Marches On. Available at http://www.medialit.org/reading_room/article415.html. Retrieved on January 18, 2004.

Dorfman, L. and Schiraldi, V., *Off Balance: Youth, Race & Crime in the News.* Available at http://www.buildingblocksforyouth.org/media/media.html. Retrieved on January 17, 2004.

Dowler, K. 2003. Media consumption and public attitudes toward crime and justice: The relationship between fear of crime, punitive attitudes, and perceived police effectiveness, *Journal of Criminal Justice and Popular Culture* 10(2).

Einstadter, W.J. 1994. Crime news in the old West, in *Media, Process, and the Social Construction of Crime*, Barak, G. (Ed.). New York, NY: Garland.

Eisfeld, R. 1995. Myths and realities of frontier violence: A look at the gunfighter saga, *Journal of Criminal Justice and Popular Culture* 3(5).

Father of the Drug War. Available at http://www.heartbone.com/no_thugs/hja.htm. Retrieved on January 24, 2004.

Freeman, R.M. 2000. *Popular Culture and Corrections,* Lanham, MD: American Correctional Association.

Huesmann, L.R. 2003. Moise-Titus, J., Podolski, C., and Eron, L.D., Longitudinal relations between children's exposure to TV violence and their aggressive and violent behavior in young adulthood: 1977–1992, *Developmental Psychology* 39(2).

Kappeler, V.E., Blumberg, M., and Potter, G.W. 2000. *The Mythology of Crime and Criminal Justice*, 3rd ed., Prospect Heights, IL: Waveland Press.

Killingbeck, D. 2001. The role of television news in the construction of school violence as a 'moral panic', *Journal of Criminal Justice and Popular Culture* 8(3).

Levine, H.G., *The Secret of World-wide Drug Prohibition: The Varieties and Uses of Drug Prohibition.* Available at http://www.cedro-uva.org/lib/levine.secret.html. Retrieved on January 22, 2004.

Maguire, B. and Weatherby, G.A. 1999. Crime stories a television news: A content analysis of national, big city, and small town newscasts, *Journal of Criminal Justice and Popular Culture* 7(1).

Maltby, R., The public enemy." Available at http://www.senseofcinema.com/contents/03/29/cteq/public_enemy.html. Retrieved on January 23, 2004.

Mediascope Issue Briefs—Local TV News and Violence. Available at http://www.mediascope.org/pubs/ibriefs/lnv.htm. Retrieved on January 18, 2004.

The motion picture production code of 1930 (Hays code). Available at http://artsreformation.com/a00l/hays-code.html. Retrieved on January 25, 2004.

Overholser, G., *If Journalism Were a Profession. ...* Available at http://www.poynter.org/dg.lts/id.54/aid.44984/column.htm. Retrieved on January 21, 2004.

Pepinsky, H.E. and Jesilow, P. 1992. *Myths That Cause Crime,* 3rd ed., Washington, DC: Seven Locks Press.

Print and War. http://xroads.virginia.edu/~CLASS/am485_98/lane/media.htm. Retrieved January 22, 2004.

Quinney, R. 1970. *The Social Reality of Crime.* Boston, MA: Little, Brown, and Co.

Ratner, L.A. and Teeter, D.L. 2003. *Fanatics & Fire-Eaters: Newspapers & the Coming of the Civil War*, Champaign, IL: University of Illinois Press.

Reefer Madness. Available at http://www.filmthreat.com/Reviews.asp?Id=2138. Retrieved on January 24, 2004e.

Research on the Effects of Media Violence. Available at http://www.media-awareness.ca/english/i...cts_media_violence.cfm?RenderforPrint=l. Retrieved on January 18, 2004.

Sands, L., *Moral Panics.* Available at http://www.aber.ac.uk/media/students/lcs9603.html. Retrieved on January 25, 2004.

Schiraldi, V., Hyping juvenile crime—a media staple, *The Christian Science Monitor, November 6, 1997.* Available at http://search.csmonitor.com/durable/1997/11/06/opin/opin.l.html. Retrieved on January 17, 2004.

Society of Professional Journalists—About SPJ. Available at http://www.spj.org/spj_about.aps. Retrieved on January 21, 2004.

Surette, R. 1998. Prologue: Some unpopular thoughts about popular culture, in *Popular Culture, Crime & Justice*, Bailey, F. and Hale, D. (Eds.) Belmont, CA: Wadsworth.

Stephens, G. 2001. *Criminal Justice in Perspective*, Columbia, SC: College of Criminal Justice, University of South Carolina.

Tepperman, J., *Toxic Lessons: What Do Children Learn from Media Lessons?* Available at http://www.4children.org/news/1-97tox1.htm. Retrieved on January 18, 2004.

Walker, S. 2001. *Sense and Nonsense about Crime and Drugs: A Policy Guide,* 5th ed., Belmont, CA: Wadsworth.

West, D., *Media Roots in the 19th Century.* Available at www.insidepolitics.org/ps111/mediaroots.html. Retrieved on January 22, 2004.

Youth Violence: A Report of the Surgeon General—Chapter 4. Available at http://www.surgeongeneral.gov/library/youthviolence/chapter4/appendix4bsec2.html. Retrieved on January 18, 2004.

See also **Internet Resources in Criminology and Criminal Justice; Obscenity; Pornography and Criminal Behavior; Public Opinion and Criminal Behavior; Public Opinion and the Criminal Justice System**

Mass Murder *See* **Homicide: Mass Murder and Serial Killings**

Matza, David

David Matza was born on May 1, 1930 in New York. Following his graduation from high school, he attended the City College of New York, receiving his baccalaureate degree in 1953. Matza's graduate career began that same year when he enrolled at Princeton University's Department of Sociology. He enjoyed a successful tenure at Princeton, earning both his master's (1955) and doctoral (1959) degrees. It was at Princeton where he first focused his academic attention on juvenile delinquency, studying under criminologist Gresham Sykes, with whom he was to collaborate, in what would become his most renowned work. While completing his graduate work, he took his first academic appointment at Temple University in 1957. He is currently a Professor Emeritus in the Department of Sociology at the University of California–Berkeley, where he has held various positions since his appointment in 1961.

Matza is best known for his theory of delinquency, Techniques of Neutralization, which he first proposed in a 1957 article coauthored with his mentor Gresham Sykes. Matza's first considerable contribution to criminology, Techniques of Neutralization, contended that psychological processes called *neutralizations* serve to reduce social control exerted over delinquents. These neutralizations allow juveniles to reconcile or justify their criminal acts, thereby alleviating any stress that may otherwise be associated with guilt proceeding delinquency. Matza and Sykes' intent was to build upon Sutherland's theory of differential association that attributed criminality to a learning process wherein juveniles were not only taught *how* to commit crime, but also were instilled with attitudes and values condoning such activity. Techniques of Neutralization represented Sykes and Matza's attempt to explain the latter, that is, how juveniles are able to justify and support their attitudes favorable to the violation of law.

Matza and Sykes identified five such techniques, including (1) denial of responsibility, (2) denial of injury, (3) denial of victim, (4) condemnation of the condemners, and (5) appeals to higher loyalties. The first, denial of responsibility, occurs when the juvenile refuses to accept responsibility for his or her actions, instead placing the blame with external factors, such as poor parenting or poverty. Denial of injury occurs when the juvenile does not deny the act itself, rather contends that there is an absence of victimization. This technique is especially used by delinquents engaging in crimes such as drug use and shoplifting. Denial of victim occurs when the juvenile believes that the victimization is justified such that the victim "deserved it" or "had it coming." Use of the technique is frequent with gang-related violence, as many members feel retaliatory acts can easily be justified in terms of "settling the score." The fourth, condemnation of the condemners, involves a view of others, particularly those in positions of power, as oppressive and even hypocritical. Delinquents will justify their criminal acts by displacing the blame on authority figures, often citing instances of the injustice dispensed at their hands. The fifth and final technique appeals to higher loyalty and occurs when delinquents rationalize their deviant acts as serving the immediate demands of the group. These demands supercede family, community, and legal obligations.

The ability to rationalize delinquent acts had been previously explored by Cohen (1955) who contended that juvenile gangs form, in part, as a reaction to middle-class values and standards. Unable to compete in a world where success is measured by a middle-class measuring rod, lower-class juveniles engage a reaction formation defined by an alternate set of values diametrically opposed to mainstream society. Miller (1958) also advocated a subcultural explanation positing that the lower class did not share the same value system as the rest of society, instead possessing focal concerns conducive to criminality. However, neither Cohen nor Miller explicated the exact process by which juveniles diffused blame or responsibility. Matza and Sykes' theory was also dissimilar to these related theories in that they did not agree that delinquents' value systems were necessarily altogether different from that of mainstream society. Contrary to both Cohen and Miller, Matza and Sykes suggest that lower-class juvenile delinquents do subscribe to the dominant values of mainstream society, but to a lesser extent than their middle- and upper-class counterparts. Matza contends "there is a subculture of delinquency, but it is not a delinquent subculture" (1964, 33).

Matza and Sykes extended their theory of juvenile delinquency with the publication of "Juvenile Delinquency and Subterranean Values" in 1961. They further described the value system of delinquents and how it compares to that of the greater society. Here, they contend that the values behind much juvenile delinquency are far less deviant than commonly portrayed and this faulty picture is because of a gross oversimplification of the middle-class value systems (p. 713). Specifically, Matza and Sykes explore the subjectivity of juvenile delinquency, arguing in a labeling theory vein that the quality of values is obscured by the particular context in which they are found. "When 'daring' turns out to be acts of daring by adolescents directed against adult figures of accepted authority, for example, we are apt to see only the flaunting of authority and not the courage that may be involved" (p. 715).

Matza and Sykes further argue that the view of the law-abiding middle class is over-simplified and leads to erroneous conclusions about differences between delinquent and mainstream values. Most values appear in most social classes; the social classes differ only in the frequency with which the values appear. Moreover, the values criticized by mainstream society are often a reflection of similar values in an alternative context. For example, delinquent values can mirror those described by Thorstein Veblen's "gentlemen of leisure," who place heavy emphasis on daring and adventure, the rejection of the discipline of work, the taste for luxury and conspicuous consumption, and the respect paid to manhood demonstrated through force. In this view, delinquency is not alien to the body of society but rather a caricature of it (Matza and Sykes, 1961).

Matza published *Delinquency and Drift* in 1964, a book that represented his attempt to incorporate his previous research on juvenile delinquency with what he observed of the various social movements of the day (e.g., civil rights movement, antiwar protests, sexual revolution). *Delinquency and Drift* analyzed the similarities between delinquency and political protest, focusing on the use of techniques of neutralization and shifting value systems. He labeled these shifting value systems as *drift*, arguing that both juveniles and adults hold conventional beliefs that at times may lapse, thereby opening the door for the emergence of delinquency and other forms of deviance. Matza believed that individuals drift between these two extremes of conventional and criminal behavior; techniques of neutralization allow for the rationalization of such behavior.

Drift is often described as soft determinism, which views criminality as partly chosen and partly determined. The will to commit crime occurs when one of two conditions is present: preparation and desperation. These allow the individual to form the decision to commit a crime. Preparation occurs when a criminal act is repeated once the person realizes that the criminal act can be achieved and is feasible; desperation activates the will to initially commit a crime because of an extraordinary occasion, or fatalism, which is the feeling of lacking control over one's surroundings (Matza, 1964). Underlying the latter is the concept of injustice. For Matza, injustice serves as a critical catalyst for much deviant behavior.

Evaluations of Matza's theories have produced mixed empirical results. An implicit assumption of drift theory is that participation in deviant acts decreases as adolescents move toward adulthood (Shoemaker, 2000), a premise strongly supported by the lifecourse perspective (see Laub and Sampson, 1993). Examination of Matza's specific concepts, however, has provided mixed support of his assertions. Hindelang (1974) failed to find support for the basic premise that juveniles are generally disapproving of delinquency. Rather, his study suggested that those juveniles who engaged in greater levels of delinquency also held more permissive attitudes regarding deviance. Giordano (1976) examined Matza's contention that delinquency is spurred by a sense of injustice on the part of the juvenile. Survey results indicated that youth who had repeated contact with the juvenile justice system (i.e., repeat offenders) actually held more favorable views of the system, contrary to Matza's prediction. Agnew (1994), in a longitudinal study of youth, found that most juveniles are disapproving of violence but are capable of neutralizing their guilt using techniques described by Matza. Agnew's study offered support for differential association in that neutralization was particularly salient when accompanied by encouragement from delinquent peers.

Matza's drift theory is essentially a social psychological explanation of crime and delinquency that incorporates conceptual elements from various criminological perspectives. Drift theory is often characterized as a control theory because it implies a weakening of social restraints that deter juveniles from delinquency. It also falls within this vein because of the implicit assumption of weak inner controls; the juvenile does not truly believe that the delinquent act is acceptable or right, but is able to rationalize their deviance. The techniques of neutralization also speak to a subcultural perspective sharing features of both Cohen's (1955) and Miller's (1958) explanations of delinquency. Additionally, Matza's assumption that both delinquency and attitudes favorable toward such dissipate as one progresses into adulthood has a distinct lifecourse flavor. Drift theory also shares many features with differential association, leading some to classify it as a learning theory.

HOLLY E. VENTURA

Biography

Born in New York, NY, May 1, 1930. Education: College of the City of New York B.A. 1953; Princeton University M.A. 1955, Sociology, Ph.D. 1959, Sociology. Instructor, Temple University, 1957–1959; Post-Doctoral Fellow, University of Chicago Law School, 1960-61; Professor of Sociology, University of California, Berkeley, 1961–present; Book Review Editor, *American Sociological Review*, 1962–1965; Book Review Editor, *Journal of Criminal Law and Police Science*, 1961–62.

References and Further Reading

Agnew, R. 1994. The techniques of neutralization and violence. *Criminology*. 32, 555–580.

Cohen, A. 1955. *Delinquent Boys: The Culture of Gang*. Glencoe, IL: The Free Press.

Coleman, J.W. 1987. Toward an integrated theory of white-collar crime. *American Journal of Sociology*. 93(2), 406–439.

Costello, B. 2000. Techniques of neutralization and self-esteem: A critical test of social control and neutralization theory. *Deviant Behavior: An Interdisciplinary Journal*. 21, 307–329.

Hagan, J. 1991. Destiny and drift: Subcultural preferences, status attainments, and the risks and rewards of youth. *American Sociological Review*. 56(5), 567–582.

Hindelang, M.J. 1970. The commitment of delinquents to their misdeed: Do delinquents drift? *Social Problems*. 17, 502–509.

Laub, J. and Sampson, R. 1993. Turning points in the life course: Why change matters to the study of crime. *Criminology*. 31, 301–326.

Martin, R., Mutchnick, R., and Austin, W.T. 1990. *Criminological Thought: Pioneer Past and Present*. New York, NY: Macmillan Publishing Company.

Matza, D. and Sykes, G. 1961. Juvenile delinquency and subterranean values. *American Sociological Review*. 26(5): 712–719.

Matza, D. 1964. *Delinquency and Drift*. New York, NY: John Wiley and Sons, Inc.

Matza, D. 1964. *Becoming Deviant*. NJ: Prentice-Hall, Inc.

McCorkle, L. and Korn, R. 1954. Resocialization within walls. *The Annals of the American Academy of Political and Social Sciences*. 293, 88–98.

Miller, W.B. 1958. Lower class culture as a generating milieu of gang delinquency. *Journal of Social Issues*. 14, 5–19.

Minor, W.W. 1980. The neutralization of criminal offense. *Criminology*. 18, 103–120.

Minor, W.W. 1981. Techniques of neutralization: A reconceptualization and empirical examination. *Journal of Research in Crime and Delinquency*. 18, 295–318.

Minor, W.W. 1984. Neutralization as a hardening process: Considerations in the modeling of change. *Social Forces*. 62, 995–1019.

Mitchell, J. and Dodder, R. 1983. Types of neutralization and types of delinquency. *Journal of Youth and Adolescence*. 12, 307–318.

Mitchell, J., Dodder, R., and Morris, T. Neutralization and delinquency: A comparison by sex ans ethnicity. *Adolescence*. 25(98), 487–497.

Pfohl, S. 1994. *Images of Deviance and Social Control*. New York, NY: McGraw-Hill, Inc.

Priest, T.B and McGrath, J. 1970. Techniques of neutralization: Young adult marijuana smokers. *Criminology*. 8, 185–194.

Shoemaker, D. 2000. *Theories of Delinquency*. New York, NY: Oxford University Press.

Sykes, G. and Matza, D. 1957. Techniques of neutralization: A theory of delinquency. *American Sociological Review*. 22(6), 664–670.

Thurman, Q. 1984. Deviance and the neutralization of moral commitment: An empirical analysis. *Deviant Behavior*. 5, 291–304.

See also **Control Theories; Gresham Sykes; Neutralization/Drift Theory**

Mediation and Dispute Resolution Programs

Most people work through a variety of interpersonal conflicts or disputes on a daily basis. The majority of these disputes are quickly resolved through a conflict resolution process that is so routine that we do not recognize the situation as a conflict. In other cases interpersonal conflicts can be so serious that friendships and relationships are threatened. These relatively serious conflicts typically include many issues and parties and may be difficult to resolve without outside assistance.

Unresolved conflict can result in stress, violence, litigation, and a variety of activities intended to prevail. Because these activities can be very destructive, it is in our best interest to develop efficient procedures that allow the parties to resolve differences peacefully.

Ideally, these dispute resolution processes will allow the parties to satisfy their interests in ways that reduce suffering while efficiently relying on positive resources. In effect, conflict provides an opportunity to communicate, to learn how the other parties define the problem, and work toward a resolution that will, in addition to addressing the issues, lead to lowered levels of stress and other emotional responses to conflict.

Litigation, Power, and ADR

Although many people are good at resolving simple conflicts, other disputes cannot be resolved without the help of outside parties. Each conflict situation offers many options for resolution and it is important to choose the proper process. In addition to processes that rely on interpersonal skills, our legal system has designed a number of methods for resolving or minimizing conflict. Choices we make when faced with conflict can result in very different results, both in terms of substance and process.

As we know, litigation is often chosen when conflict reaches a level where interpersonal skills fail to lead to a successful resolution. Unfortunately, the decision to litigate often results in a process that is mechanical and contentious. Litigation-based processes often ignore the feelings of the disputants. Although the parties reach a decision that is defined as a resolution, unresolved issues often lead the disputants to report that they are not satisfied with the results or the process. Access to litigation, and in many ways justice, is not equal. Many disputants are not able to take their disputes to court. As a result, litigation fails to address many of the most common disputes. In addition to litigation, or in the absence of other means of dispute processing, aggressive responses to conflict may be chosen. Aggressive responses to conflict are dangerous, ineffective, and in most cases unlawful. An aggressive response to conflict also demonstrates disrespect for self and others.

As in these examples, many responses to conflict involve the use of power, either personal power or reliance on state power, that can be called upon to support an individual's belief that he or she is "right." Mediation and other alternatives to litigation offer a solution to litigation and other power-based responses to conflict. Litigation and other power-based forms of conflict processing often result in a winner-take-all way of thinking. Failing to realize that a cost-free "victory" is extremely unusual, disputants may begin the litigation process with the expectation of a clear and convincing resolution in their favor. As we know, even if one party prevails on every point, the case will be extremely expensive in terms of money; relationships; and the emotional, personal, and business life of each party.

Although litigation remains an option for many parties and disputes, there are many alternatives that seek to minimize power, respect feelings, and resolve disputes in ways that leave parties with positive feelings about the process and result. Alternatives to litigation are referred to as alternative dispute resolutions, or ADR, and include a range of processes. ADR processes can be very informal. In many cases the process is limited to the disputants, and the requirements of record keeping and other protocols are relaxed in comparison to courtroom processes. At other times, the dispute is more complex and may include a multiple-stage process, with many disputants and a group of mediators. In other situations, the ADR process is strictly controlled and may closely resemble courtroom-based efforts to resolve conflict. The flexibility of these processes is one of the key strengths.

Alternative dispute resolution processes typically include a neutral third party whose role varies according to the process selected. An information sharing process, in which disputants work out the details of their dispute and work toward an agreement, is typical of most ADR processes. In mediation, a trained third party neutral works to help the parties communicate in ways that lead to resolution. The mediator generally does not have the authority to make decisions that would end the dispute. In arbitration, the neutral third party is empowered with decision-making authority. Other ADR processes include fact finding, ombudspersons, private tribunals, mini-trials, conciliation, and other processes that include a mixture of techniques.

ADR works best if it is chosen early in the life of a dispute—before the parties have committed to hard and fast positions. That is the point in time when a neutral, objective, and impartial third party may assist the parties in achieving results that can be imaginative, inventive, and not necessarily based on a monetary settlement. In contrast to litigation, which typically relies on processes that can seem very mechanical and dehumanizing, ADR has the capacity to search for, and adopt, results that meet the parties' underlying interests and overall objectives. As disputes often include multiple parties and interests, value can be attached to feelings, actions, and other things that are difficult to quantify but have value that is unique to the disputants.

ADR processes are often endorsed by the courts and are connected to court-based dispute resolution processes. The court may transfer its decision-making power or it may be used to narrow the range of issues to be addressed by the court. ADR processes can also be independent of the courts. Community mediation programs have been created to address neighborhood and other local disputes. School-based mediation programs are evident in the development of campus mediation centers and peer mediation programs. ADR processes are used in the workplace, where ombudspersons, arbitrators, and mediators are active in the resolution of employment related disputes. These processes are also used to resolve environmental and property disputes and in efforts to resolve disputes between organizations, corporations, and nations.

Mediation

ADR includes a range of processes, each sharing similar procedures, philosophy, and advantages. Mediation is one of the best known and best understood of these processes.

In mediation, the disputing parties engage a third party to assist them in coming to a mutual resolution. "Ownership" of the dispute remains with the disputants and the third party remains neutral. The mediator's goal is to help the parties work together to resolve "their" dispute.

Although the mediator is neutral with respect to outcome, he or she controls the mediation process. A primary goal of the process is to enable the disputants to communicate in a way that will lead to mutual understanding of the issues and interests that underlie positions that have been expressed by the disputants. The mediator helps the disputants discover and evaluate a range of settlement options, eventually leading to a mutually acceptable agreement.

Communication is the centerpiece of any mediation. The disputing parties each have the opportunity to tell their stories and be heard by the opposing party. Because poor communication skills and the escalation of conflict that may result from ineffective communication may be at the root of the dispute, the mediator works to encourage an open and respectful exchange of ideas. Throughout the early stages of this communication process disputants typically take "positions." These positions may be firmly held and in direct opposition to the positions expressed by the other party. The parties have expressed these positions because they see them as a means to achieve certain goals or to satisfy unexpressed "interests." The mediator assists the parties in a communication process that is intended to expose these underlying interests. If the parties listen carefully they may learn that the other party's perceptions are very different from their own. In addition to disclosure, the parties will begin to understand why these positions have been expressed and will hopefully begin to develop respect for (not necessarily agreement with) the other party's feeling and interpretations. In many cases, the process of moving from "positions" to "interests" leads the parties to realize that their goals are not as divergent as they assumed during the early stages of the conflict.

The mediator assists the parties in reaching agreement by using and encouraging active listening techniques. The mediator also asks directive and clarifying questions in an effort to expose all relevant issues. Throughout the process the mediator works to validate the parties' points of view, acknowledging the disputant's right to own his or her feelings and have these feelings be expressed and clarified in an effort to reach a shared understanding of all issues. A key advantage of the communication process is that the process often leads to the identification of common interests. Once these interests are identified the mediator helps the disputants develop and evaluate alternative solutions to the dispute.

The primary goal of mediation is for all parties to identify a solution they can live with and trust. This goal is reached through a process that encourages an honest discussion of past issues and a shared move toward a future-focused orientation in which the parties solve problems in ways that protect feelings and relationships. Mediation and other forms of ADR also have important secondary goals. In many cases disputants benefit from improved communication and an enhanced understanding and respect for the other person's point of view. Mediation also offers an opportunity to be heard, and perhaps to express anger and other emotions in a positive environment. Mediation also presents an opportunity to openly examine the strengths and weaknesses of the positions that disputants cling to as the preferred "solution" to their dispute.

Conclusion

Although mediation and other ADR processes may provide an effective alternative to litigation, it would not be accurate to suggest that these processes are always preferable or that litigation could, or should, be replaced by ADR. It may be best to think about these processes as adding to, or extending, the range of tools available in our efforts to resolve difficult disputes. Some have expressed concerns about the privatization of disputes, including disputes that may best be addressed through legislation and other processes that lead to change. Others have raised concerns about the effectiveness of informal and neutral processes in situations where judicial processes have the potential to "balance the scales" in an effort to prevent a powerful party from imposing solutions. Concerns have also been raised about training, education, and licensing of mediators and others involved with various ADR processes. Finally, some have expressed concerns about a "one size fits all" application of ADR to disputes where alternate means of dispute processing might be more appropriate.

The benefits of ADR include savings of time and money, the potential to protect ongoing relationships, increased satisfaction with the process and solution, and greater control over the dispute resolution process. The process is confidential, flexible, creates an opportunity to end a dispute without a "loser," and empowers parties to work together to resolve future disputes. These processes provide a fair and flexible alternative process that can be used to resolve disputes efficiently. When chosen correctly, and used by skilled professionals, mediation and other forms of ADR have proven to be very powerful tools in the effort to peacefully resolve disputes.

KENNETH MENTOR

References and Further Reading

Bush, R. and Folger, J. 1994. *The Promise of Mediation*. San Francisco, CA: Jossey Bass.

Carpenter, S.L. and Kennedy, W.J.D. 1998. *Managing Public Disputes: A Practical Guide to Handling Conflict and Reaching Agreements*. San Francisco, CA: Jossey Bass.

Fisher, R., Ury, W., and Patton, B. 1991. *Getting To Yes: Negotiating Agreement Without Giving In,* 2nd ed. New York, NY: Penguin Books.

Folberg, J. and Taylor, A. 1984. *Mediation: A Comprehensive Guide to Resolving Conflicts without Litigation*. San Francisco, CA: Jossey Bass.

Goldberg, S.B., Sander, F.E.A., and Rogers, N. 1992. *Dispute Resolution: Negotiation, Mediation, and Other Processes.* 2nd ed. Boston, MA: Little, Brown.

Moore, C.W. 1996. *The Mediation Process: Practical Strategies for Resolving Conflicts*. 2nd ed. San Francisco, CA: Jossey Bass.

Ury, W., Brett, J. and Goldberg, S. 1989. *Getting Disputes Resolved*. San Francisco, CA: Jossey Bass.

See also **Criminal Courts: Lower; Diversion and Diversion Programs; Peacemaking Criminology**

Medieval Europe, Crime and Justice in

The Middle Ages, or Medieval Period, in Europe is a long historical period generally seen as stretching from the fall of Rome in the 5th century CE through the beginnings of the early Modern period in the 15th century CE. The period is often further divided into the early Middle Ages (the 5th century CE through the 11th century CE) and the late Middle Ages (the 11th century CE through the 15th century CE). In this thousand-year time block, we find many important transformations and processes working to set the stage for our own modern societies and cultures—changes in law and criminal justice are no exception. Further, there is a large amount of geographic and cultural variation within Europe. Southern Europe remains more closely tied to the classical world and classical traditions (such as Roman law and justice); the English Isles go through long periods of relative isolation and develop their own historical and cultural patterns and responses. Although it is difficult to say anything that can globally be applied to a number of societies and cultures over a millennium, there are a number of significant trends that deserve close examination.

Most medievalists agree that one dominating aspect of society and culture is its pervasive and powerful Catholicism. Early in the period, Catholic Christianity not only became the predominant religion, it also became the dominant epistemology—the way in which people understood and made sense of their world and lives. This strongly influenced the predominant theory of what caused crime in the period—demonology. Essentially, criminal and deviant behavior were philosophically explained as sinful behavior, which was rooted in being influenced if not outright coerced through possession, by the Devil himself or his agents. As we will see, this also strongly influenced some criminal justice procedures as well as what was considered a crime. Until the strong consolidation of power in states, the church played a large role not only in defining crime, but also in the adjudication of justice.

With the fall of Rome, much of Europe resorted to local legal and political control. Throughout much of what is now England, France, Germany, and the low Countries, Germanic law replaced Roman law. Within Germanic law there was not a concept of crimes against the public or the state, there were only crimes against other people. Whether it was a crime of violence or property, crime was seen as an aspect of interpersonal relationships; legal and political authorities would intervene to settle the disputes. Law itself was seen in a personal manner, as protecting individual rights. Rulers and political entities did not create law as much as preserve it. The primary political (and legal) entity at this time was the kingroup (or kindred), what most modern anthropologists would today call clans—groups of related families and lineages. Crimes were personal offenses by one person against another. Thus, justice took the form of the offender paying restitution to the victim or the victim's kingroup—most frequently in the forms of monetary compensation.

Most justice proceedings involved the kingroup of the offender and the kingroup of the victim attempting to come to an agreement about what was proper recompensation for the criminal act. Another typical way in which justice was carried out was through rites of vengeance. Any kingroup who had a member killed (or injured) was entitled to take vengeance upon the kingroup of the offender. Complex social norms controlled who was allowed, and expected, to enact such vengeance.

Although much medieval literature highlights, and even romanticizes, feuding, in reality feuds were often avoided through a set of victim compensation processes. Each person in Germanic society was given a specific monetary value—a wer (or wergild); each body part was similarly given a value—a bot. Bot was highly complex, with each body part (i.e., ears, nose, fingers, hands) having separate values and with different values being set for different injuries (i.e., loss of hearing, ear cut off, ear cut through, etc.). Elites were seen as having a higher values than commoners and men having a higher value than women and children. This system of justice can be seen as the distant root of many of our own sets of criminal and civil fines. Determining a monetary damage for crime and then making payment as a form of personal and social restitution is at the heart of our current civil justice procedures and is used frequently in criminal procedures. Through the early Middle Ages, these fines were paid directly to the victim, as we see in contemporary civil cases. Later, the state itself began to impose fines for criminal activity paid to the state itself. An early form of the governmental fine, the wite, was used in some Germanic societies in crimes where the injury was intentional. A portion of the overall bot, the wite, was paid to local lord, as both payment for the adjudication processes as well as a punitive action.

Socially, this system not only creates a deterrence system of financial burden, it also serves to reintegrate the very social structure. In low population kinship-based societies, like the Germanic tribes, not only is every person almost essential to the survival of the group, but positive intergroup relations between kingroups are necessary for the survival of the entire community. Paying bot and wer not only punishes (and recompensates) for a crime, it also serves to reintegrate the offender's and victim's kingroup—allowing peace to return to the community.

When an injury occurred, the proper bot or wer was calculated. Often, if the full price could not be paid, valuable items or people might be sent to the offended kingroup to act as a form of collateral until the full debt could be paid. If the kingroups could not agree on a precise payment, or if the offender or offender's kingroup refused to pay the determined price, a blood feud would result. Here, the victim's family would exact an equivalent injury on the offender's kingroup. Blood feuds were not chaotic and without order. If a family exacted too much vengeance, they themselves would be seen as offending parties and need to recompensate the opposing kingroup. The need for peaceful cooperation in the community would override personal kingroup needs. Much of these processes was governed by the informal, though powerful, agent of public opinion. It should be realized that within Germanic law, none of these values and laws were written down. There was no legal profession and no external social institution to adjudicate disputes.

Although many disputes in the period were settled between kingroups, mediated by public opinion, there was an external body that could hear disputes—the moot. Moots were community gatherings, dominated by elders and respected community leaders, but generally open to any one in the community to hear, speak, and persuade. Moots dealt with more than just crimes and interfamily disputes, but they did provide a forum that would help mediate a conflict and generate a solution that would carry the weight of public approval. Such a collective public body reinforced community connections and opinions. Although the moot had no coercive power to enforce its decisions, unlike our contemporary criminal justice bodies, those who went against the decisions and opinions emerging from a moot faced the harshest punishment of the Early Middle Ages: banishment. An individual so labeled was seen as being dead to the community. No community member was to speak to, much less help, the outcast. The result was a slow death by exposure to the elements, facing the perils of still uncontrolled wilderness, and eventually starvation.

In addition to moots, Germanic law contained another manner of discerning truth in competing testimonies: the oath helpers. In a typical dispute, each party would give its testimony as to the nature of the events. Each party also had family members and other community figures, the oath helpers, speak for them. The prestige of the oath helpers, as well as how precisely they recited the highly poetic and formalized oaths, would lend credence to the individual's testimony.

During the middle years of the Early Middle Ages, political leaders had garnered enough power and legitimacy to issue forth and enforce law codes. These early dooms began the movement in Germanic law away from feuding and the resolution of conflict through informal norms into the codification of formal laws and formal punishments that were backed by the authority of political leaders. The systematization and enforcement of laws within a given region seems to have occured once a king consolidated enough power in his realm to do so. The earliest surviving indigenous European law codes come from Clovis (481–511 CE), the founder of the Merovengian dynasty, one of the earliest powers to arise out of the void created by Rome's fall. The *Lex Salica* lists specific fines for many common crimes including thefts, assaults, and homicides. Ethelbert (601–604 CE) issued the first recorded Anglo-Saxon laws that we have historical record of. Most of Ethelbert's laws focus on what we could call property crimes today—primarily theft. Later, Ine (688–695 CE) established dooms regulating interpersonal violence. During the early Middle Ages, these specific law codes lasted as long as the leaders did. However, by the 9th century CE, these laws (and their lawgivers) were held in enough esteem that there was a strong focus on bringing offenders and victims before the judges and courts of royal powers. As more and more cases were brought before royal authorities a key problem presented itself: how to discern truth in testimony. These early trials boiled down to competing claims of truth. One way of resolving these claims was trial by ordeal, a practice with its roots in early Germanic society.

Although it may appear barbaric to us today, trial by ordeal was widespread throughout the Middle Ages. It was based with the Christian beliefs that God was intimately involved in the daily affairs of men and women. God was seen as powerful and just, refusing to let innocent people be punished and the guilty to go unpunished. Ordeals were designed to inject God into the trial processes by making Him the final arbiter of the testimony. The accused would be forced to undergo some physically damaging and dangerous activity, the results of which would reveal God's will. There were many ordeals commonly used. In trial by cold water, the accused would be submerged in a body of water. If the accused floated, they were deemed guilty of the offense in question; if they sank, they were innocent. Care had to be taken not to allow the accused to remain submerged for long. In trial by hot water, the individual would thrust their arm into a pot of boiling water. The arm would be bandaged then inspected after 3 days; lack of injury indicated innocence. Another common trial involved hot irons. Iron rods would be heated until glowing within a fire. Then they would be placed upon the body of the accused (often on the hands or arms), then the area would be wrapped. Again, within 3 days the area would be inspected; burns and blistering indicated guilt. A variant of this practice was to make individuals walk barefoot across heated plowshares. Within all of these trials, it was expected that God would intervene to prevent injury to the innocent. Clergy were a large part of the ritual, acting as verifiers of the workings (or lack thereof) of God.

A variant on trial by ordeal, highly popular in England, was trial by combat. Widely popularized in medieval literature, here the resolution of the conflict occurred in a duel between champions appointed by each involved party. A classic example from Arthurian literature is Sir Lancelot du Lak's defense of Queen Guinevere when she is charged with adultery. Her husband, King Arthur, cannot defend her, because as king he must preside over the trial. Lancelot, as her (and Arthur's) champion, sets forward to defend the charges. Ironically, and tellingly, it is Lancelot himself who is the other party in the adultery. Even in the literature, there is a key awareness that the success and failure of the trial is not necessarily divine judgment (as in most tellings Lancelot is victorious), but martial superiority. Trial by combat had its roots deep in pre-Christian Europe. Germanic society, especially political leadership, was structured around combat and warrior codes. Elites in Germanic society, as well as nobles in later medieval society, lived in a world structured by warfare and combat. Leaders obtained and held their positions through victory on the battlefield. Resolving disputes through armed combat, as with feuding, fit strongly within the cultural beliefs of the day. Throughout Christian Europe, as with ordeals, God was expected to intervene and ensure that the champion representing the "true" testimony was victorious. The realities, as shown in the tales of Lancelot and Guinevere, were far different.

One significant event that heavily influenced issues of crime and justice in the Middle Ages was the Lateran councils, meetings held by the heads of the church to address key issues within medieval Christianity. Pope Innocent II's decrees in Lateran IV (1215 CE) had two profound effects on issues of crime and justice. First, they forbade clergy to participate in ordeal trials. As discussed above, the key power of these trials was the legitimacy conferred by clergy presence, ensuring that the trial expressed the will of God. Innocent II was not necessarily concerned with the accuracy or brutality of ordeals, though some sources show he was influenced by thinkers strongly opposed to them on such grounds; his primary concern was with corruption and the corruptibility of clergy. Regardless of the motive, after this injunction, most ordeal trials fell out of use; however, trials by battle continued, especially in England. Also, trials by water were used in cases of witchcraft into the 18th century CE.

Second, Lateran IV created a whole new class of crimes—those related to heresy. Primarily in response to the Cathars and other new Christian sects that had views that radically differed from Rome's, the church criminalized religious beliefs that differed from papal dogma. As the Vatican did not have the power and influence to completely police such crimes, enforcement often fell to local nobles and other enforcement agencies. Locals enforced such laws out of respect for and fear of the excommunication power of the papacy. Investigating and punishing religious crimes, especially witchcraft, are a significant part of Western criminal justice into the 18th century CE.

Although such crimes of religious beliefs run counter to our current beliefs about religious expression, it should be noted that because of the power of the Catholic faith on the culture of the Middle Ages, such enforcement would be seen as natural and normal. Secular institutions of government were seen as being decreed and created by God; it made sense within the medieval mind for what we would now see as secular entities to enforce religious laws. Nobles were thought to have held their position by divine grace. Many chivalric manuals of the time, most notably Geoffrey de Charni's *On Chivalry*, repeatedly emphasized to nobles that their primary duty was to uphold God's laws and rule His lands and people justly.

As Europe entered the late Middle Ages, the consolidation of political and legal power in the hands of kings also influenced the nature of criminal justice procedures throughout the region. Although early bodies like moots and oath helpers were well enshrined in criminal justice processes, around the 12th century CE we begin to see further codification and systematization of criminal justice bodies and procedures whose authority came directly from the king. Courts and juries grew out of existing bodies that had developed earlier in the period. In England, Alfred the Great (871–899 CE) established one of the early police-court systems. Under early feudalism, thanes—landowners—were responsible for keeping the peace within their lands under the king's laws. As a check on the power of the thane, tythings developed. These were groups of ten families who met frequently to discuss issues related to local politics, but who were also responsible for turning over lawbreakers in their families to the thane and for handling minor civic disturbances. Tythings were grouped into hundreds (the heads of each family from ten tythings), which were further grouped into geographic units called shires. Yearly, the hundred would meet and elect a reeve, who was responsible for law enforcement within the shire (thus the root of the term sheriff—shire reeve).

In 1066, William the Conqueror, a French Norman, defeated Harold Godwinson at the Battle of Hastings, thereby taking control of Anglo-Saxon lands. While keeping the base of the Anglo-Saxon system, William made changes to consolidate his power. He made the reeve an appointed rather than elected position, thereby ensuring that the chief law enforcement office in each shire was loyal to the king. While keeping the structure of the hundred, he changed its primary duties to that of acting as a local court dealing with minor crimes and civil disputes, renaming it the Court of Tourn. Serious cases called for different procedures, where 12 men from the hundred were selected to hear the case—the early origins of our 12-person jury of one's peers.

More serious breaches of the peace (e.g., homicides or treason) were handled by royal courts. As William (and his successors) lacked the manpower and finances to establish a royal court in every community, circuits were created whereby a judge would travel from one community to the next. Some circuits were small and a judge would reach a community several times a year; other circuits were quite large and a town could go years between judicial visits. Upon arrival, the circuit judge would call before him important people in the community to tell what serious breaches of the peace had occurred since his last visit. Often times these people were from the hundred; this most likely represents the origins of our current grand jury proceedings. The people would then relay accusations and evidence to the judge, as today a grand jury investigates allegations to determine if there is enough evidence to proceed with further legal action. These circuit judges also operated under the principle of *stare decisis* ("to stand by decided cases")—the foundation of today's principle of precedent in modern case law. In order to keep peace and loyalty in highly diverse regions, these judges would hand down punishments based upon local custom and past practice in the community. Thus, the same judge would often give different sentences for similar crimes in different communities. This is a direct outgrowth of Germanic law's emphasis on tradition in adjudication and helped maintain a sense of fairness under law within the eyes of the people in these conquered territories.

As English monarchs began to consolidate power, they began to minimize the differences in punishments for crimes throughout the kingdom, but the foundation remained the past decisions of judges. This is strongly seen during the reign of Henry II (1154–1189 CE), William's great grandson. Henry II attempted to bring all of his people under one law, a common law—where punishments and judgments would be made with uniform standards. This is the root of English common law, which serves as the basis of the legal system of most of England's ex-colonies. Henry II also attempted to bring the clergy under the lawful authority of the king. Before his Constitution of Clarendon (1164 CE), clergy were tried in church courts under canon law instead of local secular law. Penalties were typically lighter (for example, the church never imposed capital punishment, a favored punishment for a number of crimes in the Middle Ages). Henry II removed the ability to appeal to Rome and brought clergy in his lands under his law and courts.

By the 11th century, court procedures began to use another set of citizens in the decision-making process— the petty (from the French *petite* for small) jury. Previously, the judge was expected to punish (often by banishment or execution) all those taken before him by the grand jury. With the passing of ordeal trials to determine guilt, other mechanisms were sought for guilt determination and to place a check on the power of a grand jury. Once the grand jury had relayed information and accusations to the circuit judge, a body of citizens would hear the case along with the judge. Quickly, the grand and petty juries were separated. By the mid-12th century, law prohibited grand jury members from serving on petty juries. From the start, jury nullification—the practice of juries ignoring or reinterpreting laws on the spot—was widespread. Early petty juries often took into account mitigating circumstances behind the crime and were clearly not rubber stamps for the judges and grand juries. The framework for our modern trial system was well in place. Another critical aspect was also soon to be codified.

On the continent, courts began to shift their processes from assessing competing claims to find which held more truth, to establishing one set of claims as true and the other as false. Often called the inquisition method, this approach to criminal justice fundamentally changed many aspects of the legal system. First, instead of hearing competing claims from the parties involved, the inquisition system relied upon official investigators to provide data to support one set of claims over another. The judge played an active role in obtaining and sifting through the available evidence, rather than a passive role of hearing testimony. Secret hearings where the accused was not present quickly became a routine part of the system. Later outcries against this behavior helped form the basis of the Sixth Amendment of the U.S. Constitution, especially its insistence on the right of the defendant to confront his or her accusers. With this new emphasis on a single version of truth, confession became a desired element of criminal investigation. If the court could get the accused to admit that they had indeed committed the questioned act, much labor and investigation could be avoided. This lead to practice that, like ordeal trials, is viewed in a far different light today—the use of torture to obtain confessions.

Developed in the church's fight against heresy (and reaching its most well-known peak during the Spanish Inquisition), this reflects a fundamental shift more broadly in criminal justice. Instead of relying on methods of discerning truth in conflicting testimony, the focus of much judicial action became obtaining a confession from the accused, eliminating the need for sorting through counter-facts and discrepancies. Perusal of many museums shows us the artifactual legacy of this period in criminal justice. Racks, thumbscrews, iron maidens, iron pokers, and other more insidious tools of pain survive to remind us of this era. One extreme tool was the pear, a metal device shaped like its namesake with the addition of a spike on the end. It was hinged with a crank and would be inserted in the accused's mouth, anus, or vagina and opened. During the 13th century (and into the 18th century), the English were fond of extracting confessions via pressing. Here the accused's limbs were stretched out and tied, as if the individual were going to be drawn and quartered, and a board was placed upon their chest. Weights were added to the board until a confession was forthcoming. Most torture-generated confessions were not accepted outright. Typically, one had to reaffirm the confession a day or two after the torture session. However, failure to do so would initiate more torture proceedings. It was well after the Middle Ages that western criminal justice ceased to use torture as a means to discern truth in testimony.

Torture not withstanding, both approaches to trials can still be seen in our current American court system. The English emphasis on competing truth claims, which holds the basic assumption that there is truth in what both parties say, is seen at the roots of our current civil trial system. Here standards of evidence are lower and the jury only has to come to a majority decision, not a unanimous one. Criminal courts use stricter standards of evidence and decision making strongly influenced by the inquisitorial mode. The jury has to reach a unanimous, singular truth claim, or declare itself "hung."

Throughout the Middle Ages, punishments for crime were often harsh. Although fines were commonly used throughout the English Isles and on the continent, inability to pay could result in imprisonment or imposed servitude. As during the Germanic era, exile was a common sentence for theft and homicide. In addition, execution was common for both crimes, with hanging and beheading being the most common methods, though women were frequently burned alive at the stake. Unlike our contemporary era, executions were strongly public affairs. Although this may have added a level of deterrence to the proceedings, more often it was seen as a form of public entertainment. Executions would draw large, often rowdy, crowds. Frequently, if the prisoner was not harassed and tortured to the satisfaction of the crowd, the executioner himself could be the target of verbal and physical assaults.

Physical mutilations were not uncommon, with William the Conqueror insisting on mutilation of hands, feet, eyes, and genitalia over execution for its shamming and deterrence factors. Minor infractions, like slander, drunkenness, or assault, could be punished with time in the stocks or other public forms of humiliation. The stocks, also called the pillory, were hinged boards where the accused's arms, legs, or head would be inserted between the boards and held fast. While in and of itself, this seems mild compared to some other forms of punishment, time in the pillory was indeed dangerous. Not only was one exposed to the elements, but passersby were encouraged to verbally and physically assault the detained. In movies, this is typically portrayed as a good natured ribbing or scolding, but in reality it was often dangerous if not deadly. Assaulting people in the pillory is a form of social control that indeed united the community—allowing the public degradation of moral violators; the crowds drawn to the stocks were very similar to crowds drawn to public executions throughout the Middle Ages. Although many of these forms of punishment arose in the Middle Ages, many continued well into the 18th century or later.

It was also during the Middle Ages that prisons and jails began to take a large role in criminal justice processes. Early on, these facilities detained offenders before and during the trial process and were not places of punishment. Stays could be rather long, while one waited for the circuit judge to return to one's community. Typically, prisoners were responsible for their own support and health, relying on family, friends, or jailers charging excessive prices to provision them with food, water, and health care items. Needless to say, many prisoners died of illness and disease before their trials were complete. It is during this period, however, that incarceration began to be used additionally as a form of punishment, mostly for those unable to pay their court-imposed fines.

As Europe entered the late Middle Ages, many social and historical forces began to fundamentally alter the nature of life and society. The relative isolation of the early Middle Ages broke down in favor of ever-increasing political and economic relations between emergent nations. Trade becames widespread, with land and sea routes developing, linking Europe together, as well as developing relationships with the Near East, Asia, and Africa. Spurred by economic expansion, cities began to grow and expand. As a result, many of the connections we see today between crime and urban populations influence the quality of life in cities and social demands placed upon those who are charged with keeping the peace. As relationships between individuals in urban areas become more and more grounded in nonkinship and

emotional needs than is seen in smaller communities, social networks of informal control break down. Thefts, violence, vice, and other ills arise and become common occurrences in medieval cities. As the later Middle Ages drew to a close, urban populations swelled and workers found their economic power quickly diminishing. Wages were reduced and buying power deflated. In response, theft, violence, and prostitution began to proliferate in the major cities of Europe. As the early modern period dawned, the stage was set for our contemporary issues of urban crime, policing, and criminal justice.

As the cities and their governments changed, the focus of courts and criminal justice changed as well. During the later Middle Ages, violent crimes eclipsed property crimes as those most frequently handed by the courts. In Paris throughout the 14th and 15th centuries, essentially every crime listed in the court records was one of violence and the records were dominated by petty arguments and assaults. Although pickpocketing, breaking and entering, counterfeiting, and other property crimes were still present, enforcement shifted toward violent offenses. City watches and early "professional" policing forces began to take shape in the urban areas with the primary charge of keeping the public peace. The cultural practices of settling minor (and major) disputes with violence quickly became the targets of law enforcement, who found themselves filling local jails with tavern brawlers, fishwives fighting over customers, and participators in domestic violence. For most of these offenses, punishment was light: a night in jail and a minor fine. However, it again shows a key shift toward more modern policing and court efforts.

The Middle Ages were a long and fascinating period of history. Many elements of our modern criminal justice system emerged and evolved in this period. Although many medieval practices, like trial by ordeal and torture, have been generally abandoned, the roots of our current system, approaches, and ideas were developed in this period. In a sense, the modern world was crystallizing by the end of the Middle Ages, and with it our modern patterns of and approaches to crime and justice.

CHRISTOPHER W. MULLINS

References and Further Reading

Berman, H.J. 1983. *Law and Revolution: The Formation of the Western Legal Tradition*, Cambridge, MA: Harvard University Press.

Durant, W. 1950. The age of faith: A history of medieval civilization—Christian, Islamic, and Judaic—from Constantine to Dante: ad 325–1300. *Vol. 4, The Story of Civilization*. New York, NY: Simon and Schuster.

Johnson, H.A. and Wolfe, N.T. 2000. *The History of Criminal Justice*. 2nd ed., Cincinnati, OH: Anderson Publishing.

Moore, R.I. 1987. *The Formation of a Persecuting Society: Power and Deviance in Western Europe, 950–1250*, Oxford and New York, NY: Basil Blackwell.

Wormser, R.A. 1962. *The Story of Law* New York, NY: Simon and Schuster.

Zacour, N. 1969. *An Introduction to Medieval Institutions.* New York, NY: St. Martin's Press.

See also **Ecclesiastical Law and Justice; English Legal Tradition; Sheriffs**

Mens Rea (Criminal Intent)

Mens rea is Latin for "evil mind," and refers to the degree to which an offender intended to commit a crime. In the Anglo-American legal tradition, each crime requires a particular *actus reus* (evil act) and a particular *mens rea*.

Even in ancient times, the codes of law recognized that not all crimes are created equal. Not only are some acts more heinous than others, but also two identical acts may be worthy of different punishments, depending on whether the offenders intended to commit them. For example, a man who purposely plans to kill his neighbor, lies in wait for him, and attacks him with a knife is considered deserving of a more severe punishment than a second man who carelessly, but accidentally, runs over and kills his neighbor with a cart. The *actus reus* in these two examples—the killing of another human being—was the same, and the victims are equally dead, but the *mens rea* of the two offenders was very different.

The idea of differential treatment of offenders depending on their mental states was adopted into the English common law, which embraced the maxim *actus non facit reum nisi mens sit rea* (an act is not evil unless the mind is evil). Unfortunately, legal definitions of *mens rea* were complex, confusing, and often vague. In the U.S., therefore, many statutory drafters took great care to sort out and clarify the law in this area. Today, most crimes require one of four levels of *mens rea*: purposely, knowingly, recklessly, or negligently.

A person acts purposely when he or she intends to engage in a particular act or cause a particular result. For example, if a person aims her car at her enemy and runs that enemy over in order to seriously hurt him, she has purposely committed a criminal act. She might be guilty, then, of crimes such as assault with a deadly weapon.

People act knowingly when they are aware of what they are doing, or when they are aware that a particular result is practically certain. Unlike purposeful conduct, however, the offenders need not actually intend anything. For example, suppose a person is being pursued by police. Seeing that the road ahead of her is blocked, she drives her car at a very high speed onto a crowded sidewalk, striking several pedestrians, causing them to be seriously injured. She did not purposely injure anyone, but, given the nature of the situation and her behavior, she did act knowingly: she knew that very serious injury was almost certain.

Now imagine a person drinks several glasses of wine. In the past, she has been in a serious accident caused by her driving drunk. Nevertheless, she attempts to drive home much faster than the speed limit. Once again she gets into an accident; this time she crashes into another car and seriously injures the occupants. In this case, she has acted recklessly: she was aware that her behavior created a substantial risk of harm, and yet she chose to do it anyway. The primary difference between knowingly and recklessly has to do with the degree of the risk. If something is nearly inevitable, the act is knowing; if it is simply very likely, then the act is reckless.

The final level of *mens rea* is negligence. People act with criminal negligence when they should be aware of a substantial risk. Suppose our driver is cruising along a city street at 45 miles per hour (10 miles over the limit). She is so engrossed in a conversation on her cell phone that she does not notice she has entered a school zone; she fails to reduce her speed as she should and, as a result, accidentally hits two students who are walking home from high school. They are seriously hurt. Unlike the drunk driver, she was not aware of the risks her behavior was creating. However, she should have been, and an ordinary, reasonable person would have been. Therefore, she has acted negligently. In order to be criminally negligent, behaviors must be more than a little careless: they must deviate grossly from reasonable standards of care. This is a higher standard than is required for civil negligence lawsuits.

As these examples show, the distinctions between the different levels of *mens rea* are fine ones, and it is not always easy to determine the appropriate category for a particular offender. Nevertheless, it is essential that *mens rea* be ascertained, because it is an element of most crimes.

In the American legal system, each crime is composed of distinct elements. One element is the *actus reus*, or the particular conduct that is required for that crime. For most crimes, a particular level of *mens rea* is also an element; if the offender did not have the requisite *mens rea*, he cannot be found guilty of that crime. Perhaps the clearest example of this is homicide. There are several different kinds of homicide, ranging from involuntary manslaughter through first-degree murder. All of these have the same *actus reus*: the killing of another live human being. The only thing that distinguishes them is the *mens rea*. To constitute second-degree murder, for instance, a killing must usually be purposeful, whereas it need only be reckless or negligent for involuntary manslaughter. Therefore, a defendant's mental state may mean the difference between a few years in prison or a death sentence.

To complicate things even more, a particular crime may require a different *mens rea* for several different elements. Different *mentes reae* may be required for the *actus reus*, for the results of the conduct, and for other required circumstances. At common law, for example, the crime of burglary required that the offender purposely break and enter a house with the further intent of committing a crime (such as theft) once he was in the house. And murder requires not only that the offender purposely commit the deadly conduct (e.g., shooting the gun, putting the poison in the cup), but also that he intend for the victim to die; that is, he must intend both the *actus reus* and a particular result.

The law of *mens rea* is complicated even more by the fact that it is often difficult to prove. After all, we cannot read defendants' minds so as to know what their mental states were when they committed their crimes. Therefore, unless they confess, proof of *mens rea* must rely on circumstantial evidence. Sometimes, of course, the circumstantial evidence is pretty clear: if a person puts on a disguise, walks into a bank, points a gun at the teller, and demands that the teller hand over some money, it seems fairly safe to assume that that person intends to rob the bank. Frequently, however, the evidence is less clear, and it may be difficult for a jury to determine exactly what the defendant's state of mind was.

Another issue that sometimes arises regarding *mens rea* is the issue of transferred intent. Suppose that a person intends to shoot his enemy, but his aim is bad, and instead he misses his enemy and ends up shooting and killing an innocent bystander. The shooter did not purposely shoot this third person, nor did he intend for her to die. Should he be able to take advantage of luck or his own poor shooting skills in order to escape criminal liability? Clearly not, and so his intent is said to transfer from his original target to his actual victim. Therefore, he can be convicted of murder even though he meant to kill someone else.

Similarly, intent can transfer from one *actus reus* to another if they are similar in kind. For example, at common law assault was intentionally putting another person in fear of harmful or offensive contact, whereas battery was actually intentionally causing that harmful or offensive contact. Imagine a person swings her fist at another person, intending only to threaten or scare him, but not to actually hit him. However, she misjudges slightly, and her fist does hit his face. In this case, because assault and battery are such similar acts, her intent will transfer from the assault to the battery, and she can be convicted of battery. In order for this doctrine to apply, however, the intended act and the actual crime must be very similar.

There are some crimes that do not require any *mens rea* at all. These are call strict liability crimes. To convict someone of a strict liability crime, the prosecutor must merely show that he committed the requisite *actus reus*. Whether his acts were purposeful, knowing, reckless, or negligent is irrelevant. In fact, he can be convicted even if his behavior was the result of a perfectly reasonable mistake.

Most strict liability crimes involve corporate acts such as pollution and sale of unsafe products. The rationale behind these crimes is that a strong public interest is involved, and that it is often impossible to prove *mens rea* within a corporation. The penalties are usually fines, rather than incarceration. Most commentators argue that the number of strict liability crimes ought to be very limited, as it is usually inappropriate to impose criminal sanctions on a person whose intentions were innocent and who has caused harm accidentally.

Lay people, and even some people in the legal community, sometimes confuse *mens rea* with motive. Whereas *mens rea* refers to the degree to which a person intended his actions, motive refers to the reasons behind those actions. For example, suppose a person steals his neighbors' television because he wants to sell it for money to buy heroin. He has committed larceny: he has intentionally and permanently taken away another person's property. But now suppose a different person steals her neighbors' television because she believes that watching television is bad for them, and that they will lead more fulfilling lives without it. She, too, has intentionally and permanently taken another's property, and she, too, is guilty of larceny. Both offenders committed the identical *actus reus*, and both had the same *mens rea*: purposely. However, their motives, or the reasons why they took the televisions, were very different.

Motive is very rarely an element of a crime. One major exception to this rule is hate crimes, in which the defendant must not only purposely commit some criminal act, but the defendant must also have been motivated by the victim's group (e.g., the victim's race, religion, etc.). For the vast majority of crimes, however, the definition of the crime does not consider the reasons behind the acts. Motive may be considered during sentencing, during which people with less culpable motives may receive lesser sanctions. In fact, in capital cases sentencers may be required to consider a defendant's motives when they determine whether to impose a death sentence.

PHYLLIS B. GERSTENFELD

References and Further Reading

Brady, J.B. 1970. *The Doctrine of Mens Rea: A Study in Legal and Moral Responsibility,* PhD dissertation, University of Texas, Austin.
Duff, A. 1990. *Intention, Agency, and Criminal Liability: Philosophy of Action and the Criminal Law,* Cambridge, MA: Blackwell.
Finkelstein, C. 2000. The inefficiency of mens rea, *California Law Review* 88.
Gardner, M.R. 1993. The mens rea enigma: Observations on the role of motive in the criminal law past and present, *Utah Law Review.*
Katz, L. 1987. *Bad Acts and Guilty Minds: Conundrums of the Criminal Law,* Chicago, IL: University of Chicago Press.
Mendez, M.A. 1995. A Sisyphean task: The common law approach to mens rea, *University of California Davis Law Review* 28.
Pillsbury, S.H. 1998. *Judging Evil: Rethinking the Law of Murder and Manslaughter,* New York, NY: New York University Press.

See also **Actus Reus; Elements of Crime**

Mental Illness and Criminal Behavior

The relationship between mental illness and criminal behavior is often overstated and misunderstood. Many laypersons, politicians, and professionals regard the presence of mental illness as a crucial explanation for criminal behavior, especially for violence. It is often believed that if a person has a mental illness and commits a crime, the behavior is explained by, and often excused by, the mental illness. These views oversimplify the complex relationship between mental illness and criminal behavior.

Understanding the possible link between mental illness and criminal behavior has taken two paths: general theory and epidemiology. In the first instance, general theories about crime and mental illness are largely empirically untestable. Research that attempts to establish correlates of mental illness and criminal behavior is usually descriptive, although quite often informative with policy and clinical implications. Establishing correlates of mental illness, or psychopathologies, and crime among groups of persons is one task. Predicting how mental illness affects a particular individual's behavior is even more difficult. And even more challenging is establishing the mechanism, or the causal connection, among the many related characteristics.

Perhaps the first obstacle in studying the relationship between mental illness and criminal behavior is one of definition, inherent in the conflict between the two gatekeeping professions—psychiatry and law. Psychiatry determines which behaviors constitute a mental illness and periodically revises the *Diagnostic and Statistical Manual (DSM)*, defining mental illness. The legal field determines which behaviors are crimes and periodically revises the criminal laws. The two disciplines share neither a common language nor similar objectives. The source of much conflict is psychiatry's (and psychology's) view of human behavior on a continuum and the law's view of human behavior as a dichotomy.

Early studies of mental illness and criminal behavior were conducted by medical doctors and later by psychiatrists. Identifying the brain as the "organ of the mind" dates back to 500–600 BCE in ancient Greece, and it was believed that mental illnesses arose from brain disease and disorder. The belief that personalities were the product of the four humors (blood, phlegm, black bile, and yellow bile) persisted until fairly modern times. Further, emotional disorders such as melancholy, mania, hysteria, and delirium were objectively described and treatments prescribed, although by today's standards, treatments were rudimentary (e.g. leeching and trephining). Distinctions between organic and functional mental disorders were made by the 19th century, as our understanding of physical disease grew. Separating criminal behavior from mental illness is a modern development as early physicians were charged with one task—controlling dangerous and abnormal people whether as the result of mental disease or criminal behavior. Often, the two groups were confined together in asylums.

Perhaps because of the quantitative and empirical orientation of criminology, especially during the 20th century, criminologists often overlook psychological theories of criminal behavior. Empirical validation of general psychological theories is hampered by the object of study being the subjective mind rather than the objective body. Despite scientific advances in understanding the functions of the human brain, the more unique human mind (or personality) eludes empirical study. Early theories, such as the psychoanalytic model based on Freud's work, focused exclusively on the mind. More current, albeit broad theories, such as the evolutionary model are more biological in orientation and, thus, offer more promise of scientific validity. Recent empirically driven research, rather than theoretically oriented research, has made advances in identifying factors associated with violent behavior without questioning the origin of the mental disorder.

Despite criminology's wariness of the nonempirical and highly individualistic view of psychology, the psychological explanation of criminal behavior is a dominant and influential one, both in terms of the general public's perceptions of the causes of criminal behavior and the official responses to crime. Social change, the logical outcome of many macro-sociological theories of crime, is not often politically palatable. In contrast, individual change through psychotherapy, group counseling, or mandated pharmacological treatment is politically and socially manageable. So while the early psychological theories focused on the etiology of the mental disorders and the resultant bizarre or criminal behaviors, there was little empirical testing of the theories. More recent theories such as those based on cognitive-behavioral or social learning theories and evolutionary theories do hold up under empirical scrutiny. Yet, they, too, view criminal behavior as part of a behavioral continuum, not as a discrete category. The most recent empirical research linking mental illness and criminal behavior avoids etiological questions altogether and, instead focuses on identifying clinical, legal, and social factors that are analyzed in an epidemiological manner, in effect, leaving the causal connections to the theorists.

Related to the general definitional conflict between two powerful and competing professions, psychiatry and law, a corollary definition challenge is determining the range of psychopathologies to include in the category of "mental illness." If all diagnoses in the *DSM* were included, most criminal behaviors would be attributable to psychopathology. Limiting the category to only "serious psychoses" such as schizophrenia and mood disorders is probably too narrow as that would exclude substance abuse disorders and personality disorders. This leads to the other major hurdle in linking mental illness to criminal behavior: diagnosis. Aside from the clinical challenges inherent in diagnosing a "disease of the mind" where no objective medical test exists, it is an additional difficulty in aligning a psychiatric diagnosis with a legal construct such as "crime." Individuals with mental illness themselves differ as to the number and severity of symptoms at any one point in time. And, of course, there is large variation across individuals who have mental illnesses. Therefore, linking mental illness to criminal behavior is risky business. The historical context of correlating mental illness and criminal behavior can be better viewed as studying mental "disturbances" rather than actual diagnosed mental disorders as many psychologists and psychiatrists were called upon to treat (change) individuals who exhibited bizarre and sometimes dangerous behavior, regardless of criminal justice attention. Today's research relies on "best practices" of psychiatric diagnosis of mental illness and on legal designations of criminal behavior, questioning neither.

The influence of Sigmund Freud (1856–1939), the father of psychoanalysis, on the understanding of mental illness and crime cannot be overstated. He focused largely, if not exclusively, on the mind rather than the brain although trained as a physician and psychiatrist. Freud's major contribution to abnormal psychology and crime is the belief that criminal behavior arises when there is an unhealthy balance among the id (innate urges), ego (moderator between the id and superego), and superego (conscience). His perspective broke from earlier medical views that mental disorder was a brain disease and from religious views that mental illness and criminal behavior were caused by moral failings. Instead, Freud asserted that individuals who have an overdeveloped superego feel excessive guilt and may commit crimes to be caught and punished. Alternately, an individual who has an underdeveloped conscience may give into desires and urges and thus commit crimes.

As with many other psychological theories, psychoanalysts view criminal behavior as an extension of the underlying psychological disturbance, not as a distinct behavior; criminal behavior must be viewed in terms of childhood (mal)development. According to psychoanalytic theory, abnormal behavior, including criminal behavior and mental illness, arises from conflict between our unconscious desires and the conscience. A psychologically healthy individual sublimates these urges into socially acceptable behaviors; a person with a disturbed personality might express these same desires as crime. The strength of psychoanalytic theory and its derivative psychodynamic theories is that they allow for a general understanding of mental disorder and criminal behavior whether violent, property, or victimless crimes. The weakness is the inability to test the theory empirically, as much of the data are highly individualistic and interpretive, limiting generalizability.

A second major intellectual influence on the study of mental illness and criminal behavior arose from the works of behaviorists, namely from B.F. Skinner (1904–1990). Although few psychologists and criminologists adhere to the strict operant behaviorism of Skinner, his influence can be recognized throughout the cognitive-behavioral school with the work of Albert Bandura and the social learning school beginning with Edwin H. Sutherland (1883–1950) and continuing today with the work of Ronald L. Akers and others. The cognitive-behavioral model regards humans as thinking hedonists. As we develop as humans, we influence and are influenced by the world around us, shaping our behavior as we interpret reality. It is our individual perception that influences us. If the give-and-take is pleasurable, we will continue the behavior; if it is painful, we will stop.

What makes cognitive behaviorism different from Skinner's behaviorism is the role of thinking or cognition and motivation. Both cognitive behaviorists and social learning theorists view the etiology of criminal, or abnormal, behavior as not intrinsically different from normal behavior; the same processes are involved in learning prosocial and antisocial behaviors. An individual who has a highly unique, and perhaps, distorted view of reality could misinterpret environmental cues that could lead to criminal behavior. Similarly, an individual with antisocial motivations could engage in criminal behavior, especially when there are no perceived costs to the behavior. What makes this perspective critical for understanding the link between mental illness and criminal behavior is that it is one of the dominant theoretical views held by psychologists. Cognitive therapy is the prevailing type of psychotherapy today, challenging individuals to test their version of reality with relevant evidence. By changing thought and perception disturbances, criminal behavior will change. Empirical studies grounded in cognitive-behavioral or social learning theory support the basic tenets of this perspective (Akers, 1998), but mental illness as a contributing factor to criminal behavior has not been sufficiently explored by these theorists.

As most general psychological theories strive to understand and explain the development of personality and how that affects behavior, more specific applications of personality theory attempt to link a disturbance in a person's personality to criminal behavior. One focus of study has been on comparing standardized tests (e.g., personality inventories like the Minnesota Multiphasic Personality Inventory or ink blot tests like the Rorschach) of criminals and noncriminals. These tests have been used to try to predict recidivism of criminal behavior as well as to predict initial offending behavior, in neither case reliably. Summaries of research using standard psychological tests to predict criminal behavior report that if a relationship exists, it is inconsistent at best. Another vein of research on personality and criminal behavior was initiated by Hervey Cleckley (1955) when he widely introduced us to the concept of the "psychopath" in his book, *The Mask of Sanity*. As used by Cleckley and until very recently, the term "psychopath" was used interchangeably with "antisocial personality disorder" (APD) and "sociopath" to try to explain the seemingly inexplicable acts of human cruelty that have always occurred. APD is a *DSM* diagnosis used widely as a diagnosis for persistent criminal behavior. For this diagnosis to be given, the behaviors must arise in childhood or adolescence and continue into adulthood. They are believed to be caused by a personality flaw, but the APD diagnosis does not focus on personality traits as much as it does on the antisocial behaviors.

A more recent direction of personality theory has sharpened the definition of psychopathy with the development and validation of a series of assessments, the Psychopathy Checklist (PCL) by Robert Hare (1996). The PCL is a lengthy assessment and encompasses a broad spectrum of affective, interpersonal, and behavioral factors in assessing level of psychopathy. Research on the PCL is broad and cross-cultural, yielding the same conclusions—that the PCL reliably distinguishes offenders from nonoffenders. This definition of psychopathy differs substantially from Cleckley's use of the term. This new definition is a more specific clinical construct than APD and is, as a result, more effective in distinguishing persistent offenders from other offenders. Psychopathy encompasses APD, but the reverse is not true. Implicit in the studies of psychopathy is that it is a devastating disorder that envelopes all aspects of the person's personality and behavior. Although the PCL proves to be quite promising in predicting future criminal behavior based upon the levels of psychopathy, it does not offer strong theoretical arguments as to how and why the disorder exists.

A more recent addition to the general psychological approaches to studying criminal behavior is evolutionary psychology, a biologically based theory that views the social environment as an important factor in shaping human behavior. As with most contemporary studies, evolutionary psychologists have focused on aggression and violence and not on less serious criminal behavior. Further, as with earlier general psychological theories, this model does not focus on mental illness as such, but on explaining all behaviors, including abnormal behavior. The evolutionary psychologists believe that our adaption to our environment and our innate struggles (e.g., survival, reproduction) have left us with many psychological mechanisms that respond to very specific environmental inputs. Our behavior is highly context- and task-specific, regulated by very specific psychological adaptations. Evolutionary psychologists believe that behavior is the result of interaction between the underlying innate psychological mechanisms and the varying environmental inputs. Although this sounds similar to the cognitive-behavioral or social learning theorists, a major difference lies in the emphasis each places on the underlying innate structures of the personality and the environmental contexts. Evolutionary psychologists claim many empirical successes in explaining the underlying causes of violence and aggression (as well as mate selection). Because of the relative newness of this theory and the attention it is garnering, it is not without its critics who claim that it has not reached the level of empirical verification that is needed to be a general theory (c.f. Buss, 1999).

Sociology has had an impact on the study of mental illness and criminal behavior, although often not linking the two until recently. Beginning with Emile Durkheim's (1858–1917) study of suicide, sociologists have continued the tradition of placing individual-level factors such as behavior in a community context. The first study of mental disorder in the community was conducted by Robert E. Faris and H. Warren Dunham in Chicago in the 1930s. They, like Durkheim, argued that individual-level problems, such as mental illness, were also a function of social structural variables. In particular, these early studies linked mental illness (and criminal behavior) to social disorganization and especially to neighborhood poverty.

In the 1950s, August B. Hollingshead and Frederick D. Redlich (1953), a sociologist and psychiatrist, respectively, studied the prevalence of mental disorders in New Haven, Connecticut. They found that social factors were highly related to the type of mental disorders people experienced and treatment they received with the poor being the most disadvantaged. Again, although these studies do not link mental illness with criminal behavior, when coupled with research conducted on social factors and criminal behavior, the link is implicit.

In the 1980s, the National Institute of Mental Health conducted the Epidemiologic Catchment Area (ECA) study, a survey of the prevalence of mental disorders and mental health services in five U.S. communities. Subsequent analysis of data from three of the sites showed that risk of violent behavior was associated with a diagnosis of schizophrenia, especially when hallucinations and delusions were also present (Swanson, Borum, Swartz, and Monahan, 1996). Using different data, Link, Andrews, and Cullen (1992) found that even when controlling for individual factors, psychiatric patients reported higher levels of violent behavior when compared with other residents of the same New York City neighborhoods.

The MacArthur Violence Risk Assessment Study (Monahan, Steadman, Silver, Appelbaum, Robbins, Mulvey, Roth, Grisso, and Banks, 2001) published the results of their comprehensive research that sought to bring the best science possible to the task of violence risk assessment. In addition, they developed an actuarial risk assessment "tool" for use by mental health professionals. Overcoming most of the methodological limitations of prior studies, their findings contradicted some long-held beliefs about the link between mental illness and violence. For example, they established that a diagnosis of having a major mental disorder, especially schizophrenia, results in a lower rate of violence, when compared with a diagnosis of either personality disorder or adjustment disorder. Individuals with schizophrenia or substance abuse disorder were no more violent than non-mentally ill community members. Critical to this finding was that a co-occurring diagnosis of schizophrenia and substance abuse was a strong risk factor for violence. The presence of delusions was not found to be related to violence, whereas a "suspicious" attitude toward others was. Hallucinations, including "command" hallucinations, were not found to be related to violence unless the hallucinations were specific in the commanded violent act. Violent thoughts such as daydreaming about harming others and anger were associated with violence. Finally, among the 106 factors measured, psychopathy as measured on the Hare PCL showed the strongest association with violence.

Silver (2000) combined individual level characteristics from the MacArthur study with community level variables in the tradition of the early Chicago School, arguing that it is an "individualistic fallacy" to attribute all personal outcomes in terms of individual characteristics such as those listed above. Instead, by introducing rates of neighborhood disadvantage to the individual level data, Silver showed that prior analyses overstated the effect of individual characteristics in understanding the factors that are associated with violence. In other words, by not studying social contexts, researchers placed too much emphasis on individual variables. Silver's work reminds researchers who study mental illness and criminal behavior that behavior is not just a composite of individual level data, a charge leveled against psychological research for decades. Focusing on individual level data alone can result in misleading conclusions.

Understanding the correlates of mental illness and criminal behavior remains on two tracks that occasionally intersect but have yet to merge. Theories, ranging from the early works of Freud to more contemporary evolutionary theory, remain largely unverifiable although some key advances have been made. These theories seek to explain the appearance of a link between mental disorders and criminal behavior. Epidemiological studies have recently compiled an impressive list of social and clinical factors that are correlates of violent behavior, with some types of mental disorders being among the factors that increase the risk of violence. When mental disorder is present in a person involved in crime, it is among the many correlates to the behavior.

LISA A. CALLAHAN

References and Further Reading

Akers, R.L. 1998. *Social Learning and Social Structure: A General Theory of Crime and Deviance.* Boston, MA: Northeastern University Press.

Bandura, A. 1973. *Aggression: A Social Learning Analysis.* Englewood Cliffs, NJ: Prentice-Hall.

Buss, D.M. 1999. *Evolutionary Psychology: The New Science of the Mind.* Needham Heights, MA: Allyn and Bacon.

Cleckley, H. 1955. *The Mask of Sanity: An Attempt to Clarify Some Issues about the So-called Psychopathic Personality,* 3rd ed. St. Louis, MO: Mosby.

Diagnostic and Statistical Manual of Mental Disorders, 1994. 4th revised ed. Washington, DC: American Psychiatric Association.

Faris, R.E. and Dunham, H.W. 1939. *Mental Disorder in Urban Areas.* Chicago, IL: University of Chicago Press.

Hare, R.D. 1996. Psychopathy: A clinical construct whose time has come, *Criminal Justice and Behavior* 23.

Hollingshead, A.B. and Redlich, F.D. 1953. Social stratification and psychiatric disorders, *American Sociological Review* 18.

Link, B.G., Andrews, H.A., and Cullen, F.T. 1992. The violent and illegal behavior of mental patients reconsidered, *American Sociological Review* 57.

Link, B.G., Monahan, J., Stueve, A., and Cullen, F.T. 1999. Real in their consequences: A sociological approach to understanding the association between psychotic symptoms and violence, *American Sociological Review* 64.

Monahan, J., Steadman, H.J., Silver, E., Appelbaum, P.A., Robbins, P.C., Roth, L., Grisso, T.A., and Banks, S. 2001. *Rethinking Risk Assessment: The MacArthur Study of Mental Disorder and Violence.* New York, NY: Oxford University Press.

Silver, E. 2000. Extending social disorganization theory: A multi-level approach to the study of violence among persons with mental illnesses, *Criminology* 38.

Swanson, J.W., Borum, R., Swartz, M.S., and Monahan, J. 1996. Psychotic symptoms and disorders and the risk of violent behavior in the community, *Criminal Behavior and Mental Health* 6.

See also **Neurophysiological Theories of Criminal Behavior; Psychological Theories of Criminal Behavior**

Mercy Killing *See* Euthanasia and Physician-Assisted Suicide

Merton, Robert K.

Robert K. Merton is one of the most influential sociologists and theorists of the American social sciences. The life work of Merton has been inspired by some of the great sociological minds of the past two centuries, such as Emile Durkheim, Max Weber, and Talcott Parsons, and, in turn, continues to influence many new generations of social scientists both in North America and around the world, such as Albert Cohen, Richard A. Cloward, and Lloyd E. Ohlin.

One of the key influences on Merton's early work is the French sociologist Emile Durkheim, and his macrotheory of "anomie" or normlessness. Durkheim's focus in the late 19th century was upon the social structure of French society and how this structure can propel people toward violating norms. Durkheim felt that a successful social structure defined reasonable limits on desires. In other words, the desires of an individual or of a group of people were prescribed by the society in which they lived. When the social organization is unsuccessful, such as during times of war or rapid social change, insatiable desires are released. Anomie was the result of the disjunction between people's increasing aspirations and their ability to fulfill their desires. Durkheim felt that anomie would occur with the greatest frequency among the upper classes, as the aspirations set down for these groups were the most difficult to attain.

It was by building on Durkheim's notion of anomie that Merton developed his theory of deviance (strain theory), which, in turn, made an invaluable contribution to the field of criminology. Like Durkheim's, Merton's explanation of deviance is grounded in the social structure of society. Unlike Durkheim, however, who assumed that people are naturally inclined to have unlimited desires that must be socially controlled, Merton hypothesizes that these desires were socially generated. Merton felt that the notion of the "American dream," where anyone can achieve their ambitions, placed an extraordinary emphasis on the desirability of wealth, status, power, and prestige. The Protestant work ethic, which is predominant in America, has long postulated that with hard work, anyone in America can be successful. The American dream is an egalitarian belief that is fundamentally flawed, because of the inequalities of power, status, and privilege in the American social structure. In this type of a society, some segments of the population have an advantage over others. More specifically, the legitimate means for achieving success and wealth, such as education and interpersonal contacts, are differentially available throughout the class structure. Members of the lower classes, therefore, experience greater strain in their attempts to achieve wealth, owing to their limited access to the legitimate means available to aid them in reaching their goals. This strain felt in the lower classes leads some members to seek out illegitimate means of obtaining wealth, resulting in anomie, or deviancy. Thus, Merton's theory of anomie contrasts with that of Durkheim for another reason, in that anomie would be more prevalent among the lower classes, as opposed to the upper classes as postulated by Durkheim. Merton hypothesized that the structure of American society, the strong desirability for wealth, and the strain that it placed on certain members of its society, resulted in a higher crime rate than that found in other Western countries.

Not all members of society respond to strain by becoming deviant, however. Indeed, Merton developed a typology of five modes of adaptation to strain, of which three are deviant. These modes are conformity, innovation, ritualism, retreatism, and rebellion. Briefly, a conformist accepts both the goals as defined by society as well as the prescribed legitimate means of achieving these goals. An innovator accepts the societal goals, but rejects the socially prescribed means of reaching them. A ritualist conforms to the institutionalized means of pursuing goals, but does not actively pursue these goals. The retreatist rejects both the goals and the means of attaining them as dictated by society. Finally, the rebel also rejects both goals and means, but replaces them with his or her own set of goals and means of reaching them. From a criminal justice perspective, the innovators, retreatists, and rebels are the modes that result in deviant and often criminal behavior.

Merton's strain theory sparked a tremendous amount of research and theorizing on deviant behavior. His theory was tested, revised, and refined for years following its initial publication by both himself and others. Theories such as the subculture of delinquency theory find their origins in Merton's strain theory. Strain theory had immediate and tangible policy implications in the U.S., as evidenced by the policies adopted in the 1960s during the administrations of John F. Kennedy and Lyndon Johnson. During this time, the American federal government supported initiatives to combat poverty and improve educational and job opportunities. It is widely conceded that these programs failed, however, this failure may be more accurately explained by a shortcoming in the implementation of the policies rather than a shortcoming of the theory.

The influence of Merton is felt beyond the realm of criminology and indeed, beyond the world of social sciences. He is well respected and continues to enjoy a very positive reputation. His contributions to the understanding of deviance, as well as his substantive work in the areas of structural functionalism, middle-range theories, bureaucracy, mass communication, the sociology of science, and the practice of sociological research cannot be underestimated, yet it is the balance between theory and empirical research that Merton was able to maintain over the length of his career for which he continues to receive accolades from his peers. Some of Merton's concepts, such as the "self-fulfilling prophecy," "role model," "typology," "manifest" and "latent" functions, "serendipity," and the "focus group interview," have become a part of the common language and are understood by the masses.

Merton's long, prolific, and very successful career spans the rise and decline of several schools of thought in sociology and has witnessed the skeptical scrutiny of his own pioneering work. His writings remain, however, as required reading for all students of sociology and criminology and his influence in the field will continue for years to come.

NICOLA EPPRECHT

Biography

Born in Philadelphia, PA, July 5, 1910 as Meyer R. Schkolnick; son of Jewish immigrant shop keepers. Educated at Temple University, B.A. 1931; Harvard (M.A. 1932; Ph.D., 1936). Faculty member, Harvard University, 1936–1939. Faculty member, Tulane University, 1939–1941. Columbia University, 1941–1979. Became Full Professor in 1947. Associate Director of Columbia University's Bureau of Applied Social Research, 1942–1971. Honored as Giddings Professor in 1963. Awarded the National Medal of Science in 1994. Merton is Professor Emeritus at Columbia University, NY. Merton maintains several homes in New York State.

Selected Works

Social structure and anomie, *American Sociological Review* 3:672–682.
Social structure and anomie: Revisions and extensions, *The Family,* Anshen, R. (Ed.) New York, NY: Harper Brothers, pp. 226–257.
Social Theory and Social Structure (1949; enlarged editions, 1957, 1968) New York, NY: Free Press.
Social conformity, deviation, and opportunity-structures: A comment on the contributions of Dubin and Cloward, *American Sociological Review* 24:177–189.
On Theoretical Sociology (1967) New York, NY: Free Press.

The Sociology of Science: Theoretical & Empirical Investigations (1973). USA: University of Chicago Press.
On the Shoulders of Giants: A Shandean Postscript (1993) USA: University of Chicago Press, 3rd ed.

References and Further Reading

Akers, R.L. 1994. *Criminological Theories: Introduction and Evaluation.* Los Angeles, CA: Roxbury Publishing Co.
Brown, S.E., Esbensen, F.-A., and Geis, G. (Eds.) 1991. *Criminology. Explaining Crime and Its Context.* Cincinnati, OH: Anderson Publishing Co.
Encyclopedia Britannica OnLine. Available at http://members.eb.com/bol/topic? *Merton, Robert King; Alienation; Crime and Punishment; Social Structure.*
Evans, M. Available at http://www.criminology.fsu.edu/crimtheory/merton.htm.
Hunt, M. 1961. A biographical profile of Robert K. Merton, *The New Yorker* 28:39–63.
Pfohl, S. 1994. *Images of Deviance and Social Control.* New York, NY: McGraw-Hill.
Rosenberg, M.M., Shaffir, W.B., Turowetz, A., and Weinfeld, M. (Eds.) 1987. *An Introduction to Sociology, Second Edition.* Toronto, Canada: Methuen Publications.
Rosenfeld, R. 1989. Robert Merton's contributions to the sociology of deviance, *Social Inquiry* 59:453–466.

See also **Sociological Theories of Crime; Strain Theories: From Durkheim to Merton**

Micronesia, Crime and Justice in

Micronesia is comprised of over 2000 islands spreading across 3 million miles of the Pacific Ocean, north of Papua New Guinea, and south of Japan. The region includes, *inter alia*, the Caroline, Gilbert, Ellice, Marianas, and Marshall Islands groups. Many of the islands were under Japanese control at the outbreak of WWII. Following WWII the islands were placed in trust by the UN and the U.S. was named as trustee. The Trust Territory of the Pacific Islands (TTPI) included the Marshall, Marianas, and Caroline Island groups. The objective of the trust was to advance the political and economic development of the islands, eventually resulting in self-governance. Today, every island that had been a member of the TTPI is either an independent state or a semiindependent state in voluntary association with an independent state. The post-TTPI Micronesian political entities include the Commonwealth of the Northern Marianas Islands, the Republic of Palau, the Republic of the Marshall Islands, and the Federated States of Micronesia. Other Micronesian states that were not part of the TTPI include Guam, which is a territory of the U.S., the Republic of Kiribati, and the Republic of Nauru. The remainder of this article will focus on the Federated States of Micronesia (FSM).

The 600-plus islands of the FSM are divided into four states, Chuuk, Kosrae, Pohnpei, and Yap. The national capital is located at Palikir, Pohnpei. English is the official language of the national government. The official language of each state is the local language of the people (Trukese or Chuukese, Kosraen, Pohnpeian, and Yapese). The FSM is an independent state in free association with the U.S. The FSM was admitted to the UN in 1991. The islands are small and familial and traditional life greatly influences criminal and civil justice.

Even though independent, the FSM has maintained a close relationship with the U.S. in the post-TTPI years. Through a compact of free association first approved in 1982 and most recently approved with amendments in 2003, the U.S. provides military protection to the FSM and financially supports its development. In the criminal justice context, the U.S. and the FSM have agreed to mutually assist one another in the prevention and investigation of criminal activity and the enforcement of the criminal laws of both the FSM and U.S.

The government of the FSM is modeled after that of the U.S., including similar divisions of authority. The national government is divided into three branches, an executive headed by a president, a unicameral Congress, and a Supreme Court, which acts as both a trial court and an appellate court. Each of the four states has a similar structure. The national government and each state government have an attorney general who is appointed by the chief executive. The attorney general acts as the chief prosecutor, chief law enforcement officer, and chief legal advisor to the government. At the national level, there are two law enforcement agencies, the Division of Security and Investigation and the Division of Marine Surveillance. The chiefs of each of these divisions report to the attorney general. Each state has its own police department as well. A 1991 amendment to the FSM Constitution transferred the responsibility of prosecuting "major" crimes from the national government to the states. In addition to the western political and legal system, a system of traditional life continues. Custom plays an important role and traditional leaders continue to be recognized on all but one island (Kosrae).

The national and state legal systems are of the common law family, having been significantly influenced by attorneys from the U.S. The FSM Constitution, which was ratified in 1978 and became effective in 1979, contains a declaration of fundamental rights similar to that of the U.S. So, those accused of crimes enjoy freedom from self-incrimination, due process, the right to counsel, freedom from unreasonable searches and seizures, freedom from cruel and unusual punishments, and other rights. There are no juries in the FSM, so all criminal cases are heard and decided by judges.

One significant difference between U.S. law and FSM law is the latter's constitutional recognition of customary and traditional life. Article V of the FSM Constitution specifically recognizes the role and function of traditional leaders and enables the FSM Congress to recognize customs and traditions by statute, giving them constitutional, not statutory, authority. Article IX delegates the authority to define national crimes to the FSM Congress with "due regard for local custom and tradition." Additionally, Article XI contains a so-called Judicial Guidance Clause requiring decisions of the Supreme Court to "be consistent with this Constitution, Micronesian customs and traditions, and the social and geographic configuration of Micronesia." A 1991 amendment to the Judicial Guidance Clause requires the court to consult and apply Micronesian sources of law. This Amendment was a direct response to the court's history of applying U.S. law in the islands. Legal recognition of traditional leaders and of customary law is even greater in some of the states. For example, Yap has two councils of chiefs that possess the authority to veto legislation that violates custom.

Consistent with these provisions, traditional leaders continue to engage in dispute resolutions of both criminal and civil cases on nearly all of the islands. On most of the islands, traditional law gives the victim a significant role in prosecution and sentencing. For example, on Pohnpei, the traditional apology ceremony, which is commonly known as the Sakau Ceremony, continues to be recognized. An apology occurs when the family of a perpetrator tenders an apology, following specific customary procedures, to the victim's family. If the apology is accepted, and it is customary to accept an apology, the matter is completely settled under traditional law. The other islands have similar traditional settlement methods.

Many prosecutors will not prosecute a case if there has been a traditional resolution. If a case is prosecuted after a traditional settlement has occurred, the Judicial Guidance Clause of the FSM Constitution and similar state laws require judges to take the traditional settlement into consideration. This may result in the dismissal of a charge or a reduction of sentence. The judiciary employs an accusatorial, adversarial process. This has been criticized by some commentators as being inconsistent with the Micronesian nonconfrontational way of life. Although the adversarial method is employed throughout the courts of the nation, it is most strictly adhered to by the FSM Supreme Court.

Crime data are not collected in the FSM. Because the frequency of traditional dispute resolution is unknown and because underreporting of crime is likely to be more common in the FSM than in more developed nations, the number of crimes reported to police and the number of criminal cases filed in the courts are not accurate measures of crime frequency. Few criminal cases that are filed charge serious violent crimes, although simple assault, disturbing the peace, public intoxication, and mischief are prevalent. Many state authorities report that much of this crime occurs while the offenders are under the influence of alcohol. Theft, particularly theft and embezzlement from the government, is likely the most common national crime.

Although developing, the use of technology in crime control and crime prevention is low. Many law enforcement and corrections officers have not graduated from high school and their field training is minimal. A few officers have attended college and a smaller number have attended academy training in the U.S.

Generally, punishment is lenient when compared to punishment in the U.S. Incarceration, restitution, fines, community service, and public acknowledgement of misbehavior are all common. The FSM Constitution prohibits capital punishment. Corporal forms of punishment occasionally occur in traditional settings.

Each state maintains a jail. The national government contracts with the states to house its prisoners. The jails are small and security is minimal.

The professionalization of law enforcement and corrections, the establishment of a system of data collection, continued efforts to define the relationship between traditional life and the western form of criminal justice, gender equality, and other modernization and cultural preservation challenges face the Micronesian people in the early decades of the 21st century.

DANIEL E. HALL

References and Further Reading

Burch, K.M. 2002. Due process in Micronesia: Are fish due less process? *Roger Williams Law Review*, 8:43.

Hall, D. 1993. *World Factbook of Criminal Justice Systems: Federated States of Micronesia*. Department of Justice, Bureau of Justice Statistics. Available at http://www.ojp.usdoj.gov/bjs/abstract/wfcj.htm.

King, E.C. 2002. Custom and constitutionalism in the federated states of Micronesia, *Asian-Pacific Law and Policy Journal*, 3:249.

Laughlin, S.K., Jr. 1995. *The Law of United States Territories and Affiliated Jurisdictions*. Lawyers Cooperative Publishing.

Tamanaha, B.Z. 1989. A proposal for the development of a system of indigenous jurisprudence in Micronesia, *Hastings International and Comparative Law Review*, 13:71.

Tamanaha, B. 1993. *Understanding Law in Micronesia: An Interpretive Approach to Transplanted Law*. Leiden: Brill Publishing Co.

Compact of Free Association, as Amended in 2003, Between the Government of the United States and the government of the Federated States of Micronesia. See Sec. 175 and the implementing Agreement on Extradition, *Mutual Assistance in Law Enforcement Matters and Penal Sanctions*.

FSM Const. art. XI, §11 (Judicial Guidance Clause).

See also **Comparative Crime and Justice: An Overview; Customary Law**

Military Justice: The Police

The military is a social system within a society but is also an independent social system, in effect, a microsociety of its own, sometimes consisting of millions of individuals. Military social systems may, in some instances, operate quite independently of the larger society. The French Foreign Legion, for example, by law, is not permitted to even be stationed on the mainland of France. This military is essentially isolated from the larger parent society. In the People's Republic of China, the People's Liberation Army, although theoretically subordinate to the government of the country, in reality is relatively independent. The People's Army even owns and operates businesses, farms, and factories to generate food and profit. It also has significant investments in various commercial enterprises both within the PROC and abroad as well. The People's Army can often be relatively assertive in regard to the government. In some societies, the government may even be subordinate to the military, or at least very responsive to the wishes of the military.

The Military as a Normative Order

As with all social systems, the military, here and in other societies, represents a formidable population with the attendant need for appropriate mechanisms of social control. Members of the military, such as here in the U.S., are (Bryant, 1979, 6):

> … theoretically subject to the same full range of civilian legal regulations and constraints as are other citizens, including conventional civilian socio legal codes at federal, state, and local levels. As members of the military, they are also subject to the additional social control imposed by military law, and accountable under supplemental sets of legal constraints governing their occupational behavior, including the U.S. Uniform Code of Military Justice as well as various international treaties. Such constraints are normally enforced and severely sanctioned by the U.S. military establishment. In the event of violation of these prescribed rules of conduct, the offender is subject to military justice and its attendant punishments.

A military may operate in foreign countries and under conditions where civilian courts are not readily or appropriately available. Also, in time of war and peace, additional rules of conduct—not normal to civilian life—have been found necessary in the training and operation of a disciplined army. Thus, the specialized nature and mission of the military, and the setting in which it operates, all necessitate a separate and additional system of formalized social control in order to prescribe and regulate appropriate behavior for its members (Bryant, 1979, 7).

The military, as with all social systems, will experience violations of its normative structure in the form of unique, endemic, and constituent patterns of deviant behavior and crime—military crime. Accordingly, the military requires, and relies on its own system of law and justice, and its own law enforcement personnel—the military police.

Although most militaries have relied on a military police apparatus that has the missions of law enforcement, handling prisoners-of-war, traffic control, and security of bases and rear areas in combat situations, some societies have created military organizations that were more oriented toward the suppression of political dissent and the enforcement of mandated political ideology—"thought police," as it were. One such instance was Japan and its *Kempeitai*, or special military police organization. It functioned along similar lines as the German *Gestapo*, as a kind of political police, although the *Kempeitai* was formed much earlier than the *Gestapo*. In this regard (Lamont-Brown, 1998):

> The Kempeitai themselves were well established before The TOKKO [a kind of civilian political or "thought police" organization], having been founded by order of the Meiji Council of State of 4 January 1881, as an elite corps of 349 men. Their first work was to discipline army officers who resisted conscription. They not only 'policed the army' but regulated the people as well; for farmers also protested against the conscription law which took young men from the rice fields.

From its inception up through the end of World War II, the *Kempeitei* was a much dreaded police force that relied on brutality and torture in interrogation in connection with its counter-intelligence and political police functions. The *Kempeitai* was also responsible for the torture and murder of a number of allied servicemen who were prisoners-of-war of the Japanese during World War II.

The Progenitors of the Military Police

Military rules are, perhaps, as old as intergroup hostility, and the regulation of warfare dates back to the earliest civilizations, and likely even earlier. Often there were specialized military personnel assigned to enforce military rules and sanction those who violated the rules. The Greeks and the Romans had detailed systems of military justice (Knudten, 1970, 472), and the Romans even had the equivalent of modern-day military police to enforce order and military regulations (Robinson, 1971, 19). As Bryant (1979, 27) relates:

> Errant Roman legionnaires might well be fined, subjected to extra duty, or even flogged for infractions of the rules or dereliction of duty.

Military Police in the Revolutionary War

Military Police as an organizational entity in the American Army dates back to the colonial period.

When George Washington assumed command of the Continental army on July 3, 1775, he encountered little more than a "disorganized and undisciplined mob." Cognizant of the need for order and discipline in an effective army, he subsequently moved to implement the new Articles of War (that had been enacted by the U.S. Continental Congress on June 30, 1775) and vigorously effected military justice (Maurer, 1964). Robert K. Wright (1991, 4), the author of a concise history of the Military Police, relates that Congress, on May 27, 1775, authorized the formation of a provost unit to be part of the Continental Army. This unit was named the Marechaussee Corps (from the French term for provost troops) and was assigned "... to per- form those necessary police functions required in camp and in the field" (Wright, 1991, 4). More specifically, General George Washington (in an order signed by him on October 11, 1778) directed the Marechaussee Corp (U.S. Army Military Police School, 1975, 50):

> ... to patrol the Camp and its neighborhood for the purpose of apprehending Deserters, Marauders, Drunkards, Rioters, and Stragglers, and to apprehend all other soldiers that may be in a violation of General orders.

To serve as Provost Marshall of the Continental Army and Commander of the Marechaussee Corps, General Washington appointed one Bartholomew Von Heer with the rank of Captain (Wright, 1991, 3). The organization of the first Military Police unit is interesting.

All armies have some type of military police personnel, but this discussion specifically addresses only the Military Police of the U.S. Army. It consisted of (Wright, 1991, 3):

One Captain
Four Lieutenants
One Clerk
One Quartermaster Sergeant
Two Trumpeters
Two Sergeants
Five Corporals

Forty Three Provosts
Four Executioners

Aside from being somewhat "top-heavy" with rank, one can only speculate at the perceived need for four executioners and two trumpeters. Wright (1991, 3) points out that there must have been an anticipation of the Corp's need for speed and special equipment, inasmuch as it ". . . was mounted and accoultered as Light Dragoons."

What is most interesting to note, however, is the similarity of functions (missions) assigned to the Marchaussee Corps at that time and the functions (missions) of today's Military Police Corps. The latter will be explored later in the discussion. In regard to the functions of the Corps during the colonial period, Wright (1991, 3) articulates several of these functions including the responsibilities of:

1. serving as a "camp patrol" in order ". . . to detain fugitives and arrest rioters and thieves."
2. combating situations to patrol and rescue the rear area along the army's "second line," ". . . rounding up stragglers and preventing desertions."
3. patrolling the rear area and being on watch against enemy attack from behind, thereby serving as an "early warning" unit.
4. supervising relations with the sutlers [civilian merchants who sold food and merchandise to the troops], [presumably insuring honest and non-rancorous transactions].
5. "the collection, security and movement of prisoners of war."

This set of functions (missions) is remarkably similar to modern day Military Police functions, as will be noted later in this discussion.

Wright (1991, 3333–34) also relates that later in the Revolutionary War, the Commonwealth of Virginia organized a second large military police force to guard British and German soldiers captured in the Battle of Saratoga and imprisoned in a prisoner-of-war compound built at Charlottesville.

The two military police groups did not survive the Revolutionary War, however. The unit that guarded the POWs was disbanded in 1781 and the Marechaussee Corps was mustered out at the end of the war in 1783 (Wright, 1991, 3–4).

From the end of the Revolutionary War until the beginning of the American Civil War, no military police Units were authorized or organized. Inasmuch as the functions (missions) of the Marechaussee Corps remained to be fulfilled, the army relied on the expedient of temporary military police. According to one historical account (U.S. Army Military Police School, 1975, 50):

During the period between the Revolutionary War and the Civil War military police *duties* were [BD1][BD2] performed by troops temporarily selected for such duty by individual commanders. As early as 1820, a guide for commanders in determining assignment of personnel to military police duties was found in General Regulations for the Army, under Article 58, "General Police."

In other wars such as the War of 1812 and the Mexican War, army personnel from various units were temporarily assigned as military police or the "Provost Guard" to enforce military regulations and maintain order among the troops.

Military Police in the Civil War

With the beginning of the Civil War, a new era for military police opened up. During the massive mobilization on both sides immediately before the war began, "unit commanders were authorized to appoint their own Provost Marshals and establish their own Military Police Units" (U.S. Army Military Police School, 1975, 51).

With the beginning of the war, the need for a law enforcement entity within the Union Army was recognized by the War Department, which on September 24, 1861, issued general orders. Later in 1863, the U.S. Congress created the office of the Provost Marshall in the Union Army and Brigadier General James B. Fry was identified as the first Provost Marshall General.

Both the Union and the Confederacy raised large armies, and a significant proportion of both armies was used in combat units as infantry. Manpower was scarce and the Union Army conceived of the notion of generating manpower for military police service by using army veterans who had been wounded. In doing so, able-bodied men could be used in combat units. In April of 1863, the War Department established a new military entity to be known as the Invalid Corps to be made up of soldiers who had been wounded in combat or incapacitated by disease and ". . . judged unfit for further frontline service . . ." (Wright, 1991, 6).

The label of "the Invalid Corps" was subsequently changed to that of "the Veterans' Reserve Corps." The assigned function of this unit was (U.S. Army Military Police School, 1975, 51):

. . . to retain the military services for garrison, hospital, and provost duty of that class of deserving officers and men who, from wounds received in action or disease contracted in the service, were unfit for further duty in the field. . . .

The Veterans' Corps initially wore distinctive sky-blue uniforms, but they easily became dirty. Also, the men wished to retain their identity as members of the army. Accordingly, the Corps was permitted to wear regular army uniforms (U.S. Army Military Police School, 1975, 51)

Battlefield losses on both sides were enormous and while "the disadvantages of using personnel unfit for field service were recognized, but the inability to secure manpower was so severe that fit men could not be spared for these functions" (Military Police School, 1948, 1–2). The need for personnel to perform military police duties was acute, however. Large armies can often be unruly armies, especially when not engaged in combat. Drunkenness, gambling, looting, being disorderly in places of public accommodation, "marauding," fighting, desertions and going AWOL, theft, and altercations with civilians were all endemic behavior among some elements of the military. In addition to dealing with such offenses, some elements of the Veterans' Corps were also sent to New York City to help suppress the massive Draft Riots that broke out there in July of 1863 (Wright, 1991, 6). Those soldiers who were performing military police duties had their work cut out for them.

There was another exigency that dictated the need for diligent and concerted military law enforcement. The Civil War produced the Lieber Code. Francis Lieber, a scholar regarding the history of the laws of warfare, was recruited by the U.S. government to help draft ". . . a code of regulations for the usages of War." Lieber produced a draft of such a code and it was later accepted and issued in May 1863 as General Orders No. 100. *Instructions for the Government of Armies of the United States in the Field* (Bryant, 1979, 25). This code called for the regulations of military behavior with a high degree of specificity. In order to enforce the regulations constituent to this code, an appropriate law enforcement system was required.

Another significant event in military justice also occurred early in the war—holding officers responsible for the misconduct and crimes committed by their men. As Taylor (1972, xviii) relates:

> The notion of command responsibility was plainly enunciated in General McClellan's order of 1861, to the Army of the Potomac, warning his officers that they would "be held responsible for punishing aggression by those under their command" and directing that military commissions be established to punish violations "of the established rules of warfare."

Commanders were now constrained to vigorously enforce the laws and regulations of war, particularly in regard to the mistreatment of civilians by soldiers under their command. Again, this policy necessitated the need for stricter enforcement of military law and the attendant requirement for military police to accomplish this. Toward this end, General McClellan authorized his division commanders to organize their own Provost Guard units within their division. This pattern of organization became the model for today's military police structure (Wright, 1991, 5).

As had been the case at the end of the Revolutionary War, when the Civil War was over, the office of the Provost Marshall General was abolished and the Veteran Reserve Corps and all other subordinate units had been disbanded. Again, military police work became the responsibility of unit commanders (Military Police School, 1948, 2; U.S. Army Military Police School, 1975, 51).

During the period following the Civil War up to the time of the Spanish-American War, military police work was largely handled by individual military units. When the Spanish-American War broke out, the army again had need of a more formally organized military police apparatus. Brigadier General Arthur MacArthur, (the father of Douglas MacArthur) was appointed Military Governor and Provost Marshall General of Manila in the Philippines. He, in turn, authorized military personnel ("military and native police") to make arrests for various offenses (U.S. Army Military Police School, 1975, 52).

Military Police in World War I

After the U.S. entered World War I, Major General Enoch H. Crowder was appointed as Provost Marshall General. The vast mobilization of American troops dictated the need for formal military police units to enforce order and military regulations. General John J. Pershing was sent to France to command the American Expeditionary Forces (AEF). Pershing, in turn, appointed a Provost Marshal of the AEF. In May of 1917, the War Department approved plans for the establishment of ". . . a headquarters and two military police companies, a total of 316 officers and men in each division" (Wright, 1991, 7). General Pershing later went on to establish large military police units (often battalions) in each Corps and Army. A Military Police training school was established in Autun, France, to provide the necessary skills to military police personnel. In May of 1918, the War Department established another military police organization, the Criminal Investigation Division (CID). Small CID squads were assigned to a variety of larger troop units to investigate crimes such as theft, black-market activities, and the illegal sale of government supplies, to mention but some (Wright, 1991, 7). During World War II, the military police began to wear a more distinctive uniform, including scarlet tabs under the collar brass, a military police brassard, and green and gold piping on the overseas cap (U.S. Army Military Police School, 1975, 53).

In addition to enforcing military laws and regulations, the military police in the AEF. had a formidable task in controlling traffic in the rear areas and to and from the front. Military police also had the responsibility of processing and guarding prisoners of war (some 48,000) (Wright, 1991, 9). By the end of the war, military police personnel had grown to a total of 40,000 enlisted men and 1400 officers. These were organized into 138 military police companies performing "routine" duties, 122 prisoner escort companies, and 8 criminal investigation companies (U.S. Army Military School, 1975, 54).

By the end of World War I, the need for a permanent Military Police Corps was very apparent and General Pershing requested that Brigadier General Henry H. Bandholtz, the Provost Marshal General of the AEF. draft a proposal to establish a permanent Military Police Corps and submit it to congress for approval. In this proposal, General Bandholtz spoke eloquently of the need for properly trained military police personnel. In this regard, he pointed out that (Military Police School, 1948, 2):

> Maintenance of a specially organized Military Police Corps, in our peacetime military establishment, with units that may be actively engaged in Military Police duties, particularly during maneuvers and field training, whose personnel shall be carefully selected and highly rained, Having such Esprit de Corps and intelligent appreciation of their functions as will enable the individual Military Police to perform his often delicate duties with assurance and certainty, yet without offense or embarrassment. Then in case of war, we will have the nucleus to supply instructors for needed expansion and trained units to be the first troops to report at any training area.

General Bandholz's proposal went unheeded. It was brought before Congress and failed to receive approval. The National Defense Act of 1920 did, however, make provision for a Military Police Corps. The act also established a Military Police Branch of the officers' Reserve Corps and from 1921 on, Reserve Officers were commissioned in that Branch (Military Police School, 1948, 2).

Once again military police responsibilities had to be handled by units themselves who simply designated certain officers and enlisted men in the unit to perform such duties. The Army recognized the need for a military police corps should war again break out and appropriate plans were made. In 1924, the army issued a directive for the "future organization of a Military Police Corps" (U.S. Army Military Police School, 1975, 55). An Acting Provost Marshal General of the Army was identified and in December of 1937 the army published the *War Department Basic Field Manual IX, Military Police*. World War II was imminent and the army was aware of the fact that if war broke out, upwards of 20,000 civilian aliens would have to be interned. In view of this and the impending mass mobilization of the armed forces, the office of the Provost Marshal General was established in July of 1941, and on September 26 of that year, the Corps of Military Police was ordered (U.S. Army Military Police School, 1975, 55).

Military mobilization had begun before the attack on Pearl Harbor and in view of the need for well-trained military police to support the massive build-up of troops, the army established the Military Police School in January of 1941 at Arlington Cantonment (Fort Myers), Virginia (U.S. Army Military Police School, 1975, 56). During the war, military police served in all theaters of operation performing a wide variety of duties, ranging from traffic control to guarding prisoners-of-war to fighting enemy airborne troops behind the lines (Wright, 1991, 10). One historical account (U.S. Army Military Police School, 1975, 56) relates that:

> In World War II the men of the Corps fought as infantry and performed as engineers. They landed on beachheads to organize traffic control, and when the enemy broke through allied positions, they fought rearguard actions. Remagen, Salerno, and Leyte, to name but a few, proved that being an MP was not just a "white glove" operation.

By the end of the war, the Military Police Corps had grown to a size of approximately 200,000 enlisted men and 9250 officers. Some 1150 Military Police Battalions and 900 other Military Police units had been activated (U.S. Army Military Police School, 1975, 56–57).

After World War II, the size of the military was greatly reduced, including the size of the Military Police Corps. Unlike after previous wars, the Corps was retained, as was the Military Police School and the office of the Provost Marshal General. By 1947, the Military Police Corp had shrunk to 2078 officers and 19,630 enlisted men (U.S. Army Military Police School, 1975, 57).

After only a short time the war in Korea broke out and the army, including the Military Police Corps, was committed to a "police action" in that country. Military police performed their usual duties but an interesting new responsibility was added to their mission—that of uncovering and suppressing black-market activities, and apprehending both military personnel and local civilians engaged in such illegal commerce. As Wright (1991, 11) described the situation:

> The Korean War also introduced a new duty for military police. The war witnessed a dramatic increase in black market activities associated with an army fighting in a third world nation. In previous decades control of the black market fell to civil affairs units, but the massiveness

of the problem that began to appear in 1951 quickly involved the resources of the military police and, eventually, the corps added control and eradication of black market activities to its list of responsibilities.

In Korea, military police personnel secured highways and bridges, controlled the traffic flow, protected vital installations, guarded prisoners-of-war, and fought with infiltrating enemy units in the rear areas.

After the cease-fire in Korea, military troops stayed on there and were stationed in other Southeast Asian countries such as in the Philippines, as well. By 1964, the U.S. military involvement in Vietnam was significant, and for the next several years enormous numbers of troops were sent there. This necessitated the need for large numbers of military police units. Military police personnel, as in previous wars, were involved in a very wide range of military duties and activities, such as locating and destroying enemy tunnels, supervising the movement of refugees, providing convoy security, and in some instances, became frontline fighters (Wright, 1991, 11). In this latter regard, during the Tet offensive in 1968, military personnel were heavily engaged in combat especially in and around the cities of Saigon and Que. It was claimed that a military police battalion saved Saigon, and a small detachment of military police successfully defended the U.S. Embassy from capture or destruction (U.S. Army Military Police School, 1975, 60).

Since Vietnam, military police have carried out both combat and support duties in the invasion of Grenada, Panama, the Gulf War, and the Balkans, and are now doing so in Iraq.

Contemporary Military Police Doctrine[1]

Although today's military police functions (missions) still incorporate the duties and responsibilities of the Revolutionary War Marechaussee Corps, the range of their functions has expanded and diversified considerably. According to Welter (2003), current military police functions (missions) as expounded in current military police doctrine include:

1. Maneuver and Mobility Support Operations
2. Area Security
3. Law and Order Operations
4. Internment and Resettlement Operations
5. Police Intelligence Operations

---

[1] In this section of the exposition, we draw very heavily on material on military police doctrine generated and sent to us by Major Douglas M. Welter, U.S.A.F. Doctrine Division, U.S. Army Military Police School. I have essentially quoted or paraphrased this material in its entirety. I am most indebted to Major Welter for his courtesy in supplying this information.

Each of these official functions encapsulates a number of subfunctions.

Maneuver and Mobility Support Operations
The U.S. Army today is an army of rapid mobility, as evident from the very swift movement of American forces from the border of Iraq to Baghdad. To accomplish this, the Army relies on vehicles in great numbers, and an efficient military police presence to oversee, expedite, and control the movement of vehicles (and personnel) throughout the area of operation. Toward this end, the military police will reconnoiter the proposed route of military forces, and regulate and enforce traffic rules and procedures to accomplish the swift movement of troops. The military police will also provide support for river crossing, breaching operations, and the passage through the lines. Stragglers and dislocated civilians can be an impediment to the swift movement of troops and the military police attempt to control such groups (Welter, 2003).

Area Security
Military police are responsible for defending military camps and bases and providing physical security for the military forces in such locations. They are to be particularly attentive to the security needs of critical assets and sites, and high-risk personnel. Component to this task is appropriate reconnaissance and surveillance activities. In the event of damage to the base, camp, or area (such as fire or explosion), the military police are responsible for expediting the efforts of response agencies (such as firefighters) through efficient traffic control and site protection. Terrorism or guerilla attacks often occur in rear areas and, accordingly, the military police are charged with the responsibilities of antiterrorism operations and tactical combat response force operations (Welter, 2003).

Law and Order Operations
As they have traditionally done, the military police enforce laws, regulations, and rules and attempt to prevent criminal acts. Where crimes do occur, appropriate military police personnel (e.g., a CID unit) will investigate the crime and apprehend offenders. In some circumstances, the military police assume customs' inspections responsibilities (Welter, 2003).

Internment and Resettlement Operations
The military police will take charge of and guard enemy prisoners-of-war, civilian internees, and high-risk detainees. They will also assume control of the local civilian population and resources in

some circumstances (in a combat situation, for example). Combat or the needs of the U.S. military forces may dictate the need for resettling dislocated civilians or relocating them from a given location. The military police will assume responsibility for such operations (Welter, 2003).

Police Intelligence Operations

The military police will take measures ". . . to collect, analyze and disseminate information from criminal activity, law enforcement, security operations, and other incidents" (Welter, 2003). Military police will also undertake criminal investigations, and analyze data and evidence obtained from such investigations. They will collect and assess police information. Additionally, they will "support intelligence preparation of the battlefield" (Welter, 2003).

Conclusion

The military police have proven to be a durable and efficient law enforcement apparatus, capable of performing a wide variety of purely military tasks and duties, in addition to maintaining law and order, and investigating criminal activities and apprehending offenders. Some researchers (Falcone and Smith, 2000, 247) have studied both civilian law enforcement agencies and the Army Military Police and have asserted that ". . . the MPC represents [as a multitasked police agency] a distinctive modal form of policing that has borrowed heavily, albeit, from preexisting models, especially the office of the county sheriff." They go on to suggest that:

However, given recent attempts at shifting the police paradigm toward community-oriented policing, the MPC serves as a model for selective adoption.

CLIFTON D. BRYANT

References and Further Reading

Bryant, C.D. 1979. *Khaki-Collar Crime*. New York, NY: The Free Press.
Falcone, D.N. and Smith, B.A. 2002. The army military police: A neglected policing model, *Police Quarterly*, 3 (3): 247–261, September.
Knudten, R.D. 1970. The system of military justice. *Crime in a Complex Society: An Introduction to Criminology*, Ch. 19. Homewood, IL: Dorsey Press.
Lamont-Brown, R. 1980. *Kempeitai: Japan's Dreaded Military Police*. Phoenix Mill, AZ: Sutton Publishing.
Maurer, M. 1964. Military justice under General Washington, *Military Affairs* 28 (Spring), 8–16.
Robinson, H.R. 1971. Caius Largennius, *The Universal Soldier,* Windrow, M. and Wilkinson, F. (Eds.), Garden City, NY: Doubleday, pp. 17–31.
Taylor, T. 1972. Forward, *The Law of War: A Documentary History*, Friedman, L. (Ed.), 2 vols. New York, NY: Random House, pp. xiii–xxv.
The Military Police School, 1948. *History, Corps of Military Police*. Fort Gordon, Georgia: Military Police School.
U.S. Army Military Police School, 1975. Military police corps history, *Military Police Law Enforcement Journal* (Fall), 50–61.
Wright, R.I., Jr. 1991. *Military Police*. Washington, DC: Center of Military History.

See also **Military Justice: Courts, The Law, and Punishment**

Military Justice: Courts, the Law, and Punishment

The military criminal justice system has historically been one of the largest systems of justice in the U.S. The original foundation of American military law and the military justice system was the 1774 British Articles of War. In fact, our first military justice codes, the American Articles of War and the Articles for the Government of the Navy, predated the Constitution and the Declaration of Independence. The military justice system and military courts were, therefore, in existence well before the founding fathers drafted Article III of the U.S. Constitution in 1787 creating the skeletal foundation of the American court system. Courts-martial were thus among the first courts in the colonies and the newly founded U.S.

Throughout the first 100 years of existence, the U.S. had a small standing army. Those who chose to serve in the military understood that they would fall under a different system of justice with different procedures and punishments than the civilian justice system. Military justice evolved through some revisions and amendments to the codes during this century, but the system remained largely unchanged.

The 20th century proved to be a fertile time for the military justice system to undergo radical changes. At the beginning of the 1900s, a large number of Americans served in the military during World War I. As a result of the war, there were reports of individuals who had bad experiences with the military justice system as it existed at that time. Despite these complaints there was little revision in the system. This was primarily owing to the fact that after the war the U.S. reverted to a small standing army. It was not until after World War II that major changes were called for in the military justice system. In World War II, 16 million men and women served in the armed forces, and there were approximately 2 million courts-martial convened during the war years. At that time, the military justice system looked quite different than it does today. The military justice system did not offer the accused service member the protections afforded by the civilian court system. It was a system foreign to many American citizens who had volunteered or been drafted for the war effort. There was general disapproval of the way criminal law was being applied in the military. Following the war, several organizations including the American Bar Association, the American Legion, and the Judge Advocate Association studied and made proposals to improve the military justice system. As a result, congressional hearings were held on the military legal system. After unification of the armed services under the Department of Defense in 1947, Secretary Forrestal, the first Secretary of Defense, decided that there should not be separate criminal law rules for the different branches of the service, and he advocated for a uniform code that would apply to each branch of the service. His efforts set the stage for a new uniform system of justice.

The foundation of military law is the Constitution of the U.S. The Constitution provides that Congress has responsibilities to make rules to regulate the military, and further establishes the president as the commander-in-chief of the armed forces. In 1950, Congress exercised its responsibilities over military justice by enacting the Uniform Code of Military Justice (UCMJ), which is codified in Title 10 of the U.S. Code, Sections 801 through 946. The UCMJ, which became effective in 1951, was a major revision to military criminal law and the military justice system. The UCMJ is essentially a complete set of criminal laws. It includes most crimes that are found in civilian criminal statutes such as rape, murder, drug use, etc., but also includes unique military crimes for which the civilian justice

system has no counterpart. For example, military crimes include such offenses as desertion, absence without leave, disrespect toward superiors, failure to obey orders, dereliction of duty, misbehavior before the enemy, spying, and espionage to name a few.

The UCMJ is implemented through executive orders of the president of the U.S. pursuant to his authority under Article 36, UCMJ (10 USC, Section 836). The executive orders of the president form a comprehensive volume of law known as the *Manual for Courts-Martial* (*MCM*), hereafter referred to as the *Manual*.

The UCMJ has been amended on a number of occasions since becoming law in 1951. Significant changes occurred in 1968 and 1983. These changes enhanced the role of the trial judge, and also introduced the requirement that a licensed attorney be appointed as defense counsel to represent the accused at a court-martial. The *Manual* was substantially revised in 1984, and the military rules of evidence (Mil.R.Evid.) were adopted for use at court-martial proceedings. The military rules of evidence are in essence a mirror image of the federal rules of evidence used in the federal court system. The 1984 revision of the *Manual* substantially reorganized the text to follow the procedural steps of the court-martial process, and renamed and renumbered the legal requirements into what are now the rules for courts-martial (RCMs). The *Manual* is separated into five parts: Part I, the preamble; Part II, rules for court-martial; Part III, military rules of evidence; Part IV, punitive articles; and Part V, nonjudicial punishment procedures.

Like its civilian counterpart, one of the basic requirements of military law is the concept of jurisdiction. A military court-martial must have both personal jurisdiction over the accused and subject matter jurisdiction over the offense. Subject matter jurisdiction is easily shown by reference to Part IV of the *Manual*, which contains the punitive articles of the UCMJ. The punitive articles consist of Articles 77–134, which are a comprehensive list of the prohibited crimes for military personnel. Personal jurisdiction is established by reference to Article 2 of the UCMJ (Section 802 of Title 10 U.S. Code). Article 2 lists 12 categories of individuals who are subject to trial by court-martial. Court-martial jurisdiction is most commonly exercised over active-duty personnel, and personal jurisdiction begins with enlistment or commissioning and terminates with the delivery of a valid discharge certificate. The remaining categories under Article 2 cover such individuals as reserves, retired, cadets, prisoners, members of the Public Health Service, etc. Another unique aspect of military jurisdiction is that it necessarily has worldwide application. That is, the UCMJ applies wherever the military is deployed.

In the military, commanders play a unique role in the legal system. Unlike the civilian justice system, the military disciplinary system is initiated by a report of a suspected violation of the UCMJ to the service-members commanding officer. In the civilian criminal justice system, reporting and investigating crime is a function of federal, state, or local police. Once the investigation is done it is turned over for prosecution to the district attorney on the local level or the U.S attorney on the federal level. The district attorney or the U.S. attorney in the civilian system of justice has the ultimate discretion on whether or not a case is processed though the system. In the military, the commander fills this role. When the commander is acting in this role he or she is referred to as the "convening authority," which indicates that the commander has the authority and ability to convene (create) a court-martial.

The commanding officer may receive reports of an offense from various sources. They can originate from the military police, other specialized military law enforcement agencies, local law enforcement, federal law enforcement, or other members of the military. Upon receipt of a report of a suspected violation of the UCMJ the commander is required to conduct a "preliminary inquiry" into the allegations against a member of the command. Procedurally this inquiry is required under the rules for courts-martial (RCM 303). The commander can conduct this inquiry personally, appoint someone else in the command to do it, or as happens in very serious cases, request assistance from civilian or military criminal investigative agencies. The inquiry can be very informal or in more serious cases can result in a formal written report of investigation.

When the commander finishes the preliminary inquiry a decision must be made on how to resolve the case. The military commander has an arsenal of disciplinary alternatives available. These alternatives include a decision to take no action, administrative sanctions such as admonition or reprimand, punishment under Article 15, UCMJ, or the initiation of a court-martial. If the commander decides that a court-martial is appropriate charges will be "preferred" that is similar to "swearing out a complaint" in civilian jurisdictions. This preferral of charges initiates the court-martial process.

Article 15, UCMJ, or nonjudicial punishment (NJP), is the first formal procedure that may be used by a commander to discipline the members of the command. NJP proceedings are known by different terms among the services. The most common terms used to describe this procedure are "Article 15," "Office Hours," or "Captain's Mast." Article 15 is designed to allow the commander to discipline members of the command for "minor offenses" under the UCMJ. Punishments awarded by a commander using Article 15 are relatively minor and may consist of loss of pay, restriction, and under some circumstances reduction in rank. Article 15 punishment is administrative in nature and does not result in a federal conviction like a court-martial. Therefore, the servicemember is not entitled to an attorney at this proceeding. Also, the servicemember may refuse Article 15 punishment, in which case the commander will either refer the case to a court-martial, decide to drop the case, or use some alternative form of punishment. The one exception to the right to refuse Article 15 is if the servicemember is attached to a ship or vessel in which case there is no right to refuse.

In the course of the investigation or preliminary inquiry an attempt may be made to question the accused servicemember about the alleged offense. The military justice system provides an accused rights and due process that in many ways are superior to those provided a defendant in civilian criminal courts. Pursuant to Article 31, UCMJ, servicemembers have a right against self-incrimination, and are entitled to be informed of the suspected offense before questioning begins. In addition to protections against self-incrimination, servicemembers have a right to free military counsel when questioned as a suspect.

In the event that a commander decided that a court-martial is appropriate the commander may order the accused servicemember into pretrial confinement. Under the UCMJ, any military officer can order an enlisted member into confinement if the officer has information that the servicemember has committed an offense. Pretrial confinement is only appropriate when the commander feels that the accused servicemember is a flight risk, or that there is some reason to believe that the member will commit further misconduct or influence potential witnesses. The military system of pretrial confinement does not provide for bail like the civilian counterpart. Therefore, there are some strict requirements that must be followed with regard to pretrial confinement. The military justice system follows the civilian requirement that a review of the decision to confine the individual be conducted within 48 hours. Thereafter, within 72 hours, the military member is entitled to have his or her commanding officer review whether continued confinement is appropriate. If someone other than the commanding officer confined the member originally, and the commanding officer's review was actually conducted within 48 hours, then the commanding officer's review can serve to satisfy both review requirements. Within 7 days of confinement, and after the commander reviews the confinement and decides that further confinement is necessary, the accused servicemember is entitled to have the case reviewed by a neutral magistrate called the initial review officer (IRO). The IRO can order the accused servicemember released from confinement, or if deemed appropriate, retain the servicemember in confinement pending court-martial. Once the case is referred to a military judge for trial the accused can file a motion requesting that the judge release him or her from pretrial confinement.

After the preliminary inquiry, if the commander decides that a court-martial is warranted, there are three levels of court-martial to choose from. The first level of court-martial is the summary court-martial. This court is a one-officer court in which the officer appointed to conduct the court acts as prosecutor, defense counsel, and judge. The summary court-martial is designed for minor offenses and there is a jurisdictional limit on punishment. The maximum punishment of a summary court-martial is two-thirds loss of pay for 1 month, confinement for 30 days, and a reduction to the lowest enlisted grade. In the case where the enlisted member is above the fourth pay grade, a reduction of only one grade is authorized. Much like NJP a summary court-martial is administrative in nature and a finding of guilty does not carry the stigma of a conviction. Owing to the administrative nature of this proceeding the accused servicemember is not entitled to a military lawyer, but the accused may hire a civilian lawyer at his or her own expense. The servicemember can refuse a summary court-martial, in which case the commander will further consider the alternatives of dropping the case or referring the case to a special or general court-martial.

The second level of court-martial is a special court-martial. This is a court of federal criminal jurisdiction, and conviction by this court results in a federal criminal conviction. The special court-martial is composed of not less than three members. Members in a military court-martial are the equivalent of jury members in the civilian court system. In the case of an enlisted accused, one-third of the members can be enlisted members. If desired, the accused servicemember must request the enlisted members, and all members detailed to the court must be senior in grade to the accused. At a special court-martial a military judge presides over the court in the same manner as a civilian judge. If requested by the accused, the military judge may hear the case alone, in which case the judge becomes the trier of fact. In the case of a trial by a judge alone, if the accused is convicted, the military judge will award the sentence. The court is guided by the military rules of evidence and the procedures used at trial are identical to any criminal court in the U.S. This is the first level of court-martial at which the accused servicemember is entitled to a military lawyer at no expense to the accused. The accused servicemember may request a particular military attorney and that attorney will be provided if the request is considered reasonable and the attorney is available. The accused may also retain a civilian attorney at no expense to the government. The maximum punishment that a special court-martial may adjudge is: confinement for 1 year, forfeiture of two-thirds pay for 1 year, reduction to the lowest pay grade (E-1), and a bad conduct discharge. Unlike in a civilian court, in a military court-martial that is composed of members, if there is a conviction, the members decide on the sentence.

The most severe form of court-martial is the general court-martial, which is a court of unlimited jurisdiction for punishment purposes. The only limit on punishment at a general court-martial is the prescribed maximum that is listed in the *Manual* for the offense charge. For the most severe crimes the death penalty is an authorized punishment.

Unless the accused waives this right, no charge may be referred to a general court-martial until a thorough and impartial investigation into the basis for the charge has been made. This pretrial proceeding is known as an "Article 32" pretrial investigation or preliminary hearing. The Article 32 investigation essentially serves the equivalent function of a grand jury hearing in civilian jurisdictions. Normally an officer in the grade of O-3 or above is appointed by the convening authority to conduct this hearing. The accused has the right to a free military lawyer at the Article 32 and has the right to present evidence at the investigation. At the conclusion of the investigation the Article 32 officer makes recommendation to the convening authority as to the form of the charges and what type, if any, disciplinary action is recommended. Unlike a grand jury the recommendations of the Article 32 officer are advisory in nature and may be disregarded by the convening authority. A general court-martial is presided over by a military judge and consists of no less than five members. The accused servicemember has the same counsel and forum rights at a general court-martial as he or she has at a special court-martial.

If a general or special court-martial convicts an accused, there are several avenues of appeal available. A unique concept in military law is that the convening authority is required to review the record of trial and approve the court-martial. During this process the accused can submit additional matters in the way of clemency under RCM 1105/1106. The convening authority has the authority to take action on the charges and the sentence. The convening authority may approve the court entirely, or disapprove the findings on any or all charges. In addition, the convening authority may reduce the sentence as a matter of clemency. The convening authority is prohibited from attempting to change a finding of not guilty to guilty, or to increase the sentence in any way. In many cases, (approximately 90%) the convening authority and the accused may have entered into a pretrial agreement (plea bargain) prior to trial. In this case the accused has agreed to plead guilty to certain charges and in exchange the convening authority has agreed to limit the punishment. In this case, the convening authority would be required by law to reduce any sentence awarded to one that is no more severe than what was agreed to in the pretrial agreement.

If there is an approved sentence from a court-martial, which includes a sentence of death, a punitive discharge, or confinement for 1 year or more, the courts of criminal appeal of the servicemembers branch of service will automatically review the case. The court of criminal appeals can correct any legal error it finds, and it can reduce what it considers to be an excessive sentence.

The U.S. court of appeals for the armed forces (CAAF) consists of five civilian judges, appointed by the president and confirmed by Congress. The CAAF is responsible for overseeing the military justice system. In all but death penalty cases, which it reviews automatically, and cases certified by the judge advocate general, CAAF chooses upon petitions for review which cases it will consider, similar to federal courts of appeal.

Military members convicted of crimes may petition the U.S. Supreme Court for a review of their case. The military accused has a right, without cost, to the services of a military appellate defense counsel at all appellate review levels, including review by the Supreme Court. The military accused may petition the U.S. Supreme Court for a writ of *certiorari* without prepayment of fees and costs.

MARK STEVENS

References and Further Reading

Davidson, M.J. 1999. *A Guide to Military Criminal Law*, Annapolis, MD: United States Naval Institute Press.

Filbert, B.G. and Kaufman, A.G. 1998. *Naval Law: Justice and Procedure in the Sea Services*, 3rd ed., Annapolis, MD: United States Naval Institute Press.

Fidell, E.R. and Sullivan, D.H., (Eds.) 2002. *Evolving Military Justice*, Annapolis, MD: United States Naval Institute Press.

Lurie, J. 2001. *Military Justice in America: The U.S. Court of Appeals for the Armed Forces, 1775–1980,* abridged, revised edition, University Press of Kansas.

Rant, J. and Blackett, J., (Ed). 2003. *Courts Martial, Discipline, and the Criminal Process in the Armed Forces*, New York, NY: Oxford University Press.

Saltzburg, S.A., et al. 1994. *Military Evidentiary Foundations*, 2nd ed., Miamisburg, OH: Lexis Publishing.

Saltzburg, S.A., et al. 1997. *Military Rules of Evidence Manual*, 4th ed., Miamisburg, OH: Lexis Publishing.

Schlueter, D.A. 1999. *Military Criminal Justice: Practice and Procedure,* 5th ed., Miamisburg, OH: Lexis Publishing.

Shanor, C.A. and Hogue, L.L. 1996. *Military Law in a Nut Shell*, 2nd ed., St. Paul, MN: West Publishing Co.

See also **Military Justice: the Police; Warfare and Criminal Behavior**

Miller, Walter B. *See* **Subcultural Theories of Criminal Behavior**

Miranda Rights *See* **Arrest; Due Process**

Mistake of Fact as a Criminal Defense to Criminal Liability

A person is generally not guilty of a criminal offense unless that person acted with purpose, knowingly, recklessly, or negligently (Section 2.02(1), American Law Institute, *Model Penal Code and Commentaries* [1985]). Occasionally, persons may argue that they are mistaken as to a fact in existence at the time they committed an act and may then be exempt from criminal liability. Proof of such a mistake of fact can be used to prove that the person did not possess the mental state required for the commission of a particular crime.

A good example of a mistake of fact appears in the movie *Eight Heads in a Duffel Bag*. The two main characters in that movie both travel on the same airplane and both carry duffel bags that are identical on the outside. One character accidentally takes the other character's duffel bag upon departing from the plane and claiming his baggage. Although that character certainly took something that did not belong to him, which is a violation of the law, the argument can be made that he was not guilty of a crime because of his mistaken belief that the bag he was claiming was his own, not that of another person. The character was not purposefully attempting to steal luggage and did not know that he was stealing the luggage. The questions to be considered in instances such as this are whether the person was reckless or negligent in taking the luggage. Perhaps the person could have opened the luggage to see what was in it or placed some other identifying characteristic on the outside of the luggage prior to traveling, such as a tag with his name on it, in order to verify that the luggage was his before taking it with him. Although the *Model Penal Code* sets forth some instances where mistake of fact is a defense to a criminal action, state courts vary widely on whether a mistake of fact can be successfully used as a defense to a crime.

Mistake of fact is often given as a jury instruction, so that the jury is able to determine whether they believe a mistake of fact existed that is sufficient to relieve a person from criminal liability. Such a jury instruction was permitted in a California case where James Eugene Bray was being charged with violating a statute that prohibited being a felon in possession of a firearm. *People v. Bray*, 124 Cal. Rptr. 913 (Cal. App. 3d., 1975). Bray had run into some trouble with the law previously in Kansas but was not sure whether his Kansas conviction had been for a felony or not. In fact, even the California district attorney had some difficulty determining the status of the Kansas conviction. Thus, the court determined that an instruction allowing the jury to determine whether Bray's mistake of fact should relieve him from criminal liability was appropriate.

The use of mistake of fact defenses is often set forth in statutory rape cases, because statutory rape involves sexual intercourse with a person who is below a particular age. Some states provide a cutoff age under which a person cannot argue that they believed the child was old enough to consent, regardless of what the victim may have stated his or her age to be. In other words, in some states, a person can argue that they believed the victim was above a certain age, and that their mistake of fact as to the victim's age means that they did not intend to violate the law, and are therefore not criminally liable. Some states provide that the victim must have held himself or herself out to be a particular age in order for a mistake of fact defense to be valid. In these states, a mistake of fact defense is not valid regardless of the circumstances. Some states provide for strict liability in statutory rape cases, meaning that the person is guilty of a criminal offense regardless of how old they believed or were led to believe the victim was.

States that allow mistake of fact as a defense to criminal liability may require the defendant to demonstrate that the mistake of fact was reasonable. However, when a crime requires that specific intent be present, even a mistake of fact that a reasonable person might not have made could be an acceptable defense.

A second item often required by the courts in using a mistake of fact defense is that the conduct of the defendant must have been legal and moral had the facts been as the defendant believed. For example, in *White v. State*, 185 N.E. 64 (Ohio, 1933), a defendant was charged with the abandonment of his pregnant wife. The defendant argued as a defense that he was unaware that his wife was pregnant when he abandoned her. The court determined that the defendant would have violated his duty to his wife by abandoning her even if she had not been pregnant, and thus did not allow the defendant to use mistake of fact as a defense. Similarly, the *Model Penal Code* does not provide for the defense of mistake of fact if the defendant would have been guilty of a criminal offense even if he or she had not been mistaken as to the facts. However, the *Model Penal Code* does prescribe that the person would be charged with a lower offense if that offense would have been the only charge that could have been brought against the person had the facts been as the person believed.

TINA M. FRYLING

References and Further Reading

Dressler, J. 2001. *Understanding Criminal Law,* Miamisburg, OH: Lexis Publishing Co., 3rd ed.
Loewy, A.H. 2000. *Criminal Law in a Nutshell,* Saint Paul, MN: West Publishing Co., 3rd ed.

See also **Accident as a Defense to Criminal Liability**

Money Laundering

Introduction

Efforts to curb the laundering of criminally derived incomes became a high priority for governments and law enforcement agencies only during the 1990s. (The term itself is believed to date from the efforts to cover up political donations and bribes at the time of the Watergate scandal during President Richard Nixon's administration.) So it looks as if money laundering is a "new crime," somehow connected with globalization and electronic payments systems. Yet laundering has been going on since the Middle Ages, when merchants avoided the ban on usury (excessive interest) by inflating exchange rates or inventing late payment charges to compensate for any interest payments due. These subtleties have their modern equivalents in laundering.

Although money laundering may be an ancient activity, it was not until the 1980s that the act of attempting to launder criminally derived income and wealth was made a crime as such. The U.S. and U.K. were among the nations first to criminalize, but encouraged by a panoply of international bodies spawned by the Organization for Economic Cooperation and Development (OECD), as well as by the Council of Europe, the European Union and the UN, huge pressure has been exerted on all nations both to criminalize money laundering for all crimes (not just drugs) and to introduce a raft of measures aimed at making concealment of identity difficult ("Know your customer" rules) and at requiring financial institutions and—in many countries—lawyers, accountants, casinos, even car dealers to report (1) "suspicious transactions" and (2) in the U.S. and Australia, all cash deposits and wire transfers over a certain limit. Since 2000, this pressure has included economic sanctions against 15 noncooperating countries and territories, with threatened escalation unless they improved their laws and regulatory practices, as many did.

Underlying the criminalization of money laundering is the theory that strip away the proceeds of crime, and people will neither choose to become career or "organized" criminals (for they will have no hope of keeping the profits), nor will they have ready access to working criminal capital to finance crimes, as others will not find it profitable to lend for projects whose proceeds have a strong chance of being confiscated. Domestically, money-laundering laws lead to tougher sentences and more plea bargaining pressures; inter-nationally, their necessity worldwide is a reason for reducing sovereignty rights. Associated asset forfeiture laws have become core finance for antinarcotics efforts in the U.S., though less so elsewhere, and when—as in the U.S., the Irish Republic, and New South Wales, Australia, for example—proceedings can be taken on a civil standard of proof *irrespective of conviction or even prosecution*, this is a way of getting at the key organizers of crime popularly termed "Mr. Bigs."

Unless they simply spend or give away their crime proceeds soon after committing crimes, rational enterprise criminals of every sort—corporate embezzlers, drugs traffickers, stock fraudsters, and transnational corporations bribing foreign public officials—must launder the money flow for two reasons. The first is that the money trail itself can become evidence against the perpetrators of the offense; the second is that they may wish to preserve their crime proceeds against the risk of forfeiture or taxation. Money laundering should be construed as a dynamic three-stage process that requires: (1) moving the funds from direct association with the crime, whether within the country or internationally; (2) disguising the trail to make pursuit harder or impossible; and (3) making the money available to the criminal once again with its occupational and geographic origins hidden, so that it can be used as "clean money." The latter stage makes it different from merely hiding or using smuggled funds, though under Anglo-American law, anything more concealing than putting proceeds into a sock constitutes criminal laundering.

Alternatively viewed, the Financial Action Task Force divided money laundering into placement (the placing of cash into the legal economy—including simple bank deposits—or smuggling it out of the country); layering (separation from source by creating complex concealment structures such as interprivate corporation transfers); and integration (placing laundered funds back into the economy as legitimate funds).

The simplest forms of laundering take place only in the country where the crimes have been committed. If the sums are modest and infrequent, launderers can simply use their illegal cash to purchase winning racing or lottery tickets, usually paying the true winner a premium (unless they have inside information), and then present the ticket for payment, showing it as legitimate earnings from gambling.

In more sophisticated schemes, the person seeking to launder money buys spot and sells forward, or the reverse: one transaction records a capital gain, the other a capital loss. The broker destroys the record of the losing transaction, and the launderer leaves with capital gains. The cost is the double commission plus any "bonus" to ensure the broker's silence. Alternatively, they buy real estate or high-value items such as yachts, paying a publicly recorded price well below the real market value, using formal bank instruments and legitimately earned money. The rest of the purchase price is paid covertly in cash. The property is then resold for the full market value and the money recouped, with the illegal component now appearing to be capital gains on a real estate deal. (If the person is more concerned with lifestyle enjoyment, he or she can simply acquire a company from a jurisdiction friendly to the launderers to purchase the yacht, and no one will be able to discover who the beneficial owners of the company are.)

However, to handle large, ongoing flows of criminal money, cash-based retail service businesses are favored, such as laundries, video-game arcades, bars, and restaurants. The launderers inflate the apparent sales of the business, and—if they can afford to—legitimate the funds by paying tax on them. Whether funds transfers are international depends partly on the skills and contacts of the offenders, and partly on how much attention they expect to receive from domestic and international law enforcement: practices friendly to money laundering in *any* of the jurisdictions through which funds pass can spell safety. In short, the measures criminals take to conceal proceeds of crime interact dynamically with the efforts that law makers and law (including regulatory) enforcement make to deal with them.

MICHAEL LEVI

References and Further Reading

Blum, J., Levi, M., Naylor, R.T., and Williams, P. 1998. Financial havens, banking secrecy and money-laundering, issue 8, *UNDCP Technical Series*, New York, NY: United Nations.
Blumenson, E. and Nilsen, E. 1998. Policing for profit: The drug war's hidden economic agenda, *University of Chicago Law Review*, 65.
van, Duyne, P.C. 1998. Money-laundering: Pavlov's dog and beyond. *The Howard Journal of Criminal Justice*, 4.
Financial Action Task Force Reports. Available at www.oecd.int.
Gilmore, W. 1999. When accessed? *Dirty Money: the Evolution of Money-Laundering Counter-Measures*, Amsterdam, The Netherlands: Council of Europe Press.
Levi, M. 1997. Evaluating the 'New Policing': Attacking the money trail of organised crime, *Australian and New Zealand Journal of Criminology*, 30.
Levi, M. 1991. Pecunia non olet: cleansing the money launderers from the Temple, *Crime, Law, & Social Change*, 16.
Naylor, R.T. 1999. Washout: A critique of follow-the-money methods in crime control policy, *Crime, Law & Social Change*, 32.
Rider, B. 1998. Crusade against money laundering: time to think! *European Journal of Law Reform*, 1.

See also **Bribery and Graft; Drug Control Policy: Enforcement, Interdiction, and the War on Drugs; Drug Trafficking as an Occupation; Forgery; Terrorism**

Moral Panic

The concept of moral panic has furnished criminologists with a useful tool to understand crime, deviance, social problems, collective behavior, and social movements, especially in the context of pseudo-disasters. Whereas Jock Young is credited with the first use of the term, the idea of moral panic developed rapidly in the work of Stanley Cohen, who offered its enduring definition. Moral panic has occurred when: "A condition, episode, person or group of persons emerges to become defined as a threat to societal values and interest; its nature is presented in a stylized and stereotypical fashion by the mass media and politicians" (1972, 9). Cohen learned that moral panic was a key component of a moral crusade, a social enterprise he discovered while studying societal reaction to youths in England. In his groundbreaking treatise, *Folk Devils and Moral Panics* (1972, see 2003), Cohen explored the roles of the public, media, and politicians in constructing heightened concern over British youths in 1964, when the Mods and Rockers were depicted as threats not only to public peace but the social order as well. Together, the media and members of the political establishment publicized exaggerated claims of the dangers posed by the Mods and Rockers; in turn, such claims were used to justify enhanced police powers and greater investment in the traditional criminal justice apparatus.

Since the 1970s, the concept of moral panic has enjoyed growing popularity among scholars studying the social construction of crime. Among the more recent examples of moral panic are those involving crack cocaine (Chiricos, 1996; Reinarman and Levine, 1997), crack mothers (Humphries, 1999), street gangs (Zatz, 1987; McCorkle and Miethe, 1998), satanic ritual abuse in day care centers (Best, 1990), graffiti (Ferrell, 1993), flag burning (Welch, 2000), immigrants (Welch, 2002), and wilding (a form of youth violence associated with the attack of the Central Park jogger in 1989; Welch, Price, and Yankey, 2002, also see Hall, Critcher, Jefferson, Clarke, and Roberts, 1978; Welch, Fenwick, and Roberts, 1997).

The moral panic perspective explains turbulent societal reactions to crime, particularly those producing a disaster mentality in which there is a widespread perception that society is endangered. As moral panic mounts, there is a sense of urgency to do something now or else society will suffer even graver consequences later, compelling social policy to undergo significant transformation in a rash attempt to diffuse the putative threat. Moral panic typically manifests as intense public hostility and condemnation aimed at a particular group; correspondingly, it strengthens the social control apparatus with more criminal justice legislation that produces more penalties, police, and prisons.

There are five criteria of moral panic: concern, hostility, consensus, disproportionality, and volatility. Moreover, for a moral panic to exist, each of the five indicators must be supported by a high degree of convincing evidence.

Concern

The first component of moral panic is a heightened concern over the behavior of others and the consequences such conduct is believed to have on society. Criminologists insist that concern ought to be verifiable in the form of an observed and measurable manifestation, such as public opinion polls, public commentary in the form of media attention, proposed legislation, and social movement activity. Although in many cases the level of concern does not have to reach that of fear, there must be a perception that a threat exists.

American preoccupation with flag burning in the late 1980s provides evidence confirming moral panic (Welch, 2000). Public opinion polls showed that citizens were increasingly concerned for the Stars and Stripes and even supported legislation to protect it from desecration. In a national poll conducted shortly after the *Texas v. Johnson* (109 S.Ct., 1989) (granting flag burning protected speech status), 65% of Americans disagreed with the Supreme Court and 71% supported a constitutional amendment to protect the flag from desecration (*Newsweek*, July 3, 1989). Similarly,

a *New York Times*/CBS News poll found that 83% of its respondents believed that flag burning should be against the law and 59% of those polled endorsed a constitutional amendment (Greenhouse, 1990). Media attention directed at flag burning exploded, resulting in unprecedented levels of news coverage. Moral panic over flag burning also manifested in political debate, culminating in extensive and expensive congressional activity leading to additional laws and penalties designed to punish and deter flag desecration. Conservative columnist Cal Thomas likened the *Johnson* decision to "protecting pornography" that "inspires serial killers" and "tolerance of marijuana," which had "paved the way for crack cocaine," and even Elvis Presley, who had "opened the door through which heavy metal and garbage-mouth groups walked" (*New York Daily News*, August 12, 1989).

Hostility

Criminologists note that moral panic arouses hostility toward an identifiable group or category of people who, in turn, are vilified as social outcasts. Members of this category are collectively designated as the enemy of respectable society and their behavior is seen as harmful, or threatening to the values, interests, and possibly the very existence of at least as sizeable a segment of society. Unlike bona fide social problems that do not direct blame at any one group of people, such as the aftermath of natural disasters, moral panic shifts blame to unpopular people who become scapegoats and folk devils. According to Goode and Ben-Yehuda (1994), "not only must the condition, phenomenon, or behavior be seen as threatening, but a clearly identifiable group in or segment of the society must be seen as *responsible* for the threat." Moreover, a distinction is made between "us"—good, decent, respectable people—and "them"—deviants, undesirables, outsiders, villains, criminals, and disreputable people. Hostility contained in moral panic manifests in several ways. Frequently, those groups blamed for a putative social problem are criminalized, pathologized, marginalized, and scapegoated.

In an extensive study of moral panic over flag burning, Welch (2000) found that protesters who burned the flag were quickly labeled enemies of respectable society and their conduct viewed widely as offensive to the majority of Americans who revere Old Glory. Under certain circumstances, such hostility goes beyond rhetoric of aggression, manifesting in violence and victimization against flag desecrators. Occasionally, such vigilante justice is condoned not only by citizens but lawmakers as well. Consider Pennsylvania's "beat a flag burner" bill, in which a fine of 1 dollar would have replaced the existing penalties of assault and aggravated assault (i.e., a 10-year maximum prison sentence and a fine of $25,000). Although the Pennsylvania resolution failed, similar proposals were introduced—albeit unsuccessfully—in Colorado, Georgia, and Tennessee. Still, the Louisiana "beat a flag burner" bill passed the House by a 54–39 vote in 1990; that measure proposed to lower to $25 the fine for assaulting flag burners, while the existing penalty for simple assault is a $500 fine (*New York Newsday* 1989, December 16).

Consensus

In becoming a recognizable phenomenon, moral panic requires a certain consensus among members of society. By no means does such agreement need to be universal, or even representative of the majority. Still, there must be a widespread belief that the problem at hand is real, it poses a threat to society, and something should be done to correct it. Moral panic comes in different sizes: some gripping the vast majority of the general public while others affect smaller segments or regions of society.

Disproportionality

Another key component of moral panic is its disproportionality, suggesting that the perceived danger is greater than the potential harm. In essence, moral panic means that there is a consensus among many members of society that a more sizeable number of individuals is engaged in the behavior in question than actually are. Furthermore, the threat, danger, or damage believed caused by the behavior is far more substantial than a realistic appraisal could sustain.

Whereas it might be difficult to determine whether a social problem has been blown out of proportion, there are four indicators of disproportion: namely, exaggerated figures, fabricated figures, the existence of other harmful conditions, and changes over time. The presence of these indicators of disproportion coupled with stylization and political hyperbole suggest that persons and groups involved in making claims engage in disinformation campaigns whereby distorted messages are disseminated for purposes influencing public and political opinion, which, in turn, alters legislation and its enforcement.

Exaggerated Figures
The criterion of disproportion is met when figures and statistics cited to measure the scope of the problem are grossly exaggerated. Huge discrepancies among figures usually points to the emergence of moral panic; suffice to say that bona fide social problems do not

need to be exaggerated in order to convince the public that something should be done (e.g., the Great Depression, the polio epidemic). In a recent analysis of moral panic over immigrants in the U.S., Welch (2002) provides numerous examples of how exaggerated figures stoke fear of outsiders. For instance, former presidential candidate Pat Buchanan proclaimed that the U.S. is undergoing an invasion of illegal aliens who enter from Mexico: "That is what's taking place when one, two, or three million people walk across our borders every year" (Holmes, 1996). The figures on illegal entries commonly are exaggerated, thus fueling public anxiety over immigrants and the perception that American society is under siege.

Similarly, as California's controversial Proposition 187 gained momentum in 1994, Governor Wilson announced that Los Angeles County "had spent $946 million in 1991–92 on services to recent immigrants, adding that the county had only collected $139 of the $4.3 billion a year in federal, state, and local taxes paid by immigrants" (Flanigan, 1993, D1). Wilson's figures on social spending were immediately contradicted by reports published by governmental and nongovernmental groups, including the Urban Institute and the RAND Institute. Interestingly, the California Senate chided politicians "for their failure to heed admonitions that scapegoating immigrants won't begin to solve the state's economic woes" (Mata, 1998, 152; see Calavita, 1996; Welch, 2003).

Fabricated Figures
At times, claims-makers contribute to public anxiety by publicizing false claims about the putative problem, often by generating and disseminating statistics and figures. Upon closer scrutiny, however, the authenticity of such information is highly suspect. In a study of moral panic over youth violence, Welch et al. (2002) discovered an example of how government leaders manipulate public fear of crime for political leverage. In New York City amid the wilding controversy, City Councilman Andrew Stein issued the following claim without any official documentation that might verify the incident: "On Halloween last year, the fear of mob violence kept many New Yorkers at home. Thousands of teenagers went on bloody rampages in several boroughs. They moved spontaneously in packs of 20 or 30 and assaulted people at random" (Stein, 1990, 27).

The Existence of Other Harmful Conditions
The existence of other conditions contributing to the overall harm is another indicator of disproportionality. Consider, for instance, moral panic over crack

(cocaine) babies in which claims-makers deliberately failed to acknowledge that pregnant addicts also consumed alcohol, nicotine, and other drugs that adversely affected the health of the fetus; moreover, many pregnant addicts had poor nutrition and inadequate prenatal care. To place the blame solely on crack cocaine while ignoring those other harmful conditions is politically manipulative, especially if such claims about the dangers of crack are used as a basis for public policy aimed at criminalizing drug use rather than developing medical and health care programs for addicted mothers and their children (Goode, 1993; Humphries, 1999).

Changes over Time

"If the attention paid to a given condition at one point in time is vastly greater than that paid to it during a previous or later time, without any corresponding increase in objective seriousness, then, once again, the criterion of disproportionality may be said to have been met" (Goode and Ben-Yehuda, 1994, 44). In the 1980s, for example, there were widespread claims that drug abuse was on the rise, thus contributing to a series of antidrug laws and enhanced enforcement. Conversely, studies had shown that drug abuse among Americans had actually declined (Goode, 1990).

Stylization and Political Hyperbole

As is typically the case with moral panic, the threat posed by a social problem is not merely exaggerated but also stylized. By sensationalizing the problem of crime, it is hyped in a stylized manner that feeds public anxiety, reproducing criminal stereotypes predicated on race and ethnicity. Hyperbole also manifests in apocalyptic metaphors characteristic of a disaster mentality, resorting to catastrophic rhetoric emblematic in moral panic. Amid moral panic over immigrants, Welch (2002) noted that nativists and immigration restrictionists issued books with catastrophic titles, such as *The Immigration Invasion* (Lutton and Tanton, 1994), *The Immigration Time Bomb: The Fragmenting of America* (Lamm and Imhoff, 1985), *Will America Drown? Immigration and the Third World Population Explosion* (Dalton, 1993), *The Path to National Suicide: An Essay on Immigration and Multiculturalism* (Auster, 1990).

Another manifestation of disproportionality is the use of hyperbole in describing the identifiable group blamed for the problem in question. Cohen (1972, 2003) reminded us that the media relies on hyperbole in a manner that stylizes the image of a threatening group, and in doing so, adds to its menacing reputation.

In their study of moral panic over youth violence, Welch et al. (2002) found that the media delivered a steady flow of metaphors, depicting the suspects in wilding incidents as "urban terrorists" and "packs of animals." Just as the word "pack" projects a danger to society, the term "gang" also implies a similar threat. For dramatic effect, the press further stylized wilding by using the term "gang" rather than "group" in its description of several participants involved in the same crime. Whereas "group" appears to be a neutral term, "gang" is heavily loaded, conjuring potent images of predatory urban street gangs. A chief reason why a gang seems more menacing than a mere collection or group of lawbreakers is that the term implies that its members are organized, and thus more committed to violence and mayhem (Best and Hutchinson, 1996; Best, 1999; Glassner, 1999).

Because of the weight of disproportionality and stylization, moral panic typically evokes claims that certain forms of crime (e.g., youth violence) pose a much more sinister threat to the prevailing social order than is realized initially. For many claims-makers, crime is symbolic of a deeper moral decline in civilized society, a belief that punctuates the disproportionate character of moral panic.

Volatility

Criminologists have discovered that moral panic often breaks out following a major crisis or event. As the term "volatility" suggests, moral panic erupts quickly (although the problem may lie dormant or latent for long periods of time), then subsides, fades, or vanishes from the collective conscience or public psyche. Still, even though moral panic subsides, the changes made in policies and government institutions remain, eventually becoming obsolete and inappropriate for dealing with the problem. Because moral panic occurs suddenly, policies and legislation are often made in haste, driven more by emotion than rational decision making; consequently, such laws are difficult to enforce fairly and without discrimination owing to the sprawling nature of the legislation. Volatility also implies that interest in the putative threat is subject to rapid decline. As mentioned later, it is important to emphasize that moral panic fluctuates along with perceptions of economic threat.

Conclusion

Summarizing the nature of pseudo-disasters, Goode and Ben-Yehuda reiterate that moral panic: "locates a 'folk devil,' is shared, is out of synch with the measurable seriousness of the condition that generates it, and varies in intensity over time" (1994). It is crucial to emphasize, however, that moral panic does not necessarily mean that there is not the potential for a problem; rather, that societal responses to the putative problem are fundamentally inappropriate. Crime, and especially violence, certainly is a significant social issue, but to neglect its underlying sources (e.g., socioeconomic inequality and other forms of repression) merely compounds the problem. Moreover, as political and criminal justice elites enact ambitious measures of coercive social control (e.g., more penalties, police, and prisons) crime is reproduced rather than resolved. In the end, people who are easy to identify and dislike, namely, young Black (and Latino) males, are criminalized according to prevailing racial stereotypes.

Although a common view of moral panic suggests that pseudo-disasters quickly burst into formation then dissipate, there are studies that demonstrate some of the lingering effects. For example, moral panic over youth violence reinforces racial biases prevalent in criminal stereotypes, particularly the popular perception that young Black (and Latino) males constitute a dangerous class. Compounded by sensationalistic news coverage on wilding, along with carjacking, gang banging, and other stylized forms of lawlessness associated with urban teens, minority youth remain a lightning rod for public fear, anger, and anxiety over impending social disorder, all of which contribute to additional law and order campaigns (Welch, Fenwick, and Roberts, 1997; Welch, Price, and Yankey, 2002).

Whereas much of the pioneering work on moral panic emphasized its implications to the political economy, that facet of the paradigm tends to be neglected in contemporary scholarship. Still, it should be understood that moral panic symbolizes not only a threat to society at large but also to a prevailing political economy that thrives on racial and economic inequality. Underlying the hysteria over a putative social threat exists class conflict in which the source of the problem is believed to be rooted in the lower, so-called dangerous class, and in a predatory manner creeps up the social ladder.

Finally, moral panic research also tends to overlook the ironic and symbiotic relationship between moral crusaders and those they demonize. Correcting that deficiency, McRobbie and Thornton (1995) recognize that social worlds have become increasingly multimediated. Therefore, targets of moral panic and campaigns of criminalization often are able to fight back using the media to challenge the authority and legitimacy of moral guardians (see Ferrell, 1996; Welch, Sassi, and McDonough, 2002).

MICHAEL WELCH

References and Further Reading

Auster, L. 1990. *The Path to National Suicide: An Essay on Immigration and Multiculturalism.* Monterey, VA: American Immigration Control Foundation.

Best, J. 1999. *Random Violence: How We Talk about New Crimes and New Victims.* Berkeley, CA: University of California Press.

Best, J. 1991. 'Road warriors' on 'hair triggers highways': Cultural resources and the media's construction of the 1987 freeway shootings problem. *Sociological Inquiry,* 61, 3: 327–345.

Best, J. 1990. *Threatened Children: Rhetoric and Concern about Child Victims.* Chicago, IL: University of Chicago Press.

Best, J. and Hutchinson, M. 1996. The gang initiation rite as a motif in contemporary crime discourse. *Justice Quarterly,* 13, 3: 383–404.

Calavita, K. 1996. The new politics of immigration: 'Balanced-budget conservatism' and the symbolism of proposition 187. *Social Problems,* 43, 3: 285–305.

Chiricos, T. 1996. Moral panic as ideology: Drugs, violence, race and punishment in America. *Justice with Prejudice: Race and Criminal Justice in America,* Lynch, M. and Patterson, E.B. (Eds.). New York, NY: Harrow and Heston Publishers, pp. 19–48.

Cohen, S. 2003. *Folk Devils and Moral Panics: The Creation of the Mods and Rockers.* 3rd ed. London, UK: Routledge.

Cohen, S. 1972. *Folk Devils and Moral Panics: The Creation of the Mods and Rockers.* London, UK: MacGibbon & Kee Ltd.

Dalton, H. 1993. *Will America Drown? Immigration and the Third World Population Explosion.* Washington, DC: Scott-Townsend.

Ferrell, J. 1996. *Crimes of Style: Urban Graffiti and the Politics of Criminality.* Boston, MA: Northeastern University Press.

Flanigan, J. 1993. Blaming immigrants won't solve economic woes. *Los Angeles Times,* August 15: D1.

Glassner, B. 1999. *Culture of Fear: Why Americans Are Afraid of the Wrong Things.* New York, NY: Basic Books.

Goode, E. 1990. The American drug panic of the 1980s: Social construction or objective threat? *The International Journal of the Addictions,* 25, 9: 1083–1098.

Goode, E. and Ben-Yehuda, N. 1994. *Moral Panics: The Social Construction of Deviance.* Cambridge, MA: Blackwell.

Greenhouse, L. 1990. Supreme court voids flag law. *New York Times,* June 12: A1, B7.

Hall, S., Critcher, T. J., Clarke, J., and Roberts, B. 1978. *Policing the Crisis: Mugging, the State and Law and Order.* New York, NY: Holmes and Meiser.

Holmes, S.A. 1996. Candidates criticized for sound-bite approach to problem of illegal aliens. *New York Times,* March 7: B10.

Humphries, D. 1999. *Crack Mothers: Pregnancy, Drugs, and the Media.* Columbus, OH: Ohio State University Press.

Lamm, R. and Imhoff, G. 1985. *The Immigration Time Bomb.* New York, NY: Ruman Talley Books.

Lutton, W. and Tanton, J. 1994. *The Immigration Invasion.* Petoskey, MI: Social Contract Press.

Mata, A. 1998. Stereotyping by politicians: Immigrant bashing and nativist political movements. *Images of Color, Images of Crime,* Mann, R. and Zatz, M. (Eds.). Los Angeles, CA: Roxbury, pp. 145–155.

McCorkle, R. and Miethe, T. 1998. The political and organizational responses to gangs: An examination of a 'moral panic' in Nevada. *Justice Quarterly,* 15, 1: 41–64.

McRobbie, A. and Thornton, S. 1995. Rethinking moral panics for multi-mediated social worlds. *British Journal of Sociology*, 46, 4: 559–574.

New York Daily News. 1989. Flag flap. August 12: 24.

New York Newsday. 1989. Beat a flag burner, pay $1. December 16:9.

Newsweek. 1989. A fight for old glory. July 3: 18.

Reinarman, C. and Levine, H.G. 1997. *Crack in America: Demon Drugs and Social Justice.* Berkeley, CA: University of California Press.

Stein, A. 1990. Wilding is a crime, except in law. *New York Times,* January 13: 27.

Welch, M. 2003. Ironies of social control and the criminalization of immigrants. *Crime, Law & Social Change: An International Journal,* 39, 4: 319–337.

Welch, M. 2002. *Detained: Immigration Laws and the Expanding I.N.S. Jail Complex.* Philadelphia, PA: Temple University Press.

Welch, M. 2000. *Flag Burning: Moral Panic and the Criminalization of Protest.* New York, NY: de Gruyter.

Welch, M., Fenwick, M., and Roberts, M. 1997. Primary definitions of crime and moral panic: A content analysis of experts' quotes in feature newspaper articles on crime. *Journal of Research in Crime and Delinquency,* 34, 4: 474–494.

Welch, M., Price, E., and Yankey, N. 2002. Moral panic over youth violence: Wilding and the manufacture of menace in the media. *Youth & Society,* 34, 1: 3–30.

Welch, M., Sassi, J., and McDonough, A. 2002. Advances in critical cultural criminology: An analysis of reactions to avant-garde flag art. *Critical Criminology: An International Journal,* 11: 1–20.

Zatz, M. 1987. Chicago youth gangs and crime: The creation of a moral panic. *Contemporary Crisis,* 11: 129–158.

See also **Mass Media and Criminal Behavior**

Motor Vehicle Theft: Extent and Correlates

Motor vehicle theft is the unlawful taking or attempted taking of a motor vehicle such as an automobile, van, truck, or motorcycle. It does not include those cases where the motor vehicle is taken for temporary use by persons having lawful access to the vehicle, such as family members. Although the definition includes various types of motor vehicles, automobiles are stolen at a much higher rate. For example, the theft rate per 100,000 inhabitants is 336.9 for automobiles, 86.5 for trucks and buses, and 33.4 for other vehicles.

Motor vehicle theft is a form of larceny but because of its frequency and seriousness the Federal Bureau of Investigation's (FBI) Uniform Crime Report (UCR) treats it as a separate category. According to official data, motor vehicle thefts represent a large proportion of all property crimes in the U.S. For example, motor vehicle thefts accounted for 12% of all property crimes reported in the UCR (2002). Data from the UCR indicate that the overall trend in the rate of motor vehicle theft rose steadily from the 1930s to the 1960s, increased dramatically in the late 1960s and early 1970s, leveled off until the mid-1980s, and then began to rise again. It reached its high point in 1991 with a rate of 659 per 100,000 people. Since this time the rate has slowly declined. In 2001, the rate was 430.6 per 100,000 inhabitants. In general, variation in motor vehicle theft is similar to other types of property crimes.

The primary source of data for motor vehicle theft is the UCR. Although the UCR has provided great insight into the nature of motor vehicle theft, it does significantly underestimate the frequency of auto theft in two major ways. First, when counting crimes, only the most serious crime that occurred during a single incident is counted; thus, if the offender commits multiple crimes, the auto theft may not be counted. Second, the UCR generates rates of motor vehicle theft per 100,000 *people*. A more appropriate way to measure motor vehicle theft rates is per 100,000 registered *vehicles*. By measuring motor vehicle theft in this way a more accurate account of risk assessment can be obtained. For example, in 1987 the rate of auto theft per 1000 people was 5.6, whereas the rate per 1000 vehicles was 8.9 (Clarke and Harris, 1992a).

Financial Loss and Recovery Rates

With such high numbers of motor vehicle theft it is not surprising that the financial loss from it is enormous. In 2001, the estimated average value of stolen motor vehicles was $6646 and the total value lost as a result of auto theft was $8.2 billion.

Fortunately for victims, stolen vehicles are often recovered. The recovery rate of stolen vehicles was more than 90% from the 1940s until the late 1960s, when it began to gradually decline. By 1970, the recovery rate dropped to 84% and by 1980 it was at 55% percent. The percentage began to steadily rise in the 1980s, reaching 67% by 1997. It has since been declining and by 2000 the recovery rate was down to 53.1%

(UCR 2001). Although significantly lower than it once was, the recovery rate of stolen vehicles is still much higher than the recovery rate of other stolen items. For instance, the percent of miscellaneous property recovered was 35.5% in 1940 and steadily declined to 9.3% in 1997. For those vehicles recovered, 58% of them are found within 1 day and 79% are found within 6 days.

Clearance Rates

Despite the high recovery rates, motor vehicle theft has one of the lowest clearance rates of all property crimes. A crime is considered cleared when at least one person is arrested, charged with the commission of an offense, and turned over to the court for prosecution (UCR, 2002). The clearance rate for motor vehicle theft from 1940 to the 1960s stayed at about 25%. In 1970, however, clearance rates for all crimes, including motor vehicle theft, began to decline. For the last two decades the clearance rate for motor vehicle theft has been consistently around 14%, which is a percentage similar to the clearance rate for burglary. Some have argued that the drop in clearance rates suggests that there has been an increasing involvement of skilled auto thieves. This assertion may not be true as variations in clearance rates may have more to do with changing enforcement priorities than with the skill levels of offenders.

Reporting Rates

Information from the UCR and the National Crime Victimization Survey (NCVS) indicates that victims are more likely to report motor vehicle theft than any other Type I offense. The most recent estimates are that 94.2% of completed motor vehicle thefts are reported to the police. This is compared to 55.6% of completed burglaries and 68.1% of completed robberies.

The high rates of reporting are attributable to several factors. First, other than one's home, a vehicle is often the most expensive single item that people own. The loss of such a large investment is a great economic strain on nearly everyone affected by it. The hope that the police will be able to relieve this pressure by recovering the car motivates victims to report the crime. Another reason for the high levels of reporting is that insurance agencies typically require a police report. For those with theft insurance, reporting is a necessary step toward recovering their loss. A third reason for the high rate of reporting is that many people believe that their vehicle was stolen for the commission of another crime. Although this represents only a small part of all motor vehicle thefts (about 2%), the fear of being accused for someone else's crime motivates people to report the theft.

Offender Characteristics

Determining the characteristics of those who engage in motor vehicle theft is difficult because of the crime's low clearance rate. Early researchers argued that motor vehicle theft was a crime of the favored classes (Wattenberg and Balisteri, 1952; Sanders, 1976). Studies in several large U.S. cities supported the claim that juvenile car thieves were young, White, and middle class. Sanders (1976) provided an explanation for the favored group findings. He argued that adolescents living in suburban communities learned the value of cars for transportation and had the ability to drive at a relatively young age. In the inner cities, public transportation was more practical so the demand for cars and the knowledge of how to drive was not as widespread. As the majority of cars were stolen for joyrides, offenders tended to be White and middle class.

More recent studies of juvenile delinquents, however, show that social class has no significant explanatory power for motor vehicle theft (Higgins and Albrecht, 1981, 37). Current UCR (2001) data suggest that young males and minorities are disproportionately arrested for motor vehicle theft. Of those arrested for motor vehicle theft in 2000, 83.7% were male, 52.5% were under the age of 21, and 47.1% were non-White.

Motivations for Motor Vehicle Theft

Motor vehicle theft, like most other crimes, is committed for a variety of reasons. Motivations for motor vehicle theft include the desire to turn the theft into financial gain, the thrill of the theft and the possible high-speed car chase, and the means of retaliating against those who deserve it (Copes, 2003). Several researchers have used criminal motivations to create a typology of motor vehicle theft (McCaghy, Giordano, and Henson, 1977; Challinger, 1987; Clarke and Harris, 1992b). The earliest and most popular of these classification schemes groups car thieves into five categories (McCaghy et al., 1977). The first and most common form of motor vehicle theft is joyriding, which is the recreational short-term use of the stolen car. Joyriders do not steal cars for economic reasons or for transportation needs. Instead, the motivations behind joyriding are excitement, proving one's manhood, or gaining status. In short, "the car is not stolen for what it does, but for what it means" (McCaghy et al., 1977, 378).

A second motivation for motor vehicle theft is for short-term transportation. As its name implies, the car is stolen for a short time with the sole purpose of specific transportation, and not for a thrill. Usually, the short-term car thief succumbs to situational pressures where immediate transportation is seen as necessary, thus believing that the only way to relieve this stress is by stealing a car.

Long-term transportation is a third reason for stealing a vehicle. The primary goal of this type of car theft is so that the thief can keep the car. This category is unusual because if the car is recovered, it is often in better shape than when it was stolen. It may have a new paint job or some other type of detailing done to it. The offenders are also different from the other types of car thieves in that they tend to be older and from another locale.

The fourth category consists of those people who steal the car for profit. This category consists of individuals who steal to sell parts or the entire vehicle, as well as professional organizations that operate "chop shops," where automobiles are literally chopped into parts for sale. The goal for this type of theft is solely economic. Theft of the vehicle is based on the automobile as a valuable piece of property, not as a symbol or form of transportation.

The final category of motor vehicle theft is for the commission of another crime. It involves stealing a vehicle for its use in another crime, more often than not a felony. The car is stolen to conceal one's identity and move around without the authorities being able to trace him or her through motor vehicle identification. This is the rarest motivation for motor vehicle theft.

Targeted Vehicles

When an offender sets out to steal a car it is assumed that a subjective decision has been made about the kind of vehicle to steal. The most important factors in the decision-making process include the motivation for stealing the car, the car's level of security, and the ease with which the car can be concealed. A strong correlation exists between the motive of auto thieves and the vehicles they choose (Clarke and Harris, 1992b). Those who steal for joyriding tend to prefer small, high performance vehicles that present a "macho" image, such as the Chevrolet Camaro and the Pontiac Firebird. Those who plan to strip the car to sell the parts tend to prefer cars that have attractive parts for resale. For instance, the high-quality radios that come standard in many Volkswagens are a causal factor for its high rate of theft (Braga and Clarke, 1994). Cars that are stolen for permanent retention tend to be large, expensive, luxury cars such as a Porsche or Mercedes Benz. These makes are chosen because they bring a large profit and they have an appeal to professional criminals.

For the majority of car thieves, targets are chosen based upon convenience and ease. Heavy trucks, buses, and motorcycles have a significantly higher theft rate per 100,000 vehicles than do passenger cars because they are easier to steal, as evidenced by the fact that cars have a higher rate of unsuccessful thefts than do trucks or motorcycles. Many lack the necessary skills to steal most vehicles so they rely exclusively on found opportunities. Certain passenger cars are more often selected as targets because of their low level of security. The poor ignition lock of certain 1969–1974 Ford models, for example, was a major cause for their disproportionately high rate of theft. When Ford finally replaced the old locks with more secure ones in 1975, the theft rates for Fords decreased by 25% (Karmen, 1981). Similarly, the introduction of steering column locks effectively reduced car theft rates in the U.S. (Mayhew et al., 1976).

Some cars are chosen not because they can be stolen easily but because they can be concealed more effectively. Cars stolen to be exported to Mexico tend to be the same types of cars that are made and sold in that country (Field, Clarke, and Harris, 1992). By choosing cars that are common in Mexico, thieves cut their chances of being apprehended.

HEITH COPES

References and Further Reading

Braga, A.A. and Clarke, R.V. 1994. Improved radios and more stripped cars in Germany: A routine activity analysis, *Security Journal* 5.

Challinger, D. 1987. Car security hardware—How good is it? *Car Theft: Putting on the Brakes, Proceedings of Seminar on Car Theft*, May 21, Sydney, Australia: National Roads and Motorists' Association and the Australian Institute of Criminology.

Clarke, R.V. and Harris, P.M. 1992a., Auto theft and its prevention, *Crime and Justice: An Annual Review of Research*, 17, Tonry, M. and Morris, N. (Eds.), Chicago, IC: University of Chicago Press.

Clarke, R.V. and Harris, P.M. 1992b. A rational choice perspective on the targets of automobile theft, *Criminal Behavior and Mental Health* 2.

Copes, H. 2003. Streetlife and the rewards of auto theft, *Deviant Behavior* 24.

Federal Bureau of Investigation, Department of Justice, 2001. *Uniform Crime Report: Crime in the United States*, Washington, DC: Government Printing Office.

Federal Bureau of Investigation, Department of Justice, 2002. *Uniform Crime Report: Crime in the United States*, Washington, DC: Government Printing Office.

Field, S., Clarke, R.V., and Harris, P.M. 1992. The Mexican vehicle market and auto theft in border areas of the United States, *Security Journal* 2.

Higgins, P.C. and Albrecht, G.L. 1981. Cars and kids: A self-report study of juvenile auto theft and traffic violations, *Sociology and Social Research* 66.

Karmen, A. 1981. Auto theft and corporate irresponsibility. *Contemporary Crisis* 5.

Mayhew, P., Clarke, R.V., and Hough, J.M. 1986. Steering column locks and car theft. *Crime as Opportunity* (Home Office Research Study No. 34), Mayhew, P., Clarke, R.V., Struman, A., and Hough, J.M. (Eds.). London, UK: HMSO.

McCaghy, C.H., Giordano, P.C., and Henson, T.K. 1977. Auto theft: Offender and offense characteristics, *Criminology* 15.

Sanders, W. 1976. *Juvenile Delinquency,* New York, NY: Praeger.

Tremblay, P., Clermont, Y., and Cusson, M. 1994. Jockeys and joyriders: Changing patterns in car theft opportunity structures, *British Journal of Criminology* 34.

Wattenberg, W.A. and Balistrieri, J. 1952. Automobile theft: A favored group delinquency, *American Journal of Sociology,* 57.

See also **Larceny or Theft: The Law; Motor Vehicle Theft: The Law; Receiving Stolen Goods**

Motor Vehicle Theft: The Law

Motor vehicle theft is a larceny offense that involves the theft of a motor vehicle such as an automobile, van, truck, or motorcycle. It does not include those situations where a person has lawful access to the vehicle, such as a family member, and then takes the vehicle for temporary use. The earliest federal anti-motor vehicle theft legislation began in 1919 with the passage of the Dyer Act, popularly known as the National Motor Vehicle Theft Act, which made interstate transportation of stolen vehicles a federal crime. This Act imposed stiff penalties—fines and up to 10 years imprisonment—for those who transported stolen vehicles across state lines. The Dyer Act was designed to help states effectively combat automobile theft. This act was particularly needed for those areas near state lines because state law enforcement authorities were seriously hampered by car thieves' ability to transport stolen vehicles beyond the jurisdiction in which the theft occurred.

Federal legislation pertaining to motor vehicle theft ceased until the passage of the Highway Safety Act in 1966. This act led to two federal standards being implemented. The first required that most vehicles be equipped with steering column locks and that the number of combinations of key-locking systems be increased. These improvements were designed to make it more difficult for auto thieves to successfully steal the vehicle. The second standard required that manufacturers of motor vehicles and equipment items place a vehicle identification number (VIN) in all road-going motor vehicles. Beginning on January 1, 1969, all passenger cars manufactured in the U.S., or manufactured overseas and subsequently imported into the U.S., were required to have a VIN. Initially, the format of the VIN (e.g., pattern of letters and numbers) for passenger cars could be determined by each manufacturer. However, after January 1, 1980, all manufacturers were required to use a uniform 17-character VIN.

The next major piece of motor theft legislation occurred in 1984 with the passage of the Motor Vehicle Theft Law Enforcement Act. The intent of this legislation was to reduce the incidence of motor vehicle theft by increasing the tracing and recovery of stolen motor vehicles and parts. This law required manufacturers to mark 14 major components (including the engine, transmission, front fenders, hood, doors, and bumpers) in "high-theft-risk" cars with a 17-character identification number. In 1994, this regulation was amended to apply to all passenger cars, multipurpose passenger vehicles, and light-duty trucks. In addition, all replacement parts were required to be stamped with the manufacturer's registered trademark and the letter R. The Act was designed to make it more difficult for professional car thieves who operated "chop shops" to sell stolen vehicles and parts. These high theft parts were not previously marked with identification numbers and were nearly impossible to identify as stolen once separated from the vehicle. The marking of the parts made the components traceable, thereby increasing the risk associated with dealing in stolen vehicles and parts.

In addition, the 1984 Act provided criminal penalties for altering or removing motor vehicle identification numbers and allowed for the seizure and forfeiture of vehicles or components that have a falsified or removed VIN. To aid the U.S. Customs Service in preventing exportation of stolen vehicles, the 1984 Act requires that exporters of used motor vehicles submit a proof of ownership containing the VIN to the Customs Service before exporting the vehicle.

Another 1984 federal law, the Comprehensive Crime Control Act, made it a federal offense to forge or counterfeit motor vehicle title certificates. This act sets forth punishments of not more than $250,000 and/or not more than 10 years imprisonment for making or possessing a counterfeit or forged title.

The early 1990s saw increased attention to a deadly form of motor vehicle theft known as carjacking. To combat carjacking new federal laws were enacted. The first, the Anti Car Theft Act of 1992, made armed auto theft (carjacking) a federal offense. Then, in 1994, the Violent Crime Control and Law Enforcement Act made murder that resulted from a carjacking punishable by death. Many states followed suit and implemented their own anticarjacking statutes. This allowed states to prosecute armed auto theft under carjacking statutes instead of robbery or motor vehicle theft statutes.

The 1992 Act was also intended to deter trafficking in stolen vehicles by combating automobile title fraud (Title II) and by preventing chop shop related thefts (Title III). Title II of the act required that the Department of Transportation implement a National Motor Vehicle Title Information System (NMVTIS). This system enables multiple jurisdictions to verify the validity of titles, prior to issuing new ones, thus helping to reduce title fraud and theft. Junk and salvage titles must also be included in the system and the sale of salvaged vehicles without disclosing this information is prevented. Thus, it also curbs fraud associated with junk or salvage titles. This act was revised in 1995 by upgrading state motor vehicle department databases containing title information in order to facilitate their use by federal and state law enforcement officials. Title III of the Act made it a federal crime to own, operate, maintain, or control a chop shop. The penalty for operating a chop shop includes a fine and/or up to 15 years of imprisonment.

The effectiveness of these laws at deterring motor vehicle theft is often difficult to determine. Most criminal justice scholars agree that legislation that simply imposes stiffer penalties for engaging in crimes does not significantly deter offenders. Some argue that the most effective legislation is that which is imposed on automobile manufacturers to design more theft-proof vehicles (Karmen, 1981; Brill, 1982). For example, antitheft legislation that required manufacturers to install steering column locks led to decreases in the rate of auto theft in the U.S. (Webb, 1997). However, other evaluations of antitheft legislation have not been as promising. Evaluations of the Motor Vehicle Theft Law Enforcement Act's requirement of parts marking have shown it to be ineffective at reducing long-term theft rates (Harris, 1990; Harris and Clarke, 1991).

HEITH COPES

References and Further Reading

Brill, H. 1982. Auto theft and the role of big business, *Crime and Social Justice* 18.

Harris, P. 1990. Targeting the high-theft-risk automobile, *Security Journal* 1.

Harris, P. and Clarke, R. 1991. Car chopping, parts marking and the Motor Vehicle Theft Law Enforcement Act of 1984, *Social Science Research* 75.

Karmen, A. 1981. Auto theft and corporate irresponsibility, *Contemporary Crisis* 5.

Webb, B. 1997. Steering column locks and motor vehicle theft: Evaluations from three countries, *Situational Crime Prevention: Successful Case Studies*, Clarke, R.V., (Ed.) Guilderland, NY: Harrow and Heston.

See also **Larceny or Theft: The Law; Motor Vehicle Theft: Extent and Correlates**

Murder or Killing *See* Homicide

N

National Crime Victimization Survey (NCVS)

Introduction

How do criminologists determine how much crime exists in America? How do we know whether it is increasing or decreasing? Although most people get their crime information from media outlets such as television, newspapers, movies, books, and the Internet, the U.S. government collects information about crime, as well. Government sources tend to better represent the reality of crime than media sources because mainstream media focus almost exclusively on violent crimes and tend to blow crime problems out of proportion.

Criminologists gain information about crime from two main sources produced by the U.S. government. One source may be better than the other, depending on what you want to learn. Major sources of crime data in the U.S. include the Uniform Crime Reports (UCR) and the National Crime Victimization Survey (NCVS). Criminologists also utilize self-report studies when they want to get information directly from offenders.

History

The National Crime Victimization Survey (NCVS) was designed by the U.S. Department of Justice, Bureau of Justice Statistics in 1972 to explore the perceptions of American crime victims. The original name was the National Crime Survey (NCS). Its three purposes are to: develop detailed information about the victims and consequences of crime; estimate the number and types of crimes not reported to police; and provide uniform measures of selected types of crime.

The survey was redesigned in 1989 to improve validity, and the first annual results for the redesigned survey were published for the year 1993. The redesign was partly aimed at improving survey techniques to increase the ability of people to recall events, including previously undetected victimizations. According to the Bureau of Justice Statistics (2000):

> Criticism of the earlier survey's capacity to gather information about certain crimes, including sexual assaults and domestic violence, prompted numerous improvements. New questions were added to accommodate heightened interest in certain types of victimizations. Improvements in technology and survey methods were incorporated in the redesign. The survey now includes improved questions and cues that aid victims in recalling victimizations. Survey interviewers now ask more explicit questions about sexual victimizations. Advocates have also encouraged victims to talk more openly about their experiences. Together, these changes substantially improve reporting for many types of personal and household crime.

As expected and as hoped, respondents of the annual survey are now reporting more types of crime incidents and previously undetected victimizations are being captured.

NCVS versus UCR

Prior to the NCVS, first published in 1973, the only source of national crime statistics was the UCR, which is a measure of crimes known to police. The UCR is a city, county, and state law enforcement program providing a national source of crime data based on the submission of crime statistics by law enforcement agencies across the country, including nearly 18,000 city, county, and state law enforcement agencies who employ more than 800,000 officers.

Of the many limitations of the UCR, the most troubling, both in terms of crime frequencies and crime trends, is that the UCR is only a measure of crimes known to the police. As most crimes are *not* known to the police, the measure is *not* an accurate account of actual crime frequencies. Crimes *not* known to the police are commonly referred to as the "dark figure of crime." The UCR does not address this unknown crime.

Statistics from the Bureau of Justice Statistics (BJS) suggest that victims only report about one out of every three property crimes and that victims are most likely to report their victimizations to the police when they are violent in nature, when an injury results, when lost items are valued at $250 or more, or when forcible entry has occurred. In 2002, for example, 42% of victimizations were reported to the police, including 48% of personal crimes and 40% of property crimes. Robbery is typically the violent victimization most likely to be reported to the police, whereas rape or sexual assault is the least often violent victimization reported to the police. Of the property crimes, motor vehicle thefts are the most likely victimization reported to the police, at about 95%. Police are only notified in 33% of thefts, and the least likely property victimization to be reported to the police is thefts of less than $50, at 17%.

As factors that affect the UCR figures fluctuate from one year to the next, it is not entirely clear how valid the measure is of crime rates over time, known as "crime trends." For example, rates of forcible rape may appear to be increasing according to the UCR when they may in fact be decreasing or remaining steady over time. If police across the U.S. get better at detecting rape or if citizens report more rapes to the police, the UCR would show an increase in rape rates even though the actual rape rate may not have changed at all. Police departments are also to be motivated by political reasons to alter their data, for example, to gain or maintain federal funding. Some departments may want to create the appearance that crime is decreasing, while others may want to create the appearance that it is increasing.

Given such limitations, the government wanted to discover a way to assess a more valid measure of all crimes, both known to the police and not known to the police. In part to uncover some of the dark figure of crime—to assess some of the crimes not being reported to the police—the NCVS was created. The NCVS is a survey of roughly 100,000 people ages 12 years and older in approximately 50,000 households. Researches ask survey respondents a series of questions about their criminal victimizations in the past twelve months.

The sample of respondents is made up of a nationally representative group of individuals who live in U.S. households. Demographic variables such as age, sex, race, and income are used to compare victimizations of different subgroups within the population.

NCVS Results

The NCVS collects crime data on both personal crimes and property crimes. Citizens are asked about their victimization experiences twice each year from the offenses below.

Crimes Measured by the NCVS

Personal Crimes
- Rape and sexual assault (includes rape, attempted rape, and sexual assault)
- Robbery (includes with injury, without injury, and attempts with injury, and without injury)
- Assault (includes aggravated with injury and threatened with weapon, and simple with minor injury or without injury)
- Personal theft (includes pocket picking, purse snatching, and attempted purse snatching)

Property Crimes
- Household burglary (includes completed with forcible entry and entry without force, and attempted forcible entry)
- Motor vehicle theft (includes completed and attempted)
- Theft (includes completed and attempted)

As the NCVS includes both crimes that citizens reported to the police and those that they did not, it is a more valid measure of actual crime rates than the UCR. This is why the NCVS always indicates there is more crime than the UCR. The table below shows how many actually offenses of each type were reported to NCVS researchers in 2002, the latest year for which crime data are available.

Criminal Victimizations in the U.S., 2002

All crimes	23,036,030
Personal crimes	5,496,810
Rape/Sexual assault	247,730
Robbery	512,490
Assault	4,581,190
Personal theft	155,400
Property crimes	17,539,220

Burglary	3,055,720
Motor vehicle theft	988,760
Theft	13,494,750

According to the 2002 NCVS, there were more than 23 million violent and property crimes experienced by Americans ages 12 years or older. Although this may sound like a lot of crime, keep in mind that there are more than 280 million people in the U.S. Each person is a potential crime victim, as is his or her property. This means crime is not as prevalent as you might suspect. Roughly 8% of Americans can expect to be a victim of a crime measured in the NCVS, and the vast majority will be victimized by a minor property crime. For every 1000 persons ages 12 or older, only 1 rape or sexual assault occurred in 2002, only 1 assault occurred that caused injury, and only 2 robberies occurred. Whereas the NCVS does not measure murder, in 2001 only 6 murders occurred for every 100,000 people.

The NCVS shows us that at least 76% of crime in America is committed against property. The most common type of property crime is theft (accounts for 59% of all crimes in the NCVS). Relatively little crime in America is violent crime. The NCVS shows that the most common types of violent victimization in America are threats of violence and simple assault without injury.

Other than America's murder rate, which is typically ranked among the top five in the world, the nation's crime rate is comparable to other industrialized countries. Findings from the International Crime Victimization Survey (ICVS), first administered by the Dutch Ministry of Justice in 1988, suggest that crime rates are at about average in the U.S.

Characteristics of Victims

Other valuable statistics reported in the NCVS include characteristics of crime victims. From the annual victimization survey, criminologists learn who is most vulnerable to violent and property crime victimizations.

Violent Crime

Gender of Victim

Males are typically more likely to report violent victimizations than females. For example, in 2002, males experienced violent crime victimization at a rate of 25.5 per 1000 persons, versus 21 per 1000 persons for females. The only violent victimization for which females were more victimized than males was for rape and sexual assault. Since 1973, the rates of violent victimization between males and females has narrowed significantly.

Age of Victim

Generally, younger people are more susceptible to violent victimization than older people. In 2002, persons aged 12–15, 16–19, and 20–24 years experienced similar rates of overall violent victimization (45, 58, and 48 victimizations per 1000 persons, respectively). These youngest persons sustained violent crime at rates higher than persons in all other age categories. Among persons ages 25 years and older, violent victimization rates decreased as age increased. For example, in 2002, of people ages 25–34 years, 26 per 1000 persons were victimized, compared to only 3 per 1000 persons ages 65 years and greater.

Race of Victim

The most likely group to experience violent victimizations is members of the African American race. Blacks were victims of overall violent crime in 2002 at rates higher than Caucasians and than other races considered together (28 per 1000 persons, versus 23 per 1000 and 15 per 1000, respectively). Blacks were also more likely to suffer from serious violent victimization (homicide, rape, robbery, and both simple and aggravated assault)—the rate for Blacks in 2002 was 13 per 1000 persons versus 7 per 1000 persons for Caucasians.

Ethnicity of Victim

Non-Hispanics and Hispanics were victims of overall violent crime at similar rates in 2002 (24 per 1000 persons). Hispanic persons aged 12 or older experienced 12% of all violent crime in 2002 and made up 12% of the population.

Household Income

In general, higher annual household incomes are associated with lower violent victimization. For example, in 2002, individuals in households with annual incomes greater than $75,000 were victims of violent crime at rates lower than other income categories, most notably than households who earned less than $7,500 per year (19 per 1000 persons versus 46 per 1000 persons, respectively).

Marital Status

The NCVS also shows that citizens who have never been married were the most likely in 2002 to be violent crime victims (43 per 1000 persons), followed by those who are divorced or separated (31 per 1000 persons), and married individuals (11 per 1000 persons).

Region and Residence

Western and Midwestern urban dwellers had the highest rates of violent crime victimization in 2002 (42 per 1000 persons), followed by Southern urban residents (27 per 1000 persons) and Northeastern urban resident (21 per 1000 persons). Urban residents experience overall violent victimization at rates higher than suburban residents, and suburban residents experience overall violent victimization at rates higher than rural residents.

Victim-Offender Relationship

According to the NCVS, violent crime victims are victimized by people they know at about the same rate as they are by strangers. In 2002, about half (51%) of violent crime victims knew the offender(s). Rape or sexual assault victims were most likely to know the offenders (66%), whereas robbery victims were least likely to know the offenders (28%).

Property Crime

Race of Household Head

African Americans generally experience property crimes at higher rates than Caucasians. In 2002, 174 black and 158 white households per 1000 were victims of property crime overall. For example, of African American households, 41 per 1000 were burglarized, versus only 26 Caucasian households per 1000.

Persons of other races experienced overall property crime and burglaries at rates lower than African Americans, but were victims of motor vehicle theft and theft at rates equal to African Americans.

Ethnicity of Household Head

Generally, Hispanic households are characterized by higher rates of overall property crime, motor vehicle theft, and theft than non-Hispanic households. In 2002, Hispanic households were more likely to have a motor vehicle stolen than non-Hispanic households (18 versus 8 motor vehicle thefts per 1000 households). Hispanic and non-Hispanic households were burglarized at similar rates during 2002 (30 and 27 burglaries per 1000 households, respectively).

Household Income

The NCVS demonstrates that the relationship between annual household income and property crimes depends upon the type of crime being considered. Overall, no relationship between annual household income and the rate of total property crime emerged in 2002. Yet, households with incomes below $75,000 were least likely to experience a motor vehicle theft and households with annual incomes below $75,000 were most likely to be burglarized than households with higher incomes.

Region and Residence

In 2002, Western urban households had higher rates of overall property crime (268 per 1000 households) than Midwestern urban households (222 per 1000 households), Southern urban households (222 per 1000 households), or Northeastern urban households (127 per 1000 households). Although the highest rates for individual types of property crime vary by region, generally the Northeast has the lowest amount of property crime. Urban households have higher rates of overall property criminal victimization than suburban and rural households.

Home Ownership

Property crime is significantly more likely to occur in rented properties than in owned properties.

Crime Trends

The NCVS is a better measure of crime trends because the factors that affect victim recall and reporting to researchers are more constant than those which affect the UCR crime trends. According to the NCVS, crime rates are at their lowest rates since the inception of the survey. They have generally declined since 1973 and have continued a downward trend since the redesign of the survey. For example, victimization rates in 2002 were the lowest recorded since the survey's creation in 1973. The figures below show that 2002 estimates of violence continued a consistent downward trend that began in 1994, whereas those for overall property crime began declining in 1974.

Violent Crime

Between 1973 and 1994, violent crime victimization rates fluctuated. Violent crime rates have declined since 1994. This includes 10% reductions in violent crime between 1994 and 1995 and between 1995 and 1996, followed by 7% decreases between 1996 and 1997 and between 1997 and 1998. Violent crime fell even faster from 1998 to 2002.

In general, robbery trends over the last three decades paralleled overall violent crime trends. Robbery rates fell from 1974–1978 and then increased until 1981. Between 1981 and 1985, the rate rose slowly until 1994, and has decreased since then to the 2002 level of 2.2 robberies per 1000 persons (the lowest robbery rates recorded by the NCVS). The rate of aggravated assault declined starting in 1974 with some interruptions until the mid-1980s. After a few years of minimal change, the aggravated assault rate increased from 1990 to 1993 but has fallen steadily since then, reaching the 2002 level of 4.3 per 1000 persons (also the lowest ever recorded).

Simple assault, the most common form of violent crime measured by the NCVS, increased from 1974 to 1977, remained stable until 1979, then declined until 1989. Between 1990 and 1994, the rates rose to the highest levels ever recorded, 32 victimizations per 1000 persons. Yet, since 1994 simple assault rates have fallen to the lowest level ever recorded, 15.5 simple assaults per 1000 persons in 2002.

Property Crime

Aside from an increase between 1973 and 1974, the overall property crime rate has declined since the inception of the NCVS. After a period of slow decline that was interrupted by an increase from 1980 to 1981, the burglary rate fell each year through the rest of the period. The 2002 household burglary rate (28 burglaries per 1000 households) was less than a third of the adjusted rate of 1973.

Despite some periods of increases, the motor vehicle theft rate declined from 1973 through 2002. The 2002 rate (9 per 1000 households) was half that seen in 1973. In general, motor vehicle theft rates fell between 1973 and 1985. From 1985 through 1991, motor vehicle theft rates increased markedly with a peak in 1991. Between 1992 and 1994 motor vehicle theft rates remained stable, then began to decline at a slow pace.

Thefts increased between 1973 and 1974, then remained stable until 1977. From this time, the rate has declined steadily. In 2002 the theft rate (122.3 per 1000 households) was more than two-thirds lower than the adjusted rate in 1973.

Limitations of the NCVS

The main limitations of the NCVS concern four main measurement issues. First, the NCVS does *not* include statistics on homicide simply because it is impossible to ask a dead person how many times he or she has been murdered in the past 12 months. The UCR is the most valid measure of homicide available because most murders are known to the police. Second, the NCVS does not measure crimes committed against the youngest of Americans, people under the age of 12 years, arguably the most vulnerable of all victims. Third, the NCVS does not probe other types of victimizations, most notably those caused by acts of corporations, which, according to most criminologists, cause much more physical and financial harms than all street crimes

combined. As a result, criminologists must rely on their own independent studies in order to assess victimizations caused by corporations. Fourth, because the NCVS relies on self-reported victimizations from victims, the validity of the NCVS is called into question. Respondents may lie, exaggerate, distort, or simply forget past victimization experiences. Most criminologists still believe that the NCVS is a more valid measure of crime victimization than the UCR, which only measures crimes known to the police.

MATTHEW B. ROBINSON

References and Further Reading

Beckett, K. and Sasson, T. 2000. *The Politics of Injustice: Crime and Punishment in America,* Thousand Oaks, CA, Pine Forge Press.
Blumstein, A., and Wallman, J., Eds. 2000. *The Crime Drop in America,* New York, Cambridge University Press.
Bureau of Justice Statistics, Available at: http://www.ojp.usdoj.gov/bjs.
Donziger, S., Ed. 1996. *The Real War on Crime: The Report of the National Criminal Justice Commission,* New York, Harper Collins.
Friedrichs, D. 1983. Victimology: A consideration of the radical critique, *Crime & Delinquency,* 29(2), 283–294.
Friedrichs, D. 1996. *Trusted Criminals: White Collar Crime in Contemporary Society,* Belmont, CA, Wadsworth.
Gove, W., Hughes, M., and Geerken, M. 1985. Are uniform crime reports a valid indicator of the index crimes? An affirmative answer with minor qualifications, *Criminology,* 23, 451–501.
Kappeler, V., Blumberg, M., and Potter, G. 2000. *The Mythology of Crime and Criminal Justice,* 3rd ed., Prospect Heights, IL, Waveland Press.
Karmen, A. 1996. *Crime Victims: An Introduction to Victimology,* 3rd Ed., Belmont, CA, Wadsworth.
Mayhew, P., and Van Dijk, J. 1997. *Criminal Victimization in Eleven Industrialized Countries: Key Findings from the 1996 International Crime Victims Survey,* The Hague, The Netherlands, Dutch Ministry of Justice.
McCleary, R., Nienstedt, B., and Erven, J. 1982. Uniform crime reports as organizational outcomes: Three time series quasi-experiments, *Social Problems* 29, 361–372.
Miller, T., Cohen, M., and Wiersema, B. 1997. *Victim Costs and Consequences: A New Look,* Washington, DC, U.S. Department of Justice, Office of Justice Programs, National Institute of Justice.
Phipps, A. 1986. Radical criminology and criminal victimization: Proposals for the development of theory and intervention, in Matthews, R., and Young, J., Eds., *Confronting Crime,* Beverly Hills, CA, Sage.
Robinson, M. 2002. The case for a "New Victimology": Implications for policing, in L. Moriarty, Ed., *Police and Victims,* Upper Saddle River, NJ, Prentice-Hall.
Rosoff, S., Pontell, H., and Tillman, R. 1998. *Profit Without Honor: White-Collar Crime and the Looting of America,* Upper Saddle River, NJ, Prentice-Hall.

See also **Uniform Crime Reports (UCR); Victimization, Crime: Characteristics of Victims**

National Institute of Justice (NIJ)

In 1967 the President's Commission on Law Enforcement and Administration of Justice provided recommendations to Congress to take measured responses to the control of crime. As a result, in 1968 the U.S. Congress passed the Omnibus Crime Control and Safe Streets Act. This Act helped establish the Law Enforcement Assistance Administration (LEAA). The National Institute of Law Enforcement and Criminal Justice (NILECJ) was established as the research agency of the LEAA. The main purpose of the National Institute of Law Enforcement and Criminal Justice was to encourage research and development directed toward new methods of crime control and prevention. Traditionally this has meant sponsoring research in the areas of crime prevention, courts, corrections, and law enforcement. In 1978 this agency was renamed the National Institute of Justice (NIJ). The Office of Justice Programs replaced the LEAA. The NIJ now represents the official research agency of the U.S. Department of Justice and is one of six bureaus within the Office of Justice Programs.

The main mission of the NIJ is to sponsor special projects and research programs that will help improve the criminal justice system and reduce crime. The NIJ funds national demonstration projects that attempt to employ innovative or promising approaches toward improving the control of crime. Most of these research programs examine innovative practices in the areas of law enforcement, courts, and corrections. Some of these research projects are evaluations of specific criminal justice programs that hold promise and could be implemented across the country. These research products are meant to provide recommendations to federal, state, and local governments on how to improve the effectiveness of the criminal justice system. Additionally, the NIJ has funded basic research on criminal behavior.

NIJ research funding is appropriated by the Congress on an annual basis. Although the amount of funding has varied, typically the NIJ receives between $20 and $40 million a year to fund research in the area of crime and justice. The NIJ has been able to expand its research initiatives through the result of funding set aside for research under the Violent Crime Control and Law Enforcement Act of 1994. These initiatives have examined research and evaluation in the issues of community policing, violence against women, sentencing and corrections, new innovations in the court system, as well as new technologies for local law enforcement.

The NIJ director is appointed by the president and confirmed by the Senate of the U.S. The NIJ directors are nominated by each new presidential administration. Table 1 presents a chronological list of the agency's directors.

The Director of the NIJ has sole discretion over what research projects the NIJ will fund. The NIJ with guidance of the priorities set by the Office of Justice Programs, the Department of Justice, and the needs of the criminal justice field acts as an independent research program within the Department of Justice. The director of the agency reports directly to the Assistant Attorney General in charge of the Office of Justice Programs.

The agency is currently divided into three main divisions: the Office of Science and Technology (OST), the Office of Research and Evaluation (ORE), and the Office of Development and Communications (ODC). The OST funds research on innovative technologies for criminal justice agencies. The ORE division funds research and evaluation on innovative programs and practices in criminal justice. The ODC is responsible for publishing materials on the work NIJ has funded and disseminating this information to policy makers, researchers, and practitioners in criminal justice agencies. The ODC is also responsible for the institute's yearly strategic planning, where the NIJ makes its formal request to Congress for future funds.

Table 1. National Institute of Justice Directors

Name	Years as Director
Ralph Siu	1968–1969
Henry Ruth	1969–1970
Irving Slott	1970–1971
Martin Danziger	1971–1973
Gerald Caplan	1973–1977
Blair Ewing	1977–1979
Harry Bratt	1979–1981
James Underwood	1981–1982
W. Robert Burkhart	1982
James K. Stewart	1982–1990
Charles B. DeWitt	1990–1993
Michael J. Russell	1993–1994
Carol V. Petrie	1994
Jeremy Travis	1994–2000
Julie E. Samuels	2000 to Present

To promote research in the area of crime and justice the NIJ has regular solicitations for research proposals. A research proposal is a written document that clearly describes a planned research project to be conducted. These research solicitations ask for applicants to develop a research proposal to address either a specific research topic in criminal justice or to examine novel issues related to crime and justice. At least once a year the NIJ solicits proposals for investigator-initiated research. This research solicitation is an open invitation to researchers to explore innovative topics and techniques that will assist in shaping public policies to control crime or improve justice. The NIJ throughout the year also solicits proposals for research directed at specific topic areas. The solicitations for specific topics vary from year-to-year and have included such areas as research and evaluation of residential substance abuse treatment, violence against women, community policing, and forensic DNA research and development. To develop ideas for funding specific topics the institute holds regular meetings with researchers and criminal justice practitioners to discuss what areas of research need to be conducted in the field of criminal justice. Often these meetings take the form of focus groups, cluster conferences, and seminar series.

All NIJ research proposal solicitations have a firm submission deadline. Once this deadline has passed the NIJ convenes panels of experts to review the proposals. These experts include researchers, academics, and practitioners involved in the criminal justice field. The panel of experts reviews all of the proposals submitted to the NIJ for the specific solicitation and decides (without input from the NIJ staff) the proposals that merit further review by the NIJ for funding consideration. The panel writes out specific comments and criticisms of each research proposal. These comments are then given to NIJ staff for review. Applicants whose research proposals are outright rejected by the panel of experts typically receive a copy of the written comments and a rejection notice from the NIJ shortly after the panel has convened. Proposals that warrant further consideration are then reviewed internally by NIJ staff and forwarded to the NIJ Director with detailed comments on each proposal. The director of the NIJ makes the ultimate decision on which proposals to accept. After the director's decision has been made a formal award letter is written. The notice of an accepted proposal is then forwarded to the U.S. Congress so that local representatives can inform the successful applicants of their pending research award. Shortly after the notice from Congress, successful applicants receive their award letter from the NIJ. This award letter specifies the proposed project that has been funded and the special conditions that must be met.

Awarded proposals take on the form of an accepted research grant from the NIJ. This research grant is similar to those awarded by other research organizations (e.g. the National Institutes of Health, the National Institute of Mental Health, the National Science Foundation) and requires grant recipients (grantees) to accomplish the research goals stated in their proposals. The NIJ also requires that all grantees provide a final report and executive summary of their research findings, along with an electronic copy of any data that were collected for the research project. The executive summary is a brief overview of the final report. This summary is used to concisely highlight the research that the NIJ has funded. Final reports provide a thorough description of the research that was conducted, the findings from the research, and any policy implications. Shortly after receiving a final report the NIJ has anonymous researchers review the report. These anonymous reviewers then make suggestions on any modifications that are necessary before the final report should be published in its final form. Once the grantee has made the necessary revisions to the final report, both the executive summary and the final report are released for public dissemination and archived at the National Criminal Justice Reference Service (NCJRS). The NCJRS acts as the reference library for all NIJ funded projects. All NCJRS documents are open to the general public.

Over the past three decades the NIJ has funded the majority of research in the area of criminal justice policy. These NIJ funded studies have provided many research-based recommendations to public officials on how to improve issues of crime and justice.

One of the earliest major studies funded by the NIJ was the Kansas City Preventive Patrol Experiment. This study examined the crime prevention effectiveness of the widely used police practice of having patrol cars randomly patrol a given area. The results indicated that random patrol was not an effective method of crime prevention. The findings from this study were important because they challenged a widely held belief in law enforcement.

The NIJ has also funded studies that found detective work alone is not an effective method of crime control. This research suggested that information obtained by patrol officers in preliminary investigations is largely responsible for the successful apprehension of suspects. These findings indicated that patrol officers should be given a larger role in conducting preliminary crime investigations.

More recently, the NIJ has funded research examining the use of community policing and other innovative crime control strategies. The NIJ, for example, funded a number of field experiments to test whether foot patrol was an effective method of controlling crime and reducing the fear of crime in urban areas. The NIJ has also funded field experiments that examined the most appropriate option for the police in responding to calls for domestic violence. Results from this research had a substantial impact on encouraging police departments to adopt policies that require officers to make an arrest when responding to a domestic violence incident.

The NIJ also has consistently funded research in the areas of prosecution and sentencing. Research funded by the NIJ, for instance, suggested ways that prosecutors could identify career criminals and increase the likelihood of successful convictions and increased sentence lengths. The NIJ also funded research on how to improve the use of pretrial release decision-making. These research projects examined what factors courts should take into account when deciding whether or not to release suspects awaiting trial back into the community.

In the 1980s and 1990s, the NIJ supported a series of evaluations on the use of boot camps and intensive probation and parole supervision as alternatives to incarceration. Early evaluations suggested that boot camps were not more effective in reducing rearrest rates but were substantially less expensive than prison. Research on intensive probation and parole supervision suggested that it neither reduced costs nor rearrests compared to traditional sanctions.

In addition to research and evaluation of specific crime control strategies, the NIJ has also supported basic criminological research examining issues related to violence, child abuse, career criminals, drug use among arrestees, and community factors related to crime. Much of this research has been addressed through funds that the NIJ has provided to the National Research Council of the National Academy of Sciences to convene panels of experts to assess the knowledge and formulate research agendas in a variety of areas of basic criminal justice research.

The NIJ also funds an extensive amount of research on the development and use of innovative technologies for the control of crime. The NIJ's Office of Science and Technology has funded research that examines the application of computer technology to assist police investigations, the development and testing of Kevlar bullet resistant vests, and the use of model practices for the handling of DNA evidence.

Research funded by the NIJ since the early 1970s has had a profound effect on shaping the knowledge base on the effectiveness of various crime and justice policies. Through combining the concerns of both criminal justice practitioners and researchers into their funding decisions, the NIJ has provided the leading information on how to improve public policy responses to issues of crime and justice in the U.S.

JOHN M. MACDONALD

Principle Writings

Blumstein, A., and Petersilia, J. 1994. NIJ and its research program, *25 Years of Criminal Justice Research,* Washington, DC, U.S. Department of Justice, National Institute of Justice.

National Institute of Justice. Available at: http://www.ojp.usdoj.gov/nij.

National Criminal Justice Reference Service. Available at: http://www.ncjrs.org/.

Travis, J., and Blumstein, A. 2000. Departing thoughts from an NIJ director, *National Institute of Justice Journal,* 243.

Further Reading

Blumstein, A., Cohen, J., Roth, J., and Visher, C., Eds. 1986. *Criminal Careers and "Career Criminals,"* Vol. II, Washington, DC, National Academy Press.

Kelling, G.L., Pate, T., Dieckman, D., and Brown, C.E. 1974. *Kansas City Preventive Patrol Experiment—A Summary Report,* Washington, DC, Police Foundation.

MacKenzie, D.L., Shaw, J.W., Gowdy, V.B. 1993. *Evaluation of Shock Incarceration in Louisiana, Research in Brief,* Washington, DC, U.S. Department of Justice, National Institute of Justice.

National Advisory Commission on Crime Justice Standards and Goals, 1973. *Police,* Washington, DC, U.S. Government Printing Office.

Petersilia, J., Turner, S. 1993. *Evaluating Intensive Supervision Probation/Parole: Results of a Nationwide Experiment, Research in Brief,* Washington, DC, U.S. Department of Justice, National Institute of Justice.

Sherman, L.W., Schmidt, J.D., Rogan, D.P. 1992. *Policing Domestic Violence: Experiences and Dilemmas,* New York, Free Press.

See also **Law Enforcement**

Native American Crime and Justice

Native American crime and criminal justice refers to the commission and address of crime by American Indians and Alaskan natives (Eskimos and Aleutians), collectively termed Native Peoples. Native Peoples are members of 558 federally acknowledged nations that exist as relatively autonomous governmental entities within the larger nation. An additional 200 tribal groups have been officially acknowledged by the states and have petitioned for federal recognition. According to the 2000 U.S. Census, these peoples constitute almost 2% of the U.S. population. The present Native Peoples population of approximately 4.2 million people is a considerable increase since the 1900 Census total of less than 200,000, a figure reflecting the various North American Indian wars of the 19th century. This overview of American Indian and Alaskan Native crime and justice reports current crime data, identifies common stereotypes and myths specific to Indian criminality, and presents leading jurisdictional matters and policy issues.

Discussion of crime and justice in a Native Peoples context is typically characterized by the interrelated themes of cultural conflict, ethnostress, and socially constructed Indian culture. Ethnostress (Light and Martin, 1986) captures the essence of discrimination against Native Peoples, a common theme of European colonization. Discrimination against Indians is multifaceted and, historically, has assumed legal, economic, educational, sociocultural, and religious forms. Most pronounced of these is sociocultural discrimination that is often inseparable from religious practices. Spiritual rituals performed prior to fishing and hunting, rites of adulthood and at the life junctures of marriage and death have been legally prohibited and land use treaties specific to ceremonial and religious expression repeatedly violated. Much of this discrimination stems from both formal and informal assimilation efforts that, although initially successful, have elicited a general reaction formation of cultural resistance that has resulted in considerable cultural awakening and political unity across tribes, a social movement including the emergence of the Indian Country concept (Nagel, 1996). Indian Country is both a sociological and legal concept, the latter extending Indian influence beyond geographic boundaries to the larger realm of traditions, many of which are recognized and protected by federal law.

Statistics on Native American Crime

Data on Native American crime are gathered from a number of sources, including the Uniform Crime Report (UCR), FBI records, the National Crime Victim Survey (NCVS), tribal criminal records, and criminological and criminal justice science research. These various data sources all have limitations but do enable a general profile of Native American criminality, victimization, and justice outcomes. A few examples of data collection and compilation problems include: 1) UCR data reflect offenses reported to and recorded by local and state law enforcement agencies that often do not include tribal crime; 2) UCR data distort crime realities by veiling the role of ethnicity, as in hate crimes; 3) NCVS data are collected by telephone surveys, but many American Indians are impoverished and do not have phones; 4) cultural practices and historical patterns of discrimination foster mistrust and discourage participation in crime research that is typically conducted by non-Indians; 5) American Indian data are often erroneously collapsed into "other" categories; and, perhaps most importantly, 6) tribal courts do not have adequate resources to maintain accurate crime data. Researchers have also observed that large national studies collapse both offenses by Indians and victimization rates into a single category from which broad generalizations are made about the nature of Indian crime. Such an approach, it is argued, fails to acknowledge culturally-specific attitudes and practices across the many tribes. Essentially, a false assumption argument is generated (Green, 1993; Baird-Olson, 1994; Nagel, 1996).

The most current and comprehensive accounting of Indian crime is the report on "First Peoples in the 1990s" (Greenfield and Smith, 1999) that provides offense rates and extremely high rates of violent victimization. The Native American violent victimization rate of 124 per 1000 population is more than double the rate for all other races. Indian women are especially likely to experience violent victimization, more so than any other population demographic as Indians are the most likely group to experience rape or sexual assault. The pattern of experiencing violence holds true for Indians of all age groups but is especially acute for late teens and young adults. American Indians in the 18 to 24 range are twice as likely to experience violence

(332 per 100,000), a statistic that increases still for the 25 to 34 age cohort (145 per 100,000 for American Indians compared to just 61 per 100,000 for the all-race rate). Native American crime victims are typically male, socioeconomically disadvantaged, between 12 and 24, victimized by an acquaintance, and, interestingly, in an urban area despite the fact that the majority live in rural areas with 37% residing on reservations.

This finding of greater victimization holds true for most violent crimes, including sexual assault and rape, aggravated assault, and simple assault, but the homicide rate of 7 per 100,000 is only minimally higher than whites (5 per 100,000). In short, the overall Native American violent victimization rate for all offenses is 153 per 100,000 compared to only 60 per 100,000 for all races (Rennison, 2001).

American Indians, according to 1996 arrest data, commit just under 1% (0.99%) of serious crime (murder, rape, assault, and battery). American Indian youth are arrested at about the same rate as white youth (both are approximately 17%) for most violent and property offenses (Coalition for Juvenile Justice, 2000). Indian offenders are most often convicted for public disorder (39.5%), property crime (27.5%), and then violent crime (26.6%).

Native Peoples do disproportionately commit alcohol-related violations, however, at a rate that is more than twice the national average (2545 per 100,000 compared to 1079 per 100,000). Interestingly, the statistics for these alcohol offenses (DUI, public drunkenness, and lesser liquor ordinance violations) do not hold for illicit drug offenses which are actually lower for American Indians than for all other races. The role of alcohol is significant for American Indian crime, generally. The majority of offenses committed by Indians are public disorders involving alcohol and 70% convicted of violent crime had been drinking during the offense. The general trend of public order and morality offenses that largely characterizes Indian crime also explains their overrepresentation in jails, given the localized nature of disposing of peccadillo-type cases.

American Indians are overrepresented in the nation's correctional system, experiencing an incarceration rate almost 40% higher than the national average (Baird-Olson, 1994; Minton, 2001). Although comprising less than 1% of the total population, Native Peoples account for almost 8% of the federal prison population, a statistic that is not surprising given the high level of poverty within Indian Country generally and the strong positive correlation that exists between socioeconomic status and criminality. A total of 62,600 men and women were identified as under the control of the criminal justice system according to the 1998 First Peoples Report (Greenfield and Smith, 1999),

which is 4% of the Native American population. Comparatively, the incarceration rates for other races are 4% for blacks, 2% for whites, and less than 0.5% for Asians.

As of 1996, there were 135 tribal law enforcement agencies employing almost 2000 sworn officers. Additionally, the Federal Bureau of Indian Affairs allocated 340 officers. The Bureau and many reservations house jails, especially in South Dakota, Arizona, and New Mexico. Typically, tribal police exercise jurisdiction within reservation boundaries (Clinton, 1971; Greenfield and Smith, 1999). Many criminal justice services in Indian contexts, however, are delivered in conjunction with local, state, or federal law enforcement and often create jurisdictional confusion.

Today, the federal government aids in juvenile delinquency and crime prevention and law enforcement efforts extensively. The U.S. Bureau of Justice Assistance, for example, provides funding through the Indian Alcohol and Substance Abuse Program to reduce crime associated with the distribution and use of alcohol and illicit drugs in tribal communities. The alcohol or drugs and crime nexus is addressed by initiatives that mobilize tribal communities to implement and enhance collaborative efforts. Other federal funding programs facilitate environmental protection, drug court training, and law enforcement technical assistance.

In addition to prevention and policing oriented resources, funding support is provided for tribal jurisprudence. The Tribal Court Assistance Program focuses on developing new tribal courts, improving the operations of existing tribal courts, and training court staff. The primary objective of this program is to help tribal governments develop, enhance, and continue operation of tribal justice systems, including intertribal court systems. The nature of tribal courts and the justice they dispense reflects an ongoing cultural awakening and revitalization of the Indian ethos, evident by transformation in recent years. Whereas Native Peoples' criminal justice has largely reflected the European model since the turn of the 20th century, recent changes have noticeably moved away from an adversarial approach toward a peacemaking and restitution model more in sync with historic Native American ethnocentricity and culture.

J. MITCHELL MILLER

References and Further Reading

Aguirre, A. and Turner, J.H. (2001). *American Ethnicity: The Dynamics and Consequences of Discrimination*, New York, McGraw-Hill.

Bachman-Prehn, R.D. (1992). *Death and Violence on the Reservation: Homicide, Violence, and Suicide in American Indian Populations*, New York, Auburn House.

Baird-Olson, P.K. (1994). *The Survival Strategies of Plains Indian Women: Coping with Structural and Interpersonal Victimization on a Northwest Reservation,* PhD. dissertation, University of New Mexico, Albuquerque, NM.

Bureau of Indian Affairs (2001). *Tribal Court Clearinghouse: Native American Justice Systems,* Washington, DC.

Clinton, R.N. (1971). Development of criminal jurisdiction over Indian lands: The historical perspective, *Arizona Law Review,* 951, 953–954.

Coalition for Juvenile Justice (2000). *Enlarging the Healing Circle: Ensuring Justice for American Indian Children,* Washington, DC.

Deloria, V. and Lytle, C.M. (1985). American Indians, American Justice, Austin, TX, University of Texas Press.

Flowers, R.B. (1990). *Minorities and Criminality,* Westport, CT, Praeger.

Green, D.E. (1993). The contextual nature of American Indian criminality, *Culture and Research Journal,* 17, 99–119.

Light, H.K. and Martin, R.E. (1986). American Indian families, *Journal of American Indian Education,* 26(1), 1–5.

Minton, T. (2001). *Jails in Indian Country, 2000,* Washington, DC, U.S. Department of Justice, Office of Justice Programs, Bureau of Justice Statistics.

Nagel, J. (1996). *American Indian Ethnic Renewal: Red Power and the Insurgence of Identity and Culture,* New York, Oxford University Press.

Rennison, C. (2001). *Violent Victimization and Race, 1993–98,* Washington, DC, U.S. Department of Justice, Office of Justice Programs, Bureau of Justice Statistics.

Ross, L. (1998). *Inventing the Savage: The Social Construction of Native American Criminology,* Austin, TX, University of Texas Press.

See also **Genocide; Race and Ethnicity and Criminal Behavior**

Natural Law

Also referred to as the law of nature, natural law is a set of principles based on what is considered to be the nature of man. The central premise of natural law is that what naturally *is*, is what *ought* to be. Although natural law principles form a theoretical tradition, they are also a set of objective norms serving as a practical guide for governing human conduct.

Unlike positive law—legislative acts and judicial decisions set down by humans—natural law is universal and immutable. It is universal because it is discerned through an attribute shared by all human beings—human reason. It is immutable insofar as the nature of man is thought to be unchanging. Thus, although positive law is grounded in customs and conventions (*nomos*) that may potentially vary, natural law is grounded in man's unchanging nature (*physis*). Whereas positive law does not necessarily possess any intrinsic moral requirement, the law of nature as revealed through reason contains an inherent standard of morality.

Natural law principles were first expressed by the early Greek philosophers. The Stoics, such as Chrysippus (c. 280–206), held in their moral universalism that divine reason governs all parts of the universe. As part of this universal nature, man too is governed by reason. Thus for man to live naturally and virtuously, he must live in accordance with reason; it is his moral duty to do so. Even from its inception, the natural law tradition submits that what *is* human nature *ought* to direct human affairs.

Ancient Roman thought also played an important role in the development of the tradition. Adopting the Stoic belief that the universe is a rational whole governed by divine reason, the Roman statesman and orator Cicero (106–43 BCE), in his *De re publica,* proffered a definition of natural law (*jus naturale*) that has become the cornerstone of the tradition: "True law is right reason in agreement with nature; it is of universal application, unchanging and everlasting…there will not be different laws at Rome and at Athens, or different laws now and in the future, but one eternal and unchangeable law will be valid for all nations and all times."

One of the most enduring contributions to the natural law tradition was made by St. Thomas Aquinas (1225–1274). The theoretical tenets of his *Summa Theologica* form the underpinnings for most natural law theories today. Aquinas maintains several "first indemonstrable principles" of natural law. These principles are self-evident truths and there is one principle upon which all other natural law precepts rest. The first principle of practical reason, "that good is to be done and ensued, and evil is to be avoided," is knowable by the fact that God has instilled it in man's mind so that it may be known to him naturally. In Thomistic philosophy, a different approach to natural law is revealed where the Christian God is identified as the source of divine reason. Complementing the natural law is an "eternal law," God's wisdom that directs all human actions and movements. For Aquinas, it is this eternal law that provides the basis for natural law.

Unlike the earlier Christian emphasis on divine will, modern natural law of the 17th century stressed the rational nature of man and his capacity to reason. Hugo Grotius (1583–1645), for instance, not only underscored the importance of reason but more so, right reason. Similarly, Thomas Hobbes (1588–1679) maintained that the law of nature is the dictate of right reason around those affairs pertaining to the preservation of life.

The tradition of natural law was revived in the 20th century by, among others, John Finnis and his theory of goods. In *Natural Law and Natural Rights* (1980), Finnis identifies seven basic human goods that, he argues, form seven practical principles of natural law. The seven goods—life, knowledge, play, beauty, friendship, practical reasonableness, and religion—form practical principles because, following the structure of Aquinas' first principle, they are to be pursued while their opposites are to be avoided. For example, life is to be pursued while death is to be avoided. For defenders of the tradition, the pursuit and protection of the basic goods can and ought to inform the enactment of positive law.

Despite its remarkable history, natural law has not been immune from critique. The advent and influence of empiricism, historicism, legal positivism, and utilitarianism all meant serious challenges to the tradition. Regarded as a set of unscientific and disprovable tenets, critics raised many philosophical questions. Is there really a human nature? Can universal, timeless, and self-evident truths be upheld? Does the truth of natural law depend on the existence of a divine source? Proponents of the tradition were also accused of committing the naturalistic fallacy, the error of inferring from facts (*is*) to norms (*ought*). For example, that knowledge *is* good for man does not necessarily mean that man *ought* to pursue knowledge. Logical consistency mandates a second *ought* statement: man *ought* to pursue good. Natural law proponents have addressed the naturalistic fallacy in several ways. Among them is the reply, although deemed unsatisfactory for some, that there is really no *is* in the first place. That is, the first practical principles are underived and indemonstrable and are not inferred from what human nature *is*. They are self-evident and hence need no further defense.

The tradition of natural law has an impressive 2000-year old history. Its immutable and universal principles are still appealing today because they provide objective moral standards for human governance—standards that are especially appealing in light of the human atrocities of World War II. As a corrective to totalitarianism, natural law offers an ethical foundation for protecting fundamental human rights while informing important and symbolic documents such as the U.S. Declaration of Independence (1776) and the UN Universal Declaration of Human Rights (1948). At a time when relativistic theories of justice are unable to provide standards for judgment and action, the tradition of natural law continues to provide an indispensable moral framework for human affairs.

SAMANTHA S. KWAN

References and Further Reading

Aquinas, St. T. 1989. *Summa Theologiö: A Concise Translation,* translated by McDermott, T., Westminster, MD, Christian Classics.

Cicero, M.T. 1928. *De re publica,* translated by Keyes, C.W., London, Heinemann.

Finnis, J. 1980. *Natural Law and Natural Rights,* New York, Oxford University Press.

George, R.P., Ed. 1992. *Natural Law Theory: Contemporary Essays,* New York, Oxford University Press.

Hittinger, R. 1987. *A Critique of the New Natural Law Theory,* Notre Dame, IN, University of Notre Dame Press.

Maritain, J. 1943. *The Rights of Man and the Natural Law,* translated by Anson, D.C., New York, Scribner.

Rice, C.E. 1993. *50 Questions on the Natural Law: What It Is and Why We Need It,* San Francisco, CA, Ignatius Press.

Rommen, H. 1998. *The Natural Law: A Study in Legal and Social History and Philosophy,* translated by Hanley, T.R., Indianapolis, IN, Liberty Fund.

Simon, Y.R. 1965. *The Tradition of Natural Law: A Philosopher's Reflections,* New York, Fordham University Press.

Strauss, L. 1953. *Natural Right and History,* Chicago, IL, University of Chicago Press.

Veatch, H. 1981. Natural law and the 'Is'-'Ought' question, *The Catholic Lawyer,* 26(4).

Weinreb, L.L. 1987. *Natural Law and Justice,* Cambridge, MA, Harvard University Press.

Necessity as a Defense to Criminal Liability

Some form of necessity defense is recognized in every Anglo-American jurisdiction. It differs from duress in that the situation that justifies the conduct is most often created by some natural disaster rather than by human beings. Necessity is sometimes stated as "choice of evils," in that it applies to situations the law simply failed adequately to anticipate. When confronted with an unanticipated "choice of evils," an accused will have a defense when the greater evil is in obedience to the law rather than disobedience. An example is someone who breaks and enters into a residence to rescue a human being or an animal.

The weighing of the evils is up to the finder of fact, jury, or judge, unless it appears that the legislature has already weighed the evils. When the legislature has already considered the situation, the courts must follow the legislative command without regard to how the judge might weigh the same evils. For example, one who trespasses at an abortion clinic to "rescue" a fetus will not normally have a necessity justification for criminal trespass, at least when the abortion clinic is operated in a lawful manner. One who trespasses at a nuclear power plant to stop its operation or who vandalizes a selective service office cannot use the necessity defense to place nuclear power or the selective service system on trial. Without regard to whether abortion, nuclear power, or conscription constitute "evils," the legislature and the courts have already provided for their existence.

The necessity defense is further limited to situations where there is no third alternative. If it is possible to avoid both harms, the defendant must do so. For example, if a person claims a necessity defense to driving while intoxicated because of some emergency that arose unexpectedly, the defense will not apply if the defendant had the option of walking or taking public transit. A man who becomes intoxicated at home when his wife is nine months pregnant will not normally have a necessity defense if he suddenly has to drive her to the hospital. Necessity defenses to driving while intoxicated generally find little favor in the case law because driving while intoxicated is an act so clearly dangerous to human life.

When crimes more dangerous to human life than breaking and entering or trespass are at issue, the weighing of evils may become more difficult, but it is generally held that the necessity defense, when it applies, will justify any crime short of homicide. Necessity is problematic in a homicide case because both the evil sought to be prevented by the law and the evil sought to be justified are deaths of human beings. The law does not weigh the lives of some people more heavily than others. Even more difficult is the case where the unlawful death of one person might save more than one life.

Most jurisdictions respond to these moral dilemmas by simply ruling out necessity as a defense to homicide. Some jurisdictions, and the Model Penal Code of the American Law Institute, take the view that it is permissible to weigh the taking of one life as a lesser evil than the cost of many lives.

STEVE RUSSELL

References and Further Reading

Fuller, L.L. 1949. The case of the speluncean explorers, *Harvard Law Review,* 62.
Glazebrook, P.R. 1972. The necessity plea in English criminal law, *Cambridge Law Journal,* 30.
Simpson, A.W.B. 1984. *Cannibalism and the Common Law,* Chicago, IL, The University of Chicago Press.

See also **Defenses to Criminal Liability: Justifications and Excuses; Self-Defense as a Defense to Criminal Liability**

Neighborhood Watch Programs *See* **Crime Prevention**

Neo-Nazi Groups

Neo-Nazis are defined simply as groups that share a hatred for Jews, minorities, homosexuals, and sometimes Christians. Clearly, their primary enemy is the Jew, which gives reason to their love for Adolf Hitler and Nazi Germany. In 2002 the Southern Poverty Law Center declared, in the Intelligence Report from Spring 2002, the National Alliance as "the largest and most effective neo-Nazi organization in the United States" (p. 3). However, since that time the leader of the National Alliance, William Pierce, died from cancer and left the group very unstable. In 1995 Roy in "Organized Hate In America" stated that the Aryan Nations was "the Nation's most menacing neo-Nazi group." Although both groups have lost some of their luster and power over the years, there is still reason to fear and keep track of such neo-Nazi groups. In the most recent Southern Poverty Law Center's Intelligence Report (Spring, 2003), there were 708 active hate groups listed in the U.S. This is up almost 5% from 2001. This entry will address primarily the Aryan Nations and the National Alliance. While addressing these groups, other splinter or offshoot groups and members of these organizations will also be discussed.

Some Americans had vague notions of neo-Nazis or white supremacist groups prior to April of 1995. However, on April 19, 1995, the terms neo-Nazi and white supremacy became household words. On that date, Timothy McVeigh bombed the Oklahoma City federal building. By most accounts it is believed that McVeigh was inspired to bomb the federal building by a book called *The Turner Diaries,* written by William Pierce (founder of the National Alliance) under the pseudonym of Andrew McDonald.

Although April 1995 may be the date most people recall as the first time they heard about such hate groups, in reality neo-Nazi groups have a long history in the U.S. and internationally. Many of the beliefs neo-Nazi groups possess originate from the 19th century religion called British-Israelism (Ridgeway, 1995), today referred to as Christian Identity. In short, Christian Identity believes that white "Aryans" are the descendants of the biblical tribes of Israel. Furthermore, Identity believers state that Jews are the very descendants of the Devil. In other words, they believe the Jews are the literal children of the serpent (or Satan) and Eve in the Garden of Eden. Thus, those who practice Christian Identity believe the white Christians are the true "Israelites" and God's chosen people, rather than the Jews. According to Ridgeway (1995):

They [Identity believers] hold that the nonwhite races are "pre-Adamic"—that is, part of the creation finished before God created Adam and Eve. In his wisdom, they say, God fashioned the subhuman nonwhites and sent them to live outside the Garden of Eden before the Fall. When Eve broke God's original commandment, she was implanted with two seeds. From Adam's seed sprang Abel and the white race. From the serpent Satan's seed came the lazy, wicked Cain. Angered, God cast Adam, Eve, and the serpent out of the Garden of Eden and decreeded eternal racial conflict. Cain killed Abel, then ran off into the jungle to join the pre-Adamic nonwhites.

Although this interpretation of the Bible is unheard of to most Christians, it, along with many other interpretations, are the tenets of many neo-Nazi groups, most notably the Aryan Nations.

Richard Butler, founder of the Aryan Nations, is a preacher of the Church of Jesus Christ Christian and a follower of the Christian Identity religion. According to the Anti-Defamation League (2002), Butler was introduced to Christian Identity by one of the founders of the Posse Comitatus, General Douglas MacArthur, while also working under Wesley Swift, founder of the Christian Defense League. Both the Posse Comitatus and the Christian Defense League are believers in Identity.

The Posse Comitatus organized in the late 1960s in Portland, Oregon. Posse Comitatus members are considered constitutional fundamentalists. This group's basic philosophy is that the local sheriff is the most important and prominent government figure. They disregard all state and federal laws, including federal and state income tax laws, the U.S. Supreme Court, and do not agree with any international policies or treaties (Ridgeway, 1995). Although most of the Posse Comitatus members were focused on political ventures, the

Posse is also intertwined with Christian Identity beliefs. According to Ridgeway (1995), after several arrests for numerous crimes, the Posse Comitatus essentially disappeared in the 1980s.

Dr. Wesley Swift is considered by most the "father of modern racialist Christian Identity" (Kaplan, 2000, 296). Swift is most well known for his connections to the Church of Jesus Christ Christian and the Christian Defense League. Swift is also credited with the evolution of British-Israelism to Christian Identity. As a preacher of the Church of Jesus Christ Christian, Swift was able to influence many notable white supremacists over the years, including Gerald K. Smith, Richard Butler, and William Potter Gale. In 1964 Swift created the long-standing group called the Christian Defense League. Richard Butler, of the Aryan Nations, was the first to lead this group into prominence. According to the Southern Poverty Law Center (2003), the Christian Defense League currently has only one location in Louisiana. Swift died in 1970, but his legend continues through audiotaped versions of his sermons on the Christian Defense League's homepage.

When Swift died in 1971, Butler proclaimed his Church of Jesus Christ Christian to be the direct successor to Swift's ministry (Anti-Defamation League, 2002). Following Swift's death, Butler moved the organization to a 20-acre compound in Hayden Lake, Idaho. Until recently, Hayden Lake was considered the home of the racist right. During Butler's more vital years he recruited prisoners to join the Aryan Brotherhood, an offshoot Aryan Nations group for prisoners. Two of the three men who were charged and convicted of James Byrd, Jr.'s death in Jasper, Texas, are believed to be members of Richard Butler's Aryan Brotherhood.

Butler and his organization are well known for their racist gatherings at Hayden Lake. Starting in 1982, Butler invited a crew of racist, right wing supporters to the compound for a campfire and "cultural" experience. He called the gathering the first International Congress of Aryan Nations (Ridgeway, 1995) or the Aryan World Congress (Southern Poverty Law Center Intelligence Report, Fall 2000). Numerous racists attended this first Congress, including William Pierce, leader of the National Alliance, and young Bob Matthews, who later became a legend to white supremacy leaders.

Robert J. "Bob" Mathews, former member of the John Birch Society, the National Alliance and Church of Jesus Christ Christian, is also the founder of The Order (Anti-Defamation League, 2002). The Order is one of the more known splinter groups of the Aryan Nations. The Order was founded under the pretense of overthrowing the American government and establishing an Aryan homeland. The idea of forming such a group did not come from Mathews; rather it is believed to have come from Pierce's book *The Turner Diaries*.

After a crime spree in the early and mid-1980s, including the murder of radio talk show host Alan Berg, 23 of the Order's members either pled guilty or were convicted of numerous crimes. Mathews eluded capture but was eventually shot and killed during a shootout with federal agents on an island in the state of Washington.

Butler became well known among white supremacists for the festivals, otherwise known as World Congress meetings, he would have on his compound. Recruiting among young skinheads through music and other media, like the Internet, gave Butler the numbers he sought to organize and create a stable environment and membership list for the Aryan Nations. At these festivals, white power groups would play for young skinheads and older more prominent white supremacists had time to discuss recruiting tactics and financial support for their groups. The 1994 festival at Hayden Lake is considered the most successful of Butler's gatherings. During the early 1900s, the Aryan Nations had a stable and growing membership list and was financially very successful. No one could foresee the fall they were about to take.

By 1995 the Aryan Nations had emerged as the "Nations most menacing neo-nazi group" (Roy, 1995, 10). It is believed that the group was able to make such an impact during those years for two reasons: (1) the KKK and David Duke's group were unorganized and unstable; and (2) the Aryan Nations offered a common ground for many different racist and other radical organizations. Whereas the KKK was more known during that time for hatred of African Americans, the Aryan Nations allowed all extremists alike to join and become a part of the group (Roy, 1995). Although the Aryan Nations could boast being the most dangerous and menacing hate group of the mid-1990s, they soon lost that label to the National Alliance.

In July of 1998 Victoria Keenan and her son Jason stopped their car to pick up a wallet that Jason accidentally dropped out of the car window (Southern Poverty Law Center's Homepage Legal Action, 2003). Unsure exactly what provoked the men, the Keenans do know what followed. Apparently three Aryan Nations guards either heard or noticed the Keenans and jumped in a truck and started following the Keenans, firing bullets into the car. Once the Aryan guards got the car to stop, they walked up to the Keenans and put a gun to Victoria's head. Threatening them to stay away, eventually the guards backed off and left the Keenans with their bullet-riddled car.

Two of the armed guards were eventually sentenced to prison terms for their crimes against the Keenans. More notably though, Richard Butler lost a civil suit filed by Morris Dees and the Southern Poverty Law

Center with the Keenans. The court found Butler and his organization grossly negligent in selecting and supervising the guards (Southern Poverty Law Center's Homepage Legal Action, 2003). The court ordered Butler to pay the Keenans $6.3 million. Butler filed bankruptcy in an attempt to stop or slow down payment of the judgment. The property was eventually turned over to the Keenans, who then sold it to philanthropist Greg Carr. Carr had the Aryan Nations compound burned and will leave the property in its natural state to serve as a "peace park" for the local community.

Since 2001, the Aryan Nations has become less organized, partly because of the civil judgment and the declining health of leader Richard Butler. Originally in 1999 Butler turned leadership of his group over to Pastor Neumann Britton, but Butler outlived Britton, who died in August 2001. Following the death of Britton, Butler announced that Harold "Ray" Redfeairn would become his heir to the organization and August Kreis would become minister of propaganda (Anti-Defamation League, 2002).

Since the summer of 2002 it has become apparent that there are problems among the new leaders of the Aryan Nations. Since then, according to the Anti-Defamation League (2003) web page that offers updates of their 2002 publication, four different Aryan Nations organizations have appeared. According to the Anti-Defamation League: (1) the Church of Jesus Christ Christian or Aryan Nations is still headquartered in Hayden Lake, Idaho, with Richard Butler as the leader; (2) the Church of Jesus Christ Christian or Aryan Nations is based in Ulysses, Pennsylvania, with leaders August Kreis, Charles Juba, and Joshua Caleb Sutter; (3) the Church of the Sons of Yahweh is based in Dayton, Ohio, with Ray Redfeairn and Morris Gulett as their leaders; and finally (4) the Church of True Israel, headquartered in Couer d'Alene, Idaho, is run by Charles Mangels, James Dillavou, John Miller, Ed Dosh, Stanley McCollum, and John Burke. The Church of True Israel was one of the original splinter groups from the Aryan Nation in 1996. Where some would like to believe that this might be the downfall or end of the Aryan Nations, it is apparent that Richard Butler and his group(s) still have much support. After losing his compound to the Keenans in the civil suit, Vincent Bertillini bought a $107,500 home for Butler just outside of his former compound (Southern Poverty Law Center Intelligence Report, Fall 2000).

Another event affecting the existence of neo-Nazi groups that occurred during the summer of 2002 was the death of William Pierce, founder and leader of the National Alliance. However, prior to Pierce's death several sources named Pierce and his organization, the National Alliance, as the most powerful and dangerous of the neo-Nazi groups.

Pierce's organization is very similar in some ways to Butler's Aryan Nations, with the most striking difference being the religious beliefs of Pierce. Pierce does not adhere to Christian Identity; rather, he has developed his own philosophical belief, which he calls Cosmotheism. According to Griffin (2001), "Cosmotheism is a version of the religious orientation called pantheism" (Griffin, 2001, 187). Similar to the evolution of British-Israelism into Christian Identity, Pierce took Pantheism and evolved it to fit into his philosophical or religious belief of Cosmotheism. However, the *Encyclopedia of White Power* (Kaplan, 2000) states that Pierce's Cosmotheism can be attributed to Ben Klassen's Church of the Creator. Regardless of the source Pierce used to develop his religious doctrine, the religion itself is rooted in racism and anti-Semitism.

William Pierce, a former physics professor at Oregon State University, discovered the extremist movement during the early 1960s when he joined the John Birch Society (Anti-Defamation League, 2002). The John Birch Society is a radical-right political organization, sometimes referred to as an extremist group, where many would-be racists or anti-Semitists often start their extremist activities. After leaving the John Birch Society, Pierce found a home in the American Nazi Party. Although Pierce claimed to have never been a member of the American Nazi Party, he had a long association with George Lincoln Rockwell, the founder and leader of the Party. Pierce even became the editor of Rockwell's publication, the *National Socialist World*, that targeted academics. After Rockwell was assassinated in 1967, Pierce became one of the leaders of Rockwell's old American Nazi Party, then called the National Socialist White People's Party.

In 1968–69, according to the Anti-Defamation League (2002) and the *Encyclopedia of White Power* (Kaplan, 2000), Pierce left the National Socialist White People's Party to start a new extremist group with Willis Carto, called the National Youth Alliance. Carto is one of the longest standing extremists in the U.S. He has founded numerous anti-Semitic organizations over the years and has been involved with numerous racist and extremists leaders, such as, George Wallace, David Duke, Tom Metzger, and Ben Klassen, to name a few.

Willis Carto is often referred to as the most influential anti-Semitic in the U.S. (Anti-Defamation League, 2002). Although, his name is not as well know as others, Carto emerged in the white supremacist movement in the 1950s. He served as leader of the Liberty Lobby, the National Youth Alliance, and one of the organizers for George Wallace's presidential campaign in 1968. Over the years he was also the publisher for *The Spotlight*, which, for a time was the leading far right publication. Although he is a well-known anti-Semitic, he does not like himself or his groups to be referred to with that label. In the 1980s Carto sued the *Wall Street Journal* for libel when it referred to the Liberty Lobby as a "far right" and "anti-Semitic" organization (Anti-Defamation League, 2002). Remarkably Carto, born in 1926, is still alive. However, his organizations have seen better days. Regarding his work, the publication of *The Spotlight,* his work on Wallace's campaign, and the National Youth Alliance were his most prominent ventures.

The National Youth Alliance never achieved success compared to the National Alliance. In 1970–71 Pierce left the National Youth Alliance to form the new National Alliance by 1974. In 1985 Pierce relocated the National Alliance to Mill Point, West Virginia, on a 346-acre farm (Anti-Defamation League, 2002). Since that time Pierce has developed video games and published several books, articles, and magazines or journals. Pierce also acquired several white power music companies, including Resistance Records and Vinland Records. Most notably, early in the 21st century, Pierce developed a video game called "Ethnic Cleansing." The video game is aimed at children, as is the white power music, and allows them to participate in the "race war" by killing minorities and Jews, with the goal being a white nation. Finally, Pierce has published the magazine *Attack,* which later became the *National Vanguard* and *Resistance* magazines, and the books *Hunter* and *The Turner Diaries* under the pseudonym Andrew Macdonald.

Both *Hunter* and *The Turner Diaries* have been accused of being the blueprint for several crimes associated with extremist groups. Although Pierce claims not to support any violent actions committed by National Alliance group members or any other extremist group members, crimes committed by The Order and Timothy McVeigh have been found to be very similar to the crimes depicted in Pierce's books. Pierce was also found liable in a civil suit filed by Morris Dees and the Southern Poverty Law Center for the murder of a black man in North Carolina believed to be inspired by *The Turner Diaries* (Southern Poverty Law Center's Homepage Legal Action, 2003). Even with the civil suit's judgment, Pierce's group, the National Alliance, remained at the forefront of white supremacists groups until his death in 2002.

According to the Anti-Defamation League (Online updates, 2003), since Pierce's death the National Alliance has become very unstable. Erich Gliebe became the leader of the National Alliance and there appears to be arguments between him and Billy Roper. Apparently, Roper had plans to become the leader of the organization. Roper's plans included unifying the National Alliance with other American white supremacy

groups. Gliebe disagreed with this plan. Roper may have been the heir of the National Alliance, but after the September 11 attacks on the World Trade Center and the Pentagon, Pierce may have changed his mind. Roper took the liberty of stating to the press that he wished National Alliance members had "half as much testicular fortitude" as the September 11 hijackers. Pierce retracted Roper's comments by saying that his praise for the mass murderers was "ill-advised private comments" (Southern Poverty Law Center, Spring 2002).

It is also important to note that Pierce kept a distance from all other white supremacy groups because of disagreements with their tactics. Pierce ran a very strict organization. He did not agree with Nazi symbols or tattoos on members of the National Alliance. Nor did he agree with the shaved heads seen in several youth skinhead groups, or Nazi uniforms. Rather, Pierce felt that he could influence the general public of the U.S. better if he presented himself, and his members, as intellectual businessmen wanting to better the U.S. for the white race. Pierce, himself, would rarely speak to the public, but when he did he spoke in an intellectual, educated, nonextremist fashion. Most noted that Pierce was far from being charismatic, but Griffen (2001) notes that he believed he had a "very dynamic presence." Although Pierce had few media-related interviews during his life, he never gave permission for other members to speak to the public about the organization.

Another would-be leader of the National Alliance is Kevin Alfred Strom. Strom has been a long time member of the National Alliance and since Pierce's death he has taken over the radio broadcast/Internet feed "American Dissident Voice" (Southern Poverty Law Center, 2003). Earlier in the 1990s Strom disappeared from the group after getting married, but has reappeared and taken a very active role in leading the National Alliance past the change in leadership. However, it appears that Gliebe and Roper will continue to feud over the details of running such an organization. And, although the National Alliance has lost some respect and membership because of these feuds, they are still continuing to pursue recruitment campaigns and rallies waging support for anti-Semitism and racists activities.

ALEXIS J. MILLER

References and Further Reading

Anti-Defamation League, *Extremism In America: A Guide,* Anti-Defamation League, 2002. Available at: www.adl.org.

Barkun, M. 1994. *Religion and the Racist Right: Origins of the Christian Identity Movement,* Chapel Hill, NC, The University of North Carolina Press.

George, J. and Wilcox, L., *American Extremists: Suprem-acists, Klansmen, Communists, and Others,* Amherst, MA, Prometheus Books.

Griffen, R.S. 2001. *The Fame of a Dead Man's Deeds: An Up-Close Portrait of White Nationalist William Pierce,* Bloom-ington, IN, 1st Books Library.

Kaplan, J., Ed. 2000. *Encyclopedia of White Power,* Walnut Creek, CA, AltaMira Press.

Macdonald, A. 1996. *The Turner Diaries,* Hillsboro, WV, National Vanguard Books, 1978, New York, Barricade Books.

Macdonald, A. 1989. *Hunter,* Hillsboro, WV, National Vanguard Books.

Ridgeway, J. 1995. *Blood in the Face: The Ku Klux Klan, Aryan Nation, Nazi Skinhead, and the Rise of a New White Culture,* 2nd ed., New York, Thunder's Mouth Press.

Roy, J.T., Sr. 1995. Organized hate in America, *Civil Rights Journal,* 1.

Southern Poverty Law Center. 2003. *Intelligence Report,* Issue 100, Montgomery, AL, Southern Poverty Law Center, Spring.

Southern Poverty Law Center. 2000. *Intelligence Report,* Issue 109, Montgomery, AL, Southern Poverty Law Center, Fall.

Southern Poverty Law Center. 2002. *Intelligence Report,* Issue 105, Montgomery, AL, Southern Poverty Law Center, Summer.

(All Intelligence Reports of Southern Poverty Law Center, dating back to Winter of 1997 are available at: www. SPLCENTER.org.)

See also **Hate Crime**

Netherlands, Crime and Justice in the

Traditionally, the Kingdom of the Netherlands, situated in Western Europe bordering Belgium, Germany, and the North Sea, has been known in almost a stereotypical fashion for both low crime rates and a very mild penal climate. As Kommer put it, not without a touch of irony:

> [...] It used to be very simple: the Netherlands was a country of guidance, an enlightening example for the rest of the world. Our criminal law was humane, and our country was proud of having the lowest number of detainees per 100,000 inhabitants. It was therefore no wonder that criminologists from all over the world came over to see how we pulled that off (Kommer, 1994).

This picture was by and large accurate until about 1980. The Netherlands experienced a period of *decarceration* in the decades prior to 1980 yielding a prison rate of only about 35 per 100,000 population (Downes, 1988). Crime rates were relatively low as well. Crime rates have risen since then, but seem to have peaked around 1994. The same cannot be said for the prison population, which continued to rise until, at least, the end of the millennium. Today the prison rate is 85, which is close to the European average, but lower than the world average (about 125), and incomparably lower than the rates of countries such as the Russian Federation and the U.S. (Walmsley, 2002).

The increase of the prison population has been carefully documented (see Pakes, 2000). Part of its explanation lies in the aforementioned increase in criminality, in particular with regard to serious and violent crime. Secondly, researchers observed a selective increase in punitivity: violent and sexual crimes have attracted longer prison sentences whereas many perceived minor offences are not being punished more severely. Other reasons given include developments in forensic science that have improved detection and the advent of organized crime to the Netherlands (Fijnaut et al., 1998) to which the Dutch authorities have struggled to formulate a balanced and effective response.

Policing efforts to combat the new threat in the early 1990s were characterized by overzealous and unlawful investigative methods that yielded few results. Moreover, the discovery of this widespread use of radical and unsupervised investigative actions such as the controlled import of drugs and infiltration in criminal organizations led to a crisis in Dutch law enforcement. Policing had gone out of control. Judicial review by bodies such as the prosecution service, investigative magistrates, and the courts was found to be ineffective or altogether lacking. Legislation to regulate the when and how of novel investigative methods was also found to be lacking. Attitudes of sections within the police and the prosecution service that overemphasized crime fighting at the expense of due process were also criticized (Van Traa, 1995). However, a government commissioned report argued that control over criminal investigations has been regained. New legislation on investigative methods has been introduced. Another novelty is the Central Review Committee that reviews and authorizes the most radical policing action on a national basis.

The state of crime in the Netherlands gives rise to debate as it depends very much on which crimes are being considered. The homicide rate in the Netherlands seems to be very low as compared to many other countries, with a rate of 1.5 per 100,000 (Kangasputa, Joutsen, and Ollus, 1999). Firearm ownership and use are low, and quite possibly declining (Van der Leest and Luykx, 2000). The situation with regard to aggressive contact crime (robbery, sexual assaults, and assaults with force) is less favorable: the 2000 International Crime Victimization Survey (ICVS) ranked the Netherlands 12th out of 17 countries (Van Kesteren, Mayhew, and Nieuwbeerta, 2000). Property crime appears to be rife. According to the ICVS and Heuni data (Kangasputa, Joutsen, and Ollus, 1998) the Netherlands ranks very highly on this front (to which bicycle theft is a major contributor) whereas the petty crime index used by Kangasputa and colleagues even places the Netherlands at the top of the countries included in their study.

Organized crime undeniably exists in the Netherlands. However, the degree of organization has been argued to be relatively low. According to Fijnaut et al. (1998) there is no evidence for closely knit, hierarchically organized structures that are highly interwoven with legal institutions. Rather, criminal organizations tend to be loosely related friendships of people who establish contacts when useful. They are primarily involved with trafficking of humans and illegal goods, most particularly drugs.

The fact that the Netherlands is considered an attractive place for drug-related activities is no doubt related to the perceived leniency with which the authorities treat the use of so-called soft drugs, most particularly cannabis. Whereas import and wholesale trade of cannabis is illegal and can attract lengthy prison sentences, it is not always rigorously policed as a certain level of supply serves to effectuate the policy of condoning personal cannabis use as long as it is within guidelines set.

The policy on cannabis is seen to be more or less unique to the Netherlands although the ministry of justice is quick to point out that local initiatives similar to the Dutch policy occur in many countries. Other features that reinforce the Netherlands' image as a country in which matters of justice are dealt with slightly differently include the legalization of euthanasia and assisted suicide. Strict rules are in operation to regulate this practice. Such life ending acts can only be performed by a physician, following a consistent and repeated wish by a patient able to express such a wish, further to a second opinion, and subject to a notification procedure (Tak, 2002). The legalization of brothels in 1999 is another such piece of legislation that has made the newspapers throughout the world. Legislation such as those on brothels and euthanasia will serve to ensure that the Netherlands will continue to be regarded as a bit of an oddity with regard to their criminal justice policy making. However, this reputation can no longer be justified with reference to the achievements that brought it that reputation, the low crime and prison rates. As far as these are concerned, times certainly have changed.

FRANCIS J. PAKES

References and Further Reading

Downes, D. (1988). *Contrasts in Tolerance: Postwar Penal Policy in the Netherlands and England and Wales*, Oxford, U.K., Clarendon Press.

Fijnaut, C.M.C.F., Bovenkerk, F., Van de Bunt, H.G., and Bruinsma, G.J.N. (1998). *Organized Crime in the Netherlands*, The Hague, The Netherlands, Kluwer.

Kommer, M.M. (1994). Het Nederlandse strafklimaat in internationaal perspectief [The Dutch penal climate in international perspective], in Moerings, M., Ed., *Hoe punitief is Nederland?* [How punitive is the Netherlands?], Arnhem, The Netherlands, Gouda Quint.

Kangaspunta, K., Joutsen, M., and Ollus, N., Eds. (1998). *Crime and Criminal Justice in Europe and North America*, Heuni Report Publication Series no 25. Helsinki, Finland.

Pakes, F.J. (2000). League leaders in mid-table: On the major changes in Dutch prison policy, *Howard Journal of Criminal Justice*, 39, 30–39.

Tak, P.J.P. (1999). *The Dutch Criminal Justice System: Organisation and Operation*, The Hague, The Netherlands, WODC.

Tak, P.J.P. (2002). *Essays on Dutch Criminal Policy*, Nijmegen, The Netherlands, Wolf Legal Productions.

Van der Leest, W.P.E. and Luykx, F. (2000). Kruitsporen [gun powder traces], *Tijdschrift voor Criminologie* [Journal for Criminology], 42(2), 1130–1141.

Van Kesteren, J., Mayhew, P., and Nieuwbeerta, P. (2000). *Criminal Victimisation in Seventeen Industrialised Countries: Key Findings from the 2000 International Crime Victims Survey*, The Hague, The Netherlands, Ministry of Justice.

Van Traa, M. (1995). *Parlementaire Enquete Commissie Opsporingsmethoden: Inzake opsporing* [Parliamentary inquiry committee investigative methods: concerning criminal investigation], The Hague, The Netherlands, Sdu.

Walmsley, R. (2002). *World Prison List*, 3rd ed., London, HMSO.

See also **Comparative Crime and Justice; International Crime Trends**

Neurophysiological Theories of Criminal Behavior

Theories that identify some aspect of brain functioning as contributing to criminal behavior are called neurophysiological (or neurologically specific or brain-based theories). As more has been learned about how the brain controls behavior, several neurophysiological theories have been proposed. They share a common logical structure, as illustrated in the diagram below. This structure differs from the structure of the more prevalent social environmental theories not by denying that social environmental variables are important, but by asserting that social variables interact with genetic and neurological factors. As the diagram shows, both genetic influences and social environmental influences are assumed to affect how the brain of each person functions, which in turn affects his or her probabilities of violating criminal statutes.

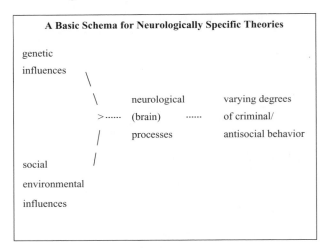

A Basic Schema for Neurologically Specific Theories

The human brain is structurally similar to that of other mammals, and consists of two distinct parts, although these parts are connected so that they continually communicate with one another. The more primitive part of the mammalian brain is called the subcortex and consists of regions of the brain that control everything from respiration and other bodily functions to the sex drive and other basic emotions. Covering this subcortex is the neocortex (meaning "new layer"). It is the part of the brain reading and understanding this article, and can be thought of as an emotionless computer that helps the subcortex satisfy its "desires" in relative efficiency.

For both genetic and environmental reasons, each of us has different strengths and weaknesses with respect to these two fundamental components of our brains. According to proponents of neurophysiological theories, these relative strengths and weaknesses can help explain why some people are more chronically involved in crime, delinquency, and other antisocial behavior patterns than other people. The six most prominent neurophysiological theories at the present time are suboptimal arousal theory, reward dominance theory, seizuring theory, frontal lobe theory, hemispheric functioning theory, and neuroandrogenic theory.

Suboptimal Arousal Theory

Midway through the 20th century, researchers began documenting that some people are inherently much less sensitive to environmental stimuli than other people. This led two psychologists, American David Lykken and Hans J. Eysenck, a German who moved to England early in his career, to speculate about how people's varying sensitivities to environmental stimuli may be responsible for antisocial behavior. Both suggested that for neurological reasons mainly having to do with subcortical arousal control, some people prefer much more intense environmental stimulation, while others prefer very little (with most preferring something in between).

If a person's arousal control center is unusually sensitive to incoming stimuli, he or she will be prone to quickly learn to avoid engaging in behavior that raises the intensity of stimuli to unpleasant levels. On the other hand, if an individual is unusually insensitive to environmental stimuli, he or she will require a high level of unpleasant stimuli before learning to avoid the same behavior. According to suboptimal arousal theory, the latter individuals will be more prone toward criminal or antisocial behavior.

In addition to predicting that offenders will be difficult to condition with punishment, suboptimal arousal theory also suggests that offenders will go out of their way to have environmental experiences that are unusually stimulating. According to the theory, this is because the higher brain centers are often being "starved" for stimulation because of the failure of the arousal control regions in the subcortex to attend to most of the incoming stimuli.

A simple way to illustrate suboptimal arousal theory is to discuss it in conjunction with ADHD (attention deficit with hyperactivity disorder), a condition that has been statistically linked to involvement in delinquent and criminal behavior. Studies have shown that in most cases the hyperactive and inattentive behavior of ADHD children can be temporarily "normalized" by giving them a stimulant drug called methylphenidate (with the brand name Ritalin). Ritalin has potency that falls roughly between two other stimulants: caffeine and amphetamines.

At first, it seems odd that a stimulant drug would have a calming effect on most ADHD children, but suboptimal arousal theory offers an explanation. Studies have shown that like many conduct-disordered children and chronic delinquents and criminals, the brains of ADHD children tend to emit unusually high proportions of slow brain waves. Theoretically, these slow brain waves are being experienced as "boredom," which in turn motivates affected individuals to seek and create environments with more things going on. Unfortunately, many of their boredom-relieving activities are irritating and disruptive to others. Stimulant drugs artificially activate the brain, and thereby temporarily diminish the symptomatic behavior.

In summary, suboptimal arousal theory asserts that a substantial amount of human behavior is oriented toward maintaining a preferred (or optimal) level of arousal. Like Goldie Locks, we all seek environmental conditions that are neither too constant nor too varied. However, as with the three bears, what is "just right" for one person may be "too much" or "too little" for someone else. As far as criminal or antisocial behavior is concerned, suboptimal arousal theory stipulates that persons who most often feel "starved" for environmental stimuli will be most likely to offend.

Reward Dominance Theory

Herbert C. Quay (1927–) and Jeffrey A. Gray (1934–) are among the main proponents of the so-called reward dominance theory. The theory is based on the idea that most voluntary behavior is regulated by the relative strength of two opposing behavior control functions in the brain. One is called the behavioral activation system (BAS) and the other is called the behavioral inhibition system (BIS). The BAS is thought to motivate or induce behavioral responses to cues of probable reward, and the BIS is believed to inhibit behavioral responses to cues of probable punishment.

When someone senses that reward is likely to be a consequence of one's actions, an individual's BAS is thought to be become engaged, and this engagement will motivate him or her to initiate the necessary action sequence. In other words, if steps A, B, and C are perceived as leading to a reward, the BAS will begin the action sequence. In contrast, when an individual perceives a high probability of being punished if a particular course of action is taken, the BIS will be engaged. This means that, if steps X, Y, and Z are seen as likely to result in punishment, an inhibitory region of the brain will prevent the action sequence from being initiated.

According to reward dominance theory, the relative strengths of the BAS and the BIS are roughly equal for most people. As a result, most people are sensitive to both the rewarding and the punishing aspects of their actions, and they learn to make decisions accordingly. In the case of criminals and psychopaths, however, reward dominance theory asserts that the BIS is relatively weak or the BAS is especially strong, or both. Consequently, criminals and psychopaths are hyperresponsive to the prospects of reward and hyporesponsive to the prospects of punishment, or reward dominant. The behavior of criminals and psychopaths, therefore, becomes skewed toward all sorts of reckless and socially inappropriate activities.

Most of the initial research undertaken to test the merit of the reward dominance theory involved computerized games. After some initial "easy wins," the computer was programmed to ensure greater and greater proportions of losses, so that it behooves players to stop playing beyond the first dozen tries. Reward dominance theory predicted that antisocial subjects would persist at these games despite increasing losses. The results of these experiments have been largely supportive of the theory.

Reward dominance theory basically asserts that people who are antisocial and criminal become easily "hooked" on the prospects of reward, and ignore the signs that response contingencies are actually not at all in their favor. Proponents of reward dominance theory have sought to identify specific aspects of brain functioning that might actually function as the theory asserts. There are some promising leads involving some neurotransmitter systems connecting subcortical and neocortical brain regions, but research is still underway.

Seizuring Theory

In the 1970s, a small group of psychiatrists and neurologists began considering the possible role of the limbic system in certain types of criminal behavior. They were drawn to study this particular region of the subcortex after noting the bizarre and seemingly senseless nature of some violent crimes, such as attacking a loved one or a drinking buddy over some utterly trivial issue, or gunning down children in a school yard.

Seizuring theory was inspired by research on epilepsy and the fact that some epileptic seizures are said to be subconvulsive, meaning that they do not result in the spastic convulsions (fits) normally associated with epilepsy. For instance, if a seizure is localized in a small region of the limbic system, it may not affect motor coordination at all, but it could have dramatic effects on emotions, because the limbic system has a great deal to do with basic social emotions such as rage and jealousy.

According to seizuring theorists, subconvulsive seizures in and around the limbic system may sometimes induce criminal behavior. The term that has often come to be used to describe this phenomenon is *episodic dyscontrol*. During these episodes, affected individuals might act with no impairment as far as basic coordination is concerned. Nevertheless, the behavior might not only be contrary to "rational thought," but could even surprise the person engaging in the behavior (as far as his or her neocortex is concerned).

The detection of subconvulsive seizures can be much more difficult than in the case of convulsive (epileptic) seizures. This is not only because subconvulsive seizures, by definition, do not cause convulsive fits, but also because subconvulsive seizures often occur too deep inside the brain to be detectable with electrodes attached to the scalp.

An area of the limbic system that has been most often implicated in the seizuring theory of violent criminality is the *amygdala*. Not only is it one of the most seizure-prone regions of the brain, but also a part of the limbic system most involved in regulating social emotions. Physical damage to this primitive region of the mammalian brain frequently unleashes a torrent of violent behavior, both in humans and in other mammals. Nevertheless, some types of damage to the amygdala can make aggressive animals more passive and docile.

One of the strongest lines of support for seizuring theory has come from research on the treatment of persons who engage in criminal behavior because of diagnosed episodic dyscontrol. Medication that is often effective in treating epilepsy—known as anticonvulsants—has also been found to be helpful in treating episodic dyscontrol. Experiments with laboratory animals also indicate that vicious attacks can be curtailed by anticonvulsants.

Full-blown epilepsy has such devastating effects upon muscular coordination that its victims would rarely be capable of criminal behavior, although some seizures are subconvulsive in the sense that they affect areas of the brain that have little direct control over muscular movement. According to seizuring theory, if seizures occur in or around the limbic system, they can trigger fairly primitive emotions that elicit acts of violence and perhaps property offenses in the form of kleptomania or vandalism.

Frontal Lobe Theory

The frontal portions of the neocortex, called the frontal lobes, are prominent in humans relative to other mammals, comprising nearly a quarter of the entire human brain. The part played by the frontal lobes in human thought and behavior control have been deduced in part from studying people with severe damage to these lobes (for example, from injuries in unrestrained automobile crashes). These studies have revealed that most people usually suffer only modest ill effects as far as basic intelligence is concerned. The sorts of effects most associated with frontal lobe injuries mainly have to do with the ability to plan and reflect upon the consequences of various courses of action needed to attain long-term goals. These planning skills are known as executive functions.

In addition to impairing realistic plans for the future, damage to the frontal lobes often results in inflexible responses to new, unfamiliar contingencies. Affected people exhibit what has been termed response preservation, meaning stubbornly sticking to the originally established response mode even though doing so is not accomplishing the subject's desired objective, and may even be counterproductive.

Another prominent function of the frontal lobes appears to be control over empathy and feelings of remorse and shame, achieved when these lobes monitor the limbic system. Damage to the prefrontal region of the frontal lobes is often associated with emotional "flatness" and an inability to feel genuine sorrow for having caused others to suffer.

Beginning primarily with Ethan Gorenstein, numerous proposals have been made regarding the possible involvement of the frontal lobes in criminal and antisocial behavior. According to this theory, the frontal lobes evolved primarily to help guide behavior that requires long-term planning and foresight, particularly within a complex social environment. The theory assumes that planning and foresight usually make it possible for people to satisfy their basic needs and desires without interfering with other people's needs and wants. This reasoning has led proponents of frontal lobe theory to attribute much antisocial behavior to failures in executive functioning.

Dysfunctioning of the prefrontal area is not only because of physical injury; more subtle causes of frontal lobe dysfunctions may include various genetic factors. In addition, damage sustained during prenatal development by mothers consuming alcohol or other drugs during critical times in fetal brain development may prevent the prefrontal lobes from developing normally.

Hemispheric Functioning Theory

The neocortex is divided into two hemispheres, the left and the right. Many studies have shown that the two hemispheres function differently, and that these functional differences manifest themselves in terms of different types of thoughts and emotions. The three best documented differences are: (1) the right hemisphere is less adept at verbal or linguistic reasoning than is the left hemisphere, tending to reason more holistically and in spatial terms; (2) the right hemisphere is responsible for more negative or unfriendly/rejecting emotions than is true of the left hemisphere; and (3) the right hemisphere appears to respond more impulsively to stimuli than is true of the left hemisphere.

According to hemispheric functioning theorists, criminal or antisocial behavior is more likely to emanate from the right hemisphere (and/or from a failure of the left hemisphere to override the right). Theoretically, this is because obeying the law is a form of prosocial behavior requiring that one understand linguistic commands and reflect upon the consequences of violating those laws. If so, left hemispheric dysfuntions might contribute to criminal behavior. The earliest proponent of this theory is a Canadian psychiatrist named Pierre Flor-Henry.

Neuroandrogenic Theory

The neuroandrogenic theory was first proposed by Lee Ellis. The theory focuses on how male sex hormones (collectively known as androgens) influence brain functioning. According to this theory, testosterone (the main androgen) in particular acts on the brain in ways that increase overtly competitive behavior. To explain *why* testosterone would have such effects on brain functioning, the theory asserts that overt competitiveness has helped males transmit their genes to future generations more than similar behavior has done in females. Theoretically, one expression of this competitiveness is criminal or antisocial behavior, especially during adolescence

To explain *how* androgens increase overt competitiveness, the theory proposes that the male brain is sexually differentiated in two stages. The first stage takes place before birth (the perinatal stage) and the second follows the onset of puberty. During the perinatal stage, exposing the brain to testosterone (and its metabolites) causes the brain to be less sensitive to stimuli. This is called the *suboptimal arousal effect*.

Theoretically, perinatal exposure of the brain to male-typical testosterone has a second effect that influences offending probabilities. This second effect involves shifting neocortical functioning away from the left hemisphere and toward the right hemisphere, a phenomenon called the *rightward shift effect*.

At puberty, the brain is again exposed to high levels of testosterone, which, Ellis believes, further accentuates and fully engages both the suboptimal arousal and the rightward shift effects. According to the neuroandrogenic theory, both of these brain functioning effects increase the probability of delinquency, criminal, and antisocial behavior.

The neuroandrogenic theory essentially combines the suboptimal arousal theory and the hemispheric functioning theory, and then adds concepts having to do with the effects of androgens on brain functioning. The exact form that overtly competitive behavior takes not only depends on brain exposure to androgens, but also on learning. Most males rather quickly learn how to express their overtly competitive behavior in ways that do not elicit legal retaliation (e.g., sports or job performance). However, males who have the greatest difficulty learning (e.g., those low in intelligence or with learning disabilities) are most likely to persist in offending beyond adolescence.

Overall, neurophysiological theories of criminal behavior emphasize that various aspects of brain functioning are at the heart of people's varying tendencies to engage in criminal and antisocial behavior. Nothing in these theories is contrary to the view that social environmental factors are also important. Neurophysiological theories merely assert that for a host of biological reasons, people vary in how readily they learn some behavior patterns relative to others, and that this variability includes behavior that is contrary to existing criminal statutes.

LEE ELLIS

References and Further Reading

Ellis, L. and Walsh, A. (2000). *Criminology: A Global Perspective,* Boston, MA, Allyn & Bacon.

Lykken, D.T. (1995). *The Antisocial Personality,* Hillsdale, NJ, Lawrence Erlbaum.

McCord, J. and Tremblay, R.E., Eds. (1995). *Preventing Antisocial Behavior,* New York, Guilford.

Raine, A. (1993). *The Psychopathology of Crime,* San Diego, CA, Academic Press.

See also **Genetic Theories of Criminal Behavior; Psychological Theories of Criminal Behavior**

Neutralization or Drift Theory

The subculture of delinquency literature suggests that criminality is learned through social interactions. Most research on subcultural theory has involved the processes through which delinquency is learned, but less is known about the *content* of what is learned when a person becomes delinquent. One view is that the delinquent learned a system of values that represented a complete inversion of the moral code held by conventional society (e.g., Cohen, 1955). If conventional society believes police officers are honorable and that crimes like theft and assault are wrong, then delinquents believe that every cop is a criminal and that all the so-called sinners are saints.

Gresham Sykes and David Matza's (1957) neutralization theory emerged as a critique of the view that delinquents held procriminal attitudes that are in opposition to the values of conventional society. Sykes and Matza argued that if this view were correct, then apprehended delinquents would likely show no feelings of guilt or shame, nor would they likely have strong attachments to noncriminal parents or role models. On the contrary, Sykes and Matza argued that at least at the point of apprehension, delinquents did frequently experience moral discomfort about their offending, and seemed to worry about how their arrest would affect their families. This internalized guilt seemed manifest most in the delinquent's use of a variety of excuses and justifications for his or her behavior.

Rather than learning an oppositional value system, therefore, Sykes and Matza argued that these rationalizations—which they termed *techniques of neutralization*—were the primary means through which delinquency was transmitted via delinquent subcultures. In this formulation, delinquents can "have their cake and eat it, too." They can embrace conventional moral values, but they also allay the pangs of guilt involved in breaking these rules by internalizing a variety of neutralizations, including:

- *Denial of responsibility*—The claim that one's actions were involuntary, accidental or the product of other influences ("They made me do it").
- *Denial of injury*—Minimizing the harm caused by one's actions ("These stores all have insurance anyway")
- *Denial of the victim*—Blaming the victim for the crime ("The bastard deserved it")

- *Condemnation of the condemners*—A reaction formation that shifts the attention away from one's own indiscretions and toward the hypocrisy, prejudice, and hidden deviance of those in power in society ("The cops are more violent than we are")
- *Appeal to higher loyalty*—Justifying deviance on the basis of some greater cause such as one's duty or honor ("I was avenging my sister's honor")

More than just after-the-fact rationalizations, the internalization of this vocabulary of motives (Mills, 1940) was thought to "precede deviant behavior and make deviant behavior possible" (Sykes and Matza, 1957, 667).

David Matza (1964) developed this idea further with his concept of "drift." He defines "drift" as a temporary period of irresponsibility or an episodic relief from moral constraint. Neutralization enables drift by freeing the individual from the moral bind of law and order. Importantly, according to Matza, the experience of drift does not "cause" delinquency in the positivist sense, but rather drift makes delinquency possible. Revisiting the classical school of criminological thought, Matza argues that delinquency is not determined by external or internal forces as in positivist criminology, but rather is the product of the delinquent's will.

Once set in a state of drift, a young person is likely to choose willfully to commit a crime under circumstances of *preparation* (or familiarity with the particular offense type) or *desperation*. Matza's concept of desperation is linked to the delinquent's central neutralization technique, the denial of responsibility, or what is referred to as a "mood of fatalism." In the mood of fatalism, common to the experience of drift, delinquents believe that they have been "helplessly propelled into new situations" like a "billiard ball" (David Matza, 1964, 667). By denying their own agency in this fashion, delinquents are able to relieve themselves of feelings of responsibility and blame. At the same time, however, this feeling of helplessness encourages the delinquent to want to "take control" of his or her situation and prove that he or she can "make something happen." Considering the limited options available to adolescents, this frequently means committing a new type of offense in order to generate excitement and no small amount of attention and even prestige. After all, at the same time that conventional society officially condemns criminal behavior, it also glorifies and glamorizes outlaws and rule-breakers.

Indeed, in an article titled "Delinquency and Subterranean Values," Matza and Sykes (1961) argue that many of the values associated with the delinquent subculture, including excitement, displays of daring, leisure, and easy wealth, are actually derived from the wider society. Although not outwardly recognized as respectable, these "subterranean values" are privately affirmed by the conventional majority, and these buried cultural beliefs help to legitimize delinquent behavior (for a recent version of this argument, see Hagan et al., 1998).

Matza and Sykes imply that the delinquent subculture might be a disturbing exaggeration, rather than an inversion, of mainstream culture with its subterranean values of manliness and conspicuous consumption. "Youth stand at the threshold of manhood, and consequently they are more obsessed by the postures and poses that symbolize and confirm it" (Matza and Sykes, 1961, 156). Adolescent males, insecure with their masculinity, can become obsessed with "the cult of cowboy masculinity" promoted in the mass media (Matza and Sykes, 1961, 62), and can become enraged at imagined affronts to their dignity or "manhood." Similarly, the disorganization of the youth gang (and the predictable loss of its membership through maturational reform) can encourage exaggerated emphasis on the conventional value of loyalty to one's friends.

Likewise, the neutralization techniques used by delinquents are not unknown to mainstream society. In fact, Matza (1964) argues that delinquent neutralizations are legitimated by a most unlikely source—the juvenile justice system itself. When agents of convention, from social workers to judges, argue that delinquents are the helpless products of their environment, they unwittingly contribute to the internalization of neutralizing excuses. Matza writes, "The subcultural delinquent is exposed to and hears—his ears are perked—pronouncements from a variety of allegedly reputable sources that confirm his viewpoint. He hears, distorts, and capitalizes on these pronouncements" (Matza, 1964, 91). The mitigation procedures built into the legal machinery itself lend credence and support to adolescent interpretations of self-defense and *mens rea*, and in this way, the "law contains the seeds of its own neutralization."

Finally, Matza argues that the perceived hypocrisy, mystification and "word magic" of the juvenile court further erodes the juvenile delinquent's belief in the legitimacy of the moral order. In particular, the message that, "It isn't your fault that you commit crimes, you are a product of your environment (or your genes or whatever), but you will be punished for what you have done anyhow" strikes most delinquents, who are "untrained

in sophistry," as terribly unjust. The sense of injustice then becomes a primary catalyst of drift. In fact, the delinquent subculture itself is, among other things, "a memory file that collects injustices," according to Matza (Matza, 1964, 102).

The Legacy and Implications of Neutralization or Drift Theory

The work of Sykes and Matza has had a profound and continuing impact on criminological theory, research, and practice. Although rooted in a symbolic interactionist perspective, the central premise of neutralization theory has been incorporated into major criminological theories as diverse as social control theory (Hirschi, 1969) and social learning theory (Akers, 1985). Nearly every year, qualitative research appears in criminology journals confirming that deviants of every nature use neutralizations when accounting for disapproved acts ranging from deer poaching, to hate crimes against the Amish, to topless dancing, to shopping on Sunday (among active Mormons), to violence against prostitutes.

The most common criticism of neutralization theory, however, involves the perplexing "chicken and egg" problem of causal ordering. Do neutralizations cause delinquency? Or does delinquency cause neutralizations? Although there is virtually no disagreement in the literature regarding the prevalent use of justifications and excuses among offenders, researchers disagree on whether these techniques of neutralization actually precede deviant behavior or whether they are just after-the-fact rationalizations unrelated to the original offending (e.g., Hindelang, 1970).

Hirschi (1969) has suggested that both positions might be true. When individuals are caught breaking some norm, they may create a retrospective justification to rationalize the act. The use and acceptance of such justifications, in turn, may allow that person to continue or even accelerate offending behavior. Hirschi describes the development of neutralizations, therefore, as a "hardening process" that facilitates continued criminal behavior, and this reconceptualization has received empirical support from Agnew (1994) and Minor (1981).

In fact, empirical research has generally supported most of the claims of neutralization theory, but the correlation between acceptance of neutralizations and delinquency tends to be small to moderate at best. Agnew (1994) has argued that this may be because of a failure to incorporate the other elements of Matza's theory into the empirical tests—"a fundamental flaw in virtually all research on neutralization" (Agnew, 1994, 560). After all, Sykes and Matza did not argue that neutralizations caused criminal behavior in a direct fashion, only that neutralizations freed an individual from moral restraints, and could allow for delinquency under specific conditions. Using a nationally representative sample and longitudinal design, Agnew (1994) included these conditioning variables into his test of neutralization theory, and found a strong and significant relationship between acceptance of neutralizations and future involvement in violence.

The notion of "drift" and its implications for positivist research have also been revised in recent years (e.g., Hagan, 1991; Henry and Milovanovic, 1996). The majority of research inspired by *Delinquency and Drift* (Matza, 1964), however, does not "test" the theory in a positivist sense. Rather, remaining in agreement with the idea of qualitative "naturalistic" research (Matza, 1969), this research seeks to understand delinquency from the perspective of the delinquent and within the context of his or her relationship to society (e.g., Maruna, 2001).

Importantly, the impact of Sykes and Matza's work has also transcended the realm of criminology. In his research on the understanding of the Holocaust among Germans, Hazani (1991) argues that neutralization techniques are "universal modes of response to inconsistency" that reveal widely shared "modes of reduction of disequilibrium that are totally unrelated to guilt or criminality" (Hazani, 1991, 137). As such, the techniques of the neutralization article anticipated the so-called "cognitive turn" or "cognitive revolution" that is said to have taken place in psychology and throughout the social sciences in the late 1950s and early 1960s. Sykes and Matza's work preceded many of the authoritative works on social cognition and personal attributions in social psychology. Sykes and Matza directly inspired Scott and Lyman's (1968) influential theory of "accounts," which also suggested that the key to understanding deviance was to understand the rationalizations of deviants. Neutralization theory even predated the groundbreaking discovery of "cognitive distortions" and the "thinking errors" (many of which sound like neutralization techniques) thought to be associated with psychopathology in the cognitive therapies of Albert Ellis and Aaron Beck.

The primary difference between this work on social cognition and the theory of neutralizations is the relative inattention to the concept of subterranean values and the subcultural nature of neutralizations in the psychological literature. Sykes and Matza would surely argue that the cognitive therapy interpretation of neutralizations is too focused on a model of individual rather than societal pathology. As such, the legacy of neutralization or drift theory is probably most fully realized in the research of Judith Rumgay (1997) on the use of intoxication excuses in the British Court system and in Diana Scully and Joseph Marolla's (1984) research on the vocabulary of motives of convicted rapists. Both studies convincingly demonstrate

that, far from being idiosyncratic or pathological, the excuses and justifications offered by offenders have their origins in widespread cultural beliefs (mainly myths) about the effects of alcohol (in Rumgay's study) and the nature of rape (in Scully and Marolla). For example, the rapist echoes sexist views in the wider culture when he claims that the sexually suggestive talk or provocative dress of his victim should excuse his crime. Like Sykes and Matza, this research suggests that efforts to curb criminal behavior should begin, not with changing individual deviants, but with the societal promotion and tolerance of these criminogenic beliefs.

SHADD MARUNA

References and Further Reading

Agnew, R. 1994. The techniques of neutralization and violence, *Criminology*, 32.

Akers, R. 1985. *Deviant Behavior: A Social Learning Approach*, 3rd ed., Belmont, CA, Wadsworth.

Cohen, A. 1955. *Delinquent Boys*, Glencoe, IL, The Free Press.

Hagan, J. 1991. Destiny and drift: Subcultural preferences, status attainments, and the risks and rewards of youth, *American Sociological Review*, 56.

Hagan, J., Hefler, G., Classen, G., Boehnke, K., and Merkens, H. 1998. Subterranean sources of delinquency beyond the American dream, *Criminology*, 36.

Hazani, M. 1991. The universal applicability of the theory of neutralization: German youth coming to terms with the holocaust: An empirical study with theoretical implications, *Crime, Law and Social Change*, 15.

Henry, S. and Milovanovic, D. 1996. *Constitutive Criminology*, Thousand Oaks, CA, Sage.

Hindelang, M. 1970. The commitment of delinquents to their misdeeds: Do delinquents drift? *Social Problems*, 17.

Hirschi, T. 1969. *Causes of Delinquency*, Berkeley, University of California Press.

Maruna, S. 2001. *Making Good: How Ex-Convicts Reform and Rebuild Their Lives*, Washington, DC, American Psychological Association Books.

Matza, D. 1964. *Delinquency and Drift*, New York, Wiley.

Matza, D. 1969. *Becoming Deviant*, Englewood Cliffs, NJ, Prentice Hall.

Matza, D. and Sykes, G. 1961. Delinquency and subterranean values, *American Sociological Review*, 26.

Mills, C.W. 1940. Situated actions and vocabularies of motive, *American Sociological Review*, 5.

Minor, W.W. 1981. Techniques of neutralization: A reconceptualization and empirical examination, *Journal of Research in Crime and Delinquency*, 18.

Rumgay, J. 1998. *Crime, Punishment and the Drinking Offender*, New York, St. Martin's Press.

Scott, M. and Lyman, S. 1968. Accounts, *American Sociological Review*, 33.

Scully, D. and Marolla, J. 1984. Convicted rapists' vocabulary of motive: Excuses and justifications, *Social Problems*, 31.

Sykes, G. and Matza, D. 1957. Techniques of neutralization: A theory of delinquency, *American Sociological Review*, 22.

See also **Defenses to Criminal Liability: Justifications and Excuses**

New Zealand, Crime and Justice in

Crime

New Zealand, a country of 3.8 million people, is an independent Pacific nation that lies about 1200 miles southeast of Australia. Although the country's reputation is one of peace and civil safety, its criminal profile is similar in many respects to other Western democracies. A 1992 international crime victimization survey found rates of theft, burglary, robbery, and sexual attacks to be comparatively high, whereas rates of assault were very high, relative to the eight other countries surveyed, including Australia, Canada, England, and the U.S. On the other hand, however, although New Zealanders are heavily armed, with possibly a million firearms in private ownership, murder rates are similar to other nations and, at about 55 a year, are only a fraction of those in the U.S. This is largely because handguns are strictly controlled in New Zealand, and numbers are low. The vast majority of firearms owned by New Zealanders are sporting rifles and shotguns. Only 25% of New Zealand murder victims are shot.

As in most other countries, white-collar crime is a problem for New Zealand, although it is of uncertain magnitude. Since 1990 a small specialized agency known as the Serious Fraud Office has existed, armed with extraordinary powers to investigate offenders suspected of stealing NZ$500,000 or more. Since 1990 the office has prosecuted fraud valued at approximately NZ$100 million, involving nearly 200 defendants. About 85% of those convicted have been sent to prison and have received an average sentence of 45 months. Other areas where fraud levels are significant are welfare benefit fraud—estimated at more than NZ$100 million per year—and tax evasion. New Zealand is similar to other countries in this respect, and from overseas estimates, it is likely that at least 10% of due tax in New Zealand, or approximately NZ$3.2 billion per year, is never paid.

Because of the huge amounts of money forfeited through white-collar crime and the impact it has on the economy through lost investor confidence, it must be considered one of New Zealand's most serious crime problems. The other area of grave concern is domestic violence, especially toward children. True levels are impossible to ascertain; however, a national survey of crime victims in 1996 found that a quarter of all reported violent incidents occurred in the home.

In 1998 about 9000 people were taken into the care of women's refuges, and 5000 of them were children. Violence toward or neglect of children is a significant problem because research indicates repeatedly that the abused and neglected children of today frequently become the criminal adults of tomorrow. Each year in New Zealand, about 3500 nonfatal violent offenses are reported against children aged under 16 years. Roughly 10% of all murder victims are under the age of 11. Native New Zealanders (Maori) and Pacific island people are grossly overrepresented in national domestic violence victim statistics, and young Maori and Pacific islanders also heavily predominate in the country's crime figures, especially those involving violence.

An area of crime to which New Zealand has low exposure is official corruption. In contrast with its closest neighbor, Australia, New Zealand's police and official agencies are relatively free of systemic improbity. Regular corruption reports by the Berlin-based agency Transparency International repeatedly find New Zealand at or near the bottom of the 85 countries surveyed. This absence of corruption, the small size of the country, and its remoteness from other nations are all important factors in keeping organized crime at a low level. Organized crime does exist, however, and the basis for most of it is drug dealing. Crime of this nature, which is now dominated by motorcycle and street gangs, has been known since the early 1970s. These gangs deal mainly in locally grown marijuana, but since the 1990s locally produced methamphetamine and imported LSD and ecstasy have made significant inroads. Very few gangs deal in heroin. The majority of heroin available in New Zealand comes from prescribed noninjectable morphine sulfate tablets that can easily be converted to injectable heroin. This is cheap to buy, but nonetheless, addiction rates are low. There are only about 2500 registered addicts in New Zealand and only about half a dozen recorded opiate fatalities each year.

As in the U.S., there has been an overall reduction in the amount of reported crime in New Zealand in recent years. Specifically, since reaching a peak in the early 1990s, police-reported thefts have fallen by 11%, burglaries by 22%, and violent crimes by 33%. Murders have dropped by 30%, and reported drug offenses (94% of them marijuana related) have stabilized. The reasons for these changes appear to have little to do with penalties. For although sentence lengths for violent crime have grown considerably since 1985, penalties for drugs and dishonesty have not. Moreover, whereas sentences for robbery increased progressively by more than 75% in the decade after 1988, reported robberies did not begin to fall until 1998. The explanation for the decline in crime rates is manifold. Significant factors include a falling unemployment rate, a reduction in the population aged 15–29, better home, business, and vehicle security systems, a drop in per capita alcohol consumption, and an increase in police powers and community resources for dealing with domestic violence.

Criminal Justice

New Zealand has a liberal tradition as far as the treatment of crime is concerned. The death penalty for murder was abolished in 1961, and the penalty for murder is now life imprisonment, with parole eligibility normally occurring after ten years. The average lifer serves about 13 years, although this is increasing as courts and parole authorities crack down on violent crime. There has been a gradual toughening of treatment for all forms of violent offending since 1985, with mandatory imprisonment, longer sentences, and tighter restrictions on parole. Apart from murder, the crime of rape receives the heaviest average penalty in New Zealand—slightly higher even than for manslaughter or attempted murder. The national starting point for a rape sentence is eight years, with no parole eligibility but release on good time likely after two-thirds of the sentence. The reason that rape is so harshly treated relative to other crimes has largely to do with the effectiveness of the feminist lobby, which has campaigned vigorously for tougher rape sentences since the late 1970s.

The hard line taken toward violent offending has had little evident effect on crime, with reductions not appearing until approximately seven years after the legislation began coming into effect. The impact on crimes of sexual violation has been even slower in coming, with convictions rising dramatically and steadily for a full decade after 1986, before commencing a sharp decline in 1997.

Dealing in heroin, LSD, or cocaine carries a maximum life term in New Zealand, but such a sentence has only been given and sustained twice since the principal legislation was passed in 1978. For dealing in other drugs, the maximum is either 8 or 14 years. The average prison sentence for dealing cannabis is 13 months; for other drugs, 33 months, with parole eligibility after one-third of the sentence. Sentences for property crimes likewise are short, with burglary, the

most heavily punished, receiving only 12 months' imprisonment on average.

In spite of this, and notwithstanding the fact that noncustodial sentencing alternatives, such as compulsory community work, are widely used, New Zealand's prison population is high relative to most other Western nations—except the U.S.—and growing. There are currently about 5800 people held in New Zealand's prisons and jails, a figure that has doubled since 1985. A principal reason for the increase is a high number of convictions for violent crime that has been maintained during the 1990s—despite the fall in reported offending—and the longer sentences awarded. Sentencing policy has also impacted on the composition of the prison population. Maori are only about 12% of the national population, but they now constitute almost 60% of the prison muster. Women, whose offending tends to be nonviolent and less serious than men's, constitute only 4% of prisoners in custody.

Conditions in New Zealand prisons are good compared to most other countries. All prisons bar one are run by the state, and most have reasonable access to work, welfare, and educational programs. Nearly all prisoners have their own cells or share a cell with one other. There are no dormitories, and homosexual rape is almost unknown. Only about 5% of sentenced inmates are held in maximum security. Sixty percent have minimum security status and are eligible to apply for weekend furloughs every two months. At 1.25% per annum, escape rates are fairly low and mostly consist of walkaways and furlough nonreturns. This is because, by and large, sentences are short, the prisons are well managed, conditions are good, and New Zealand's insularity makes getting out of the country difficult. Fugitives who remain in this small island nation are soon caught and returned to prison, typically with a six-month extension.

New Zealand's prisons are, for the most part, peaceful places where the destructive consequences of incarceration are reduced to a minimum. Relations between staff and inmates are relaxed and informal, assaults and suicides are few, and there were only five prison murders in the 20th century—all after 1979. The country has not experienced a prison riot for nearly 30 years. However, this ambience has not translated into lower recidivist rates. Conforming to the pessimistic principle that "nothing works" in corrections, recidivist rates in New Zealand are high—and no different from those of the U.S., where prison conditions are much harsher. Approximately 80% of all inmates are reconvicted of a felony within five years of release. In New Zealand, as elsewhere, it seems, a person's social background and socioeconomic circumstances are far more reliable predictors of reoffending than the treatment he or she may receive at the hands of the Department of Corrections.

GREG NEWBOLD

References and Further Reading

Harland, A. 1995. *Victimisation in New Zealand: As Measured by the 1992 International Crime Survey,* Wellington, New Zealand, Ministry of Justice.

Newbold, G. 1989. *Punishment and Politics: The Maximum Security Prison in New Zealand,* Auckland, Oxford University Press.

Newbold, G. 2000. *Crime in New Zealand,* Palmerston North, New Zealand, Dunmore Press.

Newbold, G. and Eskridge, C.W. 1996. History and development of modern correctional practices in Fields, C.B. and Moore, R.H., Jr., New Zealand, in *Comparative Criminal Justice: Traditional and Nontraditional Systems of Law and Control,* Prospect Heights, IL, Waveland Press.

Webb, P.M. 1982. *A History of Custodial and Related Penalties in New Zealand,* Wellington, New Zealand, Government Printer.

Young, W. et al. 1997. *New Zealand National Survey of Crime Victims, 1996,* Wellington, New Zealand, Victimisation Survey Committee.

See also **Australia, Crime and Justice in**

Nigeria, Corruption in

Corruption is both endemic and widespread in Nigeria. Corruption is an offense that is economically motivated and is committed by persons of power and status in the course of their occupations. Corruption is a crime that usually remains unreported in Nigeria, because of the general distrust of the criminal justice system, charged with its control, hence the attitude: why "report corruption to corruption" (Adeyemi, 1992). Moreover, victims of corruption are often actively involved in the act. Again, corruption has eaten deep into the Nigerian fabric and has even penetrated the private sector. As Justice Akanbi (2003), chairman of the Nigerian National Anti-Corruption Commission (NACC), notes, past Nigerian governments promoted graft "almost to an official state policy" and that "rulers have made corruption almost second nature in the country" (p. 1). Akanbi further observes that, "most Nigerians do not believe that there is somebody who is not corrupt" in the country (ibid). To understand the nature and extent of corruption in Nigeria, an analysis of the power structure, political culture, ethnic relations, the value system, and prevailing differential privileges and prestige is important. Laws against corruption seek to promote the integrity of government officials and to protect the society against power abuse and exploitation.

In 2002, Transparency International, in its corruption perception index, rated Nigeria one of the most corrupt nations in the world. The World Bank, in its 2002 economic report on Nigeria, has also noted that an estimated 80% of the nation's $15 billion yearly oil and gas revenues are consumed by government officials and the exigencies of running the wheel of the state. The World Bank annual report further notes that only 1% of Nigeria's population enjoys about 80% of its revenue, while the other 99% of the population is left to make do with just about 20% of the national wealth. Economic development programs are further undermined by the fact that the looted money is stashed away in foreign banks, thus worsening the unemployment situation and the economic hardship in the country. Available records, according to the Director General of the Nigerian Economic and Financial Crimes Commission (EFCC), Mr. Emmanuel Akomaye (2003), indicate that key Nigerian government officials, both past and present, have an estimated $170 billion stashed away in foreign banks. In a separate report, Alhaji Nuhu Ribadu (2003), the Chairman of the Economic and Financial Crimes Commission (EFCC), stated that he was in possession of a document that reveals 20 out of the 36 of Nigeria's currently serving governors own choice houses in various upscale areas of London.

Corruption is blamed for Nigeria's political crisis, poor economic performance, and poor human rights records. Several factors foster corruption, including unhealthy ethnic rivalry, weak institutional, economic, political, social and historical bases, and it flourishes in the absence of the rule of law, weak democratic institutions, and traditions. Corruption above all undermines the capability of the civil society in demanding and obtaining responsible, transparent, and accountable leadership. All measures put in place by successive Nigerian governments to prevent and combat corruption remain ineffective. This is partly because successive Nigerian governments lack the political will to enforce laws regulating corrupt practices of key government officials despite promises to stamp out corruption in government business. Further, contributing to the failure of all corruption controlling measures is the condoning attitude of the people towards corruption and the fact that everyone is "involved in the act," so to speak. Moreover, corruption does not attract any stigma in Nigeria. In fact, the prevailing value system in the society encourages, promotes, and celebrates corruption. Wealthy top government officials and retired public servants who apparently enriched themselves through their offices are rewarded with chieftancy titles and honorary doctorate degrees by traditional rulers and universities, respectively. The emerging moral climate is such that many who pursued and amassed wealth without work are valorized; politics is played without principles and many educated elites are lacking in character. Many Nigerians believe that the goal of the average Nigerian political office seeker is the gaining of power at all costs and retaining power by rewarding friends and relatives and punishing opponents.

It is well known in Nigeria that political tensions arise more from political appointments than from policies. This is because political institutions in Nigeria are redundant in that they fail to restrain persons occupying that office. Persons holding key government positions take precedence over rules, and politics is more personalized and less restraining. Jackson and Rosberg (1982) describe African politics as characterized by personal rule. Personal rule is the opposite of institutional rule, "where persons take precedence over rules, where the office holder is not effectively bound by his office and is able to change its authority and powers to suit his own personal or political needs" (p. 10). General Theophilus Yakubu Danjuma (2003), a former Minister of Defense of the present civilian government of Nigeria, during their first term in office alluded as much to this when he described his experience as minister as very frustrating and the most trying period in his life. According to Danjuma, "the government is run by a cartel" (p. 1). Government policies are enacted and executed outside of government institutions, by the president and a clique who were neither elected nor are accountable to the people.

Corruption is when someone holding a public office intentionally engages in illegal or unethical acts, thereby betraying public obligation for some personal objectives. The most common forms of corruption in Nigeria are bribery, embezzlement, fraud, extortion, mobilization fee racket, contract inflation or fictitious contracts, over-invoicing, and salaries to ghost workers. They can be described as follows:

1. Bribery is when a government official demands or receives cash or a valuable commodity from a citizen for services rendered or for services to be rendered in future. Bribery has become so institutionalized that government officials even demand gratification from their colleagues before they pay them their leave allowances, duty tour allowances, or gratuities to which they are entitled. The victim of the offense of bribery is considered a party and an accomplice to the offense.

2. Embezzlement is when government officials outright steal or misappropriate government funds entrusted to their care or that they have access to.

3. Fraud is part of corruption when government officials use their offices to deceive, conceal, or misrepresent facts to individuals or the government for economic benefits.

4. Extortion is when government officials obtain money or other valuable commodities through coercion, violence, or the threat of force. The citizens who import contraband goods or fail to pay taxes are blackmailed into parting with their money under duress for fear of exposure or incrimination. Unlike bribery, the payers are giving out the money against their will. Extortion is said to harm the individuals who are made to cough up their money. Bribery, on the other hand, damages the common wealth, and not the bribe giver.

5. Mobilization fee racket: Governments sometimes hire companies with specialized expertise in certain service areas to provide such services on its behalf for a fee. A company or contractor whose tender is successful is given about 25% of the contract's cost to start them off. The company director, after collecting the mobilization fee, disappears without executing the contract or connives with the officer incharge and shares the booty without executing the contract.

6. Contract inflation or fictitious contracts: Government contractors inflate the value of a contract. This could happen either at the beginning of the award of the contract, or mid-way into the execution of the contract. This could happen through contract reviews ostensibly done to accommodate inflation. Contracts can also be awarded for a fictitious project. Budgetary allocations are made for nonexistent projects. Contracts for the said project are awarded to a conniving contractor. The contractor cashes the

money for the project and shares it with the supervising officer. Contracts for a particular project can be awarded twice. Contracts for supplies that are already in stock are awarded and paid for. The contractor and the supervising officer share the money without purchasing anything.

7. Over-invoicing: Goods listed in the invoice are more than the goods purportedly supplied by the contractor. The controlling officer overlooks this discrepancy and is adequately rewarded by the contractor.

8. Salary to ghost workers: Deceased or nonexistent workers remain on the government payroll and the supervising officer embezzles the money ostensibly paid to the ghost workers. Other forms of corruption include outright stealing of government property, and illegal transfer of public funds to private accounts.

Corrupt officials employ several methods to cover their crime, including large-scale destruction of government documents and files, and setting of government buildings on fire.

The pertinent questions to ask at this stage are, why is corruption endemic and widespread in Nigeria? Why are policies put in place to control corruption ineffective? What can be done to restore trust, honesty, and accountability in the public service?

First and foremost, Nigerian government officials lack the political will to confront corruption and other aspects of the abuse of power in a systematic, organized, and consistent fashion. So far, all attempts to control corruption have often been sporadic, or done in a fire-brigade manner. In view of the fact that the corruption law could not be said to be enforced in Nigeria, those caught during the few times it is enforced believe they are unlucky or victims of ethnic or political victimization. The nonenforcement of laws against corruption also sends the wrong message of governmental approval. Many even believe government expects public servants to supplement their meager wages with the exploits of bribery and extortion.

Furthermore, available records show that the Nigerian government contributes immensely to the corruption of the system. The government uses cash, land, and political appointments to bribe traditional leaders and community opinion moulders. Bribery is a common practice of government to win the loyalty and support of influential Nigerians, political and human rights activists, and religious and ethnic groups.

The enforcement of laws regulating corruption and the abuse of power, even with the best of intentions, is a very difficult task. Sutherland (1949) identified legalism, that is, the legalistic definition of criminality,

as a major impediment to the control of corruption. The law courts can only interpret an act as criminal if the act matches with the criminal code definition. Further, the courts in prosecuting an offender must rely on the evidence provided by the prosecutors. Lack of evidence is a major handicap as those in a position to provide evidence are often parties to the crime. Moreover, African culture is anathema to imprisonment as a form of punishment. Family members of an incarcerated elite are also affected by the prison stigma. Again, the African's concept of justice is not the strict interpretation of the letter of the law. Furthermore, few African judges will incarcerate a "non-violent" offender with a dependent wife, children, and aging parents. Consideration of the effect of incarceration on an offender's family is a sufficient mitigating factor.

Public attitudes even in the Western world, according to Sutherland (1949), discourage punishment as a sanction against people convicted of corruption. Many believe punishment should be applied only to the very dangerous offenders. Sutherland observes that the laws regulating corruption often do not conform with that of societal sentiments. There is therefore no organized resentment against corruption by the general public. Again, people involved in corrupt behavior are often educated and seemingly reasonable people who do not fit the stereotype associated with criminals. In addition, it is fair to observe that it is a major challenge to enforce the laws governing corrupt practices in Nigeria because almost everyone with an opportunity to commit corruption is involved in the act.

Christie (1993) has observed that the control of the upper class of any society is a major challenge to the criminal justice system. This is because the upper economic class has enormous power, extensive social networks, and knowledge of the system such that it can circumvent the judicial processes in their favor. In the same vein, the control of the underclass is also problematic because these are often people who have nothing to lose. The poor have no money, stocks, work, social network, or even honor.

The Nigerian government's lack of political will, sincerity, and commitment to the enforcement of laws governing corruption is implicated by its failure to empower the agencies of the criminal justice system to confront the offenses of corruption head-on. For example, in 1981, the government established the "Code of Conduct Bureau" and the "Code of Conduct Tribunal," to ensure the maintenance of high standards of morality in the conduct of government business. This Bureau existed for several years without convicting anyone of corruption, because the National Assembly failed to give the Bureau the enabling legislation as required by the Constitution. In 2000, the government scrapped the Bureau and set up a panel to investigate corruption, known as the Anti-corruption Commission. Three years into the existence of the commission, Nigeria still had not convicted anyone corruption. Many Nigerians remain skeptical about government motives in establishing the commission. Aubert (1952) describes it best when he describes some legislations as more or less an attempt, pretence, or deliberate measure to strengthen the position of one group of people without weakening that of other groups.

Ekeh's 1975 thesis on the two publics in Africa further provides a plausible explanation for the condoning attitude of Nigerians towards the offense of corruption. Ekeh notes that one of the consequences of colonialism, apart from the imposition on Africa of foreign languages, morals, religion, laws, political structures, and systems of education, is the emergence of two publics in Africa. Western countries according to Ekeh have one public. The private and public realms are easily distinguishable in the West. However, both the private and public realms derive from one moral foundation, namely the Judeo-Christian belief systems.

On the other hand, in postcolonial Africa, there were two publics—primordial public and the civic public. In the *primordial public*, the individual's behavior is determined by considerations for primary relationships and ties, such as peer, family, and kingship groupings. The *civic public* is characterized by the state and its paraphernalia. The military, police, and the bureaucracy all came with the colonial state.

The state is a major agent of modernization. The state emerged in Europe to become the dominant power after a protracted struggle amongst the feudal lords, the aristocracy, the church, and the mercantile powers. In Africa, the states were imposed by the colonial powers. The major issue here is that the two publics have different "moral linkages to the private realm" unlike what obtains in the West. Within the primordial public in Africa, there is morality, accountability and transparency that are miserably lacking in the civic public. Many African elites will go the extra mile to provide and sustain their primordial publics. On the other hand, the civic public, as represented by the state and its resources, are fair game for exploitation for personal and primordial interests. Accounting for this attitude according to Ekeh is that the African derives immense benefit from the primordial public, hence the African elite feels morally obliged to be loyal to it. Such benefits are in both tangible and intangible forms, including social and psychological security. This attitude contrasts sharply with the average African's perception of the modern state as colonial creation, to exploit and oppress the African people. There is a connection between the overzealous pursuit of ethnic interests and pervasive corruption and the absence of the rule of law in Nigeria. Furthermore, in the traditional African governments, there were checks and balances such that corrupt and authoritarian chiefs could be removed by the people. Modern African governments with a monopoly over the instrument of violence can sustain themselves in power by force against the will of the people.

Though corruption is an international crime, it does not receive the same attention by the international crime control mechanism as drug and terrorism, for example. It is even fair to observe that governments of Western countries even encourage bribery of foreign officials by making it tax deductible. It is widely known that Western countries do not hesitate to freeze the bank accounts of known drug dealers, but have consistently ignored calls by poorer nations like Nigeria to freeze the bank accounts of their government officials accused of stealing money from their people. Accounting for this is the fact that drugs and terrorism are a major cause for concern in the Western countries. Drugs are widely believed to be damaging the fabric of the Western societies. Terrorism is also a major threat to life and security, and is perceived to be undermining international business. As such, greater emphasis is given to their control. On the other hand, leaders of the poorer nations have literarily looted the treasuries of their respective countries and lodged the same in their private banks in the West. The governments of the West hound and harass the governments of the weaker nations to assist them in combating terrorism and drug trafficking, but do not show any interest in helping the weaker nations control the corruption that is doing great harm and hampering economic and technological development in these countries.

This study examined some of the social factors that foster corruption in Nigeria. The same factors also militate against the control of corruption. The existence of widespread corruption and its negative effects on the socioeconomic development of Nigeria have been acknowledged. Yet there has been no moral commitment by the government to involve the Nigerian people in disapproving corruption. The result is the lack of awareness of the average Nigerian of the dangers of corruption in the society.

O. OKO ELECHI

References and Further Reading

Adeyemi, A.A. (1992). Corruption in Africa: a case study of Nigeria, in Mushanga, T. Mwene, Ed., *Criminology in Africa,* Rome, UN Interregional Crime and Justice Research Institute (UNICRI).

Akanbi, M. (2003). National Anti-Corruption Commission. Available at: http://www.nigeriabusinessinfo.com/nacc.htm. Retrieved on June 28, 2003.

Ake, C. (1989). *The Political Economy of Crisis and Development in Africa*. Lagos, Nigeria, JAD Publishers.

Akomaye, E. (2003). *Interview by Daily Trust Newspapers of November 11, 2003*. Available at: http://www.mtrustonline.com/dailytrust.htm.

Aubert, V. (1989). *Continuity and Development—in Law and Society,* Oslo, Norway, Norwegian University Press.

Aubert, V. (1969). *Sociology of Law (Selected Readings),* Middlesex, U.K., Penguin Books Ltd.

Christie, N. (1993). *Crime Control as Industry: Towards Gulags, Western Style,* London, Routledge.

Clifford, W. (1974). *An Introduction to African Criminology,* Nairobi, Kenya Oxford University Press.

Constitution of the Federal Republic of Nigeria 1999. Available at: http://www.nigeriaworld.com/focus/Republic/constitution/constitution.html. Retrieved on December, 10, 1999. (Incomplete).

Danjuma, T.Y. (2003). Interview in the Daily Trust of November 10, 2003. Available at: http://www.mtrustonline.com/dailytrust/danjuma10112003.htm.

Diamond, L., Linz, J.J., and Lipset, S.M., Eds., (1988). *Democracy in Developing Countries—Africa,* London, Adamantine Press Ltd.

Ekeh, P.P. (1975). Colonialism and the Two Publics in Africa: A Theoretical Statement, *Comparative Studies in Society and History,* Vol. 17.

El-Wathig, K. and Kursany, I. (1985). *Corruption as the "Fifth" Factor of Production in the Sudan.* Research Report No. 72; Scandinavian Institute of African Studies, Uppsala.

Jackson, R.H. and Rosberg, C.G. (1982). *Personal Rule in Black Africa: Prince, Autocrat, Prophet, Tyrant,* Los Angeles, CA, University of California Press.

Okereke, O.G. (1993). Public attitudes toward the police force in Nigeria, *Police Studies,* 16(3), 113–1121.

Ribadu, N. (2003). *Interview of the Daily Trust Newspaper of October 7, 2003.* Available at: http://www.mtrustonline.com/dailytrust.htm.

Thomas, S. and Canagaraja, S. (2002). *Poverty in a Wealthy Economy: The Case of Nigeria,* International Monetary Fund (IMF) Working Paper.

Transparency International Corruption Perception Index. Available at: wysiwyg://14http://www.infoplease.com/ipa/A0781359.html.

See also **Extortion and Blackmail; Political Crimes by the State**

Obscenity

Obscenity is generally defined as an act that is offensive to the prevailing concepts of morality or decency. The key element in this definition is the term "prevailing." Such a term accurately implies that the term is completely subjective and determined by where one is and at what time. This subjective nature of defining what obscenity is, and what it is not, has become one of the most confounding problems in modern legality.

The determination of what is obscene has likely been an issue as long as humanity has been making drawings on cave dwellings. However, documented reviews of obscenity typically begin in reviewing the works of the late medieval times and the Renaissance, likely because this is the period that sparked a new interest in human nature and the advent of the printed book. It was in the latter part of this era that Galileo, as well as a number of his contemporaries, was sentenced to lifelong imprisonment for heresy, which is a derivative term for obscenity.

In Galileo's case, he proposed that the Copernican theory—that the earth is not the center of the universe—was accurate. Shortly after this was published, Galileo was condemned to lifelong imprisonment. We now know that what he wrote was true and most people today would protest his prosecution. However, according to modern day obscenity laws, which are based completely on contemporary community values, Galileo was rightly imprisoned then, and would likely be condemned today in many communities. Such attitudes regarding brilliant works can be seen in the 20th century bans of critically

acclaimed works, such as *The Catcher in the Rye* by J. D. Salinger and James Joyce's *Ulysses*.

Contemporary issues regarding obscenity involve challenges to the constitutional protections offered under the freedom of speech and press clause of the First Amendment. Although the Constitution does not make an explicit exception for certain material, over the last 50 years the U.S. Supreme Court has ruled as though it does so. The Court has heard numerous cases, many involving pornography, and have provided no specific criteria for what is obscene and what is not. For example, perhaps the best that the Supreme Court has done in determining what is obscene is represented by Justice Potter Stewart's statement in which he proclaimed that he did not know what the definition of obscenity was, but that he knew it when he saw it. This is actually the current criteria for determining obscenity, assuming that Justice Stewart's determination of the community standards in the area of question represents the "average reasonable person."

This legal standard for determining obscenity goes back to a U.S. Supreme Court decision—*Miller v. California* (413 U.S. 15, 1973)—that emphasized the importance of determining community standards regarding various forms of obscenity. It is notable that additional court decisions have confirmed this standard. The *Miller* standard established that individual communities must determine for themselves what material is legally obscene and thus prohibited. The Court presented a three-pronged test that is based on a trier of fact (be it judge or jury) determining whether the average person, applying contemporary standards, would find that the work in question (1) appeals to the prurient interest; (2) depicts in a patently offensive way sexual or other conduct as defined by law; and (3) lacks serious literary, artistic, political, or scientific value.

Therefore, the primary implication derived from *Miller* and other court decisions is that the judge or jury from each community must attempt to distinguish material that is obscene from that which is simply free speech. Given the criteria explicitly provided by the Court, individuals (be it a judge or jury member) who make this decision are not supposed to rely on their own perceptions of what is acceptable, but rather are supposed to decide on the basis of what the average reasonable person would decide. However, empirical studies have shown that individuals interpret each of these three prongs differently, and furthermore make decisions about the obscenity of a given work that are quite different from the community in which they live. Therefore, it is not surprising that obscenity is one of the few crimes that potential offenders do not know if they are actually guilty until they are judged by a judge or jury from their community.

By relegating the decision of what is obscene to local communities, the U.S. Supreme Court has essentially relieved itself of the responsibility of developing a federal standard for determining whether materials are obscene. The Court has left it up to individual states, which results in wide variation as to how a community is defined. Some states have chosen to adopt a state standard, but many states have left it up to smaller geographical units—such as counties or cities—to determine what is obscene and what is not, which results in wide disparity across jurisdictions.

No matter where obscenity trials occur, the verdict is based on what the trier of fact (either a judge or jury) decides, based on the *Miller* test. Studies have shown that this decision is significantly influenced by the demographics, location, and region of the jurors in the case, as well as the location of the outlet sources of the materials being distributed.

Further complicating matters is the advent of the Internet, which transcends the issue of community in the sense that all localities have access to materials that are on the Internet. For example, one recent case—*U.S. v. Thomas* (74 F.3d 701, 6th Cir. 1996; cert. denied, 117 S. Ct. 74)—involved a married couple who were transmitting pornographic material from their home. Robert and Carleen Thomas were convicted in a Memphis court for violating local obscenity statutes because the material they were transmitting from their California home was accessible by citizens in the Memphis area. Although the San Jose (CA) Police Department had determined that the Thomas's material had not violated their local standards, the holding of the Memphis conviction by the courts can be interpreted as requiring the Thomas couple to know the standards of every community that could possibly download their material from the Internet.

Therefore, the definition and application of obscenity standards remain vague, and it is likely that with the proliferation of the Internet this standard will become more confusing and debated in years to come.

STEPHEN G. TIBBETTS

References and Further Reading

Blanchard, M.A. 1992. *Revolutionary Sparks: Freedom of Expression in Modern America,* New York, NY: Oxford University Press.

Hixson, R.F. 1996. *Pornography and the Justices: The Supreme Court and the Intractable Obscenity Problem,* Carbondale, IL: Southern Illinois University Press.

Randall, R.S. 1989. *Freedom and Taboo: Pornography and the Politics of a Self Divided,* Berkeley, CA: University of California Press.

Tibbetts, S.G. and Blankenship, M. 1999. Explaining citizens' attitudes toward pornography: Differential effects of predictors across levels of geographic proximity to outlet sources, *Justice Quarterly,* 16.

Ziolkowski, J.M. 1998. *Obscenity: Cultures, Beliefs and Traditions,* Boston, MA: Brill Academic Publishers.

See also **Exhibitionism and Voyeurism; Pornography and Criminal Behavior; Pornography: The Law**

Obsession

An obsession refers to a troubled mind or a mind preoccupied or haunted by certain thoughts. Obsessional thoughts can lead to a wide range of white-collar and violent criminal roles and activities. Individuals who engage in certain white-collar crimes, such as corporate theft, may be highly obsessive about details, such as accounting procedures. Obsessions over the desire to save money or increase income may lead to insider trading scandals. Obsessions over the desire to be successful also can lead to different white collar crimes that involve cheating, theft, and fraud. The process of social learning or role modeling also influences the extent to which a person's obsessions will ultimately lead to his or her participation in various white collar crimes. Moreover, social pressures to succeed that may be imposed by family members, coworkers, supervisors, and employers may trigger an individual with obsessive thoughts to eventually engage in certain white collar crimes. In the above instances, the person's obsessions, along with the process of role modeling and social pressures, disrupt their adherence to the conventional norms of society.

In terms of violent crimes, obsessive beliefs underlie a variety of violent crimes, such as rape and pedophilia. Sexual offenders, such as pedophiles, develop sexual obsessions and fantasies, and various factors, such as proximity to playgrounds, schools, the use of child pornography, and other images of children, trigger criminal activities.

One of the most prevalent forms of obsessional behaviors in daily interactions that can result in violent crimes is stalking or repeated and unwanted following, lying in wait, and other intrusive and harassing activities (Morewitz, 2003). Stalkers have been classified into three categories: (1) simple obsessional, (2) love obsessional, and (3) erotomanic (Zona et al., 1993; 1998). Simple obsessional stalkers frequently stalk intimate partners or persons in nonintimate relations. Many simple obsessional stalkers have mental problems, such as substance dependence and personality disorders. Simple obsessional stalkers who have been in intimate relations may be more likely than those in nonintimate relations to commit serious violence against their partners. These stalkers may be less likely to have psychotic disorders than those who stalk strangers. Love obsessional stalkers tend to have a fanatical love for their targets. Some love obsessional stalkers also may have the delusional belief that the target is in love with the stalker when in fact the target does not even know the perpetrator. These delusional beliefs typically are secondary to a major mental disorder. Erotomanic stalkers are persons who have the primary delusion that they are loved by a person, when in reality they may be complete strangers. In the past it was thought to be a rare disorder that primarily occurred among women who stalked higher status women. These cases are now considered fairly common and occur among both men and women. Among the three stalker types, the duration of stalking among erotomanics is the longest and the risk of violence is the lowest.

Stalkers have also been classified by their motivation. Mullen et al. (1999) classified five types of stalkers: (1) rejected, (2) intimacy seeking, (3) incompetent, (4) resentful, and (5) predatory stalkers. Rejected stalkers are those persons who become obsessed over feelings of loss, anger, and jealousy, and stalk their targets in response to these feelings associated with rejection. Intimacy-seeking persons become obsessed with the desire to gain intimacy with people they believe to be their true loves although they may be strangers. These stalkers can have erotomanic delusions and may suffer from schizophrenia and mania, morbid infatuation, and other disorders. Incompetent stalkers realize that their targets are not in love with them but have the obsessive belief that their stalking behaviors will result in an intimate relationship. Incompetent stalkers typically have restricted social and intellectual functioning and are not familiar with courtship rituals. Resentful stalkers use stalking behaviors to scare and harass their targets. They often become obsessed with their desire to scare or harass their victims because they have vendettas against them. Predatory stalkers are persons who are obsessed with achieving a sense of power over their victims. They often become familiar with a target's routines and develop fantasies about attacking them in the future.

Segregation and incarceration of offenders may help to protect some victims. However, incarceration can be ineffective, as after incarceration, the obsessive offenders may return to revictimize their targets or victimize new targets. Getting offenders with obsessions into treatment can be difficult. In some cases, their negative life histories and mental disorders make it unlikely that they will participate in therapy. In the U.S., several states now require that convicted stalkers and other perpetrators undergo psychiatric or psychological evaluation and treatment. Certain offenders with obsessions may be more amenable to criminal justice interventions than therapy. For example, rejected stalkers, except for those in child custody disputes and morbidly jealous individuals, may benefit more from criminal justice efforts than therapy. Medical treatments have also been used in the treatment of sex offenders in order to reduce their obsessions involving sexual assaults and pedophilia.

STEPHEN J. MOREWITZ

References and Further Reading

Morewitz, S.J. (2003). *Stalking and Violence—New Patterns of Trauma and Obsession,* New York, NY: Kluwer Academic/ Plenum Publishers.
Mullen, P.E., et al. (1999). Study of stalkers. *American Journal of Psychiatry,* 156(8), 1244–1249.
Zona, M., Sharma, K., and Lane, J. (1993). A comparative study of erotomanic and obsessional subjects in a forensic sample. *Journal of Forensic Sciences,* 38, 894–903.
Zona, M., Palarea, R., and Lane, J. (1998). Psychiatric diagnosis and the offender-victim typology of stalking, pp. 69–84. In Meloy, J.R. (Ed.) *The Psychology of Stalking: Clinical and Forensic Perspectives,* San Diego, CA: Academic Press.

See also **Stalking**

Obstruction of Justice

From the common law perspective, obstruction of justice was a vague, broadly defined offense. According to *Black's Law Dictionary* (1990, 742) such a crime was defined merely as the act of "impeding or obstructing those who seek justice in a court, or those who have duties or powers of administering justice therein." Although the current crime of obstruction of justice is still rather broad in nature, its components have been more readily defined. Generally, such behavior involves the "interference with the orderly processes of civil and criminal courts, such as refusing to produce evidence, intimidating witnesses, and bribing judges" (Reid, 2003). If a government official commits obstruction of justice, then the offense is termed official misconduct in office, defined as "any willful, unlawful behavior by public officials in the course of their official duties. The misconduct may be a failure to act, a wrongful act, or an act that the actor had a right to do, but that was performed improperly" (Reid, 2003).

The exact behaviors outlined as obstruction of justice were initially defined in *18 U.S.C.* §1501– 1518. Such activities may include intimidating witnesses, failing to obey a court order, obstructing criminal investigations, influencing jurors, tampering with a jury, retaliating against witnesses or victims, destroying documents, as well as attempting to or actually bribing witnesses, jurors, or judges. The scope of obstruction of justice charges under §1503 and 1505 were limited in 1995 by *U.S. v. Aguilar,* 515 U.S. 593 (1995). This U.S. Supreme Court case showed that specific intent had to be present to warrant obstruction of justice charges under §1503 and 1505. They further defined the requisite components of intent to include a specific relationship between the act and a judicial proceeding with the demonstrated ability to clearly link the act with the deliberate interference of such a proceeding. The *Sarbanes-Oxley Act of 2002* further defined the crime of obstruction of justice, through the application of document destruction to the provisions contained within §1512 and the addition of §1519, which also specifically address the act of document destruction as obstruction of justice (Polkes, 2003).

Measuring the true extent of this crime proves to be a challenge for researchers. As is the case with many white-collar crimes, the primary barrier to effective measurement is that the statistic is not included in crimes measured under the Uniform Crime Report. Thus, much of the documentation of obstruction of justice is limited to high-profile cases publicized by the media.

Correlations and Theories

There are numerous explanations for white-collar crimes such as obstruction of justice. Edwin Sutherland first offered the most widely recognized explanation of such crimes. He felt that a focus on white-collar crimes was needed, as many of the theoretical explanations of crime at the time were focused solely upon offenses dealt with in criminal courts. Sutherland's

(1995) theory, differential association, explains criminal behavior as the product of a learning process. In the corporate setting, behaviors are learned through exposure to the behavior of others within the occupational environment. The daily exposure to these behaviors often leads individuals to accept them as the norm. When those behaviors are deviant in nature, then the individual learns behaviors that are favorable to law violation, rather than law abiding. Thus, they are more likely to engage in such behaviors. Given the current climate of today's corporate world, the application of differential association to obstruction of justice is indeed conceivable.

The rational choice perspective is also a widely recognized explanation of white-collar crimes. The decision to violate laws is one based on analysis of cost versus benefit. When dealing with obstruction of justice, many offenders may believe that the benefits (i.e., usually destroying key evidence against themselves) often outweigh any risks (i.e., getting caught).

In an integrated approach, Coleman (1985) seeks to explain white-collar crime through the combined approach of opportunity theory and motivation. He argues that the crime is caused by a combination of opportunity and motivation. The individual's actions are further influenced by the use of neutralizations of any ethical or moral restraints present. The application of this theory to obstruction of justice is appropriate given that the nature of such a crime is dependent upon the opportunity to do so, as well as the increased level of motivation (i.e., eliminating evidence against oneself).

Yet another explanation of white-collar crimes was offered by Gottfredson and Hirschi (1990). They argue that the primary cause of crime is based on the simple desire to avoid pain and seek pleasure. They offer an explanation of all crime, not just street crime or white-collar crime, which combines essential components of opportunity and control theories. Basically, if individuals possess low self-control, then given an opportunity to commit a criminal act, they will be more likely to engage in such an act. Thus, it takes both the presence of low self-control in an individual as well as an opportunity to commit crime before crime will occur.

Given the prominence of highly publicized obstruction of justice charges in cases such as Arthur Andersen, Enron, and Martha Stewart, obstruction of justice can be considered today's top example of white-collar crime. This seemingly widespread appearance of actions involving obstruction of justice has not been limited solely to the corporate world. Obstruction of justice charges were brought against several governmental agents within the past few years including a federal agent involved in the Ruby Ridge incident; President Clinton for his alleged involvement in the Monica Lewinsky scandal; and charges were discussed for Congressman Gary Condit, owing to his alleged interference in the investigation into the disappearance of intern Chandra Levy. Partially in response to the influx of obstruction of justice cases publicized in the media, Congress passed the *Sarbanes-Oxley Act of 2002*. In general, this Act sought to improve deterrence through the enhancement of penalties set forth by the U.S. Sentencing Commission regarding obstruction of justice (Fenstermarker, 2003). The deterrent strategy is the primary response used by the government to combat obstruction of justice.

LISA HUTCHINSON WALLACE

References and Further Reading

Abramowitz, E. and Bohrer, B.A. 2002. White-collar crime, *New York Law Journal.*

Black, H.C. (Ed.) 1990. *Black's Law Dictionary,* St. Paul, MN: West Publishing.

Bureau of Justice Statistics. 1988. 2nd ed. *Report to the Nation on Crime and Justice,* Washington, DC: United States Department of Justice.

Gottfredson, M.R and Hirschi, T. 1990. *A General Theory of Crime,* Stanford, CA: Stanford University Press.

Lou, G. and Ro, N.M. 1999. Obstruction of justice, *American Criminal Law Review,* 36.

Polkes, J.D. 2003. Obstruction of justicer nexus requirement unclear in new statutes, *New York Law Journal.*

Reid, S.T. 2003. *Crime and Criminology,* Boston, MA: McGraw Hill.

Sutherland, E.H. 1945. Is "white-collar crime" crime? *American Sociological Review,* 10.

Sutherland, E.H. 1959. *White Collar Crime,* New York, NY: Holt, Rinehart, and Winston.

18 U.S.C.A. § 1501–1519.

See also **Bribery**

Occult Crime

Introduction

Before considering what is an occult crime, the complex question of what is the occult must be answered. In the broadest meaning, the occult concerns the hidden or obfuscated use of symbols, ideas, actions, performances, and rituals connected to supernatural beliefs and powers that can be manipulated to bring about a desired end or goal. The occult has much in common with magic where the individual is involved in attempting to force the supernatural into accomplishing tasks for the individual. Some scholars consider the occult to be a form of magic whether "white" or "positive" where the practioner seeks to enhance some aspect of themselves, others, or the world. Some who are involved with the occult are claimed to be practicing "black" magic where the alteration of the physical world is focused upon achieving a harmful or criminal result. These distinctions are a matter of some disagreement (see Cavendish, 1967) with some occultists advocating a position from a host of political and personal positions (such as gay magic). The occult is not a specific religion, although occult practice can be associated with a unique body of adherents or churches such as the Church of Satan or Temple of Set.

Many people consider occultism to be sick, perverse, heretical, dangerous, evil, and even illegal because believers' actions and identity are far removed from mainstream religious practice. Most occult activities, however, are neither illegal nor evil and are, in fact, protected under the First Amendment guaranteeing Americans freedom of religious choice. What the Constitution does not protect are illegal activities conducted by those motivated by the occult in conjunction with their belief system.

It appears that, to the occult practitioner, the type of magic practiced is largely perceptual; that is, practicing magic really involves what the practitioner believes is being invoked. To the criminal justice system, however, the practitioner's perceptions are moot; he or she is either involved in legally protected spiritual activity or in illegal criminal activity. This tension between belief and perception is critical in understanding occult crime.

Occult Crime

Just as the perception of the practitioner of what may be called the occult is central to defining their activity,

the perception of criminal justice professionals is also critically important in defining occult crime. Therefore, defining occult crime, not surprisingly, is as controversial a task as defining hate crime. Some members of the law enforcement community use definitions that place occult and occult-related criminal activity into a new category of criminal behavior specifically labeled as an occult or spiritual crime. Other legal professionals, however, strongly object to placing occult and occult-related criminal activity into a special category. To these criminal justicians, anyone of any spiritual, religious, or personal belief system who commits a crime, whether or not to further their beliefs, religion, or organization, has committed a crime and should be treated accordingly by the criminal justice system. The point that these critics raise is an important one: regardless of the label given to the crime itself, it is still a crime first and foremost.

Occult crime is criminal action as defined by local, state, and federal statutes based on spiritual, ritual, or ceremonial actions. Regardless of the specific beliefs, symbols, and values, reinforcing occult-related individual or group behavior motivates these actions. Occult crime is a generic term which, although useful in defining unusual criminal behavior, is not a complete definition of specific occult crimes. For example, satanic crime is one type of occult crime that explains only those criminal activities that may be committed by practicing satanists, not all criminals who are motivated by the occult. Similarly, ritualistic abuse is a type of occult crime involving repeated physical, sexual, psychological, or spiritual abuse that uses symbolic rituals.

In law enforcement circles today, occult crime is a hotly debated topic, not just because such criminal activities involve belief systems diametrically opposed by many Americans and are allegedly heinous in nature, but because few law enforcers agree on the extent of occult crime; the motives of perpetrators; the types of crimes perpetrated by occultists; or the veracity of adults and children who claim they are victims of occult crime, especially ritualistic abuse.

Although the vast majority of those interested in the occult are law-abiding, some step over the line between involvement in unusual spiritual activities and involvement in occult crime. Those occultists who become involved in crime frequently do so for the same reasons as nonoccult criminals. The notion that the occultist is searching for some supernatural power that leads to a world of occult crime is rare (such as Richard Ramirez, the serial killer known as the Night Stalker).

Most of those involved with the occult who commit crimes are "Dabblers." Dabblers are individuals who are often runaways or social outcasts who experiment with a variety of religions, spiritualities, and the occult. These individuals experiment their way into occult activities rather than engaging in the occult because of a systematic search for meaning and belonging. It is important to note that they also experiment with illegal drugs, prostitution, and other criminal activities. These individuals rarely form a stable social organization, church, or other vehicle for their beliefs.

Although dabblers constitute the majority of occult criminals, there are some occult organizations that advocate criminal behavior. Social organizations such as the Temple of Set and the Werewolf Order have had members who sought to encourage others within their groups to commit crimes. Much less is known about organizational support for occult crimes than we know about dabblers. The overwhelming majority of members within occult organizations and occult individuals are law-abiding citizens.

When crimes are committed for occult reasons whether by dabblers or members of occult organizations, there is frequently a perception that the crime possessed supernatural characteristics. The rise of public interest in exorcism, delivering, laying on of hands, and other unconventional spiritual beliefs and actions, have created a market for these beliefs that often hampers police investigations (see Victor, 1993; Goode, 2000; Cuneo, 2002). The hunt for paranormalism (behavior, belief, and symbols that exist beyond the normal) and ritualism (repeated actions characterized by a series of physical movements, spiritual symbols, and psychological meanings combined with a systematic use of ceremonial placement and prayer, statement, or reflection) are tied to a public interest about the occult rather than good investigative technique. The same criminal forensics used in mundane police investigations can be used to good effect in occult crimes to determine intent, causation, and violation.

This is not to dismiss the occult believers who commit crimes because such actions, based on their perceptions, are required by their particular belief systems. These persons are involved in crime primarily because of the beliefs, rituals, and accepted behavior related to their occult beliefs. However, these are their perceptions of their occult activity rather than the nature of the occult itself. We can apply this notion to several well-known organizations that engaged in criminal enterprises: The People's Temple under Jim Jones and the Aum Shakiro movement in Japan just to name two. Another form of occult crime that demonstrates the significance of perception to occult crime and has drawn the most attention and interest is the belief in a satanic ritual abuse conspiracy.

Satanic Ritual Abuse (SRA)

The belief in a satanic ritual abuse network that has been accepted by growing numbers of those in various helping professions and among some criminal justice professionals is the belief in an intergenerational, underground, international satanic conspiracy that kidnaps children, abuses them, ritually kills them, and engages in cannibalism. This rumor-panic, as the sociologist Jeffrey Victor calls it, has long historical roots but grew more prominent in the U.S. in the 1980s following the publication of books supposedly detailing the satanic underground such as *Michelle Remembers* (Smith and Pazder, 1980). When these stories first surfaced with *Michelle Remembers* and then in 1983 with the McMartin preschool case in Southern California, then the Bakersfield, California, and Jordan, Minnesota, cases, many journalists, law enforcement personnel, and mental health professionals tended to believe that SRA existed, at least hypothetically. However, the empirical evidence for these claims quickly became problematic. In the case of *Michelle Remembers*, Michelle Smith was an emotionally dysfunctional woman who with the assistance of her therapist (and later husband) discovered what they identified as previously repressed early childhood memories of horrible physical and sexual abuse in a bizarre secret satanic cult whose members included her immediate family. Although this book was widely disseminated among networks of Christian activists and churches, no physical corroborative evidence was obtained to prove Smith and Pazder's assertions.

However, books, pamphlets, and other media such as this alleged that an active cult of satanists from all walks of life kidnapped and kept thousands of women to generate babies for sacrifice. During the height of reports in the mid-1980s, these secret occult satanists were alleged to have killed 50,000 infants in the U.S. every year. The rituals of this international satanic cabal were estimated to have occurred on every continent and practiced inverted, sacrilegious parodies of Christian beliefs and practices.

Rather than being true, however, this idea was a rumor-panic (Richardson, Best, and Bromley, 1991; Victor, 1993; Wright, 1994). Rather than a substantiated series of crimes that could be proven, people assumed that the stories were true and posed a danger. Rumors, such as these, are unsubstantiated stories that convey misconceptions, misperceptions, distortions, and complete (in some cases) fabrication of actual events, even when some events actually occurred.

Federal law enforcement investigations have repeatedly shown that there is no empirical evidence for a vast international satanic conspiracy.

As we can see, the perception of the occult, occult activity, and occult symbols is as significant as any actual crime.

ARTHUR JIPSON

References and Further Reading

Cavendish, R. 1967. *The Black Arts,* New York, NY: Putnam's Sons Publishers.

Cuneo, M. 2002. *American Exorcism,* New York, NY: Broadway Books.

Goode, E. 2000. *Paranormal Belief,* Prospect Heights, IL: Waveland Press.

Richardson, J., Best, J., and Bromley, D.G. (Eds.). 1991. *The Satanism Scare,* New York, NY: Aldine De Gruyter.

Smith, M. and Pazder, L. 1980. *Michelle Remembers,* New York, NY: Pocket Books.

Victor, J. 1993. *Satanic Panic,* Chicago, IL: Open Court Press.

Wright, L. 1994. *Remembering Satan,* New York, NY: Alfred A. Knopf Publishers.

See also **Religion and Criminal Behavior; Witchcraft and Heresy**

Occupational Crime

Defining Occupational Crime

The popular image of crime most readily brings to mind such activities as murder, rape, assault, robbery, burglary, and auto theft. These activities are conventionally thought of as occurring outside the context of ordinary, legitimate occupations. Accordingly, the concept of occupational crime directly challenges stereotypical ideas about crime. The term should not be confused with the notion of criminal activity as a full-time occupation. The terms professional crime—and organized crime—address a full-fledged commitment to illegal pursuits. The term occupational deviance is a related but broader term than occupational crime, insofar as it includes forms of deviation from workplace norms such as drinking on the job, malingering, or sexual harassment; these activities may be deviant, but they are not defined as crimes (Bryant, 1974). The term workplace crime also overlaps with, but is not synonymous with, occupational crime, insofar as it includes robberies, rapes, assaults, and homicides—including mass murders committed by disgruntled or deranged employees—that occur at the workplace. Occupational crime, then, is a term most appropriately applied to illegal actions carried out in the context of a legitimate (legal) occupation for purposes of personal financial gain or to avoid financial loss (Friedrichs, 2002). It is one of the two principal forms of white-collar crime; the other is corporate crime. (Corporate crime can be most concisely defined as illegal and harmful activity carried out on behalf of a corporation to maximize gain and advantage or to minimize loss and disadvantage; Friedrichs, 2001, 89.) It includes such activities as defrauding of a customer by an auto mechanic, unnecessary surgery performed by a doctor, and embezzlement or theft of merchandise by an employee. Gary Green (1997) has called for a broader conception of the term occupational crime, and has proposed that this term replace white-collar crime. He argues that the latter term does not have a clear meaning. He defines occupational crime as "any act punishable by law that is committed through opportunity created in the course of an occupation that is legal." (Green, 1997, 15) Green contends that occupations structure opportunities for criminal behavior and this fact provides a coherent point of departure for criminological analysis.

Certainly it is true that the term white-collar crime is broadly applied to a wide range of different forms of behavior. But Green's conception of occupational crime includes correctional officers, physicians, and day care workers who sexually harass, molest, or assault inmates, patients, or children in their care, respectively. Although it may be true that their occupational status facilitates opportunities and outcomes, in the examples given, this factor would seem far less significant than the sexual deviancy involved. Green differentiates between organizational occupational crime (e.g., corporate price fixing), state authority occupational crime (e.g., genocide), professional occupational crime (e.g., lawyers padding bills), and individual occupational crime (e.g., employee theft). Again, that such diverse activities all occur within the context of legitimate occupations would seem less important than other dimensions of these activities.

Occupational crime can be found in all societies that have advanced beyond the level of primitive life, and it has become an object of research in many countries. The review in this article focuses on the American literature, although patterns for occupational crime are quite parallel across developed societies. Gerald Mars' (2001) *Occupational Crime* reprints some of the key historical and cross-cultural contributions to the literature on occupational crime.

Discovering Occupational Crime

The recognition that harmful and sometimes illegal activities are carried out in the context of legitimate occupational activities is hardly new. We can find proscriptions against crimes of traders, merchants, and skilled practitioners in ancient codes, the Old Testament of the Bible, and in Classical Greek and Roman law. Throughout medieval times various fraudulent practices were proscribed. In the 19th century critics of capitalist industrialism—such as Karl Marx and Friedrich Engels—wrote about the great harms perpetrated by the ownership class. And some early American sociologists—notably, E. A. Ross (1907), in *Sin & Society*—also addressed the crimes of businessmen, as did muckraking journalists of the early 20th century.

Within criminology Edwin H. Sutherland (1940) is given the principal credit for having directed the attention of criminologists to crimes committed in the context of middle and upper class occupations. Sutherland (1940) originally defined white-collar crime as "crime in the upper or white-collar class, composed of respectable or at least respected business and professional men ... [involving a] violation of delegated or implied trust." In his book *White Collar Crime*, however, Sutherland (1949) focused almost exclusively on corporate crime. In the mid-20th century period a small handful of criminologists inspired by Sutherland (e.g., Marshall Clinard, 1952; Donald Cressey, 1953) published studies of black marketeers and embezzlers, respectively. Richard Quinney (1963), a PhD student of Clinard, produced a dissertation on prescription violations by retail pharmacists, and subsequently published an article calling for a reformulation of the concept of white-collar crime to more fully consider occupational crime (Quinney, 1964). Clinard and Quinney (1967) subsequently published an influential book, *Criminal Behavior Systems: A Typology*, that identified occupational crime as one type of criminal behavior, and defined it as "violation of the legal codes in the course of activity in a legitimate occupation." In the second edition of this book Clinard and Quinney (1973) specifically distinguished corporate crime from occupational crime, now defined more narrowly as "the offenses committed by individuals for themselves in the course of their occupations and the offenses of employees against their employers." The dichotomy of corporate crime and occupational crime, as the principal forms of white-collar crime, came to be widely adopted in the field (Friedrichs, 1992). A parallel contrast is drawn between individualistic and organizational white-collar crime.

Types of Occupational Crime

Occupational crime itself is divided into a number of different types: small business occupational crime (retail and service); crimes of professionals (e.g., doctors and lawyers); and employee crime.

Although small businesses are often thought of as victims of crime they may also engage in a wide range of deceptive and illegal activities, including fraudulent (or misleading) advertising; illegal pricing practices; fraudulent representation of merchandise; purchase and resale of stolen goods; exploitation of employees (e.g., exposure to hazardous conditions, or nonpayment of social security taxes); evasion of sales taxes; and payoffs to inspectors and other public officials (Barlow, 1993). The most vulnerable parties—e.g., the poor, the bereaved, and the seriously afflicted or dependent elderly—are especially prone to victimization. Some studies of repair services (e.g., auto) have found that overcharging or unnecessary repairs, is the norm.

The professions enjoy considerable prestige, and generally high levels of trust, in our society; all too often this trust is violated. Illegal and unethical activities engaged in by physicians include fee-splitting, or taking and offering kickbacks; price-fixing; conflicts of interest (e.g., through ownership of clinics); unnecessary operations, tests, and other medical services; false and fraudulent billing (especially Medicaid fraud); filling of illegal prescriptions; and tax evasion. In the case of unnecessary surgery, patients may suffer physical injury, and possibly loss of life. Medicaid and Medicare fraud has been estimated to be in the billions, and contributes to the high cost of health care (Jesilow et al., 1993). Other professionals—including lawyers, professors, and scientists, and members of the clergy—sometimes violate the trust they enjoy through such activities as overbilling and embezzling from clients; plagiarism and fabrication of research data; and raising money from the faithful that is used to pay for personal extravagances rather than for legitimate spiritual purposes.

Employees collectively may account for greater losses to their employers than do outside parties (Hollinger and Clark, 1983). These losses add up to billions of dollars annually, and can contribute to business failures. Some surveys have suggested that half or more of employees engaged in some form of theft or misconduct, and that such activity is on the rise. Managerial employees are often positioned to steal on the largest scale, and may do so. Lower level employees may embezzle or steal on a fairly regular basis, although some employees will steal certain forms of company property but not other forms (Horning, 1970). The scope of employee crime against the employer has been found to vary according to a range of factors relating to the nature of the employer's business, specific circumstances, and the length of time on the job. More specifically, larger businesses are somewhat more vulnerable to employee theft than are smaller businesses (Smigel, 1970); unanticipated personal circumstances can lead an employee to theft (Cressey, 1953), but female employees were more likely to embezzle from an employer owing to family circumstances than male employees (Zietz, 1981). Workers who expect to be on the job for a shorter time were less likely to steal than others (Boye, 1991). These are, in any case, the findings of some studies on employee theft.

Cognate, Hybrid, and Marginal Types of Occupational Crime

Some other forms of criminal behavior have a generic relationship to occupational crime, although they do not fit neatly within the parameters of what is traditionally considered occupational crime. These forms include what I have designated elsewhere (Friedrichs, 1996; 2004) as: political white-collar crime; finance crime; technocrime; enterprise crime; contrepreneurial crime; and avocational crime. These types of crime are cognate, hybrid, or marginal forms of white-collar crime, or occupational crime.

Political white-collar crime refers to illegal and unethical activities of individuals in the context of public office, or government employment. This type of crime is exemplified by the taking of bribes by police officers or legislators, judges, and governors. As the term white-collar crime, as formulated by Sutherland, originally focused entirely on private sector activity, it seems appropriate to treat public sector offenses as a parallel but distinct form of occupational crime. Some would argue that such offenses are especially serious and harmful, insofar as they involve a violation of a public trust.

Finance crime refers to large-scale illegality that occurs in the world of finance and financial institutions, often involving huge stakes, entwined with corporate and financial networks, and sometimes a threat to the integrity of the financial systems. The savings and loan frauds of the 1980s, and insider trading cases, exemplify this type of crime.

Technocrime is a term used to refer to the use of computers and other forms of high tech to engage in illegal activity (Bequai, 1987). Not all such crime—for example, computer hacking—is linked with occu-

pational crime, but at least in some proportion of cases computers (and sophisticated technology) facilitate embezzlement or theft and fraud within an occupational context on an especially large scale.

Enterprise crime refers to a cooperative enterprise involving organized or syndicated (Mafia-type) crime, and legitimate businesses, or professionals. As syndicated criminal enterprises in the recent era increasingly infiltrated legitimate businesses, and became involved with such activities as securities fraud, the traditional distinctions between organized crime and white-collar crime have often become blurred. Small businessmen and lawyers who collaborate with syndicated crime members on swindles and frauds, for example, are involved in enterprise crime.

Contrepreneurial crime is a term combining confidence (professional crime) games with entrepreneurial (business) activities. A vast number of businesses, costing consumers billions of dollars annually, fall in the grey zone between outright scams and legitimate businesses, engaged in deceiving, defrauding, or swindling people to some degree. Home improvement, land sales, travel and time-share resorts, and telemarketing are just a few areas where contrepreneurial activity has been well-represented.

Finally, avocational crime refers to occasional economic crimes committed by respectable members of society outside an occupational context. If such activity is by definition not occupational crime, it requires some attention here because those involved, their motives, and the nature of the illegal activity often overlaps with and is parallel to occupational crime. Income tax evasion, insurance fraud, and false and fraudulent actions on loans, debts, and credits are examples of this type of crime.

Victims of Occupational Crime and Its Costs

Victims of conventional crime—for example, burglary, assault, rape, and robbery—are typically only too well aware that they have been victimized, and they may be quite severely traumatized by the experience. Most of those who are victims of occupational crime are not aware that they have been victimized. When someone is overcharged for services and goods, subjected to unnecessary surgery and medical procedures, or suffers losses on investments because of illegal manipulations, the individual is often not conscious of the victimization. The financial losses involved, or in some cases physical injuries, are nevertheless real, and often substantial. When people do discover that they have been defrauded—in some cases losing their life savings— we have evidence that the psychological trauma can be devastating. When they have been defrauded by someone whom they trusted—as is often the case with occupational crime—an added measure of pain may be experienced.

We have no truly reliable way to measure the full scope of victimization by occupational crime, but we have good reason to believe that it dwarfs financial losses from conventional crime. Certain forms of occupational crime—for example, performance of unnecessary operations by physicians, or sale of spoiled meat by food retailers—can cause significant physical harm, including loss of life.

When victims of occupational crime become aware of their victimization, it may be less clear to them to whom they should report the victimization than in the case of street crime victimization: The Better Business Bureau? A professional association such as the American Medical Association? A television consumer hotline? A regulatory agency? Furthermore, victims of occupational crimes are more likely to opt to sue a business or professional they believe has defrauded or harmed them, because there are potential assets for recovery. Businesses that are victims of employee crime often prefer to address the matter internally—possibly by simply firing the employee involved—rather than contending with the publicity and expenditure of time involved when a crime is reported to an official agency.

Explaining Occupational Crime

"Greed" is arguably the most concise—and most widely embraced—explanation for occupational crime. A certain proportion of occupational crime reflects need, not greed, in the sense of people attempting to extract themselves from financially desperate circumstances.

When we attempt to explain occupational crime we have to differentiate between attempting to explain criminality, crime, and criminalization: what motivates people to commit offenses; what circumstances, including opportunity, allow for the occurrence of occupational crime; what processes lead to some kinds of harmful occupational activities being defined as crimes, and others not.

To explain occupational crime we have to look to the structural level, or competitive pressures for materialistic acquisition or success; values and practices within organizational and professional subcultures privileging other interests over integrity; situational factors, such as unanticipated financial pressures or unusually easy opportunities for wrong-doing; and personal factors relating to individual character and personality. In any specific case of occupational crime some complex interaction of factors operating on these different levels may be involved. Changing conditions in the economy—for example, a recession, downsizing—can impact on motivations as well as opportunities for occupational crime (Friedrichs, 1997). Rationalizing (or neutralizing) of wrongdoing is an especially common dimension of occupational crime: for example, everybody does it; I am not really hurting anyone; I need to do this to survive in a competitive environment. At the same time it should be noted that significant forms of harm—for example, misleading people, taking advantage of vulnerable people—have not necessarily been criminalized. But any sophisticated effort to explain occupational crime is necessarily integrative, interdisciplinary, and multidimensional.

Policing, Prosecuting, and Adjudicating Occupational Crime

The police have been organized to address conventional forms of street crime, not occupational crime. However, even in the 19th century the police addressed some forms of fraud, and in the recent era more police departments have developed fraud units to respond to such crime. Regulatory agencies addressing such matters as pollution, health standards, consumer fraud, and working conditions respond to some forms of occupational crime. Self-policing plays a significant role in responding to occupational crime. For example, the Better Business Bureau is set up by local businesses to address complaints about unfair or fraudulent business practices, and professional associations or licensing boards address complaints about physicians and lawyers. Critics of self-policing have alleged that these entities are often more concerned with protecting the interests and public image of their members, rather than aggressively pursuing occupational crime.

Prosecutors, too, have traditionally found it politically more rewarding, and generally easier, to focus their time and resources on conventional forms of crime. Those who are prosecuted for occupational crime offenses are disproportionately middle class, or lower middle class, rather than upper class. Furthermore, a certain proportion of those prosecuted have past criminal records, at odds with a common perception of occupational crime offenders as one-time violators of the law. But this may well be because such offenders commit relatively low-level mail frauds and embezzlements that are especially visible to law enforcement agencies.

It is often difficult to demonstrate specific criminal intent in occupational crimes (e.g., proving that a surgical operation was unnecessary); the evidence in such cases may be buried in records that are time consuming to obtain and review; those charged with occupational crimes are especially likely to hire private lawyers who will aggressively contest the charges; judges (and juries) have historically been somewhat reluctant to impose criminal convictions on "respectable" members of society; prison has traditionally been regarded as inappropriate as a punishment for convicted occupational crime offenders. Probation, community service, fines, and restitution orders have been somewhat more common dispositions for these offenders. When occupational crime offenders are sent to prison they are likely to be sent to minimum security prisons, with a camp-like environment.

Responding to Occupational Crime

We have good reason to believe that occupational crime represents a significant ongoing challenge for our justice system, and by some estimates may increase as the population ages and new opportunities for fraud (e.g., through the Internet) arise. What is the most effective form of response to occupational crime?

Some commentators have suggested that occupational crime principally reflects a moral failure within our society, and specifically within professional or business subcultures. In this view, we should emphasize ethics and professional responsibility courses in the curriculum, and enforceable ethics codes within professional associations and businesses. However, there is little evidence that such an approach prevents unethical and illegal occupational behavior in the face of situational pressures and opportunities.

As occupational crime is regarded as instrumental and rational, it should be especially susceptible to deterrence. But clearly many occupational offenders are not deterred by the prospect of punishment, probably because they assume they will not be caught. A truly effective response to occupational crime requires a transformation of a culture that promotes extreme forms of materialism and competitiveness, as well as the reorganization of how goods and services are provided, reducing the broad structure of opportunity for doing harm and defrauding people that presently exists. Somewhat less ambitiously, we may hope to make inroads into the problem of occupational crime by increasing consciousness of and attention to it, and by enhancing procedures for policing, prosecuting, and sanctioning such activity.

DAVID O. FRIEDRICHS

References and Further Reading

Barlow, H. 1993. From fiddle factors to networks of collusion: Charting the waters of small business crime, *Crime, Law, and Social Change,* 20.

Bequai, A. 1987. *Techno-Crimes,* Lexington, MA: Lexington Books.

Boye, M.W. 1991. *Self-Reported Employee Theft and Counter-productivity as a Function of Employee Turnover Antecedents,* PhD dissertation, DePaul University.

Bryant, C.D. 1974. *Deviant Behavior: Occupational and Organizational Bases,* Chicago, IL: Rand McNally.

Clinard, M.B. 1952. *The Black Market: A Study of White Collar Crime,* New York, NY: Holt, Rinehart, and Winston.

Clinard, M. and Quinney, R. 1973. *Criminal Behavior Systems: A Typology,* New York, NY: Holt, Rinehart, and Winston, Inc.

Cressey, D.R. 1953. *Other People's Money,* New York, NY: The Free Press.

Friedrichs, D.O. 1992. White collar crime and the definitional quagmire: A provisional solution, *Journal of Human Justice,* 3(2).

Friedrichs, D.O. 2004. *Trusted Criminals: White Collar Crime in Contemporary Society,* Belmont, CA: ITP/Wadsworth.

Friedrichs, D.O. 1997. The downsizing of America: A neglected dimension of the white collar crime problem, *Crime, Law, and Social Change,* 26.

Friedrichs, D.O. 2001. Corporate crime, pp. 89–94, in Luckenbill, D. and Peck, D., (Eds.), *Encyclopedia of Criminology and Deviant Behavior: Volume II, Crime and Juvenile Delinquency,* Philadelphia, PA: Brunner-Routledge/Taylor & Francis.

Friedrichs, D.O. 2002. Occupational crime, occupational deviance, and workplace crime: Sorting out the difference, *Criminal Justice,* 2(3).

Horning, D.H. 1970. Blue-collar theft: Conceptions of property, attitudes toward pilfering, and work norms in a modern industrial plant, in Smigel, E.O. and Ross, H.L., (Eds.), *Crimes Against Bureaucracy,* New York, NY: Van Nostrand Reinhold.

Green, G.S. 1997. *Occupational Crime,* 2nd ed. Chicago, IL: Nelson Hall.

Hollinger, R.C. and Clark, J.P. 1983. *Theft by Employees,* Lexington, MA: Lexington Books.

Jesilow, P., Pontell, H.N., and Geis, G. 1993. *Prescription for Profit: How Doctors Defraud Medicaid,* Berkely, CA: University of California Press.

Mars, G., (Ed.) 2001. *Occupational Crime,* Aldershot, UK: Ashgate.

Quinney, R. 1963. Occupational structure and criminal behavior: Prescription violations by retail pharmacists, *Social Problems,* 11.

Quinney, R. 1964. The study of white collar crime: Toward a reorientation in theory and research, *Journal of Criminal Law, Criminology, and Police Science,* 55.

Ross, E.A. 1973. *Sin and Society,* New York, NY: Harper & Row.

Smigel, E.O. 2001. Public attitudes toward stealing as related to the size of the victim organization, pp. 15–28, in Smigel, E. and Ross, H.L. (Eds.), *Crimes against Bureaucracy,* New York, NY: Van Nostrand Reinhard.

Sutherland, E.H. 1940. White-collar criminality, *American Sociological Review,* 5.

Sutherland, E.H. 1949. *White Collar Crime,* New York, NY: Dryden Press.

Zietz, D. 1981. *Women Who Embezzle or Defraud: A Study of Convicted Felons,* New York, NY: Praeger.

See also **Employee Theft or Inventory Shrinkage; White-Collar Crime: Definitions**

Official and Unofficial Measures of Criminal Behavior

There are three major methods of measuring involvement in criminal behavior: (1) official statistics on criminal offending, (2) self-report measures of delinquency and crime, and (3) self-report measures of criminal victimization. In fact, today, when people talk about statistics on criminal behavior, they most often are referring to official police statistics on crime. What people do not realize, despite disclaimers in these documents, is that official and unofficial statistics each have well-known limitations. Let us look at the origins of official and unofficial measures of criminal behavior, what they measure, what they do not measure, and how each method can complement the others for identification and understanding of criminal behavior.

The first national effort to collect statistics on criminal behavior was carried out in France in 1825 (Mosher, Miethe, and Phillips, 2002). Official statistics on criminal behavior include data collected by police, judicial, and correctional organizations. Police statistics have been collected on a systematic basis in England since 1857 and in the U.S. since 1930. Most countries collect police statistics of some form but these do not necessarily provide a good measure of crime (see Council of Europe, 1999).

Statistics on crime have always faced criticism about their validity as a measure of criminality. Quetelet (1842) used data from France and Belgium to show a consistency in crimes recorded and crimes prosecuted between 1826 and 1830. Quetelet recognized that there was a difference between crimes recorded (an accusation made in court) and crimes that occurred. The *dark figure of crime* not captured by official police statistics is the difference between the true number of crimes and crimes known.

People can get information about crime from a variety of sources such as the news media, neighbors, friends, and relatives. In the U.S., the vast majority of Americans get their information about crime from their local television news (Flanagan and Longmire, 1996). A problem, however, is that crime in the news may not correspond with rates of criminal behavior. Marsh (1991) demonstrates that crime coverage in the news does not coincide with official statistics in the U.S. and other countries. On one hand, it may be that crime news may be considered irrelevant because the media overrepresents spectacular crimes that most people will never encounter (Skogan and Maxfield, 1981). On the other hand, an abundance of sensationalist crime stories may have detrimental effects of increasing fear of crime (Chiricos, Padgett, and Gertz, 2000) and may create false perceptions about the extent of crime (Vandiver and Giacopassi, 1997). Media coverage is important though it has motivated governmental agencies to collect so-called *official* measures of criminal behavior.

In the 1920s, the International Association of Chiefs of Police (IACP) was very concerned about newspaper generated crime waves (Maltz, 1977). The IACP worked to establish the Uniform Crime Reports (UCR) program in 1929 in the U.S. to collect crime data to counter media accounts (O'Brien, 1985).

A significant problem for measuring criminal behavior is that different jurisdictions (countries, states, and cities) may have different laws and organizational practices about what constitutes crime. Sellin (1931, 351) wrote that "international comparisons are particularly hazardous." Sellin, a contributor to the development of the UCR program (see Laub, 1983), argued that the use of scientific methods in collecting crime data was critical for ensuring that the crime index would be reliable and valid. International comparisons have been done but it often requires substantial work to ensure that the researcher is comparing similar information (see Archer and Gartner, 1984; Gillis, 1989).

Police agencies may have different organizational practices, rules, and even different laws in their jurisdictions. In order to reliably measure crime, scoring systems have been devised for the collection of official statistics. "Scoring" rules (how to count) have been devised to standardize the measurement of crime. Understanding how police organizations count crimes is important for establishing the internal validity of official measures of crime. A count is only as good as our understanding of how it is put together. In 2001, the Home Office changed the National Crime Recording Standard (NCRS) that had the effect of artificially increasing the number of recorded crimes in England and Wales in 2002 (Simmons and Dodd, 2003).

Using the UCR as an example of how police data are collected, a survey of local police departments was conducted in 1929 and 26 separate offenses were selected because: (1) they were most likely to be reported to the police, (2) police investigation could establish if they were well-founded (whether a crime had occurred), (3) they were serious crimes, and (4) they occurred with sufficient frequency to adequately compare jurisdictions (MacKenzie, Baunach, and Roberg, 1990). The IACP debated whether to use arrests or crimes known (reported) to the police with August Vollmer, Chief of Police of Berkeley, California, arguing that arrest data would lead to a false measure because arrest practices are biased from jurisdiction to jurisdiction (Maltz, 1977). Vollmer won out and the UCR uses crimes known to the police. Sellin's (1931, 346) dictum describes the importance of choosing crimes reported as he said "the value of a crime rate for index purposes decreases as the distance from the crime itself increases." That is crimes known to the police will be more useful as a measure of crime than arrest, prosecution, and correctional statistics because each set of statistics is subject to administrative structures.

The UCR program is a voluntary program where local police departments report their monthly *scores* to the Federal Bureau of Investigation who compile the annual report. Beginning in 1930 with 400 agencies, there were by the 1990s over 18,000 agencies reporting to the FBI. Since 1958, the FBI (annual) has reported a national estimate of crime in the U.S. (Maltz, 1999).

Each jurisdiction is to use the UCR scoring rules to count crimes in their jurisdiction on a monthly basis and to report them on an annual basis. Although there may be different laws in different jurisdictions, the UCR scoring rules were to be used to classify crimes. A hierarchical rule is present for instances where more than one crime occurs in a single incident so that the most serious crime is the one that is counted. The reports submitted to the FBI are subject to consistency checks to ensure that scoring rules were followed. These reliability checks were also present in the early UCR program with limitations of these data published in the reports.

The UCR initially classified offenses under two broad categories—part I and part II crimes. Seven offenses were selected for inclusion in the UCR (Part I) index: Murder and nonnegligent manslaughter, rape, robbery, aggravated assault, burglary, larceny, and motor vehicle theft. An eighth, arson, was added to the index in 1979. To compute the crime index the counts of each of the part I crimes are added up, divided by the population in the jurisdiction, and multiplied by 100,000. The result is a standardized crime rate per 100,000 population. A similar calculation can be done for each individual index crime (e.g., murder and nonnegligent manslaughter rate), or for violent crimes (murder, rape, robbery, assault), or for property crimes (burglary, larceny, motor vehicle theft, and arson). The UCR reports this information annually in tabular format for the U.S. as a whole, states, metropolitan areas, and cities with populations over 10,000.

By its very definition, the UCR crime index is a limited measure of crime because it does not include all possible types of crime. It simply was not intended as a measure of *all* crimes. It does not compile information about violation of federal laws, white-collar crimes, rules governing commerce and industry, other illegal activities, and little information about drug offenses (MacKenzie et al., 1990). It also was not designed to deal with incidents where more than one crime occurred in an incident. A National Incident Based Reporting System (NIBRS) is being developed to overcome this deficiency but its development has been much slower than was originally anticipated (Bureau of Justice Statistics, 1997).

Official statistics such as the UCR crime index were designed to standardize measures of criminal behavior. A standardized measure allows people and organizations to estimate whether crimes reported to the police went up or down in a particular place and to enable the possibility of comparisons across jurisdictions. We will return to a discussion of the validity of official statistics after we introduce other measures of criminal behavior.

A second measure of criminal behavior uses the self-report method to ask people about criminal offending. It is considered an *unofficial* measure of criminal behavior because these surveys are collected by an independent researcher (not a governmental official from the police, courts, or corrections). Self-report methods are commonplace in research today.

There are many historical studies using self-report methods. Porterfield (1943) published one of the first studies on crime and delinquency. He uses the self-report method to show that every one of a sample of college students had committed a delinquent act, yet few of these students had an official report with the police or in the juvenile court. Thornberry and Krohn (2000) describe Porterfield's study as a landmark effort because it alerted criminologists to the extent of hidden delinquency. Official statistics were clearly shown to be biased.

Although Porterfield pioneered self-reports, Nye and Short's work revolutionized the method (Hindelang, Hirschi, and Weiss, 1981). Nye and Short (1957) devised a scale to measure delinquent behavior in the general population. Although official records from juvenile courts document the extent of delinquency known to the court, they argued that official measures were unreliable for establishing the extent of delinquency in the general population. They devised a series of questions that they administered to official delinquents (in a training school) and to a general population of adolescents (attending school). Their initial survey (1957, 328) included 21 items from which 9 items were scaled to assess the extent of delinquency. The nine-item check list asked about behaviors such as "driven a car without a driver's license," "taken little things (worth less than $2) that did not belong to you?," drinking beer, wine or liquor, skipping school, sexual relations, defying parental authority, running away from home, and taking things of medium value (between $2 and $50). Nye and Short's research is significant because of their focus on methodological issues. They were interested in scale construction, reliability, validity, sampling, and the potential to test the relationship of social class with delinquent (criminal) behavior (Thornberry and Krohn, 2000). Nye and Short concluded that self-report studies of delinquency did not correspond with official measures of delinquency.

Nye and Short's work led to much use of the self-report method in the 1960s and 1970s. A limitation of self-report measures, however, is that they focus on a limited number of delinquent behaviors and that these were usually minor offenses. The self-report methodology advanced in the 1980s as researchers set out to tap and explain the etiology of serious delinquency (Elliot, Huzinga, and Ageton, 1985; Thornberry, 1987). The National Youth Survey in the U.S. and longitudinal studies in Rochester, Denver, Pittsburg, and Cambridge all enhanced the development of better questions for understanding delinquency and development issues related to crime.

The self-report method continues to be applied by many researchers. One large-scale effort is the "Monitoring the Future" study that is a national effort in the U.S. to document the extent of drug use and delinquency among high school students. Thornberry and Krohn (2000, 41) describe the self-report method as being used in the most innovative research in crime and delinquency. Of importance, is that the self-report method allows researchers and policy makers to measure criminal offending in areas that official statistics do not allow reliable and valid measures.

A third measure of criminal behavior uses the self-report method to gather information about criminal victimization. A sample of people from a population is surveyed about their personal experiences with criminal victimization. The major purposes of these

victimization surveys are to measure criminal behavior by estimating the extent of victimization, the circumstances of these crimes, potential methods to prevent criminal behavior, and to uncover the dark figure of crime not reported to police.

Questions on victimization surveys have been designed to measure the same kinds of crimes that official statistics seek to measure. Using a similar definition enables some comparisons of the two measures. The National Crime Victimization Survey (NCVS) in the U.S. asks people about crimes of rape, sexual assault, personal robbery, aggravated and simple assault, household burglary, theft, and motor vehicle theft. Note that homicide is not included on victimization surveys.

National crime victimization surveys are relatively new when compared to official statistics. In part, the victimization surveys have arisen because of known weaknesses in official statistics. At the same time, self-report victimization surveys and official statistics both provide valuable information about criminal behavior.

The National Crime Victimization Surveys have been collected in the U.S. on an annual basis since 1973 (Bureau of Justice Statistics, 1993) with samples of about 50,000 households or approximately 100,000 people aged 12 and older. The British Crime Survey (BCS) was collected on a periodic basis: 1982, 1984, and 1988, moved to a biennial survey in the 1990s, and became an annual survey in 2001 (Simmons and Dodd, 2003). About 40,000 people aged 16 and over are interviewed per year in the British Crime Survey. Other countries have collected national victimization surveys but these surveys are relatively rare (del Frate, Zvekic, and van Dijk, 1993). Canada's General Social Survey program uses a 5-year cycle to ask people about personal risk including criminal victimization (Sacco, 1995).

National Crime Victimization Surveys are very expensive to conduct. Although criminal behavior may occur in large numbers in a country, criminal victimization is still a relatively rare event. Thus, very large samples—tens of thousands of people—are needed if one wishes to reliably measure the extent of victimization for different types of crimes in a population.

Self-report victimization surveys are designed to measure criminal behavior seen from the victim's point of view. These surveys use questions that are presented in plain language using nonlegalistic terminology to ask questions about criminal behavior. This methodology has the potential to both broaden the measure of criminal behavior beyond what may fit into the legal definition of a criminal act and to reduce it because people may ignore some criminal behavior if they themselves do not define it as a crime.

When asking questions about criminal victimization, it is also important to anchor the questions in a specific time frame because people may telescope events. Some respondents may forget information about crimes (because they may perceive them as trivial) whereas other respondents may bring incidents that actually happened outside the time frame back into focus because their memory of these events is vivid (they perceive these events as more recent because they were very important events). Keeping a relatively short time frame such as 6 months or 1 year reduces the methodological problem of telescoping of events. Households in the NCVS are included in the sample for 3 years and household members aged 12 and older are interviewed using 6-month intervals.

The design of the NCVS and BCS where people are interviewed and then reinterviewed at regular intervals provides an opportunity to examine repeat criminal victimization. Ellingsworth, Farrell, and Ken Pease (1995) have pioneered research using the BCS to demonstrate that victims are at much higher risk of revictimization than persons in the general population are at risk for a first victimization.

The NCVS and BCS and other national victimization surveys have used standardized (the same) questions on their victimization surveys. Using standardized questions allows for trend analyses. Nonetheless, victimization surveys also need to be evaluated to determine whether their design works as a measure of crime. The BCS has used the same questions throughout its program (Simmons and Dodd, 2003). The NCVS program underwent a significant evaluation in the 1980s and in 1993 it was redesigned to measure more crimes and to measure crimes better. There has been much discussion of the problems of measuring sexual assault in the NCVS (Koss, 1993; Jensen, 1993). There also is much discussion of the importance of trend analysis and how and whether to compare the redesigned NCVS to the original program (Kinderman, Lynch, Cantor, 1997).

The three major measures of criminal behavior all have their strengths and weaknesses. Comparing each measure to the others can enrich our overall understanding of criminal behavior and how to prevent it.

There are many studies that are critical of biases in official statistics. The validity of police statistics as measures of crime and criminality was deeply questioned in the 1960s. Beattie (1960) said that the UCR was so unreliable that it should not be used at all for research purposes. Kitsuse and Cicourel (1963) published their famous article where they suggested that official statistics were simply social artifacts because police discretion in arrest procedures was of such magnitude that the official index of crime was more so a measure of police discretion than a measure of criminal behavior. Chambliss and Nagasawa (1969) suggested official statistics were so misleading as indicators of deviance (crime) that they are virtually useless as indicators of deviant behavior. Of debate was how police discretion was used differently across cultural groups and social classes so that the statistics were distorted. Skogan (1974) countered these constructionist arguments arguing in favor of the use of official statistics until we have something that could replace them. Tittle, Villemez, and Smith (1978) challenged the social-class argument as a myth. They compared empirical studies that used official statistics to self-report studies finding only a slight negative effect between class and criminality and revealing less association in studies that used official statistics. Gove, Hughes, and Gerkins (1985), comparing the UCR to victim surveys, argued that criminology cannot go forward as a science if official statistics are not treated as valid measures of serious crimes. Kitsuse and Cicourel's argument (and researchers following their methodology) continues to be important because it shook the very foundation of studies of criminal behavior as the validity of official statistics was no longer taken for granted (Duster, 2000).

Official statistics, self-report studies of offending, and self-report studies of victimization each provide unique information measuring criminal behavior. Taken together though, they may complement each other to provide a more comprehensive understanding of criminal behavior. Official statistics help us to understand fluctuations in particular jurisdictions. Self-report studies of offending have provided substantial information about the causes of serious delinquency and criminal behavior. Victimization surveys help us to understand the extent of criminal behavior, how to prevent it, why the police are (and are not) called, and the risks of repeat victimization. Although police statistics may have greater public visibility, these three measures provide complementary information to measure criminal behavior.

DAVID R. FORDE

References and Further Reading

Archer, D. and Gartner, R. 1984. *Violence and Crime in Cross-National Perspective*, New Haven, CT: Yale University Press.

Beattie, R.H. 1960. Criminal statistics in the United States, *Journal of Criminal Law, Criminology and Police Science*, 51.

Bonger, W.A. 1916. *Criminality and Economic Conditions*, New York, NY: Agathon.

Bureau of Justice Statistics. 1993. *Highlights from 20 Years of Surveying Crime Victims: The National Crime Victimization Survey*, 1973–1992, Washington, DC: Bureau of Justice Statistics.

Bureau of Justice Statistics. 1997. *Implementing the National Incident-Based Reporting System,* Washington, DC: Bureau of Justice Statistics.

Canadian Centre for Justice Statistics. Canadian crime statistics, annual. *Juristat,* Annual. Ottawa: Statistics Canada.

Chambliss, W.J. and Nagasawa, R.H. 1969. On the validity of official statistics, *Journal of Research in Crime and Delinquency,* 6, 1.

Chiricos, T., Padgett, K., and Gertz, M. 2000. Fear, TV news, and the reality of crime, *Criminology,* 38, 3.

Council of Europe, 1999. *European Sourcebook of Criminal Justice Statistics,* Available at www.europeansourcebook.org.

del Frate, A.A., Zvekic, U. and van Dijk, J.J.M. (Eds.), 1993. *Understanding Crime Experiences of Crime and Crime Control,* Rome: United Nations Interregional Crime and Justice Research Institute.

Duster, T. 2000. The epistemological challenge of the early attack on 'Rate Construction,' *Social Problems,* 48, 1.

Elliot, D.S., Huizinga, D., and Ageton, S.S. 1985. *Explaining Delinquency and Drug Use,* Beverly Hills, CA: Sage Publications.

Ellingsworth, D., Farrell, G., and Pease, K. 1995. A victim is a victim is a victim?" *British Journal of Criminology,* 35, 3.

Federal Bureau of Investigation, *Crime in the United States, Annually,* Washington, DC: Department of Justice.

Flanagan, T.J. and Longmire, D.R. (Eds.), 1996. *Americans View Crime and Justice: A National Public Opinion Survey,* Thousand Oaks, CA: Sage.

Gillis, A.R. 1989. Crime and state surveillance in nineteenth-century France, *American Journal of Sociology,* 95, 2.

Gove, W.R., Hughes, M., and Geerken, M. 1985. Are uniform crime reports a valid indicator of the index crimes? *Criminology,* 23, 3.

Hindelang, M.J, Hirschi, T., and Weis, J.G. 1979. Correlates of delinquency: The illusion of discrepancy between self-report and official measures, *American Sociological Review,* 44, 6.

Hindelang, M.J, Hirschi, T., and Weis, J.G. 1981. *Measuring Delinquency,* Beverly Hills, CA: Sage.

Jensen, G.F. 1993. Managing rape: Exploratory research on the behavior of rape statistics, *Criminology,* 31, 3.

Johnston, L.D., Bachman, J.G., and O'Malley, P.M. 2001. *Monitoring the Future: A Continuing Study of the Lifestyles and Values of Youth,* Ann Arbor, MI: University of Michigan.

Kinderman, C., Lynch, J., and Cantor, D. 1997. *Effects of the Redesign on Victimization Estimates,* Washington, DC: Bureau of Justice Statistics.

Kitsuse, J.I. and Cicourel, A.V. 1963. A note of the uses of official statistics, *Social Problems,* 11, 2.

Koss, M.P. 1993. Rape: Scope, impact, interventions, and public policy responses, *American Psychologist,* 48, 10.

Laub, J.H. 1983. *Criminology in the Making,* Boston, MA: Northeastern University Press.

MacDonald, Z. 2001. Revisiting the dark figure: A microeconomic analysis of the under-reporting of property crime and its implications, *British Journal of Criminology,* 41, 1.

MacKenzie, D.L., Baunach, P.J., and Roberg, R.R., (Eds.) 1990. *Measuring Crime,* State University of New York.

Maltz, M.D. 1977. Crime statistics: A historical perspective, *Crime and Delinquency,* 23, 1.

Maltz, M.D. 1999. *Bridging Gaps in Police Crime Data,* Washington, DC: Bureau of Justice Statistics.

Marsh, H.L. 1991. A comparative analysis of crime coverage in newspapers in the United States and other countries from 1960–1989: A review of the literature, *Journal of Criminal Justice,* 19, 1.

Mosher, C.J., Miethe, T.D., and Phillips, D.M. 2002. *The Mismeasure of Crime,* Thousand Oaks, CA: Sage.

Nye, F.I., and Short, J.F., Jr. 1957. Scaling delinquent behavior, *American Sociological Review,* 22.

O'Brien, R.M. 1985. *Crime and Victimization Data,* Beverly Hills, CA: Sage.

Porterfield, A.L. 1943. Delinquency and outcome in court and college, *American Journal of Sociology,* 49.

Quetelet, L.A.J. 1842. *Treatise on Man and the Development of his Faculties,* Edinburgh, Scotland: S.W. and R. Chambers.

Rand, M.R., Lynch, J.P., and Cantor, D. 1997. *Criminal Victimization, 1973–95,* Washington, DC: Bureau of Justice Statistics.

Rennison, C.M. and Rand, M.R. 2003. *Criminal Victimization, 2002,* Washington, DC: Bureau of Justice Statistics.

Sacco, V. 1995. Fear and personal safety, *Juristat,* 15, 9.

Sellin, T. 1931. The basis of a crime index, *Journal of Criminal Law and Criminology,* 22, 3.

Simmons, J. and Dodd, T. (Eds.), 2003. *Crime in England and Wales 2002/2003,* London, UK: Home Office.

Skogan, W.G. 1974. The validity of official crime statistics: An empirical investigation, *Social Science Quarterly,* 55, 1.

Skogan, W.G. and Maxfield, M.G. 1981. *Coping with Crime,* Beverly Hills, CA: Sage.

Thornberry, T.P. 1987. Toward an interactional theory of delinquency, *Criminology,* 25.

Thornberry, T.P. and Krohn, M.D. 2000. The self-report method for measuring delinquency and crime, Ch. 2 in Duffee, D. (Ed.), *Criminal Justice 2000: Vol. 4., Measurement and Analysis of Crime and Justice,* Washington, DC: National Institute of Justice.

Tittle, C.R., Villemez, W.J., and Smith, D.R. 1978. The myth of social class and criminality: An empirical assessment of the empirical evidence, *American Sociological Review,* 43, 5.

Vandiver, M. and Giacopassi, D. 1997. One million and counting: Students' estimates of the annual number of homicides in the U.S., *Journal of Criminal Justice Education,* 8, 2.

See also **National Crime Victimization Survey (NCVS): Self-Report Research; Uniform Crime Report**

Ohlin, Lloyd E.

Lloyd Ohlin was born in Belmont, Massachusetts on August 27, 1928, to Swedish immigrants Emil and Elise Ohlin, the second of four boys. Upon his graduation from Belmont High School in 1936, Lloyd attended Brown University in Providence, Rhode Island. At Brown, Ohlin divided his time between his academic interests in sociology and psychology and participation in track and field, graduating with honors in 1940, with an A. B. in sociology and a minor in psychology. It was during his years at Brown that he became interested in the study of crime through contact with the chair of the sociology department, whose specialization was criminology. Ohlin perceived the study of crime as a union of sociology and psychology, his two key areas of interest.

Spurred by his interest in the study of crime, after completing his undergraduate coursework at Brown, he then continued on to the graduate program at Indiana University to study with criminology's founding father, Edwin Sutherland. This contact and interaction with Sutherland was to have great influence on Ohlin's approach to criminology. Also while at Indiana, Ohlin was exposed to the ideas of Nathaniel Kantor of the psychology department. Ohlin credits Kantor as having great influence on his theorizing and work, finding his brand of psychology and social psychology extremely fascinating. Ohlin received his M.A. in Sociology in 1942.

After completing the master's program at Indiana, Ohlin took a brief hiatus from academia, joining the military and serving in the counterintelligence corps in Europe from 1942 until November 1945. After returning from his service in World War II, he married Helen Hunter, the daughter of Walter Hunter, chair of the psychology department at Brown University. In March of 1946, both Lloyd and Helen started graduate school at the University of Chicago. It was at Chicago, while working on his Ph.D. in Sociology, that Ohlin met the other person whom he credits with influencing the direction of his career, Ernest Burgess.

In the fall of 1947, Ohlin took on the job of sociologist-actuary with the Illinois Parole and Pardon Board, a position that allowed him to pursue his dissertation in the area of adult corrections. As a sociologist-actuary, Ohlin was responsible for interviewing inmates, preparing case materials for parole board dockets, and conducting research in parole prediction. He held this position until he was transferred to the Chicago office of the Board in 1950, where he served as a supervising research sociologist, researching parole board decisions, parole statistics, and prediction. Ohlin was also involved in the development of in-service training programs for correctional workers while continuing to work toward his Ph.D.

Ohlin left the Parole and Pardon Board in 1953 to take a position at the University of Chicago serving as Director of the Center for Education and Research in Corrections. The following year, he received his Ph.D. in Sociology. During that same year, Ohlin continued to hold the position of Director of the Center while also beginning a 5-year relationship with the American Bar Association as a consultant on field research for their survey of the administration of justice in the U.S. In 1955, he assisted in the reorganization of the correctional program of the Cook County (IL) Jail.

Lloyd Ohlin was appointed as a professor of sociology in 1956 at the Columbia University School of Social Work. In the fall of 1957, Ohlin, along with Richard Cloward, began a comparative study of juvenile offender institutions at Columbia's new research center. It was this project that led to the development of differential opportunity theory and the 1960 publication of *Delinquency and Opportunity: A Theory of Delinquent Gangs*.

Differential opportunity theory rests heavily on the premises put forth by Merton's strain theory (1938). Cloward and Ohlin agree, for instance, on the central premise that members of society share a common set of values emphasizing certain life goals, particularly that of material success, and that two standard avenues exist for achieving these goals— legitimate and illegitimate (Williams and McShane, 1999). They also concur with Merton in that members of the middle and upper classes have primary access to the legitimate opportunity structure (e.g., business and politics), whereas members of the lower class have primary access to illegitimate opportunity structure. Where the theory departs from Merton's version is in its treatment of access to these opportunity structures.

Delinquent subcultures, according to Cloward and Ohlin, flourish in the lower classes and take particular forms so that the means for illegitimate success are no more equally distributed than the means for legitimate success. They argue that the means for illegitimate success are dependent upon the degree of integration that exists within the particular community. This level of integration, in turn, determines the level of social disorganization the community experiences. A negative relationship therefore exists between the two—the less the level of integration, the more the level of social disorganization.

Communities with well-organized and integrated illegitimate opportunity structures provide learning environments for organized criminal behavior (Williams and McShane, 1999). Unlike classical social disorganization theory (see Park and Burgess, 1924; Shaw and McKay, 1942), which typically views crime as an important indicator of disorganization, differential opportunity contends that the presence of organized crime is analogous to the presence of organized communities. Other types of crime, manifested through the development of male youth gangs, are the result of unequal access to illegitimate means of success that in turn are predicated on the cohesiveness of the community. Based on the degree of integration and social disorganization, differing delinquent gang types will emerge.

Cloward and Ohlin propose three types of delinquent gangs: (1) the criminal gang, (2) the conflict or violent gang, and (3) the retreatist gang. The first, the criminal gang, emerge in areas where conventional as well as unconventional values of behavior are integrated by a close connection of illegitimate and legitimate businesses. Older gang members serve as role models and mentors for community youth ensuring the continuation of profit through illegal activity. This type of gang is stable and organizes its criminal activity toward realization of financial and material gain. The second type, the conflict or violent gang, is neither stable nor integrated and suffers from a lack of criminal organization. This gang strives to possess a reputation for toughness and destructive violence and has no real identifiable material goals. The third and final gang type, the retreatist gang, is equally unsuccessful in legitimate as well as illegitimate means. Members are considered double failures, thus retreating into a world of sex, drugs, and alcohol.

Cloward and Ohlin's differential opportunity theory is typically classified as a strain theory, however, it possesses elements of both structure and process. In combining the strain of anomie theory and the process of differential association theory, differential opportunity theory leans more toward structure (Williams and McShane, 1999). Apart from emphasizing one's position in the social structure, it also attempts to explicate the process by which the content of criminal lifestyles is transmitted from one generation to the next. Thus, differential opportunity theory may be considered as

an early example of an integrated theory, combining key precepts from strain, social disorganization, subcultural and learning perspectives.

Lloyd Ohlin is currently the Touroff-Glueck Professor in Criminal Justice, Emeritus at the Harvard Law School where he has served in varying capacities since his appointment in 1967.

HOLLY E. VENTURA

Biography

Born in Belmont, MA, August 27, 1928. Education: Brown University A.B. 1940, Sociology; Indiana University M.A. 1942, Sociology; University of Chicago PhD. 1954, Sociology. Supervising Research Sociologist, Chicago office of the Board, 1950; Director, Center for Education and Research in Corrections, University of Chicago, 1953; Professor of sociology, Columbia University School of Social Work, 1956; Professor of Criminology, Harvard Law School, 1967; Roscoe Pound Professor of Criminology, Harvard Law School, 1973; Touroff-Glueck Professor in Criminal Justice, Harvard Law School, 1981.

References and Further Readings

Bottoms, A.E. and Wiles, P. (1992). Explanations of crime and place. In Evans, D.J., Fyfe, N.R., and Herbert, D.T. (Eds.) *Crime, Policing and Place: Essays in Environmental Criminology*, pp. 11–35. London, UK: Routledge.

Cloward, R.A. and Ohlin, L.E. (1960). *Delinquency and Opportunity: A Theory of Delinquent Gangs.* New York, NY: Free Press.

Cohen, A.K. (1955). *Delinquent Boys: The Culture of the Gang.* New York, NY: Free Press.

Cohen, A.K. (1965). The sociology of the deviant act: Anomie theory and beyond. *American Sociological Review,* 30, 5–14.

Cullen, F.T. (1988). Were Cloward and Ohlin strain theorists? Delinquency and opportunity revisited. *Journal of Research in Crime and Delinquency,* 25, 214–241.

Felson, M. (1994). *Crime in Everyday Life: Insights and Implications for Society.* Thousand Oaks, CA: Pine Forge Press.

Merton, R.K. (1938). Social structure and anomie. *American Sociological Review,* 3, 672–682.

Messner, S.F. and Rosenberg, R. (1994). *Crime and the American dream.* Belmont, CA: Wadsworth Publishing.

Park, R.E. and Burgess, E.W. (1924). *Introduction to the Science of Sociology,* 2nd ed. Chicago, IL: University of Chicago Press.

Shaw, C.R. and McKay, H.D. (1942). *Juvenile Delinquency in Urban Areas.* Chicago, IL: University of Chicago Press.

Williams, F.P. and McShane, M.D. (1999). *Criminological Theory,* 3rd ed. Upper Saddle River, NJ: Prentice Hall.

See also **Cloward, Richard; Gangs: Theories; Subcultural Theories of Criminal Behavior; Strain Theories**

Organized Crime: Activities and Extent

Organized crime is an international phenomenon that transcends national and continental borders. It tends to thrive where government institutions and legitimacy are weak whereas traditions of corruption are strong. The secrecy of the groups involved and the scope and nature of their enterprises, makes reasonable estimates of their measurement impossible. The business of organized crime has been described as providing goods and services that happen to be illegal. Translating morality into a statute backed by legal sanctions widens the scope of the law and creates both temptation and opportunity for those willing to risk violating the law. As in any business, the better organized are usually the more successful, and organized crime is basically a business enterprise.

But the business of organized crime often includes activities that are neither "goods" nor "services" but are clearly parasitic. Organized crime may have a relationship with the purveyors of illegal goods and services that is extortionate—"protection racket." An organized crime group may simply "license" an illegal business whose operator purchases a "license" through the payment of "street taxes" to avoid being beaten or killed (or subjected to harassment by corrupt law enforcement).

The boundary between providing goods or a service and being parasitic is not clearly delineated. Thus, although professional gamblers may be required to pay street taxes to operate in a particular area, in return the organized crime group may limit market entry—competition—and provide collection and arbitration services that are vital in such enterprises. Organized criminal groups operate as a shadow government, providing policing and judicial services to a vast underworld, thereby increasing efficiency and coordination in an otherwise anarchic—Hobbesian—environment. An organized crime connection can also provide a professional criminal—burglars and armed robbers, for example—with valuable information about lucrative targets as well as the equipment they may be need—firearms, stolen cars, electronic equipment, and fencing services to dispose of stolen property. Organized crime loan sharks can finance elaborate frauds or major drug deals. With this in mind, let us review the "goods and services" of organized crime.

Gambling

Gambling includes a wide array of games of chance and sporting events on which wagers are made. Some of these are legal, for example, state licensed horse- and dog-racing tracks, government-operated offtrack betting parlors, and the lottery. At the same time, there are unauthorized (illegal) gambling operations whose control is the responsibility of these same governments. In such an ambiguous environment, it is easy to understand why gambling enforcement does not generate a great deal of public support.

The low priority given to gambling enforcement adds to its attractiveness to organized crime. Profits from drug trafficking are quite substantial; so are enforcement activities and penalties; whereas sentences for illegal gambling are minimal. Lack of enforcement resources owing to competing demands for police services, combined with advanced telephonic communications—for example, the mobile phone—explain why enforcement has declined.

Bookmaking

Bookmakers "book" bets on two types of events—horse and sometimes dog races and sporting events such as football, basketball, baseball, and boxing. In earlier days "horse parlors" or "wire rooms," neighborhood outlets, were often set up in the back of a legitimate business. Results coming in over the wire service were posted on a large chalkboard for waiting bettors. Today, most bets are placed by telephone directly or through a roving "handbook," "runner," or "sheetwriter" who transmits the bet to the bookmaker. To maintain security, some bookmakers change locations frequently, often monthly, and they may use cellular telephones. Many use a "call back" system. The bettor calls an answering service or answering machine and leaves his or her number. The bookmaker returns the call from a variety of locations, and the bet is placed.

Bets are written down and may also be tape-recorded by a machine attached to the phone. This helps avoid any discrepancies over what arrangements were actually made over the phone. The bookmaker usually employs clerks and handbooks, runners, or sheetwriters. The clerks handle the telephone, record the bets, and figure out the daily finances. The runners call the clerks and are given the day's totals for the bets they booked. Based on this information, they either collect or pay off. The runners receive a portion of the winnings, usually half, and they must also share the losses.

Lotteries or Numbers

During the 19th century, lotteries under state license or control were found throughout the U.S. Because of the negative publicity surrounding problems with the Louisiana lottery, in 1890, the U.S. enacted legislation prohibiting lotteries from using the mails and even prohibited newspapers that carried lottery advertisements from using the mails. This prohibition opened the way for the illegal exploitation of the desire to bet on lotteries through such devices as "numbers" or "policy" betting.

Policy is based on drawing numbers from 1 to 78 by spinning a wheel. During the 1920s, numbers were introduced as competition with policy. Numbers is now the prevailing form of illegal lottery. In numbers, a player selects one, two, or three digits from 0 to 9 with the odds of winning running from 10 to 1, 100 to 1, and 1000 to 1.

There are a variety of elaborate schemes for determining the winning numbers, often using the amounts for win, place, and show of the first race at a particular racetrack or the last three digits of the racetrack's "handle" (total gross receipts)—figures available in the daily newspapers. In some games the numbers are selected before an audience of bettors at a central location. In states having a legal lottery, the illegal lottery will often use the same numbers as the state lottery, although the odds in the illegal lottery may be higher than those offered by the state. Furthermore, the illegal lottery does not report winnings to the Internal Revenue Service.

The structure of the illegal lottery requires a great deal of coordination and is labor intensive, providing many jobs for unskilled individuals, making it an important source of employment in poorer communities. At the bottom of the hierarchy are those who accept wagers directly from the bettors, such as writers, runners, and sellers. These are generally individuals with ready access to the public, such as elevator operators, shoeshine boys, newspaper vendors, bartenders, and waitresses. Customarily they are paid a percentage of the wagers they write (unlike sports bookmaking, numbers wagering is done on a cash basis), usually from 15 to 30%, and frequently are given a 10% tip from winning bettors.

It is essential that wagers reach trusted hands before the winning number or any part of it is known. Sometimes this is done by telephone; other times wager records (commonly known as work, action, or business) are physically forwarded to a higher echelon by a pickup man. In a small operation, the wagers may go directly to the central processing office (commonly called the bank, clearinghouse, or countinghouse). More often, in large enterprises they are given to management's field representative (known as the field man or controller), who may be responsible for making a quick tally to determine the existence of any heavily played numbers that should be layed off. At such levels of operation one frequently finds charts consisting of 1000 spaces numbered 000 to 999 where tallies can be made for only certain wagers meeting minimum dollar values.

Near the top of the hierarchy is the *bank* where all transactions are handled. During the collection process the bank will be making decisions as to whether or not to lay off certain heavily played numbers. After the winning number is known, the bank will meticulously process the paperwork to determine how much action has been written, how many hits are present, and the controllers and writers involved.

Casino Gambling and Related Activities

Casino gambling (with a wide array of games of chance including roulette, chuck-a-luck, blackjack, and craps) requires a great deal of planning, space, personnel, equipment, and financing. In the past, casino gambling was available in "wide-open towns" such as Newport, Kentucky, and Phenix City, Alabama, and on a more discreet level in Saratoga Springs, New York and Hot Springs, Arkansas. Some cities have a tradition of holding "Las Vegas Nights," events often run under the auspices of, or with the approval and protection of, an organized crime unit, using the legitimate front of a religious or charitable organization. The operators provide gambling devices, personnel, and financing, and they share some of the profits with the sponsoring organization.

Organized operatives may also organize or sponsor card or dice games, taking a cut out of every pot for their services. These may be in a permanent location such as a social club or veterans' hall, or for security reasons, may "float" from place to place. The games may be operated in the home of a person in debt to a loan shark as a form of paying off the loan. In certain cities, gambling activities not operated under organized crime (OC) protection, "outlaw games," run the risk of being raided by the police or being held up by independent criminals or robbery teams sponsored by an OC unit.

In the past, a number of plush casinos in Las Vegas hotels were controlled (through hidden interests) by

OC bosses throughout the U.S. Typically, funds were "skimmed" before being counted for tax purposes and the money was distributed to OC bosses in proportion to their amount of (hidden) ownership. As a result of federal investigations and trials during the 1980s, Las Vegas is no longer a mob-controlled playground—casinos are major corporate entities— and OC has been moved to the fringes of the Las Vegas scene.

In Atlantic City, New Jersey, the second state to authorize casino gambling, there were intensive efforts to keep organized crime out of the casinos. The New Jersey State Police, which has extensive experience in dealing with OC, and the New Jersey Casino Control Commission, were put in charge of overseeing casino operations to prevent OC infiltration. Although there has been no information linking OC to any casino hotel in Atlantic City, OC has been able to influence the purchase of goods and services through control over key unions.

Miscellaneous Gambling

Bingo is legal in 46 states. Although played purportedly to raise funds for charitable causes, bingo is also a source of profits for OC. They may run the operations for the front (charity) or merely be connected through "licensure." In a number of localities, coin-operated video poker machines are very popular, often a staple in many bars or taverns. These machines operate like slot machines but are legal because they do not dispense money. Payoffs are provided by the proprietor (or bartender) surreptitiously. In a number of cities, distribution of these machines is controlled by organized crime.

Loan-Sharking (Usury)

The generally negative view of money lending is highlighted in the Bible, which on three separate occasions cautions against charging interest. Between 1880 and 1915 a practice known as "salary lending" thrived in the U.S. This quasi-legal business provided loans to salaried workers at usurious rates. The collection of debts was ensured by having the borrowers sign a variety of complicated legal documents that subjected them to the real possibility of being sued and losing employment. Through the efforts of the Russell Sage Foundation, states began enacting small-loan acts to combat this practice. Massachusetts was the first in 1911. These laws, which licensed small lenders and set ceilings on interest, eventually brought salary lending to an end; credit unions, savings banks, and similar institutions began to offer small loans. However, this also led to the wholesale entry of organized crime into the illicit credit business.

Loan-sharking embodies exorbitant interest rates in extending credit and the use of threats and violence in collecting debts. With the Prohibition drawing to a close and the onset of the Great Depression in 1929, persons in organized crime began searching for new areas of profit. These criminals found themselves in the enviable position of having a great deal of excess cash in a cash-starved economy, which gave them an important source of continued income. Persons in organized crime often insulate themselves from direct involvement in loan-sharking by using nonmember associates.

Many loan sharks provide loans to other criminals. Individual gamblers may also borrow from a loan shark who stays around card and dice games or accepts "referrals" from a bookmaker. Although a loan shark is not looking to take over a legitimate business, he sometimes finds himself involved with a debtor's business when the owner cannot meet the debt obligations. If an established business falls into OC control as a result of gambling or loan shark debts, the new owners may use the scam.

The Scam

The scam is a bankruptcy fraud that victimizes wholesale providers of various goods and sometimes insurance companies. Scam operations are popular in industries with merchandise that has a high turnover potential, is readily transportable, and is not easy to trace. Small orders are placed and paid for in full. Larger orders are placed, and a percentage of the balance due on such orders is paid. Using credit established as a result of the payments made for the previous orders, very large orders are placed. Items easily converted into cash, such as jewelry and appliances, usually constitute a large proportion of these orders. Thereafter, merchandise is converted into cash through a fence or a surplus-property operator, normally one with a sufficiently large legitimate inventory to easily intermix the scam merchandise into the normal inventory. The company is then forced into bankruptcy by creditors because, according to plan, all cash has been appropriated by the scam operators.

A popular time for the scam operator is just before a seasonal increase in the popularity of particular merchandise, when rush deliveries are commonplace and thorough credit checks are often overlooked. In some scams, arson is the final step: the business is "torched" for the insurance instead of declaring bankruptcy.

Theft and Fencing

Members of organized crime do not usually engage directly in theft, burglary, or robbery, although many have criminal records for such activities that typically precede their entry into organized crime. However, members of organized crime will provide information and financing, arrange for necessary firearms or stolen cars, and help link up criminals to carry out more predatory crimes such as payroll robberies, large-scale commercial burglaries, hijackings, and thefts of stocks and bonds. They will finance frauds, swindles, and any conventional criminal activity that can bring in a profit substantial enough to make the effort worthwhile. They will help market stolen merchandise such as securities, checks, and credit cards. Members of organized crime are in a unique position to provide these services. Their widespread connections to both legitimate and illegitimate outlets provide a link between conventional criminals and the business world.

The fence provides a readily available outlet for marketing stolen ("hot") merchandise. He thus provides an incentive for thieves and may also organize, finance, and direct their operations. Because of his connection with criminals (and otherwise) legitimate businessmen, the OC member is in a unique position to arrange for the disposition of stolen goods.

The Business of Sex

Organized crime's involvement in sex as a money-maker has changed with the times. House prostitution was an important social phenomenon during the days of large-scale immigration; immigrants were most often unattached males, single or traveling without their wives. Commercial sex, usually confined to infamous vice ("red light") districts in urban areas, was a target of social and religious reformers. The campaign against this activity became known as the war on the "white slavery" trade, which at the turn of the century was an international problem. There was an elaborate system for procuring and transporting women from different parts of the world and transporting them between major urban centers in the U.S.

Organized crime's interest in prostitution waned during Prohibition because money could be made more easily in bootlegging. With Prohibition drawing to a close, and with the advent of the Great Depression, OC groups began looking for new areas of income. In many cities they "organized" independent brothels: the madams were forced to pay OC middlemen for protection from the police and from violence. The brothel industry reached its peak in 1939. During World War II, and more significantly after 1945, the importance of brothels as a source of income for OC steadily declined. Today, OC members may organize or finance or be involved in an extortionate relationship with the proprietors of commercial sex establishments, ranging from brothels to bars that feature sexually explicit entertainment.

The OC pornography business, like prostitution, apparently suffers from a great deal of "amateur" involvement. Pornography, which at one time was under the exclusive control of organized crime, is widely available throughout the U.S. Liberal court decisions have virtually legalized pornography, and legitimate entrepreneurs have entered the market.

Labor Racketeering

Labor racketeering refers to the use of a union for personal benefit by illegal, violent, and fraudulent means. The array of labor rackets typically include payment to union officers for them not to organize a business, thereby allowing for payment of less than the going union wage; the sale of "strike insurance" in which the union threatens a walkout and the employer pays to assure a steady supply of labor; the "sweetheart deal" in which management pays the labor representative for contract terms unobtainable through legitimate bargaining; and the siphoning of union funds.

The union can be used for the benefit of the employer through the limitation of competition either through the refusal to work on goods or by directly enforcing illegal price agreements in an industry. Labor and racketeering distinguishes Irish, Jewish, and Italian organized crime groups from others and makes the former more influential than the latter.

The rise of organized labor and the subsequent reaction of American business generated a conflict that provided fertile ground for the seeds of racketeering and organized crime. The first step away from union democracy was a response to power wielded by employers. The leaders of organized crime provided mercenary armies to unions that were willing to use violence to organize workers, and thwart strikebreakers. They protected pickets against management goons—strong-arm personnel who were employed by licensed detective agencies. It soon became clear, however, that it was easier to hire gangsters than it was to fire them.

Unions fought not only with management, but also each other. In 1938, during struggles over jurisdiction and representation between the AFL and the CIO, both sides resorted to "muscle" from organized crime. Many locals and some internationals were delivered into the hands of organized crime, most notably, the International Brotherhood of Teamsters, Hotel and Restaurant Employees Union, Laborers International

Union of North America, and International Longshoremen's Association. In recent decades, federal government action against labor racketeering has considerably weakened the influence of organized crime in union activities.

Business Racketeering

There is no hard-and-fast line separating labor racketeering from business racketeering—one is often an integral part of the other. In some schemes, corrupt union officials and (otherwise) legitimate businessmen have willingly cooperated in order to reduce market competition. This collusion involves illegal restraint-of-trade agreements by businessmen in a highly competitive market, building construction and solid waste hauling, for example. A trade association is formed and members divide up the industry, usually allocating geographic areas (territories) or specific customers. The members (illegally) agree not to compete for another member's business. Each is thereby free to charge whatever the market will bear for its services. The illegal arrangement is policed by organized crime, keeping those not part of the illegal cartel out of the market and enforcing the restraint-of-trade agreement through intimidation and violence. Whether in the U.S., Italy, Russia, or Japan, trust is not always sufficient to enforce illegal agreements and the coercion provided by organized crime may be needed as an additional resource to punish those who would disrupt the system.

Drug Trafficking

The international and domestic traffic in illegal drugs is a multibillion-dollar-a-year industry. As in any major industry, there are various functional levels: manufacturers, importers, wholesalers, distributors, retailers, and consumers. Workers in the drug business range from leaders of powerful international cartels to street dealers whose activities support a personal drug habit. At the manufacturing and importation levels, the drug business is usually concentrated among a relatively few persons who head major trafficking organizations; at the retail level it is filled with a large, fluctuating, and open-ended number of dealers and consumers. People at the highest levels of the drug trade are often connected by kinship and ethnicity.

Drugs are smuggled into the U.S. from both source and transshipment countries. Traffickers may use circuitous routes to avoid the suspicion normally generated by shipments from source countries. For example, cocaine may be shipped from Colombia to the African continent; from there it is moved to the U.S. as part of legitimate maritime cargo. Pleasure crafts and fishing vessels blend in with normal maritime traffic, and low-profile vessels fabricated of wood or fiberglass and measuring up to 40 feet in length are difficult to spot and do not readily appear on radar. Smugglers also use aircraft, landing on isolated runways and even highways or airdropping their cargo. Motor vehicles using land routes across Canada and Mexico and "mules" carrying drugs that they have put in condoms round out the smuggling picture.

For decades, the trafficking of heroin within the U.S. was principally controlled by traditional organized crime groups that lived and operated inside the country. In a drug trafficking network that became known as the French Connection, New York City-based crime groups (families) purchased heroin from Corsican sources, who worked with French sailors operating from Marseilles, to transship the drug directly to the U.S. Ultimately, the heroin was distributed throughout the U.S. by domestic organized crime families to street-level dealers working in low-income, minority communities. However, in 1972, the French Connection was effectively dismantled by French and U.S. drug agents, ending the domestic Mafia's monopoly on heroin distribution in the U.S.

The demise of the French Connection, coupled with the subsequent emergence of criminal syndicates based in Colombia, marked a significant evolution in the international drug trade. The new trafficking organizations introduced cocaine into the U.S. on a massive scale, launching unparalleled waves of drug crimes and violence. Throughout the 1980s and 1990s, the international crime syndicates continued to increase their wealth and dominance over the U.S. drug trade, overshadowing the domestic crime families.

Today, the traffic in illegal drugs, from manufacture to final street-level sale, is controlled by international organized crime syndicates from Colombia, Mexico, and other countries. From their headquarters overseas, foreign drug lords oversee the wholesale distribution of unprecedented volumes of cocaine, heroin, and, to a lesser degree, methamphetamine, throughout the U.S. They maintain tight control of their workers through highly compartmentalized cell structures that separate production, shipment, distribution, money laundering, communications, security, and recruitment. High-level traffickers have at their disposal the most technologically advanced airplanes, boats, vehicles, radar, communications equipment, and weapons that money can buy. They have also established vast counterintelligence capabilities and transportation networks.

The enormous profits that accrue in the drug business are part of a criminal underworld where violence is always an attendant reality. Drug transactions must be accomplished without recourse to the formal mechanisms of dispute resolution that are usually available in the world of legitimate business. This reality leads to the creation of private mechanisms of enforcement and the drug world is filled with heavily armed and dangerous persons in the service of the larger cartels, although even street-level operatives are often armed. These private resources for violence serve to limit market entry, to ward off competitors and predatory criminals, and to maintain internal discipline and security within an organization.

Organized Crime, Legitimate Business, and Money-Laundering

In addition to their illegal business activities, persons involved in organized crime often own legitimate enterprises. For persons in organized crime, profit provides motivation for legitimate business activity—not all members of organized crime are able to make a "respectable" income from illicit activities. A legitimate business also provides the OC member with security of income. Although it may be subject to market and other business conditions, a legitimate enterprise is usually not a target of law enforcement efforts.

Illegitimate enterprises are difficult, if not impossible, to transfer to dependents. Investing in legitimate enterprises such as a business or real estate ensures that an estate can be legally inherited. An OC member with a legitimate business is also in a position to act as a patron for a person in need of legitimate employment—for example, persons on probation or parole or relatives he wants to shield from the stigma and risks associated with criminal enterprises. Of course, a legitimate business can provide a front or a base of operations for a host of illegal activities: loan-sharking, gambling, and drug trafficking, to name a few. Finally, a legitimate business can provide a tax cover, thereby reducing the risk of being charged with income-tax evasion. Funds from an illegitimate enterprise can be mixed with those from the legitimate business, particularly if it is a "cash" business.

Persons in organized crime have a serious problem: What to do with the large amounts of cash the business is continually generating? Ever since Al Capone was imprisoned for income-tax evasion, successful criminals have sought to launder their illegally secured money. Further complicating the problem is that this cash is frequently in small denominations. In some cases "laundering" may simply be an effort to secure $100 bills so that the sums of money are more easily handled—500 bills weigh about 1 pound; $1 million in 20s weighs about 100 pounds—or to convert them into one or more cashier's checks.

To avoid IRS reporting requirements under the Bank Secrecy Act, transfers of cash to cashier's checks or $100 bills must take place in amounts under $10,000—or through banking officials who for a fee (generally 5%) agree not to fill out a Currency Transaction Report (CTR). A CTR is required for each deposit, withdrawal, or exchange of currency or monetary instruments in excess of $10,000. It must be submitted to the IRS within 15 days of the transaction. In 1984, tax amendments extended the reporting requirements to anyone who receives more than $10,000 in cash in the course of a trade or business. A CMIR (Currency and Monetary Instrument Report) must be filed for cash or certain monetary instruments exceeding $10,000 in value that enter or leave the U.S. Federal Reserve regulations require banks to file suspicious-activity reports when they suspect possible criminal wrongdoing in transactions. Attempts to strengthen these regulations have met vigorous opposition from the banking industry.

Modern financial systems permit criminals to transfer instantly millions of dollars through personal computers and satellite dishes. Money is laundered through currency exchange houses, stock brokerage houses, gold dealers, casinos, automobile dealerships, insurance companies, and trading companies. The use of private banking facilities, offshore banking, free trade zones, wire systems, shell corporations, and trade financing all have the ability to mask illegal activities.

Money laundering has been greatly facilitated by advances in banking technology. It has become increasingly difficult for the government to effectively monitor banking transactions. An alternative to physically removing money from the country is to deposit the cash, then transfer the funds electronically to other domestic and foreign banks, financial institutions, or securities accounts. The sheer volume of wire transfers makes accounting difficult—one major bank in New York handles about 40,000 wires each business day.

A customer can instruct his or her personal computer to direct a bank's computer to transfer money from a U.S. account to one in a foreign bank. The bank's computer then tells a banking clearinghouse that assists in the transfer—no person talks to another. As depositing more than $10,000 in cash into an account requires the filing of a CTR, the government receives more than 7 million such reports annually and is hopelessly behind in reviewing them. The daily average volume of American transactions is about $7 billion.

As part of an overseas laundering scheme, a lawyer acting on behalf of a client creates a "paper" (or "boilerplate") company in any one of a number of countries that have strict privacy statutes, for example, Panama, which has over 200,000 companies registered. The funds to be laundered are transferred physically or wired to the company's account in a local bank. The company then transfers the money to the local branch of a large international bank. The paper company is then able to borrow money from the U.S. (or any other) branch of this bank, using the overseas deposit as security. Or an employment contract is set up between the launderer and his or her "paper" company for an imaginary service for which payments are made to the launderer. In some cases, the lawyer may also establish a "boilerplate bank"—like the company, this is a shell. Not only does the criminal get his money laundered, but he also earns a tax write-off for the interest on the loan.

Under the Bank Secrecy Act, however, wiring or physically transporting cash or other financial instruments out of the country in excess of $10,000 must be reported to the Customs Service. Once the money is out of the U.S., however, it may be impossible for the IRS to trace it. Liechtenstein, population 32,000, has 80,000 trust companies and associated banks whose transactions are protected by bank secrecy laws; the tiny principality has been a favorite for money laundering by the Sicilian Mafia, Colombian drug cartels, and Russian organized crime.

HOWARD ABADINSKY

References and Further Reading

Abadinsky, H. 2000. *Organized Crime,* 6th ed., Belmont, CA: Wadsworth.

Brill, S. 1978. *The Teamsters,* New York, NY: Simon and Schuster.

De Franco, E.J. 1973. *Anatomy of a Scam: A Case Study of a Planned Bankruptcy by Organized Crime,* Washington, DC: U.S. Government Printing Office.

della Porta, D. and Vannucci, A. 1999. *Corrupt Exchanges: Actors, Resources, and Mechanisms of Political Corruption,* New York, NY: Walter de Gruyter.

Goldstock, R. and Coenen, D.T., *Extortionate and Usurious Credit Transactions: Background Materials,* Ithaca, NY: Cornell Institute on Organized Crime

Jacobs, J.B. with Friel, C. and Raddick, R. 1999. *Gotham Unbound: How New York City Was Liberated From the Clutches of Cosa Nostra,* New York, NY: New York University Press.

Kelly, R.J. 1999. *The Upperworld and the Underworld: Case Studies of Racketeering and Business Infiltrations in the United States,* Hingham, MA: Kluwer.

McCoy, A.W. 1991. *The Politics of Heroin,* Brooklyn, NY: Lawrence Hill.

Morales, E. 1989. *Cocaine: White Gold Rush in Peru,* Tucson, AZ: University of Arizona Press.

Powis, R.E. 1992. *The Money Launderers,* Chicago, IL: Probus.

Reuter, P. 1987. *Racketeering in Legitimate Industries: A Study in the Economics of Intimidation,* Santa Monica, CA: RAND Corporation.

Walsh, M.E. 1977. *The Fence,* Westport, CT: Greenwood.

See also **Organized Crime: Definitions and Models; Organized Crime: Enforcement Strategies; Organized Crime: The Law; Organized Crime, Theories of**

Organized Crime: Black Mafia

The term "Black mafia" originated in the 1970s, a decade of profound change in the ethnic composition and structure of American organized crime. Almost simultaneously, scholars and journalists recognized that some African American criminals had organized illegal enterprises worthy of the label of organized crime. Arrests and convictions of Black gangsters raised questions about the relative power of Black mafia groups and partnerships they formed with Italian American crime families. Early evidence of "Black mafia" organizations suggested that African American subculture had spawned successful groups that interacted with and paralleled legitimate social institutions. Unquestionably, the degree of Black involvement in organized crime has remained elusive, but the evidence of an ethnic transformation in the urban underworld was compelling.

Formal study of underworld Blacks was first conducted by Francis A. J. Ianni, an anthropologist whose application of ethnic succession theory to Italian and Italian American crime families achieved recognition in criminology. In *Black Mafia* (1974), Ianni presented limited evidence to support the proposition that criminal involvement was a temporary pathway to legitimacy for Black gangsters. Small networks of Black criminals displayed individual patterns of enterprise and a capacity for coalitions with other ethnic groups, mainly Italian American gangsters. Relationships introduced new business opportunities based on demand for illicit goods and services. Ianni had pioneered the study of new ethnic compositions of organizations that had reached levels of criminal syndication. His innovative work, however, introduced more questions than answers, and the relative power of the "Black mafia" was not confirmed. Current theorists (Schatzberg and Kelly, 1997) have argued that continued use of a Cosa Nostra or Italian American model of organized crime has distracted attention from important issues relevant to criminal organizations emanating from different subcultures.

In recent decades, selective studies have focused on an alleged trend toward African American control of criminal enterprises, such as low-risk numbers gambling to high-risk drug dealing. Ivan Light's (1977) work on numbers gambling among urban Blacks stressed that complex and lucrative gambling enterprises served as alternative financial institutions in many Black neighborhoods, not unlike the Italian lotteries of earlier eras. Furthermore, he concluded that Black vice operators held significant control over production and distribution of quantities of drugs and other illegal products and services. As federal agents made deeper penetrations into crime groups in the late 1980s, new evidence mounted that Black gangsters had formed successful mafia-style organizations. In 1989, for example, several Black gangsters, all members of an organized group, were convicted of drug trafficking in Queens, New York City, and for the gratuitous murder of a rookie police officer. To date, however, no study has undertaken a comprehensive accounting of African American racketeers.

Images of Black gangsters appeared first in the 1970s in such films as *Shaft* (1971), *Superfly* (1972), and *Black Caesar* (1973). *Shaft*, a film portraying a larger-than-life Black detective who waged war on White and Black gangsters, was produced at low cost but it achieved box office success and a limited amount of critical acclaim. These films demonstrated popular interest in the ethnic diversity of criminal enterprises. *New Jack City* (1991), a gritty and violent film, characterized a sophisticated Black criminal organization that controlled a New York crack cocaine trafficking business. Based in part on exploits of Harlem's heroin kingpin, Leroy (Nicky) Barnes, and a loosely knit crew of associates of Italian American crime groups, the film stirred concerns for new ethnic conspiracies in organized crime. Barnes's success proved that Black gangsters had learned from others, at least until federal strike forces in the Bronx, Brooklyn, and Manhattan broke up the ring. An expanding pool of evidence indicated that Black gangsters employed sophisticated practices of distribution, territorial control, regulation of internal conflict, and funding protection for members captured by police. Barnes's mafia-style organization never achieved any independent status as an enduring crime family, especially since its leader became a protected federal witness. The story of rapid but short-lived notoriety is an oft-repeated legacy of other Black gangsters in Detroit, Los Angeles, Philadelphia, Washington, DC, and other cities. One view is that persistent use of violence and an inability to form stable internal organizations has depleted membership loyalty so essential for building the internal strength of crime groups (Kleinknecht, 1996).

A more important issue may have been the number of urban Black youths who have regarded gangs and gangsterism as avenues of upward mobility. Warring gangs, such as the Bloods and the Crips, evolved in the mid-1980s from inner city life in Los Angeles, migrating east and north to escape investigations and to establish new chapters. Estimated to have several thousand members, these groups established enterprises in extortion, vice racketeering, and violence-for-hire. Also they proved an ability to sustain criminal organizations employing top-down management controls and effective marketing strategies. Transformation of ordinary street gangs into savvy mafia-type groups appears in the elusiveness of business transactions, infrequent prosecutions, continuity of gang leadership, minimal media exposure, and focus on political influence. Somewhat older and steeped in the political myth of nationalism, Jamaican Posses were recognized mainly in eastern urban centers for cocaine distribution and gun running. These gangs formed coalitions with other Black gangs and organized crime groups of other ethnicities.

Research on the institutional characteristics of Black organized crime encounters the same methodological pitfalls as other studies in which crime and ethnicity take center stage. Scholars who investigate African American criminal enterprises may tend, therefore, to undertake historical investigations in place of research to evaluate the viability of non-Italian American crime groups in a complex global economic environment. It will be important in the future to learn more about the role of ethnicity and race in all forms of transnational crime, especially as they bear relevance to the integrity of sovereign nations and to the stability of economic systems. For now, however, "Black mafia" is regarded as an obsolete symbol of interlocking associations of crime groups. New research is needed to fill gaps in the sparse evidentiary mosaic of Black organized crime, particularly with respect to political corruption of local officials.

JAMES D. CALDER

Further Reading

Century, D. 1999. *Street Kingdom: Five Years Inside the Franklin Avenue Posse,* New York, NY: Warner.

Cook, F.J. 1971. The black mafia moves into the numbers racket, *New York Times Magazine,* April 4.

Fox, S. 1989. *Blood and Power: Organized Crime in Twentieth-Century America,* New York, NY: William Morrow.

Haller, M. 1972. Organized crime in urban society: Chicago in the twentieth century, *Journal of Social History,* 2.

Ianni, F.A.J. 1974. *Black Mafia: Ethnic Succession in Organized Crime,* New York, NY: Simon and Schuster.

Joseph, J. 1999. Jamaican posses and transnational crime, *Journal of Gang Research* 6, 4.

Kleinknecht, W. 1996. *The New Ethnic Mobs: The Changing Face of Organized Crime in America,* New York, NY: Free Press.

Light, I. 1977. The ethnic vice industry, 1880–1944, *American Sociological Review,* 42.

Light, I. 1977. Numbers as a black financial institution, *American Sociological Review,* 42.

Martens, F.T. 1990. African-American organized crime: An ignored phenonmenon, *Federal Probation,* 54.

O'Kane, J.M. 1992. *The Crooked Ladder: Gangsters, Ethnicity and the American Dream,* New Brunswick, NJ: Transaction.

Opolot, J.S.E. 1986. Organized crime as it emerges in sections of Africa, in Kelly, R.J. (Ed.). *Organized Crime: A Global Perspective,* Totowa, NJ: Rowman & Littlefield.

Pennsylvania Crime Commission. 1991. *Organized Crime in Philadelphia: A Decade of Change, 1990 Report.* Conshocken, PA: The Commission.

President's Commission on Organized Crime 1985. *Organized Crime and Heroin Trafficking* (Vol. 5), Washington, DC: Government Printing Office.

Schatzberg, R. 1993. *Black Organized Crime in Harlem: 1920–1930,* New York, NY: Garland.

Schatzberg, R. and Kelly, R.J. 1997. *African American Organized Crime: A Social History,* New Brunswick, NJ: Rutgers University.

Seibel, G. and Pincomb, R.A. 1994. From the Black P Stone Nation to the El Rukns: Reflections of a Chicago street cop, *Criminal Organizations,* 8, 3 and 4.

Yablonsky, L. 1997. *Gangsters: Fifty Years of Madness, Drugs, and Death on the Streets of America,* New York, NY: New York University Press.

See also **Organized Crime: Activities and Extent; Organized Crime: Enforcement Strategies**

Organized Crime: Chinese Tongs and Triads

History

The term *Triad* has been placed upon Chinese secret societies by the Hong Kong government. The name is based upon a triangular symbol that has been associated with, and represents, these secret societies. The symbol is the Chinese character "Hung," which is encased in a triangle representing the union of heaven, earth, and man. Because of this Triad societies are often referred to as the "Hung Society" or the "Heaven and Earth Society."

The Triads (known as Tongs if based in the U.S.) have a long rich history that is complicated by as much fiction as fact. Triads were created as secret societies with the sole purpose of overthrowing unpopular rulers. At the time of the Triad's founding when they were called the "Hung League," their sole purpose was to overthrow the Qing Empire and restore the Ming Empire back to power. The emergence of the Triad societies goes as far back as the Ming Empire, when the Manchurian neighbors invaded and seized power, thus creating the Qing Empire. As wars and invasions escalated, the Qing Empire recruited monks from monasteries to train and help fight the invaders. The monks were successful in this assignment and as a reward enjoyed appointments and honors from the Empire.

With time the Qing Empire became suspicious about the strengths of the monks and ordered them to be executed. Of the 18 original monks, only five survived after the famous burning of the monastery. The five remaining monks became the "Five Ancestors" to the modern Triads. The subsequent generations continued with the cause of overthrowing and Qing Empire. Their motto became "Crush the Ch'ing, Establish the Ming." After the fall of the Qing Empire, the Triads realigned their goals and some of these organizations became criminal in nature.

Structure

The strict structure of the organization has diminished since the political crackdown on the Triads in the 1950s. At the basic level there exists a "big brother" (Dai-Lo) and a "little brother" (Sai-Lo). The big brothers provide advice, counsel, and protection whereas little brothers return loyalty and financial support. Although this is the simplest relationship in the Triad structure, it is the most important.

All official positions begin with the number four (4), representing the four oceans that once surrounded China; thus placing it at the center of the universe. At the top of the organization is the 489. This man is formally known as the Mountain Lord, First Route Marshal, or Dragon Head. The 489 is an elected position that oversees the entire Triad. The word of the 489 stands as the law of the Triad, and he is sometimes referred to as 21 (4 + 8 + 9), the character for which means "Hung."

Next in command is the 438, commonly referred to as "The Assistant Mountain Lord," Incense Master, and the Vanguard. The 438 replaces the 489 in times of absence and is expected to provide counsel. The 438 holds the additional responsibility of maintaining tradition and preserving the power and prestige of the organization.

Next in line are the 426, or the Red Poles. Originally, the Red Poles were military units, but have evolved into criminal ring leaders. The Red Poles usually oversee a group of approximately 50 men and are responsible for criminal activities. At the same level as the Red Poles are the 415, or the White Paper Fan. The 415 represent the administrative officers responsible for keeping the books. The 415 are usually educated men who provide counsel to the Red Poles in times of need and are not considered fighters. Also at the same level are the 432, or Straw Sandals, who represent the messengers of the organization and handle ransoms, gang fights, and branch meetings.

At the bottom of the Triad are the 49s (foot soldiers). Historically, almost every Triad member belongs to this group. The number 49 is often referred to as 36 (4 × 9), the number of oaths a new recruit must swear before joining the Triad. According to recent reports, most of these positions have been eliminated leaving mainly the Red Poles as the leadership structure and the rest falling into the 49s.

Current Triad Operations

There is evidence that a Triad organization exists in most countries. It is estimated that there are at least 50 Triad societies with a membership of around 8000 in Hong Kong alone. Of the 50 societies, it is reported that 15 are criminally active. Sun Yee On is the largest Triad in Hong Kong with an estimated membership of 25,000, and is reported to be in control of the government of the Guangdon Province on the mainland since 1994. The Wo group is the second largest with nine specialized subgroups and maintains

an estimated membership of 20,000. The 14K Triad also has around 20,000 members and is considered the most powerful international Triad today. The Big Circle Gang is a group of former Red Army guards and PLA soldiers. It is estimated that 5–10% of all detected crime in Hong Kong is connected with the Triad societies.

Criminal Activities

The main criminal activities of the Triad societies include extortion, human smuggling, drug trafficking, loan-sharking, credit-card fraud, and video piracy (the most prominent criminal activity being extortion). Many Triads have become so powerful and wealthy as to move into legitimate businesses, including the film industry. Reports of extortion and violence have surfaced during the casting and production of movies. One reported account tells of an actress who refused to participate in a film directed by a known Triad. This actress was later shooting a scene for a different movie when five men beat her in front of the camera crew. None of the camera crew helped her and she later worked on the Triad movie.

One of the most significant forms of criminal activity perpetrated by the Triads is the human smuggling business. It is estimated that 100,000 illegal Chinese immigrants are smuggled into the U.S. every year, many of them forced into involuntary servitude to pay the $40,000 charge to smuggle them to the U.S.

NATHAN R. MORAN

References and Further Reading

Chin, K.-L. (1995). Triad societies in Hong Kong. *Transnational Organized Crime* 1 (Spring): 47–64.

Chin, K.-L. (1990). *Chinese Subculture and Criminality: Non-Traditional Crime Groups in America*. Westport, CT: Greenwood.

Chin, K.-L., Kelly, R.J., and Fagan, J. (1994). Chinese organized crime in America, pp. 213–243 in *Handbook of Organized Crime in the United States,* Kelly, R.J. (Ed.) Chin, K.-L. and Schatzberg, R. Westport, CT: Greenwood.

Sheldon Z., Kelly, R.J., and Chin, K.-L. (1998). Transnational Chinese organized crime activities: Patterns and emerging trends. *Transnational Organized Crime* 4 (Autumn/Winter): 127–154.

See also **Organized Crime: Activities and Extent**

Organized Crime: Colombian Cartels

Introduction

The Colombian drug cartels represent some of the wealthiest transnational organizations in existence (Lupsha and Cho, 1999; Thoumi, 1999). The UN estimates that trafficking in narcotics is a $400 billion a year business that has doubled in size since 1987 (U.S. Department of State, 1997). The Andes drug organizations in Bolivia and Peru act as subcontractors to the Colombian cartels. They perform the first stages in the drug manufacturing process of refining the raw coca into a cocaine paste or base. The Colombians then provide the transportation to move the products to the final processing labs, bringing with them large sums of cash to pay for the raw narcotics. According to Godson and Olson (1999), "Until recently the Colombians generally did not involve themselves directly in these regional efforts, but with increased law enforcement successes, particularly in Bolivia, that have rolled up whole local organizations, the Colombians have begun to take more control" (157).

To move cocaine to the U.S. the Colombians have established vast networks with the Mexican cartels, which represent only arrangements of convenience. Indeed, the Colombians reportedly complain of incompetence on behalf of the Mexicans, "but they need the Mexicans to run the network of local landing strips, safe houses, and logistical-support systems—including the network of corrupt officials that the Mexican organizations had developed over the years—necessary to sustain huge long-range drug-trafficking operations" (Godson and Olson, 1999, 157).

Similarly, as the Colombians develop ties with the Mexicans, they are also developing ties with the Sicilian Mafia and other organized crime and transnational organized crime groups in Europe (Jamieson, 1994; Hess, Meyers, Gideon, Gomez, and Daly, 1999; Jamieson, 2000; Paoli, 1999). They are also establishing contacts in Eastern Europe and the Commonwealth of Independent States to launder money (Den Boer, 1999; Edelbacher, 1999). The Colombians are colluding with Asian (primarily Chinese) heroin traffickers, occasionally exchanging heroin for cocaine, and are studying the potential to grow poppies in the Andes Mountains, studies that have relied largely on the importation of technicians and agricultural experts from Asia (Lee III, 1999).

The Emerging Relationship between Drugs and Terror in Colombia

In recent years an emerging relationship between the money and power of the international drug trade and paramilitary terrorist organizations has been observed (Lee, 1999; Ward, 2000; Mueller, 2001). The connection between paramilitary terrorist groups and the illicit drug industry was highlighted in August 2001 when the Colombian government arrested Niall Connolly (a 36-year-old Sinn Fein member), Martin McCauley (a 37-year-old IRA member previously convicted of weapons possession), and James Monaghan (a 56-year-old IRA member convicted in 1971 of conspiring to cause an explosive charge and is purported to have invented the mortar bomb), charging them with providing explosives and terrorist training to the Revolutionary Armed Forces of Colombia (FARC). The three were arrested at Bogotá International Airport while attempting to leave the country. Colombian authorities initially planned to deport the trio for false passports, but the Attorney General decided there was enough evidence for the FARC-related charges. Since the arrests, the Colombian government, including President Alvaro Uribe, has publicly stated that the three are members of the Provisional Irish Republican Army (PIRA). (Hereafter, the PIRA will be referred to as the IRA. It should be noted, however, that significant ideological differences exist between the PIRA and the Real IRA, although both are commonly referred to simply as IRA.)

The trial, which began in December 2002, has been controversial from its inception. Not only is the presiding judge, Jairo Acosta (who specializes in drug and terrorism trials), hearing the case without a jury, he is also hearing it without the accused being present because Connolly, McCauley, and Monaghan refuse to appear in court in protest of how the case is being handled (Murray, 2002). On the surface, this might be just another trial, but closer inspection reveals a complexity that involves the IRA, FARC, Colombia, the U.S. government, the international drug trade, and global terrorism. The situation clearly illustrates the effect of the burgeoning relationship between drugs and terrorism, as well as the globalization of organized crime and terrorism. To understand the implications of this trial and the impact of its outcome, three questions must be answered:

1. What does the FARC gain by receiving IRA support?
2. What does the Colombian government gain by convicting these men?
3. What does the U.S. government gain by supporting Colombia?

What Does the FARC Gain by Receiving IRA Support?

The Colombian government and FARC rebels have fought to a virtual stalemate, but the staunch resolve of President Uribe and increased U.S. funding are likely to turn the tide in the government's favor. To combat this new threat FARC appears to be pursuing three key objectives: (1) move the war into the cities, (2) terrorize the social elite (thereby bringing greater pressure to bear on the government), and (3) force the government out of FARC-controlled jungles.

Move the War into the Cities

The shifting objectives of the FARC and the IRA's role in the change became painfully apparent with the recent release of an IRA-FARC intelligence report. The dossier, published by a Colombian counter-terrorism unit, provides evidence that bombs developed by FARC match those of the IRA used against the British government (Sharrock, 2003). The dossier goes on to state that a recent change in the methods employed by FARC rebels shows all the signs of international assistance, including "clear advances…in the FARC's mortar production" (Sharrock, 2003). The report also reveals that from 2001, the year that Monaghan, McCauley, and Connolly were arrested, FARC attacks using improvised devices rose sevenfold. Clearly the FARC is developing the ability move the war out of the jungles and into the cities, placing the Colombian government on the defensive.

Terrorize the Social Elite

FARC revealed the true impact of their newly acquired abilities earlier this year when they moved the war into the enclaves of Colombia's social elite. IRA weaponry is suspected to have been used in a 330-pound car bomb detonated outside a Bogotá nightclub in February 2003. The explosion killed 35 people and wounded more than 160 (Thornton, 2003). According to Defense Minister Martha Lucia Ramirez, the device was "something more sophisticated than we have seen in the past" (Thornton, 2003). Like many terrorist attacks, the target

chosen for this incident is just as devastating as the loss of human life. According to Wilson (2003a), "The car bombing at Club El Nogal, a fortified precinct of exclusivity and power, has brought the brutality of Colombia's war closer to the urban elite than at any time in the 39-year conflict." Until the bombing of the El Nogal, Colombia's wealthiest citizens were insulated from the devastation of FARC attacks. Now that the war has appeared on their doorstep, the Colombian government is beginning to feel new pressure to resolve the situation.

Force the Government out of the Jungles

As Colombia's social elite come to terms with the war that has ravaged the country for decades, the FARC is using its new found power in an attempt to force the Colombian government to abandon efforts to encroach into FARC-controlled territory. The FARC's latest attempt involves both the Colombian and U.S. governments. In February, FARC claimed responsibility for kidnapping for ransom three U.S. government contractors, calling them CIA agents and demanding the military halt a search and rescue operation. The FARC seized the three on February 13 after their U.S. government light aircraft crashed on a hillside in southern Colombia during what Colombian officials said was a reconnaissance mission to discover coca bushes. The FARC also demanded the removal of U.S. trained troops, the cessation of U.S. over flights, and the elimination of the U.S. sponsored coca eradication effort for several months. As the American led search and rescue operation intensified, FARC expanded their demands to include the removal of military personnel from a cluster of eight towns. According to the FARC, "The life and the physical integrity of the three gringo officials is in our power, we will only be able to guarantee [their safety] if the Colombian army immediately suspends military operations as well as over flights" (Webb, 2003b). In making such a request the guerrillas indicated that the rescue operation was getting close to accomplishing its mission.

With improvements in technique and technology provided by international terrorist organizations such as the IRA, the FARC is increasingly capable of taking its war out of the jungle and into the centers of Colombian wealth and power. With the strength of this new bargaining chip the FARC is positioned to demand that the Colombian government remove all presence from FARC-controlled jungles, thereby allowing the FARC to operate with absolute impunity. Combined with their penchant for taking hostages, the multimillion-dollar IRA-FARC partnership seems to be paying dividends.

What Does the Colombian Government Gain by Convicting These Men?

As the line between the counterinsurgency war and combating the overwhelming illegal drug trade in Colombia continues to blur, the Colombian government becomes more dependent on financial aid, military training, and equipment from the U.S. The trial of Connolly, McCauley, and Monaghan provides the Colombians with an opportunity to simultaneously accomplish two objectives: (1) reenergize the U.S. commitment to Colombia and (2) increase the level of aid, thereby offsetting the declining Colombian economy.

Reenergize U.S. Commitment to Colombia

Until 2001, all money provided by the U.S. was earmarked for fighting the war on drugs and could not be used by the Colombian government to aid efforts to combat the FARC. In 2002, the Bush administration modified the U.S. military mission in Colombia from antidrug activities to assistance in the country's counterinsurgency wars. This change allowed U.S. supplied equipment, intelligence, and training to be used in counterinsurgency operations for the first time. According to DeYoung (2003), the U.S. has appropriated almost $2 billion in military assistance to Colombia since 2001, and the 2003 Congressional budget adds another $500 million.

Although U.S. aid to help Colombia reduce the flow of illegal drugs has been unwavering for many years, statements made by Washington officials in March 2003 indicate this may not continue to be the case. The Bush administration has recently made it clear that Colombia will have to "shoulder more of the military and financial burden of fighting its guerrilla war" (Wilson, 2003c). U.S. officials have recently begun to use such words as "exit strategy" and "endgame" to describe Washington's philosophical shift toward Colombia, even as President Uribe asks for more help. According to Marc Grossman, U.S. Undersecretary of State for Political Affairs, "We're not looking to put more people in [Colombia]...This is a Colombian problem that the Colombians will have to solve" (Wilson, 2003c). Although President Uribe is appealing to Washington to view Colombia's guerrillas as part of the larger war on terrorism, so far it has not worked.

A change in U.S. policy toward reducing aid to Colombia would have devastating effects on the Colombian economy as well as its ability to counter FARC advances. The Colombian government stands to lose roughly $1 billion a year in aid. They also risk losing the ability to spend the substantial U.S. contributions in their ongoing war against the FARC, which would have a negative impact on President Uribe's ability to pacify the newly terrorized social elite within Colombia. In response, high-ranking members of the Colombian government have been on the political offensive, contending that the FARC now represents global terrorist activity. Colombian Defense Minister Martha Lucía Ramírez made this point very clear during a recent trip to Washington D.C. Ramírez contends that Colombia should be considered a battleground in the war on terrorism, and that Bogotá needs more U.S. assistance to fight it. While speaking, Secretary of State Colin Powell was asking Congress for $574.6 million to help President Alvaro Uribe with his war against terrorism and the illicit drug trade. According to Powell, the aim "is to secure democracy, extend security and restore economic prosperity to Colombia, and to prevent the narco-terrorists from spreading instability to the broader Andean region" (Johnson, 2003). Secretary Powell's distinction between terrorists and the "drug trade that fuels terrorist activity" is significant. Combined with U.S. statements regarding a Colombian exit strategy and an unwillingness to fund the Colombian counterinsurgency problem, the Colombian government needs to clearly link drugs, the FARC, and global terrorism or risk a reduction in funding.

The impact of the current U.S. aid package was explained by Acting Assistant Secretary of State for Western Hemisphere Affairs, J. Curtis Struble, in April 2003. According to Struble, the U.S. has provided Colombia with nearly $2 billion since July 2000 to combat the emerging relationship between organized crime and terrorism (U.S. Department of State, 2003). According to the State Department (2003), this funding has "strengthened Colombia's democratic institutions, protected human rights, fostered socio-economic development, and mitigated the effect of violence on civilians." Thus, extending security, restoring prosperity, preventing instability, fostering development, and creating jobs are compelling reasons for the Colombian government to highlight the link between the FARC and global terrorism, thereby extending the flow of money, equipment, and training from the U.S.

With the kidnapping of three American contractors in February 2003, the level of U.S. involvement in Colombia has increased dramatically. In response to the abductions, an unprecedented search-and-rescue operation was conducted including 7000 Colombian soldiers, dozens of U.S. military personnel, as well as FBI investigators (at a cost of more than a half-million dollars a week). According to Sanchez (2003), "The United States is pushing hard to improve the Colombians' communication capabilities and their human intelligence gathering, interrogation and investigative techniques." Hence, $500,000 per week is currently being spent on training, improved communications, interrogation techniques, and new equipment; all of which are desperately needed by the Colombian government. But according to key administration officials, the influx of funds may be short lived. According to State Department officials, "The increased U.S. participation in Colombia's decades-old guerrilla war is likely to last only as long as the Americans are missing" (Wilson, 2003c). Colombian Vice President Francisco Santos summed up the impact of reduced U.S. presence by asserting "An exit strategy now is a disaster strategy" (Wilson, 2003c).

Help for the Declining Colombian Economy

Colombia has become dependent on the enormous amount of U.S. aid as both the war against the FARC and a declining coffee market wrack the Colombian economy. One of the most dramatic effects has been the paramilitary's ability to stop coffee bean cultivation. According to Toro (2003), during coffee harvest 2003, peasants needed to pick the beans were missing from the plantations. In fact, more than 2500 took refuge in remote villages after right-wing paramilitary fighters (Peasant Self-Defense Forces of Casanar, or ACC) threatened to kill anyone working with or for FARC in the region. Recently the ACC hacked a peasant to death and kidnapped eight others, including a 14-year-old girl (Toro, 2003).

The threat of paramilitary organizations such as the FARC and ACC is not limited to direct attacks against the government or the military, but also involve attacks on the nation's economy (that is heavily based in agriculture). In response, farmers who are unable to make a living from growing coffee often turn to coca production. According to Villelabeitia (2003), "Coca needs less care and yields four harvests a year; coffee trees require expensive fertilizer, are labor-intensive and can be harvested twice a year." In Samana, Colombia, a single hectare of coffee will produce an estimated $700 per year, whereas a single hectare of coca pays 15 times as much. In addition, the reduction in coffee bean prices by $70 billion globally is disastrous when combined with the increasing demand and return on coca production.

An increased dependence on U.S. aid and a failing coffee market provide more reason for the Colombian government to clearly establish the relationship between their counterinsurgency war with the FARC and global terrorism. However, with the corresponding shift from fighting the war on drugs to the war on terrorism, the Colombian government will likely continue to receive aid from not only the U.S. and the UN, but from other countries as well.

What Does the U.S. Gain by Supporting Colombia?

From a global perspective, Colombia is the most logical front on which to fight a war against drugs. Although President Uribe was elected on a firm anti-drug platform, the fact remains that Colombia is the number one exporter of both cocaine and heroin to the U.S. (Moran, 2002). By continuing to provide monetary and military support the U.S. gains two distinct advantages: (1) reduce the flow of drugs and (2) protect vital U.S. interests.

Reduce the Flow of Drugs

John Walters, director of the White House Office of National Drug Control Policy (ONDCP), summarized the effects of Colombian drug imports when he testified before the House Committee on International Relations, Subcommittee on the Western Hemisphere. According to Walters, the U.S. now has

> …an unprecedented opportunity in cooperation with allied nations' to achieve a long-term reduction in the supply of illegal drugs because leaders throughout the Western Hemisphere are acutely aware that drug-funded terrorism is the greatest threat to national security and stability…Drug production and trafficking provides around $300–$500 million per year to illegal armed groups in Colombia. These well-financed narco-terrorists pose a threat to U.S. interests and stability in Colombia and the entire Andean region (Walters, 2003).

As the epicenter of heroine and cocaine trafficking, the U.S. has a vested interest in helping the Colombians control the production and manufacture of illegal drugs. However, Director Walters also points out the need to counter threats to vital U.S. interests.

Protecting Vital U.S. Interests

One of the primary U.S. interests is Colombia's oil pipelines, which commonly come under leftist guerilla attack. The 490-mile Caño Limón pipeline (second largest in Colombia), which services oil fields operated by California-based Occidental Petroleum Corp., is capable of producing 120,000 barrels per day.

As of June 2003, the line has suffered 34 attacks (much lower than the 170 attacks in 2001) (Stewart, 2003). U.S. Ambassador Ann Patterson revealed the importance of the Caño Limón when she stated, "Protecting the pipeline is about more than just helping the Colombians fight rebels—it's also about oil security for the United States after Sept. 11" (Brodzinsky, 2003). In 2002 Colombia was the source of only 2% of U.S. oil imports (or 600,000 barrels a day). According to Ambassador Patterson, given the current state of international affairs, "now more than ever it's important for us to diversify our sources of oil."

Conclusion

The arrest of Niall Connolly, Martin McCauley, and James Monaghan provides the backdrop for the globalization of organized crime and narco-terrorism. As the IRA forms ties with the FARC, the range and complexity of their terrorist efforts increases exponentially. Similarly, as the FARC gains the equipment and experience necessary to move their war into the cities of Colombia, their ability to force concessions from the government increases dramatically.

With the heightened effectiveness of the FARC terror campaign (that now includes such terrorist organizations as the IRA), Colombia has become more dependent on the U.S. to provide additional monetary aid, military training, and equipment. At the same time, the U.S. is inundated by the ceaseless flow of cocaine and heroin churned out by FARC protected drug cartels each year; thus forcing the U.S. to dedicate even greater amounts of manpower and money in an effort to maintain the status quo. As terrorist groups and drug cartels around the world begin to replicate this design, governments, the rule of law, and the viability of transitioning toward democracy are threatened.

NATHAN R. MORAN

References and Further Reading

Brodzinsky, S. (2003, February 14). *U.S. Crosses a Line in Colombia,* MSNBC. Available at http://www.msnbc.com/news/705583.asp?cp1=1#BODY.

Clawson, P. and Lee III, R.W. (1996). *The Andean Cocaine Industry.* New York, NY: St. Martin's Press.

DeYoung, K. (2003, February 21). *Bush Uses Exemption on Colombia Forces.* Washington Post. Available at http://www.washingtonpost.com/wp-dyn/articles/A44614-2003Feb21.html.

Hill, S.D. and Ward, R.H. (2002). *Extremist Groups: An International Compilation of Terrorist Organizations, Violent Political Groups and Issue-Oriented Militant Movements.* Huntsville, TX: OICJ.

Johnson, T. (2003, February 12). Experts: Colombia bombers had help. *Miami Herald.* Available at http://www.miami.com/mld/miamiherald/5160052.htm.

Lee III, R.W. (1999). International organized crime: An Overview. In Farer, T. (Ed.), *International Crime in the Americas,* pp. 1–38. New York, NY: Routledge.

Moran, N.R. (2002). *The Globalization of Russian, Colombian, and Chinese Organized Crime from 1991–2001: A Time-Series Analysis.* Unpublished dissertation.

Mueller, G.O.W. (2001). Transnational Crime: Definitions and Concepts. In *Combating Transnational Crime: Concepts, Activities, and Responses,* Williams, P. and Vlassis, D. (Eds.) London, UK: Frank Cass, pp. 13–22.

Murray, D. (2002, December 3). *Court Reporting, Colombian style.* BBC News. Available at http://news.bbc.co.uk/1/hi/northern_ireland/2537219.stm.

Padgett, T. (2003, February 24). The next terror nexus? Colombia fears the IRA and ETA may be using the country for a base for weapons testing and training. *Time.* Available at http://www.time.com/time/europe/magazine/article/0,13005,901030224423493,00.html.

Rowan, B. (2002, June 13). IRA 'tested weapons' in Colombia. *BBC News.* Available at http://newsvote.bbc.co.uk/1/hi/northern_ireland/2043156.stm.

Sanchez, M. (2003, March 8). Forgotten manhunt in Colombia. *Washington Post.* Available at http://www.washingtonpost.com/wp-dyn/articles/A24484-2003Apr3.html.

Sharrock, D. (2003, February 8). Rebel weapons 'have IRA hallmark'. *The Times.* Available at http://www.timesonline.co.uk/article/0,,3-570124,00.html.

Staff Writer. (2003, April 3). U.S. Department of State. *The Washington File.* Available at http://usinfo.state.gov/cgibin/washfile/display.pl?p=/products/washfile/geog/ar&f=03040202.lar&t=/products/ washfile/newsitem.shtml.

Stewart, P. (2003, February 6). Colombian rebels bomb oil pipeline near US troops. *Forbes.* Available at http://www.forbes.com/business/energy/newswire/2003/02/06/rtr872356.html.

Thornton, C. (2003, February 13). IRA link to FARC bomb is probed Minister claims help went to rebels. *Belfast Telegraph.* Available at http://www.belfasttelegraph.co.uk/news/story.jsp?story=377986.

Thoumi, F.E. (1999). The impact of the illegal drug industry on Colombia. In Farer, T. (Ed.), *International Crime in the Americas.* New York, NY: Routledge.

Toro, J.P. (2003, April 4). Colombian peasants flee fields at harvest. *Mississipi Sun Herald.* Available at http://www.sunherald.com/mld/sunherald/news/breaking_news/5554769.htm.

U.S. State Department. (2003, February). National strategy for combating terrorism. Available at http://usinfo.state.gov/topical/pol/terror/strategy/.

Villelabeitia, I. (2003, March 11). Coca fueling violence in Colombia's coffee fields. *Forbes.* Available at http://www.forbes.com/business/newswire/2003/03/11/rtr903540.html.

Walters, J. (2003, February 27). U.S. drug czar offers overview of U.S. drug policy in western hemisphere. *Office of the National Drug Control Policy (ONDCP).* Available at http://www.usembassy.it/file2003_02/alia/ a3022715.htm.

Ward, R.H. (2000). The internationalization of criminal justice. In Friel, C.M. (Ed.), *Boundary Changes in Criminal Justice Organizations,* Vol. 2, pp. 267–322. Washington, DC: National Institute of Justice.

Webb, J. (2003, February 22). Colombia rebels say holding three 'CIA agents.' *Reuters News*. Available at http://www.reuters.com/newsArticle.jhtml;jsessionid=HO2RLTP2HXUKYCRBAEZSFEY?type=topNews&storyID=2271210.

Wilson, S. (2003a, February 9). Bombing brings war to Colombia's elite toll at club rises to 33; Officials blame rebels. *Washington Post*. Available at http://www.washingtonpost.com/wp-dyn/articles/A45655-2003Feb8.html.

Wilson, S. (2003b, February 23). Colombian rebels link hostage safety to pullback. *Washington Post*. Available at http://www.washingtonpost.com/wp-dyn/articles/A50031-2003Feb22.html.

Wilson, S. (2003c, March 8). U.S. seeks to avoid deeper Role in Colombia involvement likely to decline after hunt ends for Americans. *Washington Post*. Available at http://www.washingtonpost.com/ac2/wp-dyn?pagename=article&node=&contentId=A63201-2003Mar8&notFound=true.

See also **Drug Control Policy: Enforcement, Interdiction, and the War on Drugs; Organized Crime: Definitions and Models; Organized Crime: The Law**

Organized Crime: Cuban Gangs

Introduction

When Fidel Castro overthrew Fulgencio Batista in 1959, he sentenced to exile many of the American Mafioso who ran the casinos in Havana. When this occurred many of the American Cuban crime associations fled the country as well in fear that Castro would be coming after them. Upon fleeing the country many of these exiled criminals moved to South Florida, most notably Miami. It was not long before the organized crime businesses operated in Cuba were started in the U.S. During the 40 years since Castro's rebellion, several Cuban gangs have spawned based on a similar ideology: a hatred for Fidel Castro. The most notable of these is the *Armed Forces of National Liberation (FALN)*.

FALN

FALN (the Armed Forces of National Liberation) a Puerto Rican terrorist group, founded by the Cuban Intelligence Officer Filiberto Ojeda Rios in Havana, Cuba in 1974, has ties to both the government of Fidel Castro and the Italian Mafia (Szigethy, 1999). Its main goal was for Puerto Rico to become an independent Communist nation through a violent overthrow of the imperialist U.S. commonwealth government. The rebellion was to be funded by cocaine and heroin shipments from South America trafficked through Cuba into Florida, in addition to some shipments ending up in the hands of the Italian Mafia (Szigethy, 1999). During the 1970s and 1980s the FALN, and another group known as the Macheteros, took responsibility for a number of bombings and robberies in both the U.S. and Puerto Rico, mainly on political and military sites. The two rebel groups fought against other signs of U.S. authority, which included attacks against members of the Puerto Rican and U.S. military and police (Intelligence Resource Program, 1999), as well as threats and failed conspiracies that called for the assassination of then President Ronald Reagan (James, 1981). On October 26, 1974, FALN took credit for five bombings in New York, and continued its bombing campaign throughout the next decade to claim a total of 72 bombings, 40 fire attacks, 8 attempted bombings, and 10 bomb threats. The results included 5 deaths, 83 injuries, and over $3 million in property damage. This period became known as the "Reign of Terror." After key convictions of FALN and Macheteros members the "Reign of Terror" came to an end, with the exception of a few sparse instances of violence, mostly in Puerto Rico (Intelligence Resource Program, 1999).

At the closing of the 20th century FALN was in the media spotlight once more. This time the attention was owing to the highly controversial decision of former President Bill Clinton to offer clemency to 16 FALN terrorists incarcerated in U.S. federal prisons with the stipulation that they renounce the use of violence. None of these prisoners in question were convicted of any crimes that resulted in injury or death (Avala, 1999). Although four federal law enforcement agencies opposed President Clinton's decision, 11 of these prisoners were released on September 21, 1999 (U.S. Senate Republican Policy Committee, 1999).

Smuggling Cubans into the U.S.

As organized crime has become drawn into the immigrant trade, the number of Cubans being smuggled into the U.S. quadrupled in 2003. According to John Hamilton, deputy assistant to the Secretary of State, in 1997 to the first 11 months into 1998, the number of illegal Cubans reaching U.S. shores increased from 186 to 732. One reason it has become more difficult to catch Cubans immigrating illegally is owing to a shift from the use of rickety rafts to high-powered speedboats. As a result the U.S. has had to step up patrols across the 90-mile stretch of water on the Florida shore. Another contributing factor to the increase of immigrants is because Cuba has lowered the charge for processing legal exit permits. In 1997, it cost $700 to get an exit permit processed, but in 1998 the charge was reduced to $500. In addition the U.S. has increased the number of non-immigrant visas for Cubans (from 5361 in 1997 to 8078 in 1998).

Drawing Gangs to God

Mario Forte, 31, is a former gang recruiter for one of Miami's biggest gangs. Now he is a recruiter for God. Forte started a congregation, called Jesus' Disciples, otherwise known as God's Nation, to save troubled young people from jail and possible death (Decker, 1999). He wanted to exchange the guns and drugs in the gangs with the Christian Bible. Forte approached this by using the same methods gangs use to recruit kids. Thus, Forte offers gang members a way out of the gang life that would not otherwise be possible.

During the 1990s, the Latin Kings, an intense rival of Forte's former gang, sent Jorge Lopez to spy on Forte and to find out what he was doing with this new congregation. In the process, Lopez stated, "Forte won his soul." Attempts by gang members to leave a gang without going to jail or dying are almost always unsuccessful.

A member who leaves is often brutally beaten or killed for fear that he or she may try and contact the authorities and become "snitches" for the police. According to Forte, if gang members state that they have truly found God, their gang will let them leave without serious retribution.

Forte also sees a positive side to gangs. He believes that they produce a measure of self-esteem and brotherhood that is valuable to minorities. Forte says that kids like to identify and associate with something. According to him an example of this association lies in the colorful logos painted on the walls of buildings throughout the city. As a result, Forte gives his followers (when they prove they are truly serving God) strands of red, gold, and white beads to wear around their necks.

NATHAN R. MORAN

References and Further Reading

Avala, C. (1999). *Puerto Rico: FALN bombs or US Bombs?* Available at solidarity.igc.org/atc/83Ayala.html-16k. Retrieved on December 9, 2003.
Decker, T. (July 27, 2003). Drawing gangs to God. *St. Petersburg Times.* (1999). Available at www.sptimes.com/news/42599/Floridian/Drawing_gangs_to_God.shtml.
James, D. (1981). *Puerto Rican Terrorists Also Threaten Reagan Assassination.* Available at www.rose-hulman.edu/~delacova/faln.htm. Retrieved on December 9, 2003 (July 25, 2003). *Intelligence Resource Program.* Armed Forces of Puerto Rican National Liberation (1999). Available at www.fas.org/irp/world/para/faln.hym.
Leet, D.A., Rush, G.E., and Smith, A.M. (2000). *Gangs, Graffiti, and Violence: A Realistic Guide to the Scope and Nature of Gangs in America,* 2nd ed. Incline Village, NV: Copperhouse.
Szigethy, de J.R. (July 25, 2003). *American Mafia.* Puerto Rican terrorist group tied to Castro, mafia (1999). Available at www.americanmafia.com/news/9-8-99_Tied_To_Castro.html.
United States Senate Republican Policy Committee. (1999). Coddling Terrorists? Available at http://www.senate.gov/~rpc/releases/1999/eb3092199.htm.

See also **Organized Crime, Theories of**

Organized Crime: Definitions and Models

Although there is no general agreement on the definition of organized crime—the federal Organized Crime Control Act of 1970 fails to provide a definition—there have been some efforts to define the phenomenon. The FBI offers this definition: "Any group having some manner of formalized structure and whose primary objective is to obtain money through illegal activities. Such groups maintain their position through the use of violence or threats of violence, corrupt public officials, graft or extortion and generally have a significant impact on the people in their locales or region of the country."

The lack of an accepted definition is highlighted by the variety of definitions, ranging from the simple definition of the state of Mississippi—"Two or more persons conspiring together to commit crimes for profit on a continuing basis"—to the more elaborate definition offered by the state of California, which stresses the types of activities that fall under the term "organized crime":

Organized crime consists of two or more persons who with continuity of purpose, engage in one or more of the following activities: (1) The supplying of illegal goods and services, that is, vice, loan-sharking, etc.; (2) Predatory crime, that is, theft, assault, etc. Several distinct types of criminal activity fall within this definition of organized crime. The types may be grouped into five general categories:

1. *Racketeering.* Groups of individuals that organize more than one of the following types of criminal activities for their combined profit.
2. *Vice operations.* Individuals operating a continuing business of providing illegal goods or services such as narcotics, prostitution, loan-sharking, and gambling.
3. *Theft/fence rings.* Groups of individuals who engage in a particular kind of theft on a continuing basis, such as fraud and bunco schemes, fraudulent documents, burglary, car theft, and truck hijackings, and associated individuals engaged in the business of purchasing stolen merchandise for resale and profit.
4. *Gangs.* Groups of individuals with common interests or backgrounds who band together and collectively engage in unlawful activity to enhance their group identity and influence, such as youth gangs, outlaw motorcycle clubs, and prison gangs.
5. *Terrorists.* Groups of individuals who combine to commit spectacular criminal acts, such as assassination and kidnapping of public figures to undermine public confidence in established government for political reasons or to avenge some grievance.

Attributes of Organized Crime

Although there is no generally accepted definition of organized crime, there is some agreement on its attributes:

1. *Nonideological.* An organized crime group is not motivated by social doctrine, political beliefs, or ideological concerns; its goals are money and power. This distinguishes organized crime from groups of persons who may be organized and violating the law to further their political agenda.
2. *Hierarchical.* An organized crime group has a vertical power structure with at least three permanent ranks, each with authority over the level beneath. The authority is inherent in the position and does not depend on who happens to be occupying it at any given time.
3. *Limited or exclusive membership.* An organized crime group significantly limits membership. Qualifications may be based on ethnic background, kinship, race, criminal record, or similar considerations. Those who meet the basic qualification(s) for membership usually require a sponsor, typically a ranking member, and must also prove qualified for membership by their behavior—for example, willingness to commit criminal acts, obey rules, follow orders, and maintain secrets. There is a period of apprenticeship, which may range from several months to several years. If the OC group is to remain viable, there must be considerably more persons who desire membership than the OC group is willing to accept. Exclusivity of membership serves to indicate that belonging is indeed something to be valued.
4. *Perpetuates itself.* An organized crime group constitutes an ongoing criminal conspiracy designed to persist through time, that is, beyond the life of the current membership. Permanence is assumed by the members, and this provides an important basis for attracting qualified persons to the group, thus perpetuating the group's existence.
5. *Willingness to use illegal violence and bribery.* In an organized crime group, violence is a readily available and routinely accepted resource. Access to private violence is an important dimension that allows the group to actively pursue its goals. When necessary, the OC group will resort to bribery in order to protect its operations or members.
6. *Specialization/Division of labor.* An organized crime group will have certain functional positions filled by qualified members.
7. *Monopolistic.* An organized crime group eschews competition. It strives for hegemony over a particular geographic area (a metropolitan area or section of a city), a particular

"industry," legitimate or illegitimate (e.g., gambling, trucking, loan-sharking), or a combination of both (for example, loan-sharking in a particular area).

Models of Organized Crime

The attributes of organized crime can fit two contrasting organizational models: the *bureaucratic* and the *patrimonial or patron–client network.*

Bureaucratic Model

The corporation, the police, and the military are examples of bureaucracies, that mode of organization essential for efficiently carrying out large-scale tasks. All bureaucracies are rational organizations sharing a number of attributes:

- A complicated hierarchy
- An extensive division of labor
- Positions assigned on the basis of skill
- Responsibilities carried out in an impersonal manner
- Extensive written rules and regulations
- Communication from the top of the hierarchy to persons on the bottom, usually in written (memo) form

The quintessential bureaucratic model of organized crime is the outlaw motorcycle club such as the Hell's Angels. The outlaw motorcycle club exhibits a number of characteristics that are bureaucratic. Given the military background of the founders and many members of the outlaw biker subculture, this is to be expected. There is a rather elaborate hierarchy, specialization, advancement based on skill, and extensive rules and regulations that are in written form. There is general uniformity in style of dress, colors, and motorcycles—large Harley-Davidsons. Minutes of meetings are recorded and dues are collected and maintained by a secretary-treasurer. Each member contributes weekly dues to the chapter, and the chapter pays into the national treasury. The Hell's Angels also maintain a multimillion-dollar fund to which members and chapters are occasionally asked to contribute. The fund goes for legal expenses and to help support the families of imprisoned members.

Each chapter has a president, vice president, secretary-treasurer, enforcer, and sergeant-at-arms. The "colors" are the official club insignia and a member typically wears colors on the back of a denim jacket with the sleeves cut off or, in colder climes, a leather jacket. Consistent with a military orientation, various offenses can result in the "pulling of patches."

The Clubs' Activities

A criminal organization can exhibit a formal structure whereas its economic activities may actually involve small firms or partnerships among members and include nonmember associates. This is often the case with leading outlaw motorcycle clubs. Each member is reputed to have about ten associates and his own network of friends. For business purposes, each member is at the center of an action group that, although tied to every other member through the structure of the club, operates independently or in partnership. In other words, the formal structure of the motorcycle club is not necessarily the same as its economic structure. Although there is a relatively clear hierarchy within each of the four outlaw clubs, income-generating activities involve several smaller operationally independent units. But members can call upon the muscle of the club in the event of conflict, making them formidable entrepreneurs. Lavigne (1996, 246) notes: "The Hell's Angels are truthful when they say they are not a criminal organization. Rather, they are an organization of criminals. They go out of their way to maintain a barrier between the Hell's Angels as a club and the Hell's Angels as a business. Criminal matters are discussed among members of many cliques within the gang."

Patrimonial or Patron–Client Networks

Francis Ianni states that the Italian American version of organized crime is a traditional social system organized by action and by cultural values that have nothing to do with modern bureaucratic or corporate principles. He maintains that Italian American crime syndicates are better explained through an examination of kinship networks: the subtitle of Ianni's 1972 book is *Kinship and Social Control in Organized Crime*. In other words, their structure is based on the traditions and experiences of southern Italy. Italian American OC can be seen as *patrimonial* (Collins, 1975, 65n):

Patrimonial organization, most characteristic of traditional societies, centers on families, patrons and their clients, and other personalistic networks. The emphasis is on traditional rituals that demonstrate the emotional bonds among men; the world is divided into those whom one can trust because of strongly legitimated personal connections and the rest from whom nothing is to be expected that cannot be exacted by cold-blooded bargaining or force. In modern bureaucratic organization, by contrast, personal ties are weaker, less ritualized, and less emotionally demonstrative; in their place is the allegiance to a set of abstract rules and positions. The different class cultures in patrimonial and bureaucratic organizations are accordingly affected. Patrimonial elites are more ceremonious and personalistic. Bureaucratic elites emphasize a colder set of ideals.

Many aspects of bureaucracy are impractical for organized crime, because there must be constant concern with the very real possibility that communications are being monitored. The use of the telephone must be limited (often only to arrange for in-person meetings), and written communication is avoided. Information as well as orders, money, and other goods are transmitted on an intimate, face-to-face basis. Lengthy chains of command characteristic of modern bureaucracy, are impractical for organized crime, and this limits the span of control. Randall Collins (1975, 293) points out that control is a special problem for patrimonial organizations. Bureaucracies develop, he argues, to overcome such problems: "Patrimonial organizations cannot be very well controlled much beyond the sight of the master." He notes that when the geographic range becomes too great, the organization collapses into feudalism.

In fact, says Mark Moore (1987, 53), a highly centralized organization "tends to make the enterprise too dependent on the knowledge and judgment of the top management, and wastes the knowledge and initiative of subordinate managers who know more about their own capabilities and how they fit into a local environment of risks and opportunities."

Decentralization in a criminal organization can be advantageous for both business and security reasons, notes Joseph Albini (1971, 285). He points out that the bureaucratic model would be a relatively easy target to move against: "All that would be necessary to destroy it would be to remove its top echelon." Instead, Albini argues, the syndicate's real power lies in its amorphous quality: "If a powerful syndicate figure is incarcerated, all that has really been severed is his position as a patron to his clients." If it so happens that another individual is in a position to assume this role, the clients may continue in the enterprise. The alternative is to find a new patron.

Every person is embedded in a social network, notes Jeremy Boissevain (1974, 24), "the chains of persons with whom a given person is in contact." As contact can be through a chain of persons, an individual can send "messages" to far more people than he or she actually knows directly. These are the "friends of friends," a phrase that in Sicily refers to *mafiosi.* "Every individual provides a point at which networks interact. But not everyone displays the same interest in and talent for cultivating relationships with strategic persons for profit" (Boissevain, 1974, 147). To be successful, each member of organized crime from the boss down to a soldier—just like Sicilian *mafiosi*—must display such interest and talent. This is done by acting as a *patron.*

The patron "provides economic aid and protection against both the legal and illegal exaction of authority. The client, in turn, pays back in more intangible assets" for example, esteem and loyalty. He may also offer political or other important support, thus making the relationship reciprocal (Wolf, 1966, 16–17). The patron acts as a power broker between the client and the wider society, both legitimate and illegitimate.

The member of an organized crime unit, acting as a patron, controls certain resources as well as strategic contacts with people who control other resources directly or who have access to such persons. The member-as-patron can put a client "in touch with the right people." He can bridge communication gaps between the police and criminals, between businessmen and syndicate-connected union leaders; he can transcend the world of business and the world of the illegitimate entrepreneur. He is able to perform important favors and be rewarded in return with money or power. There is a network surrounding the patron, a circle of dyadic relationships orbiting the organized crime member in which most clients have no relations with each other except through the patron.

The patron needs a great deal of time to manage his network adequately, to develop and maintain contacts, provide services, enhance power and income, and keep himself well-informed. As organized crime members do not usually have to maintain conventional schedules, they are free to "hang around," to pick up and disseminate important information. An organized crime member, as patron, may dominate a particular geographic area or industry. He will have available a network of informants and connections; for example, with the police and other officials, as well as with specialized criminal operatives such as *papermen* (persons who convert stolen "paper," such as stocks, bonds, and checks, into cash), *torches* (professional arsonists), musclemen or legbreakers, and enforcers. He is in a position to fence large amounts of stolen goods—he can truly "get it for you wholesale"—or to lend out various amounts of money at usurious interest—loan-sharking. He will act as a center for information (providing targets for professional burglars, for example), "license" criminal activities (e.g., enable a high-stakes dice game to operate), and use his position to assist criminals in linking up for specialized operations (e.g., finding a driver for a robbery or hijack team). He can provide stolen firearms and autos and other items necessary for conventional criminal activity. Thus, despite their relatively small numbers, persons in organized crime can present a significant public threat—a single member can be at the center of, and act as a catalyst for, an extraordinary amount of criminal activity. This crime unit is tied together in a network that includes nonmember associates who are clients of each of the members, including the boss and captains. In the Italian American version of OC, each of the bosses is connected (by kinship, friendship, mutual respect) to every other boss.

HOWARD ABADINSKY

References and Further Reading

Abadinsky, H. 2000. *Organized Crime*, 6th ed., Belmont, CA: Wadsworth.

Albini, J.L. 1971. *The American Mafia: Genesis of a Legend*, New York, NY: Appleton-Century-Crofts.

Arlacchi, P. 1986. *Mafia Business: The Mafia Ethic and the Spirit of Capitalism*, London, UK: Verso.

Boissevain, J. 1974. *Friends of Friends: Networks, Manipulators and Coalitions*, Oxford, UK: Basil Blackwell.

Collins, R. 1975. *Conflict Sociology*, New York, NY: Academic Press.

Cressey, D.R. 1972. *Criminal Organization: Its Elementary Forms*, New York, NY: Harper & Row.

Ianni, F.A.J. 1972. *A Family Business: Kinship and Social Control in Organized Crime*, New York, NY: Russell Sage Foundation.

Lavigne, Y. 1987. *Hells Angels: Into the Abyss*, New York, NY: HarperCollins, 1996; *Hells Angels: Taking Care of Business*, Toronto, Canada: Deneua and Wayne.

Moore, M.H. 1987. Organized crime as a business enterprise, in *Major Issues in Organized Crime Control*, pp. 51–64, Edelhertz, H. (Ed.), Washington, DC: U.S. Government Printing Office.

See also **Organized Crime: Activities and Extent; Organized Crime, Theories of**

Organized Crime: Enforcement Strategies

Introduction

The nature of organized crime has changed over the last half century. In this era of economic and cultural globalization, organized crime has quickly become international in nature. As such, law enforcement agencies (as well as their enforcement strategies) must become global and collaboration between countries is integral.

This entry will assess enforcement strategies commonly used in the fight against organized crime (both national and international). These strategies include, but are not exclusive to, traditional surveillance, electronic surveillance, relatively new technologies such as Carnivore, and recent legislation including the USA Patriot Act and the Foreign Intelligence Surveillance Act (each of which will be discussed in greater detail below).

Traditional Surveillance

Surveillance is the oldest and most used method of preliminary investigation into organized crime activity. Traditional surveillance consists of covert observation to obtain information about identities or activities of a criminal suspect or group. Surveillance is effectively used to detect criminal activities, obtain evidence, and prevent crime. A popular technique is automobile surveillance in which a transmitter (a.k.a., "beeper") is attached to the underside of a car frame. A receiver is placed in a surveillance car allowing investigators to follow at a safe distance to prevent detection (O'Hara and O'Hara, 1988). Recorders hidden in suitcases or brief cases and mini-recorders concealed on the body are also used as surveillance devices. Closed-circuit television allows observation of subjects.

Electronic Surveillance

Electronic surveillance is probably the most prevalent strategy used by law enforcement agencies to acquire evidence in complex organized crime investigations. Electronic surveillance has proven to be so successful because organized crime depends on telecommunications to plan and execute criminal activities. More than 25,600 felons have been convicted in the last 13 years using electronic surveillance (Carnivore Diagnostic Tool, 2000). The Task Force on Organized Crime has noted that "because of their [organized crime] organization and methods organization, organized crime activities require sophisticated means of evidence gathering. Often witnesses will not come forward, and members are bound by either an oath of silence or threats of violence. Often the use of informants is of limited value, and many organizations are difficult, if not impossible, for undercover agents to penetrate to the point where they can obtain useful information" (Task Force on Organized Crime, 1976, 148).

Wiretaps are an often used electronic surveillance tool. A wiretap is an electronic device that picks up both ends of a conversation. Telephone taps can be wired along the line; in a direct tap placed in the phone company's bridge box; in a "parasite tap" consisting of a transmitter wired into the phone line; and in an induction coil (O'Hara and O'Hara, 1998). In 1996, the Administrative Office of the U.S. Courts and the Department of Justice recorded 2.2 million conversations.

Another electronic surveillance strategy is "bugging." A bug is a self-contained receiver and transmitter as small as a fingernail that is located in a hidden place (O'Hara and O'Hara, 1998, 222). The bug relays audio (and occasionally video) radio waves to a recording device. Cameras, satellites, and lasers are also common devices used in surveillance. The laser is frequently used to listen to conversations inside a room in which there is not already a listening device in place (such as a bug). The laser works by being aimed at a window of the room that reflects the laser back to the operator. Sound waves in the room, produced as a by-product of normal conversation, collide with the window, and then travel through the laser back to the operator. A computer then translates the audio waves back into the conversation taking place into the room.

Carnivore

In response to increased Internet usage by organized crime groups, the FBI developed Carnivore, an Internet wiretapping system. Wiretapping on the Internet can only be conducted with a search warrant. An application for interception must be authorized by the Department of Justice. Then the U.S. Attorney's Office applies for an order. Interception orders are filed in federal district courts. The application must demonstrate probable cause that the stated offense has, is, or will occur. The application must also be specific as to the offense under investigation, the place where the intercept will take place, types of communications to be intercepted, and identities of persons involved (Carnivore Diagnostic Tool, 2000; U.S. Constitution, Fourth Amendment).

Carnivore uses an intercept operation that allows an authorized investigator to pick a single electronic

communication from a stream of millions of messages. Carnivore is currently being used in the fight against both organized crime and terrorism (of which the two are merging into a new "gray" form of criminal activities). A typical Internet wiretap lasts 45 days. The FBI uses Carnivore on infrastructure protection, hackers, counter terrorism, and drug trafficking cases (Bridis and Bridis, 2000).

A criticism of Carnivore is that the FBI can intercept electronic (e-mail) communication with seemingly little or no oversight (although a Title III Search Warrant is required). Additionally, Carnivore is troubling to countries that compete with multinational U.S.-based corporations. Many foreign companies have complained that the Carnivore system has been used to give an unfair trade advantage to American companies operating on the global marketplace by way of spying on intracompany e-mails.

Regional Information Sharing System (RISS)

Because of the abundance of intelligence available (sometimes overwhelming) to law enforcement organizations, the Regional Information Sharing System (RISS) was developed. RISS is a multijurisdictional criminal intelligence network that supports the sharing of information between more than 5000 agencies at the federal, state, and local levels. RISS is funded by the Department of Justice (DOJ) with the goal of identifying, targeting, and removing criminal conspiracies that extend beyond jurisdictional boundaries. There are six regional RISS centers that are staffed by intelligence analysts, field operatives, and computer personnel. RISS centers provide investigative support, intelligence dissemination, and training and loan specialized surveillance equipment (Regional Information Sharing Systems, 1998).

USA Patriot Act of 2001 (USAPA)

Legislation expanding police powers in response to emerging forms of criminal activity (specifically international crime activity related to organized crime and terrorism) is an increasingly common strategy used in the fight against organized crime. The USA Patriot Act of 2001, signed by President Bush on October 26, 2001, broadly expanded surveillance procedures (wiretaps, search warrants, pen or trap orders, and subpoenas) and legislative powers.

The USAPA is based on the Anti-Terrorism Act (ATA) of 2001. The ATA expanded the law enforcement and intelligence agencies authority to monitor private communications and personal information.

Some of the more significant provisions of the USAPA are that it:

> Gives federal law enforcement and intelligence officers greater authority (at least temporarily) to gather and share evidence, particularly with respect to wire and electronic communications; Creates new federal crimes, increases the penalties for existing federal crimes, and adjusts existing federal criminal procedure, particularly with respect to acts of terrorism; modifies immigration law, increasing the ability of federal authorities to prevent foreign terrorists from entering the U.S., to detain foreign terrorist suspects, to deport foreign terrorists, and to mitigate the adverse immigration consequences for the foreign victims of September 11; and authorizes appropriations to enhance the capacity of immigration, law enforcement, and intelligence agencies to more effectively respond to the threats of terrorism (Doyle, 2001).

The USA Patriot Act quickly became one of the most controversial laws ever passed by the U.S. Congress. The impact of this law upon Supreme Court decisions interpreting the Fourth Amendment is yet to be told. The USAPA is set to expire in October 2005 unless renewed by Congress; but it must first survive the scrutiny of the courts.

Foreign Intelligence Surveillance Act (FISA)

The Foreign Intelligence Surveillance Act, passed in 1978, regulates the collection of intelligence on foreign entities. In 1998, the FISA was amended to permit pen or trap orders to gather foreign information. The USA PATRIOT Act expanded the government's surveillance authority through the FISA where foreign intelligence is a significant purpose of the investigation. The FISA also permits a "roving wiretap," defined as the interception of any communications made without specifying the particular phone line or computer to be monitored (Foreign Intelligence Surveillance Act, June 30, 2003). The roving wiretap is probably the most controversial aspect of both the USAPA and the FISA.

Foreign Intelligence Surveillance Court (FISC)

The Foreign Intelligence Surveillance Court, or "spy court," is a relatively new tool in the fight against organized crime. The FISC is concerned with intelligence requests about suspected spies, terrorists, and foreign agents (Associated Press, March 24, 2003). The Court consists of seven district court judges appointed by the Chief Justice of the U.S. Supreme Court. They meet every 2 weeks to review warrant applications. The records are sealed and proceedings are secret (Scheers, May 9, 2003).

Applications to the Court must include:

- A statement that the target of surveillance is a foreign power,
- A certificate from the executive branch stating that the information is from foreign intelligence,
- Statements including all previous applications involving the target,
- Details about the nature of the information, type of communication, and the subject of surveillance,
- Length of surveillance,
- If physical entry will occur, and
- Procedures to reduce the possession, use, and retaining of information about disagreeable U.S. persons.

The FISC can approve surveillance of a foreign agent for up to a year before review (Foreign Intelligence Surveillance Act, June 30, 2003).

In May 2002, the FISC ruled that the USA Patriot Act does not allow federal investigators in terrorism cases to be given evidence gathered under special search warrants. The Court held that evidence gathered in spy cases could not be used in criminal investigations because it undermined a suspect's constitutional rights (Chatterjee, 2002). However, Attorney General Ashcroft appealed to a three-judge panel of the Foreign Intelligence Surveillance Court of Review. This review said that government officials did not have to limit monitoring of foreign intelligence, and that law enforcement agencies could use this information to build cases for prosecution. This allowed the federal, state, and local law enforcement agencies to coordinate their efforts toward foreign threats.

To get a warrant from the spy court, the government must demonstrate that the suspect is a foreign power or agent. Emergency warrants authorized by the FISA have allowed authorities to tap phones and faxes and conduct searches 72 hours before they are subject to review by the FISC. As of March 2003, Attorney General John Ashcroft cleared more than 170 spying warrants (Associated Press, March 24, 2003).

The most prevalent and lucrative activity of international organized crime groups is that of drug production and trafficking (Moran, 2002). The U.S. Drug Enforcement Administration (DEA) uses intervention strategies to enforce the Controlled Substances Act, thus combating the trafficking of drugs into the U.S. Specifically, the DEA is tasked to investigate those organizations or individuals involved in the growing, manufacturing, and distribution of controlled substances. The DEA's strategic plan for fighting drug trafficking combines three levels (international, national or regional, and local) of drug trade by focusing on specific aspects of drug production and trafficking. Drug Enforcement Administration (DEA)

On March 19, 2002, Attorney General Ashcroft presented a drug plan for the Department of Justice designed to reduce the availability of illegal drugs. He announced the following six strategies:

- Decrease supply of drugs by 10% in the U.S.;
- Originate a national list of drug targets—the consolidated priority organization target (CPOT) list;
- Focus on financial investigations that would eliminate and get rid of drug organizations and their profits;
- Attempt to redirect resources of drug imports;
- Lead investigations that work together in various districts against the targeted groups to limit the supplying of illegal drugs; and
- Under the Organized Crime Drug Enforcement Task Force (OCDETF), combine all of the abilities of the federal law enforcement agencies to focus on the major drug organizations that supply illegal drugs to the U.S. (Aftergood, 2003).

The Organized Crime Enforcement Task Force

A common strategy in the fight against organized crime is the use of task forces. The Organized Crime Drug Enforcement Task Force (OCDETF) is one such unit (overseen by the attorney general). Its goal is the disruption of drug trafficking organizations. The OCDETF works at federal, state, and local levels to target organizations that deal in illegal narcotics and related crimes such as money laundering, tax evasion, corruption, illegal immigration, and violations of weapons laws. The OCDETF has led to the prosecution and conviction of 44,000 members of organized crime groups and the seizure of cash and assets of more than 3 billion dollars. There are currently more than 2500 federal agents and prosecutors working under OCDETF. In addition, there are 6000 state and local law enforcement officers engaged in cases with the OCDETF (Executive Office for the Organized Crime Drug Enforcement Task Force, 2001).

Organized Crime and Racketeering Section (OCRS), Department of Justice

The Organized Crime and Racketeering Section (OCRS) of the Department of Justice organizes and coordinates programs to combat organized crime. Its efforts are aimed at traditional groups such as the La Cosa Nostra families and Russian organized crime (as opposed to nontraditional groups such as outlaw motorcycle gangs). It uses strike force units under the U.S. Attorney's Office, which includes 21 federal districts. The OCRS investigates extortion, murder, drug trafficking, and racketeering activities. The OCRS coordinates with the FBI and the Drug Enforcement Administration through the Attorney General's Organized Crime Council. It advises prosecutors on the Racketeer Influenced and Corrupt Organizations (RICO) statutes. The OCRS also reviews labor management disputes, employee pension and welfare benefits, and internal affairs of labor unions. The OCRS has a litigation unit composed of experienced attorneys who are mobile and able to travel to assist in the prosecution of organized crime cases across the U.S. (Organized Crime and Racketeering Section, 2001).

RICO

Hailed as the single most significant piece of legislation in the fight against organized crime, the Racketeer Influenced and Corrupt Organizations statute (18 U.S.C. Sections 1961–1968), known as RICO, defines racketeering broadly to include "any act or threat involving murder, kidnapping, gambling, arson, robbery, bribery, extortion, or dealing in narcotic or other dangerous drugs, which is chargeable under state law and punishable by imprisonment for more than one year." Additionally, there are a plethora of federal offenses defined as racketeering under this statute, including:

- Hobbs Act violations
- Bribery
- Sports bribery
- Counterfeiting
- Embezzlement from union funds
- Loan-sharking
- Mail fraud
- Wire fraud
- Obstruction of justice (federal or state)
- Contraband cigarettes
- White slavery (Mann Act violations)
- Bankruptcy fraud
- Drug violations
- Obscenity (added in 1984)

In order for an organized crime activity to be considered for prosecution under RICO, there must appear a "pattern" requiring only the commission of two crimes listed under the statute within a 10-year window. Thus, single criminal acts cannot be prosecuted under RICO.

The penalties upon conviction under the RICO statute are substantial: "Whoever violates any provision of section 1962 of this chapter shall be fined not more than $25,000 or imprisoned not more than 20 years, or both." Additionally, and possibly more importantly, there exist civil forfeiture provisions, requiring the convicted violator to forfeit to the government any business, property, or monetary funds he or she acquired while violating the RICO statute. RICO also carries provisions allowing private citizens to sue for damages: "Any person injured in his business or property by reason of a violation of section 1962 of this chapter may sue therefore in any appropriate United States district court and shall recover threefold damages he sustains and the cost of the suit, including a reasonable attorney's fee."

With all the power of RICO, there are criticisms. Four of the most often raised criticisms of RICO include the following:

1. RICO is overreaching, leading to the prosecution of persons who, although involved in criminal acts, are not connected to organized crime.
2. Invoking RICO can result in assets being frozen before a trial can begin. Such action can effectively put a company out of business. This threat can induce corporate defendants to plead guilty even when they may be innocent.
3. A RICO conviction brings with it the stigma of being labeled a "racketeer," which may be inappropriate for the circumstances of the case.
4. RICO allows for the possibility of triple damages when ordinary business transactions, or organized crime activity, are at issue.

Conclusion

In a globalized world, many new challenges have appeared and crime and corruption have expanded to an international level. New world criminals have expert knowledge of global technology and law enforcement agencies must keep abreast of organized crime by constantly learning and adapting.

The most effective strategy against organized crime is the legal system. Laws must constantly be updated as criminal activity changes. The U.S. Department of Justice and Department of State have coordinated efforts to develop international law enforcement procedures on a global basis to fight organized crime. Legislators are passing complex legislation to combat criminal networks (such as the USAPA and the FISA). Organized crime may never be eliminated, but it can be controlled through the coordinated efforts of government and law enforcement officials.

NATHAN R. MORAN

References and Further Reading

Abadinsky, H. (2002). *Organized Crime in America.* Cincinatti, OH: Anderson.

Aftergood, S. (2003). *Drug Enforcement Administration.* Available at http://fas.org/irp/agency/doj/dea/. Accessed on July 25, 2003.

Bassiouni, M.C. and Vetere, E. (1998). *Organized Crime: A Compilation of UN Documents, 1975–1998.* New York, NY: Transnational.

Big Brother in the Wires: Wiretapping in the Digital Age. (1998). *American Civil Liberties Union Freedom Network.* Available at http://archive.aclu.org/issues/cyber/wiretap_brother.html. Accessed on July 24, 2003.

Bridis, N. and Bridis, T. FBI system covertly searches e-mail. (2000). *The Wall Street Journal Online.* Available at http://zdnet.com.com/2100-11-522071.html?legacy=zdnn. Accessed on July 24, 2003.

Carnivore Diagnostic Tool. (2000). FBI Programs and Initiatives. Available at http://www.fbi.gov/hq/lab/carnivore/carnivore2.htm. Accessed on July 24, 2003.

Carter, D.L. (1997). International Organized Crime: Emerging Trends in Entrepreneurial Crime. In Ryan, P.J. and Rush, G.E. (Eds.), *Understanding Organized Crime in Global Perspective: A Reader.* Thousand Oaks, CA: Sage.

Chatterjee, S. Ashcroft, judges clash over FBI terror probe tactics. (2002). *Knight Ridder Newspapers.* Available at http://www.kentucky.com/mld/kentucky/3926286.htm?template=contentModules/print. Accessed on July 23, 2003.

Doyle, C. (Updated December 10, 2001). *CRS Report for Congress, Terrorism: Section by Section Analysis of the USA Patriot Act,* Congressional Research Service, The Library of Congress.

Diplomatic Strategies to Fight Transnational Organized Crime. (2001). *Washington File.* Available at http://usinfo. org/wf/2001/010124/epf305.htm. Accessed on July 24, 2003.

EFF Analysis of the Provisions of the USA PATRIOT Act. (2001). *Electronic Frontier Foundation.* Available at http://www.eff.org/Privacy/Surveillance/Terrorism_militias/20011031_eff_usa_patriot. Accessed on July 25, 2003.

Einstein, S. and Amir, M. (1999). *Organized Crime: Uncertainties and Dilemmas.* Chicago, IL: Office of International Criminal Justice.

Executive Office for the Organized Crime Drug Enforcement Task Force. (2001). *Department of Justice Criminal Division.* Available at http://www.usdoj.gov/criminal/ocdetf.html. Accessed on July 23, 2003.

Foreign Intelligence Surveillance Act (FISA). (2003). *EPIC Archive.* Available at http://www.epic.org/privacy/terrorism/fisa/. Accessed on July 25, 2003.

Moran, N.R. (2002). *The Globalization of Russian, Colombian, and Chinese Organized Crime from 1991–2001: A Time-Series Analysis.* Sam Houston State University Press: Huntsville, TX.

O'Hara, C. and O'Hara, G. (1988). *Fundamentals of Criminal Investigation,* 5th ed. Springfield, IL: Charles C. Thomas.

Organized Crime and Racketeering Section. (2001). Department of Justice Criminal Division. Available at http://www.usdoj.gov/criminal/ocrs.html. Accessed on July 22, 2003.

Regional Information Sharing Systems Program (1998). Washington, DC: Bureau of Justice Statistics.

Scheeres, J. Feds Doing More Secret Searches. (2003). *Wired News*. Available at http://www. wired.com/news/print/0,1294, 58774, 00.html. Accessed on July 24, 2003.

Supremes Uphold U.S. Spy Power. (2003). *Associated Press*. Available at http://www.wired.com/news/print/0,1294,58186, 00.html. Accessed on July 24, 2003.

Task Force on Organized Crime (1976). *Organized Crime*. Washington, DC: U.S. Government Printing Office.

The USA PATRIOT Act. (2003). EPIC Archive. Available at http://www.epic.org/privacy/terrorism/usapatriot/. Accessed on July 25, 2003.

Organized Crime: Irish and Jewish Mobsters

Although public perceptions tend to identify organized crime in the U.S. with the Italian "Mafia," closer analysis reveals that numerous ethno-racial groups have participated in it for much of the country's history. In addition to Italians, two ethnic groups with a history of involvement in organized crime are Jewish and Irish Americans. Both were oppressed peoples in their home countries: Jews in the anti-Semitic societies of Eastern Europe, the Irish in English-dominated Ireland. The hostile attitudes of the authorities instilled in each a suspicion of central government and a willingness to seek local, informal solutions to social problems. These attitudes, bred over many years of suffering and persecution in Europe, accompanied them when they immigrated to the U.S.

British repression and the failure of Ireland's potato crop combined to produce a boom in Irish immigration to the U.S. in the 1840s. Between 1840 and 1854, almost 2 million Irish Catholics poured into the country. They settled predominantly in northeastern cities, in which their numbers sometimes reached two-thirds of the population. In Ireland many of these immigrants had worked in agriculture. In the U.S., however, they were confined in urban ghettoes that prevented access to their former occupations. Vigorous bigotry within the Protestant Anglo population sharply limited Irish social mobility. In the old country, they had countered British repression by resorting to informal methods of resolving conflicts and addressing social problems. In this manner, an unofficial shadow government responsive to Irish citizens came into being alongside the British-administered system of colonial rule, law, and education. When newly arrived immigrants encountered Anglo prejudice in the U.S., they fell back on their default strategy of localism and communal self-help.

Irish organized crime flourished in the seedbed of thwarted mobility and 19th century urban politics. Realizing that large Irish populations could become a powerful base of electoral politics, northern Democrats courted the favor of the new immigrants, and soon a firm alliance between the two groups was forged. Local leaders of Irish wards mobilized the vote on behalf of Democratic politicians. In exchange, successful Democrats provided jobs, housing, and government aid to Irish voters. In time political "machines" arose in the cities of the Northeast that throve on this alliance of Democratic politicians and Irish urban dwellers. The "bosses" of the machines were often Irish immigrants or their children. By the 1860s, the Irish had gained control of Tammany Hall, a political machine that fed on the electoral support of Irish New Yorkers. Under William March Tweed, the Tammany machine orchestrated the election of its candidates to New York's board of aldermen and to the state legislature. Soon Tammany freely disposed of New York City's treasury, plundering city coffers with phony bid deals, fictitious payrolls, and inflated goods and services provided by its "employees." It also shielded vice operations within the city from molestation by the police. Tammany's power as a political and criminal force in New York City continued until 1932, when the Tammany candidate for president failed to garner support in Manhattan. Official investigations subsequently exposed the endemic corruption of the Tammany machine. Tammany lingered until the 1960s, when it finally disappeared from the landscape of American politics.

The era of Prohibition that began in 1919 was a boon to Irish American mobsters. Organized criminals throughout the U.S. reaped enormous profits as they strove to meet the demand for illegal liquor through bootlegging, speakeasies, and smuggling. Irish mobsters played a significant role in Boston, where until the 1930s the "Gustin gang," led by Frank Wallace, dominated the city's criminal underworld. Despite Irish preeminence, the Jewish mob under Charles "King" Solomon also flourished in Boston during this period. By the 1930s, Italian mobsters, supported by Charles "Lucky" Luciano in New York City, had muscled into Boston, murdered Wallace and Solomon, and displaced the Irish as the leading ethnic mob in the city. This *coup d'etat* notwithstanding, Irish mobsters continued to operate in Boston. The two groups settled their differences, and when Italian mob leaders relocated their headquarters to Providence, Rhode Island, Irish gangsters worked for them as enforcers.

As in Boston, the Irish were a formidable presence in the organized crime scene of Philadelphia. Between 1917 and 1960, a network led by Irish and Jewish mobsters controlled the city's illegal rackets. As early as 1900, the Irish dominated Philadelphia's illegal gambling industry. With the onset of Prohibition in 1919, a bootlegging syndicate under largely Jewish and Irish leadership arose. The Rosen mob (see below) had formed by 1930, led by Jewish mobster Nig Rosen but comprising numerous Irish members. From 1930 to 1960, the Rosen gang presided over Philadelphia's gambling and heroin importation rackets. In the post-World War II era, the influence of Irish mobsters declined as Italians assumed the dominant role in American organized crime.

A snapshot of U.S. organized crime circa 1900 would show the Irish in control of political machines like Tammany Hall. Increasingly, however, the dominance of Irish mobsters was contested by Jewish racketeers, who gradually gained a toehold in illegal gambling and prostitution. The turning point for Jewish organized crime occurred after 1919, when Jewish gangs flocked into bootlegging during the Prohibition era. By the 1920s as many as 50% of the leading "entrepreneurs" in the illegal liquor industry were Jewish.

Arguably, the most important Jewish mobster was Arnold "the Brain" Rothstein, a figure swathed in legend for his role in the Chicago Black Sox scandal of 1919. The son of an Orthodox Jew, Rothstein accumulated capital at a young age as a billiards "shark," which he then loaned at usurious interest rates. Thereafter he diversified his rackets, purchasing a gambling establishment and working as a bookmaker. At the same time, he developed a relationship with machine boss Tim Sullivan. The contact proved valuable for Rothstein, because Sullivan protected him from police investigation. He retained a gang of Jewish gangsters led by Jacob Orgen to be his strikebreakers in New York unions—a gang that included Lewis "Lepke" Buchalter and Jacob Shapiro. Rothstein also mingled his rackets with legal business pursuits in insurance, real estate, and the bail-bond industry.

Dalliances with legitimate business to the contrary, the lure of illegal profits was irresistible for Rothstein. Prohibition afforded him the opportunity to import liquor into the U.S. In order to maximize profits, he smuggled diamonds and narcotics in the cargo holds of his liquor ships; out of this smuggling operation, Rothstein assembled an international narcotics syndicate. The syndicate received the drugs from foreign suppliers, which, after importation into the U.S., were distributed to mobsters like Johnny Torrio and Al Capone in Chicago, Rosen in Philadelphia, Solomon in Boston, and Luciano in New York. In 1928, Rothstein died from a gunshot wound without divulging the name of his killer. Records discovered in his apartment proved his connections with the nation's largest drug syndicate.

Rothstein may have been the most administratively sophisticated of Jewish mobsters, but he was by no means the only one. A salient example is "Dutch" Schultz, who controlled the illegal liquor market in the Bronx and Manhattan and the Harlem numbers racket. The proceeds of his lucrative rackets—he was a millionaire by 1930—were invested in slot machines, which he distributed throughout the state of New York. Schultz was an excessively violent mobster, even by the gaudy standards of his day. When a former employee of Schultz, Jack "Legs" Diamond, began hijacking Schultz's beer trucks, he had Diamond killed. He dealt in a similar way with the Coll brothers, two Irish mobsters who intimidated buyers of Schultz's liquor. On Schultz's orders, his thugs machine-gunned Vincent Coll in a New York drugstore. Schultz's brazen and remorseless use of violence proved to be his undoing. After U.S. Attorney Thomas Dewey unsuccessfully prosecuted him for tax evasion, Schultz resolved to have Dewey murdered. Other New York mobsters feared that Dewey's murder would mean an all-out law enforcement crusade against organized crime in New York City. They contacted Murder, Inc. (the enforcement arm of the mob) about killing Schultz. The contract was accepted, and in October 1935, Schultz and three of his assistants were gunned down in the Palace Chop House in Newark, New Jersey.

Another infamous Jewish crime figure, Louis "Lepke" Buchalter, would become the only significant gangster in U.S. history to suffer capital punishment for his crimes. After his release from prison in 1922, Buchalter joined Jacob Shapiro as enforcer for labor racketeer Jacob Orgen, whose organization Buchalter and Shapiro took over in 1927. In the aftermath, the two mobsters became pioneers of modern industrial racketeering by infiltrating labor unions and controlling them from within. Buchalter's racket not only controlled labor unions in New York City, but extorted money from the firms that retained him as a union buster. From the late 1920s until 1940, Buchalter received millions in extortion proceeds from various New York industries.

By 1937, Thomas Dewey was on Buchalter and Shapiro's trail. Shapiro was indicted, convicted on extortion charges, and sent to prison, where he died in 1947. In hiding, Buchalter ordered the assassinations of members of his organization who could turn state's witnesses against him. A bloodbath ensued that claimed between 60 and 80 lives. Far from cowing potential witnesses into silence, however, the rampage stampeded Buchalter's henchmen into the arms of the police. He was arrested in 1939 and convicted first in federal court of antitrust and drug violations, then in New York state court for murder. In March 1944, Buchalter was electrocuted.

Whereas Buchalter amassed his fortune in labor racketeering, the Jewish mobsters Meyer Lansky and Ben ("Bugsy") Siegel became wealthy men through the illegal liquor racket in the era of Prohibition. Their organization furnished guards to protect the liquor shipments of high-profile gangsters. They also conducted bootlegging and gambling operations that generated opulent profits. By the 1930s, Siegel and Lansky were among the elite of the American *demimonde*.

In 1936, Siegel lighted off for the West Coast, where with mobsters from Cleveland, Chicago, and New York he formed new rackets in offshore gambling, prostitution, and labor racketeering. During his California period, Siegel established the Screen Extras Guild and the mob-owned "Trans-America Wire Service." (The latter relayed the results of horse races around the country.) Siegel's ambition to build a sumptuous hotel and gambling resort in the Nevada desert, however, would paradoxically both result in his death and ensure his immortality in American popular culture. With financing provided by Nevada gamblers and East Coast mobsters, he built a casino hotel called "The Flamingo" in Las Vegas, the first of its kind in the desert town. Siegel's errant management of The Flamingo alarmed his gangster investors. In 1947, he was assassinated in Beverly Hills.

Lansky, on the other hand, pursued a more long-lived if less glamorous career in organized crime after he parted ways with Siegel. He established gambling syndicates in Havana, Cuba, which he controlled until Fidel Castro ousted him in 1959. He added to these revenues by fencing the ill-gotten gains of other mobsters, ploughing them into licit businesses like the jukebox industry. After years of cat-and-mouse with federal authorities, he retired to Miami Beach and died of cancer in 1983.

In addition to New York City, Jewish mobsters were among the leading figures in the criminal underworld of Philadelphia. A coalition of Irish and Jewish gangsters dominated Philadelphia's bootlegging rackets during Prohibition. In 1930, a New York Jew, Nig Rosen, formed the "69th Street Gang" in Philadelphia, trafficking in illegal liquor and gambling. By 1939, his organization had captured the numbers racket in the city. In subsequent years Rosen became involved in the "French connection" heroin trade, for which he served a 5-year prison term in 1958. The Rosen gang was notable for its multiethnic composition: Jews held the top leadership positions, Irish and Italians were the rank-and-file. When Rosen retired to Florida in the 1960s, he was succeeded by notorious Italian mobster Angelo Bruno. The example of the Rosen gang, when considered along with the careers of other powerful Jewish and Irish mobsters, belies the popular misconception that equates American organized crime with Italian *mafiosi*.

MICHAEL BRYANT

References and Further Reading

Block, A. and Chambliss, W.J. 1981. *Organizing Crime,* New York, NY: Elsevier.

Fried, A. 1980. *The Rise and Fall of the Jewish Gangster in America,* New York, NY: Holt, Rinehart and Winston.

Joselit, J. 1983. *Our Gang: Jewish Crime and the New York Jewish Community,* 1900–1940, Bloomington, IN: Indiana University Press.

Lacey, R. 1991. *Little Man: Meyer Lansky and the Gangster Life,* Boston, MA: Little, Brown.

Levine, E.M. 1966. *The Irish and Irish Politicians,* Notre Dame, IN: University of Notre Dame Press.

Peterson, V.W. 1983. *The Mob: 200 Years of Organized Crime in New York,* Ottawa, IL: Green Hill.

See also **Organized Crime: Activities and Extent; Organized Crime: Theories of**

Organized Crime: Italian American Mafia

Most Italians who came to the U.S. did so during the years 1875–1920. More than 80% were from south of Rome—the *Mezzogiorno*. Every important Italian American organized crime figure has had cultural roots in the *Mezzogiorno*, especially Sicily, home of the Mafia. These poor, uneducated immigrants faced enormous social and economic hardship exacerbated by ethnic prejudice and American nativism. As with earlier generations of immigrants, a small number sought to succeed by bending and breaking both moral and legal codes. These criminals adapted their southern Italian culture to the American experience.

As a result, there were Mafia gangs in every American city that had a sizable Sicilian population. With secret rituals and membership ceremonies, these *mafiosi* lived as parasites off of the toil of honest Italians from whom they extorted "protection" money. They were also involved in the manufacture of low-cost, high-proof, untaxed alcohol, a business that prepared them well for Prohibition (1920–1933).

Prohibition

Prior to Prohibition, organized crime was restricted to the local community. Prohibition enabled the Mafia gangs to break out of the bounds of "Little Italy" and operate in the wider society—booze-hungry Americans were not fussy about the source of their liquor. Prohibition enabled these loosely linked but otherwise independent and uncoordinated "crime families" to expand throughout urban America. The ban on alcoholic beverages did not reduce demand, but encouraged the creation of city- and region-wide criminal organizations that allowed Italian gangsters to consolidate their power.

Prohibition also unleashed an unparalleled level of violence, as competing criminal gangs sought to gain advantages over their competitors. In Chicago, the infamous "beer wars" turned the Windy City into a battleground from which America's most notorious gang leader, Al Capone, would emerge dominant.

Elsewhere, by 1930 there were two major Mafia factions; one headed by Giuseppe ("Joe the Boss") Masseria operating out of the Little Italy of East Harlem and the other by Salvatore Maranzano whose business office was in midtown Manhattan. Their struggle for domination became known as the Castellammarese war because Maranzano and many of his supporters came from the small Sicilian coastal town of Castellammare del Golfo. The Maranzano group consisted mainly of Sicilians, especially the "moustache Petes," Old World types, many of whom had fled from Benito Mussolini's persecution of the Sicilian Mafia. After his own escape, Maranzano had helped to smuggle many of his compatriots into the U.S., and they in turn gave support to their protector. The Masseria group had both Sicilian and non-Sicilian members, most notably, Lucky Luciano. Through ties developed by Luciano, they were allied with non-Italians, Jewish gang leaders such as Meyer Lansky and Ben ("Bugsy") Siegel. As the war turned against Masseria—the Maranzano forces were reinforced by a continuing supply of Sicilian exiles—five of his leading men, including Luciano, went over to the other side. In 1931, Masseria was murdered and the Castellammarese war was over. Later that year, acting on orders from Luciano, Marranzano was murdered by killers dispatched by Lansky and Siegel.

A National Syndicate Emerges

In the aftermath of the Castellammarese war, 24 Italian American crime families emerged, scattered throughout most large cities with significant Italian populations. In cooperation with some Irish but primarily Jewish gangs, they constituted a syndicate that dominated bootlegging and related enterprises. When Prohibition was repealed in 1933, the syndicate moved into other criminal enterprises, sometimes pushing aside weaker groups who had been active in gambling, loan-sharking, prostitution, drug trafficking, and labor racketeering. Syndicate leaders continued to maintain important political ties that provided a great deal of protection against law enforcement efforts. Nevertheless, Luciano was successfully prosecuted for controlling a widespread prostitution ring—a dubious charge—by special New York State prosecutor, Thomas E. Dewey, and spent World War II in prison. After the war, he was pardoned by then Governor Dewey who cited Luciano's efforts to assist the Navy during the war. Luciano was immediately deported back to Italy where he died in 1962.

During the decades following World War II, organized crime underwent considerable change. It became increasingly clear that organized crime was dominated mainly by Italians—the Irish, except for small pockets in New York and Boston, were no longer involved. And although the sons of Jewish immigrants played a vital role in organized crime, by the third generation, the Jews had moved out.

In most of urban America, the Mafia maintained hegemony over organized criminal activity. They influenced or controlled important labor unions, dominated illegal gambling operations, extorted from legitimate and illegitimate entrepreneurs, and, in some areas, were involved in wholesale drug trafficking. They moved into legitimate business, sometimes as a result of debtors being unable to meet their obligations and sacrificing their businesses. For decades, they skimmed profits from the gambling casinos of Las Vegas, in which they had a secret ownership. Until Fidel Castro drove them out in 1957, they enjoyed a government-authorized monopoly over gambling in Cuba.

The Structure of the American Mafia

American Mafia groups are patrimonial organizations centered around patrons and their clients, and other personal networks. Whereas every person provides a point at which networks interact, *mafiosi* reveal an interest in and talent for cultivating relationships with strategic persons for profit. This is done by acting as a *patron*.

The patron provides economic aid and protection against both the legal and illegal exaction of authority. The client, in turn, pays back in more intangible assets; for example, esteem and loyalty. He may also offer political or other important support, thus making the relationship reciprocal. The patron acts as a power broker between the client and the wider society, both legitimate and illegitimate.

The member of an organized crime (OC) unit, acting as a patron, controls certain resources as well as strategic contacts with people who control other resources directly or who have access to such persons. The member-as-patron can put a client "in touch with the right people." He can bridge communication gaps between the police and criminals, between businessmen and syndicate-connected union leaders; he can transcend the world of business and the world of the illegitimate entrepreneur. He is able to perform important favors and be rewarded in return with money or power. There is a network surrounding the patron, a circle of dyadic relationships orbiting the OC member in which most clients have no relations with each other except through the patron.

An OC patron may dominate a particular geographic area or industry. He will have available a network of informants and connections; for example, with the police and other officials, as well as with specialized criminal operatives. He is in a position to fence large amounts of stolen goods or to lend out various amounts of money at usurious interest. He will act as a center for information (providing targets for professional burglars, for example), "license" criminal activities (e.g., enable a high-stakes dice game to operate), and use his position to assist criminals in linking up for specialized operations (for example, finding a driver for a robbery or hijack team). Thus, despite their relatively small numbers, persons in organized crime can present a significant public threat—a single member can be at the center of, and act as a catalyst for, an extraordinary amount of criminal activity.

The actual name by which a Mafia group is known varies. In New England, for example, it is the "Office"; in Chicago, it is the "Outfit." In New York City there are five "families." Although any number of members may be related, the term *family* does not imply kinship by blood or marriage. Each crime unit is composed of members and associates.

To be eligible for membership, a young man (there are no female members) must be of Italian descent. The prospective member requires a sponsor and must have a long history of successful criminal activity or possess certain skills required by the group. Every potential member, however, is expected to participate in a murder—although not necessarily as the actual executioner. Such participation serves to more closely bind the person to the ongoing conspiracy that is organized crime, and it precludes government agents from becoming members. An OC group is also interested in criminals who have proven to be moneymakers, "earners" who can increase the group's income.

In New York, each member is an independent operator, not an employee—he receives no salary from the group. Instead, the member—made guy—has a form of "franchise": he is authorized by the group to make money by using the family connections that come with membership, bolstered by the status (that is, fear) that membership generates. Although part of a particular crew, he is an independent entrepreneur, violent, aggressive, and constantly on the prowl for moneymaking opportunities. In a typical pattern, a made guy, or franchised member, will attract nonmembers who are eager to associate with him, to become "connected," because an associate enjoys some of the status and connections that the crime family enjoys. If the member is able to generate considerable income, he gains greater status in the family and can become a candidate for advancement to captain. If successful associates are Italian, they become candidates for membership. Each new member is a potential threat to the security of the group—a potential informant—so new members are selected with caution and great care. A prospective member may have to serve the group for many years before achieving membership status. Members and associates are organized into crews, semi-independent units, nominally headed by a captain, a street boss, or even a soldier. Crews generate finances that they share with their crew chief; he then shares it with the captain or with the boss.

In the past, the boss usually was a senior citizen— it took many years to gain the respect of members and the knowledge and connections needed by the group. It is a sign of weakness that many of the current heads of important Italian American crime groups are relatively young, as well as volatile and violent.

Typically, the boss operates out of a fixed location: a restaurant, a private club, or his own business office. The boss, like many other members of a crime family, has investments in illegitimate and legitimate enterprises, often in partnership with other members of his own or other crime groups or with nonmember associates. He receives a portion of the illegal earnings of all of the members of his family, roughly between 10% and 15% if he had no stake in the activities. With activities that he directs personally, the share will be considerably higher. Soldiers will share their earnings with their captain, who will pass on a portion to the boss.

Organized crime—the Outfit—in Chicago differs from that found in New York and other East Coast cities. The Chicago Outfit was always a cooperative venture with other groups, although the Italians were dominant. There is an absence of independent entrepreneurs in the Chicago Outfit, and all important decisions are made at the executive level. Moving into a new business or new territory is determined at the top of a truly hierarchical organization.

The Outfit is led by a boss who at various times has actually been akin to a chief executive officer responsible to one or more persons constituting an informal board of directors. Assisted by his underboss and advisors—older and influential members of the Outfit who assume some type of senior status—the boss controls three area bosses. Each area boss has responsibility for a particular part of the Chicago land area (the city and nearby counties). He oversees the activities of street bosses who direct the day-to-day activities of crew members.

Each of the crews is associated with a particular geographic area, although these areas have undergone change over the years. In addition, there are subgroups nominally attached to crews. Thus, major gambling operations are the responsibility of a specialty crew whose members report to the Outfit hierarchy, not a street boss.

In Chicago, made guys are supervisors and the people they supervise are associates. Associates are assigned to activities for which they are equipped: someone with numbers skills would, for example, work as a clerk for a bookmaker; someone with a tough-guy reputation would be assigned to collections. There is no evidence of an initiation ceremony involving oaths of secrecy and obedience, the drawing of blood, and the burning of a saint's portrait.

The American Mafia in the 21st Century

In recent decades, the ranks of the Mafia have been thinned by successful federal prosecutions using the Racketeer Influenced and Corrupt Organizations statute of 1970, particularly the long, double-digit sentences typically handed down. Once ruled by an iron code of silence, the Mafia has become riddled with informants seeking to gain leniency from federal prosecutors. Government estimates indicate that there are now less than 1500 Mafia members—although they have thousands of associates—with about 80% in the New York City metropolitan area. Although New York and Chicago contain the strongest crime families, Mafia groups operate in other cities, such as Buffalo, Detroit, New Orleans, Southern California, and particularly Philadelphia, where there has been a great deal of violence in recent years for domination of that city's Mafia family.

Italian Americans are now being overshadowed by emerging criminal groups—Asian, Latino, African American—who are using the drug trade much as their organized crime predecessors did bootlegging during Prohibition.

HOWARD ABADINSKY

References and Further Reading

Abadinsky, H. 2000. *Organized Crime,* 6th ed., Belmont, CA: Wadsworth.
Albini, J.L. 1971. *The American Mafia: Genesis of a Legend,* New York, NY: Appleton-Century-Crofts.
Boissevain, J. 1974. *Friends of Friends: Networks, Manipulators and Coalitions,* Oxford, UK: Basil Blackwell.
Cressey, D.R. 1969. *Theft of the Nation,* New York, NY: Harper & Row.
Ianni, F.A.J. 1972. *A Family Business: Kinship and Social Control in Organized Crime,* New York, NY: Russell Sage Foundation.
Nelli, H.S. 1981. *The Business of Crime.* New York, NY: Oxford University Press.
President's Commission on Organized Crime. 1986. *The Impact: Organized Crime Today.* Washington, DC: U.S. Government Printing Office.

See also **Organized Crime: The Sicilian Mafia**

Organized Crime: Japanese Mobsters

Boryokudan, the Japanese mobsters' (called Yakuza) organization, is generally defined as an organization or group engaged in habitual and collective criminal activities involving violence. The categories of professional gamblers, street peddlers, delinquent youth groups, stevedore gangs, and unscrupulous constructors are examples of mobsters. These groups emerged through the cracks during periods of social disorganization and economic instability. They have repeatedly split and merged among themselves and survived persistently over the ages.

In 1998, the number of arrested regular and associate members of Boryokudan was 32,985, an increase of 2.7% over the previous year. The breakdown of arrests consists of 20,207 offenders of the Penal Code and 12,778 offenders of special laws. Although Penal Code offenders increased by 9% over the previous year, those of special laws decreased by 5.8%. In terms of types of crime, those arrested for violation of the Stimulant Drug Control Law topped the list with 7193 (21.8%), followed by those arrested for inflicting a bodily injury 4882 (14.8%), those for larceny 3062 (9.3%), and those for extortion 3044 (9.2%).

Boryokudan initially emerged and rapidly grew amid the chaos that had developed after World War II. By the mid-1950s, Boryokudan controlled the black market economy in Japan, engaging in the illicit trafficking of Philopon (a stimulant drug), arranging and holding various kinds of concerts and shows, and repurchasing and reselling pachinko prizes. (Pachinko is a gambling game that resembles a cross between slot machines and pinball.) In particular, the widespread abuse of stimulant drugs distributed by Boryokudan created serious social problems.

Since the mid-1960s, in addition to the traditional ways of income generation such as the trafficking of stimulant drugs, extortion, gambling, and bookmaking, Boryokudan has sought to raise funds by intervening in private disputes or civil affairs with violence. During years of rapid expansion (1986–1991), when land prices soared in urban areas, Boryokudan intervened in real estate deals and sought to make money through securities transactions. Then, after the economic bubble burst, they used violence on corporate executives and were implicated in unlawful lending and unlawful disposal of bad loans. Gradually, the money-making activities of Boryokudan have grown increasingly complex and sophisticated.

With strict crackdowns on Boryokudan carried out through "crush-the-leadership" campaigns, the number of Yokuza declined, whereas remaining Boryokudan members increasingly turned to violence. Even after the conflicts between two rival factions (the Yamaguchi-gumi and Ichiwa-kai) wound down in the second half of the 1980s, turf wars among Boryokudan groups continued, causing the accidental deaths of citizens and policemen.

In the middle of this situation, a popular outcry for a tougher crackdown on Boryokudan mounted. Facing the growing seriousness of the situation, the government enacted the Anti-Boryokudan Law (formally called the Law for Preventing Gangsters' Unlawful Actions) in 1991. This legislation enabled the police to take administrative measures (called "discontinuance" and "recurrence prevention" orders) against Yakuza maintaining offices and other acts previously unpunishable under the existing Penal Code and regulations. The total number of discontinuance and recurrence prevention orders issued since the enactment of the Anti-Boryokudan Law was 8607 by the end of 1998.

In 1992, the First Prefectural Centers for the Elimination of Boryokudan were created under the Anti-Boryokudan Law. These centers have carried out activities with a view to eliminate Boryokudan from communities in cooperation with the police and other neighborhood agencies and organizations. In these circumstances, lawsuits have been filed against Boryokudan in various parts of the country, seeking a court order to relocate Boryokudan offices, injunctions against the use of such offices, and compensation for damages resulting from the illegal acts of Yakuza.

In addition, police actively help businesses keep Yakuza racketeers at bay in various ways. For example, the national and local governments are working hard to exclude undesirable contractors, including Boryokudan groups and those hiring Boryokudan members, from public work projects.

In recent years, the internationalization of Boryokudan has been noted as an important trend in gang syndicates. Crimes involving drugs and weapons, such as violations of the Stimulant Drug Control Law and the Firearms and Swords Control Law, now are committed globally. Cooperation between Boryokudan and other foreign criminal syndicates has increased. For example, Boryokudan and foreign criminal organizations are involved in their entries of illegal foreign workers into countries, residences, and employments. Undoubtedly, Boryokudan will strengthen ties with foreign syndicates through these activities.

NORIYOSHI TAKEMURA

References and Further Reading

Iwai, H. 1986. Organized crime in Japan, in Kelly, R. (Ed.), *Organized Crime: A Grobal Perspective*, Totowa, NJ: Rowan and Littlefield.

Kaplan, D.E. and Dubro, A. 1986. *Yakuza: Japan's Criminal Underworld*, Boston, MA: Addison-Wesley Publishing Company Inc.

Kato, H. and Hanzai, S. 1992. *no Kenkyuu: Mafia, La Cosa Nostra, Boryokudan no Hikaku-Kennkyuu* (Research on Organized Crime: Comparative Research on Mafia, La Cosa Nostra and Boryokudan), Tokyo: Seibundo.

National Police Agency, 2000. Government of Japan, *White Paper on Police 1999* (Excerpt), Tokyo: The Japan Times.

Raz, J. 1996. *Anthropology of Yakuza: Japan as Seen from Its "Back Door."*

Ryan, P.J. and George, E.R. 1997. (Eds.), *Understanding Organized Crime in Global Perspective: A Reader*, Thousand Oaks, CA, London, UK, and New Delhi, India: Sage.

Yokoyama, M. 1999. Trends of organized crime by Boryokudan in Japan, in Einstein, S. and Amir, M. (Eds.), *Organized Crime: Uncertainties and Dilemmas*, Chicago, IL: The University of Illinois Press.

See also **Japan, Crime and Justice in**

Organized Crime: Mexican Mafia

Between 1956 and 1957, the EME or Mexican Mafia (MM) prison gang was formed within the California Department of Corrections (CDC) at the Deuel Vocational Institution. "EME" refers to the letter "M" and its proper pronunciation in Spanish. Cox (1986) reports that the Mexican Mafia originated in the East Los Angeles barrio of Maravilla and, unlike some of the other major prison gangs, has no known constitution. The prison gang, as the name implies, consists primarily of Mexicans. Members of the EME reside in the southern part of California whereas their arch enemy, the Nuestra Familia, reside in the northern part of the state. Throughout the 1960s, the Mexican Mafia grew rapidly and expanded its control of prison narcotics traffic, gambling, debt collection, extortion, and most other inmate black market activity. The gang spread throughout the CDC and eventually expanded its activities outside the prison walls. Its primary objective is to control all illicit activities within the CDC and to expand its influence to the community. The MM is wholly directed to organized crime with no specific political goals, except when certain politicians can be used to enhance their criminal goals.

The structure of the MM involves a chain of command whereby orders from the generals are implemented by captains, lieutenants, and the rank and file troops or "soldiers." Leadership within the MM is usually based on past performance and the respect paid him by other "carnales" (Spanish for brother). This term, "carnal," is frequently used by members and associates as a means of signifying membership. Status within the organization and moving up in power and leadership within the MM is based largely on the number of violent incidents in which a member has engaged. Each institutional chapter of the EME tends to have its own separate leadership while remaining bound to the primary leaders who may be housed elsewhere in the CDC system. Generally, when an MM member is transferred from one prison to another he does not retain the status and rank that he possessed at the previous institution. This is not always the case, however, as a member of high rank with considerable status and prestige may assume a high leadership role at the new facility. As the "Mafia" name implies, the MM imitates the traditional Italian Mafia and is considered to be well-organized and disciplined. The MM has its origins in the CDC. However, it is also active to a lesser extent in the federal prison system and several of the prison systems located in the southwest, such as Arizona, New Mexico, Colorado, and Texas. In the 1970s, the MM was known to have infiltrated publicly funded community jobs, drug, and halfway house programs in East Los Angeles, obtaining administrative positions that allowed them access to program funds. As noted, the MM has historically drawn its members from Los Angeles generally, East Los Angeles specifically, as well as from southern California Latino gangs. The members are made up almost entirely of first or second generation American-born Mexicans or Latinos. Sponsorship is normally required if someone wants to join the organization. The "wannabe" member is expected to perform some specific tasks. Once in, membership is for life and voluntary withdrawal as a member is strictly prohibited (Fong, 1990).

The MM has historically maintained an alliance with the Aryan Brotherhood (AB) that serves to the mutual advantage of both gangs. The EME is also aligned with La Cosa Nostra (LCN) and the New Mexico Syndicate, the latter being New Mexico's equivalent to the MM. The EME and AB frequently have been known to take contract "hits" for each other, to have mutual drug connections, and to work closely with each other in prison narcotic trafficking. The Black Guerrilla Family (BGF), the northern Mexicans (Nuestra Familia), and one faction of the Texas Syndicate, as well as all "Nortenos" (Mexican northerners) are MM enemies. The MM tends to recruit urban, barrio Latinos, whereas the Nuestra Familia recruits mainly Mexicans from primarily agricultural and rural California (Porter, 1982).

If an MM member disobeys an order or otherwise demonstrates disrespect or cowardice, he receives a physical beating or minor stabbing as a warning. Serious transgressions can result in death or having a contract placed on the offending member. Once a member is placed on a "hit" list usually he cannot usually remain in the general population and must be placed in protective custody. Transfer to another institution is not a viable means to avoid harm because the "contract" will follow him to whichever prison or system he is sent. EME members have been known to take on the guise of a "dropout" in order to obtain access to the protective custody unit to carry out a "hit." In order to convince institutional staff of their need for protective custody, an MM member seeking to be placed in protective custody may actually undergo a bogus assault by other EME members.

Institutional prisons or systems may confuse the MM with the Mexikanemi from Texas and care should be taken in evaluating these distinct prison gangs. Some prison staff members believe that Mexikanemi share identical tattoos with the MM, however, there are subtle differences that must be considered in classifying members from each of these groups. As noted above, MM members often refer to each other as "carnal" or brother, which is a slang term used by many working-class Latinos. The letter "M" (pronounced EME in Spanish) has historically been used to refer to the MM. Sometimes the "M" is tattooed or placed over a person's name in written correspondence to signify membership. In the past, many, if not most, MM members tattooed the letter "M" or the letters "EME" on their bodies to reflect membership. However, as correctional officers, probation or parole officers, and the police have come to use these tattoos as means of identifying MM member, many in the gang have chosen to use other symbols or merely shy away from tattooing anything that may be used to link them to the organization (U.S. Department of Justice, 1994).

SAM TORRES

References and Further Reading

Buentello, S., Robert, S., and Fong, R.E. 1991. Prison gang development: A theoretical model, *The Prison Journal,* 71, 2 (Fall-Winter), 3–14.

Champion, D.J. 1990. *Corrections in the United States: A Contemporary Perspective,* Englewood Cliffs, NJ: Prentice Hall Inc.

Clear, T.R. and Cole, G.F. 2000. *American Corrections,* Belmont, CA: Wadsworth/Thomson.

Cox, V. 1986. Prison gangs: Inmates battle for control, *Corrections Compendium,* 10, 9 (April), 1, 6–9.

Earley, P. 1992. *The Hot House: Life Inside Leavenworth Prison,* New York, NY: Bantam Books.

Fong, R.S. 1990. Organizational structure of prison gangs: A Texas case study, *Federal Probation Quarterly,* 54, 1 (March), 36–43.

Fong, R.S. and Buentello, S. 1991. Detection of prison gang development: An empirical assessment, *Federal Probation Quarterly,* 55, 1 (March), 66–69.

Buentello, S., Fong, R.S., and Vogel, R.E. 1991. Prison gang development: A theoretical model, *The Prison Journal,* 71, 2 (Fall-Winter), 3–14.

Fox, V.B. and Stinchcomb, J.B. 1994. *Introduction to Corrections,* Englewood Cliffs, NJ: Prentice Hall Career & Technology.

National Institute of Corrections 1991. *Management Strategies in Disturbances and with Gangs/Disruptive Groups,* Washington, DC: U.S. Government Printing Office, (October).

Porter, B. 1982. California prison gangs: The price of control, *Corrections Magazine,* 8, 6 (December), 6–19.

Quinn, J.F. 1999. *Corrections: A Concise Introduction,* Prospect Heights, IL: Waveland Press, Inc.

Silverman, I.J. 2001. *Corrections: A Comprehensive View,* Belmont, CA: Wadsworth/Thomson Learning.

U.S. Department of Justice 1994. *Security Threat Groups Symbols & Terminology Manual,* Washington, DC: U.S. Federal Bureau of Prisons Intelligence Section (September).

See also **Mexico, Crime and Justice in**

Organized Crime: Outlaw Motorcycle Clubs

Outlaw motorcycle clubs in the U.S. date from the years after World War II, when many combat veterans, particularly those residing in California, sought new outlets for feelings of hostility and alienation. Some found release in riding and in associating with others in motorcycle clubs. These clubs became a means of continued quasi-military camaraderie. And the motorcycle became a symbol of freedom from social responsibilities and restraints.

In 1948, in San Bernardino County, California, dedicated outlaws formed a new group and adopted a name favored by World War II fighter plane pilots—Hells Angels. In the early 1960s, police harassment and legal fees left the club on the brink of extinction. Thus, the Hells Angels, who had been exposed to the drug subculture through a tenuous relationship with the counterculture movement, turned to the sale of methamphetamine. The outlaw bikers, former military veterans who were rabid hawks, eventually broke with the counterculture over the Vietnam War. But the easy money they had found in drugs eventually moved the Hells Angels beyond the biker subculture and into organized crime.

The Outlaw Motorcycle Club and Organized Crime

The Hells Angels and the outlaw clubs that copied them have important attributes that equip them for organized crime: paramilitary organization, a strong sense of brotherhood, a code of secrecy, and a subcultural orientation that militates against cooperation with the police.

During the late 1960s and early 1970s, interest and membership in outlaw motorcycle clubs swelled because of the return of disgruntled veterans from the Vietnam War. The Hells Angels expanded rapidly, and the organization became international in scope, with about 85 chapters in 15 countries. In 1973, the club president, Ralph "Sonny" Barger, was convicted and imprisoned for the possession and sale of drugs. He was released in 1977, but other indictments against the Hells Angels soon followed. In 1985, more than a hundred Hells Angels across the U.S. were arrested in a major federal effort against the club's drug trafficking.

From the fun-loving and hell-raising clubs of the immediate post-World War II era, the Hells Angels and some other outlaw motorcycle clubs have developed into self-perpetuating, highly structured, disciplined organizations whose major source of income is from criminal activity. But not all of the estimated 500 outlaw motorcycle clubs are sophisticated criminal organizations. According to law enforcement officials in the U.S., only four clubs actually fit the definition: Hells Angels, Outlaws, Pagans, and Bandidos.

Hells Angels chapters are centered in California and the East Coast. The Outlaws were founded in 1959 in Chicago, and chapters are scattered in Michigan, Illinois, western New York, Ohio, western Pennsylvania, Oklahoma, Arkansas, Kentucky, North Carolina, Georgia, and Florida. The Pagans were founded in 1959 in Prince George's County, Maryland; chapters are centered on the East Coast. Although there are Pagan chapters in West Virginia and New Orleans, most are located in Pennsylvania. It is the only one of the "Big Four" that does not have international chapters, although it does have ties to outlaw bikers in Canada. The Bandidos were founded in 1966 in Houston. Chapters are centered in the far Northwest and in the South, particularly in Texas. Together these four groups have a combined membership of about 4000 white males. The Bandidos have been allied with the Outlaws, whereas the Hells Angels and the Outlaws have been at war since 1974.

Structure

Consistent with their founders' background as military veterans, the Hells Angels and outlaw clubs that have copied them exhibit a bureaucratic structure. Each has a written constitution and bylaws as well as a mother club that serves as the national or international headquarters. Any problems that involve a national outlaw club as a whole will usually be submitted to the mother club. The national secretary–treasurer is responsible for the club's finances, makes revisions in the club bylaws and records; and maintains the minutes and other club records. The national enforcer answers directly to the national president or to the mother club and may act as the president's bodyguard. In addition, he handles all special situations involving violations of club rules.

Each club chapter has a president, vice president, secretary–treasurer, enforcer, and sergeant at arms. There is also the road captain, who fulfills the role of logistician and security chief for club-sponsored runs, or motorcycle outings. Outlaw motorcycle clubs have several mandatory runs per year, and all members not otherwise incapacitated must participate with motorcycles (only large Harley-Davidson models) and full colors.

"Colors" are the official club insignia worn on the back of a denim jacket with the sleeves cut off or, in colder climes, a leather jacket. Colors may also be worn as a tattoo. Also sewed or pinned on the jacket are other "authorized" patches, which are usually quite offensive to conventional society. The clubs practice precision riding, and club runs are accomplished in a military-style formation.

Activities

The outlaw clubs are involved in distributing automatic weapons, explosives, and stolen motorcycles and motorcycle parts; providing exotic dancers and prostitutes for various sex-oriented establishments; and trafficking in LSD, PCP, cocaine, and methamphetamine. They have been particularly successful in exerting control over the methamphetamine market.

Although most bikers operate along the lines of short-term hedonism, some profits have been invested in a vast array of legitimate businesses, often for profit and sometimes as fronts for illegal activities. The outlaw clubs have a reliable pipeline of members and chapters for the flow of illicit goods, and the members are highly mobile and able to find support and safety in any city that has a club chapter.

The structure of criminal activities is not necessarily the same as its organizational structure. Economic activities may actually involve partnerships among members and include nonmember associates. For business purposes, each member is at the center of an action group that, although tied to every other member through the structure of the club, operates independently or in partnership—the formal structure of the motorcycle club is not necessarily the same as its economic structure. Although there is a relatively clear hierarchy within each of the four outlaw clubs, income-generating activities involve several smaller operationally independent units. Thus, outlaw motorcycle clubs are not criminal organizations; rather, they are organizations of criminals.

HOWARD ABADINSKY

References and Further Reading

Abadinsky, H. 1999. *Organized Crime,* Boston, MA: Allyn and Bacon, 1981; 6th ed., Belmont, CA: Wadsworth.
Lavigne, Y. 1987. *Hell's Angels: Taking Care of Business,* Toronto, Canada: Deneau and Wayne.
Lavigne, Y. 1997. *Hell's Angels: Into the Abyss,* Toronto, Canada: HarperCollins, 1996; New York, NY: HarperPaperbacks.
Wolf, D.R. 1991. *The Rebels: A Brotherhood of Outlaw Bikers,* Toronto, Canada: University of Toronto Press.

See also **Organized Crime: Activities and Extent; Organized Crime: Definitions and Models**

Organized Crime: Russian Mafia

Definition of Terms

To set the parameters for a discussion of the so-called Russian "mafia"—the popular characterization of Russian organized crime—it is necessary that three elemental terms be defined. The first is Russian. As was the case during the time of the Soviet Union, most Americans at least think of persons from that part of the world (i.e., from the countries that made up the USSR) as being Russians. Although Russia is the largest of the former Soviet states and there are many ethnic Russians who have immigrated, indeed including some who are criminals, not all of those popularly characterized as being part of the Russian mafia are actually Russian. Instead, some are, for example, Armenian, Georgian, Ukrainian, Azeri, or Chechen, or they are actually from Eastern Europe, such as Albanians. Thus, the phenomenon, known as the Russian mafia, is not strictly Russian.

The next term, organized crime, is best thought of as that crime committed by criminal groups whose existence has continuity over time and across crimes. Such organizations use systematic violence and corruption to facilitate their criminal activities, but unauthorized use of violence or attempts to corrupt public officials is discouraged and indeed may be punished. Organized crime is engaged in by criminal organizations that have the capacity to commit serious economic, physical, psychological, and societal harms.

Third, there is the notion of mafia. Strictly speaking, mafia is a very particular kind of organized crime, especially associated with Sicily and southern Italy. Made members of the mafia—inducted in formal ceremonies—are considered to be men of honor. They are bound by traditions that have been passed down for generations, such as respecting *omerta*, or the vow of silence. The Sicilian Mafia's traditional business has been providing protection and acting in quasi-governmental roles. Although the term mafia has come to be used indiscriminately to refer to all kinds of criminal organizations, mafia is not synonymous with organized crime.

Origins

Organized crime has a 400-year history in Russia. This history is characterized by blurred distinctions between what was legal and illegal and what was public versus private. It is also characterized by a rather feeble commitment to the rule-of-law. Stealing the Russian czar's timber, for example, was not considered criminal, whereas one peasant stealing anything from another was. During the Russian Revolution of 1917, Marxist political revolutionaries called Bolsheviks collaborated closely with professional criminals to overthrow first the czar and then the first short-lived revolutionary government.

Russian organized crime evolved and was shaped by the peculiar characteristics of the Soviet economy and politics. In most instances, organized crime arises to meet market demands for goods and services that are either illegal, regulated, or simply in short supply. The demand for illegal drugs is one example, but arms, cigarettes, sex workers, and even babies could be included. Fulfilling the demand requires organizational capacity—thus the need for criminal organization. From the perspective of the criminals themselves, the base instinct of greed and the thirst for money and power propels organized crime.

Goods and services were in chronically short supply during the seven decades of Soviet power. This led to or fed the emergence of what was known as a shadow economy, and to a black market. That shadow economy produced legal goods "off the books," to be sold or bartered illegally. The black market usually dealt in illegal goods, such as prohibited items from the West or drugs. Practitioners in a variety of these activities during the Soviet period were referred to as mafias. Soviet citizens used *blat*—connections and informal networks—to access the black market and shadow economy. Years of experience with these practices had at least two effects that are relevant to the current nature of Russian organized crime: they created a distinct mentality about conniving to survive and they stimulated the development of a shadowy entrepreneurial class used to operating outside the law.

The offshoots of this unusual history include the current monetarization of organized crime in Russia, as dealing in goods and services has been shifting to dealing in currency. This inheritance also extends to the crony capitalism and pervasive corruption that are so characteristic of Russia's economy and politics today.

During the 1960s, organized crime in Soviet Russia evolved into a three-tiered, pyramid structure. The top tier was made up of high-level government and Communist Party bureaucrats—those referred to as the *apparatchiks* and the *nomenklatura*. The middle tier was composed of the shadow economy (underground) operators and the black marketeers. The bottom tier consisted of professional criminals. The latter included the *vory v zakone* or thieves-in-law. The *vory* were products of the Soviet gulag or prison system, and were the most sophisticated of the professional criminals. They lived within a set of rules known as the thieves' law, dedicated themselves to a life of crime, and rejected involvement with the legitimate world. In many respects, although not all, they bore a resemblance to the traditional notion of mafia—more so than any other form of Russian organized crime.

Russian Organized Crime Today

Organized crime has been able to penetrate Russian business and state enterprises to a degree that is unheard of in most other countries of the world. This penetration takes place in a variety of ways. Protection rackets are operated by what are called *kryshas*, Russian for "roofs." Nearly every business in cities such as Moscow and St. Petersburg and Ekaterinburg must make extortion payments for "protection" by a *krysha*. This protection sometimes comes in the form of acquiring unwanted partners who use their muscle to grab shares of businesses.

As the former Soviet Union has moved to privatize its vast state holdings, selling to private owners what was previously owned by the central government, organized crime in partnership with corrupt officials has engaged in the wholesale exploitation of the process. They have collaborated to buy up valuable properties at fire sale prices via insider trading information. What has resulted from these perversions of economic reform is thus not an economy governed by market principles but instead a predatory economy.

Russian organized crime is currently evolving into new forms that are diminishing the role of the old *vory v zakone*. Professionalization, globalization, legalization, and patrimonialism characterize these new forms. Their skill at white-collar crimes (especially offenses against banking and financial institutions) give witness to the professionalism of the new Russian criminals. At the same time, a Russian diaspora is developing—particularly in Canada, Israel, and the U.S. This diaspora provides the critical mass for the development of organized crime in these countries. Globalization is also evident in such activities as worldwide money laundering and in the trafficking of a variety of goods and persons. Through effective use of the mass media and charitable donations, and through heavy donations to political campaigns and electing their own candidates to political office, Russian organized crime has also moved to legalize or legitimize itself. Finally, patrimonialism—for example, via insider trading, the issuance of preferential licenses, and the illegal banking of state funds—is the other major force driving organized crime into the center of "normal" political activity. Whereas in most societies organized crime is an outside threat external to the society, in Russia organized crime is an internal threat, pervasive and centered on the political and economic mainstream.

Needs and Problems in Combating Russian Organized Crime

The current environment in Russia is very conducive to the emergence and sustenance of organized crime. In the manner of hyenas and vultures, corrupt officials and criminals demonstrate their greed in carving up the body of the old Soviet State. The supply or demand factor is also very apparent in such criminal activities as drug smuggling, arms trafficking, and human trafficking. Moscow is a crossroads in the thriving flesh trade in young women and girls. Corruption is widespread, as is violence, appearing in such chilling forms as contract killings. Business or political rivals are often the victims of these contract killings that are carried out by professional killers.

Among the structural tools any society needs to resist and combat organized crime are an aware and active civil society, a culture of lawfulness, and a strong public disgust for crime and corruption. Such society and culture do not now exist in Russia. Also needed, but likewise in still quite an anemic state, is an independent and incorruptible legal and judicial system.

Russia does not have effective legal tools for fighting organized crime, nor does it have an effective law enforcement system. The police are out-manned, out-gunned, and under-resourced. They are also hobbled by corruption of both a systemic (system-wide) and a situational kind. The latter refers to individual instances of corruption that arise out of immediate circumstances, for example, a very poorly paid policeman with a family to feed accepts a small bribe to ignore a traffic violation.

The legacy of the *nomenklatura* is the absence of a viable, independent, and professional civil service. The symbiotic relationship among business, crime, and government presents an enormous challenge that so far shows no signs of being overcome. Until these fundamental problems are solved, Russia will not be able to effectively excise its organized crime cancer.

Impact in the U.S.

Russian criminals are known to have been active in the U.S. since the mid-1970s. Their criminal activity in the beginning was, however, quite limited, and localized in the main Russian speaking community of Brighton Beach in Brooklyn, New York. During the 1980s, the numbers of emigres to the U.S. from the former Soviet Union grew, and the numbers allegedly involved in crime likewise increased. The nature of their crimes also began to change, becoming more sophisticated and organized. For instance, a series of bootleg gasoline tax evasion schemes netted their perpetrators millions of dollars. Interestingly, although these types of crimes required organization to carry them off, the criminal networks engaged in them did not possess the characteristics of organized crime groups described earlier. They did not have continuity over time and hierarchical structures. They did not attempt to gain monopolization of the criminal market, nor did they systematically use violence and corruption to further their ends. They also did not then, and most importantly do not now, have any of the characteristics associated with traditional notions of what is the mafia (especially *omerta*).

It is estimated that there are approximately 12–15 "Russian" criminal groups currently operating in the U.S. that have international ties. Their estimated total size is 500–600 members. Because of their propensity for engaging in extortion and protection rackets, violence is one of their defining characteristics. But not surprising given their history, the predominant crimes of persons from the former Soviet Union in the U.S. are frauds and scams. The criminal networks they have established are diverse in the criminal opportunities they exploit, and they reflect a blend of legal and illegal activities. In sum, their crimes reflect their ancestry in the old system of *blat,* the black market, and the shadow economy.

Is there a Russian Mafia? In Russia itself there are criminal organizations that look and act like a mafia. Many others that are similarly labeled, however, do not. And it is clearly the case that what we see in the U.S. is neither Russian nor Mafia. The promiscuous and inappropriate application of this label obscures distinctions among criminal networks and lends to some relatively minor criminal groups an air of criminal importance they do not deserve. The results only make the job of law enforcement more difficult. In the end, it is important to keep in mind that we are still in the early stages of the evolution of Russian crime in America. Time and the degree of success of law enforcement in combating it will tell us where this evolution will ultimately lead.

JIM FINCKENAUER

References and Further Reading

Finckenauer, J.O. and Voronin, Y.A. 2001. *The Threat of Russian Organized Crime,* Washington, DC: National Institute of Justice International Series on Crime and Justice.

Finckenauer, J.O. and Waring, E. 1998. *Russian Mafia in America: Immigration, Culture, and Crime,* Boston, MA: Northeastern University Press.

Ledeneva, A.V. and Kurkchiyan, M., Eds. 2000. *Economic Crime in Russia,* The Hague, the Netherlands: Kluwer Law International.

Robinson, J. 2000. *The Merger,* Woodstock, NY: The Overlook Press.

Vaksberg, A. 1991. *The Soviet Mafia,* London, UK: Weidenfeld.

Williams, P., Ed. 1997. *Russian Organized Crime: The New Threat?* London, UK: Frank Cass.

See also **Organized Crime: Activities and Extent; Organized Crime: Definitions and Models; Russia, Crime, and Justice in Modern; Soviet Union: Crime and Justice in the**

Organized Crime: Sicilian Mafia

The Mafia is a phenomenon that evolved out of the cultural history of the Southern Italian island of Sicily. For more than 1000 years, Sicily was ruled by foreigners: Byzantine, Arab, Norman, and Spanish. This history led to the development of a culture that stresses the variables necessary for survival in a hostile environment. Sicilians developed an ideal of manliness, *omertá,* that included noncooperation with authorities, self-control in the face of adversity, and the *vendetta,* which dictated that any offense or slight to the family (*famiglia*) had to be avenged, no matter what the consequences or how long it took. Neither government nor church was to be trusted. The only basis of loyalty was *famiglia,* an extended clan composed of blood relatives, including distant cousins, aunts, and uncles. The clan was supplemented through godparenthood, through which carefully selected outsiders became members of the family.

The family consisted of a structural hierarchy headed by a patriarch, the *capo di famiglia,* who demanded absolute loyalty from clan members. In the *famiglia,* physical aggression was rewarded and the strongest member of the domestic group assumed the dominant status. The family was to be made prosperous, respected, and feared. Enlarged by strategic marriages and strengthened by alliances with families of equal status, the most powerful family constellation dominated a particular geographic area. Although foreigners controlled the outward symbols of authority—the police and courts—de facto rule remained in the hands of the *capo* of the leading *famiglia.*

The Italian Renaissance had little impact on Sicily, which remained mired in feudalism and dependent on agriculture. The succession of foreign rulers ended in 1860 with a revolution against (Spanish) Bourbon rule that eventually united Italy. For the *contadini* (peasants) of Sicily, however, little changed. Instead of foreign repression, they were repressed through an alliance between the northern industrial bourgeoisie and the Sicilian landed aristocracy.

Mafia Emerges

The government in Rome imposed an onerous tax policy on Sicily—landowners escaped heavy taxation, which fell disproportionately on the peasants. Meanwhile, the landed aristocracy, actually absentee landlords, either hired or rented their estates to a *gabelloto,* a manager who was often a representative of the dominant *famiglia*. The *gabelloto* ruled over the estate with brute force, protecting it from bandits, peasant organizations, and unions. He was assisted by *famiglia* and *amici* (friends) who were hired because they were "men of respect," quick to use violence and widely feared. The *gabelloto* did not usually perform his overseer's functions in person—often he did not even show up on the estate that had been entrusted to his custody. He simply allowed his name to be mentioned, with the declaration that the estate was under his protection. Control over access to farmland allowed the *gabelloto* to act as a patron to his peasants, a mediator between them and official power. In league with the landlords, he fought land reform, labor unions, and revolution. The *gabelloto* and the network of relationships surrounding him became known as the Mafia, which protected and ripped off the owners of the great estates while protecting and exploiting the sharecroppers who worked the estates.

The term *mafia* is apparently Sicilian Arabic derived from terms meaning to protect and to act as guardian; it connotes power, integrity, and strength. A *mafioso* does resort to police or courts in his private quarrels, but makes himself safe by gaining a reputation for toughness—he settles his differences by violence. He recognizes no obligation except those of the code of *omertá*. Thus, *mafia* is a state of mind, a way of life—not a secret criminal organization. The culture of *mafia* is shared by all Sicilians, the honest and the criminal: that they must side with friends, defend dignity at all costs, and never allow the smallest slight to go unavenged; they must keep secrets and be wary of government authorities. Mafia, the criminal organization, could not flourish without the culture of *mafia*.

The Mafia *Cosca*

At the center of the Mafia, the criminal organization is the *capomafioso*, around whom other *mafiosi* gather, forming a *cosca*. The word *cosca* refers to the leaves of an artichoke, the *capomafioso* being the globe's heart. The typical *cosca* rarely has more than 15 or 20 members, and at the center are four or five blood relatives. The *cosca* is devoid of any rigid organization; it is simply the "friends of friends."

Standardized rituals around the Mafia developed in the 1870s. Once initiated into the *cosca*, the *mafioso* became a *compadre*; this practice is based on the custom fictional kinship or godparenthood. Each village has its own *cosca*, larger ones have more. The *cosca* establishes working relationships with other *cosche*, respecting territories and boundaries. Collectively they are the Mafia.

The Role of the Mafia

Mafiosi were often not only tolerated by their communities but respected as standard bearers of a more equitable system of justice than that provided by the state. The *mafioso* is in a position to provide protection where the state is unwilling or unable to provide arbitration services superior to those available from local judges, especially to the poor person who cannot afford a lawyer, or for those whose justice is of a social, not a legal, nature—the pregnant daughter whose seducer refuses to marry her.

In southern Italy an aura of mistrust and suspicion pervades personal and business relationships—a dilemma the *mafioso* could overcome by offering himself as a guarantor—"Mafia insurance." The *mafioso* serves as a guarantor for price rigging and collusive bidding on building projects. For legitimate entrepreneurs he provides insurance against otherwise untrustworthy suppliers or customers and will limit competition by restricting market entry. He acts as a guarantor so that persons who do not trust one another can transact business with a significant degree of confidence; this refers to legitimate entrepreneurs and, most particularly, the illegitimate, who cannot turn to the police or courts to remedy their grievances.

The Mafia became the only political force that mattered in Sicily, and governments in Rome eagerly courted their aid. In return, the Mafia was able to operate without any significant interference from government authority. The situation remained unchanged until the rise of Benito Mussolini and the Fascist state.

Mussolini and the Mafia

Mussolini's rise to power in the 1920s had important implications for the Mafia. Cosca leaders attempted to win Mussolini's support by influencing the election of Fascists. Thus, in the elections of 1922, no Fascist was elected to Parliament from Sicily. In the elections of 1924, with Mafia support, 38 Fascists were elected out of the 57 representatives from Sicily.

Nevertheless, a totalitarian regime does not tolerate pockets of authority that are not under its control, and Mussolini moved to destroy the Mafia. Elections were abolished in 1925, depriving the Mafia of its major instrument of alliance with government and an important basis for its immunity from criminal justice. The other important basis was intimidation. However, Fascist courts trying criminal cases in which members of the Mafia were implicated found it just as impossible to obtain convictions. Mussolini responded by investing Prefect Cesare Mori of Lombardy, a career police officer, with emergency police powers and sending him after the Mafia.

Mori assembled a small army and set about the task of purging the island of *mafiosi*; repression became savage. Many *mafiosi* were sent to prison, killed, or tortured, but also many left-wingers were called *mafiosi* for political expediency. The Fascists replaced the Mafia as intermediaries and maintainers of Sicilian law and order.

Many Mafia bosses assumed important positions within the regime, and the Fascists failed to significantly transform social and economic conditions upon which the Mafia depended. Many *mafiosi* awaited "liberation," which came in the form of the Allied landing in 1943. The Mafia quickly reemerged as soon as fascism fell. The campaign against the Mafia did succeed in driving some important *mafiosi* out of Sicily. They traveled to the U.S. at an opportune time, during the Prohibition era, and took up important positions in a newly emerging form of organized crime.

Nuovo Mafia or Cosa Nostra

The end of the World War II brought a Mafia renaissance in Sicily as a vacuum in local leadership was filled by former *capimafiosi*. Many became town mayors under the allied military government, and they violently thwarted the efforts of trade unionists, socialists, communists, and land reformers. A brief flirtation with Separatism—seceding from the mainland in favor of affiliation with the U.S.—was discarded in 1946, when the government in Rome announced Sicilian autonomy. In return, the most important *capomafioso*, Calògero Vizzini ("Don Calò"), the illiterate son of a peasant father, pledged support for the Christian Democratic Party. In return, *capimafiosi* were frequently accorded places of honor in the party.

When Don Calò died of natural causes in 1954, he left an estate worth several million dollars. He was the last of the old-style *capomafiosi*, characterized by modesty in both speech and dress, a rural animal holding sway over the countryside. The behavior of the old *mafioso* had power as his primary goal. The modern *mafioso*, is a materialist for whom power is simply a means to achieve wealth; and he exudes conspicuous consumption. The new *mafioso* is not bound by the traditions of the rural *cosca*. He dresses like a successful businessman, sometimes a bit flashy, like the American gangster whose pattern he seems to have adopted. The New Mafia—often called *Cosa Nostra* ("our thing") by its members—has a distinctly American tint, the result of American gangsters being deported to Sicily and interacting with their Sicilian counterparts.

Cosa Nostra resorted to robbery and kidnapping to accumulate the capital necessary to be a player in legal endeavors such as the construction industry and in the illicit heroin and cocaine marketplaces. Drug money has changed the functioning and mode of organization of the Mafia in which luxury and extravagant consumerism has become the norm. The New Mafia also has continued the *pizzo*, protection money extorted from large and small businesses. But financial considerations reportedly play a secondary role in this enterprise, being primarily a Mafia way of maintaining territorial domination.

The contrast between the "Two Mafias" is evidenced by a conflict between the *capomafiosi* of Corleone in the immediate postwar years. Michele Navarra was a medical doctor and a representative of the Old Mafia. Luciano Liggio, born in 1925, represented the New Mafia. At the age of 19, Liggio became the youngest *gabelloto* in the history of Sicily (his predecessor was murdered). Navarra was the inspector of health for the area, head of the town's only hospital (his predecessor was also mysteriously murdered). In the tradition of Don Calò, he also trafficked in stolen beef and served as chairman of the local branch of the Christian Democratic Party. Luciano Liggio was his most violent assistant. Liggio and an associate hanged a trade unionist who was a threat to Navarra's power, and the murder was witnessed by a shepherd boy. In a state of shock after telling his story, the boy fainted and was taken to the hospital. There, an injection from Dr. Navarra ended the boy's life. Navarra was convicted of the murder and sentenced to 5-year exile in Calabria—he returned home after a few months.

With his followers, Liggio began to develop activities of his own. Having little in common with the Mafia presided over by Don Calò except its laws of secrecy and the vendetta, Liggio chose to control the supply of meat to the Palermo market rather than raising livestock. He drove out all of the tenant farmers on the estate under his protection, burning down their houses, and replaced them with day laborers. He recruited gunmen, and anybody who crossed him was summarily shot.

The old Mafia benefited from feudal conditions, living off the control of the land and cheap labor. When a dam was proposed for the town of Corleone to harness the river water flowing to the ocean, Dr. Navarra vetoed it because he made money from the water pumped from artesian wells. *Cosa Nostra*, oriented toward capitalistic change, recognized the profits that could be earned from control over building projects. Although Navarra and his followers were living in the 19th century, Liggio was a man of the times. With Navarra in control, nothing would change, and the New Mafia recognized this reality. In 1958, 15 of Liggio's men ambushed Dr. Navarra's car; 210 bullets were found in his body. One by one, the remaining followers of Navarra were murdered, and Luciano Liggio became the undisputed *capomafioso* of the Corleone *cosca*.

Mafia Warfare

During the 1960s, the emerging Mafia clans engaged in a bitter struggle for dominance. The struggle led to an emigration of *mafiosi* similar to that experienced during the reign of Mussolini. This proved to be quite beneficial as these overseas *mafiosi* provided the links for greater international operations, including a wholesale entry into the lucrative cocaine trade.

In 1967, the Mafia war led to the trial of 114 *mafiosi*, and Luciano Liggio emerged as the most powerful *capomafioso*. In 1974, Liggio was convicted of the murder of Dr. Navarra and sentenced to life imprisonment. His right-hand man, Salvatore (Totò) Riina, became head of the Corleone *cosca*. A short, stocky man, the son of poor farmers with only an elementary school education, Riina is known as "The Beast" for ordering mass killings and personally participating in some of them. He formed private alliances with rising members of many Mafia clans, planted his own men in others, and then with a reign of terror came to dominate the Mafia—at a cost of nearly 1000 lives. Many members of his *cosca* are close relatives, including his son Giovanni and his nephew Mario Salvatore Grizzaffi.

After being tried in absentia and sentenced to life imprisonment for murder and drug trafficking, Riina became the most wanted man in Italy. He was able to avoid authorities for more than 23 years, partly because photographs of him were out of date. While living as a fugitive, Riina was married to the sister of a powerful *mafioso* by a Mafia priest (who was eventually defrocked), honeymooned in Venice, sired four children, and continued to oversee the activities of his Mafia clan.

One of the victims of Riina's campaign to centralize and control the Mafia was *capomafioso* Tommaso Buscetta, who lost ten relatives, including two sons, a brother, a nephew, a son-in-law, and two brothers-in-law. In 1995, another Buscetta relative, his 45-year-old nephew, was murdered in Palermo. In 1983, Buscetta who had escaped to Brazil, was arrested on an international warrant. He attempted to commit suicide with a strychnine pill. When he recovered, Buscetta agreed to cooperate with American and Italian authorities. In 1987, with the help of Buscetta and other informants, the Italian government convicted 338 *mafiosi* in the largest mass trial (452

defendants—referred to as the maxitrial) of its kind ever held in Italy.

Cosa Nostra Offensive

The Christian Democratic Party had ruled Italy from the end of the Second World War and the party's bedrock of support was in southern Italy, in particular the *mafiosi* and their circle of friends in Sicily. In 1987, angry over the government's maxitrial and the failure of the Christian Democrats to intervene, Totò Riina ordered a switch in votes: although the Christian Democrats increased their strength throughout the rest of Italy, in Palermo only Mafia-backed candidates won.

As the political role of *mafiosi* changed, so too did their ability to act as brokers between peasant and officialdom. The *mafioso* was no longer *un uomo di rispetto* but simply an urban gangster in the American tradition; that is, a predatory criminal without popular roots or popular backing. The New Mafia reflects the emerging *Mezzogiorno*. The south is changing; modernization, fed by government-sponsored public works, is slowly encroaching on feudal ways. Above all, the mark of respect has more to do with one's wealth than with one's name or reputation. It was power, not wealth, that the traditional *mafioso* pursued: "The possession of wealth, regarded by the traditional *mafioso* as one among the proofs and results of a man's capacity to make himself respected, becomes, in the 1960s and 1970s, meritorious in itself." Family wealth, not family honor, is a reason for violence: "Wealth, in a word, becomes intrinsically honourable and confers honour on its possessors" (Arlacchi, 1986, 60).

Beginning in 1971, the Mafia has assassinated investigative, judicial, and political officials, something that was anathema to the old Mafia. Offenses against symbols of authority were foreign to the methods of a Mafia that, considering itself an authority and surrogate for the state, wanted to preserve and respect certain values, in particular, respect for authority. In 1992, the prosecutor who helped gather evidence for the Mafia maxitrial, Judge Giovanni Falcone, was killed along with his wife and three bodyguards, when a half ton of TNT was detonated by remote control on a road near Palermo. The killers obviously had inside information about Falcone's movements. His murder led to an anti-Mafia demonstration by about 40,000 persons in Palermo, a remarkable occurrence for that city. But it did not prevent the Mafia from striking again. On July 20, 1992, Paolo Borsellino, Falcone's replacement as Palermo's chief public prosecutor and head of a new anti-Mafia superagency, was killed along with five police bodyguards; 175 pounds of a

Czech-made plastic explosive placed under a car was detonated while Borsellino was walking outside an apartment building where his mother and sister resided. The government responded by dispatching 7000 troops to Sicily in a highly publicized anti-Mafia campaign, and Palermo reelected a crusading anti-Mafia mayor. The soldiers were withdrawn in 1998 because Italy wanted to cast off an image of a European nation requiring a peacekeeping force to occupy its own territory. The day after troops were withdrawn, the police arrested scores of *mafiosi*, including 20 members of the Corleone *cosca*, whose boss, Vito Vitale, was already in custody. And there have been results: murders in Palermo that averaged 130–140 annually, fell to fewer than 10 in 1997.

The violence that gained Riina his nickname also drove *mafiosi* to the authorities seeking protection from "the Beast." In 1992, Italy enacted a witness protection law. The cooperation of *mafiosi* is believed to be behind the capture of the 62-year-old Don Totò, arrested in his car on a Palermo street on January 16, 1993. He and his driver were unarmed. Later that year, Riina was ordered imprisoned for life by a Palermo court and, like Palermo, his home city of Corleone elected an anti-Mafia mayor. Officials arrested other leading *mafiosi*, including Riina's heir apparent, who had been a fugitive for 11 years; the heads of the Neapolitan Camorra and Calabrian *'Ndrangheta* and hundreds of their followers were also arrested. Two years later, Leoluca Bagarella, 53, Riina's brother-in-law and boss of the Corleone *cosca*, was captured. He had been a fugitive since 1991 and is reputed to be behind attacks against the state, including the bombing of the Uffizi. He is believed responsible for moving the Corleone *cosca* into drug trafficking. Riina's commanding role in the Mafia was taken by Giovanni Brusca, who with his brothers are part of a *cosca* in the region of San Giuseppe Iato, just outside Palermo, once headed by their father. In 1996, at age 39, Giovanni was arrested for a 1992 murder—he is alleged to have pushed the remote control button that set off the bomb that killed prosecutor Falcone.

As a result of the assassinations of government officials, the New Mafia lost the support of important elements of Italian society. In 1982, Salvatore Cardinal Pappalardo, the Sicilian-born archbishop of Palermo, led Sicilian priests in a vocal campaign against the Mafia, reversing decades of church indifference toward and even tolerance of local dons. Later that year, while on a visit to the island of Sicily, Pope John Paul issued an attack on the Mafia. In 1993, the Mafia struck back at its critics in the Church: a 56-year-old priest who spoke out against the Mafia was shot to death in front of his rectory in a Palermo slum. And as part of its campaign of terror, the Mafia bombed two of Rome's most venerable churches, in addition to other bombings in Rome, Milan, and Florence that killed ten people and left dozens injured. By 1993, increasing scandal and the collapse of European communism finally led to the demise of the Christian Democratic Party, which, despite its corruption and ties to the Mafia, had been the only viable alternative to the Communist Party. As a sign of its current weakness, in 1999, the president of Italy led an anti-Mafia demonstration in the notorious city of Corleone on a day dedicated to the victims of the Mafia. Despite its weakened condition, the pool of Mafia prospects remains strong, the result of an unemployment rate approaching 60% among the youth of Sicily.

The greater political and economic unity that emerged with the formation of the European Community and the breakup of the Communist bloc provides new opportunities for Mafia, Camorra, and *'Ndrangheta* clans to move drugs, firearms, extortionate practices, and laundered money into northern Italy and across national boundaries. The old Mafia was "hampered by the *cult of honour,* which obligated them to squander their time and resources in gaining supremacy over their rivals, and by the fact that their income was drawn from parasitic activities: in consequence, they were unable to amass the large cash sums needed to get involved at the highest levels of the world drugs import–export circuit" (Arlacchi, 1986, 203). The New Mafia is under no such cultural constraints, and activities in the construction industry allowed New Mafia firms to amass the money necessary to invest in large-scale drug trafficking.

Profits from drug trafficking have put the Mafia all over Italy. The profits generated from its illegal business, particularly drugs, cannot easily be reinvested in these same enterprises, so these cash-rich criminals have spread their investments throughout Europe. For example, 14 Camorra members were arrested for using drug money to purchase restaurants and supermarkets in Germany and Spain, whereas others invested in casinos and real estate in France. There is hardly a European city without mob representatives who have forged profitable ties with local criminals. As if to emphasize this point, in 1992, Italy issued arrest warrants for fugitive Mafia suspects in the Netherlands, France, and Germany. There are indications of *mafiosi* forming ties with criminal groups in Eastern Europe, as they had with Colombia cocaine organizations. But excesses at home, the vigorous government response, and the increasing number of informers has weakened the Mafia.

HOWARD ABADINSKY

References and Further Reading

Arlacchi, P. 1993. *Men of Dishonor: Inside the Sicilian Mafia,* New York, NY: William Morrow.

Arlacchi, P. 1986. *Mafia Business: The Mafia Ethic and the Spirit of Capitalism,* London, UK: Verso.

Barzini, L. 1972. *The Italians,* New York, NY: Bantam.

Blok, A. 1974. *The Mafia of a Sicilian Village, 1860–1960: A Study of Violent Peasant Entrepreneurs,* New York, NY: Harper and Row.

Boissevain, J. 1974. *Friends of Friends: Networks, Manipulators and Coalitions,* Oxford, UK: Basil Blackwell.

Catanzaro, R. 1992. *Men of Respect: A Social History of the Sicilian Mafia.* New York, NY: Free Press.

della Porta, D. and Vannucci, A. 1999. *Corrupt Exchanges: Actors, Resources, and Mechanisms of Political Corruption,* New York, NY: Walter de Gruyter.

Gambetta, D. 1993. *The Sicilian Mafia: The Business of Private Protection,* Cambridge, MA: Harvard University Press.

Hess, H. 1973. *Mafia and Mafiosi: The Structure of Power,* Lexington, MA: D.C. Heath.

Pantaleone, M. 1966. *The Mafia and Politics,* New York, NY: Coward and McCann.

Stille, A. 1995. *Exquisite Cadavers: The Mafia and the Death of the First Italian Republic,* New York, NY: Pantheon.

See also **Organized Crime: Italian American Mafia**

Organized Crime: The Law

Introduction

Organized crime has become as familiar throughout the world as McDonald's and running water. It can be found in every industrialized country and has intertwined itself among legitimate commerce and government to the extent that actual size and figures of its prevalence cannot be determined. Thus, enforcing the laws passed to fight organized crime is analogous to treating cancer—you eradicate it in one area only to have it appear in another. As a result, today more than ever federal law enforcement and investigatory agencies find themselves collaborating as partners because of the complex nature of 21st century organized crime.

Current Conditions

Significant federal prosecutions in the 1980s and 1990s have placed the "old-time" Italian and Sicilian Mafia bosses of the 26 major U.S. Mafia "families" in prison or exile because of the Racketeer Influenced and Corrupt Organizations (RICO) Act of 1970. The new face of organized crime has become much more multicultural to include the Russian Mafia, Colombian drug cartels, Japanese yakuza, Chinese Triads, and a multitude of ethnic inner-city street gangs. This new form of organized crime is much smarter, sophisticated, and technologically savvy than the Mustache Petes of Hollywood's yesteryear.

Crimes and Laws

Changes in the face of organized crime also calls for changes in how organized crime is investigated and prosecuted. As will be seen below, many of the laws promulgated do not specifically address "organized crime," but rather address "organized crime activity." Three organized crime activities and their corresponding laws will be discussed as well as mutual legal assistance and issues pertaining to extradition will be discussed.

Trafficking in Persons

Millions of men, women, and children around the world are being held captive because of the illegal trafficking in persons for labor and sex. Organized crime (OC) groups lure these victims with promises of legitimate and rewarding jobs, benefits, and travel. The victims soon realize that their travel and ID papers are seized upon arrival at their destination, they are obligated to pay an enormous debt for relocation, and are subject to brutal beatings if their income is not satisfactory to their owners. The victims do not know where to go for help to get out of this situation, and are afraid of the local police authorities and the gangsters who placed them in this situation. A recent U.S. government estimate states that between 800,000 and 900,000 people per year are trafficked worldwide.

The Trafficking Victims Protection Act of 2000 defines a "severe form of trafficking in persons" as:

a. sex trafficking in which a commercial sex act is induced by force, fraud, or coercion, or in which the person inducted to perform such act has not attained 18 years of age; or

b. the recruitment, harboring, transportation, provision, or obtaining of a person for labor or services, through the use of force, fraud, or coercion for the purpose of subjection to involuntary servitude and peonage, debt bondage, or slavery.

Countries are rated as follows according to the Trafficking Victims Protection Act: Tier I: countries whose governments fully comply with the Act's minimum standards; Tier II: countries whose governments do not fully comply with the Act's minimum standards but are making significant efforts to bring themselves into compliance with those standards; and Tier III: countries whose governments do not fully comply with the minimum standards and are not making significant efforts to do so.

Money Laundering

Section 326 of the USA Patriot Act (USAPA), enacted after 9/11, is now a new and important part of the Bank Secrecy Act (BSA) and Anti-Money Laundering (AML) compliance programs. This section is intended to be both a sword and a shield against international money laundering and terrorist financing, and should also help in preventing forms of fraud (including identity theft). Institutions may adopt the minimum elements of a customer identification program (CIP) set forth in this section, but may also develop their own risk-based CIP.

An institution's CIP will be triggered any time a new customer, whether an individual or legal entity, opens a new account. This applies to owners of the account, not signatories. The section requires four minimum elements:

1. Identity verification procedures;
2. Verification record keeping;
3. Government list comparison (procedures for determining whether a customer appears on any list of known or suspected terrorist organizations issued by the federal government); and
4. Notice to customers (procedures for providing customers with adequate notice that the financial institution is requesting information to verify their identities).

Attus Technologies provides regulatory compliance software called "WatchDOG SSN," "WatchDOG PHOTO ID," and WatchDOG CIP."

Highlights Include:

Nearly half of all Federal money laundering matters were referred in the six geographic areas defined as High Intensity Financial Crimes Areas by the U.S. Departments of Treasury and Justice; About 60% of laundering/racketeering (Title 18) offenses prosecuted involved an underlying property offense (embezzlement or fraud); about 17% involved drug trafficking; and about 7% involved racketeering or violations of customs laws.

Offenders convicted of money laundering face prison terms of up to 20 years, fines up to $500,000.00 or twice the value of the property involved, and possible criminal and civil forfeiture related to the value of the property or funds involved." (U.S. Dept. of Justice)

The bulk of Federal money laundering investigations and enforcement strategies focus on the underlying criminal offenses that produce the illicit funds. Law enforcement uses a "follow-the-money" approach to trace illegal monies from such crimes as drug trafficking, health care fraud, and terrorism. U.S. attorneys may apply the laundering/racketeering statutes when a financial transaction involved the proceeds and/or concealment of the money source for any of over 250 offenses or specified unlawful activities (SUA's).

Other acts passed to aid in the prosecution of money-laundering or illegal banking operations include:

- The Bank Secrecy Act of 1970 (BSA)
- The Money Laundering Control Act (1986)
- The Anti-Drug Abuse Act (1988)
- The Money Laundering Suppression Act (1994)
- The Money Laundering and Financial Crimes Strategy Act (1998)
- The Strengthening America Act by Providing Appropriate Tools; Required to Intercept and Obstruct Terrorism (USA PATRIOT) Act of 2001

Gambling or Gaming

Gambling or gaming can be defined as the betting of valuables on games of chance. In England and the U.S., gambling was not a common law crime if conducted privately. Even in colonial America, however, gambling was liable to rankle public opinion because it was often associated with rowdy activities and could produce debtors that would burden society.

Although there is no general consensus, many theorists feel that illegal industries such as gambling, are very important to local economies and play a large role in community decision making. According to Liddick, a recognized organized crime expert, "In some instances, criminal industries have even been the source of local political change. The case can be made that OC is a "community social institution," and is in many ways functional. Providing highly demanded products and services like sex, gambling, and drugs provides jobs for the unemployed, capital for re-investment in the community, and a non-violent alternative to more predatory crimes like robbery and burglary." (Liddick, 1999)

Along the early U.S. western frontier, gambling and prostitution enterprises kept cattle and mining towns such as Abilene and Dodge wild and lawless. Faro, a game where "the dealer drew only two cards, paying off those who held similar cards on the first draw and collecting from card holders on the second," (Liddick, 1999) was extremely popular and has been credited with being one of the main reasons gambling was transformed into a widespread form of OC activity.

The proliferation of businesses catering to the pursuit of human pleasure has been tightly regulated by states, "creating a climate for criminal conspiracies that thrive on the systematic avoidance of regulations, i.e. gambling, prostitution, and illicit drugs" (Liddick, 1999).

At the end of World War II, Las Vegas had a population of 20,000 and not much in the way of a thriving industry. Twenty years later, the town had grown to ten times its post-WWII size, nurtured and built by shrewd and calculating mobsters like Benjamin Siegel, Frank Costello, Hyman Abrams, and Meyer Lansky. Labor union pension fund loans were given to "front men" to build these empires into seemingly legitimate businesses. As to enterprises peripheral to the casino business, in Arizona, the New York City Bonnano Family grossed $13 million in a single year from only one licensed junket service.

Large-scale gambling is heavily regulated and has now become part of corporate America. In 1990, under the federal asset forfeiture program, the U.S. Marshal's Service took over the daily operations of the Bicycle Club Casino, a legal enterprise in California that was used by Asian OC to launder illicit drug profits. In 1996, the Senate Governmental Affairs committee learned that the casino lost money and illegal procedures continued after the Marshal's Service took control. The highest paid employee of the casino was convicted of conspiracy, loan-sharking, and extortion of casino customers.

The "wave of the future" of gambling appears to be by Internet. As of 1998, there existed approximately 140 Internet casinos (Liddick, 1999). The gambling economy has mushroomed 1600% since the mid-1970s, with revenues of some $50 billion.

Mutual Legal Assistance and Extradition

Presently there are various transnational crimes, including the three mentioned above, which are being committed by a host of organized criminal organizations. The UN has begun to emphasize the importance of international cooperation in the fight against organized crime with the passing of several resolutions, including:

- The Model Treaty on Extradition (General Assembly Resolution No. 45/116 of December 14, 1990)
- The Model Treaty on Mutual Assistance in Criminal Matters (General Assembly Resolution No. 45/117 of December 14, 1990)
- Resolution No. 49/159 on December 23, 1994 (emphasizing collaboration). The Resolution urged member states to implement the Political Declaration and the Global Action Plan against OC at Naples

Reciprocity forms the legal basis for extradition. Thus, if there is no treaty, no legal extraditions may take place (according to U.S. law). However, the state considering extradition of a suspect may refuse to extradite on the basis that certain aspects of the requesting state's criminal process are so alien to its legal system as to lack any basis of reciprocity (generally pertains to human rights and capital punishment).

The general rule for "double criminality" is that the offense committed must be an "extraditable crime" under the laws of both states involved. There are three elements to determine where the crime, even though criminal in both states, falls within the meaning of double criminality:

1. Whether the act is chargeable in both states as a criminal offense regardless of its prosecutability;
2. Whether the act is chargeable and also prosecutable in both states; and
3. Whether the act if chargeable and prosecutable, could also result in the conviction in both states.

The following substantive criteria must be met for an extradition to take place:

1. If a treaty exists, the offense must be listed or designated;
2. If no treaty exists, the respective states will reciprocate for the same type of offense;
3. If no treaty or reciprocity exists, but the request is based on comity, the requested state will rely on its customary practice; and
4. Furthermore, in all three instances, the offense charged must also constitute the offense in the requested state (i.e. double criminality).

Summary

Organized crime impacts all industrialized nations and states to some degree. Although there are numerous laws designed to combat organized crime, severe short-comings have prevented their success. These short-comings include:

- Underfunding of the specified programs, such as the UN International Drug Program,
- Underfunding at local, regional, and national levels,
- The emphasis on fighting drug trafficking differs greatly from one country to the next,
- High levels of corruption in countries that produce and export most of the illegal drugs,
- And the serious issue that developing and nascent democracies lack the legal infrastructure to implement effective programs.

NATHAN R. MORAN

References and Further Reading

Einstein, S. and Amir, M. (1999). *Organized Crime: Uncertainties and Dilemmas*. Chicago, IL: Office of International Criminal Justice.

Gilmore, W.C. (1992). *International Efforts to Combat Money Laundering*. Washington, DC: Society.

Helleiner, E. (1999). State Power and the Regulation of Illicit Activity in Global Finance. In Friman, H.R. and Andreas, P. (Eds.) *The illicit global economy and state power*, pp. 53–90. Boston, MA: Rowan and Littlefield.

Liddick, D. (1999). *An Empirical, Theoretical and Historical Overview of Organized Crime*. Lewiston, NY: Edwin Mellen.

Moran, N.R. (2002). *The Globalization of Russian, Colombian, and Chinese Organized Crime from 1991–2001: A Time-Series Analysis*. An unpublished dissertation. Sam Houston State University, College of Criminal Justice.

U.S. Dept of Justice, Federal Justice Statistics Program, Money Laundering Offenders, 1994–2001. Available at www.usdoj.gov.

See also **Organized Crime: Activities and Extent; Organized Crime: Definitions and Models; Organized Crime: Theories of**

Organized Crime: Theories

Explanations for the existence of organized crime have, for the most part, been borrowed from theories that attempt to explain criminal behavior in general. Despite the widespread interest in organized crime in popular culture, scholars have been reticent, their interest either fleeting or nonexistent. The reason for this can easily be understood when we consider the secrecy and violence that permeates the universe of organized criminals. One of the earliest attempts to explain organized crime was offered by sociologist Robert K. Merton.

Anomie

Building on a concept originated by the French sociologist Emile Durkheim in the 19th century, in 1938, Merton set forth a social and cultural explanation—anomie—for deviant behavior in the U.S. Anomie results when the pressure to achieve economic success is not matched by corresponding opportunity. The pers an thereby become estranged from society.

Merton conceived of organized crime as a normal response to pressures exerted on certain persons by the social structure. He pointed to an American preoccu-pation with economic success—pathological material-ism—in which it is the goal that is emphasized, not the means. This being the case, the only factors limiting goal achievement are technical, not moral or legal—the-ends-justifies-the-means doctrine becomes a guiding tenet for action. This was exemplified by the activities of earlier "godfathers," the "robber barons" of the 19th and early 20th century who took advantage of every (legitimate and illegitimate) opportunity. These men became the embodiment of the great American success story. However, the opportunity for economic success is not equally distributed, and the immigrants who followed these men to America found many avenues from "rags to riches" significantly limited if not already closed. Culture conflict, however, offered an opportunity for latter-day adventurers.

Culture Conflict

In the same year as Merton wrote his seminal essay on anomie, Thorsten Sellin pointed out that conduct norms express cultural values of a group, and the content of those norms varies from culture to culture. In a homogeneous society, the conduct norms express the consensus of the group: few people disagree about what is right and wrong. The same is not true of more heterogeneous societies, where disagreements abound with what is right and wrong, what is to be valued, and what is to be demeaned. In a heterogeneous society, laws represent the conduct norms of the dominant group. Whenever immigrants leave one culture for another, they run the risk of cultural conflict as their imported norms accompany them.

In the U.S., culture conflict between earlier and later immigrants created a demand from the latter for goods and services outlawed by the former. Some immigrants recognized that the cards were stacked against them, and as a result, organized crime flourished. This led to the creation of gambling syndicates and infamous criminal organizations of the Prohibition era. Today, alcohol and various forms of gambling are legally available in most areas of the country, whereas the outlawing of certain chemicals enjoyed by a large minority of the population provides continuing incentive and opportunity for organized crime.

If, as Merton believed, anomie is widespread, particularly in areas of social and economic deprivation, why do some persons suffering from anomie turn to organized crime, whereas others do not? Edwin Sutherland provides an answer: differential association.

Differential Association

According to Sutherland, all behavior—lawful and criminal—is learned. The principal part of learning occurs within intimate personal groups. What is learned depends on the intensity, frequency, and duration of the association. When these variables are sufficient and the associations are criminal, the actor learns the techniques of committing crimes and the drives, attitudes, and rationalizations that add up to a favorable precondition to criminal behavior. The balance between noncriminal and criminal behaviors is tipped in favor of the latter.

Learning the techniques of sophisticated criminality requires the proper environment—ecological niches or *enclaves* where delinquent or criminal subcultures flourish and this education is available. In a capitalist society, socioeconomic differentials relegate some persons to an environment wherein they experience a compelling sense of strain—anomie—as well as differential association. In the environment where organized crime has traditionally thrived, strain is intense. Conditions of severe deprivation are coupled with readily available success models and associations that are innovative, such as racketeers and drug dealers. This makes certain enclaves characterized by social disorganization and delinquent or criminal subcultures spawning grounds for organized crime.

Subcultures and Social Disorganization

Instead of conforming to conventional norms, some persons, through differential association, organize their behavior according to the norms of a delinquent or criminal group to which they belong or with which they identify. This is most likely to occur in environments characterized by relative social disorganization, where familial and communal controls are ineffective in exerting a conforming influence. In enclaves with strong traditions of organized crime, young persons stand a greater chance of being exposed to criminal norms. In these areas persons exhibiting criminal norms are often well-integrated into the community, and such areas are the breeding ground for delinquent subcultures and entrants into organized crime.

In a *subculture*, the values of its members are separate from the wider society. From the viewpoint of the larger dominant culture, the values of the subculture set it apart and prevent total integration, occasionally causing open or covert conflicts. Subcultural theory explains criminal behavior as learned; the subcultural delinquent has learned values that are deviant. Ideas about society lead to criminal behavior. Being right or wrong in terms of the wider society is simply not a guidepost for behavior. Instead, nonconventional behavior, the ability to fight, to win at gambling, to deceive outsiders, is admired.

Clifford Shaw and Henry McKay, sociologists at the University of Chicago, used that city as a laboratory for their study of patterns of criminality during the 1920s and 1930s. They found that certain clearly identifiable neighborhoods maintained a high level of criminality over many decades despite changes in ethnic composition. Thus, although one ethnic group replaced another, the rate of criminality remained constant.

According to Shaw and McKay such neighborhoods are characterized by attitudes and values that are conducive to delinquency and crime, particularly organized crime where the presence of a large number of adult criminals means that children are in contact with crime as a career, symbolized by organized crime. In this type of organization can be seen the delegation of authority, the division of labor, the specialization of function, and all the other characteristics common to well-organized business institutions, wherever found. The heavy concentration of delinquency in certain areas means that boys living in these areas are in contact not only with individuals who engage in proscribed activity but also with groups that sanction such behavior and exert pressure upon their members to conform to group standards.

A disruption of the social order is associated with high rates of delinquency in a community, the result of a breakdown in mechanisms of social control. In many U.S. cities around the turn of the 20th century, the social order was disrupted by the combined interactive effects of industrialization, immigration, and urbanization. Deviant traditions developed and competed with conventional norms; in some communities, deviant norms won out. Once established, these indigenous norms took root in areas that, according to Shaw and McKay, are characterized by attitudes and values that are conducive to delinquency and crime, thus creating a subculture of crime. The attitudes and values, as well as the techniques of organized criminality, are transmitted culturally.

Back in the 1920s, John Landesco found that organized crime in Chicago could be explained by the prevalence of social disorganization in the wider society (during the period of Prohibition) and by the distinct social organization of urban slums from which members of organized crime emerge. Once a set of cultural values is created and established they tend to become autonomous in their impact. In other words, the roots and culture of particular neighborhoods explain why gangsters come from clearly delineated areas where the gang tradition is old and where adolescents, through differential association, can absorb the attitudes and skills necessary to enter the world of adult organized crime.

Inadequate familial socialization prevents some persons from conforming to the conventional norms of the wider society. Through differential association, some of these persons organize their behavior according to the norms of a delinquent or criminal subculture with which they identify or to which they belong. This is most likely to occur in environments characterized by relative social disorganization, where familial and communal controls are ineffective in exerting a conforming influence.

In order for an organized crime group to survive, it must have "an institutionalized process for inducting new members and inculcating them with the values and ways of behaving of the social system" (Cressey, 1969, 263). Donald Cressey notes that "in some neighborhoods all three of the essential ingredients of an effective recruiting process are in operation: inspiring aspiration for membership, training for membership and selection for membership" (1969). In his research, Gerald Suttles (1968) refers to areas from which members of organized crime have typically emerged as *defended neighborhoods*: recognized ecological niches whose inhabitants form cohesive groupings and seal themselves off through the efforts of delinquent gangs, restrictive covenants, and a forbidding reputation. Such neighborhoods have traditionally provided the recruiting grounds that ensure the continuity of organized crime.

In such communities, the conventional and criminal value systems are highly integrated. Leaders of organized criminal enterprises will often maintain membership in conventional institutions in their local communities such as churches, fraternal and mutual benefit societies, and political parties. These formal and informal political, economic, and religious ties provide both illegitimate and legitimate opportunities. Furthermore, these leaders are effective instruments of social control, able to control delinquent behavior and predatory crime in their domain, strengthening their value to the community.

Recruitment into organized crime is made viable because "in the type of community under discussion boys may more or less realistically recognize the potentialities for personal progress in the local society through success in delinquency. In a general way, therefore, delinquent activity in these areas constitutes a training ground for the acquisition of skill in the use of violence, concealment of offense, evasion of detection and arrest, and the purchase of immunity from punishment" (Kobrin, 1966).

According to Irving Spergel, in such communities life in OC is considered acceptable and therefore a legitimate aspiration for young persons. Although these communities provide an appropriate learning environment for the acquisition of values and skills associated with the performance of criminal roles, integration into OC requires selection and tutelage in the process of acquiring recognition—and only a select few are given recognition by those who control admission. Entry into organized crime is characterized by *differential opportunity*.

Differential Opportunity

In agreement with Merton, Richard Cloward and Lloyd Ohlin note that American preoccupation with economic success, coupled with socioeconomic stratification, relegates many persons to an environment wherein they experience strain: "Many lower-class male adolescents experience extreme deprivation born of the certainty that their position in the economic structure is relatively fixed and immutable—a desperation made all the more poignant by their exposure to a cultural ideology in which failure to orient oneself upward is regarded as a moral defect and failure to become mobile as proof of it" (1960, 107).

Conditions of severe deprivation with extremely limited access to ladders of legitimate success result in collective adaptations in the form of delinquent subcultures. Cloward and Ohlin distinguish three types, including the *criminal or rackets subculture*: Gang activity devoted to utilitarian criminal pursuits, an adaptation that begins to approximate organized crime.

Anomie alone, note Cloward and Ohlin, is not sufficient to explain participation in organized crime: what is necessary is cultural transmission (Shaw and McKay) through differential association (Sutherland). However, Cloward and Ohlin point out that illegitimate opportunity for success, like legitimate opportunity, is not equally distributed throughout society (1960, 145): "Having decided that he 'can't make it legitimately,' he cannot simply choose from an array of illegitimate means, all equally available to him." In other words, access to criminal ladders of success are no more freely available than are noncriminal alternatives.

Only those neighborhoods in which crime flourishes as a stable, indigenous institution are fertile learning environments for the young. Because these environments afford integration of different age-levels of offender, selected young people are exposed to "differential association" through which tutelage is provided and criminal values and skills are acquired. To be prepared for the role may not, however, ensure that the individual will ever discharge it. One important limitation is that more youngsters are recruited into these patterns of differential association than the adult criminal structure can possibly absorb. As there is a surplus of contenders for these elite positions, criteria and mechanisms of selection must be evolved. Hence a certain proportion of those who aspire may not be permitted to engage in the behavior for which they have prepared themselves. (1960, 148)

Ethnic Succession

During the decades following World War II, organized crime underwent considerable change. It became increasingly clear that in the U.S. the phenomenon was dominated mainly by Italians—the Irish, except for small pockets in New York and Boston, were no longer involved. And although the sons of Jewish immigrants played a vital role in organized crime, by the third generation, the Jews had moved out.

Although the pool of available candidates for membership in organized crime dwindled in Jewish communities, in Italian communities it remained adequate enough; the large-scale organizations needed to profit from Prohibition were no longer necessary. Thus, for example, although Al Capone is reputed to have employed 700 gunmen for an organization that involved thousands of persons, more contemporary estimates of the size of the traditional Chicago organized crime unit, have ranged only as high as 130. The largest of the crime families, the Genovese family of New York, is estimated to have no more than 400 members. These core members, however, have associates, and the total number of criminal actors participating directly or indirectly in a crime group's enterprises is many times the size of the core membership at any given time.

As Nicholas Gage (1971, 113) points out in *The Mafia Is Not an Equal Opportunity Employer*, no door is more firmly locked to blacks than the one that leads to the halls of power in organized crime." He states that Irish, Jewish, and Italian mobsters have tended to recruit and promote from within their own ethnic groups, while cooperating with one another. Organized crime is no less stratified than the wider "legitimate" society, and the dominant groups in both have always been white. This leads to the issue of *ethnic succession* in organized crime.

Daniel Bell (1964, 116) refers to crime as an American way of life, "A Queer Ladder of Social Mobility." He points out that the "jungle quality of the American business community, particularly at the turn of the century, was reflected in the mode of 'business' practiced by the coarse gangster elements, most of them from new immigrant families, who were 'getting ahead' just as Horatio Alger had urged." Francis Ianni (1974) notes that this "queer ladder" had organized crime as the first few rungs.

The Irish came first, and early in this century they dominated crime as well as big-city political machinations. As they came to control the political machinery of large cities they won wealth, power, and respectability through subsequent control of construction, trucking, public utilities, and the waterfront. By the 1920s and the period of prohibition and speculation in the money markets and real estate, the Irish were succeeded by the Jews in organized crime, and Arnold Rothstein, Lepke Buchalter, and Gurrah Shapiro dominated gambling and labor racketeering for over a decade. The Jews quickly moved into the world of business and the professions as more legitimate avenues to economic and social mobility. The Italians came next.

According to this thesis, each successive immigrant group experienced *strain* to which some members reacted by *innovating* in accord with a tradition that had been established by earlier American entrepreneurs such as the "robber barons" of earlier centuries. Ethnic succession results when a group experiences success in crime and legitimate opportunities thereby become more readily available. Strain subsides, and the group moves out of organized crime, creating an opportunity for innovation for the succeeding immigrant group. According to this thesis, persons involved in organized crime are not committed to a deviant subculture but are merely using available, albeit illegal, opportunity to achieve economic success.

Ianni states that ethnic succession is continuing, that "the Italians are leaving or being pushed out of organized crime [and] they are being replaced by the next wave of migrants to the city: blacks and Puerto Ricans" (1974, 14). Although they may not have been obvious to Ianni when he was conducting his research in New York during the early 1970s, today we would have to add other ethnic groups: Cubans, Chinese, Colombians, Dominicans, Jamaicans, Mexicans, Nigerians, Russians, and outlaw motorcycle clubs. According to the ethnic succession thesis, involvement in organized crime is simply a rational response to economic conditions.

Other theorists reject this one-dimensional view. Organized crime, they argue, provides important psychic rewards and meaningful social structures. Young Italian American males from middle-class circumstances continue to be drawn by the allure of organized crime, a romaticization of the mob kept alive in certain neighborhoods—enclaves—and reinforced by media representations. Being "connected" to organized crime brings prestige, and in the social environment inhabited by "wiseguys"—bars, restaurants, night clubs—a privileged status is evident. The would-be outlaw is socialized into an exciting world where he eagerly adopts the attitude, behavior pattern, and even the clothing styles exemplified by the "wiseguys" of organized crime.

Ianni describes the "Lupollos," the Italian OC family he studied, whose core members are all related by blood or marriage. In the fourth generation, "only four out of twenty-seven males are involved in the family business organization. The rest are doctors, lawyers, college teachers, or run their own businesses" (1972, 193). Ianni argues that ethnic succession continues (1974, 12): "We shall witness over the next decade the systematic development of what is now a scattered and loosely organized pattern of emerging black control in organized crime into the Black Mafia."

Peter Lupsha (1981, 22) questions the "ethnic succession" thesis. He argues that despite Ianni's limited findings, Italian American organized crime figures who have gained economic status are not leaving organized crime and, in many instances, their progeny have followed them into OC—there are dozens of contemporary OC members whose children have followed them into "the life." An additional development affecting ethnic succession in organized crime has been the arrival of relatively large numbers of southern Italian immigrants into the New York metropolitan area during the 1960s, some of them members of Italian criminal organizations fleeing prosecution or internecine warfare. They have developed ties to or have become members of existing organizations.

In the meantime, new criminal groups are emerging that may prove to be more powerful and difficult to combat than those of traditional organized crime. Gary

Potter concludes that, historically, "ethnic succession" appears to be a dubious concept. Instead, he argues, new groups become part of organized crime, but they do not necessarily *replace* the older groups. This would appear to be the case with members of Italian American organized crime, whose strong subcultural orientations have resisted changes in their economic status. Chinese, Japanese, Mexican, outlaw bikers, Russian crime units—whose perpetuity appears insured by the strong subcultural atmosphere pervading their environment.

Although *strain* can help explain why some persons from disadvantaged groups become involved in organized crime, it fails to provide a satisfying explanation for the continued existence of traditional organized crime. In other words, although poverty and limited economic opportunity can certainly impel one toward innovative activities, they do not explain why middle-class youngsters become involved in organized crime or why crimes by the wealthy and the powerful—for example, massive savings and loan industry fraud, securities fraud, insider trading, collusive agreements—continue to be a problem in the U.S. In fact, organized criminal activity on a rather outrageous scale, without necessarily being connected to conditions of *strain*, has been an important part of American history.

The increasing scale and complexity of modern life has altered the social structure of urban communities. Greater social mobility has marked the end of many ethnically defined neighborhoods. Racket subcultures vanished as residents found jobs, became educated, and moved to the suburbs. Although it may signal the beginning of the end of traditional Italian American organized crime, it does not signal the end of organized crime as a method of crime or as a means by which members on the lowest rungs of the American ladder of social mobility achieve wealth. Italian Americans are now being overshadowed by emerging criminal groups who are using the drug trade much as their organized crime predecessors did bootlegging. But these criminal groups lack the incubation provided by corrupt urban political machines and ineffective federal law enforcement.

HOWARD ABADINSKY

References and Further Reading

Cloward, R.A. and Ohlin, L.E. 1960. *Delinquency and Opportunity.* New York, NY: Free Press.

Bell, D. 1964. *The End of Ideology.* Glencoe, IL: Free Press.

Cressey, D.R. 1972. *Criminal Organization. Its Elementary Forms.* New York, NY: Harper & Row.

Cressey, D.R. 1969. *Theft of the Nation: The Structure and Operations of Organized Crime in America.* New York, NY: Harper & Row.

Elliott, D.S., Huizinga, D., and Ageton, S.S. 1985. *Explaining Delinquency and Drug Use,* Beverly Hills, CA: Sage.

Gage, N. 1971. *The Mafia Is Not an Equal Opportunity Employer,* New York, NY: McGraw-Hill.

Nicholas, I. and Francis, A.J. 1974. *The Black Mafia: Ethnic Succession in Organized Crime.* New York, NY: Simon and Schuster.

Nicholas, I. and Francis, A.J. 1972. *A Family Business: Kinship and Social Control in Organized Crime.* New York, NY: Russell Sage Foundation.

Kobrin, S. 1966. The conflict of values in delinquency areas. pp. 151–160 in *Juvenile Delinquency: A Book of Readings,* Giallombardo, R. (Ed.) New York, NY: Wiley.

Landesco, J. 1968. *Organized Crime in Chicago,* Chicago, IL: University of Chicago Press.

Lupsha, P.A. 1981. Individual choice, material culture, and organized crime. *Criminology* 19: 3–24.

Merton, R. 1967. *On Theoretical Sociology.* New York, NY: Free Press.

Merton, R. 1938. Social structure and anomie. *American Sociological Review* 3: 672–682.

Potter, G. 1994. *Criminal Organizations: Vice, Racketeering, and Politics in an American City.* Prospect Heights, IL: Waveland.

Saney, P. 1986. *Crime and Culture in America: A Comparative Perspective,* New York, NY: Greenwood.

Sellin, T. 1938. *Culture Conflict and Crime.* New York, NY: Social Science Research Council.

Spergel, I. 1964. *Racketville, Slumtown, Haulberg,* Chicago, IL: University of Chicago Press.

Sutherland, E.H. 1973. *Edwin H. Sutherland: On Analyzing Crime,* Schuessler, K. (Ed.) Chicago, IL: University of Chicago Press.

Suttles, G.D. 1968. *The Social Order of the Slum,* Chicago, IL: University of Chicago Press.

Wolfgang, M.E. and Ferracuti, F. 1967. *The Subculture of Violence: Toward an Integrated Theory in Criminology,* London, UK: Tavistock.

See also **Organized Crime: Activities and Extent; Organized Crime: Definitions and Models**

P

Parole

Parole is defined by Clear and Cole (2000) as the "conditional release of an offender from incarceration but not from the legal custody of the state." Offenders who comply with the conditions of supervision, violate no laws, and otherwise complete their period of supervision satisfactorily will receive a favorable termination or discharge from parole. Most states also provide for an early termination from supervision when the parolee has maintained an "exemplary" adjustment in the community. The practice of parole, historically, has been justified by one or more of the three concepts. Parole as a "grace or privilege" views early release from prison as simply a privilege or benefit granted by the state for the offender's good behavior. Following this reasoning, parole is a privilege that is granted by the benevolence of the state that can be revoked or taken away by the offender's misbehavior or failure to comply with the conditions of supervision. Parole supervision as a "contract" holds that the offender and the state enter into an agreement that, so long as the parolee complies with the terms of his or her contract, the conditions of parole, he or she will be allowed to remain in the community under supervision. However, if the offenders fail to abide by the terms of the contract and violate the terms of parole, they may have the contract revoked, whereby the offenders can be returned to prison to complete the remaining time left on their sentence. The last justification for parole is that parole is simply another form of "custody" along the classification continuum of security levels. Institutions are commonly classified as super-maximum, maximum, medium, and minimum. Parole in this scheme would be viewed as minimum, open, or community custody. Just as an inmate who can be reclassified to a maximum custody prison if he or she experiences serious misconduct in a medium or minimum security facility, the offender on community custody or parole can be reclassified to closed custody and returned to the confines of an institution.

It should be noted that the overwhelming number of prisoners (95%) will be returned to the community. Furthermore, parole can be differentiated from probation in that parolees have been convicted of a felony and sentenced to a period of imprisonment in excess of 1 year. Probationers may have committed a felony or a misdemeanor, and if they have served any time in custody as part of their sentence, such time will normally not exceed 1 year in a local or county jail. Although probation can be administered at the local or county level, as is the case in California, or combined with parole in a state agency, as is the case in Nevada, parole is almost always a state or federal government function. The administration of parole usually falls within a larger state department of corrections, with some states having a parole board that is an autonomous agency whose members are appointed by the governor. Although some counties use the concept of parole as in releasing an inmate early from a county jail sentence, any period of supervision that follows is most often monitored by probation officers, and therefore, more appropriately considered probation. Parole may thus be considered both a type of supervision that is carried out in the open community and also as a method whereby prisoners are released prior to the completion of their full sentences.

Parole has its origins in England during the 19th century when Alexander Maconochie (1787–1860), warden of the Norfolk Island penal colony off the coast of Australia, created a system whereby prisoners would progress through several stages, ultimately leading to their gradual return to the community. Maconochie, considered the father of parole, established five stages leading to their freedom. The first stage was strict imprisonment, followed by hard labor on chain gangs, freedom within a specified area, ticket-of-leave or supervision in the community, and finally full liberty or release from the jurisdiction of the state. This process of gradual release formed the basis of the modern-day parole system when Maconochie held that offenders could be prepared gradually for their reintegration back into society. Later, in Ireland, Sir Walter Crofton (1815–1897) employed Maconochie's "mark system," allowing prisoners to earn "marks" toward their early release from imprisonment through hard work, education, and good behavior. Offenders who earned sufficient "marks" allowing their early release were required to abide by a number of conditions. Compliance with release conditions was normally overseen by local police officials. In the U.S., the indeterminate sentence and parole were intricately linked with the principles of rehabilitation and reform, and in 1930, the U.S. Board of Parole, later changed to the U.S. Parole Commission, was established by Congress.

Parole, therefore, is a discretionary release of an offender from imprisonment by the state. As noted, parole has historically been closely aligned with the principles of rehabilitation and the indeterminate sentence wherein a parole board conditionally releases offenders to supervision in the community when it is concluded that the prisoners have demonstrated that they have been rehabilitated and can be safely released to the community. In making their decision to release a prisoner conditionally on supervision, parole boards generally consider the seriousness of the crime committed, prior criminal record, institutional adjustment, prior adjustment on probation or parole, mental stability, and the suitability of the parole or release plan. Eligibility for parole is normally determined by the minimum term established by the court, less time spent in jail prior to sentencing as well as good time and other meritorious time earned.

Parole has been criticized by both liberals and conservatives, as well as prisoners, because the decision-making process for release has been excessively subjective and arbitrary. For example, how does a parole board determine when a prisoner is actually rehabilitated and no longer poses a danger to the community? How does the parole board determine whether the changes that appear to have occurred have actually occurred and that the prisoner is not simply "programming" or pretending to change in order to impress the board? If, in fact, the prisoner appears to have made major positive changes through prison programs, how can a parole board be assured that these changes will be sustained after release, especially when most offenders return to the same criminogenic environment that contributed to the criminality in the first place?

In an attempt to address the charges of too much subjectivity and thus arbitrariness, many states and the federal government established objective guidelines to aid in the parole decision. One such instrument, the salient factor score, used by the U.S. Parole Commission, measures offender risk along six dimensions including prior convictions, prior commitments, age, current offense, recent commitment-free period, whether the person was on probation or parole at the instant the offense was committed, and lastly, whether the offender has a history of heroin or opiate dependence. Each item is scored from zero to three points with low scores representing a higher risk. The maximum number of points in the salient factor scale would be ten. A score of eight, nine, or ten would represent a low risk and, thus, a probable suitable candidate for parole. Likewise, the U.S. parole officer would also use the salient factor score to assess the level of supervision that should be provided. Parolees with scores of nine or ten might be classified minimum supervision whereas those with scores of three, two, one, or zero would likely be placed on maximum supervision.

The success of the correctional system generally, and parole specifically, is usually measured by the extent of recidivism or reoffending. It is difficult to determine the exact level of reoffending following release from prison because jurisdictions vary in how they define recidivism. Furthermore, some violations are not acted upon and other violations that occur are not detected. A combined failure rate of approximately 25% within the first 3 years of release has been reported for years, however, reports do not clearly distinguish between technical violations and new criminal conduct. According to Clear and Dammer (2000), the recidivism rates among jurisdictions range from about 25% to well over 50%. However, some jurisdictions put their recidivism rates considerably higher than noted by Clear and Dammer. For example, the California Department of Corrections reports a violation or "return rate" of almost 68% (67.7). Of this 68%, 13.2% of parolees are returned to prison as a result of a new prison term whereas 54.5% are returned for committing technical violations of their parole conditions.

Parole officers, like those who work in probation, experience what many feel is a significant "role conflict" between the social worker and law-enforcement responsibilities of the job. As a social worker, the parole officer is expected to identify the offender's needs and provide assistance in such areas as employment, mental health counseling, substance-abuse treatment, housing, and family problems. In some jurisdictions, the parole officer provides these supportive services directly, however in other jurisdictions the officer serves as a "broker" of services, referring the offender to an agency in the community that is better suited to meet specific needs. In this regard, parole officers, like probation officers, are expected to be knowledgeable about community resources. It should be noted that in some jurisdictions parole and probation functions are differentiated and provided by separate agencies, whereas in other jurisdictions the functions are combined, generally into one state agency under the department of corrections.

In the role of law enforcer, the parole officer is expected to enforce the general and specific conditions of parole and to report serious violations to the parole board. General or standard conditions are those conditions that apply to all prisoners released on parole. These include requirements to obey all laws, maintain employment, truthfully respond to all parole officer inquiries, report to the parole officer as directed, notify the parole officer of any change in residence, not leave the jurisdiction without permission, and not use drugs. Special or specific conditions include conditions applicable to only certain offenders based on the crime committed or special needs identified. These could include requirements to submit to drug testing, participate in mental health or sex offender treatment, participate in electronic monitoring, not associate with gang members, and, in some jurisdictions, take medications or hormones as part of a chemical castration program to reduce the sex drive of sex offenders. The supervising parole officer is frequently given a great deal of discretion in enforcing the conditions of parole, and in many jurisdictions, parole boards may require offenders to participate "as directed by the parole officer."

In the role of law enforcer the parole officer or agent emphasizes surveillance and monitoring activities, requiring the offender to report to the office, provide financial data, employment check stubs, or other documentation confirming that he or she is fulfilling the requirements of parole. The officer will usually make announced or unannounced home visits to observe how the parolee is functioning in the home and community. Collateral contacts with family members, employers, drug or mental health counselors are also necessary to assess the offender's adjustment to community supervision.

Historically, parole agencies have tended to emphasize either the social worker or law enforcer role.

During the rehabilitation era spanning the period from about 1930 to the early 1970s the social worker role was emphasized. The medical-model view of criminality took the rehabilitation emphasis to its logical conclusion. That is, criminality was a type of social illness or disease that required a thorough assessment in order to identify or diagnose the root causes of the deviant behavior. Once the underlying causes were diagnosed, usually through the presentence report prepared by a probation officer, an appropriate treatment plan would be presented to the court, and if the convict were placed on probation, the plan would be implemented by the supervision officer. However, if the convict were committed to state or federal prison, the presentence report containing diagnostic information would follow the offender to his or her designated institution. Later, this document would be used by the parole board to assist in the parole granting decision. Furthermore, if granted parole, a copy of the presentence report was sent to the field officer to assist him or her in establishing a supervision plan.

As civil unrest swept the U.S. in the 1960s, coupled with soaring crime rates, the rehabilitation model of probation began to lose favor and public attitudes shifted toward a more punitive approach to dealing with criminal offenders and, perhaps, this was more so with parolees than probationers because offenders on parole are considered to be greater risks. Instead of emphasizing rehabilitation, the public now wanted the criminal justice system, including probation and parole, to emphasize deterrence, retribution, and incapacitation. Several things fueled the dramatic shift from rehabilitation to a conservative crime control strategy beginning in the mid-1970s and continuing to the present time. These included high crime rates, Robert Martinson's landmark study in 1976 concluding that rehabilitation efforts were generally ineffective, and Ronald Reagan's election as president in 1980. Although many probation departments still continue to emphasize a rehabilitation approach, parole agencies in the U.S. today are more likely to stress a law enforcement role. This is most notable in some states like California that have required their parole agents to be armed since the 1970s. Furthermore, parole agents in California work very closely with local police departments on task forces, joint raids, even riding with police on patrol and conducting joint raids.

Parole supervision assignments frequently are specialized by offender type. For example, it is common for parole agencies to have officers who have specialized caseloads of violent offenders, gang members, drug offenders, or mental health cases. Proponents of specialization argue that parole officers will develop a high level of skill in supervising certain types of offenders and therefore will be able to enhance the services and supervision provided. Specialized caseloads are often designated as a higher grade with an increased level of pay. Those who argue against specialized caseloads suggest that specialists are not "well-rounded" and prolonged supervision of only one type of offender will distort an officer's perspective. Furthermore, dealing with only one type of offender over an extended period of time may result in a higher level of burnout among officers.

For many years it was thought that parole supervision would be more effective if only caseloads could be reduced to manageable levels. Parole and probation officers, as well as administrators, argued that lower caseloads would allow officers to devote more time and attention to each case, thus enhancing the level of surveillance, monitoring, and rehabilitative support services. It was suggested that an ideal caseload size was somewhere between 35 and 50 cases per officer. However, studies conducted in the 1960s and 1970s concluded that recidivism, as measured by new criminal conduct, did not decrease significantly with reduced caseloads. Some studies did find that the rate of technical violations (violations of the rules of probation) increased because officers had more time to monitor compliance with parole conditions. With reduced caseloads, parole and probation officers devoted more time to monitoring compliance with the conditions of supervision and were able to detect noncompliance with general and specific conditions at a higher level.

It should be noted that a distinction is made between caseload and workload. Caseload refers to the raw number of cases supervised by a parole officer whereas workload represents the amount of time devoted to any given case. For example, most parole officers recognize that drug offenders, mental health cases, and violent offenders require more of an officer's time. Furthermore, parole supervision is a continuous process of classifying and reclassifying parolees depending on their adjustment to supervision. A stable, first time offender, who may initially be classified as requiring only minimum supervision, can be reclassified to maximum supervision because of drug use, unemployment, or failure to comply with treatment orders. Likewise, a parolee initially classified as a maximum supervision case may later be reduced to medium, and then minimum, because of a favorable response to supervision. With extremely stable cases the parole officer may require no face-to-face contact and simply allow the parolee to submit written monthly reports. If the stability continues, the parole officer may recommend to the parole board that the offender be discharged early from parole.

Parole supervision may be terminated when the offender successfully completes his or her full term of supervision. Most jurisdictions also allow for an early termination if the parolee performs in an exemplary manner and appears to no longer be in need of supervision. Supervision may also be terminated or revoked as a result of violations that occur during the period of parole. Violations are of two types, technical and legal. Legal violations, also called new criminal conduct, occur when the parolee is arrested or convicted of a new crime. Although most parole officers prefer that a conviction occur before initiating revocation proceedings, officers may commence revocation proceedings prior to a conviction. If the parolee is in custody awaiting trial, it is common for parole officers to lodge a warrant detainer requiring that the holding agency does not release the offender when the case is completed or the offender has served the period of imprisonment ordered by the judge. The burden of proof for conviction of a crime is beyond a reasonable doubt, but the preponderance of the evidence is sufficient in a revocation hearing. If violation proceedings are initiated, the parole officer need not arrest the offender and may ask that he or she be cited or summoned to appear before the parole board. Because of the gravity of their offenses, a parolee (more so than a probationer) may also be taken into custody pending his or her appearance before the parole board. If found in violation, the parole board may reinstate the offender to supervision, may reinstate with additional conditions, or may revoke parole and order that additional time be served on the sentence.

In 1972, the Supreme Court in the case of *Morrissey v. Brewer* 408, US 471, provided parole violators with minimal due process rights including:

- Written notice of the claimed violations of parole;
- Disclosure to the parolee of evidence against him;
- Opportunity to be heard in person and to present witnesses and documentary evidence;
- Right to confront and cross-examine adverse witnesses (unless the hearing officer specifically finds good cause for not allowing confrontation);
- A "neutral and detached" hearing body such as a traditional parole board, the members of which need not be judicial officers or lawyers; and
- A written statement by the fact-finders as to the evidence relied on and reasons for revoking parole (del Carmen, Ritter, Witt, 1998, 143).

Morrissey is significant because, for the first time, the Court determined that parolees are entitled to some form of due process, at least in the parole revocation process, noting that parole represents a "grievous loss" that triggers due process guarantees. Aside from the six due process rights outlined above, the Court also said that there are two important stages in most parole revocation hearings: (1) the preliminary hearing, and (2) the revocation hearing. In both of these stages the Court held that the parolee is entitled to the due process rights mentioned in this case. Although the Court indicated in its opinion that there are two important stages in the parole revocation, hearing it did not hold that in all revocation proceedings the two stages must be present. In fact, in many jurisdictions the preliminary, revocation and dispositional hearings are all integrated into one hearing. This is most often the case when the parolee does not dispute the violations, presents an explanation, and is then informed by the parole board of the action to be taken (144). With respect to the right to counsel, the Court was ambiguous and simply noted that "we think that the decision as to the need for counsel must be made on a case-by-case basis" (Abadinsky, 2000, 130). In many jurisdictions however, counsel is routinely allowed at the parole revocation hearing.

Although release from imprisonment can be a euphoric experience for offenders, it can subsequently result in considerable disappointment and frustration. The parolee's memories of family, friends, and loved ones represent snapshots frozen in time, but in reality, everyone has changed, moved away, taken a new job, grown up, or perhaps most disappointingly have become almost strangers. The attempts to restore old relationships can be very threatening and eventually disappointing (Clear and Cole, 2000, 377). In addition, the presence of almost complete freedom after years of living in a structured, confined prison setting can also add tremendous stress to adjusting to the open community where the offender must now assume major responsibilities of transportation, obtaining a driver's licence, finding a job, reporting for drug testing, and so on. If married, with children, the spouse may unrealistically expect the offender to immediately begin providing financial relief to the family that perhaps has endured financial hardships while the breadwinner was away. Other barriers to success include civil disabili-

ties that prohibit a felon from voting, holding public office, and most importantly, from being employed in certain occupations.

SAM TORRES

References and Further Reading

Abadinsky, H. 2000. *Probation and Parole,* 7th ed., Upper Saddle River, NJ, Prentice-Hall, Inc.

Augustus, J. 1972. *John Augustus: First Probation Officer,* Montclair, NJ, Patterson-Smith. (First published in 1939 by the National Probation Association under the title, *A Report: Labors of John Augustus for the First Ten Years in the Aid of the Unfortunate.*)

Allen, H.E. and Simonsen, C.E. 2001. *Corrections in America: An Introduction,* 9th ed., Upper Saddle River, NJ, Prentice-Hall, Inc.

Carter, R.M. and Wilkins, L.T. 1976. *Probation, Parole, and Community Corrections,* 2nd ed., New York, John Wiley and Sons, Inc.

Champion, D.J. 1996. *Probation, Parole, and Community Corrections,* 2nd ed., Upper Saddle River, N.J. Prentice-Hall, Inc.

Clear, T.R. and Dammer, H.R. 2000. *The Offender and the Community,* Belmont, CA, Wadsworth/Thomas Learning.

Clear, T.R. and Cole, G.F. 2000. *American Corrections,* 5th ed., Belmont, CA, Wadsworth/Thomas Learning.

Cromwell, P.F. and Del Carmen, R.V. 1999. *Community-Based Corrections* 4th ed., Belmont, CA, West/Wadsworth.

Del Carmen, R.V., Ritter, S.E. and Witt, B.A. 1998. *Briefs of Leading Cases in Corrections,* 2nd ed., Cincinatti, OH, Anderson Publishing Company.

Dressler, D. 1959. *Practice and Theory of Probation and Parole,* New York, Colombia University Press.

McCarthy, B.R. and Bernard J. McCarthy, Jr. 1997. *Community-Based Corrections,* 3rd ed., Belmont, CA, Wadsworth Publishing Company.

McCleary, R. 1992. *Dangerous Men: The Sociology of Parole,* 2nd ed., New York, Harrow and Heston Publishers.

Morris, N. and Tonry, M. 1990. *Between Prison and Probation,* New York, Oxford University Press.

Silverman, I.J. 2001. *Corrections: A Comprehensive View,* 2nd ed., Belmont, CA, Wadsworth/Thomas Learning.

See also **Careers in Probation and Parole; Probation; Rehabilitation and Treatment**

Peacemaking Criminology

A new perspective has been developing in criminology as a response to the perceived failures of the war on crime. Termed peacemaking criminology, this critical perspective examines the processes of the criminal justice system in ways different from the traditional "get tough on crime" perspective. Peacemaking criminology is concerned with relieving the suffering caused by crime (Quinney, 1991). The victim, the offender, their families, and the community are all impacted by unlawful behavior. By reducing the harm caused to all these parties by crime, the peacemaking perspective strives to break the cycle of violence and retribution by addressing the underlying issues that perpetuate crime. By promoting social justice and repairing the relationships between the offender and the community, it is possible to strengthen the social fabric and ensure that there is a reasonable chance to heal the wounds caused by crime (Fuller, 1998).

Peacemaking criminology is a new term based on some very old ideas and practices. It first made its way into the discipline with the publication of Harold Pepinsky and Richard Quinney's collection of essays, *Criminology as Peacemaking* in 1991. This seminal work with contributions by some of the leading critical criminologists quickly spurred the interests of many scholars who were dissatisfied with the way traditional criminology theorized about crime and crime control. Paper sessions and roundtables concerning peacemaking criminology have become a common feature at criminology meetings and new books on the subject are appearing. Additionally, in 2001, a major university in the U.S., San Diego State, listed peacemaking criminology as an area of expertise it was looking for in potential faculty candidates. In the space of a decade, peacemaking criminology has established itself as a viable approach for thinking about the problems of crime and crime control.

According to Pepinsky and Quinney (1991), peacemaking criminology draws on three intellectual traditions for its foundation: religious and humanist, feminist, and critical. It is useful to look at each of these intellectual traditions to see which ideas peacemaking criminology borrows. Religion and spirituality were, at one time, important features in explaining and responding to crime. With the move to make criminology more scientific, religion has not been viewed as an important area of public policy in regard to crime. Peacemaking criminology recognizes the importance of individual self-esteem and how this is often linked to some form of religious or humanist system of ethics. By recognizing the role played by ancient traditions such as the major religions, peacemaking criminology attempts to include in the study of crime how offenders are bonded to conventional behavior. Religion is a major institution in society and any comprehensive look at crime must include how religion affects decisions by individuals to adopt unlawful lifestyles. It is important to add that peacemaking criminology does not promote one type of religion or humanism over another, but it simply tries to understand how these intellectual traditions have influenced behavior in the

past and how they might do so in the future (Braswell et al., 2001).

Feminism is the second intellectual tradition that supplies peacemaking criminology with its foundation. Although there are many variations of feminism, it is fair to say that all require social, economic, and political equality between men and women. Feminists have made major contributions to the study of crime, and peacemaking criminology includes these critiques of gender relations in its canon (Harris, 1991). The promotion of social justice requires that opportunities for advancement be available to women, that the patriarchy ingrained in our history be recognized, and that women be accorded the full range of rights and freedoms available to men.

Finally, peacemaking criminology draws on a critical tradition (Arrigo, 1999). Critical criminology traces its roots to the economic critique of society made by Karl Marx. Expanding on Marx, the critical tradition looks at a variety of methods that are used both economically and politically to reinforce the domination of those in powerful positions. Critical criminology has a rich heritage in looking at how laws are made and enforced to promote the interests of those who have the money and power to promote their wishes. Peacemaking criminology includes this critique in its examination of how social equality can be included in society's reaction to crime.

Although peacemaking criminology draws from each of these intellectual traditions, it is important to note that they are interrelated. This means that criminologists would consider themselves as critical and feminist scholars and that these distinctions are made only to show how peacemaking criminology is linked to other ways of theorizing about crime. Additionally, peacemaking criminology does not borrow these other intellectual traditions *in toto*, but merely draws from them aspects that support the ideals of relieving suffering and promoting social justice. For example, Marx advocated the overthrow of the capitalist class, by violence if necessary (Akers, 2000), and some well-established religions believe there are appropriate roles for men and women that are based on patriarchy. Peacemaking criminology does not incorporate these views in how it envisions a just and effective criminal justice system.

In order to understand how peacemaking criminology can be applied to the problems of crime and the criminal justice system it is useful to look at Fuller's (1998) "peacemaking pyramid paradigm." Fuller envisions solutions to criminal justice issues to be peacemaking to the extent that they are able to include the factors that comprise the pyramid. At the base of the pyramid is nonviolence. Any criminal justice policy that uses violence as its core cannot be considered a peacemaking option. For example, peacemaking criminologists are opposed to capital punishment because it teaches that violence by the state is justified. Likewise, the use of corporal punishment in the school through the practice of paddling would be opposed by peacemaking criminologists. The use of violence as a means of social control is doomed to be repeated by those at the receiving end of such policies, according to the views of peacemaking criminology.

The second factor in the peacemaking pyramid is social justice. It is not enough for a solution to a problem to be nonviolent if it leaves social injustice unexamined. Fuller (1998) provides the example of the juvenile who bullies his classmates. Simply moving the bully to another classroom would not solve the whole problem. Peacemaking criminology would suggest that the relationship between the bully and his victims be repaired. The bully should be enlightened by how his actions cause pain and suffering to his victims, and he should be given the opportunity to apologize. This does not mean that the young man should be coerced into offering an apology that he does not really mean, but rather, that he should be given the chance to understand how his behavior harms others and limits his relationships.

The third factor in the pyramid is inclusion. When crafting a solution to a criminal justice problem, all the affected parties should have a say in the outcome. Presently, the offender is pitted against the state and the victim. The families and the community are excluded from the process to a great degree. Restorative justice practices such as family conferencing and alternative dispute resolution allow the victim and the offender to exchange viewpoints in a controlled yet productive setting. Additionally, the families of the victim and offender are given the opportunity for input. This inclusion is very important because many times the families are necessary for the agreed upon sentence to be implemented successfully.

Correct means as the fourth factor is an idea that suggests that the path to a peaceful solution is as important as the solution itself. If deception, trickery, and force are used to arrive at a solution to a criminal justice problem, then that solution cannot be considered a peacemaking solution. The process used to arrive at the solution should be a model of the solution itself. If the solution is expected to last, then it must be based on a method that all can agree is just, fair, and inclusive.

The next factor in the pyramid is ascertainable criteria. This simply means that people should understand what is being said and why decisions are being made. The legalese in the criminal justice system renders everyone, except the attorneys and the judge, unable to understand the process. Offenders are often required

to make decisions without fully understanding the full implications. Although there will be illiterate offenders who will not be able to read even the simplest explanations, ascertainable criteria is still a goal. Every effort should be made to attempt to explain the process of the criminal justice system and the ramifications of any decisions such as plea-bargaining.

The final step in the pyramid is the categorical imperative. This is a term used by the philosopher Immanuel Kant (1995) that every decision should be considered as if it would become a universal law. This requires that decision makers, such as judges or law-enforcement officers, look beyond the specific circumstances of the case and consider how the reasoning for their decision might be applied to other cases. This would help delineate where the boundaries of appropriate behavior are drawn and ensure a consistency in how the law is enforced.

This peacemaking pyramid reflects the features of an alternative method for dealing with crime. When the war on crime metaphor is used, it sets up a process that is not only ineffective, but often counterproductive. The war on crime approach views crime as a discreet event that can be detected, punished, and forgotten. The war on crime approach does not recognize the interconnectedness of criminal behavior and criminal justice system policy. Peacemaking criminologists focus on the offender, victim, and the community in fashioning policy (Braswell et al., 2001). The war on crime criminologist focuses on the punishment of the offender with the hope that the punishment will act as a deterrent.

So what is wrong with the deterrent idea? According to the peacemaking criminologist, deterrence is not effective in solving the underlying conditions that foster crime. Deterrence works best for those who have a stake in society. It does not work very well for those with little to lose if they are caught breaking the law. Furthermore, deterrence based on punishment does not prepare the offender for a productive life once released from prison. The war on crime perspective has resulted in long sentences with little treatment coupled with overcrowded prisons where violence is common. The result is that the offender comes back to society unskilled, bitter, and with a proclivity for violent behavior to meet his needs (Gilligan, 1996).

One reason the peacemaking perspective is thought to be superior to the war on crime perspective is because of its optimistic view of human behavior. With the goal of relieving suffering for the offender as well as the victim, and the attempt to repair the harm done to all by the crime, the peacemaking perspective attempts to break the cycle of violence. The war on crime perspective views the offender as the enemy and treats the control of crime as a war. This war metaphor is ill-suited for the task of social control, because it results in all citizens being treated as suspects and the singling out of those who are the least powerful for extra surveillance and punishment. By treating citizens as the enemy, the criminal justice system loses the support of many individuals. Even though some people commit crimes and need to be arrested, the criminal justice system is not very good at deciding which individuals, reasonably, can be considered the enemy. Offenders are indistinguishable from law-abiding citizens, so the police can only act on broad stereotypes in deciding whom to treat as the enemy. Given the fact that many citizens have committed some offense for which they could be brought into the criminal justice system, the label of "criminal" is really a function of which citizens get caught and which citizens manage to escape detection. If we factor into this equation the differential treatment we accord to citizens based on race, social class, gender, and age, we can begin to understand why many people deem the criminal justice system and its war on crime as biased and discriminatory (Fuller, 1998).

To fully appreciate the peacemaking perspective, it is necessary to understand that it operates at many levels. One common misconception about peacemaking criminology is that it is simply a personal philosophy. Some critics dismiss it as a nice, feel-good, theory about individual transformation that has little use in crafting criminal justice policy. Peacemaking criminology actually operates at many levels. Fuller (1998) identifies the intrapersonal, interpersonal, institutional or societal, and the international or global levels as arenas where the peacemaking perspective is effective. All these levels are interconnected, and a peacemaking criminologist can find issues in all of them to practice the perspective. At the intrapersonal level, one should realize that self-esteem comes from personal effort and satisfaction. Henry David Thoreau said "the mass of men lead lives of quiet desperation." The intrapersonal level of peacemaking would have each of us examine the factors that cause us our discomfort and stress and decide how we incorporate these factors into our personality. Michael Foucault alerts us to how grids of self-imposed discipline are adopted by individuals without them actually realizing why. The intrapersonal dimension of peacemaking would have each of us make peace with ourselves as we attempt to make peace with others.

At the interpersonal level, the peacemaking perspective would have us treat other people as we would wish to be treated. By treating others with respect and dignity, many of the problems of interpersonal relations can be avoided. In the criminal justice system, practitioners such as law enforcement officers and correctional personnel can deal with offenders in ways that do not demean and humiliate them. Common respect and courtesy can go a long way in helping to forge healthy relationships in the community and in the prison.

At the institutional or societal level, the peacemaking perspective moves beyond a personal philosophy and attempts to influence criminal justice policy. The peacemaking perspective aims at getting the institutions of society (such as families and schools.) to treat individuals in democratic ways that allow for social justice. The peacemaking perspective would take positions on public policy that are consistent with the idea that society should do everything possible to relieve suffering and promote social justice. To that end, peacemaking would oppose capital punishment, support gun control, and denounce practices such as racial profiling. Although the peacemaking perspective can be applied to other institutions, peacemaking criminology is mainly concerned with the criminal justice system. One of its strengths, however, is its relationship to other levels of analysis (intrapersonal) and to other institutions. In this way, peacemaking criminology operates in a broad context that treats problems as multidimensional.

Finally, peacemaking criminology can be viewed in an international or global perspective. Respect for the environment and cooperation with other nations in ensuring that all people are accorded human rights is a goal of the peacemaking perspective. Although peacemaking criminology is not fully developed at this level, there are criminologists who have spoken on many of these issues. For example, Larry Tifft and Lyn Markham (1991) have made the connection between the society and international levels with their chapter in *Criminology as Peacemaking*, "Battering Women and Battering Central Americans." In this remarkable work, Tifft and Markham show the similarities between battering women and U.S. policy toward Central America, which, they contend, is similar to battering. They make these comparisons in terms of (1) the nature of these types of battering, (2) social and structural sources of battering, (3) the social processes and vocabularies for accepting and defending these behaviors, and (4) the issues that need to be addressed in ending violence and initiating peacemaking processes.

It is because of the applicability of peacemaking criminology to these four levels of analysis that it has such potential to transform the way justice is done in the U.S. Peacemaking criminology does not operate in a limited manner in only the criminal justice system. It examines how crime is connected to other features and institutions in society. Additionally, it holds the individual responsible for incorporating peacemaking processes into his or her own life and relationships. Peacemaking criminology is not a "soft on crime" policy. Rather, it holds both individuals and institutions responsible for addressing the issues that cause human suffering and misery. By insisting on nonviolence from both the offender and institutions, the peacemaking perspective attempts to break the cycle of violence that seems so much a part of the criminal justice system. Additionally, by bringing all the affected parties to the table, (offender, victim, families, and attorneys), peacemaking criminology provides a forum for long-term solutions based on social justice and the healing of relationships. Because peacemaking criminology is relatively recent in its development, it will be years before the empirical studies will be done that can gauge its effectiveness. Until then, we can expect peacemaking criminology to grow in visibility and stature within the discipline.

JOHN R. FULLER

References and Further Reading

Akers, R. 2000. *Criminological Theories: Introduction, Evaluation, and Application,* Los Angeles, CA, Roxbury.

Arrigo, B.A. 1999. *Social Justice or Criminal Justice: The Maturation of Critical Theory in Law, Crime, and Deviance,* Belmont, CA, Wadsworth.

Braswell, M., Fuller, J. and Lozoff, B. 2001. *Corrections, Peacemaking, and Restorative Justice: Transforming Individuals and Institutions,* Cincinnati, OH, Anderson.

Fuller, J. 1998. *Criminal Justice: A Peacemaking Perspective,* Boston, MA, Allyn and Bacon.

Gilligan, J. 1996. *Violence: Reflections on a National Epidemic,* New York, Vintage Books.

Harris, M.K. 1991. Moving into a new millennium: Toward a feminist vision of justice, in Pepinsky, H.E. and Quinney, R., Ed., *Criminology as Peacemaking,* Bloomington, IN, Indiana University Press.

Kant, I., in Close, D. and Meier, N. 1995. *The Categorical Imperative, in Morality in Criminal Justice: An Introduction,* Belmont, CA, Wadsworth.

Pepinsky, H.E. and Quinney, R. 1991. *Criminology as Peacemaking,* Bloomington, IN, Indiana University Press.

Quinney, R. 1991. The way of peace: On crime, suffering, and service, in Pepinsky, H.E. and Quinney, R., Ed., *Criminology as Peacemaking,* Bloomington, IN, Indiana University Press.

Tifft, L.L. and Markham, L. 1991. Battering women and battering central Americans: A peacemaking synthesis, in Pepinsky, H.E. and Quinney, R., Ed., *Criminology as Peacemaking,* Bloomington, IN, Indiana University Press.

See also **Marxist Theories of Criminal Behavior; Radical Theories of Criminal Behavior**

Peel, Sir Robert

Sir Robert Peel was a major political figure in England during a period that saw important changes as a result of the Industrial Revolution. Society across Europe was shifting from an agriculture-based structure to one reliant upon manufacturing. It was also a time that witnessed a political shift whereby power was wrested from the monarchy to a more democratic mode of governing. His father, Sir Robert Peel I, was a wealthy industrialist who served in Parliament. From his earliest years, Sir Robert Peel II was groomed to assume a major political role. He was an excellent student, and though a relatively private man, developed keen political skills for getting things done. It was this practical side that played a large role in finding Peel a significant place in history. Although from a conservative and aristocratic family, belonging to the dominant Anglican Church, he ultimately contributed to important changes that were often contrary to those conservative roots. In short,

Peel displayed an inclination to change his own outlook for practical reasons and frequently played the role of a change agent in the political realm. He was a leader of the more liberal wing of the Tory Party, and later in his career, led the new Conservative Party. It was in this context of facilitating reforms that Peel had a very important impact upon the administration of law and criminal justice.

Peel's political career was launched immediately after his graduation from Oxford. At the age of 21 he was elected to Parliament, serving in the House of Commons with his father. After only 3 years he was appointed to serve as the Chief Secretary for Ireland, a role to which he devoted 6 years. After a 3-year interim, he was then appointed to the politically powerful position of Home Secretary of England. The pinnacle of his career came with his service as Prime Minister of the country from 1841 to 1846.

Although a collapse of political support within his own Tory Party brought his ministry to a close, the remaining years of his life, 1846–1850, saw him in a leading role as a statesman. His unexpected death, coming as the result of a horse-riding accident, brought extensive mourning to the country.

To understand Peel's rise to power, as well as his major political setbacks along the way, it is necessary to note his reversals of positions on several major issues. Although he was a conservative, he facilitated critical changes that were most often motivated by practical concerns. First, in chairing the Bullion Committee in 1819, he supported the introduction of a metallic standard for currency, going against the leanings of his Tory Party. Another significant shift in Peel's career came in his decision to advocate the Catholic Relief Bill of 1829. Although he had generally not been attuned to the wishes of the Catholic minority, nor was the Tory Party, the extension of political rights to Catholics may have prevented England from falling into civil war. Peel's conservative leanings also led him to be unsympathetic to significantly opening the political process, but again, he ultimately compromised by supporting the Reform Act of 1832, leading to a restructuring of Parliament that allowed for broader class representation. This reform also led to the demise of the Tory Party, to be replaced by the Conservative Party. Thus Peel fell into the position of leading a new minority party, which he did with great success; he is remembered in England as the "founder of modern conservatism" (Gash, 1972, 709). Ironically, Peel's final shift of position on a major issue led to the end of his 5-year stint as Prime Minister and the falling of the Conservative Party from power. In this case, it was the Corn and Customs Bill of 1846, repealing the tax on corn and opening the country for free trade. Repeal of the Corn Laws headed off a crisis wrought by a famine in Ireland and growing class resentment, but led advocates of protectionism to seek vengeance against Peel (Gash, 1972). Adding to the irony, however, Peel remained popular and was regarded as the leading statesmen in England in the years following his ministry (1846–1850).

Somewhat less controversial by comparison, but representing substantial accomplishments indeed, were the reforms that Peel brought to the justice system throughout his career. It is for these contributions that criminologists extend an important place in history to Sir Robert Peel. He was much influenced by classical thought about crime and justice as reflected in Cesare Beccaria's *On Crimes and Punishments*. This was the very time that classical propositions were spreading throughout the Western world and being incorporated into legal reforms. Peel followed in the footsteps of

Sir Samuel Romilly, a colleague in the House of Commons, who was an impassioned advocate of the humanitarian reforms called for by classical thinking. The flavor of the era is captured in words that Romilly spoke to English Parliament in 1813:

> I cannot but confess that I feel some disappointment and much mortification at the resistance to the bill now before us. I had flattered myself that at least in this one instance I should have secured your unanimous concurrence. I certainly did not foresee that in an English House of Commons in the nineteenth century, one voice would have been heard in defense of a law that requires the tearing out of the heart and bowels from the body of a human being, while he is yet alive, and burning them in his sight (Phillipson, 1970, 274).

Peel similarly sought criminal reform, albeit in a more measured and politically astute tone, and when Romilly died prematurely by suicide in 1818, Peel carried on with the cause.

Early in his career, while serving as the Chief Secretary for Ireland, Peel sponsored reform legislation to improve policing by spreading the Dublin model of policing, eventually known as the Royal Irish Constabulary, across all of Ireland. These constables were well-received and nicknamed "Bobbies" and "Peelers" as namesake to Secretary Robert Peel. Later, as Home Secretary, he successfully advocated the removal of some 100 felonies from England's capital punishment laws. During Peel's nine years as Secretary, he oversaw modification or repeal of close to 300 criminal statutes.

Sir Robert Peel is best known in criminological circles for his dogged advocacy of the London Metropolitan Police Act of 1829. There was staunch resistance to police reform on a large scale because the police in other European countries, notably the French *Gendarmerie*, had been used as political tools of powerful central governments. Thus there was resistance to organizing the police on a wide scale and developing efficient policing. For these reasons Peel had to very carefully maneuver around political resistance to developing a centralized and professional police force. He finally succeeded in passage of this major reform bill after several years of effort. The small Scotland Yard section of London was also exempted from the act to gain support of members of Parliament who did not wish to be subjected to the same style of policing as the remainder of the metropolitan area. Still, the public's response was initially very negative. The "Peelers" or "Bobbies," as the name was adopted from Ireland, were at first ridiculed. They were sometimes subjected to insults and physical abuse publicly. There were even cases where officers were killed and their murderers not brought to justice because the officers were held in such low regard.

Peel's police reform remained quite true to Beccarian principles. The force was founded on the notion of deterrence, consistent with the logic of other reforms of the era. In indoctrinating his first two commissioners of the London Metropolitan Police, Peel closely followed Beccaria in asserting that "the principal object to be attained is the prevention of crime ... The absence of crime will be considered the best proof of the complete efficiency of the police" (Lyman, 1964, 133). Visible uniforms were required to maximize the appearance of police presence, whereas plain clothes were prohibited, largely to alleviate suspicions that the police might be used to infiltrate political meetings, as the *Gendarmerie* were noted for doing. Peel's concern with disassociating policing from the military was a second factor that had a major impact on the characteristics of the new professional police. The suits worn were quite distinct from those associated with military service. They wore blue civilian-style suits marked only by brass buttons emblazoned "police" and top hats. A marked feature was the absence of firearms. A third theme of Peel's new police was incorporation of features designed to project a positive image of professionalism, good character, and discipline. Selection of personnel emphasized detachment from the local citizenry, with rural backgrounds and retired noncommissioned military officers preferred as recruits. Drinking alcohol while on duty and acceptance of gratuities were prohibited. The Peelian reform provided the model of policing that spread to America and has persisted with only relatively minor adjustments in recent years. Thus the reform instituted by Peel with the London police became the classical model of policing that has endured in the Western world for nearly two centuries.

An attempt to assassinate Peel during his tenure as Prime Minister indirectly involved him in a significant reconceptualization of criminal responsibility (see Moran, 1977). Although the classical principles that he had so strongly identified, which envisioned all people as rational beings making free-willed choices to commit or not to commit criminal acts, the incident provided shape to the emerging concept of insanity that had come to exempt individuals from the assumptions of rationality and free will. In the 1843 incident, Daniel M'Naghten fatally shot Peel's secretary, having mistaken him for Peel. The courts found M'Naghten not guilty by reason of insanity and formulated the M'Naghten Rule, focusing on whether the defendant could distinguish right from wrong at the time of the offense, as a new test for insanity. This "right–wrong test" has since persisted as one of the most common legal insanity criteria in England and the U.S.

STEPHEN E. BROWN

Biography

Born in London, England, July 5, 1788; son of a wealthy manufacturer. Educated at Oxford University where he graduated in 1808 with Honors in mathematics and the classics. Served in House of Commons, 1809 through most of his pre-ministry career Served as Chief Secretary for Ireland from 1812–1818. Served as Home Secretary of England, 1821–1830. Served as Prime Minister of England, 1841–1846. Died in his Whitehall Gardens home, London, July 2, 1850.

References and Further Reading

Crosby, T.L. 1976. *Sir Robert Peel's Administration, 1841–1846,* Hamden, CN, Archon Books.
Gash, N. 1972. *Sir Robert Peel: The Life of Sir Robert Peel After 1830,* Totowa, NJ, Rowman and Littlefield.
Lyman, J.L. 1964. The Metropolitan Police Act of 1829, *Journal of Criminal Law, Criminology and Police Science,* 55.
Moran, R. 1978. Awaiting the crown's pleasure: The case of Daniel M'Naghten, *Criminology,* 15.
Morrow, J. 1997. The paradox of peel as Carlylean hero, *The Historical Journal,* 40.
Phillipson, C. 1970. *Three Criminal Law Reformers,* Montclair, NJ, Patterson Smith.
Thursfield, J.R. 1972. *Peel,* Freeport, New York, Books for Libraries Press.

See also **Police: History in England**

Penal Colonies

Penal colonies are remote locales to which convicts are sent for punishment and, arguably, rehabilitation purposes. With very few exceptions, they were established and conducted throughout the 18th and 19th centuries and are of general historical significance. Several nations have experimented with penal colonies as a solution to their crime and correctional problems at various points throughout their histories including

Portugal, France, Mexico, Holland, Spain, Russia, Denmark, and, most notably, England. The English experience with penal colonies is consequential in several respects in that it: (1) was one of the earliest efforts of its kind, (2) was coupled with the larger governmental objective of colonization, (3) exemplified, during its evolution, and at times simultaneously; the goals of punishment, deterrence, and reform; and (4) impacted the development of correctional philosophy.

Penal colonies constituted an alternative to imprisonment and were originally embraced as a means by which to address crime in society. During late 18th century England, the penal colony concept emerged as an answer to the pressing question of what to do about prison overcrowding (Eriksson, 1976). It was a subject that generated considerable philosophical debate concerning the efficiency and effectiveness of banishing prisoners, an approach that was weighed against another, eventually more lasting option, the penitentiary. Penitentiaries originally proved to be too expensive an approach, so penal colonies emerged as the dominant crime control mechanism for two centuries.

Banishment to a penal colony was known by the term *transportation*, which then carried a negative connotation, as convicts were transported to American and Australian colonies. The American Revolution ended the sending of convicts across the Atlantic Ocean and there is little historical reference to early American settlers as criminals, save "pilgrims" whose religious practices were prohibited and prosecuted. Although the penal colony concept furthered the colonization and settlement of frontier areas of America, most notably Georgia and New Orleans, rapid migration minimized general characterizations of territories as being of a penal colony origin. Australia, in turn, became the world's largest and most successful penal colony and comprises the bulk of most discussions on the topic.

The transportation of prisoners from England to Australia dates back to 1718, when felons sentenced to 3 years or more were banished to New South Wales (Robson, 1965). There is disagreement among scholars as to the manifest function of populating the Australian colony with convicts. In addition to using transportation as a means of effecting criminal justice, it has been contended that the primary purpose of establishing a penal colony, especially in New South Wales, was to realize greater economic benefit for the mother country. Convicts were a cheap labor source that developed the territory by building towns, bridges, and roads. From Botany Bay, where the first Australian penal colony was established, convicts' efforts served the interests of English trade and military prowess (Martin, 1978).

The more straightforward purpose of the penal colony, that of crime policy, is perhaps the foremost incapacitation initiative in criminal justice history. By sending vast numbers of convicts to the penal colony, it was thought that the bulk of England's criminal class could literally be removed. Augmenting this extreme form of incapacitation was the belief that the penal colony would generate a deterrent effect. Life in the penal colonies was intended to be a harsh and punitive existence characterized by unrelenting hard labor and virtually no luxuries.

Penal colonies were intended to be self-supporting, primarily through convict labor or public farms. Agriculture originally failed, owing to convicts' lack of farming skills, and management and control issues resulting from too few authorities to regulate an ever-growing convict population. Starvation was a constant concern and tales of inadequate food supplies added to both the misery of penal colony life and the perception of such, theoretically generating the desired deterrent effect.

Criminals originally did come to fear a sentence of transportation. In addition to the obvious punishments of hard work, potential starvation, the fear of the unknown, and never seeing friends, family or homeland again, the journey to Australia was more often than not characterized by both peril and cruelty. Hunger, thirst, and shipwrecks were common, as was inhumane treatment, sometimes to the point of torture by private contractors hired by the government to transport the convicts, who were also subjected to considerable moral degradation (Robson, 1965; Hughes, 1987).

Life in the early penal colonies was characterized by considerable misery, social disorganization, and a constantly changing authority system as drastically outnumbered officials tried to manage a population already at odds with law and order (Hirst, 1983). Conditions were so bad, especially in the penal colony known as Van Diemen's Land, an island off the Australian coast where prisoners were sent when New South Wales became overpopulated, that many turned to blinding or maiming themselves to avoid work. Others chose suicide.

Despite the horrific realities of the first penal colonies, there appeared to be little evidence of the desired deterrent effect. In fact, the penal colonies evolved to the point that prisoners actually wanted to be transported. Officials, constantly faced with the threat of revolt and the problem of fast-paced population growth, did away with the barbaric treatment of prisoners and instigated perhaps the first broad-scale initiative of reintegrating the prisoners into society. Many were pardoned by governors, either upon arrival or over time through an earned mark system. Prisoners in England, faced with either lengthy incarceration or the trapping of basement socioeconomic status with no hopes of upward mobility, came to see the penal colonies as opportunity.

Although agriculture and other labor dimensions were initially conducted by state agents and private citizens who migrated to Australia in an entrepreneurial spirit, convicts came to escape these masters by saving wages and becoming property owners in a free-market economy—a reality that would have never been more than a dream for them in England. A natural question about the penal colonies is the ability to effect an orderly society among a population of felons. By allowing and enabling convicts to better their conditions, they realized a vested stake in social affairs in a system that encouraged responsibility and a certain requisite level of social bonding. The ultimate success of the penal colonies demonstrated the logic of reintegrative correctional philosophy.

The English practice of transportation ended in the mid-1800s to be replaced with Jeremy Bentham's penitentiary concept. Other nations have temporarily used penal colonies but with less notoriety or success than the Australian experience. As England gave up using penal colonies as correctional policy, the French embraced it. The most famous French penal colony was Devil's Island, aptly named for both its criminal population and the extremely cruel treatment served there. The French continued using penal colonies into the 20th century, as did Mexico, but most nations had abandoned the practice. The banishment of criminals and political dissidents in Russia to Siberia at the turn of the 20th century is the most contemporary reality approximating penal colony life.

J. MITCHELL MILLER

References and Further Reading

Clark, C.M.H. (1962). *A History of Australia*. London, UK, Cambridge University Press.

Eriksson, T. (1976). *The Reformers: An Historical Survey of Pioneer Experiments in the Treatment of Prisoners*. New York, Elsevier.

Hirst, J.B. (1983). *Convict Society and Its Enemies: A History of Early New South Wales*, Sydney, Australia, G. Allen & Unwin.

Howard, D.L. (1960). *The English Prisons*, London, Frome & Tanner, Ltd.

Hughes, R. (1987). *The Fatal Shore*, New York, Alfred Knopf.

Martin, G., Ed. (1978). *The Founding of Australia: The Argument about Australia's Origins*, Sydney, Australia, Hale & Iremonger.

Nicholas, S. Ed. (1988). *Convict Workers: Reinterpreting Australia's Past.* Cambridge, UK, Cambridge University Press.

Robson, L.L. (1965). *The Convict Settlers of Australia*, Melbourne, Australia, Melbourne University Press.

Shaw, A.G.L. (1966). *Convicts and the Colonies*, London, Faber & Faber.

See also **Australia, Crime and Justice in; U.K., Crime and Justice in**

Penitentiaries *See* **Jails; Prisons**

Perjury

Considered an affront to the integrity and proper functions of the courts, perjury occurs when a defendant knowingly makes false statements under oath of material matters in any proceeding before or ancillary (actions conducted by judicial representatives or actions conducted pursuant to explicit statutory or judicial procedures) to any court or grand jury of the U.S. Laws governing perjury were established to prevent the legitimacy of court proceedings from being compromised by individuals who knowingly and deliberately provide false testimony in a material matter. Defined as a criminal offense, statutes addressing perjury were enacted by Congress under Title 18, § 1621, 1622, and 1623. The goals of the statutes were to prevent and deter individuals from presenting false testimony or making false declarations in any judicial setting and to proscribe sanctions for that offense. The broadest statute regarding perjury, Section 1621, applies to all material statements or evidence provided under oath and addresses the essential elements of perjury. Section 1622 relates to subordination of perjury that requires that the defendant induce a witness to falsely testify and that the witness must actually commit perjury. Section 1623 addresses prosecutorial sanctions for committing perjury or subordination of perjury and requires that the government provide proof beyond a reasonable doubt for conviction. Based on these statutes, both perjury and subordination of perjury require that: (1) the individual is under oath, (2) testimony is given in a judicial setting, (3) the witness knowingly makes false statements, and (4) the testimony is material to the proceeding before the court.

Oath

Under Title 18, perjury requires that an oath or affirmation (legally recognized equivalent of an oath that is permitted or required by statute) has been administered by a duly appointed officer. An oath is the swearing to the truth of a statement or affidavit administered by the government in proceedings before or ancillary to any court or grand jury. The statute requires that the defendant understand the obligations of the oath and the associated penalties for perjury. To constitute perjury, the oath requirement of Title 18 must be met at the time testimony is given.

Knowingly False

Under Section 1621, the element of "knowing" focuses on the intent of the defendant and whether the defendant willfully stated or subscribed to testimony with the knowledge that the testimony was false. Knowing involves a requisite mental state that coexists with the doing of a proscribed act. Section 1623 only requires that the testimony is knowingly stated or subscribed to and is not limited to willfully (intentional, deliberate) stated testimony. Both sections require that the defendant know the testimony is false or does not believe it to be true and that the information is material to the proceedings to constitute perjury. However, a defendant cannot be convicted of perjury when false statements are not attributable to corrupt intention, but to an error of judgment or mistake of law or fact. Statements given that are expressions of belief or opinion, literally truthful, unambiguous, inadvertent, evasive, honest mistakes, carelessness, negligent, or contradictory do not constitute perjury, even if they are intended to mislead.

Materiality

Materiality relates to any information or evidence that is important or relevant to legally proving or disproving the issue before the court. Any false testimony given under oath is material only if it is germane to the investigation. Broadly constructed to incorporate a wide range of information, materiality and the effect of the false testimony are weighed in terms of the potential to impede or hinder the investigative efforts of the courts. The standard of materiality does not require only that the false testimony be material to the main issue or primary subject under investigation, but also includes collateral matters and subsidiary issues that have the tendency to influence, impede, or hamper the court's investigation. The government does not have to prove that the testimony actually impeded the investigation, only that the testimony was relevant to any issue before the grand jury with the potential to influence or mislead the court.

Section 1863 also requires two witnesses or one witness with corroborating evidence to support single-witness testimony to convict a defendant of perjury. Corroborating evidence to support perjury can include testimony, books, papers, documents, records, recordings, or other material that is knowingly false or contains false information. The burden of proof is met by the government when materiality is proven by transcripts of prior proceedings, testimony from witnesses of the proceeding, or the prior testimony of the defendant. Although perjury requires proof beyond a reasonable doubt, the government only has to show that the testimony is false in one or more material facts. This evidence must show by clear, convincing, and direct evidence to a moral certainty and beyond a reasonable doubt that the defendant's actions were willful and corrupt. The court is required to examine the nature of the inquiry and the evidence introduced at trial to determine whether a truthful answer would have aided the court's investigation.

Subordination of Perjury

Subordination of perjury occurs when a defendant corruptly induces another witness to present false testimony in a court proceeding. Essentially relying on the elements of perjury (oath, testimony in court, knowingly false statements, and material), subordination of perjury requires actual testimony under oath that is perjured and knowledge by the defendant and the witness that the testimony is false. Evidence must show that the defendant knew or should have known that the testimony was false and that he knowingly induced the witness to give false testimony. In addition, the witness must falsely testify with the knowledge that the information provided is in fact false. As with perjury, it is not necessary that the false testimony be relevant to the main issue, only that the testimony in question has the potential of proving or disproving a material fact in the proceedings. Based on Section 1623, proof of subordination of perjury also requires proof beyond a reasonable doubt, two independent witnesses or a single witness whose testimony is corroborated by other evidence for a perjury conviction.

PATRICIA GRANT

References and Further Reading

Chamelin, N. and Evans, K. (1995). *Criminal Law for Police Officers,* 6th ed., Englewood Cliffs, NJ, Prentice Hall.

Cunningham, L. (1999). Taking on testilying: The prosecutor's response to in-court police deception, *Criminal Justice Ethics,*18(1), 26.

Dorfman, D. (1999). Proving the lie: Litigating police credibility, *American Journal of Criminal Law,* 26(3), 455–504.

Klotter, J. (2001). *Criminal Law,* 6th ed. Cincinnati, OH, Anderson Publishing Company.

Muraskin, R. and Muraskin, M. (2001). *Morality and the Law,* Upper Saddle River, NJ, Prentice Hall.

Scanlon, H. (2002). False statements, *American Criminal Law Review,* 39(2), 507–527.

18 USCS § 1621. (2003).

18 USCS § 1622. (2003).

18 USCS § 1623. (2003).

See also **Criminal Courts, Problems in**

Personality Theories of Criminal Behavior

Introduction

The study of personality is well rooted in psychological and criminological theory and universally defined as the various emotions, behaviors, and attitudes that distinguish each person and make him or her unique from others. It is the interaction between personality and behavior that makes it a fundamental issue in criminology today. More specifically, the understanding of the link between personality and criminal behavior is of such interest to criminologists because it offers a unique perspective on creating crime prevention interventions that connect individual traits to behaviors. In this essay the various personality theories will be discussed and then examined within the realm of criminal justice.

Psychological Theories of Personality Development

Many personality theorists believe that personality development is an early construction that when formed is difficult to change. Whether it is in an academic or a criminal justice setting, personality plays a role in all of our actions and reactions in life. It impacts how we respond to others, how we approach our decisions, our motivation levels, our success in attaining life goals, and in handling life disappointments and decisions (Fontana, 2000). Consequently, research has acknowledged that personality has a significant bearing on behavior.

The traditional theories of personality are based on learning and psychoanalytic theory. Traditional learning theorists state that personality is developed from the experience that children have as their parents punish and reinforce their behaviors. Early learning theorist John Watson explained that by age three, parents' interactions with their children determine what type of adult that child will become in the future. Furthermore, Watson believed that the development of the personality of the child and ultimately the adult that he will become is the direct responsibility of the parent(s) (Goldstein, 1994).

A more elaborate traditionalist theory is Allport's (1961) Trait Approach, which focuses specifically on the individual's uniqueness, suggests that an individual can be depicted as possessing three types of traits: cardinal trait, central traits, and secondary traits. Cardinal trait is described when a person possesses a strong dominant trait such as altruism. Central traits are described when a person possesses several observable characteristic traits such as honesty and creativity. Secondary traits are described as characteristic traits that are observed only in specific circumstances such as artistic ability. Expanding upon Allport's trait approach, Eysenck (1952b) suggested that traits are inherited when he proposed that people possessed three personality dimensions, introversion–extraversion, neuroticism–stability, and psychotocism. In contrast to Allport's ideographic approach to traits, Eysenck argued for a nomothetic trait approach. Eysenck (1952b) proposed that individuals possess the same traits but in differing degrees.

Goldstein (1994), on the other hand, argued that the personality trait approach assumes individuals are classified as a result of their behavioral tendencies. The behavioral tendencies include consistency and individual differences. Consistency is the predisposed way that individuals act, thus allowing predictions to be made, whereas individual differences suggest the uniqueness of each person, thus their traits.

Based on Goldstein's work the Trait Approach to personality development was then expanded into personality categories. Tupes and Christal (1961) were the first to create these categories, known as the five-factor model. The five-factor model, referred to as the Big Five, consists of five basic personality dimensions. They are neuroticism, extraversion, openness to experiences, agreeableness, and conscientiousness (Costa and McCrae, 1985; Mount and Barrick, 1995).

Neuroticism is characterized by exhibiting fear, anxiety, depression, and moodiness, suggesting an imbalance between adjustment and emotional stability. Neurotic individuals are also perceived as lacking self-esteem and self-confidence. Extraversion exemplifies outgoing, assertive, talkative, and excitement seeking tendencies. Those scoring low on extraversion tend to be introverted, reserved, and task-oriented. Openness to experiences is characterized by expressing a desire to search for new experiences and challenges, possessing creativity, and thoughtfulness. Those scoring low on openness to experiences tend to be unartistic and conservative. Agreeableness is defined as one's geniality specifically, whether one is kind, trusted, trustworthy, and warm. Those scoring low on agreeableness tend to be suspicious, rude, and manipulative. Lastly, conscientiousness suggests an achievement oriented focus expressed through organizational skills, persistence, and motivation (McCrae and Costa, 1991). The five-factor model attempted to explain cognitive, clinical, and social theories and has been the framework for connecting criminal behaviors and motivations with personality.

Personality Theory and Criminology

A significant amount of criminal justice research has examined the impact of personality on crime and criminal behavior. The previous sections of this essay displayed a universal definition of personality, one that is more often used in attempting to explain criminal behavior is "all biological influences, psychological traits and cognitive features of the human being that psychologists have identified as important in the mediation and control of behavior" (Megargee, 1966, 18). In recent research, criminologists, specifically criminal psychologists, have shifted their focus around the connection between personality development and criminal behavior to concentrate on the cognitive aspects of personality development, as it relates to criminal offending.

In the late 1960s Edwin Megargee developed a theoretical perspective of explaining violence through

personality. After researching a highly assaultive population, Megargee developed two distinct personalities, under-controlled and the chronically over-controlled, based on the behaviors that he saw in this population (Megargee, 1966).

Chronically Over-Controlled Personality Type

The chronically over-controlled personality, in complete contrast, is more established in his or her inhibitions against aggressive behavior and rigidly adheres to them, even in the face of provocation. According to Megargee, those who were identified to have chronically over-controlled personalities have learned through experience about the consequences, both real and imagined, of engaging in any type of violent behavior (1966). Megargee (1966) believed that those who had a chronically over-controlled personality were likely to have been over-socialized to the extent that they believe that any violation of any social rule would end in punishment.

Even further, Megargee hypothesized that when the chronically over-controlled person becomes so overwhelmed and frustrated, it is likely that he or she may respond violently. Megargee (1966) also believed that when frustrated enough, the person displaying the chronically over-controlled personality type might strike out even more violently than a person displaying an under-controlled personality type. He also described their criminal behaviors as being more brutal and unexpectely violent acts. Ultimately, Megargee (1966) believed that criminals displaying an under-controlled personality type were likely to include such extremely violent criminals as those who commit such acts as family mass murders.

Under-Controlled Personality Type

Megargee (1966) also developed a typology for the under-controlled personality. A person who displays an under-controlled personality has few inhibitions with regards to aggressive behavior. These individuals are likely to regularly engage in violent behavior when provoked or frustrated. According to Megargee (1966), in people with the under-controlled personality type, aggression becomes a habitual response to volatile situations, especially when the person becomes upset or angry.

The Violent Personality

Toch (1969) was able to expand on Megargee's under-controlled personality type and develop a subcategory known as the violent personality type. He theorized in his book *Violent Men* that most violent episodes can be explained by the past success that individuals have had in dealing with conflicted, interpersonal relationships. Toch (1969) was stating that the violent acts displayed by some individuals are not just a simple lack of impulse control but instead are acts of those who historically responded violently to similar situations. Ultimately, Toch's (1969) research showed that if one were to examine the history of people who were incarcerated for violent acts, he would see that most of those incarcerated had a history of responding violently to interpersonal conflicts in their past.

Following Toch's (1969) theory further, people who have committed violent acts have done so because the violence has allowed them to receive the positive or negative reinforcement needed to acquire what was wanted or to avoid taking part in a particular situation. Ultimately, the individuals who had a violent history and who responded violently when frustrated were thought to have a violent personality, according to Toch (1969).

Toch (1966) expanded his theory further and stated that those individuals who have a violent personality were likely to have been humiliated or threatened in a way that made them feel that their reputation or status was in question. Ultimately, these individuals with violent personalities have few social skills and are unable to handle the day-to-day strikes at their self-esteem without acting out. The person with the violent personality is even more likely to be provoked into aggression when he or she comes from a subculture that is more approving of aggressive acts.

Conditioned Violence Personality

Berkowitz (1970) expanded on Toch's theory by stating that people are likely to react violently not because they anticipate some type of negative reaction but because "situational stimuli have evoked the response that they are predisposed to make in the given situation" (Berkowitz, 1970, 140). Berkowitz believed that people who are prone toward violence are classically conditioned to react violently because of prior experiences in similar situations. According to Berkowitz (1970) powerful environmental stimuli can "trigger" a response in persons who have a personality prone to violence. The environmental stimuli in these situations vary from person to person and can be as clear as abuse or as simple as a facial expression. No matter what the trigger, it is likely the individual who causes the violent response has had similar reactions in the past in which they did respond violently and received some type of positive reinforcement.

Research connecting personality and criminal behavior did not stop with the work of Toch (1969), Berkowitz (1970), and the other early theorists. The connection between personality and crime is still of interest to psychologists and criminologists today. Researchers continue to acquire evidence that offers theoretical premises for the "psychological sources of behavioral propensities that have high social costs and benefits in the population at large (i.e. partner violence, crime, and altruism)" (Krueger, 2002, 566). Hans Eysenck was one of the first personality theorists to begin to examine the impact of the interaction between personality development and environment in the creation of antisocial personality theory.

Eysenck's Biological Typology

Hans Eysenck defined personality as a "more or less stable and enduring organization of a person's character, temperament, intellect, and physique which determine his unique adjustment to the environment" (Eysenck, 1970). Based on Eysenck's definition, traits are emphasized and used to create a typology. His typology includes three dimensions: extraversion or introversion, stability or neuroticism, and impulse control or psychotocism. All three of Eysenck's personality dimensions are directly related to various aspects of crime; however, Eysenck felt that it was the stability or neurotic and control or psychotocism dimensions that were of the greatest relevance to criminologists. Generalized neurotics are those individuals who have unreasonable fears of various objects, places, persons, open spaces, or heights. Most often generalized neurotics have an anxiety level that is disproportionate to the realities of the situation. The generalized neurotics are of little concern to criminologists because in most cases their fears do not allow them to act in a criminal manner; however, there are a few in this group who are "unable to assess the consequences of their actions and who behave in an asocial or antisocial manner regardless of the punishment meted out by others" (Eysenck, 1965, 100).

The second personality dimension that Eysenck felt directly related to criminal behavior is the control or psychotic. Psychotics show extreme levels of psychopathology and in many cases are insensitive to others, hostile, cruel, and inhumane, with a strong need to make fools of other people or upset them. Along with these varied deviant traits, psychotics according to Eysenck can also be extremely creative. It is the combination of these two characteristics that make many psychotics likely to not only take part in criminal behavior but also in many times violent crimes. It is in this category that psychopaths and serial killers are often found.

Violence Subculture and Personality

Wolfgang and Ferracuti (1967) expanded on the work of Eysenck by creating a more concrete integration of psychological and criminological theory in an attempted understanding of the development of criminal behavior with the subculture of violence theory. According to Wolfgang, citizens in poor urban communities (ghettoes) develop a subcultural value system that accepts the use of violence to obtain what one wants from the community (Wolfgang and Ferracuti, 1967). Wolfgang and Ferracuti (1967) believed that those who are raised in such a subculture develop a personality that allows them to condone "physical toughness, sexual exploitation, shrewdness, thrill seeking, and aggressive behavior as a result of racial oppression and economic marginality" (Curtis, 1975, 124).

The norms and values of this subculture are adopted and somewhat accepted by the members of these communities and in this internalization process they develop a personality type that condones criminal behavior (Curtis, 1975). The "criminal personality" that develops from the subculture of violence can most clearly be seen in the young males of the community. The criminal personality developed from the subculture enables them to use illegal means to attempt to gain what they do not have (Rosenfield, 1997). The values of the subculture are passed on to others in the community. This eventually causes the citizens of these communities to submit to accepting the system and not becoming a victim to it (Rosenfield, 1997).

Multifactor Personality Theory

A second personality theory that begins to merge the development of personality with criminal behavior is the Multifactor Personality Theory developed by Krueger and colleagues (2001). They have been able to build on the earlier works of Toch (1969) and more clearly conceptualize the relationship between personality and crime. Moffitt et al. (2000) conducted an extensive longitudinal–epidemiological study of a birth cohort of persons at ages 18, 21, and 26 in an attempt to establish a stable relationship between personality and crime. Through this extensive examination, three personality factors were found to be directly related to criminal behavior. The first personality factor was one's tendency to constrain one's expression of impulses. This factor was found to manifest in a tendency to obey the law three years in the future. The second personality factor reflected negative emotionality and was most often seen in the expression of anxiety and alienation. The third personality factor was one that reflected a tendency to experience positive emotions most often through achievement. Moffitt et al.'s (2000) study showed that these factors were strongly correlated with personality scales at age 18 and as strongly correlated with criminal behavior at age 21. Overall, this was one of the first longitudinal analyses providing empirical evidence for the theoretical claim that "personality measures and measures of criminal behavior are both a manifestation of a latent and stable tendency to act in an unconstrained manner" (Moffitt et al., 2000, p. 220).

Summary

In conclusion, the blending of the fields of criminal justice and psychology is the best way to fully understand the impact that personality development has on criminal behavior. Unfortunately, for many years, the two disciplines, psychology and criminology, have not been integrated in their perspective but instead acted in separation. The lack of a multidisciplinary approach to understanding the impact of personality theory on criminal behavior has left many unanswered questions. However, it is the hope that through the current trend of more actively blending these two fields, we will be able to more fully understand the multifaceted relationship that exists between personality theory and criminal behavior.

ROBYN D. LACKS AND HEATHER WILLIAMSON

References and Further Reading

Allport, G.W. (1961). *Patterns and Growth in Personality*, New York, Holt.

Barrick, M.R. and Mount, M.K. (1991). The big 5 personality dimensions and job performance: A meta-analysis, *Personnel Psychology*, 44, 1–26.

Berkowitz, L. (1970). The contagion of violence: An S-R mediational analysis of some effects of observed aggression, *Nebraska Symposium on Motivation*, Lincoln, NE, University of Nebraska Press.

Bouchard, T.J., Lykken, D.T., McGue, M., Segal, N.L. and Tellegen, A. (1990). Sources of human psychological differences: The Minnesota study of twins reared apart, *Science*, 250, 223–228.

Douglas, J., Burgess, A., Burgess, A. and Ressler, R. (1992). *Crime Classification Manual*, New York, Lexington Books.

Eysenck, H.J. (1952). *The Scientific Study of Personality*, New York, Macmillan.

Eysenck, H. (1965). *The Causes and Cures of Neurosis*, San Diego, CA, Robert R. Knapp.

Eysenck, S. (1970). Crime and personality: An empirical study of the three-factor theory, *British Journal of Social and Clinical Psychology*, 10, 225–239.

Fontana, D. (2000). *Personality in the Workplace*, Lewiston, NY, Macmillan Press.

Goldstein, E.B. (1994). *Psychology*, Belmont, CA, Brooks or Cole Publishing.

Hogan, J. and Ones, D.S. (1997). Conscientiousness and integrity at work, in R. Hogan, J. Johnson, and so Briggs, Eds., *Handbook of Personality Psychology*, pp. 849–870, San Diego, CA, Academic Press.

Jackson, J. and Berkerian, D. (1997). *Offender Profiling: Theory, Research and Practice*, New York, Wiley.

Kenny, D.A. (1991). A general model of consensus and accuracy in interpersonal perception, *Psychological Review*, 98, 155–163.

Krueger, R. (1999). The structure of common mental disorder, *Archives of General Psychiatry*, 56, 541–568.

Krueger, R. (2002). Personality from a realist's perspective: Personality traits, criminal behaviors, and the externalizing spectrum, *Journal of Research in Personality*, 36, 564–572.

McCrae, R.R. and Costa, P.T., Jr., (1990). *Personality in Adulthood*, New York, Guilford.

Megargee, E. (1966). Undercontrolled and overcontrolled personality types in extreme antisocial aggression, *Psychological Monographs*, 80, 15–27.

Mount, M.K. and Barrick, M.R. (1995). The big five personality dimensions: Implications for research and practice in human resources management, in G.R. Ferris, Ed., *Research in Personnel and Human Resources Management*, Vol. 13, pp. 153–200, Greenwich, CT, JAI Press.

Toch, H. (1969). *Violent Men: An Inquiry into the Psychology of Violence*, Chicago, IL, Aldine.

Pinizzotto, A. (1984). Forensic psychology: Criminal personality profiling, *Journal of Police Science and Administration*, 12, 32–40.

Pinizzotto, A. and Finkel, N. (1990). Criminal personality profiling: An outcome and process study, *Law and Human Behavior*, 14, 215–234.

Shoham, S. (2000). *Personality and Deviance: Development and Core Dynamics*, New York, New York Press.

Tupes, E.C. and Christal, R.E. (1961). *Recurrent Personality Factors Based on Trait Ratings* (USAF ASD Tech. Rep. No. 61–97), Lackland Air Force Base, TX, U.S. Air Force.

See also **Psychological Theories of Criminal Behavior; Psychopathy and Crime**

Petersilia, Joan

It was through serendipity that Joan Petersilia initially became a criminal justice researcher and consequently became one of the most well-known criminologists and corrections scholars in the world. In 1974, she had just finished her master's degree in sociology at Ohio State University (OSU) and now was back in the Los Angeles area looking for a job. While at Ohio State, she had taken courses from Simon Dinitz, a highly regarded criminologist, and had participated in research at a halfway house for female parolees. Both of these experiences had sparked an interest in corrections issues and led her to question the effectiveness of correctional programs. However, she was frustrated by what she then saw as a "disconnect" between academic research and what was going on in the real world. She wanted to use her life to help people who entered the criminal justice system and initially intended to work as a probation officer in Los Angeles. But before probation had a job opening, she was offered a position as a research assistant for Peter Greenwood at RAND in Santa Monica, California. Greenwood triggered her interest in criminal justice policy research, showing her ways to bridge research and real world issues. She went on to work for RAND for over 20 years.

It was RAND's empirically based, policy-oriented, collaborative approach to criminal justice research that influenced Petersilia most. Throughout her applied research career she has focused on the "hot" corrections topics—the issues that people in the field are currently struggling to address. In the 1970s, she worked with Peter Greenwood and other colleagues on the *Criminal Careers of Habitual Felons* project, which was one of the first attempts to track repeat offenders over their life course and measure their crime commission rates (later known as "lambdas.") This project served as a pilot test for obtaining self-report data from inmates and other high-risk repeat offenders. It was a precursor to the now-famous RAND Inmate Survey, where researchers interviewed 2190 inmates and identified ten types of offenders and their characteristics. These early RAND projects introduced the notion of "selective incapacitation" and inspired future research on the effects of correctional policies on crime and criminal careers.

While at RAND, Petersilia quickly became a well-known and respected expert in correctional program evaluation. Beginning in the 1980s, Petersilia and her long-time research and writing colleague, Susan Turner, focused on community corrections issues. *Granting Felons Probation: Public Risks and Alternatives*, funded by the National Institute of Justice (NIJ), was the first empirical study of the costs of and risks posed by placing serious offenders on probation. This California study showed that most felons granted probation were rearrested and that many of them therefore posed a serious threat to public safety. It prompted practitioners nationwide to study their own felony probation practices (spawning many replications of the study nationwide) and to rethink their sentencing practices. Probation officials, under a storm of criticism for the high recidivism rates, asked: would these offenders have done better if sentenced to prison?

To answer this question, Petersilia and Turner conducted another NIJ-funded study, *Prison versus Probation in California,* in which they studied the recidivism rates of matched cohorts of prisoners and probationers. The offenders were matched on as many background and crime characteristics as possible to allow the researchers to focus on the effects of the sanctions. They found that most probationers and prisoners failed within the follow-up period, but that prisoners had higher recidivism rates. They were arrested more, had more charges filed, and were convicted more often. The study suggested that prison did not deter or incapacitate as well as some had hoped. Rather than be deterred, offenders seem to make up for lost time. The researchers also discovered that, in this sample, about a quarter of those sentenced to prison could not be statistically distinguished from those sentenced to probation. Prison was also increasingly expensive, leading the researchers to conclude that intermediate community sanctions, such as intensive supervision, electronic monitoring, and house arrest, might incapacitate many offenders while avoiding the direct and collateral costs of prison.

Looking for alternatives was particularly important in the late 1980s. Policymakers were facing the practical problems of prison crowding, as "get tough" policies and pro-punishment attitudes grew. Neither felony probation nor prison seemed effective, and many wondered whether some middle-range sanction might better control crime and corrections costs while delivering just punishment. To help policymakers address this dilemma, Petersilia wrote a RAND report in 1987 entitled *Expanding Options for Criminal Sentencing* in which she described intermediate sanctions, elaborated on specific model programs, and discussed the advantages and disadvantages of using these sentencing options. At that time, there was great enthusiasm about intermediate sanctions—the anecdotal evidence suggested such programs reduced recidivism and saved money. Unfortunately, there were no rigorous evaluations of their impacts.

For the next five years, Petersilia and Turner conducted rigorous, experimental-design evaluations of a variety of intermediate sanction programs (e.g., electronic monitoring, intensive supervision, work release, drug testing). From 1987 through 1991, the U.S. Department of Justice funded a nationwide field test of intensive supervision probation and parole (ISP),

and Petersilia and Turner were chosen as the national evaluators. Each participating site was required to participate in a randomized field experiment, where eligible offenders would be assigned to routine or intensive supervision. This was the first time researchers had designed and implemented a multisite experiment using random assignment "in the field" (within the working criminal justice system). It demonstrated that it was possible to use rigorous methodological designs to evaluate correctional programs and illustrated the benefits of researchers and practitioners working together. The results were published in dozens of reports and articles and demonstrated conclusively that offenders sentenced to intensive supervision (ISP) had *higher* recidivism rates than people on routine supervision, in part because they were watched more and their misbehaviors therefore were more likely to be detected. Officials had hoped that ISP would decrease system costs by decreasing arrests and incarceration, but the opposite was true. Many ISP programs were subsequently dismantled, because program proponents could no longer persuasively argue that the programs saved money or diverted people from prison. However, the study also importantly showed that intensive supervision *did* reduce recidivism when it was able to *combine* surveillance and treatment activities. This finding caused some ISP programs to increase their treatment services or focus on juveniles, where rehabilitation was a greater part of the mission. Petersilia was asked by the Department of Justice to summarize the results of her extensive research on intermediate sanctions, which she did in the publication, *A Decade of Experimenting with Intermediate Sanctions: What Have We Learned?*

During the 1990s, the get-tough sentencing movement continued. States imprisoned a record number of people and many abolished traditional parole services. The late 1990s, therefore, brought another major issue to the policymaking forefront. Many inmates were returning to their communities without correctional programming to ease their transition. Petersilia quickly became one of the academic leaders working with correctional practitioners and policymakers to consider these reentry challenges. One of her recent publications, *When Prisoners Return to the Community: Political, Economic, and Social Consequences*, discusses the effects of releasing offenders without giving them the skills and support necessary for success. Petersilia continues to examine the issues surrounding "prisoner reentry" and to focus on finding solutions to the problems it creates.

True to her original aspirations, Petersilia has maintained her connection to the real world of sentencing and corrections policy. She has produced many research findings that have influenced the decisions of policymakers who struggle daily to design more effective programs and improve public safety. Many look to her for guidance, because she is able to translate complicated research findings in a way that makes them accessible and useful to practitioners. She is also respected by scholars, who recognize that she does not compromise her rigorous research and evaluation standards in order to do research in operational settings. Some academics refer to her as an "applied criminologist," (as opposed to a more theoretically-oriented one). She welcomes this description and sees herself as testing ideas that come directly from those who work within the criminal justice system. She also has a unique ability to sense the emerging issues, trying to lend data and empirical understanding to them before they hit the crisis point. Her lasting legacy likely will be that she had built bridges between academics and correctional leaders, and has had a major impact on the way probation, prison, and parole programs are implemented and evaluated. Her empirical studies and balanced writings have produced objective data that can be used to inform the too-often political and philosophical debates over corrections policy. She says she would be most gratified if she had accomplished a rather simple career goal: having practitioners use empirically grounded findings for their policy and program decisions.

JODI LANE

Biography

Born in Pittsburgh, Pennsylvania, January 2, 1951; daughter of Air Force General and an Army nurse. Educated at Loyola Marymount University in Los Angeles, California, B.A., 1972; The Ohio State University, M.A. in Sociology, 1974; University of California, Irvine, Ph.D. in Social Ecology (Criminology), 1990. Senior Researcher, RAND Corporation Criminal Justice Program, 1974–1989; Director RAND Corporation Criminal Justice Program, 1989–1994; Corporate Fellow, RAND Corporation, 1991–1994; Professor of Criminology, Law and Society, University of California, Irvine, 1992 to present. Vice-Chair, Law and Justice Committee, National Research Council, 1997-present; President of Association for Criminal Justice Research in California, 1984–1985; President of American Society of Criminology, 1989–1990. Elected Fellow of Western Society of Criminology, 1988; Elected Fellow, American Society of Criminology, 1990; Vollmer Award, American Society of Criminology, 1994, Academy of Experimental Criminology, 2000; Resides in Santa Barbara, California.

Selected Works

Criminal Careers of Habitual Felons, with Peter Greenwood and Marvin Lavin. The RAND Corporation (1978).

Criminal Career Research: A Review of Recent Evidence, in *Crime and Justice: Annual Review of Research,* Vol. 2, edited by Norval Morris and Michael Tonry (1980).

Granting Felons Probation: Public Risks and Alternatives, *Crime and Delinquency* 31 (1985).

Prison versus Probation in California: Implications for Crime and Offender Recidivism, with Susan Turner. The RAND Corporation (1986).

Expanding Options for Criminal Sentencing. The RAND Corporation (1987).

Implementing Randomized Experiments: Lessons from BJA's Intensive Supervision Project, *Evaluation Review* 13 no 5 (1989).

An Evaluation of Intensive Probation in California, with Susan Turner, *The Journal of Criminal Law and Criminology* 82 (1991).

Policy Relevance and the Future of Criminology, *Criminology* 29 (1991).

Evaluating Intensive Supervision Probation and Parole: Results of a Nationwide Experiment, with Susan Turner. National Institute of Justice (1993).

A Crime Control Rationale for Reinvesting in Community Corrections, *The Prison Journal* 74 no 4 (1995).

A Decade of Experimenting with Intermediate Sanctions: What Have We Learned? *Federal Probation* 62 (1998).

Parole and Prisoner Reentry in the U.S., in *Prisons,* edited by Michael Tonry and Joan Petersilia (1999).

When Prisoners Return to the Community: Political, Economic, and Social Consequences, National Institute of Justice (2000).

References and Further Reading

Blumstein, A., Cohen, J., Roth, J.A. and Visher, C., Ed. 1986. *Criminal Careers and "Career Criminals,"* Washington, DC, National Academy Press.

Byrne, J.M., Lurigio, A.J. and Petersilia, J., Ed. 1992. *Smart Sentencing: The Emergence of Intermediate Sanctions,* Newbury Park, Sage Publications.

Chaiken, M.R. and Chaiken, J.M. 1984. Offender types and public policy, *Crime and Delinquency,* 30(2).

Champion, D.J. 1988. *Felony Probation: Problems and Prospects,* New York, Praeger Publishers.

Clear, T.R. 1994. *Harm in American Penology,* Albany, NY, State University of New York Press.

Clear, T.R. and Dammer, H. 2000. *The Offender in the Community,* Belmont, CA, Wadsworth.

Currie, E. 1998. *Crime and Punishment in America: Why the Solutions to America's Most Stubborn Social Crisis Have Not Worked—And What Will,* New York, Metropolitan Books.

Harland, A.T. 1996. ed. *Choosing Correctional Options that Work:* Defining the Demand and Evaluating the Supply, Thousand Oaks, CA, Sage Publications.

McCarthy, B.R., McCarthy, B.J., Jr. and Leone, M.C. 2001. *Community-Based Corrections,* 4th ed., Belmont, CA, Wadsworth.

Morris, N. and Tonry, M. 1990. *Between Prison and Probation: Intermediate Punishments in a Rational Sentencing System,* New York, Oxford University Press.

Tonry, M. 1996. *Sentencing Matters,* New York, Oxford University Press.

Tonry, M. and Hamilton, K., Eds. 1995. *Intermediate Sanctions in Over-crowded Times,* Boston, MA, Northeastern University Press.

Wilson, J.Q. and Petersilia, J., Eds. 2001. *Crime: Public Policies for Crime Control,* San Francisco, CA, Institute for Contemporary Studies Press.

See also **Prisons: Problems and Recent Developments in**

Phrenology

In the mid-1800s the positivism movement was begun by Auguste Comte, who believed that human knowledge should be limited to those observable facts that can be determined by scientific methods. Other than the observable, we cannot be sure of anything (Mill, 1907). Positivist theories were developed soon after to attribute observable biological and environmental factors of crime and criminality. Italian criminologist Cesare Lombroso proposed developing a science of the criminal man. He believed that criminals could be detected by their physical abnormalities such as facial asymmetries or distinctive features (e.g., high cheek bones, indentations on the head, and protruding ears), and that these features would signal potential social dangers. Simply put, it was believed by Lombroso and his followers that one should be able to look at another person and identify him or her as either a criminal or not. Throughout his career Lombroso collected skull and head measurements of living and deceased criminals and compared them to noncriminals. He also attempted to develop a system for subcategorizing criminal types (Horn, 2003).

Around this time, other researchers were collecting anthropomorphic data, which are essentially the measurement of how people differ physically. Devices were designed to measure such attributes as skin and hair color, eye pigment, lip thickness, and skull capacity. It was believed that the larger the skull capacity of an individual, the more evolved that individual was. Thus, the larger headed person was deemed more civilized and more intelligent. These studies have been criticized as being ethnocentric and racially biased (Guthrie, 1998).

Because the spirit of the time was to examine physical differences, what was then thought to be an upcoming science of measuring bumps and depressions on the head gained attention. This "science" was known as phrenology. Phrenology began as a legitimate science studying human "faculties," but is now regarded as a pseudoscience and outright quackery promoted by charlatans (Goodwin, 1999).

The beginnings of phrenology can be traced to Franz Josef Gall, who was trained as a physician skilled in anatomy. Gall was interested in the functioning of the brain. He compared the brains of many animal species and argued that the size of brain structures corresponded with the species' mental abilities. Gall further argued that the brain was the organ of intellect and emotion and that these faculties were located within distinct regions in the brain. Although the location of the faculty was thought to remain constant, the amount of each faculty possessed varied from one individual to the next. Increased capacity or development of these cerebral parts was thought to result in a prominent protrusion. Likewise, a corresponding deficit would result in depression or indentation of the individual's skull.

Gall's work was initially referred to as "cranioscopy," and would later be known as phrenology (where "phrenos" refers to the mind and "-ology" refers to the study of) when Johann Spurzheim coined the term (Spurzhiem, 1832). Whereas Gall is credited with discovering phrenology, Spurzheim is best known for popularizing phrenology in America and in parts of Europe. In Spurzheim's (1832) *Outlines of Phrenology* he detailed five main principles of phrenology:

1. The brain functions as the organ of the mind.
2. The mind is composed of intellectual and emotional facilities.
3. Each facility is located in a specific region of the brain.
4. The amount of brain tissue for any given facility varies across individuals.
5. As the skull conforms to the shape of the brain, the strength of the facility can be determined by the skull's shape.

Spurzheim took Gall's ideas and began to tour abroad. He lectured on the subject in America and phrenology gradually caught on. As the phrenology movement gained momentum and spread to America, more localized areas were "discovered." For example, in the 1840s, American physician Silas Hubbard claimed to have discovered bumps that he labeled no. 41 and no. 25 that were thought to measure consciousness and conjugal love, respectively (Heath, 1929).

Phrenology captured the public's interest. Elaborate machines were developed to measure head shape. Practitioners of phrenology, such as the Fowlers of New York, often provided group and private phrenology readings. It was not uncommon for individuals to get a reading to help them determine their abilities and other attributes along with their compatibility with others. Phrenological "readings" of famous 19th century Americans were developed and published. For example, Edgar Allen Poe was described in the following manner: "How broad in the region of the temples, where Ideality, Constructiveness and Sublimity are located! And the region of Spirituality was also enormously developed!" (Stern, 1982).

By the 1920s, phrenology was viewed with skepticism and largely denounced as a pseudoscience and ultimately dismissed by the scientific community. Mary Hubbard Heath (1929) provides an excellent anecdotal account of a phrenological reading her father gave during a public meeting that illustrates phrenology's subjective nature. Silas Hubbard was trained as a physician but practiced phrenology to supplement his income. Hubbard describes a reading where her father was blindfolded and asked to read the skull of the local hooligan. Unknown to Hubbard, the town minister was swapped in at the last minute, and became the new subject of the reading. The crowd roared to Hubbard's embarrassment when he began to reveal the negative facilities possessed by the minister. This story sheds light on both the subjectivity inherent in phrenology and on the public interest it fostered. Because of its widespread acceptance, however, phrenology retained popular acceptance for some time.

Even though phrenology ultimately became viewed as quackery, it indirectly benefited science in promoting the notion of localization of cerebral function. Researchers during this time period discovered the localization of language production and comprehension, whereas others discovered the localized areas of the sensorimotor cortex (Solso, MacLin, and MacLin, 2004). In the history of criminal justice, the contributions of phrenology are less illustrious and perhaps deleterious to those individuals unfortunate enough to have been misshapen. Yet, truly it is an interesting chapter in the history of criminology, psychology, and brain sciences.

Otto H. MacLin

References and Further Reading

Guthrie, R.V. (1998). *Even the Rat Was White,* Boston, MA, Allyn and Bacon.

Goodwin, C.J. (1999). *A History of Modern Psychology,* New York, John Wiley & Sons.

Heath, M.H. (1929). *Elbert Hubbard I knew: An Intimate Biography,* New York, Roycrofters.

Horn, D.G. (2003). *The Criminal Body,* New York, Routledge.

Mill, J.S. (1907). *Auguste Comte and Positivism,* London, Kegan Paul, Trench, Trubner & Co.

Solso, R.L., MacLin, M.K. and MacLin, O.H. (2004). *Cognitive Psychology,* Boston, Allyn and Bacon, Inc.

Spurzheim, J. (1978). Outlines of phrenology, in Robinson, D.N., Ed., *Significant contributions to the history of psychology. Series E. Vol II,* Washington, DC, University Publications of America.

Stern, M.B. (1982). *A Phrenological Dictionary of Nineteenth-Century Americans,* Westport, CT, Greenwood Press.

Gould, S.J. (1981). *The Mismeasurement of Man,* New York, W. W. Norton & Co.

Leahey, T.H. and Leahey, G.E. (1983). *Psychology's Occult Doubles: Psychology and the Problem of Pseudoscience,* Chicago, IL, Nelson-Hall.

See also **Biological Theories of Criminal Behavior; Body-Type Theories of Criminal Behavior; Intelligence (IQ) and Criminal Behavior**

Physical Attractiveness and Criminal Behavior

Physical unattractiveness, deformity, and disfigurement have been associated with evil since antiquity. In the *Iliad,* Homer described the wicked Thersites as possessing thin hair over a "misshapen head," with one blinking eye, and a lame leg. Physiognomy (the "science" of reading personality characteristics into facial features) traces its practice to Homer's Greece. When Socrates was convicted for heresy and the corruption of youth in the 5th century BC, a physiognomist charged that his face betrayed a brutal disposition. Greek culture embraced the notion that mind and body were interconnected; if a sound mind went together with a sound body, the implication was that a twisted mind resided in a deformed body. Aristotle confirmed this view in his *Metaphysics* when he reasoned that the essence of the body is contained in the soul.

These opinions were ensconced into law in medieval Europe. Among those accused of demonic possession, ecclesiastical edicts interpreted large warts and moles on the skin as physical signs of the entry point of the devil into the soul (Einstadter and Henry, 1995). Secular law directed jurists to convict the uglier of two people who were under equal suspicion for a crime (Wilson and Herrnstein, 1985). In an echo of these sentiments some years later, Shakespeare's Cassius, in *Julius Caesar* (Act I, Scene II), is judged a dangerous man by his "lean and hungry look."

The link between unattractiveness and criminal behavior remained alive and well in 20th century American popular culture. In his famous comic strip and in the movies it inspired, cartoonist Chester Gould sharply contrasted the square-jawed, clean-cut good looks of detective Dick Tracy with cutthroat criminals like the flat-headed "Flattop," the pointy-snouted "Mole," the wrinkle-cheeked "Pruneface," and the big-bottomed "Pear Shape." Hollywood imitated science in *Johnny Handsome* (1989), a feature film about a robber with grotesque facial deformities who reforms after receiving extensive cosmetic surgery.

Some of the earliest criminological researchers shared this thinking. Physiognomy persisted throughout the 18th century, most notably in the work of Swiss scholar Johan Casper Lavater, whose influential *Physiognomical Fragments* appeared in 1775. One hundred years later, Italian prison physician Cesare Lombroso published *Criminal Man* (1876), a famous study that attributed criminal behavior to what he termed "atavism," an inherited condition that made offenders evolutionary throwbacks to more primitive humans. By conducting autopsies on 66 deceased criminals, and comparing 832 living prison inmates with 390 soldiers, Lombroso created a list of physical features that he believed were associated with criminal behavior. These "stigmata" included sloping foreheads, asymmetrical faces, large jaws, receding chins, abundant wrinkles, extra fingers, toes, and nipples, long arms, short legs, and excessive body hair—hardly the image of handsome men.

The notion that criminal behavior was related to physical anomalies was dealt a severe blow by the publication of Charles B. Goring's *The English Convict* in 1913. This study subjected 37 of Lombroso's stigmata to empirical testing by comparing 2348 London convicts to a control group that represented a cross section of young Englishmen. Goring found little support for Lombroso's arguments, concluding that criminal behavior is caused by inherited feeblemindedness, not physical appearance.

Undaunted by these results, Harvard anthropologist Earnest A. Hooton conducted an ambitious 12-year study that compared 13,873 male prisoners in 10 states with a haphazard sample of 3023 men drawn from the general population, searching once more for physical differences. Hooton published his findings in *The American Criminal* and *Crime and the Man*, both books appearing in 1939. The books attributed criminal behavior to biological inferiority and "degeneration," ascribing a variety of unattractive physical characteristics to criminals (including sloping foreheads, compressed facial features, drooping eyelids, small, protruding ears, projecting cheekbones, narrow jaws, pointy chins, and rounded shoulders).

By the 1930s, however, biological research was rapidly losing favor, as criminologists increasingly argued that social factors alone cause criminal behavior. Hooton's research was ridiculed in particular, one sociologist dismissing his findings as comically inept in historic proportions (or "the funniest academic performance ... since the invention of movable type" (Reuter, 1939)). Hooton was condemned for his circular reasoning: offenders were assumed to be biologically inferior, so whatever features differentiated criminals from noncriminals were interpreted as indications of biological inferiority.

Despite the skepticism of many sociologists regarding these attempts to link physical unattractiveness to criminal conduct, self-derogation, and general strain theories can explain this relationship. Self-derogation theory asserts that youth who are ridiculed by peers lose self-esteem and the motivation to conform (Kaplan, 1980). General strain theory claims that repeated "noxious," unwanted interactions produce disappointment, depression, frustration, and anger (Agnew, 1992). Both theories see delinquency and crime as means of retaliation that boosts one's self-worth or vents one's anger. Certainly, unattractive youths are prime candidates for noxious ridicule that results in low self-esteem and emotional strain.

Only a handful of modern studies have tested the relationships among attractiveness, criminal behavior, and perceptions about crime. Saladin, Saper, and Breen (1988), for example, asked 28 students in one undergraduate psychology class to judge the physical attractiveness of a group of photographs of young men. Forty students in another psychology class were asked to examine the same photographs and then assess the probability that those pictured would commit either robbery or murder. The researchers found that men rated as less attractive also were perceived to be prone to commit future violent crimes, suggesting that unattractive people are more likely to be branded as criminals.

Another study randomly scrambled 159 photographs of young men incarcerated in juvenile reformatories with 134 photographs of male high school seniors (Cavior and Howard, 1973). College sophomores in psychology courses were asked to rate the facial attractiveness of these youth. Significantly more high school seniors were judged attractive than males from the reformatories.

In the fascinating policy-oriented research that became the basis for the movie *Johnny Handsome*, surgeons performed plastic surgery to correct deformities and disfigurements (e.g., protruding ears, broken noses, unsightly tattoos, and needle track marks from intravenous drug use) on the faces, hands, and arms of 100 physically unattractive men at the time of their release from Rikers Island jail in New York

City (Kurtzberg et al., 1978). These exconvicts were matched against a control group of equally unattractive inmates released from the jail who received no reconstructive surgery. When the researchers compared recidivism rates 1 year later, those who received the surgery had significantly fewer rearrests. Apparently, improved appearance resulted in improved behavior.

These research findings are preliminary and suggestive; more definitive studies using better measurements are needed. In particular, future research should relate ratings of physical attractiveness to the self-reported criminal behavior of persons taken from the general population. Such studies would rule out the possibility that unattractive offenders are more likely to appear in jails and reformatories simply owing to the prejudices of the police and prosecutors.

Nevertheless, existing research hints that the folk wisdom dating back to the ancient Greeks may have some basis in reality. Physical appearance is related to self-worth and behavior; as the adage goes, "pretty is as pretty does." When it comes to criminal behavior, the opposite may be true as well.

RICHARD A. WRIGHT

References and Further Reading

Agnew, R. 1992. Foundation for a general strain theory of crime and delinquency, *Criminology*, 30(1).

Cavior, N. and Howard, L.R. 1973. Facial attractiveness and juvenile delinquency among Black and White offenders, *Journal of Abnormal Child Psychology* 1(2).

Einstadter, W. and Henry, S. 1995. *Criminological Theory: An Analysis of Its Underlying Assumptions*, Fort Worth, Texas, Harcourt Brace College.

Goring, C.B. 1972. *The English Convict: A Statistical Study*, London, H.M.S.O., 1913. Reprint, Montclair, NJ, Patterson Smith.

Hooton, E.A. 1939. *The American Criminal*, Cambridge, MA, Harvard University Press.

Hooton, E.A. 1939. *Crime and the Man*, Cambridge, MA, Harvard University Press.

Kaplan, H.B. 1980. *Deviant Behavior in Defense of Self*, New York, Academic Press.

Kurtzberg, R.L., et al. 1978. Plastic surgery on offenders, in Johnston, N. and Savitz, L.D., *Justice and Corrections*, New York, Wiley.

Lombroso, C. 1972. *L'uomo Delinquente*, Milan, Hoepli, 1876. Reprint, Rome, Napoleone Editore, 1971. Translated as *Criminal Man*, New York, Putnam, 1911. Reprint, Montclair, NJ, Patterson Smith.

Reuter, E.B. 1939. Book review of Earnest A. Hooton's "Crime and the Man," *The American Journal of Sociology*, 45(1).

Saladin, M., Saper, Z. and Breen, L. 1988. Perceived attractiveness and attributions of criminality: What is beautiful is not criminal, *Canadian Journal of Criminology*, 30(3).

Wilson, J.Q. and Herrnstein, R.J. 1985. *Crime and Human Nature*, New York, Simon and Schuster.

See also **Biological Theories of Criminal Behavior; Body-Type Theories of Criminal Behavior; Genetic Theories of Criminal Behavior**

Physicians and the Pharmaceutical Industry, Crimes by

Crimes that are committed by medical doctors, as well as those that occur within the context of the pharmaceutical industry, are commonly referred to as "white-collar" offenses. The term white-collar crime, first introduced by Edwin Sutherland (1995) over 50 years ago, is used to identify a broad category of behaviors that are fundamentally different from traditional street crimes. Unlike traditional street crimes, white-collar offenses are typically perpetrated by means of fraud or deception, and white-collar offenders include persons primarily from the occupational professions and corporate ranks. In this regard, crimes that are committed specifically by physicians are often referred to as "professional" or "occupational" crimes, whereas crimes that occur within the pharmaceutical industry fall under the general rubric of "corporate" offenses.

Criminal justice practitioners, researchers, and the general public have historically downplayed the significance of white-collar crime in favor of highlighting the more visceral impact associated with street crimes such as rape, robbery, or homicide (Reiman, 1995). This reluctance to identify, prosecute, and punish white-collar offenders in general has certainly occurred in response to wrongdoing committed within the trillion dollar a year healthcare industry. Estimates of the cost of healthcare fraud range from 50 to 80 billion dollars annually, and the consequences related to unnecessary medical procedures, negligent care, and prescription violations exact an enormous physical toll as well (Witkin, Friedman, and Doran, 1992; Liederbach, 2001a).

Crimes by Physicians

Physicians are generally recognized as an elite occupational group in American society (Rosoff, 1987). Their status derives from years of highly specialized training, lucrative salaries, and the much admired ability to remedy physical ailments. The prestige afforded to medical professionals has not, however, shielded the profession from criminal wrongdoing. Prominent crimes committed by doctors include medical kickbacks, unnecessary treatments, fraud, and prescription violations.

The term "kickback" refers to payments from one party to another in exchange for referred business or other income-producing deals. The state has an interest in controlling these practices through legal codes, because physicians who are primarily concerned with obtaining financial gains through kickbacks may compromise their loyalty to patients and their professional decision making (Liederbach, 2001b). Two well-recognized types of medical kickbacks are self-referrals and fee-splitting. Self-referrals involve sending patients to specialized medical facilities in which the doctor has a personal financial interest. It has been estimated that between 50,000 and 75,000 physicians have a financial stake in auxiliary medical practices (Rosoff, Pontell, and Tillman, 1998). A more traditional form of kickback is the fee-split. Fee-splitting occurs when a general practitioner physician receives payment from a surgeon or other medical specialist in exchange for referred business. The acceptance of medical kickbacks by doctors is considered unethical, and most states had declared the practice of fee-splitting illegal by the 1950s (Rodwin, 1992).

The infliction of unnecessary medical treatments on patients can be considered illegal because these treatments needlessly expose patients to physical risks (a form of assault) and they result in compensation that has been deceptively gained (fraud) (Lanza-Kaduce, 1980). In light of the uncertain nature of medical diagnoses, however, it is often difficult to determine when a particular medical procedure can be deemed "unnecessary." Green (1997) has outlined several methods used by researchers to determine the extent of the problem, including comparing geographical variations in surgical rates, variations in surgical rates among insurance plans, and expert opinions. For example, one government study discovered a 120% higher surgical rate for patients enrolled in traditional fee-for-service medical plans versus patients enrolled in more cost-conscious health maintenance organizations (Green, 1997).

Fraudulent billing schemes that can include billing for services not rendered, charging for nonexistent office visits, and the illegal distribution of prescription drugs constitute an additional form of medical crime (Liederbach, 2001b). These schemes initially developed and continue to flourish in association with the Medicaid program that extended government sponsored health coverage to needy Americans beginning in 1965. The program provided unscrupulous doctors unique opportunities for fraud and abuse because government legislators failed to provide adequate cost-containment policies to the original plan and enforcement of violations was often lax (Jesilow, Pontell, and Geis, 1993). Perhaps the most prominent form of Medicaid fraud is the development of "Medicaid mills," where a number of Medicaid service providers collaborate to perform unnecessary tests and procedures, as well as serve the illicit drug trade through the illegal dispensing of prescription drugs (Jesilow, Pontell, and Geis, 1993).

The unlawful dispensing of prescription drugs is one of the most common forms of crime by physicians. Although the vast majority of physicians uphold their responsibilities concerning dangerous and addictive drugs including tranquilizers, amphetamines, and narcotics, a considerable number of doctors do not. Between 1988 and 1996, 1521 doctors were disciplined by state medical boards for misprescribing or overprescribing drugs (Wolfe et al., 1998). A report documenting the prescription of drugs in one large Albany, NY, hospital reported that doctors made 2.5 prescription errors *per day* (quoted in Green, 1997). Unfortunately, the medical profession has largely failed to adequately discipline doctors who violate prescription laws. At least 69% of the doctors cited between 1988 and 1996 were not even temporarily suspended from practicing medicine (Wolfe et al., 1998).

Crimes by the Pharmaceutical Industry

Large-scale pharmaceutical companies have created a vast global marketplace for the development, manufacture, promotion, and sale of prescription drugs. Many of the drugs developed by pharmaceutical companies have proven to be "miracles" in terms of their ability to reverse deadly illnesses and diseases, and the drugs have surely contributed to increasing life spans. Many of the companies responsible for creating these miracle cures, however, have also produced a dubious track record of illegal and unethical activities far surpassing those found in other industries. These crimes are often committed in conjunction with physicians, since they are involved in the testing and distribution of these substances. The most prominent corporate crimes that have occurred within the industry include fraudulent drug safety testing, unsafe manufacturing practices, bribery of foreign nationals, and graft involving physicians (Braithwaite, 1984; Braithwaite, 1995).

Pharmaceutical firms have used fraudulent means to obtain safety approval for the sale of dangerous drugs. Pharmaceutical manufacturers spend billions of dollars in the production of new drugs. This massive investment of research and development funds has the potential to create conflicts of interest whereby drug manufacturers aim to obtain safety approvals by any means necessary, including concealing unfavorable testing data or aiding in the production of fraudulent testing data in clinical trials.

The conflict between the need for drug approval and safety interests has produced disastrous results in some cases. For example, during the 1960s the Merrill Co. introduced MER/29, a drug intended to reduce cholesterol. 300,000 American used MER/29 during its initial year of introduction (Silverman, 1976). The drug had been approved for use on the basis of positive clinical trials, however, the company had concealed unfavorable testing data related to the drug's side-effects, including baldness, changes in reproductive organs, and the development of cataracts (Braithwaite, 1984). Hundreds of patients filed civil lawsuits against Merrill after experiencing adverse reactions to the drug, and corporate executives plead no contest to criminal fraud charges (Knightly et al., 1979).

This case was followed later that same decade by the thalidomide disaster. Thalidomide was introduced as a sleep aid and widely distributed in many European nations. Shortly after introduction of the drug, clinicians began reporting dangerous side-effects including peripheral neuritis, a condition that causes irreversible numbness in the limbs (Braithwaite, 1984). Although some countries (including the U.S.) failed to approve the drug for sale or banned its use, there was no international mechanism for the exchange of adverse drug information. So too, the manufacturer harassed physicians who sought to publish unfavorable information concerning the drug (Braithwaite, 1984). Thalidomide was eventually prescribed to expectant mothers, thousands of whom gave birth to children with horrendous birth defects related to thalidomide use (Knightly et al., 1979). Most of the civil cases eventually brought against the manufacturer were settled out of court, and criminal charges were suspended after payments were made to the families of thalidomide victims (Braithwaite, 1984).

The thalidomide case resulted in the enactment of laws designed to regulate the international drug market; however, more recent failures suggest the need for continued vigilance in the area of drug testing. For example, the introduction of the arthritis drug Oraflex by Eli-Lilly Corp. in the 1980s has been linked to 49 deaths and over 900 injuries. The company had concealed information pertaining to the deaths of 29 patients overseas prior to the drug's approval in the U.S. (Rosoff, Pontell, and Tillman, 1998).

Some pharmaceutical companies have been guilty of distributing unsafe drugs by substituting less expensive ingredients in the production process or by failing to prevent contamination during drug manufacturing. The most prevalent abuses in this area now occur in third world nations that lack effective drug regulations. Most industrialized countries now require drug manufacturers to abide by "Good Manufacturing Practices" (GMPs) that have been mutually agreed upon industry-wide. In fact, regulatory controls in the manufacture of drugs date to 1938 and the enactment of the Food, Drug, and Cosmetic Act. The act was adopted in response to over 100 deaths attributed to the drug Elixir Sulfanilamide during the 1930s.

A more recent and widely-cited example of unsafe manufacturing involved the production of sterile intravenous solutions by Abbott Laboratories during the 1970s (Braithwaite, 1984). The company was subjected to 38 recalls related to poorly manufactured solutions, including the mislabeling of products, contamination, and over 40 cases of blood poisoning. The case resulted in the rare criminal prosecution of company executives for the deaths of several patients (Braithwaite, 1984).

In addition to fraudulent testing and unsafe manufacturing, the industry has a well documented history of illegal and unethical payoffs to foreign nationals as a means to promote the use of prescription drugs. These payoffs are a violation of U.S. foreign aid regulations first enacted as part of the 1977 Foreign Corrupt Practices Act. Pharmaceutical companies are able to conceal illegal foreign payoffs because of the industry's complex transnational organization and the difficulties involved in regulating corporations across national boundaries (Braithwaite, 1984). Payoffs have been employed in order to persuade foreign health officials to allow dangerous drugs on the market or convince customs officials to allow the shipment of banned substances (Braithwaite, 1984). The pharmaceutical industry has historically been the most commonly cited for violations of illegal foreign payments.

Finally, industry sales representatives have used gifts to physicians as a means to promote drug prescriptions. Doctors who accept such gifts in exchange for increased future prescriptions of a particular drug are guilty of "graft," whereby individuals use their occupational position and influence in order to elicit monetary payoffs. Researchers estimate that drug companies spend an average of $5000 per doctor (or two billion dollars) annually in order to convince doctors to use a particular brand of prescription drug (quoted in Green, 1997). These payoffs can involve medical supplies and equipment, free drug samples, consumer products, or entertainment expenses.

Despite the industry's poor regulatory history, significant progress has been made over the course of the last half century in monitoring the production and development of prescription drugs and curbing abuses (Braithwaite, 1995). The original Food, Drug, and Cosmetic Act of 1938 was augmented in 1962 following the thalidomide case. The 1962 Act provided an industry-wide, transnational reporting system for adverse drug reactions. Today, the Food and Drug Administration (FDA) is charged with ensuring drug safety and effectiveness prior to company marketing and distribution. The World Health Organization (WHO) provides additional regulatory controls on the international level. In 1993, the FDA implemented the voluntary Medical Products Reporting System ("MedWatch") as a way to monitor the safety of prescription drugs after they enter the marketplace. The system has resulted in over 10,000 reports of adverse drug reactions and the removal of several dangerous prescription drugs that had been previously approved for sale in the U.S. (Ropp, 1995).

JOHN LIEDERBACH

References and Further Reading

Braithwaite, J. (1984). *Corporate Crime in the Pharmaceutical Industry,* Boston, Routledge & Kegan Paul.

Brathwaite, J. (1995). Transnational regulation of the pharmaceutical industry, in Geis, G., Meier, R.F. and Salinger, L.M., Eds., *White Collar Criminality: Classic and Contemporary Views,* pp. 299–315, New York, The Free Press.

Green, G.S. (1997). *Occupational Crime,* 2nd ed., Chicago, IL, Nelson-Hall.

Jesilow, P., Pontell, H.N. and Geis, G. (1993). *Prescription For Profit: How Doctors Defraud Medicaid,* Berkeley, CA, University of California Press.

Knightly, P., Evans, H., Potter, E. and Wallace, M. (1979). *Suffer the Children: The Story of Thalidomide,* New York, Viking.

Lanza-Kaduce, L. (1980). Deviance among professionals: The case of unnecessary surgery, *Deviant Behavior,* 1, 333–359.

Liederbach, J., Cullen, F.T., Sundt, J.L. and Geis, G. (2001a). The criminalization of physician violence: Social control in transformation, *Justice Quarterly,* 18(1), 141–170.

Liederbach, J. (2001b). Opportunity and crime in the medical profession, in Shover, N. and Wright, J.P., Eds., *Crimes of Privilege: Readings in White Collar Crime,* pp. 144–156. New York, Oxford.

Reiman, J. (1995). *The Rich Get Richer and the Poor Get Prison,* Boston, MA, Allyn & Bacon.

Rodwin, M.A. (1992). The organized American medical profession's response to financial conflicts of interest: 1890–1992, *Millbank Quarterly,* 70(4), 703–741.

Ropp, K.L. (January, 1995). *MedWatch: On the lookout for medical product problems,* US Food and Drug Administration Special Report.

Rosoff, S.M. (1987). *Physicians as Criminal Defendants: Specialty Status and Sanctions,* PhD. dissertation, Department of Criminology, Law, and Society, University of California, Irvine, CA.

Rosoff, S.M., Pontell, H.N. and Tillman, R. (1998). *Profit Without Honor: White-Collar Crime and the Looting of America,* Upper Saddle River, NJ, Prentice Hall.

Silverman, M. (1976). *The Drugging of America,* Berkeley, CA, University of California Press.

Sutherland, E.H. (1995). White-collar criminality, in Geis, G., Meier, R.F. and Salinger, L.M., Eds., *White Collar Criminality: Classic and Contemporary Views,* pp. 29–39, New York, The Free Press.

Witkin, G.D., Friedman, D. and Doran, G. (1992). Health Care Fraud, *US News and World Report,* 24, pp. 34–43.

Wolfe, S., Franklin, K.M., McCarthy, P., Bame, P. and Adler, B.M. (1998). *16,638 Questionable Doctors Disciplined by State and Federal Governments,* Washington, DC, Public Citizens Health Research Group.

See also **Consumers, Crimes Against; White-Collar Crime: Definitions**

Pistols *See* **Firearms**

Poland, Crime and Justice in

Introduction

Poland is situated in Central Europe on the Baltic coast. It occupies an area of 312,685 km² (the ninth largest country in Europe) and has a population of about 39 million. The administrative division consists of 16 voivodeships, 308 counties (including 65 towns with county status), and 2478 communes.

The 1989 downfall of the totalitarian system undoubtedly influenced the dynamics and structure of crime in Poland. Political and economic transformations are increasingly exploited by offenders. References made to data concerning the years 1970–2000 (Table 1) illustrate the dimension of crime and its development tendencies. Between the year 1991 and 2000 the average number of crimes was 983,240, that is,

twice the number during the 1980s and two and a half times the rate from the 1970s. Expanding crime exerts an impact on the growing pathologization of public life in Poland. This situation is becoming increasingly menacing owing to the considerable rise of the gravest crimes (Table 2).

The highest growth rate occurred in the cases of assault, which in 1997 was more than four times higher than in 1989. The characteristic feature of Central-Eastern Europe during the 1990s was spontaneously developing migration movements that also affected the quantitative transformations of offences committed by foreigners. In 1989–1999 the number of foreigners suspected of having perpetrated a crime in Poland grew systematically: from 957 in 1989 and 719 in 1990 to

Table 1. Crime, convictions, and prisoners in Poland in 1970–2000

Year	Crime		Convictions			Prisoners	
	Number of Crimes in Poland	Rate Per 1000 Population	Number of Convictions	Males	Females	Number of Prisoners	Rate Per 100,000 Population
1970	427,217	1304.2	166,049	148,405	17,644	82,436	253.4
1971	475,411	1449.2	197,334	176,685	20,649	102,902	313.7
1972	379,086	1146.4	169,321	150,020	19,301	115,343	348.8
1973	355,125	1064.4	152,176	135,247	16,929	124,685	373.7
1974	339,542	1007.8	147,469	130,073	17,396	81,075	240.6
1975	340,440	1000.6	161,286	143,143	18,143	96,242	282.9
1976	324,181	934.4	159,363	142,208	17,155	97,748	284.5
1977	344,506	992.9	137,847	123,788	14,059	85,262	245.7
1978	355,492	1017.8	157,463	141,312	16,151	97,849	280.2
1979	337,302	956.7	153,026	136,592	16,434	106,243	301.3
1980	337,935	949.8	151,958	135,861	16,097	99,638	280.1
1981	379,762	1057.8	12,6403	114,132	12,271	74,807	208.4
1982	436,206	1204.1	148,456	132,480	15,976	79,783	220.2
1983	466,205	1274.8	141,768	127,679	14,089	85,295	233.2
1984	538,930	1460.0	125,132	111,741	13,391	76,164	206.3
1985	544,361	L463.2	149,414	132,099	17,315	110,182	296.2
1986	507,913	1356.0	153,037	133,386	19,651	99,427	265.5
1987	508,533	L350.2	166,753	146,515	20,238	91,140	242.0
1988	475,273	1255.3	137,159	122,699	14,460	67,824	179.1
1989	547,589	L442.4	93,373	84,849	8,524	40,321	106.2
1990	883,346	2317.3	106,464	100,189	6,275	50,165	131.6
1991	866,095	2264.6	152,333	144,021	8,312	58,619	153.3
1992	881,076	2296.6	160,703	151,091	9,612	61,409	160.1
1993	852,507	2216.7	171,622	160,772	10,850	61,562	160.1
1994	906,157	2351.0	185,065	173,327	11,738	62,719	162.7
1995	974,941	2526.6	195,455	183,196	12,259	61,136	158.4
1996	897,751	2324.7	227,731	212,586	15,145	55,487	143.7
1997	992,373	2567.6	210,600	195,693	14,907	57,382	148.5
1998	1,073,042	2774.1	219,064	203,710	15,354	54,373	140.6
1999	1,121,545	2900.5	207,607	192,944	14,663	56,765	146.8
2000	1,266,910	3277.6	222,815	206,041	16,774	70,544	182.5

Table 2. Committed crimes according to selected categories, juvenile suspects, and penalties in Poland in 1989–2000

Committed Crimes–Selected Categories	1989	1990	1991	1992	1993	1994	1995	1996	1997	1998	1999	2000
Murder	556	730	971	989	1106	1160	1134	1134	1093	1072	1048	1269
Rape	1660	1840	1921	1919	1976	2039	2267	1985	2260	2174	2029	2399
Serious assault	8588	10,415	12,956	13,795	16,646	18,454	18,901	19,371	20,506	19,496	17,849	18,429
Other assault	2988	3935	5553	6060	7285	9223	10,600	11,575	13,005	13,034	12,576	14,363
Theft	106,061	159,988	139,507	125,074	134,089	180,514	211,602	157,479	184,368	211,651	243,537	309,846
Violent theft	9067	16,217	17,094	17,715	21,034	23,574	26,858	26,257	30,063	34,225	44,775	53,533
Burglary	218,581	431,056	355,896	330,741	314,338	304,293	304,899	305,703	324,017	355,176	369,235	364,786
Drug related crime	2278	1105	2468	2442	5457	4000	4284	6780	7915	16,432	15,628	19,649
Others	197,810	258,060	329,729	382,341	350,576	362,900	394,396	367,467	409,146	419,782	414,868	482,636
Number of juvenile suspects	29,841	37,534	41,433	41,573	43,039	61,109	68,349	57,240	58,730	58,151	52,674	56,345
Rate per 1000 population aged 13–16	1242.2	1519.0	1641.8	1621.6	1660.3	2339.3	2590.7	2139.1	21,72.7	2143.1	1964.4	2174.6
Penalties	92,686	106,464	152,333	160,703	171,622	185,065	195,455	227,731	210,600	219,064	207,607	222,815
Unconditional imprisonment	24,733	29,140	40,635	39,671	36,989	33,659	33,324	31,303	25,806	25,942	26,171	30,748
Conditional imprisonment	41,007	52,030	76,579	84,350	91,295	99,856	105,796	123,669	116,159	123,410	127,437	143,497
Restriction of liberty	9758	5230	5291	5405	6389	7223	7306	10,612	10,934	13,263	15,648	14,796
Fine	17,188	19,487	29,714	31,259	36,920	44,308	49,997	62,082	57,689	56,400	38,209	33,699

8306 in 1997 and 6017 in 1999. In other words, in 1999 the number of foreign suspects rose more than six times in comparison to 1989.

Unfavorable phenomena within the structure of crime had became more frequent by 1993; in particular, this concerned the threat of crimes against life, health, and property, combined with aggression, violence, and ruthlessness toward the victims. Juvenile crime also demonstrates a disturbing growth rate (see Table 2).

In 1989–1990 juvenile offenders constituted from 13% to 16% of all suspects, and in 2000 they made up 14% of all suspects (56,345). The number of juvenile suspects in 2000 was twice as large as in 1989. The greatest number of murders (51) was perpetrated by juvenile offenders in 1994.

The number of convicts is shown in Table 1.

An analysis of tendencies disclosed by convictions in 1970–1992 should take into consideration amnesties carried out in 1974, 1977, 1981, 1984, 1986, and 1989. The period under examination witnessed distinct changes within the structure of convictions according to types of imposed penalties (Table 1). The amnesties also influenced the number of persons imprisoned (Table 2). In 2000, the size of the prison population totaled 70,544 convicts.

Organized Crime

At the beginning of the 1990s, Poland became the scene of developing organized crime. Statistical data from January 2001 show the activity of more than 400 crime groups, including 170 international groups whose members originate from 30 states. More than 50 groups deal with the illegal production and distribution of narcotics, 40 groups focus on the theft and smuggling of cars, more than 40 groups collect protection money, 30 groups trade in arms and explosives, and 15 groups concentrate on criminal terrorism. New criminal phenomena are associated with securities turnover and insurance. The most frequently occurring forms of malversations (appropriation of someone else's belongings entrusted with perpetrator) involve:

- The granting of fictitious bank guarantees, enabling the financial inauguration of new economic subjects;
- The nonobservation of principles established in banking law, enabling persons and companies to obtain credit upon the basis of false guarantees;
- The illicit obtaining of credit by nonexistent companies and persons while using overissue checks;

- The illicit obtaining of undue insurance benefits: both property and social insurance (i. e., unemployment benefits).

Further malversations include:

- The retransfer abroad of gathered funds and the signing of fictitious contracts with foreign firms concerning the organization of economic activity, counseling, and marketing;
- The opening abroad—without suitable currency permission—of registered accounts used for transferring payments from foreign partners;
- The emission of obligations while violating regulations of the law on obligations, and in particular sums exceeding the value of company capital;
- The exploitation of the insurance on nonexistent commodities in order to obtain insurance cession for the credit bank.

The increase in crime is connected with the international turnover, realized by physical persons and companies as well as foreign persons and firms.

At present, organized criminal groups specialize in the smuggling of alcohol, cigarettes, electronic equipment, and other commodities. An equally great threat is posed by the fictitious export, reexport, and transit of goods actually intended for the domestic market; in this procedure, frequent use is made of contracts with foreign firms and individuals, as well as forged documents. The export of commodities continues being confirmed in return for bribes.

Groups and firms specializing in the organization of smuggling into Poland use this country as an open market. The organizers are frequently Polish citizens, or former Polish citizens living in Germany or Austria—the source of the largest demand for such commodities as alcohol, cigarettes, and electronic appliances. Criminal contacts across the eastern border are also growing. In this instance, smuggling usually encompasses cars, nonferrous metals, mercury, and works of art. Moreover, Poland constitutes a transit area for commodities intended for the expanding markets of the former Soviet republics.

Poland is becoming known worldwide as an amphetamine producer. According to data provided by Interpol, 10% of this narcotic confiscated in Europe originates from Poland, which supplies 25% of the amphetamine market in Germany and Scandinavia. Twenty Polish laboratories specialize in amphetamine production.

In its capacity as a transit country and the destination of smuggled drugs, Poland is in the very center of the interests pursued by international crime groups (i.e., Colombian). Annually, about 150 Polish citizens are intercepted abroad for their participation in drug trafficking. This particular variety of smuggling contributes to the development of drug addiction at home, which at present affects about 300,000 persons (17% of school students have had experience with narcotics). Criminal groups also steal and smuggle art—about 1500 museum exhibits and sacral objects are stolen annually.

Organized crime continues to expand regarding the quality and the quantity of goods stolen and smuggled, and it feeds on the dangerous phenomenon of cooperation between criminals, businessmen, and politicians. Furthermore, international currency links, global financial transactions, the exchange of goods and commodities, as well as freedom of movement generate an even greater internationalization and professionalization of Polish criminal groups.

The Main Causes of Crime

Crime is a phenomenon delineated by the course of assorted economic, social, political, and cultural processes; hence there is a great number of factors determining its dynamic and structure. Economic factors are a particularly dominant force in relation to crime. In January 2001 about 2,700,000 people—as much as 15% of the production-age population—could not find work. Disturbing traits of Polish unemployment include the considerable number of people unemployed for more than 12 months (about 45%), the high rate among young people under 24 years of age (approximately 33%), and the extremely large spatial differentiation of the unemployment level, combined with the low spatial mobility of the unemployed.

The actual income of the population has declined since 1990, and the relations between employment incomes and those obtained from social benefits changed essentially. Circumstances conducive for the functioning of the "grey zone" (grey zone includes the turnover of goods whose purchase and sale are forbidden for ethical and economic reasons or transactions in which the goods are legal, but their origin or conditions of sale are not consistent with law regulation) are the result of the nonadaptation of the mechanisms (systems) of the economy and administration to altering social and economic-political reality as well as the imperfection of legal solutions and technical delays. They include the following factors:

- The weakness of the fiscal apparatus that does not have at its disposal sufficient legal and technical instruments;
- The legal restrictions of the functioning of organs dealing with the detection and investigation of economic pathologies, including the police as well as fiscal and control organs;

- The transference of the burden of proving the legality of the origin of property onto the fiscal organs instead of the owner;
- The absence of technical possibilities for circulating and exploiting information about expenses and other events connected with the possession and transference of property rights;
- The total lack of protection of domestic currency resources against their export;
- The absence of activity on the part of banks for the protection of financial resources, as well as the concealment of losses suffered in the credit system;
- The generally low efficiency of information circulation between the state and economic institutions and organs, including control and prosecution organs;
- The low level of information and communication within the entire economy and administration;
- Social tolerance for activities circumventing the law or outright violating its norms within the fiscal sphere as a result of long-term practice and experience as well as a misunderstanding of the consequences of this type of thinking and conduct, especially within the conditions of the market economy.

Furthermore, emphasis should be placed on organizational factors associated with the functioning of the police force, the prosecutor's office, and the courts.

The Polish police force is undergoing a financial and staff crisis. The Central Headquarters was turned into an organizational giant, which in the year 2000 employed 2500 police officers and gradually lost its fundamental nature of a planning-coordination center. Wages are tragically low—police officers earn about 300 U.S. dollars (gross), which means that some 30% of their families live on the brink of the social minimum. For several years now, Polish courts and the prosecutor's office have been experiencing a difficult staff, organizational, and financial situation. The functioning of the common courts is deteriorating systematically. The duration of trials is becoming longer, the registered number of cases awaiting identification is rising, and the effectiveness of verdicts is diminishing.

The number of posts held by prosecutors does not grow proportionally to the number of conducted inquiries.

Life in new systemic conditions has also affected the system of values shared by Polish society. The dominating life model is focused on consumption, with money constituting the supreme value. This is the reason why such axiology, together with other factors (e.g., the weakness of the state apparatus, the still-encountered nonnative chaos, the liberalization of regulations, and the excessively liberal policy of the courts), constitutes an essential source of the etiology of criminal behavior.

Crime Control

The institutions of the incognito witness (1995) and the chief witness (1997) have been introduced into Polish legislation in order to render the struggle against crime, particularly its organized variety, more effective. Since 1995, the operational-identification activity conducted by the police force and the Office for the Protection of the State also encompasses unconventional methods of obtaining testimony, such as controlled purchase, the institution of the secret agent, and so-called covert surveillance of the transportation, storage, and turnover of crime objects.

Recent years have been particularly significant for the Polish justice system. A new constitution was finally enacted on April 2, 1997. An important step in the codification of penal law was made when on June 6, 1997, a new Penal Code, the Criminal Procedure Act, and a Sanctions Enforcement Code were approved.

Attempts to restrict crime were made at the beginning of the 1990s: in 1994 the Central Police Headquarters created an Organized Crime Squad; a Second Squad was established, also at the central level, in 1997. In 1998–2000 the police force embarked upon an intensified combat of organized crime; the Central Police Headquarters organized a Central Investigation Bureau (2000). The Ministry of Justice established a Coordination department for the Pursuit of Organized Crime (1994), transformed in 1996 into the Organized Crime Bureau. In January 1998, the Ministry of Finances inaugurated the activity of the General Customs Inspectorate, which predominantly combats crime connected with lowering the customs value of imported articles. The Bureau of Fiscal Documentation at the Ministry of Finances (active since July 1998) deals with penal proceedings conducted in treasury control offices.

In the wake of organizational transformations generated in 1999 by the administrative reform of the country, the basic tasks of trade inspection are performed by the Chief Inspectorate of Trade Inspection, supervised by the chairman of the Office for the Protection of Competition and Consumers as well as voivodes, assisted by 16 voivodeship inspectors and 33 delegate offices.

The chairman of the Office of Public Commissions (since 1994) controls contracts warded by tenders in order to limit corruption and ascertain eventual violations of the discipline of public finances.

It is foreseen that a program of the technical modernization of the police force will be implemented in 2001–2004. Priority requirements in this domain include further information, the modernization of communication systems, the construction of systems of command support, and the introduction of modem systems enabling the detection of perpetrators.

Presumably, the year 2001 witnessed the establishment of a Criminal Information Centre that will perform the role of gathering information essential from the vantage point of the efficacy of assorted activities intent on combating crime.

The purpose of the National Court Register that began functioning on January 1, 2000 is to limit opportunities for committing economic crimes by guaranteeing the participants of the economic turnover and prosecution organs access to information about enterprises and other subjects of economic life, including insolvent debtors.

The best known among the numerous crime prevention programs realized in Poland in 1955–2000 was the "Safe City" program, whose subdivisions include the "Safe Home," "Safe Business," and "Safe School" projects. The "ATOMIUM" program, introduced in 1998, could also play a considerable part in prophylaxis because it promotes standards applied by the police forces of the European Union member states. Local communities are embarking upon crime prevention, resorting, among others, to the experiences of the American police force and so-called community policing.

The effectiveness of these attempts to curb criminal activity will improve once the Polish Parliament (Sejm) passes a statute (Prevention Act) concerning the prevention of crime and other negative social phenomena.

BRUNON HOTYST

References and Further Reading

Hotyst, B. 2000. *Kryminologia* (Criminology), Wydawnictwa Prawnicze PWN, 9th ed., Warsaw, Poland.
Ministry of Internal Affairs and Administration (edited) 2000. *Bezpieczeństwo i porz̨adek publiczny w Polsce* (Public Security and Order in Poland), Warsaw, Poland.
Siemaszko, A., Ed. 2000. Crime and Law Enforcement in Poland on the Threshold of the list Century, Oficyna Naukowa, Warsaw, Poland.

Police: Administration and Organization

Police administration can be understood in a narrow sense or in a broad sense. Narrowly, it refers to the tasks and issues involved in managing a police organization—that is, the responsibilities of police chiefs, sheriffs, and their subordinate managers. This narrower perspective brings to mind such topics as recruitment, training, discipline, allocation of resources, information technology, supervision, and leadership. Alternatively, and more broadly, police administration can encompass the challenges facing a community or an entire society in seeking to create and sustain a system for providing police services that is effective, equitable, and accountable. This perspective on police administration focuses our attention on different issues, such as fragmentation versus consolidation of police departments, elected versus appointed law enforcement executives, the role of the federal government, civil service systems, and civilian review boards.

Both perspectives are important. The narrower view tends to dominate the attention of practicing law enforcement officials as well as city managers, who are the immediate supervisors of many police chiefs. This perspective is typically reflected in police administration textbooks, college courses, executive development programs, and supervisor training programs. The focus is on the practical problems associated with managing people within a police organization and administering the organization itself. Although there have been police administration textbooks for about 50 years, many ideas and approaches can also be drawn from the literature and practice of management in general, drawing on such fields as business administration, public administration, and applied psychology. Many journals and magazines support these fields, and dozens of new management books are published each year, so there is never a shortage of new theories, principles, and programs awaiting application to law enforcement organizations.

The broader view of police administration is less affected by popular new management ideas and more focused on fundamental, endemic issues. Some of these are literally universal. Everywhere, police have power and authority, leading them inevitably into controversies over whether their use of authority is proper and adequately regulated, and into conflicts with other powerful groups in the political contest for influence and control within the society.

Additional issues arise in democratic societies, because individual liberties are emphasized and government authority is substantially restricted. In free societies, coercive governmental action is frowned upon in favor of open discussion, debate, negotiation, deliberation, elections, and similar political and judicial processes designed to support majority rule while protecting minority rights—the police are called in, though, whenever prompt coercive action is needed to quell a disturbance, restore order, or enforce the law. As such, the police are the principal mechanism for "the distribution of non-negotiably coercive force" in otherwise noncoercive societies. These issues are particularly prominent in the U.S. because of federalism, separation of powers, and the fragmentation of police authority. In a country largely founded on the principle that government should be weak, issues surrounding the administration of an institution as potentially powerful as the police are bound to be vexing.

Police Organizations

The three most basic features of American police organizations are that they are predominantly small, local, and nonmilitary. The U.S. has approximately 17,000 police agencies with an average (mean) size of 40–50 sworn officers. Because of the preponderance of very small police and sheriff departments, though, the *median* size is closer to 10–15 officers. About 75% of U.S. police officers work for counties, cities, or towns, compared to 25% who work for the state or federal government. Most other countries have only a few police agencies, located at the national or state level, each with thousands of officers, and in many countries the police and the military are indistinguishable.

The small size of most American police agencies has implications for police administration. Most chiefs and sheriffs administer rather small organizations. These small departments have few levels of hierarchy and only limited specialization. The chief or sheriff of a small department has to "wear more hats" than an executive in a larger agency, with fewer opportunities to delegate tasks to staff or subordinates. On the plus side, though, it is easier to disseminate information throughout a smaller organization, and it is a real advantage to be able to manage and lead directly, instead of through layers of middle managers.

Police agencies usually make an organizational distinction between operations and administration. Operations, sometimes called field services, include those personnel and units engaged in providing direct service to the public, such as patrol, traffic, and investigations. Administration includes staff and units that provide internal support to operations, such as personnel, training, and information systems. In larger police departments, a further distinction is sometimes made between administration and support services. The latter includes those internal activities in support of field operations that must be made available on a continuous basis, such as communications (radio systems), detention, and records, as contrasted with more 9–5 types of administration, such as personnel and training.

The five basic functions performed by police managers are planning, organizing, staffing, directing, and controlling. Planning includes setting goals, designing strategies for accomplishing goals, and preparing for contingencies. Organizing involves creating a structure of authority, responsibility, units, and positions that can carry out plans and strategies and respond to contingencies. Staffing is aimed at securing and preparing the people the organization needs to fill positions, do the work, carry out the plans, and accomplish goals. Directing includes leading and training and is focused on communicating to employees what they are supposed to do and accomplish and encouraging them to do it well. Controlling supports directing. Through methods such as supervision and discipline, employees get feedback about their performance and the organization tries to assure that directions are followed, that plans are implemented, and that goals are accomplished.

Within most organizations, higher-level administrators tend to devote relatively more time and attention to planning, organizing, and staffing issues, while lower-level managers tend to be consumed with directing and controlling their immediate subordinates. This is generally true in police organizations as well, except that directing and controlling probably demand more attention of top police executives than is true in most other types of organizations. As discussed below, this is because of the nature of police work, in which low-ranking employees make very significant decisions that have dramatic consequences. This feature of police work makes police executives very conscious of the extent to which their success is dependent on the good will and good judgment of ordinary police officers, and thus inclines them toward giving substantial attention to the directing and controlling functions of management.

Police work and police organizations are labor-intensive. In the typical police budget, 80–90% of expenditures are for salaries and benefits, leaving little money for discretionary spending. As a result, managing budgets has traditionally lagged far behind managing people as a major focus of police administration training and practice. Several factors have raised the attention given to financial management within police administration in recent years, however. These include increased fiscal scrutiny from city managers, closer supervision of police overtime expenditures, greater interest in purchasing new law enforcement and information technology, and the availability of federal and state grant funds that can augment otherwise tight budgets.

Important Characteristics of Police Work

An important tenet of organization theory is that structure, administration, and management vary depending on the nature of the work performed in organizations. Routine, repetitive work and highly creative work, for example, typically are, or should be, organized and managed differently. Police work has several characteristics that profoundly affect how it is administered. One is that police officers exercise substantial authority—they can stop and detain people, arrest them, and use force against them, including deadly force. These are serious matters with serious consequences. Because so much is at stake, police organizations tend to emphasize *control*. Officers are sworn to duty and required to complete reports on all kinds of activities. Departments have extensive policies, procedures, and rules with punishments attached if the rules are violated. They provide layers of supervisors and managers and emphasize the chain of command. Larger police organizations also have internal affairs units to investigate complaints against officers and inspections units to conduct internal audits to assure compliance with policies and procedures.

Ironically, despite the emphasis on control within police administration, police officers are not tightly controlled in the actual performance of their duties. The biggest reason is *discretion*. Despite the highly codified criminal law and extensive organizational regulations, when officers respond to calls and initiate proactive efforts they have much leeway in how to handle them. This includes decisions about whether to stop and detain, whether to ticket, whether to arrest, and whether to use force. It also includes decisions about which parts of the beat to spend time in, whether or not to investigate a suspicious situation, whether to stop that expensive car with three minority youths in it, whether to seek consent to search following a minor traffic stop, whether to contact code compliance about the house with the junk car in the yard, and so on.

There are several reasons for all this discretion. One is that so many violations of the criminal law and the traffic law occur that the courts and jails would be totally overwhelmed if police practiced strict enforcement. Moreover, most violations are so minor (disturbing the peace, speeding 1 mile over the speed limit) that few would really want the police to enforce all the laws all the time. So the police decide which laws to enforce when. Next, the police organization is frustrated in directing its officers about "which laws to enforce when" because situations vary so much. Arrests for disturbing the peace are advisable in some circumstances but not in others. Strict speed enforcement is sometimes justified, but impractical and unwise as a general policy. Minority youths in an expensive car might justify a vehicle stop in some situations, but as a common practice such stops give rise to concerns about racial profiling. Finally, the police organization is greatly constrained in its ability to supervise officers' use of discretion because police work goes on 24 hours a day, 7 days a week, out in the field, and mostly away from supervisors' eyes. Much of police work involves "low visibility decisions" made by individual officers acting alone.

To be sure, officer use of discretion is not totally unregulated. Officer actions that result in reports, tickets, or arrests are usually reviewed by supervisors after the fact, though this is often merely a review of paperwork. Arrests must pass legal scrutiny at several levels. Citizens can complain against officers. At the scene, the presence of complainants, witnesses, and other officers has been found to influence officer decision making. The ubiquitous "low visibility" situation has become somewhat less common in recent years with the advent of video cameras in police patrol cars, officer-carried audio recorders, closed-circuit surveillance cameras deployed by businesses and governments, and camcorders wielded by citizens. Legislatures have moved to reduce discretion in the handling of certain offenses, such as domestic violence, and police departments have constrained the use of discretion in high-risk situations, such as pursuit driving.

Despite these constraints, police officers still have substantial discretion in how they do their work. Because of this fundamental characteristic of police work, the single most important challenge for police administrators is guiding and controlling officer use of discretion. This is significantly different from the primary challenges faced by top managers in most other types of organizations. More typical challenges in non-police organizations include motivating employees to work harder, getting employees to work together as a team, spurring employees to be more creative, finding cheaper ways to manufacture products, or finding new markets for products and services.

Managing Discretion

As a key feature of police work is making discretionary decisions, a key focus of police administration is guiding and controlling the decisions that officers make. This is done successfully when the choices that officers make about where within their beats to patrol, whether to arrest a particular disorderly person, when to engage the community in problem solving, and so forth are exactly the choices that the department's top executives would make if they were in the same situations. It is done unsuccessfully when officers make different choices than their superiors would prefer, whether because of ignorance, bad decision making, or other reasons.

One ingredient of correct decision making is information. Police organizations seek to assure that officers know what information to take into consideration when making decisions, and that this information is available to officers when it is needed. For example, officers are taught to use crime analysis information and repeat call data in order to direct their patrolling time and activities within their beats. To make this approach to patrol and problem solving practical and compelling, departments design computer systems and create analysis units so that officers can get accurate and up-to-date information. Optimal decision making will fall short in this example if officers fail to use the information, if the information is inaccurate, or if it is not timely.

Some organizations solve the challenge of assuring that employees know what they need to know by hiring people who possess the requisite knowledge—hospitals hire doctors and nurses who have already completed educational programs, for example. Police reformers have dreamed of implementing this model for decades, but the college degree requirement for police employment has not been widely adopted by police agencies, nor has the higher education system developed models of police education that would fully prepare students for police employment. Instead, police departments have come to rely on training, both recruit and in-service, as the primary means of providing employees with the knowledge and information needed to make good decisions.

The other main ingredient of correct decision making is values. Police departments want officers to know and accept the organization's approved goals, objectives, principles, and values, so that they are pursuing the right ends and choosing ethical and proper means when they make decisions. For example, when officers are deciding how much force to use in arresting an unruly and uncooperative person, the department wants the officers to choose the least-force option that will secure the arrest, even if officers might be tempted to use a little extra force out of frustration or anger. Similarly, a department might want its officers to choose to employ creative problem solving and community-based alternatives to deal with a neighborhood gang problem, even though officers might personally prefer to rely solely on intimidation and enforcement.

Police agencies employ several techniques to get officers to accept the organization's approved values as guides to their decision making. One is to recruit and select officers who bring with them certain values. Another is to socialize new officers during initial classroom and field training periods. Departments also publish and display their codes of ethics, mission statements, and core values. They attempt to reinforce these values through the administration of the organization, especially with awards, performance evaluations, special assignments, and promotions. Police executives try to exemplify the values through their own behavior. And on the other side of the coin, supervision and discipline are used to identify and punish officers who fail to use the official values as guides to their decision making.

In practice, however, most police agencies fall far short of this ideal. Often, the values of street officers and the police "subculture" differ significantly from the organization's approved values. New officers find themselves caught between the administration and the subculture; the subculture frequently wins, because new officers crave acceptance from their peers and in fact must rely on their fellow officers for assistance in dangerous situations on the street. Police administrators sometimes unwittingly contribute to this situation when their own actions and decisions are seen as arbitrary and capricious, and when they seem to support new philosophies and strategies, such as community policing, only half-heartedly. Because officer values often end up in conflict with the organization's official values, police managers largely resort to supervision and discipline to force officers to do the right things and make the right decisions. This creates even more conflict within the police organization and results in decisions that are only minimally compliant with the organization's values, at best, and evasive and counterproductive, at worst.

The best decisions occur within organizations when the decision maker takes the correct ingredients (information and values) into consideration and then "calculates" which available alternative would have the most beneficial outcome. This decision-making process combines creativity, analysis, and judgment. For example, the police officer confronting a neighborhood gang problem needs to (1) combine creativity with information in order to "imagine" a range of possible responses to the gang problem, (2) assess the evidence in favor of the likely effectiveness of each of the potential responses, and then (3) use judgment in weighing the pros and cons of each response, in relation to the police department's approved values and principles, in the context of the specific neighborhood situation being confronted. Targeted enforcement actions might be the most promising response in some neighborhood gang situations, whereas elsewhere, community mobilization, organized-crime style investigations, youth programs, partnerships with schools, mediation or negotiation, and environmental changes may be more effective. Police officers do the best job when they consider a wide range of alternatives like this and then rationally choose the most promising responses for the particular circumstances at hand.

The same decision-making process applies in narrower situations. When the driver of a speeding car refuses to stop for an officer and instead accelerates to a high speed, the officer has to decide what to do. In some departments, pursuit policies specify a number of factors for the officer to consider, such as weather conditions, traffic conditions, and the known offense involved, in deciding whether to pursue. In other departments, policies largely prohibit all high-speed pursuits. In either case, however, the officer has to (1) take into account the correct information about the offense and the situation, (2) take into account the department's values and principles as expressed in the pursuit policy and other guiding documents, and then (3) identify and "imagine" a range of appropriate responses within the parameters of the applicable information and values, (4) assess the likely effectiveness of each of those responses, and (5) choose a response. Even where high-speed pursuits are prohibited, there may be alternatives available for consideration, such as airborne surveillance, following from a distance, anticipating the vehicle's destination, or searching for the vehicle and driver later.

The important point for this discussion is that, to be successful, police organizations must influence the decision-making processes used by officers. Just as they take steps to assure that officers get and use the correct information when making decisions, and just as they attempt to assure that officer decisions are guided by the right values, so too must police administrators assure that officers consider an appropriate range of responses in each decision situation, that they correctly assess the pros and cons of each response, and that they then use sound judgment in selecting which response(s) to employ. Unfortunately, this process is not typically recognized or taught in police education or training programs. At best, departments try to hire people who already have "good judgment," expose them during recruit training to new information and approved values, tell them some stories that illustrate good decision making, attach them to an experienced officer for a period of time, and hope that they learn to make good decisions on their own. Given the centrality of decision making and discretion in police work, this is not an adequate approach. In the coming decades, as police administrators become more aware that their key challenge is managing discretion, it is anticipated that teaching officers how to make good decisions, and developing other organizational systems in support of that objective, will be given even greater emphasis in the field of police administration.

Contemporary Issues

Over and above the endemic issue of managing discretion, police administration faces a number of contemporary challenges and opportunities. One relates to increasing diversity. The growing complexity of American society creates some significant challenges for police officers, requiring greater sensitivity to different cultures and greater skill in communicating with people who speak languages other than English. Preparing officers to deal effectively with this diversity is a challenge for police administration, with implications for recruitment, selection, training, and other organizational systems. Additionally, increased diversity of personnel within police agencies creates its own set of challenges for police management.

Recruiting is always challenging for police organizations, but the driving issues change from time to time. Fundamentally, police agencies need sufficient numbers of applicants so they can be reasonably choosy in hiring. Preferably, they would also like to have numerous applicants with the specific qualities they are looking for. In the 1960s and 1970s, many police departments were particularly keen on attracting college graduates. In the 1970s and 1980s, increased emphasis was also placed on attracting women and racial or ethnic minorities into police work. These emphases continue to the present, of course, but the nation's commitment to affirmative action, as reflected in legislation and court decisions, seemed to wane in the 1990s. Then, in the later 1990s and into the new millennium, the strong economy in the U.S. resulted in substantially fewer applicants for police positions, and thus a renewed focus on recruiting simply aimed at producing sufficient applicants for the agency to choose from. Early in the new millennium, recruiting challenges are among the greatest concerns of police executives.

Another particularly challenging issue for police administration in recent years is racial disparity in vehicle stops and use of force. These are actually long-standing issues, of course, and connected to the key police administration challenge of managing the discretion that police officers exercise in the course of their duties. Since the Rodney King and O.J. Simpson episodes in Los Angeles, though, racial disparity in police decision making has stayed at the very forefront of public and political concern. Almost every use of deadly force by the police sparks controversy, and patterns of police shootings of African American youth have been observed in several cities. The phenomenon of racial profiling (pejoratively termed "driving while black") has garnered enormous national and local attention. Police administrators all over the country have been put on the defensive in trying to account for, and respond to, data indicating disproportionate vehicle stops and use of force against African Americans and other people of color.

New technology presents both challenges and opportunities for police administrators. Police executives are rarely technology experts to begin with, let alone experts in rapidly changing technologies. To make matters worse, technology is expensive, and police administrators fear making the wrong purchases. On the opportunity side, though, new technologies in the areas of less-than-lethal force and vehicle stopping have helped police agencies reduce risks by giving officers additional options for handling dangerous situations. Also, developments in information technology (especially in computer systems) have enhanced both police officer decision making and the organization's ability to direct and control officers in the field. Additionally, as illustrated by the COMP-STAT process pioneered in New York, information technology can assist top police executives in holding mid-level managers, such as precinct captains, accountable for using their resources efficiently and addressing the most serious problems in their areas of responsibility. In bigger police organizations, especially, this has been a major accomplishment, dramatically altering certain aspects of large-agency police administration.

In both the broad sense and the narrow sense, police administration remains a very challenging enterprise. As did their predecessors, modern police administrators wrestle with endemic and contemporary issues in their efforts to lead their organizations and provide their communities with fair and effective police services.

GARY CORDNER

References and Further Reading

Cordner, G.W., Scarborough, K. and Sheehan, R. 2004. *Police Administration*, 5th ed., Cincinnati, OH, Anderson.
Fyfe, J.J., Greene, J.R., Walsh, W.F., Wilson, O.W. and McClaren, R.C. 1997. *Police Administration*, 5th ed., New York, McGraw-Hill.
Geller, W.A., Ed. 1985. *Police Leadership in America: Crisis and Opportunity*, New York, Praeger.

Geller, W.A. Ed. 1991. *Local Government Police Management*, 3rd ed., Washington, DC, International City Management Association.

Hoover, L.T., Ed. 1992. *Police Management: Issues and Perspectives*, Washington, DC, Police Executive Research Forum.

Hoover, L.T., Ed. 1996. *Quantifying Quality in Policing*, Washington, DC, Police Executive Research Forum.

Moore, M.H. and Stephens, D.W. 1991. *Beyond Command and Control: The Strategic Management of Police Departments*, Washington, DC, Police Executive Research Forum.

Wilson, J.Q. 1968. *Varieties of Police Behavior: The Management of Law and Order in Eight Communities*, Cambridge, MA, Harvard University Press.

See also **Police and the Rule of Law**

Police: Brutality and Corruption

Modern democratic societies have slowly come to the view that brutality and corruption are inevitable in police work unless strong preventive measures are in place. This conclusion is based on a scientific understanding of the many intense and conflicting pressures placed on police that lead to unlawful and unethical behavior. Although there are established strategies to prevent abuses of power, the nature of police work makes comprehensive prevention very difficult.

Definitions

There is a great deal of variation and overlap of terminology in describing and categorizing police brutality and corruption. The word "corruption," for example, can be used very broadly—along with "misconduct" and "deviance"—to cover all types of malpractice. The word also has a much more specific usage referring to soliciting or accepting a bribe. Four main types of misconduct can be identified, although it should be kept in mind that different typologies are possible and considerable blurring of categories occurs in usage and in practice.

1. "Corruption," in the sense of "bribery" or "graft," is the classic type of misconduct and involves a police officer receiving a personal benefit for not doing their duty. This may be organized—as in a "protection racket" where police receive a regular fee from a brothel or gambling den for not raiding and prosecuting the premises. Alternatively, it may be opportunistic and irregular—such as a traffic officer accepting a bribe offered by a motorist stopped for speeding. Some critics describe gifts and discounts (or "gratuities") offered to police as "petty corruption" because gifts may involve an expectation of favorable treatment in return.

   "Corruption" in this sense may also include obtaining a personal benefit through theft of goods in police custody, reselling seized drugs, or selling confidential information.

2. "Process corruption" describes the fabrication of evidence. The victims may be innocent or guilty but police seek their conviction in court through fraudulent means. This sometimes includes illegal searches or wiretaps, but usually involves coercing suspects into making confessions, lying in the witness box, or withholding contrary evidence.

3. "Brutality" or "excessive force" covers the full range of violence from heavy-handed frisking or prodding with a baton through assault to murder. Some writers include threats of violence and verbal abuse in this category. Police work is frequently defined in terms of the right to use force. However, police use of force, like citizens' legal use of force, is highly circumscribed. Normally, only the use of reasonable force is permitted when arresting suspects, stopping fights, directing people, breaking into premises, or acting in self-defense. Most jurisdictions prohibit actions such as shooting fleeing suspects or frisking people at random. Inevitably, however, conflicting interpretations arise over differences between justified force and brutality.

4. The remaining types of deviance could be considered as "miscellaneous misconduct," or are sometimes grouped together in such typologies as "misconduct" or "disciplinary offenses." These can include harassment, discriminatory law enforcement, incivility, inaction, drug abuse and intoxication, abuse of sick leave, dangerous high-speed vehicle pursuits, abuse of strip searching, racist or sexist slurs, and neglect of

1159

detainees. It also covers forms of internal corruption or misconduct such as sexual harassment and discrimination in assignment and promotion.

What all these categories share in common is a breach of occupational duty and misuse of police powers. It is only when an offense is committed in relation to employment as a police officer that this becomes a form of "corruption" or "occupational deviance." However, many departments possess authority to discipline officers for any conduct that brings the police organization into disrepute.

Discovering Brutality and Corruption

Knowledge about police misconduct comes from a number of sources. Judicial commissions of inquiry have been the most important. There is a long history of failure on the part of such inquiries to either expose corruption or to affect permanent reforms that would prevent recurrences. However, this failure has usually resulted from inadequate powers and resources. It is mainly in the last three decades of the 20th century that public pressure and political maturity have led to the establishment of properly equipped inquiries. The success of modern inquiries has been based on the use of carefully selected investigators, reasonable time limits for completion, broad jurisdiction on matters to be pursued, the availability of indemnities to witnesses, and power to demand answers to questions. The capacity to use covert surveillance and simulated misconduct opportunities (or "stings") has also been important. A key weapon is the ability to "turn" corrupt officers to become witnesses, usually through offers of indemnities from prosecution.

The Knapp Commission in New York City, from 1970 to 1972, best marks the turning point in modern consciousness about police misconduct. It provided a model set of investigative methods and reform recommendations for many subsequent inquiries in different countries. People around the world became familiar with the bureaucratically organized subculture of corruption in the NYPD through the dramatized books and films Serpico and Prince of the City, based on the experiences of key informants. The extensive, almost universal, corrupt practices in the NYPD at the time were based on the exploitation of routine police functions such as prosecution of traffic violations, illegal gambling, and drug trafficking. Officers abused their authority to create an extensive system of extortionate gratuities from restaurant and other business owners. Law enforcement was highly selective, as Robert Daley recounts of detectives in the Special Investigating Unit in the NYPD:

They chose their own targets and roamed New York at will. Someone once called them the Princes of the City, for they operated with the impunity, and sometimes with the arrogance, of Renaissance princes. They could enforce any law or not enforce it, arrest anyone or accord freedom. They were immune to arrest themselves (1978, 6).

Since the Knapp Commission, many other jurisdictions have undergone similar painful processes of investigation and exposure of corruption. Some inquiries have been focused more on harassment and racism—such as the 1981 Scarman Inquiry into the Metropolitan Police in London, following the Brixton riots. The 1991 Christopher Commission in Los Angeles was focused on brutality, following the infamous police bashing of Rodney King revealed through a citizen's videorecording. Other inquiries, such as the large-scale Wood Commission in the Australian state of New South Wales (1994–1997), have been more in the mold of Knapp, uncovering diverse forms of misconduct as well as a hard core of organized graft.

Other factors have contributed to growing awareness about police abuses. The period from the 1960s to the 1980s saw large numbers of mass demonstrations over issues such as the Vietnam War, conscription, racism, and pollution. In many cases, these protests were brutally suppressed by police, often in full view of television news cameras. In Britain in the 1980s, the antiunion policies of the Thatcher government also provoked bitter public fighting between police and striking workers. Peaceful protest was seen as an essential condition of democracy, and repressive tactics made police appear as agents of antidemocratic social élites. Many people who would ordinarily have little contact with police began to see them as the enemy, often through personal experience. This conflict was exacerbated by the growing social acceptance of drug use and police targeting of minor drug users. Public trust in police was further eroded by revelations of miscarriages of justice, usually as a result of the dogged efforts of defense lawyers. The most notorious cases occurred in Britain in the 1980s, when groups such as the Guildford Four and Birmingham Six were wrongfully convicted of terrorism-related charges. The failure to find political solutions to social problems, such as the civil war in Northern Ireland, has been a major factor in police malpractice.

International human rights groups and political dissidents are another source of knowledge about police abuses. Following a review of excessive force cases in 14 major cities in the U.S., the 1998 report by Human Rights Watch described police brutality as "one of the most serious, enduring, and divisive human rights violations in the United States" (1998, 1). It is not surprising then that nondemocratic countries or those with less developed democratic institutions typically have enormous problems with entrenched police malpractice. For example, much of the sexual exploitation of women and children in impoverished nations is either committed by the police or occurs through police protection. In many countries, police still serve a dual function of general law enforcement and repressive protection of dictatorial regimes—both right and left wing—through the routine use of torture, summary execution, fabricated prosecutions, and suppression of demonstrations. Hence the continued currency of the term "police state."

Explaining Brutality and Corruption

The findings of numerous inquiries have contributed to more objective knowledge about the causes of police corruption. This knowledge has been further advanced by social scientists using observational studies, surveys, and interviews. Increasing use is being made of ethics surveys to identify attitudes that may support corrupt behavior. Surveys of police, and people who have had contact with police, can also be useful in providing indicators of levels and types of misconduct. Different studies focus on different causes of brutality and corruption, but the approaches primarily center on "structural" and "cultural" theoretical orientations.

The New York City Knapp Commission report explicitly attacked what it termed the "rotten apple" theory of corruption, supporting instead a concept of systemic corruption. The rotten apple theory claims that corruption involves only a few officers who are guilty of moral failure and that the organizational "barrel" remains sound. Many police chiefs, politicians, and police unions have used this stock argument to defend the status quo and their own role in failing to prevent corruption. Although it is certainly the case that police misconduct can be confined to one individual or a few, most modern inquiries have identified widespread problems. This is why corruption is often described by scholars as "endemic" or "pervasive" in policing. Nonetheless, it must be kept in mind that corruption levels can vary substantially between departments, as well as varying within departments over time and across different sections. However, even where police deviance is isolated, its continuation is likely to be related to inadequate management strategies.

A structural perspective on malpractice focuses on the nature of police work—or the "task environment." Corruption opportunities derive directly from the law enforcement function. Police work involves frequent contact with criminals who are motivated to trade money and other benefits for immunity from prosecution, and officers are able to threaten prosecution when soliciting bribes. Patrol officers and detectives enjoy very low levels of supervision and high levels of discretion that give them wide scope to bend or break laws and evade detection. Failure to prosecute criminals who bribe police can be explained away in terms of lack of evidence or as a necessary tradeoff for information from informants about serious crime.

The demand and supply scenario applies to any criminal conduct or regulatory breaches coming to police attention, and may result in corruption in limited forms with individuals acting opportunistically. The scenario has also led to acute problems of long-standing corruption networks, particularly where there is a high demand for illegal commerce in drugs, liquor, prostitution, abortion, and gambling, or information held on police databases. Hence, corruption is a major unintended consequence of well-intentioned efforts to prohibit "vice." A task-environment approach also explains variations in deviance related to specific tasks. Patrol officers, for example, may be more likely to engage in brutality, whereas detectives may be more prone to fabricate evidence. Officers in licensing or vice squads are more likely to engage in organized corruption.

A structural perspective is also useful for explaining process corruption. Pressure to fabricate evidence comes from a number of sources including political and administrative pressure to improve clearance rates for crime, and political and community pressure to bring offenders to justice—particularly for more terrifying or repugnant crimes. Corrupt process may also follow from police frustration with due process constraints such as the right to silence, the inadmissibility in court of certain evidence, or the high standard of proof in criminal cases. This has given rise to the concept of the "Dirty Harry syndrome," based on the methods of a Hollywood screen detective who feels compelled to break the law to protect innocent citizens from predatory criminals. Similarly, police brutality is influenced by perceived or actual pressures for summary punishment associated with public cynicism about defendant safeguards and sentencing policies. It can also be argued that brutality follows from the fact that police are given an impossible task of controlling crime caused by social factors such as unemployment and poverty. Officers who feel powerless may therefore be tempted to exceed their powers and use threats, harassment, and beatings to deter criminal behavior. "Brutality" is in fact not a one-way process, but also involves provocation of police. Operational officers are routinely subject to insults, threats, and assaults—sometimes life-threatening—that require extraordinary self-restraint in response.

The second main area of theory concerns the concept of organizational culture. The distinctiveness of the police occupational subculture is easily overstated. Many other occupations have problems of unethical practices and protective solidarity. However, attention to "culture"—to attitudes, practices, traditions, and unwritten codes of practice—is useful for understanding processes through which misconduct is facilitated and reinforced. Secrecy and solidarity are central in cultural perspectives on police misconduct, and the most extreme expression of this is the persecution of police whistleblowers. The concept of a police subculture includes the "slippery slope" perspective on corruption. In this view, rookie officers are first encouraged to accept gratuities and then through peer pressure and threats are gradually socialized into participating in more and more serious types of corruption.

A deviant police subculture has also developed from recruitment and training processes that produced a narrow conformist type of officer. Historically, in western countries, police recruitment has been almost exclusively from among poorly educated lower-class white males. Training focused on rote learning of law, fitness, and physical control techniques. It is little wonder that police developed a "macho" culture of isolation and antiintellectualism that encouraged and supported violence and disdain for formal procedures and civil rights. Many aspects of the traditional or negative police subculture are closely associated with "structural" influences, such as the need for confidentiality to protect sensitive operations or the camaraderie deriving from the stress and danger of police work. The problem occurs when these positive values mutate and become reinforcers of unethical practices. The common problem of racism is similarly closely related to the sociopolitical "structuring" of conflict between police and minority groups in the arena of street crime. But brutality and discriminatory policing also follow from the "cultural" dimension of ethnically biased police recruitment, use of racist and sexist jokes and stereotypes, and inadequate training in cultural sensitivity.

Prevention

It follows from both structural and cultural perspectives that strong and permanent measures are needed to guard against the numerous constant pressures for policing to slide into misconduct. One of the outcomes of this acceptance of the need for prevention has been the creation of dedicated "internal affairs" units, with responsibility for integrity management and complaints investigations across the whole police department. From the point of view of prevention strategies, the corollary of a structural approach is to modify the task environment. Some options include legalization or decriminalization of vice; removal of police responsibility

for regulation of particular offences, such as prostitution; the introduction of tape recording of interviews with suspects; and circulation of officers through corruption-prone squads to avoid the development of unlawful networks. There are, however, major limitations on the extent to which the task environment can be altered without eroding police powers and responsibilities in crime control. Consequently, increasing attention is being given to advanced methods of detection and deterrence. These include integrity tests ("stings") targeted on officers or sections where there are continuing suspicions about misconduct. Hidden cameras or recording devices provide evidence of either "failing" or "passing" the test. There is also a trend toward both targeted and random drug and alcohol tests.

Prevention initiatives deriving from cultural perspectives include recruitment strategies aimed at creating more points of resistance to group pressures. This entails diversifying the personnel profile with more women and minority group members, and older and more educated people. Women appear to be resistant to corruption, act less aggressively and are more capable in diffusing conflict. More attention is being given to ethical assessments in recruitment, as well as psychological testing to screen out people who may have a predisposition toward violence or crime. Training initiatives include more attention to ethics, to communication skills, and to cultural sensitivity. These strategies are designed to develop officers who have internalized high ethical standards and are resistant to misconduct opportunities. Many jurisdictions have also introduced compulsory reporting of observed or suspected misconduct as well as informant protection legislation in an effort to break down the code of silence. The concepts of problem-oriented policing and, especially, community policing are in part designed to reduce police violence through greater community consultation, especially in dealing with public order issues and minority groups. Many police departments now train specialist negotiators who are highly skilled in diffusing the potential for an escalation of violence in siege situations. More sophisticated physical restraint techniques have been developed for situations where force is unavoidable.

Although the reforms described above have often been enthusiastically supported, there is growing recognition of the power of the informal organizational culture to undermine such initiatives (combined with the opportunities and pressures in the task environment). More advanced control strategies initiated in some jurisdictions have included profiling of officers by using complaints databases about possible misconduct. This allows for the introduction of interventions, such as retraining or counseling, to address problem behaviors. In some cases it may be necessary to remove violence-prone officers or others who appear resistant to remedial interventions. A key element of many reform programs has been to hold line managers responsible for misconduct problems in their section in order in inculcate a management prevention approach to corruption. Finally, the problem of police solidarity has prompted the increasing use of civilian watchdog agencies to review police investigations of complaints. There is also a trend toward the independent investigation and adjudication of complaints by civilian agencies.

Conclusion

It is now an accepted tenet of police studies that the nature of police work makes it an extremely high-risk occupation for misconduct. Revelations of police brutality and corruption have been so frequent and widespread that no accountable government can trust police to keep their own house in order. Police managers must take prime responsibility for misconduct prevention, but it is also essential to have a strong and independent oversight agency to investigate serious matters and to assess the quality of police strategies for developing ethical conduct. The numerous pressures and opportunities for brutality and corruption in policing, and the diverse forms of possible misconduct, mean that constant vigilance is required to protect democratic liberties and prevent police abusing their authority.

TIM PRENZLER

References and Further Reading

Barker, T. and Carter, D.L., Ed. 1991. *Police Deviance,* Cincinnati, OH, Anderson.
Daley, R.1978 *Prince of the City,* Boston, MA, Houghton Mifflin.
Dixon, D., Ed. 1999. *A Culture of Corruption: Changing an Australia Police Service,* Sydney, Australia, Hawkins Press.
Geller, W.A. and Toch, H., Eds. 1996. *Police Violence: Understanding and Controlling Police Abuse of Force,* London, Yale University Press.
Goldstein, H. 1975. *Police Corruption: A Perspective on its Nature and Control,* Washington, DC, Police Foundation.
Human Rights Watch 1998. *Shielded from Justice: Police Brutality and Accountability in the U.S.* New York, Human Rights Watch
Kappeler, V., Sluder, R. and Alpert, G. 1994. *Forces of Deviance: Understanding the Dark Side of Policing,* Prospect Heights, IL, Waveland Press.
Kleinig, J. 1996. *The Ethics of Policing,* New York, Cambridge University Press.
Maas, P., *Serpico* 1973. New York, Viking Press.
Newburn, T. 1997. *Understanding and Preventing Police Corruption,* London, Home Office.
Punch, M. 1985. *Conduct Unbecoming: The Social Construction of Police Deviance and Control,* London, Tavistock.
Shearing, C. 1981. *Organisational Police Deviance: Its Structure And Control,* Toronto, Canada, Butterworths.
Sherman, L.W. 1978. *Scandal and Reform—Controlling Police Corruption,* Los Angeles, CA, University of California Press.
Skolnick, J.H. 1994. *Justice Without Trial: Law Enforcement in Democratic Society,* 3rd ed., New York, Macmillan.

See also **Police Crime; Police: Race and Racial Profiling; Police: Use of Deadly Force**

Police: Contemporary Developments

The concept of "policing" is often conflated with the institution of the public police. This is a misguided notion. Despite the fact that one of the central projects of modern government was to secure a monopoly over the business of governing security within the nation-state, this project has in no nation of the modern world been successfully completed. Private and civil bodies, such as paid security agencies and local citizens' initiatives, have always been active in the process of policing (Johnston, 2000).

The involvement of nonstate agencies was for a significant time obscured from the academic researcher's eye through the rise to dominance of the public police that reached its high point in both democratic and authoritarian states over the early and middle decades of the 20th century. In more recent years, however, the politics of social service provision (i.e., "welfare liberalism") in Western democracies and the centralized repression of authoritarian states that characterized the era of public police dominance have been undermined through significant economic, political, and social challenges associated with globalization (Johnston, 2000; O'Malley and Palmer, 1996; Mawby, 1999). Accordingly, the "monopoly" of the public police over the process of policing collective life—which was tenuous even at its heyday—has collapsed in both established liberal and transitional societies.

This realization has prompted a significant redefinition of the concept of "policing," away from an *institutional* focus on the public police in favor of an examination of the *processes* through which individuals and agencies act—whether directly or through designating others—to produce and offer assurances of safety and security (Bayley and Shearing, 1996). Some early progress has subsequently been made into understanding the ways in which public policing agencies *interact* with non-state policing agencies in the process of governing security. Rather than being eclipsed by nonstate agencies, it has been documented that the public police are themselves reorganizing—shifting their guiding mentalities, institutional forms, and ground-level practices—to meet the challenges associated with contemporary shifts in policing and governance.

In a political climate characterized by shrinking state services, the police have been pressed by governments to adopt the market rationality of competitive business management and efficient institutional organization. A key component of this logic is the principle of "subsidiarity," a concept taken from business management that posits that tasks and decision making ought to be devolved to the lowest possible level within an organization. This logic has been associated with the devolution of authority in both carrying out operational matters and mid-range planning in public policing organizations. This is in marked contrast with the dominant rationale of past decades, wherein authority over police operations and planning was concentrated at the upper levels of the "professionalized" police organization.

In subjecting the police-to-market discipline, much "streamlining" of the services provided has taken place. Public police agencies have contracted out to the private sector services that do not require the exercise of police powers or are otherwise not seen as essential state functions, such as the radar monitoring of speeding traffic, response to security alarms in private property, and the transportation of prisoners. Significantly, this devolution of functions has not been restricted to "peripheral" policing activities. In some locales, such as Australia, private agencies have assumed such "core" policing functions as investigations in drug trafficking, fraud, and political corruption (O'Malley and Palmer, 1996).

This shift in dominant policing rationalities is given expression in many practical public policing programs. Of particular significance is the rise of "community policing" as the dominant framework for policing in North America and Western Europe. Similar approaches are also in development in many states that are in transition to liberal democracy, notable among them Thailand, Singapore, Japan, South Africa, and Northern Ireland. Though policing programs assume distinct characteristics in different locales, most share essential features that can be distinguished from the "professional"

and "authoritarian" models of policing that previously characterized Western democracies and transitional states, respectively.

In the West, professional policing was associated with the primacy of the public police in addressing crime and problems of disorder within the social body. The rationale was to have a highly efficient public police organization that would, through adherence to ideal patrol and incident-response protocols, successfully combat crime. The public was viewed as passive beneficiaries of professional police crime-fighting expertise and service provision (Bayley, 1994; Johnston, 2000). Similarly, in authoritarian regimes, the police were paramount, though they directly served the interests of the state over the rule of law in many instances (Mawby, 1999).

Community policing sets much of this logic on its head. Its fundamental premise is that the public police cannot combat the problem of crime alone. The public police are understood to be *dependent* upon the public. What differs in various locales and continues to change over time is the *nature* and *degree* of this police dependency upon the public. In some of its earlier Western incarnations, community policing simply involved improving communication between the police and the public. It was considered that this would have the immediate effect of improving police–community relations, with the grander benefit of increasing the capacity of the police to combat crime through improving their ability to collect the information necessary for efficient criminal prosecution. Thus, within such early approaches to community policing, the public was very much considered to be the "junior partner" of the police.

This early approach has given way in many locales to a deepened notion of police–community partnership, in which the public takes an active role in guiding the activity of the public police (Johnston, 2000). Within such schemes, the public is reconceived as the "equal partner" to the public police in the business of governing security. This trend in part reflects the "marketization" of public policing at the local level. The intention is to render the police responsive to the public in much the same manner that paid private security agents are to their customers.

This deepened notion of partnership reflects a more fundamental reorientation of the approach to governing security. Rather than relying exclusively upon the familiar mechanism of law enforcement and arrest to fight crime, the advanced model of community policing seeks to manage future risks through a high degree of surveillance and constant informal correction of problematic behavior. This policing approach has been rendered possible through recent innovations in surveillance, communications, and data-processing technologies. In this connection, Richard Ericson and Kevin Haggerty (1997) have postulated that the public police have come to fill the role of information brokers in a broader network of agencies that engage in surveillance and instrumental control, such as private security agencies, insurance companies, health agencies, as well as others. Through cooperating with nonstate policing agencies and relying on more sophisticated surveillance technology, the public police have to a significant degree adopted the logic and practices of risk-management that characterize the private sector.

It must be stressed, however, that law enforcement remains an integral component of contemporary public policing. This is obvious not only in states that are in transition to democracy from authoritarian systems of rule but also in the established democracies of the West. With regard to the former, policing practices are often harsh in Russia and the states of the former Soviet Union (Mawby, 1999). Many nations of the suddenly collapsed USSR are struggling to reform the authoritarian, demoralized, and corrupted police structures of the Soviet era, with varying levels of success. Whereas East Germany, Hungary, and Estonia have managed to raise and devote substantial resources toward this end, other less well-off successor states, such as Uzbekistan and Tadzikistan, have achieved a much smaller degree of change. Indeed, it has been suggested that policing in these states is much more authoritarian than in the final years of the Soviet Union (Mawby, 1999).

Research suggests that policing also retains authoritarian elements in Asia (Mawby, 1999). Although Japanese police services are firmly rooted in their communities, they are not held directly accountable to those communities in the same ways as in the community-policing programs of Western democratic states. Many Asian police services operate in an ideological and cultural environment that places an emphasis upon group responsibility and obligation over individual rights. Thus, police services in Japan combine a community-service orientation with tight centralized control. There is some evidence that the community-service orientation is increasing in Japan in recent years, with the effect that the "democratization" of policing has gone further here than in surrounding Asian states. Further, some researchers consider that developments in policing in Asia will tend toward further democratization in the coming years, with Japan, Singapore, and Thailand taking the lead (Mawby, 1999).

Public order policing also remains a central component of policing programs in the liberal democracies of the West. Indeed, the policing of social protest boils over in many instances into police violence against the public in established democracies and transitional states alike. This is true not only in "divided" Western societies like Northern Ireland, which are characterized by entrenched sectarian conflict and violence (Francis, Davies, and Jupp, 1997; Johnston, 2000), but in other nations as well. Indeed, recent police violence in Canada directed toward persons protesting trade with the (now collapsed) authoritarian Suharto regime of Indonesia reveals that policing can be very harsh in even the established democracies with the most pacific of reputations (Ericson and Doyle, 1999). This has implications for the advisory role democratic nations often play in reforming police services abroad.

The survival of law-enforcement-oriented modes of policing illustrates that risk- and market-oriented thinking are not the only influences behind innovations in policing. As Les Johnston (2000) and Pat O'Malley and Darren Palmer (1996) have highlighted, risk-based forms of policing are often combined with traditional "disciplinary" styles. This process of combination is influenced by political conditions. For instance, although community policing is in part oriented toward the market principles of community satisfaction and involvement in the process of governing security, it can also be seen as intimately connected with the emergence of a broader "neo-liberal" political program that calls for the paring down of government services and concomitant political "responsibilization" of self-sufficient individuals to fill this service-provision vacuum (O'Malley and Palmer, 1996).

One of the major problems associated with recent incarnations of partnership-oriented policing is that it evokes the imagery of harmonious and geographically-defined "communities" where members share values and security priorities. It is doubtful that such arrangements have ever existed, and they certainly do not in the present. Indeed, recent decades have seen a diversification of communities on two principle levels. First, "communities" of the traditional residential type—which are situated in physical space and comprise some relatively stable number of individuals—are becoming increasingly heterogeneous in their cultural and socioeconomic makeup. Second, the present is witness to a multiplication in the form of "communities," some of which have no representation in physical space whatsoever, such as "virtual" communities in cyberspace, "contractual" communities of consumers subscribing to particular services, and "lifestyle" communities, where people share a passion for a particular pursuit (e.g., sports or leisure).

These dual processes pose tremendous challenges to the project of community policing. It has been pointed out that where community consensus does not exist, the police are forced to fabricate one (Johnston, 2000). This poses substantial problems for issues of representation and inclusion, raising the question of on whose behalf and interests policing is being exercised. It has been documented that in many instances, the "community" is represented, and thereby the police are directed, by wealthy, socially conservative members of the ethnic majority. Closely tied in with this phenomenon is the idea that community policing is increasingly coming to represent the control of "risky" segments of the population, the so-called "dangerous classes" that are made up of the poor and socially marginalized ethnic minorities (Ericson and Haggerty, 1997; Johnston, 2000).

An illustrative example of the confluence of these processes is the "zero-tolerance" approach to "community policing" that has taken hold in New York City. Within this framework, "quality of life" offenses such as panhandling and loitering are targeted through a relentless program of law enforcement. The ideology underlying this approach is that such minor offenses create a disorderly context in which more serious forms of crime are likely to occur. Thus, it is considered that eliminating these offenses creates safety for the community at large. It is apparent, however, that such a program targets the less wealthy segments of the "community," and by extension, disproportionately brings ethnic minorities into harsher contact with the police (Johnston, 2000). The security created by the police thereby does not amount to a "social benefit"—or a "democratic right"—in the traditional sense of a good that is equally distributed.

The emergent market-oriented logic of local policing is also given practical expression in recent shifts in the ways in which the police are held accountable (Johnston, 2000; Leishman, Loveday, and Savage, 2000; Loader, 2000; O'Malley and Palmer, 1996). In the late 1960s and throughout the 1970s, increasing pressures were exerted upon the police to be more open to such traditional modes of police accountability as media criticism, governmental review, and revised approaches to internal review wherein the police themselves take responsibility for investigating and adjudicating alleged abuses of authority.

In more recent years, the behavior of the police is increasingly monitored and adjudicated by independent external agencies. This process involves increased use of audits—standardized empirical assessments—of community desires and levels of satisfaction with the police (Johnston, 2000; Loader, 2000). Such innovations in "marketized" police-community interaction and accountability are most advanced in Britain, but similar initiatives are also commonplace in the U.S., New Zealand, and Australia (Johnston, 2000; Loader, 2000). As community-based policing continues to spread to transitional democracies, such innovations in approaches to accountability will similarly spread and take hold. Significant developments in this regard

have occurred in the new democratic South Africa (Bayley and Shearing, 1996) and are emerging in Northern Ireland.

Although local level policing is increasingly characterized by "subsidiarity," national-level policing has been increasingly become centralized. Principally, this has occurred in the areas of "high-policing" practice, which address the security of the state and other politically-oriented crimes, such as illegal migration, drug trafficking, and public order concerns. Thus the devolution of policing practice has been restricted to relatively routine police work. The nationalization of "high policing" practice is especially pronounced in the context of the member states emergent of the European Union (Johnston, 2000).

The centralization of national police forces is highly intertwined with the third major trend in contemporary policing: increasing cooperation of police agencies at the transnational level. Although cooperation among police forces of different nations is not in itself a new development, such collaboration presently takes place to a degree that is qualitatively distinct from what has gone before (Sheptycki, 2000). Indeed, it is true that Interpol—an international communications system and legal advisory agency linking police agencies around the world—dates back to 1923. In recent years, however, there has been a multiplication in number of transnational links between existing police forces as well as the creation of specialized transnational policing bodies.

With regard to the former, of particular note are the arrangements that have emerged from the Shengen Convention, which are designed to facilitate policing objectives across Europe's borders, such as coordinated border surveillance, the right of "hot pursuit" of criminals across borders, and the coordination and sharing of information between police forces of member states (which includes the establishment of a computerized data exchange system). An important instance of novel specialized transnational bodies is the Trevi Group, a high-level ministerial association composed of senior police officers from the 12 member states of the European Union and the "friends of Trevi" who attend its meetings as observers (Austria, Canada, Morocco, Norway, Sweden, and the U.S.), that seeks to facilitate European police cooperation (Johnston, 2000). Thus, these novel forms of transnational policing cooperation are especially well-developed in the context of the emergent European Union.

A major preoccupation of transnational policing has been "cross-border crime," particularly terrorism, drug-trafficking, and illegal migration. These developments raise serious concerns regarding accountability, legal jurisdiction, and the violation of individual rights. To begin, there is the question of which nation's legal rules ought to apply where an offender from one state is being investigated in another. Related to this is the individual rights concern of whether law-enforcement agencies are aware of and sensitive to the legal and constitutional restrictions on policing activity in other locales (Sheptycki, 2000).

Secondly, transnational policing creates the potential for abuse of authority. Transnational policing initiatives are presently directed by nonelected bureaucrats and police professionals, and so are largely unaccountable to the public. It has been suggested that the desire to maintain "international trust" between cooperating police agencies provides a motivation or justification for secrecy in transnational law enforcement in much the same way that the notion of "national security" does in the more traditional modes of law enforcement that takes place within nation–states (Sheptycki, 2000). Such "invisible" policing action raises the problem of "plausible deniability" of involvement in abuse of authority on the part of publicly-accountable figures.

Thirdly, the concern has been raised that the focus on "high-policing" at the national and transnational levels might distort the quality of policing in general (Johnston, 2000). For instance, the concern has been raised that a preoccupation with the "war on drugs" at the transnational level in the emergent European Union might contribute to an intolerant attitude and set of policing practices affecting immigrants from less developed regions of South and Eastern Europe, and Northern Africa (Sheptycki, 2000).

Transnational cooperation between police agencies has also prompted policing reform within nations, especially in the postcommunist societies of Eastern Europe. Although during the time of authoritarian rule these police systems were characterized by a highly militaristic structure and an emphasis upon political rather than more mundane forms of crime, efforts to integrate into transnational policing networks with the West have led to substantial demilitarization and depoliticization of the police in many of these locales, although, these processes are far from complete.

MICHAEL KEMPA

Further Reading

Bayley, D. 1996. *Police for the Future,* New York, Oxford University Press.
Bayley, D. and Shearing, C. 1996. The future of policing, *Law and Society Review,* 30(3), 585–606.
Ericson, R. and Doyle, A. 1999. Globalization and the policing of protest: The case of APEC 1997, *The British Journal of Sociology,* 50(4), 589–608.
Ericson, R. and Haggerty, K. 1997. *Policing the Risk Society,* Buffalo, New York, University of Toronto Press.
Francis, P., Davies, P. and Jupp, V. 1997. *Policing Futures: The Police, Law Enforcement and the Twenty-First Century,* London, MacMillan Press; New York, St. Martin's Press.
Johnston, L. 2000. *Policing Britain: Risk, Security, and Governance,* Harlow, U.K., Pearson Education.
Loader, I. 2000. Plural policing and democratic governance, *Social and Legal Studies,* 9(3), 323–245.
Mawby, R.I., Ed. 1999. *Policing Across the World: Issues for the 21st Century,* London, UCL Press.
O'Malley, P. and Palmer, D. 1996. Post-keynesian policing, *Economy and Society,* 25(2), 137–155.
Saulsbury, W., Mott, J. and Newburn, T., Eds. 1996. *Themes in Contemporary Policing,* London, Independent Inquiry Into the Roles and Responsibilities of the Public Police.
Sheptycki, J., Ed. 2000. *Issues in Transnational Policing,* London, Routledge.
Leishman, F., Loveday, B. and Savage, S. 2000. *Core Issues in Policing,* 2nd ed., Harlow, U.K., Pearson Education.

See also **International Policing: Cooperation Among Nations in the European Union; International Policing: Interpol; Law Enforcement: Community Policing; Police: Municipal/Urban**

Police Crime

Society passes rules or behavioral standards to protect individuals and groups from other individuals and groups who want to harm them. This rules and behaviors standard makes some behavior unacceptable. The unacceptable social behavior rules are referred to as "laws of society." These rules, which are referred to as laws, are defined as a crime. A crime can be defined as "an intentional act or omission in violation of criminal law, committed without the defense or justification, and sanctioned by the state as a felony or misdemeanor" (Inciardi, 2002, 662).

To maintain social order in society and to observe the behavior of citizens a formal mechanism has been put into place to hold accountable those who violate the law. The police in American society have been given the responsibility to arrest those who violate society's laws. Each year the American police arrest thousands of individuals who commit crimes ranging from shoplifting to premeditated murder. However, periodically it occurs that those responsible for maintaining social order and to enforce society's laws are the law violators. Students of social history readily recognize that those responsible for enforcing the standards established by society are often the ones who violate society's standards. Periodically this occurs with the police, who have the duty and responsibility for being society's law enforcers. As the police are the enforcers of crimes designated by society it is difficult to accept the police as law violators.

The U.S. being originally a British colony has inherited the English concept of policing. Initially, the male citizen was given the duty of maintaining social order, as was the custom in England. With the development of the Industrial Revolution in England and in the U.S., and with an influx of the population from rural areas to the cities, disorder and crime increased substantially. The mechanism to maintain social order and to enforce laws was not working. Often those responsible for maintaining social order and enforcing the law were law violators committing acts of violence and theft. For example, in England private citizens known as thief-takes, who were involved in the investigation of thieves, were often the thieves. The thief-taker would only receive payment for recovering stolen property. What better way to receive a payment for recovering stolen goods than to receive payment for recovering the stolen goods one has stolen?

In addition to the poor reputation of the thief-taker, the citizens appointed to maintain social order and enforce the laws would not enforce the laws. Of course these individuals were poorly trained and were not compensated. In order to correct the situations a movement existed in England to establish a permanent government to curtail the disorder and get the crime rate under control.

In 1829, Sir Robert Peel was able to get the approval of the British Parliament to establish the London Metropolitan Police. This was the beginning of modern policing, as we know it today. Because of the high crime rate in New York City, the New York state legislature established modern policing in America in 1845, based on the London Metropolitan Model.

Police history in America is full of criminal acts committed by police officers. In addition to police corruption, which includes acts of bribery, selling confidential police information, and protecting criminal activities, police officers are involved in every conceivable criminal act committed by the average citizen. The criminal acts include murder, rape, robbery,

assault, drug trafficking, domestic violence, child abuse, and theft.

In 1967, the President's Commission on Law Enforcement and Administration reported that police officers have operated burglary rings, stolen items from burglarized premises and from drunks (115). For example, in Denver, Colorado, approximately 30 police officers assigned to the night shift were found to be involved in a burglary ring. In Chicago, police officers served as planners and lookouts for a burglar for a share of the theft (Bopp and Schultz, 1972, 137).

A 1972 study found that one of every three police officers in Chicago was found guilty of a criminal act; in Boston it was one in four; and in Washington, DC, it was one in five (McCafferty and McCafferty, 1998, 59). As police departments do not maintain crime statistics on crimes committed by police officers it is difficult to obtain an accurate account of crimes committed by police officers.

Just like any violent criminal there are police officers who commit crimes of violence. During the 1980s, numerous Miami police officers were arrested for criminal acts. Nineteen Hispanic Miami police officers were arrested during this period, but seven of them were known as the River Cops. The River Cops were police officers who committed violent criminal acts. The crimes the River Cops committed and were convicted of consisted of murder, threats involving murder, civil rights violations, robbery, possession of narcotics, and conspiracy.

On November 5, 1992, four Detroit, Michigan, police officers were involved in the beating death of a black motorist. All four police officers were charged and convicted of murder. Two of the police officers were convicted of beating the victim to death with flashlights (Conser and Russel, 2000). Although the officers were on duty when they committed this act, it was an act of murder. The victim did nothing to justify being murdered by the police officers.

A crime committed by a police officer that was even difficult for police officers to comprehend occurred shortly after 1:00 AM on April 4, 1995. An off-duty New Orleans police officer, Antoinette Frank, burst into the Kim Anh Vietnamese restaurant with her crime partner. Frank shot and killed fellow off-duty police officer Ronald Williams, who she knew and once partnered with in her police precinct. Two members of the Vietnamese family restaurant were pistol-whipped, with Frank and her partner demanding the day's receipts. Both victims begged for mercy before they were murdered execution style by Frank and her partner. The crime came to the attention of authorities because two of the family members hid in the restaurant's cooler and could identify Frank and her partner. The brutality of the crime was shocking and even more so because a female police officer was involved in acts of cold-blooded premeditated murder. Frank and her partner were convicted of capital murder. It should be noted that, from October 31, 1994 to October 2, 1995, 31 New Orleans police officers were arrested for crimes including rape, homicide, and drug trafficking. Frank was the fourth New Orleans police officer arrested within a year's time (People, 1995, 131–134). In December of 2002 Antoinette was denied a new sentencing hearing by an Orleans Parish judge. Another New Orleans police officer was sentenced to death for ordering the shooting that resulted in the death of a woman (Times-Picayune, 1996, B3).

Los Angeles, California, is another city where police officers were involved in murders and attempted murders. In one killing, Los Angeles police officers shot ten rounds into a 44-year-old man with no criminal record when they mistook him for a drug dealer. To justify their wrongful actions the officers planted a gun on the victim and reported that he pointed a gun at them. In a 1996 incident, officers fired ten rounds into a 19-year-old man in the head and chest and planted a gun on him. In another incident, police officers opened fire on two holiday travelers. Eventually an officer familiar with the incident reported that the officers were out "hunting" that night, meaning they were out hunting human beings for sport. The travelers were arrested on false charges. There are additional unjustifiable shootings by Los Angels police officers (Knowland and Nebbia, 2000, 2).

Police officers have been charged with rapes, robberies, domestic violence, child abuse, burglaries, and larceny. In Savannah, Georgia, a police officer placed his own child in scalding hot water. In Wichita, Kansas, a police officer was charged with child molestation. In Galesburg, Illinois, a police officer was charged with bank robbery, and in Chatham County, Georgia, a police officer was caught robbing convenience stores, including a convenience store on his own beat.

While attending a law enforcement conference in Cincinnati, Ohio, a New Jersey police officer robbed a bank. After a lengthy chase the officer was finally apprehended. This officer, known as the Camouflage Bandit, was believed to have robbed seven banks in New Jersey. Police officers have patronized prostitutes. A Seattle, Washington, police officer was arrested for such an act. Similarly, an Arizona police officer was arrested for releasing a prostitute in exchange for having sex with him. In 1999, a Denver, Colorado, police lieutenant was arrested for sexual assault of a child. The lieutenant, who had 25 years of police service, was on medical leave when he assaulted the child (Birzer, 2001, 174). A 15-year police sergeant veteran in a suburban department in St. Louis, Missouri, was convicted of sex acts with a teenage girl. The girl, an Explorer Scout, testified that she had eight or nine sexual encounters with the police sergeant (O'Neal and Lhotka, 1999, C1).

With drug trafficking and drug use a crime problem in the U.S., it should come as no surprise that police officers are periodically involved in drug crimes. This includes drug trafficking, selling, stealing, and using illegal drugs. For example, in the mid-1990s, Savannah, Georgia, had a police sergeant who operated a drug-trafficking ring. In a drug-sting operation conducted by the Chicago Police Department a Chicago police officer was among 57 people arrested. The officer was charged with possession of a controlled substance (News, 1994, 49). In another incident, a Glen Falls police officer was sentenced to 3 years probation and 120 hours of community service for attempting to purchase cocaine. This same officer was previously arrested for altering prescriptions for pain medication and charged with forgery and criminal possession of a forged substance (Capital Region, 1999, B7).

Police officers also commit property crimes such as theft and shoplifting. A suburban Milwaukee police officer stole enough building materials from an apartment complex that he was able to fill a pickup truck and minivan. The officer stole power tools, a sliding door security bar, light bulbs, rolls of paper towels, a ceiling fan, and various light fixtures (Sussman, 2001, 01B). Police officers have been involved in shoplifting and extortion. A Wichita, Kansas, police officer was fired because he attempted to collect money from an insurance company on items already collected on. There is no end to the crimes police officers commit.

Police officers who reflect society values may also violate society laws. As no statistics are maintained on police crimes, there exists no way to determine how many crimes are committed by police officers. Police crimes provide a negative image in the community's perception of the police. Just as crime in America may be unstoppable, so it seems is police crime. Police criminals should be a category of crime—like career criminals or juvenile crime. Crimes committed by police officers do exist and statistical records need to be maintained.

MICHAEL J. PALMIOTTO

References and Further Reading

Birzer, M. (2001). Crimes committed by police officers, in Palmiotto, M.J., Ed., *Police Misconduct,* Upper Saddle River, Prentice-Hall.

Bobbs, W.J. and Schultz, D.O. (1972). *A Short History of American Law Enforcement,* Springfield, IL, Charles C. Thomas.

Capital Region. (June 23, 1999). A 3-year probation for ex-cop in drug-charge guilty plea, *The Times Union,* Albany, NY.

Conser, J.A. and Russel, G.D. (2000). *Law Enforcement in the U.S.,* Gaithersburg, MD, Aspen Publishers.

Inciardi, J.A. (2002). *Criminal Justice,* 7th ed., Fort Worth, TX, Harcourt Press.

McCafferty, F.L. and McCafferty, M.A. (1998). Corruption in law enforcement: A paradigm of occupational stress and deviancy, *Journal of American Academic Psychiatry Law*, 26(1).

News (October 4, 1996). Cop arrested in drug sting, *Chicago Sun-Times*.

O'Neil, T. and Lhotka, W. (June, 4, 1999). Jury convicts eureka officer of sex act with teen; verdict follows detailed testimony from the explorer scout, *St. Louis Post-Dispatch*.

O'Neil, T. and Lhotka, W. (October 2, 1995). A killer in blue, *People*.

Times-Picayune (1996). Former police officer sentenced to death, The President's Commission on Law Enforcement and Administration of Justice (1967)

The Challenge of Crime in a Free America, Washington, DC, Government Printing Office.

Sussman, L. (December 20, 2001). Officer accused of stealing to build home; disciplinary hearing begins in Thiensville, *Milwaukee Journal Sentinel*.

See also **Police: Brutality and Corruption; Police: Disciplinary Actions and Internal Affairs**

Police: Detectives

According to the *Oxford English Dictionary*, the word "detective" entered the English language in 1843, when Sir James Graham, then Home Secretary, announced that a "few especially intelligent men have been recently selected to form a body called the 'detective police.'" It would take another dozen years for the adjective "detective" to mature into a noun and more than another quarter of a century before the Metropolitan Police of London would permit its detective unit to grow into a bureau of any meaningful size. The reason for this reticence was that at the time of its creation, the role of detective was among the most suspect, feared, and despised of all police roles.

The basis for the early hostility to the detective was that, unlike the uniformed constables who were confined to patrol beats, the detectives dressed in civilian clothes and were free to move about with their police identity concealed. The detective provoked images of the undercover, informer-riddled police of France, and the English feared that such detectives could be used to spy on citizens as weapons of political control by the administrative branch of government. To counter these fears about the potential political uses of the detective, the early architects of the detective role, the first commissioners of the Metropolitan Police, Charles Rowan and especially Richard Mayne, imposed controls on their detectives that would comfort the public. During his 40-year term as commissioner, Mayne kept the number of detectives very small, no more than 15 detectives in a police force of more than 3500 employees in a London of nearly 2 million residents. He appointed as detectives only constables of sergeant rank or above, personally supervised their work, and carefully managed his detectives' public appearances.

He assigned them, as the elite of the police service, to investigate only the most high-profile cases.

Mayne's early efforts to construct a favorable image for the detective were augmented by the simultaneous development in literature of the genre of detective fiction. In 1841, the first detective story, Edgar Allen Poe's *Murders in the Rue Morgue*, appeared. It was followed quickly by Poe's *Purloined Letter* (1842) and his *Mystery of Marie Roget* (1843). In 1852, in *Bleak House*, Charles Dickens, a police buff who wrote very favorably about real detectives he had met, introduced Inspector Bucket, the first Metropolitan Police detective to appear in English fiction.

It was, however, not until Mayne retired that his successor, Sir Edmund Henderson, felt comfortable enough with the idea of detectives to increase the number to 200. Unfortunately, within a few short years the detective division for whom Mayne had worked so hard to cultivate an exemplary reputation found itself embroiled in a corruption scandal, with three of Henderson's chief inspectors convicted of taking bribes. As a reform measure, in 1878 the CID was formed and the number of detectives in the Metropolitan Police grew to about 800 by 1887. That was the year that Sherlock Holmes, the most famous fictional detective of all time, and quite possibly the most famous character in all of literature, entered the scene in Arthur Conan Doyle's *Study in Scarlet*.

Sherlock Holmes would go on to dominate the world of detective fiction for the next century and created a nearly insatiable public appetite for the hundreds of classical detective heroes who would follow in his image. The image he bequeathed was not the legendary deerstalker cap and Calabash pipe but of special genius in the application of logic, observation, study, science, and analysis in the solution of the most challenging crimes. It was their use of these morally exemplary and culturally cherished means of solving cases that defined the classical detectives, made them cultural heroes, and joined Holmes with the otherwise very different likes of Father Brown, Charlie Chan, Lt. Columbo, Jessica Fletcher, Miss Marple, Perry Mason, Hercule Poirot, Virgil Tibbs, Philo Vance, Ellery Queen, Lord Peter Wimsey, and Nero Wolfe.

The classical detective hero was not the only literary figure who enhanced the popular image of the detective. In the 1930s, in distinction to Holmes and the classical detectives, there emerged a detective of a totally different sort. The adult, hard-boiled, tough-guy detective was a creature of depression America who was not confined to the use of morally exemplary means. A man who walked the city's meanest streets, the adult, hard-boiled, tough guy detective was willing and able to employ both force and fraud to solve a case. But despite the fact that this type of detective hero could employ enormous violence, he was restrained in its use by an inward, spiritual code of honor. It was this inward, spiritual code that defined the hard-boiled detectives, guided them in their use of dirty means, and joined them in a collection of street-savvy individualists as varied as Sam Spade, the Continental Op, Philip Marlowe, Mike Hammer, Lew Archer, "Dirty Harry" Callahan, Axel Foley, and Spenser (For Hire).

Images of both types of fictional detective heroes continue to feed both public and police expectations about what real detectives could and should be. However, what detectives are and what detection actually is prove to be rather different stories. The ennobling restraints of culture and character that defined classical and adult detectives often failed to control their real-world counterparts. From the corruption scandal that prompted the formation of the Metropolitan Police CID to the most contemporary incidents of police misconduct, detectives have disproportionately been the source of misbehavior that shamed and embarrassed the police. Historically, only undercover drug investigators have proven more vulnerable than detectives to temptations that invite corruption.

The vulnerability of the detective role to abuse and corruption is inseparable from the difficulty of supervising the work of detectives. Because the working world of detectives is fundamentally structured by the cases they are assigned, detectives must be given two types of discretion to solve them. The first is discretion over the means they use to solve the cases they are assigned. Such means may range from relatively benign interviews of victims and witnesses through collection and analysis of crime scene physical evidence to more precarious practices of interrogation and confession, searches of suspect places, and creation and development of informants by rewarding them for the information they provide. The second type of discretion detectives must enjoy is discretion over the time they allocate to different portions of their caseload. Both freedoms provide considerable cover for misconduct.

To add to the problems associated with the detective role, empirical research, beginning with the now classic study by the Rand Corporation, *The Criminal Investigation Process* (1975), has thrown considerable doubt about the value of the detective role and its actual contribution to the criminal justice process. Despite long-standing myths to the contrary, detectives actually spend only a small proportion of their time, less than 10%, in efforts dedicated to solving cases. Most of detectives' work time is devoted to postarrest processing, assembling information for trial, or recollecting information that has already been collected by patrol officers.

The nature and contribution of the case-solving efforts that detectives do make are also rather different than the heroes of detective fiction would lead one to believe. Perhaps the most common misperception is the failure to recognize how much the case-solving efforts of detectives depend directly on the work of patrol officers. In a substantial proportion of cases, detectives "solve" cases after patrol officers arrest the perpetrator at the scene. An equally important means of "solving" cases is simply to have the victim or a witness tell the detective "whodunit." Despite myths to the contrary, in only a relatively small proportion of cases does physical evidence play a direct role in solving cases. When physical evidence is available, it is typically used by detectives to strengthen their position for obtaining confessions from suspects.

Recognizing these and other limits on the detective role, many police agencies have reduced their allocation of detectives. Other agencies have sought to manage detective efforts more efficiently. The most common method of doing so has been to develop systems for screening cases and assigning for detective follow-up only those cases with sufficient probabilities of solution. Cases that do not survive such a screening are simply filed away and receive no further investigative attention. If new information becomes available, a case may then be recalled and reconsidered for detective assignment.

Reduction in the number of detective employees and the use of case screening methods can be justified as rational improvements in police agency efficiency and economy. Such measures save money and actually improve agency case-solution rates. However, these measures must be balanced by the need to maintain a relatively small number of police officers who must be given time and discretion in the choice of methods they use to investigate some cases. Those same officers should be expected to develop some specialized skills and knowledge to conduct the special investigations that require them. Although most police agencies would be well-advised to reduce the number of detectives to these minimal levels, such reductions exact a public relations cost that many police agencies remain unwilling to pay. For more than a century, both literary and organizational detective myths have sponsored the impression that a police agency that truly cares about serious crimes will send its best detectives to investigate them. Many agencies continue to support that impression with the full knowledge that the detectives will do little more than repeat the efforts of the patrol officers.

CARL B. KLOCKARS

References and Further Reading

Cawelti, J.G. 1976. *Adventure, Mystery, and Romance*, Chicago, IL, University of Chicago Press.

Eck, J. 1983. *Solving Crimes: The Investigation of Burglary and Robbery*, Washington, DC, Police Executive Research Forum.

Ericson, R. 1993. *Making Crime: A Study in Detective Work*, 2nd ed., Toronto, Canada, University of Toronto Press.

Greenwood, P. and Petersilia, J. 1975. *The Criminal Investigation Process, Vol. 1: Summary and Policy Implications*; Chaiken, J.M., *The Criminal Investigation Process, Vol II: Survey of Municipal and County Police Departments*; Greenwood, P.W., Chaiken, J.M., Petersilia, J. and Prusoff, L., *The Criminal Investigation Process, Vol. III: Observations and Analysis*, Santa Monica, CA, The Rand Corporation.

Horvath, F. and Meesig, R. 1998. The criminal investigation process and the role of forensic evidence: a review of empirical findings, *Journal of Forensic Sciences,* 43, 1.

Klockars, C. 1985. *Idea of Police*, Newbury Park, CA, Sage.

Manning, P. 1980. *The Narc's Game: Organizational and Informational Limits on Drug Law Enforcement*, Cambridge, MA, MIT Press.

Lock, J. 1993. *Scotland Yard Casebook: The Making of the CID 1865–1935*, London, Robert Hale.

Marx, G. 1988. *Undercover: Police Surveillance in America*, Berkeley, CA, University of California Press.

Morgan, J.B. 1990. *The Police Function and the Investigation of Crime*, Hants, U.K., Gower.

Petrow, S. 1994. The rise of the detective in London, 1869-1914, in Knafla L.A., et al., Eds., *Criminal Justice History: An International Annual*, Vol. 14, Westport, CT, Greenwood Press, pp 91–108.

Thorwald, J. 1965. *The Century of the Detective*, Harcourt, New York, Brace & World.

Wilson, J.Q. 1978. *The Investigators: Managing FBI and Narcotics Agents*, New York, Basic Books.

See also **Federal Bureau of Investigation (FBI); Police Investigation**

Police: Disciplinary Actions and Internal Affairs

Since the very beginning of formalized, professional law enforcement agencies, there has been police misconduct. Although it is important to remember that the vast majority of police officers are honest, law abiding professionals, there are some officers who engage in inappropriate behavior. When acts of police misconduct do occur, the behavior is usually viewed as much more serious than if a "regular" citizen had violated a policy, procedure, or law. Police officers hold a special place in our society. Not only are they charged with enforcing the laws of the land, but they also have the right to use deadly force, if need be, in order to gain compliance. As a result, their behavior is held to a higher standard.

Depending on the severity of the infraction, acts of police misconduct may result in a number of public reactions including feelings of violation, anger, and mistrust. These feelings are often directed not only at the police themselves, but at the criminal justice system as a whole. In the most extreme cases, real or perceived acts of police misconduct have been identified as the triggering incident in many riots in the U.S., especially during the turbulent era of the 1960s. Because of the serious nature of police misconduct, internal affairs bureaus have been developed to monitor the behavior of officers, investigate allegations of misconduct, and recommend disciplinary actions.

An internal affairs bureau (IAB) is generally viewed as an integral component of a modern, professional police agency. An IAB is staffed with sworn departmental personnel who are charged with investigating allegations of misconduct that have been made against their fellow officers. It must be recognized that the actual size, duties, and scope of an IAB vary greatly. Most municipal law enforcement agencies in the U.S. are actually quite small. Nearly 80% of local police departments employ fewer than 25 sworn personnel. In very small agencies, there may not be a separate, internal division that exclusively investigates allegations of misconduct. Instead, the chief of police or a high ranking member of the senior staff may assume such duties. Conversely, large agencies will have a separate division with a number of full time detectives or other investigators assigned.

Most internal affairs bureaus are reactive in nature. That is, an employee, citizen, or supervisor contacts the IAB to report an allegation of misconduct. The case is then assigned to an investigator, who speaks with the interested parties and makes a determination whether or not an act of misconduct has in fact occurred. Conversely, there are some IABs that are more proactive in nature. In large agencies, IAB investigators may work in undercover sting operations to test the integrity of the officers with respect to buying drugs, taking bribes or protection money from citizens, or other acts of corruption.

It is important to note that acts of police misconduct may take on a variety of forms that vary greatly in severity and impact. For example, a police officer may show up late for work, miss a required court appointment, speak rudely to a citizen, or fail to adequately investigate a crime. A police officer may also commit perjury, plant drugs or weapons on an innocent person, actively pursue "payoffs" or bribes, or shoot an unarmed suspect. In rare cases, police officers have also been convicted of robbery, rape, drug trafficking, murder, and other serious violations of criminal law. Police officers must follow internal departmental rules and regulations as well as local, state, and federal guidelines concerning such issues as the search and seizure of evidence and the treatment of suspects. Because of the wide range of actions that may be labeled as police misconduct, we will classify acts of police misconduct very generally as either internal violations or external violations. As we shall see, the type of misconduct an officer has been accused of has implications for the investigation, the determination of guilt or innocence, and any disciplinary action that may ultimately result from the complaint.

Internal acts of police misconduct involve violations of departmental policy. Police agencies provide their personnel with extensive manuals full of rules, regulations, and procedures. As is the case with most places of employment, some of the rules are strongly enforced and others, while "on the books," may be violated regularly without a negative consequence. There may be written policies governing where an officer may live, restrictions on personal grooming (hair length, color, facial hair), and even whether or not an officer may accept a free cup of coffee from a citizen. In addition to violations of these policies, internal acts of police misconduct may also involve such behaviors as showing up late for work, failure to appear in court, insubordination, use of illegal drugs, sexual harassment, abuse of sick or leave time, sleeping or drinking on duty, or incompetence. Whereas another employee who witnessed the questionable action may report allegations of internal misconduct directly to the IAB, the accused officer's direct supervisor makes most internal allegations.

External acts of misconduct involve behaviors that have been directed toward citizens. This category is quite broad and includes a variety of behaviors, including harassment, poor investigations, rudeness, indifference or other demeanor-related behaviors, illegal searches, improper touching, hitting, and other varieties of lethal and nonlethal force. Most allegations of external misconduct come to the attention of internal affairs through citizen complaints.

Generally speaking, allegations of internal acts of misconduct are much easier to sustain by internal affairs investigators. If an investigation is ruled "sustained," this means that there was sufficient evidence to prove the allegations made in the complaint. Oftentimes investigations of internal acts of misconduct are fairly straightforward. If an officer has been referred to internal affairs for missing work, court, or other assigned duties, the supervisor would easily be able to produce time sheets, schedules, subpoenas, and other evidence to support the allegations.

Conversely, allegations of external acts of misconduct can be very difficult to sustain. The majority of these allegations come to the attention of IAB through citizen complaints. Citizen complaints of misconduct can be very difficult to investigate and to substantiate. Nationally, on average, 10% or fewer complaints are ruled sustained by internal affairs investigators. This is not to say that the IAB investigators are not conscientiously performing their duties. In many cases, a behavior that a citizen perceives to be an act of misconduct may actually have been the only legal course of action available to the responding officer. Most citizens do not understand the complexity of the criminal law. Citizens may demand that an officer make an arrest, conduct a search, or demand other actions that an officer simply cannot do given the legal constraints of the U.S. Constitution. When an officer does not comply with the wishes of the citizen, the citizen may file a complaint alleging incompetence or other charge of misconduct.

There are other factors that make the investigation of citizen complaints difficult. The investigation of the complaint may result in a hopeless stalemate as the allegations of a citizen are evaluated against the defensive response of a known sworn law enforcement officer. Many police–citizen encounters occur out of the public eye in private homes, darkened alleys, at isolated traffic stops, or other secluded locations. This implies that there are few independent witnesses available for questioning by IAB to uphold or reject the allegations made in a complaint. A citizen may allege that an officer cursed at him during a traffic stop. Without a reliable witness or other supporting evidence IA investigators cannot sustain the complaint unless, of course, the officer admits his or her inappropriate conduct.

Another related challenge to Internal Affairs investigators searching for the truth is the "Blue Wall of Silence." It is very rare to find an officer willing to testify against another officer. There are strong norms that support a culture of silence among police officers. The vast majority of officers simply will not "rat" on a fellow officer, even if an act of misconduct has occurred.

If an individual filing a complaint of misconduct has a criminal record or is engaging in illegal activities, then the allegation may be not be taken as seriously as complaints filed by "innocent" civilians. The allegations made by a known drug dealer, prostitute, or gang member may be evaluated as unreliable. This is especially true for allegations such as harassment. Consider the case where a patrol officer regularly stops and questions a group of known gang members. The gang members may complain that they are being persecuted for no good reason. Internal affairs investigators must determine whether or not the officer is simply an aggressive officer who is actively seeking out crime and criminals, or if the officer has crossed the line and is in fact harassing the gang members. These types of investigations are challenging for IAB detectives, especially because there is a positive correlation between officer productivity and citizen complaints. That is, officers who handle a large number of calls for service, initiate high numbers of arrests, issue numerous traffic citations, and otherwise find themselves in a high number of potentially negative contacts with the public have more complaints than officers with lower levels of productivity.

Whether the IAB investigation stemmed from an internal or external allegation of misconduct, the accused officer is afforded due process rights during the investigation. Many of these rights parallel the rights given to private citizens accused of law violations, including the right to an attorney or other representative during questioning, the right to confront witnesses, the right to call witnesses on the behalf of the accused, and the right against self-incrimination.

If, in fact, the investigation finds enough evidence to sustain the allegations of the complaint, disciplinary action may be taken against the guilty officer. In assessing the appropriate level of discipline, the agency will consider a number of factors including the severity of harm that resulted from the action, the experience and past record of the officer, and whether or not the act of misconduct resulted from an intentional act or a mistake. Disciplinary actions may involve rather minor punishment such as written or verbal reprimands, or they may be more serious in nature. Officers may be suspended without pay, demoted in rank, terminated, or face decertification. If an officer's conduct has violated the criminal law, he or she may face other penalties, including fines, probation, imprisonment, or other legal recourse.

Given the difficulties in investigating allegations of misconduct, IABs are turning to a number of innovative methods of monitoring the behavior of police officers. For example, in order to support or negate allegations of misconduct stemming from traffic stops, more agencies are using video recorders that are mounted on the dashboards of patrol vehicles. If a citizen files a complaint of rudeness, IAB investigators need only view the tape to determine if the allegations are true. Additionally, other agencies are using videotaping to ensure compliance with departmental procedures. High-speed pursuits are very dangerous, high-liability activities. As a result, some agencies are requiring that high-speed pursuits be videotaped by personnel assigned to the helicopter or aviation unit. The tape is then viewed by supervisory personnel to ensure that all departmental procedures were followed.

The newest trend in monitoring police behavior involves the establishment of early warning systems (EWS). Sometimes known as early intervention programs, this proactive management tool is designed to identify potentially problematic officers before a serious incident occurs. On a regular basis, IAB personnel monitor a number of indicators to see if an officer has accumulated a larger than normal number of events. These indicators may include such things as citizen complaints, number of use of force reports, abuse of sick time, or weapons discharges. Once an officer has been identified by the EWS, the behavior of the officer is then evaluated more carefully to determine whether or not the officer's actions were appropriate under the circumstances, or if additional training, reassignment, or other intervention is necessary.

KIM MICHELLE LERSCH

References and Further Reading

Dunham, R.G. and Alpert, G.P., Eds. (2001). *Critical Issues in Policing,* 4th ed., Prospect Heights, IL, Waveland Press.
Greene, J.R., Piquero, A.R. and Hickman, M.J., Eds. (2004). *Supporting Police Integrity,* Belmont, CA, Wadsworth.

Kappeler, V.E., Sluder, R.D. and Alpert, G.P. (1998). *Forces of Deviance: Understanding the Dark Side of Policing,* 2nd ed., Prospect Heights, IL, Waveland Press.

Lersch, K.M., Ed. (2002). *Policing and Misconduct,* Upper Saddle River, NJ, Prentice Hall.

Report to the Honorable Charles B. Rangel, House of Representatives, Law Enforcement (May, 1998). *Information on Drug-related Police Corruption, Report of the GAO* [GAO/GGD-98–11], Washington, DC, U.S. Government Printing Office.

Thurman, Q. and Zhao, J., Eds. (2003). *Contemporary Policing: Controversies, Challenges, and Solutions,* Los Angeles, CA, Roxbury.

Walker, S. (2001) *Police Accountability: The Role of Citizen Oversight,* Belmont, CA, Wadsworth Publishing Company.

Walker, S. and Katz, C. (2002). *The Police in America,* 4th ed., New York, McGraw Hill.

See also **Police Crime; Police: Brutality and Corruption**

Police: Forensic Evidence

For every crime committed, there is a crime scene that contains potential physical evidence that often provides information to the criminal investigator about the "who, what, when, where, how, and why" of a crime. The scene is essentially twofold in that it presents not only answers about the crime, but also poses questions for the investigator that may lead or hinder his or her investigation. It is ultimately the primary investigator's responsibility to determine which questions and answers are relevant in reconstructing the crime; identify the victim(s) and perpetrator(s); determine why, when, and where the crime occurred; determine the possibility of a secondary crime scene; protect the integrity of the crime scene; and recognize potential evidence. Dependent upon the investigators' departmental policies and procedures, they may also be responsible for the collection and preservation of evidence. Large agencies generally have a division specifically designated to process crime scenes and manage evidence, unlike small- to mid-sized agencies. In either case, the primary investigator must keep in mind the basic fundamental principle that the success or failure of an investigation is contingent upon the recognition, collection, preservation, development, and interpretation of the physical evidence.

In this article, our discussion will begin with an overview of crime scenes and the responsibility of law enforcement personnel. Continuing, this article will explain what physical or forensic evidence is and present specific types of evidence. Further, the responsibility of forensic scientists or criminalists, the forensic laboratory, and related case law will be presented.

With an increase in the crime rate, technological advances, and the more knowledgeable criminal, criminal investigators have had to expand their resources to use the knowledge, expertise, and advanced technology of science to solve crimes. The application of the various fields of the physical and natural sciences to crime analysis is referred to as forensic science. Forensic science is an interdisciplinary approach to putting the puzzle pieces of a crime together, with the finished product being a dynamic and true picture of what happened, why it happened, and, of course, who is responsible. Forensic science has become an all-encompassing field of study that includes not only criminology and criminal justice, but also uses psychology, chemistry, anthropology, biology, entomology, engineering, medicine (pathology and odontology), physics, and geology, to name a few, to solve crimes.

The point where criminal investigation meets forensic science can be referred to as criminalistics. After crime-scene investigators collect and preserve the evidence, it is generally transported to a forensics laboratory, where the chain of custody is extended to the criminalist. Criminalists are generally scientists from the various fields of study previously mentioned who apply scientific methods to the development, examination, recording, and interpretation of physical evidence collected from a crime scene. Some of the various types of evidence presented to a criminalist for examination include: impression evidence, biological evidence, firearm evidence, trace evidence, questioned documents, arson and explosive evidence, and drug and toxicological evidence.

The basic premise of forensic science is that criminal investigators and scientists work hand-in-hand to obtain accurate interpretations of physical evidence through objective analyses. This fundamental premise is more than 189 years old and is the origin of existing principles and techniques used by the disciplines that constitute forensic science.

The forensic chain of events begins at the scene of a crime. As previously mentioned, for every crime committed there is a crime scene that contains physical evidence that may or may not be pertinent to the investigation. Essentially, a crime scene is the place of origin of a criminal act. It is the responsibility of the first patrol officer on scene to protect the scene until the notification and arrival of a criminal investigator. First and foremost, the primary patrol officer should approach every crime scene with care and caution so as not to destroy potential evidence. After clearing the scene by searching for suspects and checking the welfare of the victim, the primary patrol officer should protect the scene by establishing a perimeter by using barrier tape, additional personnel, or barricades. The perimeter should be protected by officers to assure that nonessential personnel, on-lookers, and the media are kept at a distance so as not to interfere with the scene or the investigation. An officer should begin an entry and exit log to document who comes and goes from the scene. The log should contain the name of every person entering and leaving the scene, the time, the person's agency, and the reason they entered or exited the perimeter.

Upon arrival of the investigator, he or she will begin the criminal investigation. A criminal investigation is "a lawful search for people and things useful in reconstructing an illegal act or omission and the mental state accompanying it. It is a probing from the known to the unknown, backward in time" (Weston and Lushbaugh, 2003). The investigation should be conducted in a methodical manner so as to not disturb the crime scene. The investigator should be briefed by the primary patrol officer before beginning the investigation. The investigator may also want to speak with the victim, witnesses, and the perpetrator, if applicable, before processing the crime scene or contacting the crime-scene unit. In conducting interviews or briefings, the investigator must keep in mind their primary responsibilities during and after the on-scene investigation. The primary responsibilities of the criminal investigator are to determine whether or not a crime has actually been committed; answer questions regarding jurisdiction; identify perpetrators, victims, and witnesses; apprehend perpetrators, develop and follow up on leads; gather various types of evidence; recover stolen property; notify victims of criminal procedures; testify in court; and assist in the prosecution of perpetrators (Osterburg and Ward, 2000).

Upon completion of interviews and briefings, the investigator should begin by noting the condition of the overall scene. The preliminary assessment of the scene may fall within one of two classifications: organized or disorganized. An organized crime scene "reflects a methodical, well-organized subject who leaves little physical evidence behind. The scene appears to have been well thought out" (Lyman, 2002). An organized crime scene generally establishes that the perpetrator was comfortable with the environment where the crime was committed. To the contrary, a disorganized crime scene represents an opportunist who happened upon the area where the crime was committed. The perpetrator leaves the scene in disarray. Although the crime might have been planned, the perpetrator did not plan well and appears to have been uncomfortable with the location or his or her surroundings (Lyman, 2002).

After categorizing the crime scene, the investigator should photograph, sketch, or video the scene to have a pictorial representation of the crime scene. It is important for the investigator to remember that any visual documentation may eventually be used as evidence. The investigator should begin photographing from the outside of the scene and work inward (general to specific). For large outside crime scenes, aerial photographs could prove to be very useful. A photograph log should be maintained of the pictures taken at the scene, to include the type of film and camera used. Sketching the crime scene aids in showing the relationship of one object to another by including measurements. Once again, if the crime scene is out of doors, a crime scene diagram of the area, to include landmarks, would prove to be more useful than a sketch. Videotaping the scene is useful in that an investigator may make investigative comments (verbal notes) while recording the scene. The investigator should always keep in mind that everything they or other personnel on scene are saying may be recorded and used by defense attorneys at trial.

Upon completion of the visual documentation of the scene, a search of the scene should be conducted in a very precise and methodical manner. The search pattern that the investigator chooses to use is generally based on the type of crime scene they are working. The ever-widening circle technique begins at the center of the crime scene, or a designated focal point, and extends outward in a circular manner. The ever-narrowing technique begins on the outside of the crime scene and continues, in a circular manner, toward the center of the crime scene, or other designated focal point (Weston and Lushbaugh, 2003). The zone or grid search is the breaking down of the scene into small segments. Each segment is searched, individually. A grid or strip search is useful when searching large areas. The area is boxed off and the investigator begins at one corner of the box and walks back and forth until they have reached the opposite side of the box. If possible, after the initial search has been completed, a different investigator should conduct a search of the scene as well. This adds a different perspective to the search and will serve as a "double-check" of the area for physical evidence. Should evidence be located during the search, the item should be marked with a flag or marker. The area should then be rephotographed or visually documented. Upon completion of the area search, the collection of physical or forensic evidence should begin.

The collection and preservation of physical evidence must be completed in a methodical and logical manner and may prove to be very time consuming. The most crucial and fragile objects of evidence should be collected first so as to prevent destruction or contamination. An evidence log should be maintained to document what object was collected and from where it was collected. Photographs of the object of evidence, as well as the location of discovery, should be taken before the object is collected. The collection techniques that may be used are contingent upon the type of physical evidence the object is or the condition of the piece of evidence. A review of various collection and preservation techniques used will be provided after a short introduction of physical evidence.

Physical evidence is any tangible material, however microscopic, that can prove whether or not a crime has actually been committed, identify anyone that may be associated with the crime (victim, suspect, witnesses, etc.), prove that a suspect has had contact with the victim, or place the suspect at the scene of the crime (Swanson, Chamelin, and Territo, 1998). Physical evidence collected at the scene of a crime may also corroborate a victim or witnesses' accounts of the crime and may prove that a potential suspect is actually innocent. Further, physical evidence is much more reliable than witness statements and may be used as a tool in obtaining a confession from a suspect during an interview or interrogation.

Physical evidence can take the form of a liquid, solid, or gaseous material and is obtained from three main sources: the crime scene itself, the suspect, or the victim. In a perfect world, physical evidence would always be objects that could be seen with the naked eye versus a magnifying glass and collected by hand versus tweezers. Trace evidence, however, are very important pieces of evidence that prove to be very difficult to locate and thus easy to overlook. Trace evidence are very small bits of matter or material that are not generally apparent to the naked eye and are either carried away from or to a crime scene by the victim, suspect, or even witnesses. Carrying evidence away from or to is referred to as a cross-transfer, also known as Locard's Exchange Principle. The principle states: "Wherever he steps, whatever he touches, whatever he leaves, even unconsciously, will serve as silent witness against him. Not only his fingerprints or his footprints, but his hair, the fibers from his clothes, the

glass he breaks, the tool marks he leaves, the paint he scratches, the blood or semen he deposits or collects, all these and more bear witness against him. This is evidence that does not forget, it is not confused by excitement of the moment, it is not absent because human witnesses are. It is factual evidence. Physical evidence cannot be wrong, it cannot perjure itself, and it cannot be wholly absent. Only its interpretation can err. Only human failure to find it, study and understand it, can diminish its value" (FBI, 1998).

According to the U.S. Department of Justice (1992), physical evidence may fall into one of nine known categories: weapons, body fluids, friction ridge impressions, shoe and tire impressions, tool marks, questioned documents, soil, glass, and miscellaneous trace evidence (gunshot residue, fibers, paint chips, hair). In addition to belonging to a particular category, physical evidence can further be classified as either evidence with identification characteristics or with class characteristics. Evidence with identification characteristics can be defined as "evidence which can positively be identified with an individual or source, whenever sufficient quantities or identifiable markings are present, to the exclusion of all other sources" (FBI, 1998). In sum, this type of evidence is unique. Some examples of this type of evidence include body fluids, friction ridge impressions (fingerprints), tool, tire, and shoe impressions. Evidence with class characteristics can be defined as "evidence that has the possibility of more than one source of questioned material" (FBI, 1998). Some examples of this type of evidence are generally trace evidence such as paint chips, gunshot residue, fibers, and glass.

As discussed, physical evidence can be any material found at a crime scene and is critical in every aspect of the investigation. Care must be given at all stages of the investigation to protect the integrity of all evidence. The first patrol officer on scene must protect it until the arrival of an investigator. He or she must continue to methodically collect and preserve the evidence until it can be transported to the forensics lab for analysis. Criminalists must continue with care while developing and interpreting the evidence. This delicate chain of custody is crucial to a successful prosecution. Below, specific types of evidence are discussed as well as the various collection and preservation techniques.

Firearms

In the 1920s, Calvin Goddard presented the theory that a spent casing or bullet could be linked to the firearm from which it was fired, by comparing the casings to those produced by a test-fire of the suspect firearm. To aid in comparison, he developed and refined his theory by producing the comparison microscope, which is still widely used today (Osterburg and Ward, 2000).

As previously mentioned, spent casings and bullets can be linked to a particular firearm by the damage the casing receives during loading, firing, and ejection or extraction, with the most evidence occurring during the firing stage. Before continuing, it is important to understand the composition of a bullet. The bullet consists of a cartridge or case, which is considered the "body" of the bullet that holds the gunpowder. This portion is ejected after firing in semiautomatic and automatic firearms, unlike revolvers. The primer is located at the bottom or "seat" of the casing and is the area the firing pin strikes to ignite the gunpowder. The "head" of the casing is the bullet. It is generally made of lead or a higher strength metal jacket (Swanson, Chamelin, and Territo, 1988). When the firing pin strikes the primer, an impression is recorded. This recording can occur in both centerfire and rimfire ammunition. As the bullet continues through the barrel of the firearm, striations are carved in the casing. The striations are unique to the general make and model of the firearm and are referred to as a class characteristic. In addition to class characteristics, every weapon has distinctive or individual characteristics that are unique to that particular weapon. Distinctive or individual characteristics are generally microscopic in nature and are engraved on the bullet by the barrel markings, firing pin impressions, and the breech face impressions (Saferstein, 2000). When the casing is ejected, as in semiautomatic and automatic firearms, additional markings can be seen on the spent casing.

The Federal Bureau of Investigations (FBI) has developed a database, known as DRUGFIRE, that contains information regarding the unique markings or surface characteristics of casings and bullets. The Bureau of Alcohol, Tobacco, and Firearms (ATF) uses a similar system called Integrated Ballistic Identification System (IBIS) (Saferstein, 2000). Although these databases have proven useful to the criminalist, there are times when traditional laboratory analysis will be required.

With an increased occurrence of crimes involving the use of a firearm, criminalists in the science of firearm identification have had to expand their knowledge beyond casing and bullet comparisons to include the restoration of firearm serial numbers, characterizations of gunpowder or gunshot residue, bullet trajectory, and shooting distance. Many firearms that are used to commit a crime have the serial numbers damaged to impede law enforcement officials from tracing the weapon and linking it to a particular owner. However, today an etching process exists that makes it possible to recover a filed or otherwise damaged serial number. The criminalist cleans and polishes the area and applies a specific type of regent with a cotton swab. The etching may be recovered "because the original stamping process sets up a strain in the metal by compressing the area underneath the stamp, the etching rate for the metal under pressure and that not so compressed is not the same" (Osterburg and Ward, 2000).

Gunshot residue (GSR) can be burnt or unburnt gunpowder, or pieces of the primer that can be recovered from items in the area where the suspect was standing at the time he or she fired a weapon. More importantly, GSR can also be found on the subject's person, particularly the hand that fired the gun, or clothing. Techniques have been developed that aid criminalists in determining whether or not an individual, usually the suspect, has fired a weapon. There are several techniques that may be used to determine if the subject has fired a gun. Some of the techniques used are neutron activation analysis (NAA), dermal nitrate, dilute acid, atomic absorption, fluorescence test, and scanning electron microscopy (Osterburg and Ward, 2000). Either type of analysis should be conducted within a few hours after shooting; however, certain analyses are able to produce a positive identification of GSR for up to 6 hours after the incident. Some techniques, such as NAA, have been successful even after hand washing.

Criminalists can use laser light sources or rods to determine the bullet's trajectory. The location of the subject at the time they fired the weapon and the line of travel of the bullet may be determined by locating the point where the light beams or rods cross or meet at a common point. Criminalists are also able to determine the distance between the subject and victim. The closer the subject is to the victim, the more dense the tattooing is, the more singeing by the fire from the barrel, and the smoke halo is more apparent. Tattooing, or powder pattern, is the collection of burnt and unburnt gunpowder and primer pieces and varies in density that aids in the determination of distance.

When collecting firearm evidence from the scene, the firearm should be secured in a cardboard box, paper envelope, or bag. When picking up the firearm, it should be handled by a textured surface on the gun. Before packaging, the firearm should be rendered safe. Ideally, the casing should be wrapped in cotton and secured in an evidence box. Any ammunition found should be secured in a paper bag or envelope.

Biological Fluids

Some of the body fluids that are useful evidence include blood, semen, urine, vaginal secretions, saliva, feces, and vomit (Lyman, 2002). Blood, semen, vaginal secretions, and saliva are susceptible to deoxyribonucleic acid (DNA) analysis. Urine may serve as valuable evidence when the alcohol content or blood type of a subject is important. A significant amount of urine is needed for testing. Fecal analysis may also be able to provide the blood type of the subject. An analysis of vomit can tell investigators the contents and time of the subject's last meal and may also provide information regarding the subject's medical history.

DNA analysis was developed in the 1970s, but was not applied to forensics until 1985, and was not available for law enforcement use until 1989 (Eckert and James, 1989). The FBI created the Combined DNA Index System (CODIS) around this time. Even with the advent of CODIS, the FBI would only receive evidence for DNA analysis from certain cases. The types of cases they would accept for conducting DNA analysis are limited to homicides, seriously aggravated assaults, and sexual assaults, where a suspect had been developed and a blood sample, from the suspect, was available for comparison purposes (Osterburg and Ward, 2000). Besides DNA analysis, blood may provide answers to other investigative questions through blood splatter analysis and blood typing.

The techniques for the collection of body fluids as evidence is contingent upon several factors. If the body fluid is dried, the investigator or CSI may store the item on which the body fluid is dried in a paper envelope or bag. Under no circumstances should the specimen be secured in a plastic bag. If the body fluid is wet and a significant amount is available, the sample may be taken with an eyedropper and put in a specifically marked tube. If the sample is small, it may be absorbed by a cotton swab or similar type fabric, air dried, and secured in a paper bag or envelope. If the body fluid sample is on an item that is too large to transport or store, the area where the body fluid was located may be cut from the larger item. All items containing body fluids should be packaged separately to prevent cross-contamination and refrigerated until they can be transported to the forensics lab.

Impression Evidence (Friction Ridge Impressions, Shoeprints, Tool Marks, Tire Tracks, Teeth Marks)

The use of friction ridge impressions as a means of identification began in 1883 by Alphonse Bertillon. It was not used in the U.S. until approximately 1901 (Saferstein, 2000). Friction ridge impressions (fingerprints, palm prints, foot prints) are one of the most common and valuable types of physical evidence discovered at a crime scene. A fingerprint is an impression of the friction ridges on the skin of the fingers. "In leaving an impression, an outline of the ridges is transferred and duplicated by the deposit of perspiration and other substances on the objects handled" (Osterburg and Ward, 2000). This process also occurs with the palm of the hand and the soles of the feet. Friction ridge impressions are very useful tools in identifying a subject because no two individuals, not even identical twins, can produce the same fingerprints. Further, no one individual has duplicate ridge details. Each finger has its own distinct pattern. These unique patterns develop before birth and never change. In fingerprint analysis, criminalists are concerned with the ridge-line details as well as with the ridge-line detail deviations. The various types of ridge lines are used for classification details, whereas the ridge-line details are considered individual characteristics (Fisher, 1993). The ridge details are classified by three distinct patterns: arches, loops, and whorls, which are then further divided as plain or tented arches; radial or ulnar patterned loops; and plain, central pocket, double, and accidental loops (Osterburg and Ward, 2000). Various techniques are used to develop and collect friction ridge prints. The technique used is contingent upon the type and condition of the surface being tested. For smooth, nonporous surfaces, latent powders, small particle regent, cyanocrylate or fluorescent dyes; for rough, nonporous surfaces, small particle regent, cyanocrylate or fluorescent dyes; for paper and cardboard surfaces iodine, ninhydrin, DFO, silver nitrate, physical developer, latent powders; for plastics, iodine, small particle regent, cyanocrylate or fluorescent dyes, latent powders; for soft vinyl, rubber, and leather-iodine small particle regent, cyanocrylate or fluorescent dyes, latent powders; for untreated metals, small particle regent, latent powders, cyanocrylate or fluorescent dyes; for unfinished wood, ninhydrin, latent powders, silver nitrate, physical developer; waxed surfaces, nonmetallic powders, cyanocrylate or fluorescent dyes; and for adhesive surfaces, adhesive side powders (Sirchie, 2002). After the use of the appropriate development product, the prints are lifted using a variety lifting tapes, once again contingent upon the type of item from which the latent print is to be lifted. Same products and techniques are used in developing and collecting palm- and foot-print impressions. After the prints are lifted, the latent prints may be transported to the forensics lab for analysis through the Automated Fingerprint Information System (AFIS). The study of friction ridge impressions requires and deserves a length of discussion that far exceeds the scope of this entry. Shoeprints, tool marks, and tire tracks are also very important items of evidence. The normal wear and tear of the aforementioned items is what makes them unique from other like products and can link a suspect to the scene of the crime. Criminalists may analyze the castings or lifts collected at the scene and can provide the make or model (where applicable) of the shoe or tire mark (McDonald, 1989). The shoe and tire impressions may be cast, using a plaster-of-paris type product or dental stone. After the casting dries, it should be secured in paper. Impressions of the same can be lifted from hard surfaces in a similar manner as fingerprints.

Tool marks left at a scene can provide information regarding the type and size of the tool used, and may contain more specific evidence by unique irregularities and specific characteristics. Further, tool fragments may be located at the scene and matched to a suspect's tool. Ideally, the item that contains the tool mark can possibly be transported to the forensics lab for analysis. If the item is too large to be transported and stored, a casting may be made of the marks by using dental stone. Other types of materials such as dental stone creams, molding putty, polysulfide rubber-based material, and silicone rubber are also used to record tool marks (Fisher, 1993). Once again, the cast should be wrapped in paper and transported to the forensics lab for analysis.

Teeth marks, by the same token, may be cast and compared to a dental cast or dental x-rays of the suspect. The cast made of the dental impression should also be secured in paper.

Trace Evidence (Hair, Fibers, Glass, Paint Chips)

Hair evidence may prove to be very useful physical evidence. If the hair contains the root or sheath, then a DNA analysis may be conducted. The DNA analysis can provide information that the hair came from an individual within a certain class of people. Hair is a class evidence, not individual; thus the ability to say that the hair came from a specific subject with 100% certainty, at this point, is impossible. The first step a criminalist takes is to determine whether the hair is human or nonhuman. Through microscopic observations, the criminalist will be able to provide the following information: the part of the body the hair came from; if the hair had been bleached or dyed; the race of the individual; the color, length, and diameter of the hair; how the hair was removed (cut or forced); and whether or not the individual suffered from disease or deficiencies (Saferstein, 2000). The age of the individual cannot be determined, unless the individual is an infant. Criminalists have also been unable to provide information regarding the sex of the individual through hair analysis. A representative or comparative sample, generally 25–50 hairs, is needed for laboratory comparison through the card coding system. Hair evidence must be collected using tweezers and stored in a folded piece of paper or a pill box.

Fibers also may be located at the scene of the crime, on the victim, or on the perpetrator. An analysis of fiber may provide class characteristics such as the type (natural or man-made material) and color of an article. Representative or comparison samples should be collected, if possible, for laboratory comparison. Fiber evidence should be collected and secured using the same techniques and methods as hair.

Glass and paint are also class characteristic in that a criminalist will be able to conclude that the scene sample matches a sample taken from the suspect, by identifying the type and color of the sample (FBI, 1998). Paint samples from vehicles may be able to provide the make of a vehicle. Once again, a known or controlled sample should be submitted to the lab. Paint and glass evidence should be collected and stored in a paper envelope or bag.

Questioned Documents

In analyzing questioned documents, criminalists are able to examine the letter characteristics of a subject's handwriting. Known exemplars containing the subject's handwriting should be submitted to the forensics lab with the questioned document. Additionally, documents may be examined for fingerprints (see techniques listed under friction ridge impression section). Questioned documents should be handled with care and stored in a paper envelope to be submitted to the lab.

It is important to note that there are many additional types of evidence, such as drugs, alcohol, arson, and explosive evidence, that require extensive discussion, which once again is beyond the scope of this article.

After the evidence is collected, the items are transported to a forensics lab for analysis and interpretation. The forensics lab may consist of physical science, biology, firearms, photography, document examination, toxicology, latent fingerprint, voiceprint analysis, polygraph, and toxicology units (Saferstein, 2000). As previously mentioned, the forensics lab is composed of individuals from various disciplines of the natural and physical sciences to include, but certainly not limited to: chemistry, anthropology, geology, medicine, toxicology, pathology, entomology, psychiatry or psychology, odontology, serology, criminology, and physics, to name but a few. These individuals conduct a variety of analyses and examinations on the physical evidence and provide lab reports to the investigating officer. Further, they also serve as expert witnesses at trial.

In conducting laboratory analyses of potential physical evidence, criminalists must be ever cognizant of the judicial rules of evidence. The landmark case *Frye v. U.S.* (Circuit Court, 1923) set the standard and provided guidelines for "determining the judicial admissibility of scientific examinations by stating the following: Just when a scientific principle or discovery crosses the line between the experimental and demonstrable stages is difficult to define. Somewhere in this twilight zone the evidential force of the principle must be recognized, and while the courts will go a long way in admitting expert testimony deduced from a well-recognized scientific principle or discovery, the thing from which the deduction is made must be sufficiently established to have gained general acceptance in the particular field in which it belongs" (Saferstein, 2000). From the circuit courts statement, a plethora of proceeding cases emerged, such as *Daubert v. Merrell Dow Pharmaceutical, Inc.*, and *Kumbo Tire Co., Ltd. v. Carmichael*, to name but a few (Saferstein, 2000). As with every aspect of a criminal trial, forensics are held to specific judicial and legal standards with certain limitations. Forensic scientists, as well as forensic evidence, will be challenged by the defense attorney, even as much as the criminal investigator and facts of law.

Forensic scientists have become as commonplace in the courtroom as attorneys and investigators, because they are important in the process of crime solving. As the scientific community and technology continue to advance, more and more new techniques and scientific principles are becoming available to law enforcement personnel to use in the discovery, collection, preservation, identification, and interpretation of forensic evidence.

DAWN CALDWELL

References and Further Reading

Eckert, W. and James, S. (1989). *Interpretation of Bloodstain Evidence at Crime Scenes,* New York, Elsevier Science Publishing.

Eliopulos, L. (1993). *Death Investigator's Handbook: A Field Guide to Crime Scene Processing,* Boulder, CO, Paladin Press.

Federal Bureau of Investigations (1998). *Handbook of Forensic Science,* Washington, DC, U.S. Printing Office.

Fisher, B. (1993). *Techniques of Crime Scene Investigation,* 5th ed., Boca Raton, FL, CRC Press.

Lyman, M. (2002). *Criminal Investigation—The Art and Science,* 3rd ed., Upper Saddle River, NJ, Prentice-Hall.

McDonald, P. (1989). *Tire Imprint Evidence,* New York, Elsevier Science Publishing.

Osterburg, J. and Ward, R. (2000). *Criminal Investigation: A Method for Reconstructing the Past,* 3rd ed., Cincinnati, OH, Anderson Publishing.

Saferstein, R. (2000). *Criminalistics—An Introduction to Forensic Science,* 7th ed., Upper Saddle River, NJ, Prentice-Hall.

Sirchie (2002). *Criminal Investigation Equipment,* Youngsville, NC, Laboratories.

Swanson, C., Chamelin, N. and Territo, L. (1988). *Criminal Investigation,* 4th ed., New York, Random House.

U.S. Department of Justice (1992). *Collection and Preservation of Physical Evidence,* Washington, DC, U.S. Printing Office.

Weston, P. and Lushbaugh, C. (2003). *Criminal Investigation: Basic Perspectives,* 9th ed., Upper Saddle River, NJ, Prentice Hall.

See also **Police Detectives**

Police History: England

Introduction

To avoid confusion it is convenient to organize and discuss the history of policing in England in a context that covers a wide degree of locales as well as very broad periods of history in terms of time. As such, it is important to cover eras that are critical to the development of policing in general and also those that are specific to the development of policing in England. To more cogently organize the discussion and to make it as clear as possible, one can reference the discussion in terms of several general periods of time that many scholars have felt free to address (Gaines and Kappeler, 2003). More specifically, many who have written on the topic of police history in England have tended to categorize their discussion using broad swaths of time such as "antiquity" (Langworthy and Travis, 2003),

and "policing in ancient times" (Champion and Hooper, 2003). For the purposes of this discussion, those periods of time will cover ancient policing, early policing in England, early English police reform, and the "Bobbies."

In fact, the police as we know them today did not begin to develop until communities organized themselves into more formalized political states (Gaines and Kappler, 2003). More specifically, political organization and the subsequent development of the police seemed to follow four general themes: (1) the creation of formal legal systems; (2) the emergence or recognition of different social classes; (3) the production and distribution of excess materials and resources; and (4) the general emergence of political states (p. 57). The developments of police as we know it followed this pattern as the emergence of ancient empires and city–states are responsible for the founding of the first police forces. Specifically, the geographic locales of Mesopotamia, Egypt, Greece, and Rome were among the first to create organized systems of police.

Ancient Policing

However, prior to the existence of these rudiments of modern English policing was the establishment of what has come to be known as kin policing. At this point of time, the primary unit of social organization was the tribe or clan. Laws as we know them today did not exist, and, in fact, unwritten traditions guided the behavior of members of the tribe. Because no organized system of policing existed, some method had to be used to control criminal activity. As a means to address this need, societies gave wide latitude in terms of the inflic-tion of punishment to the victims of criminals (Berg, 1999). This method relied upon family members of the victim, their "kin," to control individuals, and this prac-tice has been likened to the old Biblical adage, "I am my brother's keeper" (Uchida, 1997).

Using this method, each member of the clan or tribe was accorded a degree of authority and therefore took it upon themselves to track down those who broke the rules and or violated a member of their respective tribe. As one might assume, this system was fraught with difficulty as punishments, even for relatively minor offenses, were often severe (p. 16). In addition, track-ing down these ancient criminals often ignited argu-ments between the tribes involved that frequently resulted in long-standing feuds between clans.

However, these methods of controlling criminals began to evolve with the development of more sophis-ticated social relationships. The beginning of this gen-eral trend began in the region of Mesopotamia around 3500 BCE in the area between the Tigris and Euphrates Rivers in what is modern day Iraq (Berg, 1999). King Sargon conquered a number of cities in this region and consolidated his authority into a political city–state (Gaines and Kappeler, 2003). Not long after his reign, King Hammurabi created a code of laws that addressed legal protection for the citizens of his empire that, although severe, was organized and considered some-what humane. Further, this code provided specifics in terms of what acts were deemed illegal and what the subsequent punishments for those actions were to be. In an attempt to make the code enforceable, Ham-marubi declared that the kings "messengers" were given the authority to enforce the laws (Champion and Hooper, 2003) and thus these servants of the king were one of the first organized groups affiliated with the state and given the role of police (p. 41).

Around the same time that the Babylonians were developing their written codes, villages along the coast of North Africa along the Nile River were beginning to consolidate into ancient Egypt. In the earliest part of its history, Egypt created official positions called Judges Commandment of the Police that were respon-sible for the general security of the Egyptian provinces (Gaines and Kappeler, 2003). As time passed, some individuals were given the specialized task of enforc-ing the laws of a particular jurisdiction. Like many nations that exploited their access to the water, Egypt also developed an organized group of police that has been equated with modern customs officers to monitor its international trade routes (Berg, 2002). In fact, the River Security Unit had the specific duties of control-ling piracy and smuggling. Finally, the Egyptians also moved to control the problem of grave robbing as King Ramses III increased the responsibility of the police by ordering their around-the-clock presence at impor-tant tombs (Champion and Hooper, 2003).

However, as Egypt grew in size and political orga-nization, policing became increasingly associated with the military and specific units. At this point, the pri-mary responsibility of the police was shifted to that of protecting the political leader from both internal and external threats against his life or authority (Lyman, 2002). More specifically, Egyptian pharaohs created the position of Vizier in order to delegate broad author-ity to loyal officials while they conducted their military engagements (Gaines and Kappeler, 2003). Primary among their responsibilities were the oversight of the high court, collecting taxes, supervising the military, and finally, acting as "chief of police" for the kingdom (Champion and Hooper, 2003). Although Egypt cer-tainly played a role in the development of ancient policing, that influence certainly did not take place in a vacuum as other political entities such as ancient Greece also had an impact on early policing.

In ancient Greece much of what passed for policing in its earliest history was similar to the "kin police" system that in practice made everyone a police officer by granting them a limited amount of authority to initiate prosecutions (Sheldon, 2001). However, as time passed, Greece realized a good deal of population growth and the kin police system failed to be effective in controlling large groups of people and as a result it was discarded (Gaines and Kappeler, 2003). To address the problem, the Greeks granted authority to Draco to reform the law but the process proved a failure because of his increased reliance upon the death penalty, even for minor offenses, and for the allowance of debtors to be sold into slavery (Champion and Hooper, 2003).

As a crisis developed, Pisistratus, the ruler of Athens, staged an attack on himself in an attempt to create sympathy for his desire to create an organized force to protect the city (Champion and Hooper, 2003). His trick proved successful and he was granted the authority to create a force of bodyguards that he and his successors used to establish control over the population (Berg, 2002). Following the rule of Pisistratus in Athens, Pericles created a police force that was supervised and maintained by a small group of administrators called The Eleven (Champion and Hooper, 2003). These individuals shouldered the responsibility of helping the police apprehend criminals and performing executions (p. 44). Although the Greeks had a definitive impact upon the development of policing, the citizens of Rome had reform ideas of their own.

The earliest methods to subdue the population in that city were undertaken by the Roman legions. These were Roman soldiers who conquered various lands and, when needed, were used to maintain control over their defeated foes. However, owing to the fact that the Roman empire grew to encompass most of the known world, the legions were needed to maintain order in many places, and, as a result, they never stayed in one area for long periods of time (Gaines and Kappeler, 2003), which increased the opportunities for conquered peoples to revolt.

Dealing with increased violence in Rome and in the other provinces of the empire, Caesar Augustus created three separate forces used to police the empire: the Praetorian Guard, the urban cohort, and the vigils. First, the Praetorian Guard mirrored earlier societies in that its primary function was to protect the life, property, and palaces of the emperor. In fact, the Praetorian Guard has been referenced as one of the first examples of presidential protection (Champion and Hooper, 2003). The size of the guard was large, as it was composed of nine units of 1000 men who were drawn from Rome (Lyman, 2002). This force often attracted the best applicants to the special benefits that went along with membership. More specifically, members of this special force were given higher pay than most soldiers, private lodging, and did not have to wear uniforms (Gaines and Kappeler, 2003; Champion and Hooper, 2003). Second, the urban cohort had the responsibility to maintain the peace within Rome and was smaller than The Praetorian Guard. Finally, the vigils were basically a combination of firemen and night watchmen (Shelden, 2001) and they were organized into seven groups of 1000 men and were assigned to police at least two regions of the empire each (Champion and Hooper, 2003).

While these developments were occurring in what is modern-day Continental Europe and the Middle East, these events as they pertain to the development of policing were not confined to these places. France's system of policing developed separately from these places and along different lines, with much of its development reliant upon political and military events. In addition, England developed along similar lines as some of the ancient world early on, but as time passed its police forces became more and more organized and less involved with the surveillance and protection of a political figure.

Early English Policing

From the earliest organization of forces to maintain the "King's Peace" in England, the frankpledge system was put in place (Critchley, 1972). The system was based upon local control and it was the smallest of those localities, called vills or tuns (Summerson, 1979), that bore the greatest responsibility of the early policing in England. The tithing was a group of ten families and every male adolescent 12 years of age or older was required to serve as a policeman for the purposes of that tithing. Therefore, any member of the group who committed an offense was to be brought before the proper authorities by the tithing for punishment. If the tithing failed to produce the individual, the group itself could be fined. The next layer of organizational structure was called a hundred and consisted of a group of ten tithings. The administrator over the hundred was called a hundred man. Other titles for this bureaucratic overseer included the reeve or headborough and it was these early organizational positions that are thought to be the first examples of English constables (Brown, 1956).

Several small measures were undertaken as a means to improve upon this system and many scholars point to the Norman Conquest where such changes were made. For example, the Assize of Clarendon, the "Conservators of the Peace" (Brown, 1956), and the Statute of Winchester are all thought to have been alterations to or legal confirmation of the frankpledge system. The Assize is important because it required males aged 15–60 to maintain a weapon for maintenance of the peace (Wall, 1998). Secondly, the "hue and cry" was implemented to foster cooperation between sheriffs so that they were encouraged to help one another capture escaping criminals. The "Conservators of the Peace" originated as administrators until gradually their authority was increased and they became what have come to be known as the justices of the peace (Brown, 1956). Finally, in 1285, the Statute of Winchester basically codified many of these proposals. In fact, the principles set out in the law can be summarized in the following way: (1) all of the subjects of the kingdom had a degree of authority to arrest an offender; (2) the constable had a degree of help from the "watchman," whose job it was to patrol the divisions of the "watch and ward" on foot; and to (3) alert bystanders, constables, and other watchman to the "hue and cry" when an offense took place or when an offender was fleeing or the official needed help; (4) all males above a certain age were required to maintain a weapon with which to maintain the peace and respond to the hue and cry.

This system of policing persisted for several centuries and evolved into additional bureaucratic structures that supported the ancient methods. For example, at the beginning of the 18th century in metropolitan London and in the larger towns the earlier methods of policing were not enough to stem the growing crime rates that have been attributed to the Industrial Revolution. Although policing in general really did not change as a result of these advances, new police forces saddled with the same tasks were created to deal with the problem. Two of the more widely recognized forces are the beadles (Tobias, 1979) and the night watchmen.

Essentially, the beadle was a paid officer and took over some of the less appealing activities that were given to the constable (Smith, 1985). These officials sometimes acted as town crier, maintained order in the church courtyard during services, and arrested beggars and vagabonds (Reynolds, 1998). Initially, their pay was quite minimal but around 1735 localities were given permission to impose a "rate" (fee) on their residents for the purpose of providing a full-time, paid police force that was basically the official institution of the beadle as the local police officer (Tobias, 1979). The night watchmen, as the name implies, operated strictly at night. These officers were not very effective and usually comprised individuals who could not obtain employment in another way. Generally, they would report to their headquarters at dusk, pick up their small truncheon and lantern and report to their post. After a set period of time, they would patrol along their assigned street. Unfortunately, because of the fact that the watchman often served as the town crier, he gave ample warning of his presence to any would-be criminal.

Unfortunately, the early system of policing is more widely known for its corruption and ineffectiveness than its efficiency. Part of the problem lay in the fact that the constables were burdened with so many tasks, which included the housing of prisoners, keeping the nightly watch, initiation of the hue and cry, and participation in the imposition of punishments (Critchley, 1972), that no one really wanted the position. These officers were also required to document every violation of the law and do so for very little in the form of wages or for none at all. As a result, those who were assigned to serve often sought out opportunities to avoid the appointment altogether.

Practically, one could avoid having to serve as constable in three ways. First, the appointee could pay his way out by paying a fine to the parish (Tobias, 1979). Additionally, some people exercised their option on what was called a "Tyburn Ticket" (Pringle, 1958).

These certificates exempted the holder from having to serve as an officeholder for the parish and could be sold by those who possessed them and bought by those who wanted to avoid having to serve (Pringle, 19). The third mechanism for shunning an appointment was to actually accept it. However, once officially sworn in, one could then pay another individual to act as a "deputy" and that person would then perform all the duties required of the original appointee. One can easily determine that over time the office became highly undesirable and ample opportunities for corruption arose as the office itself degraded.

However, the difficulties of the constables are not thought to be solely responsible for the decline of the office. Some researchers have asserted that the Justice of the Peace also hastened the demise of the early police officer in England (Critchley, 1972). Although the initial role of the justices was to enforce the law as delineated in the Statute of Winchester (Pike, 1968), they were also given additional responsibilities over time which may have contributed to the demise of the system of policing as it existed.

By the early 18th century, the justices of the peace were the local administrators. They were required to maintain roads but they also were thought of as one of the highest local officials that dealt with law enforcement and crime. They had active roles in the criminal process as they tried minor offenses and investigated (in a preliminary way) other serious crimes. They were also responsible for issuing search and arrest warrants (Hart, 1951). At that time, the justice had more authority than he does today, as they often took direct control of investigations and ordered the police under their authority to accomplish tasks related to an investigation. Additionally, it was also the responsibility of the justice of the peace to "preserve public order." This particular function addressed the problem of rioting, and when one occurred the justice of the peace directed his police forces or called in the army to restore order.

As a result of their enhanced authority over time, scholars assert that the office of Justice of the Peace hastened the demise of the office of constable in several ways. First, this additional layer of administrative control did nothing to stem the tide of disorder that already existed. Second, it is also thought that the justice of the peace was given some of the authority of the constable and that the constable was to now report violations of law directly to the justice (Wrightson, 1980). Finally, as many view the two offices working together, it is also said that the two were equally corrupt. In fact, those justices who were involved in the practice of accepting contributions by offenders prior to a judicial decision came to be known as "trading" or "basket" justices (Tobias, 1979). Unfortunately, these individuals used the office they occupied for personal financial gain and were despised by the general public. In an effort to combat the problem, justices of the peace were eventually given salaries. This helped the problem, but it was the effort of several magistrates and their reputation for honesty and diligence in the pursuit of criminals that changed the perception of the magistrates and also helped to reform policing in England.

Early English Police Reform

The first magistrate among these was Thomas de Veil, who was a trading justice like many of his counterparts but was vigorous in his quest to catch offenders and to prevent further opportunities for criminal activity (Ascoli, 1979). He was eventually promoted to the top magistrate post in London and continued his pursuit of criminals until his death in 1746 (Tobias, 1979). It was de Veil who moved into the now famous 4 Bow Street in 1739 and began reforms that would later transform policing in London (Ascoli, 1979). However, his successor was given most of the credit for popularizing the Bow Street model.

Henry Fielding was a playwright and novelist who became intrigued with the idea of organized policing. He published *An Enquiry into the Cause of the Late Increase of Robbers* and argued that policing should be a preventative enterprise, not reactive, as it was, and largely still is, and that social conditions played an important role in crime causation (Ascoli, 1979). He and his brother John are noted for their tireless work ethic and publication of the *Covent Garden Gazette,* which identified suspected and known criminals in the area (Johnson and Wolfe, 2003). In addition, Fielding convinced a small group of honest men to join him in his crusade against crime and submit themselves to his authority as Bow Street Magistrate. The primary purpose of these men was to catch thieves, and they were variously called "thief-takers," "Mr. Fielding's People," (Pringle, 1955) and the "Bow Street Runners."

However, shortly after the creation of this force, Henry died, so it was left to his brother John to carry on the duties of the office and to continue on with the ideas initiated by the Bow Street office. John did not disappoint, as his career was just as illustrious as Henry's. During his tenure, John Fielding is credited with the creation of the Bow Street Horse Patrol and the addition of several groups of detectives who served in various places in and around London as a means to protect travelers from robbers (Johnson and Wolfe, 2003). John continued to publish the *Gazette* and at the dawning of the 19th century his Bow Street Runners were cheered as the best law enforcement organization in London. As a result of the immense popularity and success of his programs, John was knighted at the end of his career (Johnson and Wolfe, 158).

Around the same time that popularity for Sir John Fielding's Bow Street Runners and Horse Patrol was peaking, Patrick Colquhoun arrived in London. Although Colquhoun was popular in his native Scotland, he came to London to find trading opportunities for Scottish businesses and to address his interest in social and police reforms (Reith, 1975). Soon after his arrival he was appointed one of the first paid magistrates in London and used this platform to argue for the expansion of the programs created and initiated by the Fieldings. As an example, in his book—*A Treatise on the Police of the Metropolis,* explaining the various crimes and misdemeanors that at present are felt as a pressure upon the community, and suggesting remedies for their prevention—he argued that the Fielding's ideas concerning crime prevention and the role of the police should be wedded into one large police force covering the entire city of London (Johnson and Wolfe, 2003).

Although Colquhoun did not survive to see such a force, he did see the creation of the River Police instituted by the Thames Police Act. In response to his book, several traders approached Colquhoun about creating a plan to police the shipping port of London (Reynolds, 1998). They were losing a great deal of money to robbery and theft but had no means to counteract the criminal activity. Colquhoun created a plan, funded by the merchants, which allowed for the hiring of about 1200 men to help unload the ships and patrol the docks (Reith, 1975). This force is said to have been the first organized police force in London and was so successful at controlling crime on the river that the government took control over it. Unfortunately for Colquhoun, the government ignored his requests to create independent forces in English towns and ports and, as a result, unified policing in England had to wait until 1829, several decades later.

The Bobbies

However, when organized policing came to England, it came with a great deal of controversy. The British were keenly aware of the ways in which unified, government controlled police forces could be used by observing their neighbors across the English Channel. At the time, France was using its police forces to spy on the populace and to maintain control of its citizenry by using an extensive network of informants and surveillance techniques designed to collect as much information about individuals as possible. These methods naturally raised fears in England that institutionalizing the police would lead to the same injustices and infractions upon the liberties of the British citizenry (Philips and Storch, 1999). As a consequence of such fears, the

English population, as well as many of its representatives, was highly distrustful of the ability of the national government to carry out the police function in a unified, organized way.

Those fears were somewhat mollified by Robert Peel. To stem the tide of criticism he faced in creating a unified force for the City of London, he agreed to exclude the city proper from his proposed bill titled *Bill for Improving the Police in and near the Metropolis*. As a result, only the rural areas that encompassed the city were included in the implementation of the new law in 1829, so much of the political resistance to the proposal was eliminated. From an organizational perspective, the "new police," as they were sometimes called, were really the amalgamation of all the existing forces in these areas at the time. More specifically, the Bow Street Runners, the Dismounted Horse Patrol, and the Day Patrol were all affected by the passage of the Bill. At a later date, the Horse Patrol and the Thames Police were also folded into this new force (Tobias, 1979). For a time distrust of the police was strong, and the new officers were distastefully referred to as "Peel's Bloody Gang" (Miller, 1999), but that mistrust waned over time as the new force held its own during various riots and disturbances. As a result, they were given a new nickname, the "Bobbies," after their founder Robert Peel. However, time and actions taken by the police were not the only means by which people slowly began to trust their new overseers.

Soon after the passage of the Bill, Peel appointed the first two police commissioners: Col. Charles Rowan and Richard Mayne. These three men instituted restraints on the police that likely contributed to their eventual acceptance: (1) they were to carry only a small, concealed truncheon under their coat as their weapon; (2) they wore uniforms; and (3) they were deployed for the purpose of crime prevention (Klockars, 1985). As the force developed, Peel faded into the background and the commissioners exerted their influence by emphasizing the following principles, taken from *The Blind Eye of History* by Charles Reith, as the basis for the creation of the force and its extension: (1) prevent crime and disorder; (2) the power of the police to fulfill their functions is dependent upon public approval; (3) to maintain the respect of the public means to secure their cooperation; (4) the extent to which the cooperation of the public can be secured diminishes the necessity to use force; (5) demonstrate impartial service to the law; (6) use physical force only when the exercise of persuasion is unsuccessful; (7) maintain a relationship with the public; (8) refrain from usurping the powers of the judiciary; (9) the test of efficiency is the absence of crime.

It is these principles that the commissioners argued should be the guiding light of the new force. These ideals model fairness, evenhandedness, prevention, and only the minimal use of force when resistance is encountered. It was the commissioners' demand that new officers adhere to these rules and as a result of any lack of such, the officer could be (any or many times was) relieved of his position. Such strict adherence and the restraint evidenced by the new police helped to diminish the concerns of the citizenry. Although it is true that the new force experienced a great deal of turnover in the first decade of its existence, it decreased significantly over time as the "Bobbies" settled into their new role and began to allay the fears of much of the public that it served.

In conclusion, modern policing has a long and varied history throughout much of the world and in England as well. Ancient forces did not resemble those of today but were organized around family ties that accorded responsibility to those individuals in punishing criminals and bringing individual offenders to justice. As time passed, these forces evolved as groups of individuals whose primary mission it was to protect a political leader and to help maintain his control over the population over which he ruled. Although this process evolved in many ancient societies it did not take place in a vacuum, as other societies, such as England, also made attempts at policing its population.

In England, groups of families with administrative leaders became the first known policemen. Over time, these individuals were organized as rudimentary forces that had specific roles but were not very effective at controlling crime. An additional layer of administrative control, called the justice of the peace, further addressed the crime problem but because of their expanded authority and corrupt activities, they further exacerbated the decline of the office of constable. However, a series of justices contributed to the reform of policing in England, particularly in and around London. It was their efforts that led to the protection of the citizenry from robbery and theft in rural London and on its outer highways. Finally, a unified police was created that subsumed many of the forces in existence under its control in 1829. Although the "Bobbies" were met with a great deal of resistance, they eventually were accepted owing to their diligence and the scrupulous ideals of their commissioners.

MICHAEL CRETACCI

References and Further Reading

Ascoli, D. 1979. *The Queen's Peace,* London, David and Charles.

Berg, B.L. 1999. *Policing in Modern Society,* Boston, MA, Butterworth and Heinemann.

Brown, D. 1956. *The Rise of Scotland Yard,* New York, G.P Putnam's Sons.

Champion, Sr., Darl, H. and Hooper, M.K. 2003. *Introduction to American Policing,* New York, Glencoe McGraw-Hill.

Critchley, T.A. 1972. *A History of Police in England and Wales,* 2nd ed., Montclair, NJ, Pattersen Smith.

Gaines, L.K. and Kappler, V.E. 2003. *Policing in America,* 4th ed., Cincinnati, OH, Anderson Publishing Company.

Hart, J.M. 1951. *The British Police,* London, Allen and Unwin.

Klockars, C.B. 1985. *The Idea of Police,* Beverly Hills, CA, Sage Publications, Inc.

Langworthy, R.H. and Travis, L.F., III 2003. *Policing in America: A Balance of Forces,* 3rd ed., Upper Saddle River, NJ, Prentice Hall.

Lyman, M.D. 2002. *The Police: An Introduction,* 2nd ed., Upper Saddle River, NJ, Prentice Hall.

Miller, W.R. 1999. *Cops and Bobbies: Police Authority in New York and London, 1830–1870,* 2nd ed., Columbus, OH, Ohio State University Press.

Philips, D. and Storch, R.D. 1999. *Policing Provincial England 1829–1856: The Politics of Reform,* London, Leicester University Press.

Pike, L.O. 1968. *A History of Crime in England Illustrating the Changes in the Laws in the Progress of Civilization,* London, Smith, Elder and Co.

Pringle, P. 1958. *The Thief Takers,* London, Museum Press Limited.

Pringle, P. 1955. *Hue and Cry; The Story of Henry and John Fielding and the Bow Street Runners,* Bungay, U.K., William Morrow and Company.

Reith, C. 1975. *The Blind Eye of History,* Montclair, NJ, Pattersen Smith.

Reynolds, E.A. 1998. *Before the Bobbies,* Stanford, CA, Stanford University Press.

Shelden, R.G. 2001. *Controlling the Dangerous Classes: A Critical Introduction to the History of Criminal Justice,* Boston, MA, Allyn and Bacon.

Smith, P.T. 1985. *Policing Victorian London,* Westport, CN, Greenwood Press.

Tobias, J.J. 1979. *Crime and Police in England, 1700–1900,* New York, St. Martin's Press.

Uchida, C.D. 1997. The development of the American police: An historical overview, in Dunham, R.G. and Alpert, G.P., Eds., *Critical Issues in Policing: Contemporary Readings,* 3rd ed., Prospect Heights, IL, Waveland Press, Inc.

Wall, D.S. 1998. *The Chief Constables of England and Wales: The Sociolegal History of a Criminal Justice Elite,* Brookfield, VT, Ashgate Publishing Limited.

See also **English Legal Traditions; U.K., Crime and Justice in**

Police History: U.S.

The development of policing in the U.S. closely followed the development of the English system. In the early colonies policing took two forms. It was either informal and communal (the "Watch") or private-for-profit policing ("The Big Stick") (Spitzer, 1979). The watch system was composed of community volunteers whose primary duty was to warn of impending danger. Boston created a night watch in 1636, New York in 1658, and Philadelphia in 1700. The night watch was not a particularly effective crime control device. Watchmen often slept or drank on duty. Although the watch was theoretically voluntary, many "volunteers" were simply attempting to evade military service, were conscripts forced into service by their town, or were performing watch duties as a form of punishment. Philadelphia created the first day watch in 1833 and New York instituted a day watch in 1844 as a supplement to its new municipal police force (Gaines, Kappeler, and Vaughn, 1999).

Augmenting the watch system was a system of constables, official law enforcement officers, usually paid by the fee-system for warrants they served. Constables had a variety of nonlaw enforcement functions to perform as well, including serving as land surveyors and verifying the accuracy of weights and measures. In many cities constables were given the responsibility of supervising the activities of the night watch.

These informal modalities of policing continued well after the American Revolution. It was not until the 1830s that the idea of a centralized municipal police department first emerged in the U.S. In 1838, the city of Boston established the first American police force, followed by New York City in 1845; Albany, NY, and Chicago in 1851; New Orleans and Cincinnati in 1853; Philadelphia in 1855; and Newark, NJ, and Baltimore in 1857 (Lundman, 1980; Harring, 1983; Lynch, 1984). By the 1880s, all major U.S. cities had municipal police forces in place. These "modern police" organizations shared similar characteristics: (1) they were publicly supported and bureaucratic in form; (2) police officers were full-time employees, not community volunteers or case-by-case fee retainers; (3) departments had permanent and fixed rules and procedures, and employment as a police officer was continuous; and (4) police departments were accountable to a central governmental authority (Lundman, 1980).

In the Southern states the development of American policing followed a different path. The genesis of the modern police organization in the South was the "Slave Patrol" (Platt, 1982). The first formal slave patrol was created in the Carolina colonies in 1704 (Reichel, 1992). Slave patrols had three primary functions: (1) to chase down, apprehend, and return runaway slaves to their owners; (2) to provide a form of organized terror to deter slave revolts; and (3) to maintain a form of discipline for slave-workers who were subject to summary justice, outside of the law, if they violated any plantation rules. Following the Civil War, these vigilante-style organizations evolved into modern Southern police departments primarily as a means of controlling freed slaves who were now laborers working in an agricultural caste system and enforcing "Jim Crow" segregation laws, designed to deny freed slaves equal rights and access to the political system.

The key question, of course, is what was it about the U.S. in the 1830s that necessitated the development of local, centralized, bureaucratic police forces? One answer is that cities were growing. The U.S. was no longer a collection of small cities and rural hamlets. Urbanization was occurring at an ever-quickening pace and the old informal watch and constable system was no longer adequate to control disorder. Anecdotal accounts suggested increasing crime and vice in urban centers. Mob violence, particularly violence directed at immigrants and African Americans by white youths, occurred with some frequency. Public disorder, mostly public drunkenness and sometimes prostitution, was more visible and less easily controlled in growing urban centers than it had been in rural villages (Walker, 1996). But evidence of an actual crime wave is lacking. So, if the modern American police force was not a direct response to crime, then what was it a response to?

More than crime, modern police forces in the U.S. emerged as a response to "disorder." What constitutes social and public order depends largely on who is defining those terms, and in the cities of 19th century America they were defined by the mercantile interests, who through taxes and political influence supported the development of bureaucratic policing institutions. These economic interests were more concerned with social control than crime control. Private and "for profit" policing was too disorganized and too "crime-specific" in form to fulfill these needs. The emerging commercial elites needed a mechanism to ensure a stable and orderly work force, a stable and orderly environment for the conduct of business, and the maintenance of what they referred to as the "collective good" (Spitzer and Scull, 1977). These mercantile interests also wanted to divest themselves of the cost of protecting their own enterprises, transferring those costs from the private sector to the state.

Maintaining a stable and disciplined work force for the developing system of factory production and ensuring a safe and tranquil community for the conduct of commerce required an organized system of social control. The developing profit-based system of production antagonized social tensions in the community. Inequality was increasing rapidly; the exploitation of workers through long hours, dangerous working conditions, and low pay was endemic; and the dominance of local governments by economic elites was creating political unrest. The only effective political strategy available to exploited workers was what economic elites referred to as "rioting," which was actually a primitive form of what would become union strikes against employers (Silver, 1967). The modern police force not only provided an organized, centralized body of men legally authorized to use force to maintain order, it also provided the illusion that this order was being maintained under the rule of law, not at the whim of those with economic power.

Defining social control as crime control was accomplished by raising the specter of the "dangerous classes." The suggestion was that public drunkenness, crime, hooliganism, political protests, and worker "riots" were the products of a biologically inferior, morally intemperate, unskilled, and uneducated underclass. The consumption of alcohol was widely seen as the major cause of crime and public disorder. The irony, of course, is that public drunkenness did not exist until mercantile and commercial interests created venues for and encouraged the commercial sale of alcohol in public places. This underclass was easily identifiable because it consisted primarily of the poor, foreign immigrants, and free blacks (Lundman, 1980, 29). This isolation of the "dangerous classes" as the embodiment of the crime problem created a focus in crime control that persists to today, the idea that policing should be directed toward bad individuals, rather than social and economic conditions that are criminogenic in their social outcomes.

In addition, the creation of the modern police force in the U.S. also immutably altered the definition of the police function. Policing had always been a reactive enterprise, occurring only in response to a specific criminal act. Centralized and bureaucratic police departments focusing on the alleged crime-producing qualities of the "dangerous classes" began to emphasize preventative crime control. The presence of police authorized to use force could stop crime before it started by subjecting everyone to surveillance and observation. The concept of the police patrol as a preventative control mechanism routinized the insertion of police into the normal daily events of everyone's life, a previously unknown and highly feared concept in both England and the U.S. (Parks, 1976).

Early American police departments shared two primary characteristics: they were notoriously corrupt and flagrantly brutal. This should come as no surprise in that the police were under the control of local politicians. The local political party ward leader in most cities appointed the police executive in charge of the ward leader's neighborhood. The ward leader, also, most often was the neighborhood tavern owner, sometimes the neighborhood purveyor of gambling and prostitution, and usually the controlling influence over neighborhood youth gangs who were used to getting out the vote and intimidatting opposition party voters. In this system of vice, organized violence, and political corruption, it is inconceivable that the police could be anything but corrupt (Walker, 1996). Police systematically took payoffs to allow illegal drinking, gambling, and prostitution. Police organized professional criminals, like thieves and pickpockets, trading immunity for bribes or information. They actively participated in vote buying and ballot-box-stuffing. Loyal political operatives became police officers. They had no discernable qualifications for policing and little, if any, training in policing. Promotions within the police departments were sold, not earned. Police drank while on patrol, they protected their patrons' vice operations, and they were quick to use peremptory force. Walker goes so far as to call municipal police "delegated vigilantes," entrusted with the power to use overwhelming force against the "dangerous classes" as a means of deterring criminality.

In the post-Civil War era, municipal police departments increasingly turned their attention to strike breaking. By the late 19th century union organizing and labor unrest were widespread in the U.S. New York City had 5090 strikes, involving almost a million workers, from 1880 to 1900; Chicago had 1737 strikes, involving over half a million workers in the same period (Harring, 1983; Barkan, 2001). Many of the "riots" that so concerned local economic elites were actually strikes called against specific companies. The use of public employees to serve private economic interests and to use legally-ordained force against organizing workers was both cost-effective for manufacturing concerns and politically useful, in that it confused the issue of workers' rights with the issue of crime (Harring, 1981; 1983).

Police strike breaking took two distinct forms. The first was the most obvious: the forced dispersal of demonstrating workers, usually through the use of extreme violence (Harring, 1981). The second was more subtle: In order to prevent the organization of workers in the first place, municipal police made staggering numbers of "public order" arrests. In fact, Harring concludes that 80% of all arrests were of workers for "public order" crimes (Harring, 1983). In Chicago, according to Harring, the police force was "viciously anti-labor … On a day-to-day basis it hauled nearly a million workers

off to jail between 1875 and 1900 … for trivial public order offenses" (Harring, 1981). In other cities police made use of ambiguous vagrancy laws, called the "Tramp Acts," to arrest both union organized and unemployed workers (Harring, 1977).

Antilabor activity also compelled major changes in the organization of police departments. Alarm boxes were set up throughout cities, and respectable citizens, meaning businessmen, were given keys so that they could call out the police force at a moment's notice. The patrol wagon system was instituted so that large numbers of people could be arrested and transported all at once. Horseback patrols, particularly effective against strikers and demonstrators, and new, improved, longer nightsticks became standard issue.

Three compelling issues faced by early American police departments were, (1) should police be uniformed; (2) should they carry firearms; and (3) how much force could they use to carry out their duties. The local merchants and businessmen, who had pushed the development of municipal policing, wanted the police uniformed so that they could be easily identified by persons seeking their assistance and so they would create an obvious police presence on the streets. Some police officers themselves opposed uniforms. They felt that uniforms would subject them to public ridicule and make them too easily identifiable to the majority of citizens who bore the brunt of police power, perhaps making them targets for mob violence. Early police officers began carrying firearms even when this was not department policy, despite widespread public fear that this gave the police and the state much too much power. Police departments formally armed their officers only after officers had informally armed themselves. The use of force to effect an arrest was as controversial in the 1830s and 1840s as it is today. Because the police were primarily engaged in enforcing public order laws against gambling and drunkenness, surveilling immigrants and freed slaves, and harassing labor organizers, public opinion favored restrictions on the use of force. But the value of an armed, paramilitary presence, authorized to use deadly force, served the interests of local economic elites who had wanted organized police departments in the first place. The presence of a paramilitary force occupying the streets was regarded as essential because such "organizations intervened between the propertied elites and propertyless masses who were regarded as politically dangerous as a class" (Bordua and Reiss, 1967).

State police agencies emerged for many of the same reasons. The Pennsylvania State Police were modeled after the Phillipine Constabulary, the occupation force placed in the Philipine Islands following the Spanish American War. This all-white, all-"native" paramilitary force was created specifically to break strikes in the coal fields of Pennsylvania and to control local towns composed predominantly of Catholic, Irish, German, and Eastern European immigrants. State "troopers" were housed in barracks outside the towns so that they would not mingle with or develop friendships with local residents. In addition to strike-breaking they frequently engaged in antiimmigrant and anti-Catholic violence, such as attacking community social events on horseback, under the pretense of the enforcement of public order laws. Similarly, the Texas Rangers were originally created as a quasi-official group of vigilantes and guerillas used to suppress Mexican communities and to drive the Commanche off their lands.

By the end of 19th century, municipal police departments were firmly entrenched in the day-to-day political affairs of big-city political machines. Police provided services and assistance to political allies of the machine, and harassed, arrested, and interfered with the political activities of machine opponents. This was a curious dichotomy for an organization that ostensibly had the purpose of crime control. Political machines at the turn of the century were in fact the primary modality through which crime was organized in urban areas. Politicians ran or supervised gambling, prostitution, drug distribution, and racketeering. In fact, organized crime and the dominant political parties of American cities were one and the same. Politicians also employed and protected the many white-youth gangs that roamed the cities, using them to intimidate opponents, to get out the vote (by force if necessary), and to extort "political contributions" from local businesses. At the dawn of the 20th century, police were, at least *de facto*, acting as the enforcement arm of organized crime in virtually every big city.

Police also engaged in and helped organize widespread election fraud in their role as political functionaries for the machine. In return, police had virtual carte blanche in the use of force and had as their primary business not crime control, but the solicitation and acceptance of bribes. It is an understatement to say that in late 19th and early 20th centuries police simply were corrupt; they were the primary instruments for the creation of corruption in the first place.

Police departments during the machine era provided a variety of community services other than law enforcement. In New York and Boston they sheltered the homeless, kept tabs on infectious epidemics, such as cholera, and even emptied public privies. Although these service functions of police continues to be important today, it is important to recall that in the context of political machines, government services were traded for votes and political loyalty. And although there is no doubt that these police services were of public value, they must be viewed as primarily political acts designed to curry public favor and ensure the continued dominance of their political patrons.

The advent of Prohibition (1919–1933) only made the situation worse. The outlawing of alcohol combined with the fact that the overwhelming majority of urban residents drank and wished to continue to drink, not only created new opportunities for police corruption but substantially changed the focus of that corruption. During Prohibition lawlessness became more open, more organized, and more blatant. Major cities like New York, Chicago, and Philadelphia had upward of 20,000 speakeasies operating in them. Overlooking that level of publicly displayed crime required that corruption become total. But most important to policing, Prohibition marked a change in how corruption was organized. Criminal syndicates, set up to deliver alcohol to all those illegal outlets, acquired enormous sums of money and political power in their own right; these groups were no longer dependent on the machine's largesse and respectability. Organized crime was able to emerge from the shadows and deal directly with corrupt police. In many cities police became little more than watchmen for organized crime enterprises, or, on a more sinister vein, enforcement squads to harass the competition of the syndicate paying the corruption bill. By the end of Prohibition, the corruption of American policing was almost total.

The outrages perpetrated by municipal police departments in the ensuing years inevitably brought cries for reform. Initially, reform efforts took the form of investigative commissions looking into both police and political corruption. As is the case today, these commissions usually were formed in response to a specific act of outrageous conduct by the police. And, like today, those commissions, upon investigating the specific incident in their charge, uncovered widespread corruption, misfeasance, and malfeasance. Examples of such specific outrages spawning investigatory bodies included: (1) the formation of a prostitution syndicate by Los Angeles Mayor Arthur Harper, Police Chief Edward Kerns, and a local organized crime figure, combined with subsequent instructions to the police to harass this syndicate's competitors in the prostitution industry; (2) the assassination of organized crime figure Arnold Rothstein by police lieutenant Charles Becker, head of the NYPD's vice squad; and (3) a dispute between the mayor and district attorney of Philadelphia, each of whom controlled rival gambling syndicates and each of whom used loyal factions of police to harass the other (Fogelson, 1977; Potter and Jenkins, 1985).

One of the earliest of these investigative commissions was the Lenox Committee, formed in 1894 to investigate police corruption related to gambling and prostitution and to investigate charges of police extortion. The Lenox Committee also determined that promotion within the New York Police Department required a bribe of $1600 to be promoted to sergeant and up to $15,000 to be promoted to captain. Subsequent investigatory commissions in New York City included the Curren Committee (1913), which investigated police collusion with gambling and prostitution; the Seabury Committee (1932), which investigated Prohibition-related corruption; the 1949 Brooklyn grand jury that investigated gambling payoffs; the 1972 Knapp Commission, which looked into corruption related to gambling and drugs; and the 1993 Mollen Commission, which exposed massive drug corruption, organized theft by police officers, excessive use of force, and use of drugs by the police (Kappeler, Sluder and Alpert, 1998).

In Philadelphia, a series of investigative grand juries exposed massive police collaboration with gambling and prostitution enterprises. Commissions also investigated police corruption in Louisville, San Francisco, Milwaukee, New Orleans, Indianapolis, Atlanta, and Los Angeles. Recently, the Christopher Commission investigated police misconduct in Los Angeles related to the widespread use of excessive force by the LAPD and racism within the ranks of that department.

On a national basis, President Hoover appointed the Wickersham Commission in 1929 to examine what was perceived as a rising crime rate and police ineffectiveness in dealing with crime. It is no accident that in looking at those issues, the Wickersham Commission also became the first official governmental body to investigate organized crime.

Commissions, though shedding light on the extent of corruption and serving to inform the public, have little lasting impact on police practices. As external organizations, they report, recommend, and then dissolve. The police department continues on as a bureaucratic entity resistant to both outside influence and reform.

Other attempts to reform policing have come from within the ranks of the departments themselves. Reform police commissioners and chiefs, often appointed in the wake of various scandals, made efforts to change the nature of the police bureaucracy itself. Among the reforms instituted within police organizations were the establishment of selection standards, training for new recruits, placing police under civil service, and awarding promotion as a result of testing procedures. The purpose of these reforms was to lessen the hold of politicians, and particularly ward leaders on police officers. If the recruitment, selection, and promotion processes were housed within the department and governed by objective criteria, the hope was that officers would no longer owe their jobs and their ranks to political operatives.

Similarly, reform-minded police executives began to try to restructure the department itself, making it more bureaucratic, with an internal clear chain-of-command. Once again, the hope was to structurally isolate police officers from politicians. In this vein, many police departments added a middle level of management to their organizational charts, changed the geographic lines of police precincts so they would no longer be contiguous with political wards, and created special squads to perform specific duties within the departments. One of the ironies of this reform effort was that the creation of centralized special squads—such as traffic, criminal investigation, vice and narcotics units—had the effect over time of reducing organized crime's corruption costs. Rather than spreading through an entire department, narcotics and prostitution operators could now corrupt a smaller, more discreet unit and still maintain a high level of immunity from police interference with their illegal businesses.

By the 1950s, police professionalism was being widely touted as better way to improve police effectiveness and reform policing as an institution. O.W. Wilson set the standard for the professionalism movement when he published his book, *Police Administration*, which quickly became a blueprint for professionalizing policing. Wilson argued for greater centralization of the police function, with an emphasis on military-style organization and discipline. Central themes for police administration were to become crime control and efficiency in achieving crime control. Closer supervision of police officers was recommended, foot patrols were replaced by motorized patrols, precinct houses were consolidated and more central police facilities constructed, and command functions were centralized in a headquarters staff (Uchida, 1993).

Police professionalism, however, did not turn out to be the panacea Wilson had envisaged. In some cities, professionalism increased tensions between the police and the communities they served and created rancor and dissension within the departments themselves. The crime control tactics recommended by the professionalism movement, such as aggressive stop-and-frisk procedures, created widespread community resentment, particularly among young, minority males who were most frequently targeted. Police professionalism and the military model of policing became synonymous with police repression. Furthermore, "a half century of professionalization had created police departments that were vast bureaucracies, inward looking, isolated from the public, and defensive in the face of any criticism" (Walker, 1996). In addition, professionalization did nothing to rectify racist and sexist hiring practices that had been in effect since police departments were created in the 1830s.

Within police departments professionalization meant an emphasis on bureaucratic efficiency. Police administrators centralized authority; tightened the chain-of-command; and tried to run their departments through the application of arcane, contradictory, and often inapplicable rules. A highly authoritarian police bureaucracy not only isolated itself from the public, but from the very police officers whose conduct it was trying to control. By the mid-1960s police officers had responded with an aggressive and widespread police unionization campaign. Aided by court rulings more favorable to the organizing of public employees; fueled by resentment of the authoritarian organization of departments; and united in a common resistance to increasing charges of police brutality, corruption, and other forms of misconduct, nearly every large-city police department had been unionized by the early 1970s. Police officers struck in New York City in 1971, in Baltimore in 1974, and in San Francisco in 1975. "Job actions" such as the "blue flu" and work slow-downs (i.e., not writing tickets, making few arrests) were common in other cities.

Initially, the response to this union activity was to reduce centralization in the police bureaucracy and to include officers in discussions of rules, procedures, and departmental practices. What had been the exclusive fiefdom of the police executive was now subject to negotiation with a union. But reduced municipal tax bases, caused primarily by the exodus of white, afflu-ent executives and professionals to the suburbs in the 1970s; a prolonged economic recession in the 1970s and early 1980s; and fiscal mismanagement in many cities led to layoffs of police and other municipal workers, and rollbacks in benefits. In fact, unions became an attractive scapegoat for municipal prob-lems. Politicians, administrators, and the media all blamed demands by public workers for the financial straits in which the cities had been floundering. Despite the fact that the fiscal crises had been caused by much larger social and economic trends, blaming police and other workers allowed police administrators and poli-ticians to once again reorganize the police. This reor-ganization has been dubbed the "Taylorization of the police" by historian Sydney Harring (1981).

Under the "Taylorization" reforms, police depart-ments reduced the size of their forces, went from two-person to one-person patrol cars, and increased the division of labor within police departments. Police work was broken down into ever more specific highly specialized tasks, patrols became more reactive, tech-nology was used to restore the control of police admin-istrators (i.e., 911 emergency lines, computerization), and some traditional police tasks were turned over to civilian employees. All of this served to further isolate the police from the citizenry, to further reduce the effectiveness of police practices, and to continually justify ever more "Taylorization" as a response to increasing inefficiency.

Concurrent with reform efforts aimed at profes-sionalization was an increased reliance on technology and the scientific aspects of police investigation. The idea of police as scientific crime fighters had origi-nated with August Vollmer as early as 1916, with the introduction of the crime laboratory. By 1921, Voll-mer was advocating the widespread use of lie detec-tors and the establishment of a database for collecting national crime data (Crank and Langworthy, 1992). Over the years, science became synonymous with professionalism for many police executives. The use of fingerprints, serology, toxicology, chemistry, and scientific means for collecting evidence were empha-sized as part of a professional police force. In terms of technological advancements, new ways of main-taining police record systems and enhancing police communications, such as the police radio, became priorities. The emphasis was on efficiency and crime fighting, with the social work aspects of policing deemphasized and discouraged. The hope was also that the professional, scientific crime fighters would be less susceptible to corruption. It is therefore a further irony of policing that in Philadelphia new communications technologies were put to use in establishing what was arguably the first "call girl" system in the U.S., calling out for prostitutes using police communications systems.

By the 1960s, massive social and political changes were occurring in the U.S. The civil rights movement was challenging white dominance in the South and rac-ist social policies in the North. The use of professional police forces to suppress the Civil Rights movement, often by brute force, damaged the image of American police. From 1964 to 1968, riots, often sparked by incidents of police brutality or oppression, rocked the major cities in the U.S. Campus protests were common: in the 1967–1968 school year alone, there were 292 mass demonstrations against the Vietnam War on 163 college campuses across the country. All of this polit-ical instability was further antagonized by a series of political assassinations, including President John Kennedy in 1963 and Martin Luther King, Jr. and Senator Robert Kennedy in 1968. National commis-sions created to investigate riots and political instabil-ity frequently pointed to the police as a source of social tension.

The police and criminal justice system response was twofold. First in 1968, as part of the Omnibus Crime Control and Safe Streets Act, large sums of federal money were made available for rather cosmetic police–community relations programs, which were mostly media focused attempts to improve the image of the police. By the 1980s, many police departments had begun to consider a new strategy, community policing. Community policing emphasized close working relations with the community, police responsiveness to the community, and common efforts to alleviate a wide variety of community problems, many of which were social in nature. Community policing is the latest iteration in efforts to (1) improve relations between the police and the community, (2) decentralize the police, and (3) provide a means to make citizens feel more comfortable about the seemingly insoluable problem of crime in America.

From the beginning, American policing has been intimately tied to the exigencies and demands of the American political establishment. From the attacks on immigrants by early police forces, to the strike breaking of the later 1800s, to the massive corruption of the early 20th century, through professionalism, Taylorization, and now attempts at amelioration through community policing, the role of the police in the U.S. has been defined more by economics and politics than by crime or crime control.

GARY W. POTTER

References and Further Reading

Barkan, S. 2001. *Criminology: A Sociological Understanding,* 2nd ed., Upper Saddle River, NJ, Prentice-Hall.

Bordua, D. and Reiss, A., Jr. 1967. Law enforcement, in Lazarsfeld, P., Sewell, W. and Wilensky, H., Eds., *The Uses of Sociology,* New York, Basic Books.

Crank, J. and Langworthy, R. 1992. An institutional perspective of policing, *The Journal of Criminal Law and Criminology,* 83(2).

Fogelson, R. 1977. *Big-City Police,* Cambridge, MA, Harvard University Press.

Gaines, L., Kappeler, V. and Vaughn, J. 1999. *Policing in America,* 3rd ed., Cincinnati, OH, Anderson Publishing Company.

Harring, S. 1977. Class conflict and the suppression of tramps in Buffalo, 1892–1894, *Law and Society Review,* 11(5).

Harring, S. 1981. Policing in a class society: The expansion of the urban police in the later nineteenth and early twentieth centuries, in Greenberg, D., Ed., *Crime and Capitalism,* Palo Alto, CA, Mayfield.

Harring, S., 1981. The Taylorization of police work: Policing in the 1980s, *The Insurgent Sociologist,* 10(4).

Harring, S. 1983. *Policing in a Class Society: The Experience of American Cities, 1865–1915,* New Brunswick, NJ, Rutgers University Press.

Kappeler, V., Sluder, R. and Alpert, G. 1998. *Forces of Deviance: Understanding the Dark Side of Policing,* 2nd ed., Prospect Heights, IL, Waveland Press.

Lundman, R.J. 1980. *Police and Policing: an Introduction,* New York, Holt, Rinehart & Winston.

Lynch, M. 1984. *Class Based Justice: A History of the Origins of Policing in Albany,* Albany, NY, Michael J. Hindelang Criminal Research Justice Center.

Parks, E. 1976. From constabulary to police society: Implications for social control, in Chambliss, W. and Mankoff, M., Eds., *Whose Law? What Order?* New York, Wiley.

Platt, T. 1982. Crime and punishment in the U.S.: Immediate and long-term reforms from a Marxist perspective, *Crime and Social Justice,* 18.

Potter, G. and Jenkins, P. 1985. *The City and the Syndicate: Organizing Crime in Philadelphia,* Boston, MA, Ginn Press.

Reichel, P.L. 1992. The misplaced emphasis on urbanization in police development, *Policing and Society,* 3(1).

Silver, A. 1967. The demand for order in civil society: A review of some important themes in the history of urban crime, police and riot, in Bordua, D., Ed., *The Police: Six Sociological Essays,* New York, Wiley.

Spitzer, S. 1979. The rationalization of crime control in capitalist society, *Contemporary Crises,* 3(1).

Spitzer, S. and Scull, A. 1977. Privatization and capitalist development: The case of the private police, *Social Problems,* 25(1).

Uchida, C. 1993. The development of American police: An historical overview, in Dunham, R. and Alpert, G., Eds., *Critical Issues in Policing: Contemporary Readings,* Prospect Heights, IL, Waveland Press.

Walker, S. 1996. *The Police in America: An Introduction,* New York, McGraw-Hill.

See also **Police: Administration and Organization; Police: Brutality and Corruption; Police Crime; Police: Municipal or Urban; Police: Patrol; Police: Race and Racial Profiling; Police and the Rule of Law; Police: Rural**

Police: Municipal or Urban

Often referred to as the "thin blue line," owing to the dark navy hue of their uniforms, the function of the police in the U.S. is a paradox existing within a free democracy. The role and function of police in the U.S. have progressed through the years from the original hue and cry of the colonial era, to the slave patrols of the deep south, up to contemporary law enforcement. Not only has the role of the police changed over the years, but as America becomes an increasingly pluralistic society the face of policing is charging as well.

Police officers in the U.S. hail from a variety of racial, ethnic, and religious backgrounds. Men and women work together in daily patrol efforts to curb the rising tide of crime, maintain order, keep the peace, and assist the citizenry as they protect constitutionally guaranteed rights and freedoms.

Police officers in the U.S. face a daily role confusion because of the myriad of tasks they are required to perform as peacekeepers, crime fighters, and community liaisons. Not only are police officers required to perform a variety of intricate tasks in the course of their daily operations, but they also face the additional dilemma of balancing the need to maintain order, keep the peace, and protect individuals' rights with the duty of depriving some citizens of their freedom if their actions violate the law. The need to protect the rights of the general population also means, at times, depriving others of freedom, through arrest, as the need to protect overrides the desire to be free. As Herman Goldstein has pointed out, "The police, by the very nature of their function, are an anomaly in a free society" (1977).

The first attempt at law enforcement in the U.S. was brought with the colonists as they left England in search of religious freedom and an end to persecution. Few instances of criminal activity can be traced historically to the American colonies. Most crimes involved individuals running afoul of the law by working on the Sabbath, engaging in adultery, or violating some moral principle. One noteworthy crime wave occurred in the Massachusetts colony in 1692 in which several individuals were executed on charges of witchcraft.

Eventually the American colonies began to grow as more Europeans flocked to the new land. As the population grew so did the need for some type of law enforcement. Over time, local ordinances provided for the office of constable to patrol the villages and towns of the newly formed colonial districts. In more rural areas county governors, drawing upon the English system, appointed sheriffs to guard the countryside. The office of the sheriff was considered by most to be the single most important law enforcement office, owing to the predominantly rural nature of most of the American landscape. The sheriffs, named after the English "shire reeve," was an obligatory position whose duties included enforcing the law, apprehending criminals, collecting taxes, appearing in court, and serving subpoenas (Walker, 1999). The sheriff was paid according to the amount of work he performed. The more taxes he collected or the more tasks he performed, the higher his pay.

As time marched on and the colonies grew in population and area, the office of sheriff became an increasingly difficult position. As more and more people evaded their duty of acting as sheriff it became clear

to government officials and citizens alike that a new method of law enforcement was needed. It would be the colony of New Amsterdam that introduced the concept of a paid watch in 1658. The City of Boston attempted the same innovation in 1663, however, the expense ultimately proved too much for the meager colonial government budgets and the paid watch soon became a thing of the past.

During the decades of the late 1700s, the American colonies began experiencing massive social and political unrest as revolution loomed ever closer. It became apparent that some form of organized law enforcement was desperately needed in the colonies. As the French and Indian War came to a close the colonies experienced massive economic depression. Many families were entrenched in poverty and soon property and street crime began to increase. Another depression struck in 1783, after the close of the American Revolution, and lasted until approximately 1790 (Walker, 1999). As irony would have it, the new American government would look to England for aid in developing some form of organized law enforcement for the fledgling nation.

The history of the police is long and fails to follow any neatly organized path as is so often depicted in many history texts. The first true police force as we know it today was formed in London in 1829 by Sir Robert Peel. It was the desire of Sir Robert to devise some sort of organized, professional police force capable of enforcing the law and protecting the general populace while not appearing to be an armed, occupying army. The police were to serve and protect the citizens of London, not act as a military force.

This concept of an organized, professional police force eventually found its way over the Atlantic to the newly formed U.S. Because of the colonial history of the U.S., citizens were suspicious of any organized, armed, law enforcement attempt. ⌐owing to this inherent cynicism, the roots of American policing followed three primary paths of evolution. Policing in the U.S. would become a fragmented system of smaller law enforcement organizations, with limited authority and jurisdiction, each possessing its own local control. This jurisdictional limitation is still observed in American law enforcement.

As the U.S. began to grow, various regions of the nation took on their own distinct flares. In the South the immense cotton and tobacco plantations required large labor supplies. This much needed labor came in the form of African slaves captured and enslaved in order to furnish plantation owners with workers and servants. Over time the slave population would grow to far surpass that of the white plantation masters. This situation required supervisors to oversee the slaves and to ensure that the slaves worked at a proper pace in the fields. This led to the development of the slave patrols.

The slave patrol was a distinctly American phenomenon. In states with a large slave population the slave patrols were charged with the duties of guarding against slave revolts and capturing runaway slaves. These slave patrols gradually grew in size and were probably the first modern police forces in the nation. In Charleston, South Carolina, the slave patrol had approximately 100 officers in 1837 and far outsized even the largest metropolitan law enforcement organizations (Hadden, 2001).

After the close of the Civil War the great northern industrial capitals began to rapidly increase their population. With ever increasing numbers of immigrants the populations of many northern cities grew at alarmingly rapid rates. Finally, in 1845, New York City established the first full-time, paid police force. This law enforcement organization was modeled after the paramilitary style first envisioned by Sir Robert Peel in the creation of his London Metropolitan Police Force. Boston and Philadelphia soon followed the New York example and by 1850 most major cities had police departments (Cole and Smith, 2001).

The development of contemporary law enforcement did not come without its price. In many cities the police organizations were rampant with corruption. Bribery was common and rank was quite often available to the highest bidder. In some cities, such as New York and Chicago, the police worked for the mayor's political party rather than for the citizens. This era, replete with political intrigue, corruption, and bribery, came to be referred to as the political era. This time in the history of policing lasted from approximately 1840 to 1920 (Walker, 1977).

As the nation continued to grow and prosper there was a push westward. With thousands of people moving into the western territories the hazards they faced soon became cause for some form of law enforcement to be developed for the unique needs of the open frontier lands. Apart from Indian attacks, there was a general atmosphere of lawlessness in the American west. Individuals were required to take legal matters into their own hands and vigilantism was often the only form of organized legal resort. Soon after the end of the Civil War the U.S. government appointed marshals to enforce the law in all western territories. Men such as Bat Masters, Wyatt Earp, and Wild Bill Hickok acted in the scope of U.S. Marshals, protecting the citizenry and arresting law violators.

Eventually the west was tamed, the south rebuilt after the Civil War, and the northern industrial capitals' populations began to level out. The political era of the late 1800s and early 1900s would slowly give rise to what became known as the professional era.

The professional era, lasting from approximately 1920 to 1970, was marked by an increased concern and overt demand for efficient and effective government offices. Refocusing the attention of law enforcement organizations on tasks associated with crime fighting would radically change American policing (Gaines and Kappeler, 2003).

The professional era saw an increased use of technological advancements to assist officers in fighting crime and disorder. Police officers began to receive better training and personnel advancements were based on merit. No longer was rank for sale for the highest price. However, with the advent of professional policing, officers began to patrol the streets of America's cities in squad cars. This removed the officer from the neighborhoods' streets, resulting in many minority communities experiencing feelings of resentment and abandonment as the police came to be seen as instruments of oppression rather than protectors and servants of the people.

As the feelings of bitterness and indignation gave way to urban violence it became apparent that police–community relations were in drastic need of improvement. For the vast majority of U.S. history police officers were white males. With the great migration of African Americans to northern cities in search of employment and opportunity, the mostly-white police force was considered by many as nothing more than a modern day slave patrol. Not only were most of the police officers white men but they no longer patrolled on foot. The squad car effectively removed the officer from all citizen contact. The only personal encounters with the minority community were in instances of arrest or criminal investigation.

With the passage of the Equal Employment Opportunities Act in 1972 many police agencies began recruiting female and minority officers. Unfortunately, although women and minorities were recruited as police officers, frequently patrol assignments for these new officers were in areas white officers were afraid to venture. Minority officers were frequently assigned to minority neighborhoods in efforts to improve community relations and female officers were generally assigned to juvenile divisions as it was believed that "real" police work was too dangerous for women.

As time progressed the professional era gradually gave way to what has become known as the community policing era. This era began in 1970 and continues to the present day. Community policing is an attempt to put officers back in neighborhoods, improve community relations, and integrate the police firmly into American society. Officers have been removed from squad cars and new forms of patrols have been integrated into daily operations in many jurisdictions. In larger urban areas foot patrols, bicycle patrols, and horse patrols have supplanted automobile patrols in some areas. Community policing was intended not simply as another patrol strategy, but as a completely new and enlightened method of law enforcement. Officers were to act as servants of the citizenry. Traditional law enforcement is, of course, still very much a duty of police in the U.S. However, with the new community policing strategies it was necessary for officers to become familiar with the people they policed and protected (Das, 2003).

In 1982, the theory of Broken Windows was devised by James Q. Wilson and George Kelling. Their influential, new theory would again alter the patrol strategy of police officers in a way that had yet to be envisioned. The theory of Broken Windows stated quite plainly that neighborhood deterioration resulted in citizen apathy, which in turn led to increased crime and fear among residents. This theory broadened the scope of community policing even farther than initially believed. After the publication of Broken Windows, police officers, although endeavoring to become more integrated into the communities they patrolled, now had a much larger task of locating and stopping what would have been considered minor nuisances years earlier. Now police officers reported instances of disarray in neighborhoods. Dilapidated buildings, rowdy juveniles on street corners, rubbish, and even weeds now became potential sources for criminal enterprises that could ultimately lead to citizen fear and increased violent crime.

Although patrol strategies have changed significantly over the years, the very face and nature of the police professional have also undergone many alterations. The police are indoctrinated into the policing profession not only through their experiences in recruiting and training but also less obviously through the very subculture of the police. Officers begin to experience this effect of the police subculture immediately upon entry into the recruitment and training processes. A subculture comprises symbols, beliefs, values, and attitudes shared by the various members of a smaller group existing within the larger society. A subculture can be anything from medical doctors, college professors, lawyers, or, in this case, police officers. Newly recruited officers are indoctrinated into the various beliefs and values shared by their peers informally through personal interactions as well as formally through training and their academy experience.

The police subculture is marked by the concept of the "working personality" of the police officer. Officers are expected to be physically and mentally tough and to be able to take charge of situations when the need arises. The police subculture is also marked by the role of police morality. In the field of policing, it is the moral duty of each officer to uphold the letter of the law and to protect the innocent. Officers are expected to apprehend law violators and to "always get their man." This subculture is also characterized by the isolation experienced by many law enforcement officers. Police officers are usually required to socialize with other officers as many people in society are frightened by the presumed dangerous and violent world of policing. Many people are overcome by the media's and Hollywood's portrayal of police officers as existing in *Miami Vice* or *Dirty Harry*. Few people actually take the time to learn what the real daily lives of police officers entail. As a result officers experience a sense of isolation, whether real or imagined (Klockars, 1985).

Finally, the police subculture is marked by stress. The profession of policing is replete with stress. Depending upon the jurisdiction, some officers rarely experience large-scale violence or high crime rates. However, there are those areas of the country where murder, rape, and other violent crimes are frequent. This creates a stressful working environment as officers are forced to confront criminals and those engaged in unlawful activities on a daily basis (Walker, 1999).

There have been certain noteworthy court cases that have served to alter the daily patrol operations of police over the years. In 1966, the Supreme Court ruled, in *Miranda v. Arizona* (384 U.S. 436), that confessions made by suspects who have not been properly notified of their constitutional rights cannot be admitted into evidence. This case would result in the ground-breaking development of the *Miranda* warning. Suspects now were required to be read their rights before being taken into custody. Initially police organizations were outraged. The belief was that this stipulation would result in diminished effectiveness and efficiency for the police. However, fears and concerns of those in opposition to the *Miranda* ruling never developed and to this day suspects are read the *Miranda* warning before being taken into police custody.

In 1985, the Supreme Court would again rule on an issue altering the very fabric of the policing profession in *Tennessee v. Garner* (471 U.S. 1). In October 1974, two Memphis police officers were dispatched to a burglar call in which the suspect turned out to be a 15-year-old, unarmed, black male. As the officers arrived at the scene, one officer proceeded to the rear of the house, where he saw the suspect trying to escape by scaling a chain link fence. Certain that the suspect would escape if allowed to climb over the fence, the officer ordered the young man to stop. The suspect failed to stop and he was shot and killed by the officer. The Court would later rule in 1985 that, despite the fact that the officer was acting in accord with state law and departmental procedure, the use of deadly force to stop a fleeing felon was unconstitutional. The Court stated that it is not better that all felony suspects die than they escape.

Today modern policing has changed radically from the simple watchman strategy of the colonial era. Contemporary police officers are now able to communicate with dispatch, other law enforcement organizations, and even international agencies via lap top or desktop computers. The Internet has enabled police from many different nations to coordinate criminal investigations across broad expanses. No longer are police officers relegated to their "beats." Policing is now very much an international effort. Police cruisers are often equipped with satellite technology enabling patrol officers to investigate suspects and crimes in the comfort of their patrol cars. These technological advancements increase effectiveness and efficiency among police officers.

However, the increasing use of computers and satellite relays also requires that police officers be equipped with the mental and intellectual prowess to use and understand this technology. Officers are now required in most jurisdictions to undergo at least 2 years of college training or education. In some jurisdictions officers are required to hold a college degree such as a B.S. or B.A. In addition, foreign language skills are very much in demand in many jurisdictions in the U.S. The U.S. is continuing to become a pluralistic society. There are a variety of ethnicities and languages spoken across America. The increased use of high tech devices also makes it logical for law enforcement personnel to have knowledge of a foreign language.

As is evident from the preceding paragraphs, the profession of policing is complex as officers strive to maintain order, keep the peace, fight crime, and find their proper role in the contemporary U.S. As technological and social science advancements are shaped, the field of policing will, undoubtedly, grow and develop as well.

WENDY L. HICKS

References and Further Reading

Bittner, E. 1990. *Aspects of Police Work,* Boston, MA, Northeastern University Press.
Cole, G.F. and Wilson, J.Q. 1998. Broken windows: The police and neighborhood safety, in Cole, G.F. and Gertz, M.G., Eds., *Criminal Justice System: Politics and Policies,* 7th ed., Belmont, CA, Wadsworth.
Das, D.K. and Verma, A. 2003. *Police Mission: Challenges and Responses,* Lanham, MD, Scarecrow Press.
Gaines, L.K. and Kappeler, V.E. 2003. *Policing in America,* Cincinnati, OH, Anderson Publishing.
Goldstein, H. 1977. *Policing a Free Society,* Cambridge, MA, Ballinger Publishing Co.
Hadden, S.E. 2001. *Slave Patrols: Law and Violence in Virginia and the Carolinas,* Cambridge, MA, Harvard University Press.
Kelling, G.L. 1974. *The Kansas City Preventive Patrol Experiment: A Technical Report,* Washington, DC, Police Foundation.
Klockars, C.B. 1985. *The Idea of Police,* Beverly Hills, CA, Sage Publications.
Shusta, R.M. 2002. *Multicultural Law Enforcement: Strategies for Peacekeeping in a Diverse Society,* Upper Saddle River, NJ, Prentice Hall.
Walker, S. 1977. *A Critical History of Police Reform: The Emergence of Professionalism,* Lexington, MA, Lexington Books.
Walker, S. 1999. *The Police in America: An Introduction,* Boston, MA, McGraw-Hill College.
Websdale, N. 2001. *Policing the Poor: From Slave Plantation to Public Housing,* Boston, MA, Northeastern University Press.

See also **Police: Administration and Organization; Police: History of**

Police: Occupational Problems

The police occupation has consistently ranked among the highest in terms of occupational danger. In fact, the National Institute for Occupational Safety and Health ranks only one occupational group, taxicab drivers or chauffeurs, as more dangerous than police work in terms of occupational homicides. According to the Uniform Crime Reports publication, *Law Enforcement Officers Killed and Assaulted* (2001), 220 law enforcement officers were killed in the line of duty (including the 72 officers killed in the tragedy of September 11, 2001) by either a felonious slaying or by an accident, whereas 56,666 officers were assaulted on duty. Therefore, the physical hazards of police work are very real and well-documented realities of the job.

Whereas the physical hazards of police work, such as homicide, assaults, or injury either by offenders or in accidents, are common occurrences and perceptions of the occupation, other types of hazards are less often depicted and generally less discussed regarding the role of police officers. Psychological hazards of police work, such as stress and cynicism, are more common than the physical dangers. These psychological hazards of police work have direct physical implications for law enforcement officers and impact the officer's ability to enforce the law. Recently, these hazards of police work have been receiving increased attention by researchers and police departments across the country and around the world.

In order to combat the ever-present physical dangers of their occupation, it is believed that police officers have developed methods of dealing with the dangers of their job. In fact, it is commonly believed that the police have their own subculture and personality. It is through the development of the police personality and the banding together within the subculture that the police are able to shield themselves from the negatives of the job (e.g., suffering and pain and isolation from community). It is also this subculture that breeds and teaches the psychological hazards that are endemic to the police occupation.

There is much debate as to how officers develop the police personality. Some scholars argue that police officers learn the attitudes and beliefs on the job whereas other scholars contend that individuals who possess the traits associated with the police personality are drawn to the profession (i.e., self-selection). Regardless of how the traits became instilled in the individual officer, there are two common hazards associated with police officers: cynical attitudes and stress. These two hazards are noteworthy because of the effects they have on all aspects of the police officer's life. Not only do these traits surface on the job; they also permeate the officer's entire life.

Cynicism

Police officers are frequently accused of having cynical attitudes. Cynicism is commonly referred to as the inability to observe any good in the motives of others or the belief that people are motivated by evil and selfishness. The seminal piece of research examining the attitudes of police officers was conducted by Arthur Niederhoffer (1967). He believed that young police recruits began their careers with eager professional excitement but were quickly faced with on-the-job experiences of failure and more often frustration that would force a shift in their attitudes from ambitious to cynical. Therefore, he hypothesized that the degree of cynicism experienced by police officers would increase with the age of the officer and with years of on-the-job experience. In order to examine this hypothesis, he surveyed male police officers in the New York Police Department and found a curvilinear effect in the degree of cynicism experienced by police officers. More specifically, the findings revealed that the least cynical police officers were those who were on the first day of their job. The degree of cynicism cumulatively increased with job experience and peaked with the group of police officers who had 7–10 years experience. Levels of cynical attitudes then began to decrease as the police officers reached retirement. In addition to the length of service, Niederhoffer examined other correlates of cynicism such as officer rank (supervisor versus patrol officer) and level of education (college educated versus noncollege educated) and found that supervisors were less cynical than patrol officers and that college educated police officers were more cynical than noncollege educated officers. In sum, Niederhoffer's analysis revealed that cynicism was not strictly a function of years of experience, but rather that cynicism is multidimensional with a variety of influential factors.

There have been several attempts made to replicate and extend the original work of Niederhoffer with specific attention to examining the differences in police attitudes by officer rank, level of education, department size, race, and gender. Results from these various extensions have been mixed. For example, support has further extended Niederhoffer's finding of the relationship between increased cynicism levels and length of police service (O'Connell et al., 1986) and level of education (Regoli, 1976); however, other research has been unable to show a statistical relationship between officer rank, education, and cynicism levels. Additionally, research also appears to suggest that there are differences in the attitudes of police officers by race and gender.

The extent of cynical attitudes is important to understand and control. Long-term consequences of cynicism can affect every aspect of the individual officer's life as well as produce adverse effects for the department. When one part of the organization is jaded, it can have negative effects upon the entire organization. For example, the quality of work performance and morale can be harmed by a single officer with a cynical attitude. The poor work performance of this one officer can cause a cancer within the department and impact not only the cynic but also the other officers who are counting on that officer for backup or support. A cynical attitude may begin to permeate the entire force and negatively impact department morale while crushing the enthusiasm and idealism of individual officers (Graves, 1996, 107).

Police Stress

As noted above, policing in general is a physically as well as psychologically demanding profession.

Many elements of the job such as working unusual hours, structured rules and regulations, lack of appreciation, and differential treatment from the public as well as the ever-present potential for danger make policing a high-pressure and stressful occupation. Few scholars would debate that policing does not rank high among one of the most stressful occupations. In fact, relatively few occupations have the variety of stressors that police officers must face on an almost daily basis (Anderson et al., 1995).

Much research attention has focused on identifying and ranking the type of stressors present in police work. Leading the way in identifying stressors was research conducted by William Kroes and his colleagues (1974). They examined 100 male officers as well as 30 police administrators in order to gain a better understanding of the stressors involved in police work. Subjects were asked to identify what was bothersome about their jobs and what they believed others in the same position perceived as bothersome. The top five categories of both groups included administrators, lack of equipment or manpower, strained community relations, courts, and shift work, though not necessarily in the same order. Numerous other scholars have also examined the presence of police stressors and have found categories similar to those uncovered by Kroes and his colleagues.

Typically research has uncovered that the categories of stressors within policing have been quite consistent and include: organizational or administrative stressors, personal stressors, stressors that are inherent to police work, stressors stemming from the criminal justice system, and those stemming from the public. Stressors stemming from the organization or administrative stressors refer to those items that are related to the pressures put upon officers from the department. Items in this category would include things such as departmental rules and regulations, relationships among officer and supervisors, as well as officers' perceptions of support by the department. Personal stressors relate to the factors in the officers' lives that are unrelated to the job. These would include things such as belief in one's own ability as well as items affecting the personal lives of the officers (e.g., family demands and strained relations with loved ones). Stressors inherent to police work are those items that are directly associated with the job demands of a police officer. These would include things such as the constant threat of danger, shift work, drawing and possibly shooting one's firearm, and high-speed chases. Stressors from the criminal justice system relate to the effectiveness of the judicial and correctional systems. These other components of the criminal justice system can create feelings of frustration in police officers who often view the other segments of the system as nonappreciative

of the work they have done. Finally, public stressors relate to the ways in which police feel the public views them. As most contact between police officers and the public tends to be negative, the negative contacts the police have with the public instills in them that they are undervalued and not appreciated by the very people they serve. Despite the fact that most of the public respect and view the police positively, officers tend to believe that the public is apathetic toward them.

The police stress literature has also examined stress in terms of officer demographics and career variables. Studies have examined the relationships of stress to police experience and age. In general, the findings from these studies yield results similar to those found with cynicism: a curvilinear relationship with stress being pronounced in the middle of an officer's career or life. Numerous scholars have speculated on this peak and subsequent decline. Explanations include a greater immersion into the police subculture, reality shock, learning to cope with stress through emotional attachment, or a mellowing as experience increases (Lotz and Regoli, 1977; Violanti and Aron, 1995). Additional police stress research reveals that married officers suffer from greater levels of stress than do single officers and that race and gender have little if any effect on police stress (Violanti and Aron, 1995).

Research on police stress and its effect on officers has also been conducted cross-culturally. For example, research has examined officers in the U.K., Australia, Germany, and Korea. It appears that, despite culture differences, officers experience the same types of stressors identified in American officers, primarily those that stem directly from the police organization or administration, those that are inherent to police work, those stemming from the public and personal stressors. Demographic variables also appear to yield similar conclusions to the studies conducted on American officers with the exception of length of service. It appears that officers with more years of experience in both Australia and Germany report higher levels of stress than the less experienced officers, even though the junior officers are typically assigned to work general patrols (Savery et al., 1993; Haward, 1994).

The impact of stress on officers has been examined in a variety of outcome areas. Finn and Tomz (1997, 14) report that effects of police stress commonly include the following ailments: emotional detachment, posttraumatic stress disorder, heart attacks, ulcers, weight gain, suicide, reduced efficiency in performing duties, reduced morale, excessive aggressiveness, alcoholism and other substance abuse, and marital or family problems. Thus, police stress influences not only the physical but also the mental being of the police officer. These negative effects influence the work performance as well as the family functioning of the officers.

Conclusion

Psychological hazards such as cynical attitudes and stress are important to understanding the well-being of not only the individual police officer but also the officer's family and the department as a whole. Early identification and recognition of these factors are important for police administrators, researchers, and departments. Oftentimes intervention at early stages can help officers and their families find ways to cope with the stressors that arise because of the role of the police officer. Unfortunately, if left unattended and uncared for, these conditions can manifest into other physical and emotional problems such as burnout, fatigue, and even suicide.

NICOLE LEEPER PIQUERO

References and Further Readings

Anderson, W., Swenson, D. and Clay, D. (1995). *Stress Management for Law Enforcement Officers,* Englewood Cliffs, NJ, Prentice Hall.

Finn, P. and Tomaz, J.E. (1997). *Developing a Law Enforcement Stress Program for Officers and Their Families,* Washington, DC, National Institute of Justice.

Graves, W. (1996). Police cynicism: Causes and cures, *FBI Law Enforcement Bulletin,* 65, 16–20.

Haward, L.R.C. (1994). Stress and strain in the polizei, *The Police Journal,* October, 347–350.

Kroes, W.M., Hurrell, J.J. and Margolis, B. (1974). Job stress in police administrators, *Journal of Police Science and Administration,* 2, 381–387.

Kroes, W.M., Margolis, B. and Hurrell, J.J. (1974). Job stress in policemen, *Journal of Police Science and Administration,* 2, 145–155.

Lotz, R. and Regoli, R. (1977). Police cynicism and professionalism, *Human Relations,* 30, 175–186.

Neiderhoffer, A. (1967). *Behind the Shield: The Police in Urban Society,* Garden City, NY, Doubleday.

O'Connell, B., Holzman, H. and Armandi, B. (1986). Police cynicism and the modes of adaptation, *Journal of Police Science and Administration,* 14, 307–313.

Regoli, R.M. (1976). An empirical assessment of Niederhoffer's police cynicism scale, *Journal of Criminal Justice,* 4, 231–241.

Savery, L., Soutar, G. and Weaver, J. (1993). Stress and the police officer: Some West Australian evidence, *The Police Journal,* July, 277–290.

Violanti, J.M. and Aron, F. (1995). Police stressors: Variations in perceptions among police personnel, *Journal of Criminal Justice,* 23, 287–294.

See also **Police: Personalities and Subcultures**

Police: Patrol

We closely associate the term "patrol" with the police today. New police officers are usually assigned to patrol duties and are often called patrol officers. The largest unit in most police departments is the patrol division; in small police departments, everyone patrols. When we call for police assistance, whether for an emergency, to report a crime, to quell a disturbance, or to request some type of routine service, a patrol officer is typically dispatched. And when we encounter the police in that most ubiquitous of all enforcement situations, a traffic stop, it is usually an officer on patrol who has stopped us.

Before the advent of two-way radios, police on patrol had one primary purpose—*watching*. It was (and is) expected that police on patrol will prevent some crime and disorder by their watchfulness, and also that they will effectively intervene when they discover law breaking in progress. In the middle ages, the military and quasi-military precursors of modern police patrolled Europe watching for highway robbers. In England, the sheriff and his men patrolled on the lookout for Robin Hood and others who poached game on lands owned by the king and other nobles. In the American South in the 1700s, slave patrols watched for runaway slaves. As urbanization took hold in the early 1800s and 1900s, uniformed foot patrol officers watched for all kinds of crime and disorder in cities and towns.

Automobiles and two-way radios dramatically affected police patrol in the 20th century, especially in the U.S. As more and more of the public used cars to go shopping, to travel to neighboring towns, and to commute to and from work in the city from homes in the suburbs, the police had to use cars as well. Motorized police patrols were deemed necessary to pursue motorized criminals and to enforce traffic laws. Motorized patrols also came to be seen as more efficient than foot patrols, because a larger area could be watched by police in cars. Then, the addition of the two-way radio made it possible for personnel at police headquarters to contact patrol officers in the field and dispatch them to respond to citizen requests for assistance. The impact of these two basic technologies should not be underestimated. Before cars and radios, police response to emergencies and other crises was more like the fire department model—from the station. Officers on patrol were out on the streets watching, but they were not in continuous communication with headquarters.

As the 20th century progressed, police patrols became more and more dependent on the car and the radio. The public learned to call the police whenever crime or disorder was suspected, and calls for police assistance increased steadily. Over time, that portion of the workload of police patrol officers represented by call handling increased. By the 1970s, a second fundamental purpose of patrol had taken root—*waiting*. Many patrol officers came to see their jobs primarily as handling calls, and when they were not "on a call" they were waiting for one. As waiting joined watching as a purpose of patrol, and in some cases largely replaced it, patrol became a more reactive and passive activity.

Careful research on the practice and effectiveness of police patrols started slowly in the 1950s and began to flourish in the 1970s. Early findings focused primarily on the discovery that patrol officers exercised wide discretion when enforcing the law and maintaining order. It was found that police invoke the law much less often than they could, often preferring to handle situations informally. Police officers' discretionary decisions about whether to enforce the law are affected by such factors as department policy, victim or complainant preferences, suspect demeanor, and the seriousness of the offense.

Research on the make-up of patrol officer workload indicates about a 50–50 split between time spent handling calls and time spent patrolling, although, of course, this varies widely between jurisdictions and across different shifts. Officers on the day shift handle relatively more routine crime reporting and public service duties; evening shift officers handle more disorders, disputes, and crimes in progress; and night shift officers have less human interaction and focus more of their attention on the few businesses open during those hours and the security of the many businesses closed for the night.

Patrol workload is neither all crime fighting, as media portrayals might suggest, nor all mundane public service, as some early studies seemed to indicate. The best studies have shown that patrol work combines a variety of crime control, order maintenance (relating to such complaints as drunk and disorderly conduct), traffic enforcement, and service duties and requests. Of these four commonly used categories, crime control seems to account for the largest portion of calls handled by the police as well as police encounters with citizens, and pure service accounts for the smallest portion. However, it must quickly be emphasized that most crime-related calls and encounters involve minor offenses, routine report taking, and no arrests (often because a suspect is never identified). Patrol officers are more likely to take enforcement actions, in the form or arrests or citations, in order maintenance and traffic situations than in crime-related situations.

The seminal study of patrol effectiveness was the Kansas City Preventive Patrol Experiment, conducted by the Police Foundation and published in 1974. This experiment tested the impact of three levels of patrolling strength, ranging from no patrol to twice the normal level, in 15 patrol beats over the course of a year. The results were surprising—no differences in victimization, reported crime, fear of crime, public perception of police presence, arrests, traffic accidents, or anything else that was measured. Police patrols (not all police presence, just regular patrols) were virtually eliminated from five beats for an entire year and nobody noticed. Similarly, patrols were doubled in five other beats and nobody noticed.

The internal and external validities of the Kansas City study have been debated for years by researchers, and its implications have been hotly debated by police practitioners. Regardless of the outcome of these debates, though, the theory and practice of police patrol have been changed forever. Few are willing to assume any longer that mere "visibility" and "omnipresence" are sufficient patrol strategies for reducing crime or fear of crime. Many are willing to take a more strategic approach to patrol deployment and tactics, as it no longer seems absolutely necessary to assign a patrol car to every beat on every shift just to provide police visibility.

Two other significant research contributions affecting police patrol came along in the 1970s and early 1980s. First, studies of police response times revealed, much to everyone's surprise, that immediate police response to reported crimes rarely leads to an arrest, nor is it the crucial factor in victim satisfaction. Immediate response rarely leads to arrests because the vast majority of crimes are property crimes reported after they have occurred—the suspect is long gone and the victim has no idea who did it. Moreover, victim satisfaction depends more on how empathetic and competent the officers are once they arrive than merely on how quickly they arrive. These findings had substantial practical implications precisely because, by the early 1980s, the primary purpose of police patrols had become one of waiting for calls and then responding rapidly.

The second major research contribution in the early 1980s was the rediscovery of foot patrols in the U.S. (it had never been abandoned in most other countries). Studies in Newark, New Jersey, and Flint, Michigan, each indicated that foot patrols might have some of the positive effects that had been found wanting in Kansas

City when motorized patrols were tested. Both studies suggested that foot patrols make residents feel safer and enhance the public's regard for the police. The Flint study also claimed that foot patrols reduced crime, but the Newark study did not. Still, in the aftermath of the Kansas City experiment, just finding that foot patrols had beneficial effects on fear of crime and attitudes toward police was enough to renew police interest in foot patrols.

The rediscovery of foot patrols contributed to the development of the broken windows thesis. In a nutshell, this thesis holds as follows: foot patrol officers, as contrasted with motor patrol officers, are more likely to address minor crime and disorder problems on their beats, such as drunks, panhandlers, prostitutes, loud youths, and small-time drug dealers; when officers address these kinds of problems, residents notice, they feel safer, and they appreciate it; residents who feel safer and who have more confidence in the police are then more likely to assert informal social control, which makes the neighborhood even safer; reduced fear and enhanced safety encourages residents to remain in the neighborhood, spurs them to improve their properties, and attracts other residents and investors to the area; and a positive cycle of improvement continues. It should be emphasized that this broken windows thesis is far from proven, but it has had a powerful impact on police strategies, crime prevention programming, and urban renewal over the last 15–20 years.

The rediscovery of foot patrols also contributed directly to the rise of community policing. As a metaphor, foot patrols symbolized a police officer well-known to neighborhood residents working closely with them to address neighborhood problems, in contrast to the motorized patrol metaphor of an officer wearing reflector sunglasses darting into a neighborhood to enforce a law and then either disappearing or driving around staring at residents. This contrast had long been recognized and debated, of course, but prior to the several studies noted above the police had been able to argue that motorized patrols and rapid responses, though perhaps not warm and fuzzy, were effective and necessary. Research made these claims untenable and opened the door to a variety of strategic innovations, most notably community policing.

The practical impact of community policing on police patrols can be described in terms of purpose and workload. Instead of driving around in patrol cars watching and waiting, community policing officers are supposed to be working in partnership with neighborhood residents and other agencies to identify and solve specific local problems. This approach to patrolling is more collaborative and more proactive than previous models. Naturally, these patrol officers still must handle reported crimes and other calls for assistance, but when not handling calls they emphasize problem solving more than watching or waiting.

Another strategic direction that patrolling has taken in the last 20 years is toward a more focused or directed approach. One might think of traditional motorized patrols as the mayonnaise approach—spread evenly over the entire jurisdiction. Directed patrols, by contrast, try to apply patrols in a more focused manner to particular locations where crimes or other problems are occurring. Enhancements in crime analysis and crime mapping in recent years have made this approach more feasible.

Technology continues to affect police patrols. Officers now commonly have computers in their cars through which they can check vehicle registrations, driving records, criminal records, warrant files, and a host of other databases in seconds. Technology has also affected police weaponry, police protective gear, audio and video taping of police–citizen encounters, night vision, evidence location and collection, handling of high-speed pursuits, and many other conditions and aspects of the patrol officer's job.

Despite significant changes over the past century or two, the work of patrol officers remains very challenging and controversial. Most use-of-force incidents, including deadly force, involve patrol officers responding to calls or investigating suspicious situations. Most high-speed chases involve patrol officers. The current controversy in the U.S. surrounding racial profiling centers primarily on the practices of patrol officers in stopping and searching vehicles and pedestrians.

Police patrol officers are among the most powerful and visible agents of government. Police work, including patrol work, inherently entails the use of government authority to regulate and restrict peoples' behavior. Most of us resent such restrictions when they are applied to us, plus errors are bound to be made when using such authority. More seriously, perhaps, the institutions that exercise such authority are unlikely to avoid the prejudices that permeate the societies in which they operate. New technologies, and new strategies such as community policing, have some potential for reducing abuses of authority and preventing use-of-force tragedies, but it is unlikely that the necessity for split-second life-or-death decision making can ever be completely eliminated from police patrol work.

GARY CORDNER

References and Further Reading

Cordner, G.W. 1989. The police on patrol, in Kenney, D.J., Ed., *Police and Policing: Contemporary Issues*, New York, Praeger.
Kelling, G.L., Pate, T., Dieckman, D. and Brown, C.E. 1974. *The Kansas City Preventive Patrol Experiment: A Summary Report*, Washington, DC, Police Foundation.

McGarrell, E.F., Chermak, S. and Weiss, A. 1999. *Targeting Firearm Violence Through Directed Police Patrol,* Indianapolis, IN, Hudson Institute.

Police Foundation 1981. *The Newark Foot Patrol Experiment,* Washington, DC, Police Foundation.

Reichel, P. 1988. Southern slave patrols as a transitional police style, *American Journal of Police,* 7.

Sherman, L.W. and Weisburd, D. 1995. General deterrent effects of police patrol in crime hot spots: A randomized, controlled trial, *Justice Quarterly,* 12.

Spelman, W. and Brown, D.K. 1981. *Calling the Police: Citizen Reporting of Serious Crime,* Washington, DC, Police Executive Research Forum.

Trojanowicz, R. 1982. *An Evaluation of the Neighborhood Foot Patrol Program in Flint, Michigan,* East Lansing, MI, National Center for Community Policing, Michigan State University.

Wilson, J.Q. and Kelling, G.L. 1982. Police and neighborhood safety: Broken windows, *Atlantic Monthly,* March.

See also **Police: Community Policing**

Police: Personalities and Subcultures

Ask police officers why they joined the force and you may get responses such as, "to help people," "to make a difference," "to lock up scum bags," "to give back to society," "job security," or "for the excitement." Regardless of the reason, thousands of men and women choose to join the ranks every year. Law enforcement agencies in the U.S. employ over a million full-time and part-time sworn officers. A "brotherhood" of sorts unites these officers in one of the most distinct of all occupational subcultures. Not all police officers share the personality traits or adhere to the ethos of the police subculture discussed in this article. Interestingly, though, the great majority of sworn officers do adopt the "police persona" and the subcultural philosophies, despite having come from all walks of life (male and female, wealthy and poor, skilled and unskilled, educated and uneducated, etc.), varying backgrounds, differing motivations, and diverse ethnic and racial cultures.

Police personalities and subcultures were first researched and written about in 1950, by William Westley. Since then, a significant amount of research has studied this unique subculture to determine the typology of personality of those who choose careers in law enforcement, as well as to explain the facets and functions of the police subculture. Other notable researchers of police personality and subculture include John Van Maanen, Jerome Skolnick, Arthur Neiderhoffer, and James Q. Wilson. Although a majority of the research occurred between the 1950s and mid-1970s, these researchers defined characteristics of the police culture and officer personality that persevere today, over 30 years later.

Occupations in law enforcement are significantly different from other occupations in relation to the inherent complex dynamics and working environment. Police officers are symbolically the "thin blue line" separating order from disorder, and as such are called upon to create order out of disorder via report writing, investigation, mediation, arrest, and use of force. Although a minimal amount of an officer's job is actually spent conducting crime-fighting duties, they are typically deployed to work among, and interact with, the apprehensive, hostile, and mean people within a community. As police officers patrol their beats and respond to calls for service, they most often encounter individuals who are experiencing fear, pain, anger, frustration, confusion, and occasionally mourning. Infrequently, officers will respond to a call or happen upon a situation that is pleasurable. This dark and dismal nature of police work has led some researchers to theorize that individuals must be born with the police personality, and subsequently drawn to law enforcement as a career. Such theories, however, are not widely accepted; rather, it is believed that those who choose and are accepted into police work as a profession espouse the police persona through socialization and work-related experiences.

The socialization process comprises two "instructional" paths, informal and formal. The informal channel usually begins prior to an individual choosing to enter the policing field, meaning that potential candidates gain an often-skewed perception of police work through media outlets. Fictional and "reality" shows depict police officers living in a world of chronic excitement and power, or authority. Newscasts are frequently headlined by extraordinary incidents during which the police were required to use some type of force. The reality of police work as predominantly report takers and information gatherers is rarely, if ever, depicted in popular culture.

For whatever reason the choice is made to pursue a police career, a candidate must then compete with other candidates through a battery of procedures law enforcement agencies use to select whom they believe will make good police officers. Often times, these procedures have little to do with the knowledge, skills, and abilities to perform the duties of a police officer; however, they assist those making the selection to determine a level of morality and discretion that are important attributes of police officers. Included in many selection processes are background investigations, physical fitness screenings, written tests, financial credit screenings, polygraph examinations, and oral review boards. Some researchers argue that these processes are designed to result in the selection of homogeneous candidates, explaining such as the reason for the predominance of middle-class white males in police work.

Upon admittance as a police recruit, successful candidates typically begin their formal socialization via police training academies. This introduction phase of socialization involves police recruits being subjected to a series of academic examinations to evaluate their knowledge of the material taught to them more often than not by veteran police officers trained as instructors. A result of having veteran officers as instructors is that the formal socialization, or learning the facets of the job, is often side-tracked with informal socialization, as instructors share, often inflated, stories of their experiences. These "war stories" often sensationalize police work, and are typically told about extraordinary events or experiences the officer had. Few, if any, veteran officers engage in long discussions about how they patrolled their beat for 4 hours without responding to a call. Such is not as interesting as the incident that involved a chase or fight or shooting.

Formal socialization continues during a rookie officer's Field Training and Evaluation (FTE) program, or Field Training Officer (FTO) program. Varying in length from 4 to 20 weeks, depending on the department, the FTO program affords the new officer the opportunity to partner with an experienced veteran officer to learn the department's policies, procedures, and accepted practices. Often times, however, this phase of training is also riddled with informal socialization, as the rookie not only learns how he or she should conduct, but is also exposed to how officers actually perform their duties, despite rules and boundaries established by law or policy.

As new officers progress through the encountering phase of police work, the informal and formal socialization processes inundate the officer with the traditional personality and subcultural characteristics. Whether the officer adopts or adheres to the accepted practices of his or her colleagues is a personal choice; however, when the majority of one's waking day is spent in the company of a particular group, human nature tends to take over. Subsequently, the individual assumes the norms and beliefs of those with whom they are associated.

Traditionally, police officers develop over time a mindset of us versus them, or police versus citizens, as a result of the isolationism officers experience in consequence of various characteristics of the job that reinforce the adversarial philosophy initiated through the socialization process. Among these characteristics are the identifiable uniform and distinguishable mobile patrol platform, or patrol vehicle. These items tend to isolate police officers from citizens. It is not uncommon for other occupations to require their employees to wear identifiable uniforms, however, few uniforms include a shield, or badge, and utility belt equipped with tools to inflict pain or death. It is also extremely uncommon for citizens to operate automobiles donning reflective tape and decals and flashing emergency lights. These articles of power and authority are often viewed as intimidating, resulting in a perception that officers are unapproachable. Aside from the aspect of the uniform, the job itself fosters elements that further isolate police officers from the citizenry. Duty hours most often rotate through a system of shifts on a monthly and sometimes weekly cycle. Daily hours typically comprise 12-hour shifts, but extra time is routinely put in to complete daily reports and other obligations prior to going off-duty.

Danger, perceived and actual, is another facet of police work that sets it apart from most other occupations. Although law enforcement does not rank as the most dangerous of occupations, the potential for an officer to be injured on the job is very real. Law enforcement professionals, media, and citizens often describe the police as putting their lives on the line on a daily basis. Although it is true that police frequently face unknown, and potentially dangerous, environments (i.e., making traffic stops, especially at night, entering and clearing buildings, and responding to calls), the likelihood that a police officer will be killed in the line of duty is nominal. Officers are assaulted and injured in the line of duty at a much higher frequency. The problem for police officers is they do not know when a situation may become or is threatening; therefore, exercising caution is of utmost importance. Using caution at all times leads to yet another aspect of police work that differentiates the job from others—suspicion.

Via a recruit officer's formal and informal socialization, the threat of danger is constantly emphasized with "officer safety" being a fundamental idiom that becomes ingrained in the officer's subconscious. As a facet of the police-working environment, suspicion results in officers being apprehensive during most encounters with citizens. The uneasiness is expressed through the officers' verbal and nonverbal communications and is interpreted by citizens on many occasions as aggressive or overzealous. In the interest of practicality, however, police officers are trained to focus on situations or circumstances that are unnatural, or that seem out-of-place (i.e., suspicious activity). Such suspicious conditions are often the basis of police-initiated activity.

Probably the most distinguishing characteristic of police work is the power, or authority, the job is responsible for and the capability to use force legally to assert such power. Police officers assume a delicate balancing act in their strife to create order from disorder. They must perform their duties as law enforcers, public servants, and protectors in such a manner that meets or exceeds the expectations of the police department's administration, as well as those of the citizenry; however, officers must do so delicately so as not to infringe upon any individual's constitutional rights. Police are the only element of society that exercises the right to take someone's freedom or life, and do so legally, if justified. Such is an awesome responsibility, and police officers are prepared mentally and physically to assume the responsibility through formal and informal socialization phases. Officers-in-training are inundated with various tactics, techniques, and skills to implement force when the situation dictates, to include the use of deadly force.

The characteristics of police work described previously foster the development of the police persona. Various researchers have offered typologies and attributes of police personalities, possibly the most prevalent of which is Jerome Skolnick's (1975, 1966) "working personality." The elements of the working personality have been referenced earlier in this article—danger and authority that lead to suspicion and social isolation. The potential of danger is ever present in police work by the inherent nature of the job. Police officers are tasked with enforcing laws and ordinances, whether or not the officer agrees with the law. Rarely do individuals desire to be arrested, spend time in jail, or receive a ticket; however, it is also rare to identify anyone who never breaks the law in some form, typically traffic law infractions. As a result, police officers exercising their given authority naturally inspire stress, anxiety, apprehension, and fear—emotions that have powerful effects on the human brain and body. Officers are trained formally and informally to recognize and empathize with the various emotions faced on a daily basis, as well as those most often associated with active resistance. Citizens become "symbolic assailants" if they exude particular demeanors, or if they exhibit certain characteristics considered by police to be those of potentially "bad" people. In essence, officers respond to citizen behavior by taking some type of

enforcement action which rouses emotion in the citizen, fostering a potentially dangerous situation for the officer. This scenario is frequent in police work and tends to generate cynicism for the police officer, leading to the officer becoming isolated from non-police under the belief that non-police don't understand and cannot empathize with the life of a police officer. Officers tend to have a sense of aloneness within their community and typically associate only with other law enforcement officers, if with anyone.

Other descriptors of the police personality are authoritarian, aggressive, cynical, dogmatic, secretive, rigid, and stereotypical. The police, by the inherent nature of their job, must exert authority to complete fundamental duties. As described earlier, police are given the power to enforce laws and maintain order, and society expects the police to do so. When such authority is used, however, society often condemns the police for being overzealous, discourteous, or aggressive. Officers face a paradox which predicates police cynicism. Cynicism breeds dogmatism as officers become critical of a perceived ungrateful society. As a result, police generally do not share their activities with the public and maintain an aura of secrecy in matters concerning police operations. Ironically, doing so fuels the social condemnation of the police. Police officers tend to withdraw from society and gravitate toward social lives exclusively among other police in an us-versus-them (police-versus-citizens) worldview. Police officers often see the world in rigid shades of black and white, with little deviation. Prejudice and stereotypical beliefs emerge as officers become absorbed in the police culture. Officers find themselves balancing prejudgment based on experience or on personal biases. Such beliefs are not necessarily founded on racial lines, but rather on types of deviant behaviors (i.e., "thugs," "crack heads," "gang bangers," "perps," etc.)

It must be emphasized again that individuals who choose police work do not necessarily adopt, or reject, the traditional personality and subcultural attributes equally. Because of this, the police subculture comprises different types of officers. As noted, some researchers have offered typologies of police. John Broderick (1987) compared and contrasted the works of other researchers and compiled a general typology of police officers, categorizing officers as *enforcers, idealists, realists,* and *optimists.* Enforcers are described as those officers who take great pleasure in the enforcement aspect of the job. Although sympathetic of "good people," they tend to have great discord for those perceived as thugs or the dregs of society. Enforcers focus their efforts on social order, their sense of which is based on personal values and morality. They tend to be dissatisfied, generally, with the criminal justice system and unhappy with their jobs, but are motivated more by police solidarity than their categorized counterparts. This type of officer is more cynical and resentful of society than other types of police, but desires enforcing the law.

Idealists derive their label because of their belief in the ideals of law enforcement, expressed through the Police Officer Code of Ethics. Although they may not constantly adhere to the ideals, they understand them and strive to uphold them. They value human rights and believe in the criminal justice system, but experience frustration as they perceive society generally dislikes and is unappreciative of the efforts of police officers. They tend to be more satisfied with their occupations than enforcers, but less so than optimists.

Realists, on the other hand, tend to share the dissatisfaction with the job with the idealists, however, for different reasons. Realists maintain a pessimistic view of society and respond to it most often in a resentful and cynical fashion. Realists are quick to identify problems in society, in the criminal justice system, in police work, or within their agency, but offer few solutions or suggestions of how to resolve the problems. Still, they continue to do the job, but do so in an apathetic manner, taking police action when called upon, and only when absolutely necessary.

Optimists take a different approach to police work than those in other categories. Optimists focus on the majority of time police officers spend not actually fighting crime and use this time to connect with the community. Optimists find doing so satisfying and rewarding. The enforcement side of police work is not seen as insignificant; rather, optimists believe that such is a small part of the job and that service to the public is most important. Optimists tend to be more well-rounded than enforcers, idealists, or realists, which affords them a better perspective about the function of police work. They face the same frustrating and discouraging circumstances that the other types of officers resent, but view the situations on a less personal basis, keeping in mind that service to the public is priority one.

Regardless of the personality type, or even of specific traits an officer may assume, police are members of a distinct occupational subculture that harbors specific themes, philosophies, and informal rules. John Crank (1998) describes the police culture as a "confluence" and the "carrier of institutionalized values." Metaphorically, police officers are streams that converge into the sea, or culture. The streams are shaped differently and have varying characteristics, but merge to form a larger body of water encompassing a combination of qualities. The police subculture remains intact despite the uniquely high turnover experienced in the profession, and subcultural ideals are passed on to new generations of officers. Cultural themes of isolation and solidarity mimic those of individual personalities. As officers disenchant themselves from society on a personal basis, they tend to fulfill their psychological need of belonging through relationships with other police. It is through these relationships and the occupational nature of relying on one another for assistance that crystallizes police solidarity. Police support, protect, and rely on each other, binding the "brotherhood" and strengthening *esprit de corps*. An unfortunate consequence of the police culture unity is the capacity for it to breed deviant behavior by police officers. Elizabeth Reuss-Ianni (1983) identified informal rules, or "postulates," for police to live by in relation to police culture. In relation to secrecy and solidarity, police are expected to not "give up another cop," "watch out for your partner first and then the rest of the guys working that tour," "don't implicate anybody else," and "hold up your end of the work."

Kappeler, Sluder, and Alpert (1998) describe the principles of police work, or "ethos." Similar to the isolation and solidarity themes, the *ethos of secrecy* governs police in the aspect of privatizing the operations of police as well as the internal functions of the police subculture. The *ethos of bravery* characterizes police work in relation to the danger aspect, as described previously in this article. The idea of potential danger and officer safety is purposefully ingrained in a police officer's psyche as a self-protection function. Reuss-Ianni (1983) explains that within the police subculture, officers are expected to abstain from showing any form of cowardice. Police should "be aggressive" when necessary, but not "too eager." In other words, officers should not go looking for trouble, but should be able to handle themselves when trouble occurs. Police also share the *ethos of autonomy*. Police officers often work by themselves under extremely limited supervision. This autonomy dictates that officers exercise a great amount of discretion; therefore, officers must be skilled decision makers and practice exercising good judgment.

The police profession is unique to most other professions in regard to the personality of its members and the ideals of the subculture. Despite facing complex challenges, police officers believe in their work and in the constructs of law and order. They share a sense of morality and believe in order maintenance. Individuals are not inherently born with the personality traits of a police officer, but rather adopt the police persona during socialization in the field and membership in the police subculture. In this essay, an attempt has been made to introduce the reader to the police culture on a tertiary level. Readers are encouraged to refer to the reference section materials for more detailed information.

M. Patrick Long

References and Further Reading

Broderick, J.J. (1987). *Police in a Time of Change,* 2nd ed., Waveland Press, Inc., Prospect Heights, IL.

Crank, J.P. (1998). *Understanding Police Culture,* Anderson Publishing Company, Cincinnati, OH.

Dunham, R.G. and Alpert, G.P. (2001). *Critical Issues in Policing,* 4th ed., Waveland Press, Inc., Prospect Heights, IL.

Kappeler, V.E., Sluder, R.D. and Alpert, G.P. (1998). *Forces of Deviance: Understanding the Dark Side of Policing,* 2nd ed., Waveland Press, Inc., Prospect Heights, IL.

Langworthy, R.H. and Travis L.F., III (1994). *Policing in America: A Balance of Forces,* Chap. 10: Police Officers, MacMillan Publishing Company, New York.

Peak, K.J. (2003). *Policing America: Methods, Issues, Challenges,* 4th ed. Chap. 3: Police subculture: The making of a cop, Prentice Hall, Upper Saddle River, NJ.

Van Maanan, J. (1973). Observations on the making of policemen, in Manning, P. K. and Van Maanan, J. (1978) *Policing: a view from the street.* Goodyear Publishing Company, Inc.: Santa Monica, CA.

Skolnick, J.H. (1975). *Justice Without Trial,* 2nd ed., Chap. 3: A sketch of the policeman's "working personality," John Wiley and Sons, Inc., New York.

Walker, S. and Katz, C.M. (2002). *The Police in America: An Introduction,* 4th ed., Part 4: Officers and organizations, McGraw-Hill Companies, Inc., New York.

Wilson, J.Q. (1978). *Varieties of Police Behavior: The Management of Law and Order in Eight Communities,* Chap. 2: The patrolman, Harvard University Press, Cambridge, MA.

See also **Police: Administration and Organization; Police: Occupational Problems**

Police: Private Security Forces

In the U.S., it is commonly believed that public police as part of the criminal justice system represent the first line of defense against crime and disorder. Yet, current estimates suggest that the number of private security personnel, including private security officers or private police, outnumber sworn public law enforcement officers by about three to one, and outspend public law enforcement by as much as 50%. During the past 40 years there has been extraordinary growth in the private security industry, particularly in contract guard services. The reasons for the growth of private security include: (1) an increase in third-party liability suits in which crime victims place a greater responsibility on businesses to provide protection over and above traditional law enforcement; (2) increased public fear of crime and awareness of safety issues resulting in a greater demand for crime prevention and protection; (3) a greater responsibility of businesses to ensure safe environments for both patrons and employees; (4) an increase in crimes in the workplace; (5) the increasing costs of providing public law enforcement to communities; (6) an increased public and business awareness of the cost effectiveness of private security services; and (7) response to September 11, 2001, terrorist attacks and fear of future incidents. Problems affecting the private security industry involve inadequate training and education, lack of standardization within the industry, and the legal functions of private security personnel in relation to public law enforcement.

Private security personnel are used in such diverse settings as public and private schools and universities; hotels; apartments; shopping centers; parking garages; parks; airports; hospitals; factories; corporations; nuclear power plants; and local, state, and federal government buildings and facilities. Some metropolitan police departments now contract out some of their services to private security for traffic control; the protection of public property such as buildings, parks, and other recreation sites; animal control; prisoner transport; housing development patrols; city and county code violations; and court security. Private security has become such an integral part of the auxiliary protection system in the U.S. that some people suggest that it comprises what might be called a "private justice system," which provides protection for most of the assets, people, and property in corporate and industrial America. As noted in a 1985 U.S. Department of Justice study, this private justice system handles countless incidents, many of which meet the statutory definitions of crime, which otherwise would overwhelm the resources of the criminal justice system. Although the duties of private security guards and public police overlap in some ways, distinctive differences between the two exist. Municipal and state police, who have a mission to protect the public from crime, primarily through the investigation and apprehension of alleged offenders, derive their mandated authority from local, country, or state legislation, and are funded by taxes. Private security personnel, on the other hand, protect people and property only within the clear limits of their sphere of influence (e.g., in a particular business or building) and with some exceptions have no greater legal authority than private citizens in their ability to detain, investigate, or make arrests. Private security operations are usually funded by the private businesses that they service; however, when private security personnel are contracted by governmental entities the funding is through public taxes.

History of Public and Private Policing

The institution of public police empowered by state authority is a relatively new phenomenon, coming into existence in the first three decades of the 19th century. Indeed, specialized institutions of formal social control such as state mandated police forces were invented when societies had grown so complex in social structure and diverse in population and normative composition that the older mechanisms of informal social control ceased to be effective in maintaining social order. For many centuries, ordinary individuals secured their own families, villages, and businesses. In England, at least from the time of Alfred the Great (871–899), primary responsibility for keeping the peace in communities fell on all able-bodied males over age 12, according to an ancient code of collective responsibility known as the "mutual pledge" system. Groups of citizens were required without pay to apprehend offenders and form posses to track down fugitives. Later, following passage of the Statute of Westminister in 1285, local security was provided by a system of "watch and ward," where all "able-bodied" men were required to patrol and protect English towns against criminal elements. Crime became such a problem in cities such as London through the 1700s that merchants and tradesmen organized private forces of ex-soldiers and cavalrymen to police the warehouse and trade districts of the city. Essentially bounty hunters, these private police were paid a fee for apprehending or killing the most dangerous criminals. Because of increasing crime and violent civil disorders, the inadequacy of the "watch" system, and the inability of military forces to quell mob violence, the first formal public police department was authorized in London in 1829 by the London Metropolitan Police Act.

When British colonists arrived in America, they brought with them the police system as it existed in 16th and 17th century England, including the "watch and ward" in the larger villages and towns, and the concept of collective responsibility for law enforcement. Following the American Revolution, however, increased urbanization during the first decades of the 19th century brought increases in crime and disorder as small homogenous villages turned into larger and more diverse centers of trade and commerce. In short, what was happening in London was also taking place in the major American cities. The first public police

force was established in New York City in 1844, followed by other cities such as Chicago, Boston, Baltimore, San Francisco, Philadelphia, and New Orleans.

Despite the creation of public police departments in virtually every major city in the U.S. by 1890, increases in crime and the particular need for industrial and business organizations to protect their assets stimulated the growth of the private security industry. Alan Pinkerton formed the North West Police Agency in 1855 to provide private protection for Midwest railroads, and the Pinkerton Protection Patrol in 1857 to provide a private guard service to businesses, particularly large industrial concerns. The Pinkerton Company remains one of the largest private guard services in the world. Other security practitioners of the 1850s included Washington Perry Brinks, who started a truck and delivery service that became Brinks Armored Car Service, and Henry Wells and William G. Fargo, who likewise developed a major firm to offer security for the transportation of valuables and money. The 20th century saw the use of private security hired by factory owners to protect their people and property from labor disturbances and union rallies. Overzealous and uncontrolled security forces beat and shot strikers in several controversial encounters during the depression years. Both World Wars I and II stimulated the use of proprietary or "in-house" security in the protection of defense plants from domestic and foreign sabotage and espionage. The Defense Industrial Security Program (DISP) was created by the federal government to better train private police to improve plant security. Most authorities believe, however, that private security did not become a nationwide industry until the late 1940s. The use of both contract and proprietary security personnel to protect the vast defense industry complex in the U.S. dramatically expanded during the past 50 years. Most major corporations and businesses now have security, loss prevention, or risk assessment divisions engaging in any number of asset protection programs, many of which involve the deployment of private security officers to protect people and property. Current figures estimate that there are about 2 million contract private security officers in the U.S. today with unknown numbers of proprietary security personnel working in various organizations.

The Role of the Private Security Officer

Private security officers routinely perform some of the tasks traditionally performed by public law enforcement officers including guard, patrol, and investigative services. The degree of these and other services often depends on whether the security officer is working in the capacity as a *contract guard* employed by a large company such as Wackenhut or Burn's International

Security Services, Inc., or as a *proprietary* or in-house officer employed by a specific business. Contract security personnel are contracted by a business to provide specific and often specialized security functions, whereas in-house officers usually perform a broader diversity of security activities such as engaging in crime prevention practices, crisis prevention and disaster management, fire and safety monitoring, and follow-up investigations of security breaches that occur on the property.

Guard services include a number of duties such as access control, or ensuring that only authorized individuals enter the premises and that unauthorized people are kept out. Other activities along these lines may require officers to check identification badges of employees or assign special passes to other individuals who have legitimate business on a property. Officers may also monitor and check motor vehicles and other means of conveyance on to a property for proper admittance. Officers may also guard specific types of property such as merchandise in a retail store, money in a bank, company computers and data, or vehicles in a parking lot. They also guard people, including employees and customers in businesses. Specialized security guards engage in "executive protection," where wealthy persons or top executives vulnerable to abduction or kidnapping are given exclusive protection. Private security officers guarding specialized facilities such as airports or nuclear power plants may engage in elaborate procedures in protecting the perimeter and boundaries of the property. The patrol duties of private police involve the monitoring and observation of a specific property, which can range from high-rise office buildings to shopping centers. Officers usually patrol premises based on the nature of the property or business and the degree of risk that the property is subjected to. Special post orders are usually given to security personnel, requiring them to give special attention to particularly vulnerable areas of a property. Personnel may be assigned to foot or walking patrols, bicycle patrols, or to vehicular patrols. In all instances, patrol duty involves monitoring a facility for anything that might be out of the ordinary and threaten the operation, including such things as attempted illegal entry, harm to individuals, the movement of unauthorized personnel, fire, malfunctioning of equipment, or any other potentially disruptive problem. Large properties may also be "video patrolled," where private security officers monitor closed circuit television surveillance systems around a property, and then physically respond when problems occur. Officers are usually required to document through internal incident reports or logs problems that occur during their patrol shifts. This information is used by business owners in periodic security assessments of their property to determine if their level of security is adequate or inadequate over time.

Some private security officers engage in various types of investigations connected with their work such as investigating internal and external thefts, employee sabotage, workplace violence incidents, and other acts that affect the safety and security of the premises that they are protecting. However, company rules and regulations do not have the same force as law. Employees may be investigated by security for breaking rules or regulations, but when violations of the law occur, including allegations of charges and investigations, cases come under the jurisdiction of local, state, and federal law enforcement agencies. The security guard must leave law enforcement to the responsible agency.

Private Security Officer Standards and Training

A 1972 study of private policing by James Kakalik and Wildhorn Sorrel characterized the average security guard in this country as underscreened, undertrained, undersupervised, underpaid, and in need of licensing and regulation to upgrade both personnel and services. Since this study, there have been significant advances made in the larger field of private security and particularly in the area of training security officers. Still, efforts to provide national statutory standards for operating private security firms and minimum guidelines for security officer training have been slow in coming. No doubt, part of the slowness can be attributed to the costs associated with educating and training private security officers.

Numerous studies have made recommendations for improvement. In 1976, the federal government issued *Private Security: Report of the Task Force Report on Private Security*, which proposed a number of goals and standards for private security (including recommendations for 32–40 hours of training for armed security guards), but the report neglected training criteria for other types of security guards. In 1998, the International Association of Chiefs of Police in conjunction with several national security associations issued guidelines for the selection, training, and licensing of private security officers. Different types of licenses or certifications for private security officers (e.g., armed, unarmed, and armored car officers) were proposed and training topics (e.g., legal, operational, firearms, administrative, electronic, armored transport, and use of force) were offered as minimum basic training requirements for state private security regulatory agencies. Currently, about half of the states have minimum standard guidelines for the certifying or licensing of private security officers. Criteria vary substantially by state but include such things as minimum classroom hours devoted to security topics such as law, legal powers, general duties, and report writing as well as additional instruction for armed guards. In some states with minimum requirements, guidelines apply only to contract security officers and not proprietary personnel.

Several professional security associations, some industry specific, have developed their own security officer training and certification programs. For example, the International Foundation for Protection Officers (FOP) provides training for officers through the Certified Protection Officer (CPO) program. The International Association for Healthcare Security and Safety (AIMS) offers a Basic Security Officer Training Standard consisting of a 40-hour course of instruction. In addition, the American Hotel and Motel Association, through their Educational Institute Lodging Security Officer program, offers a Certified Lodging Security Officer (CLSO) designation. There is no doubt that efforts to better train, certify, and license private security personnel will continue in the 21st century.

Legal Authority of Private Officers

Some of the duties of private security officers are similar to commissioned law enforcement officers, although their overall powers are very different. Under special circumstances private security officers working under the authority vested in them through state legislation or local ordinances may have similar legal authority as traditional law enforcement officers. For example, public housing authorities and public transit systems in cities may employ private security officers who have special officer commissions that allow them to have police powers only on their respective premises. Likewise, all states have shoplifting statutes that give merchants and their employees, including private security, the right to detain suspected shoplifters in a reasonable manner and for a reasonable length of time when there is probable cause to think that a person has stolen money or merchandise from their place of business. This type of detention is not considered an unlawful arrest, and the security officer is not criminally or civilly liable.

With these exceptions, private security officers basically have the same legal powers as citizens in terms of detaining and arresting individuals for crimes (generally limited to felony offenses that occur in their presence). Private police officers have more confidence than private citizens when making arrests because the former have the consent and knowledge of their superiors. This distinction has important consequences in terms of the civil liability of the arresting individual. The amount of force that can be used to make an arrest must be the amount necessary only to complete the arrest. Deadly force can be used only when the arresting individual has reason to believe that his or her life is in danger and the danger is imminent. State laws regarding the powers of private individuals and security officers to conduct searches, even pursuant to a legitimate arrest, vary and often are ambiguous. Most private security officers are trained to ask for a suspect's permission before conducting a search of their person or property. However, even if an illegal search takes place, any evidence obtained from the search is admissible in a criminal proceeding. Businesses that employ private security guards are subject to vicarious liability whereby the employer may be liable under civil law for the inappropriate behaviors (e.g., unlawful arrest) of their officers. Because of increases in premise liability cases over the years (where individuals have sued businesses for the tortuous actions of negligent security officers) it is incumbent upon a business owner to make sure that he or she is hiring well-trained security personnel.

Public and Private Police Cooperation

In the past, relations between the traditional police and private security officers have been strained. Private security guards were often depicted as nothing more than "door rattlers" and "wanna be" cops. Today, about 20% of commissioned law enforcement officers regularly supplement their salaries by performing off-duty private security details for a variety of businesses. As the budgets of large metropolitan police departments have been reduced, making it difficult to maintain personnel and resources necessary to provide crime control, and as the field of private security has undergone professonalization, cooperation between public and private police has been enhanced. Furthermore, it is quite common now in large cities to find police commanders meeting regularly with private security directors of major businesses in an effort to share information and keep one another mutually informed about such things as known criminal offenders, "hot spots" or problem areas for criminal behavior, and special events (e.g., conventions and concerts) that affect crime. The sharing of this information enhances crime prevention and control efforts throughout the community.

The Growth of Private Security Internationally

The growth of the private security industry in many other countries has been unprecedented in the last decade. Countries such as Canada and Australia are very similar in their dependence on private security personnel for the protection of people and property. Canada, for example, has a ratio of private security to public police approaching that of the U.S., and some private security companies provide guards who offer quasi-police services for low-income public housing developments and upper class neighborhoods, and carry out complex white-collar investigations.

Since the dismantling of the Soviet Union and *perestroika* (restructuring), the Russian Federation has experienced both increases in crime, decreases in state security organizations, and a growing private security industry. Two major types of security agencies exist in Russia: (1) *chastnye sluzhby bezopasnoti*, private company security services (PSS) that protect businesses including large banks and companies often handling state financial assets, and (2) *chastnye okhrannye predpriyatiya*, private protection companies (PPC) providing security services to smaller businesses on a contractual basis. The expansion of new businesses especially in cities such as Moscow and St. Petersburg no doubt has stimulated private security enterprises (Volkov, 2001).

Future of Private Security

The Hallcrest Report II (1990) made predictions about the future role of private security in the control of crime. This well-known report suggests that private security will continue to surpass public law enforcement in terms of spending and the number of individuals employed, and that greater cooperation between traditional law enforcement and private security will occur in the protection of people and property. In addition, emerging new security technologies such as electronic surveillance, access control systems, and sophisticated alarm systems will no doubt have an affect on the continued growth of private security throughout the 21st century.

WILLIAM E. THORNTON

References and Further Reading

Bilek, A.J., Klotter, J.C. and Federal, K.R. 1980. *Legal Aspects of Private Security*, Cincinnati, OH, Anderson Publishing Co.
Crinchley, T., The *History of Police in England and Wales*, Montclair, NJ, Patterson Smith.
Cunningham, W.C., Strauchs, J.J. and Van Meter, C.W. 1990. *Private Security Trends 1970 to 2000: The Hallcrest Report II*, Boston, MA, Butterworth-Heinemann.
Cunningham, W.C. and Taylor, T.H. 1985. *Private Security and Police in America: The Hallcrest Report I*, Boston, MA, Butterworth-Heinemann.
DeWitt, C.B. 1991. *Private Security: Patterns and Trends, Research in Brief*, Washington, DC, U.S. Department of Justice.
Fischer, R.J. and Green, G. 1998. *Introduction to Security*, Boston, MA, Butterworth-Heinemann.
Forst, B. 2000. The privatization and civilianization of policing, in *Boundary Changes in Criminal Justice Organizations*, Washington, DC, National Criminal Justice Reference Service.
Jacobs, J.B. 1983. Private police and security forces, in Kadish, S.H., Ed., *Encyclopedia of Crime and Justice*, New York, The Free Press.
Gray, B.M. 1989. History and principles of crime prevention, in Fennelly, L.J., Ed., *Handbook of Loss Prevention and Crime Prevention*, Boston, MA, Butterworth-Heinemann.
Hamill, W. 1991. *National Laws and Statutes for Private Investigators and Security Guard Agencies*, Edmond, OK, Oklahoma Investigators.
Kakalik, J.S. and Wildhorn, S. 1972. *Private Policing in the U.S.: Findings and Recommendations*, LEAA, Washington, DC, Department of Justice.
National Advisory Committee on Criminal Justice Standards and Goals 1976. *Private Security Report of the Task Force on Private Security*, Washington, DC, U.S. Government Printing Office.
Private Security Officer Selection, *Training and Licensing Guidelines*, Alexandria, VA, International Association of Chiefs of Police, 1998. Available at: www.theiacp.org/pubinfo/Pubs/PSLC/psic6.toc.htm.
Purpura, P.P. 1993. Private Security: History and Development in the U.S., in Fay, J.J., Ed., *Encyclopedia of Security Management*, Boston, MA, Butterworth-Heinemann.
Shearing, C. and Stenning, P. 1987. *Private Policing*, Beverly Hills, CA, Sage Publications.
Simonsen, C.E. 1998. *Private Security in America*, Upper Saddle River, NJ, Prentice Hall.
Voigt, L., Thornton, W., Barrile, L. and Seaman, J.M. 1994. *Criminology and Justice*, New York, McGraw Hill.
Volkov, V. 2001. Security and enforcement as private business: The conversion of Russia's power ministries and its institutional consequences, in Bonnell, V., Ed., *New Entrepreneurs in Russia and China*, New York, West View Press.
U.S. Department of Justice 1985. *Crime and Protection in America: A Study of Private Security and Law Enforcement Resources and Relationships*, Washington, DC, U.S. Department of Justice.
Williams, T.L. *Guard Operation, Protection of Assets*, Santa Monica, CA, Merritt Publishing, 1007.

See also **Police: Recent Developments**

Policing: Police and Racial Profiling

For several decades, profiling has been used as a strategy to fight crime by law enforcement agencies. Consequently, this method has resulted in treating some minority groups as possible offenders on the assumption that doing so will increase the likelihood of catching more criminals. This approach is based on data suggesting that minorities, e.g., blacks, commit more crimes than whites. Some police officials have argued that such a practice is legitimated because of the strong observed correlation between race and crime, resulting in the idea that skin color should be one indicator of an increased propensity to engage in criminal acts, especially drug crimes (see Harris, 2002). Profiling practices have been exposed, mainly resulting in allegations of discrimination.

During the past decade, allegations of racial profiling during police–citizen encounters for both pedestrian and traffic stops have been abundant and widely publicized. Media coverage of racial profiling has largely contributed to the growing national concerns of this phenomenon among the public, government officials, and civil liberty groups. Social scientists and law scholars, moreover, have become devoted to a sustained dialogue concerning implementation and analysis of data collection systems on these particular encounters and the unfolding of events that occur during them.

In light of emerging interests concerning racial profiling, this essay intends to accomplish several tasks. First, racial profiling is defined and a brief account of its historical roots in policing is unraveled. Second, some empirical evidence that has informed the debate on racial profiling is discussed. Finally, some methodological limitations and problems with prior racial profiling studies are identified.

Racial Profiling: Definition and History

Racial profiling has been variably defined by police agencies, academics, and law scholars. Harris (2002) stated that racial profiling is a crime fighting tool used to single out members of minority groups as criminal suspects assuming that such methods will result in an increased likelihood of apprehending criminal offenders, particularly drug offenders. Kennedy (1997) echoes this by stating that, unfortunately, race is used as a proxy for criminality where police wrongly place minorities groups in general categories that are at an increased risk for engaging in criminal activity. Others, such as the acclaimed criminal justice scholar Dr. Samuel Walker, have stated that racial profiling exists when race or ethnicity is used independently or jointly with other indicators that go into police officers discretionary decision making to stop a motor vehicle or person. Others, such as the American Civil Liberties Union (ACLU) definition, specifically allowed the use of race when identifying a particular suspect in a particular crime. Although no consensus has been reached concerning the appropriate definition, many feel that racial profiling is an institutionalized practice.

Generally, profiling has been a tactic or strategy used by law enforcement officers for decades. In the 1980s the drug courier profile surfaced in both airports and highways designed to be predictive of crime and not individual criminals. Although receiving scrutiny over the years, the drug courier profile in airports was upheld, without rigorous empirical evidence of its effectiveness, as a constitutionally acceptable basis for the temporary detention of a suspect in an airport to investigate possible drug trafficking.

Bob Vogel, who may be one of the most devoted practitioners and supporters of profiling to emerge from law enforcement, is a former Florida State Trooper and sheriff in Volusia County Sheriffs department in central Florida. Vogel has been identified as one of the first to create a profiling strategy on American highways. During routine drug busts Vogel noticed a so-called pattern of similar characteristics emerge among offenders that he documented, eventually leading him to generate a profile based on approximately 30 cases. Once the Drug Enforcement Agency (DEA) became aware of Vogel's profiling success, they bought into his system and launched Operation Pipeline in the late 1980s, which was the DEA's persistent effort to convert law enforcement agencies around the country to employ Vogel's profiling strategy as an effective crime-fighting strategy (Harris, 2002).

Until recently, profiling strategies were not subjected to scientific investigations to gauge whether they have been successful crime-fighting tools. Such investigations were needed to provide answers to some important questions. First, is profiling a rational strategy for combating crime, specifically the war on drugs? Second, do profiling strategies lead to negative consequences for minority citizens? The opposing position to the effectiveness of profiling as a crime-fighting strategy is the fear that minorities are being discriminated against.

Some have argued that discretion allotted to officers has played a critical role in racial profiling, influencing racially motivated traffic stops, stops and frisks, and searches. Pretextual traffic stops are one important example. Police discretion over traffic stops is practically unlimited, as hundreds of pages of law have been documented describing vehicle standards and moving infractions that allow officers to stop drivers as they please. Therefore, it would not be hard for an officer to find a justifiable excuse for stopping a driver because of a "hunch" (Harris, 2002). In sum, the arguments for and against racial profiling, from both liberal and conservative camps (see MacDonald, 2003), have framed the research questions in today's data collection efforts of traffic stops, stops and frisks, and searches.

Evidence of Racial Profiling by Police

The fundamental question in the profiling debate concerns the disproportionate representation of blacks and Hispanics, relative to whites, in traffic and pedestrian stops and searches. In other words, does this disproportionate representation reflect discrimination by law enforcement officials or disparities reflecting true differences? Alleged evidence for racial discrimination is derived from two sources: anecdotal, which is of limited value to social scientists, and statistical, which encompasses a large number of systematic observations of events or incidences (MacDonald, 2003). Data collection and analysis by social scientists have been the most important ways of addressing the above questions, as well as the main reform effort to increase police accountability and eradicate racial profiling (Walker, 2000).

To date, collection efforts at the federal, local, and state levels have produced many important findings and have led to the identification of many methodological weaknesses that inhibit drawing definitive conclusions. Studies published from available data have largely focused on a set of variables during police-initiated interactions with citizens including: the initial contact (e.g., racial differences in traffic or pedestrian stops), whether a search of the vehicle or person occurred, and if contraband was found on the person.

Since the mid-1990s several aggregate and individual level studies have uncovered racial disparities in stops (Ramirez, McDevitt, and Farrell, 2001), indicating that both Hispanics and blacks are disproportionately represented in such encounters relative to their percentages in the population at risk of being stopped. Results from studies focusing particularly on searches for contraband during stops have produced the most compelling evidence of racial discrimination and, moreover, have countered claims that argue racial profiling is a justified law enforcement strategy. Several of these studies have shown that although blacks and Hispanics are at a disproportionate risk of being searched they are less likely to be found toting contraband. In some studies these groups are even less likely to have contraband than whites.

Early studies conducted on racial profiling were largely in response to law suits that were pressed by civilians, in concert with civil liberty groups, claiming to be racially discriminated against by police during traffic stops. Historically, one landmark case, that is, *State v. Pedro Soto* (734 A. 2d 350, N.J. Super. Ct. Law. Div. 1996), led to the well publicized New Jersey Turnpike study that assessed aggregate level data to observe patterns in traffic stops by race. Dr. John Lamberth of Temple University was employed by the defense to study the problem. Querying randomly selected data from patrol activity and police radio logs, he observed rates at which troopers stopped, ticketed, and arrested blacks on the pertinent stretch of highway during April 1988 through May 1991. In addition, Lamberth used direct observational methods to measure the racial composition of the turnpike's driving population and used a rolling survey to measure speeding violations by race, which included over 42,000 cars. Although Lamberth concluded that blacks and whites violate some traffic laws at the same rate, it was estimated that 13.5% of cars on the turnpike had black drivers and 35% and 70% of those stopped and arrested were black, respectively. These findings were used to support the notion that discriminatory law enforcement practices were being used by the New Jersey State Troopers (see Harris, 2002; MacDonald, 2003).

A similar investigation was undertaken by Lamberth in response to a case in 1996 that involved allegation of civil rights violations for an illegal stop and detention based on a racial profile while the defendant was driving along I-95 in Maryland. Based on the outcome of this case, Lamberth was retained once again by the ACLU to analyze data on traffic stops that were required to be collected by the Maryland police. Maryland police were required to collect data on all traffic stops that included searches. Lamberth concluded that whereas blacks represented 17% of the driving population they accounted for approximately 72% of all those who were stopped and searched. In addition, racial minorities were present in 80% of cases involving a stop and search. Such large disparities led Lamberth to conclude that these data showed racial dsicrimination. Once again, it was argued that law enforcement officers targeted minorities for stops and investigation (see Harris, 2002).

Some of the most revealing data supporting the argument that racial profiling is an ineffective law enforcement strategy come from studies that have empirically assessed "hit rates" after stops and searches have been made, rates at which officers actually find drugs, guns, or other evidence of crime when they perform stops and searches. Although several studies have revealed that minorities are disproportionately stopped and searched by police, they show that minorities are less or equally likely to be carrying illegal drugs or weapons relative to whites. Several data collection efforts have now incorporated opportunities to investigate "hit rates," consistently revealing that racial profiling is an inefficient and ineffective crime-fighting strategy.

The Maryland stop-and-search data, analyzed by Lamberth, were some of the first to assess the distribution of "hit rates" by race. Surprisingly, these data showed quite different patterns in that, of those who were searched, a relatively small percentage were found with contraband. More interestingly, blacks and whites had approximately equivalent "hit rates" among those who were searched, 28.4% of the time for blacks and 28.8% of the time for whites. Recent data from New Jersey reveal a similar pattern. Despite efforts to minimize racial profiling on the New Jersey Turnpike, data from 2000 indicated that blacks and Latinos were still at a disproportionate risk of being stopped and searched, even though they were less likely to be in possession of contraband. Specifically, of those searched on the turnpike, whites had contraband 25% of the time, blacks 13% of the time, and Latinos only 5% of the time (see Harris, 2002). Patterns found in New Jersey and Maryland have also been discovered in other studies including traffic-stops studies in North Carolina, stop-and-frisks studies in New York City, and studies on airline passengers coming into the U.S. (U.S. General Accounting Office, 2000).

General Problems of Past Studies on Racial Profiling

Despite conclusions from studies on racial profiling, some inherent problems exist regarding data collection, base rate calculations, and lack of academic review of past reports. First, researchers have identified that more data need to be collected before the extent, nature, and consequences of racial profiling can be understood. Such data would include date, time, and location of stop; length of stop; identity of officer; identity of individuals stopped (e.g., age, gender, and demeanor); type of stop (e.g., reason for stop and outcome of stop); and search information (e.g., performed or not, legal basis for search, consensual search or not, description of contraband found, and quantity of contraband) (Ramirez et al., 2000). Furthermore, additional data need to be collected to make sure that other legal factors do not account for the observed disparities between race and traffic stops. Second, the base rate or denominator in prior studies has been very

questionable, which in addition has been one of the most damaging criticisms of prior studies. The base rate problem concerns the population of minorities at risk of being stopped by police, which has not been adequately addressed. The base rate is important because it allows comparisons and calculations of the number of minorities stopped relative to the number at risk of being stopped in the population (Walker, 2000). Third, it is important to note that several studies reported in this essay have not been subjected to "blind" academic review by trained social scientists and therefore have not been published in scientific journals. The absence of such review and publication can lead to the questioning of the merit of prior studies. Although these limitations are definitely problematic for understanding racial profiling and its consequences, social scientists are now in the process of addressing such concerns, among others, to advance knowledge concerning this high priority societal issue.

Similar to prior studies, this essay also has its limitations. Given space restrictions, some important issues surrounding the racial profiling debate went unaddressed. For example, this essay did not discuss citizens' attitudes toward racial profiling and the police; policies for dealing with racial profiling such as major consent decrees; consequences of racial profiling for minority communities; the psychological and behavioral consequences of racial profiling for those who have been victims of these practices; and theories that might help explain racial disparities in traffic and pedestrian stops, as well as, searches. For a more exhaustive review of some of these issues we refer readers to books published by David Harris (2002) and Heather MacDonald (2003).

CHRIS GIBSON AND AMY RECKDENWALD

References and Further Reading

Harris, D. (2002). *Profiles in Injustice: Why Racial Profiling Cannot Work,* New York, The New Press.

Kennedy, R. (1997). *Race, Crime, and the Law,* New York, Random House.

MacDonald, H. (2003). *Are Cops Racist?* Chicago, IL, Ivan R. Dee Publishers.

Ramirez, D., McDevitt, J. and Farrell, A. (2000). *A Resource Guide on Racial Profiling Data Collection Systems,* Washington, DC, U.S. Department of Justice.

U.S. General Accounting Office. (2000). *U.S. Customs Services: Better Targeting of Airline Passengers for Personal Searches Could Produce Better Results,* Washington DC, U.S. General Accounting Office.

Walker, S. (2000). *Searching for the Denominator: Problems with Police Traffic Stop Data and an Early Warning System Solution,* Washington, DC, National Institute of Justice.

See also **Discrimination in Justice; Police: Brutality and Corruption; Race and Ethnicity and Criminal Behavior**

Policing: Rural

Rural policing has attracted a great deal of attention during the last decade. The realities of *The Andy Griffith* television show—with Sheriff Andy Taylor and Deputy Barney Fife languishing in the Mayberry, North Carolina, Courthouse waiting for the telephone to ring, dispatching them to a traffic accident or assisting some citizen with a personal problem—are long gone. Although still understaffed, most rural police departments are overwhelmed with calls for service and the complexity of these crimes can be far reaching. Furthermore, most rural police officers are exposed to even greater danger than their urban counterparts owing to an increase in violent crime and a lack of rapid assistance (back-up).

Rural policing has traditionally centered on the protection of livestock, agricultural equipment, and the occasional disorder, whether domestic or public. Prior to the arrival of illicit drugs, the local substance abuse problems centered on underaged consumption or the sale and distribution of untaxed liquor (moonshining). With the saturation of urban centers by drug traffickers in the 1980s, the more enterprising and profit-oriented dealers moved their product to the rural areas. In these rural markets drug dealers found a ready supply of consumers and could raise their prices owing to a lack of competition. Naturally, as the demand for these illicit drugs increased, so did the prices. Thus, rural law enforcement agencies began to see a rise in the local crime rate as a result of these new consumers attempting to meet the escalating cost of these drugs. Reported cases of crimes against property began to rise as well as cases of crimes against persons.

To place this issue in the proper perspective, a definition of what constitutes a rural area and rural policing is appropriate. Population estimates and geographic size would appear to be the most logical standards for assessment; however, these criteria were often traditionally subordinate to the number of full-time sworn law enforcement personnel employed by the local agency. Although this measurement of department size seemed inappropriate, most scholars and practitioners agreed that departments that employed fewer than 15 full-time sworn personnel were rural in nature. The more stringent definition referred to departments that employed ten members or fewer. This measurement by number of officers employed is the result of a 1973 publication by the National Advisory Commission entitled *Report on Police* that divided the

police departments into six categories: 1–15, 16–75, 76–150, 151–400, 401–1000, and more than 1000.

In a 1994 National Institute of Justice Bulletin, Weisheit, Falcone, and Wells seriously question a proposition made in the *Local Government Police Management* guidebook (published in 1982 by the International City Management Association) that "the distinctions between urban and rural policing are considered nominal and are rapidly disappearing." Weissheit et al. add: "Clearly, there is an urban emphasis in research efforts concerning police organizations, management, operations, and methods in America." Unable to offer a more accurate or more succinct definition of rural policing, these authors return to the traditional measure of full-time sworn personnel for reporting and comparison purposes. However, Weisheit et al. do shed light on the difficulty in defining rural departments and small departments and the misperception that rural departments are small and small departments are rural because the geographic complexion of an area may dictate not only the nature of policing required, but also the number of personnel necessary in order to adequately safeguard the community and its property.

Departments that employ larger numbers of officers are frequently less centralized in their operation and have the luxury of highly trained specialists. An example of this specialization would be (evidence) forensic technicians, sexual violence units, or specialized tasks forces (for example, on drugs or gangs). Smaller or more rural departments must rely on their personnel to be law enforcement generalists trained in a variety of crime-solving techniques. Even though the rural officer is required to possess a broader general knowledge of crime-solving techniques than the more urban counterpart, respect and competence are all too often associated with the "big city" officer. These negative stereotypes may be a remnant of the "big-bellied sheriff" era, when cronyism and political nepotism dictated rural politics. Although small-town politics are still prevalent in certain areas, better training and state mandates more closely regulate local policing.

Another problem confronting rural law enforcement is that crimes frequently go unreported simply because the victims never call the police. Even when crimes such as simple assault, larceny, and burglary are reported, the local investigating agency may not forward those crime statistics to the state or federal crime databases. Therefore, no true picture of criminal activity in rural areas exists.

Not all police departments in the U.S. were fortunate enough to benefit from the prosperity of the 1990s. Although larger more urban departments were able to enjoy increased funding as a result of tax surpluses and increased revenues owing to new economic development and commercial growth, rural departments were not as fortunate. The majority of rural jurisdictions had to cope with a substantially smaller tax base and little or no additional revenue from unfamiliar investors.

Because funding was scarce, many rural law enforcement agencies came to rely upon "special, reserve, or part-time officers." These supplemental officers, although not counted as a part of the department's regular complement, do have a significant impact on local rural law enforcement. Only within the last decade have special or reserve officers been required by state legislatures to have the same amount of initial training as full-time sworn personnel. Some jurisdictions that lack sufficient funding for full-time law enforcement officers retain individuals who have acquired basic certification at their own expense, on a part-time basis. These officers are paid an hourly wage, receive no benefits, work less than 40 hours per week, and desire to obtain a full-time position in another agency.

In an effort to increase the number of law enforcement officers nationwide and to insure quality personnel, President Clinton, as part of his Crime Bill Initiative, created the Police Corps. Individual states are allocated federal funds to recruit, train, and distribute newly qualified personnel within their borders. The major recipients of these new potential police officers are rural law enforcement agencies, because these agencies are generally unable to hire additional officers owing to local fiscal constraints or to compete effectively with their urban counterparts when offering salaries and benefits for qualified new personnel. The Police Corps provides scholarships, stipends, and law enforcement training for qualified college students who desire to pursue careers in criminal justice. Once formally educated and trained at a state or regional academy, these new recruits are employed by agencies within the state and a generous annual stipend is awarded to the agencies that employ these individuals. After a period of 4 years these officers may remain with the agency, seek employment with another law enforcement agency, or leave the field of criminal justice. Early empirical data suggest that most officers remain in law enforcement and that a distinct number remain with their original agency.

In Wynne, Arkansas, local authorities, realizing that traditional policing methods were ineffective, turned to the community to help control crime. Much like the "Four Track" approach used in the U.K., the Cross County Sheriff's Department established a partnership with the community's farming population and held "problem-solving" public meetings at the local feed and grain stores. These public meetings allowed the Sheriff's Department to tailor the type of police service, residents felt, was necessary to ensure their safety and protect their property. Farmers felt more comfortable in these informal surroundings and were more open to expressing their concerns to the local deputy and to receiving information on how to protect their agricultural equipment and livestock. Furthermore, this type of cooperative venture allowed the Sheriff's Department to receive federal and state grant funds for expanding its programs.

In Richmond, a small town located in Sagadhoc County, Maine, several rural law enforcement agencies banded together in order to overcome the enormous cost of local policing and improve the service to the community. A decision was made to develop something known as enhanced neighborhood policing (ENP). This program allows communities and law enforcement to work together in a regional manner and yet local control is still maintained by the various members. Most satisfying is the regional vision adopted by the individual members of each community. These individuals refuse to allow local politics to interfere with the welfare of the region. The U.S. Attorney's Office in Alabama is expected to test pilot the enhanced neighborhood policing model to determine if it would be an appropriate program for their area.

Law enforcement agencies in the state of California are nationally recognized as leaders in innovative concepts and technological advances. The Kings County Sheriff's Department was plagued with the same problems mentioned previously. However, their approach to these problems was to grant broader discretion to the local deputies who helped to design and implement the following programs: Citizen Police Academies, Citizens on Patrol, "Are You OK?", and Farm Watch. These programs enlisted the aid of the local citizens in a more proactive manner. Citizens would help patrol this vast county and alert police when necessary. The elderly and infirm were called daily to ensure their health and well-being were intact and citizens were able to attend "mini" police academies to better inform them of the rationale involved in an officer's decision making. Farm Watch is particularly creative because it contains certain elements of the traditional crime watch model and adapts other elements to an agricultural setting. For instance, farmers in their fields or in remote areas of the county use cell phones to call police directly. The deputy assigned to a specific area has a cell phone in the patrol vehicle and can therefore respond more rapidly and receive better information directly from the complainant (farmer) rather than have the information relayed through a dispatcher.

Problems of rural policing affect countries other than the U.S. For instance, the Telford Division of West Mercia Constabulary in the U.K. is a high technology town located within the pastoral setting of Shropshire. Modern industry has arrived in the area and presented some interesting challenges with regard to adequate staffing and appropriate planning. The Division covers 874 square kilometers or 524 square miles and the local constabulary uses the "Four Track" approach to police this vast and diverse community. This "Four Track" style allows them to prioritize the allocation of their officers by first responding to emergencies, then concentrating their efforts in areas with repetitive problems, maintaining good relationships with the citizens, and finally encouraging partnership ventures with community groups to increase the quality of police service.

In rural Essex (in the U.K.), several smaller police stations were closed and community policing teams were created in an effort to more efficiently police this sprawling landscape. These teams will share facilities with other organizations in an effort to conserve resources for more appropriate police use such as forensic examinations and criminal prosecutions.

Resources are even more precious in South Africa, where nearly 50% of the population resides in rural areas and roughly 75% are considered impoverished. The majority of these individuals lack the means to protect themselves or their property and have come to expect little from local law enforcement because the nearest officer may be many miles away. Occurrences of theft and violence are frequent and expected. Law enforcement in this environment is clearly reactive and quite often ineffective.

In the U.S., the economy enjoyed unprecedented growth in the 1990s. Yet rural law enforcement agencies have struggled with limited resources and inadequate staffing. Whereas the national crime rate exhibits an overall decline, rural crime has declined at a much slower pacer. This reported decline in rural crime may not exist because many smaller agencies either lack the ability or the will to report criminal offenses to state or federal crime databases. Continuing to cloud the issue of rural policing is the lack of scholarly research in the area. Although contemporary information does exist, most of it is anecdotal. This does not invalidate its use, however, because clearly many departments are ingenious in their approach to providing the best service possible with limited resources. Furthermore, it would appear that state and federal agencies are not as reluctant as they once were to fund innovative strategies proposed by small or rural agencies.

Rural policing will continue to pose a problem to scholars and practitioners alike because large amounts of land will continue to be serviced by small numbers of officers. Proactive programs combined with local community involvement will be crucial to any successful strategy to reduce crime in this environment.

ROBERT E. GRUBB JR.

References and Further Reading

Brinkworth, B. (1998). Rural justice: The challenge of policing an agricultural community, *Sheriff Times*, V(6). Available at: http://www.communitypolicing.org/publications/shtimes/s6_wi98/s6brin.htm. [Retrieved on November 14, 2000].

Churchill, N. (1996). Rural Maine communities adopt a joint approach, *Sheriff Times*, 1(1). Available at: http://www.communitypolicing.org/publications/shtimes/s1church.htm [Retrieved on November 15, 2000].

Coblentz, B. (1999). Locked doors replace trust in rural areas, *Mississippi Community News*, Starkville, MS, Mississippi State University, Office of Agricultural Communications.

Donnermeyer, J.F. (1995). *Crime and Violence in Rural Communities*, North Central Regional Educational Laboratory. Available at: http://www.ncrel.org/sdrs/areas/issues/envrnmnt/drugfree/v1donner.htm. [Retrieved on December 18, 2000].

Estes, J. (1999). Rural county tops the field in innovation. *Sheriff Times*, 2(9). Available at: http://www.communitypolicing.org/publications/shtimes/s9_su99/s9estes.htm. [Retrieved on November 15, 2000].

Ntuli, S. and Louw, A. (1999). *The Challenge of Policing Rural Crime*, Institute for Security Studies. Available at: http://www.iss.co.za/Pubs/Crime%201Index/2.5/The%20challenge.html. [Retrieved on December 18, 2000].

Policing Rural Essex: Launch of Community Policing Teams (April 16, 1999). Available at: http://www.essex.police.uk/pages/about/a_rural3.htm [Retrieved on November 14, 2000].

Sims, V.H. (1988). *Small Town and Rural Police*, Springfield, IL, Charles C. Thomas.

Weisheit, R.A., Falcone, D.N. and Wells, L.E. (1994). *Rural Crime and Rural Policing*, National Institute of Justice: Research in Action. U.S. Department of Justice, Office of Justice Programs.

Welcome to the Telford Division of West Mercia Constabulary Home Page (November 1, 1999). Available at: http://www.wwestmercia.police.uk/telford/contents.htm [Retrieved on November 14, 2000].

See also **Police: Administration and Organization; Police: Community Policing; Police: Municipal or Urban; Police: Patrol**

Police: Use of Deadly Force

American police officers possess a great amount of discretion in the use of deadly force. Under English common law, upon which American law is based, a police officer was authorized to use deadly force in self-defense or to prevent a felon from escaping apprehension. This "fleeing felon rule" dates back to the Middle Ages, when virtually all felons were punished by death after trial. For practical purposes, it made little difference whether the felon died before or after the trial.

Many crimes considered felonies under common law were only misdemeanors by the turn of the 20th century. As a result, some states and police departments adopted stricter guidelines governing police use of deadly force, including such measures as the "forcible felony rule" that allowed officers to use deadly force only in cases of violent crimes such as rape or murder. By the 1970s, there was a movement to use guidelines established by the Model Penal Code as a basis for police use of deadly force. The Model Penal Code stated that the use of deadly force was not justifiable unless the arrest was for a felony and the officer reasonably believed that the crime for which the arrest was being made involved the use of deadly force or that there was a substantial risk that the person being arrested would cause death or bodily harm if not immediately apprehended.

Most states and the federal government, however, refused to lessen the discretion of the police to use deadly force. The events that occurred on October 3, 1974, changed all of that. On that night, police officers in Memphis, Tennessee, responded to a house prowler call. Upon arriving, the officers obtained information from a neighbor who stated she heard glass breaking in the adjacent house. While one officer radioed for assistance, the other investigated the situation, where he heard a door slam and saw a person run across the back yard. When the fleeing suspect stopped by a 6-feet fence, the officer observed that the suspect was a 17- or 18-year-old male and unarmed. The officer was sure that if the suspect climbed the fence he would escape; thus he made known his intent to arrest. When the suspect did not stop, the officer shot him in the back of the head. The young man later died on the operating table. Ten dollars and a purse taken from the house were found on the body of Edward Garner.

Garner's father filed a lawsuit against the officer, the police department, and the city. The case took over 10 years to decide (and the civil suit took 20 years to decide). The decision of the Supreme Court in this case became a landmark in police law that altered police practices nationwide. The Supreme Court did not declare the use of deadly force unconstitutional, only that its use to prevent the escape of a felon who posed no threat of death or grievous bodily harm was unconstitutional.

In deciding under what circumstances the use of deadly force might be appropriate, the Court relied heavily on the Model Penal Code's version of police use of force. In the end, the Court held that the police use of deadly force was not appropriate "unless it is necessary to prevent the escape and the officer has probable cause to believe that the suspect poses significant threat of death or serious physical injury to the officer or others."

This case set a standard for police use of deadly force, although many questions still remained concerning the practical application of the rule. Lower courts decided most of these issues. Most of these decisions required the courts to determine under what circumstances the decision in *Garner* would be applied. The greatest number of these cases centered on whether or not a seizure had occurred. The Fourth Amendment states that "The right of people to be secure in their persons, houses, papers, and effects against unreasonable searches and seizures shall not be violated ...," which means that police must obey certain rules when seizing people or their things.

One of the cases in this area dealt with unapprehended individuals killed in chases by the police. In *Galas v. McKee* 801 F.2d. 200 (1986), the court ruled that an individual who is killed in an automobile accident while fleeing the police is not "seized" and not entitled to a Fourth Amendment claim. In a similar case, *Cameron v. City of Pontiac, Michigan* 813 F.2d 782 (1987), the court held that even though shot at by police officers during a chase, an offender who runs into traffic while being chased by police is not seized under the Fourth Amendment. This issue was ultimately addressed by the Supreme Court in *Brower v. County of Inyo* 489 U.S. 593 (1987). In this case, Brower had stolen a car and was driving at a high speed to elude police. An 18-wheeled tractor-trailer was placed in the road behind a hill that blocked it from view. The police also positioned a police car with its lights on to blind Brower. Brower was killed in the crash as a result of the roadblock. His family sued the police department, arguing that the roadblock was an excessive use of force. The Supreme Court ruled that the government's intentional termination of an individual's freedom of movement is a form of seizure; thus, any forcible action taken by the police results in a seizure subject to Fourth Amendment provisions, and any injury or death that results from that seizure will be judged concerning the proper use of deadly force.

In the *Garner* decision, the Court stated that the use of force is unconstitutional unless "... the officer has probable cause to believe that the suspect poses a significant threat of death or serious physical injury to the officer or others." The Court, however, did not delineate what would constitute a threat of death or serious physical injury. Lower courts have made several rulings that further defined what is to be considered adequate threat. One of the cases was *Ryder v. City of Topeka* 814 F.2d. 1412 (1987). In this case, a young female was involved in the robbery of a pizza parlor. The police had prior knowledge of the robbery but did not know if the suspects were armed. At the scene, an officer saw one of the suspects with a knife, but he did not know if the others were armed. When the suspects fled, one officer chased Ryder. As they neared a residential area, the officer shot Ryder, stating he was afraid if she made it into one of the houses she might take a hostage or injure residents. Ryder was not armed when she was shot. The issue brought before the Court was whether using deadly force based on possible future actions is a violation of the Fourth Amendment. The Court ruled the officer reasonably could have believed that the lives of others were in danger if Ryder escaped, so the use of deadly force was authorized. This established the "future dangerousness" rule concerning the use of deadly force.

In a similar case, the Court addressed what constituted imminent danger to the officer or others. In *Hinojosa v. City of Terrell, Texas* 834 F.2d 1223 (1985), the police were called to a pool hall fight. At the scene, officers used force on one of the persons fighting. The owner of the pool hall stated that he tried to refrain the officers from using force and they pointed a gun at him. Hinojosa filed suit against the officers. The court found that an officer does not make a seizure or use excessive force when using a weapon to make someone back off with no intent to arrest him or her.

The appellate courts also decided on whether other police weapons could be considered deadly force when used. In *Garcia v. Wyckoff* 615 F.Supp. 217 (1985), a police officer threw a flashlight at Garcia as he was fleeing the police. Garcia stated he sustained serious injuries as a result. The Tenth Circuit Court of Appeals ruled that an individual who was not killed in an incident with the police could not use *Garner* as the basis for a suit against them.

The response to *Tennessee v. Garner* 471 U.S. 1 (1985) by police officers was split. Many were outraged that their discretion on use of force was limited. They saw it as a severe restriction on effective law enforcement because, by removing an officer's right to use deadly force on fleeing felons, offenders would be allowed to escape justice because the police could not use force to effect the arrest. Other police officers welcomed the strict guidelines. With the rise in lawsuits against officers for wrongful deaths, many welcomed a definite court ruling governing the practice. With respect to the use of deadly force against fleeing felons, officers were less likely to have to make a split-second decision on whether to shoot or not and have to worry if the courts would support the decision.

Despite initial claims of injustice, it would appear that the *Garner* decision has had a significant and positive influence on police officers. The police now have a firm basis for determining when and when not to use deadly force under many circumstances. In situations where split-second decisions are made concerning life and death, no rule can be adequate. In some situations, a violent offender who could have been apprehended with deadly force may escape. Likewise, some nonthreatening offenders may be unnecessarily subjected to deadly force. However, simply knowing when the use of deadly force is not permissible under law may prevent an officer from taking actions that could lead to unnecessary injury and litigation.

Probably the greatest, and least recognized, impact of the *Garner* decision is its influence upon the police departments and supervisory personnel. Although many large police departments already had deadly force policies in effect—many of which were at least as strict as the ruling in *Garner*—that decision set a standard by which smaller departments could base their policies. Additionally, it gave guidance as to where the deadly force lines were to be drawn for those departments that had more lenient guidelines than those of the *Garner* decision. This took the burden off supervisors and policy makers concerning police use of deadly force as the courts' rulings spelled out what was and was not allowed. Furthermore, knowing what actions the courts would consider constitutional and what would be considered violate could save the department and the supervisors lost time and money in lawsuits.

Other countries around the world vary in terms of violence and, therefore, the expectations of law enforcement are varied. In some countries in the

Caribbean, community policing is a matter of policy and the people of these countries are very interested in the actions of their police officers. In 1960, references to use of force by police officers stated that officers should use only as much force as necessary, whereas by 2001 any reference to the use of force by police was omitted. This has caused a great deal of public discourse in Trinidad. For example, early in 2000, an officer in Trinidad shot and killed a young woman who the police claimed had entered the station cursing and threatening the officer who had arrested a relative of hers. An inquest was ordered into her death and the officer was subsequently charged with murder.

Conversely, Brazil, which has one of the worst records of urban police violence in the Americas, is also struggling with this issue. In 1992, in the greater metropolitan area of São Paulo alone, police killed 1470 civilians. When comparing citizen killings by Brazilian police with those in U.S. cities, the Rio police annually kill almost as many citizens as all U.S. police forces combined. The comparison is more dramatic when you consider that Rio's population is 5.5 million and the U.S. population is over 250 million. Another country struggling with this issue is Guyana. As in the U.S., police use of deadly force in Guyana is only lawful in certain circumstances, which include defense of property, arrest and detention of dangerous felonies, and prevention of minor crimes.

JEFFERY T. WALKER AND AMY C. VANHOUTEN

References and Further Reading

Blackstone, W. 1765. *Commentaries on English Common Law.* Oxford, U.K., Clarendon Press.

Deosaran, R. 2002. Community policing in the Carribbean: Context, community and police capability, *Policing* 25(1), 125–146.

Fyfe, J.J. 1988. Police use of deadly force: Research and reform, *Justice Quarterly,* 5(2), 165–205.

Fyfe, J.J. and Walker. J.T. 1991. Garner plus five years: An examination of supreme court intervention and legislative prerogatives, *American Journal of Criminal Justice,* 14(2), 167–188.

Geller, William A. and Michael S. Scott. 1992. *Deadly Force: What We Know.* Washington, DC: Police Executive Research Forum.

Hall, J.C. 1988. Police use of deadly force to arrest: A constitutional standard, *FBI Law Enforcement Bulletin,* 20–29.

Huggins, M.K. 2000. Urban violence and police privatization in brazil: Blended invisibility, *Social Justice,* 27(2), 113–134.

American Law Institute. 1962. *Model Penal Code.*

See also **Police: Brutality and Corruption; Police: Disciplinary Actions and Internal Affairs**

Police: Vice and Special Units

Policing in America is portrayed in the popular media as glamorous work carried out mostly by specialists, such as detectives, undercover officers, and specially trained crime scene investigators. Although this media image is often more a caricature than an accurate depiction of *real* police work, the portrayal of law enforcement organizations as being centered on trained specialists is actually a keen observation. This entry focuses on police specialization in general and about vice specialization in particular. It attempts to explain the origins of special policing units and gives emphasis to the activities of a vice unit. The essay also considers current trends in police specialization and speculates whether this mode of organization will be effective into the future given the changes is modern policing philosophies.

Specialization in Policing

In order to understand why modern American policing is organized by functional specialties, like vice and juvenile delinquency, it is necessary to look back to the early 20th century, a period marked by rationalism, widespread immigration, and urbanization. These are the philosophical and social conditions out of which police professionalism and the development of the modern police organization emerged.

Police Professionalism

The popular explanation for the movement toward police professionalism in the early 20th century has been that it was a response to widespread police corruption of the previous century. During the 19th century, local politics influenced all aspects of American policing. Police officers were often portrayed as corrupt and ineffective. Much of the corruption was related to police involvement in noncriminal matters such as the issuing of licenses and managing elections (Fosdick, 1920). The corruption also included regular payoffs to police to ensure the nonenforcement of sumptuary laws like gambling, prostitution, and after-hour liquor sales. The average citizen thought of the police as "political hacks" and, therefore, the police were afforded little or no respect.

An alternative view of this period presents the origins of police professionalism in America as a class struggle (Deakin, 1988). In the late 19th century waves of immigrants landed on the shores of the U.S. The growth of industrialization led many of these newcomers to settle in large cities like Chicago and New York. Between 1825 and 1855, New York's population jumped from 166,000 to 630,000. The U.S., as a whole, saw a 500% increase in urbanization between 1870 and 1916. In many U.S. cities, the political machines found power in their immigrant constituency; political power in the inner city was used to improve conditions and social mobility of the immigrants. Police corruption was simply a tool used by the political machinery to accomplish this goal.

The Progressive Movement, of which police professionalism was a part, was a response to these emerging political forces that some believed would result in a deterioration of American values. Deakin (1988) had this to say about the Progressive Movement:

> The progressive movement campaign, a loose alliance of Protestant clergy, lawyers, doctors, bankers, insurance men, business men and other established American reformers, set up societies for the suppression of vice and associations for the maintenance of law and order to accomplish a moral regeneration of America. They pressed municipal officials to enforce laws on drinking, gambling, prostitution, and Sunday business. (p. 23)

Progressive reformers believed that if they could release the police from the influence of the local political machinery they would be better able to enforce laws against behaviors that violated traditional moral codes. They believed that only an apolitical, professional police department could be effective. Toward this end, reformers believed that through better training; upgrading the quality of personnel; and management efficiency, policing could assume a place among the other more established professions such as law and medicine.

Organizing for Professionalism

For the progressives, police reform meant creating organizations that eliminated politics and citizen influence.

The progressives were guided by the work of Max Weber, who noted two ideal ways of organizing social relationships: (1) by developing strong personal ties, and (2) by setting up general rules (Collins and Makowsky, 1998). The earliest forms of police organization in America come from the first model. They were based on a sense of communal obligation, consisting of a night watch and constabulary, without any single specialized agency of social control. Under the constabulary all able-bodied men were responsible for assuming a period of service, during the daytime hours, addressing the legal complaints of their neighbors. With the night watch, adult men took turns spending the evening looking for fires, while also reporting on the exact time and weather. Both of these roles were voluntary and considered a part of the onus of the community.

However, the social and economic conditions of the 19th century led to a breakdown of these strong social bonds, which, in turn, necessitated the second form of organization, popularly known as a bureaucracy. Weber's model of bureaucracy included a hierarchical structure; management by rules (that applied to everyone); specialization in the division of labor; and the maintenance of impersonal relations, so that decisions could be made rationally and without emotional influences (Gerth and Mills, 1946; Munro, 1974; Johnston, 1993). The reformers chose a military form of bureaucracy because it was thought to provide both discipline *and* efficiency. The controls provided by the military discipline would help deter influences of local politics whereas the bureaucratic organization, particularly in terms of specialized work tasks, would maximize efficiency.

Vice as a Specialty Area in Police Organizations

Vice activity was of special interest to early police organizations. Vice laws are those that prohibit behaviors that offend the community's moral code. They include transgressions that lack an easily identifiable victim and are generally related to commerce in illegal goods and services such as drugs, gambling, and prostitution. Vice squads—historically referred to as purity squads—are specialized police units made up of plainclothes officers who investigate and enforce laws aimed at protecting the moral welfare and physical health of citizens (Mijares and Klinger, 2002). From this perspective the vice squad is charged with upholding the moral and social order, a mandate with inherent problems as reflected in Wilbur Miller's discussion of "blue laws," that is, prohibitions against secular business or amusements on Sunday.

The "victim" is not any individual, but the community's standard of proper behavior. People in small towns may agree on moral standards, but in heterogeneous cities behavior varies according to social class and ethnic group, particularly on how to spend one's time on Sunday. The policeman is required to enforce laws that seem to dictate cultural or religious conformity instead of protecting individuals against crime. Whenever he enforces or ignores the laws, somebody is bound to complain of oppression or negligence of duty (Miller, 1977, 127–28).

Above, Miller is recognizing that the vice laws are an issue of morals rather than a prevention of, or protection from, some sort of immediate harm to the citizenry. Because some are offended by the behavior whereas others enjoy it, a conflict is inevitable. From this conflict a system of policing evolves with a manifest function of eliminating vice and a latent function of actually perpetuating and managing it. In an extensive study of the vice industry in a large American city Chambliss (1975) explicitly describes this process.

> I saw a bet made and called for a $1000 in one of these games. During this game, the highest stakes game I witnessed in 6 years of the study, the police lieutenant in charge of the vice squad was called in to supervise the game—not, need I add, to break up the game or make any arrests, but only to insure against violence. (Chambliss, 1975, 149)

In this scenario vice squads are like referees who keep the game proceeding in an orderly fashion rather than putting an end to it.

Over the years the integrity of many police departments has been tarnished by the corruption stemming from the enforcement (or lack thereof) of vice laws. In fact, Chambliss (1975) argues that the vice industry has historically been orchestrated by members of local business, political, and law enforcement communities in conjunction with more conventional criminals. He writes of "cabals," comprising corrupt public officials and powerful community members who operate regional crime syndicates. Ironically, this corruption results from moral crusades against behaviors labeled as vice. Middle-class moral entrepreneurs seize on a behavior, typically of the lower class, that offends their sensibilities and seek to stamp it out (Ranulf, 1938; Gusfield, 1963). If they are successful in their campaign against the specified depravity, new sanctions are established, or older ones better enforced, against the offending behavior. However, because the vices are victimless crimes, it is hard to achieve a real consensus with regard to their social detriment. No matter how convincing the crusaders, there will be dissent within the community with regard to the proper enforcement of the law.

More recently, many police officers have come to view vice activities not so much as problems in and of themselves, but as the *cause* of more serious problems.

Based on the Wilson and Kelling (1982) article in the *Atlantic Monthly* entitled "Broken Windows: The Police and Neighborhood Safety," the police today often see vice activity simply as a visible sign of community disorder which, if not fixed, will result in the appearance of more serious violent crimes. From this perspective, the police are more apt to vigorously enforce vice laws.

Vice Work

The nature of vice crimes, such as prostitution, gambling, and the sale of illegal drugs, presents special difficulties for the police. For example, citizens do not readily report these crimes as they would a violent crime, like robbery, or a property crime, like burglary because they are viewed as "victimless" crimes. In order to uncover and investigate vice crimes, the police are often forced to use covert methods such as wiretaps, undercover operations, and informants. Even when maximally effective, these covert tactics can present ethical problems and unintended consequences for police and citizens.

Wiretaps

Wiretaps are one form of electronic surveillance that can be particularly useful to vice officers. These investigations involve the monitoring of telephone conversations from a particular phone or phones that are subscribed to by one or more people involved in an ongoing conspiracy to commit vice crimes. By listening in on conversations, and confirming the information through informants, other forms of surveillance, and the execution of search warrants, the police are able to build solid cases on entire criminal networks. One problem with wiretap investigations is that the police sometimes must listen to private, personal conversations involving individuals not even involved in the investigation. Therefore, it is sometimes difficult to know where to best strike the balance between the community's right to safety (i.e., from vice offenders) and the individual's right to privacy (i.e., from government intrusion).

Undercover Operations

Undercover work involves police officers pretending to be someone other than who they really are in order to gather intelligence, catch people engaged in vice activities, and infiltrate illegal networks. For example, one strategy used by the police to investigate alleged prostitution, particularly when it occurs in open areas such as along city streets, is the use of "decoys." Decoys are often young female police officers who dress provocatively and stand visibly in open areas frequented by prostitutes and those who solicit them, known as "johns." If a decoy is approached by a prospective male customer, she must engage in a conversation with him to confirm whether he will actually solicit her for sex. If during the conversation the male offers to pay the decoy some amount of money in return for sex, he is arrested, either immediately or as he leaves the area. Likewise, male vice squad officers are sometimes used to solicit female prostitutes. Like the female decoys, the male undercover solicitors must present themselves as being interested in sex and willing to pay for it. It has been reported that male vice officers have even gone so far as to actually have sex with prostitutes in order to prove they (the prostitutes) were engaged in illegal activities (Marx, 1988).

Undercover vice investigations can present a variety of moral dilemmas for the officers. For example, undercover officers are often required to lie about who they are. In doing so, the officers sometimes develop (then betray) close friendship bonds with those they are investigating and later have to arrest (Nolan, 2002). Marx (1988) suggests that officers often resolve these dilemmas by focusing on the good that will come from the law enforcement activity. Walker (1992) argues that an unintended consequence of this undercover deception is that the officers can become untrustworthy. Once police officers become accustomed to lying in one context, perhaps they will find it easier to lie in others, such as during court testimony.

There are more undesirable consequences of undercover work for the vice officer. For example, the odd (and long) hours can strain personal relationships, and the frequent contacts with those in a criminal environment can affect the officer's moral and ethical judgments and his or her own sense of identity (Marx, 1988). In addition, undercover vice work often involves less supervision and more opportunities for officer discretion. This situation can also result in negative consequences for the target of a vice investigation, such as when the undercover officers use excessive coercion or trickery in order to "instigate" the crime. Innocent third parties may also be exposed to direct harm during an undercover investigation, such as when undercover officers participate in crimes (such as theft) so that their true identity is not revealed prematurely (Marx, 1988).

Informants

The use of informants is an important aspect of vice investigations. In many cases it is an informant who first notifies the police about the nature and extent of a particular vice activity. Informants have a variety of motivations for coming forward to help the police; however, most are not altruistic. Many informants are trying to avoid criminal charges, eliminate competition in a particular vice market, or simply trying to earn money to support a drug habit (Marx, 1988). The police may use the informant in several ways. In many cases an informant simply provides as much information as possible about the vice activity and those individuals involved. Less frequently, informants introduce undercover officers into the criminal network or to someone they know outside the network who, in turn, becomes an unwitting informant for the police. Some informants are requested to wear electronic monitoring equipment while they engage in an illegal vice activity like gambling or to make a controlled purchase of an illegal drug. There are many problems associated with the use of informants in police work in general and vice investigations in particular. These problems include the following: (a) informants sometimes go beyond what is legal or ethical to make a particular case, (b) informants sometimes lie to the officers about the facts, and (c) informants are rarely called to testify in court regarding the integrity and accuracy of the information they provide.

Since the early 20th century vice control has been an important part of American policing. It was one of the first forms of specialization in modern police organizations and remains an important focus in many departments even today. Clearly, vice investigations present unique challenges for the police and require special training, tactics, and organizational policies to prepare officers to successfully deal with them.

Current Trends in Police Specialization

Vice control is but one of many areas of police specialization that have emerged over the past 100 years or more. The earliest police bureaucracies included only a few areas of specialization. For example, in the early 1900s the Philadelphia Police Department had only three operational specialties: uniform patrol, traffic, and criminal investigations. Likewise, the St. Louis Police Department had the same three specialized units, but the criminal investigations unit included squads specializing in gambling and "morality" (Fosdick, 1920). In 1967 the President's Commission on Law Enforcement and the Administration of Justice published its recommendations for improving the quality of policing in the U.S. The report provided an organizational chart of a "well organized" municipal police department that included patrol, traffic, detectives, juvenile, and vice units (Presidents Commission on Law Enforcement and Administration of Justice (1967)).

In most police organizations today, these areas of specialization are still very important. However, many more forms of specialization have emerged over the years. Data collected by the Bureau of Justice Statistics reveal that 82% of the municipal police departments in the U.S. that serve populations of 100,000 or more have

Table 1. Specialized Units in Major Municipal Police Agencies and in State Police Agencies, 2000

Specialized Units	Municipal Police (N = 227)		State Police (N = 49)	
	Number	%	Number	%
Bias crime	25	11%	1	2%
Child abuse	135	60%	4	8%
Community crime prevention	180	80%	10	20%
Community policing	148	65%	12	25%
Crime analysis	188	83%	23	47%
Cyber crime	45	20%	17	35%
Domestic violence	140	62%	5	10%
Drug education in school	161	71%	19	39%
Drunk drivers	72	32%	17	35%
Environmental crime	14	6%	7	14%
Gangs	154	68%	9	18%
Juvenile crime	161	71%	5	10%
Missing children	107	47%	15	31%
Prosecutor relations	72	32%	7	14%
Repeat offenders	51	23%	2	4%
Victim assistance	93	41%	9	18%
Youth outreach	95	42%	3	6%

Source: Bureau of Justice Statistics, Law Enforcement Management and Administrative Statistics (LEMAS): 2000 Sample Survey of Law Enforcement Agencies (Computer file). ICPSR version. Washington, DC: U.S. Dept. of Commerce, Bureau of the Census (producer), 2001. Ann Arbor, MI: Inter-university Consortium for Political and Social Research (distributor), 2003.

full-time drug enforcement units. Other specialized units in these agencies include the following: community crime prevention (80%), gangs (68%), child abuse (60%), community policing (65%), domestic violence (62%), drug education in schools (71%), and juvenile crime (71%). These same specialty units can be found in state police units too, albeit at a lower frequency (see Table 1) (Bureau of Justice Statistics, 2003).

The Effectiveness of Police Specialization

It is clear that policing has become more complex over the years and police organizations have responded by adding new areas of specialization. For the early reformers, making police organizations more professional was the solution to the problem of crime in a modern society. However, by the late 1970s and early 1980s, crime in the U.S. was continuing to rise, citizens were more fearful than ever before, and minorities believed they were not being treated fairly by the police or the criminal justice system (Kelling and Moore, 1988). In response to these growing problems, a new perspective on policing emerged that challenged

the "professional" policing paradigm. Community policing is based on the belief that the police and the community should work together to solve mutual problems related to crime and quality of life (Thurman, Zhoa, and Giacomazzi, 2001). From this perspective one might ask whether a bureaucratic form of organization, as Weber described, is still needed. Remember, Weber's model included a hierarchical structure, impersonal relations with employees and customers (so that everyone is treated equally and fairly), and the division of labor by functional specialty. It seems that to be successful in community policing, officers must be close to the citizens and free to make decisions, commit resources, and take actions that might normally require higher levels of authority. In order to accomplish this goal, organizational hierarchies must be flattened. In addition, community policing necessitates the development of strong ties between the police and the community. Therefore, the bureaucratic principle, that relations between police and citizens should be "purposely impersonal," must be abandoned. But, what about the third aspect of bureaucracy: the division of labor into functional specialties? Should that be abandoned too? The bureaucratic assumption that organizational effectiveness and efficiency are maximized with the division of labor into functional specialties is not necessarily inconsistent with the community policing philosophy. It simply requires that police are able to pull resources from specialized units as needed in order to deal in a coordinated way with specific problems in specific neighborhoods (see Alpert and Dunham, 1997).

The Impact of Accreditation on Police Organization

A growing trend in policing today is that of accreditation. In 1979, the four leading law enforcement organizations in the U.S.—the International Association of Chiefs of Police (IACP), National Organization of Black Law Enforcement Officers (NOBLE), National Sheriffs' Association (NSA), and the Police Executive Research Forum (PERF)—joined forces to develop national law enforcement standards and accreditation. The Commission on Accreditation for Law Enforcement Agencies (CALEA) was established as an independent accrediting agency. The accreditation process is voluntary, but provides enough benefits to law enforcement organizations that many have joined in. According to James D. Brown, the Associate Director of COLEA, two-thirds of all law enforcement agencies in the U.S. with more that 1000 officers are either accredited or in the process for being accredited (Nolan and Brown, 2003). Accreditation is based on a set of standards for the organization, management, and administration of a police agency. It also sets standards for the implementation of specialized operational units within the agency, including criminal investigations; drugs, vice, and organized crime; juvenile operations; crime prevention and community relations; and unusual occurrences and special operations.

The impact of accreditation on the future of police organizations (particularly, special units and on the movement toward community policing as an organizing philosophy) is yet to be seen. One might speculate that if accreditation standards remove the counterproductive components of bureaucracy (i.e., hierarchy and impersonal relations) and yet maintain the elements of specialization that work in the community policing paradigm, accreditation itself might be a facilitator of future change. However, accreditation standards that maintain elements of the professional bureaucratic model work will clearly work against this change.

JAMES J. NOLAN AND NORMAN CONTI

References and Further Reading

Alpert, G. and Dunham, R. 1997. *Policing Urban America*, 3rd ed., Prospect Heights, IL, Waveland Press.

Bureau of Justice Statistics 2003. *Law Enforcement Management and Administrative Statistics (LEMAS), 2000 Sample Survey of Law Enforcement Agencies*, [Computer file], ICPSR version; Washington, DC, U.S. Dept. of Commerce, Bureau of the Census [producer], 2001; Ann Arbor, MI, Inter-university Consortium for Political and Social Research [distributor].

Chambliss, W.J. 1975. Vice, corruption, bureaucracy, and power, in Chambliss, W., Ed., *Criminal Law in Action*, New York, Hamilton Publishing Company.

Collins, Randall and Michael Makowsky 1998. *Discovery Society*, 6th edition. Boston: McGraw Hill.

Deakin, T.J. 1988. *Police Professionalism: The Renaissance of American Law Enforcement*, Springfield, IL, Charles C. Thomas Publishers.

Fosdick, R.B. 1920. *American Police Systems*, New York, The Century Co.

Gerth, H.H. and Mills, C.W. 1946. *From Max Weber: Essays in Sociology*, New York, Oxford University Press.

Gusfield, J.R. 1963. *Symbolic Crusade*, Urbana, IL, University of Illinois Press.

Johnston, K. 1993. *Beyond Bureaucracy: A Blueprint and Vision for Government That Works*, Homewood, IL, Business One Irwin.

Kelling, G.L. and Moore, M. 1988. The evolving strategy of policing, in *Perspectives on Policing*, No. 4, Washington, DC, National Institute of Justice and Harvard University.

Marx, G.T. 1988. *Undercover: Police Surveillance in America*, Berkley, CA, University of California Press.

Mijares, T. and Klinger, D. 2002. Police: Policing complainant-less crimes, in Dressler, J., Ed., *The Encyclopedia of Crime and Justice*, 2nd ed., New York, McMillan Reference USA.

Miller, W.R. 1977. Never on Sunday: Moralistic reformers and police in London and New York City, 1830–1870, in Bayley, D.H., Ed., *Police and Society*, Beverly Hills, CA, Sage Publications.

Munro, J.L. 1974. *Administrative Behavior and Police Organization*. Cincinnati, OH, Anderson.

Nolan, J.J. 2002. From vice cop to sociology prof.: A long journey to a familiar place, *The American Sociologist*, 33(2).

Personal telephone conversation between James J. Nolan and Mr. Brown on August 26, 2003.

Presidents Commission on Law Enforcement and Administration of Justice 1967. *Task Force Report: The Police*, Washington, DC, U.S. Government Printing Office.

Ranulf, S. 1938. *Moral Indignation and Middle Class Psychology: A Sociological Study*, Copenhagen, Denmark, Levin & Munksgaard.

Thurman, Q., Zhao, J. and Giacomazzi, A. 2001. *Community Policing in a Community Era: An Introduction and Exploration*, Los Angeles, CA, Roxbury.

Walker, S. 1992. *The Police in America: An Introduction*, New York, McGraw Hill.

Wilson, J.Q. and Kelling, G.L. 1982. Broken windows: Police and neighborhood safety, *The Atlantic Monthly*, 249.

See also **Police: Brutality and Corruption; Law Enforcement: Electronic Surveillance and Wiretapping**

Political Crimes against the State

Oppositional (or antisystemic) political crime refers to those actions committed by individuals, groups, and countries that want to change or dismantle a particular political or economic system, its institutions, the state, or interests aligned with the state (e.g., major corporations) (Ross, 2002).

Political crimes against the state can be either domestic or international. A domestic political crime includes a correctional officer violating a prisoner's civil, human, or constitutional rights here in the U.S. (Welch, 1996, 343–344). On the other hand, an international political crime would cover the 1998 bombing of the U.S. embassies in Kenya and Tanzania, allegedly committed by followers of Osama bin Laden (Reeve, 1999, Chap. 1).

In an effort to improve definitions of political crime and move toward a more analytic perspective, some experts have outlined acts that can and should be subsumed by political crimes. Others (Packer, 1962; Ingraham and Tokoro, 1969; Kittrie, 1972; Sagarin, 1973; Roebuck and Weeber, 1978; Beirne and Messerschmidt, 1992) have marshaled typologies. Additionally, various categories of political criminals (or perpetrators) (e.g., organizational, occupational, and individual) exist (Roebuck and Weeber, 1978, 7–8). There is, however, considerable debate over which political crimes in general, and which antisystemic political crimes in particular, to include in these categories.

In sum, typologies of political crime, albeit primarily antisystemic political crime, have categorized these actions based on: intent, target, degree of harm done to the state, situational location or profession of the violators, and degree of violence associated with the crime.

Types of Crimes against the State

Five major crimes against the state have been recognized in criminal law: subversion, sedition, treason, espionage, and terrorism. All of these practices have existed since the creation of the first state; however, the legal codification of them has varied with the growth of countries, sophistication of legal codes, and power of various constituencies inside states.

Oppositional political crimes can be regarded as a subset of "crimes against the administration of government" (Schmalleger, 2002, 454–463). This broader rubric includes such violations as: treason, misprision of treason, rebellion, espionage, sedition, subordination of perjury, false swearing, bribery, contempt, obstruction of justice, resisting arrest, escape, and misconduct in office. Some, but not all, of these crimes have a political motivation. In general, treason, misprision of treason, rebellion, espionage, sedition, bribery, and misconduct in office are traditionally considered to be political crimes.

Although the labels and actions that individuals, organizations, and states have ascribed to antisystemic political crime differ, this type of action has existed since the birth of the first state. Historically these oppositional political offenses have often exacted the most repressive responses by the government.

The lion's share of political crime definitions focus on its antigovernment nature. And it is safe to say that most people are familiar and comfortable with this interpretation. By the same token, definitions and the characteristics attributed to political crime have varied considerably over time. Because of a variety of factors, since the late 19th century, the doctrine of political crime has become increasingly limited in its scope and application and hedged with exceptions in those European democracies and constitutional monarchies that had adopted it into their codes (Ingraham and Tokoro, 1969, 147).

Nonviolent Oppositional Political Crimes

Although most criminal justice agencies sanction "political" offenders under traditional criminal laws (Kittrie and Wedlock, 1986, xi), there are four nonviolent antisystemic political crimes against the state that in contemporary times have been recognized inconsistently by some, but not all, scholars, policy makers, politicians, activists, and jurists.

In general, subversion, sedition, treason, and espionage are typically included in many of the criminal codes or legislation governing security and intelligence agencies of advanced industrialized countries. All of these actions have existed since the creation of the first state, however, their codification in legal statutes has varied among countries and may be associated with alternative mechanisms for quelling dissent and the sophistication of legal codes. Although misprision of treason and criminal syndicalism have been recognized as oppositional political crimes, in the last three decades these charges have been rarely applied in courts against so-called political criminal defendants.

Before reviewing the different antisystemic political crimes, a conceptualization of dissent (which is relevant and easily and typically confused with oppositional political crimes) is provided as a necessary backdrop.

Dissent

The simplest definition of dissent is a difference of opinion. Dissent, however, has been defined elsewhere as "the ideological label ascribed by national security agencies or those assuming this mandate to social conducts or opinion held by citizens of diverging political learning. It follows ... that dissent cannot be recognized by a determined behavior of social actors, but rather by the limits (of either an ethical or a formal nature) set to what is considered acceptable social and political behavior" (Faucher and Fitzgibbons, 1989, xx).

Further complicating matters is the awareness that the word dissent, and the behaviors it refers to, are embedded with other political crime concepts and practices. According to Turk (1982, 100), "[d]issent includes any mode of speaking out against the personages, actions, or structures of authority ... Each form of resistance may vary in regard to whether it is calculated or spontaneous (or instrumental versus expressive) and organized."

Undoubtedly, both governments and states have flexible criteria for identifying and responding to "acceptable and unacceptable dissent." Franks (1989) suggests that dissent can be classified into four categories based on the dimensions of legal–illegal and legitimate–illegitimate. According to him, "the state's response to it can be illustrated by classifying dissent along two dimensions: legal–illegal and legitimate–illegitimate."

The legal mechanisms for controlling dissent have been criticized because they typically "directly sanction or prohibit unwanted behavior by labelling it illegal. Instead, the law permits authorities to investigate, study, and report. This results in indirect penalizing" (Franks, 1989, 1), or what Whyte and MacDonald (1989) term "partial sanctioning."

This includes "hidden penalties such as negative personnel reports, or refusal to hire. ... These sorts of activities do not fit within the liberal-democratic legal tradition. They are outside standard legal and judicial concepts and practices" (Franks, 1989, 1). Whyte and MacDonald (1989) conclude that Western democracies have lost the ability to use legal concepts in the field of national security regarding dissent. Consequently, "this leads to extreme problems in making a distinction between legal and illegal dissent" (Franks, 1989, 11).

Subversion

Subversion refers to the act of "overthrow[ing] that which is established or existing" and is a term "used to delegitimize ideas and activities opposed to the established order, and hence to legitimize the states' acting against them, even through those ideas and activities are lawful" (Franks, 1989, 10). Building on Franks' (1989, 10–11) typology, the state defines subversion as an action that is "legal but illegitimate. Subversion is largely defined through a supposed link between internal dissent and so-called deviant foreign influences." In Great Britain, the 1989 Security Service Act defines subversion as "actions intended to overthrow or undermine parliamentary democracy by political, industrial or violent means" (s.1(2). "This definition clearly includes political and industrial activity that is both peaceful and lawful" (Gill, 1995, 91).

Sedition

Sedition has been defined as the "incitement of resistance to or insurrection against lawful authority" (Websters, 1980, 1037). In other contexts it is "communication or agreement intended to defame the government or to incite treason" (Schmalleger, 2002, 456). In the U.S., individuals judged to be engaging in sedition have been charged with violating the Sedition Act of 1798, ch. 74, 1 Stat. 596. In essence, it criminalizes any scandalous article written about the President or Congress. Later federal law defined seditious conspiracy as "If two or more persons in any State or Territory, or in any place subject to the jurisdiction of the United States, conspire to overthrow, put down, or destroy by force of authority, thereof, or by force to prevent, hinder, or delay the execution of any law of the United States, or by force to seize, take, or possess any property of the United States contrary to the authority thereof..." (18 U.S.C., Section 2384).

More commonly, those determined by authorities to have engaged in sedition are charged with seditious libel. Thus, the problem is embedded in the larger discussion of freedom of speech, especially that which criticizes government (Borovoy, 1985; Foerstel, 1998, Ch. 1). Furthermore, the criteria for defining acts as seditious libel are dynamic and subject to changes in political, economic, and social conditions. In its most expansive form, however, seditious libel may be said to embrace any criticism—true or false—of the form, constitution, policies, laws, officers, symbols, or conduct of government (Stone, 1983, 1425).

Understandably, the biggest difficulty with the crime of sedition is being able to specify "at what point in the continuum between the thought and the deed is it appropriate for the law to intervene" (Borovoy, 1985, 156). In general, "Speech which is likely to result in imminent violence is arguably dangerous enough to warrant legal intervention. On the other hand, speech which is not likely to culminate in this way does not warrant such intervention" (Borovoy, 1985, 156). In 1918, in an effort to shore up support for the entrance of the U.S. into World War I, and to prevent criticism of the war, which would damage recruiting efforts, the act was amended, becoming more specific, and was popularly referred to as the Sedition Act.

Occasionally, individuals are charged with seditious conspiracy. "Conspiracy is established by inference from the conduct of the parties. It is very rare that the agreement between the parties can be established by direct evidence; the evidence offered is usually purely circumstantial. To prove the agreement, evidence such as hearsay which would normally be inadmissible to establish any other criminal offense, may be admitted to show links in a chain of circumstances form which the common agreement may be inferred" (Grosman, 1972, 142).

Because of the cumbersome nature of the Sedition Act, the government has found it more convenient to charge and convict individuals under a number of acts that exist that virtually put a gag order on the statements of exemployees.

Treason

Treason refers to overt (i.e., nonsymbolic) acts aimed at overthrowing one's own government or state or murdering or personally injuring the sovereign (king or queen) or their family.

In the U.S., the Constitution (Article III, Section 3) specifically outlines what is meant by treason. According to this document, "Treason against the United States, shall consist only in levying War against them, or in adhering to their Enemies, giving them Aid and Comfort." Federal statutes use similar language, such as "Whoever, owing allegiance to the United States, levied war against them or adheres to their enemies, giving them aid and comfort within the United States or elsewhere is guilty of treason and shall suffer death, or shall be imprisoned not less than five years and fined under this title but not less than ten thousand dollars ($10,000); and shall be incapable of holding any office under the United States…" (18 U.S.C., Section 2381). And, many states either in their legislation or constitutions have specific sections which refer to treason (Schmalleger, 2002, 455).

Thus, it is "a criminal offense to publish false, scandalous, and malicious writings against the government, if done with intent to defame, or to excite the hatred of the people, or to stir up sedition or to excite resistance to law, or to aid the hostile designs of any foreign nation against the United States" (Packer, 1962, 82).

The appropriateness of the charge is always debatable. Historically treason has been a slippery concept for it is often recognized as criminal, whereas at other times it is not. Furthermore, prosecuting individuals and organizations for treason has been applied by the state in an erratic fashion.

Most importantly, because treason is a violation of allegiance, for the charge to have merit, one must be a citizen of the U.S. Thus, if you have lost, renounced, or were never a citizen of the U.S., the charge of treason does not apply (Schmalleger, 2002, 455).

Normally the offense is committed inside the U.S., but jurisdiction has expanded to outside America; several persons were successfully prosecuted for broadcasts deemed treasonous made from Axis countries during World War II (Packer, 1962, 80). "Most insurrections have been local affairs and have usually been handled under state treason, sedition, or subversive conspiracy statutes or under statutes designed to control riots and public disturbances" (Ingraham and Tokoro, 1969, 148).

Espionage or Spying

Spying, also called *sub rosa* crime or espionage (the act or practice of spying), is one of the most well-known acts of treason. It refers primarily to secretly obtaining information or intelligence about another, and typically hostile, country, its military or weaponry (Bryan, 1943; Laqueur, 1988). In short, espionage occurs when "gathering, transmitting, or losing information or secrets related to national defense with the intent or the reasonable belief that such information will be used against the United States" (Schmalleger, 2002, 455).

Various types of espionage exist, including "black espionage," a term for such things as "covert agents" involved in classical forms of spying, and "white espionage," referring to spying via space satellites, through code-breaking, or technical collection" (Hagan, 1990, 444). In 1917, the U.S. Congress passed the Espionage Act (18 U.S.C., Section 2384).

Violent Oppositional Political Crimes: Terrorism

During recent times, the majority of oppositional political crimes and those that have garnered the most amount of academic, government, and media attention are violent.

Although the crime of rebellion defined as "deliberate, organized resistance by force and arms, to the laws or operations of the government committed by a subject" exists in federal legislation (Schmalleger, 2002, 455), over the past three decades it has been rarely applied. Since the early 1960s, however, anti-systemic political terrorism has generated considerable attention. By far the greatest number of incidents of oppositional political crime during recent times fall under the rubric of terrorism.

Definitional and Conceptual Issues

Following Schmid's (1983) conceptualization, better and more concretely defined, terrorism is a method of combat in which random or symbolic victims become targets of violence. Through the use or threat of violence, other members of that group (e.g., class, nation, etc.) are placed in a state of chronic fear. The victimization of the target is considered extranormal by most observers, which creates an audience beyond the target of terror. According to Schmid, the purpose of terrorism is either to immobilize the target of terror in order to produce disorientation or compliance, or to mobilize secondary targets of demands (e.g., government) or targets of attention (e.g., public opinion) (Schmid, 1983, 100). This definition has many advantages and, with four qualifications, it is relatively appropriate (Ross, 1988a; 1988b).

Typologies

Several different types of oppositional terrorism (i.e., domestic, state-sponsored, and international) exist. Thus, it seems logical that each has a slightly different pattern of causation, and the relative importance of each contributing factor varies according to the type of terrorist act, the group that commits it, and its location across space and time.

Advanced industrialized democracies (especially Western Europe and Latin America) have been the political and economic systems most frequently targeted by oppositional terrorism during the contemporary period. Groups that have engaged in such antiregime terrorism have subscribed to a wide spectrum of ideologies. Terrorism has existed throughout the history of most of the advanced industrialized countries, however, it was most prominent during the 1960s and 1970s.

How Widespread Is the Problem?

Since the mid-1970s, there has been an increase in attempts to systematically collect data on terrorism. The prevailing impression given by the mass media, public officials, and experts concerned with international terrorism is that it is on the increase. In the main, the increase in terrorism is genuine and is not an artifact created by both better media and academic attention. Over the past two-and-a-half decades there has been a ragged increase with several peaks and valleys.

The increase in the volume of terrorist activity has been matched by its geographic spread. The number of countries experiencing some sort of terrorist activity each year has gradually increased. Terrorists operate with a fairly limited repertoire of attacks. Six basic tactics have accounted for 95% of all terrorist incidents including: bombings, assassinations, armed assaults, kidnappings, hijackings, and barricade and hostage incidents. In short, terrorists blow up things, kill people, or seize hostages. Every terrorist incident is essentially a variation on these three activities.

Theoretical Explanations of Political Crime

Few scholars have developed a theory of political crime. Merton (1964; 1966; 1968) provided one of the earliest explanations that, in part, touches on political crime. His anomic theory of deviance that partially explains political crime is used by Kelly (1972) and Alexander (1992a; 1992b).

An alternative perspective has been offered by Turk (1982). His structural conflict theory posits that although power and inequality are important factors in explaining political crime, the cultural gap between offenders and authorities is what establishes this divide. Although Turk's theory is interesting, it is limited in its explanatory power. Both Merton's and Turk's theories are useful in describing, and in some cases explaining, various types of political crime, but are not very helpful in accounting for all the vagaries of this phenomenon. What needs to be understood is the dynamic nature, the importance of context, and linking macro-with micro-level processes in political crime.

The New Explanation

Like so many other phenomena in the social and natural sciences, the process of political crime follows an interactive, iterative, or what I call "dynamic" pattern. One of the central hypotheses underlying contemporary research (Ross, 2002) is that political crime results from the interaction between antisystemic and state crime. More important to the understanding of political crime, however, is the relationship among situations or opportunities, organizations, and resource adequacy (i.e., the SOR relationship) (Ross, 2002, Ch. 2).

Political crime does not exist in a vacuum. Rather, it is affected by a series of factors that are endemic to the individuals who commit the crimes, the occupations they hold, the organizations that employ them (or they are members of), and more generally the context in which a particular crime exists. Thus, political crime is a response to a variety of subtle, ongoing, interacting, and changing psychological and structural factors manifested by perpetrators, victims, state agencies, and audiences.

JEFFREY IAN ROSS

References and Further Reading

Alexander, D. (1992a). *Applying Merton's Theory of Anomie to Political Criminality,* Paper presented to the American Society of Criminology Annual Meetings, New Orleans, LA.

Alexander, D. (1992b). *Political Crime: An Application of Merton's Theory of Social Structure and Anomie,* Masters Thesis, Virginia Polytechnic Institute and State University, VA.

Beirne, P. and Messerschmidt, J. (1992). *Criminology.* New York, Harcourt Brace Jovanovich.

Borovoy, A. (1985). Freedom of expression: Some recurring impediments, in Abella, R. and Rothman, M.L., Eds., *Justice Beyond Orwell,* Montreal, Canada, Les Editions Yvon Blais, pp. 125–160,

Bryan, G.S. (1943). *The Spy in America,* Philadelphia, PA, Lippincott.

Gill, P. (1995). Controlling state crimes by national security agencies, in Ross, J.I., Ed., *Controlling State Crime: An Introduction,* New York, Garland Publishing, pp. 81–114.

Laqueur, W. (1985). *A World of Secrets,* New York, The Twentieth Century Fund.

Faucher, P. and Fitzgibbins, K. (1989). Dissent and the state in Latin America, in Franks, C.E.S., Ed., *Dissent and the State,* Don Mills, Ontario, CA, Oxford University Press, pp. 138–168.

Foerstel, H.N. (1997). *Free Expression and Censorship in America,* Westport, CT, Greenwood Publishing.

Foerstel, H.N. (1998). *Banned in the Media,* Westport, CT, Greenwood Publishing.

Franks, C.E.S. (1989). *Dissent and the State,* Toronto, Canada, Oxford University Press.

Grosman, B.A., (1972). Political crime and emergency measures in Canada, in Adler, F. and Mueller, G.O.W., Eds. *Politics, Crime and the American Scene,* San Juan, Puerto Rico, North-South Center Press, pp. 141–146.

Hagan, F. (1990). *Introduction to Criminology: Theories, Methods, and Criminal Behavior,* Chicago, IL, Nelson-Hall.

Ingraham, B.L. and Tokoro, K. (1969). Political crime in the U.S. and Japan, *Issues in Criminology,* 4(2), 145–169.

Kelly, R.J. (1972). New political crimes and the emergence of revolutionary nationalist ideologies, in Adler, F. and Mueller, G.O.W., Eds. *Politics, Crime and the International Scene: An Inter-American Focus,* San Juan, Puerto Rico, North-South Center Press, pp. 23–35.

Kittrie, N.N. (1972). International law and political crime, in Adler F. and Mueller, G.O.W., Eds., *Politics, Crime and the International Scene: An Inter-American Focus,* San Juan, Puerto Rico, North-South Centre Press. pp. 91–95.

Kittrie, N.N. and Wedlock, E.D., Jr. (1986). *The Tree of Liberty: A Documentary History of Rebellion and Political Crime in America,* Baltimore, MD, Johns Hopkins University.

Laqueur, W. (1985). *A World of Secrets,* New York, The Twentieth Century Fund.

Packer, H.L. (1962). Offenses against the state, *The Annals of the American Academy,* 339, 77–89.

Reeve, S. (1999). *The New Jackaels.* Boston, MA, Northeastern University Press.

Roebuck, J. and Weeber, S.C. (1978). *Political Crime in the U.S.,* New York, Praeger.

Ross, J.I. (1988a). An events data base on political terrorism in Canada: Some conceptual and methodological problems, *Conflict Quarterly,* 8(2), 47–65.

Ross, J.I. (1988b). Attributes of political terrorism in Canada, 1960–1985, *Terrorism: An International Journal,* 11(3), 213–233.

Ross, J.I. (2000). *Controlling State Crime,* 2nd ed., NJ, Transaction Books.

Ross, J.I., Ed., (2000a). *Varieties of State Crime and Its Control,* Monsey, NY, Criminal Justice Press.

Ross, J.I. (2002). *The Dynamics of Political Crime,* Thousand Oaks, CA, Sage Publications.

Sagarin, E. (1973). Introduction, in Proal, L., Author, *Political Crime,* Reprint ed., Montclair, NJ, Paterson Smith, pp. v–xvi.

Schmalleger, F. (2002). *Criminal Law Today,* Upper Saddle River, NJ, Prentice Hall.

Schmid, A. (1983). *Political Terrorism: A Guide to Concepts, Theories, Data Bases and Literature,* New Brunswick, NJ, Transaction Books.

Stone, G.R. (1983). Sedition in *Encyclopedia of Crime and Justice,* New York: Free Press, Vol. 4, 1425–1431.

Turk, A.T. (1982). *Political Criminality,* Beverly Hills, CA, Sage.

Welch, M. (1996). *Corrections: A Critical Approach,* New York, McGraw Hill.

See also **Political Crimes by the State; Politics and Crime Policies; Sedition and Treason**

Political Crimes of the State

Research and theory in criminology historically have been guided by a conception of crime as a phenomenon performed by a single person for their personal goals, need, or profit in violation of state or federal criminal law. Most of the field of criminology continues to study such behaviors, but a few criminologists recently have devoted attention to the harmful conduct of states, state agencies, and political bodies. These political crimes by the state differ from the traditional form and popular conception of crime in two ways: (1) They are committed by legitimate bodies of governance in the pursuit of organizational goals, and (2) the actions may be considered criminal even though they do not violate domestic criminal law.

The contemporary criminological understanding of political crimes by the state (more commonly referred to as state crime by those studying the phenomenon) is built on a long tradition of scholarly critique and iconoclasm. Many years ago, Edwin H. Sutherland criticized criminologists for studying only crimes prohibited by the criminal law. He argued that criminologists had categorically ignored a more ominous form of crime—white-collar crime—which he defined as crime committed by respectable members of society (often of high social status) in the context of a legitimate occupation. Once the term white-collar crime was introduced into academic criminology, the phenomenon was studied by only a few scholars, and it took over two decades before it became a widely recognized subfield of study within criminology. In the 1970s, the concept was bifurcated into corporate crimes, which are crimes organizationally based and directed toward corporate goals, and occupational crimes, which are crimes committed by individuals in the course of their occupation for their own personal gain. Soon other sociologists followed suit and began advancing the argument that crime and criminal activity can be located on a higher level of abstraction, the organizational level. These theorists rejected the atomistic notion that only individuals could be considered "criminal," and advanced the idea that organizations are social actors in their own right that can be studied criminologically because, among other things, the organization can persist and act despite changes in personnel. Thus, it was maintained that organizations themselves can and should be the unit of analysis rather than the individual or an individual member of the organization (Gross, 1978). This led to the realization that many white-collar crimes are in fact organizational crimes. Although it is acknowledged that the specific decisions and activities leading to organizational crime are often the product of the choices made by individuals, these choices are made within an organizational context for organizational goals, and therefore often have a different genesis than occupational crimes for purely individual gain.

As a form of organizational crime, political crimes by the state may be defined as those crimes committed by a state, state agency, or political body for the advancement of organizational goals. Such goals may be facilitative, as when the state engages in crime to advance the interests of elites or special interest groups, or the goals may be direct, as when states engage in genocide or massive human rights abuses. Crimes committed for the personal benefit of a politician (e.g., bribe taking) are best thought of as examples of political white-collar crime (Friedrichs, 2002).

There are two basic ways criminologists recognize a state action as criminal. One school of thought holds that a state or state agency is only criminal if it violates a particular law, such as the internationally recognized Geneva Convention or the Genocide Convention. Genocidal state actions like those found at various points in the history of Armenia, Cambodia, Germany, Kosovo, Rwanda, and the former Yugoslavia are examples. A state can also violate its own law, such as when state officials (e.g., the police or military) systematically harm its citizens in violation of constitutional protections to due process, freedom of speech, freedom of assembly, and search and seizure. A second major way political crimes by the state have been defined is via the social harms perspective. This approach holds that social harm, injury, exclusion, and exploitation caused by the state or its organs should be considered criminal, even though no law may have been violated. There are dozens of state crimes that would fit under this definition, including the state's role in the institutional oppression of racial and ethnic groups, religious minority groups, women, children, and nonmainstream or radical political parties and groups. Some criminologists have gone even further, arguing that it is criminal for a state to allow such things as homelessness and poverty. There is some debate over this approach, both from the left and the right, as recently exemplified in the definition of state crime offered by Green and Ward (2000), which calls for some form of organizational deviance to be involved in human rights violations, not just the existence of social harm or injury that can somehow be traced back to the state.

Now that state crimes have been defined and conceptualized as organizational crimes, we can identify three basic forms of state crime: state crimes of commission, state crimes of negligence, and state crimes of omission. State crimes of commission occur when states or state agencies engage in direct, overt, and purposeful action that violates law or produces social injury. This form of state crime is perhaps the most visible to the casual observer and the least contentious use of the term state crime. Examples include illegal wars and aggression, systematic violations of human rights, and the oppression of minority groups. But there are other types of state crimes of commission. The U.S., for example, has violated international laws and caused considerable physical harm to people as a result of reckless environmental policies, fraudulent "medical" experiments on humans, drug experiments on military soldiers and prisoners, and funding of oppressive governments in Latin America. In particular, during its 50 years of nuclear weapons programs, the U.S. government (admittedly) has been involved in dangerous and unethical plutonium and uranium tests and experiments, many of which have had negative consequences on groups of women, children, the poor, the developmentally disabled, and mentally ill, and people of color (Kauzlarich and Kramer, 1998).

States can also be involved in crimes of negligence that result when the state or a state agency disregards unsafe and dangerous conditions, *when it has a clear mandate and responsibility to make a situation or context safe.* Many times this form of crime is related to bureaucratic failures and institutional dysfunction, and often becomes visible in the context of consumer, worker, and environmental affairs. The archetypical case of state crimes of negligence is the 1996 crash of ValuJet flight 592. Although the technical cause of the crash, which killed 110 people, was a fire that erupted after one or more oxygen generators exploded in a cargo compartment, both ValuJet and SabreTech (an airline maintenance company) failed to comply with a host of regulations concerning the presentation, storage, and transportation of hazardous materials by air. Although most criminologists would consider this an example of corporate crime, there is more to the story. What makes the tragedy an instance of state negligence is that the Federal Aviation Administration (FAA) was woefully inadequate in its oversight of some airlines, especially ValuJet, failing to monitor the safety of individual commercial aircraft (Matthews and Kauzlarich, 2000). People rely on government regulators to make sure planes, automobiles, food, and the workplace are reasonably safe. When they are not, and when this causes injury, the state should bear some degree of responsibility. Another example of state negligence is found in the 1991 Imperial Food Products fire in North Carolina (Aulette and Michalowski, 1993, 203). Although the proximal cause of the death of over two dozen workers was Imperial Food Products' decision to lock fire doors, Aulette and Michalowski (1993) argued that greater federal funding for the Occupational Safety and Health Administration (OSHA) could have reduced the likelihood of this type of tragedy. Framing the case in this manner also reveals how specific interactions between the state and private corporations can produce social harm. This has been called state–corporate crime, defined by Aulette and Michalowski as "illegal or socially injurious actions that result from a mutually reinforcing interaction between (1) policies and practices in pursuit of the goals of one or more institutions of political governance, and (2) policies and practices in pursuit of the goals of one or more institutions of economic production and distribution."

Perhaps the most contentious use of the term state crime is when it is applied to social problems such as economic, racial, and gender inequality. Several scholars have argued that such problems can be traced to state crimes of omission: by doing nothing, or next to nothing, to solve or decrease the damage of avoidable human suffering some argue, the state is engaged in crime. This approach highlights state complicity in these wider and more abstract, but nonetheless injurious, structural and institutional relationships. The archetype of this form of state crime is the unequal distribution of wealth in capitalist nations, resulting in class, race, and gender inequalities (Henry, 1991). For example, Susan Caulfield and Nancy Wonders (1993) have employed the notion of state negligence to implicate the

U.S. government's complicity in violence against women. They argue much violence against women is a result of state crimes of omission; a large proportion of such violence is directly related to the state's active choice not to intervene or limit serious harms if they are directed primarily toward women. This includes the failure to create laws to address known harms, as well as the differential application of existing laws to harms committed against women.

The major difference between state crimes of negligence and state crimes of omission is whether a state or state agency has a clear, identifiable responsibility to act to reduce the likelihood of harm. Crimes of negligence can be thought of as the result of a conscious choice on the part of state agents and agencies not do to something about an observable or potentially observable harm. Crimes of omission are the result of tacit state support for patriarchy or capitalist political and economic organizations, leading to social injury.

What often makes state crimes different from corporate crime or other forms of organizational crime is that the primary motivational factors are political, not economic. Political goals relate to the state's interest in exercising power and authority in a variety of contexts, such as:

- Establishing a favorable climate for a given economic mode of production (e.g., capitalism);
- Protecting economic and political climates abroad through interventions, unethical sanctions and embargos, and military guidance;
- Stifling dissent or alternative political movements;
- Supporting social inequality (e.g., social stratification systems); and
- Legitimizing the theft of resources for the benefit of political and economic elites.

Given the tremendous variety of actions, policies, and behaviors that have been studied as state crimes by criminologists, it is a particularly daunting task to explain the phenomenon. It is also important to note that state crime is a relatively new field of study within criminology, with most work conducted on the phenomenon by critical criminologists. Although a handful of volumes exist on the topic (e.g., Barak 1991; Tunnell, 1993; Friedrichs, 1998; Kauzlarich and Kramer, 1998; Ross, 1995; 2000) the majority of the work has been conceptual, not theoretical. In very recent years, however, there have been some steps taken to develop general theories about the causes and control of state crimes.

David Kauzlarich and Ronald C. Kramer have integrated organizational crime theory and some traditional criminological theories into a theoretical model of state crime. Recognizing the multidimensional and multifactor nature of the phenomenon, they propose that state crime is related to three "catalysts for action, including 1) motivation or performance emphasis, 2) opportunity structure, and 3) the operationality of social control" (Kauzlarich and Kramer, 1998, 176). Each catalyst functions at the individual, organizational, and structural–cultural level to produce conditions that facilitate state crime. The model proposes that "criminal behavior on the organizational level results from a coincidence of pressure for goal attainment, availability and perceived attractiveness of illegitimate means, and an absence or weakness of social control mechanisms" (Kauzlarich and Kramer, 1998, 148). In other words, state crime is more likely to occur when states, state agencies, and state officials: (1) are highly motivated to achieve structural, organizational, and individual goals; (2) find legitimate means for goal achievement blocked or unattractive; and (3) are not constrained by external oversight and regulation. The theory is highly influenced by sociological organizational theory (e.g., Gross, 1978), organizational crime theory, Mertonian strain theory, and Sutherland's differential association theory.

Jeffery Ian Ross (1995; 2000) has developed a line of theoretical inquiry that focuses on the control of state crime, not the causes. Ross' (1995) model suggests that there are a number of bodies that can regulate the affairs of the state and therefore decrease its ability to engage in crime. There are both international and domestic controls available, as well as internal and external controls. External controls may be exercised by the media, special interest groups, alternative political parties, social movements, human rights courts, the International Court of Justice, and the body of international human rights law. Internal controls are important as well, for sometimes external controls increase the likelihood of cover-ups and obstruction of justice. Internal controls include more culturally diverse membership in state agencies, training and education in human rights for state managers, and the creation of regulatory agencies within organizations, such as internal affairs investigative bodies or review boards (Ross, 2000).

Some real world attempts to control, regulate, or criminalize harmful state behaviors include the 1996 International Court of Justice opinion (that the use and threat to use nuclear weapons are inconsistent with international law). This generated a renewed interest in the effort to end nuclear proliferation and to limit the amount of nuclear weapons tests conducted around the world. The recently enacted International Criminal Court, also an external control agency, has raised hopes that a permanent court to indict, try, and sentence criminal government officials

and war criminals may help victims of state crime recover from their losses and act as a deterrent to other state managers and agents. Evidence from some European Human Rights Courts and the UN Human Rights Commission suggests that such an initiative may be successful, provided it has reliable funding and sufficient resources.

Political crimes by the state represent one of the greatest threats to the health, well-being, and happiness of people around the world. Illegal wars, imperialism, and genocide alone have caused the deaths of and injuries to millions, and perhaps billions of persons throughout history. Add that volume of harm to the injuries caused by state supported racism, sexism, classism, environmental degradation, and the violation of political and civil rights, and it is not difficult to conclude that the overall physical, emotional, and economic losses of state crime easily dwarf those engendered by "traditional" street crimes (such as homicide, sex offenses, aggravated assault, and arson property offenses). Even street crimes happen in the context of some state crime, when people's houses are burned, women and children are abused and raped, and innocent people die in gunfire or explosions during warfare (all of which has happened in the 1999 Serbian campaign against ethnic Albanians). The immense potential for political states to affect human life and experience for better or for worse suggests that the problem of state crime should receive further empirical and theoretical investigation in criminology (Kauzlarich and Friedrichs, 2001).

DAVID KAUZLARICH

References and Further Reading

Aulette, J.R. and Michalowski, R.J. 1993. Fire in Hamlet: A case study of state-corporate crime, in Tunnell, K., Ed., *Political Crime in Contemporary America,* New York, Garland.

Barak, G. 1991. *Crimes by the Capitalist State,* Albany, NY, State University of New York Press.

Caulfield, S.L. and Wonders, N. 1993. Personal and political: Violence against women and the role of the state, in in Tunnell, K., Ed., *Political Crime in Contemporary America,* New York, Garland.

Friedrichs, D.O. 2002. *Trusted Criminals: White Collar Crime in Contemporary Society,* 2nd ed., New York, Wadsworth.

Friedrichs, D.O. 1998. *State Crime Volumes I and II,* Aldershot, U.K., Dartmouth.

Green, P.J. and Ward, T. 2000. State crime, human rights, and the limits of criminology, *Social Justice,* 27.

Henry, S. 1991. The informal economy: A crime of omission by the state, in Barak, G., Ed., *Crimes by the Capitalist State,* Albany, NY, State University of New York Press.

Kauzlarich, D. and Friedrichs, D.O. 2002. Crimes of the state, in Schwartz, M.D. and Hatty, S., *Controversial Issues in Critical Criminology,* Cincinnati, OH, Anderson.

Kauzlarich, D. and Kramer, R.C. 1998. *Crimes of the American Nuclear State,* Boston, MA, Northeastern University Press.

Gross, E. 1978. Organizational crime: A theoretical perspective, in Greenwich, D.N., Ed., *Studies of Symbolic Interaction,* Greenwich, CT, Jai Press.

Matthews, R.A. and Kauzlarich, D. 2000. The crash of Valujet flight 592: A case study in state-corporate crime, *Sociological Focus,* 3.

Tunnell, K. 1993. *Political Crime in Contemporary America,* New York, Garland.

Ross, J.I. 1995. *Controlling State Crime,* New York, Garland.

Ross, J.I. 2000. *Varieties of State Crime and its Control,* Monsey, NY, Criminal Justice Press.

See also **Environmental Crimes; War Crimes**

Politics and Crime Policies

Politics is very important in the criminal justice system. Politicians in the U.S. define what constitutes criminal behavior in writing the statutes. Also, politicians in passing a budget decide how much money will be spent on government's response to crime. Crime can also be very important for political elites when they run for election. Crime issues and symbols can help politicians construct the winning margin in an election. The masses of voters in the U.S. generally indicate considerable fear of crime and thus will respond to campaign rhetoric that assures a significant attempt to control crime.

"Politics, in its broadest sense, is concerned with the distribution of advantages and disadvantages among people" (Froman, 1962). Politicians, then, are the people who decide how many advantages and disadvantages are to be distributed. Legislators, in writing criminal statutes, define certain behavior as illegal and thus place perpetrators of such behavior at a disadvantage. Deciding which behavior is criminal may place certain socioeconomic groups at a disadvantage because the forbidden behavior pattern may be more closely identified with one class grouping such as the lower class.

The advantages or rewards that politicians distribute can be tangible or symbolic. Tangible or material rewards have a direct monetary value. Politicians will decide how much money is to be spent on police personnel and equipment. Politicians decide how much money will be spent on judges' salaries. Also, politicians decide how much money will be required of those who must pay a fine because of a finding of guilt in a criminal case. In recent years, legislators in American states have decided to spend increasing amounts of money on privatizing some prisons. Thus companies in the business of building and running prisons are rewarded with significant contracts. The passing of a budget is one of the most important ways in which politicians distribute tangible or material rewards.

Symbolic rewards are distributed through the use of political symbols. Political symbols are shorthand methods of referring to reality. Because they evoke emotions in the perceiver, symbols are used a great deal by politicians. Symbols help politicians build support for themselves. On the one hand, if the public is apathetic about a problem such as crime, politicians can use symbolic phrases like "law and order" or "rape and pillage in the streets" to get the attention of the public. On the other hand, if the public is very distraught about a particular problem, such as the potential for racial riots, politicians can use symbols like "law and order" to assure the population that an adequate response is being made to any potential rioters.

Language is used by government to define and respond to problems. In using language politically, government leaders set up a situation that provides symbolic rewards and allows for the distribution of tangible rewards:

> If political language both excites and mollifies fear, language is an integral part of the political scene: not simply an instrument for describing events but itself a part of the events, shaping their meaning and helping to shape the political roles officials and the general public play (Edelman, 1977).

Language thus provides the categorization of political events and problems. Because neither the public nor the media can directly experience all political actions, they are dependent upon how politicians characterize any given situation. Language is one important way in which people structure the world for others. Because the issue of crime raises so many emotions, the manipulation of language by government is particularly important in the criminal justice system.

The political manipulation of language does not cause people to behave in identical ways because individuals respond differently to events. Also, individuals' perceptions of reality vary; they react to events in terms of their interests, their experiences, and their roles. For example, a police officer and a psychiatrist may have quite different perceptions of crime and its related problems. This does not imply that players are so defined by their roles that individual variations do not exist. For instance, some prosecutors are very sensitive to the human implications of their work whereas others are not. Some prisoners adjust to their new environment whereas others never do. Some police officers are corrupt; others are not.

The situation of multiple perceptions of reality is made more complex by the pervasiveness of contradictory beliefs about issues that is particularly evident in the area of crime. There are a variety of beliefs about the causes of the crime problem, the proper roles of criminal justice authorities, and the effectiveness of solutions (Edelman, 1977). Some, for instance, would attribute an individual's criminal behavior to a lack of self-control or to immorality, whereas others would explain such behavior by citing the influence of socioeconomic deprivation or racial discrimination. The existence of such contradictory beliefs brings about contradictions in public policies dealing with crime. The result is that "the coexistence of contradictory reactions to a 'problem' from which many benefit helps assure that it will be deplored but tolerated, rather than attacked in a resolute way" (Edelman, 1977). The contradictory beliefs, in other words, are tied to the distribution of advantages for some of the players; the continual flow of symbolic or tangible rewards may be more influential than solving problems. Such beliefs, however, do aid in the proliferation of views concerning the criminal justice system.

Thus there are numerous policy options that could be pursued by politicians in an attempt to address the problem of crime. However, Scheingold (1991) observes "that the political will to tackle the problem of street crime is more apparent than real." He points out that there are two opposing explanations for crime. One he calls "structural." In that view, crime results from social disorganization. Social disorganization results from hierarchy, deprivation, coercion, and alienation. The other explanation he calls "volitional." Criminal behavior is seen as a matter of personal choice.

> (V)olitional criminology discounts the economic causes of crime and thus puts less stress on the capabilities of the state. By identifying criminality with pathological individuals, volitional criminology stigmatizes criminals and validates punitive responses to them, and punishment is simply less costly across the board than structural transformation (Scheingold, 1991).

Legislators will have significant choices to make in voting for a particular policy option—whether it be systemic or volitional. The process by which legislators decide to vote on the American national level has been identified by John Kingdon (1989). His "consensus mode of decision" theory emphasizes that if a bill is noncontroversial, legislators vote with the consensus. If a bill is controversial, they look on their own personal "field of forces" that includes personal policy attitudes as well as those of constituents, party leaders, trusted colleagues, staff members, the administration, and important interest groups. If there is conflict within the field of forces, the congressperson will consider his or her goals, the most important of which is his or her own attitudes (Kingdon, 1989). Similar findings exist on the state level. A study of Oklahoma and Kansas state legislatures found attitudes and values to be consistently important in the choice of voting cues for all issues examined except redistricting (Songer et al., 1986). Thus the policy coming out of the legislative process will reflect the priorities of the public if constituents are sending messages to their legislators. In fact, Kingdon, in discussing the impact of constituency, points out that legislators are likely to respond to those issues that are highly salient. Kingdon operationalizes a highly salient issue as one that involves messages coming from the masses in the constituency as well as from elites or those with decision-making power in an organization in the home district (Kingdon, 1989). Chambliss has documented the activities of interest groups in their efforts since the 1960s to make crime a central issue in the minds of American citizens (Chambliss, 1999). Interest groups are adept at giving their members incentive to contact legislators and thus make an issue highly salient in the minds of the legislators. Thus volitional approaches to crime policy have been the predominant approach to the problem of crime.

Schiengold (1991) argues that crime and criminals are important symbolic enemies in American politics. He points out that politicians have financial incentives for framing structural problems with the American economy as crime control issues with the accompanying war on crime or drugs. Politicians see that it would be far more costly to declare war on "poverty, unemployment, homelessness, economic deprivation or other sources of deviant behavior." The individualistic culture of the U.S. places considerable stress on material attainments. It also, as Barbara Ehrenreich suggests, brings with it a "fear of falling" (1989). Many are fearful of their inability to achieve material success or to continue maintaining a particular level of affluence in the U.S. Thus considerable anxiety and anger about abilities and attainments will result in scapegoats being sought against whom the anger can be discharged.

> My argument is that street criminals, conceived of as predatory strangers, are among the scapegoats – along

with others who threaten to subvert the social order: communists, welfare cheaters, and drug addicts. Here are people we are entitled to hate – but only so long as we think of them as victimizers rather than victims ... (T)he point is that street crime as a spectator sport provides a way of sublimating the anger, anxiety and guilt generated by American social life. (Scheingold, 1991)

Thus crime is an important symbol allowing politicians not to address the so-called root causes of the anxiety citizens have about the "fear of falling" in the economic structure of the U.S. and similar societies.

As policies designed to respond to crime come out of legislatures, it is necessary to look at the nature of public policies passed by legislative bodies. Ripley (1988) characterizes the normal state of business in the U.S. Congress as one of fragmentation. "Fragmentation is characterized by a decentralized organization and by a lack of planned coherence" (Ripley, 1988). Ripley identifies eight facets of congressional life that are conducive to fragmentation:

Members are popularly elected from specific geographical constituencies in which they must reside. There are two separate and quite different houses of Congress. The federal government has a large and diverse agenda. Congress shares power with a large and disaggregated bureaucracy. Congress is open to the activities and influence of a large number of diverse organized interest groups. Congress organizes itself into a very large number of committees and subcommittees in order to process its business. The national political parties are generally weak, although they do offer significant campaign finance help, especially in the case of the Republicans. Many members are ambitious primarily in terms of personal influence, re-election, and/or advancement to more prestigious elective office. (Ripley, 1988)

The type of public policy resulting from a state of fragmentation is characterized by Ripley as stable in terms of policy content with slow and small policy changes (Ripley, 1988). Most domestic policy is characterized as distributive and thus provides subsidy and support for private activity rather than protective regulatory or redistributive policy (Ripley, 1988). Policies to address systemic conditions conducive to crime would be redistributive in nature because such policies would take resources from those with wealth and reallocate them to the poor. Ripley also suggests that there is a low degree of bureaucratic oversight in a fragmented system. There is little evaluation of the impact of policies. Thus the inability of correctional facilities to rehabilitate criminals comes under little review. Serious review of the impact of imprisonment on the inmates generally is not carried out by legislators on

an ongoing basis even though one of the duties of legislatures in the American context is to execute bureaucratic oversight on a regular basis. Also, Ripley (1998) indicates that fragmentation in Congress is accompanied by passivity among the members toward their policy role. The status quo in terms of criminal justice policy continues to operate because of the state of fragmented decision making that constitutes business as usual in Congress. Ripley (1988) indicates that "(c)hange in policies is difficult in a highly fragmented situation."

The volitional approach is the predominant one in the American criminal justice system. A variety of arguments are presented by scholars and policy researchers to bolster the volitional approach. Wilson and Herrenstein (1985) see that some are more inclined to criminality. They cite a correlation between crime and personality, gender, age, and intelligence. This stress on the individual component in crime genesis was reinforced by the work of Becker (1968). His is an "economic model of crime." He posits a situation in which a potential criminal uses all available information to select actions and thus be a rational utility maximizer. One assumption of the model is that the potential perpetrator knows the precise likelihood of apprehension. Although the Becker model was not intended to be an accurate reflection of the world, it did provide significant support for a stress on the deterrent impact of punishment. In an economic model of deterrence such as Becker's, certainty and severity of punishment will be equally important in deterring potential perpetrators from engaging in their criminal acts. Thus Becker provided an important intellectual support for public policy pronouncements that criminal punishment should be severe and certain. Dye (2002) in his analysis of this model of deterrence points out that the American system of criminal justice is remiss in delivering certain and severe punishment.

Nonetheless, Wilson and Herrenstein (1985) placed significant stress on individual responsibility for deciding to carry out a crime. They pointed out that:

(c)rime is held in check not only by the objective risk of punishment but by the subjective sense of wrongdoing. Punishment as moral education almost certainly reduces more crime than punishment as deterrence. An internalized prohibition against offending is like an additional cost of crime, possibly strong enough to prevent its occurrence even when there is no risk of being caught and punished by society.

This stress on individual responsibility for criminal wrongdoing brought with it a major policy commitment in the 1980s to increase the punitive nature of correctional systems in the U.S. The assumption appeared to be that most criminals are dangerous people who need to be locked up. Increasing the length of incarceration will keep dangerous criminals off the streets and will deter potential criminals when they contemplate a crime (Austin and Irwin, 2001).

A number of studies in the 1980s suggested that there were "career criminals" from whom society needed to be protected (Greenwood and Abrahamse, 1982; Blumstein, Cohen, and Farrington, 1988). A cohort of individuals was identified who continued to commit crime over a long period of their lives. These "careers criminal" engendered fear in the public. The politicians with reinforcement from media portrayals of crime responded to this perceived concern by increasing the length of prison terms as well as multiplying the numbers of people being incarcerated.

Miller (1974) identified an ideology that developed to support an evil person perspective on crime. In this view

(t)he bulk of serious crime is committed by members of certain ethnic and social class categories characterized by defective self-control, self-indulgence, limited time horizons, and undeveloped moral conscience. The criminal propensities of these classes, which appear repeatedly in successive generations, are nurtured and encouraged by the enormous reluctance of authorities to apply the degree of firm, swift and decisive punishment which could serve effectively to curb crime.

In this view society must use punishment to protect itself from these reprobates.

An alternative view is the evil society view or the structural view as identified by Schiengold. The responsibility for the crime problem is placed on an unfair and unjust society. In this view, society is faulted for allocating insufficient resources to address such root causes of crime as "poverty, urban deterioration, blocked educational and job opportunities" (Miller, 1974). The problem is further compounded by "widespread systems of segregation—separating race from race, the poor from the affluent, the deviant from the conventional, and the criminal from the law abiding" (Miller, 1974)

In this view those committing street crime are basically forced into such behavior by a destructive set of social conditions. Flaherty (1995), for example, argues that:

(i)t is unrealistic to expect most of the eight- and ten-year-olds playing tag in the ruins of the abandoned buildings or the pre-teenagers sifting through mounds of garbage piled on the sidewalks to develop healthy notions of public good and personal responsibility. The 'common sense' emerging among this newest generation is that 'The System' hates them.

Currie (1985) also stresses the role of the inequality in the American social structure in the genesis of crime in his analysis of cities in the U.S. with high violent crime rates, he finds a distinct correlation with high rates of poverty. He found covariance of crime and inequality when he did a comparative analysis of the U.S., Japan, Holland, and Sweden.

Linsky and Strauss (1986) investigated the relationship between the crime rate and social stress in the American states. They found that states with higher rates of social stress had higher crime rates. They identified the following indicators of social stress to be predictive of higher violent crime rates: business failures, unemployment claims, workers on strike, personal bankruptcies, mortgage foreclosures, divorces, abortions, illegitimate births, infant deaths, fetal deaths, disaster assistance, state residency of less than 5 years, new houses authorized, new welfare cases, and high school dropout rates. Their work suggests a significant relationship between structural factors and the genesis of crime.

William Julius Wilson (1987), in his work *The Truly Disadvantaged*, identified those poor people in American census tracts in which at least 40% of the population consists of people living below the official definition of poverty. He suggested a variety of structural reforms or macroeconomic reforms that he felt would reduce the proportion of the population in the U.S. that he classified as the "truly disadvantaged." He advocated the promotion of balanced economic growth by the federal government in the U.S. as well as the creation of a tight labor market situation. He suggested the importance of a national labor market strategy along with government assurance of child support. In addition, he advocated the establishment of programs assuring childcare as well as a program of family allowance. Such programs would reduce poverty and the social stresses attached to it.

Jargowsky (2003) analyzed census tract data from the 1990 and 2000 census. He was particularly interested in those census tracts with 40% or more residents officially defined as poor in the U.S. He found that there was a 24% decline in the number of people living in high poverty census tracts. In addition, the number of census tracts with a poverty rate of 40% or more declined by 25% in the 10-year period. This change was found across the U.S., suggesting that structural reforms in the economy can have an impact on poverty rates and the social stress related to high crime rates. Jargowsky's work suggests one possible explanation for the falling crime rates that were seen in the 1990s in the U.S. and provides possible support to those advocating structural approaches to the reduction of crime.

The predominance of the volitional approach has brought with it some significant problems in the U.S. The U.S. now has the highest rate of imprisonment of industrialized countries. The rate of imprisonment continued to rise in the 1990s even though crime rates were in decline. California now is spending more on corrections than on higher education (Justice Policy Institute, 1998a). New York, also, is spending more on corrections than on higher education (Justice Policy Institute, 1998b). Austin and Irwin (2001) point out that this expensive imprisonment remedy is being imposed predominantly on people of the lower class. At the same time, economic policies are causing the gap between the wealthy and the poor to widen. In addition, Austin and Irwin posit that another generation of poor children is being produced who will probably enter the correctional system as they mature.

There is evidence that the media and the public play a significant role in heightening the saliency of punishment in the minds of legislators. Haghighi and Sorenson (1996), in analyzing results of the 1995 National Opinion Survey on Crime and Justice executed at Sam Houston State University, indicated that media crime coverage was significantly related to fear of crime. Those respondents who felt the media gave too much coverage to crime were more fearful of sexual assault, robbery, aggravated assault, and burglary. Flanagan (1996) indicates that political elites are prone to misperceive citizen attitudes toward criminal justice issues. The citizens are seen as conservative and resistant to change and innovation in the area of criminal justice policy.

Flanagan (1996), in reviewing studies of public opinion in the U.S. on crime, indicates that the public is supportive of the following measures: the hiring of more police, broader use of the death penalty, "three strikes and you're out" legislation to increase penalties for repeat offenders, stronger penalties in the juvenile justice arena, the reduction of delay and perceived leniency in the courts, tougher prisons. All of these measures indicate support for a volitional approach to crime. However, Flanagan (1996) also identified public support for measures that are more indicative of a structural approach to crime: programs to ameliorate the living conditions of high-risk children such as early intervention programs and positive social programs, education, training, and counseling options within correctional institutions, and community-based programs for nonviolent offenders. Austin and Irwin (2001), in their critique of contemporary correctional policies, pointed out that fully 52.6% of the prisoners in their ethnographic study of males incarcerated in Washington, Nevada, and Illinois were petty criminals who were convicted for nonviolent offenses. There is some indication that state legislators are beginning to see that the volitional approach is not cost-effective and that some aspects of the structural approach to policy would help to reduce the costs of the present approach (Baker and Meyer, 1998).

However, the message about crime presented in the media is generally supportive of volitional crime policy. Lawrence (2000), in doing a content analysis of police brutality stories in the *New York Times* and the *Los Angeles Times* over a 10-year period, pointed out that the news is a socially constructed representation of reality in which public policy problems are defined. Thus the social construction of the news involves competition between interested groups to define a public problem in a way that is most advantageous to their interest. The way in which a particular problem is defined will determine the distribution of political resources or who wins and who loses in the political process. Police brutality incidents present a challenge to police bureaucracies because brutality is an accidental event that cannot be planned as a regular event in the life of the police organization. The consistent pattern that Lawrence found in police explanations of the brutality event in the news placed blame on the individual who experienced the brutality. The official response to police brutality incidents generally involved the process of "individualizing" the incident. The person experiencing the brutality brought the incident upon himself or herself with deviant or violent behavior. Nonofficial responses to the incident were generally of a systemic nature. Eighty percent of the stories in the *New York Times* and the *Los Angeles Times* relied on official sources. Lawrence provides confirmation that the message presented in the more prestigious media in the U.S. reinforces volitional policy, thus making it more difficult to pursue structural approaches to crime policy.

FRED MEYER AND RALPH BAKER

References and Further Reading

Austin, J. and Irwin, J., Eds. 2001. *It's About Time,* 3rd ed., Belmont, CA, Wadsworth.

Baker, R. and Meyer, F. 1998. *Criminal Justice and Overcriminalization: The Potential for Legislative Change,* Paper presented at Southern Political Science Association meeting, Atlanta, GA.

Becker, G., Crime and punishment: An economic approach, *Journal of Political Economy,* 76, 169–217.

Blumstein, A., Cohen, J. and Farrington, D.P., Criminal Career Research: Its value for criminology, *Criminology,* 26(1), 1–35.

Chambliss, W.J. 1999. *Power, Politics and Crime,* Boulder, CO, Westview Press.

Dye, T.R. 2002. *Understanding Public Policy,* 10th ed., Upper Saddle River, NJ, Prentice Hall.

Edelman, M. 1977. *Political Language,* New York, Academic Press.

Ehrenreich, B. 1989. *Fear of Falling: The Inner Life of the Middle Class,* New York, Pantheon.

Flanagan, T.J. 1996. Public opinion and public policy in criminal justice, in Flanagan, T. and Longmire, D.R., Eds., *Americans View Crime and Justice,* Thousand Oaks, CA, Sage Publications, Inc.

Froman, L.A., Jr. 1962. *People and Politics,* Englewood Cliffs, NJ, Prentice-Hall.

Greenwood, P. and Abrahamse, A. 1982. *Selective Incapacitation,* Santa Monica, CA, Rand Corporation.

Haghighi, B. and Sorenson, J. 1996. America's fear of crime, in Flanagan, T. and Longmire, D.R., Eds., *Americans View Crime and Justice,* Thousand Oaks, CA, Sage Publications, Inc.

Jargowsky, P.A. 2003. *Stunning Progress, Hidden Problems: The Dramatic Decline of Concentrated Poverty in the 1990s,* Center on Urban and Metropolitan Policy, Washington, DC, The Brookings Institution.

Justice Policy Institute 1998a. *Class Dismissed: Higher Education vs. Corrections During the Wilson Years,* Washington, DC, Justice Policy Institute.

Justice Policy Institute 1998b. *New York State of Mind? Higher Education vs. Prison Funding in the Empire State, 1988–1998,* Washington, DC, Justice Policy Institute.

Kingdon, J.W. 1989. *Congressmen's Voting Decisions,* 3rd ed., Ann Arbor, MI, University of Michigan Press.

Lawrence, R.G. 2000. *The Politics of Force,* Berkeley, CA, University of California Press.

Linsky, A.S. and Strauss, M. 1986. *Social Stress in the U.S.,* Dover, MA, Auburn House.

Miller, W.B. 1974. Ideology and criminal justice policy: Some current issues, in Reasons, C.E., Ed., *The Criminologist: Crime and the Criminal,* Pacific Palisades, CA, Goodyear Publishing.

Ripley, R.B. 1988. *Congress,* 4th ed., New York, Norton.

Scheingold, S.A. 1991. *The Politics of Street Crime,* Philadelphia, PA, Temple University Press.

Songer, D.R., Dillon, S.G., White, D., Jameson, P.E. and Underwood, J.M. 1986. The influence of issues on choice of voting cues utilized by state legislators, *Western Political Quarterly,* 39, 118–125.

Wilson, J.Q. and Herrenstein, R. 1985. *Crime and Human Nature: The Definitive Study of the Causes of Crime,* New York, Simon and Schuster.

Wilson, W.J. 1987. *The Truly Disadvantaged: The Inner City, the Underclass and Public Policy,* Chicago, IL, University of Chicago Press.

See also **Criminal Justice Funding: The State Role; National Institute of Justice**

Pornography and Criminal Behavior

The impact of pornography on criminal behavior, sexual aggression, and rape in particular has been a source of debate in criminology and criminal justice for several decades. Overall, the research findings surrounding the crime causing nature of pornography have been mixed, with substantial criticism leveled at the ability of current research methodology to thresh out the connection between the two phenomena. Moreover, as the nature of pornography continues to evolve, and its methods of exposure to the public are expanding, past research findings may be less applicable to those at present. Thus, efforts to build on and improve the research on the pornography–crime relationship will likely remain at the forefront of the analysis of sexual offenses and rape.

Pornography is certainly not a new occurrence in the U.S. or other countries around the world. The general public's familiarity with pornography is changing, however, largely because of the computerization of the workplace, schools, and homes across the world. Long hidden in the underground community, it is difficult for adults and adolescents alike to avoid exposure to pornographic materials today. Indeed, in 1994, only 38% of public schools in the U.S. had access to the Internet, whereas 98% had it by the year 2000 (Thornburgh and Lin, 2002). Similarly, over 95% of public libraries had access to Internet connections, while nearly 18 million had access to the Internet at their homes (Thornburgh and Lin, 2002). Because the large majority (76%) of teens do indeed use the Internet (Thornburgh and Lin, 2002), it is highly likely that they will encounter pornography of some type. Such Internet pornography today may come in the form of spam e-mails, bulletin boards, chat rooms, and so on.

The potential for growth and exposure of pornography makes it critical that its potential negative impact on society be examined. However, there are a number of difficulties in undertaking this endeavor, and these difficulties have led to controversy over the available evidence on the subject. Some of these controversies surround the definition of pornography, the theoretical underpinnings for pornography's impact on crime, and the methodology used in research studies analyzing pornography and crime.

Although most people use the term pornography as if it has cut and dry boundaries, there is no definition that perfectly explains this complex phenomenon. Aiding to the confusion is that differences exist between legal definitions of pornography, definitions found in the dictionary, and those found in common language. Looking at the origins of the term, the Greeks characterized it as literature relating to prostitution (Easton, 1998). Though evolved, a number of modern definitions are also exceedingly restrictive. For instance, it has been defined as sexually explicit material that uses pictures or words in a manner that show women to be subordinates (Easton, 1998). Certainly, materials do not have to include females to be considered pornography by most scholars today.

Perhaps the best method by which to define pornography is by making a distinction between sexually explicit material, obscene material, and pornography. For example, material that is obscene is not always pornographic. Rather, obscene material is only sometimes pornographic, and includes behavior that is illegal because it poses a threat to society, violates common morality, has no redeeming social value, and so on (Conklin, 2001). The determination of what is obscene is increasingly being left to the decision of the local jurisdictions (Tibbetts and Blankenship, 1999). Pornography can be, but certainly is not always, illegal behavior, as a number of pornographic materials are sold legally at stores and online.

Although sexually explicit material and pornography are both viewed as materials that depict sexually explicit acts or illustrate the reproductive organs of the human body, there are also differences between the two. Although sexually explicit materials can be used for education, art, science, sexual gratification, fantasy, etc., many argue that pornography is material that is intended to arouse people sexually through the portrayal of sexuality (Conklin, 2001; Thornburgh and Lin, 1998). This popular definition does not provide a perfect distinction between these two concepts, however, as sexual material that is intended for science, art, or education may generate a sexual arousal from the audience. Unfortunately, the tendency of researchers to measure pornography through distinct definitions has undoubtedly contributed to the mixed findings surrounding its impact on crime and sexual offenses. Readers are advised to note this methodological difficulty when reading any literature review of pornography research.

Theories focusing on the detrimental impact of pornography can be differentiated based upon the behavior that they are intended to explain. Specifically, pornography has been theorized to have an impact on crime in general as well as more specific sexual offenses, and the theories differ accordingly.

Although it is popular for the general public to equate pornography as a determinate of crime, there is little theoretical justification to indicate that one's exposure to pornography places a person at greater risk of obtaining a criminal record. In fact, there is probably greater justification for pornography's influence on general crime at the aggregate rather than individual level. Indeed, Wilson's (1983) broken window theory can be applied to pornography as an incivility just as it can be applied to any other incivility within a community. Accordingly, incivilities within a community, whether it be prostitution, drugs, abandoned buildings, strip clubs, pornography stores, etc., lead to a downward cycle within an area, ultimately attracting the criminal element and increasing crime rates.

There is a little more theoretical support for a link between pornography exposure and sexual offending. For example, Zillmann (1982) theorized that sexually explicit material, whether it is viewed on television or in magazines, may produce emotional and physiological arousal. Although Zillmann's arousal theory did not take a definitive stand on the exact nature of explicit material on behavior, it does suggest that exposure to sexual material can have short-term impacts on sex drives and aggression.

Differential Association Theory, introduced by Sutherland in 1939, may provide even stronger theoretical grounds for the potential impact of pornography on crime (Sutherland and Cressey, 1978). Accordingly, criminal behavior is learned through a process identical to conventional behavior. When a person's ideas or definitions that are favorable to committing a criminal act become stronger than their definitions against it, crime is likely to occur (Sutherland and Cressey, 1978). Factors such as the intensity, duration, and frequency of exposure to ideas that are in contrast with the laws also play strong roles.

Some theorists have expanded the ideas of Sutherland to other more specific types of learning. For instance, Bandura (1971) focused on the potentially strong impact that the media can have on human behavior. Specific to sexual behavior, Bandura theorized that exposure to sexual content in the media can have long-term ramifications on ones' motivations and opinions toward sexual conduct. In fact, within the proper context, subjects may imitate the sexual behavior to which they are exposed (Bandura, 1971).

As criminologists have repeatedly determined, theory does not always translate into practice, nor does it always translate into congruent research findings. Theory on the pornography–crime relationship does not completely contrast with the available research in the area, yet there are plenty of researchers whose findings undermine the link between the two. Again, these findings need to be considered within the context of their findings, and the specific types of crime, pornography, and samples that they examine.

Perhaps the controversy over the pornography or crime relationship has been fueled most by contrasting opinions in governmental studies on the topic. For instance, a 1970 presidential panel found no link between violence and sexually explicit material. In 1986, however, the final report of the Commission on Pornography concluded that there is a causal link between many forms of aggressive behavior and pornography. This study drew much attention owing to the controversy surrounding its findings, with much criticism by researchers directed at the research methods used in forming the conclusion (Donnerstein and Linz, 1986; Wilcox, 1987). In fact, a few of the commission members made strong dissenting remarks concerning the validity of the study.

Just as there are fewer theoretical links between pornography and general crime, there are also fewer research studies testing these proposed links. Perhaps this is a result of the difficulty in trying to rationalize causal order in a correlation between nonsexual criminal behavior and pornography. In theory, pornography may impact general crime rates through the degradation of morality and civilities within neighborhoods and larger communities. But, other than large-scale aggregate level theories testing the correlation between crime and pornography, there are few quantitative methods through which to test this relationship. Thus, the large majority of empirical tests analyze the impact of pornography on some type of sexual offense or deviance. Sexual behavior measures tested against pornography exposure have included sexual aggression, verbal and sexual abuse and humiliation, domestic violence, and rape of adults and minors. Moreover, research methodology has consisted of both aggregate and individual level analysis, with cross-sectional studies taken at one point in time being far more abundant than longitudinal studies that track individuals' pornography use against their sexual offenses.

As a whole, macro-level studies focusing on the relationship between pornography and crime have been heavily scrutinized (Nemes, 1992). Though they have the strength of testing a larger group of people and findings that can be generalized to wider sections of the country, studies focusing on the aggregate or macro-level of study have not escaped criticism. As these studies measure neighborhood, city, county, or even state differences in pornography use in comparison to crime, the congruence between the crime and pornography measures comes into question.

The key question in macro-level studies of pornography and crime is whether both measures being tested are equally valid and encompass the same number of people. For instance, Diamond and Ayako (1999) compared trends in the availability of pornography against sex crimes in Japan from 1972 to 1995 and found that as pornography availability increased over the years, sex crimes actually decreased. Similarly, Kutchinsky (1991) analyzed the same relationship in the U.S., Denmark, Sweden, and Germany from 1964 to 1984 and found that increases in pornography availability had no more impact on rape than other nonsexual violent crimes in any of the countries. In fact, similar to Diamond and Ayako's (1999) more recent analysis on Japan, they found that in all countries but the U.S., pornography had a lesser impact on rape than nonsexual violent crimes.

The drawbacks of such longitudinal macro-level studies include the change in measurement of, and reporting tendencies of, sexual offenses over time and the difficulties in measuring pornography aggregately. For instance, Kutchinsky (1991) used circulation of pornography magazines as a proxy for pornography use. Diamond and Ayako (1999) noted their difficulty in finding adequate measures of pornography availability, and had to put together a combination of measures including surveys concerning sex materials, sexually explicit books in libraries, adult videos, magazines, and so on. Because much of the pornography industry still operates underground, it is difficult to pinpoint the extent to which its circulation increases each year. More problematic is the difficulty that faces any measure of availability, including the availability of drugs, guns, and so on. The problem is that increased availability does not necessarily translate into increased use by consumers. Indeed, the ability of researchers to thresh out the relationship between availability and use of pornography remains one of the more serious concerns in aggregate level analysis.

The majority of studies on pornography have focused on its micro- or individual-level impact on sexual behavior. Specifically, a large number of studies have surveyed either victims or offenders of sexual assault and asked them what role pornography played in the offense. Another popular form of study has been to correlate individuals' exposure to pornography with their attitudes toward women, relationships, and sexually aggressive behavior. Furthermore, there have been a number of experimental studies that expose subjects to different levels of pornography and note the differences in attitudes concerning women and sexual aggressive behavior.

As with most studies on the pornography–crime link, results of experimental studies have been mixed. For instance, Malamuth and Ceniti (1986) assigned male university students to sexually violent pornography, sexually nonviolent material, and control group conditions during a 4-week period. The conditions included feature-length films and written and pictorial depictions, and the researchers concluded that the pornographic material did increase the likelihood of rape ratings of the students. Fischer and Greneir (1994), however, found that males exposed to sexually violent pornography did not have antiwoman aggression, fantasies, or attitudes.

Again, there has been an abundance of pornography research that survey victims and offenders of sexual assault. Similar to experimental studies, the results of this research are also mixed. For instance, Langevin (1988) interviewed 227 male sex offenders and a control group of nonoffenders in Canada and found that their purchase of, and involvement with, pornographic materials did not have an impact on sexual offending. On the other hand, Carter (1987) interviewed convicted child molesters and rapists and found that both groups had significant exposure to pornography in youth, whereas child molesters had more during adulthood.

More, though no less controversial, support for the rape or pornography correlation can be found in surveys of women concerning the impact of their partner's pornography use on his sexual battery. Somers and Check (1987) compared 44 sexually battered women from shelters with a comparison group and found that the spouses of the battered women had significantly higher exposure to pornographic materials than the comparison group. More recent studies by Cramer, McFarlane, Parker, et al. (1998) and Bergen and Bogle (2000) partially support this assertion, with the studies finding that a sizeable percentage of rape victims (41% and 28%, respectively) report that their assaulters used pornography.

Some other research studies do not test the direct link between exposure and behavior of experiments or surveys of victims and offenders, but their findings are relevant to decisions surrounding policy in the field. For instance, support for less stringent laws on pornography is found in studies such as Baron (1990), who examined pornography circulation in 50 states in comparison to gender equality. Baron found that increases in pornography were actually related to increases in gender equality in politics, economics, and legal rights. Although pornography is not said to cause more liberal attitudes toward gender, Baron said that communities that support pornography have similar liberal attitudes about women's role in society. Similar to Baron's study, Thompson (1990) surveyed college students and found that while 65% of them stated that pornography should be protected through freedom of speech, females tended to view pornography as having a negative impact on the relations between the genders.

In conclusion, the debate over the pornography–crime connection is still apparent in the literature today and will likely continue well into this century.

There are a number of questions still to be answered. For instance, if pornography exposure does enhance sexually aggressive attitudes toward women, is it only for males who already have aggressive attitudes caused by other factors? Will money be available for more longitudinal studies that follow the potential long-term impacts of pornography on crime? What are the potential benefits of pornography for society? What are the ramifications of increased technology on the pornography–crime relationship? What type of challenges will this technology continue to bring for the enforcement of pornography laws? Research surrounding these questions will have far reaching impacts on the future of pornography related policies in the U.S.

BRION SEVER

References and Further Reading

Bandura, A. (1971). *Social Learning Theory.* General Learning Press, New York.

Baron, L. (1990). Feminist perspectives on pornography, *Journal of Sex Research,* 27, 363–380.

Bergen, R. and Bogle, K. (2000). Exploring the connection between pornography and sexual violence, *Violence and Victims,* 15, 227–234.

Conklin, J. (2001). *Criminology,* 7th ed., Boston, MA, Allyn and Bacon.

Cramer, E., McFarlane, J., Parker, B., et al., (1998). Violent pornography and abuse of women: Theory to practice, *Violence and Victims,* 13, 319–332.

Diamond, M. and Uchiyama, A. (1999). Pornography, rape, and sex crimes in Japan, *International Journal of Law and Psychiatry,* 22(1), 1–22.

Donnerstein, E. and Linz, D. (1986). The question of pornography, *Psychology Today,* 20, 56–59.

Easton, S. (1998). *Encyclopedia of Applied Ethics,* Toronto, Canada, Academic Press.

Fischer, W. and Greneir, G. (1994). Violent pornography, antiwoman thoughts, and antiwoman acts: In search of reliable effects, *Sex Research,* 31, 23–29.

Gentry, C. (1991). Pornography and rape: An empirical analysis, *Deviant Behavior,* 12(3), 277–288.

Kutchinsky, B. (1991). Pornography and rape: Theory and practice? Evidence from crime data in four countries where pornography is easily available, *International Journal of Law and Psychiatry,* 14(1/2), 47–64.

Malamuth, N. and Ceniti, J. (1986). Repeated exposure to violent and nonviolent pornography: Likelihood of raping ratings and laboratory aggression against women, *Aggressive Behavior,* 12, 129–137.

Nemes, I. (1992). The relationship between pornography and sex crimes, *Journal of Psychiatry and Law,* 20(4), 459–481.

Sommers, E. and Check, J. (1987). An empirical investigation of the role of pornography in the verbal and physical abuse of women, *Violence and Victims,* 2, 189–209.

Sutherland, E. and Cressey, D. (1978). *Criminology,* 10th ed., Philadelphia, PA, Lippincott.

Thompson, E. (1990). Regulating pornography: A public dilemma, *Communication,* 40, 73–83.

Thornburgh, D. and Lin, H., Eds. (2002). *Youth, Pornography, and the Internet,* Washington, DC, National Academy Press.

Tibbetts, S. and Blankenship, M. (1999). Explaining citizens' attitudes toward pornography: Differential effects of predictors across levels of geographic proximity to outlet sources, *Justice Quarterly,* 16(4), 735–763.

Wilcox, B. (1987). Pornography, social science and politics: When research and ideology collide, *American Psychology,* 42, 941–943.

Wilson, J. (1983). *Thinking About Crime,* New York, Basic Books.

Zillman, D. (1982). Transfer of excitation in emotional behavior, in Cacioppo, J. and Petty, R., Eds., *Social Psychophysiology,* New York, Guilford.

See also **Pornography: The Law; Rape, Forcible: Theories**

Pornography: The Law

The distribution and receipt of pornography has historically fallen under the First Amendment, which provides a constitutional right to freedom of speech. Obscene material for personal use by adults has been deemed as constitutional (*Stanley v. Georgia,* 394 U.S. 557, 1969); however the sale, transportation, or mailing of such material to children is not constitutionally protected. Involving children in the production of obscene material is also prohibited. Defining what is "obscene" or "pornographic" has posed difficulty for lawmakers and judges. In 1964, Justice Stewart made the statement, "I know it when I see it" when defining pornography (*Jacobellis v. Ohio,* 378 U.S. 184, 197, 1964). Although this test lacked objectivity, it was not long before a more objective test was created. In 1966, obscenity was defined as something that lacked "redeeming social value" (*Memoirs v. Massachusetts,* 383 U.S. 413, 1966). A subsequent decision, however, made by the U.S. Supreme Court in the case of *Miller v. California* (413 U.S. 15, 1973) became a landmark case in terms of how pornography would be defined. In a five to four decision, the *Memoirs* standard was rejected and the *Miller* test was applied. The *Miller* test defined obscene material as that which "... the average person, applying contemporary community standards, would find that the work, taken as a whole, appealed to the prurient interest, [and] ... the work depicted or described, in a patently offensive way, sexual conduct specifically defined by the applicable state law, as written or authoritatively construed, and whether the work, taken as a whole lacked serious literary, artistic, political, or scientific value" (p. 15).

One constant prohibition has been portraying minors in pornographic material and allowing minors to access pornographic material. Although most states had laws prohibiting minors to view or be the objects of pornographic material, the U.S. Supreme Court addressed the issue in 1968, which established precedence for all states (*Ginsberg v. New York,* 390 U.S. 629, 1968). In *Ginsberg*, the defendant was convicted for selling a "girlie" magazine to someone under the age of 17, which violated a state statute. The Court, in a five to four decision, found that the New York statute that prohibited knowingly selling material "harmful to minors" did not violate the constitutional rights of minors. Minors, therefore, have not been extended the same First Amendment rights as adults.

Minors and pornographic material was again addressed in the U.S. Supreme Court case, *New York v. Ferber* (458 U.S. 747, 1982). In this case the owner of a bookstore was convicted of selling two films that depicted young boys masturbating. This violated a New York statute that prohibited anyone from knowingly promoting sexual activity involving children under the age of 16. It was held that "child pornography, like obscenity, is *un*protected by the First Amendment if it involves ... a visual depiction of sexual conduct by children without serious literary, artistic, political, or scientific value" (italics added for emphasis) (p. 747). This case reinforced the notion that the selling or promoting of material involving children as objects of pornography was not protected by the Constitution.

Although it would seem that the issues surrounding pornography had been addressed either through state laws or U.S. Supreme Court cases, the issue of pornography is still in fact debated in the courtroom. One of the more current issues involves the availability of pornography on the Internet, where nude photographs and videos have become commonplace. Congress attempted to regulate pornography on the Internet by passing the Communications Decency Act (CDA) in 1996. Even though adults have the right to access such material, minors do not. Given that the Internet provides a great deal of anonymity, those who provide such images have few options to restrict minors, while providing adults full access. The CDA required criminal penalties for anyone who "(i) makes, creates, or solicits, and (ii) initiates the transmission of, any comment, request, suggestion, proposal, image, or other communication which is obscene or child pornography, knowing that the recipient of the communication is under 18 years of age, regardless of whether the maker of such communication placed the call or initiated the communication" (§223(b)(i)(ii)). Internet service providers, however, were exempt from prosecution. Additionally, those who show "good faith" by taking "reasonable, effective and appropriate" action in preventing minors from accessing pornographic material would not face civil or criminal charges (§223(e)(6)).

Not long after the president signed the statute, several petitioners filed a lawsuit against the attorney general, challenging the legality of the CDA. They made that the CDA has the potential to censor speech that falls outside the scope of the statute. For instance, while prohibiting minors from accessing pornographic material, adults may also be kept from material that they have the right to view. It was also argued that the technology did not exist to provide an effective method to deny minors access without denying the material to adults. After a preliminary injunction was issued the case was appealed to the U.S. Supreme Court. In a seven to two decision, the Court held the contested provisions of the CDA were unconstitutional. Because the contested statutes were vague and not carefully tailored to meet the goal of protecting minors from harmful material, the contested statutes of the CDA were held unconstitutional.

In another attempt to prevent minors from accessing pornographic material on the Internet, Congress passed the Child Online Protection Act (COPA) in November of 1998. Again, a long list of plaintiffs filed a lawsuit challenging its constitutionality. COPA was an attempt to address the shortcomings of the CDA and was more carefully tailored. It prohibited commercial entities from knowingly making harmful material available to minors and mandated fines of no more than $50,000 for each violation (each day constitutes a separate violation) (§231(a)(2–3)). It also subjected those who were convicted of this crime to face a civil penalty of no more than $50,000. This act only pertains to commercial businesses and not to individuals who provide minors with material that is considered "harmful." The definition of "harmful" mirrored the definition applied in *Miller*, by including the following factors: appealing to the prurient interests, depicts, describes, or represents actual or simulated sexual act or contact and is patently offense to minors, lacks serious literary, artistic, political, or scientific value for minors (§231(e)(6)(A–C)). The act also provides

protection from prosecution for those who require information verifying the person accessing pornographic material is an adult (i.e., use of a credit card, debit account, adult access code, adult personal identification number, or digital certificate verifying the person's age). It was speculated, however, such implementations would have a dramatic effect on businesses that provided pornographic material and would make it difficult for adults to access material, which they had a constitutional right to access (*ACLU v. Reno*, 217 F.3d 162, 2000). After arguments were heard a preliminary injunction was granted, restricting the implementation of COPA. The appellate court was asked to lift the injunction and a three-judge panel denied the request. Later, the U.S. Supreme Court heard the case and vacated and remanded the case back to the Third Circuit Court of Appeals. The appellate level court reaffirmed the injunction; thus, the specific statutes of COPA that addressed regulating pornographic material on the Internet were never enforced. The Court found that COPA was still overbroad and was not narrowly tailored. The statutes that have been specifically tailored to address pornography on the Internet have not been successful; the laws that existed prior to the rapid growth of the Internet are relied upon to regulate pornographic material on the Internet.

The U.S. Supreme Court addressed an additional aspect of pornography on the Internet in *Ashcroft v. Free Speech* (535, U.S. 234, 2002). The case dealt with the Child Pornography Prevention Act of 1996, which banned "virtual pornography" of children. Virtual pornography refers to computer-generated images of children; thus, it does not involve actual children, but rather computer-generated depictions of children. The U.S. Supreme Court affirmed the Ninth Circuit Court of Appeals' decision, which held that the Act violated the First Amendment. It was noted that virtual pornography was not like real child pornography, in that it was not related to the sexual abuse of children. It was stated that some virtual images may have literary or artistic value and that the ban of virtual child pornography was not justified. The Court, therefore, ruled that the Child Pornography Prevention Act that banned virtual child pornography was unconstitutional. Virtual child pornography is legal to portray and view; it is not seen as a violation of individual liberties.

Although legislation passed by Congress has not been upheld when challenged, alternative means of restricting pornographic images on the Internet have been pursued. One alternative avenue involves denying federal funds to public libraries that do not use filters that restrict access to pornographic material on the Internet. Congress had enacted the Children's Internet Protection Act (CIPA), which prohibited public libraries from receiving federal funds unless software blocking obscene or pornographic material had been installed (*U.S. v. American Library Association*, 156 L. Ed. 2d 221, 2003). The Eastern District Court of Pennsylvania held that CIPA violated the First Amendment. The case was appealed to the U.S. Supreme Court and the decision was reversed in a six to three decision. Precedent had established that Congress has a great deal of latitude in attaching contingencies in providing federal funds. The Court disagreed with the district court's finding that CIPA was not narrowly tailored and violated First Amendment rights. Thus, denying federal funds to libraries that do not install pornography filters is allowed and does not violate any constitutional rights.

Legal issues surrounding pornography and First Amendment rights have always been controversial. Although adults have been extended the right of creating and viewing pornographic material for personal use, children have not been extended the same rights. Allowing adults to exercise this right whereas denying it to minors has been a difficult balance. This became especially true after the Internet became widely accessible. Although stores that sell pornography can clearly restrict minors from accessing the stores, the Internet has no "storekeeper" to view all those who enter the area. The Internet provides a great deal of anonymity to its users. Congress has attempted to restrict minors accessing pornographic material on the Internet by passing the Communications Decency Act (47 USCS § 223, 2000). After it was found unconstitutional, Congress passed the Child Online Protection Act (47 USCS § 231, 2001), which targeted only commercial websites and mandated some sort of age verification process. Again, this act was ruled as unconstitutional.

In an attempt to prohibit virtual child pornography, the Child Pornography Prevention Act was passed, which the U.S. Supreme Court found unconstitutional because it did not violate anyone's individual rights. This has allowed virtual child pornography to be portrayed on the Internet. Congress also attempted to regulate accessing pornographic material on computers provided by public libraries; Congress was successful in this attempt. The U.S. Supreme Court found that Congress could attach such a contingency on federal funding. This appears to be the first successful attempt to regulate pornographic material on the Internet. It is likely that pornography will always be a controversial issue and as technology improves, it will likely be a topic the U.S. Supreme Court will address again.

DONNA M. VANDIVER

References and Further Reading

Baird, R.M. and Rosenbaum, S.E., Eds., (1991). *Pornography: Private Right or Public Menace?* New York, Prometheus Books.

Elias, J.E., Bullough, V.L. and Jarvis, W. (1999). *Porn 101: Eroticism, Pornography and the First Amendment*, New York, Prometheus Books.

Hawkins, G. and Zimring, F.E. (1989). *Pornography in a Free Society*, New York, Cambridge University Press.

Jenkins, P. (2001). *Beyond Tolerance: Child Pornography on the Internet*, New York, New York University Press.

Richard, P. and Simon, R.J. (2003). *Global Perspectives on Social Issues: Pornography, Lanham*, MD, Lexington Books.

Taylor, M. and Quayle, E. (2003). *Child Pornography: An Internet crime*, New York, Brunner-Routledge.

See also **Pornography and Criminal Behavior**

Postmodernism and Constitutive Theories of Criminal Behavior

Postmodernism is a movement among social theorists and philosophers that is skeptical of science and the scientific method and its promise to deliver progress. Postmodernism transcends disciplinary boundaries, and indeed began in the arts and the humanities before arriving in the social sciences. It did not reach criminology until the late 1980s. The basic position of those termed postmodernist is found in a cluster of ideas, which include the following: truth is unknowable;

rational thought is merely one way of thinking, and not necessarily a superior way; rational thought is a form of power; knowledge is not cumulative; facts are merely social constructions that are supported by various claims to truth that constitute a discourse or way of talking about phenomena; and criticism assumes an alternative truth and should be replaced by "critique" or "deconstruction," which is the continuous attempt to expose the constructed nature of knowledge by revealing the assumptions on which it is based. In criminology, this cluster of postmodernist ideas was seen as valuable but too "skeptical." An alternative version, called "affirmative postmodernism," accepted the basic tenets of postmodernism but argued that deconstruction also implies "reconstruction." In other words, if the world was socially constructed through discourse, it is possible to reconstruct it through different discourse. Such reconstruction or "replacement discourse" is no more truthful, and no less contingent, but can be attended to in such a way that the consequences for those investing their energy in the construction of the social world could be less harmful and less painful. Such reconstruction implies a continuous ongoing societal process of struggle to replace harmful social constructions with less harmful ones.

The affirmative postmodern position in criminology draws on several other strands of social theory including Ferdinand de Saussure's semiotics, Jacques Lacan's psychoanalysis, Alfred Schutz's sociological phenomenology, Harold Garfinkel's ethnomethodology, Michel Foucault's poststructuralism, Peter L. Berger and Thomas Luckmann's social constructionism, Anthony Gidden's structuration theory, Paulo Freire and Henry A. Giroux's critical pedagogy, and it also incorporates the diverse ideas from the mathematics of Benoit Mandlebrot, as well as topology theory and chaos and catastrophe theory. Leading theorists introducing aspects of postmodernist theory into criminology include Bruce Arrigo, Gregg Barak, Stuart Henry, Ronnie Lippens, Dragan Milovanovic, Peter Manning, Rob Schehr, and T. R. Young, however, the fullest development of these ideas into an integrated theoretical perspective is with Stuart Henry and Dragan Milovanovic's *Constitutive Criminology*.

Constitutive Criminology

Constitutive criminology, consistent with its postmodernist roots, believes that crime and its control cannot be viewed separately from the historical, cultural, and social contexts within which it is generated. Constitutive theory rejects the arguments in mainstream criminology that see crime and offenders as disconnected from the wider society or the result of individuals acting independently from the context of which they are a part. Constitutive criminologists argue that it is relationships of power, constructed by humans through their discourse, that provide the motivation, the scripts, and the props for the play that creates the harms that are labeled "crime." Humans, they argue, are active coconstructors of their worlds. They construct their worlds by transforming their surroundings through social interaction, not least via discourse or language use. Through language and symbols humans identify

differences, construct categories, and share a belief in the reality of their world that gives apparent order to otherwise chaotic states. It is toward these social constructions of reality that humans act. Insofar as our world is socially produced by our collective actions, we also coproduce the harm in our world. Thus constitutive criminology shifts the criminological focus away from narrow dichotomized issues focusing either on the individual offender or on the social environment. Crime is not parasitic behavior on our social world perpetrated by evil individuals, nor is it the result of uncontrollable forces of our social environment. Rather it is an integral part of our relationships with the world we create.

Constitutive criminology thus takes a holistic conception of the relationship between the "individual" and "society" that examines their mutuality and interrelationship. In the process of investing energy in socially constructed categories of order, humans not only shape their social world, but are also shaped by it. They are coproducers and coproductions of their own and others' agency. Constitutive criminology is about how some of this socially constructed order, as well as the humans constituted within it, can be harmed, impaired, and destroyed by both the process and by what is built during that process: ultimately by each other as fellow humans.

Constitutive theorists argue that the coproduction of harmful relations occurs through society's structure and culture, as these are energized by human actions. Constitutive criminologists look at what it is about the psycho-social-cultural matrix that provides the medium through which humans construct "meaningful" harms to others. They find that this medium is to be found in relations of inequality and power.

Constitutive criminologists argue that relationships of inequality established throughout the whole of society and reflected in its organizational and cultural arrangements translate into specific harmful relationships between the powerful and the powerless. Social processes of inequality not only produce directly harmful outcomes, but they also provide a blueprint for how all relationships operate. To the constitutive criminologist, human relationships in hierarchically ordered societies as different as those in the U.S., Europe, China, or India are first and foremost relationships of power and relationships about power.

The power that frames human relationships may be formal and stabilized in social institutions, such as corporations, government agencies, marriage, and the family. This power may be traditionally established as part of a historical and cultural context, as in relations between different races, ethnicities, and genders. It may be informal and fluctuating, as in subcultural groups or within interpersonal relationships among otherwise similar individuals. In any of these frames of power, and particularly in the interrelations of all three, harm is either a manifest or dormant outcome. Harm is not so much caused by inequality as it is embedded in relations of inequality. Thus, rather than identifying specific causes of crime, constitutive criminology seeks to demonstrate the ways in which harm is the frequent outcome of unequal power relationships, and to demonstrate the ways that some of this harm is labeled as crime.

Constitutive criminology sees crime as the outcome of humans investing energy in harm producing, socially constructed relations of power, based on inequalities constructed around differences. Crimes are nothing less than people being disrespected for being different. People are disrespected in numerous ways, but all have to do with denying or preventing us from becoming fully social beings. What is human is to make a difference to the world, to act on it, to interact with others, and together to transform the environment and ourselves. If this process is prevented or limited we become less than human; we are harmed. Thus constitutive criminologists define crime as "the power to deny others their ability to make a difference." The paradox of constitutive criminology is that although the making of difference constitutes what it is to be human, the use of difference to deny others the right to be different and make a difference constitutes the harm that is crime.

Constitutive criminology divides crime into two types: "crimes of reduction" and "crimes of repression." Crimes of reduction occur when those offended experience a loss of some quality relative to their present standing. They could have property stolen from them, but they could also have dignity stripped from them as in hate crime. Crimes of repression occur when people experience a limit, or restriction, preventing them from achieving a desired position or standing or realizing an accomplishment as occurs in sexism or racism. Considered along a continuum of deprivation, crimes of reduction or repression may be based on an infinite number of constructed differences.

In Western industrial societies such crimes or harms cluster around familiar socially and discursively constructed differences: economic (class, property), gender (sexism), race and ethnicity (racism, hate), political (power, corruption), morality, human rights, social position (status or prestige, inequality), psychological state (security, well-being), self-realization or actualization, biological integrity, etc. Whatever the construction, actions are harms either because they move an offended away from a position or state they currently occupy, or because they prevent them from occupying a position or state that they desire, the achievement of which does not deny or deprive another. However, actions and processes are not considered harms of

repression when they limit the attempts by some person or social process to make a difference that themselves limit others' attempts to do the same. Where attempts to achieve a desired position or standing are themselves limiting to others, then the repression of these attempts might be more correctly called control. Such control is to some extent also always a crime of repression, but the manner in which control is achieved can be more or less harmful or more or less justified.

This reconception of crime, offender, and victim leads to a different notion of crime causation. To the constitutive criminologist crime is not so much caused as discursively constructed through human processes of which it is one. However, there is something uniquely concentrated about those designated as criminals. Whether single human beings or human groups, constitutive criminology sees such people as "excessive investors" in the power to impose order (i.e., discursive constructions) on others. The offender is viewed as an "excessive investor" in the power to dominate others. Excessive investors put energy into creating and magnifying differences between themselves and others. This investment of energy disadvantages, disables, and destroys others' human potentialities. The investor's "crime" is to limit others' freedom. Their crime is that they act toward others as objects for domination such that, in the process, the victim loses some of their humanity, or the ability to make a difference or to be different. Victims, from this perspective, are disabled by the excessive investor and suffer loss. Victims suffer the pain of being denied their own humanity. The victim of crime is thus rendered a nonperson, a nonhuman, or a less complete being.

Constitutive criminology envisions criminal justice, as it is traditionally practiced, as part of the very problem it claims to control. Its practitioners act toward the discursively constructed categories of crime and crime control as if they were real. Criminal justice is an exercise in the investment of energy that perpetuates further harm. Criminal justice is a major excessive investor in harm. Both the discursive fear of the victimized and the system of criminal justice thus feed crime. Both fuel the energies that drive our notions of crime. Indeed, as indicated above, agencies of law and criminal justice, the official social control institutions of society, are themselves organizations that exercise power (and, therefore, harm). Agencies of justice and law not only accomplish both crimes of reduction (of liberty, of property, of life) and repression (incapacitation), they also deepen the problem by labeling and categorizing only some harmful behavior of power relationships as "crime," leaving other harmful behavior unlabeled, as though it were acceptable, legal, legitimate, or "not crime." In this process of societal social control, harmful behavior and those who produce it become colonized by criminal justice; they become subject to justice's own powerful relations. The results are amplification, concentration, and multiple layering of powerful relations and from these emerge multiple possibilities for harm.

Contributing further to the excessive investment in harm are crime shows, crime dramas, crime documentaries, crime news, crime books, crime films, crime precautions, agencies of criminal justice, lawyers, and academic criminologists. Each contributes to the continuous coproduction of crime by exploiting the relations of power and by perpetuating the discourse of crime (domination).

Language is a key ingredient in the coproduction of the relations of power that produce harm. It is through discourse (language and symbol use) that we conceive of and act to produce our world. Therefore, discourse is a major means of achieving social change, changes in structures of powerful relations and, through this, crime (harm) reduction. Constitutive criminology suggests alternative ways to deal with the harm that is "crime" that build on the central role of language. This involves reorganizing society to minimize the harm that is based on differences of power. Part of this reorganization comes from a deconstruction of the language or "discourse" of power. To help bring about such reorganization and social change, constitutive criminologists suggest developing "replacement discourses." These are alternative ways of describing the world that do not perpetuate existing relations of power, nor create new relations of power, but help constitute relationships founded on human interconnectedness. Here difference is the basis for greater understanding rather than a foundation for inequality. Developing such replacement discourses will be a key practical action in the reconstruction of human relations toward minimizing harm.

Given the continuous coproduction of crime, and its compounding by the criminal justice process, and the mass media's discursive reproduction of the very relations of power that affirm their reality, what can be done? Constitutive criminology suggests that crime must be deconstructed as an ongoing discursive process, and that reconstruction must take place. The emphasis is on creating replacement discourses that provide the linguistic materials out of which new conceptualizations of being human in society may appear.

The new constructions are designed to displace crime as moments in the exercise of power and as control. They offer an alternative medium by which social constructions of reality can take place. Beyond resistance, the concept of replacement discourse offers a celebration of unofficial, informal, discounted, and ignored knowledge through its discursive diversity.

In terms of diminishing the harm experienced from all types of crime (street, corporate, state, hate, etc.), constitutive criminology talks of "liberating" replacement discourses that seek transformation of both the prevailing political economies and the associated practices of crime and social control. Constitutive criminology thus simultaneously argues for ideological as well as materialistic changes; one without the other renders change only in part.

Replacement discourse can be implemented through attempts by constitutive criminologists to reconstruct popular images of crime in the mass media through engaging in what Barak (1998) has called "newsmaking criminology." It can also be induced through what Parry and Doan (1994) call "narrative therapy." Narrative therapy developed as part of family therapy to enable offenders (excessive investors in power) to construct more liberating life narratives and through these reconstitute themselves.

Evaluation

Constitutive criminology has raised much discussion in recent literature and several arguments have been levied against it, although most share Thomson's (1997) view that this theory is stimulating, "raising issues that must be confronted by scholars in the empirical, romantic, and Marxist traditions of modern theorizing." Several of the criticisms of constitutive criminology relate to its postmodernist leanings. For example, a central theme is that postmodern or constitutive prose is excessively complex, difficult and "esoteric." Constitutive theorists counter that it is only difficult because of the narrow range of discourse that mainstream criminologists are exposed to. A second issue is to challenge the value of using integrative methodology. The general charge here is that constitutive theorizing attempts artificial integration of incompatible theoretical positions such as modernism and postmodernism or idealism and materialism. Constitutive theorists believe that these positions are interrelated, and the mistake is to separate and prioritize one over the other. Unlike much of modernism's dualisms such as "free will versus determinism," "conflict versus consensus" and "order versus chaos," constitutive theory sees that each of these is operative. Indeed, according to the insights generated by chaos theory, we can have order and disorder in the same system.

Third, some critics disparage constitutive criminology's embrace of social constructionist concepts. They assume that because of constitutive criminology's claim that crime is socially constructed, advocates also believe crime does not have any real consequences. However, constitutive theorists believe that real harm comes from people acting toward constructions as if they are realities, as is clearly demonstrated in the example of crimes committed in the name of religion.

Fourth, others have criticized the constitutive redefinition of crime as harm, saying that this expands crime beyond its real scope, but constitutive theorists point to the arbitrary nature defining only some harm as crime.

Fifth, questions have been raised over whether a set of causal assumptions still really underlie the analysis, and if so whether this can be measured. For example, critiques have been levied against constitutive criminology's use of nonlinear logic, especially the use of chaos theory rather than conventional causal analysis. Leading mainstream modernist theorists like Ron Akers complain that "constitutive criminology has not yet offered a testable explanation of either crime or criminal justice."

Sixth, given the various forms of repressive practices in society, the question of what to do about crime that we address above through replacement discourse has also led to significant reaction. Here critics often feel that they have the last word against constitutive criminology, claiming that such theorizing "can too easily lead toward nihilism, cynicism, and conservatism." Others challenge the policy of constitutive criminology for being naïve in believing changes in discourse can change power structures. Some point out that there is nothing sacrosanct about the idea of "replacement discourse" as a form of reconstruction that limits its strategic use to progressive and harm reducing objectives. Nor is replacement discourse the prerogative of one particular political persuasion. Indeed, even some sympathetic supporters indicate that replacement discourse may itself be harm producing, and that while affording a means of resistance it can also allow new negative constructions to occur. Finally, there are critics who believe that the constitutive approach to social change implies a vanguard of intellectuals rather than workers, which they claim, embodies a pacifism that is likely to be ineffective against the powerful excessive investors. The problem for constitutive theorists, however, is not to remove existing institutional and social structures that reproduce the differences whose investment with power results in oppression and inequality. Instead, the problem is how to cease our nonreflexive rebuilding of these social forms and structures while reinvesting energy in alternative, connective interrelational social forms. They suggest that structures that are extremely sensitive to their environment and its perturbations and consequently undergo continuous change while still providing provisionally stable horizons for social action may become the basis of political action and social policy. Whether these reconstructed contingent orders will be able to replace existing more harmful ones is the challenge to constitutive criminology.

STUART HENRY AND DRAGAN MILOVANOVIC

Further Reading

Barak, G. (1998). *Integrating Criminologies*, Boston, MA, Allyn and Bacon.

Henry, S. and Milovanovic, D. (1999). *Constitutive Criminology at Work: Applications to Crime and Justice*, Albany, NY, SUNY Press.

Henry, S. and Milovanovic, D. (1996). *Constitutive Criminology: Beyond Postmodernism*, London, Sage.

Milovanovic, D. Ed., (1996a). *Chaos, Criminology and Social Justice*, Westport, CT, Praeger.

Milovanovic, D. (1998). *Postmodern Criminology*, New York, Garland.

Parry, A. and Doan, R. E. (1994). *Story Re-Visions: Narrative Therapy in the Postmodern World*, New York, Guilford Publications.

Rosenau, P.M. (1992). *Postmodernism and the Social Sciences*, Princeton, NJ, Princeton University Press.

The Journal of Postmodern Criminology. Red feather Institute website.

Thomson, A. (1997). *Post-Modernism and Social Justice*, Paper presented at the Annual Meeting of the Society of Socialist Studies, St. John's, Newfoundland. Also available at: A shorter version is published in *Canadian Journal of Sociology*, 23, 109–113 (1998).

See also **Psychoanalytic Theories of Criminal Behavior; Psychological Theories of Criminal Behavior; Social Control Theories of Criminal Behavior; Sociological Theories of Criminal Behavior**

Presentence Investigation Reports (PSIR)

The presentence investigation report (PSIR) is a key document in the correctional process and it forms the nucleus for several subsequent reports made on a convictee as he or she travels through the criminal justice system. It is a prominent feature of the American judiciary and is to be found in other countries as well, notably the U.K.

The PSIR is mainly a social investigation of an offender who has been convicted of a crime but is awaiting sentencing. It is conducted by a probation officer and is primarily designed to assist a judge in imposing a sentence appropriate to both the crime committed and to the individual circumstances of the convictee. The probation officer preparing the PSIR does so under the supervision of that specific court and is often an employee of the court although there are many jurisdictions that use a centralized probation agency that serves all the courts within a political jurisdiction. There are other investigations conducted by probation officers that resemble the PSIR but are not primarily used to aid in postconviction sentencing. Examples of these are reports used in juvenile courts as a precursor to a finding of delinquency and reports used in making various pretrial diversion decisions.

The typical PSIR contains information that can be listed under such categories as: description of the offense; convictee's statement regarding the offense; prior criminal record; convictee's developmental history, including school and early family life; present family and living conditions; employment history; physical and mental condition; and financial status. Mitigating and aggravating circumstances to the current offense are described in detail. Other categories of information may be included on a case-by-case basis. The basic aim is to provide an instrument to the court that can be used in arriving at a sentence that meets the need for just punishment, for deterrence, for possible incapacitation, and for the potential rehabilitation of the offender. The aforementioned four goals are difficult to balance in all cases and there are times when one goal assumes a preeminence in the attitude of the community or in the case of a particular offender. For example, around the 1960s offender rehabilitation was the dominant goal in the criminal justice process and the idea was to fit the sentence to the rehabilitation needs of the offender whenever feasible. That began to change in the 1970s and 1980s when fitting the sentence to the crime became the ascendant objective.

As the fundamental goals of sentencing have shifted, so have the typical structure and content of the PSIR. As a means of achieving fairness and reasonable uniformity in sentencing (i.e., similarly situated convictees should receive similar sentences for similar crimes), various jurisdictions have developed sentencing guidelines. These guidelines usually involve numerical scoring-based weights given to such things as seriousness of offense and prior criminal record. Some sentencing guidelines also include social factors related to rehabilitation or recidivism. This has resulted in the probation officer having to include in the PSIR a numerical score derived from an arithmetical calculation of specifically weighted factors. This score, in turn, leads to a limited range of sentences that the judge can impose. Thus, in addition to limitations set by statute in regard to a specific offense, further limitations emerge from official and binding sentencing guidelines. Consequently, discretion in sentencing is significantly restricted and, with reduced discretion, the goal of rehabilitation is undermined. Many judges and probation officers have chafed in trying to work with sentencing guidelines especially when faced with the exceptional cases that are bound to appear. The PSIR of today is less freewheeling, less diagnostic, and less creative than it was prior to the device of sentencing guidelines with its accompanying shift away from a rehabilitation focus.

Further affecting the character of the PSIR is the changing orientation of the probation officer. Partially brought about by sentencing guidelines and the decline of the rehabilitation ideal, the style of the probation officer has changed from a therapist or social worker outlook to a law enforcement one. The tools available to probation officers for supervising those placed on probation, including electronic monitoring, are in accord with popular policies of strict supervision marked by severe restrictions on the activities of the probationer. This overall change in attitude is reflected in the PSIR becoming more of a legal document than a document seeking psychological and sociological explanations of a particular convictee's criminal behavior.

There is great variation in the practice of the PSIR providing more or less specific recommendations as to a sentence. In many cases, the numerical score calculated by the probation officer, operating under statutorily defined guidelines, establishes a legally mandated sentence. In cases where sentencing guidelines are minimally restrictive or actually nonexistent, some judges insist upon having a sentencing recommendation from the probation officer contained in the PSIR. Other judges want only an oral recommendation, or no recommendation, thereby avoiding the obvious pitfall of possibly seeming to have made a mistake by going against a recorded recommendation.

Although initiated by the court working in its own behalf, the PSIR, depending on the sentence imposed, is used in other capacities. It becomes the nucleus for the record that is developed and maintained by prison authorities on a convictee sentenced to imprisonment. It is also the nucleus for the record maintained on a convict placed under probation supervision. Parole boards use the PSIR as part of their independent file on a prisoner eligible for parole consideration. Clemency authorities use the PSIR in deciding whether to grant pardons, commutations, reprieves, or restoration of lost civil rights.

Despite the wide use of the PSIR in the criminal justice system, there are concerns relating to confidentiality. Some jurisdictions attach a copy of the PSIR to the court papers, thus virtually making the PSIR a public document. Other jurisdictions have denied the defendant access to the PSIR. Among the arguments in favor of allowing the defendant access to his or her own PSIR are points of simple fairness. Reviewing the PSIR also enables a convictee to protect against the errors that probation officers sometimes make in these reports. Arguments against lifting confidentiality, usually made by probation officers are that sources of information would dry up without the promise of confidentiality. Nevertheless, the trend is away from confidentiality in most jurisdictions.

EUGENE H. CZAJKOSKI

References and Further Reading

Adair, D.N., Jr. 1993. Discovery of probation officer files, *Federal Probation*, 57(3), 76–80 (Sept).

Adair, D.N., Jr. and Slawsky, T.D. 1991. Fact-finding in sentencing, (The Sentencing Reform Act of 1984 and Sentencing Guidelines), *Federal Probation*, 55(4), 58–72, (Dec).

Campbell, C., McCoy, C. and Osigweh, C.A.B. 1990. The influence of probation recommendations on sentencing decisions and their predictive accuracy, *Federal Probation*, 54(4), 13–21 (Dec).

Clear, T.R., Clear, V.B. and Burrell, W.D. 1989. *Offender Assessment and Evaluation: The Presentence Investigation Report*, Cincinnati, OH, Anderson Publishing Co.

Cohn, A.W. and Ferriter, M.M. 1990. The presentence investigation report: An old saw with new teeth, *Federal Probation*, 54(3), 15–25 (Sept).

Gaines, L.K., Kaune, M. and Miller, R.L. 1999. *Criminal Justice in Action*, Belmont, CA, Wadsworth or Thomson Learning.

Jaffe, H.J. 1989. The presentence report, probation officer accountability, and recruitment practices: Some influences of guidelines sentencing, *Federal Probation*, 53(3), 12–14 (Sept).

Schmalleger, F. 1999. *Criminal Justice: A Brief Introduction*, 4th ed., Upper Saddle River, NJ, Prentice Hall.

See also **Sentences and Sentencing: Guidelines; Sentences and Sentencing: Types**

Prediction of Criminal Behavior (Risk Assessment)

"If you can look into the seeds of time, and say which grain will grow and which will not, speak then unto me."
(William Shakespeare)

Throughout history, humans have shared a fascination with the art of prediction—from simple predictions such as projecting winners of sporting events and political races, to even more complex predictions, such as calculating the expected lifespan of a human being. At the core of many prediction models is a formulation of the probability of risk, that is, whether there is a possibility that something may be gained, or lost (Kemshall, 1998). Based upon the prediction made, a particular course of action is then taken. If there is a greater probability that the proposed outcome will be positive, it is more likely the risk will be taken. Conversely, if there is a greater likelihood that the outcome will be negative, it is more likely that the risk will be avoided. Although the concept of risk incorporates both positive and negative outcomes, it has increasingly become synonymous with predicting harmful consequences (Kemshall, 1998). This is seen in the criminal justice system, where the practice of risk assessment focuses on the likelihood that an individual will engage in a variety of negative behaviors.

The Principle of Prediction

Prediction is based on the premise that by identifying patterns of behavior within groups of individuals, one can estimate the risk of whether an individual who shares characteristics with the group will also engage in that behavior. Traditionally, the most common outcome predicted in risk assessment is recidivism. However, risk assessment has also been used for other purposes, such as estimating the likelihood that an individual will fail to appear for assigned court dates, escape from custody, pose a security risk within the institution, or violate conditions of supervision in the community (Van Voorhis and Brown, 1997). In Texas and Oregon, risk assessments are mandated by the legislature before jurors can impose the death penalty (Cunningham and Reidy, 1999; Sorensen and Pilgrim, 2002). Risk assessments guide severity of community controls in Washington State. The premise supporting these uses of risk assessment is that if these types of behavior can be predicted, they can be averted (Gottfredson, 1987a).

In today's climate of fiscal constraint and increased public scrutiny, agencies are being held accountable for their decisions and how they allocate their resources. Consequently, prediction has become fundamental to the operation of the criminal justice system (Bonta et al., 1996; Kemshall, 1999). If an agency can accurately assess risk, it can "match" offenders to the appropriate level of supervision and reserve resources for those identified as high-risk (Andrews and Bonta, 1994). However, the manner in which agencies calculate this risk remains an elusive mixture of art and science.

Types of Risk Assessment

Traditionally, criminal justice agencies have relied upon either subjective (e.g., "clinical") or objective (e.g., "actuarial") criteria to help guide decision making (Bonta, 1996). Agencies that rely on a clinical approach to risk assessment gather information about the offender through unstructured interviews and case file reviews, which must then be synthesized in some meaningful way. Case management decisions are based on intuitive evaluations and can vary from one clinician to another. Not surprisingly, this practice has been sharply criticized by researchers and civil libertarians for its idiosyncratic approach to decision making and its potential for "personal prejudices and biases to operate [which] may contribute to decisions inconsistent with the objectives of the system" (Hoge, 2002, 382). Although this is the most commonly used method of assessment, it has been found largely incapable of accurately predicting future criminal behavior (Glaser, 1987; Groves and Meehl, 1996). Consequently, many agencies have pursued a more objective approach to decision making.

The practice of standardized risk assessment is rooted in the same methodology the insurance industry employs when creating "actuarial tables." Risk factors are first identified statistically by studying patterns of behavior in the general population, and then systematic comparisons are made between an individual and the reference group (Gottfredson, 1987a).

The first attempt at adapting this methodology to a criminal justice population was completed by Burgess (1928) in his study of parolees. After identifying a set of factors correlated with parole failure, Burgess scored subjects on each item, assigning a 1 or 0 based on its presence or absence. Items were then summed to create a composite risk score that could serve as an indicator of the offender's likelihood of future criminality. Burgess hypothesized the higher the score, the greater the "risk" the individual posed to society.

Although this model brings a greater level of objectivity to how decisions are formulated, it has been challenged as being too simplistic because it assumes all risk factors are equally predictive (Gottfredson, 1987a; Gottfredson, 1987b; Jones, 1996).

A more sophisticated scoring technique was developed by the Gluecks (1958). Specifically, they used multivariant analysis techniques to assign "weights" to each risk factor based upon the strength of its relationship with the outcome measure. Although this approach has been touted to be the superior method for developing prediction models, numerous studies have failed to find significant improvements in models based upon multiple regression techniques over those that used the simpler Burgess method (Farrington and Tarling, 1985; Gottfredson and Gottfredson, 1986).

Currently, there are two kinds of actuarial risk instruments used by criminal justice agencies (Bonta, 1996). The first, static risk scales, rely exclusively on risk factors that do not change over time (e.g., demographics) or are unidirectional (e.g., criminal history). The most widely used instrument of this kind is the salient factor score (SFS). Developed in the late 1960s by the U.S. Parole Commission, the SFS was designed to bring greater structure to parole board decisions. Using this instrument, offenders are scored on six items, including prior convictions or adjudications, prior commitments ≥ 30 days, and age at current offense. In the federal system, this score is used in combination with the severity of offense rating at sentencing to determine the amount of time an offender must serve before becoming eligible for parole.

Although instruments, such as the SFS, increased the validity, structure, and consistency of decision making from those derived from clinical assessments, they have been criticized on a number of levels. First, by focusing exclusively on an offender's criminal history, risk is conceptualized as a one-dimensional construct, although crime is multidimensional (Andrews and Bonta, 1994). In addition, such an approach limits the use of the instrument to only being capable of making recommendations about supervision or confinement (Bonta, 2002).

As a result of this shortcoming, a new generation of instruments was developed that includes a broader range of correlates of crime. These "risk-needs" instruments include criminal history variables, as well as a select number of social and contextual variables that are shown to contribute or diminish an individual's likelihood of reoffending (Andrews, Bonta, and Hoge, 1990). Often referred to within the literature as "criminogenic needs," these factors typically focus on areas within the offender's life that are amenable to change, such as family functioning, deviant associations, and drug use. Researchers and practitioners argue that by modifying or diminishing these risk factors through specific individualized treatment plans, agencies can help reduce an offender's probability of recidivism (Bonta, 1996).

One instrument that has demonstrated a great deal of promise is the level of service inventory—revised (LSI) (Andrews and Bonta, 1994). Originally developed in the late 1970s and later revised in the mid-1980s, the LSI-R incorporates both static and dynamic risk factors. The instrument includes 54 items broken down into ten domains. Each domain is theoretically linked to offending behavior, such as criminal history, education and employment, family and marital relationships, attitudes and orientations, and alcohol and drug problems. Currently, the LSI-R is used to guide sentencing decisions, match offenders to appropriate correctional treatment programs, and structure parole recommendations (Bonta, 2002). It has also been adapted for a juvenile justice population (e.g., youth level of service inventory). Most importantly, the LSI-R is one of the few assessment instruments that has been cross-validated and found to demonstrate dynamic validity (Andrews and Bonta, 1995; 1998; Gendreau, Little, and Goggin, 1996; Harris, Rice, and Quinsey, 1993).

Unlike those instruments that focus exclusively on the offender's criminal history, "risk-needs" instruments enable an agency to monitor *change* within the offender. Through regular reassessment, agencies can make adjustments to security classifications or programming that will best reflect the offender's current level of risk (Bonta, 2002). As a result, agencies are in a stronger position to manage their resources more effectively and uphold their promise to protect the public.

The Challenges of Predictive Efficiency

Despite the advances made in risk assessment over the past 40 years, the predictive efficiency of these instruments has often been jeopardized by a number of methodological and practical issues. In particular, some agencies have mistakenly adopted an existing instrument developed by another agency without first cross-validating it on their own population. Other agencies have developed an instrument with one population and then applied it unilaterally. Unfortunately, such "shortcuts" have produced a significant proportion of prediction error.

There are two types of prediction errors that are found in every risk instrument. The first type of error occurs when an instrument predicts that an individual will reoffend, but in reality he or she does not. These errors are referred to as "false positives." The second type of error occurs when an instrument predicts that an individual will not reoffend, but in reality he or she does. These errors are referred to as "false negatives." Each of these errors create a number of practical and ethical dilemmas for agencies.

When instruments produce a high proportion of false positives a "net-widening" effect is triggered, causing a large number of low-risk offenders to be assigned more stringent or intrusive conditions of supervision than they would have ordinarily received. In the worst-case scenario, this type of error could result in the unnecessary detention of an individual. Because agency resources are limited, assigning more intensive measures to low-risk offenders is not only fiscally irresponsible, but may also cause more harm in the long run. In particular, research has shown that low-risk offenders assigned to intensive services were more likely to recidivate than those who received no intervention (Andrews et al., 1990; Coulson et al., 1996; Van Voorhis and Brown, 1997).

The second type of issue presented occurs when instruments produce false negatives. In particular, instruments that produce a high proportion of false negatives inappropriately release high-risk offenders back into the community, thereby raising concerns from a public safety perspective. In the worst-case scenario, such an individual could commit a serious, violent crime. This occurred when Richard Allen Davis, a convicted sex offender, kidnapped and murdered 12-year-old Polly Klaas while he was on parole ("Guilty Verdict," 1996).

In either case, both types of prediction errors jeopardize the instrument's validity from the perspective of both the stakeholders and the line-staff who are responsible for implementing the protocol, which may in turn cause agencies to become more resistant to adopting such practices (Kemsall, 1999; Pfeifer, Taxman, and Young, 2001). Accordingly, the challenge to researchers is to determine a way to balance these two errors without compromising the instrument's overall predictive efficiency. Unfortunately, creating such a model is a mixture of art and science.

Risk instruments are evaluated not only on how well they can accurately predict recidivism, but also on how well they are able to distinguish between different levels of risk. Ideally, offenders who are classified as "medium" risk should be twice as likely to recidivate as "low" risk offenders, and half as likely to recidivate as "high" risk offenders. To create such classifications, researchers select "cut-off points" along a predictive scale to group offenders into different risk classifications. Unfortunately, this decision is often made subjectively (Bonta et al., 1996). To introduce more objectivity to this process, researchers have turned to mathematical models to identify optimum combinations of cut-off points that will minimize the proportion of prediction errors while maximizing the instrument's predictive efficiency.

One such method is to calculate the model's "Relative Improvement over Chance" (RIOC) score (Loeber and Dishion, 1982; Gottfredson and Gottfredson, 1986). The RIOC tests the efficiency of the instrument by determining how a model performs relative to its expected performance and its best possible performance. Scores range from zero, indicating no improvement, to one, indicating absolute improvement. The closer the score is to one, the more efficient the model. One of the advantages of the RIOC is that it takes into account the model's base rate and selection ratio, thereby allowing researchers to assess the predictive efficiency of models whose criteria variables have skewed distributions (Copas and Tarling, 1986; Gottfredson and Gottfredson, 1986; Jones, 1996). The weakness of the statistic, however, is that it creates a two-way classification scheme assigning youth to only "high" or "low" risk categories, when most instruments classify offenders into three or more risk levels. In addition, it has been criticized for its sensitivity to changes in the instrument's selection ratios (Bonta et al., 1996)

A more sophisticated analysis that enables researchers to measure an instrument's predictive efficiency independent of base rates and selection ratios is the "Receiver Operating Characteristics" (ROC) test statistic (Swets, 1986). ROC estimates an instrument's sensitivity at discriminating between true positives (TP) and false positives (FP) (Bonta et al., 1996). The cumulative frequencies of TP and FP for each score are plotted graphically to produce a curve. The "Area under the Curve" (AUC) is then calculated and given a numeric value. Scores range from zero, indicating perfect negative prediction, to one, indicating perfect positive prediction. The larger the value, the greater the difference between the proportion of TP and FP, and hence the better the model's predictive efficiency. As the ratio between TP and FP shifts as each score is plotted along the curve, researchers can then pinpoint where the cut-off scores should be assigned.

Although each of the aforementioned techniques help researchers construct the most statistically sound prediction model, LeBlanc (2000) cautions that researchers should not overlook the importance of also evaluating the instrument from a social utility perspective. Specifically, researchers should assess the proportion of prediction errors produced by various cut-off scores against the seriousness of the behavior the instrument is designed to predict. For example, when predicting violent behavior, it may be more acceptable to construct a model that minimizes the proportion of false negatives given the threat this type of offender poses to society. In contrast, when predicting institutional misbehavior, it may be more acceptable to minimize the proportion of false positives because a significant proportion of such behavior often involves minor infractions. Although this may not produce the most optimally predictive instrument, it will yield a model that will balance the goals of the agency, manage resources efficiently, and protect the public (Pfeifer, Taxman, and Young, 2003.).

Risk Assessment and Special Populations

As researchers have become more proficient in risk assessment, there has been a marked increase in the development of instruments used to predict more elusive behaviors, such as violent or sexual offenses. Given that the base rate for such behaviors is low, it is exceedingly difficult for risk instruments to derive accurate predictions about those behaviors (Bonta et al., 1996). Within the past few years, however, a number of specialized instruments have been developed that have shown some promise (Bonta, 2002). For example, the Violence Risk Appraisal Guide (VRAG) (Harris, Rice, and Quinsey, 1993) has been shown to predict violent recidivism within both a general offending population and among mentally disordered offenders (Bonta, Law, and Hanson, 1998; Quinsey et al., 1998). Researchers have also identified a set of risk factors that predict sexual recidivism, which in turn, have been used to construct the sex offender need assessment rating (SONAR) (Hanson and Harris, 2000).

Although most of the research on risk assessment has occurred within the adult offending population, there has also been increased interest within the juvenile justice system to incorporate a more formalized approach to risk assessment. To date, at least 16 states have developed some type of formal risk assessment measure for juveniles (Towberman, 1992). In the process, researchers have discovered that predicting juvenile recidivism is similar to trying to hit a moving target. Not only do youth have a shorter criminal history to base predictions upon, they are also undergoing significant physical, intellectual, and emotional changes, making it difficult to identify a set of uniform risk factors (Ashford and LeCroy, 1990; Altschuler and Armstrong, 1991; Kazdin, 2000). Consequently, researchers have argued that these instrument need to be revalidated every few years (Gottfredson, 1987a).

Researchers are also now beginning to explore the impact of protective factors on youth's risk levels. These factors include personal, familial, or environmental conditions that can help offset or moderate the negative effects of risk factors (Hoge, Andrews, and Leschied, 1996; Carr and Vandiver, 2001). These factors encapsulate such things as: the youth's sense of self-worth or self-efficacy, the degree of closeness shared with parents and family members, and the number of attachments to supportive adults in the community. Preliminary findings have shown that juveniles with a greater number of protective factors are less likely to recidivate than those with fewer protective factors (Carr and Vandiver, 2001).

The process of developing specialized risk instruments for juvenile offenders and specific adult offending populations has been a lengthy and expensive process. However, such an approach is essential. Each of these populations has specific needs that agencies must address. If agencies fail to do so by adopting a "one size fits all" attitude toward risk assessment, they are at greater risk of misclassifying offenders. This may result in a lack of appropriate treatment for all offenders, in an increased threat to public safety for violent and sexual offenders.

Conclusion

For nearly two decades, researchers and policymakers have touted the importance of using valid risk screening tools in the adult and juvenile systems. During this period, significant advances have been made, particularly in how researchers and agencies have conceptualized and measured risk. By including dynamic, as well as historical factors on risk instruments, agencies are now able to calculate changes in an offender's risk level, as well as the progress he or she makes in assigned interventions. As a result, agencies have become more effective at managing their resources. These instruments have also helped introduce a greater level of accountability for those agencies by reducing the amount of discretion allowed in the decision-making process.

In sum, the key to success of risk assessment lies in the ability of agencies and researchers to recognize that it is a process, rather than a task to be completed in a short period of time. Like crime, risk is a dynamic construct. By continually refining our definition of risk, researchers will make greater strides in accurately predicting future criminal behavior.

HEATHER PFEIFER AND FAYE TAXMAN

References and Further Reading

Altschuler, D. and Armstrong, T. (1991). Intensive aftercare for the high risk juvenile parolee: Issues and approaches in reintegration and community supervision, in Armstrong. T., Ed., *Intensive Interventions with High-Risk Youth: Promising Approaches in Juvenile Probation and Parole,* Monsey, NY, Willow Tree Press.

Andrews, D.A. and Bonta, J. (1995). *The Level of Services Inventory-Revised,* Toronto, Canada, Multi-Health Systems.

Andrews, D.A. and Bonta, J. (1998). *The Psychology of Criminal Conduct,* 2nd ed., Cincinnati, OH, Anderson.

Andrews, D.A., Bonta, J.L. and Hoge, H.D. (1990). Classification for effective rehabilitation: Rediscovering psychology, *Criminal Justice and Behavior,* 17, 19–52.

Ashford, J.B. and LeCroy, C.W. (1990). Juvenile recidivism: A comparison of three prediction instruments, *Adolescence,* 25(98), 441–450.

Bonta, J. (1996). Risk-needs assessment and treatment, in Harland, A., Ed., *Choosing Correctional Options that Work: Defining the Demand and Evaluating the Supply,* Thousand Oaks, CA, Sage, pp. 18–32.

Bonta, J. (2002). Offender risk assessment: Guidelines for selection and use, *Criminal Justice and Behavior,* 29(4), 355–379.

Bonta, J., Law, M. and Hanson, R.K. (1998). The prediction of criminal and violent recidivism among mentally disordered offenders, *Psychological Bulletin,* 123, 123–142.

Bonta, J., Harman, W.G., Hann, R.G. and Cormier, R.B. (1996). The prediction of recidivism among federally sentenced offenders: A re-validation of the SIR scale, *Canadian Journal of Criminology,* 38(1), 61–79.

Burgess, E.W. (1928). Factors determining success or failure on parole. in Bruce, A.A., Harno, A.J., Burgess, E.W. and Landesco, J., Eds., *The workings of the Indeterminate Sentence Law and the parole System in Illinois,* Springfield, IL, State Board of Parole.

Carr, M.B. and Vandiver, T.A. (2001). Risk and protective factors among youth Offenders, *Adolescence,* 36(143), 409–426.

Coulson, G., Ilacqua, G., Nutbrown, V., Giulekas, D. and Cudjoe, F. (1996). Predictive utility of the LSI for incarcerated female offenders, *Criminal Justice and Behavior,* 23(3), 427–439.

Copas, J.B. and Tarling, R. (1986). Some methodological issues in making predictions., in Blumstein, A., Cohen, J., Roth, J. and Visher, C., Eds., *Criminal Careers and 'Career Criminals',* Washington, DC, National Academy Press, pp. 291–355.

Criminal law database—parole, Available at: http://www.pdsdc.org/CriminalLawDatabase/parole.asp?ID=1. Retrieved on August 15, 2002.

Cunningham, M.D. and Reidy, T.J. (2002). Violence risk assessment at federal capital sentencing: Individualization, generalization, relevance, and scientific standards. *Criminal Justice and Behavior,* 29(5), 512–537.

Farrington, D. and Tarling, R., Eds., (1985). *Prediction in criminology,* New York, State University of New York Press.

Gendreau, P., Little, T. and Goggin, C. (1996). A meta-analysis of the predictors of adult recidivism: What works! *Criminology,* 34, 401–433.

Glaser, D. (1987). Classification for risk, in Gottferdson, D.M. and Tonry, M., Eds., *Prediction and Classification,* Chicago, IL, University of Chicago Press.

Gottfredson, D.M. (1987a). Prediction and classification in criminal justice decision making, in Gottfredson, D. and Tonry, M., Eds., *Crime and Justice: A Review of Research,* Chicago, IL, University of Chicago Press, pp. 1–20.

Gottfredson, S.D. (1987b). Prediction: An overview of selected methodological issues, in. Gottfredson, D. and Tonry, M., Eds., *Crime and Justice: A Review of Research,* Washington, DC, National Academy Press, pp. 212–290.

Gottfredson, S.D. and Gottfredson, D.M. (1986). Accuracy of prediction models, in Blumstein, A., Cohen, J, Roth, J. and Visher, C., Eds., *Criminal Careers and 'Career Criminals',* Washington, DC, National Academy Press, pp. 212–290.

Grove, W.M. and Meehl, P.E. (1996). Comparative efficiency of informal (subjective, impressionistic) and formal (mechanical, algorithmic) prediction procedures: The clinical-statistical controversy, *Psychology, Public Policy, and Law,* 2, 293–323.

Guilty Verdict in Klaas Murder, Killer Could Face Death Penalty (1996, June 18). Available at: http://www.cnn.com/US/9606/18/klaas.verdict. Retrieved on August 15, 2003.

Hanson, R.K. and Harris, A.J. (2000). *The Sex Offender Need Assessment Rating (SONAR): A method for measuring change in risk levels*, User Report No. 2000–01. Ottawa, Canada, Solicitor General Canada.

Harris, G.T., Rice, M.E. and Quinsey, V.L. (1993). Violent recidivism of mentally disordered offenders: The development of a statistical prediction instrument, *Criminal Justice and Behavior*, 20, 315–335.

Hoge, R.D. (2002). Standardized instruments for assessing risk and need in youthful offenders, *Criminal Justice and Behavior*, 29(4), 380–396.

Hoge, R.D. Andrews, D.A. and Leschied, A. (1996). An investigation of risk and protective factors in a sample of youthful offenders, *Journal of Child Psychology and Psychiatry*, 37, 419–424.

Jones, P.R. (1996). Risk prediction in criminal justice, in Harland, A.T., Ed., *Choosing Correctional Options That Work*, Thousand Oaks, CA, Sage. pp. 33–68.

Jung, S. and Rawana, E.P. (1999). Risk and need assessment of juvenile offenders, *Criminal Justice and Behavior*, 26(1), 69–89.

Kemshall, H. (1998). *Risk in Probation Practice*, Aldershot, U.K., Ashgate.

Kazdin, A.E. (2000). Adolescent development, mental disorders, and decision making of delinquent youths, in Grisso, T. and Schwartz, R.G., Eds., *Youth on Trial: A Developmental Perspective on Juvenile Justice*, Chicago, IL, University of Chicago Press, pp. 33–65.

LeBlanc, M. (2000). *Review of Screening, Decision-Making, and Clinical Assessments Strategies and Instruments for Adolescent Offenders*, Paper presented at NATO Advanced Research Workshop, Crakow, Poland.

Loeber, R. and Dishion, T. (1982). Early predictors of male delinquency: A review, *Psychological Bulletin*, 94, 68–99.

Pfeifer, H.L., Taxman, F. and Young, D. (2001). *Six of One, Half a Dozen of the Other: The Benefits and Challenges Associated with Risk Classification Tools*, Paper presented at annual American Society of Criminology meeting, Atlanta, GA.

Quinsey, V.L., Harris, G.T., Rice, M.E. and Cormeir, C.A. (1998). *Violent Offenders: Appraising and Managing Risk*, Washington, DC, American Psychological Association.

Sorenson, J.R. and Pilgrim, R.L. (2002). An actuarial risk assessment of violence posed by capital murder defendants, *The Journal of Criminal Law and Criminology*, 90(4), 1251–1270.

Swets, J.A. (1986). Indices of discrimination or diagnostic accuracy: Their ROCs and implied models, *Psychological Bulletin*, 99, 100–117.

Towberman, D.B. (1992). A national survey of juvenile risk assessment, *Juvenile and Family Court Journal*, 61–67.

Van Voorhis, P. and Brown, K. (1997). *Risk Classification in the 1990s*, Washington, DC, National Institute of Corrections.

See also **Biological Theories of Criminal Behavior; Cohort Research; Psychological Theories of Criminal Behavior; Sociological Theories of Criminal Research**

Preliminary Hearings

The preliminary hearing (preliminary examination) is one of several pretrial procedures afforded to criminal defendants. It usually occurs 10–30 days after the initial appearance, the Gerstein determination, and the bail hearing, and serves as an opportunity for a judicial review of a prosecutor's charging decision.

Although the preliminary hearing is not constitutionally mandated, most jurisdictions provide for it by either statute or court rule. The role of the preliminary hearing, however, differs between those jurisdictions that use grand juries and those which do not. Jurisdictions requiring prosecution by indictment, including the federal courts that are bound by the Fifth Amendment grand jury requirement, provide preliminary hearings to determine whether a case should be bound over to the grand jury. (See Fed. Rule Crim. Pro., 5.1 (2003).) These jurisdictions commonly render the requirement for a preliminary hearing moot when the prosecutor secures an indictment prior to the date of the preliminary hearing. In jurisdictions allowing prosecution to proceed by information, the defendant is usually entitled to a preliminary hearing before the information is filed by the prosecutor. In these jurisdictions the purpose of a preliminary hearing is for a judge, rather than the grand jury, to determine whether probable cause exists to support the charges. Some of these jurisdictions, however, also allow the prosecutor to bypass a preliminary hearing and ask for a judicial predetermination of probable cause. (See, example. e.g., *State v. Farnsworth*, 240 Mont. 328, 783 P.2d 1365, 1989 Mont. LEXIS 353 (1989).)

The preliminary hearing is not a trial to determine the defendant's guilt or innocence. It is an adversarial proceeding before a magistrate to determine whether a defendant should be bound over for trial. Thus, the amount of proof that the prosecution must present at a preliminary hearing is much less than what is necessary to support a conviction. At the preliminary hearing the burden is on the prosecution to provide enough evidence to show that there is probable cause to believe that an offense has been committed and probable cause to believe that the defendant committed it. The definition of the concept of probable cause applicable at a preliminary hearing varies from state to state. As probable cause to arrest is determined earlier in the process, at either a Gerstein hearing or prior to issuance of an arrest warrant, redetermination of that issue seems repetitive. Some states are attempting to heighten this standard. For example, the Pennsylvania Supreme Court has determined that "at a preliminary hearing, the Commonwealth bears the burden of making a prima facie showing that a crime has been committed and that the accused is the person who committed it" (*Commonwealth v. Prado,* 481 Pa. 485, 393 A.2d 8 (1978)).

As a preliminary hearing is an adversarial proceeding, defendants are provided an opportunity to challenge the prosecution's case. In order to effectively challenge the prosecution and protect their own rights the Supreme Court has held that defendants are entitled to counsel (*Coleman v. Alabama,* 399 US 1, 26 L Ed 2d 387, 90 S Ct 1999, 1970 US Lexis 17 (1970)). That Court found that an attorney plays an important role at a preliminary hearing by assisting in the impeachment of witnesses, helping with discovery of evidence, and by recognizing evidentiary weaknesses that can be exploited at trial. The Court further found that the preliminary hearing is a critical stage of the criminal process. Thus, indigent defendants have a right to counsel. The Coleman Court supported its decision by stating that "the guiding hand of counsel at the preliminary hearing is essential to protect the indigent accused against an erroneous or improper prosecution" (Id, p. 9).

Each state and the federal government has developed a separate evidentiary standard applicable to preliminary hearings. The Federal Rules of Criminal Procedure provide that "the defendant may cross-examine adverse witnesses and may introduce evidence but may not object to evidence on the ground that it was unlawfully acquired" (Fed. Rule Crim. Pro., 5.1(e), (2003); see also, *U.S. v. Blue,* 384 U.S. 251, 255 (1966) holding that "[u]se at a [pretrial] hearing of such tainted evidence does not violate the United States Constitution because the proper remedy for unconstitutional acquisition of evidence is exclusion at trial, not suppression in a probable cause proceeding."). State courts have also allowed hearsay evidence and unconstitutionally obtained evidence to be admitted at preliminary hearings. These courts have found support for their decision both in their own state laws and constitutions and in Supreme Court decisions regarding the use of such evidence for grand jury purposes. Because the purpose of a preliminary hearing and the purpose of a grand jury proceeding is to determine whether probable cause exists to bind an accused over for trial, courts have inferred that the same evidentiary standards are applicable to both types of hearings (*Wisconsin v. Moats,* 156 Wis. 2d 74, 457 N.W.2d 299, 1990 Wisc. LEXIS 269 (1989)).

After hearing the evidence the magistrate must determine whether both prongs of the probable cause test have been satisfied. If the magistrate decides that evidence supports a finding of probable cause the accused is bound over for trial. If not, the complaint is dismissed and the defendant is discharged from custody. Neither decision is a finding of guilt or an acquittal; a preliminary examination is merely an inquiry into whether enough evidence exists to justify a trial of the defendant. Still, states often limit the circumstances under which such charges may be refiled.

ALISON MCKENNEY BROWN

References and Further Reading

Black, H.C. et al. (1979). *Black's Law Dictionary,* 5th ed., 1062 (5th Edition). St. Paul, MN, West Publishing.

Federal Rules of Criminal Procedure, 5.1(e), (2003).

Moore, R.L. (2002). Thirty-first Annual Review of Criminal Procedure: II. Preliminary Proceedings: Preliminary Hearings, 90 Geo. L.J. 1295.

Whitebread, C.H. and Slobogin, C. (2000). Criminal procedure: An analysis of cases and concepts. *Preliminary Hearings.* New York, Foundation Press.

See also **Presentence Investigation Reports; Pretrial Detention**

Pretrial Detention or Preventive Detention

Pretrial detention is the holding of the accused in a secure facility (usually a jail) prior to the adjudication of his or her case. Pretrial detention occurs when the accused cannot afford to pay the monetary bail, or when bail is not granted to the accused.

Bail may not be granted to the accused for one of several reasons. It may be believed that the individual is a flight risk and thus will not appear at the next step in the adjudicatory process. Typically, some evidence would have been presented at a bail hearing to suggest that this is the case, or the accused would have had to have a history of flight or appear ready for flight before bail would be withheld on that basis (i.e., cash in his or her pocket and a passport and airplane ticket on his or her person). Bail may not be granted because it is believed the offender is a danger to the community, and that the only safe place for that offender to be is behind bars. Holding the offender in jail prior to trial for this reason is referred to as preventive detention.

The concept of preventive detention was established in The Bail Reform Act of 1984. According to the U.S. Supreme Court in *U.S. v. Salerno* (1987).

The Bail Reform Act of 1984 (Act) requires courts to detain prior to trial arrestees charged with certain serious felonies if the government demonstrates by clear and convincing evidence after an adversary hearing that no release conditions "will reasonably assure ... the safety of any other person and the community" 18 U.S.C. 3142(e) (1982 ed., Supp. III). The Act provides arrestees with a number of procedural rights at the detention hearing, including the right to request counsel, to testify, to present witnesses, to proffer evidence, and to cross-examine other witnesses. The Act also specifies the factors to be considered in making the detention decision, including the nature and seriousness of the charges, the substantiality of the government's evidence, the arrestee's background and characteristics, and the nature and seriousness of the danger posed by his release.

This contains several points from the above worth noting. First, the Act does require that the safety of the community be taken into consideration. It is clear that the intent of the government was to ensure the protection of the community as a primary concern.

Second, the Act outlines specific procedural rights that the accused would have at the detention hearing, including the right to cross-examine some witnesses. The hearing must be initiated by the government and it may apply only in the case of certain crimes (i.e., a violent crime, a crime punishable by death or life imprisonment, certain drug crimes, etc.). Finally, there are four factors that are to be taken into consideration when making detention decisions including the nature and seriousness of the charges and the nature and seriousness of the danger posed by the release of the accused. After the Bail Reform Act of 1984, the government could (and was required to) consider dangerousness as a factor in determining whether or not bail would be granted. Although this was done informally prior to the Act, the Bail Reform Act of 1984 codified the practice in federal law.

Shortly after its implementation, the Bail Reform Act of 1984 was tested by *U.S. v. Salerno*, (481 US 739, 1987). Salerno, an organized crime figure, was given a detention hearing under the provisions of the Bail Reform Act (although not permitted to cross-examine government witnesses) and was found to be a danger to the community. Thus, he was argued that the 1984 Bail Reform Act violated the Fifth Amendment due process clause and the excessive bail clause of the Eighth Amendment. In upholding the Bail Reform Act of 1984, the U.S. Supreme Court reasoned that the Act places a heavy burden on the government to prove that the accused posed significant threats to society. It further reasoned that the speedy trial provision would not be affected. The bottom line was that, according to the Supreme Court, the interest in protecting the community from dangerous persons outweighs the interest in liberty for the accused.

Thus the largest and most significant argument in favor of preventive detention is that it provides a legal means by which dangerous persons may be held prior to trial so they do not harm others and society will be kept safe until their trial.

Preventive detention is a controversial topic. On one hand, the protection of the community is a concept that the vast majority of citizens support. It would be difficult to find anyone who does not believe that a guilty defendant who is a violent offender should not be detained prior to trial. The controversy enters the picture in that until the trial is held, the American criminal justice system operates under a presumption of innocence. To assume an offender should be incarcerated prior to his or her trial may be to operate under an assumption of guilt. The Supreme Court did address this point to some degree in its reasoning in *Salerno*, finding that pretrial detention was not punishment prior to a guilty finding but rather, a legitimate regulatory goal.

Those who see preventive detention as problematic argue that the party who is accused of a crime is detained (incarcerated) prior to the trial, even though legally he or she is still presumed to be innocent. Although detained, the accused is subject to adverse consequences such as the loss of employment, strained family relations, loss of social standing, and damage to the reputation. In addition, incarceration, even for a short time, may cause psychological and physical harm to the individual. Often, the family of the detained party suffers as well since the loss of one income may create severe financial hardships, such as utilities being shut off or family evictions.

There has been some research to suggest that pretrial detainees have other disadvantages. When in detention, defendants are subject to the schedules of the jail administrators and are not free to meet with their counsel or witnesses who may be beneficial to them at their leisure. They may not be as able to help with their own defense, nor may they be as flexible when it comes to preparing themselves for court. Pretrial detainees are much more likely to "appear" guilty, as they typically wear jail jumpsuits and give juries the impression that they must be dangerous since they have to be incarcerated. Thus, they may be more likely than defendants who are out on bail to be convicted (Ares, Rankin, and Sturz, 1963).

But beyond these considerations, there are some other perhaps larger issues associated with preventive detention that have been the subject of some concern and speculation.

In his dissent in *U.S. v. Salerno*, Justice Thurgood Marshall, joined by Justice Brennen, expressed grave concern over preventive detention. He wrote:

> This case brings before the Court for the first time a statute in which Congress declares that a person innocent of any crime may be jailed indefinitely, pending the trial of allegations which are legally presumed to be untrue, if the Government shows to the satisfaction of a judge that the accused is likely to commit crimes, unrelated to the pending charges, at any time in the future. Such statutes, consistent with the usages of tyranny and the excesses of what bitter experience teaches us to call the police state, have long been thought incompatible with the fundamental human rights protected by our Constitution.

Taken as a whole, the foregoing points support the notion that the largest and most significant argument in opposition to pretrial detention is that it violates a fundamental principle of our criminal justice system: the presumption of innocence.

Balancing these two interests (fairness to the defendant and safety to the community) creates a need to know who is a danger to the community. However, predicting dangerousness is not easy. In deciding who is likely to offend and consequently, who should not be released prior to trial, judges may use some form of prerelease (bail) guidelines. Like sentencing guidelines, these are based on prediction models and take into consideration variables that are likely to decrease failure rates. Research suggests that some such variables are the nature and extent of the defendant's criminal record, the defendant's prior involvement with drugs, age of defendant, and employment of defendant (Gottfredson and Gottfredson, 1988). As most people are willing to err on the side of caution when it comes to the safety of the community, even if prediction models are not accurate, there is an assumption that some guidance is better than none, even if the accuracy of the prediction is questionable. Most citizens, as well as most judges, would rather err on the side of caution when it comes to releasing potentially dangerous offenders into the community.

One of the consequences of pretrial detention is jail overcrowding. The Bail Reform Act of 1984 was not passed in a vacuum. Rather, it was conceived within the framework of the war on drugs. As such, it became just one of several contributing factors to jail and prison overcrowding. In efforts to address jail overcrowding that has been precipitated by pretrial detention, programs of intensive supervision have been implemented. Pretrial intensive supervision is an alternative to incarceration that allows the defendant to be released in the community under very strict supervision conditions. The federal courts as well as some state jurisdictions use pretrial supervision services, combined with electronic monitoring, to detain defendants at home prior to trial. This has created the need for more probation officers and a bureaucracy to implement supervision services.

Juvenile Pretrial Detention

The juvenile justice system was established in the latter part of the 19th century (1899), with the establishment of the Illinois Juvenile Justice Act. After its implementation, there were a series of U.S. Supreme Court decisions based upon the philosophy of *parens patriae*, which recognized the role of the state as a "father" or benevolent paternal image to the juvenile. These Supreme Court decisions reached into the middle and late 20th century, as the "Due Process Revolution" spread throughout the criminal and juvenile systems. One such decision, *Schall v. Martin* (467 U.S. 253, 1984), addressed the issue of pretrial detention.

Prior to the implementation of the Bail Reform Act of 1984, the U.S. Supreme Court was asked to decide on pretrial detention as it related to juveniles. At that time, even without a provision for such a procedure for adults in criminal court, the Court determined that pretrial detention was appropriate and that it served a regulatory, rather than punitive function. In *Schall v. Martin*, the Court stated,

> Secure detention is more restrictive, but it is still consistent with the regulatory and *parens patriae* objectives relied upon by the State. Children are assigned to separate dorms based on age, size, and behavior. They wear street clothes provided by the institution and partake in educational and recreational programs and counseling sessions run by trained social workers. Misbehavior is punished by confinement to one's room. See Testimony of Mr. Kelly, id., 292–297. We cannot conclude from this record that the controlled environment briefly imposed by the State on juveniles in secure pretrial detention "is imposed for the purpose of punishment," rather than as "an incident of some other legitimate governmental purpose" (*Schall v. Martin*, 255).

The legitimate government function, cited later in the opinion, is the protection of the community. This theme was followed later by the Court in its decision related to criminal defendants in *Salerno*.

Preventive Detention of Accused Terrorists

As controversial as preventive detention has been as a criminal court issue and as an issue applied to juvenile defendants, the most controversial application of the concept of preventive detention has been the detention of those persons who are military combatants and accused terrorists. Enemy combatants are detained under the provisions of the Geneva Convention; however, those suspected terrorists who have been detained across the country because of their ambiguous status as immigration violators or material witnesses, have been detained under the preventive detention provisions. The "war on terrorism" has provided new opportunities for the use of preventive detention, particularly under the USA Patriot Act, which allows considerable latitude for the designation and incarceration of "terrorist threats."

Controversy has surrounded aspects of detaining immigrants under this policy because many of the detainees did not have the opportunity to speak with counsel and charges were ambiguous, if made at all. There were accusations that the preventive detention was a disguise for the incarceration of suspicious individuals, particularly those who were classified as "material witnesses," where there was considerable secrecy and little access to counsel. Material witnesses, under the USA Patriot Act, may not have committed a crime at all, but may be detained nonetheless. Although they may have done nothing illegal, they may know of someone else who has and that in itself may create a compelling government interest to hold them under the law. Levinson (2002) notes that such material witnesses are often unlikely to testify before grand juries when called, partially out of fear. Charges are then likely to change from "material witness" to "obstruction of justice," because of their refusal to cooperate.

Some have expressed fears that the decision in *Salerno* has been stretched to fit the need to restrict the movement of possible or suspected terrorists. Levinson (2002) has articulated these reservations as follows:

> These words have become a justification for the aggressive use of both the immigration laws and material witness warrants to detain individuals suspected of, but not charged with, terrorist acts and sympathies. In the name of security, we have pushed the legal envelope by using laws that were created for other purposes to assist in detaining perceived enemies (p. 1225).

Conclusion

There has been an evolution of the concept of preventive detention from its inception to its present applications. As with most concepts that are constitutionally defined and monitored by the system of checks and balances, there can probably be an expectation that any abuses or perceived abuses will not be permitted to continue for long. The principle of a "balance of interests" is one that has been established to be in the best interests of both the public and a reasonable justice system. If the implementation of a policy that was meant to protect is found to harm, it can be expected that the tipped scales will force divergent action.

MARY ANN EASTEP

References and Further Reading

Ares, C., Rankin, A. and Sturz, H. (1963). The Manhattan bail project: An interim report on the use of pretrial parole, *New York University Law Review*, 39, 67–92.

Gottfredson, M. and Gottfredson, D. (1988). *Decision-Making in Criminal Justice*, 2nd ed., New York, Plenum.

Levinson, L., Detention, witnesses and Terrorism, *Loyola of Los Angeles Law Review*, 35, 1217.

See also **Bail, The Right to; Trial, The Right to**

Prison History: Continental Europe and England

When examining historical accounts of European and English prisons, two acknowledgements are useful: social advancements practiced in present-day Western civilization are outcomes of an evolution started some 10,000 years ago in the Near East (Drapkin, 1989).

And, history is written from records left by the privileged (Zinn, 1990). One implication is that generations are products of previous generational experiences, and the significance of those experiences depends upon who is reading the records. Some time ago, individuals responded to antisocial behavior by a simple means: revenge. Wrongdoers received a retaliatory or a punitive response throughout history (Durkheim, 1958). Durkheim argues that crime is a natural kind of social activity and as such as, "an integral part of all healthy societies" (p. 67).

Therefore, elements of justice grew from seeds of private vengeance (Oppenheimer, 1975–1913). Pietro Marongiu and Graeme Newman (1987) argue, "All acts of vengeance arise from an elementary sense of injustice, a primitive feeling that one has been arbitrarily subjected to a tyrannical power against which one is powerless to act" (p. 9). Vengeance or retribution toward criminals or wrongdoers can be traced to the early development of societies. Yet, consequences changed overtime and were administered by the state, publicly. State revenge is the origin of public justice, which gradually displaced all other forms of justice (Drapkin, 1989).

In preliterate societies, the law of retaliation or *lex talionis* (an eye for an eye) was the consequence of most violations (von Hirsch, 1976, 6). Natural law is the law of the strongest, and it dominates history (Drapkin, 1989, 9). Violators broke the standards established by those strong enough to develop and enforce standards or laws, and "strong enough to carryout imposed sanctions or consequences of standard violations" (Erikson, 1966, 6). A crime cannot exist without criminal law. It follows that criminal law is the formal statement of authority exercised by the state (Zelman and Siegel, 1994). With that said, what is known about prison is it is the consequence of a legal system regardless of its level of sophistication as influenced through resources, policy, and management (Stevens, 2001). Yet, history is unclear on how consequences or prison affects violators (Reiman, 1995; Shelden, 2001). Prison has been an option throughout history but not in the way expected.

Ancient Athens

Around 700 BC, it was believed that the capacity to live prescribed by law is what makes human beings uniquely human. Justice was seen as a set of dispute-settling procedures reducing inequalities of wealth, power, and status between contestants, and allowed for a decision centered on the disputed issue (Peters, 1998; Morris and Rothman, 2003). The *polis*, the autonomous city–state, created a public authority that produced laws and a set of consequences for violators: stoning to death (lapidation), throwing offenders from cliffs (precipitation), binding them to stakes to suffer a slow death from public abuse while dying (apotympanismos, crucifixion); and the forbidding of all communication with offenders.

Imprisonment was rarely considered punishment, yet idealized as typified in Athenian entertainment. Zeus' anger at the titan Prometheus who stole fire from heaven and gave it to humans, illustrates this thought. Zeus chained Prometheus to a mountain and subjected him to insufferable torments. The play illustrated epic confinement and even the title: *Prometheus desmotes* means "chained." An early Athenian prison was named Desmoterion—the place of chains.

Plato and Socrates endorse two functions for prisons:

1. Punishment should make those imprisoned better for it because they will learn their lesson from the experience (specific deterrence).
2. Others see individual suffering and fear their own imprisonment (general deterrence) (Peters, 1998).

Plato proposes "three models of confinement" depending on incorrigibility of an offender (Peters, 1998, 4–5).

1. A public building near the marketplace would imprison common violators for less than 2 years.
2. As "evil acts" are committed out of "foolishness" or ignorance rather than intrinsic qualities, imprisonment should last 5 years or less for serious violators. Reform through instruction is the primary goal.
3. The incorrigible (habitual) should be imprisoned for life, have no visitors, and be guarded and fed by slaves. At death, remains are cast beyond the frontiers (Peters, 1998, 8).

Ancient Rome

In 451 BC, the Twelve Tables of Rome dealt with private disputes: assault, theft, insult, the theft or destruction of crops, perjury, and offenses against the state. Compensation was the usual punishment. During the process, violators were imprisoned. Those who could not or would not pay were sold into slavery or executed. Other confinement consisted of private "cells" to discipline family members. Roman law prohibited involuntary confinement as punishment.

In the mid-second century BC, Rome established courts in an attempt to limit private justice and executions. But, the focus of the empire centered on the antiquarian-minded power of Sassanian Persians in the east, on Germanic tribes in the Danube and Rhine frontiers, and in North Africa Roman power was eroding (Collins, 1991, 1–3). At home, the Roman economy overheated—prices were spiraling, and government reduced the value of silver in coinage. By 415, armies were recalled owing to civil upheavals, and violators were held in makeshift quarry prisons.

Quarry prisons were located on the southern slope of Capitoline Hills where rock had been quarried and a primitive sewer system flowed through small underground chambers (Peters, 1998, 16–17; Hennington, Johnson, and Wells, 1999). Those underground chambers functioned as Mamertine Prison. The goal was to control prisoners and to produce as much suffering as possible (Johnson, 1987, 1–6). Mamertine was "repulsive and fearful, because of the neglect, the darkness, and the stench" (Peck, 1922, 279).

Rome saw threats to public health posed by human waste and human deviance as one in the same, and expelled both from sight and consciousness (Johnson, 1987). Edicts such as Constantine's Theodosian Code in 320 sponsored reform.

Early Medieval Prisons

Germanic kingdoms carved from old imperial provinces—kingdoms of Visigoths in the Iberian (Spain and Portugal) peninsula, Franks in Gaul, Lombards in Italy, and Angles and Saxons in Britain, wrote laws influenced by Roman standards. But English common law escaped Rome's influence, and many parts of Europe, especially Germany, centered justice upon local custom, resulting in fragmentation. Nobles, ecclesiastical rulers, and cities wielded unchecked local power limiting royal justice (Peters, 1998, 33). Imprisonment was typified by private quarters within estates for family members and servants; underground dungeons for common offenders soon to be executed, sold into slavery, or released upon paying their debts; or monasteries and convents for prisoners-of-war. The Franks illustrated typical punishment of the era: fines, enslavement, mutilation, and capital punishment. Antiquity laid the groundwork for early medieval prisons, but medieval experiences had not done the same for Middle Age prisons.

The Middle Ages

Middle Age fortresses, castles, bridge abutments, and town gates were strongly and securely built for defense. But, bubonic plague and gunpowder reduced the significance of fortress cities as protectors. For instance, two-thirds of the population of many European cities succumbed to the destruction of the plague (Burckhardt, 1878). Women lepers and Jews were thought to have deliberately spread plague or, because of their "innate dishonor," to have polluted society and brought out "God's" vengeance. Needless to say, they were executed. As for the massive fortresses, eventually sections were converted to prisons. By the 12th century, prison chambers were specifically included in castle plans.

For example, London was anciently a walled city, with four gates. One gate was the site of a prison for almost a thousand years. The first prison was nearly as old as the Tower of London and much older than the Bastille in Paris. It is first mentioned in the reign of King John and in the following reign of Henry III. After the Cathedral of St. Paul and the gate used for confinement were destroyed in 1086, once rebuilt, the gate was called Newgate Prison. Newgate was cold and dark, and the smell of human waste filled the air. Living conditions were foul (Griffith, 1896). Many met death at Newgate and at similar facilities throughout Europe. One estimate is that one in seven offenders died at Newgate. It is calculated that for the average period of confinement in 1827, there was 1 death to 22 sentenced in the central houses of imprisonment of France; and the average mortality rate was 1 in 16 for the men, and 1 in 26 for the women.

One way to determine the effectiveness of early prisons of the 19th century might be to look at mortality rates among prisoners. For instance, France's mortality in the central houses (*maisons centrales*) and of thosse of justice and correction were 1 in N number of prisoners:

Central Houses	Mortality Rates (N)
Montpellier	9.33
Riom, 1821–1827	9.87
Baulieu near Caen, 1814–1825	11.59
Melun, 1817–1825	14.81
Gaillon, 1817–1825	11.86
Metz, 1801	18.43
Toulouse, 1822–1824	35.07*
Lyons, 1820–1826	43.00†
Saint-flour, 1813–1826	47.00

* In 1814, 1 prisoner died out of 8.

‡ The infirmaries have been better organized, and the nursing better conducted. The mortality in 1812, 1813, and 1814, was 1 in 4.006.

However, prisons were designed with various accommodations. In the royal prisons of England those accommodations varied from foul to comfortable—the latter reserved for prisoners with funds.

Inquisitor Prisons: Prisons were rarely used for long-term until inquisition prisons appeared. It was argued that long confinement would change heretic perspectives and promote repentance. However, other motives promoted long-term imprisonment, too. For instance, the chief source of royal income was land tax based on a valuation, taxes on articles of consumption, and duties on exported and imported goods that were added to the private fortune of the ruling house (Burckhardt, 1878). One possible increase could be derived from business growth and general prosperity, but the plague limited those potentials. Another way was to enhance the royal treasury through a well-planned confiscation and plundering strategy especially in France and Spain. Execution meant a transfer of property to heirs.

But, long-term imprisonment enhanced inquisitor treasuries since heretic property was confiscated, Megan Cassidy-Welch (2002) argues. Similar information is contained in a manuscript now held in the Vatican Secret Archive.

Inquisitor authorities said they were eradicating heresies, but often met sabotage, resistance, and public anger. For example, the Bishop of Albi, Bernard de Castanet, distinguished himself by arresting and imprisoning a number of the town's leading citizens in 1299. Townspeople marched on the prison, Mur at Carcassonne, and liberated its prisoners. Royal intervention brought peace after discovering the prison was used for beatings and torture and to feed the sexual appetite of the bishop. The bishop was guilty of abduction and murder of women and when their remains were discovered, some had been dismembered.

Iberian Peninsula: In the Christian kingdoms after the fall of Muslims, law was local and customary. Legal procedures were similar to those of other European societies: privately initiated, supervised by royally appointed judges, "largely oral, and unlearned" (Peters, 1998, 37). When defendants failed to make a court appearance, once found, they were thrown into prison to await trial. As royal power prevailed, uniform legal systems were established within Aragon, Castile, and Portugal. Local resistance dissipated. The most impressive legal system was *Las Siete Partidas* (the collection in Seven Parts) that included provisions associated with prison process's and prohibited the development of new prisons without royal permission.

Italy: The kingdom of Sicily, the Papal States, and the powerful city republics of Venice, Florence, Milan, and Genoa were highly advanced. A law center was in Bologna and Naples hosted a university. Although various jurisdictions existed across Italy, customs guided justice. In 1297, Florence renovated a castle into a prison, Le Stinche. Men, women, children, and business owners whose companies failed were imprisoned together, but separately housed. Five large rooms provided for over 100 prisoners (Old Florence, 1799–1859). Prisoners were charged from their accommodations at Le Stinche. The northern Italian city–republics by the 14th century overcame the objections of Roman law and used prison as punishment.

Amsterdam: The 16th century produced "workhouses or houses of correction" throughout Northwestern Europe (Shichor, 1995, 23). Amsterdam forced prisoners to rasp wood, resulting in the name "rasphouses." Prisoners pulverized redwood logs with heavy saws producing a dye-stuff (Spierenburg, 1991, 217).

Beggars and vagabonds were arrested (but not tried) and sent to rasphouses. Wealthy but undesirable residents and difficult to educate children were incarcerated, too (Spierenburg, 1991, 218). Visitors, for a fee, could watch prisoners work. Prison workhouses or comparable institutions modeled after rasphouses opened throughout Europe. The Bridewells in England were the best known.

England: The breakup of feudalism and rural migration to urban centers created an idle population. English philosophy was, "It's of little advantage to restrain the bad by punishment, unless you render them good by discipline" (Walker, 1980, 42). Bridewell trained and housed England's unemployed. Male prisoners labored on public projects and in military campaigns without pay or recognition. Females worked at spinning, weaving, clothmaking, milling of grains, and baking.

Because of Bridewell's success, parliament promoted construction of a Bridewell in every English county. However, they became catchall institutions for the mad, vagrants, prostitutes, and unruly family members whose families petitioned their admission (Shichor, 1995). Bridewells became gaols (jails). They held defendants in pretrial detainment until they paid gaol keeper services. Squalid and unhealthy conditions gave rise to epidemics of jail fever (typhus) that spread throughout England and killed many people. Prisoners were blamed for the epidemic.

By the 17th century, convicts throughout Europe worked in shipyards and were chained to their beds at night. By the end of the 18th century, conditions of workhouses throughout England and Europe were appalling. Privacy was nonexistent. Those without money, starved. Sanitary conditions were deplorable. The exploitation of inmates by other inmates and jailers resulted in the most vicious acts of violence imaginable.

Transportation of English Prisoners: Transportation emerged during the 17th century as a humane alternative to public beatings and execution (British Public Record Office, 2003). Some say transportation was not prompted by humanitarian sentiments but demand for free laborer (Early Forms of Punishment, 2003). Transportation was an effective tool used to control prisoners because jails were overcrowded. America received an estimated 1000 convicts every year between 1596 and 1776. After the Revolutionary War to 1875, England transported approximately 160,000 prisoners to Australia, Tasmania, and Norfolk Island prison colonies. It is estimated that one-third of those transported died en route (Early Forms of Punishment, 2003).

Germany and Scandinavia: Prisons consisted of holes in foundations of local fortifications, in cellars of town halls, and in subterranean chambers. The Bornheimer Loch was a prison in Frankfort under the Bornheim gate. Imprisonment was a local matter until the early modern period (Peters, 1998).

> The Scandinavian countries promoted punishment entailing property loss, death, or mutilation and occasionally in Iceland, penal servitude. In Northern Europe prison was used for temporary confinement linked to canon law courts until the 16th century when forced labor was introduced.

France: The best known prison in France was Chatelet, a fortress on the right bank of the Seine. Around 1200, it housed court, provost (royal governor), and prisoners confined in one of its towers. Outside Paris, there were few standards of prisons except in royal castles where provosts kept prisoners until transferred to Chatelet. The Bastille, the most famous royal prison, was originally one of the gates in the fortifications constructed for Paris' defense. The French national holiday commemorates the storming of the Bastille, which took place on July 14, 1789, and marked the beginning of the French Revolution. The Bastille was both a prison and a symbol of the absolute and arbitrary power of Louis the 16th's Ancient Regime. By capturing this symbol, the people signaled that the king's power was no longer absolute: power should be based on the nation and be limited by a separation of powers. It marked the end of absolute monarchy, the birth of the sovereign nation, and, eventually, the creation of the (First) Republic, in 1792. From 1370 to the 15th century, it had dungeons, eight towers with holes inside stonewalls, and physically debilitating living conditions. Prisoners were also assigned to French warships as galley slaves.

Lepers in Europe: In the 12th century, France had approximately 2000 facilities housing lepers, and England and Scotland about 220 facilities. From the 14th century through the Crusades, leprosariums "had multiplied their cities of the damned over the entire face of Europe" (Foucault, 1965, 3). There were approximately 19,000 lepers throughout Europe. As lepers vanished because of segregation toward the end of the Crusades and the break with Eastern sources of the infection, a "moral void" developed (Erikson, 1966). The "moral void" needed a scapegoat. Vagabonds and the unemployed became substitutes for lepers in Western Europe and Great Britain, and as such they filled prisons. Social exclusion and isolation was a strategy used to control undesirables.

Madness in France and Germany: In Paris, the Hospital General was created to suppress beggary. Similar hospitals operated throughout Europe. Many were converted into factories through prison labor. Another group filled the "moral void"—those with "deranged minds." In a sense, it could be implied that asylums replaced lazar houses "in the geography of haunted places as in the landscape of the moral universe" (Foucault, 1965, 57). One-tenth of all arrests in Paris consisted of the insane and "completely mad" individuals. In the 16th century, Germany mandated "madmen" to register with authorities and were quickly confined at Narrturmer Hospital. It was a facility with barred windows allowing outsiders, for a price, to observe "madmen" chained to walls. But nowhere was madness as compelling as when "madmen" were placed on ships. Sometimes, seamen would disembark their passengers sooner than promised. Other times, upon reaching a port designation, residents denied the "ship of fools" access to the docks (Foucault, 1965, vi).

Age of Enlightenment

Rebellion was commonplace as evidenced by the storming of the Bastille in 1789, but justice was respected, too—when it was fair. For instance, in Northern Burgundy in the 18th century, local courts played a vital role in everyday disputes. This thought is in opposition to many historians who argue that people resented intervention of the court and used it as a last resort. The reason villagers cooperated with local authority was that judges provided a fair resolution of disputes, with verdicts with which people agreed, Hayhoe (2003) offered.

It goes without saying that there were many who saw torture, death, and transportation as inhumane and ineffective in controlling crime. The age of the "birth of the prison" starting in the 18th century looked upon the experiences of prisons with horror, fascination, and contempt. There were others who saw punishment as providing too much state control. For example, warships used as prisons and prisoners laboring to enhance state property.

Galleys as Prison Ships: Transportation at first was provided by a great number of the English Royal Navy's fighting ships, many ending their days as prison galleys defined as old ships ("hulks") moored in coastal waters stripped of sailing gear, upper decks roofed over, and lower decks converted to cells. One such hulk was the *Dromedary*, a ship of 20 guns that arrived in Bermuda in 1826 and docked for 37 years. Its cargo was 100 convicts joined a few years later by 400 more prisoners. They built a dock, a bridge, and barracks, which they eventually used in 1851. The *Caramando* joined the *Dromedary* after several years.

Brutal punishment and degrading labor bred moral degeneration among the imprisoned and their keepers regardless of where they were confined. And when free labor worked, paid labor did not. As a result, humanitarians came forward in Western Europe in the 18th century and rallied for human dignity, human rights, and separation of state power. Although many contributed, three very influential practitioners were John Howard, Alexander Maconochie, and Walter Crofton.

John Howard's reforms still thrive two centuries later (Howard History, 2003). The John Howard Society's public educational programs promote crime prevention through constructive changes in the criminal justice process (Godber, 1977, 1–2). In 1773, Howard learned that prisoners who owed "gaoler fees," were imprisoned even after an innocent verdict. Howard persuaded English Parliament to prohibit those sanctions and improved the health issues throughout England (Godber, 1977, 10).

Alexander Maconochie

Alexander Maconochie, in 1840, was the superintendent of 2000 twice-convicted prisoners on Norfolk Island. Prisoners on Norfolk Island had committed capital felonies in Australia and England and received a capital sentence. Maconochie's plan was an incentive system that he called a "mark system" leading to a "ticket-of-leave." Once enough "marks" were earned through good behavior and hard work, the inmate was released. Maconochie did not see the ticket-of-leave as parole because he believed that a "reformed" prisoner should not be supervised (Morris, 2002).

Sir Walter Crofton

In 1854, Crofton was in charge of the Irish prisons. There were many pressing problems, yet the most serious was overcrowding. Crofton implemented an incentive system guided by the "mark system" originally developed on Norfolk Island, a prison colony a thousand miles from Australia (Morris, 2002). As a historical matter, Crofton's system impacted the way European prisons were operated by introducing the parole system. The Irish system punished prisoners for their crimes but prepared them for release by giving them options over release dates through good behavior. Then, too, American prisons were impacted too because it was Crofton who introduced Zebulon Brockway, head of Detroit's House of Corrections (later Brockway became the warden of Elmira Reformatory, New York) and other American wardens to the Irish Prison System at the 1st annual meeting of the National Prison Association in 1870, Cincinnati, OH (Dooley, 1981).

Early Modern Europe, 1865–1965

The rise of imprisonment in the previous era was associated with beliefs that prisons were a place of punishment and punishment meant forced labor (O'Brien, 1995). Little changed however: some observers added that prison populations disproportionately represented specific groups. For example, French prison populations in the 19th century were typical of those of the continent as a whole: two out of every five French male prisoners were between the ages of 21 and 30, most were single, without children, and city dwellers (Spierenburg, 1995). They possessed few job skills, and women prisoners were less skilled than males. Also, custodial demographics and social-class perspectives resembled those in custody.

Shifts in social thought about culpability of crime and treatment linked with excessive costs of incarceration, high recidivism rates, overcrowded facilities, and fears of growing homosexual promiscuity among prisoners, produced changes in public sentiment (Fairchild and Dammer, 2001). By 1900, the efficacy of isolating prisoners for long periods of time was called into question across Europe despite successful prison manufacturing that produced goods such as shoes, bedding, and baskets. Labor was the central and organizing factor of the daily life (O'Brien, 1995). On a typical day in a Belgian prison, prisoners arose at 5:00 AM to organ music as a call to prayer; breakfast and work within the hour. After dinner, work continued till 9:00 pm clock.

Some reformers argued, profitable and productive prison labor were immoral. Their reasoning was couched in unfair competition because of differences in labor-wage scales. Many countries ignored those claims continuing prison labor as a self-sustaining enterprise. Bavaria, Italy, and Spain prisons allowed inmates to choose trades. However, some prisoners forced prisoners to labor at places such as Devil's Island until they died. It was a desolate place in French Guiana and between 1884–1946 over 56,000 prisoners were transported there from France.

Despite entrepreneur successes, prison culture promoted crime, and therefore, the growing presence of recidivism in European prison populations after 1865 spurred changes. The length of prison sentences and rehabilitation were less associated than expected. The longer a prisoner was incarcerated, the more likely the prisoner would resort to crime, once released (Stevens, 1994; Morris, 1995). As a result, change came in the form of suspended sentences. Courts determined the length of a prison sentence and then suspended it, allowing a first timer to enjoy freedom as long as he remained crime free.

Belgium led the way in 1888. After World War I, suspended sentences were adapted by many European nations including "Eastern Europe: the Russian Socialist Federated Republic, Czechoslovakia, Romania and Poland and spread to Asia, Latin America, Africa and the Middle East" (Spierenburg, 1995, 189).

Supervised parole, another noncustodial sanction, was used among juveniles in France around 1830. Portugal used a form of supervised parole among adult offenders in 1861. Saxony, Germany, and Denmark developed an offender classification system allowing furlough and conditional release for prisoners by 1871. Even Russia abolished courts and prisons for children and raised the age for criminal liability from 10 to 17. European nations moved toward noncustodial sanctions.

Modern Europe 1965–2003

In 1965, Sweden enacted a new criminal code emphasizing noninstitutional alternatives. By 1970, over two-thirds of Swedish defendants received sentences of less than 4 months (McConville, 1995). Treatment and reintegration models of noncustodial care were primary practices among most European nations. Socialist countries in contrast, maintained longer prison sentences but with an emphasis on reform. English prisons mirrored America's incarceration rates and doubled their prison populations between 1950 and 1980 whereas the number declined rapidly in the open-prison countries of the Netherlands and Scandinavia (McConville, 1995). Life sentences and sentences longer than penal specialists viewed 5 years as unrealistic.

Despite suspended sentences and noncustodial care as the first choice among many European nations, in 2003, one European council comprised of 16 nations revisited old problems: the sharp rise in the prison populations, overcrowding, and deterioration of conditions of detention in European prisons and pretrial detention centers as of March 2003 (Parliamentary Assembly, 2003). Another source indicates prisons are hostile and violent places in which violators coming from lower classes and ethnic and social minorities were over-represented. Drug users and migrants make the bulk of these prisoners, despite the fact that within the chain of justice options, imprisonment is the last resort (Literaturverz, 2002). Also, although preventive measures have been established to combat HIV/AIDS, little progress has been (Soz Praventivmed, 1995). Finally, the key issues facing approximately 350,000 prisoners in European prisons is the high cost of incarceration and uncontrolled violence and drugs (Spierenburg, 1991).

Summary

From antiquity to the Middle Ages, prison was used as a temporary holding facility until execution or debts were paid. The Middle Ages witnessed the function of prisons as punishment associated with hard labor lifting Roman prohibitions. Inquisitor prisons signaled acceptance of long prison terms. Punishment and forced labor gave way to suspended sentences and treatment in modern European prison systems. Presently, prisons are under scrutiny owing to overcrowding, high recidivism rates, and drug problems.

Conclusions

Up until the early modern Europe, the business of life, the beautiful and the ugly alike, were played out in public. For a long time, offenders were punished with the community playing an active role. The public attended and paid for the spectacle of punishment. They paid to see chained madmen and executions. The "staging of executions, the ceremonial behavior of magistrates and the adornment of scaffolds" can be called social rituals (Spierenburg, 1991).

The village, into the 18th century, intervened in the life of its members. Privacy was motivated by changes in family affairs (i.e, the development of the nuclear family), communities (i.e., old villages disintegrated and impersonal urban realities predominated), and punishment (public execution and beatings were replaced by incarceration). Prior to early modern Europe, punishment was physical and public. Yet, the criminalization of lepers, vagabonds, those with "deranged minds," and the poor was obvious. Isolation was used as way to segregate alleged wrongdoers. Treating those unfortunates of physical, economic, or psychological conditions was couched in imprisonment at "hospitals." Prison as punishment coincides with the rise of powerful states and "treatment" was consistent with political ideological strategies or smoke screens. This thought reveals that treatment simply coincided with state exclusion. Imprisonment continues to be a vehicle of social control, and it may have little to do with crime trends. To bring evidence to this thought simply recall Apartie in South Africa, Nazi Germany or Kosovo. Perhaps, it could be argued that in a similar way that the fear of natural phenomena such as solar eclipse or tornados created religion and magic, the fear of enemies and private property created autocratic government and it provided justification to imprison targeted groups. Yet, throughout history, little if any compelling evidence exists demonstrating prison or punishment eradicates criminal patterns. Eventually the current crisis in Western European prisons is an echo from past generations—private vengeance.

DENNIS J. STEVENS

References and Further Reading

British Public Record Office. 2003. Available at: http://catalogue.pro.gov.uk/ExternalRequest.asp?RequestReference=ri2235. Retrieved on October.

Burckhardt, J., *The Civilization of the Renaissance in Italy,* translated by Middlemore, S.G.C., 1878. Available at: http://www.boisestate.edu/courses/hy309.

Cassidy-Welch, M. 2002. Testimonies from a Fourteenth-Century prison: Rumour, evidence and truth in the midi, *French History,* 16(1), 3–27.

Collins, R. 1991. *History of Early Medieval Europe,* NY, Marlin Press.

Dooley, E.E. 1981. Sir Walter Crofton and the Irish or intermediate system of prison discipline, *New England Journal of Prison Law,* 72(summer).

Drapkin, I. 1989. *Crime and Punishment in the Ancient World,* Washington DC, Lexington Books.

Durkheim, E. 1958. *The Rules of Sociological Method,* translated by Solovay, S.A. and Mueller, J.H., Glencoe, IL, The Free Press.

Early Forms of Punishment. Available at: http://notfrisco.com/prisonhistory/origins. Retrieved on October 2003.

Erikson, K.T. *Wayward Puritans: A Study in the Sociology of Deviance,* New York, John Wiley and Sons, Inc., 1966.

European Monitoring Centre for Drugs and Drug Addiction. Available at: http://www.emcdda.org/responses/themes/assistance_prisons.shtml.

Fairchild, E. and Dammer, H.R. 2001. *Comparative Criminal Justice Systems,* Wadsworth.

Foucault, M. 1965. *Madness and Civilization: A History of Insanity in the Age of Reason,* Translated by Howard, R., New York, Random House.

Godber, J. 1977. *John Howard the Philanthropist,* Bedfordshire, U.K., Bedfordshire County Council Arts and Recreation Department.

Griffith, A., *The Chronicles of Newgate,* 1896, Available at: http://www.fred.net/jefalvey/newgate.html.

Hayhoe, J.D. 2003. Neighbours before the court: Crime, village communities and seigneurial justice in northern Burgundy, 1750–1790, *French History,* 17(2), 127–148.

Hennington, R., Johnson, W. and Wells, T. 1999. Supermax prisons: Panacea or desperation, *Corrections Management Quarterly,* 3(2), 53–59.

Howard History. Available at: http://www.johnhoward.nf.ca/org/jh_hstry.HTM#JOHN. Retrieved on October, 2003.

Johnson, R. 1987. *Hard Time: Understanding and the Reforming the Prison,* New York, Wadsworth.

Literaturverz, S. 2002. Drug and HIV AIDS services in European prisons, Heino Stöver. Oldenburg: Bibliotheks—und Informationssystem der Univ., 248S (Schriftenreihe "Gesundheitsförderung im Justizvollzug ; 8), 217–239.

Marongiu, P. and Newman, G. 1987. *Vengeance: The fight against Injustice,* Totowa, NJ, Rowman and Littlefield.

McConville, S. 1995. The Victorian Prison: England, 1865–1965, in Morris, N. and Rothman, D.J., Ed., *The Oxford History of the Prison: The Practice of Punishment in Western Society,* New York, Oxford University Press, pp. 117–177.

Morris, N. 2002. *Maconochie's Gentlemen: The Story of Norfolk Island and the Roots of Modern Prison Reform,* New York, Oxford Press.

Morris, N. 1995. The Contemporary Prison 1965-Present, in Morris, N. and Rothman, D.J., Eds., *The Oxford History of the Prison: The Practice of Punishment in Western Society,* New York., Oxford University Press, pp. 178–201.

O'Brien, P. 1995. The Prison on the Continent: Europe, 1865–1965, in Morris, N. and Rothman, D.J., Eds., *The Oxford History of the Prison: The Practice of Punishment in Western Society,* New York, Oxford University Press, pp. 178–201.

Old Florence. (1799–1859). History Anecdotal Report-Customs. Giuseppe Conti. Available at: http://translate.google.com/translate.

Oppenheimer, H., *The Rationale of Punishment,* Montclair, NJ, Patterson Smith, (1975–1913).

Peck, H.T., Ed. 1922. *Harper's Dictionary of Classical Literature and Antiquity,* New York, American Books, p. 279.

Peters, E. 1998. Prison before the prison: The ancient and medieval worlds, in Morris, N. and Rothman, D.J., *The Oxford History of the Prison: The Practice of Punishment in Western Society,* New York, Oxford University Press, pp. 3–43.

Reiman, J. 1995. *The Rich Get Richer, the Poor Get Prison,* Boston, MA, Allyn Bacon.

Shelden, R.G. 2001. *Controlling the Dangerous Classes: A Critical Introduction to the History of Criminal Justice,* Boston, MA, Allyn Bacon.

Shichor, D. 1995. *Punishment for Profit,* Thousand Oaks, CA, Sage,

Situation of Parliamentary Assembly, Available at: http://assembly.coe.int/Documents/WorkingDocs/Doc03/EDOC9729.htm.

Spierenburg, P. 1995. The body and the state, in Morris, N. and Rothman, D.J., Eds., *The Oxford History of the Prison: The Practice of Punishment in Western Society,* New York, Oxford University Press, pp. 45–70.

Spierenburg, P. 1991. *The Broken Spell: A Cultural and Anthropological History of Preindustrial Europe,* New Brunswick, NJ, Rutgers University Press.

Stevens, D.J. 1994. The depth of imprisonment and prisonization: Levels of security and prisoners' anticipation of future violence, *The Howard Journal of Criminal Justice,* 33(2), 137–157.

Stevens, D.J., Time, custody level, and inmate attitudes on crime, *Forum on Corrections Research,* 3, 12–14 (1995). Available at: http://198.103.98.138/crd/forum/e073/e073d.htm.

Stevens, D.J. 2001. Education programming for offenders, in Compendium of Corrections, *Compendium 2000: On Effective Correctional Programming,* Provincial Government of Canada, Correctional Service of Canada, pp. 57–64.

Soz Praventivmed. 40(5), 298–301 (1995). Unique Identifier: AIDSLINE MED/96076560.

Schaller, G. and Harding, T.W., *Institut universitaire de medecine legale,* Geneve, Available at: http://www.aegis.com/pubs/aidsline/1996/mar/M9630629.html.

von Hirsch, A. 1976. *Doing Justice: The Choice of Punishment,* New York, Hill and Wang.

Walker, S. 1980. *Popular Justice: A History of American Criminal Justice,* New York, Oxford University Press.

Zalman, M. and Siegel, L.J. 1994. *Cases and Comments on Criminal Procedure,* St. Paul, MN, West.

Zinn, H. 1990. *The Politics of History,* Urbana, IL, University of Illinois Press.

See also **Eastern and Central Europe, Crime and Justice in**

Prison History: U.S.

The first form of imprisonment in colonial America was the jail. Nearly every colony established some sort of small jail to hold debtors and people awaiting trial or execution. However, jails were not designed to maintain any standard of security or hold prisoners for a long period of time; nor did they resemble our current jails or prisons. The various colonies had different laws for dealing with felons (serious offenders) but generally speaking, their criminal laws imposed punishments that inflicted pain, not the loss of freedom. The colonies administered physical punishments that involved flogging, stoning, branding, public humiliation, hanging, and mutilation. For less serious offenders banishment was often the accepted form of punishment.

Some of the first makeshift prisons began to appear throughout the eastern part of the U.S. in the 1770s. The earliest forms of imprisonment included the use of former mines, abandoned ships, pillories, hot boxes, and jails. The Newgate Prison in Simsbury, Connecticut, established in 1773, was one of the first examples. A former copper mine, Newgate was an underground prison that resembled the earliest forms of European imprisonment, similar to the sulphur pits found in ancient Rome. Prisoners were housed in long mine shafts, typically chained to the walls with iron bars holding their feet. They were subjected to the cold and damp conditions of living underground, severe overcrowding and abuse inflicted by their guards. For many prisoners, Newgate would ultimately become their place of death. Soon after opening, the Newgate Prison came under the scrutiny of the local community, concerning the inhumane conditions and poor treatment of prisoners.

After the Revolutionary War, leaders of the new U.S. began to rethink issues of crime and punishment. Proud of achieving liberty from England and stressing the importance of self-government, they established a new punishment system built on fair and just treatment. They began to view deprivation of liberty as a better type of punishment rather than the old-fashioned physical punishments of Europe.

William Penn, the leader of the Pennsylvania Quakers, introduced the shift to more humane forms of punishment. In 1682, the colony of Pennsylvania adopted the Quaker principles that emphasized humane treatment and reform as guidelines for criminal punishments. The Quakers developed the first prison, as we know it today,

by expanding their local jail. Like other jails, the Walnut Street Jail had been constructed with a central hallway that separated large open rooms where prisoners were detained. The Walnut Street Jail was converted into a prison in 1790. The original jail structure was added on to, creating a row of single cells for the most serious offenders to be held in solitary confinement, separate from the general prison population. The concept of solitary confinement was based on the Quakers' belief that solitude would help offenders repent and discover a new sense of morality and emerge reformed. The new Walnut Street Prison was the birthplace of the American prison system.

The Quakers were not only influenced by their own religious principles on how to treat offenders, but they were also influenced by the work of European philosophers and penal reformers. In 1764, an Italian philosopher named Cesare Beccaria stirred interest throughout much of the western world with his essays *On Crimes and Punishments*. Beccaria argued that imprisonment should replace harsh physical punishments, and that the amount of punishment should fit the crime. The Quakers embraced Beccaria's concepts that the certainty of punishment is more effective in controlling crime than the actual severity of the punishment. The Quakers also supported his theory that the seriousness of the punishment should be proportionate to the crime, and that deterrence was an important goal of punishment. Easing away from earlier beliefs that those who violated the law required corporal or capital punishment, the Quakers came to believe that solitary confinement to serve penance would be more influential in altering one's behavior in the future. Moreover, they decided that while local communities should continue to be responsible for the punishment and correction of misdemeanants (minor offenders), states should mete out the consequences for felons.

Although the transition to a new form of punishment was slow, by the turn of the 19th century most states had begun to develop a prison system for felons. The new state prisons supported the goals of incapacitation and deterrence; a system that still exists today. Although these prisons were designed to improve the level of security for long-term imprisonment and confine prisoners to solitary confinement, few states actually followed the single cell model. Instead they were designed much like the European workhouses with large dormitory style rooms that did not accommodate the separation of prisoners. Most of the early prisons were relatively small, built for 50–100 prisoners. The prison population was mixed together in large rooms, with men, women, and children and violent and nonviolent felons all confined together. Early prisons also were not very secure and it was difficult to prevent escapes.

The demise of these first prisons happened very quickly. With a shift toward imprisonment as the preferred method of punishment, more prisoners filled the small prisons. Most states found that severe overcrowding ultimately led to the failure to reform prisoners. Prisons were unable to maintain any level of discipline or control of prisoners; rather than a place of repentance and reform, they became a training ground for learning about crime. To reduce overcrowding, states increased the number of pardons and early releases to prisoners who often served only a very short portion of their sentence. Physical structures soon proved to be inadequate, and new architectural designs were sought to improve security. Several decades into the 19th century, a prison reform movement led to the start of the new penitentiary movement. In 1824, Connecticut closed Newgate and opened a new more secure and modern prison. By the late 1820s, most states had begun to close their original prisons, and build larger and more secure facilities referred to as penitentiaries.

The penitentiary movement was an attempt to solidify the goal of retribution, increasing the security of prisoners, while encouraging repentance with the hope that some prisoners would successfully return to the community. The purpose of this more secure institution was to punish criminals proportionately to the seriousness of their offense. A determinate sentencing model was used as a way to guarantee that the punishment would fit the crime. Offenders were sentenced to a fixed amount of time based on the seriousness of the offense committed. However, with a set amount of time to be served and no opportunity to be released early, prisoners had no incentive to change their behavior. As an incentive to reform their behavior, prison administrators lobbied for "good-time" laws. These laws gave discretion to prison administrators to release prisoners before the completion of their sentence for earned good behavior. Although most states passed good-time laws, prison administrators never lost sight of the primary goal of retribution.

The concept of incapacitation was not new when the first penitentiaries were established; it was the physical structures and living conditions that changed. The new penitentiaries were large enclosed institutions where prisoners were cut off from the outside world and lived in solitary confinement. The penitentiary was designed like a fortress with the main structure enclosed by large walls with a well-secured main entrance gate. These large, walled institutions were meant to isolate prisoners from the corrupting effects of society. The administrative offices were generally located near the front entrance and separate from the prisoners' living quarters. A centralized watch tower made it possible for the officers to observe the entire facility at the same time. The prisoners' quarters generally consisted of long cellblocks that extended in a straight line from the base of the tower. The prisoners were forbidden to speak and were encouraged to read the Bible in their cells. With close monitoring and discipline when necessary, it was believed that some prisoners would be reformed.

There were two punishment models implemented in the penitentiary movement. The first model, developed by the Quakers in Pennsylvania, was referred to as the "segregate" model, requiring prisoners to be held in 24-hours-a-day solitary confinement for the full term of their sentence. Prisoners were forbidden to speak, their only reading material was the Bible, and the only "occasional" visitor permitted was a religious leader. The segregate model was used in the first two penitentiaries established in the Pennsylvania prison system, the Eastern Penitentiary at Cherry Hill and the Western Penitentiary located outside of Pittsburgh.

The opening of the Eastern Penitentiary in 1829 marked the birth of the penitentiary movement in the U.S. Each cell had a workbench where the prisoner could make things to sell as a way to help contribute to their support while in prison. The primary emphasis of the early Pennsylvania penitentiaries was repentance, with the concept of reform rooted in religion. Prison administrators also put some hope in training through rigid routines, harsh discipline, and heavy labor. They tried to instill better work habits that along with repentance might lead criminals to mend their ways. However, reliance on solitary confinement in the segregate model of imprisonment proved to be too harsh psychologically on the prisoners and expensive (requiring larger cells). For these reasons, few states modeled the Pennsylvania prison system.

The second model of punishment was referred to as the "congregate" model, or "silent system," first employed in the New York prison system. When the first New York Penitentiary was built in Auburn, prison administrators conducted an experiment to assess the effectiveness of 24-hours-a-day solitary confinement. The results showed a drastic increase in the rate of prison suicides, sickness, and mental breakdown, suggesting that exclusive solitary confinement was a failure. The New York Prison System switched to the congregate model. Prisoners were allowed to leave their cell and work (at hard labor) during the day, had congregate meals, and remained in solitary confinement in the evening. A rule forbidding any talk was maintained, causing some to call this the silent system. In the congregate model there were three divisions marking the level of solitary confinement assigned to a prisoner. The first division required 24-hour solitary confinement for the full sentence of hardened and seasoned criminals. The second division was for the younger, less hardened criminals, and required solitary confinement until they showed signs of repentance. The third division was for the very young juveniles and for petty criminals, with no solitary confinement.

The early stages of the New York Prison movement followed a similar pattern to the Pennsylvania prison movement. Former jails were converted into penitentiaries, and eventually new prisons were constructed. The Auburn State Prison was the first penitentiary built in New York. Auburn was a large, walled structure with congregate working and eating areas, five stories of interior cell blocks, with small single-person cells designed only for sleeping. Auburn became noted for its strict disciplinarian practices, so that some critics claimed that its policies were harsher than the 24-hour solitary confinement model. At Auburn, routine practices included the lock step march as prisoners traveled through the prison, hard labor, and prisoner silence throughout the day. Harsh punishments for rule infractions were whippings and the "shot carry," where inmates were forced to walk through the prison grounds with cannonballs strapped to their hands.

The Auburn congregate model was viewed as a more efficient and economical system than the Pennsylvania system. It was notorious for exploiting prison labor, functioning as a factory to earn a profit for the state to defray the costs of the institution. Because it was much cheaper to build and to operate congregate penitentiaries, most states patterned their own systems after the Auburn model. In addition, prisoners could produce more products in congregate work areas creating more profit for the state. Cells were built much smaller because the prisoners were not confined 24 hours a day. By 1870, most states had duplicated the New York Prison System, establishing their own penitentiaries using the congregate model. Furthermore, separate prisons gradually emerged to confine men, women, and juvenile offenders.

However, a major turning point in the reformation of prisons occurred during the American Civil War when prison labor was heavily relied upon to produce equipment and clothing for the Civil War soldiers. The post–civil War period continued to rely on the much needed resource of prison labor, creating numerous prison industry systems, and altering the management and structure of prison life. Overcrowding became a major problem, prisoners were living in cramped and overcrowded cells, sanitation was minimal, and disease and abuse were major problems. With overcrowded conditions, the system of silence and solitary confinement began to deteriorate, and corruption became widespread in most state penitentiaries. Prisoners had little motivation to change their behavior; therefore, upon completion of their sentence, most returned to the community and committed more crime. Many of the penitentiaries built in the first half of the 19th century had become overcrowded and run down. By 1870, the country experienced a second major prison reform movement, one that focused on the reform and rehabilitation of prisoners.

Shortly after the Civil War, reformers began to address the issues of overcrowding, recidivism, and the run down conditions of the penitentiaries. For the first time, the quality of life in prison was under investigation. The reformers also questioned the validity of retribution and incapacitation as the primary goals of punishment. In the late 1860s, two leaders in the reform movement, Enoch Wines and Theodore Dwight, inspected all the penal institutions in the U.S. and Canada on behalf of a private reform organization, the Prison Association of New York. In their *Report on the Prisons and Reformatories of the U.S. and Canada* (1867), Wines and Dwight exposed the poor physical conditions of most prisons, lack of prison reformation, high recidivism rates, and mistreatment of prisoners. They found that severe prison overcrowding had led to a breakdown in prisoner management, leading prison administrators to use physical punishments in an effort to control prisoners and maintain labor production. The evidence in the *Report* strongly motivated other reformers from around the country to come together to review the state of American prisons.

In 1870, the first annual meeting of the National Congress on Penitentiary and Reformatory Discipline (this group is known today as the American Correctional Association) met in Cincinnati, Ohio, for a conference on improving the nation's prisons. The congress, with delegates representing 24 states, addressed the problems and failings of the penitentiary system. Wines and Dwight opened the meetings with a summary of their findings on the state of prisons. Zebulon Brockway, the third major leader in this prison reform movement, addressed the need for a new type of prison that would operate under the goal of reformation, or what we know today as rehabilitation. He argued for scientific methods of prison administration that would deemphasize the traditional goal of punishment.

The final outcome of this meeting was the approval of a document titled "A Declaration of Principles," that became the philosophical foundation of American prison management for the next 100 years. The Declaration of Principles radically underscored that the basic priority of punishment is to reform the criminal. Members of the congress recommended that prisons shift away from the former goals of retribution and harsh punishment; the declaration underscored that the basic priority of punishment was to reform the criminal. The delegation called for a new structure of indeterminate sentencing (with terms from one day to life) that would take into account the reform of the prisoner. It was believed that indeterminate sentencing would advance the goal of changing prisoners' behavior and attitudes by keeping them in prison until they were reformed.

The delegates proposed the adoption of Sir Walter Crofton's Irish "mark" system of rewards as an incentive for prisoners to improve their behavior. The "mark system" would allow a prisoner to earn time off their sentence for good behavior, permitting early release. Prisoners released early for good behavior were monitored during their early stages of adjustment to the outside world using a system similar to what is now known as parole. The Declaration of Principles also emphasized the importance of religious, educational, and vocational programs as basic steps toward reform and in preparation for returning to the community. In addition, the delegates recommended an early version of prisoner classification, separating different types of offenders based on the seriousness of their criminal behavior, gender, age, and mental capacity.

The Declaration of Principles soon led to the construction of a new type of prison, known as the "reformatory." Altering the physical design of prisons, the reformatory shifted the focus of prison management from solitary confinement and hard labor toward reformation, including education, vocational, and religious programs. The first facility, established in 1876, was the Elmira Reformatory in New York; it was designed for first time youthful offenders (between 16 and 30 years of age). As the first male reformatory in the U.S., Elmira was considered a model for other states. Elmira adopted a philosophy that emphasized prisoner classification, individualized treatment, education, vocational training, religion, indeterminate sentencing, and early release.

The Indiana State Reformatory for Women was one of the first independent women's prisons, and the first female-operated prison system for women. Female reformatories strongly emphasized religious and moral education. The first reformatories for women offered vocational programs, although they were generally gender-specific programs restricted to traditional female-oriented domestic jobs. Educational programs were either nonexistent or limited in scope. The earliest female reformatories did not operate under the "true" reformatory model because the goal of retribution remained the primary focus.

As womens reformatories began to spread across the country, a new standard developed that, in general, punish women more severely than men. State legislatures passed new laws that changed sentencing policies, permitting female juveniles and misdemeanants to serve time in the state women's reformatory for several years. There was no male counterpart to this policy. Because the new laws were based on the goal of rehabilitation and not punishment, the extended length of female misdemeanant sentences seemed reasonable to lawmakers and judges.

Most reformatories placed a strong emphasis on the reform of prisoners, although the traditional retribution model lingered in the background. For some facilities, overcrowding occurred very rapidly, forcing administrators to resort to strict disciplinary policies as a means to maintain social control. Within the first decade of operation, Elmira had twice the number of prisoners as it was designed to hold. This overcrowding reduced the effectiveness of reformation. As a means to maintain control of this large population, the administration resorted to strict adherence to corporal punishment for prisoners who misbehaved or did not cooperate. Severe beatings, whippings, and confinement to isolated areas were common punishments.

Although the initial stages of the reformatory movement did not attain all the goals set out in the Declaration of Principles, major changes did occur throughout the American prison system. The indeterminate sentence, separate male and female facilities, prisoner classification, reform programs, and early release programs were implemented in most states. However, more changes would come soon after 1900.

The first two decades of the 20th century, known as the "Age of Reform," brought major industrialization, urbanization, and advanced technological developments across America. The growth of industrialism drove massive migration to urban centers, translating into substantial social problems. Progressive reformers focused on the social problems of modern society and the need for government to manage the various populations and maintain social control. These concerns led to continued support for prison reform, although actual changes took years to materialize.

The progressive reformers were strongly influenced by the Positivist School of Criminology, which argued that offenders were a product of their social environment, biological makeup, or psychological abnormalities. This change in philosophy led prison reformers to revisit the earlier principles of rehabilitation that evolved from the 1870 Declaration of Principle's Doctrine. The progressives believed that treatment designed to capture the individual's specific needs would lead to rehabilitation. They promoted a new "Medical Model" of treatment, as well as other new alternatives to incarceration that emphasized treatment. The medical model was an extension of the Reformatory Movement; it maintained the goal of reform using a new approach to treating offenders. According to this model, people who violate the law do so because they are physically or mentally ill. Therefore, criminals were to be viewed as patients in need of treatment and medical care who when properly treated were capable of rehabilitation.

One of the driving forces behind the progressives' medical model was the development of the Federal Bureau of Prisons and its rapid transition toward a rehabilitation model. As state prisons became overcrowded and policies for contracting federal prisoners became more stringent, large federal prison facilities were constructed sporadically throughout the U.S. The construction of the first federal prison began in 1897, at Ft. Leavenworth, Kansas, and took more than 30 years to complete. The federal government maintains prisons for the purpose of housing offenders who have committed federal violations. The earliest federal prisons (c. 1927) adopted the 18th century philosophy of retribution, with solitary confinement as a primary goal of incapacitation. However, by 1929, the Federal Bureau of Prisons began moving toward the goal of rehabilitation when congress authorized the development of institutions with proper prisoner classification systems and treatment programs. Today most federal prisons are diversified, with multiple levels of security classification within one facility.

The medical model also gained support through the widely endorsed eugenics movement that sought to prevent the "inferior classes" from reproducing. The eugenicists believed that criminality was often an inherited trait, passed on through the generations, and for some, an incurable disease. They suggested that criminals were genetically defective and concluded that the best way to eliminate criminality and other social problems was to prevent the "inferior" from breeding. Those who believed in the eugenics theory also supported the sterilization of prisoners. In some states, prisoners who were diagnosed as genetically defective were sterilized or confined for life or until they could no longer have children. The influence of the eugenics movement and forced sterilization remained a prominent component of the medical model until the 1950s.

The progressives also argued for the return of indeterminate sentences, allowing prison officials flexibility in releasing prisoners, only when they were rehabilitated, indefinitely holding those who did not change their behavior. The medical model implied that curing the disease of crime was a difficult task; some offenders would never recover. Supporters of the medical model believed that the power to decide when to release a prisoner should be given to prison administrators, not judges.

By the 1920s, the psychotherapeutic model had been introduced in most state prisons. Psychiatrists were hired to diagnose prisoners' mental illnesses and to administer therapeutic treatment as a means of rehabilitation. Prisons hired psychologists to administer intelligence tests to determine which prisoners were intellectually too incompetent. The medical model also promoted a classification system that encouraged the segregation of mentally ill prisoners and those who were not capable of changing their behavior. The medical model lasted well into the 1950s and remnants of therapeutic treatment remained prominent through much of the 1970s. Today, various treatment models are integrated into a more diverse punishment strategy that also includes elements of retribution, deterrence, and incapacitation.

A major failing with the medical model was its narrow focus on the offender that ignored the institutional problems and issues of incarceration and security. The lack of a clear definition of the mentally disabled or the "mentally defective" also led to problems associated with the decision of when to release prisoners and when to declare someone "rehabilitated." On close examination of the various treatment models implemented in different state prisons, few led to actual treatment; most programs never went beyond the diagnostic stage. At the same time, a large number of young prisoners were diagnosed with "genetic disorders," considered not treatable, and sterilized. The sterilization of young offenders was viewed by prison administrators as a solution to control the expanding crime problem and decrease the prison population.

In light of the failings of the medical model a new treatment method developed that not only focused on rehabilitation, but emphasized the reintegration of prisoners into the community. The reintegration model focused on community treatment and preparing prisoners for their postincarceration return to the community. Vocational and educational programs were developed in prisons and jails to help prisoners begin the process of returning to the community. In the 1960s, treatment and rehabilitation for less serious, nonviolent offenders expanded to community-based corrections. Community corrections is based on the premise that rehabilitation is best accomplished in the community; offenders who receive treatment while maintaining their ties to the community will be more successful than their incarcerated counterparts. An increase in the number of people serving sentences in local communities (and especially probation) expanded to more than two-thirds of the total number of offenders under the jurisdiction of state and local correctional systems. The number of sentenced offenders to community corrections continues to be the largest segment of state and local correctional populations. The reintegration model was the predominant goal of rehabilitation throughout the

1970s, and continues to be a competing goal of the American prison system today.

By the 1980s, the American public became increasingly concerned as crime rates began to rise and recidivism rates grew. In the early 1970s, the overall prison population was just over 200,000, by the mid-1980s it had doubled to 400,000, in 1990 the population had risen to 800,000, and in 1994 it exceeded the 1 million mark. Although the rehabilitation model remained the primary goal of state prison systems for more than 100 years, as crime and recidivism rates continued to escalate, the rehabilitative model came under attack. The problems associated with an overburdened system led to a shift back to a retribution model in the philosophy of the American prison system.

The warehousing of offenders in and out of state prisons, longer sentences, and increasing violent crime rates caused severe overcrowding in the American prison system. Prisons became breeding grounds for problems; the combination of overcrowding, violent repeat offenders, and inadequate rehabilitation services and treatment led to a decade of major prison riots throughout the 1970s. The Attica New York State Prison riot in 1971 was the first of many violent outbursts. Eleven prison guards and 32 prisoners were killed during the Attica riot. Riots spread like wildfires throughout prisons across the country causing millions of dollars worth of damage, and loss of life. For the first time, the American public had a view of the inside of the prison system. Journalists learned firsthand about the failing rehabilitation system and the deteriorating conditions of aging facilities, and conveyed on "live TV from inside the prisons" that immediate solutions were imminent. During negotiations to end the riot at Attica, two of the most important inmate concerns involved the issue of racism in the prison and the indeterminate sentencing structure that left great uncertainty about sentencing release dates. General disillusionment toward the rehabilitation model was mounting across the country.

Also in the 1970s research involving an extensive evaluation of correctional treatment programs was completed by Lipton, Martinson, and Wilks (1975). This extensive analysis involved more than 231 correctional treatment program evaluations from across the country. The report suggested that most prison treatment did not work; rehabilitation had little or no effect on changing an offender's future criminal tendencies. This study left a lingering impact on the American correctional community, leading toward a shift in philosophical thinking and a reversion back to the retribution model. A demand for sentencing reform became both a political and a social agenda.

Since the late 1970s, retribution has been the most common rationale for punishment. Still, the American prison system operates under the competing goals of retribution, incapacitation, rehabilitation, deterrence, and reintegration. Harsher sentencing laws for drug-related activities and violent crime have had a major effect on the growth of the prison population. Increasing numbers of inmates led to prison expansion and construction and early release mechanisms to reduce overcrowding. The return of the penitentiary appeared in the form of the new "super-max" prisons that use a modified version of solitary confinement. In response to the overcrowding problem, the privatization of prisons has helped to take the burden off state and federal systems. Private corporations began contracting with states to build and manage new prisons in the 1980s. In addition, renewed alternative solutions to incarceration for less serious and first-time offenders have led to expanded community correctional and residential treatment programs.

Stricter and longer minimum sentences continue to be enacted as a response to crime. Guidelines were developed to achieve "truth-in-sentencing" policies, by which 85% of the sentence administered by the court is the minimum sentence to be served. Truth-in-sentencing also demands fairer, proportionate, and predictable sentences for specific criminal violations, ultimately increasing the actual time served. It also reduces the disparity in sentencing from one jurisdiction to another for similar crimes.

As we move into the 21st century, the American prison system is at a crossroads, with competing goals and philosophies regarding punishment and social control. The system has reached a point where a decision needs to be made about the proper blend of punishment philosophies that will effectively and efficiently address the problems of crime and prison overcrowding. Today, states are spending more than $30 billion annually on incarceration, double the rate of a decade ago. The American prison system has transformed more in the past 30 years than over the previous 100 years. The momentum to build more prisons continues even with crime rates dropping. Harsher sentencing and high recidivism rates support the need for more prison space.

DEBRA L. STANLEY

References and Further Reading

Freedman, E.B. 1981. *Their Sisters' Keepers: Women's Prison Reform in America, 1830–1930,* Ann Arbor, MI, University of Michigan Press.

Friedman, L.M. 1993. *Crime and Punishment in American History,* New York, Basic Books, Harper-Collins Publishers, Inc.

Keve, P.W. 1991. *Prisons and the American Conscience: A History of U.S. Federal Corrections,* Carbondale, IL, Southern Illinois University Press.

Lipton, D., Martinson, R. and Wilks, J. 1975. *The Effectiveness of Correctional Treatment: A Survey of Treatment Evaluation Studies*, New York, Praeger.

McShane, M.D. and Williams, F.P., Eds. 1996. *Encyclopedia of American Prisons*, New York, Garland Publishing, Inc.

Morris, N. and Rothman, D., Eds. 1995. *The Oxford History of the Prison*, New York, Oxford University Press.

Phelps, R.H. 1996. *Newgate of Connecticut, Its Origin and Early History*, Camden, ME, Picton Press.

Rafter, N.H. 1992. *Partial Justice: Women, Prisons, and Social Control*, 2nd ed., New Brunswick, NJ, Transaction Publishers.

Sutherland, E., Cressey, D. and Luckinbill, D. 1992. *Principles of Criminology*, 11th ed., Dix Hills, NY, General Hall, Inc.

Wines, F.H. 1919. *Punishment and Reformation*, New York, Thomas Y. Crowell Company.

See also **Prison Riots; Prisons, Problems and Recent Developments in; Prisons: Administration and Organization; Prisons: Inmate Populations and Subcultures; Prisons, Privatized; Prisons: Women's Facilities**

Prison Riots

Introduction

Correctional riots are not a new phenomenon in the history of American correctional institutions. The first correctional riot reportedly took place in Simsbury, Connecticut, in 1774, at a prison that had been constructed over an abandoned mine in 1773 (Fox, 1972). George Nicholson (1922) described an incident involving inmates in 1866 as "On the Saturday following the Charleston, South Carolina, earthquake the inmates at the jail became mutinous and refused for a time to be locked in their cells for fear of being trapped victims of any future aftershocks. Under Col. Lipscomb's careful supervision and peculiar power of persuasion, he finally quelled the trouble without bloodshed" (p. 42). However, whereas 69 prisoners had been hastened into the yard, 36 others escaped through a breach in the high brick fence. These inmates were later captured.

In 1923, a special South Carolina joint legislative committee reported to the General Assembly on a riot that took place in the state penitentiary during the month of May 1922. Several inmates were injured and one was killed after a confrontation with correctional officers.

A riot between inmates and correctional officers occurred at the Central Correctional Institution in Columbia, South Carolina, on April 1, 1968. An article in *The State* newspaper stated that two inmates jumped two guards as the officers were planning another inmate in his cell on suspicion of being drunk. A crowd of 75 inmates then joined the struggle. A tear gas canister was used to break the riot (McCuen, 1968).

Definition of a Riot

Throughout history and study of prison riots, experts have developed various definitions with respect to describing the elements of a "riot." The South Carolina Department of Corrections conducted a national study of American prison riots between the time periods of 1900 and 1971. In this study the definition of a riot was defined as "an incident involving 15 or more inmates and resulting in property damage or personal injury." The results of their findings produced a level of consistency when comparing statistics (number of inmates, time of year, "cause," property damage, action taken to end the riot, etc.). The resulting level of uniformity was one of the first federally funded studies of riots and has become a model for many studies that were to follow (Catoe and Harvey, 1996).

In 1998, the American Correctional Association suggested that there are three categories of violence and disorder that may occur within a correctional institution. These are: (1) an incident, (2) a disturbance, and (3) a riot. These definitions range from an occurrence, which is least severe in terms of damage, time, number of inmates, frequency, etc. to those of the greatest magnitude (Crews, Gordon, and Montgomery, 1998).

Range of Riot Causation

There are many theories about why riots occur in correctional institutions. Some of the most popular theories will be discussed in brief here. The first of these is the "conflict theory of riots" as proposed by Dr. Emerson Smith (Braswell, Montgomery, and Lombardo, 1994). He believes that prison riots are a result of unresolved conflicts.

Another regularly cited theory is the "power vacuum" theory (Braswell et al., 1994). This explanation revolves around the idea dealing with abrupt changes to a structured system. It is believed that when sudden revisions or reorganization takes place that the network of formal control mechanisms is disrupted. The disturbances may result in institution friction and finally in some consequential shifts in the power relationships of the system.

Perhaps the most basic of the theories used when discussing prison riots is the "deprivation theory" (Braswell et al., 1994). This notion argues the commonsense position that riots and protests come in response to "bad" or unacceptable conditions from the vantage point of those sponsoring the action.

Dr. Vernon Fox (1972) developed the "time bomb" theory. His theory of prison riots is broken down into five stages, four during the riot and one following the riot. Fox's (1972) first stage involved a period of undirected violence by inmates. An excellent example of this stage can be witnessed in the Kirkland Correctional Institution (KCI) riot, which occurred on April 1, 1986, in Columbia, South Carolina. Ken McKellar was the warden at the time of the riot. This incident, also known as the April Fool's Day riot, had started at 7:00 PM when an inmate jumped a correctional officer and obtained the cell door keys. The inmate unlocked 30 doors and released 32 high security inmates. The rebellious inmates broke open a large toolbox, which contained crowbars, sledgehammers, bolt cutters, and acetylene torches. Using these tools the inmates freed an additional 700 inmates. Twenty-two employees were either taken hostage or trapped in dorms. By 7:40 PM fires had been set in the treatment building, library, education building, and dorm offices (Catoe, 1986).

Another example of this first stage of the "time bomb" theory took place at the Polk Youth Institution in Raleigh, North Carolina, on January 1, 1994. This riot had begun as a New Year's Eve celebration. The party got out of hand because of a lack of proper supervision. Another contributing factor was a lack of proper lighting. Three staff and 60 inmates were injured during the riot, which lasted 8 hours. The Prison Emergency Response Team ended the riot as some inmates had to be removed by force (Crews et al., 1996).

Dr. Fox (Crews et al., 1996) believed that prisons were time bombs waiting to go off. It would only take a spark (e.g., fist fight) to set a riot in motion. Pontiac State Penitentiary, for example, had a prison riot on October 4, 1971. This Illinois prison riot began with a fight between two inmates. The riot involved 200 inmates by its end after 4 hours. Eleven inmates and ten guards were injured. Damages to the institution amounted to $65,000.

Rumors can also be the "spark" to a riot (Crews et al., 1996). The Green Bay Reformatory, for example, exploded on November 12, 1971. Rumors had spread among the inmates that guards had beaten prisoners. The ensuing riot lasted only 30 minutes, however, over 200 inmates were involved in this Wisconsin riot, which resulted in injuries to both guards and inmates.

Dr. Fox's (1972) second stage involved the emergence of inmate leaders who determine inmate policy during a riot. A fine example of stage two can be seen in the riot that took place at the Central Utah Correctional Facility in Gunnison, Utah, on August 9, 1993. Five inmates started the riot. Ten other inmates followed these riot leaders into an escalated event, which lasted 5 hours. The damages totaled out at over $50,000.

On April 11, 1993, at 3:00 PM a riot took place at the Southern Ohio Correctional Facility in Lucasville, Ohio. This riot, also known as the Easter Riot, lasted 11 days. Four inmate gang leaders influenced the progression of the riot, which resulted in the deaths of nine inmates and one correctional officer. Twelve officers were taken hostage and were freed through negotiations. Officer Bobby Vallandingham was the one officer killed by the inmates. L-block was destroyed and it cost approximately $26 million to rebuild the institution. The riot ended through negotiation.

A major cause of complaint for the rioting inmates was the requirement by prison officials that inmates take part in a tuberculin skin test program.

Inmate leaders can and often do exert a great deal of power in a prison riot. At Attica, for example, inmate leaders imposed rules on fellow inmates. Inmates were not allowed to use drugs, leave D yard, engage in fighting, or take part in sexual behavior.

Inmate leaders who are effective can bring about a peaceful conclusion to a riot. For example, inmate leaders who emerged during the West Virginia Penitentiary riot in 1986 were able to end the riot after both parties reached an agreement. Part of the agreement was a face-to-face meeting with the governor of the state. A unique feature of the agreement was a provision that the inmates had an opportunity to clean up their living areas before returning the institution to prison authorities (Crews et al., 1996).

Dr. Fox's (1972) third stage involves a period of interaction between inmates and prison authorities. This interaction may involve either negotiations or the expression of force on either actor's part. A classic example of stage three was the prison riot at the Atlanta Federal Penitentiary, which began on November 26, 1987, at 10:00 AM. Cuban inmates at the institution were upset about a U.S. State Department agreement to return Cuban inmates to Cuba. Except for the first day of the riot, which involved violence, the method of interaction between inmates and authorities was one of negotiation. This riot lasted for 11 days (Crews et al., 1996).

A unique aspect of this riot was the involvement of Agustin Roman, Auxiliary Bishop of Miami. He encouraged inmates to take part in negotiations, which eventually resulted in a final agreement. A major point agreed to was the review of every inmate's case by the Department of Justice (Crews et al., 1996).

Another riot took place at the Cross City Correctional Institution in Florida, on January 23, 1983. The cause of this riot, which involved 200 inmates, was the shooting of an inmate attempting to escape. During the 4 hours of riot a total of $81,451.03, in damages incurred. Correctional officers chose not to negotiate and used force to regain control of the institution (Crews et al., 1996).

Dr. Fox's (1972) fourth stage was the surrender of inmates by a negotiation of force. On June 23, 1986, a riot broke out at the Kentucky State Penitentiary in Eddyville, Kentucky. A total of 41 inmates took part in this riot because of concern over the quality of food at the institution. This riot lasted 3 hours and was ended when a riot squad regained control of the institution. The squad used shotgun blasts and tear gas to end the riot (Crews et al., 1996).

Another example was the riot at the Central Facility in Lorton, Virginia. This riot involved 363 inmates who surrendered after 1 hour when correctional officer armed with tear gas and shotguns arrived at the institution. The riot occurred on September 23, 1985, as a result of a work stoppage by inmates (Crews et al., 1996).

On October 31, 1952 (Halloween riot), inmates rioted at the Ohio Penitentiary. Prisoners were upset about the lack of privacy, crowded conditions, lack of proper food, and procedures of the parole board. Fire damage to the institution amounted to $1 million dollars. The institution was retaken by force. One inmate was killed and five were wounded in the retaking of the prison (Crews et al., 1996).

At this same institution inmates rioted on August 20, 1968. Nine guards were held in this 30-hour siege. The prison was retaken when the correctional officers blasted holes in the roof and walls of the cellblock. Five inmates were killed by gunfire. The hostages were freed (Crews et al., 1996).

The Attica (New York) prison riot in 1971 and the Santa Fe (New Mexico) prison riot in 1980 provided a sharp contrast in how riots were brought to an end. The Attica riot ended when state troopers opened fire on the inmates. Inmates at Santa Fe, on the other hand, surrendered after 36 hours in a peaceful manner.

The fifth stage of a riot, according to Dr. Fox (1972), is the investigations, prosecutions, and administrative changes which follow the riot. A good example of this stage was the previously mentioned Kirkland Correctional Institution riot. A grand jury returned 36 indictments against 25 inmates on May 13, 1986. Charges ranged from "inciting a riot" to the "taking of hostages" (Crews et al., 1996).

Another example was the Federal Prison riot in Atlanta, Georgia, on November 26, 1987. After this riot the Federal Bureau of Prisons conducted an investigation. A report recommended that Congress add $33.7 million dollars to the Federal Bureau of Prisons budget to repair property damages at Atlanta (Report to the Attorney General, 1988).

On June 24, 1968, inmates rioted at the Ohio Penitentiary. Fires were started by inmates, which damaged prison property to the tune of $1 million dollars. There were injuries, but no deaths. Crowded conditions were named as a major cause of the riot. Forty-four prisoners were charged with inciting the riot.

The Attica (New York) prison riot in 1971 and the Santa Fe (New Mexico) prison riot in 1980 both resulted in investigations, which produced reports describing the respective riots. The New York State Special Commission on Attica published its finding in 1972. The Attorney General of New Mexico produced his report on Santa Fe in 1980 (Crews et al., 1996).

Riot Prevention Strategies

The author feels more strategies must be tried in order to prevent more prison riots. One strategy to prevent riots is the use of *grievance mechanisms* by the prison systems. A grievance mechanism is a device for resolving inmate grievances. A grievance usually involves a complaint about the substance or application of a written or unwritten policy or regulation. A hearing is held where the grievance is resolved.

Another strategy for correctional departments is the use of an *ombudsman*. Such a person performs in a capacity similar to an inspector general in the military. This person has the power to ameliorate problem situations and render satisfactory responses to legitimate problems.

Inmate councils are an effective strategy for allowing inmates to express their concerns. Inmate representatives are inmates who have been elected to their positions by fellow inmates. Arrangements are typically made for representatives to discuss with other inmates their major concerns and anxieties. Inmates who have suggestions, problems, complaints, or grievances are able to communicate them to the inmate representative, who in turn relays the information to the inmate council. Concerns are related to the warden for resolution.

Inmate inventories are written instruments, which can be used by wardens to detect riot-prone conditions. The inmate inventory uses a Likert scale of measurement. For example, one item might be "chance to see warden."

The inmate is provided two words at the opposite ends of the scale. One word is the word "easy" and the other word is the word "difficult." Five spaces numbered one to five are provided for the inmate to mark his or her feelings on this particular item.

A warden can administer the inmate inventory at his or her institution to a random sample of inmates (e.g. 100 inmates). If, for example, 90% of the inmates marked dissatisfied with the medical treatment, then the warden would have a definite need to investigate and correct the perceived problem area.

Another process, which is effective in preventing prison violence, is the use of *post-occupancy evaluations (POE)*. POE's collect data on facility design and policy in an organized, systematic, and reliable manner and present the findings clearly. The findings come directly from users of the institution. For example, inmates, line staff, maintenance staff, and management would provide input. Systematic observations, interviews, and surveys are the main tools used to evaluate a facility. The POE's help prison administrators correct current problems as well as influence design improvements for new institutions.

Correctional personnel should receive training in how to recognize signs of tension in their prisons. One such course is entitled "containment of prison violence," which was created by the National Institute of Corrections. For example, if inmates were to start buying items from the commissary in an increased amount this might be a sign that the inmates feel a riot is going to happen in the near future. They know they will not be served meals during a prison riot.

Many experts feel that the proper way to prevent prison riots is to have prison administrators who are effective. Dr. Ellis MacDougall (1985) feels a major contributor to institutional violence is insufficient prison space. Inmates are impacted every day by this problem. Tensions arise from this close confinement. The solution is more cell space per inmate.

Boredom and the absence of meaningful employment, educational, and vocational opportunities contribute to the potential for prison violence and riots. Inmates must feel there is hope for them. Thus, antiquated prisons packed with populations of violent individuals lacking in productive activities or programs and devoid of hope pose serious threats to institutional safety and tranquility.

Change is also an important factor that must be understood by administrators managing their prisons. Causal and hasty rule changes may cause ripples of discontent that soon increase in magnitude. Changes should be announced in advance so that the potential obstacles may be identified and appropriate adjustments made.

Qualities of leadership cannot be overestimated in managing prisons. People will follow a leader who has consistent policies and follows them without bias, and is willing to bend or depart from rigid enforcement when an exception or compassionate departure is in order.

Communication is another concern that is frequently mentioned in corrections, but rarely understood or systematically developed within correctional operations. A prison administrator who communicates with his entire organization and regularly deals with surfacing problems is likely to avoid prison disturbances through early detection and diffusion practices (Crews et al., 1996).

Prison Security and Technological Innovations

A big factor that must not be overlooked is that of prison security. Correctional officers and prison administrators must have riot plans in place if a riot breaks out. It is important to stop a riot as soon as possible. Modern technology can play a part in developing an effective riot prevention plan. One example is that of video visitation.

Traditional visitation within a penal institution is replaced by communication between the inmate and another actor via videoconference. This method proves itself worthy in many respects. It eliminates the amount of contraband that is typically smuggled in during face-to-face visitations, and provides a greater sense of security for the visitor, inmate, and correctional staff involved. Video visitation also allows prisoners to communicate with individuals they otherwise may not have had access to for long periods of time (such as relatives living great distances, busy lawyers, and so forth).

The benefits that technology bring are not just limited to the concept of visitation but, rather, they also may play a large role in courtroom appearances and investigation. This new ability to communicate via phone or satellite also would allow the building of prisons in more remote areas without raising the cost of transportation or reducing the number of visitors who feasibly can travel such a distance (Crews et al., 1996).

Another useful technology is that of face-prints to produce positive identification. Inmates who are classified as dangerous, generally, do not move freely inside an institution. "Face-prints" would allow correctional staff to identify inmates immediately and determine if an inmate is in the proper location. This system uses infrared sensors that can recognize an individual's facial thermogram. The heat-emitting veins and arteries on the face create a person's pattern, which the computer then stores in its memory. This system consists of a camera and a computer database of facial thermograms. For identification, and individual stands in front of the camera and types a personal identification number into the computer. Using the identification number, the computer calls up a stored image and matches it with the live image of the person standing before the camera. The technology is so advanced that persons who have had plastic surgery will not confuse the system (Crews et al., 1996).

Bar codes could be a part of an effective prison security system. These codes would be scanned and a corresponding computer would access the inmate's information file. A correctional officer using a scanner can check whether an inmate should have a razor or not. If inmates were on suicide watch, they would not be allowed to have a razor. Using a scanner, a correctional officer could check if an inmate should be in certain locations. Also, the correctional officer could check on inmate property to prevent theft by other inmates.

Ultrasound might be a technique useful to end prison riots in matter of seconds. Sound devices could be installed in correctional facilities. These devices would produce high-intensity sound waves. Rioting inmates would be knocked unconscious for several minutes when the sound waves hit their eardrums. Correctional officers, on the other hand, would wear special helmets to protect their eardrums (Crews et al., 1996).

One way to control inmates who become violent would be for the correctional officer to spray them with sticky foam. This technology currently is being tested at various police departments and by the U.S. Marine Corps. Sticky foam stops a suspect because everything it touches becomes stuck to it, immobilizing the subject's legs and arms like contact cement. Sticky foam might help to capture rioters if exits were blocked with large bags filled with the substance through which a rioter would have to pass to escape riot squads. If rioters broke the bag, they would be engulfed in sticky foam (Crews et al., 1996).

Looking toward the Future

Right now it sounds far out, but as property for the sites of prisons becomes more valuable, innovative systems may consider undersea prisons. Huge prisons built on the floor of the ocean would present little opportunity for prisoners to escape. Inmates in these correctional facilities could be used to harvest sea vegetation and drill for oil. Even greater security could be achieved by building space prisons. Few inmates would want to take part in a riot that possibly could damage their supply of oxygen.

Treatment based approaches might also be a part of the effort to prevent prison riots. Prison experts have found that aggressive inmates relax when they take part in pet therapy programs. Taking care of animals teaches them to behave gently while in a harsh environment. Such therapeutic techniques will reduce an individual's predisposition to violence and work to rehabilitate an inmate, preparing the inmate for the eventual return to society (Crews et al., 1996).

Correctional institutions might use subliminal messages to influence inmate behavior. Subliminal antiriot messages might include the following: "Do the right thing," "Obey the prison rules," "Don't take part in a riot," "Do your own time; don't let others influence you the wrong way." These subliminal messages could be mixed with background music 24 hours a day in jails and prisons. Courts even might sentence offenders to have subliminal antiriot micro-players implanted.

Correctional institutions in the future should emphasize improved use of space, color, and lighting. The double-bunked, crowded cells evident in correctional institutions could be modified greatly, allowing each inmate more humane living conditions. Correctional institutions in the future should implement structural changes such as the more frequent use of plexiglass in the place of bricks and bars, and a greater use of skylights. As a result, inmates' perceptions of their confinement may be more positive; they will feel less like caged animals and more like human beings. When they feel they are treated better, they may react in a less hostile manner. Prisons in the future also should emphasize constructive use of color. Recent studies indicate the calming effects of soft pastel colors on inmates (Crew et al., 1996). In the correctional setting, color should serve as a control mechanism, calming the inmates and, hence, preventing disruptive behavior.

Medically trained correctional personnel might use brain peptides and chemicals to control an inmate's emotional behavior. It is known, for example, that high levels of serotonin can control aggression. With the aid of a peptide implant, this chemical could be released automatically, lowering a person's level of aggression. Through the implanting of brain chemicals, undesired behavior could be controlled. Implementation of ideas such as this will serve as fertile grounds for court litigation in the near future.

As the number of inmates continue to increase in the U.S., it is clear "new" strategies will need to be used to prevent prison riots. It is hoped that some of the nonlethal strategies mentioned in this paper will be effective in preventing or ending future prison riots.

REID MONTGOMERY

References and Further Reading

ACA. (1998). *Standards supplement,* Lanham, MD, American Correctional Association.

Braswell, M.C., Montgomery, R.H., Jr. and Lombardo, L.X. (1994). *Prison Violence in America*, 2nd ed., Cincinnati, OH, Anderson Publishing Company.

Catoe, W.D. and Harvey, L. (1986). *A Review of the Kirkland Correctional Institution Disturbance on April 1, 1986*, Columbia, SC, South Carolina Department of Corrections.

Crews, G.A., Montgomery, R.H., Jr. and Garris, W.R. (1996). *Faces of Violence in America*, Needham Heights, MA, Simon & Schuster Publishing.

Crews, G. and Montgomery, R. (1998). *A History of Correctional Violence: An Examination of Reported Causes of Riots and Disturbances*, Lanham, MD, American Correctional Association.

Fox, V. (August, 1972). Prison riots in a democratic society, *Police*, 16(35).

MacDougall, E. (1985). Foreword, *Prison Violence in America*, 1st ed., Cincinnati, OH, Anderson Publishing Company.

McCuen, S.E. (April, 2, 1968). *Guards Quickly Put Down Prison Inmate Disturbance*, The State, p. 1.

Montgomery, R. (1923). *South Carolina Report of the Special Joint Legislative Committee to Investigate Conditions at the State Penitentiary*, Columbia, SC.

National Institute of Corrections, U.S. Department of Justice (1982). *Containment of Prison Violence*, Washington, DC, U.S. Government Printing Office.

Nicholson, G. (1922). The South Carolina Penitentiary, Master's thesis, University of South Carolina, SC. (Unpublished).

See also **Prisons, Problems and Recent Developments in; Riots: Extent and Correlates; Riots: The Law**

Prisons: Administration and Organization

Introduction

At mid-year 2003 there were approximately 2 million men and women locked up in our prisons and jails. This is a substantial investment by our taxpayers and governments and we continue to build more prisons and lock people up in order to deter them from committing further crimes in spite of evidence that, other than incapacitation, there may be no benefits to such a crime control policy. As a consequence, it is important that we understand how prisons and jails are organized and managed. The organization and administration of prisons can be viewed from several different levels: social organization, governmental organization, organization by purpose, and administrative organization.

Social organization

Prisons are characterized by both an informal inmate organizational structure and a formal staff structure. The informal inmate structure is best viewed as a social organization characterized by the "pains of imprisonment" (Sykes, 1958). Sykes observed that the uniqueness of the frustrations imposed on the inmates, or what he calls, "the pains of imprisonment," as well as the prisoners' previous training in deviance, results in a social group characterized by a high degree of exploitation, where other inmates as victims are scorned even more than the prison staff as oppressors.

Sykes asserts that the prison is characterized by a single-value system that dominates the social fabric of the inmates' lives. In addition, the inmate culture and staff culture seem to be a mirror image of one another, each with its own values and without any points of interpenetration. Sykes states that the inmate code is situational and in response to the "pains of imprisonment." Those pains are:

Deprivation of liberty. The inmate is allowed access to a few small acres of land and confined within that area. The resulting boredom and loneliness are a problem, but more importantly, confinement represents a deliberate rejection of the prisoner by the free community.

Deprivation of goods and services. Prisoners are kept in a painfully Spartan environment. They are made poor by virtue of being confined, and in a culture that equates material goods with personal worth, prisoners have the additional burden of being poor for no edifying reasons such as religious principles, deferred gratification, or the good of the community they live in. They are poor by their own misdeeds, which they perceive as a bitter attack on their self-image.

Deprivation of heterosexual relationships. The psychological problems caused by being confined with only members of the same sex are far more damaging to the self-concept than mere deprivation of physical relationships. The absence of half of the audience to whom one normally relates and from whom one draws a good portion of one's self-concept causes the self-image to become cracked and distorted from the lack of contrast.

Deprivation of autonomy. The prisoner's inability to make choices, along with the administration's refusal to explain decisions and commands, threatens the inmate's self-image by reducing her or him to the weak, helpless, and dependent status of early childhood.

Deprivation of security. The prisoner's being locked up with others whom he views as "dangerous" or "unstable" arouses great anxiety, not so much because of violence and exploitation, but because he knows that sooner or later he will be tested. The waiting and stress call into question his ability to cope—"Can he take it?"

The staff, on the other hand, sees itself as alienated and misunderstood. Kaufman (1988) found that the officer code governed much of the behavior of staff. Injunctions such as always go to the aid of an officer and never countermand the orders of another officer in front of an inmate are important guides to behavior and contributed to officer solidarity.

Governmental Organization

There are three levels of governmental prison organization: federal, state, and local. The U.S. Bureau of Prisons is responsible for holding all prisoners sentenced for violation of U.S. laws and statutes. Today the Bureau of Prisons holds more than 140,000 prisoners in 102 facilities spread across the nation. This includes community treatment centers (community work release centers), metropolitan correctional centers (federal jails), camps, medium, and close custody prisons as well as super-maximum prisons. State prisons are for the imprisonment of prisoners who have been found guilty of violating a state law and are sentenced to the custody of the Department of Corrections. Today, state prisons hold more than 1.5 million prisoners in minimum, medium, and maximum custody prisons. There are also jails, which hold in excess of 665,000 inmates awaiting trial or serving sentences of less than 1 year. Jails are considered either small (less than 40 beds, medium (between 40 and 1500 beds), and large jails (over 1500 beds).

The U.S. Bureau of Prisons and the various state prisons are organized like a pyramid with the Director or Commissioner sitting at the top of the pyramid with the lines of communication and authority flowing downward to staff and departments. The central office is responsible for establishing policy and assuring that the desires of the attorney general (in the case of the U.S. Bureau of Prisons) and the Governors and Director or Commissioner of the Department of Corrections (in the case of state prisons). Each prison is in turn under the management of a warden or superintendent. The warden has at least two assistant wardens working for

him or her and one is usually responsible for operations and the other is responsible for programs. All prisons are organized by department, that is, one department will be responsible for security, another responsible for counseling and case management, and another for food service for example. Jails usually fall under the responsibility of the sheriff and he or she in turn will appoint a jail commander. The jail commander will assure that the jail is safe, humane, and that it protects the community from individuals accused of crimes, but not yet brought to trial.

Since the early 1970s, there has arisen a new way of managing prisons and jails. In prison, unit management has proven itself as an effective way of managing a prison in order to strengthen security and improve program delivery. In jails, the new approach is called direct supervision. Both approaches rely upon the staff being in the unit or pod (as they are called in jails) directly supervising prisoners without one being separated from the other by bars or window. This approach is proactive and allows staff to prevent problems before they get out of control and the approach has proven itself to be effective (see Houston, 1998; Levinson, 1999).

Organization by Purpose

As mentioned above, most prisons are organized along departmental lines, that is, like functions are grouped together: custody of prisoners is the responsibility of the correctional officers, case management is the responsibility of the social services department, medical care is the responsibility of medical services and so on. However, unit management is responsible for breaking down some of the communication and authority problems found in some prisons because it redistributes power and alters the lines of communication.

A unit (and by inference a pod in a direct supervision jail) is staffed by a multidisciplinary team composed of a unit manager, a psychologist, a case manager or social worker, a teacher assigned part-time to the team, and correctional officers. They are responsible for all in-unit functions of the inmate and also make in-unit policy and develop programs and implement programs.

Administrative Organization

The well-managed prison will be governed by a policies and procedures manual to govern the management of the prison. The purpose of a policies and procedures manual is to guide staff training, to provide guidance and uniformity of actions of staff, and to act as a buffer in the event of lawsuits. From the policies and procedures flow a management by objectives program, which in turn will drive staff training and serve as a yardstick to measure activities within the prison over time.

Overall the administration of prisons can be broken down into operations and management. Operations (under the direct supervision of the assistant warden–operations) refers to the management of inmates and assuring the care, custody, and control of prison and jail inmates as they go about their daily life behind bars. Such things as counts (counting inmates several times a day), feeding them, providing some kind of work to occupy their time, supervision, contraband control, and movement of inmates within the jail or prison and outside to court.

Programs (under the supervision of the assistant warden of programs) refer to the delivery of services to inmates in the form of case management, spiritual programming, counseling, medical care, recreation, and psychological assessment. In the newer prisons the assistant warden of programs is aided by the implementation of unit management. In all instances, however, both assistant wardens work together to assure that the wishes of the warden are carried out.

An International Perspective

Most other countries in the industrialized world and many in the third world rely on a centralized form of government and find our decentralized approach to prisons and jails to be quite confusing. For example, the countries of Slovenia, South Africa, and the U.K. are all quite centralized and all policy and orders come from Ljubljana, Pretoria, or London, respectively. Slovenia is a small country and currently has a prison population of approximately 800, the Republic of South Africa has a prison population of approximately 190,000 (of which approximately 58,000 are unsentenced prisoners), and the U.K. has a prison population of approximately 73,000.

The primary difference between Slovenia, South Africa, and the U.K. is that the prison population includes both sentenced and unsentenced prisoners. In their systems, there are no jails managed by anyone approximating our elected position of sheriff who is responsible for the county jail. Instead, many prisons in Slovenia and South Africa will serve as a regional prison for unsentenced prisoners under the supervision of the department of correctional services. In the U.K., there are a number of "city prisons" that are responsible for holding unsentenced prisoners. Other than this big difference, the prisons in the above mentioned countries have the same level of programs and are organized and managed about the same as prisons in the U.S.

Summary

The management of a prison is a difficult and frustrating task. In many instances the Department of Corrections is underfunded and is beset with a host of problems ranging from gangs to increasing numbers of elderly inmates. At present there are approximately 2 million inmates locked up in prison or jail with newly constructed prisons coming on line with regularity.

JAMES HOUSTON

References and Further Reading

Houston, J. (1999). *Correctional Management: Functions, Skills, and Systems,* 2nd ed., Chicago, Nelson-Hall, Inc.
Kaufman, K. (1988). *Prison Officers and Their World,* Cambridge, MA, Harvard University Press.
Levinson, R. (1999). *Unit Management in Prisons and Jails,* Laurell, MD, American Correctional Association.
Sykes, G. (1958) *Society of Captives,* Princeton, NJ, Princeton University Press.
Jail Statistics (2003). Bureau of Justice Statistics. Available at: www.ojp.usdoj.gov/bjs.
Prison Statistics (2003). Bureau of Justice Statistics. Available at: www.ojp.usdoj.gov/bjs.

See also **Prisons and the Rule of Law; Prisons: Correctional Officers and Staff**

Prisons and the Rule of Law

Introduction

There are two dominant schools of thought regarding judicial intervention in prison administration. Proponents of "judicial activism" maintain that judicial intervention has been both "constitutionally proper and highly effective" (DiIulio, 1990, 4). When governmental officials, both elected and appointed, fail to provide for safe and humane conditions within correctional facilities, judges have a responsibility to intervene and uphold inmates' legal and constitutional rights. Judicial intervention, or so the argument goes, is consistent with the principle of "checks and balances." With the assistance of individuals who are knowledgeable about correctional issues, judges can shape progressive correctional polices and practices and oversee their implementation. Legal scholars argue that judicial intervention has resulted in an overall improvement in prison conditions (DiIulio, 1990; Farrar, 1996; Anderson and Dyson, 2001; Minor, Wells, and Soderstrom, 2003).

Conversely, opponents of "judicial activism" argue that judicial intervention has been both constitutionally irresponsible and, for the most part, ineffective (DiIulio, 1990). Instead, this school of thought endorses "judicial restraint" as the proper role of the judiciary. Proponents of judicial restraint believe that judges are authorized to interpret the law, not to create and administer it. Accordingly, activist judges have been accused of violating the principle of "separation of powers." In other words, judges lack the expertise and resources to determine appropriate correctional policies and practices, and therefore should defer to prison administrators. Legal scholars contend that judicial intervention has resulted in increased prison administrative costs, an escalation in prison violence, and other problems (DiIulio, 1990).

During the past four decades, the judicial pendulum has continued to swing back and forth between judicial restraint and judicial activism. Prior to the 1960s, the courts practiced a judicial restraint or hands-off policy regarding correctional matters. The period between the 1960s and 1980s was marked by judicial activism or what is also known as a hands-on philosophy. The period of the latter 1980s to present has been deemed the "due deference" era, which can be best characterized as a move back toward judicial restraint.

Historical Background

Hands-off Phase
Throughout judicial history in the U.S., the courts have been largely unconcerned with the operation of prisons and the treatment of prisoners. As noted, prior to the 1960s, the judicial system practiced a "hands-off" policy with regards to prisons. During this phase, judicial officials were reluctant to get involved in correctional issues. Judges claimed that they lacked the authority and expertise to intervene in correctional matters, and court intervention likely would result in undermining the work of correctional authorities.

Although judges may have lacked expertise regarding correctional matters, scholars have argued, judges also were guided by legal precedents, such as the 1871 case of *Ruffin v. Commonwealth* (62 Va. 790, 796, 1871) (Clear and Cole, 1994). In this case, a Virginia court noted that, "the prisoner has, as a consequence of his crime, not only forfeited his liberty, but all his personal rights except those which the law in its humanity accords him. He is for the time being a slave of the state" (p. 796). By equating prisoners to slaves, the language of the case made it seem as if prisoners had no rights (Farrar, 1996; Minor et al., 2003). In response, a number of states enacted "civil death statutes," which denied inmates certain civil rights. As a result, correctional officials became the sole determiners regarding the treatment of prisoners.

The lack of judicial intervention or court deference to prison administrators resulted in a number of abuses. Inmates had no avenue to seek relief from conditions of confinement, even if the conditions were inhumane. Inmates frequently experienced serious physical and psychological abuses at the hands of both prison officials and "elite inmates" who were chosen by the warden to assist in controlling and maintaining prison security (Anderson and Dyson, 2001). In addition, many prisoners were denied the opportunity to practice and exercise their religious beliefs. Others were routinely denied the most basic standard of medical care and treatment. Some were placed in solitary confinement for extended periods of time without being afforded due process of law or the opportunity to defend themselves against alleged rule violations.

Hands-on Phase
The hands-off philosophy of the courts eventually gave way to the hands-on approach, which was due in large part to the Civil Rights Movement of the 1960s (see Krantz, 1976; Anderson and Dyson, 2001; Minor et al., 2003). The Civil Rights Movement gained momentum when many marginalized groups (e.g., ethnic minorities and women) began to assert their rights to due process and equal protection of the laws. During this same time period, prison populations became more ethnically diverse, less educated, increasingly violent, and more likely to be substance abusers. Like minorities within the free society, prisoners began to assert their rights to equal protection and due process of the laws, and for the first time, the courts began to take notice.

Most legal scholars agree that *Cooper v. Pate* (378 U.S. 546, 1964) signaled a move away from the hands-off philosophy the courts had traditionally practiced. In *Cooper*, the U.S. Supreme Court ruled that prisoners were entitled to the protections specified in the Civil Rights Act of 1871. This legislation, known as Section 1983, imposes civil liability on anyone acting "under color of law" who denies someone in their custody of a constitutional right or federal protection. In *Cooper*, the Court recognized that prisoners could sue state officials over the conditions of their confinement. This meant that constitutional violations were more likely to result in inmates invoking Section 1983 as a legal remedy. *Cooper* significantly reduced the power and control correctional administrators had once enjoyed regarding the treatment of prisoners. *Cooper* marked the beginning of the hands-on era of prison litigation and the courts began to recognize prisoners' rights.

Prisoners' Rights

During the hands-on period, the Supreme Court began to aggressively rule on constitutional issues regarding prison operations and prisoners rights. The first order of business for the Court was to establish that prisoners would no longer be regarded as "slaves of the state." Instead the Court moved quickly and decisively to establish that prisoners were entitled to certain constitutional protections. For example, in *Wolff v. McDonnell* (418 U.S. 539, 1974) the Supreme Court held that although prisoners' rights may be diminished, prisoners are not "wholly stripped of constitutional protections." In addition, the American Bar Association Joint Committee on the Legal Status of Prisoners (1977) reported:

> Prisoners retain all the rights of free citizens except those on which restriction is necessary to assure their orderly confinement or to provide reasonable protection for the rights and physical safety of all members of the prison community (p. 25).

Because prisoners retain most of the rights enjoyed by citizens in the free community, the American Bar Association (ABA) outlined three governmental interests, which may justify some prison policies that limit prisoners' rights. These restrictions may include policies and practices that are designed to (1) preserve order and discipline, (2) prevent prison escape, and (3) assist in the rehabilitation of the offender. Prison policies that are designed to accomplish one or all of the preceding rationales will prevail even if the policies infringe upon constitutionally established rights. In other words, when a case comes before the Supreme Court, it conducts a balancing test between prisoners' rights and governmental interests. Each case is examined on a case-by-case basis. Prison officials should ask themselves whether the established policy or practice accomplishes one of the three justifications of infringement of an inmate's constitutional rights (Anderson and Dyson, 2001). If the answer is yes, the Court will generally rule that governmental interests legitimately outweigh an inmate's constitutional rights. However, the burden of establishing the necessity of a policy or regulation is on prison administrators.

Civil Rights Act or Section 1983

Although prison officials must establish the necessity of a constitutionally restrictive policy, prisoners have the burden of proof of establishing that a constitutional violation has occurred. Before prisoners can succeed in a Section 1983 claim, they must demonstrate two essential elements. First, prisoners must show that a person acted under the color of state law, which means that officers derived their authority from their position as prison officials clothed with state power (Vaughn and del Carmen, 1996). Second, inmates must show that prison officials caused a violation of a clearly established constitutional or federal right. The majority of Section 1983 litigation raises constitutional issues related to the First, Fourth, Eighth, and Fourteenth Amendments.

First Amendment

The First Amendment guarantees individuals the right to free speech, religious freedom, and freedom of the press. Although the First Amendment is hailed as one of society's most valued rights, it is subject to some restriction in prison. Prisoners commonly filed claims encompassed by the First Amendment including access to the courts, access to mail, and freedom of religion.

Access to Courts

The First Amendment provides that the people have a constitutional right to petition the government for federal redress of grievance. This provision suggests that prisoners must be afforded the opportunity to bring claims before the courts if they have grounds to initiate a complaint. The Supreme Court ruled on this very issue in the case of *Ex parte Hull* (312 U.S. 546, 1941). Specifically, the Supreme Court invalidated a Michigan rule, which prohibited state inmates from filing *habeas corpus* petitions unless the petitions were found to be "properly drawn" by an institutional welfare office and the legal investigator of the parole board. The Supreme Court emphasized that the state and prison officials may not hinder an inmate's right to apply to a federal court for *habeas corpus* relief (1941, 549). In other words, prisoners have a constitutional right to court access.

Additionally, the Court has gone even further in determining whether prison officials are providing inmates adequate opportunities to access the courts. For example, the Supreme Court ruled that unless states provided some effective means for helping illiterate or poorly educated prisoners for postrelease conviction relief, they could not prohibit the use of "jail house lawyers" by inmates in need of legal assistance (*Johnson v. Avery,* 393 U.S. 483, 1969). Rejecting such a practice without providing an alternative would, in essence, violate the prisoner's First Amendment right to court access by denying those prisoners who could not prepare legal documents themselves. In *Avery,* the Court enumerated alternative services that had been adopted in other states: (1) a public defender system that supplied trained attorneys paid for by public funds, (2) employing senior law students to interview and advise inmates, and (3) volunteer programs whereby members of the local state bar make periodic visits to prisons and consult with prisoners concerning their cases.

The Court extended the *Avery* decision in the case of *Bounds v. Smith* (430 U.S. 817, 1977). In *Bounds,* state prisoners in North Carolina brought a federal lawsuit alleging that the prison system had denied them reasonable access to the courts. The Court asserted that prisoners have a constitutional right to access the courts and that protecting that right requires prison authorities to assist inmates in the preparation and filing of "meaningful legal papers" by providing adequate law libraries for the prisoners' use or legal assistance from persons trained in the law. The court articulated alternatives that prisons may use to provide access to courts including: (1) training prisoners as paralegal assistants to work under lawyers, (2) using para-professionals or volunteer law students, (3) hiring lawyers on a part-time basis, and (4) organizing volunteer attorneys from other groups to assist prisoners.

Access to the Mail

As noted earlier, penal institutions must demonstrate a "compelling state interest" prior to the restriction of any constitutional right (ABA, 1977). The judiciary has consistently ruled that prisons have a compelling interest in controlling and regulating use of the mail system by inmates. Two general rationales have been advanced by both prison officials and the judiciary to justify placing restrictions on an inmate's right to the use of the mail system. First, prison safety and security require such restrictions. For example, contraband must be keep out of prisons; escape plans must be detected; and material that might incite a riot must be prevented from entering the prison.

The second rationale for placing restrictions on inmate mail has to do with the orderly administration of the prison. Correctional institutions have a limited number of correctional staff to enforce mail restrictions. But the safety and security of the institution requires that inmate mail be opened, inspected for contraband, read, and some sections of the content deleted. Therefore, some limit on the amount of mail

to be checked must be established. Thus, prison officials have a justified interest in placing restrictions on the quantity of mail an inmate may receive.

However, courts have been less sympathetic when penal institutions restrict the flow of mail for arbitrary reasons. For example, an administrator's refusal to mail correspondence, which does not contain contraband or illegal schemes, has been ruled as unconstitutional. In *McNamara v. Moody* (606 F.2d 621 (5th Cir. 1970)), prison officials were held to have violated a prisoner's constitutional rights by refusing to mail a letter to his girlfriend. The court held that censorship must be limited to concrete violations such as escape plans, plans for disruption of the prison system or work routine, or to prevent the introduction of contraband.

In the case of *Procunier v. Martinez* (416 U.S. 396, 1974), the inmate–plaintiffs attacked the validity of a California prison mail regulation that authorized prison officials to refuse to send inmate mail, and to refuse to distribute mail to inmates. The Supreme Court ruled the regulation void for vagueness and overbreadth. *Procunier* helped establish guidelines for regulating prison mail. In addition, *Procunier* enunciated the minimum procedure that must be followed when prison officials censor or withhold mail. Prisoners must be notified of the rejection of their letters, the letter's author must be allowed to dispute the refusal, and the complaint must be decided by a correctional official other than the one who made the original decision to refuse delivery.

Free Exercise of Religion

The free exercise clause of the First Amendment states that the government cannot prohibit the free exercise of religious practices. Although prison administrators cannot prohibit the free exercise of religion, the courts have granted them some latitude in regulating religious practices in order to maintain the safety and security in prisons. However, civil suits may be brought against prison officials who violate the free exercise clause provisions.

In the case of *Cruz v. Beto* (405 U.S. 319, 1972), the Supreme Court held that inmates must be given a reasonable opportunity to exercise their religious beliefs. In *Cruz,* the Texas Department of Corrections encouraged participation in Catholic, Jewish, and Protestant faiths by providing chaplains, Bibles, and Sunday school classes but failed to offer religious services or access to religious advisers for inmates practicing Buddhism. The court ruled that prison officials must afford equal treatment to inmates of all religions, including unconventional religions.

Although the courts have ruled that free exercise violations do occur, this does not mean that every action of prison administrators will be ruled a violation. For example, in the case of *Theriault v. Silber* (331 F. Supp 578 (W.D. Tex. 1975)), Theriault and other inmates created a religion called the Church of the New Song (CONS). They created scriptures and requested group meetings and other activities. Members of CONS also requested, as part of their religious practice in a special ceremony, to have steak (filet mignon) and wine (sherry). The Court ruled that although CONS had a right to free exercise of their religion, the request for steak and wine went too far, and therefore was denied. In a previous ruling, CONS in Texas was found to be masquerading as a religion and was viewed as nothing more than prisoners attempting to disrupt the orderly flow of the Texas Department of Corrections. Therefore, it was not entitled to First Amendment protection.

In *O'Lone v. Shabazz* (482 U.S. 342, 1987), respondents, prison inmates, and members of the Islamic faith brought suit alleging that New Jersey prison officials violated the free exercise clause of the First Amendment by adopting policies that prevented inmates from attending Jumu'ah, a Muslim congregational service held on Friday afternoons. The prison required inmates classified as "gang minimum" to work outside the buildings where they were housed and where religious services were held. For security reasons, prison officials prohibited inmates who worked outside from returning to these buildings during the day. As a result, inmates were prohibited from attending Jumu'ah. The court held that no free exercise clause violation had occurred because the policies reasonably related to legitimate penological interests (i.e., security of the facility).

Fourth Amendment

The Fourth Amendment is a constitutional right designed to protect individuals against unreasonable searches and seizures. However, according to the courts, prisoners retain few Fourth Amendment rights once they enter the prison system. The most common challenges involve the constitutionality of cell and strip searches.

Cell Searches

The Court has held that prison cells are not protected under the Fourth Amendment; cells may be searched without a warrant or probable cause (see *Hudson v. Palmer*, 468 U.S. 517, 1984). The Court concluded that inmates have no reasonable expectation of privacy in their prison cells. In these cases, the Supreme Court balances the constitutional rights of inmates against the institutional needs of the prison. As in other cases

involving the infringement of inmates' constitutional rights, the state must demonstrate that its policies and practices are related to compelling state interest. In this instance, the safety and security needs of the institution far exceed the right of inmates to be free from unreasonable searches and seizures. Although prison officials are granted a great deal of latitude in conducting cell searches, these searches cannot be used as a form of harassment.

Strip Searches

Strip searches have been upheld as constitutional owing to the overwhelming interests in safety and security of correctional facilities, personnel, and other inmates (*Goff v. Nix*, 803 F.2d 358 (8th Cir. 1968)). However, strip searches have constitutional limits. In *Goff*, a federal district court banned strip searches that occurred after inmates received medical attention and after visits from their lawyers. The Court reasoned that to subject inmates to strip searches after visits from their lawyers or after receiving medical treatment would only serve to discourage them from participating in these constitutionally protected areas.

Eighth Amendment

The Eighth Amendment prohibits cruel and unusual punishment. Prisoners frequently file claims under this amendment, especially concerning conditions of confinement (Vaughn and del Carmen, 1996). Class action lawsuits challenging the conditions of confinement have met with a great deal of success. In addition, under the Eighth Amendment, inmates may file suits alleging inadequate medical treatment. These cases have been met with less success, but have helped establish minimal standards of health care within correctional facilities.

Conditions of Confinement

The standard that the courts have adopted in determining whether conditions are cruel and unusual "must draw its meaning from the evolving standards of decency that mark the progress of a maturing society" (*Rhodes v. Chapman*, 452 U.S. 337, 1981). However, the Supreme Court clearly articulated in *Wilson v. Seiter* (501 U.S. 294, 1991), that the Constitution does not mandate comfortable prisons and that only deprivations denying the "minimal civilized measure of life's necessities" form the basis of an Eighth Amendment violation (Vaughn and del Carmen, 1996).

In order to successfully bring a civil claim, prisoners must be able to articulate facts, which demonstrate that prison officials acted with a culpable state of mind, or in other words, "deliberate indifference" (*Wilson v. Seiter*). Prisoners must be able to show that prison officials were deliberately indifferent, not merely that conditions were constitutionally insufficient.

Conditions of confinement may rise to the level of deliberate indifference when considering the "totality of the conditions." In *Holt v. Sarver* (309 F. Supp 362, 1970), for example, the federal district court ruled that the Arkansas Prison System was in violation of the Eighth Amendment because of the totality of the conditions. The court stated that confinement may amount to cruel and unusual punishment where confinement is characterized by conditions and practices that are so bad that they would shock the conscience of a reasonably civilized society.

Likewise, in *Ruiz v. Estelle*, (460 U.S. 1042, 1983), the Texas Department of Corrections was found to be in violation of the Eighth Amendment for permitting grossly deficient and unconstitutional prison conditions. The Court looked at the totality of the conditions that included brutality by guards, extreme overcrowding, inadequate medical care, a lack of staff training, disciplinary hearing violations, a trustee system that allegedly delegated security functions to inmates, and interfering with inmate access to the courts.

Medical Care

The Court has also ruled that deliberate indifference to the seriously ill may amount to cruel and unusual punishment. Because prisoners are in the custody of the state, the state must afford prisoners with a level of medical treatment that is consistent with medical treatment available to those in the general public. The Court has been generally sympathetic to the medical needs of inmates. However, it has not intervened much with regards to individual complaints of negligence or inadequate treatment.

In order for inmates to bring a claim of inadequate medical treatment under Section 1983, an inmate must demonstrate that a failure to provide treatment or inadequate treatment was shocking, barbaric, intentional, or involved deliberate indifference to the request for needed medical attention (Anderson and Dyson, 2001). Dissatisfaction with the quality of medical attention is not enough to bring an action under Section 1983.

In the case of *Estelle v. Gamble* (429 U.S. 97, 1976), the Court adopted the "deliberate indifference" standard with regards to medical treatment of inmates. Gamble was an inmate in the Texas Department of Corrections. He received a back injury during a work assignment. Over a period of 3 months, medical staff continued to examine and treat Gamble's injury.

Gamble was eventually ordered back to work but he refused. He claimed that his treatment amounted to cruel and unusual punishment. The Court ruled that his treatment, at most, would rise to the level of medical malpractice but it did not constitute cruel and unusual punishment. However, the Court took the opportunity to rule that "deliberate indifference to the serious medical needs of inmates" was a violation of the Eighth Amendment's ban on cruel and unusual punishment. The Court reasoned that because prisoners are wholly dependent on the state for their needs, the state is obligated to provide for the serious medical needs of prisoners in their care.

Fourteenth Amendment

There are two basic rights under the Fourteenth Amendment, the right to equal protection and the right to due process of law. Equal protection requires that every individual must be treated in the same manner, unless there are justifications for differential treatment. Due process is concerned with fundamental fairness of legal proceedings, which include the right to appear and be heard, the right to effective assistance of counsel, and a fair and impartial jury. The Courts have reviewed a significant number of cases involving the equal protection and due process rights of inmates.

Equal Protection of the Law

Historically, equal protection claims have been raised in prison cases involving racial discrimination. In 1968, the Court ruled in *Lee v. Washington* (390 U.S. 333, 1968) that racial segregation in prisons was unconstitutional. More recently, the courts have considered cases involving the segregation of HIV-positive inmates. For example, an appellate court in New Jersey ruled that one's HIV-positive status alone is not sufficient to place someone in solitary confinement (see *Roe v. Fauver*, 43 Cr.L. 2174, 1988). However, the policy was implemented to address prison safety and therefore prison safety considerations take priority over inconveniencing one inmate.

Due Process of Law

The most noteworthy case on due process is *Wolff v. McDonnell* (1974), which involved disciplinary hearings. Respondents, prison inmates within the Nebraska Department of Corrections, brought suit alleging that Nebraska prison disciplinary procedures violated the due process clause because inmates were given only limited rights by prison officials prior to being disciplined. The Court ruled that inmates are entitled to due process in prison disciplinary proceedings that can result in the loss of good time or in punitive segregation. The Court set the following guidelines for disciplinary proceedings:

1. Advanced written notice of the charges must be given to the inmate within 24 hours before appearing in front the disciplinary board.
2. There must be a written statement by the fact finders as to the evidence relied on and the reason for the disciplinary action.
3. The inmates must be allowed to call witnesses and present evidence in their defense, as long as it does not jeopardize the safety and security or goals of the institution.
4. Counsel substitute (either a fellow inmate or staff) will be allowed when the inmate is illiterate or when the complexity of the issues makes it unlikely that the inmate will be able to collect and present evidence for an adequate comprehension of the case.
5. The prison disciplinary board must be impartial.

Due Deference Phase

Currently, the courts have shifted back toward a judicial restraint stance. This era has also been referred to as "due deference" in which the courts generally, although not always, defer to the discretion of prison officials. Many legal scholars argue that the need no longer exists for the federal courts to intervene in order to ensure constitutional protections and safeguards for inmates (Vaughn and del Carmen, 1996; Anderson and Dyson, 2001). For example, the majority of prisoners' rights cases (a total of 45 cases) were decided between 1969 and 1995 (del Carmen, Ritter and Witt, 1998). Since 1995, the Court has not decided any cases in the areas of prisoners' rights. This may be because of a general feeling by the Court and Congress that the majority of prisoners' rights cases have been decided and policies consistent with these rulings have been established. As a result, there is little need for judicial intervention.

KIMBERLY D. DODSON

References and Further Reading

American Bar Association Joint Committee on the Legal Status of Prisoners (1977). Standards relating to the legal status of criminals. *American Law Review,* 14, 1–63.

Anderson, J.F. and Dyson, L. (2001). *Legal Rights of Prisoners: Cases and Comments,* New York, University Press of America, Inc.

Clear, T.R. and Cole, G.F. (1994). *American Corrections,* 3rd ed. Belmont, CA, Wadsworth Publishing Company.

del Carmen, R.V., Ritter, SE. and Wit, B.A. (1998). *Briefs of Leading Cases in Corrections,* 2nd ed., Cincinnati, OH, Anderson Publishing Company.

DiIulio, J.J. (1990). Introduction: Enhancing judicial capacity, in DiIulio, J.J., Ed., *Courts, Corrections, and the Constitution,* New York, Oxford University Press.

Farrar, J.R. (1996). Legal issues, in McShane, M.D. and Williams, F.P., III, Eds., *Encyclopedia of American Prisons,* New York, Garland Publishing, Inc.

Krantz, S. (1976). *The Law of Corrections and Prisoners' Rights in a Nutshell,* Saint Paul, MN, West Publishing Company.

Minor, K., Wells, J.B. and Soderstrom, I.R. (2003) Corrections and the courts, in Whitehead, J.T., Pollock, J.M. and Braswell, M.C., Eds., *Exploring Corrections in America,* Cincinnati, OH, Anderson Publishing.

Vaughn, M.S. and del Carmen, R.V. (1996). Constitutional issues in prison operations, in McShane, M.D. and Williams, F.P., III, Eds., *Encyclopedia of American Prisons,* New York, Garland Publishing, Inc.

See also **Prisons, Problems and Recent Developments in; Prisons: Administration and Organization; Prisons: History in the U.S.**

Prisons: Correctional Officers and Staff

Delving into the past we often find striking similarities to situations in the present. In the wake of the Attica (New York) Penitentiary riot in 1971, the social structure of American prisons changed drastically around the issues of race and the prisoner rights movement. Today, the racial demographics of the American prison population once again mirror deeper social problems, problems that correctional agencies and correctional staff are increasingly being asked to address. Moreover, the massive reemergence of contractual private-for-profit prisons raises important new questions about the purpose and scope of incarceration in the U.S.

Other problems such as overcrowding, gang activities, institutional violence, forced overtime, complexity of operational technology, and insufficient training are listed as key factors in the increasing work-related stress of correctional officers. In this sense, many officers and staff feel that correctional work is more stressful now than ever before. The modern correctional environment, no matter whether by choice or circumstance, confines both its employees and the inmates.

Principally members of the social and economic underclass constitute the contemporary inmate population; these are often people with acute nutritional, developmental, neurological, and mental and general health problems. Primarily minorities and women, typically they have had little or no previous access to consistent health care services, thus making them prone to a wide range of communicable diseases such as substance abuse and drug addiction, sexually transmitted disease groups (STDs), hepatitis, tuberculosis, HIV/AIDS, and a full range of psychological health problems. Practical information has led in recent years to efforts that seek to identify bases for assisting staff in classifying and treating high-risk from low-risk offenders. In this respect, the value of policy-relevant research has become increasingly apparent to first-line officers and staff.

As a major factor in American life, the corrections system can no longer survive as a closed system but instead needs to be able to anticipate change and respond rapidly to fluctuating resources, demographics, and demands. The bi-polar prison of the past has been transformed into a modern-day and complex tri-polar prison consisting of inmates, officers or staff, and the administration, now drawn together in the interplay of custodial exigencies. Moreover, the concerns of both internal employees and external communities must also be accommodated. There is an emergent and important awareness of the organizational development of modern prisons. Specifically, the conditions-of-confinement for inmates, and thus the conditions-of-work for correctional officers and staff, provide the vital framework for building a workforce that better serves the mission of modern corrections—maintaining secure, safe, and humane correctional facilities.

New Directions

The Attica uprising made it abundantly clear that the correctional officers and staff of the nation's state and local correctional facilities were not being appropriately selected and trained. At that turbulent time, the prison was viewed from the perspective of society, inmates, administration, scholars, victims, or from a philosophical standpoint. Rarely, if at all, were the views of correctional officers and staff included in these perspectives. Nonetheless, the American civil rights movement of the 1960s and 1970s was destined to permeate the prison walls and to profoundly effect both the keeper and the kept. In the prisons, it was the

Black Muslims who carried the torch of black protest behind the prison walls.

The Attica uprising also added considerable impetus to the nascent prisoner rights movement. However, the new prisoner rights movement was not comprised solely of prisoners. It depended heavily on the involvement and efforts of free citizens, particularly lawyers and reinvigorated prison reform groups. Heretofore, the federal judiciary had adhered to a "hands-off" attitude toward prison cases out of concern for federalism and separation of powers. The ensuing cases that served to reverse this judicial "hands off" purview have permanently altered both the legal status of inmates and correctional officers and staff. They serve as the primogeniture of modern penology. (See: *Wolff v. McDonnell*, 418 U.S. 539 (1974); *Dothard v. Rawlison*, 433 U.S. 321 (1977); *Bell v. Wolfish*, 520 (1979); *Ruiz v. Estelle*, 503 F.Supp. 1265 (S.D. Tex. 1980); *Rhodes v. Chapman*, 452 U.S. 337 (1981).)

In the throes of these dynamic times, the correctional officer became at last a legitimate subject of scholarly research and interest. David Fogel's *We are the Living Proof*, Leo Carroll's *Hacks, Blacks and Cons*, James B. Jacobs' *Stateville: The Penitentiary in Mass Society*, Lucien Lombardo's *Guards Imprisoned: Correctional Officers at Work*, Robert Johnson and Shelly Price, *The Complete Correctional Officer, Human Service and the Human Environment of Prison*, and Lynn Zimmer's, *Women Guarding Men* are hallmarks of the early scholarly research on the correctional officer. In fact, the very term "correctional officer" was adopted during the 1970s as the official occupational reference term used by the U.S. Department of Labor replacing the archaic denomination of "keeper" and "guard." Today there is a growing and viable interest in further developing an appropriate role for correctional officers and staff.

The job of the correctional officer has remained essentially the same for the past 150 years: care, custody, and control. The preferred ways of performing this job, however, have undergone considerable stress and role definition in the development of modern penology. The occupational correctional officer is now available to both men and women, and officially established with defined rules and regulations (Civil Rights Act, Title VII, as Amended—1972).

Formal oversight is given to the recruitment and qualifications for employment and the hiring system itself, especially as it involves civil service exams, the use of merit boards, or direct hiring by institutions. A specific hiring process has a profound effect on the retention of correctional officers. Likewise, the matters of entry salary, increments, overtime and hazardous duty pay, pension plans, and recognition as public safety "peace officer" status by state law also shape the process of recruitment and long-term retention.

Care, Custody, and Control

Where do correctional officers and staff come from? What are their social and occupational aspirations? How are they selected, nurtured, and trained to perform their duties? How are they socialized into the occupation of correctional officer? What is the influence of the occupational culture on the individual officer? These are some of the most compelling questions guiding the research on men and women correctional staff both in the U.S. and globally.

Correctional officers and staff ensure the public safety by providing for the care, custody, control, and maintenance of inmates. Most institutions require that correctional officers be at least 18 years or 21 years of age, have a high school education or its equivalent, have no felony convictions, and be a U.S. citizen. As with the police, many correctional departments are placing greater emphasis on bachelors and masters degree attainment in the hiring and promotional process. Institutions of higher education are developing specific correctional degree programs, especially at the master degree level.

Correctional officers are charged with overseeing individuals who have been arrested, are awaiting trial or other hearing, or who have been convicted of a crime and sentenced to serve time in a jail, reformatory, or penitentiary. They maintain security and observe inmate conduct and behavior to prevent disturbances and escapes. The more general duties of correctional officers and staff require them to manage and communicate with inmates, peers, and supervisors, direct inmate movement, maintain key, tool, and equipment control, distribute authorized items to inmates, as well as maintain health, safety, and sanitation.

Federal, state, and local departments of corrections provide training for correctional officers based on standards and guidelines promulgated by the American Correctional Association, the American Jail Association, and the National Sheriffs Association. Among the numerous demands on the special training correctional officers have to undergo, the development of interpersonal communication skills have become the life-blood of effective correctional officer performance. This includes the capacity to understand the full range of inmate (verbal and nonverbal) modes of communication: the culture, the slang, the signals, the threat, and the fear that abounds.

Correctional officer and staff training programs include a wide array of instruction. Typical training topics are constitutional law and cultural awareness, inmate behavior, contraband control, custody and security procedures, fire and safety; inmate legal rights, written and oral communication, use-of-force, first aid, including cardiopulmonary resuscitation (CPR), and physical fitness training.

Ecology and Performance

The correctional facility itself serves as a tangible frame of reference for orienting new staff and maintaining standards of performance for both new and incumbent staff. The architectural design and built-environment of correctional facilities, both traditional and new generation facilities, govern the interactions of all people—inmates and staff—within the confines of prison walls.

These physical plant features are often conducive to the development of the training process, providing innovative resources for on-the-job training, field applications, simulation, and emergency preparedness training. Conversely, the physical plant uniquely defines the requirements of custodial regimentation, the institutional security level, the inmate classification system, and the deployment of correctional staff (officers and support personnel).

The fact that correctional officers are *locked-in* and *unarmed* as they maintain daily custodial control is perceived only as an occupational responsibility. Moreover, the simple fact that correctional officers cannot walk away from a confrontation or crisis within the institutional setting is often overlooked. Thus, proper training and deployment of correctional officers, including the proper mix of new and seasoned officers, is of paramount importance.

The deployment of the correctional officer workforce has also been directly affected by overcrowding. The development of custodial control mechanisms and classification systems is increasingly correlated for the containment of institutional violence. Accurate, aggressive, and highly flexible inmate classification is crucial to institutional safety and inmate welfare. In this context, custodial control is not unlike the current initiatives to reinvent law enforcement through community policing programs, thus enabling both officers and inmates to perceive the mutuality of their safety concerns.

The level of tension in a prison only rarely reflects the relative comfort of physical facilities or the number and extent of vocational and recreational programs; almost always it is a measure of the ability of the corrections staff to supervise and interact with inmates firmly and fairly. Correctional officers are in a unique position because, by the nature of their job, they know the inmates and have perceptions of the inmates' treatment needs. Historically, limitations were placed on the correctional officer by their inherently limited role created in the juxtaposition among professions. Correctional officers were not encouraged to exercise discretion. Until recently, the counselors and program staff were often not interested in receiving the input of correctional officers.

In the last decade both correctional officers and staff training programs have developed a core body of knowledge for inmate-contact positions. These roles are now becoming more diffused through the implementation of unit management and special housing units within correctional facilities. Such programs require officers and staff to use a triage approach to care, custody, and control of inmates. Topics covered in these core value curricula are:

- Inmate population characteristics (including a description of sociological, ethnic and racial, cultural, psychological backgrounds, and differences) and a discussion of inmate subcultures.
- Inmate population problems, including health difficulties arising from substance abuse, HIV immune-response deficiencies, malnourishment, possible detoxification and emotional difficulties resulting in attempted suicides, severe depression and antisocial and aggressive behavior, education deficiencies.
- Basic human relations, including the development of effective communication skills (e.g., listening and nonjudgmental speech) and humane methods of control and supervision.
- Methods for dealing effectively with crisis and emergency situations.

When contemplating the tenets of care, custody, and control, officers and staff must keep in mind that they are constantly being observed by inmates. In this context, it is critical that officers and staff understand they either represent a role model to emulate or to avoid. It is the correctional employees—custody and program staff—who must offer encouragement and help to those inmates who sincerely wish to rehabilitate their lives.

New Generation Trends

The corrections system is a residual agency. Positioned downstream from all other components of the criminal justice system, it often operates under the prey of politicians. The political nature of the correctional systems, reporting to the executive branch of government at the local, state, and federal levels, leaves it vulnerable to a host of external forces, particularly with respect to budget and operational philosophy issues. For example, during the 1990s a strong conservative political camp succeeded in achieving cutbacks in inmate educational and recreational programs and a return to more stringent custodial control, including chain gangs and forced labor. This conservative climate is also putting to the test the viability of centralized training for officers and staff. In many jurisdictions training is under the threat of cost-cutting decisions by conservative budgeteers.

The traditional program staff positions of educators, chaplains, counselors, nurses, doctors, and psychologists are now fully complemented with an array of new generation staff. Many of these new positions are the direct by-products of the prisoner rights movement. These include: law librarians, inmate grievance officers, lawyers, legal aides and paralegal clerks, substance abuse counselors, AIDS counselors, parenting counselors, anger-management counselors, recreation supervisors, nutritionists, environmental health monitors, affirmative action officers, restorative-justice programmers, standards and accreditation officers, public relations officers, lobbyists, construction and contracting officers, private-prison liaison officers, U.S. Office of Safety, Health Administration (OSHA), and collective bargaining administrators.

Additionally, new generation correctional facilities are also identified with corresponding institutional staffing and environmental problems. For example, many such problems are associated with the increasing incorporation of sophisticated cyber-surveillance video-technology and the construction of super-max prisons. Veteran correctional officers and staff are now expressing concerns that these new generation facilities are becoming "incubators"—sealed prisons—where there is little to no internal human interaction. Communication is done through microphones and wall speakers, while inmate wristbands trigger door and gate movements and provide access to inmate programs and services. These trends portend extreme psychological deprivation on both sides of the bars.

Today, most American correctional systems are also providing psychological services to correctional officers and staff. These programs provide expertise in the areas of job stress, self-image, domestic-violence intervention, and alcohol abuse. In addition, correctional officer unions and the courts are intervening where legislatures and prison administrators are unresponsive to enlisting safe and secure working environments as a requirement for a correctional facility's legal operation (e.g., training, retention, and supervision of staff).

Contemporary Workforce Demographics

In the U.S. the current national (state and local) correctional workforce is approximately 617,000 officers and program staff. The federal correctional workforce is approximately 28,500 officers and correctional staff.

This does not include the personnel of private-for-profit prisons. At the state level, there is a higher ratio of nonwhite to white correction officers mostly in the southern states, with the exception of the District of Columbia (96.8%). On average, women cover 20.5% of the employees in corrections, but the rates vary from as low as 6.6% (Maine) to almost half (49.9%) in Mississippi. The situation is a bit different at the federal level according to the Federal Bureau of Prisons (U.S. Department of Justice, 1999), with only 12.5% women correctional officers and only 38.5% nonwhite employees working in the federal correctional justice system. The impact of the new generation of mixed-gender and multiracial staff is having a positive influence on staff–inmate interactions.

Correctional officers can understand simple fairness and reasonableness better than most people. They must work in a highly distilled environment where such factors are crucial to safety and cooperation. Correctional officers can also understand the need to build structure to ensure justice. Measuring the inmates' progress by their lawful behavior is as plausible to correctional officers as is measuring their own work program and upward mobility. The promulgation of the *Correctional Officers' Creed* by the International Association of Correctional Officers (IACO) illustrates the spirit and elan of this new generation workforce.

Correctional Officers' Creed

To speak sparingly ... to act, not to argue ... to be in authority through personal presence ... to correct without nagging ... to speak with the calm voice of certainty ... to see everything, know what is significant and what not to notice ... to be neither insensitive to distress nor so distracted by pity as to miss what must elsewhere be seen ...

To do neither that which is unkind nor self-indulgent in its misplaced charity ... never to obey the impulse to tongue lash that silent insolence which in times past could receive the lash ... to be both firm and fair...to know I cannot be fair simply be being firm, nor firm simply by being fair ...

To support the reputations of associates and confront them without anger, should they stand short of professional conduct ... to reach for knowledge of the continuing mysteries of human motivation ... to think; always to think ... to be dependable ... to be dependable first to my charges and associates, and thereafter to my duty as employee and citizen ... to keep fit ... to keep forever alert...to listen to what is meant as well as what is said with words and with silences ...

To expect respect from my charges and my superiors yet never to abuse the one for abuses from the other ... for eight hours each working day to be an example of the person I could be at all times ... to acquiesce in no dishonest act ... to cultivate patience under boredom and calm during confusion ... to understand the why of every order I take or give ...

To hold freedom among the highest values though I deny it to those I guard ... to deny it with dignity that in my example they find no reason to lose their dignity ... to be prompt ... to be honest with all who practice deceit that they not find in me excuse for themselves ... to privately face down my fear that I not signal it ... to privately cool my anger that I not displace it on others ... to hold in confidence what I see and hear, which by the telling could harm or humiliate to no good purpose ... to keep my outside problems outside ... to leave inside that which should stay inside ... to do my duty. (Barrington, 1998)

Unlike public safety officers such as police and fire fighters, who interact with the public on a daily basis, correctional officers and staff operate behind the walls and are, essentially, out of sight and out of mind. Their problems and concerns are rarely a matter of public interest. They find it difficult to lobby for improved salaries, benefits, and working conditions and are often viewed with the same disinterest as the inmates they supervise.

Globally, the correctional occupational field is hungry for professional development and a respected and legitimate identity as a public safety occupation. As in the U.S., the inherent political character of prisons in any society both compounds and enlightens these comparisons. In 1979, Foucault noted, the formidable right to punish "concretely" continues to fully influence the management of prisons in all societies. So, too, does the need to establish a principle of moderation for the *power of punishment* through on-going professional training and the establishment of programs for ensuring the well-being of correctional officers and staff.

JESS MAGHAN

References and Further Reading

Barrington, B. 1998. Correctional officers' creed, *The Keepers' Voice*, 19(2), 8.

Bureau of Justice Statistics, 1999. *Sourcebook of Criminal Justice Statistics*, U.S. Department of Justice, Washington DC.

Bureau of Labor Statistics, 1999. Correctional officers, *Occupational Outlook Handbook*, U.S. Department of Labor, Washington DC.

Carroll, L. 1974. *Hacks, Blacks, and Cons: Race Relations in a Maximum Security Prison*, Lexington, MA, D. C. Heath and Co.

Conover, T. 2000. *Newjack, Guarding Sing Sing*, New York, Random House.

Fogel, D. 1975. *We Are the Living Proof*, Cincinnati, OH, Anderson Publishers.

Foucault, M. 1979. *Discipline and Punish: The Birth of the Prison*, New York, Vintage.

Jacobs, J.B. 1977. *Stateville: The Penitentiary in Mass Society*, Chicago, IL, University of Chicago Press.

Johnson, R. and Price, S. 1981. The complete correctional officer: Human service and the human environment of prison, *Criminal Justice and Behavior*, 8(3).

Lombardo, L.X. 1986. *Guards Imprisoned: Correctional Officers at Work*, New York, Elsevier.

Maghan, J. 1982. Guarding in prison, in David, F. and Hudson, J., Eds., *Justice as Fairness: Perspectives on the Justice Model*, Cincinnati, OH, Anderson Publishing Company,

Maghan, J. 1995. Common ground: Comparative correctional programming, *International Journal of Offender Therapy and Comparative Criminology*, 39(2).

Zimmer, L. 1986. *Women Guarding Men*, Chicago, IL, University of Chicago Press.

See also **Careers in Corrections; Prisons: Administration and Organization**

Prisons: Inmate Populations and Subcultures

There are approximately 1.5 million prisoners in the U.S., over 90% of whom are male. Men are approximately 15 times more likely to go to prison than females, and just less than 1% of all males in the U.S. are in prison. Although less than 7% of those in prison are women, the number of women prisoners has been growing faster than the number of men for nearly 30 years and the absolute number is considerably larger than the entire prison populations of France, Germany, and England. Although little data are available about prison populations and prisons in other countries (particularly nonindustrialized countries), most scholars agree that the U.S. has the highest incarceration rate in the world.

Approximately half of those in prison in the U.S. are sentenced for violent offenses (robbery, murder, rape, assault), whereas one in five are sentenced for property (particularly burglary) or drug crimes (particularly possession and distribution of crack cocaine). Additionally, one in ten are in prison for public order offenses (primarily chronic offenders). Almost half of those in prison are black, non-Hispanic, whereas just over one in three is white, non-Hispanic, and approximately one in six is of Hispanic origin. In the U.S., Texas has the largest prison population and Louisiana has the highest rate of prisoners per 100,000. Most prisoners in the U.S. are between 20 and 39, although the mean age of prisoners in the U.S. appears to be increasing.

The first prisons in the U.S. were built at the turn of the 20th century, and a steady increase in prison populations began at the turn of the 20th century and continued until the early 1970s, when the prison population in the U.S. began growing rapidly. This rapid growth, which began in the early 1970s and continued to the end of the 20th century, was caused by a number of factors, including the implementation of a number of policies designed to enhance crime control. Parole was abolished in the federal system and in most states, and new determinate sentencing laws were enacted to incarcerate offenders for longer periods of time. Additionally, new sentencing policies gave harsher sentences to violent and career offenders and mandatory sentences for certain offenses or habitual offenders. Finally, intensive supervision of probationers and parolees and detention without bail for serious offenders believed to be a risk to the community combined to bring about this tremendous increase.

By the end of the 1980s, prison populations across the U.S. held record numbers of persons incarcerated. Additionally, correctional administrators have become more punitive toward prisoners. Evidence of this fact is the implementation and then withdrawal of chain gangs in some states during the 1990s and the ban of weight training and cigarette smoking in many prisons throughout the country.

In the U.S., prisoners are incarcerated in one of two systems: federal and state. Each is discussed below.

Federal Prisoners

The federal prison system is a highly centralized system with one director appointed by the president, six regional directors, and a staff of over 25,000. Federal prisons house offenders whose crimes involve interstate commerce, bank robbery, kidnapping, violations of other federal laws, and crimes committed on federal property. Sixty percent of those in federal prisons are incarcerated for drug-related offenses.

In 1895, the U.S. government opened the first federal prison for men at Leavenworth, Kansas, whereas the first federal prison for women was built in Alderson, West Virginia in 1927. Today, there are over 100 federal prisons throughout the U.S, with five security levels, ranging from the most restrictive, the administrative maximum (ADMAX) prison in Florence, Colorado, to the least restrictive, federal prison camps (e.g., Eglin Air Force Base, Florida) that have barracks like housing and no fencing.

State Prisons

There are approximately 1300 state adult correctional institutions, or prisons, in the U.S. This number does not include jails, detention centers, or juvenile institutions. Each state has its own prison system, with each state having at least two prisons and one state (Texas) having more than 100 prisons.

Upon entry into the prison system, most states assign custody levels based upon the perceived dangerousness of the offender, his escape risk, and type of offense. Inmates move through one of five or six custody levels (very similar to the federal levels mentioned earlier) according to the progress they are judged to have made in behavior and self-control. Serious offenders can move up as long as they do not cause trouble. Approximately half of all prisoners in state prisons are in medium security institutions, whereas one in four are in maximum or high security institutions, and about that same proportion are in minimum or community institutions.

Facts about Prisoners

Most prisoners in the U.S. are poor, young adult males with less than a high school education. Most have been incarcerated before, either as an adult or a juvenile, and have a history of drug and alcohol abuse. Most have been incarcerated or placed on probation at least twice before, and one in five has been on probation or incarcerated more than five times.

The Prison Experience

Most scholars agree that, despite the best efforts by correctional administrators and staff to provide rehabilitative opportunities, prisons remain "schools for crime," as younger and less experienced prisoners are socialized into antisocial and oppositional attitudes and as a result exit the prison more likely to commit crimes than when they entered. Nevertheless, evaluation research indicates that, under some conditions, some cognitive skills, drug-treatment, vocational training, educational, and other programs in adult prisons appear to reduce recidivism. These programs work most often when the programs are carefully matched to each prisoner's needs and risks, well-implemented and well-funded, and have compatible aftercare programs in the community available to sustain treatment upon release.

We know that the imprisonment experience has a number of "collateral effects" on prisoners' lives, both while they are incarcerated and afterward as well. There are at least three that have been identified, including: (1) imprisonment reduces exoffenders' subsequent incomes and employment; (2) exoffenders usually lose the right to vote or hold public office; and (3) imprisonment often leads to the breakup of families and less parental involvement with their children.

A prison is considered a total institution, a place where the same people work, play, eat, sleep, and recreate together on a daily basis. Sykes argues that incarceration within prison brings about five difficulties for the prisoner, which he labels as the "pains of imprisonment." These pains are as follows:

1. Deprivation of Liberty—The prisoner loses liberty in two ways: confinement to the institution and confinement within the institution. Confinement to the institution makes the inmate lose contact with friends and family and also lets the offender know that the community has abandoned him. Confinement within the institution serves as an additional punishment, as the offender has little control over his movement throughout the institution.

2. Deprivation of Goods and Services—Prisoners, particularly those in maximum-security prisons, have very few luxuries. Basic material needs are met but prisoners are not given the same amenities as people not incarcerated. Because of this, the prisoner often feels devalued and angry, and blames the system for this and not themselves,

3. Deprivation of Heterosexual Relationships— Most prisoners are not allowed conjugal visitation, where they can spend time alone with their wife or girlfriend. As such, heterosexual contact is not available for the vast majority of prisoners. Prisoners are constantly exposed to contraband pornography, sex in the media, and continual discussions of sex among prisoners, which often stimulates their sexual interests. Although some prisoners engage willingly in homosexual activity in prison, most do not. This makes many men question their masculinity, and those who do engage in homosexual behavior often question their psyche and self-image afterward.

4. Deprivation of Autonomy—Most prisoners experience hostility regarding their restricted ability to make choices within the prison. Prisoners experience a total loss of autonomy in prison, and often have to obey rules that do not make sense to them. They are forbidden to take food to their cells, denied parole, and denied mail, often without justification from the administration and staff. Additionally, many decisions are made that affect prisoners without receiving input from those same prisoners affected by the decisions. As such, prisoners experience a total loss of autonomy, often making the adjustment to the "outside" more difficult for them upon release.

5. Deprivation of Security—In prison, individuals (often regardless of their conviction offense) are thrown in with a group of violent men. Inmates realize that sooner or later they will be tested; if they fail the test, they are thereafter looked at as weak. If they win, they may become the target of prisoners wishing to prove themselves. Prisons make prisoners permanently aware of their level of courage; often, they question the very idea of their manhood. This deprivation of security, in conjunction with the previously mentioned deprivation of heterosexual relationships, creates a definition of a "man" among prisoners that revolves around his aggressiveness and his ability to protect himself.

Cultural Importation versus Deprivation

Although few deny that deprivations abound in prison, there is heated debate over the ramifications of these deprivations. Those following the "deprivation model" argue that the pains of imprisonment discussed earlier cause inmates to form a society with its own rules, beliefs, and roles—in other words, a prison subculture. Deprivation theorists argue that prison subcultures are a natural reaction to the pains of imprisonment; thus, their origin is within the prison's walls.

The counter to this argument, the "importation model," suggests that the prison subculture is brought into the prison from the streets. Those following the importation model suggest that one's preprison experiences are the most important factors shaping the prison subculture. An example of the importation model is found below in the discussion of prison gangs.

Whether it be as a result of these deprivations within the institution, or a result of one's preprison experiences, prisoners develop their own values, norms, and expectations. Thus, over time, there has developed a distinctive prison subculture. A prison subculture is defined as the values, norms, and roles characteristic of prison inmates while incarcerated in the institution.

Until 1970, prison subcultures and the socialization experience in prisons were well-documented in sociological literature. Some argue that this is no longer the case; compared with earlier times, prisons are much larger, inmate populations and staffs have higher proportions of blacks and Hispanics, many more officers and administrators are female, gangs are prevalent and powerful, and judicial intervention in prisons is greater. The sentencing policy changes referred to earlier have also produced larger fractions of prisoners serving very long sentences and with them have come increased demands for medical care and other services for the aging and elderly. Additionally, the arrival of AIDS and HIV has had a tremendous impact in prison as well; in fact, estimates indicate that between one in twenty and one in ten prisoners are HIV positive.

Despite the wide variety of prisons and prisoners throughout the country, others argue that the prison subculture has been found to be surprisingly consistent. These prison subcultures develop independently of prison authorities, and create a network of expectations into which inmates step in and participate. Prisoners are socialized into this subculture through a process known as prisonization, which refers to the learning of convict roles, attitudes, values, and language. Additionally, prisoners develop their own argot, or language. Along with this new language come new roles.

In prisons, there are a number of argot roles. The most common roles are listed below.

Fish—a brand new inmate.

Rat (or Snitch)—a prisoner who betrays his or her fellow inmates to the guards. Although this name is used regularly outside prison, it is a much more serious label in prison. Some prisoners are rats because they hope to win preferential treatment; others are rats because they want to get rid of a competitor or settle a grudge. The rat is despised by fellow prisoners, and is often one of the first victims of violence in prison riots.

Fag—a male inmate who is believed to be a "natural" homosexual, or one who engages in homosexual activity willingly.

Gorilla—an inmate who takes what he wants from others by force, including cigarettes, food, and clothing. The gorilla does not always have to use force; the threat of force is often simply enough to do it.

Pruno—alcoholic beverages made in prison from materials stolen from the dining facility or brought in as contraband.

Square John—a middle class inmate with no experience of the prison subculture prior to entry into prison.

Old Heads—older, more experienced prisoners who have already served a lengthy prison sentence.

Homey—friend from the neighborhood.

Merchant (Swag Man)—inmates who sell contraband to other prisoners.

Wolf (Pitcher)—prisoners who play the masculine role in homosexual activity. These individuals are often the rapists. Homosexuality carries no stigma for wolves.

Punk (Catcher)—inmates who submit to the wolves without displaying open signs of homosexuality. Most prisoners view punks as cowards.

Turn Out—forcing a victim to participate in homosexual activity.

The Hole—solitary confinement, or disciplinary segregation. Prisoners are isolated from other inmates, often allowed out of the cell for only 1 hour per day.

The Man (Hack, Bull, Screw)—a correctional officer.

Playing it Cool—telling staff members to their faces what they want to hear, while ridiculing them behind their backs.

Playing the Opposites—occurs when inmates lie to staff members when asked to present a preference or a desire. Inmates tell staff the opposite of how they truly feel, rationalizing that the staff do not want them to be content, and thus will do the opposite of what the inmate confesses they desire.

Inmate Code of Conduct

In most prisons, inmates develop a "code of conduct" by which they live. The code often goes as follows: Don't gamble, don't mess with drugs, don't mess with homosexuals, don't steal, don't borrow or lend, don't cooperate with correctional staff, and do your own time. Evidence indicates that most prisoners attempt to abide by this code; nevertheless, there are a number of others who do not.

Prisons also have a flourishing underground economy. In this economy, cigarettes, drugs, and other items are used to barter for services or for other items, such as food, or services, such as haircuts, laundry, etc.

Rape in Prison

Although there are no entirely accurate estimates of the number of prisoners who are raped, few scholars deny that rape goes on in prison, although they do disagree on its prevalence. Prisoners rape other prisoners for a number of reasons, including sexual gratification, extortion, to generate fear, and to maintain power over other inmates. Victims of prison rape

tend to be small in stature, white, young, and nonviolent.

Prison gangs also have received a tremendous amount of notoriety over the past few years. Even though prisons have been desegregated since the 1960s, race and ethnicity are still important criteria in prisons, particularly when it comes to gang membership. Prison gangs are one of the areas where this competition between races is most evident. Most research indicates that, particularly in maximum-security prisons, gangs are prevalent parts of the prison subculture, and are often organized with the same structure, hierarchy, and leadership as their counterparts outside of prison. Gangs compete with one another for turf and the control of contraband sales. Gangs usually are divided along ethnic lines. Minority (e.g., African American, Hispanic, and Asian) gang members often make a seamless transition from life on the streets to life in prisons, as many of their "homeboys" are already in prison and they are embraced in prison by their former partners on the street. White gangs, with the exception of outlaw motorcycle gangs, appear to be formed within prisons, often as a mechanism for protection from other, more well-established prison gangs.

Females in Prison

Although numerous works have been devoted to life inside prison for males, scant literature exists examining the inmate subculture of female prisons. What little research that exists suggests that there are a number of differences between female and male prisons and prisoners. First and foremost, female prisons are less violent than male prisons. Females are less likely to be incarcerated for violent crimes than males, and, as such, there are larger proportions of drug and property prisoners who are female than male. Second, although homosexual behavior is found among female prisoners, male prisoners appear to engage in homosexual behavior for physical satisfaction or owing to aggressive tendencies, whereas female prisoners engage in homosexual behavior for emotional satisfaction and to satisfy a need for affection denied to prisoners. Third, female prisoners are much more likely to be housed in minimum- to low-security units than are males; as such, they have more freedom of movement and often less rigorous rules regulating their behavior. Finally, as three in four female prisoners are mothers, and two in three of the mothers have children under 18, the family is much more important to female prisoners. Visits occur more often and are more likely to be contact visits (where inmates are allowed to touch visitors) than found in male prisons.

DAVID C. MAY

References and Further Reading

Abbot, J.H. 1982. *In the Belly of the Beast: Letters from Prison,* New York, Vintage.

Caroll, L. 1988. *Hacks, Blacks, and Cons: Race Relations in a Maximum Security Prison,* Prospect Heights, IL, Waveland.

Clemmer, D. 1940. *The Prison Community,* New York, Holt, Rinehart, and Winston.

Cressey, D.R., Ed. 1961. *The Prison: Studies in Institutional Organization and Change,* New York, Rinehart and Wilson.

Goffman, E. 1961. *Asylums: Essays on the Social Situation of Mental Patients and Other Inmates,* Garden City, NY, Anchor.

Hassine, V. 1999. *Life Without Parole: Living in Prison Today,* 2nd ed., Los Angeles, CA, Roxbury.

Irwin, J. 1980. *Prisons in Turmoil,* Boston, MA, Little, Brown.

Irwin, J. and Cressey, D.R. 1962. Thieves, convicts, and the inmate culture, *Social Problems,* 10.

Sykes, G.M. 1958. *The Society of Captives: A Study of Maximum Security Prisons,* Princeton, NJ, Princeton University Press.

Tonry, M. and Petersilia, J., Eds., Prisons, Vol. 26, *Crime and Justice: A Review of the Research,* Chicago, IL, University of Chicago Press.

See also **Prison Riots; Prisons: History in the U.S.**

Prisons, Privatized

Except perhaps for capital punishment, no corrections issue more than private prisons has affected so few people in the U.S. but has been so symbolically and politically important. The field is difficult to easily summarize because such prisons range from the carefully monitored and overseen to some of the most unsupervised prisons in the industrialized west. The latter are at times promoted by politicians' intent on bypassing state constitutional requirements.

The basic idea of privatization is not new, and the notion of selling prison labor for state profit was much more widespread in the 19th century than today. Further, prison services have been privatized for many years. It has long been accepted that private and nonprofit firms can provide such services as garbage hauling, drug counseling, food preparation, or medical services. In some states and countries plagued by idle prisoners private industry has been allowed to set up shop within prison walls because the first large prisons were opened more than 150 years ago. Many states find it easier to pay others to provide basic services than to hire and supervise competent employees themselves.

Today few find ethical issues in hiring out these types of services. In the past there has been more concern in the literature over whether the state has the right to delegate to a private entrepreneur such basic responsibilities as incarceration, in-prison punishment, classification, and transfer. Most commentators agree that the state can delegate some authority, but few have taken on the thornier question of just where the line should be drawn, if indeed there is any line. How much can be privatized? In an American criminal justice system that allows private, for-profit security, legal aid, victim services agencies, presentence report investigators, drug testers, electronic monitors, and probation officers, is there some area of justice that cannot or should not be privatized? Courts are as crowded or more crowded than prisons. Because some private firms are now allowed to adjudicate prison violations that can result in more prison time, is it substantially different to allow the basic sentencing function to be given to Sentencing Corporation of America? Can states with few executions farm out those they put to death to a professional firm staffed by, say, highly experienced former Texas and Florida executioners?

Although various ethical issues remain to be resolved, one can make both the arguments that private prisons are spreading rapidly, and also that they still do not amount to very many beds. Some places are heavily invested in privatization, of course. For example, under a politically conservative regime the Australian state of Victoria privatized fully half of all prison beds. A major proposed expansion of private beds throughout the rest of Australia would allow for, if fully used, fully 20% of all beds to be private. Yet, because Australia does not imprison people in the way that the U.S. does, this amounts only to a private capacity of about 7500 beds. Few political entities imprison people at the rates of Americans, which is why no matter how invested any country gets in privatization, most of the beds will be in the U.S. Yet, at the same time, well under 5% of American prison beds are in private hands.

The argument that privatization is advancing is simple. Worldwide, there were only 3100 private beds in 1987, but by early 2001 there were over 140,000 beds.

About 85% of these beds are in the U.S. Both in terms of facilities and beds, there has been a large increase in American privatization.

The origin or impetus for much of this increase has been attributed by most scholars to the massive prison overcrowding in the U.S. since 1980. Just to pick two examples, in 1998 and 1999 American states increased prison populations by about 115,000. The total state increase from 1990 to 1999 was 74%, and this is on top of the record 1980s increase. Of course, this need not be a problem in that any state that wished to increase incarceration needed only to spend more money to pay for incarceration. This is what has generally happened. However, many politicians have noticed that the same voters who demand longer sentences are also demanding that they not be taxed to pay for locking up these prisoners. In a climate wherein the 1990s court commitments to prison remained flat, some politicians found themselves promising the same voters longer sentences, increased numbers of people in prison, tax cuts, and reduced budgets to run prisons. Politicians have been eagerly seeking solutions to this dilemma.

Discovering the truth about private prisons has been hampered by the high-flown rhetoric of supporters and opponents. Those in favor of privatization claim that industry is inherently more cost effective and better run than government. The nature of competition and desire for profit provides the motivation to seek cheaper methods to deliver the product. In the U.S. literature this seems to be just about the only justification for private prisons, and about the only claim studied by government agencies. Interestingly, it is not as important an argument in the rest of the world, where it has long been argued that with proper management public employees can perform as well as private employees. Of course, public employees can also perform poorly. Private prisons would have to be terrible indeed to begin to match the excesses of many American prisons of the past.

Are private prisons cheaper? Politicians, eager to support their decisions, have most often cited the (essentially unsupported) finding that all private prisons both turn a profit and save the state at least 10–15%. Of course, in a climate where the need is for the fastest method to build a prison, few politicians have been interested in carefully designed, time-consuming studies of costs. This has left evaluators comparing what may not be comparable, and drawing conclusions based on missing data. For example, brand new private prisons may be easier and cheaper to run than elderly state prisons, but the proper comparison is to brand new state prisons. Overall, the best studies that have been done have concluded that there is no reason to believe that private prisons, or private juvenile detention, can or are saving money as compared to public facilities. Worse, few studies have included the cost of monitoring staff. If this were included, would a state save money? More important, in an American atmosphere that insists that even long sentences are a slap on the wrist, and declining crime rates require ever increasing incarceration, few politicians are willing to call for less incarceration. With cost often irrelevant, the problem may become how to build the most prisons in the fastest manner.

One problem faced by many state politicians is that all U.S. states require that the budget be annually balanced. Many require voter approval to borrow large amounts of money for construction projects such as new prisons. If voters will not approve massive new debt, but have been promised a new prison, how can this be resolved? Interestingly, the solution is "creative financing," which is not a secret, or ever discussed in the privatization literature as an ethical dilemma. Those most in favor of locking up those who evade the law in the U.S. are sometimes publicly very proud of their ability to evade the law. In some states, there is a loophole to constitutionally required balanced budgets and taxpayer accountability that allows private companies to build prisons, and then lease them back to the state. Thus, costs show up as current expenditures rather than capital construction. This bypassing of constitutional controls is invariably termed "cutting red tape." Arguments differ on whether or not taxpayers save or pay more money this way, but supporters are unanimous in asserting that prisons get built faster.

The most extreme practice of this sort can only be found in the U.S. Here a private company builds at its own expense a "spec prison" without any customers or contract. The private company builds it to any design or specification it wishes. Then, the company makes it known that the spec prison can take prisoners from any location across the nation, at any classification level, for a per diem fee. With no contract involved, there may be no government agency to monitor these prisons, giving them more free rein than any other private prison in the world. They can mix security levels, provide little to no services, cut back on security, build unsafe structures, all free from any monitoring. Even private prison proponents agree that it would be impossible to build such prisons in other Western industrialized countries.

The reason why this is a particularly American problem is that most countries have been careful to develop accountability schemes as part of privatization. Although the problem has not been completely solved in other countries, Americans have been on the whole loath to provide for performance monitors and guarantees. The best contracts are not particularly valuable without compliance mechanisms, and this is where American contracts have traditionally been very weak. Although states such as New Mexico debate at length whether noncomplying corporations might possibly owe them a refund, England and Australia regularly and easily collect such refunds.

In the U.S. context where cost is the main concern, and often the only item up for discussion, a wide variety of ethical issues at best get short shrift. Virtually all of the debate in the American field today is technical: Can nonunion, lesser-trained, lower-paid guards provide adequate supervision? Which mathematical methodology is best for comparing private and public prisons? Even within this debate, the focus is almost completely on procedural goals, both within performance contracts and within the privatization literature. Little attention has been paid in the U.S. to outcome measures, such as whether recidivism or rehabilitative outcome is different (better or worse) in private prisons. Other ethical issues, long rehearsed in the literature, do not so far seem to be a problem: that private administrators might be more corrupt than public ones, that private firms might lobby legislators to increase incarceration rates, or that private officials might find more prisoners in violation of rules to influence parole boards to keep them in longer. Of course, in an American context of constantly increasing prison populations such measures have hardly been necessary.

Interestingly, privatized prisons seem to have lost some of their appeal as scandals have affected the industry. As suggested above, cost may not be the most important issue to many legislators, but scandal has the potential to stir up people who vote. Murders at private prisons in Youngstown, Ohio, New Mexico, and other locations have begun to concern state officials in at least several states to the point of slowing down or cutting back on privatization growth. Worst of all, investigations seem to suggest that the cause of many of these murders, assaults, and escapes is "cutting corners," exactly what American proponents have long claimed would not be the case.

The most important ethical problem remains whether the state can delegate the responsibility of dealing with punishment to the low bidder. Many political theorists still believe that the administration of punishment is at the very core of the reason for the existence of the state. Dr. Ted Strickland, an Ohio congressman who worked in a maximum-security prison for a number of years, commented on this in a Washington Post article (1999, p. 3): "It sickens me to think that individuals sit in corporate boardrooms talking about increasing their bottom line when the commodity they are dealing with is captive human lives."

MARTIN D. SCHWARTZ AND DANA M. NURGE

References and Further Reading

Austin, J. and Coventry, G. 1999. Are we better off? Comparing private and public prisons in the United States, *Current Issues in Criminal Justice*, 11.

Benson, B.L. 1998. *To Serve and Protect: Privatization and Community in Criminal Justice*, New York, New York University Press.

Bottomsley, A.K. and James, A.L. 1997. Evaluating private prisons: Comparisons, competition and cross-fertilization, *Australian and New Zealand Journal of Criminology*, 30.

Durham, A.M. 1989. Origins of interest in the privatization of punishment, *Criminology*, 27.

Dyer, J. 2000. *The Perpetual Prisoner Machine: How America Profits from Crime*, Boulder, CO, Westview Press.

Harding, R.W. 1997. *Private Prisons and Public Accountability*, Buckinghamshire, U.K., Open University Press.

McDonald, D., Fournier, E., Russell-Einhourn, M. and Crawford, S. 1998. *Private Prisons in the United States: An Assessment of Current Practice*, Cambridge, MA.

Moyle, P. 1999. Separating the allocation of punishment from its administration: Theoretical and empirical observations, *Current Issues in Criminal Justice*, 11.

Pratt, T.C. and Maahs, J. 1999. Are private prisons more cost-effective than public prisons? A meta-analysis of evaluation research studies, *Crime and Delinquency*, 45.

Shichor, D. 1995. *Punishment for Profit*, Thousand Oaks, CA, Sage.

Shichor, D. and Gilbert, M.J., Eds. 2001. *Privatization in Criminal Justice—Past, Present and Future*, Cincinnati, OH, Anderson.

Strickland, T., *Private Prisons: The Bottom Line*, 1999. Available at: http://www.house.gov/strickland/prisons.htm.

Thomas, C.W. *Private Adult Correctional Facility Census*, 2000. Available at: http://www.crim.ufl.edu/pep/census/2000.

See also **Prisons, Problems and Recent Developments in**

Prisons, Problems and Recent Developments in

Prisons command a substantial amount of academic and popular attention. It is within these institutional sites that the project of "punishing" criminal offenders is concentrated in modern society. As Michel Foucault (1995) has detailed in his examination of the birth of the modern prison, punishment has been transformed from a spectacular public ritual, involving the acute application of physical pain, into a relatively hidden process of discipline and chronic suffering. The prison is associated with the dual notions of justice and public security through its promise to both deal with criminal actors as well as prevent future crimes. Despite these putative symbolic and instrumental benefits, research addressing the modern prison has exposed many problems associated with this historically-unique way of responding to crime. Principally, these problems center on the efficacy of the prison in achieving its stated objectives and the tremendous cost, both in economic and human terms, associated with its growth and development as "the" institution for punishment.

This essay addresses the debates surrounding the failure of the prison to meet its principal objectives to deter and rehabilitate offenders, and the consequent embrace of incapacitation and retribution (i.e., "just deserts") as the primary justifications for contemporary prisons. The objective of incapacitating risky segments of the population reflects the emergence of what Malcolm Feeley and Jonathan Simon have termed a "new penology" (Feeley and Simon, 1992). The new penology, it is argued, represents a major shift in penal philosophy, away from dealing with individual offenders and toward the efficient management of aggregate populations that takes place in a highly politicized context. This installment will proceed to situate several recent global trends in prisons within this emergent logic.

Although there is some divergence of opinion, much of the literature stresses the inadequacies of the modern prison and sets forth arguments for reducing its use. These arguments, which are synthesized in Thomas Mathiesen's (1990) *Prison on Trial*, address the failure of modern prisons to meet any of the major utilitarian objectives of modern sentencing: deterrence, retribution (i.e., "just deserts"), rehabilitation, and incapacitation (for an alternate perspective, see Wright 1994).

The primary justification for the physical deprivation of liberty in liberal democratic states is that such suffering deters future criminal behavior, both in the particular case of the individual offender (i.e., "specific deterrence"), and in the sense of dissuading crime among the population at large (i.e., "general deterrence"). In both cases, research suggests that prison fails to meet the deterrent objective to any significant degree. In terms of specific deterrence, research addressing the motivation of criminal actors reveals that many crimes are in fact not premeditated, and in those instances where premeditation does occur, the *severity* of sentence does not figure prominently in decision making of the potential offender (Mathieson, 1990). It must be stressed, however, that other studies have shown that the perception of the *certainty* of punishment may have a deterrent effect (Wright, 1994).

The limits of general deterrence are borne out in both international comparative and domestic longitudinal research, which shows that aggressive carceral programs are not associated with reductions in crime. Indeed, the example of the U.S. suggests the very opposite: that severe carcereal programs are associated with *escalations* in crime rates (Mathieson, 1990; Mauer, 1999).

Similarly, it is widely regarded that prisons have failed to meet the objective of rehabilitating criminal offenders. To begin, earlier studies have indicated limited success for the rehabilitative programs of the middle decades of this century. Inmates who participated in rehabilitative programs involving job and other "life skills" training, substance abuse counseling, and other "social" interventions were shown to be just as likely as nonparticipants to reoffend (Mathieson, 1990). As both proponents and opponents of rehabilitation will concede, the nature of the disciplinary prison setting—a "complete institution" that strips inmates of their capacity for personal responsibility—is poorly suited to efforts for resocialization. Similarly, living conditions in most prisons of the world—a culture and daily experience that is characterized by violence, drug addiction, and alternately massive overcrowding and dehabilitating isolation—in many instances counteracts any positive effect of rehabilitative efforts. Many researchers thereby indict the prison system itself, and call for the development of more humane correctional settings in which they consider—drawing upon the positive findings of more recent studies—that rehabilitation might flourish (Mathieson, 1990; Stern, 1998; Weiss and South, 1998; Mauer, 1999).

Although studies discounting the effectiveness of rehabilitation have subsequently been subjected to overwhelming methodological criticism—most particularly related to the notion that it is inappropriate to evaluate the "success" of these programs in terms of recidivism rates—the early dismal findings culminated in the popular (though still contested) academic thesis and later dominant political lament of the 1980s that "nothing works" in prison rehabilitation (Wright, 1994). This emergent ideology coincided with the collapse of the social-welfare political system in Western democratic states, and the rise of "pared down" government in the increasingly conservative fiscal and ideological climate that characterized the global order of economics that gained momentum in the latter decades of the 20th century (Feeley and Simon, 1992; Garland, 1995).

The ideology that "nothing works" in prison rehabilitation thereby took hold in a political climate of reduced government spending and an associated neoconservative discourse that promised to "get tough" on crime through emphasizing the punishment of criminals. The result has been the turning away from rehabilitative programs in many nations. Although rehabilitation has by no means been abandoned—it remains a central component of penal approaches in the Netherlands, and retains a significant yet diminishing role in Britain, Canada, and Australia (Weiss and South, 1998)—it is being eclipsed by incapacitation in many locales as the dominant rationale for incarceration (Feeley and Simon, 1992). This transition is most developed in the U.S., where such initiatives as "three strikes and you're out" legislation—wherein repeat offenders are locked up for indefinite periods of time—are coupled with the development of "mega-prisons" in which offenders are isolated within single cells without the benefit of rehabilitative programs (Mathieson, 1990; Stern, 1998).

Incapacitation is premised upon the construct of "career criminals," who, it is postulated, commit a disproportionate number of violent as well as petty crimes. According to this view, if this criminal segment of the population can be contained for a substantial period of time—even if it is for minor offences committed subsequent to an initial major offense—the violent crime rate will drop. At the level of operation, however, approaches to incapacitation have tended to function as programs for long-term mass incarceration of ethnic minority groups and other "problem populations." This has led many academics to propose that prisons function as sites for human warehousing of society's unwanted (Christie, 1993).

Putting more people in prison for longer periods of time with the purpose of isolating risky groups constitutes a rationale for incarceration that is very different from what has gone before. This rationale has had very tangible impacts upon recent trends in prisons practice. Three of these trends are of particular import and are in many ways reflective of the characteristics of the new penology postulated by Feeley and Simon (1992).

The first relates to the global expansion in the number of prisons and persons incarcerated over the last two decades after a period of decrease or at least stability in most nations of the world over the middle decades of the 20th century. As Marc Mauer (1999) details in *The Race to Incarcerate*, this trend is most exaggerated in the U.S. The number of inmates in state and federal prisons veritably exploded from 196,000 in 1972 to 1,159,000 by 1998. This amounts to an astonishing increase of 500% over a 26-year time period, a figure that massively exceeds the overall population increase of 28% in the U.S. Similarly, the total population of local jails has swelled over the same time period from 130,000 to 567,000 inmates. By Mauer's (1999) recent count there are in total more than 1.7 millions persons incarcerated in the U.S.

Although rates of incarceration have also been expanding in most other nations, the speed and extent of expansion have not been constant. Indeed, one of the most striking features of the contemporary international penal landscape is the tremendous difference in imprisonment rates between seemingly similar countries (Stern, 1998; Weiss and South, 1998).

The nations of Western Europe, despite showing in some instances significant increases in numbers of persons incarcerated, have maintained the lowest rates of incarceration in the world. This is in no small part because of constitutional arrangements that insulate sentencing and corrections policies from partisan and populist politics. Specifically, in many Western European nations, the judiciary maintains a high degree of autonomy and discretion in many areas of sentencing policy relative to the North American context—preventing crime from becoming an emotive lever that can be manipulated in the symbolic discourse of everyday politics. The Netherlands is an exemplar of a Western European nation that maintains a low rate of incarceration at 65 per 100,000 population, which is reflective of that nation's rejection of a carcereal "war on drugs" (Stern, 1998; Weiss and South 1998; Mauer, 1999).

Central and Eastern Europe have not fared as well as their Western European counterparts. Russia maintains its position as the world leader in incarcerating citizens, with a rate of 690 per 100,000 population (Mauer, 1999). Poland and the other new democratic nations of Eastern and Central Europe have shown similar continuity with the trends in high incarceration and deplorable prison conditions that characterized the period of communist domination. This continuity with the past has been linked to the persistence of the communist elite at higher levels of government (South and Weiss, 1998). There are important parallels here with the transitions to democracy underway in South Africa and several Latin American nations—where the continuance of the authoritarian elite is associated with the persistence and in some cases regeneration of repressive and inhumane imprisonment practices, and disproportionate incarceration of ethnic minorities and persons of lower economic standing (South and Weiss, 1998).

One of the most important trends regarding prisons in the Latin American context concerns booming rates of incarceration that are associated with the influence of the international "war on drugs." In nations such as Mexico, Chile, Peru, and Colombia, the efforts of the U.S. to limit drug importation through the contribution of law-enforcement resources have led to massive prison overcrowding (Stern, 1998; Weiss and South, 1998).

Although incarceration rates are also increasing in much of Asia, a notable aberration is Japan. In this nation, overall incarceration rates fell most of this century, sitting at last count at the low rate of 36 prisoners per 100,000 population (Weiss and South, 1998). This has been partly attributed to separation of crime control and political posturing in Japan. Observers have noted, however, that economic and social pressures are beginning to mount in this nation, with the effect that crime is becoming a more politically symbolic and volatile issue. Accordingly, researchers postulate an increase in rates of incarceration in Japan in the near future.

The second major trend in prisons—also consistent with the new penology—concerns *whom* is being locked up. International research chronicles the warehousing of ethnic minorities, opponents of established political orders, and other "problem populations" around the globe (Stern, 1998; Mauer, 1999). In the U.S., the number of black persons and other ethnic minorities, notably Hispanic persons, incarcerated is massively disproportionate to the total percentage these groups constitute of the population at large (Stern, 1998; Weiss and South, 1998; Mauer, 1999). Black persons constitute over half of all prison inmates in the U.S., but only 13% of the total population. Equally horrifying is the fact the chances of a young African American male coming under the control of the criminal justice system is higher than his chances of going to college (Mauer, 1999).

Many studies and empirical reviews have shown these massive increases and biases in sentencing rates to be linked to the "war on drugs" that selectively targets for prison sentence those substances used by ethnic minorities (Mathieson, 1990; Mauer, 1999). Of particular importance is the fact that far harsher prison sentences attach to possession and sales of crack cocaine than to powder cocaine (despite the pharmacological equivalence of these two narcotics). Although white persons consume both of these drugs in greater absolute terms than either black or Hispanic persons, a higher proportion of these ethnic minorities use crack relative to powder cocaine. Thus, targeting crack results in a disproportionate number of arrests and prison sentences for ethnic minorities in the U.S., a striking example of the harm caused by systemic forms of racism.

The demographic profile of prisons in many other nations of the developed world, notably Canada, Australia, and New Zealand, bears unfortunate parallels to that of the U.S. A disproportionate number of indigenous peoples—Native Americans, Aborigines, and Maori—are incarcerated in each of these nations, respectively (Stern, 1998). Further, such systemic discrimination is not limited to the North American or Western democratic states. In many European states, the fiscal conservatism that has been spawned by the admission requirements for prospective member states of the European Union has been marked by a rise in xenophobia and an intolerant sentencing policy that has led to an increase in rates of incarceration of nonwhite Europeans and migrants. Perhaps the most shocking example is the Roma (or "gypsies") of Central Europe, who constitute half of the prisoners in Hungary but only 5% of that nation's population (Stern, 1998).

The disproportionate incarceration of minorities around the globe, although a long-standing practice, has been given a thin veneer of legitimacy under the banner of incapacitation. It achieves this by making appeals to the management of criminally risky aggregates and behaviors rather than being premised upon controlling racial or ethnic groups *per se*. Thus it amounts to a form of systemic racism that is prejudiced in its outcomes rather than directly in its intentions.

The final and related trend is the emergence of private prisons. Led by the example of the U.S., several nations—notable among them England, Australia, and several of the emergent democracies of Eastern Europe and Latin America, are opening private prisons (Shichor, 1995). Nils Christie (1993), in his leading monograph *Crime Control as Industry*, raises a number of important warnings about the potential implications of private prisons. Fundamentally, the attachment of the profit motive to the incarceration of persons produces what has been termed a "prison industrial complex," where adherence to business logic generates continued growth in the numbers of persons incarcerated. Rising rates of incarceration are furthered through privatization in two principle ways. First, private prisons provide the physical capacity to hold more prisoners while cutting the financial costs to the state. This raises the important question of whether life may be worse for prisoners in private rather than public corrections settings because of "competitive" cost cutting in the former.

Second, Christie posits that the privatization of prisons helps to constitute an ideological context, or popular will, that is not only more tolerant, but in fact supportive, of mass incarceration. The industry achieves this by marketing itself through a discourse of commodification that is premised upon empirical forecasts of doom. Specifically, the concept of having hundreds of thousands and even millions of persons warehoused in prison loses some of its shock value where people are warned of this "eventuality" over many years. To use Christie's parlance, these forecasts of doom acclimatize us to treating people (criminals) as *commodities* to be *managed* in a risk market.

Further, Christie suggests that putting a person who has violated society's laws in the controlling hands of a private entity severs the effective connection that otherwise exists between society and *its* prisoner. Thus, privatizing prisons contributes to a culture of punitiveness where criminals are more easily viewed as alien "others" for whom the mainstream bears no attachment or responsibility.

Empirical research into these concerns is somewhat limited. David Shichor (1995) echoes some of these concerns in his recent volume, *Punishment for Profit*, and begins to flesh out these arguments through empirical testing. With regard to physical conditions within private prisons, the limited research thus far produced suggests that life in many private prisons may be no worse off than in public institutions (Shichor, 1995). Indeed, there is a small amount of evidence that rehabilitation has been introduced into some private prisons, with good effect (Sellers, 1993).

It remains to be determined, however, what the impacts of private prisons upon collective consciousness and overall levels of public punitiveness presently are or will be. It bears mention that state governments around the globe have themselves contributed to a culture of public intolerance and punitiveness, through engaging the discourse of a "war on crime" at the level of everyday party politics. It has been pointed out that the private prison movement is to a large degree a response to the state's inability to sustain its *own* long-running and highly politicized prison boom (Garland, 1995; Thomas, 1998). Thus, the record of the public sector does not support the contention that privatization is the singular driving force behind mass incarceration and exclusionary penal policies.

A sentiment that dominates academia and is suggested in studies that probe beyond the surface of public opinion is that the contemporary prison serves as the "detestable solution" to crime: expensive, ineffective, and disliked by many, yet the only feasible way at present of dealing with criminals. As such, there has been a concerted effort to implement a range of alternate community corrections programs to replace the use of prison in all but extreme cases of criminal offending. There is some significant level of public support for community corrections. Lacking clearly-defined sentencing guidelines, however, judges have been unwilling to sentence all but a few offenders to alternative sanctions. Without clear guidelines stating that the principles of sentencing would in most cases be better served through alternative sanctions, we will be faced with an expanding and ineffective prison system for years to come.

MICHAEL KEMPA

References and Further Reading

Christie, N. 1993. *Crime Control as Industry: Towards Gulags, Western Style*, London, Routledge.

Feeley, M. and Simon, J. 2000. The new penology: Notes on the emerging strategy of corrections and its implications, *Criminology*, 30, 449–474.

Foucault, M. 1975. *Surveiller et Punir: Naissance de la Prison*, Paris, Editions Gallimard. As *Discipline and Punish: The Birth of the Prison*, translated by Sheridan, A., New York, Vintage Books, a Division of Random House, 1995.

Garland, D. 1995. Penal modernism and post-modernism, in Blomberg, T. and Cohen, Eds., S., *Punishment and Social Control: Essays in Honour of Sheldon L. Messinger*, New York, Aldine De Gruyter.

Mathiesen, T. 1990. *Prison on Trial: A Critical Assessment*, Newbury Park, CA, Sage.

Mauer, M. 1999. *Race to Incarcerate: The Sentencing Project*, New York, New Press.

Sellers, M.P. 1993. *The History and Politics of Private Prisons: A Comparative Analysis*, London, Associated University Presses.

Shichor, D. 1995. *Punishment for Profit: Private Prisons or Public Concerns*, Thousand Oaks, CA, Sage.

Stern, V. 1998. *A Sin Against the Future: Imprisonment in the World*, New York, Penguin Books.

Thomas, C., Issues and evidence from the United States, in Easton, S., *Privatising Correctional Services*, Vancouver, Canada, The Frasier Institute.

Weiss, R.P. and South, N., Eds. 1998. Comparing prison systems: Toward a comparative and international penology, *International Studies in Global Change*, Vol. 8, Amsterdam, the Netherlands, Gordon and Breach.

Wright, R. 1994. *Defense of Prisons*, London, Greenwood Press.

See also **Prisons, Privatized; Prisons: Inmate Populations and Subcultures**

Prisons: Women's Facilities

In recent years, the number of female prison inmates has increased, creating a greater need for programs, services, and treatment alternatives for female offenders. This population comprises women who have been convicted of a variety of crimes, ranging from drug offenses to murder. The incarceration of female offenders presents some unique issues and concerns in terms of facilities and programs provided within correctional institutions including pregnancy, women's health care, birth control, drug treatment, child care, and educational and vocational training. Today, state departments of correction and the Federal Bureau of Prisons operate women's correctional facilities around the country. These facilities range from minimal or low security institutions for offenders convicted of less serious offenses to medium and high security institutions for more dangerous offenders. In addition to traditional correctional institutions, the federal system also operates federal prison camps for minimum-security female inmates, as well as federal medical centers for prisoners.

Brief Historical Background

Historically, state correctional institutions in the U.S. were designed to house male offenders. Until the early 20th century, female offenders were not held in separate facilities. Rather, female offenders were often given alternative punishments to incarceration or, in cases where a term of imprisonment was imposed, female inmates were housed in segregated areas within male institutions. Within these facilities, women were often subjected to dismal and unsanitary conditions. For example, at the New York Penitentiary at Auburn, women were often subjected to beatings, deprived of food, and raped by male prison guards. As a result of such treatment at Auburn and other facilities, a reform movement began to take shape to improve the conditions female inmates were subjected to and to establish separate facilities that were specifically designed for women. Prison reformers sought to develop "feminine" institutions operated by women, with a focus on the needs of female offenders.

Throughout the late 19th and early 20th centuries, a wave of organized imprisonment of women swept across the U.S. During the late 1800s, state reformatories opened around the country to house female offenders. The first of these facilities, known as the House of Shelter, opened in Detroit following the Civil War. Reformatories were designed to foster a more familial environment, whose design mirrored a school campus more than a fortress-like prison. These facilities consisted of several cottages surrounding a central administration building. Here, women were housed in private rooms rather than cells and provided opportunities to develop traditional "domestic skills" such as sewing and cooking. This design was also implemented in the federal system in the early 20th century. The first federal institution for women opened in Alderson, West Virginia, in 1927. Alderson comprised 14 cottages set in a horseshoe pattern, with each cottage containing a kitchen and quarters for approximately 30 women who were segregated by race. Alderson is still in operation today as a federal prison camp for minimum-security-level female inmates.

As the 1800s drew to a close, a new chapter in prison reform began to take shape. In the early 1900s, prison administrators began to shift from the religious and philanthropic approach fostered by previous reformers to a more feminist approach. This generation of reformers rejected the traditional stereotypical roles and vocational undertakings that women were encouraged to assume in earlier years. Rather, the focus of reformers at this time was on low wages and the lack of education and vocational opportunities for women in general at this time. In addition, attention began to be paid to the use of other professionals such as physicians and psychologists in addressing the needs of female inmates.

By the mid-1930s, the reformatory movement began to dissolve as changes in legislation, offender populations, and an emphasis on secure custody rather than personal reform became more prominent. During the 1940s and 1950s, many custodial institutions were closed and women were once again housed in reformatories. However, at this point, the reformatories had begun to discard the vestiges of femininity that they once fostered and instead began to develop more custodial regimes. In addition, rehabilitative programs began to be implemented in some facilities.

During the 1960s, the prison reform movement was somewhat stagnant. With the rise of feminism in the 1970s, however, there was a renewed interest in women's penal reform. Reformers began to reevaluate the use of single sex institutions and the implications of gender stereotyping that had been fostered in earlier years.

As the number of women being incarcerated began to rise during the late 1970s and early 1980s, the need for more facilities and programs became apparent. Between 1983 and 1998, the number of women received into state and federal correctional institutions increased by 344%, for a total inmate population 84,427 at the end of 1998. By June 2002, that number increased to 96,099 women in the custody of a state or federal prison. This enormous growth in the female inmate population has been precipitated by changes in sentencing laws, particularly those sentencing guidelines providing for mandatory minimum sentences, stricter penalties for drug offenses, economic hardship, and an increased frequency of violent crimes by women. As a result, this trend has necessitated expansion by state departments of correction and the Federal Bureau of Prisons to accommodate the number of inmates and to provide necessary treatment services.

Facilities and Institutional Staffing

There are currently over 110 correctional institutions for women in operation in the U.S. In addition to traditional prisons, the Federal Bureau of Prisons also operates several types of facilities to house women convicted of federal offenses including federal prison camps and federal medical centers. At the end of 1997, there were over 100 secure state facilities housing female inmates in the U.S., with 40 state departments of correction operating 92 facilities that housed exclusively women, and approximately, 10 states operating at least 16 facilities housing both male and female inmates. Institutions housing both male and female inmates are known as "co-correctional" facilities. Co-correctional facilities are operated by several state departments of correction as well as the Federal Bureau of Prisons, with more than 70 such facilities now in use. Some states, including Alaska, Kansas, North Dakota, and West Virginia, house female inmates exclusively in co-correctional institutions, whereas others like New Hampshire, Oregon, Hawaii, and Illinois operate one facility exclusively for women, as well as one or more co-correctional facilities. These complexes typically have separate self-contained areas for male and female inmates. However, some contact between inmates of the opposite sex is permissible at some institutions. For example, for minimum-security inmates, some prisons operate programs in which inmates of both sexes may participate and allow for work assignments with an integrated group of inmates. Other facilities only permit interaction with inmates of the opposite sex in designated areas such as the dining hall or classrooms, with physical contact prohibited.

The trend towards using a co-correctional model harkens back to the early days of correctional history when women were housed in segregated areas of male institutions. However, conditions in today's facilities are somewhat better than those which women were subjected to in the late 19th and early 20th centuries. Co-correctional institutions have been advocated for a number of reasons. First, they are viewed as a means of lessening the disparity between programs and services available at male institutions versus female institutions. Second, it is hypothesized that they aid in reducing the tension and violence commonly found in same-sex prisons and help prepare inmates for reintegration into mainstream society upon their release. Third, co-correctional facilities are thought to be more cost effective by using available space at existing institutions.

The majority of institutional staff in women's prisons is female. On average, women comprise more than 50% of these positions in women's state prisons. Female staff also hold the majority of correctional officer and security staff positions, as well as program or services providers within these facilities.

As to institutional policies, there are some differences between male and female prisons. The two areas where differences in formal policy are most pronounced are in those relating to the range of health and beauty items inmates may purchase from the prison commissary and the types of items of personal property inmates are permitted to have in their cells. Generally, female inmates are permitted to have more of these items than male inmates. In addition, rules relating to personal grooming, hair length, and the availability of programs on parenting are different between male and female prisons. In other areas, however, institutional policies for both male and female inmates are similar. For example, policies relating to visitation, telephone use, meals and special diets, security and transportation procedures, and pat down searches are generally the same for both inmate populations.

Characteristics of Inmates in Women's Prisons

Studies have identified the "typical" female state inmate as a woman of color, between the ages of 24 and 29, unmarried, with at least one child, likely to have been the victim of physical or sexual abuse, is addicted to drugs or alcohol, has a prior arrest history, has a low educational level and few occupational skills, has held primarily low-wage jobs, and is in need of educational programs and treatment services such as substance abuse counseling, mental health counseling, and assistance with parenting skills.

The types of offenses women are incarcerated for vary. Generally, women are serving sentences for nonviolent offenses. According to the Bureau of Justice Statistics, approximately 17% of women committed to state correctional institutions are serving sentences for violent offenses, 36% are incarcerated for property offenses, and 39% for drug offenses.

Issues in Administration, Services, and Treatment in Women's Prisons

One of the major issues in the administration of female prisons is the need for specialized medical care. Female inmates generally have a higher demand for both medical and mental health services than male inmates. One of the foremost medical concerns arising in female institutions is the care of pregnant inmates. Pregnancy presents numerous issues requiring specialized medical treatment. Among the issues facing prison administrators in developing correctional policy are the needs for special diets for pregnant inmates, access to abortion services, treatment and monitoring of women with high-risk pregnancies, pre- and postnatal care, and access to outside medical facilities and medical specialists. In addition to the normal risks and concerns associated with pregnancy, prison administrators must also be concerned with women who enter a facility with other complications impacting their pregnancy such as prior drug or alcohol abuse, sexually transmitted diseases, and a history of prior abortions.

In addition to pregnancy, female inmates also present other issues related to child care. After delivery, incarcerated mothers are often given only a brief time to see their newborn children. Concerns about mother–child bonding, child rearing, and the ability to reestablish relationships after incarceration are just some of the issues facing women who give birth while in prison. For those women entering prison who already have children, many are single parents and have the sole responsibility of caring for their children. Upon entering prison, the inmate's children are often forced to live with other family members or must be placed in the custody of the state for placement with foster families. In some cases, this separation can lead to the termination of the mother's parental rights. Such circumstances create problems not only for the children involved, but also for the incarcerated mothers who find themselves in need of mental health counseling for conditions such as depression and anxiety.

There are many programs offered in various prison facilities to foster healthy parent–child relationships. The goal of these programs is to help establish strong family relationships and to provide inmates with the skills necessary to provide an appropriate home environment and care for themselves and their children upon their release from custody. One example is the mothers and infants together (MINT) program offered at some facilities within the Federal Bureau of Prisons. MINT is a residential program for minimum-security level inmates who are pregnant at the time of their sentencing. Women who participate in this program serve their sentences at a community corrections center during the final months of their pregnancy. MINT provides instruction on parenting skills as well as treatment services related to substance abuse, self-esteem, physical and sexual abuse, and other life skills. Once the inmate has given birth, she is permitted to spend 3 months with her child, after which she must return to a correctional facility to complete the remainder of her sentence. Prior to admission to the MINT program, the inmate is required to make arrangements for the care of the child while she finishes her sentence.

Another area of concern in women's prisons is the high number of inmates with HIV and AIDS. In December 2000, a reported 2243 female inmates in state prisons were known to be HIV positive. This number accounted for 3.6% of the female inmate population, as compared to 2.2% of the male inmate population with HIV. The rate of HIV infection is higher among female inmates than males inmates in all regions of the country. Furthermore, in every year since 1991, the rate of confirmed cases of AIDS has been higher among all prison inmates than the general public population. By the end of 2000, the rate of confirmed cases of AIDS was approximately four times higher in state and federal prisons than in the total population of the U.S. This phenomenon may be attributed, at least in part, to the fact that many female inmates were engaged in prostitution or drug abuse prior to entering prison. Here again, the need for appropriate medical care for female inmates is evident.

Drug abuse is particularly high among female inmates. As such, substance abuse counseling and treatment programs are offered in many state prisons. Studies have shown that women have more substance abuse problems than men and that the number of women imprisoned for drug-related offenses such as sale, possession, distribution, and trafficking has increased dramatically in recent years. Research shows that approximately half of all state female inmates were under the influence of drugs, alcohol, or both at the time of the commission of the offense they were incarcerated for. Research also indicates that offenders who abuse drugs have a higher rate of recidivism upon release than nondependent offenders. As a result, substance abuse services within women's prisons become particularly important given the impact that drug dependency has on other aspects of the inmate's life and her chances of returning to prison. There are a variety of substance abuse treatment programs available in women's state prisons around the country. In the federal system, the Federal Bureau of Prisons offers several types of programs including drug abuse education, residential drug abuse treatments programs, nonresidential drug abuse treatment programs, and transitional services for those offenders transferred to halfway houses or placed on probation with the U.S. Probation Service. Residential treatment programs for women are operated at several different federal facilities including federal prison camps and federal correctional institutions.

In addition to medical concerns, educational and vocational training programs are also an important component of prison life for many inmates. There have traditionally been few vocational and rehabilitation programs offered in women's prisons. Of those programs that are offered, they tend to focus on "traditional" female occupations such as food service work, clerical or secretarial skills, cosmetology and hair styling, and sewing. Although improvements have been made in some institutions, there is still a low availability of "non-traditional" programs that prepare women to secure jobs in other fields upon their release from prison. Such training opportunities are important in lessening the likelihood of recidivism and for preparing women to pursue legitimate careers rather than returning to criminal activity. With nearly 70% of female prisoners having been on probation or incarcerated prior to the commitment of the current offense for which they are imprisoned, the need for education, vocational training, and life skills programs is very apparent.

Another issue in state and federal correctional policy in recent years has been a growing concern surrounding the abuse of female inmates. Although statistics show that a majority of the staff at women's prisons is female, there is still a large percentage of the staff that is male. As a result, some female inmates report that they are the victims of sexual abuse and sexual harassment by guards within the institution. This has led to a number of lawsuits filed by both state and federal inmates against various institutions and individual correctional officers. In response, state departments of corrections and the Federal Bureau of Prisons have implemented staff training programs specifically addressing these issues and applicable institutional policies relating to the appropriate treatment of inmates.

Female Inmates and the Death Penalty

Finally, another issue in the administration of women's prisons is the housing of female inmates who have been sentenced to death. As of April 1, 2003, there were 48 women awaiting execution. This number accounts for approximately 1.4% of the total population of inmates on death row. There are currently 38 states that have the death penalty, as well as the federal government and the U.S. military (though there are currently no women facing a federal death sentence). Generally, each state having the death penalty has a designated prison where female death row inmates are housed. These inmates are often subject to strict institutional policies and procedures and are segregated from the general population inmates.

Conclusion

The administration of women's prisons and correctional policies for female inmates present a variety of issues and concerns unique to this offender population. Prison policies, treatment programs, vocational training, education, and child care are just some of the areas that women's prisons focus on to facilitate the orderly operation of the institutions, as well as the treatment of female inmates. As the population of female inmates continues to grow, the need for more facilities to house them and the availability of institutional programs will escalate as well. As such, common issues relevant to male prisons such as overcrowding and scarcity of resources will also become critical in women's institutions.

KRISTINE A. BROWN

References and Further Reading

Austin, J. and Irwin, J. (2001). *It's About Time: America's Imprisonment Binge,* 3rd ed., Belmont, CA, Wadsworth Publishing Co.

Belknap, J. (2001). *The Invisible Woman: Gender, Crime and Justice,* 2nd ed., Belmont, CA, Wadsworth Publishing Co.

Bosworth, M. (2002). *The U.S. Federal Prison System,* Thousand Oaks, CA, Sage Publications, Inc.

Chesney-Lind, M. (1997). *The Female Offender: Girls, Women and Crime,* Thousand oaks, CA, Sage Publications, Inc.

Clear, T.R. and Cole, G.F., (1994). *American Corrections,* 3rd ed., Belmont, CA, Wadsworth Publishing Co.

Curry, L. (2001). Tougher sentencing, economic hardships and rising violence, in Herman, P.G., Ed., *The American Prison System,* Vol. 73(5), The H. W. Wilson, Co., pp. 126–129.

Death Penalty Information Center. (2003). *Women and the Death Penalty.* Available at: www.deathpenaltyinfo.org.

Federal Bureau of Prisons. (1999). *Substance Abuse Treatment Programs in the Federal Bureau of Prisons—Report to Congress.* Available at: www.bop.gov.

Feinman, C. (1994). *Women in the Criminal Justice System,* 3rd ed., Westport, CT, Praeger.

Flowers, R.B. (1995). *Female Crime, Criminals and Cellmates,* Jefferson, NC, McFarland & Co., Inc.

Greene, S. (2002). Women in prison, in *The Encyclopedia of Crime and Justice,* 2nd ed., Vol. 4, New York, Macmillan Reference USA, pp. 1729–1732.

Harrison, P.M. and Beck, A.J. 2002. *Prisoners in 2001,* Washington, DC, U.S. Department of Justice, Bureau of Justice Statistics, July.

Heffernan, E. (1993). Alderson: The early years, in *Female Offenders: Meeting the Needs of a Neglected Population,* American Correctional Association, pp. 17–18.

Maruschak, L.M. 2002. *HIV in Prisons,* Washington, DC, U.S. Department of Justice, Bureau of Justice Statistics, October.

Moon, D.G., Thompson, R.J. and Bennett, R. (1993). Patterns of substance use among women in prison, in Fletcher, B.R., Shaver, L.D. and Moon, D.G., Eds., *Women Prisoners: A Forgotten Population,* Westport, CT, Praeger, pp. 45–49.

National Institute of Corrections. (1998). *Current Issues in the Operation of Women's Prisons, September 1998,* Longmont, CO, U.S. Department of Justice, National Institute of Corrections.

Sims, A. (1992). Women's prisons: Their social and cultural environment, *Federal Prison Journal,* 3(1), 44–48. Available at: www.bop.gov.

U.S. Department of Justice, *About the Federal Bureau of Prisons.* Available at: www.bop.gov.

See also **Prisons: History in the U.S.; Prisons: Inmate Population and Subcultures**

Private Investigators

Private investigators (and associated inquiry agents) are an established component of the broad complex of private and public law enforcement and crime prevention. They have a mixed record in regard to integrity, but arguably serve an essential function in supplying a market for justice that is not adequately met by the public sector. Private investigators have a high profile in the murder mystery and suspense genre in novels and films. Research on their activities suggests a more mundane working life than is evoked by fictional representations, but not without moments of suspense and danger.

Definitions, Dimensions, and Functions

The term "private investigator" has both generic and specific meanings. In its broadest usage it relates to any person, outside government, who conducts enquiries for a customer or employer—also "PI," "private eye," "private detective," or "gumshoe." The enquiry process may extend to serving legal notices or repossessing property after locating a person. Alternatively, these latter activities are sometimes separated, as in government licensing categories that distinguish between "private investigators," on the one hand, and "commercial agents," "process servers," or "bailiffs," on the other hand. Often, however, the activities merge into one another. The adjective "private" is also somewhat limiting. It tends to imply an independent operator, but private or public sector employees can carry out the same functions. "Inquiry agent" may be a more useful term in that it can be used to cover sole operators, companies, and private and public sector employees; and can be extended to include process servers, debt recovery agents, and associated agents such as arson investigators. "Inquiry agent" has a growing currency—

along with the term "investigation services" to describe the industry sector. Nonetheless, "private investigator" persists as a popular generic term.

Reliable statistics on PIs are difficult to obtain because of different licensing systems and employment census categories, and little is known about the longer-term history of this group. Some notable developments, primarily in the 19th century, included bounty hunters, thief takers, and recovery agents, especially in frontier societies where public law enforcement was thin. Private detectives also became an important part of labor discipline, mainly in the U.S. in the same period. The private investigation sector appears to have experienced significant growth in the period from the 1960s to the 1990s, consistent with the rapid growth of the larger security industry. The *Hallcrest Report* in the U.S. estimated that in 1990 there were about 70,000 private investigator employees and about 15,000 companies, taking about 10% of security market revenues. Most companies were small with an average size of about 2.5 investigators. This would seem a typical profile for the sector in advanced industrial societies.

The private detective novel has contributed to a stereotypical image of the lone operator in a seedy second floor office taking the occasional case from a client concerned about their spouse's fidelity. This image may have applied widely at times and may still have some relevance. A major factor behind the image was strict divorce laws that required evidence of infidelity. But, since the 1970s, "personal cases" have been a minor part of the work of most private investigators. The current profile is one of high volume routine work from insurance companies, government welfare departments, law firms, financial institutions, and courts. These contracts involve surveillance on insurance claimants suspected of fraudulent injuries, obtaining evidence in criminal and civil cases, locating debtors or people under court orders, and serving notices or repossessing property. All of these activities involve a degree of risk of conflict and assault. Despite the standardization of most work, clients' requirements can be highly diverse, including searching for missing persons, investigating employee malpractice, de-bugging offices, locating heirs and assets, tracing missing persons, investigating suspected arson or unfair trading, and occasionally going undercover.

Ethics and Regulation

The image of private detectives in novels and films is also somewhat contradictory. They tend to be portrayed either as shady characters willing to engage in any kind of deceitful practices to make money and serve their scheming clients or as saintly masters of the investigative art who deliver up the guilty party in the wake of the bumbling failure of the police. The latter applies more when the PI is the protagonist of the story, but in both cases the breaking of laws and ethical standards is a focus of narrative interest. The principle that the end justifies the means, whether considered favorably or not, extends to trespass, breaking and entering, theft, intercepting and opening mail, obtaining confidential information and eavesdropping, deceptive conduct (such as obtaining entry by appearing to be a market researcher), or using threats or inducements. The scale of such practices in reality is difficult to assess. Many such breaches are opportunistic and rarely reach the courts. Other forms of malpractice, such as accessing confidential information, have at times developed into corrupt networks involving public servants and police, and have been exposed by official inquiries.

The problem of misconduct has been recognized by industry members and underlies support for government regulation. However, effective regulation is a difficult task because of the obvious problems in monitoring conduct. Many victims, for example, will not even be aware their privacy has been violated. Nonetheless, there is a trend toward government's taking a greater role in underwriting the protection of clients and the public through licensing schemes with integrity checks, compulsory training, and systems to investigate complaints, and sanction breaches of law and codes of conduct. Normally, PIs do not have any legal powers beyond those of ordinary citizens. Some industry associations argue that increased accountability should be matched by enhanced powers for licensed private investigators, such as access to government held information under strictly controlled conditions. This follows from the argument that inquiry agents account for an important and legitimate specialist part of the network of justice and law enforcement services, and fill a crucial gap in public provision of detection, recovery, and prosecution services.

TIM PRENZLER

References and Further Reading

Cunningham, W.C., Strauchs, J.J., Van Meter, C.W. 1990. *Hallcrest II: Private Security Trends 1970–2000,* Stoneham, MA, Butterworth-Heinemann.
Gill, M. and Hart, J. 1997. Exploring investigative policing: A study of private detectives in Britain, *British Journal of Criminology,* 37.
Johnston, L. 1992. *The Rebirth of Private Policing,* London, Routledge.
Jones, T. and Newburn, T. 1998. *Private Security and Public Policing,* Oxford, Clarendon Press.
McDermid, V. 1995. *A Suitable Job for a Woman: Inside the World of Women Private Eyes,* London, HarperCollins.
Morn, F. 1982. *The Eye That Never Sleeps: A History of the Pinkerton National Detective Agency,* Westport, CT, Greenwood.
Pileggi, N. 1976. *Blye, Private Eye,* Chicago, Playboy Press.
Weiss, Robert. 1986. Private detective agencies and labour discipline in the United States, 1855–1946, *The Historical Journal,* 29.

See also **Police: Detectives; Police Investigation**

Probation

In the U.S. today, approximately 65% of offenders under the authority of local, state, or federal correctional officials are on probation supervision. This represents over 3 million people, or about three times the number of people in jails and prisons. Although probation is the most extensive criminal justice sanction in use in the U.S., it continues to be viewed as a lenient, "slap on the wrist" consequence or punishment for crime, and therefore does not elicit a great deal of support from the general public. Probation in the U.S. is traced to the work of John Augustus, a bootmaker from Boston, who is credited with coining the term "probation" for his practice of having judges defer sentencing and releasing offenders into his custody for a period of time. John Augustus began his work in the Boston Police Court in 1841 when he posted bail for a man charged with being with a common drunkard. During the period of deferred sentencing or "probation," Augustus would assist the offender in becoming sober and obtaining employment. Augustus would frequently provide room and board while attempting to reform the offender. Later, when Augustus returned to court with the offender he was usually able to convince the judge that he had reformed the defendant and only a small fine would be imposed (Augustus, 1972).

At the beginning, Augustus focused his efforts on working with common drunkards, however, he later expanded his work to juvenile offenders and those adults charged with violating Boston's temperance laws. Between 1842 and 1858 he bailed out 1152 men and 794 women. He reported great success, noting that of the 1100 offenders he bailed out, only one had forfeited bond. John Augustus also developed the practice of preparing reports for the court, today referred to as presentence investigation reports, which have become an integral part of the sentencing process in all jurisdictions. Other practices initiated by Augustus that have become a major part of contemporary probation include social casework, progress reports to the court, and the revocation process. As is the practice today, Augustus was careful to screen the offenders "to ascertain whether the prisoners were promising subjects for probation and to this end it was necessary to take into consideration the previous character of the person, his age, and the influences by which he would in the future be likely to be surrounded" (Augustus, 1972).

Although John Augustus' efforts emphasized reformation, the later development of probation emphasized a law enforcement approach as probation officers were drawn from the ranks of retired police officers. Later, probation officers came to incorporate what many feel is a significant "role conflict" between the social worker and law-enforcement responsibilities of the job. As a social worker, the probation officer is expected to identify the offender's needs and provide assistance in such areas as employment, mental health counseling, substance-abuse treatment, housing, and family problems. In some jurisdictions, the probation officer provides these supportive services directly, however in many jurisdictions, the officers serve as a "broker," referring the offender to an agency in the community that is better suited to meet specific needs. In this regard, the probation officer is expected to be knowledgeable in community resources.

In the role of law enforcer, the probation officer is expected to enforce the general and specific conditions of probation and to report serious violations back to the court. General or standard conditions are those conditions that apply to all offenders placed on probation. These include requirements to obey all laws, maintain employment, report to the probation officer as directed, notify the probation officer of a change in residence, not leave the jurisdiction without permission, and not use drugs. Special or specific conditions include conditions applicable to only certain offenders based on the crime committed or special needs of the offender. These could include requirements to make restitution or pay a fine, to perform community service, attend Alcoholics Anonymous meetings or participate in an outpatient or inpatient substance abuse program, participate in a home confinement or electronic monitoring program, participate in mental health counseling, or submit to drug testing. The supervising probation officer is frequently given a great deal of latitude in enforcing the conditions of probation, and in many jurisdictions, the judge will require offenders to participate "as directed by the probation." Financial orders are frequently written ordering the offender to pay restitution or a fine in "an amount and manner to be determined by the probation officer." In the case of financial orders, it is the responsibility of the officer to make an assessment of the probationer's ability to pay and to establish a payment schedule based on this financial assessment.

In the role of law enforcer the probation officer emphasizes surveillance and monitoring activities requiring the offender to report to the office, provide financial information, employment check stubs, or other documentation confirming that he or she is meeting the requirements of probation. The officer will usually make announced or unannounced home visits to observe how the probationer is functioning in the home and community. Collateral contacts with family members, employers, and drug or mental health counselors is also necessary to assess the offenders adjustment to probation.

Historically, probation agencies have tended to emphasize one model over the other. During the rehabilitation era spanning the period from about 1930 to the early 1970s the social worker role of probation officers was clearly emphasized. The medical model view of criminality took the rehabilitation emphasis to its logical conclusion. That is, criminality was a type of social illness or disease that required a thorough assessment in order to identify or diagnosis the root causes of the deviant behavior. Once the underlying causes were diagnosed, usually through the presentence investigation report, an appropriate treatment plan would be presented to the court, and if placed on probation, would then be implemented by the supervision officer. As civil unrest swept the country in the 1960s coupled with soaring crime rates, the rehabilitation model of probation began to lose favor and public attitudes shifted toward a more punitive punishment approach to dealing with the criminal offender. Rather than emphasizing rehabilitation, the public wanted the criminal justice system, including probation and parole, to emphasize deterrence, retribution, and incapacitation. Several things fueled the dramatic shift from rehabilitation to a conservative crime control strategy beginning in the mid-1970s and continuing to the present time. These included high crime rates, Robert Martinson's landmark study in 1976 concluding that rehabilitation effort were generally ineffective, and Ronald Reagan's election as president in 1980.

Probation services in the U.S. may take on either a centralized or decentralized form of administration. In a decentralized form of administration, management of probation services is located in the community where the services and supervision are provided. For example, California has a decentralized form of administration wherein each county maintains its own probation department. Probation in California administers local juvenile facilities and camps along with performing the major functions of presentence investigations and supervision of adult and juvenile offenders. In contrast, some states combine probation and parole services and management is administered from a centralized location, usually the state capital. There is also some debate about whether probation services should be administered by the courts (judiciary) or the executive branch of government. Those who advocate administration by the courts argue that under the courts, probation will be more responsive to the wishes of sentencing judges who are more likely to scrutinize supervision when it is performed by court employees. Furthermore, advocates of judicial administration of probation services also argue that morale will be higher when probation officers work closely with judges (Clear and Cole, 2000).

In contrast, those who maintain that probation services should be located under the executive branch of government, argue that the courts are ill-equipped to be administrators of human services operations. As noted, in some states probation and parole services are separated with probation usually being administered by the counties and parole administered by state government. Those who argue for maintaining this separation report that probationers and parolees are considerably different with parolees exhibiting more severe forms of criminal and maladaptive behaviors and these differences require different approaches.

Probation officers perform two major functions, the presentence investigation report (PSIR) and supervision. The PSIR is usually prepared by a probation investigator after conviction but before sentencing. The major purpose of the presentence report is to assist the court in sentencing. Other purposes of the PSIR include helping the supervision officer formulate a plan, facilitating classification of an inmate to an appropriate institution if committed to prison, assisting parole boards to determine parole suitability, and assisting the parole officer in implementing a supervision strategy once released from prison. The PSIR contains a great deal of social information about criminal offenders and thus is also used for research purposes by correctional agencies and researchers. In large urban probation departments, the investigation and supervision functions are usually separated with some officers assigned to investigation units performing only PSIRs, whereas other officers are assigned to field services responsible for the supervision of a caseload of probationers. However, in small departments, probation officers may perform both investigation and supervision functions. For example, in the federal system in large probation offices like Los Angeles, federal probation officers are assigned to either the investigation supervision units whereas in Montana officers will conduct PSIs and will also supervise a caseload of probationers.

It should be noted that the quality of PSIRs may vary significantly depending on the volume of cases referred for investigation and the resources available to hire probation staff. In large jurisdictions, the PSIR may be quite superficial, with one hurried interview of the defendant, a criminal record check, a review of the crime reports, and then dictation of the report. Often, there is little time for verification of the information provided by the offender. However, in other jurisdictions, the PSIR may involve multiple interviews with the defendant, interviews with spouses, parents, and family members along with verification of employment, educational, and financial status. If the offender has previously been on probation or parole, a thorough investigation will involve obtaining existing probation, parole, or prison records to assess the offender's prior response under supervision. The reliability of the PSIR will be enhanced through verification of the information obtained from the various sources. Judges have historically given considerable weight to the conclusions of the probation officer and tend to follow the recommendation in 90% or more of the cases. The courts are not required to disclose the report to the defendant, but most jurisdictions follow a practice of full disclosure unless disclosing sensitive information may endanger the source. In the federal system, a rule has been established requiring full disclosure of the presentence report to the defendant. Most probation administrators tend to place a higher priority on the investigative function because the final report is a visible product that is read by several people and agencies including the judge, the prosecutor, defense attorney or public defender, prison staff, parole boards, parole officers, and researchers. The quality of these reports therefore will impact the reputation of the agency and the chief probation officer.

The supervision function in contrast is largely invisible. The type of supervision or quality of the supervision provided by probation officers is usually not seen and is difficult to measure. Supervision assignments, especially in large jurisdictions, frequently are specialized by offender type. For example, it is common for large probation offices to have officers that supervise caseloads of violent or sex offenders, drug offenders, mental health cases, white-collar offenders, or juvenile offenders who have been identified as belonging to a gang. Proponents of specialization argue that probation officers will develop specific skills associated with a certain category of offender and therefore will be able to provide enhanced services and supervision. Specialized caseloads are often designated as a higher grade with an increased level of pay. Those who argue against specialized caseloads suggest that specialists are not well-rounded and prolonged supervision of only one type of offender will distort an officer's perspective. Furthermore, dealing with only one type of offender over an extended period of time may result in a higher frequency of burnout.

For many years it was thought that probation supervision would be more effective if only caseloads could be reduced to manageable levels. Probation officers and managers argued that lower caseloads would allow officers to devote more time and attention to each case thus enhancing the level of surveillance and monitoring as well as the level of rehabilitative support services. It was suggested that an ideal caseload size was somewhere between 35 and 50 cases per officer. However, studies conducted during the 1960s and 1970s concluded that recidivism, as measured by new criminal conduct, did not decrease significantly. Some studies did find that the rate of technical violations (violation of the rules of probation) increased because officers had more time to monitor compliance with probation conditions. With reduced caseloads, probation officers devoted more time to monitoring compliance with the conditions of supervision and therefore were able to detect more violations.

It should be noted that a distinction is made between caseload and workload. Caseload refers to the raw number of cases supervised by a probation officer whereas workload represents the amount of time or work devoted to any given case. For example, most

probation officers recognize that drug offenders, mental health cases, and violent offenders require more of an officer's time. Furthermore, probation supervision is a continuous process of classifying and reclassifying probationers depending on their adjustment to supervision. A stable, first-time offender may initially be classified as requiring only minimum supervision, however, is reclassified to maximum supervision because of drug use, unemployment, or failure to comply with financial or treatment orders. Likewise, a probationer initially classified as maximum supervision may later be reduced to medium and then minimum owing to a favorable response to supervision. With extremely stable cases the probation officer may require no face-to-face contact and simply allow the probationer to submit written monthly reports.

Probation supervision may be terminated when the offender successfully completes his or her full term of supervision. Most jurisdictions allow for an early termination if the probationer performs in an exemplary manner and appears to no longer be in need of supervision. Supervision may also be terminated or revoked as a result of violations that occur during the period of probation. Violations are of two types, technical and legal. Legal violations, also called new criminal conduct, occur when the probationer is arrested are convicted for committing a new crime. Although most probation officers prefer that a conviction occur before initiating revocation proceedings, officers may return an offender to court for an arrest. The burden of proof necessary to convict for a crime is beyond a reasonable doubt, however, the preponderance of evidence is sufficient in a probation or parole proceeding. If violation proceedings are initiated, the probation officer may ask that the offender be cited or summoned to appear in court. The, the probationer may also be arrested in the case of more serious violations. If found in violation, the court may reinstate the offender to probation, may reinstate with additional conditions, may extend the period of supervision, or make revoke probation and impose a period of imprisonment. Technical violations involve noncompliance with the general or specific conditions of probation.

The Supreme Court in *Gagnon v. Scarpelli* (411 US 778, 1973) provided probation violators with minimal due process rights including the right to be presented with the charges in writing, disclosure of the evidence supporting the violations, the right to testify on one's own behalf, the right to cross examine witnesses, the right to call witnesses on one's own behalf, the right to have the violation hearing heard by a neutral hearing officer, and a right to have the decision in writing. The Court also found that unless unusual grounds exist to deny the probationer an attorney, he or she has a right to legal representation. The Supreme

Court also established a two-stage process for the hearing. The first stage, the preliminary revocation hearing, allows the court to examine whether there is sufficient evidence or probable cause to believe the probationer has violated the terms and conditions of his or her probation. If probable cause exists, the matter is set for a formal revocation hearing. In practice, usually only one hearing is necessary when the probationer admits to the violation. At the initial hearing, the charges are read and if the offender admits to the charges he or she is allowed to make a statement to the court explaining the circumstances leading to the violations. In most instances the probation officers is also present in court and either has made a recommendation in the violation report or is asked to make a recommendation in open court at the hearing.

In the public's mind probation and parole are frequently used interchangeably, however there are significant differences. In many jurisdictions probation is a county function whereas parole is a state function. Persons placed on probation are generally less serious offenders whereas persons released on parole are more serious criminals having been committed to a period of imprisonment in excess of 1 year. Many parolees are released to parole supervision sometimes after serving many years in prison. Although probation is frequently viewed as an alternative to incarceration, supervision frequently follows a split sentence wherein probation is combined with a short period of incarceration in the local jail. Although there are considerable differences in the approaches taken by probation and parole agencies, probation officers are more likely to stress the social worker role whereas parole officers are more likely to be law-enforcement oriented. Many parole jurisdictions also require that their officers carry weapons. However, in some jurisdictions the probation and parole functions are combined and officers will supervise both probationers and parolees as is the case in the U.S. probation system.

Although there are a number of indicators to use in evaluating the success of probation in the U.S., historically, rearrest rates or recidivism has been the major factor used to determine effectiveness. In this regard, probation has not proven to significantly reduce recidivism rates.

SAM TORRES

References and Further Reading

Abadinsky, Howard, 2000. *Probation and Parole* (7th Ed.), Upper Saddle River, NJ, Prentice-Hall, Inc.

Augustus, John, 1972. *John Augustus: First Probation Officer*, Montclair, NJ, Patterson-Smith. (First published in 1939 by the National Probation Association under the title *A Report: Labors of John Augustus for the First Ten Years in the Aid of the Unfortunate*).

Allen, Harry E. and Clifford E. Simonsen, 2001. *Corrections in America: An Introduction* (9th Ed.), Upper Saddle River, NJ, Prentice-Hall, Inc.

Carter, Robert M. and Leslie T. Wilkins, 1976. *Probation, Parole, and Community Corrections* (2nd Ed.). New York, John Wiley and Sons, Inc.

Champion, Dean J. 1996. *Probation, Parole, and Community Corrections* (2nd Ed.), Upper Saddle River, NJ, Prentice-Hall, Inc.

Clear, Todd R. and Harry R. Dammer, 2000. *The Offender and the Community*, Belmont, CA, Wadsworth/Thomas Learning.

Clear, Todd R. and George F. Cole, 2000. *American Corrections* (5th Ed.), Belmont, CA, Wadsworth/Thomas Learning.

Cromwell, Paul F. and Rolando V. Del Carmen 1999. *Community-Based Corrections* (4th Ed.), Belmont, CA, West/Wadsworth.

Dressler, David, 1959. *Practice and Theory of Probation and Parole*, New York, New York: Colombia University Press.

McCarthy, Belinda R. and Bernard J. McCarthy, Jr., 1997. *Community-Based Corrections* (3rd Ed.), Belmont, CA, Wadsworth Publishing Company.

Morris, Norval and Michael Tonry, 1990. *Between Prison and Probation*, New York, New York: Oxford University Press.

Silverman, Ira J. 2001. *Corrections: A Comprehensive View* (2nd Ed.), Belmont, CA, Wadsworth/Thomas Learning.

See also **Careers in Probation and Parole; Presentence Investigation Reports**

Probation and Parole: Careers

The American Correctional Association sets the following standard for entry-level probation and parole field positions: "An entry-level probation or parole officer possesses a minimum of a bachelor's degree or has completed a career development program that includes work-related experience, training, or college credits [and provides] a level of achievement equivalent to a bachelor's degree." Virtually all probation and parole agencies require at least a bachelor's degree, usually in a relevant major: sociology, criminal justice, psychology, or social work. Some require graduate education in a relevant field or counseling experience, and some agencies permit relevant experience to substitute for up to 2 years of the educational requirement (Abadinsky, 2000, 332).

Probation and parole officers have a common goal to protect the public. In some jurisdictions, like California, the functions are separated with each county having its own probation department whereas the state department of corrections administers the prison and parole system. Therefore, in California one has, for example, Los Angeles County probation officers preparing presentence investigation reports and supervising juvenile and adult probationers. Parole agents, in contrast, are employed by the California Department of Corrections (CDC) and supervise persons released from state prison. Another state agency, the California Youth Authority (CYA) supervises juvenile offenders who have been released from state institutions. Other states, such as Arkansas, Delaware, and Missouri, combine probation and parole functions into state departments of corrections or community corrections.

Probation and parole officers are responsible to supervise and assist in the offenders' adjustment to the community without becoming engaged in further criminal activity. An offender on probation may or may not have served a period of time in a local jail or juvenile hall. Once released from custody the offender is typically placed on probation if released from jail or given parole if released from state or federal prison. The majority of offenders are supervised by some combination of county or state probation or parole officers since the overwhelming number of offenders commit state crimes. However, if an offender is convicted of a federal offense he or she will be supervised by a U.S. probation officer. Probation officers in the federal system are, in effect, both probation and parole officers, and supervise offenders who have been placed on probation with little or no custody and also supervise persons who are released from federal prison, often after serving many years of imprisonment. Federal probation or parole officers supervise almost exclusively adult offenders, whereas county and state officers are assigned to either adult or juvenile caseloads. In large, urban, metropolitan areas, probation officers may be assigned to a juvenile facility, conduct presentence investigation reports, or be assigned to a variety of field supervision units. In smaller jurisdictions, probation officers will perform both presentence investigation and supervision functions.

As officers of the court, a major responsibility of probation officers is to prepare presentence reports to aid the court in sentencing. They also are charged with

enforcing general and specific conditions of probation as may be ordered by the court. Parole agents, although not involved in the preparation of presentence reports also prepare different types of investigative reports, like the prerelease investigation, and also must enforce conditions of release as ordered by parole boards. In conducting the presentence investigation, probation officers will interview offenders, families, victims, witnesses, police officers, and others concerned to assess a defendant's suitability for probation. The presentence investigation officer may also recommend prison sentences. The probation or parole officer has a dual role of being a social worker and law enforcer.

As a social worker, the officer provides assistance as may be needed by the offender. As law enforcers they may be required to administer urine drug tests, conduct searches, seize evidence, conduct surveillance, verify residence and employment, and possibly make arrests. Parole officers develop recommendations and plans for inmates before they are released from prison and also arrange for services, such as employment, housing, medical care, counseling, education, and social activities.

Probation and parole officers supervise offenders who may be violent, use drugs and alcohol, manifest mental problems, and possess minimal job skills. The neighborhoods in which they work may also be dangerous and in some jurisdictions officers are required to carry a firearm. In California, state parole agents are required to carry a weapon although most county probation departments do not authorize the carrying of firearms. Some counties do, however, allow some officers to carry a weapon if they are assigned to a high risk function, like an inner city gang unit. In the federal system, out of 94 judicial districts, all but 11 allow federal probation officers to carry firearms. Probation officers are frequently required to appear in court at the time of sentencing or when a probationer is returned to court for a probation violation. Parole agents, although generally not required to appear in court, are frequently required to attend parole board violation hearings. In both instances, probation and parole officers may be required to testify in court or at a parole board hearing as to the facts of a violation. An important part of a probation or parole officer's work is necessary to go into the community and become knowledgeable of the resources available to offenders. Probation and parole officers are also responsible for supervising offenders on electronic monitoring or home confinement and other community control programs. Caseloads vary significantly by jurisdiction. County probation officers may be assigned 60–150 juvenile cases. Adult caseloads can vary from 25, for intensive supervision, to well over 300 or more in some counties. When caseloads exceed 100, the job of a probation officer becomes little more that processing necessary paperwork with little meaningful supervision and assistance to offenders. The amount of time spent in travel and field work varies, depending on the assignment and geographic area covered. In rural areas, a great deal of travel is usually necessary.

The average caseload for parole officers is between 80 and 120 active cases. Like probation officers, parole officer or agents are subject to calendar deadlines and this can be a source of great stress. Presentence investigation reports have specific deadlines and must be available to the judge, district attorney, and defense counsel by a certain date prior to sentencing. For parole agents, parole plans must be returned to the institution by certain dates and a variety of reports must also be submitted to parole boards in a timely fashion. Most probation agencies expect the number of probation officers to grow rapidly because of prison overcrowding and the greater use of community-based sanctions, such as electronic monitoring, drug treatment, day treatment, and work furlough programs. State correctional agencies also indicate that there will be a need for additional parole officer over the next few years, however, the actual number of openings will depend on the funding of these agencies.

Salaries vary considerably from jurisdiction to jurisdiction, with some salaries starting as low as $20,000. Most salaries for probation and parole officers range from $30,000 to $60,000. Salaries throughout California vary with the size of the county and with the amount of education and experience required. Starting salaries for counties in California range from $2200 to $2500 a month with increases to $4800 a month or more. A California state parole agent I starts at $3299 a month and can reach $4642 a month. State parole agents are also provided with a state vehicle for use on the job. A federal probation or parole officer starts at approximately $2465, however, after a few years can earn between $50,000 and $85,000 depending on years employed and promotion to a senior officer position. These figures are for line officer positions and do not include higher levels. For example, a California parole agent can be promoted to agent II, III, or higher administrative positions. Federal probation or parole officers can be promoted to a senior officer position, supervisor, deputy assistant chief, deputy chief, and ultimately chief probation officer. Benefits include medical, dental, pension plan, vacation, sick leave, and life insurance plans. In some jurisdictions, like the federal system, safety retirement allows early retirement at age 50 with 20 years of service. The federal system has mandatory retirement at age 57. The normal work week is 40 hours, however, probation and parole officers typically experience a great deal of flexibility in their work schedules because evening and weekend work may be required.

Probation and parole applicants should be in good physical condition and experience sound emotional stability because the work is demanding, stressful, and oftentimes rigorous. As noted, there is often considerable pressure from deadlines and a heavy workload. In addition, probation and parole officers must work with generally uncooperative clients who are agitated, antagonistic, violent, and manipulative offenders and their families. For both probation and parole officers graduation from an accredited 4-year college or university with a major in one of the social sciences is necessary. Although a degree in the social sciences is preferred by most agencies, some will accept applicants with a degree in other majors like English, history, or communications. Excellent people, writing, and analytical skills are also required. Applicants are usually given a written and oral test and may be required to submit to a psychological examination. In California, probation officers are also required to complete, within the first year of employment, the 200-hour basic core probation officer training course certified by the California State Board of Corrections. Parole agent applicants must pass a physical abilities test, have an additional year of supervised casework experience, and complete a 4-week training session at the academy in addition to the degree. Many federal districts require a graduate degree, some graduate level courses, or prior probation or parole experience. Most probation and parole-officer positions begin at the entry-level position of probation officer or parole agent I and later advancing to probation officer II. Further promotional opportunities may include probation or parole officer III, supervisor, or administrative positions.

Major benefits of the probation- or parole-officer position include satisfaction obtained from helping others, providing a service to the community, good-to-excellent pay depending on jurisdiction, excellent benefits, and a flexible work schedule. The probation or parole officer also has a great deal of discretion in deciding whether to work in the office on a particular day or instead do field work. Officers also interact with a variety of people including offenders, employers, social agencies, local, state, or federal police, judges, defense attorneys, and district attorneys to name only a few. With reasonable parameters, probation or parole officers also exercise a great deal of discretion in determining how to address probation or parole violations. Occupational problems include low pay in some jurisdictions, working with dangerous offenders, burn-out, stress from deadlines, confrontation with offenders and their families, and a tremendous amount of paperwork.

SAM TORRES

References and Further Reading

Abadinsky, Howard, 2000. *Probation and Parole* (7th Ed.), Upper-Saddle River, NJ, Prentice-Hall, Inc.

Allen, Harry E. and Clifford E. Simonsen, 2001. *Corrections in America: An Introduction* (9th Ed.), Upper-Saddle River, NJ, Prentice-Hall, Inc., 2001.

Champion, Dean J. 1996. *Probation, Parole, and Community Corrections* (2nd Ed.), Upper-Saddle River, NJ, Prentice-Hall, Inc.

Clear, Todd R. and Harry R. Dammer, 2000. *The Offender and the Community,* Belmont, CA, Wadsworth or Thomas Learning.

Clear, Todd R. and George F. Cole, 2000. *American Corrections* (5th Ed.), Belmont, CA, Wadsworth or Thomas Learning.

Cromwell, Paul F. and Rolando V. Del Carmen, 1996. *Community-Based Corrections* (4th Ed.), Belmont, CA, West or Wadsworth.

Harr, J. Scott, and Karen M. Hess, 2000. *Seeking Employment in Criminal Justice and Related Fields,* Belmont, CA, Wadsworth or Thomas Learning.

Hutton, Donald B. and Anna Mydlarz, 1997. *Guide to Law Enforcement Careers,* Hauppauge, New York: Barron's Educational Series, Inc.

Silverman, Ira J., 2001. *Corrections: A Comprehensive View* (2nd Ed.), Belmont, CA, Wadsworth or Thomas Learning.

Stephens, W. Richard Jr., 1999. *Careers in Criminal Justice,* Needham Heights, MA, Allyn & Bacon.

See also **Corrections: Careers**

Problem-Oriented Policing: Crime Prevention *See* **Police: Contemporary Developments**

Prohibition

Prohibition was a nationwide effort in the U.S. that forbade, by law, the manufacture, importation, exportation, transportation, and sale of alcoholic beverages. It began on January 16, 1920, in compliance with the Eighteenth Amendment (National Prohibition) to the U.S. Constitution and ended 13 years later with the repeal of that Amendment. Prohibition also refers to the era during which the Eighteenth Amendment was in force.

The history of alcohol use in America shows that there was no widespread condemnation of spirituous liquor during the 17th and 18th centuries. Nor was there any organized attempt to restrict its use. Throughout the American colonies alcoholic drink, in the form of beer, rum, wine, and hard cider, was part of the staple of daily diet. Alcoholic beverages were more abundant, safer, and less expensive than impure water, unpasteurized milk, tea, or coffee. Although they denounced individual excesses, the colonists agreed that, because of its medicinal properties, the use of alcoholic beverages was beneficial. They did not regard the high level of consumption as problematic. Restraint was necessary only for those individuals who openly displayed their over-indulgence. Preventing public drunkenness was the main reason why the governing authorities in the 13 colonies enacted laws to restrict the liquor traffic. In Puritan New England intemperance was seen as contrary to the Calvinist principles of self-denial. Legislative measures were attempts at suppressing excessive drinking. Nevertheless, the colonists did not intend to completely prohibit the consumption of alcohol.

Another reason for the regulation of the liquor trade during this time was to collect revenue for the public treasury. This was done by imposing duties on the importation of wines and distilled spirits as well as imposing an excise tax on the domestic production of liquor. After the American Revolution the liquor laws did not change much when they were reenacted by the new state governments.

The concept of alcohol addiction was unknown to most Americans during the 18th century. Dr. Benjamin Rush, in his pamphlet, *An Inquiry into the Effects of Ardent Spirits upon the Human Body and Mind* (1784), popularized the idea that distilled spirits were addictive to everyone. He argued that disease, nervous affection, and mental derangement were caused by the excessive use of intoxicants. Various social problems were also attributed to the high consumption of alcohol. Rush wrote in his pamphlet: "We see poverty and misery, crimes and infamy, diseases and death, are all the natural and usual consequences of the intemperate use of ardent spirits." Rush's views were quickly and widely accepted.

Thoroughly disgusted with the drinking habits of the clergy in his own religion, Presbyterian pastor Lyman Beecher recommended in 1812, that the use of ardent spirits be restricted at all church meetings. Soon thereafter, Beecher and his associates formed the Connecticut Society for the Reformation of Morals and attacked a wide range of social problems including overindulgence in drink. The following year saw the creation of the Massachusetts Society for the Suppression of Intemperance. Its leadership consisted of distinguished politicians, clergy, and businessmen who were defenders of Calvinist theology. Both societies saw their first task as that of education. It was believed that, through moral suasion and example, individuals could learn to achieve temperance, that is, the moderate use of alcoholic beverages. Before long, the campaign for reform had extended far beyond Connecticut and Massachusetts.

During the first two decades of the 19th century, the idea of temperance was zealously embraced by several evangelical Protestant ministers who preached against the ravages of ardent spirits. Temperance was a middle-class reform because it articulated most forcefully the theme of self-control that constituted the foundation of the middle-class lifestyle at that time. Soon many of these reformers attacked not intemperance, but moderate drinking. They argued that nothing less than full prohibition could be the objective of the reform movement.

The American Society for the Promotion of Temperance was formed in 1826 for the purpose of carrying a nationwide campaign. The reform movement began to gain most of its support from organized religion including the Presbyterian, Congregational, Dutch Reformed, Methodist, and Baptist congregations. Other supporters were recruited from the ranks of medicine, business, and agriculture. By 1835, the movement could claim a membership of 1.5 million members in more than 8000 auxiliaries.

In 1836, the American Temperance Union was created as a national organization. That same year legislative temperance societies were established in the various states. Politicians quickly joined these societies, believing that they had something to gain by accepting the standards of the reformers. The temperance movement had a following, which was well-organized, and reformers felt confident that their objective was within reach. Some of them began calling for legislative enactments against manufacturers and sellers of intoxicating liquor. Prohibition through legal coercion quickly gathered force.

In 1838, Massachusetts passed a statute, the "15 gallon law," that served as a model for similar legislation in other states. The statute forbade the retail sale of spirituous liquors in less quantity than 15 gallons. The law was directly aimed at severely curtailing the sale of distilled spirits in taverns and saloons. However, in the late 1840s, massive immigration to America from countries with strong drinking cultures led to a rise in the drinking population. Indulgent attitudes toward drink became more popular as Irish, German, Polish, Italian, Greek, and Jewish immigrants arrived in the U.S. Accustomed by their cultures to drink some

kind of alcoholic beverage, these immigrant groups had set back the progress that the temperance forces had made. Believing that drinking was a threat to society, the strategy of legislative reform became increasingly important to the prohibitionists, or "drys."

The state of Maine led the way in making illegal the retail sale of intoxicants. In 1851, the governor of Maine approved a statewide prohibition act that forbade the manufacture and sale of intoxicating liquors. The Maine Law served as a sign that the temperance movement based on moral suasion had been transformed into a movement for prohibition through the coercive power of legislation. By 1855, 12 more states had adopted prohibition laws.

The dry movement gradually attained increasing importance in the political arena when the Prohibition party was organized in 1869. The Prohibition party aspired to the status of a third political party alongside Republicans and Democrats. Promising a stronger legislative effort than the Maine law, the Prohibition party campaigned to get its officers elected to Congress, the state legislatures, and the presidency. It wanted prohibition adopted by the various states in the form of a constitutional amendment.

During the 1870s, more and more women became involved in the crusade as they blamed alcohol for the neglect by husbands of their wives and children. With the founding of the Woman's Christian Temperance Union (WCTU) in 1874, women eventually took the lead in the movement and called for universal abstinence. WCTU member Carry A. Nation waged her one-woman campaign against Demon Rum by destroying saloons with a hatchet. Before long, women all over the country, fired by Nation's example, also began wielding hatchets and reducing saloons to shards.

The belief that women's nature was inherently more moral and ethical than that of men allowed them to be seen as uniquely fitted to bring about a better society. Frances E. Willard was elected president of the WCTU in 1879 and during the next two decades the organization prospered under her leadership. The WCTU had a new aim than that previously taken by the movement: constitutional prohibition in the states adopted by statewide referendum. By 1890, the organization could claim nearly 150,000 members.

Although the eradication of the liquor trade was the ultimate goal of the dry forces, banishment of the saloon became their first strategy. Founded in 1893, the Anti-Saloon League became a national organization 2 years later. The League's general counsel and legislative superintendent was Wayne B. Wheeler. In 1913, the Anti-Saloon League launched the campaign for national prohibition and sought to severely dismantle the liquor industry by constitutional amendment.

The liquor industry comprised the manufacture of beer, wine, and spirits by brewers, vintners, and distillers, as well as its sale by wholesalers and retailers.

The Anti-Saloon League achieved its goal in 1920 when the 18th Amendment, which Wheeler helped draft, took effect. Approved by Congress and ratified by the states, the Eighteenth Amendment banned "the manufacture, sale, or transportation of intoxicating liquors." An intoxicating liquor was defined as one with 0.5% alcohol content. Most alcohol production was therefore rendered illegal. Alcohol could still be used for certain legitimate purposes. Industrial alcohol was used in the manufacturing of such products as paints, explosives, photographic film, and vacuum tubes. Whiskey was allowed for medicinal purposes when prescribed by a physician. Altar wine was used legally for sacramental purposes in church communion. The breweries could manufacture only "near beer," a product that consisted of 0.5% alcohol per volume.

Despite these strict regulations, alcohol was illegally obtained in a variety of ways: first, by converting denatured (poisoned) alcohol for use in industry into drinkable liquor that was later sold at exorbitant prices in speakeasies, or unlicensed saloons. The production of industrial alcohol had increased from 57 million gallons in 1923, to 92 million gallons in 1928. Much of the denatured alcohol was not thoroughly cleaned and often contained traces of one or more poisons including wood alcohol, hydrochloric acid, phenol, benzol, and iodine.

A second source of alcohol was "moonshining," or home brewing from illicit stills. The mash from which moonshine was distilled consisted of a blend of sugar, water, yeast, and garbage. "Bathtub gin" was made from a mixture of alcohol, glycerin, and oil of juniper. In 1929 alone, 27,336 stills had been seized by federal agents. The low-quality liquor obtained from diverted industrial alcohol and home brewing led to alcoholic poisoning that caused blindness, paralysis, jakitis, gingerfoot, internal bleeding, and death. By 1927, over 11,000 deaths had been attributed to poisoned alcohol.

Another way of obtaining liquor was by "rum running," or smuggling it into the U.S. from Canada, Mexico, and the West Indies. The smuggling was done by land, air, and sea. Attempting to avoid the U.S. Coast Guard, fleets of rum-running vessels were stationed along the coastal "Rum Row" between Atlantic City and New York. They sold their cargo—mainly scotch and rye—to customers in speedboats who would meet the contrabandists just outside American territorial waters. The Department of Justice reported in 1928 that smuggling from Canada had increased by more than 75% since 1925. It is estimated that by the end of the 1920s more than 1 million gallons of Canadian liquor per year were smuggled into the U.S. People found

many innovative ways of concealing small quantities of the contraband: in extra-deep pockets in specially tailored clothing, in Christmas trees, hot-water bottles, hidden compartments in cars, hollow books, and the like.

Alcohol could also be obtained by medical prescription. The Willis-Campbell Act of 1921 prohibited physicians from prescribing beer as medicine, wine with more than 24% alcohol, or more than a half pint of hard liquor to any patient within a 10-day period. Furthermore, doctors could only write 100 prescriptions for alcohol every 90 days. Nevertheless, on average, 10 million of these prescriptions were issued by physicians every year of prohibition. In the first 6 months of prohibition more than 72,000 physicians, druggists, and drug manufacturers applied for licenses to prescribe and sell medicinal liquor.

Finally, intoxicating drink could be had either by increasing the alcohol content of near beer or just continuing traditional brewing. The process of making near beer involved the manufacture of the genuine product and then reducing its alcohol content to the legal limit of 0.5%. Some brewers simply sold real beer directly to bootleggers.

Enforcement of the amendment was provided by the Volstead Act which indicated that, "any person who manufactures or sells liquor … shall for a first offense be fined no more than $1,000 or imprisoned not exceeding six months, and for a second offense shall be fined not less than $20 nor more than $2,000 and be imprisoned not less than one month nor more than five years." Volstead also devised the Prohibition Unit (later called the Prohibition Bureau), a federal agency with a total number of agents that never exceeded more than 2300. Two of the Bureau's more colorful agents, Isadore "Izzy" Einstein and Moe Smith, had by 1925 made nearly 5000 arrests and confiscated 5 million bottles of liquor. Thousands of people were regarded as criminals for making, distributing, and selling alcohol.

The Jones Act of 1929 made Volstead violations a felony as it increased the minimum penalties to 5-year imprisonment or a fine of $10,000 or both. That year the Census Bureau showed that the number of prisoners in federal and state penitentiaries had risen disproportionately to the increases in population and was continuing to rise. There was little doubt that Prohibition had increased lawlessness.

National prohibition proved to be virtually unenforceable because a sizeable segment of the American population ignored the federal ban. Most people could not equate having a drink with committing a crime. In addition, they were curious and found drinking more appealing than when it was legal.

The problems of enforcement were major and they included the bootlegging of industrial alcohol;

overburdened judicial and penal systems; the corruption of police and city government; insufficient funds; and although the 18th Amendment had called for "concurrent" enforcement by the federal government and the states, there was a great reluctance on the part of the states to share in the cost of enforcement. The law led to seizures of property, violence, and killings by law enforcement agents and bootleggers alike. It is estimated that between 1920 and 1929, 135 criminals and 55 prohibition officers were killed as a direct consequence of the enforcement laws.

Aware of the immense profits that prohibition could provide, gangsters and racketeers became involved in the illicit liquor business. In Chicago, Johnny Torrio, Al Capone, and other leaders in organized crime began to supply public demand for alcohol. They did so by protecting its production and consumption, usually by bribing politicians, police, and other officials.

As a result of constant internecine fighting between competing criminal gangs—like the Terrible Gennas, the South Side O'Donnell's, and Capone's syndicate—the beer wars in Chicago led to the death of about 484 gangsters between 1922 and 1930. Another 220 were killed by police between 1922 and 1926. Some of the gangsters involved in the beer wars included Dion O'Banion, Earl "Hymie" Weiss, George "Bugs" Moran, Jake "Greasy Thumb" Guzik, and Frank "The Enforcer" Nitti. Capone paid bribes of approximately $30 million a year to about half the police force of Chicago. The gang warfare in that city reached a climax with the St. Valentine's Day Massacre of February 14, 1929, when six members of the O'Banion gang were killed in a warehouse. They were lured there by an offer of highjacked whiskey smuggled in from Canada. As the gangsters were waiting for the shipment to arrive, a Cadillac with a driver and four passengers, two of whom were wearing police uniforms, entered the warehouse, lined up the six hoodlums against the wall and shot them. No one was ever convicted of the crime but most police officials believed it had been orchestrated by Al Capone.

Another underworld figure who profited from prohibition was Arnold Rothstein. He employed gangsters such as Frank Costello, Charles "Lucky" Luciano, and Meyer Lansky in setting up his bootleg business in New York. Rothstein became the most important dealer in illegal liquor along the Atlantic seaboard.

As a result of the Great Depression that had begun to sweep the country in 1929, the idea of repealing prohibition as a possible solution to the economic crisis had a renewed appeal. Consequently, the most pressing reason for resurrecting the liquor business was financial. The anti-Prohibitionists, or "wets," argued that the liquor business would give people the opportunity to work in breweries, distilleries, wine presses, and liquor stores. Another argument was that farmers would benefit economically if the supply of grain to breweries were begun again. The wet forces also popularized the idea that criminal activity, government corruption, and general disrespect for the law had increased as a direct result of Prohibition.

Several anti-Prohibition organizations gained strength throughout the 1920s. These included the National Association Opposed to Prohibition, the Moderation League, the American Veterans' Association for Repeal of the 18th Amendment, the Association against the Prohibition Movement, and the Women's Organization for National Prohibition Reform that brought into question the WCTU's right to speak for women on the issue of liquor control.

Franklin D. Roosevelt, as governor of New York, continued to straddle the issue of Prohibition until the summer of 1930. By then public sentiment against the 18th Amendment had grown sufficiently strong for him to feel confident in supporting its repeal. In 1932, when Roosevelt was nominated the presidential candidate of the Democratic party, he endorsed the nullification of Prohibition. His election in November all but ensured its total defeat. On December 6, 1932, Senator John J. Blaine introduced to Congress S. J. Resolution 211 (the Twenty-First Amendment), the abolition of the Eighteenth Amendment. It is the only amendment to the Federal Constitution that has ever been repealed. The Twenty-First Amendment became law and national prohibition ended on December 5, 1933.

A. JAVIER TREVIÑO

References and Further Reading

Behr, E. 1996. *Prohibition: Thirteen Years that Changed America*, New York, Arcade Publishers.

Cashman, S.D. 1981. *Prohibition: The Lie of the Land*, New York, Free Press.

Clark, N.H. 1676. *Deliver Us from Evil: An Interpretation of American Prohibition*, New York, Norton.

Gusfield, J.R. 1986. *Symbolic Crusade: Status Politics and the American Temperance Movement*, 2nd ed., Chicago, University of Illinois Press.

Hintz, M. 1996. *Farewell, John Barleycorn: Prohibition in the U.S.*, Minneapolis, Lerner Publications Co.

Kobler, J. 1993. *Ardent Spirits: The Rise and Fall of Prohibition*, New York, Da Capo Press.

Krout, J.A. 1925. *The Origins of Prohibition*, New York, Knopf.

Pegram, T.R. 1999. *Battling Demon Rum: The Struggle for a Dry America, 1800–1933*, Chicago, IL, Ivan R. Dee.

Sinclair, A. 1986. *Prohibition: The Era of Excess*, Norwalk, CT, Easton Press.

See also **Disorderly Conduct or Disturbing the Peace; Organized Crime: Activities and Extent; Organized Crime: Irish, Jewish, and German Mobsters; Organized Crime: Italian American Mafia; Public Drunkenness**

Prosecuting Attorneys

Introduction

Prosecuting attorneys have authority to initiate, handle, and terminate court procedures to invoke the formal sanctioning powers of criminal laws. Prosecutors are law enforcement officers and part of the immense criminal justice system's mechanism of social control. Prosecutors typically receive cases from police officers, who have investigated incidents and made arrests. Prosecutors then pursue the case toward its final disposition, whether it be conviction or dismissal, fine, probation, jail, or even death. Prosecutors make daily decisions that dramatically affect individual lives.

In state courts, prosecuting attorneys are found at differing levels. The nominal head of prosecution is the state attorney general, who is typically an elected official. The attorney general has a staff of assistants who handle a limited number of criminal cases. The vast majority of state court felony prosecution is conducted in individual districts or circuits, under the supervision of a chief prosecuting attorney, often called the district attorney. This attorney is typically an elected official who has virtually unfettered discretion over prosecution in the district. The district attorney generally hires a staff of young assistants to handle the majority of cases. In 2001, nearly 25% of all state court felony cases involved violent crimes, such as assault (12.1%), robbery (5.4%), murder (1.6%), and rape (0.9%) (Bureau of Justice Statistics 2003 III). Drug offenses during the same year constituted about 37% of total felonies. These prosecutions are handled by individual districts in a fragmented system that typically does not share prosecuting resources. The state prosecution system's decentralization is problematic as overburdened districts cannot shift their burden to other districts. As a consequence, within a state, case age may vary dramatically from district to district.

At the municipal level, city attorneys are city employees who handle minor, magistrate-level offenses such as alcohol offenses, disorderly conduct, and vagrancy. Like district attorneys, the city attorney's office functions as an independent unit and may employ a staff of assistants. There are at least 5000 city attorneys nationwide.

Federal courts, by contrast, are centralized under the control of the U.S. Attorney General, the nation's chief law enforcement officer, who heads the Department of Justice. Federal court prosecution is handled by attorneys in the 93 U.S. Attorneys' offices, as well as the Department of Justice's Criminal Division. Although federal court jurisdiction extends throughout the U.S., state felony caseloads far exceed their federal counterparts. For example, in 2000, state court prosecutors secured 920,000 felony convictions, compared to just 60,000 felony convictions by federal prosecutors (Bureau of Justice Statistics 2003 I). Federal jurisdiction typically involves crimes that are interstate in character or involve federal property, so, unsurprisingly, federal prosecutors handle different types of cases than their state counterparts. In 2001, nearly one-third of federal cases were drug related and approximately one-fourth were property related, whereas only 5% involved violence (Bureau of Justice Statistics 2003 IV). Immigration (13%) and weapons (7%) crimes comprised a significant portion of federal prosecutions (ibid). Federal crimes often have concurrent jurisdiction with state crimes, that is, an offender may be violating state and federal law at the same time. In most cases, however, federal courts do not prosecute after a state court prosecution.

The Changing Face of Prosecution

Prosecution offices have experienced considerable strain in the last 20 years. Even though overall crime rates have generally decreased over the last 15 years, court dockets continued to grow. There was a 65% increase in state court felony filings between 1984 and 1998 (Ostrom and Kauder, 1999). The increase in felony filings increased prosecutor caseloads and clogged court dockets. The court system's failure to manage the increased volume led to an onerous condition: Each year, prosecution offices are disposing of fewer cases than are filed (Neubauer, 2002, 250). Consequently, the average age of a case from arrest to disposition has increased. Prosecutors typically cannot try a case prior to 1 year from arrest; trials for out-of-jail defendants often stretch to 2 years from arrest. Delayed cases have a variety of costs: Prosecutors are more likely to dismiss older cases or give them a lenient disposition. Witnesses may disappear, evidence may be lost, or new prosecutors may arrive, with no desire to handle another prosecutor's problem. Jailed defendants typically remain in jail, and the community suffers higher jail bills and a loss of productivity. Bonded defendants, at a defense attorney's advice, are often in no hurry to settle their cases, as the defense attorney recognizes the favorable outcome that may result from an aging case.

As the size of prosecution offices increases, prosecutorial functions are becoming increasingly technical. Scientific evidence is increasingly commonplace in serious cases, requiring greater technical sophistication from prosecutors. For example, in 2001, two-thirds of prosecution offices handled DNA evidence, compared to approximately half in 1996 (Bureau of Justice Statistics, 2001). Drug prosecution requires at least elementary knowledge of chemistry in handling expert witnesses. Driving under the influence prosecution necessitates knowing basics of blood chemistry and breath-testing procedures. Sex crime prosecutors must be able to intelligently assess fluid and rape trauma evidence and be able to interact with relevant experts. In all these specialized prosecution scenarios, the attorney must have sufficient command of the subject matter to be able to effectively cross-examine defense experts. Increasingly, urban crimes are migrating to rural areas, as evidenced by the spread of methamphetamine production and gangs. Such new criminal activities place increased demands on smaller, nonspecialized offices. At the same time, legal and criminal record-keeping databases are proliferating, allowing electronic research and coordination to an unprecedented degree. Many offices research legal issues online and run rap sheets electronically.

The enormous increases in felony filings prompted a 39% increase in prosecution staff between 1992 and 2001 (Bureau of Justice Statistics, 2001). In 2001, there were 2341 state court prosecutors' offices employing nearly 80,000 attorneys, investigators, and support staff (Ibid). Large-district offices (those serving districts comprising at least 250,000 people) moved 1,000,000 felony cases while maintaining an 85% conviction rate. Despite the increases in office size and caseloads, prosecution frequently has a small-town face. Nearly 25% of all prosecution offices employed only part-time prosecutors, approximately 50% had nine or fewer attorneys, and 90% served districts of less than 250,000 people.

Prosecution has progressively become a less viable long-term career choice. Increased caseloads have contributed to prosecutor turnover by increasing job strain (Gomme and Hall, 1995). Prosecutors may tire of the daily exposure to the harsh realities of victimization or the stresses of the courtroom. Larger bureaucratic structures may discourage young attorneys by creating impediments to high-level promotions. But financial security is likely the biggest reason for the experience drain (see, e.g., Glater, 2003). Between 1987 and 1997, the cost of law schools nearly doubled, whereas typical indebtedness doubled to between $70,000 and $80,000 (NAPIL, 2000). Some young attorneys assumed loan debts of $150,000 (ibid). Like a second mortgage, the enormous monthly payment on student loans makes public service work a financial strain. Although assistant prosecutors typically make more than public defenders, they make considerably less than individuals in private practice, and the wage gulf widens each year. Compounding the wage problem is potential job instability. If a new district attorney is elected, the incumbent's entire staff may be looking for work. In Colorado, as an extreme, district attorney term limits have forced district attorneys to seek other careers. In light of all these factors, assistant prosecutors typically stay between 1 and 5 years before moving to other jobs with higher salaries. The resulting turnover has created an experience rift in many offices, with a small number of highly experienced prosecutors with 10 or more years of experience, a large number of prosecutors with 2 or less years of experience, and few prosecutors in between (Glater, 2003).

Prosecutorial offices have responded to the problems of volume, specialization, and turnover by increased bureaucratization and specialization. Large districts often have numerous prosecutor teams who are specially trained to handle particular types of cases. Inexperienced prosecutors may, for example, handle only misdemeanors and minor felonies under the supervision of an experienced prosecutor. The most serious cases would be handled by specialized teams. Many offices have created drug, homicide, and sex-crime prosecution units.

Federal prosecution offices expanded even more rapidly than their state counterparts. Between 1981 and 1993, Justice Department staff increased fourfold (McGee and Duffy, 1997). Even after this period of explosive growth, federal felony convictions increased nearly 40% between 1994 and 2001 (from 50,701 to 68,533) (Federal Justice Statistics, 2003). In general, federal offices have more personnel stability: Federal prosecutors tend to be more experienced, better compensated, and more likely to be career prosecutors. Many federal prosecutors are, in fact, former state prosecutors.

The Day-to-Day Routine

Assistant district attorneys are graduates from 3-year law schools and have passed the bar, the state's comprehensive licensing examination. There is scant academic training available to prepare prospective prosecutors, who typically begin their prosecutorial careers as neophyte generalists forced to learn on the job. Young prosecutors undergo a socialization process wherein they internalize workgroup norms.

Prosecutors handle individual caseloads and must prioritize which cases to pursue over others. In handling their caseloads, prosecutors perform a wide variety of functions. They often represent the state at initial appearances, bail hearings, preliminary hearings, and arraignments. They handle trials and pleas. At all stages, their recommendations tend to carry great weight with judges. Additionally, prosecutors may initiate investigations and pursue warrants. In many jurisdictions, prosecutors also may issue grand jury subpoenas and question witnesses before juries. In preparing a case for trial, a prosecutor typically supplements police investigations with further investigation and may even employ police officers to pursue new investigatory avenues.

The vast majority of criminal cases are resolved by plea, and, specifically, by plea bargains. Federal prosecutors, for example, settled 95% of their cases by plea in 2001 (Bureau of Justice Statistics, 2003 IV). A plea bargain is an agreement by a prosecutor to give a favorable recommendation or arrangement in exchange for a defendant's acceptance of guilt. The plea bargain could result in a sentencing recommendation or the reduction or dismissal of one or more charges. A prosecutor often relies on plea bargaining as a means of disposing of cases. This reliance is pragmatic and necessary considering the stark realities of caseloads, especially for young prosecutors handling high volumes: Prosecutors are typically outnumbered by defense attorneys. Jury trials are costly and cumbersome processes that are difficult to schedule. When trials occur, they typically take at least a day and often consume the entire work week. At many courthouses, juries are often not available every week, and, when they are, the prosecutor must compete for court time with other prosecutors. Once a case begins, the prosecutor is not moving other cases, the prosecutor's caseload grows, and jailed defendants remain in jail. Trial preparation is time consuming: A 3-day trial may take weeks of preparation. A prosecutor may also have a number of weak cases, often old and inherited, which would entail high risk at trial while absorbing valuable court time. Moreover, the caseload may have numerous old cases that must be moved. The riskiness of trials also necessitates compromise. Trials are often zero-sum games involving complete wins or complete losses; maximizing the use of court resources in such situations demands trying good cases. In this environment, if forced to try all cases, the prosecutor would not move enough cases to keep up with the influx of new cases, and the system would simply break down.

Plea bargains are a controversial aspect of prosecution work, especially as they often lead to disproportionate or unduly lenient sentences. Some defendants committing the same crime may be punished harshly, whereas others receive light sentences. In extraordinary cases, prosecutors may offer absolute immunity to one defendant in exchange for favorable testimony against another defendant. By the mid-1970s, many lawmakers, including Edward Kennedy, blamed plea bargaining for rising crime rates and advocated taking steps to reduce prosecutorial and judicial sentencing discretion.

The congressional solution was the creation of sentencing guidelines to eliminate sentencing disparities and undue leniency. Through the Sentencing Reform Act of 1984, Congress established the U.S. Sentencing Commission. The Commission formulated the Federal Sentencing Guidelines, which set a sentencing range for all federal crimes. The guidelines employ a 256-box grid through which a judge can plot a sentencing range based on offense severity and offender criminal history. The Federal Sentencing Guidelines technocratized sentencing, in that the sentencing system required training and expertise to apply; the sentencing regulations have grown to over 1000 pages. Downward departures from the guidelines are only allowed in specifically created exceptions. A primary benefit of the guidelines is that they have eliminated the consideration of extralegal factors such as race and ethnicity. However, procedural purity has come at the cost of increased punitiveness: Most individuals sentenced under the guidelines go to jail. Critics have expressed great dismay over the guidelines' undue harshness, which do not allow for leniency in unusual cases (see, e.g., Stith and Cabranes, 1998). An odd byproduct of the guidelines is that they actually serve to increase prosecutorial power relative to judicial power. Prosecutors can reduce charges or substitute other charges to achieve desired sentencing results, whereas judges must sentence from the range indicating by the charge.

State legislatures have taken steps to reduce disproportionality and leniency as well. Many states have established mandatory minimum sentences, no-probation offenses, violent offenses, and no-parole offenses. The effect of these laws is to limit the heretofore unfettered sentencing discretion of prosecutors and judges. Despite these new sentencing restrictions, however, only a handful of states have created mandatory sentencing guidelines.

Prosecutorial Decision Making

Through their use of sanctioning powers, prosecutors are tools of social control and become a touchstone for the perceived legitimacy of court power. Criminal courts are social control mechanisms that not only preserve order, but a particular power structure and the interests and values of those within the power structure (Crystal, 2001). By appearing fair and impartial, prosecutors help maintain the legitimacy of the court system. Prosecutorial actions that are perceived as unfair may undermine the public's confidence in the court system and even lead to social instability. The fairness of prosecutorial action has become particularly crucial in the contemporary criminal justice system because incarceration is increasingly relied on as a tool of social control. The prison population is at an all-time high of more than 2,000,000, and 6,700,000 individuals were either in prison, on probation, or on parole in 2002. Although prisons were filling, a demographic shift occurred involving more than half a million African Americans (Butterfield, 2002): In 1980, there were 463,700 African American male college students, compared to 143,000 African American male prisoners; by 1990, there were more African American males in prison than in college (791,600–603,032). In this newly punitive atmosphere, fair prosecutorial decisions are increasingly essential.

New criminal sentencing laws have increased the power of prosecutors. Many states have life-without-parole statutes that prosecutors may invoke at their discretion. Mandatory minimums, no-parole offenses, violent offenses, and recidivist statutes have created a sentencing arsenal that prosecutors can use either to incapacitate defendants or to terrify defendants into accepting a plea bargain.

Recognizing the critical function of prosecutors, courts hold prosecuting attorneys to higher standards than their fellow attorneys. All attorneys are officers of the court and must be candid toward the tribunal, while maintaining loosely held standards of decorum. Criminal defense attorneys are ethically required to be zealous advocates and pursue all available avenues of defense (Code of Professional Responsibility, Canon 7 1969). Under this ethical mandate, most or any trial tactic short of perpetrating a fraud is acceptable. Zealous advocates may bring the court system into disrepute by arguing for issues that they know to be false and by pursuing a despised client's benefit, regardless of social costs to victims. However, courts view the zealous advocacy ethic as an indispensable check on government abuses. Thus, for defense attorneys, the truth-finding function is subordinated to a client's interests. Surprise witnesses, evidence, and ambush tactics are not merely acceptable but expected.

In stark contrast, prosecutors are ministers of justice with special responsibility for the quality of justice in the courts. Truth seeking is the prosecutor's central ethic. Prosecutors, like judges, must abide by special ethical rules. Under the ABA Rules of Professional Conduct, Rule 3.8 (2002), a prosecutor may not prosecute a charge that is not supported by probable cause. Rule 3.8 also makes prosecutors responsible for particular rights of defendants. A prosecutor must make reasonable efforts to advise defendants not only of their right to counsel but how they can exercise that right. A prosecutor may not force a defendant to waive important pretrial rights. A prosecutor's ethical duties also extend to the court system. Rule 3.6 requires the prosecutor to avoid extrajudicial statements that may taint judicial proceedings. For example, a prosecutor, in talking to the media, must restrict comments to matters of public record and general statements about the case. Rule 3.8 requires prosecutors to take reasonable steps to limit their associates' extrajudicial statements.

The prosecutor's role is characterized by broad discretion: As an arm of law enforcement, a prosecutor must decide whether to invoke the sanctioning powers of the criminal justice system, and to what degree. A prosecutor has the authority to dismiss a case or reduce a charge, and a prosecutor's sentencing recommendations are typically accepted by the judge.

Having broad discretion places a premium on making fair and impartial decisions. Unfortunately, there is a growing body of evidence suggesting that prosecutorial decision making is influenced by extralegal factors, such as race and socioeconomic status. Studies have found, for example, that victim race affected prosecutorial decisions to seek the death penalty (Smith, 1987; Paternoster and Kazyaka, 1991; Sorenson and Wallace, 1999). Moreover, Black (1994) linked criminal court outcomes to socioeconomic status. Unfortunately, the public perception of prosecutors, along with all lawyers, is low. In a recent University of Connecticut survey of 1000 respondents (Veilleux, 2000), 80% felt that prosecutors would sometimes bend the rules to obtain confessions.

In holding prosecutors to higher standards, courts have identified types of prosecutorial misconduct, which can lead to sanctions such as mistrials, dismissals, contempt sanctions, public reprimands, and even disbarment. In pretrial contexts, prosecutors must respect a defendant's right to a fair trial by divulging potentially exculpatory evidence. Upon receiving a discovery motion, prosecutors typically must turn over most of their investigative documents, such as warrants, incident reports, witness statements, and copies of evidence to be submitted in the prosecution's case in chief. At the same time, the prosecution must allow the defense to inspect tangible evidence such as pistols, hairs, and fibers. On reciprocal prosecution motion, defense attorneys must turn over some of their evidence as well, including recorded witness statements and evidence to be used at trial. This information system is notoriously incomplete: Discovery does not even require basic information such as witness lists, interrogatories, depositions, or even interviews. Both sides often proceed to trial without knowing exactly what evidence the other side has or what tactics they will choose. The other party's ignorance may leave them vulnerable to ambush tactics, such as surprise witnesses, motions, and hidden evidence. Such tactics may pervert the trial procedure's fact-finding function by giving one side an unfair advantage. In a larger context, ambush-style procedures may harm the system's integrity by undermining public confidence in the system.

Courts have partially addressed this incomplete discovery process in favor of the defense, rather than the prosecution. Rule 3.8 requires prosecutors to give the defense any evidence that is either exculpatory or mitigates the offense. In sentencing contexts, the prosecutor must turn over all unprivileged mitigating information. Furthermore, under *Brady v. Maryland*, 373 U.S. 63 (1963), the U.S. Supreme Court held that a defendant has a constitutional right to be informed of the existence of exculpatory evidence; failure to provide such evidence violates the defendant's right to a fair trial and constitutes prosecutorial misconduct. The *Brady* rule has no defense correlate: The defense attorney has no duty to turn over inculpatory evidence.

Prosecutorial misconduct can occur in a number of contexts in addition to those mentioned in Rules 3.6 and 3.8. A prosecutor may initiate an investigation, such as an unauthorized wiretap, that violates an individual's constitutional rights. A prosecutor may vindictively prosecute an individual as part of a personal vendetta. A prosecutor may take actions at trial that taint the trial procedure, such as making improper comments about a defendant's character, referring to facts not in evidence, or by making unduly inflammatory comments. The consequences of prosecutorial misconduct can be serious, as criminal investigations and procedures involve individuals' reputations, livelihoods, and liberties. Unsurprisingly, some instances of misconduct have led to lawsuits.

As a public policy concern, courts became concerned over how to balance the corrective effect of lawsuits with a corresponding chilling effect on prosecution. Lawsuits could discourage vigorous prosecution of the laws, as well as bankrupt entire offices. *Burns v. Reed*, 500 U.S. 478 (1990), provided a bright-line prosecution standard: Prosecutors have absolute immunity for traditional prosecution actions taken while in the courtroom, whether or not such action is in bad faith. Thus improper comments or suppression of evidence will not expose a prosecutor to civil damages. However, *Burns* does not shield a prosecutor from civil liability when performing nontraditional prosecutorial functions, such as pretrial investigations or giving advice to police officers concerning such investigations. In response, prosecution offices have commonly developed in-house procedures to ensure that they will be not exposed to liability from bad advice or investigative procedures.

J. EAGLE SHUTT

References and Further Reading

ABA Model Rules of Professional Conduct, 2002. Available at: http://www.law.onu.edu/ModelRules2002.pdf. Retrieved on January 4, 2004.

Black, D., 1994. *The Social Structure of Right and Wrong,* San Diego, CA, Academic Press.

Bureau of Justice Statistics, 2001. Prosecution statistics, Available at: http://www.ojp.usdoj.gov/bjs/pros.htm. Retrieved on January 4, 2004.

Bureau of Justice Statistics, 2003. Corrections statistics. Available at: http://www.ojp.usdoj.gov/bjs/correct.htm. Retrieved on January 1, 2004.

Bureau of Justice Statistics, 2003. Criminal Case Prosecuting Statistics. Available at: http://www.ojp.usdoj.gov/bjs/fed.htm. Retrieved on January 4, 2004.

Code of Professional Responsibility, 1969. American Bar Association.

Federal Justice Statistics, 2003. Available at: http://fjsrc.urban.org. Retrieved on January 4, 2004.

Glater, J.D., Hight tuition debts and low pay drain public interest law, *New York Times,* September 12, 2003.

Gomme, I.M. and Hall, M.P., 1995. Prosecutors at work: Role overload and strain, *Journal of Criminal Justice,* 23(2), 191–200.

McGee, J. and Duffy, B., 1997. *Main Justice: The Men and Women Who Enforce the Nation's Criminal Laws and Guard Its Liberties.* New York, Simon & Schuster.

NAPIL, 2000. *Executive Summary of Financing the Future: The 2000 Report on Law School Loan Repayment Assistance and Public Interest Scholarship Programs,* Available at: http://www.equaljusticeworks.org/finance/index.php?view=detail&id=1210. Retrieved on January 4, 2004.

Paternoster, R. and Kazyaka, A.M., 1991. An examination of comparatively excessive death sentences in South Carolina 1979–1987, *New York University Review of Law and Social Change,* 17, 101–159.

Ostrom, B. and Kauder, N., 1999. *Examining the Work of State Courts, 1998,* Williamsburg, VA, National Center for State Courts.

Sentencing Reform Act of 1984. S. Rep. No. 225, 98th Cong., 1st Sess. 52, 56.

Smith, M.D., 1987. Patterns of discrimination in assessments of the death penalty: The case of Louisiana, *Journal of Criminal Justice,* 15(4), 279–286.

Sorenson, J. and Wallace, D.H., 1999. Prosecutorial discretion in seeking death: An analysis of racial disparity in the pretrial stages of case processing in a midwestern couty, *Justice Quarterly,* 16(3), 559–578.

Veilleux, R., 2000. Criminal justice poll shows distrust of America's legal system. Available at: http://www.news.uconn.edu/REL00069.htm. Retrieved online January 1, 2004.

See also **Courts in the U.S.: Structure and Function; Defense Attorneys; Law and Legal Services: Careers**

Prostitution as an Occupation

Prostitution, as defined by *Merriam-Webster's Dictionary of Law*, is the act or practice of engaging in sexual activity indiscriminately, especially for money. Although often referred to as the world's oldest profession, this occupation remains illegal in most parts of the U.S. and carries a maximum penalty of 1-year confinement.

Because of the illegal nature of this occupation determining the exact number of persons who are in the occupation of prostitution is much more difficult than determining the exact number of persons in other, "legal" occupations. In 1998, the FBI Uniform Crime Reports indicated that 63,090 persons were arrested for the crime of prostitution and commercialized vice. However, we must use caution with these statistics. For example, when law enforcement agents target only the prostitute for arrest, others who are involved in prostitution and commercialized vice, such as the pimp or the madam, are left out of the statistics. Or, when law enforcement agents target street walkers, prostitutes who work through escort services, bars, or massage parlors are not included. This then explains why some scholars have suggested that as many as 500,000 persons may be involved in prostitution at any given time, and the National Task Force on Prostitution has indicated that as many as 1 million persons in the U.S. have, at one time or another, worked as prostitutes. A cautious conclusion might simply be that a significant number of persons have been in the occupation of prostitution, but only a small percentage have devoted a lifetime to this pursuit.

Although exact numbers of persons in this occupation are difficult to determine, there is consistent agreement among scholars that prostitution is an occupation dominated by adult women. In fact, the category of prostitution and commercialized vice is one of only two categories of offenses that show higher rates of arrests for women than men, 57.8% vs. 42.2% comparatively. This is not to suggest that men and children are not working as prostitutes. As indicated above, almost 43% of all persons arrested for prostitution and criminalized vice are male. Further, the International Relief Organization suggests there are as many as 300,000 children working as prostitutes in the U.S. However, the male prostitute, like the child prostitute, is not usually included in general discussions of prostitution as an occupation. For example, when addressing the male prostitute it is important to include discussions of homosexuality or transgenderism, issues that are not easily generalized to adult women in the occupation of prostitution. And, when addressing the child prostitute, it is terribly difficult to argue that children, some as young as ten, choose prostitution as an occupation. Thus, the focus of this essay will be upon adult women, those who have been the focus of much research on prostitution as an occupation.

Though an "illegal" occupation in most parts of the U.S. prostitution has many of the same characteristics associated with other, legal occupations. For example, within many occupations there exists a hierarchy, where those at the top of the hierarchy are afforded more rewards and privileges than those at the bottom of the hierarchy. Too, linked to one's occupation are levels of income, levels of autonomy, differing working conditions, and varying levels of prestige and status.

Escorts, or call girls, are prostitutes at the top of the occupational hierarchy of prostitution. As such, escorts command higher fees, sometimes as much as several hundred dollars for a single evening. Escorts also have more control over both their clientele and their working conditions. Most escorts, or the madams for whom they work, selectively screen the client and often establish a list of regular clients. Escorts are also less visible to the public primarily because clients are met discreetly in private locales. Within this stratum of prostitutes exists a majority of white, middle class women, who are noted as being more professional in both appearance and eroticism.

Heidi Fleiss, dubbed as the Hollywood Madam by the media, garnered attention in the 1990s when she was arrested, prosecuted, and sentenced for tax evasion, money laundering, and conspiracy while operating a call girl ring in Los Angeles, California. Fueled by the speculation that she might make her list of customers public, the media coverage of Heidi Fleiss allowed the reader a glimpse into the life of prostitutes at the top of the occupational hierarchy. Through testimony, prostitutes who worked for Fleiss told of extensive national and international travel and charging as much as $10,000.00 per date.

Strippers, dancers, and, most notably, bar girls are prostitutes who find themselves below escorts in the occupational hierarchy, yet in the middle rung of the strata. Bar girls do not earn as much money as do escorts, nor are their lifestyles as flamboyant and expensive. Although bar girls may have some control over their working conditions, as in client selection, the control that they do have is more limited in nature. Most bar girls work out of clubs, bars, even hotels, and sometimes have made financial agreements with the management or employees of these establishments for referrals of customers. Most interesting is the fact that many bar girls were once in the stratum of the escort, but through the years lost their appeal and, by default, their position in the upper stratum.

Toward the lower end of the strata of prostitutes we find prostitutes who work in brothels, commonly referred to as house girls. In some counties in the state of Nevada—where brothels are legal—such establishments are run by madams. Like any other business owner, the madam (or pimp) hires, trains, and supervises the house girls. This organizational structure also limits the earnings of the house girl, as she is now financially obligated to the madam, who takes a percentage of her earnings. Secondly, the house girl loses much of the control over client selection. In states where prostitution is not legal, house girls often work out of massage parlors or other private clubs.

At the lowest level of the strata of prostitutes are street-walkers, composed primarily of poor women and women of color, who publicly solicit customers for sex. Street walkers do not command the same earnings as do other prostitutes and are not in a position to be selective with clientele. As a result, street-walkers provide comparatively cheap services to a multiple of customers, and do so in relatively short periods of time so that they can return to the streets. As indicated earlier, street walkers are more often targeted for arrest, mostly because of their higher levels of visibility. As being in the streets makes one more vulnerable to arrest, prostitutes who work the streets are also placed in many more dangerous situations. Without the security provided by madams or a more select clientele, street walkers often secure a pimp for protection. However, women at the bottom of the stratum continue to face such serious problems as physical abuse, rape, and even murder.

Most recently scholars have added another stratum of prostitutes, women who work in crack houses, exchanging sex for crack cocaine. Although little more than mention is made of this new stratum of prostitute, it is safe to argue that these prostitutes make few dollars, have little choice over customers, are subjected to some of the most severe and dangerous working conditions, and constitute those prostitutes at the very bottom of the occupational hierarchy.

Although differences are found between prostitutes in each of the stratum, there are some commonalities. As discussed, it is common for prostitutes in all strata to work for, or through, a third party. As a result, many prostitutes are turning a portion of their earnings, sometimes as much as 50%, over to a madam, a pimp, or the owner of the private club. Another commonality focuses on the prestige and status, if any, a prostitute derives from her occupation. Obviously, deriving prestige from an occupation that many find distasteful or morally wrong is challenging. However, accounts from some prostitutes, specifically escorts, reveal that they enjoy their work, their pay, and their associations. Further, many prostitutes view themselves as having healthy levels of self-esteem and define themselves as less hypocritical than the general public. For example, prostitutes often argue that they are providing a service for many married individuals who claim to be "faithful spouses."

Speculating who might choose prostitution as an occupation is not an easy task. Some might argue that it is easier to explain participation in prostitution when focusing upon the escort, who receives relatively high pay for few hours of work. But what about the violence, sexually transmitted diseases, and public contempt that is associated with this occupation? Certainly we cannot argue that one would voluntarily choose such an occupation, and rarely do we hear family members or friends indicate that they aspire to be a prostitute.

There exists no single reason to explain why women choose prostitution as an occupation. Instead, we find a multiple of accounts from these women explaining their reasons for engaging in prostitution. Many of these women knew others who were already involved in the business and through these associations learned about the business. Others report early and frequent sexual encounters, as well as sexual abuse as a children. Some studies have reported that as many as 75% of all prostitutes were raped at a young age. As such, one who has been sexually victimized by others may come to believe that this is her plight in life. Some women, as in the case of the crack house prostitute, engage in prostitution to support a drug habit. Most frequently mentioned, however, is the economic position of these women. That is, many women turn to prostitution because they are poor and live in poverty and prostitution is one of the only ways that they can generate an income.

Interestingly, Meier and Geis argue that when one reviews laws against victimless crimes, only laws against prostitution have been resistant to change. Consider the evolution of both laws and social attitudes toward other victimless crimes, such as gambling. Once criminalized throughout most of the U.S., today adults can gamble at many grocery stores and gas stations through the purchase of lottery tickets. Further, many groups who once opposed state run lotteries have silenced their opposition and now allow such activity to flourish freely and without obstruction. Comparatively, however, little movement has been made in regard to changes in either law or social attitudes regarding prostitution. Indeed, the general public has very firm opinions about the occupation of prostitution. The *Sourcebook of Criminal Justice Statistics* reports that 70% of those surveyed in the U.S. report that prostitution involving adults should remain illegal. Within these statistics women, African Americans, persons over the age of 65, persons without a college education, and persons in lower income brackets are more opposed to a change in the legal statutes surrounding prostitution.

Why such resistance to change? Meier and Geis argue that one reason for such resistance is that prostitution is a controversial sexual issue that simply does not fare well in our society. In fact, authors have often argued that our society exploits sexuality, whereas at the same time, represses it. Young adults, even children, are exposed to sexually explicit images through television, film, music, and advertisement on a daily basis. However, it remains a challenge to engage some parents, even educators, in frank and open discussions about sexuality. As a consequence, laws surrounding prostitution, which demand open and frank discussions about issues of sexuality, have not undergone the same extent of change as have laws regarding other victimless crimes. Secondly, prostitution taps into issues of morality—our ideas of what is considered to be right and what is considered to be wrong. As such, many believe that sex without the conditions of love and commitment is morally wrong.

Though not a movement of the same magnitude as the civil rights, gay rights, or women's rights movements, there have been organized efforts around the issue of prostitution with prostitutes at the forefront. For example, some groups have made the argument for the legalization of prostitution. "Hooking is Real Employment," (HIRE), an Atlanta-based group founded by Dolores French, is one group that works toward the legalization of prostitution. Specifically, legalization would allow for state control and regulation. That is, the state could impose a tax on the earnings from this occupation, require licensing of both prostitutes and places of prostitution, or set occupational standards. Supporters of the initiative for legalization often use the state of Nevada as an example. In a majority of counties in Nevada, houses of prostitution have been legalized and state controls have been placed over the occupation. In Nevada, prostitutes can be screened and tested for sexually transmitted diseases, brothels are taxed, and monies previously used for the arrest and prosecution of prostitutes diverted to other issues. This means that as much as several million dollars can be funneled into other law enforcement areas.

Other groups, however, call for the decriminalization of prostitution. That is, these groups do not want state regulation and control of prostitution, but instead argue for a removal of all laws against prostitution. In 1972, a group of San Francisco prostitutes founded "Call Off Your Old Tired Ethics" (COYOTE) to promote the decriminalization, destigmitization, and unionization of prostitution. In this regard, prostitutes are arguing for the recognition that their work is a legitimate form of service work and should be free of criminal sanctions. Further, because prostitution is a legitimate form of service work, the stigma attached to such work should be eliminated so as to allow prostitutes the same rights to organize as other service workers.

However, not all organizations call for either the legalization or decriminalization of prostitution. One case in point is the group "Women Hurt in Systems of Prostitution Engaged in Revolt." WHISPER members maintain that prostitution is not a chosen occupation or a legitimate form of work, but the result of life circumstances, such as poverty, that afford women few choices for survival. As a result, many women are left to sell their bodies to earn a living, an activity that is simply exploitive in nature and constitutes another form of violence against women. Thus WHISPER members work toward the goal of eliminating prostitution.

The discussion surrounding prostitution is not limited to the organizations mentioned above. Many, including educators, politicians, and feminists have been involved in the debates over prostitution. And, like the organized efforts mentioned above, there is not a unified position from any of these camps. Take for example feminists. On one side of the debate are feminists who argue that prostitution is nothing less than the exploitation of women, which logically follows from the sexual objectification of women within our society. Simply stated, when we treat women as sex objects, we then create conditions for prostitution. On the other side, some feminists argue that prostitution is a choice and those who make such a choice should be afforded the same occupational rights as those who choose any other profession. Somewhere in the middle are feminists who will defend a prostitute's rights to do such work, but must wonder if there were not gender inequalities in the world of work, such as sex segregated occupations and pay inequities, if many women would really choose prostitution as an occupation.

As we have witnessed a variety of debates within organizations addressing issues specific to prostitution, so too have there emerged debates over the appropriate response to this occupational pursuit. It must be noted at the outset that, according to official arrest records, there has been a decline in the actual number of persons arrested for the crime of prostitution and commercialized vice in recent years. It might then be argued that little change is necessary as the traditional response of arrest, jail, and release seems to be working to eradicate the occupation. However, as has already been discussed, this pattern of arrest, jail, and release has been most often imposed upon prostitutes, not madams; street walkers, and not escorts. The end result is that this approach has done little more than inconvenience a small segment of the population. Thus, new initiatives are beginning to replace the traditional response. One example is found in the city of San Francisco, where the District Attorney's Office offers a program that focuses upon counseling and other assistance for prostitutes. It has been reported that fewer than 1% of those prostitutes who participate in the program have been rearrested for prostitution.

It is reasonable to assume that the occupation of prostitution will undergo some change in the future. However, to speculate on how significant such change will be, is difficult. Debating whether current laws against prostitution and commercialized vice are a violation of an individual's civil and human rights or simply a protection of a society's morality has a long history. From the UN to our local communities, the debate continues as we have yet to decide if prostitution is an activity that must be eradicated, contained, or allowed to operate freely in the competitive marketplace. Considering that it has taken us this long to arrive at multiple debates, the probability that this debate will be resolved in the near future is small at best.

N. JANE McCANDLESS

References and Further Reading

Aggleton, P., Ed. 1999. *Men who Sell Sex: International Perspectives on Male Prostitution and HIV/AIDS*, Philadeliphia PA, Temple University Press.

Dank, B., Ed. 1999. *Sex Work and Sex Workers, Somerset*, NJ, Transaction Publishing.

Davis, N., Ed. 1993. *Prostitution: An International Handbook on Trends, Problems, and Policies*, Westport, CT, Greenwood Press.

Delacoste, F. and Alexander, P., Eds. 1998. *Sex Work: Writings by Women in the Sex Industry, San Francisco*, CA, Cleis Press.

Elias, J.E., Ed. 1998. *Prostitution: On Whores, Hustlers, and Johns*, New York, Prometheus Books.

Flowers, R.B. 1998. *The Prostitution of Women and Girls, Jefferson*, NC, McFarland and Co.

McNamara, R. 1994. *The Times Square Hustler: Male Prostitution in New York City*, Westcost, CT, Praeger.

Meier, R. and Geis, G. 1997. *Victimless Crime? Prostitution, Drugs, Homosexuality, Abortion, Los Angeles*, CA, Roxbury Publishing Co.

Prostitutes Education Network. Available at: http.//www. bayswan.org.

Pastore, A.L. and Maguire, K., Eds. 2000. *Sourcebook of Criminal Justice Statistics*, U.S. Department of Justice, Bureau of Justice Statistics, Washington, DC, USGPO.

Weitzer, R., Ed. 2000. *Sex For Sale: Prostitution, Pornography, and the Sex Industry*, New York, Routledge.

See also **Prostitution: Extent, Correlates, and Forms; Prostitution: The Law**

Prostitution: Extent, Correlates, and Forms

Prostitution is generally defined as the immediate exchange of sex for money, although the exchange may be for anything of value considered to be payment. Historically, prostitution has been documented as far back as antiquity (Bullough and Bullough, 1987). Ancient Babylonian women were required to offer themselves on the temple steps to a stranger who would afterward make a contribution to the temple. The practice has been referred to as "temple duty." In ancient Greece, several classes of prostitutes existed, with the *hetaerae* (courtesans) holding the highest social status. Licensed brothels also appeared in ancient Greece. Prostitution was widespread in the Middle Ages. By the 16th century, the accompanying problem of the spread of venereal disease engendered a crusade to control prostitution in Europe. Since then, efforts to control or eliminate prostitution have been undertaken in virtually all parts of the world.

In the U.S. and elsewhere, female prostitutes outnumber male prostitutes. In 1999, of the nearly 64,000 U.S. arrests for prostitution and commercialized vice, almost 61% were of females (U.S. Department of Justice, Federal Bureau of Investigation, 2000). The customers of both female and male prostitutes are most often males. The criminology literature tends to ignore male prostitution or regard it more appropriately under the study of homosexuality. Consequently, we know a great deal more about the patterns of female prostitutes than we do about their male counterparts.

There are varieties of prostitution that differ with regard to income, working conditions, and occupational hazards. At the top of the status hierarchy for females is the "call girl," who is extremely selective in accepting clients and able to command the highest fees. The successful call girl develops an address or phone book of carefully screened or referred clients. Appointments are made via telephone calls and are arranged at either party's residence or a hotel room. James Bryan's study of call girls (1965) depicts the apprenticeship-like process they may go through. Though call girls are less circumspect and vulnerable to arrest than other types of prostitutes, the solitariness of their work leaves them relatively unprotected if a client becomes abusive. The upscale backgrounds of the call girl's clients, however, almost assures well-mannered individuals.

The "escort service worker" also enjoys relatively comfortable working conditions and a relatively safe clientele, as well as a good fee to accompany the client on a date. Some escort services (advertised in the yellow pages of telephone directories) are legitimate dating services, although most serve as fronts for prostitution. Even within the legitimate escort businesses, individual workers may offer "extras" on their own time. Online escort services have recently made their appearance. There are thousands of websites, each linked to hundreds of individuals advertising their rates and services on their own web pages. The advertisements do not mention sex acts, but vaguely refer to hourly rates (of $300–$500) depending on whether the service is "outcall" (at the customer's place) or "incall" (at the escort's place).

Illegal houses of prostitution (also known as bordellos or brothels) provide a setting for yet another type of prostitution. The "house prostitute" working in such a setting is usually mentored by the "madam" who runs the house and books the customers. The madam is often a retired prostitute who recruits, trains, and supervises the women who work for her (Heyl, 1977). Over the past three decades there has been a decline in houses of prostitution, which have given way to massage parlors, the latter having the advantage of being able to more easily disguise their activities. It is almost impossible to distinguish between the legitimate massage parlor and the type serving as a front for prostitution, until the customer makes requests for "extras."

"Bar girls" (B-girls) represent another form of prostitution further down the status hierarchy. They sit in bars (usually near military bases) making themselves available for drinks, conversation, and whatever may follow. Many have an arrangement with the bar owner whereby they are served watered-down drinks for which their companion pays high prices.

"Streetwalkers" (also known as "hookers") are generally considered to be at the lowest rung of the ladder of the profession of prostitution. They are the most visible, lowest paid, and most vulnerable to arrest, as well as health and safety risks. They blatantly walk the street and seductively stand on corners in areas that are known for prostitution. Once they have engaged a customer, they take him to a nearby cheap hotel room for the actual transaction. Of all the types of prostitutes, streetwalkers bring forth the largest public outcry for police to do something about the prostitution problem. Consequently, most arrests for prostitution occur for this type.

Modern variants of the streetwalker include the "lot lizard" and the "skeezer." "Lot lizards" (truck stop and highway rest area prostitutes) solicit long-haul truckers over the citizens band radio. The actual sex act takes place in the cab of the truck. "Skeezers" are prostitutes who trade sex for crack cocaine. They set up shop in crack houses, working out an arrangement with the owner.

Male prostitutes are generally "street hustlers," although some are bar hustlers, escort service workers, erotic masseurs, strippers, and "call men." Male cruising areas for street hustling are often out of view of the heterosexual community and, therefore, less likely to offend the general public. The threat of the spread of the human immune deficiency virus (HIV), believed to cause acquired immune deficiency (AIDS), fuels some public concern.

Factors associated with entrance into prostitution are varied, although common themes have appeared, such as early sexual experience and sexual abuse victimization. An in-depth study of 200 female juvenile and adult prostitutes (Silbert and Pines, 1982) revealed that negative circumstances appeared to play more of a role than did an attraction to this line of work. For the unskilled and uneducated, the choice appears to be between a low paying job and the perceived relatively better income expected from prostitution.

In 1999, almost 1.5% of those arrested for prostitution and commercialized vice in the U.S. were under the age of 18 (U.S. Department of Justice, Federal Bureau of Investigation, 2000). Teen prostitution among both males and females is most often associated with being a runaway and having no other means of supporting oneself.

Not all prostitutes willingly enter this line of work. Forced prostitution is the enslavement into prostitution of predominantly women and children. It is a worldwide problem, with Thailand, Vietnam, China, Mexico, Russia, and the Czech Republic considered to be the biggest sources of such trafficking. Women are sold by their husbands to traffickers, as are female children sold by their parents. In other cases, an outright abduction occurs or the promise of a job or marriage lures an unsuspecting victim into this form of slave trading. The victim is, in turn, sold to a brothel in another country, where she must turn over her earnings until she has compensated someone for her transportation and board.

Streetwalkers constitute the greatest number of prostitutes. They are more likely than other types of prostitutes to have a pimp, whose primary role is that of business manager. (The madam serves this role in house prostitution.) Pimps take a good share of the prostitute's earnings in return for providing a number of services. Pimps can fulfill any of the following roles: protector against the police, bodyguard, bouncer, lover, companion, husband, panderer or recruiter, purveyor of drugs, procurer for clients, coach or trainer, employment agent, and bail provider.

Streetwalkers, compared to other types of prostitutes, are more likely to be drug addicts. In fact, streetwalking appears to be a logical means to support an individual's drug addiction. Epidemiological studies of HIV among female prostitutes in the U.S. have indicated that infection with the virus is associated with injection drug use among streetwalkers, rather than with their sexual practices with their male customers. In licensed brothels in Nevada, preemployment screening and routine periodic testing for drug use are conducted—and employment is denied or terminated upon testing positive for drugs.

Streetwalkers, rather than other types of prostitutes, are most likely to be associated with ancillary street crimes, such as robbery and assault. Drug trafficking (commonly associated with pimping) is also a crime that often accompanies prostitution.

Arguments for the legalization of prostitution include the ability to regulate the practice. Regulation would mean the screening of prostitutes for injection drug use, sexually transmitted infections, and HIV. As legitimate businesses, these legal settings for prostitution would be taxed. Legalization would also eliminate the underworld nature of the activity and, therefore, most of the ancillary crimes. Money would also be saved that would have been used for arrests, prosecutions, and incarcerations. Although some countries have legalized prostitution and certain counties in

Nevada have done so, it seems unlikely that the U.S. will move any further toward legalization. To the contrary, many states have enacted penalty enhancement statutes for HIV-positive prostitutes. Such laws make it a felony for those who know they are HIV positive to continue to engage in prostitution. These laws have been enacted despite the lack of evidence that prostitutes in the U.S. are spreading HIV through sexual practices with their customers.

Prostitution is likely to remain a crime in the U.S. and elsewhere, as long as societies view the exchange of sex for money as morally wrong. Prostitutes' rights groups such as COYOTE ("Call Off Your Old Tired Ethics") have succeeded in convincing some that prostitution should be considered a legitimate occupation like any other chosen line of work. However, the public's image of the streetwalker or male hustler loitering and soliciting on street corners detracts from COYOTE's argument. Public policy in the U.S. is also guided by the belief that prostitutes are a major gateway for the spread of HIV to the heterosexual community.

JOAN LUXENBURG

Further Reading

Armstrong, E.G. 1978. Massage parlors and their customers, *Archives of Sexual Behavior,* 7.

Bryan, J.H. 1965. The sociology of prostitution, *Social Problems,* 12.

Bryant, C.D. and Palmer, C.E. 1975. Massage parlors and 'Hand Whores': Some sociological observations, *Journal of Sex Research,* 11.

Bullough, V.L. and Bullough, B. 1987. *Women and Prostitution: A Social History,* New York, Prometheus.

Davis, K. 1937. The sociology of prostitution, *American Sociological Review,* 2.

Heyl, B.S. 1977. The madam as teacher: The training of house prostitutes, *Social Problems,* 24.

McNamara, R.P. 1994. *The Times Square Hustler: Male Prostitution in New York City,* Westport, CT, Praeger.

Silbert, M.H. and Pines, A.M. 1982. Entrance into prostitution, *Youth and Society,* 13.

U.S. Department of Justice, Federal Bureau of Investigation 2000. *Crime in the United States 1999: Uniform Crime Reports,* Washington, DC, U.S. Government Printing Office.

Winick, C. and Kinsie, P. 1971. *The Lively Commerce,* Chicago, IL, Quadrangle.

See also **Prostitution as an Occupation; Prostitution: Law**

Prostitution: The Law

Introduction

Prostitution is often called the world's oldest profession. What to do about it has been debated for thousands of years. Prostitution is historically defined as a "sex specific act or offense, or related to women selling sexual favors as prostitutes. Today, prostitution is recognized as including child prostitutes, male prostitutes, and various types of pimps, madams, and customers" (Flowers, 2001a, 143) Recently, however, it has been noted that some 30 million women around the world have been sold into sexual slavery by their parents or others. Likewise, many runaway children turn to prostitution as a means of survival, perceiving they have no other means of earning money except to turn to this and perhaps other forms of criminal activity. Moreover, many women engaged in prostitution are addicted to cocaine, heroin, and other drugs, and view engaging in sex for money as one of the few ways to obtain enough means to acquire the drugs they crave. Finally, the common "street walker" is often kept in prostitution by pimps, who threaten to kill their whores unless the prostitutes do what they are told. Thus the element of free will is often suspected when the decision to enter into prostitution is involved.

Prostitution in Western Societies

Likewise, today the laws regulating prostitution are frequently contradictory, hypocritical, and vary widely from one location to another, even within the same states. All 50 of the U.S. have laws against prostitution, usually based on the notion that it is a sexual offense "involving female and male prostitutes and mostly male clients" (Flowers, 2001a, 144). Yet, the laws regarding prostitution are enforced with a distinct sexist bias. It has been said that prostitution is the only crime in the criminal law "where two people are doing a thing mutually agreed upon and yet only one, the female partner, is subject to arrest" (Millet, 1971, 79). Thus, more often than not, it is the prostitutes that are arrested whereas the client (sometimes called "the john") goes free. Nor is this the only contradiction concerning these laws in America.

While prostitution is illegal in all 50 states, it is not illegal in all parts of all states. In Nevada, prostitution laws are set by each county, and in certain counties, it is legal to engage in prostitution. And in some American cities, even where it is illegal, certain vice zones (sometimes called combat zones) have been set aside for certain vice activities (including prostitution) to take place.

Table 1 presents the prostitution law definitions, crimes, and penalties in New Jersey, which are typical of other states. First arrests for prostitution are usually treated as minor offenses (misdemeanors) whereas repeated arrests may lead to felony charges (crimes for which the penalty is at least a year in prison).

There have been times in American history when certain prostitution laws were based on what sociologists term a "moral panic." One such law was the White Slave Traffic Act, or Mann Act of 1910. Supposedly, there was an outbreak of newly arrived young white immigrant women from Europe being kidnapped and sold into forced prostitution, hence the name white slavery. Despite the fact that no objective study found such a white-slavery outbreak involving young white immigrant women, the Mann Act made transporting a female across state lines for any immoral purpose, including prostitution, a federal crime. The way the ambiguously written law was enforced, however, had little to do with prostitution.

The first black heavyweight boxing champion, Jack Johnson, spent a year in prison for transporting a white woman across a state line. Many male fiancés were prosecuted for simply being disapproved of by their future in-laws, once they had transported their future brides across a state line. In 1986, Congress finally amended the Mann Act in ways that made it gender neutral and changed its "immoral practice" clause to "any sexual activity in which one can be charged with a crime" (Flowers, 2001b, 169).

In 1980, the Racketeer Influenced and Corrupt Organizations Act (RICO) was passed by Congress. The RICO act made it a federal crime to participate in a variety of criminal enterprises, including those that affect interstate commerce and constitute a pattern of racketeering activity. Included in these activities are those crimes defined under the Mann Act. The RICO statute allows prosecutors to charge individuals with being members of prostitution rings, even if they are only in indirect control of an inter state sexual trafficking enterprise. The act also allows victims of such rings to seek restitution via civil suit.

Likewise, in 1998 Congress passed the Protection of Children from Sexual Predators Act, Section 2425

Table 1. Prostitution: New Jersey Statutes 2C:34–1: Prostitution and related offenses

Definitions

Prostitution is sexual activity with another person in exchange for something of economic value, or the offer or acceptance of an offer to engage in sexual activity in exchange for something of economic value.

Sexual activity includes, but is not limited to, sexual intercourse, including genital genital, oral genital, anal genital, and oral anal contact, whether between persons of the same or opposite sex; masturbation; touching of the genitals, buttocks, or female breasts; sadistic or masochistic abuse and other deviate sexual relations.

House of prostitution is any place where prostitution or promotion of prostitution is regularly carried on by one person under the control, management or supervision of another.

Promoting prostitution is:

- Owning, controlling, managing, supervising or otherwise keeping, alone or in association with another, a house of prostitution or a prostitution business;
- Procuring an inmate for a house of prostitution or place in a house of prostitution for one who would be an inmate;
- Encouraging, inducing, or otherwise purposely causing another to become or remain a prostitute;
- Soliciting a person to patronize a prostitute;
- Procuring a prostitute for a patron;
- Transporting a person into or within this State with purpose to promote that person's engaging in prostitution, or procuring or paying for transportation with that purpose; or
- Leasing or otherwise permitting a place controlled by the actor, alone or in association with others, to be regularly used for prostitution or promotion of prostitution, or failure to make a reasonable effort to abate such use by ejecting the tenant, notifying law enforcement authorities, or other legally available means.

Crimes and Offenses

The following are prostitution crimes:

- Engaging in prostitution;
- Promoting prostitution;
- Knowingly promoting prostitution of a child under 18;
- Knowingly promoting prostitution of one's own child, ward, or other person for whose care the actor is responsible;
- Compelling someone else to engage in or promote prostitution;
- Promoting prostitution of one's spouse;
- Knowingly engaging in prostitution with a person younger than 18;
- Entering or remaining in a house of prostitution for the purpose of engaging in sexual activity with a child under the age of 18;
- Soliciting or requesting a child under the age of 18 to engage in sexual activity.

Prostitution crimes and offenses are graded as follows:

- Engaging in prostitution:
- First offense: Disorderly persons offense;
- Second offense: Fourth Degree;
- Promoting prostitution: Fourth Degree;
- The following specific types of Promoting are Third Degree crimes:
- Owning, controlling, managing, supervising or otherwise keeping, alone or in association with another, a house of prostitution or a prostitution business;
- Procuring an inmate for a house of prostitution or place in a house of prostitution for one who would be an inmate;
- Encouraging, inducing, or otherwise purposely causing another to become or remain a prostitute;
- Knowingly promoting prostitution of a child under 18: Second Degree;
- Knowingly promoting prostitution of one's own child, ward, or other person for whose care the actor is responsible: Second Degree;
- Compelling someone else to engage in or promote prostitution: Third Degree;
- Promoting prostitution of one's spouse: Third Degree;
- Knowingly engaging in prostitution with a person younger than 18: Third Degree;
- Entering or remaining in a house of prostitution for the purpose of engaging in sexual activity with a child under the age of 18: Third Degree;
- Soliciting or requesting a child under the age of 18 to engage in sexual activity: Third Degree

Second degree crimes are punishable by:

- Imprisonment for five to ten years;
- A fine of up to $150,000; or
- Both.

Third degree crimes are punishable by:

- Imprisonment for three to five years;
- A fine of up to $15,000; or
- Both.

(continued)

Table 1. (*Continued*)

Fourth degree crimes are punishable by:

- Imprisonment for up to eighteen months;
- A fine of up to $10,000; or
- Both.

Disorderly persons offenses are punishable by:

- Imprisonment for up to six months;
- A fine of up to $1,000; or
- Both; and
- Anyone guilty of "engaging in prostitution" will also have their Driver's License suspended for six months.

of Title 18, which prohibits the use of foreign or inter-state commerce "for transmitting information about a minor for purposes of enticing, encouraging, or soliciting anyone to participate in criminal sexual conduct" (Flowers, 2001b, 169).

Internationally, prostitution laws differ widely. In most countries in Western Europe, voluntary prostitution is a legal enterprise and many middle-class college students pay for their college educations working in the "skin trade." In many of these nations, prostitutes are required to have scheduled medical checkups and be certified as free from sexually transmitted diseased. For the last century or so, many nations of the world have established conventions and agreements aimed at ending the international trade in sexual work (known today as trafficking or sexual slavery). According to the 1949 Convention for the Suppression of the Traffic in Persons, "prostitution and traffic in persons for the purposes of prostitution are incompatible with the dignity and worth of the human person (in Hernandez-Truyol and Larson, 2002, 183). In 1979, the UN adopted Elimination of All Forms of Discrimination against Women, supporting the abolition of sexual trafficking, although recently it has moved toward a position supporting voluntary prostitution as a victimless crime acceptable to human rights standards.

Prostitution in Western History

If all of this reads as confusing, it should. For thousands of years the world's civilizations have waxed and waned about the nature of prostitution and its place within society. The fight over prostitution within Christendom is illustrative of these contradictory tendencies. Originally, Jesus took pity on Mary Magdalene, who was a prostitute before she met Jesus. She played a major role in Christianity. Mary was among those who discovered Jesus' grave was empty and was the first to see Jesus after his resurrection. Jesus was also protective of prostitutes, informing the Pharisees that prostitutes would enter heaven before they would. Using

Jesus' example, the early Christians went to great lengths to convert prostitutes. In Jesus' time sexual sinners were often stoned to death. Today, in certain Asian nations, prostitutes who contract AIDS are stoned to death as part of a public health policy designed to eradicate the disease.

With the beginning of the Christian era, the debate over prostitution raged. The official position of the Christian church was first crafted by St. Augustine in the fifth century. "Even though there was more sordid...more full of shame...if they (prostitutes) were removed entirely from society, everything would be polluted by lust" (Burlough and Burlough, 1995, 206). Prostitutes, however, were excluded from the church as long as they were active in their profession. St. Thomas Aquinas reinforced this stance by claiming that prostitution functioned as a sewer in a palace, noting that without the sewer, the palace would be flooded with filth. Likewise, if prostitutes were eliminated, the world would be filled with sexual sin (i.e., sodomy).

With the emergence of Protestantism, the attitude toward prostitution once again changed. Early Protestants, such as Philip Stubbs, wanted all prostitution eliminated, and advocated that prostitutes be cauterized with red hot irons on various visible body parts. Martin Luther, however, suggested that city governments take care in closing down houses of prostitution, less they might unleash even greater evils in eradicating prostitution. This was because without a husband there were very few ways women could support themselves independently.

In the 1560s, brothels in Zurich were policed to see that no married men were customers, which proved a next-to-impossible task. London and Rome were all ordered closed, but these orders were rescinded in Rome when 25,000 prostitutes and their dependents packed up were preparing to leave the city. Many prostitutes in Rome were often seen in the company of priests from the 1490s onward (Tannahill, 1992, 280). Most cities rescinded their orders to close down the brothels or ignored the prohibition on prostitution completely, until various outbreaks of sexually transmitted diseases began to occur.

DAVID R. SIMON

References and Further Reading

Burlough, V. and Burlough, B. (1995). *Sexual Attitudes,* Amherst, New York Prometheus.

Flowers, R.B. (2001a). *Sex Crimes, Predators, Prostitutes and Victims,* Springfield, IL, Charles C. Thomas.

Flowers, R.B. (2001b). *Runaway Kida and Teenage Prostitution,* Springfield, IL, Charles C. Thomas.

Hernandez-Truyol, Espernanza, B. and Larson, J.E. (2002). in Espernanza, B. and Hernandez-Truyol, Eds., *Moral Imperialism: A Critical Anthology,* New York, New York University Press.

Millet, K. (1971). Prostitution: A quartet for female voices, in Gornick, V. and Moran, B.K., *Women in a Sexist Society,* New York, New American Library. *New Jersey Statutes 2C:34–1: Prostitution and related offenses* (ND). Available at: http://www.google.com/search?q=New+Jersey+Prostitution+Laws&hl=en&lr=&ie=UTF-8&start=20&sa=N.

Tannahill, R. (1992). *Sex in History,* Revised ed., New York, Scarborough House.

See also **Prostitution as an Occupation; Prostitution: Extent, Correlates, and Forms**

Psychological Autopsy

A psychological autopsy is a postmortem investigation into the psychological state of the deceased prior to his or her death. Such investigations are useful to forensic investigators to help determine the context in which suspicious deaths occur, and serve as an adjunct to police and coroner investigations, as they provide information about mental health issues.

Unlike medical autopsies, performed by physicians, and forensic investigations, performed by detectives, psychological autopsies are performed by mental health clinicians, such as psychologists and psychiatrists. The psychological autopsy is not meant to take the place of a forensic investigation, only to provide supplemental information about the state of mind of the decedent. These data are gathered mainly by interviewing survivors and by reviewing the victim's records. The clinician must always make clear that he or she is only making an expert opinion on the case, and must leave the final determination of manner of death to the legal fact finder.

"Equivocal death" is an expression used to mean that the forensic evidence does not provide a conclusive explanation for the manner of death. LaFon (1999) discusses five possible conclusions in determining the manner of an equivocal death: natural (e.g., heart attack, stroke); accident (e.g., fell asleep while driving, slipped off of a rooftop); suicide (an act performed deliberately to end one's life); homicide (the death was directly or indirectly caused by another person); and undetermined (when all the available evidence is inconclusive). Ebert (1991) uses the example of a parachutist who falls to his death. The death itself is obviously owing to the injuries sustained by hitting the ground. However, the person may have inadvertently fallen out of the plane (accident), purposely jumped out of the plane (suicide), gotten pushed out of the plane (homicide), or died of a heart attack before the parachute could be opened (natural causes).

Determination of manner of death may be important to establish for several reasons. The investigator focuses on an understanding of the victim's intention in order to distinguish between suicide and accidental death. This may be crucial for surviving family members, as most life insurance policies are void for cases of suicide. If the results of a psychological autopsy suggest homicide, a police investigation will be triggered.

Why conduct a psychological autopsy when law enforcement detectives and pathologists are well-trained in issues regarding manner of death? Though cause of death can usually be precisely determined, the psychologist explores the context of the death. For example, was the victim likely to engage in frequent suicidal ideation? Did the victim have a history of impulsive behavior? What types of relationships did the victim have, and could any of these interactions foster homicidal intentions in others? Did the victim have a known psychological disorder, and what impact if any did the diagnosis have on his or her daily functioning? These questions are vitally important, and it is crucial to enlist the aid of someone trained in psychological issues to avoid misinterpretation of the victim's mental health history.

Interviewing skills used with relatives and acquaintances of survivors can add crucial contextual information to an investigation. Clinicians are traditionally trained to gather and synthesize background information from significant others. Clinicians are also trained to deal with the challenging task of discussing difficult and sensitive topics with grieving survivors. The information gathering interview may also serve as a therapeutic intervention, assisting the survivor in understanding that feelings such as guilt and helplessness are quite normal in the grieving process. Discussing the death with a professional can help a survivor cope with the need to understand why and how the death occurred.

LaFon (1999) proposes that psychological autopsies be divided into two basic types: the suicide psychological autopsy and the equivocal death psychological autopsy. In the case where the manner of death is already known to be suicide, the suicide psychological autopsy focuses on collecting data about the circumstances leading to the suicide, in order to help suicidology researchers in future prevention efforts.

Ebert (1991) offered a comprehensive list of 26 factors to consider in conducting a psychological autopsy:

1. Alcohol history
2. Suicide notes
3. Writings of the deceased
4. Books owned or read by the deceased
5. Interpersonal relationships with friends, acquaintances, parents, siblings, coworkers, supervisors, relatives, physicians, mental health professionals, and teachers
6. Marital relationship
7. Mood
8. Psychosocial stressors
9. Presuicidal behavior
10. Language, that is, analyze tapes, recollections of conversation, and writings for morbid content
11. Drugs used—assess interactional effects of legal and illegal drugs.
12. Medical history
13. Mental status exam of deceased's condition before death—assess orientation, memory, attention, concentration, mood and affect, hallucinations or delusions, cognition, IQ, language, and judgment
14. Psychological history
15. Laboratory studies
16. Coroner's report
17. Motive assessment
18. Reconstruction of events occurring on the day before the deceased's death
19. Assess feelings regarding death as well as preoccupations and fantasies.
20. Military history
21. Death history of family
22. Family history
23. Employment history
24. Educational history
25. Familiarity with methods of death
26. Police reports

Though at present there are no universally accepted training or procedural guidelines for conducting a psychological autopsy, LaFon (1999) has surveyed investigators on which items are considered essential in a psychological autopsy investigation.

Once the data are gathered and analyzed, a psychological autopsy written report is created. Blau (1994) suggests dividing reports into six sections: (1) purpose of the evaluation, (2) sources of information, (3) summary of the facts, (4) significant factors, (5) psychological analysis of the deceased's functioning, and (6) conclusions.

Psychological autopsies are a relatively recent investigative aid. Although authors disagree as to when the first psychological autopsy was done, estimates tend not to go back earlier than the 1950s. In the late 1960s, with Edwin Shneidman's work on the subject at the Los Angeles Suicide Prevention Center, the practice became more recognized and popular.

Though adding a psychological autopsy to postmortem forensic investigations is likely to add significant new information to a case, and further research will allow for more refined reliability and validity studies, funding shortages in law enforcement agencies will likely leave this investigative aid underutilized in the foreseeable future.

RICHARD W. SEARS

References and Further Reading

Blau, T. 1994. *Psychological Services for Law Enforcement,* New York, John Wiley & Sons, Inc.

Ebert, B. 1991. Guide to conducting a psychological autopsy, in Lewiston, K.N.A., Ed., *Handbook of Medical Psychotherapy,* New York, Hogrefe & Huber Publishers.

Gelles, M. 1995. Psychological autopsy: An investigative aid, in Kurke, K. and Scrivner, E., *Police Psychology into the 21st Century,* Hillsdale, NJ, Lawrence Erlbaum Associates, Inc.

LaFon, D. 2002. The Psychological Autopsy, in Turvey, B., *Criminal Profiling,* San Diego, Academic Press.

LaFon, D. 1999. Psychological autopsies for equivocal deaths, *International Journal of Emergency Mental Health,* 3.

Leenaars, A., Ed. 1999. *Lives and Deaths: Selections from the Works of Edwin S. Shneidman,* Philadelphia, PA, Brunner/Mazel.

Leenaars, A., Ed. 1993. *Suicidology: Essays in Honor of Edwin S. Shneidman,* Northvale, NJ, Jason Aronson Inc.

Litman, R. 1988. Psychological autopsies, mental illness and intention in suicide, in J. Nolan, L., Ed., *The Suicide Case: Investigation and Trial of Insurance Claims,* Chicago, IL, American Bar Association.

Ogloff, J. and Otto, R. 1993. Psychological autopsy: Clinical and legal perspectives, *Saint Louis University Law Journal,* 37.

Selkin, J. 1987. *The Psychological Autopsy in the Courtroom: Contributions of the Social Sciences to Resolving Issues Surrounding Equivocal Deaths,* Denver, CO, James Selkin, Ph.D.

Simon, R. 2002. Murder, suicide, accident, or natural death? Assessment of suicide risk factors at the time of death, in Simon, R.I. and Shuman, D.W., Eds., *Retrospective Assessment of Mental States in Litigation,* Washington, DC, American Psychiatric Publishing, Inc.

Young, T. 1992. Procedures and problems in conducting a psychological autopsy, *International Journal of Offender Therapy and Comparative Criminology,* 36(1).

See also **Psychopathy and Crime**

Psychological Theories of Criminal Behavior

Theories of crime aid in the understanding of crime and criminals, the assessment of criminals and criminal behavior, and treatment. What differentiates psychological theories of crime from other discipline's theories of crime (like sociology, biology, etc.) is the focus on the individual. A psychological approach considers the mental processes and behaviors of individuals in an effort to explain or predict the crimes he or she commits (Bartol, 1991).

Although psychological theories globally focus on the individual, the content of those theories varies tremendously. Many areas central to psychology provide their own views on crime and criminals (Shoham and Seis, 1993). For instance, psychobiology (Sheldon's linkage of body type to personality characteristics), behavioral genetics (twin studies, genealogy studies), and neuroscience (brain injuries, testosterone, and aggression) all are within the domain of psychological science, but are covered elsewhere in this volume. The two main categories of psychological theories that will be covered here include social psychological explanations and clinical (or psychopathological) explanations. A review of the possible causes of crime from these perspectives necessarily raises the question of "what is crime?" In some circumstances, the behavior is a crime because there is a law that dictates such (e.g., suicide; Sutherland, 1947; Tappan, 1947;). In other circumstances, it may appear more clearly criminal owing to the violent nature of the behavior and the presence of a person perpetuating that violence on another (e.g., murder). These approaches each contribute to answer the question of whether criminals are born or made.

Social psychological theories of crime focus on how criminal behavior may derive from the complex interactions between individuals and their social environment. Research psychologists have focused intently on understanding the mechanism underlying how humans (and animals) learn, that is, how their experience changes their future behaviors. Learning theories show us that the stimuli in the environment can trigger certain responses (classical conditioning; Pavlov, 1960; Rescorla, 1988) and that our behaviors our rewarded or punished (operant conditioning; Skinner, 1938). Social learning theory (also called observational learning) focuses on learning by observing others (Bandura, 1965). You don't have to be punished directly to learn that something is wrong; you can learn that consequence by watching someone else punished for that behavior. The converse is true as well; we are more likely to engage in behaviors that we see others rewarded for. In social psychological terms this is called modeling. In other words, people may learn to do what they see everyday.

Our bonds with others (attachment to our caregivers, commitment to friends and loved ones) as well as social pressures and rules help control crime by providing frameworks for acceptable behavior. The development of morality, guilt, and conscience, which are normal social-developmental processes, may go awry as a result of poor parenting, abuse, or neglect, and produce children more likely to engage in criminal behavior. Such children may not recognize or feel the need to prescribe to society's rules. Further, their particular life experiences may have taught them that the gains associated with criminal activity outweigh the consequences.

Another social psychological perspective deals with the role of frustration in aggressive acts. The frustration or aggression hypothesis posits that frustrating situations lead to aggressive acts (Dollard et al., 1939). Frustration usually derives from some need or want being thwarted. We know that frustration is not the only precipitating factor to aggressive behavior, and that not all frustrating situations lead to aggression. However, intense frustration can lead to aggressive and even criminal behavior.

Clinical psychology, on the other hand, focuses on the mental state and functioning of the individual. Mental disease or maladaptive personality traits may be at the root of many of these disorders. Certainly not all mentally ill individuals are dangerous or engage in criminal behavior. Approximately 16% of inmates in U.S. jails and prisons are mentally ill. There is no definitive way to determine how many of their crimes were committed as a result of their mental illness, but the fact still remains that they are mentally ill. However, as concerning as it may be to have those 283,800 mentally ill inmates incarcerated, the fact remains that 1,489,950 inmates are not mentally ill, and thus the causes of their crime are from other sources.

Many personality and mental disorders may have crime as a component. As mentioned above, the behavior must be evaluated in terms of the rules of law to determine if it is "criminal." Any disorder that results in aggressive behavior could under certain circumstances be criminal (assault, rape, child abuse, homicide). Others, lead to behaviors that are illegal but not violent (stealing). Some disorders though have closer ties with criminal behavior than others. Those will be presented here (see also DSM IV-TR, 2000).

The notion of the "psychotic killer" is overused and the term psychosis is misunderstood. Clinical psychologists define psychosis as the gross distortion of reality. This distortion is evidenced by delusions or hallucinations. Not all people who are psychotic become violent or are criminals. The presence of psychotic episodes though does reflect a subset of individuals who engage in criminal behavior. Psychosis is present in disorders such as schizophrenia, and although criminal activity by this subset of the population may seem elevated (owing to media attention) it is not known whether schizophrenics engage in violent criminal behavior any more than the rest of the population; in fact, it is unlikely. Paranoid schizophrenics may engage in criminal behavior if their delusions (at least those whose action would result in criminal activity) are acted upon. Paranoid disorder of the jealous or persecutory types may result in assault or homicide if action is taken against the people who are perceived to be the source of the jealousy or the instigators of the persecution.

Mood disorders are those that are characterized by sustained emotion that affects all aspects of daily life. Manic episodes are features of several mood disorders. These episodes include elevated, irritable mood, decreased need for sleep, talkativeness, and flighty ideas (among others). In a few cases, this prolonged mood state may result in criminal activities such as assault or shop lifting.

Dissociative disorders are characterized by disruption of a person's normal identity, memory, and conscious experience. Dissociative identity disorder (commonly referred to as multiple personality disorder) has as its central features two or more identities or personality states within the same person. The individual identities often are very different, comprising different patterns of behavior, attitudes, and even eye-glass prescriptions. Criminal activity, when associated with this disorder, is usually in the form of violence to others (rape, assault, child abuse). It should be noted, however, that the very existence of this disorder is up for debate in the clinical community.

Impulse control disorders are those that are characterized by the inability to resist impulses or temptations that are harmful to the person or others. There is typically a sense of tension prior to the act, and a sense of release at the time of committing the act. Some of these disorders can result in violent criminal behaviors, others to illegal behavior that by virtue of particular state or federal laws, result in a crime. Intermittent explosive disorder is characterized by loss of control of aggressive impulses that often result in assault or destruction of property. Kleptomania is the inability to resist impulses to steal. The items stolen are not needed in terms of their function or their worth. Pathological gambling results from the failure to resist impulses to gamble despite family, work, and financial disruptions that result. Illegal activities may result as a function of trying to finance the gambling addiction. Pyromania is the deliberate and purposeful setting of fires. This may result in the crime of arson. With the exception of pathological gambling that may afflict anywhere from 1–3% of the adult population, these other impulse control disorders are extremely rare.

Paraphilias are those disorders that are characterized by arousal toward objects or inappropriate situations. These sexual disorders can lead to criminal acts when the subjects of the intense sexual urges are nonconsenting, are minors, or the situation itself is illegal regardless of others present. Sexual sadism is characterized by intense sexual urges in which the psychological or physical suffering of the victim is sexually exciting. This aberrant (and criminal) behavior is likely to be repeated until the person is apprehended. The severity of the behavior typically increases over time, and victims may be seriously injured or even killed. It is not uncommon for these individuals to commit rape and other sexual assaults. Frotteurism is a disorder characterized by rubbing or fondling a nonconsenting person in a crowded place. Exhibitionism involves showing one's genitals to a stranger. This illegal activity is done to shock or surprise the observer. Pedophilia is a disorder characterized by recurrent, intense sexual attraction to prepubescent children.

Personality disorders are another consideration for causes of crime that fall within the realm of clinical psychology. Personality is what distinguishes each of us from other people. It is your own individual pattern of perceiving, thinking, feeling, and behaving. Personality traits are what make us who we are. They tend to be stable over time and situation (though we certainly can act differently in the library vs. the night club—many of our core attributes remain stable). When personality traits become maladaptive, we enter the realm of personality disorders. Take for example shyness. Shyness is a normal characteristic for some people. If that characteristic becomes extremely maladaptive (avoiding a contact with others, great fear of being embarrassed) we have entered the realm of a personality disorder (in this case avoidant personality disorder). These maladaptive traits often become part of the person's long-term functioning, and generally cause a great deal of disruption and stress for the individual. There are some particular personality disorders that can (but not always) lead to criminal behavior (Freud, 1961; Eysenck, 1964; DSM IV-TR, 2000). These are described below.

Antisocial personality disorder is evidenced by a pattern of irresponsible and antisocial behavior, usually beginning in childhood. About 3% of the male population and 1% of the female population exhibit this disorder. Irritability and aggressiveness are hallmarks of the individual with antisocial personality disorder (sometimes referred to as psychopaths or sociopaths, though neither of these are technical terms). This disorder often causes the individual to engage in activities that are criminal in nature, for example, assaults, destroying property, harassment, stealing, drunk driving, etc. Other benchmarks are promiscuity, disregard for personal safety, as well as others' welfare. Typically, the person with antisocial personality disorder shows no remorse. There is often a general failure to conform to social norms and stay within the bounds of lawful behavior.

Other personality disorders that can lead to criminal behavior are borderline personality disorder (physical fights, illegal substance abuse, reckless driving, shoplifting), and paranoid personality disorder (aggressiveness, self-protective behaviors). Borderline personality disorder occurs in about 2% of the general population, with paranoid personality disorder being rarer, occurring in only 0.5–2.5% of the general population.

Clinical psychologists (and psychiatrists) are often called upon to determine if a defendant is "insane." Insanity is a legal term (not a psychological one) that refers to the inability of a person to recognize that their behavior at the time of a crime was wrong. Black's Law Dictionary defines "insane" as "mentally deranged; suffering from one or more delusions or false beliefs that (1) have not foundation in reason or reality, (2) are not credible to any reasonable person of sound mind, and (3) cannot be overcome in a sufferer's mind by any amount of evidence or argument." Insanity is "any mental disorder severe enough that it prevents a person from having legal capacity and excuses the person from criminal or civil responsibility." Temporary insanity exists only at the time of the criminal act. This allows for what is called an affirmative defense: I did it but I'm not responsible. Mental illness caused the act. Competency is a related legal concept that has to do with mental capacity to understand problems and make decisions. The person must have the ability to stand trial and understand the proceedings and consult meaningfully with counsel to assist in his or her own defense.

Whether mental illness is considered an excuse, a cause, or an explanation, most people in and out of the criminal justice and legal systems want to know their role in crime. Are criminals born? Are they made? The answer of course is not so simple. Psychological theories of crime provide just one piece of the puzzle, with biology, social environment, and societal influences combining to produce the people and circumstances for crime to occur.

M. KIMBERLY MACLIN

References and Further Reading

Bandura, A. 1965. Influence of models' reinforcement contingencies on the acquisition of imitative responses, *Journal of Social and Personality Psychology*.

Bartol, C.R. 1991. *Criminal Behavior: A Psychosocial Approach*, NJ, Prentice Hall.

DSM IV-TR 2000. *Diagnostic and Statistical Manual of Mental Disorders*, Washington, DC, American Psychiatric Association.

Dollard, J., Doob, L., Miller, N., Mowrer, O. and Sears, R. 1939. *Frustration and Aggression*, New Haven, CT, Yale University Press.

Eysenck, H.J. 1964. *Crime and Personality*, Boston, MA, Houghton Mifflin.

Freud, S. 1961. *The Complete Psychological works of Sigmund Freud*, London, Hogarth.

Pavlov, I.P. 1960. *Conditioned Reflexes*, translated by Anrep, G.V., Dover reprint.

Rescorla, R.A. 1988. Pavlovian conditioning: It's not what you think it is, *American Psychologist*, 43, 151–161.

Shoham S.G. and Seis, M.C. 1993. *A Primer in the Psychology of Crime*, New York, Harrow and Heston.

Skinner, B.F. 1938. *The Behavior of Organisms*, New York, Appleton-Century-Crofts.

Sutherland, E. 1947. *Principles of Criminology*, New York, J.B. Lippincott.

Tappan, P.W. 1947. Who is the criminal? in Geis, G. and Meier, R.F., Eds., *White Collar Crime*, New York, Free Press.

Psychopathy and Criminal Behavior

Psychopaths commit some of the most horrific, disturbing serial crimes. Consequently, many psychopaths receive intensive media attention and may achieve celebrity status. A pertinent example is Ted Bundy, whose spree of abduction, rape, and murder has been the subject of books and movies. However, Mr. Bundy represents only one of a variety of subtypes of psychopaths. A full understanding of the relationship between psychopathy and crime requires an appreciation of the various subtypes of psychopaths. It is also important to understand how psychopaths compare to other types of criminals. Another crucial insight is the subtle distinction between psychopaths and sociopaths. This entry addresses each of these important issues.

A Psychological Taxonomy of Criminals

One of the leading experts on psychopathy, David Lykken, divides criminals into three groups based on psychological health: Those for whom a psychiatric condition is not the direct cause of criminal behavior, those who are psychotic, and those who meet criteria for antisocial personality disorder (Lykken, 1995). For over 90% of individuals convicted of crimes, there is no mental health diagnosis that explains their criminal behavior. These individuals tend to be one-time offenders who may be victims of circumstances, such as a crime of passion or a lapse in judgment. The recidivism rate among these individuals is low, probably owing to the transient nature of the circumstances surrounding their crime. Repeat offenders among this group may include career criminals who make a reasoned choice to pursue crime as a profession. These career criminals appear to be normal in terms of their appetites, expressed morals, and psychological functioning. Examples of this group may include drug dealers who are faced with the choice between a low paying, menial job and the lucrative drug trade.

It is important to note that many offenders in the above noted group will have a diagnosable psychiatric condition. Usually these diagnosable conditions, such as major depression, are not seen as a direct cause of the criminal behavior. Nevertheless, some conditions may help to motivate criminal behavior. For example, someone who has a psychoactive substance-use disorder might steal to support their drug habit. The important consideration here is that substance dependence

is an indirect contributing factor or circumstance, rather than a cause of the criminal behavior.

Another group in Lykken's psychological taxonomy of criminals is persons who are psychotic at the time they commit a crime. An example of a psychotic individual who might be mistaken for a psychopath is Norman Bates from the movie *Psycho*. A real-life example of a psychotic serial murder is David "Son of Sam" Berkowitz.

Psychotic individuals probably account for less than 5% of persons convicted of crimes. An important cause of psychotic conditions is poorly controlled chronic mental health disorders such as schizophrenia or bipolar affective disorder (Julien, 2001). Although only a minority of seriously mentally ill persons commit crimes, a noteworthy minority of these individuals have repeated contact with police, are difficult to manage in both community and institutional settings, and have a high recidivism rate. With proper monitoring and treatment, which is not easy to accomplish in many cases, these individuals can avoid further criminal convictions (Julien, 2001).

An important cause of psychotic states is abuse of powerful drugs such as methamphetamine, crack cocaine, and PCP. Indeed, the leading cause of psychiatric states leading to emergency admission into a psychiatric hospital is psychosis related to drug abuse (Maisto, Galizio, and Conners, 1995). As with the seriously mentally ill, proper treatment for psychoactive substance use disorders can effectively reduce the incidence of psychosis and crime.

The third group in Lykken's psychological taxonomy of criminals are those who meet criteria for a mental health diagnosis called antisocial personality disorder (ASPD). According to the American Psychiatric Association (1994), ASPD is characterized by a pervasive pattern of disregard for and violation of basic societal rules or the rights of others. The technical diagnosis of ASPD requires the presence of three or more of the following symptoms: (1) repeated criminal behavior resulting in arrests, (2) repeated lying or other deceitfulness, (3) impulsivity or failure to plan ahead, (4) repeated physical fights or assaults, (5) reckless disregard for the safety of self or others, (6) consistent irresponsibility, such as failing to sustain gainful employment or meet financial obligations, or (7) lack of remorse. An individual must be at least 18 years old to be diagnosed with ASPD but the pattern of behavior must be evident prior to the age of 15 and be serious enough to receive a diagnosis of conduct disorder during childhood or adolescence. Finally, a person should not be diagnosed with ASPD if they only exhibit antisocial behavior during manic or psychotic episodes.

A well-known finding in criminology research is that a minority of criminals commit the majority of crimes. For example, in a study where 6–8% of the sample meet criteria for ASPD, the individuals accounted for 60–70% of all uniform crime report index crimes and 70–80% of violent crimes (Lykken, 1995). Among teenagers, most high-rate offenders meet criteria of the necessary precursor to ASPD, namely conduct disorder (Frick, 1998). All psychopaths should meet criteria for ASPD, but not all individuals with ASPD are psychopaths. Indeed, most individuals who meet criteria for ASPD are best described as sociopaths (Lyken, 1995). The distinction between psychopaths and sociopaths will receive more attention later in this entry, following a discussion of subtypes of psychopaths.

Subtypes of Psychopaths

There appear to be two major types of psychopaths, plus a variety of less frequent subtypes. The major subtypes are often called primary and secondary psychopaths. The defining feature of the primary psychopath is callous/unemotional disregard for the rights and well-being or others. Primary psychopaths do not appear to be driven by abnormal appetites or uncontrollable rage or other urges (Lykken, 1995). Therefore, this type of psychopath may be cruel to others, not out of a perverse sadistic pleasure, but because they do not care about the suffering or well-being of others. However, they do seem to care deeply about their own well-being. Therefore, bright and socially competent psychopaths of this type may hide their antisocial behavior behind a charming and convincing façade. They may rise to prominence in industry, government, or organized crime. Less intelligent or socially skilled psychopaths may spend their lives brutalizing others without advancing their social station.

They key feature of the primary or callous or unemotional psychopath relevant to understanding crime and punishment is that primary psychopaths show little or no shame or guilt. They may feel sorry for themselves if they get caught and threatened with punishment for doing something wrong, but there is no genuine remorse or caring empathy for their victims. This does not suggest that they are incapable of empathy. They can be very good at assessing the thoughts and feelings of others and acting effectively on this knowledge. Unfortunately, the empathic psychopath uses this understanding of others to manipulate or prey upon others. Thus, their empathy is

directed for self-gain, such as confidence schemes. They seem to live by the twisted golden rule "do what is good for me, who cares what happens to others."

Unlike primary psychopaths, secondary psychopaths may express genuine concern for others and true remorse when their actions cause harm to others. Nevertheless, they repeatedly engage in a pattern of behavior that breaks major societal rules or harms others. This may happen because secondary psychopaths tend to over-focus on rewards relative to punishment (Newman, 1987). This problem has been labeled the "reward-dominant" response. These individuals are not completely unaffected by punishment, rather they are much more aware of and motivated by rewards than they are by punishment (Frick, 1998). This leads to impaired decision making and may explain some of the impulsivity, excessive risk taking, and irresponsible behavior of psychopaths.

Both the reward-dominant and the callous or unemotional style have been associated with a tendency for psychopaths to be remarkably resistant to the effects of punishment. The root cause of the resistance to punishment may be neurological. Primary psychopaths are thought to have an under-active behavioral inhibition system (Lykken, 1995). Compared to others, they show less pronounced physiological responses to stress and therefore may be less influenced by anxiety and other restraining emotions than most persons (Frick, 1998). This is akin to having a car with faulty brakes.

Secondary psychopaths are thought to have an over-active behavioral activation system (Lykken, 1995). This may contribute to a behavioral style that leads to over-focusing on cues for rewards whereas under-focusing on cues for punishment (Newman, 1987). This is akin to having a car with a very powerful engine and a driver with a propensity to speed while failing to attend to road hazards. Regardless of the cause, reckless driving or weak brakes, the results of these deficits can be disastrous.

To summarize, primary and secondary psychopaths appear to have normal appetites and drives, but lack proper inhibitory controls on their behavior. They are difficult to socialize because they are relatively insensitive to punishment. In contrast, there may be another type of psychopaths that have abnormal drives or neurological functioning. Lykken (1995) calls this group the "distempered" subtypes.

One subtype of distempered psychopaths may be well-socialized individuals who become imbalanced owing to neurological illness or abnormality (Lykken, 1995). Thus, a brain tumor or hormonal problems may account for some sprees of violent, psychopathic behavior. Some psychopaths may have "choleric temperament" such that their neurological makeup results in extreme rage readiness or rage intensity. When their rage is triggered, these individuals may engage in psychopathic violence. Another type of distempered psychopath may have pathological cravings such as pedophilia and kleptomania. Still another group is psychopaths for whom the crime may be its own reward, and this subtype of psychopath may experience a perverse pleasure in the antisocial risk taking. Finally, for some psychopathic sex offenders, there may be a short-circuiting of the brain mechanisms for sex and violence. The infamous psychopath Ted Bundy may fit into this category.

The reader should be advised that the notion of the "distempered" psychopath is speculative and is currently the subject of case studies and ongoing investigation. However, extensive research dating back to the 1950s provides strong support for the primary and secondary subtypes. A defining characteristic of the primary and secondary types appears to be insensitivity to punishment, which is possibly related callous or unemotional traits and over-focusing on rewards relative to consequences. Understanding these phenomena is the key to understanding most psychopaths. Another key consideration is impulsivity because impulsivity combined with callous or emotional traits can be a particularly pathological combination (Frick, 1998).

Psychopathy versus Sociopathy

The key distinction between psychopaths and sociopaths is their response to the surrounding social environment. Psychopaths and sociopaths are cheaters in the cultural game as they bend or break societal rules to their advantage, ruthlessly capitalize on others' altruism or naiveté, and often use violence as a tool to get what they want. Although it may be difficult to distinguish the behavior of psychopaths and sociopaths, there are some key distinctions.

Psychopaths appear to have fundamental neurological, emotional, or cognitive deficits that make them highly resistant to normal socialization pressures. Thus, psychopaths may be playing by a different set of psychological rules than sociopaths. Thus, psychopaths' propensity to break rules or harm others seems to be a feature of temperament rather than defective socialization.

Sociopaths are often described as individuals whose criminal behavior is primarily because of unsocialized behavior owing to ineffective environments and is not because of inherent temperament or personality characteristics. This suggests that the behavior of sociopaths might be due to ignorance of acceptable cultural behavior or skill deficits. Although some sociopaths may be truly undersocialized, a more accurate explanation is that sociopaths are improperly socialized and become members of a deviant subculture, such as a gang. Thus, sociopathy is best explained by the individual's external environment whereas psychopathy might be best explained by the individual's internal psychological functioning.

Sociopathy can often be traced back to poor parental monitoring or ineffective discipline that eventually results in association with a deviant peer group (Patterson, Reid, and Dishion, 1992). If they are not managed properly by their parents, children may have serious problems with aggression, defiance, noncompliance, lying, and stealing. Children with these early onset conduct problems are typically rejected by the main-stream, relatively prosocial peer group. Rejected individuals typically gravitate toward a deviant peer group. This deviant peer group tends to reinforce antisocial behavior, which promotes an escalating cycle of antisocial behavior. In adolescence, the behavior problems may escalate to include resistance to parental supervision, truancy, substance abuse, promiscuous sexual behavior, and delinquency. Continuation of a pattern of behavior that violates the rights of others and repeatedly breaks major societal rules results in a diagnosis of ASPD in adulthood.

There are some early warning signs of a high potential to develop into a psychopath, including an early onset of conduct disorder. Children with early onset conduct disorder tend to have difficult temperaments that are evident in infancy or very early childhood (Patterson et al., 1992). Early signs of trouble may be infants and toddlers who are difficult to soothe or get into a steady routine. These dispositional characteristics can interact with environmental influences, such as chaotic home environments, to produce an escalating course of antisocial behavior (Frick, 1998). If children continue to have an escalating course of antisocial behavior despite appropriate prosocial socialization influences, such as high-quality parenting and school environments, this may distinguish them as psychopaths.

Another potential early warning sign of psychopathy is cruelty or callous disregard for the well-being of others. Examples of childhood expression of callous or unemotional traits include bullying peers, cruelty to siblings or other family members, repeated instances of overly rough play with pets, and torture or killing of animals. If these behaviors are not clearly reinforced by the environment or continue despite appropriate monitoring and punishment, this pattern of cruel behavior may distinguish the individual as a psychopath.

A final but very important consideration in this discussion of psychopathy and sociopathy is the distinction between proactive and reactive aggression (Patterson et al., 1992). Reactive aggression refers to a tendency to respond emotionally to provocation with aggression. Many psychologically normal individuals may respond to provocation with legitimate self-defense that may sometimes include violence. However, primary psychopaths are expected to show a cold and calculating response to provocation. They may deny feeling angry even after seriously injuring or killing someone in response to provocation. Secondary psychopaths are expected to over-react emotionally to provocation and exhibit extreme violence that is out of proportion with the provocation, such as giving someone a severe beating for a minor verbal slight. Sociopaths are expected to respond emotionally to provocation and retaliate in a manner consistent with environmental rewards for reactive aggression.

Proactive aggression refers to planned attacks on others. A psychopath or sociopath might consider proactive aggression to be perfectly legitimate tool for getting what they want. In addition to the tangible rewards from proactive aggression, psychopaths and sociopaths may enjoy the power and control that stems from proactive aggression. Owing to their callous or unemotional traits, primary psychopaths should experience little or no caring for the suffering of their victims of proactive aggression. Secondary psychopaths may not notice the downside of violence, including victim suffering, as they over-focus on rewards rather than costs of their behavior, Thus, if they are unrestrained by their environment, psychopaths are expected to show an escalating use of proactive aggression. Sociopaths may engage in some very violent, disturbing behavior, but they should be more restrained than psychopaths because sociopaths should have a higher capacity for remorse, fear, and sensitivity to punishment. Sociopathic violence should fit with the cultural mores of a deviant subgroup, whereas sociopathic violence would seem to be excessive even by deviant standards.

Conclusion

In conclusion, the dictionary definition of a psychopath is a mentally unbalanced individual, especially a person who is violent or dangerous. Fortunately psychopathy is rare. Nevertheless, this phenomenon is important to understand because psychopaths tend to commit many more crimes than would be expected for their small numbers in the population. Many of these crimes are spectacular for their violence or callous cunning, such as sadistic murders, extended crime sprees, involvement in organized crime, or elaborate confidence schemes including corporate or governmental corruption. There are two major types of psychopaths. One type, commonly known as primary, suffers from an imbalance owing to lack of emotional caring for others or response to punishment. They show reckless disregard for the safety of others, deliberately fail to honor obligations, and lack true remorse when their actions harm others. Another type, commonly known as secondary psychopaths, are imbalanced regarding their ability to weigh the costs and benefits of their actions. They put far too much emphasis on attending to rewards relative to potential negative consequences of their actions. The behavior of the primary and secondary psychopaths may be very similar to each other and to sociopaths. The key difference is that sociopaths have a better prognosis for intervention assuming that they can be provided with proper socialization. On the other hand, psychopaths are highly resistant to normal socialization pressures and therefore are much more dangerous, expected to have a chronic course, and may require powerful and sophisticated environmental controls to keep them from harming others.

BRAD SMITH

References and Further Reading

American Psychiatric Association. (1994). *Diagnostic and Statistical Manual of Mental Disorders*, 4th ed., Washington, DC.

Frick, P.J. (1998). *Conduct Disorders and Severe Antisocial Behavior*, New York, Plenham.

Julien, R.M. (2001). *A Primer of Drug Action*, 9th ed. New York, Worth.

Lykken, D.T. (1995). *The Antisocial Personalities*, Hillsdale, NJ, Lawrence Erlbaum Associates, Inc.

Maisto, S.A., Galizio, M. and Connors, G.J. (1995). *Drug Use and Abuse*, 2nd ed., Fort Worth, TX, Harcourt.

Newman, J.P. (1987). Reaction to punishment in extroverts and psychopaths: Implications for the impulsive behavior of disinhibited individuals, *Journal of Research in Personality*, 21, 464–480.

Patterson, G.R., Reid, J.B. and Dishion, T.J. (1992). *A Social Learning Approach IV: Antisocial Boys*, Eugene, OR, Casstalia.

See also **Psychological Theories of Crime**

Public Drunkenness

Although drunkenness was not an offense at early common law it was made a misdemeanor in England in 1606 by act of Parliament. The best view is that it was made a part of the common law of the states in the U.S. as a misdemeanor and was considered *malum in se* or morally wrong. Historically, it has been common practice for states to adopt statutes prohibiting public drunkenness or intoxication. It has also been a usual practice for local units of government to adopt ordinances with the same prohibition. The intoxication can be caused by alcohol or other drugs or by a combination of alcohol and other drugs.

Frequently, someone arrested for being drunk in public is a chronic alcoholic. Alcoholism is considered to be a disease and in 1962 in *Robinson v. California,* 370 U.S. 660, the U.S. Supreme Court declared that a California statute making it a crime to be a drug addict was unconstitutional as cruel and unusual punishment under the Eighth Amendment because the statute had made a sickness punishable. This raised the question of what is the criminal responsibility of a chronic alcoholic who is drunk in public. In 1966, the U.S. Court of Appeals for the Fourth Circuit considered this issue under a North Carolina public intoxication statute. In *Driver v. Hinnant,* 356 F.2d 761, the Court found that because of the disease of alcoholism, Driver was "powerless to stop drinking" and, therefore, the disease acted as a compulsion to be drunk (and in public). Consequently, the statute was found to be cruel and unusual punishment and was unconstitutional.

This issue finally reached the U.S. Supreme Court in 1968 in *Powell v. Texas,* 392 U.S. 514. The High Court concluded that even a chronic alcoholic made a voluntary choice to drink even though there was a compulsion which was "strong" but "not completely overpowering." The closely divided Court held the statute to be constitutional and not cruel and unusual punishment.

The current view is that chronic alcoholics (and other drug addicts) do make choices and can be held legally accountable for those choices (Boldt, 1992). There is "massive descriptive evidence...that individuals often make choices to abandon addictive conduct or abstain from drug use permanently or temporarily" (Fingarette, 1975, 443).

But alcoholism is still considered a disease that is medically treatable and there is no convincing evidence that arrest and jail terms, without treatment,

effect a cure. Consequently, most states, like West Virginia, have decriminalized drunkenness (LaFave, 2003, 484). Other states, although not adopting decriminalization, have adopted methods of diversion from the criminal justice process (LaFave, 2003). A typical diversionary practice is for the police to take the public inebriate to a detoxification center instead of to jail. There he is detoxified and offered, usually on a voluntary basis, treatment. Consequently, there is still statutory authority to remove a public drunk but the process is civil rather than criminal. Along with this system of diversion, jurisdictions can still retain their criminal, public drunkenness statute.

As a crime, public drunkenness or intoxication is considered a misdemeanor by state statute or local ordinance. Although it typically does permit a custodial arrest, it is usually considered a lesser misdemeanor in a state's statutory classification system. For example, a state might have four classes of misdemeanors with a class one misdemeanor being the most serious and carrying both a jail term (typically up to 1 year) and a fine, whereas, the class four misdemeanor would only carry a maximum fine of $100–$200 and no jail time. Public drunkenness would likely be the class four misdemeanor imposing a fine only.

There are two elements in the crime of public intoxication or drunkenness. First the offender must be intoxicated and secondly, she must be in public while intoxicated. One statutory definition of intoxicated from Virginia is that it "means a condition in which a person has drunk enough alcoholic beverages to observably affect his manner, disposition, speech, muscular movement, general appearance, or behavior" (Va. Code, Sec. 4.1–100). Of course, as noted earlier, one can be intoxicated from drugs other than alcohol or by alcohol and other drugs in combination. Black's Law Dictionary defines intoxication as a "diminished ability to act with full mental and physical capabilities because of alcohol or other drug consumption." Proof of intoxication includes such things as "slurred speech, swaying from side to side, smelling of alcohol, bloodshot and glassey eyes" (*Wilson v. Commonwealth,* 2002 Va. App. Lexis 322) as well as the results of field tests such as walk and turn, the gaze nastagmus test, blood tests, and the breathalyzer.

The second element of the crime is that the person's intoxication must take place in public. Black's Law Dictionary describes this as "The appearance of a person who is under the influence of drugs or alcohol in a place open to the general public." A place open "to the general public" or a public place includes streets, highways, hotels buses, trains, and places of public transportation, public parks, police headquarters, schools, and other places "visited by many persons and usually accessible to the ... public" (Perkins, 1997). Ordinarily, drunkenness is not public or in a public place when in the privacy of one's home or within the curtilage (e.g., in ones own yard) surrounding ones home. However, even though one is on his own property, for example, in his front yard but which fronts a public street, and is intoxicated, some states consider that public because the intoxicated person is "in open view visible to the community" (*Crislip v. Commonwealth*, 554 S.E. 2d 96, 2001).

Ordinarily, intoxication and public are the only two elements required for public drunkenness. However, some states do add other elements to the offense. In other words, the two elements alone do not constitute a crime but some other element must be added such as profane swearing or disorderly conduct (C.J.S., Sec. 8).

Although the general rule that must be satisfied to constitute a crime is that crimes must include *mens rea* (intent) and *actus reus* (the criminal act), this is not so for public intoxication. The prosecution need not prove the "intent to become and be found intoxicated" (C.J.S., Sec. 6).

JAMES L. HAGUE

References and Further Reading

Boldt, 1992. The Construction of Responsibility in the Criminal Law, 140 U. Pa. L. Rev. 2245.
Code of Virginia 1950, Sec. 4.1–100.
14 Corpus Juris Secundum, *Chemical Dependents*, Sec. 6.
14 Corpus Juris Secundum, *Chemical Dependents*, Sec. 8.
Fingarette, 1975. Addiction and criminal responsibility, *Yale Law Journal*, 84, 413.
Garner, B.A., Ed. 2003. *Black's Law Dictionary*, 7th ed., West Group, St. Paul, MN.
LaFave, W.R. 2003. *Criminal Law*, 4th ed., Thompson-West, St. Paul, MN.
Perkins, R.M. and Boyce, R.N. 1982. *Criminal Law*, 3rd ed., Foundation Press, Mineola, NY.

See also **Alcohol Use and Criminal Behavior; Alcohol Use: The Law**

Public Opinion and Criminal Behavior

Public opinion is a critical variable in understanding how we understand criminal behavior. Public opinion is even more critical in determining our response to criminal behavior. As Emile Durkheim (1982) noted, every society has its sinners and saints. However, what constitutes a "sin" and raises the moral outrage that accompanies sins or crimes varies throughout history and from society to society. Before we can look at public attitudes toward crime and criminal behavior, we must first understand how society shapes what we define as a crime and how we should react to it. This has attracted the interest of criminologists for over a century since Durkheim's seminal work. This study has examined how sentiments about a behavior form, what functions these sentiments play for the society in general, and how various institutions then use these. Although this sociological examination of the meaning of public attitudes dominates discussion there are other types of inquiry into public opinion and criminal behavior. As a way of understanding the variety and levels of investigation we can consider six intersecting and overlapping questions that have stimulated study.

First we can examine public opinion on responses to crime and criminals. Variously described as the study of public attitudes to punishment, sentencing, or crime, this area of study taps the rich vein of indignation that Durkheim first described. The public opinion associated with crime largely concerns the outrage that crime evokes. This moral indignation is indeed what draws public attention to crime and makes it so interesting to people.

Associated with this field of study, but more specific, are those investigations that focus on public attitudes to the law and the courts. Some of these studies explore the degree to which the law and the courts, through their decisions, can guide or direct public attitudes to certain behaviors. However, the direction of the causal link can vary. This emerges particularly in the highly contested nature of some crimes such as abortion. Public opinion reflected in general cultural values also has the potential to have a great influence on criminal behavior through the decision making of offenders. Indeed major criminological theories can be distinguished by their explanation of how this influence operates. Sutherland's theory of differential association is predicated on the operation of separate values or norms of criminals that permit the offending behavior. Strain theory proposes that offenders share mainstream goals but reject mainstream methods of achieving them. Neutralization theory argues that mainstream values are selectively "neutralized" by offenders. This process, Matza later argued, reflects not a permanent but rather a temporary "drift" away from group norms, typically in adolescence.

A third question concerns public attitudes to the group referred to as "criminals" or "offenders." Studies have identified "attractiveness" as a relevant variable affecting attributions of culpability and others have found the social class of the offender also affects these judgments. These studies obviously merge with the large current of research in social psychology examining processes such as scapegoating and prejudice.

Fourth is the question of attitudes toward specific types of offenses and offenders (e.g., crime-seriousness studies). Studies addressing this question will typically tap into generalized sentiments toward crime and punishment. Shifts in attitudes toward certain types of offense and offenders can reflect changing social values and priorities as will be discussed below. Current social concerns are focused mainly on minimizing personal risks and thus the distinction between violent and nonviolent offences is a major dividing line in the extent of disapproval (see Cullen et al., 2000; Garland, 2000).

A fifth question concerns public beliefs regarding the causes of crime and its remedies. The concern here is how individuals conceptualize crime, mainly because this has implications for (and helps explain) the responses to crime that individuals endorse.

Finally there are studies looking at specific types of punishment, the most important being attitudes toward the death penalty but more recently public attitudes toward mandatory sentencing. Interestingly, the continued focus on the death penalty issue has remained a concern in the U.S. only because that nation remains alone in the western world in employing it. This is not because opinions in other western countries on the death penalty are that different from those in the U.S.; rather this reflects the different political priorities of these countries (see Savelsberg, 1994).

These six lines of inquiry cover a diverse range of study from public attitudes toward criminal behavior to the possible influence of criminal behavior on public attitude. The focus here will be on the central question that is usually associated with public opinion and criminal behavior—that is public opinion *about* criminal behavior.

Apart from the subjects of study outlined above there are also different orientations adopted by different scholars. Most common is a sociological approach similar to Durkheim's, which seeks to understand the social functions and processes involved in labeling and reacting to crime. The focus is to understand the symbolic meaning of crime and punishment as an explanation of public attitudes (e.g., Tyler and Boeckmann, 1997). Closely associated with this have been more recent attempts to investigate, at a sociological level, the changing social exigencies shaping these responses (e.g., Garland, 2000). The goal here is to "situate" public opinion on crime by describing its most current and relevant social functions.

A second type of scholarship can be defined by an attempt to make sense of the empirical information available on public opinion. These studies aim to derive a meaningful picture of public opinion as a "print out" of public thinking, mood, and concern. These studies are primarily guided by an attempt to determine the implications of public opinion for policy. Scholars in this area are seeking to understand the empirical dimensions and nature of public opinion, its underlying dynamics and, therefore, its malleability. Scholars such as Roberts (see Roberts, 1992; Roberts and Stalans, 1998), Cullen (e.g., Cullen et al., 2000), and Applegate (e.g., Applegate et al., 1996) have made significant strides in this endeavor over the last two decades. Among other things these studies highlight the misunderstandings and misperceptions underlying most people's opinions about crime.

A third line of scholarship seeks to understand the political processes associated with public opinion (e.g., Savelsberg, 1994; Scheingold, 1995; Beckett, 1997). There is some contention as to whether political initiative follows or leads public opinion. The simple view that most members of the public would likely subscribe to is that political action does, and should, follow public opinion on crime. However, Beckett (1997) provides considerable evidence to suggest that public opinion on crime and drugs in the U.S. has *followed* rather than led political initiative and associated media attention. Some scholars argue that public opinion is not viewed by policy makers as a fixed reality but a set of sensitivities that are constantly shifting and changing responding to the way political initiatives are framed.

The interest with this third line of inquiry is not so much in understanding public opinion on crime but the use of this opinion by political institutions. The use and shaping of public opinion by political organizations as well as media and commercial interests is also the subject of this inquiry. Also of interest is how criminal justice workers and policy makers are influenced by what they perceive public opinion to be—and this is often based on information they gain from the media. The intricate interplay between political initiative, media treatments, and public concern have the potential to create "crime waves" and spirals of increasing concern and reaction to crime quite independent of the underlying trends in crime.

It should be stressed that these three lines of inquiry are hardly mutually exclusive but instead represent different interests and foci in the study of public attitudes on crime. Both the sociological and the psychological or empirical inquiries inform the critical issue of political implications as a practical outcome. The remainder of this article will focus on the sociological inquiry into the role of public opinion and the psychological inquiry into the nature of public opinion and how this informs the development of criminal justice policy.

Public Opinion and Society

Durkhiem was important in establishing the symbolic importance of labeling certain behaviors as "criminal." Furthermore, he described the functions (or benefits) that the associated moral outrage plays for a society. Durkheim argued that expressing outrage at those behaviors that offend societies' standard functions to increase social cohesion or solidarity. Because of its capacity to excite strong passions about fundamental aspects of social life that affect everyone, crime and punishment clearly serve functions in the community. Thus criminal justice policies and practices are often pursued with this in mind rather than being justified or evaluated in terms of their effect in reducing crime. For example, practices like capital punishment are justified not for their crime control effects, but because they are seen as necessary expressions of public sentiment. These functions become more critical at times of social and economic insecurity. A number of scholars have shown how repressive policies flourish in these times. For example, a classic work by Kai Erikson's (Wayward Puritans) showed how the Salem witch hunts drew the foundering New England communities together and served to build social solidarity. Similarly, other scholars documented how lynching of Blacks in the southern states of the U.S. increased during the economic recession of the 1890s. Some European scholars linked the desire to punish—punitiveness—to the particular social pressures felt by the social sector (lower-middle class) feeling the most frustration in their efforts to progress in society. Members of this sector typically favor the strictest rules and the most draconian punishments for transgressions in both religious and secular life.

The study of punitiveness conjoins psychological and sociological perspectives and represents a deep core of study. German scholars attempting to come to

terms with the frightening descent into authoritarianism of the Nazi era undertook much of this study. Scholars from the Frankfurt school such as such as Theodor Adorno and Erich Fromm sought to analyze the tendency to intolerance and authoritarianism as a kind of pathology. Much of the psychological work typical of studies from the 1950s through the 1970s was informed by psychoanalytic theories or saw authoritarianism and punitiveness as problematic aspects of personality.

Public concern about crime certainly emerged as a constant feature of the policy landscape in the western world in the 1990s. Garland (2000) talks about a distinct shift in the last quarter of the 20th century toward a concern with "risk management" and a reduced tolerance to offenders and a disinterest in social reform and offender rehabilitation. Notable citizen initiated or citizen-facilitated actions include public notification laws—most notably Megans' Law in the U.S. and the outcry about the unofficial publication of pedophiles names in the U.K. In terms of sentencing and legislation, longer sentences and reducing judicial discretion was endorsed in all the English speaking countries (Roberts et al., 2001).

Analyzing the Nature and Dimensions of Public Opinion

Sociological analyses have illustrated the important way that public opinion on crime reflects and shapes the values of a society. Crime seriousness studies measure the relative seriousness with which crime is viewed within a particular group at a particular time. Fortunately we have the results of a very early study of crime seriousness that was carried out by the pioneering psychometrician, Louis L. Thurstone in 1927. By comparing the results of this study with later studies of crime seriousness, significant shifts in the relative ordering of perceptions of crime seriousness have been observed. Behaviors considered quite serious previously fell down in the order of seriousness 50 years later and were replaced by other crimes. This is important as it indicates how malleable public reaction can be. The status of behaviors such as drug taking, prostitution, abortion, adultery, and so forth are highly contested. Moral indignation in regard to these offences experienced by individuals is to a large degree a function of the symbolic meaning of the offence for the individual and dominant social constructions. The mechanisms by which certain crimes are elevated in importance and moral outrage and thus change in perceived seriousness over time have been described by various students of public opinion and deviance.

The study of public attitudes to sentencing reached a critical departure with the work of Canadian criminologists

Anthony Doob and Julian Roberts. These researchers demonstrated that public knowledge was an important variable because much of public opinion about sentencing was based on misinformation and misunderstandings. Doob and Roberts (see chapter in Walker and Hough, 1988) demonstrated that as the level of public knowledge and involvement in a particular case increased public attitudes generally became less severe and indeed the disparity between the courts and public attitudes virtually disappeared. This research exposed the disparity between knowledge and attitude in a meaningful way that has now become part of criminological wisdom. Another important insight is the difference between global and specific opinions (Applegate et al., 1996). Focusing on global opinions can lead to the overestimation of public punitiveness. It is now clear from these studies that we must look critically at the results of simple questions posed to the public in a general way in opinion polls.

Studies have consistently demonstrated that the public is almost entirely reliant on the media for information about crime. This has important implications as other studies have clearly documented the subjective and selective nature of media reporting of crime. In particular as stories about crime increased in the media in the U.S. throughout the 1990s, public concern about crime also increased despite falling or static crime rates.

Public knowledge is thus an essential aspect to understanding public attitudes—underlying beliefs and assumptions inform attitudes. Also understanding attitudes requires more sophisticated measurement devices such as gauging openness to alternatives and what range of preferences the public has regarding punishment. For example, it appears that support for the death penalty can be substantially diminished when offenders receive "life without parole" sentences. The public is open to a range of options if sufficient justifications for sentences are provided. This means that rather than seeing public attitude as leading and dictating public policy it may be more appropriate to see it as providing a field of receptivity and expectations to which sound policy aiming to respect victims, ensure a safe community, and punish offenders is placed (Cullen et al., 2000).

Although there have been few cross-national studies of public opinion there are some notable exceptions (e.g., Walker and Hough, 1988; Roberts et al., 2001). The international crime victimization surveys also include questions on public opinion and these can be useful in illuminating the extent of differences between the Western countries. Comparative studies of public opinion combined with analysis of punishment practices, can be useful in illuminating the large question of whether these different practices are a reflection of underlying attitudes or whether we should look to the functions of institutions to understand the observed differences (see Savelsberg, 1994).

Conclusion

Public attitude on criminal behavior fulfils important social functions for the community but is not a good basis for the construction of effective crime policy or mechanisms to actually reduce crime. Such policies must be formed on the basis of the existing knowledge about criminal behavior and evidence about what is effective in reducing crime. Public fears and expressive issues in regard to crime and punishment certainly need to be addressed, although politicians should resist the temptation to exploit public fears. Those programs that have been developed on the basis of good evidence to prevent crime need to be effectively explained to the public to engender public participation in an effective crime policy. Criminologists have a distinct role in pointing out the nature of public opinion on crime and its limits in informing and effective crime policy.

DAVID INDERMAUR

References and Further Reading

Applegate, B., Cullen, F., Turner, M. and Sundt, J. (1996). Assessing public support for 'Three-Strikes-and-You're-Out' laws: Global versus specific attitudes. *Crime and Delinquency, 42*, 517–534.

Beckett, K. (1997). *Making Crime Pay: Law and Order in Contemporary American Politics*, New York, Oxford University Press.

Cullen, F., Fisher, B. and Applegate, B. (2000). Public opinion about punishment and corrections, in Tonry, M., Ed., *Crime and Justice: A Review of the Research*, Vol. 27, Chicago, IL, University of Chicago Press.

Durkheim, E. (1982). *The Rules of Sociological Method*, [1895], London, Macmillan.

Erikson, K.T. (1966). *Wayward Puritans: A Study in the Sociology of Deviance*, New York, Wiley.

Flanagan, T. and Longmire, D., Eds. (1996). *Americans View Crime and Justice: A National Public Opinion Survey*, Thousand Oaks, CA, Sage.

Garland, D. (2000). The culture of high crime societies: Some preconditions of recent 'Law and Order' policies, *British Journal of Criminology, 40*, 347–375.

Roberts, J. (1992). Public opinion, crime and criminal justice, in Tonry, M. Ed., *Crime and Justice: A Review of the Research*, Vol. 16, Chicago, IL, University of Chicago Press.

Roberts, J. and Stalans, L. (1998). *Public Opinion, Crime and Criminal Justice*, Boulder, CO, Westview Press.

Roberts, J., Stalans, L., Hough, M. and Indermaur, D. (2001). *Penal Populism and Public Opinion*, Oxford, U.K., Oxford University Press.

Savelsberg, J. (1994). Knowledge, domination and criminal punishment, *American Journal of Sociology, 99*, 911–943.

Scheingold, S., Ed., (1997). *Politics, Crime Control and Culture*, Aldershot, VT, Ashgate.

Tyler, T. and Boeckmann, R. (1997). Three strikes and you are out, but why? The psychology of public support for punishing rule breakers, *Law and Society Review, 31*, 237–265.

Walker, N. and Hough, M., Eds. (1988). *Public Attitudes to Sentencing: Surveys from Five Countries,* Gower, U.K., Aldershot.

Warr, M. (1994). Public perceptions and reactions to violent offending and victimization, in Reiss, A. and Roth, J., Eds., *Understanding and Preventing Violence: Consequences and Control,* Vol. 4, Washington, DC, National Academy Press.

See also **Capital Punishment: Controversies Surrounding; Physical Attractiveness and Criminal Behavior; Public Opinion and the Criminal Justice System**

Public Opinion and the Criminal Justice System

The views of the public exercise an important direct and indirect influence on the criminal justice system. Politicians in all western nations cite the results of opinion polls (if they support the position being advocated) when introducing specific penal reforms. Public perceptions of the relative seriousness of different crimes can affect the sentence ranges found in sentencing guideline systems. Judges sometimes consider the views of the community when imposing sentence and so do parole boards when making decisions about early release from prison. It is important therefore to understand the nature of public opinion with respect to crime and punishment.

The justice system attempts to inform the public about the criminal process, and to maintain public confidence in the administration of justice. If the public have little or no confidence in the criminal justice system, people will cease to participate by reporting crimes and serving as witnesses, and the system will become even less effective as a response to crime.

Attempts to inform and educate the public about crime are not always successful. Research over the past few decades has demonstrated that the public in America (as elsewhere) knows little about the justice system, and, with the exception of the police, has little confidence in most criminal justice professions. Also, the misperceptions that people have of the justice system tend to be interrelated and to reflect a view that the system protects the rights of the suspect, accused, or offender, usually at the expense of the interests of crime victims.

Surveys in several countries have documented some of the misperceptions about crime, offenders, and the justice system. With respect to crime, most people tend to overestimate the amount of crime that involves violence, and believe that crimes rates are constantly increasing (even when they are declining in reality). In the late 1990s, although crime rates were falling in America, Canada, and other western nations, most people persisted in believing the opposite. The constant emphasis in the news media on serious crime must be responsible for this systematic public misperception.

Stereotypes of offenders are widespread. People tend to believe that crime is committed by a small, easily-identifiable minority of people ("criminals"), who are very likely to commit further crimes in the future. They believe that the major causes of crimes are illegal drug use, the breakdown of the family, and a general lack of morals and values, particularly among the young. This may explain some of the difficulties that exoffenders experience in finding employment. There is also a tendency to associate criminality with certain racial minorities. These stereotypes can have negative consequences for African American defendants, if members of juries are predisposed to believe that they are more likely to be guilty. Stereotypes of offenders also affect public preferences with respect to crime control. If crime is a result of "bad people," there will be a desire to punish, rather than to rehabilitate.

Specific provisions of the criminal law are widely misperceived. For example, almost all Americans disapprove of the insanity defense; yet one survey found that when asked to provide an approximate definition of the defense, less than 1% of respondents came close to providing a legally correct definition. Most people also hold an inaccurate view of the meaning of "beyond a reasonable doubt." Other critical procedures are misunderstood. Over one-third of respondents to an American Bar Association Survey in 1998 held incorrect views that defendants in criminal trials must prove their innocence, that the civil and criminal justice system operate according to the same rules of evidence and procedure, and that all judges are appointed. Research also shows that a substantial proportion of the public do not know that they have the right to remain silent when questioned by the police.

Most people, however, know that they have a right to a lawyer, that they can still be sued for damages if found "not guilty" in criminal court, and that appellate courts can overturn decisions made in trial courts. Less knowledgeable individuals tend to have less formal education and are in the lower income brackets. This is important as these individuals are more likely to be defendants in criminal court.

Misperceptions of criminal justice statistics abound. The average member of the public tends to underestimate the severity of the sentencing process as well as the parole system. When asked to estimate the average sentence for a particular crime, many people provide a response that is lower than the actual level. This finding has emerged from research conducted in America, England, Canada, as well as Australia. In those countries that have not abolished parole, most people assume that almost all offenders get parole, when in fact only a fraction are released from prison early. Most people also overestimate the percentage of offenders released from prison that commit another serious crime. Because only a small percentage of the public has ever visited a prison, perceptions of prison life tend to be inaccurate as well; prisons are seen as being too easy on offenders.

Few members of the public have a positive opinion about the professionals that run the justice system. The exception to this rule is the police, who routinely receive the highest approval ratings in public surveys that ask people to rate the performance of criminal justice professionals. Although the police generally receive high approval ratings, many members of the public (in America at least) believe that the police use excessive force more often than is necessary. In addition, members of racial minorities in the U.S., Canada, and the U.K. believe that the police act in discriminatory ways, and are more likely to stop, question, and arrest Blacks.

The public reserves its harshest criticism for judges and parole boards. Most people regard the judiciary as unbiased and professional. Negative perceptions of the court are concentrated around efficiency and effectiveness issues such as excessive delay, expense of representation, and leniency toward criminal offenders. Judges are seen as being out of touch with the views of the general public, and this explains in the public mind why they impose lenient sentences. The public, however, have more positive perceptions of courts when they have actually been to a court. Surveys have shown that those with recent court experiences have more positive attitudes toward the court than do those who have never been to court. Parole boards also are seen as being excessively lenient, releasing too many offenders out of prison too early in their sentence.

Americans, Canadians, and Britons believe that they have the best justice systems towing to the pivotal role of juries in deciding guilt. The public overwhelmingly supports trial by jury when they are the victim or defendant of a crime. They believe that trial by jury is more accurate, more thorough, and more likely to minimize bias, and more likely to represent the opinion of minority groups. Public views of jury trials are that they are just as fair or fairer than trial by judges, even though sometimes jury trials render inaccurate verdicts. Although the law requires juries to reach verdicts based on the evidence, the public also supports allowing juries to use their conscience to arrive at a fair verdict. (This is known as "jury nullification.") The public approves of juries acquitting defendants who have committed crimes if a guilty verdict would be an unjust outcome. (Juries have acquitted defendants who were proven guilty in cases of assisted suicide, drug possession cases facing overly severe punishment, "three strikes and you're out" cases involving property or drug offenders, and cases involving violence against abortion clinics.)

Politicians and policy makers set much store by the findings of public opinion surveys that pose general questions about issues in criminal justice, such as "*Are you in favor of or opposed to capital punishment?*" However, researchers have demonstrated that such surveys are a rather inadequate way of documenting the nature of public opinion toward complex problems in the area of criminal justice.

People tend to have complex, nuanced opinions about these issues, and these opinions cannot be captured by a simplistic question on a poll. In answering simplistic, general questions, members of the public often have in mind the most severe forms of criminal offending involving repeat violent offenders. Public opinion toward general questions typically represent fleeting, "off the top of the head" answers. Public responses when given sufficient detail about criminal cases are quite different. For this reason, researchers in the field of criminal justice use a variety of research techniques, including qualitative methods such as focus groups, experimental manipulations, and more sophisticated survey methods such as computer-assisted surveys, factorial surveys, and deliberative polls. There is general agreement that an accurate portrait of public opinion can only be achieved by employing a variety of complementary research techniques.

One of the most robust findings in the literature concerns public sentencing preferences. Opinion polls conducted in all western nations over the past 25 years have routinely shown that approximately three-quarters of the public say that sentences should be harsher. But responses to such a question should be interpreted with caution. When people are asked about sentencing, they have the most serious crimes in mind. Serious crimes of violence represent only a small minority of all crimes committed. When asked specifically about other forms of criminality, public views change.

It is important, therefore, to pose specific rather than general questions to the public. This can be clearly illustrated with respect to the "three strikes" sentencing statutes in America. Applegate, Cullen, Turner, and Sundt (1996) found strong, general support for a law, which would mandate a lifetime prison sentence for an offender convicted of a serious felony for the third time. However, when confronted with specific cases, support for imposing such a law declined considerably. In addition, the respondents in this survey supported the existence of many exceptions to such a law.

Though many members of the public believe that harsher sentencing is necessary to respond to crime, it seems clear that people are aware that crime is a social problem, which cannot be addressed solely by the criminal justice system. Surveys in several countries have asked the public to identify the most effective crime reduction strategies. The results indicate that making the justice system tougher is only one option in the eyes of the public, and not necessarily the most important. Increasing discipline in the home and reducing the level of unemployment attract more support as strategies.

One critical question that has been repeatedly addressed in the literature concerns the purpose of sentencing. Researchers have attempted to ascertain which of the many purposes of sentencing (retribution, rehabilitation, deterrence, or incapacitation) generates most support among members of the public. The results of surveys in which people are asked to indicate their degree of support for one of these purposes shows that support is substantial for all options. There appears to be a bedrock of support for punishing adult offenders based on the seriousness of their offense, particularly those convicted of serious crimes of violence (e.g., Darley, Carlsmith, and Robinson, 2000). Most people believe that a "life sentence" should actually mean that the offender spends the rest of his natural life in prison. However, the public also strongly supports the rehabilitation of offenders, particularly non-violent offenders. Notwithstanding the movement toward harsher, mandatory sentencing over the past few decades, rehabilitation remains important to the public as a goal of sentencing and corrections.

The public make a clear distinction between the punishment of adult and juvenile offenders, with far greater support for rehabilitation emerging for juveniles. When asked to choose between punishment and rehabilitation, at least two-thirds of Americans choose rehabilitation and prevention programs. As well, most Americans oppose the automatic transfer of juvenile offenders to the adult court system for trial and punishment. Americans want judges to decide which juveniles will be tried as adults, and disapprove of trying accused persons under 15 as adults. Although most Americans believe that sentences imposed on juvenile offenders should be tougher, they also believe that sentences imposed on juveniles should be less severe than those imposed on adults convicted of similar crimes.

The importance of interpreting public opinion by posing detailed questions about specific scenarios also emerges as a principal finding in the vast literature on American attitudes toward capital punishment. Most polls conducted over the past three decades have shown that upward of three-quarters of the American public supports the death penalty. Support for capital punishment has been consistently strong since the first survey was conducted in America in 1936 (see Zeisel and Gallup, 1989). This general conclusion, however, fails to capture the reality that there are many forms of murder for which the public do not support the execution of the offender. For example, most American states have laws that permit the execution of people convicted of a murder occurring in the course of the commission of another crime (such as robbery). This is known as "felony murder." The public does not favor the execution of people convicted of felony murder. The public also disapproves of the execution of mentally ill offenders, mentally deficient offenders, and juvenile offenders. Moreover, when given a choice, the majority of the public supports life in prison without the possibility of parole and restitution to the family rather than the death penalty. It appears that between one-third to two-fifths of the public can be persuaded to change their support for the death penalty.

Public attitudes toward sentencing also change rapidly when people are given more information about the case or about sentencing options other than prison. Researchers in one study divided subjects at random into two smaller groups. One group was given a brief description of a case, and was asked to provide an evaluation of the sentence that had been imposed. The second group was given a more complete description of the same case. Subjects in the second group were far more satisfied with the sentence that had been imposed (Doob and Roberts, 1988).

Polls seem to show considerable public support for the use of imprisonment. When asked to "sentence" an offender, the typical public response is a period of imprisonment. As with so many findings in this area, it is important to qualify this statement. One reason why people react to crime by endorsing prison is that they typically do not think about alternative sanctions. When the public is reminded (or informed) of the existence of alternatives to incarceration, support for imprisoning offenders declines considerably.

This was dramatically illustrated by Doble and Klein (1989). Subjects were asked first to sentence offenders in a series of cases. Support for imprisonment was high. The same people were then given information about alternative ways of punishing offenders (e.g., probation and boot camps). After learning about these alternative sanctions, support for prison dropped. For example, in one case involving an armed robbery, at first over 80% of the subjects wanted the offender to go to prison. Upon hearing about the alternatives, less than half the group still wanted to imprison the offender. Other studies have asked respondents to choose between community-based alternatives or prison in sentencing specific criminal offenders. These studies find wide support for alternatives. For example, in the 1996 international victimization survey, about half of Americans, Canadians, and Britons, two-thirds of Australians, and almost three-fourth of New Zealanders recommended community-based alternatives (typically a community service order) for a repeat 21-year-old burglar.

In the past two decades, the American government has engaged in a "war on drugs." The public is quite skeptical that this government effort will reduce crime rates. The government effort to impose severe penalties for drug possession also is out of touch with public opinion. The public is more rehabilitation-oriented than government policies allow. Americans recommended probation as the penalty for possession of marijuana. This response is more lenient than the U.S. sentencing guideline punishment for this crime. The public are also willing to recommend treatment programs to small-time drug dealers, but want prison terms for major drug dealers or small-time drug dealers who fail a second time. Americans also disagreed with the additional 9-year prison term for trafficking crack cocaine required by the U.S. sentencing guidelines, and believe that drug traffickers should receive similar prison terms if they are selling heroin, cocaine, or crack cocaine. The public supports punitive penal policies only when violence is associated with the drug trafficking.

The public views certain criminal laws as unjust. The majority of respondents in several surveys support a law allowing patients (under the supervision of a physician) to use marijuana to relieve their symptoms. Even after referendums have been passed in some American states, the federal government has attempted to block the implementation of medically prescribed marijuana. This is a clear illustration that politicians listen to public opinion only when such opinion is consistent with their views.

Other criminal codes are inconsistent with public views. The public supports allowing people to use more force for the defense of property and for citizens apprehending fleeing criminals than the law allows. Although the criminal law assigns the same liability to accomplices and perpetrators, the public believes accomplices should receive less punishment. The criminal law's definition of an attempted crime also is incongruent with public view, which requires more actual action before a person can be convicted of an attempted crime.

There is no simple answer to the question "What do the public think about crime and punishment?" As with criminal justice professionals, laypersons have complex reactions to what are difficult questions. It is important to remember when discussing the nature of public views that the public derive their information about crime and criminal justice almost exclusively from the news media. In order to obtain a "true" sounding of public opinion, we need to first correct some of the misperceptions associated with crime and punishment. We also need to educate legislators and professionals about the biases associated with general polls in order to generate a more accurate reading of public opinion.

JULIAN V. ROBERTS AND LORETTA J. STALANS

References and Further Reading

Applegate, B., Cullen, F., Turner, M. and Sundt, J. 1996. Assessing public support for Three-Strikes-and-You're-Out laws: Global versus specific attitudes, *Crime and Delinquency,* 42, 517–534.

Applegate, B., Cullen, F. and Fisher, B. 1997. Public support for correctional treatment: The continuing appeal of the rehabilitative ideal, *The Prison Journal,* 77, 237–258.

Darley, J., Carlsmith, K. and Robinson, P., Incapacitation and just deserts as motives for punishment, *Law and Human Behavior,* 24, 659–683.

Doble, J. and Klein, J. 1989. *Punishing Criminals. The Public's View,* New York, Edna McConnell Clark Foundation.

Doob, A. and Roberts, J.V. 1988. Public punitiveness and public knowledge of the facts: some Canadian surveys, in Walker, N. and Hough, M., Eds., *Public Attitudes to Sentencing. Surveys from Five Countries,* Aldershot, Gower, U.K.

Finkel, N. 1996. *Commonsense Justice,* Boston, MA, Harvard University Press.

Flanagan, T. and Longmire, D., Eds. 1996. *Americans View Crime and Justice,* Thousand Oaks, CA, Sage.

Hough, M. 1996. People talking about punishment, *The Howard Journal,* 35, 191–214.

Roberts, J.V. 1992. Public opinion, crime and criminal Justice, in Tonry, M., Ed., *Crime and Justice. An Annual Review of Research,* Chicago, University of Chicago Press.

Roberts, J.V. and Stalans, L. 1997. *Public Opinion, Crime and Criminal Justice,* Boulder, CO, Westview Press.

Robinson, P.H. and Darley, J.M. 1995. *Justice, Liability and Blame: Community Views and the Criminal Law,* Boulder, CO, Westview Press.

Rossi, P. and Berk, R. 1997. *Just Punishments,* New York, Aldine de Gruyter.

Stalans, L. and Diamond, S. 1990. Formation and change in lay evaluations of criminal sentencing, *Law and Human Behavior,* 14, 199–214.

Stalans, L. and Lurigio, A. 1996. Special issue on public opinion on justice in the criminal justice system, *American Behavioral Scientist,* 39(4).

Walker, N. and Hough, M., Eds. 1988. *Public Attitudes to Sentencing,* Cambridge Studies in Criminology, LIX, Aldershot, Gower, U.K.

Zeisel, H. and Gallup, G. 1989. Death penalty sentiment in the United States, *Journal of Quantitative Criminology,* 5, 285–296.

See also **Public Opinion and Criminal Behavior**

Publications in Criminal Law

Publications in criminal law narrowly refers to publications on the subject of substantive criminal law. Criminal law may also refer to criminal procedure and evidence law. Substantive criminal law is a branch of public law that defines crimes (e.g., manslaughter, larceny), authorizes doctrinal defenses to crime (e.g., insanity), specifies the jurisdiction of criminal courts, and establishes general rules of criminal liability (e.g., voluntary act). Criminal procedure law guides the process by which criminal justice officials enforce the substantive criminal law. Its topics include arrest, search and seizure, interrogation, eyewitness identification, the conduct of pretrial stages including preliminary hearings and grand juries, the conduct of trials, sentencing, and appeals. The law of evidence includes rules that relate to the introduction of facts into consideration before the trier of fact at a trial and generally concerns the proof of facts. Another related area is the law of prisoners' rights. In addition to these legal subjects, the discipline of criminology is closely related to the subject matter of criminal law. Criminological studies provide great insight into questions concerning the causation of criminal behavior in individuals, the political and social factors that lead to officially declaring that certain behaviors are or are not crimes, the way in which specific crimes are enforced, and the effects of criminal behavior and criminalization on society (Hall, 1960). Criminalistics, the discipline of scientific crime detection, is also related to criminal law. This essay focuses on publications in substantive criminal law.

Publications in criminal law, like all legal literature, are hierarchically ordered into primary and secondary publications. Primary legal literature includes the texts of constitutions, statutes, and court cases that constitute "law" proper or the primary sources of law. In addition, executive orders, administrative agency rules, local ordinances, and court rules have the force of law.

Primary legal texts are "authorized statements" of law made by government institutions that express the formal authority of the state (Jacobstein et al., 1994). All other legal writing, including professional literature, educational materials, and legal scholarship, is secondary legal literature. Secondary publications in law are the work of independent writers or scholars, and expresses their private opinions. Legal scholarship cannot have the force of law although it is often highly authoritative and relied upon by judges and lawmakers; legal scholarship has been highly influential in stimulating law reform.

Primary legal texts are themselves hierarchically ordered in accordance with the authority status of the governmental institutions that produce them (Jacobstein et al., 1994). State constitutions and the U.S. Constitution are drafted by elected or appointed conventions and are ratified by special elections that require a supermajority of votes for passage; they are amended by special rules included within each constitution. Constitutions are deemed to issue from the people. Statutes (also called legislation or acts) are passed by elected representatives of the people and are signed by the chief executive of the state or the nation, in accord with rules specified in their respective constitutions. Case law (also called common law) consists of legal doctrines established by appellate courts in the absence of legislation, and also include authoritative interpretations of statutes and constitutions. Common law rules are established by duly elected or appointed judges. Law enacted or established by "lower" political sources must conform to law created by "higher" sources. Constitutions are superior law and any statutory or common law rule inconsistent with the Constitution is void and unenforceable. This is determined by judges whose decisions comprise constitutional law. A rule of constitutional law cannot be modified by legislation. Legislation is hierarchically superior to rules established by judges, and so statutes may abolish or modify common law rules of criminal law (except for constitutional law).

As authority, primary sources of law are designed to guide the actions of government officials and civilians. A criminal statute is more than a suggested guide to conduct—it is a rule backed up by state coercion, subjecting a violator to lawful punishment. It speaks to every person who comes under the jurisdiction of the state as a prohibition on behavior that is specified by its words. A criminal statute is also a general directive to state officials who have authority to enforce, prosecute, and adjudge whether a person's behavior amounted to the prohibited action of the criminal law. Upon an authoritative finding of guilt the statute authorizes other state officers to inflict punishments on the convicted defendant. In this way, the entirety of a jurisdiction's criminal law, found in the state's penal code and additional criminal statutes, may be seen as a blueprint for authorized action by police, prosecutors, judges, and correctional officials: they may act against persons only for those behaviors that are prohibited by law and for none other. Therefore, the criminal law both authorizes *and* limits the punitive power of the state. This principle of legality, known by the Latin slogan *nulla poena sine lege*—no punishment without law—is one of the most important attributes of the rule of law.

Official texts of statutes appear in sessions laws and codifications. Sessions laws are volumes that contain the individual statutes passed by a session of the state legislature or Congress in chronological order. Federal sessions laws are included in numbered volumes entitled *U.S. Statutes at Large*. Statutes that are currently in force (i.e., that have not been repealed) are collated by subject matter into codifications, e.g., the *U.S. Code* (abbreviated: *USC*). State codifications often include the name of the publisher, for example, *Page's Ohio Revised Code Annotated* (Anderson), (abbreviated: *Ohio Rev. Code Ann.* (Anderson)). The federal penal law is found in Title 18 of the *U.S. Code*. A constitution is a special form of statute, and the most common source for the text of a state or federal constitution is the constitution volume of the state code or the *U.S. Code*, respectively (Jacobstein et al., 1994). Each state has its own penal code or criminal code.

The reports of appellate court decisions (the essays in which the decisions are found are called "opinions") are found in numbered volumes called court reports or case reporters. Each state has an official case reporter that includes cases decided by the state supreme and another reporting intermediate appellate courts cases in chronological order (e.g., *Missouri Reports, Missouri Appeals Reports*, respectively). A few states selectively report the opinions of trial courts. Several commercial publishers publish parallel volumes of case reports. The National Reporter System collects state cases into seven regional reporters (e.g., *Atlantic Reporter*). The official case reporter for U.S. Supreme Court cases is the *U.S. Reports*. Parallel reporters for Supreme Court decision include the *Supreme Court Reporter* (abbreviated *S.Ct.*) And the *U.S. Reports, Lawyer's Edition, Second Series* (abbreviated *L.Ed.2d*). Decisions of federal Courts of Appeal and District Courts are reported, respectively, in the *Federal Reports, Third Series* and the *Federal Supplement, Second Series* (abbreviated *F.3d* and *F. Supp.2d*). Statutes and cases are also available from various electronic sources, including the LEXIS and WESTLAW databases that also include much secondary legal literature.

A primary limitation on penalization is the U.S. Constitution. Art. I, § 9 prohibits Congress, and Art. I, § 10 prohibits the states from passing particularly tyrannous forms of crimes: bills of attainder (acts of the legislature convicting specific persons) and *ex post facto* laws (laws criminalizing lawful behavior *retrospectively*). Article III, § 3 defines the crime of treason (essentially, making war on the U.S. and giving "aid and comfort" to those engaged in war against the U.S.), and limits the punishment for treason. This prevents Congress from expanding the definition of treason to encompass political enemies, a practice common among tyrannies. Civil rights found in the First and Fourteenth Amendments (e.g., freedom of assembly, due process) also limit what behaviors may be made criminal.

Primary legal publications as sources of law raise an important question of jurisprudence (legal philosophy). The text of penal statutes is commonly referred to as *the* criminal law. However, sociological jurisprudence posits that law should be understood as the *action* taken by state officers that has a tangible impact on an individual, rather than the *words* of a constitution, statute, or legal case. In this view, the text is a "source" of law. This view comports with the common observation that discretion in the administration of criminal law by police, prosecutors, judges, and juries modifies the outcomes of cases that a "strict" reading of the penal code calls for. Nevertheless, as authoritative sources, the primary texts of criminal law retain special importance as the focus of criminal law enforcement and scholarship.

Secondary legal publications include technical research publications designed for legal practitioners, educational books, model codes, and legal scholarship. Many research publications (and electronic databases) assist attorneys in finding relevant authority from among the large number of statutes and cases. These works include citators (e.g., *Shepard's Citations*), digests (e.g., *Michigan Digest, Atlantic Digest, West's Federal Practice Digest*), legal encyclopedias (e.g., *American Jurisprudence, Second Series*), and loose-leaf services (e.g., *BNA Criminal Law Reporter*). The *BNA Criminal Law Reporter* provides, on a weekly basis, excerpts of the most significant recent state and federal cases on criminal law, procedure, and evidence; important legislative developments; the docket of the U.S. Supreme Court; and the full text of Supreme Court cases related to criminal jurisprudence. These kinds of publication are described in detail in texts on legal research (Jacobstein et al., 1994). The accepted abbreviations for all legal texts are found in *The Bluebook: A Uniform System of Citation*, a volume produced by a consortium of four law reviews (also called law journals) and updated periodically.

Educational materials on criminal law for law students generally include casebooks and textbooks. Casebooks contain excerpts of appellate court opinions that illustrate various issues and principles, along with a variety of questions, comments, and supplementary material. An example is Joshua Dressler's *Cases and Materials on Criminal Law* (1999). Textbooks, also called "horn-books," may be somewhat abbreviated versions of lengthier treatises, which provide an encyclopedic coverage of all of the rules of criminal law, supported by numerous citations to relevant cases and statutes. An example is *Criminal Law, Third Edition* (2000) by Wayne R. LaFave, a one-volume student edition that is an updated abridgement of LaFave and Scott's two volume *Substantive Criminal Law*. These texts are often kept up to date with annual supplements or with annual "pocket parts" that may be slid into a pocket in the back cover of the book. Casebooks and textbooks are also written for undergraduate criminal law courses in criminal justice programs, typically covering the subject in less depth than the law school texts.

Criminal law scholarship, like all legal scholarship, is prescriptive as well as descriptive, may include interdisciplinary scholarship, and tends to focus on applied problems. Much scholarship analyzes criminal cases and statutes, and runs the gamut from simple description and summarization to abstract philosophical inquiry. It may be comparative (comparing the law of various American jurisdictions or comparing American law to foreign law), sociological (e.g., examining the impact of criminal legislation), and may draw on a variety of other disciplines (e.g., philosophy, sociology, psychology, psychiatry) and theoretical perspectives (e.g., legal liberalism, feminist theory, postmodern theory). Much criminal law scholarship critiques new cases and legislation, explores particularly difficult or interesting questions, and offers recommendations as to the best approaches that ought to be followed. All criminal law scholarship, including the most abstract,

is designed to influence and improve the primary sources, that is, to influence legislators and judges in making decisions about the criminal law (Mueller, 1969).

At the apex of criminal law scholarship lies criminal law theory. But even the theory of criminal law, which George Fletcher (1978) describes "as a species of political and moral philosophy," has practical goals, for the foundational work of penal law theorists helps guide the decisions of legislators and judges in shaping the primary texts of criminal law (Hall, 1960; Mueller, 1969). Penal theory explains criminal law at a high level of abstraction. Hall (1960) has noted that issues in criminal law were discussed in Plato's *Laws* (e.g., mental disease, intentional and negligent harm-doing) and in medieval theological speculation (e.g., *mens rea*—criminal intent). The professional and theoretical literature of Anglo-American criminal law developed over the centuries in the writings of systematizers. These authors sought to explain the mass of case law decisions that defined criminal behavior and that established criminal defenses, by framing them into coherent categories and by discerning logically consistent principles to explain the decisions. These writers included Bracton's *On the Laws and Constitution of England* (13th century), Hale's *Pleas of the Crown* (1682), and Blackstone's *Commentaries on the Laws of England*, Vol. 4 (1769). In the U.S. this work was carried forward in the 19th century by Joel P. Bishop's *Commentaries on the Criminal Law* (1856) and Francis W. Wharton's *Treatise on the Criminal Law of the U.S.* (1847). These writers did not simply collate the law of crimes but imposed order on the cases, drew on philosophical currents to explain implicit principles of penal liability, and resolved intellectual problems generated by discordant cases. Oliver Wendell Holmes' *Common Law* (1881) contributed a powerful utilitarian logic to the understanding of the development of the common law of crimes.

All these currents came together in a grand synthesis of criminal law theory, Jerome Hall's *General Principles of Criminal Law* (1960; first edition: 1947). This work, drawing on the primary literature of criminal law (statutes and cases) and on the most advanced currents in European and American legal philosophy, saw that criminal law can be viewed as consisting of three layers of propositions: rules (specific definitions of crime), doctrines (intermediate propositions that relate to penal liability, e.g., insanity defense, ignorance and mistake, criminal attempt), and seven ultimate principles, which together, summarize the entire body of criminal law: *mens rea*, act, concurrence of *mens rea* and act, harm, causation, punishment, and legality. In this book and in other articles, Hall expounded on the issues and problems concerning doctrines and principles of criminal law. In doing so, he raised the level of understanding of criminal law among practitioners, judges, and scholars. All later publications in criminal law theory owe an enormous debt to Hall's seminal work.

The way in which criminal law scholarship influences the primary sources of law is exemplified by the career of the late Professor Herbert Wechsler (1909–2000) of Columbia University Law School. In the late 1930s, he collaborated with a mentor, Professor Jerome Michael of Columbia, to write a seminal two-part law review article on the law of homicide (Michael and Wechsler, 1937) and the most sophisticated casebook to that date, *Criminal Law and Its Administration—Cases, Statutes and Commentaries* (1940). These works brought together a wide range of materials that explored criminal law in its institutional setting. This scholarship was put to good use in 1952, when Prof. Wechsler was named to head the collaborative project, sponsored by the American Law Institute that led to the publication of the *Model Penal Code* (MPC) (American Law Institute, 1985). The MPC was the most significant American publication in criminal law in the 20th century. The MPC was designed to remedy many problems with penal codes noted by jurists in the first half of the 20th century: that the texts of penal codes of most states were poorly organized, failed to establish general principles of criminal liability, were replete with archaic and unenforceable provisions, and included poorly worded and conflicting sections. The MPC, which appeared in a draft with commentaries in 1962 and in a final form in 1985, corrected these problems and was immediately hailed as a monumental work. Its overall philosophy was utilitarian. The committee that prepared it under Professor Wechsler's direction patiently reviewed a variety of issues concerning each provision that had to be included in a penal code and drafted provisions that could be adopted by various states. Although not a perfect product, since the mid-1960s, the MPC has been adopted in whole or in part by the legislatures of 34 states.

Important work on criminal law theory has continued, drawing on and modifying Jerome Hall's synthesis, and exploring the ramifications of the MPC. A book equal in scope to Hall (1960) is *Rethinking Criminal Law* (1978) by George Fletcher. This work draws heavily on ideas and examples from German, Russian, and English criminal law and on the MPC. It seeks to better explain and guide the law of homicide and theft, and the "general part" of criminal law (principles of liability). Fletcher was motivated in changing how

lawyers and jurists think about criminal law, away from the utilitarian social control basis of the MPC and toward a revival of normative penal theory based on theories of justice advanced by leading contemporary philosophers. Another important study of penal theory, *Structure and Function in Criminal Law* (1997) by Paul Robinson, proposes that just as criminal law scholars accept the idea that doctrinal criminal law defenses are rooted in a common idea of *mens rea,* there are common links in doctrines of imputation, which helps to explain the way in which criminal liability is often found despite the lack of one of the standard principles of liability. Much recent scholarship in criminal law theory has been collected in an anthology, *Foundations of Criminal Law,* by Katz et al. (1999).

A substantial amount of criminal law scholarship appears in law reviews. There are more than 500 law reviews, most published by law schools and edited by law students. A few law reviews specialize in criminal law, such as the *American Criminal Law Review, Buffalo Law Review,* and the *Criminal Law Bulletin.* However, articles on criminal law may appear in any law journal, so that it is necessary for those interested in criminal law scholarship to examine indexes to find relevant scholarship. Some law review articles are descriptions and analyses of recent cases written by law students; others are examination of practical and theoretical issues written by law professors or judges.

MARVIN ZALMAN

References and Further Reading

American Law Institute. 1985. *Model Penal Code: Official Draft and Explanatory Notes* (7 vols.), Philadelphia, PA, The American Law Institute.

Dressler, J. 1999. *Cases and Materials on Criminal Law,* 2nd ed., St. Paul, MN, West.

Fletcher, G.P. 1978. *Rethinking Criminal Law,* Boston, MA, Little, Brown.

Hall, J. 1960. *General Principles of Criminal Law,* 2nd ed., Indianapolis, IN, Bobbs-Merrill.

Hall, J. 1952. *Theft, Law and Society,* 2nd ed., Indianapolis, IN, Bobbs-Merrill.

Jacobstein, J.M., Mersky, R.M. and Dunn, D.J. 1994. *Legal Research Illustrated,* 6th ed., Westbury, NY, Foundation Press.

Katz, L., Moore, M.S. and Morse, S.J., eds. 1999. *Foundations of Criminal Law,* New York, Oxford University Press.

LaFave, W.R. 2000. *Criminal Law,* 3rd ed., St. Paul, MN, West.

Mueller, G.O.W. 1969. *Crime, Law and the Scholars: A History of Scholarship in American Law,* Seattle, WA, University of Washington Press.

Michael, J. and Wechsler, H. 1937. A rationale of the law of homicide, *Columbia Law Review,* 37.

Robinson, P.H. 1997. *Structure and Function in Criminal Law,* Oxford, U.K., Clarendon Press.

Punishment Justifications

It is in the nature of punishment that it harms people—typically depriving them of life, liberty, or property. Such harms require justification; these are things that we ought not to do to people unless we have a very good reason for doing so. The two main strands of justification are the utilitarian, comprising deterrence, incapacitation, and rehabilitation, and the Kantian, which includes both retributive and moral reform models.

Utilitarians such as Jeremy Bentham argue that punishment is justified when the harm that it does to offenders is outweighed by the good that it brings to society in the form of crime prevention. Punishment may prevent crime by deterring both the person punished and others from engaging in similar acts; it may incapacitate offenders, disabling them from committing crimes for at least some period of time; or it may be used to rehabilitate offenders, thus preventing them from committing more crimes in the future. For the utilitarian argument to succeed in justifying punishment—either the institution as a whole or a specific penalty for a particular type of crime—the pain that it causes to offenders must be less than the pain that it prevents by reducing the crime rate. Punishment that causes more pain than it prevents is not justified on this view. Thus, the utilitarian argument depends on a comparison that can only be made by using empirical evidence. The weakness of most empirical studies of deterrence, from the utilitarian point of view, is that they do not consider harm to offenders as a "cost" of punishment; instead, the only cost considered is monetary cost to taxpayers. For the utilitarian, punishment that is "cost-effective" when only monetary costs are considered may yet be unjustified if the harm to offenders exceeds the harm prevented.

Because the utilitarian approach aggregates harms and benefits across the population, it has often been criticized for failing to take proper account of individual rights. Harm to one individual—even grave harm such as death—can seemingly be justified if counterbalanced by benefits to others. If punishment is justified whenever it does more good than harm, then under some circumstances punishment of the innocent might also be justified.

It is possible, for example, that vicarious punishment—perhaps punishing the families of offenders—could be found to have stronger deterrent effects than punishment of the offenders themselves. If so, it would seem to follow from the utilitarian principle of promoting the greatest total good that vicarious punishment is preferable. Utilitarians respond to this type of criticism by arguing that any such system of punishment is likely to produce widespread fear and anxiety resulting from the inability to control one's own liability to punishment, so that it would not in fact promote the greatest total good. But this in turn seems to give the wrong kind of reason for not punishing the innocent; surely the right not to be punished for the crimes of others does not turn on contingent facts about how society at large will react to such an eventuality.

A more basic criticism of the utilitarian approach is that, at bottom, it seeks simply to use offenders as tools to promote social goals. Essentially, if punishment is carried out for the purpose of deterring others from criminal behavior, those punished are required to bear a great burden in order that others may benefit. How, the critic asks, is this different from other ways in which we could benefit society by sacrificing a few—perhaps by enslaving a minority of the population? This question is especially provocative given the fact that prison populations typically consist disproportionately of those who are already on the margins of society. The obvious answer is that punishment is different because those punished are guilty of crimes; but under utilitarian theory, guilty persons are selected for punishment only because (or insofar as) punishment will be more effective in achieving its social goals if they are the individuals selected. The guilt of the offender does not, by itself, constitute a reason to punish him on the utilitarian view.

This criticism may seem not to apply where the purpose of punishment is incapacitation or rehabilitation. If what we are doing is incapacitating criminals, then criminal behavior will be a precondition of punishment. But because guilt is predicated on past acts, and incapacitation on projected future ones, the guilt of the offender is still not required for punishment to be justified on utilitarian grounds. All that is required for the justification to go through is a reliable prediction of future crimes—which need not be grounded in past criminal acts. Similarly, because the focus of rehabilitative efforts is on the molding of future behavior, a theory that holds punishment justified where it succeeds in inducing enough individuals to conform their future behavior to the law would seem equally to justify the "rehabilitation" of individuals who have not yet committed crimes, but who can reliably be predicted to do so.

A recent variation on the traditional utilitarian approach to deterrence is the self-defense theory of punishment. Self-defense theory seeks to meet the criticisms of utilitarianism explained above by drawing an analogy between punishment and self-defense. Inflicting harm on an attacker in self-defense is obviously permissible, at least as long as the harm done is proportional to the harm threatened by the attacker. Offhand, punishment is different from self-defense in that punishment, which is inflicted after the attacker has already done his harm, seems merely to add to that harm, rather than preventing it. Self-defense theorists point out, however, that the *threat* of punishment may serve the same harm-preventive purpose as self-defense. The problem then is to justify the carrying out of the threat, which of course takes place after the attacker has already done his harm. Daniel Farrell analyzes self-defense as permissible because the attacker forces his target to choose between harm to the attacker and harm to himself. Similarly, Farrell argues, the offender who ignores our justified threat of punishment forces us to choose between harm to him (by carrying out the threat) and increased risk of harm to ourselves (by losing the credibility of our threats, thus inviting new attacks). Thus, he concludes, carrying out our justified threats in order to preserve credibility is also justified. One disturbing implication of this theory is that there need be no guarantee of efficacy; as with self-defense, force may be used as long as it is both proportional to the harm threatened and has some possibility of averting that harm. Unlike traditional deterrence theory, self-defense theory does tie the justification of punishment directly to the guilt of the offender; it must be the person punished who chooses to increase the risk of harm to us by ignoring our justified threats. The self-defense justification thus stands between traditional deterrence and retributive theories, requiring both the guilt of the person punished and some possibility of a positive social effect.

Traditional retributivists, beginning with Kant, reject the idea that punishment should serve crime-preventive ends, arguing instead that the guilt of the offender is both a necessary and a sufficient condition for punishment—in other words, punishment is justified because it is deserved. Kant's specific observations about punishment have been less influential than his general ethical theory, which, with its injunction against using persons as mere means to the ends of others, is the foundation of the most telling criticisms of utilitarian theories. Herbert Morris's influential article, "Persons and Punishment," uses Kantian precepts both to argue against the rehabilitative model of punishment and to argue in favor of retributivism.

Morris suggests that the rehabilitative model, because it tends to portray offenders as pawns of forces beyond their control and their criminal acts as symptoms of a pathological condition, fails to assign responsibility to offenders for choosing their acts and thus fails to treat them as moral agents. Punishment, on the other hand, respects the choices of offenders, assigns them responsibility for those choices, and does not seek to mold them to be more compliant with social goals. Offenders have a right to be punished, Morris suggests, rather than to be treated as manipulable objects. In place of the rehabilitative model of punishment, Morris proposes a social-contract model under which those who have freely chosen to violate a set of rules that are for the advantage of all are subjected to punishment as a way of restoring the proper balance of benefits and burdens in society. Such a model (as Morris recognizes) justifies punishment only to the extent that the preexisting balance of benefits and burdens is fair, the rules are in fact for the advantage of all, and the offender's choice to break them suitably unconstrained. Its applicability under current conditions is therefore in doubt. Even given ideal social conditions, it is not clear how punishment can serve to restore the balance of benefits and burdens disturbed by the offense. For most citizens, refraining from tax evasion or jaywalking is more difficult than refraining from serious crimes like murder. If the burden to be matched by punishment is that of self-restraint, it would then follow that tax evasion should get a more severe penalty than murder. If we instead focus on the advantages gained by the offender from the crime, we face the same problem: there is no necessary correspondence between the seriousness of the crime and the benefit it brings to the offender, so the penalty needed to cancel out the benefit gained from successful larceny might well be greater than that needed to cancel out the benefit gained from a bungled armed robbery in which people were killed.

Other retributivists have proposed different reasons for harming offenders. One school of thought is that punishment constitutes an authoritative statement on the part of society that the offender's behavior in committing the crime was wrong. Following Hegel's suggestion that punishment serves to "annul" the crime, Jean Hampton argues that the crime can be understood as making a false statement about the relative values of the offender and the victim; the purpose of punishment, in her view, is to refute that statement through an authoritative declaration that the offender is not more valuable than the victim, thus vindicating those rights of the victim violated by the crime.

A similar line of thought is found in moral reform theories, but with the focus on conveying a message to the offender rather than to society as a whole. R.A.

Duff, for example, argues that respect for the offender as a moral agent requires that we attempt to convey to him the moral wrongness of his conduct with the purpose of inducing him to repent of his wrongful behavior and so to improve his moral character. Mere words will not suffice for this effort; instead, we must show the offender, through hard treatment, what degree of penance his conduct requires, in the hope that he will thus be induced to reflect on his behavior and to adopt the penance as voluntary. Duff and other moral reform theorists emphasize that the point is not to coerce compliance; on the contrary, the point is to induce the offender to choose voluntarily to change his behavior. Thus, penalties that are inconsistent with voluntary choice are ruled out. Similarly, punishments that are disproportionate to the severity of the crime are inappropriate because part of the point of the punishment is to convey the seriousness of the crime. Punishment, on this model, is for the benefit of the offender because it is imposed out of concern for his moral character; to serve this end, it must neither overbear the offender's will nor be disproportionate to his offense. Like other theories rooted in Kantian thought, moral reform theory justifies punishment only where social conditions meet requirements of fairness; for Duff, the purpose of moral reform will justify punishment only where the crime separates the offender from a community whose values he shares, and where the punishment aims at restoring him to that community by gaining his assent to the penance initially forced on him.

DEIRDRE GOLASH

References and Further Reading

Jeremy B. 1988. *Introduction to the Principles of Morals and Legislation,* 1789, New York, Prometheus Books.

Brandt, R.B. 1959. *Ethical Theory: The Problems of Normative and Critical Ethics,* Englewood Cliffs, NJ, Prentice-Hall.

Burgh, R. 1986. Do the guilty deserve punishment? *Journal of Philosophy,* 79 (1982). Duff, R.A., *Trials and Punishments,* Cambridgeshire, U.K., Cambridge University Press.

Farrell, D. 1991. The justification of deterrent violence, *Ethics,* 100.

Hegel, G.W.F. 1966. *Grundlinien der Philosophie des Rechts,* 1821, as *Hegel's Philosophy of Right,* translated by Knox, T.M., New York, Oxford University Press.

Kant, I. 1997. *Grundlegen zur Metaphysik der Sitten,* 1785, as *Foundations of the Metaphysics of Morals,* translated by Beck, L.W., 2nd ed. (revised), Upper Saddle River, NJ, Prentice-Hall, Inc.

Montague, P. 1995. *Punishment as Societal-Defense,* Lanham, MD, Rowman, Littlefield.

Morris, H. 1968. Persons and punishment, *Monist,* 52.

Murphy, J., Ed. 1994. *Punishment and Rehabilitation,* 3rd ed., Belmont, CA, Wadworth Publishing Co.

Murphy, J. and Hampton, J. 1988. *Forgiveness and Mercy,* Cambridgeshire, Cambridge University Press.

See also **Bentham, Jeremy; Deterrence, Specific; Retribution**